Lunch-Bucket Lives

Remaking the Workers' City

CRAIG HERON

Between the Lines
Toronto

Lunch-Bucket Lives

© 2015 Craig Heron

First published in 2015 by
Between the Lines
401 Richmond Street West
Studio 277
Toronto, Ontario M5V 3A8
Canada
1-800-718-7201
www.btlbooks.com

Library and Archives Canada Cataloguing in Publication

Heron, Craig, author
  Lunch-bucket lives : remaking the workers' city /
  Craig Heron.

Includes bibliographical references and index.
Issued in print and electronic formats.
ISBN 978-1-77113-212-1 (pbk.).—ISBN 978-1-77113-213-8 (epub).—
ISBN 978-1-77113-214-5 (pdf)

  1. Working class—Ontario—Hamilton—Social conditions—19th century. 2. Working class—Ontario—Hamilton—Social conditions—20th century. 3. Hamilton (Ont.)—Social conditions—19th century. 4. Hamilton (Ont.)—Social conditions—20th century. I. Title.

HD8110.H352H47   2015   305.56'20971352   C2014-906720-8
                                              C2014-906721-6

Text and cover design by David Vereschagin,
  Quadrat Communications
Cover art by Carol Condé and Karl Beveridge
Printed in Canada

This book has been published with the help of a grant from the Federation for the Humanities and Social Sciences, through the Awards to Scholarly Publications Program, using funds provided by the Social Sciences and Humanities Research Council of Canada.

As winner of the 2012 Wilson Prize for Publishing in Canadian History, Between the Lines thanks the Wilson Institute for Canadian History for its recognition of our contribution to Canadian history and its generous support of this book.

Between the Lines gratefully acknowledges assistance for its publishing activities from the Canada Council for the Arts, the Ontario Arts Council, the Government of Ontario through the Ontario Book Publishers Tax Credit program and through the Ontario Book Initiative, and the Government of Canada through the Canada Book Fund.

Canada Council   Conseil des Arts
for the Arts   du Canada

Canada

ONTARIO ARTS COUNCIL
CONSEIL DES ARTS DE L'ONTARIO
an Ontario government agency
un organisme du gouvernement de l'Ontario

RECYCLED
Paper made from
recycled material
FSC® C103567
FSC
www.fsc.org

Contents

Part IV: The Ties That Bind

Preface

THE WRITING OF THIS BOOK has been a long intellectual journey. I have been thinking about the working people of Hamilton for decades. Way back in the fall of 1977 I first walked through the doors of the Hamilton Public Library to begin a PhD dissertation on work and politics in that city in the early 20th century. I completed it four years later, but set it aside for several years before deciding to rework and expand it into a more wide-ranging study of Canada's best-known factory town. That work proceeded in fits and starts, and was interrupted repeatedly by other projects, all of which, over time, influenced what I wanted to say here.

When I started this project more specifically in the late 1980s, I had the goal of bringing together the insights of several distinct fields of research to inform the history of working people in Canada. In addition to the work on the wage-earning experience, unions, and working-class politics that had originally inspired me, writers and scholars were producing wonderful new studies of working women, family economies, children, schooling, health care, sexuality, religion, ethnic and racial groups, popular culture, social policy and practice, and a variety of state programs, many of which illuminated particular aspects of working-class life. The fragmentation and dispersion were frustrating, and I thought all these new voices needed to sing in the same choir, to produce a richer oratorio of working-class history. I kept my focus on the half-century before World War Two because that was a period of profound change in the lives of Canada's working people. I also continued to believe that only in a close reading of the experience in one community could I find the fine-grained detail that would reveal the complexities of class experience. Those ideas took me back, again and again, to Hamilton.

I have no personal connection to Hamilton. I was not born there, and have spent few nights there. Like millions of Canadians, I grew up with a stark visual image of Hamilton as seen across its large, murky harbour from the heights of the Burlington Skyway – a conglomeration of dark, menacing structures belching smoke and spitting huge flames into the night sky. As a PhD student in the late 1970s, I chose Hamilton as a subject for my dissertation because of its status as one of the country's leading industrial centres. Eventually I would visit it countless times for research purposes and, later, for heritage work. I made friends there and became a sympathetic outsider and staunch defender of the self-styled "Lunch-Bucket Town."

I hope the people of Hamilton will find much here to appreciate. Their city's fascinating history deserves a thorough study. Yet I also hope that all readers will see a larger picture in which Hamilton stands in for many other communities in Canada and elsewhere. The relevance of what is discussed here grows with every year of this new century, as so many of Canada's working people now face the kinds of precarious uncertainty that Hamilton's workers and their families had to cope with a century ago.

Acknowledgements

INTELLECTUAL WORK is necessarily a co-operative enterprise, and this project would not have been possible without the kind, valuable assistance, encouragement, and inspiration of many people. The doctoral dissertation that preceded this book took shape in the stimulating environment of the Dalhousie University History Department in the late 1970s, where I was particularly grateful to Ian McKay, David Frank, Nolan Reilly, John Manley, Bruce Tucker, Michael Cross, David Sutherland, Judy Fingard, John O'Brien, Tina Simmons, and Linda Kealey for an exciting atmosphere of rigorous discussion and critique, as well as critical engagement with my work. At that stage, I benefited above all from the support and helpful guidance of my enthusiastic supervisor, Greg Kealey.

As I was completing the dissertation, I was drawn into an ambitious project in the McMaster University Labour Studies Program, which aimed to collect interviews and images of Hamilton working-class life and ultimately produced a beautiful book. We reached out across the city for photographs and stories and visited the archives of many of the city's largest employers. That process brought me into regular contact with the incomparable Wayne Roberts, a superb historian (and now an outstanding journalist) whose intellectual nimbleness and wacky sense of humour were a huge influence on me and my writing. That project also led to a deeply rewarding friendship with Bob Storey, my sociological sidekick, with whom I shared intellectual inspiration, political commitment, and endless good fun for years to come.

In the early 1980s, as I settled into a new teaching job at York University, I found myself immersed in new networks of imaginative scholars in the Division of Social Science, eventually including Paul Axelrod, Linda Briskin, Eduardo Canel, Paul Craven, Gina Feldberg, Pablo Idahosa, Engin Isin, and Harriet Rosenberg, and in the Department of History, especially Stephen Brooke, Ramsay Cook, Susan Houston, Kate McPherson, Nick Rogers, Adrian Shubert, and Marc Stein. Starting in the early 1990s, I also had the pleasure of working with a steady flow of outstanding graduate students, from whom I learned so much.

There were also important connections beyond York. In 1981 I began participating in a remarkable reading group, the Labour Studies Research Group (casually renamed the Toronto Labour Studies Group in the 1990s), which has met monthly ever since to discuss unpublished papers (including many of the chapters that appear here). The group has brought together a stellar series of nearly 100 graduate students and faculty in history, sociology, economics, law, and women's studies. Among those, I owe special debts to the critical insights of Franca Iacovetta, Ian Radforth, Eric Tucker, and Steve Penfold. For a few years in the 1980s I was also part of a large group of like-minded political economists who met regularly for richly rewarding discussions of labour relations in capitalist society. A decade later another short-lived but lively and engaging reading group met monthly to discuss the history of masculinities; it included Mike Birke, Stephen Brooke, Rob Kristofferson, Steven Maynard, Carolyn Podruchny, Steve Penfold, Mark Rosenfeld, and Marc Stein. My continuing friendship with Steven Maynard remained a valuable source of intellectual inspiration and comradeship.

At the same moment that I decided to write this book, I was swept up into a new project in public history, the Workers' Arts and Heritage

Centre, which provided many years of incomparable learning experiences with some of the finest minds I have ever encountered: Carol Anderson, Karl Beveridge, Carole Condé, Rosemary Donegan, Jim Miller, Glen Richards, D'Arcy Martin, David Sobel, and Renée Wetselaar, among many others. Much that appears in this book passed through the analytical lenses that I developed through those amazing associations. After the Centre opened in Hamilton in 1996, I was able to deepen my contact with many fine people in that city, notably "Fast Eddie" Thomas and Wayne Marston.

Researching this book took me to many libraries and archival repositories, where I was always fortunate to find competent, helpful staff. Large public institutions were important: the Archives of Ontario (Toronto), Library and Archives Canada (Ottawa), Provincial Archives of Manitoba (Winnipeg), and several university libraries – the Killam Library at Dalhousie University, the York University libraries, the Mills Library at McMaster University, the many University of Toronto libraries (including the Thomas Fisher Rare Books Library), the Special Collections Department at the University of British Columbia Library, Industrial Relations Library of Cornell University, and Littauer Library of Harvard University. I also benefited from the services of the Multicultural History Society of Ontario, the Presbyterian Church of Canada Archives, and the United Church of Canada Archives. In Hamilton I was grateful to several private organizations that opened their collections to me: the Ambrose McGhee Medical Museum, Big Brothers Association of Hamilton, Educational Archives and Heritage Centre, Girl Guides of Canada (Escarpment Branch), Greening-Donald, the Hamilton Group, the Hamilton YWCA, Imperial Order Daughters of the Empire (Municipal Chapter), International Harvester, Westinghouse Canada, and Workers' Arts and Heritage Centre. It would be impossible to exaggerate how important the Hamilton Public Library's Local History and Archives Department (formerly Special Collections) was for this project. I am most grateful to Bruce Shaw, Bryan Henley, and Margaret Houghton for years of unfailing help and support. I am also grateful to Myer Siemiatycki, Gene Homel, and Nathan Smith for sharing their own research material and to John Weaver for giving me access to his archive of student papers on Hamilton history. In finding my way through much of the voluminous material, I was aided by a string of excellent research assistants: Will Baker, Emily Bradbury, Rob Kristofferson, Alfonso Licata, Lynne Marks, Vienna Paolantonio, Glenda Peard, Steve Penfold, David Sobel, Peter Stevens, Eric Strikwerda, Ryan Targa, and Melissa Turkstra.

I owe a large debt to the many people whose writing on Hamilton made my work much easier. They include many scholars who were also interested in Hamilton: George Addison, Catherine Annau, Peter Archibald, Peter Baskerville, John Benson, Pat Bird, Nancy Bouchier, Dianne Brandino, June Corman, Mark Cortiula, Ken Cruikshank, Enrico Cumbo, Dianne Dodd, Michael Doucet, Kenneth Draper, Karen Dubinsky, Bill Freeman, Rosemary Gagan, Michael Gauvreau, Jason Gilliland, Adam Givertz, Carolyn Gray, Richard Harris, Peter Hanlon, Ann Herring, Andrew Holman, Michael Katz, Rob Kristofferson, Patricia Lilley, David Livingstone, Richard Lucas, Meg Luxton, Douglas McCalla, Diana J. Middleton, Cheryl MacDonald, Bryan Palmer, Doris Ragonetti, Wayne Roberts, Wally Seccombe, Matt Sendheuhler, Adrienne Shadd, Zofia Shahrodi, Myer Siemiatycki, Ted Smith, Elizabeth Smyth, Mark J. Stern, Robert Storey, R.M. Stott, James Sturgis, Jane Synge, Nicholas Terpstra, Melissa Turkstra, David F. Walker, and, above all, John Weaver. Hamilton has also had several excellent local historians whose writings have kept the history of their city alive for many years and helped orient me to its past: Mel Bailey, Marjorie Freeman Campbell, Gary Evans, Lois C. Evans, Robert Fraser, Brian Henley, Margaret Houghton, Bill Manson, John M. Mills, and Dennis Missett. I also benefited enormously from five oral-history projects conducted in Hamilton at various times beginning in the 1970s by the late Jane Synge, McMaster University Labour Studies Program, Multicultural History Society of Ontario, Peter Archibald, and Workers' Arts and Heritage Centre. I am standing on the broad shoulders of all these people.

This book came together with relatively little financial support. I am grateful to the Social Sciences and Humanities Council for a doctoral fellowship that sustained me in preparing the dissertation that started it all, and to the Association for Canadian Studies for a Writing Award that helped to sustain the momentum. At York University a Research Development Leave also gave me a year without teaching to push on.

When I finally completed a draft of a huge manuscript, I was fortunate to have five friends who volunteered to read and comment on it: Bettina Bradbury, Franca Iacovetta, Ian McKay, Steve Penfold, and Ian Radforth. After many weeks of reading, they convened for a rigorous discussion of my project. I was deeply touched by their encouragement, invigorated by their challenges, and nourished by their supportiveness. It was a wonderful privilege to be able to share in the intellectual comradeship that would bring people together in this way.

I am indebted to Carol Condé and Karl Beveridge for their skill and imagination in turning my loose ideas into a wonderful cover image. I am also grateful to my friends at Between the Lines, whose enthusiasm for this book was heart-warming. Robert Clarke once again performed his copy-editing magic in tightening up and smoothing out a dauntingly huge manuscript.

Along the way I have had personal support from some important people in my life, including my parents, the late Harold and Margaret Heron; my daughters, Anna and Emily Bradbury; and my partner, Randy Goldman, all of whom were somewhat mystified by what I did with my time, but nonetheless showed they cared. Most important was the loving support I have enjoyed from Bettina Bradbury, a remarkable scholar in her own right, who understood what I was trying to do and urged me on. It wouldn't have been possible without her.

Tables

A series of 44 tables are available to back up and supplement the information and points made in this book. The tables can be found at https://btlbooks.com/book/lunch-bucket-lives.

Hamilton c. 1930

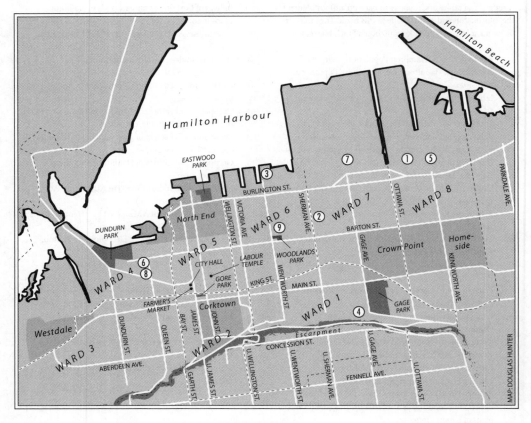

1 Dominion Foundries and Steel
2 Imperial Cotton
3 International Harvester
4 Mercury Mills
5 National Steel Car
6 Ontario Rolling Mills (Ontario Works, Steel Company of Canada)
7 Steel Company of Canada
8 Tuckett Tobacco
9 Westinghouse

1

(*LN*, 5 Jan. 1912, 2)

Opening the Lunch Bucket

THE SCREECH OF THE NOON WHISTLE pierced the din inside the factory walls. A sudden silence quickly spread across the plant as workers downed their tools and turned off their machines. The next half-hour would be theirs. Some pulled together rough benches near their work stations. Some headed outside. Others looked for a table in the company lunchroom. Wherever they went, almost all of them sat down in small groups and opened their lunch buckets.

Those simple, unadorned metal containers, also known as dinner or lunch pails, have long been as symbolic as they were practical. Most commonly, whether tucked under an arm or swinging from a fist, they marked working people who could not afford to buy lunch at work or had too little time at noon to get home for a meal. The lunch buckets were visible reminders of the material constraints of being a wage-earner. They were a public display of class identity.

Just as often they were symbols of manhood, as teenage boys quickly learned after they left

(*HS*, 12 April 1917, 16)

school and went off to work. Carrying a lunch bucket gave men the mature, respected status of a breadwinner for their families. When they left their doorsteps each morning with one in hand, their neighbours would know they had a job and were helping to support their families. Politicians who promised a "full dinner pail" recognized this concern.[1] "Handing in his dinner pail" became a popular euphemism for dying.[2] For manual workers lunch buckets often served as badges of distinction that separated their valuable labour from that of the pasty-faced office clerk or frail professional. Many "working girls" also carried some kind of lunch bucket, announcing to neighbours that they too were factory workers who were bringing home much-needed wages.[3] Yet, not surprisingly, many other women preferred to avoid threats to their femininity by hiding their lunches in their handbags.[4]

The symbolism also operated less publicly. Workers opened their lunch buckets to find a nourishing meal prepared by wives or mothers with care, skill, and usually at least a modicum of love. The term "dinner pail" suggested that the container held the big meal of the wage-earner's day.[5] What went into it had to refuel the body at the halfway point of the nine or ten hours on

the job. Wives and mothers prided themselves on packing good lunches, and family members used the quality of the meal provided as an indication of how well their womenfolk managed the household budget, even when low wages or underemployment severely taxed abilities to make ends meet. The lunch bucket, then, was a link in the family circle and a reminder of the unpaid domestic labour that sustained wage-earners through long working days. It brought a small breath of domestic nurturing into the rough harshness of the factory environment.

The time allowed to open a lunch bucket was also time away from the intense pressures of the job. It represented an island of free time in the middle of a lengthy work shift. It was a moment to relax and let the senses savour the food and drink. In the lunch bucket a worker might also have stowed away a newspaper, a religious tract, a political pamphlet, or a novel, along with some tobacco or even illicit alcohol. Briefly freed from factory production's multiple assaults on the senses, the mind, body, and spirit might get nourished in various ways.

Opening a lunch bucket was also almost always done with others – it was a symbolically social act. On the one hand, it exposed a worker to scrutiny. Did the contents reveal what good wages and regular employment could provide, or was the food meagre, cheap, and stale – a sign, perhaps, of problems at home with a lazy or angry wife, or of a worker's drinking problem that ate away at family income? Was the food familiar to the ethnic group gathered together, or did the Englishman's soft white bread or the Italian's garlicky sausage make the other workers cringe? A worker's respectability could be at stake.

Yet, on the other hand, opening lunch buckets together was a quiet, everyday ritual of communal sociability, creating a small oasis of humanity and togetherness, which was implicitly a tiny nucleus of subversion that pushed back the harsh indignities of wage labour. As often the case in human experience, food and drink brought people together. When wage-earners consumed their noon meal with workmates, they used the occasion to discuss sports, politics, courtship, shop-floor problems, and much more. The storytelling and speechifying in these moments helped to knit together a sense of community among workers – an experience that might well continue after the final whistle blew, whether in a saloon, church basement, or union hall, or outside on a playing field.

The lunch bucket encapsulates what this book is about. It is a symbol of both the hard-metal reality of surviving on wage labour and the many practices that workers engaged in to make a life worth living. In its stark simplicity, it conveys both subordination and resistance. It was a little package of determined independence and high aspirations carried into the tightly structured world of capitalist waged labour. It also contained the bonds and tensions of gender, ethnicity, and race.

Over many years the lunch bucket became a prominent symbol of Hamilton, Ontario, and its workers. Outsiders often used the lunch-bucket label to disparage Hamilton's allegedly rough urban culture. Over more recent decades, as smokestack industries declined, civic leaders tried to slough off that identity, even publishing an official commemorative book in 1971 entitled *Pardon My Lunch Bucket*.[6] This book invites the people of Hamilton (and other industrial cities) to look more closely at the rich complexities of their lunch-bucket history and, perhaps, to embrace it with considerably more enthusiasm.

Studying Workers

Writers and scholars carry into their studies of working people some deeply etched, often

Keeps fresh longer!

Put it in the lunch box!

The lunch hour can't come too soon when you know there are sandwiches of Browns' *OLD HOME Potato LOAF* in the lunch-box. How delicious—and how thoroughly satisfying they are!

This richer, better loaf is simply wonderful for making up lunches because it keeps fresh so long! Sandwiches taste delightfully fresh even if made up the night before.

Browns' *OLD HOME Potato LOAF* is made with *specially prepared* potato flour added to the wheat flour in it, in just the way mother used to bake her bread. There's *extra milk, extra sugar* and *Bowes' Creamery Butter* in it, too, to add to its richness.

Order a loaf to-day and you'll exclaim with so many others "That bread *is* just like mother used to bake!"

Phone
Regent 190
Roy G. Moffat
Manager

BROWNS' BREAD LIMITED

The **OLD HOME** *Potato* **LOAF**

(*HS*, 23 June 1925, 11)

contradictory stereotypes, around which they all too often assemble their evidence – the male clenched fist waving above an angry crowd of strikers, the slumped figure of the drunkard sprawling across a sidewalk, the weary face of the overworked housewife, the spindly limbs of the ragged street urchin, the hard expression of the adolescent delinquent, and many more such stark representations of working-class life. These are images that have been created for the most part by activists of one kind or another, most often from outside the working class – crusading journalists and photographers, child-savers and other social workers, public-health advocates and sundry urban reformers, socialist and feminist organizers, and many more. Each image captures an element of what it means to be subordinated in a society based on wage labour, but most of them remain too rigid, lacking movement, flexibility, and human resourcefulness and frailty. None adequately conveys the complexities of class relationships in capitalist societies.[7]

The image of the wage-earner with a lunch bucket can, by itself, be just as limited, but, even if it doesn't capture the full range of working-class experience, it does get at something basic and unavoidable. At the crack of dawn, six days a week, workers clutching lunch buckets or handbags stepped across the thresholds of thousands of households in cities like Hamilton. They muttered goodbyes to those left behind to keep house and trudged off to workplaces where someone had agreed to pay them for their ability to labour. These individual acts added up to a massive movement of humanity around a city every day (repeated nine or ten hours later for the homeward trek). They made starkly visible the central, unifying commonality that wage-earning and dependence on wages provide to all working people. No matter how inevitably varied were their experiences, no matter how much they squabbled and disagreed about what makes life worth living, no matter how much they avoided each other and went their own ways, they all knew that they had to work for wages to ensure the survival of themselves and their families. A shared sense of necessity sent them all into the streets at the same time.

So much in working-class households hinged on what those people earned – the size of the house they lived in, the quality of the food they ate, the health care they received, the years their children could spend in school, the pleasures they could enjoy, the confidence to stand up to the boss. Good wages opened up possibilities. Bad or insecure wages put up real barriers and constraints. No wages at all threatened a family's very survival. A dependence on wages set workers apart from the self-employed and others with substantial incomes.

Earnings, however, were the result of the class experience, not its central definition. For a deeper understanding we have to look at the role of power. As wage-earners entered their workplaces, they had to set aside their lunch buckets and give themselves over to the control of owners and managers. Their time was no longer theirs, and their bodies and minds were at the service of those who paid their wages. Until the whistle blew to turn them loose many hours later, they were subordinate in a rigid authority system. They and their families were also subordinate outside those workplaces. Political and legal bodies (cabinets, legislatures, courts) and social and cultural institutions (schools and hospitals) were largely beyond their control. Laws and the enforcement of laws by police and courts regulated public behaviour, whether it was playing or flirting in the street, drinking and fighting, setting up a picket line, or mounting a soapbox on a street corner to deliver a socialist speech.

Those forms of subordination arose from the relationships that workers had with other classes. Broadly speaking, workers encountered two major social groups in their daily lives. An upper class (or "bourgeoisie") controlled the key economic levers and had the capacity to organize large projects of capital accumulation that brought other classes into a state of subordination. The members of that class had built a distinctive class solidarity through their economic alliances and closed, exclusive social networks (separate residential areas, schooling, summer resorts, clubs, church congregations, and cultural activities, such as art, symphony, or opera).[8] Workers also engaged with members of a loosely defined middle class – the shopkeepers who sold them goods, doctors who lectured them on their children's health, clergymen who exhorted them to moral purity, engineers who set performance standards in factories, plant superintendents who oversaw production, school teachers who filled their children's heads with odd ideas, or wives in certain households who supervised servant girls from working-class families. In contrast to workers, middle-class people had more independence in organizing their own economic and social lives, and they exercised more authority over others. They were not as well off as the upper class, but their material prosperity was generally sufficient to allow them to enjoy comfortable respectability.[9]

Power was imbedded in these social relationships between classes, but it did not flow only from a single, centralized source. Capitalists did not dictate all working-class behaviour in any mechanistic way, and, despite plenty of evidence of strikebreaking and red-baiting, state policy has seldom relied simply on overt coercion. Power confronted workers in many sites in their daily lives – workplaces, schools, churches, streets, parks, courtrooms, immigration offices, public-health clinics, and more.[10]

These inequalities of wealth and power are what many writers refer to as the economic or "material" dimension of working-class lives, a dimension that provided the crucial structure of their existence.[11] Yet other major structuring forces also limited the earning capacities, employment possibilities, and other social entitlements of particular groups of working people. For the housewives who lingered by the door watching their family members heading off to work, or the working girls who joined the throngs of men carrying their lunches through a plant gate, gender expectations kept them tied to a destiny within domesticity and under patriarchal authority. Immigrant workers and people of colour found their options similarly constrained by racializing theories and practices. Class, gender, and ethnicity/race inevitably intersected; class was always present and may have predominated in particular moments, but it was not always primary and was always shaped by the other forces. Most importantly,

structure meant dynamic relationships – between the broad social classes, genders, and racial and ethnic groups, and among people within those categories. None of these structural patterns was fixed; they were constantly shifting and changing, being reconstructed and reformulated.[12]

Living within a realm of pressures and constraints undoubtedly had a strong impact on how members of particular classes (and groups within classes) conceived of themselves and their material situations. People in such circumstances were strongly disposed to similar behaviour and attitudes.[13] Yet their structural situation did not lead predictably and straightforwardly to any particular way of thinking and acting, whether it was to hunker down in compliance or rise up in resistance. Individually and collectively, people engaged in some independent reflection and assessment, and exercised some degree of agency, albeit within the narrative limitations of the language through which those actions were expressed.[14]

Workers used familiar cultural lenses to assess their experience within the structural constraints on their lives. The meaning that they drew could vary, particularly because there were always many different discourses at work attempting to ascribe that meaning, often through symbolic representation, and to encourage particular behaviour or action. Some of those discourses were dominant, or "hegemonic," and most often flowed through institutionalized channels such as the government, mass media, or education system. They encouraged workers' consent to the apparently intuitive "common sense" of the status quo.[15] Sometimes workers seized upon those hegemonic ideas and gave them a twist that emphasized their own needs and concerns. Other discourses arising perhaps from workers' movements or through informal modes and practices of communication over their lunch buckets, in their neighbourhoods, or around their kitchen tables challenged hegemonic ideas and practices more directly. Discourses might mutually reinforce a compelling social vision, but the divergences among them could create plenty of cross-currents. Workers listened and accepted, complied and ignored, confronted and rejected, mixed and integrated the discursive elements swirling around them. They therefore understood the world around them through a complex kind of awareness shaped by the structured patterns of their daily lives, the information, ideas, and language available to make sense of them, and their own willingness and ability to accept, reject, or adapt those understandings.

Class awareness varied among the major social classes depending on the power and resources (or "capacities") at their disposal.[16] Class-consciousness has always been particularly vigorous among the upper and middle classes, but workers have always constituted the loosest, least coherent, least unified of the social classes, the one least able to express its own sense of itself. New patterns of labour-market recruitment regularly brought people into wage-earning from pre-industrial backgrounds or experiences outside wage-earning. They brought with them values and practices rooted in those previous class locations that persisted in the new proletarian context. Others, such as young women or Sicilian or Polish peasants in the early 20th century, saw wage-earning as only short-term episodes that they would soon leave behind, even though their collective labour sustained whole industries – in one case, clothing and textiles, food production, and retailing, and, in the other, mining, resource-processing, and construction.[17] Even among those who settled into wage-earning, the struggle to survive typically took priority over developing larger political strategies, and followed an individualized course, which could be reinforced by segmented labour markets, industrial paternalism, charity and social work practices, and more. Workers brought together as the raw material of a working class generally had to learn over time to co-operate, and could be highly vulnerable to constructions of their experience from elsewhere.

Class, then, is rooted in the material reality of the wage relationship and all that flowed from it, but has different meanings depending on gender and ethnicity or race. But class awareness can be expressed in many diverse ways and can be eclipsed by competing perspectives on social realities, especially where class-based organizations are weak (union, co-ops, political parties). Certainly, to determine what workers thought about their situations we can look back to find often articulate proletarian voices set forth in writing, whether manifestos and editorials, or poetry and song. In working-class history, where the material and cultural resources to produce intellectual statements can be limited, however, words may often be less important than behaviour and actions – that is, practices. Beyond the spoken and written text, we may well find insights in such compliant habits as willingly accepting the direction of a priest, factory foreman, and Conservative politician, or in such contrary behaviour as quitting jobs, striking, dropping out of school, refusing to attend church, and avoiding baby clinics. Workers also expressed their attitudes in informal but ritualized performances in their daily lives.[18] The street gangs' swagger, the working girls' promenades, the workingmen's barroom treats, the families' holiday frolicking, the factory workers' initiations, the picket line's manoeuvres, the angry crowd's disciplined movements in the streets – all were part of the repertoire of collective action in which working people used their bodies to make public statements.[19]

Workers also revealed a good deal through their use of space in the city: from the arrangements of their households to the patterns of interaction in their immediate neighbourhoods and then across the city. Thanks to real-estate markets and limited incomes, working people most often lived apart from other social classes. Yet they also lived a good deal of their lives in public. They travelled to and from work, and they gathered for many purposes on street corners, in parks, at factory gates, and in such quasi-public settings as stores, churches, theatres, sports arenas, dance halls, saloons, and bingo halls. Their behaviour in those places was often governed by moral regulations of various kinds and subject to police oversight. But they repeatedly challenged limitations on their use of all that space and created new modes of collective behaviour that made the city more theirs.

Given that they lived and worked alongside so many other workers, they are often assumed to have built tight-knit working-class "communities." Certainly working-class neighbourhoods and workplaces brought them into regular contact and facilitated exchange. But that does not necessarily imply homogeneity and unanimity. Just as inside the working-class household, where sparks could fly among men, women, and children, tensions could burst out among people associating together in neighbourhoods every day. Cross-class networks based on bonds of gender, ethnicity, religion, and more could also reach outward. "Community" must be demonstrated, not assumed.[20]

The extensive writing on the diversity of working-class practice suggests a loose consistency running through all of it – what I like to call working-class realism. While it was not a fixed political position and certainly not a synonym for conservatism, the practice suggests a propensity among workers across the past century and a half to evaluate what is possible and realizable in any given context and to act on that understanding. The practice was not all a matter of individual judgments, but generally followed widespread patterns across the working class in the same period. Workers tended to work out this class awareness, at least in part, through their social networks of family and kin, workmates, neighbours, and others they met through sports, church, lodge meetings, union activities, and politics. At such historic moments as 1886, 1919, or 1946, the scope of "realistic" possibilities could expand dramatically. At other times it contracted just as abruptly. The differences in those moments related to how workers evaluated their social circumstances through the cultural and discursive lenses available to them.[21]

This book, then, looks at how workers dealt with the profound changes in their lives as wage-earners, family members, and participants in various social networks. It builds on the large body of writing focused directly on working-class experience in Canada and elsewhere, and on the many other studies that looked at workers through the lenses of such people as industrialists and engineers, public-health and social workers, civil servants and politicians, and retailers and showmen. The book turns the lens around to investigate how workers engaged with all these outside forces and managed to negotiate their way through the constraints and opportunities that confronted them in a period – lasting roughly from 1890 to 1940 – of broad and deep social change. The study takes wage-earning as a central element in working-class life, but also looks beyond the workplace into the households and neighbourhoods in which so much more of workers' lives were lived.

A Moment in Time

Industrial capitalism is inherently unstable. Individual enterprises often have short lives, and wildly fluctuating business cycles can drag down many more operations. Yet since the mid-19th century capitalist development has tended to fall into distinct phases, running close to half a century at a time. Each phase involved significantly new investment patterns, managerial systems, state institutions and policies, social programs and practices, and cultural resources – what has been called "social structures of accumulation."[22]

A distinct phase, which began in the 1890s, is often referred to as the age of "monopoly" or corporate capitalism and the era of the Second Industrial Revolution. Towards the close of the 19th century the industrial world reflected huge changes that had taken place since the first stirring of an Industrial Revolution in the 1840s. The craft workshop and family household had already been replaced as the primary sites of production for a wide range of goods, which were now turned out in larger, more centralized workplaces known as "manufactories" or factories. New modes of work and work discipline were solidly established. New recruitment patterns for a workforce of wage-earners had drawn in many newcomers, including women and children. New household economies had emerged to sustain those wage-earners. New state policies had been put in place to promote all this development and to guarantee the untrammelled rights of private property. New forces reshaped cultural life, emphasizing individual self-discipline and constraint. New classes emerged. As more people settled into a life of more or less full-time wage-earning, the first working-class organizations appeared to promote and defend their class interests. By the 1890s a particular kind of industrial-capitalist society had congealed.[23]

This book is concerned with the ways in which the key elements of that first phase of industrial capitalism were reconstructed, starting with the emergence of the corporation as the dominant economic unit in much of the economy. That phenomenon quickly extended to new workplace regimes, new social programs and state policies, new cultural forces, and new working-class responses at home, in the paid workplace, and in public life, so much so that by the 1920s a starkly different kind of industrial-capitalist society had taken shape in Canada. Yet its instability persisted, and the economic slumps of the years between the two world wars provoked widespread concern and debate. A solution was ultimately found in a new, more interventionist role for the state during World War Two, which continued to some extent after the war. A new phase of capitalist development thus began in the 1940s.

To understand the distinctiveness of the years between 1890 and 1940, then, is to be constantly aware of what went before and what followed. Much historical writing in Canada and other industrialized countries has tended to assume some kind of dramatic watershed at the turn of the 20th century that brought the working class to its knees, under the combined onslaught of mass production and mass culture.[24] But studies of the onset of industrialization decades earlier should make us suspicious of that perspective. We now know that the First Industrial Revolution involved many continuities with the past – industrial paternalism, limited mechanization, survival of craft skills, and older patterns of domestic production, for example.[25] As we turn to the early 20th century, we will be watching for the ways in which social change was not simply imposed, but negotiated, so that, by the end of the period, changes in working-class life might not seem quite so catastrophic.

Why Hamilton?

What is the most appropriate framework for a study in working-class history? Biographies can sometimes allow for a sensitive treatment of the social context in which a particular figure operated.[26] At the other extreme, nationwide studies allow writers to make broad strokes on a vast canvas and to fashion compelling international comparisons.[27] But it is difficult to synthesize the diversity of working-class experience within one nation-state into a single picture. Some writers preferred to narrow their focus to workers across a single industry. They got closer to the rhythms of particular occupational groups, but their gaze seldom left the world of wage-earning.[28] Many other writers chose single towns or cities for tightly focused "community studies," addressing various aspects of working and living in particular towns and cities. Many thought they were writing case studies of a larger social experience that could be easily generalized. Others insisted on the integrity and distinctiveness of particular local experiences that could be no more than suggestive of broader trends.[29]

I chose to study Hamilton initially because it was the largest of Canada's predominantly industrial centres in the early 20th century and nurtured key new industries of Canada's Second Industrial Revolution. It is the largest of a cluster of manufacturing centres in south-central and southwestern Ontario, and thus conveys a taste of the regional flavour of such communities as Peterborough, Brantford, Kitchener-Waterloo, and Windsor. Through a wider lens, its industrial specialization makes it similar to other larger sites of heavy industry scattered around the Great Lakes, such as Cleveland and Buffalo, and to some extent at least, with some industrial centres on other continents. Its large population also puts it into the range of the big-city experience

in Canada alongside Montreal, Toronto, Winnipeg, and Vancouver. So, in many ways, Hamilton resembled many other North American towns and cities in which a substantial portion of the population relied on wage-earning for survival. This book is therefore self-consciously comparative and draws insights from a huge variety of studies of comparable geographical entities on both sides of the Atlantic (and beyond).

Hamilton was like other places in part because it was exposed to countless outside influences. It encountered the same new trends in management, retailing, social reform, public health, and popular culture that percolated throughout the continent in the early 20th century. Its workers also felt the effects of such state policies and programs as tariffs, immigration, industrial relations, and warfare. Moreover, the early 20th century was a period of human migration on an enormous scale. Workers moved into a city like Hamilton and often moved on again, looking for new jobs or heading home. People arrived with diverse experiences – from British and US industrial centres to Polish and Italian peasant villages. They carried with them distinctive practices, but also, as they moved about, helped to generalize certain kinds of social and cultural processes. Many settled residents maintained close links with kin in a previous homeland, or travelled outside the city – and the country – often for conferences and conventions. They read newspapers and magazines that connected them with ideas and events far away. Hamilton's workers were certainly part of a much larger world.

The city at the western head of Lake Ontario nonetheless also stood on its own. Its workforce was unusually dependent on factory jobs. Labour had its own particular ethnic and racial complexion and a distinctive history of social conflict and accommodation. The city differed sharply from coal-mining towns, company-owned mill towns, or major ports. It was not a metropolitan centre with radiating transportation links or a government town brimming with goods and services for state officials and closely related voluntary associations. Moreover, on a daily basis, its working people, like those in all other industrial centres, did not operate on a national or regional scale (unlike their corporate employers), but were enmeshed in local practices and relationships. Life was lived locally. Arguably, class awareness most often found voice primarily at this level. For all the similarities and cross-influences, there was no "typical" industrial centre with a "typical" working-class population. National or continental working-class experience was the sum of these small parts, with their mixture of similarities and striking diversity.

This book is a local study, not a case study, but it attempts to draw out how Hamilton workers shared the larger working-class experience across Canada and the United States in the years between 1890 and 1940. It attempts to reveal local variations and adaptations within the larger picture – and thus to speak not just about one city's workers but also about many more who lived hundreds of miles away.

PART I

The View from the Mountain

2

Hobson's Hamilton

HAMILTON WAS NEVER A COMPANY TOWN, nor was it ever in the grip of a single industry. So all eyes were not on one industrial patriarch who dominated the city's life, as they might have been in a British Columbia coal town or the auto town of Oshawa, Ontario.[1] Yet between the 1890s and the 1920s, one man stood out as a particularly influential figure in shaping the industrial landscape of Hamilton.

Robert Hobson acquired a social and economic stature within the local business community to match his robust, dignified, six-foot-four frame and jaunty, convivial manner. Hobson, trained as a civil engineer, married the daughter of a prominent iron merchant who was at the centre of the city's new primary iron and steel company in the mid-1890s. He moved quickly to the top of that firm, joined the boards of several other local and national corporations, and gave time to promoting local economic and social development. He filled high offices in broader business organizations concerned with public policy, and was consulted by national governments. He was certainly "a great captain of industry," with a high ranking across the continent, but, even more, he was a kind of industrial statesman who, along with a handful of others, gave leadership to Hamilton's version of the Canadian bourgeoisie in the early 20th century.[2]

A new Hamilton emerged after 1900 – new industries, new structures of economic power, new arrangements of urban space, new public and private cultures, all of which reflected the aspirations of the small circle of men and

Robert Hobson. (HPL)

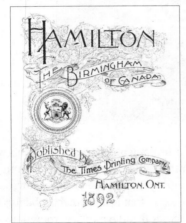

This 1892 promotional booklet was the first in Hamilton to feature photographs of industrial and commercial buildings and public institutions.

Over the years bourgeois Hamiltonians would re-create the city in countless ways and lay down the broad terrain on which other social groups had to build a life that met their own needs and concerns – from middle-class doctors to street-corner shopkeepers to wage-earning factory workers and working-class housewives. The growing power of the bourgeois elite enabled them to remain in the driver's seat, but the road could be rough and unpredictable as they encountered many challenges from below.[3]

The Ambitious City

At the turn of the century, Robert Hobson volunteered to help Hamilton civic officials coax new manufacturers to set up factories in the city. He no doubt handed them promotional literature that advertised the area's distinctive advantages and virtues. The pamphlets and booklets that the city fathers produced over the years are far from objective studies of local resources, but they are benchmarks of the city's development. In 1892, for instance – despite being in the midst of a decade that brought hard times to Hamilton, as it did throughout most of urban Canada[4] – civic boosters were not deterred from producing a glossy, oversized booklet that staked out the city's claim to industrial prominence as "The Birmingham of Canada." The booklet was chock full of detail about individual firms and their owners, products, and, inevitably, successes.

Anyone leafing through these pages would have been struck by how most of the Hamilton success stories were factories. Few other business activities of any size found their way into the publication – only a few wholesaling or financial firms, no railways shops, and no major port facilities, despite the city's location at the head of Lake Ontario. Even more striking was how many different commodities were being turned out. After four decades of industrialization, Hamilton's

women who shared Hobson's vision. To be sure, this was a story of how a dominant class enhanced its power and wealth, but it also involved their successful reframing of popular "common sense" about economy, politics, culture, and society. In particular, the vision of this group cast the most important new institution of industrial capitalism, the privately owned corporation, as the quintessence of progressive modernity. They made its promotion and protection central to the development of the surrounding community and raised its highly undemocratic internal dynamics to the status of universal template for the rest of society.

entrepreneurs were producing goods to satisfy almost every consumer taste – beer, pork, glass, furniture, cutlery, carriages and wagons, lamps, wooden ware, sundry leather goods, vinegar, coffins, pianos and organs, drugs, shoe polish, and countless other products. Some of the larger enterprises, such as Senator W.E. Sanford's ready-made clothing company, two good-size cotton mills, John McPherson's shoe factory, and George Tuckett's tobacco plant, were even reaching out to a national market. The reader did not have to look too hard to discover why the city was being compared to Birmingham. Metal goods were particularly prominent. Among the city's most distinctive products were cast-iron stoves and furnaces, especially those manufactured by the Gurney-Tilden Company, one of the country's biggest foundries. The Sawyer-Massey Company, a subsidiary of the Massey firm in Toronto since 1889, turned out farm machinery, and other local firms manufactured engines, wire products, iron pipes, tin cans, and structural iron. The Ontario Rolling Mills also kept up a flow of heavier producer-goods (materials to be used by other industries). The heads of these firms were almost all local men who had built up their businesses over the previous 40 years.[5]

In 1913, in honour of Hamilton's centennial, the city council proudly produced a smaller but fatter book that reveals how much could change in two decades. The thick 200-page volume informed visitors of the city's astonishing industrial achievements on display in the Centennial Industrial Exposition. There was now a small railway, the Toronto, Hamilton, and Buffalo, to connect with the major lines running through the region and to service local industry. Still, although many firms found the harbour useful for their own shipping needs, Hamilton was not a major transportation hub. Nor did this book report any new growth of financial institutions.

Instead, it presented a picture of a city dominated even more thoroughly by factories. There were many more of them – in the previous three years alone, over 30 new plants worth more than $6 million had started up production. The visitor clutching this handbook would certainly have been encouraged to ride a streetcar out into the new east-end district on the narrow plain below Hamilton Mountain, where the largest and newest factories were locating.[6]

The centrepiece of the factory district was the sprawling plant of the Steel Company of Canada, eventually known as Stelco. Since the turn of the century, many large new firms had located production facilities near that site, notably the massive plants of International Harvester and Canadian Westinghouse. Mostly these newcomers turned out heavy producer-goods. A few of the older firms serving the consumer market, especially Tuckett Tobacco and Sawyer-Massey, had grown and expanded. A few large canning operations benefited from the city's place in the heart of Ontario's market-gardening area. The ready-made clothing business was larger, and the textile industry now included booming knit-goods factories. Yet it was metalworking and metal fabrication that now overshadowed all else in the city's industrial life. All this production was facilitated by the huge hydro-electric facilities that the centennial book highlighted. Dominion Power (initially as Cataract Power) had been transmitting cheap power from DeCew Falls just outside the city since 1897 and had won for Hamilton the new nickname of "The Electric City of Canada."

The city's handbook would also have confirmed visitors' visual impressions that many new names had appeared over the factory gates. The city boasted that its 45 US-owned companies worth over $35 million had brought in "more United States capital . . . than any other Canadian city, and more than likely, in all the cities of Ontario combined." Corporations, both domestic and foreign, now seemed much more important than did individual entrepreneurs. Hamilton had evidently moved into a new phase of industrial development based on much larger units of production, much more specialization on a narrower range of producer-goods, and much more external control.[7]

By the late 1920s the city's industrial commissioner was routinely publishing smaller booklets to promote the city's assets. By then, revealingly, most of the older consumer-goods industries that had dotted the industrial landscape of the 1890s, including the venerable Sanford clothing firm and all the old stove foundries, had disappeared from the printed pages. In the commissioner's glowing reports on industrial success, the original downtown manufacturing district figured hardly at all. The survivors were the local enterprises that had joined in the specialization in iron and steel production and fabrication and, to a lesser degree, in textile production. The east-end factory district had several large new plants, most of them US branch operations. Generally, the trends evident in 1913 had been consolidated, though some surprising postwar newcomers, notably Firestone Tire and Rubber, were present. The commissioner had even dropped references to Hamilton as the Canadian Birmingham, now using the more appropriate title of "The Pittsburgh of Canada."[8]

A great transformation had clearly taken place over the decades.[9] How had such massive changes come about? The driving force behind industrial growth in the second half of the 19th century had been the remarkable aggressiveness of the city's capitalists, who had won for Hamilton yet another long-standing nickname, "The Ambitious City." At mid-century they had aspired to turn the community that nurtured their businesses into a commercial metropolis rivalling Toronto, but by the 1870s that vision had been shattered. Instead their goal became to create the country's pre-eminent industrial centre. In that process, local capitalists not only expanded their own enterprises but co-operated with other local businessmen to promote the competitive advantage of the city's industries generally. This was a pattern of economic development attempted in many Canadian towns and cities in the late 19th and early 20th centuries, but Hamilton's businessmen had an unusually strong collective identity. Within the general context of national tariff protection and industrial development through import substitution, they had shown an early readiness to pool their resources in local business projects. A web of interlocking directorships provided solid evidence of their commitment to capitalist co-operation for community development. The Bank of Hamilton, founded in 1872, had been one of the first examples of this spirit, as was the promotion of the Hamilton and Ontario cotton companies a decade later. But the most dramatic evidence of capitalist solidarity came in the 1890s.[10]

Local iron merchants, foundrymen, and other industrialists in the metal shops had concluded that the city needed a primary iron and steel producer to supply their needs, to reach the wider Canadian market, and to attract other manufacturers into their midst. With new federal and provincial bounties on the domestic production of iron and steel, the Hamilton capitalists lost no time in promoting such an enterprise. The city's treasury was raided in 1892 to provide a generous grant of $100,000, a free 75-acre site, and long-term tax reductions. A group of US businessmen who had been scouting several Canadian cities, including Toronto, responded promptly but encountered recurrent financial problems over the following three years. Gradually more and more Hamilton capital was drawn into the project, until by December 1895 the Americans had been displaced and all the directors were local merchants and manufacturers, including Robert Hobson's father-in-law, A.T. Wood.[11] The elaborate festivities held to mark the opening of a new iron "smelter" that month left no doubt that the venture – then known as the Hamilton Blast Furnace Company – would be the core of a vast new industrial expansion. A local member of Parliament told the celebratory banquet: "Many other industries of a similar character must necessarily follow in its train, and make this the iron manufacturing center of the Dominion."[12] Some five years later all of Hamilton's leading businessmen again joined forces, this time in collaboration with US and British capitalists, to open a nickel refinery and nickel-steel plant in the city.[13] The project collapsed, but local industrialists and financiers had demonstrated their eagerness to use primary iron and steel production as the basis for diversification into technologically more sophisticated industries.[14]

In the first decade of the 20th century it was increasingly clear that Toronto and Montreal were the big winners in this urban rivalry. Financier-industrialists in those two cities were consolidating control over larger expanses of the Canadian economy through powerful new corporations that absorbed independent units of production, distribution, and finance. That process has often been described as the dawn of "monopoly" capitalism since there was a drive within each industry to eliminate as much competition as possible and to consolidate monopolistic or, more commonly, oligopolistic control of particular markets. The concentration and centralization of economic activity that resulted reshaped the Canadian economy towards more national integration and regional specialization.

The small plant of the Hamilton Steel and Iron Company, shown here around 1900, had begun production a year earlier. (HPL)

The Maritimes were reduced to colonial status, the West was restricted to a resource-extraction role, and the economic independence of individual cities within a region like Southern Ontario was increasingly eroded.[15] Many Hamilton firms were coaxed into mergers organized from Montreal and Toronto,[16] but in general the consolidation movement of the pre-war years had a more limited effect on industry in Hamilton than it did in Toronto. When the next wave of corporate mergers hit in the 1920s, however, several more concerns were swallowed up into larger corporations, most notably the Bank of Hamilton, which was absorbed into the Bank of Commerce in 1924, and Dominion Power, which merged into Power Corporation. Thus two of Hamilton's largest independent bases of economic power passed into outside hands.[17]

Hamilton's capitalists viewed this process of national integration cautiously but with a keen eye on opportunities for themselves. In general, although many of them would remain locally based, they accepted the new economic order of continental corporate capitalism and looked for a secure, profitable place within it. Several enterprising local men set out to join the merger mania. The first, and most controversial,

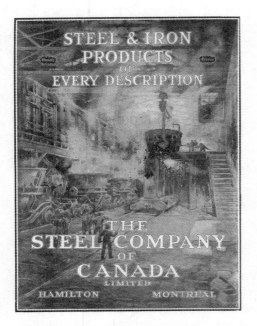

By the end of World War One the Steel Company of Canada had become the largest, most diversified manufacturer of primary steel products in the country. (*CM*, 3 July 1919, 3)

corporate giant created in Hamilton had been Cataract Power, organized in 1897 and rechristened Dominion Power in 1907. By that date the company not only controlled extensive facilities for generating and distributing hydro-electric power in Hamilton's hinterland, but also owned the Hamilton Street Railway and all the local electric railway lines.[18] Equally well publicized were mergers in the iron and steel industry. In 1899 Hamilton Blast Furnace and Ontario Rolling Mills joined forces to establish the Hamilton Steel and Iron Company, and eight years later the Ontario Tack Company and Canada Screw Company merged under the latter's name. All of these firms were then swallowed up in the creation of the Steel Company of Canada in 1910, which brought together most of the existing companies in the finishing end of Ontario's iron and steel production located in Hamilton,

Montreal, Belleville, Gananoque, Swansea, and Brantford. Montreal and Hamilton capital held the dominant interest in the new corporation, but initially effective control rested with Hamilton's experienced ironmasters.[19]

Playing the merger game was only a small part of the local business community's defensive strategy in the face of emergent corporate capitalism. Plenty of room remained for competition between urban communities to attract and hold fragments of the new corporations or to nourish smaller, related enterprises. In these efforts Hamilton's capitalists found ready and willing allies south of the border in the form of large manufacturing corporations that were eager to expand into Canada in search of new markets.[20] The Hamilton men simply had to convince those firms to locate their branch plants in the Ambitious City rather than elsewhere in the region. The city's advantages for US capitalists were its available land – especially harbourfront locations for convenient shipping on the Great Lakes – good railway connections, its central location in North America's industrial heartland, cheap electric power, primary iron and steel industry, a pool of diversified labour, and ready access to consumers in Canada and the British Empire more broadly.

The National Policy had been designed, in part, to entice US capital to leap over the tariff wall,[21] but, while a few US capitalists had invested in Hamilton in the 1880s, no significant branch plants arrived before the opening of the small Westinghouse Air Brake works in 1897. There was nonetheless a well-developed policy of municipal bonuses and tax concessions that could be used to entice more manufacturers.[22] The first major catch after the turn of the century was the Deering Harvester Company. In 1902 Hobson was among the civic and business leaders who convinced the Chicago-based company to locate its Canadian operations in Hamilton, and plans were announced to construct a huge plant next to the Hamilton Steel and Iron Company. Negotiations for a $50,000 bonus from the city ended abruptly when a referendum vote failed to give the necessary bylaw enough positive votes, thanks in large part to the campaign of the local Trades and Labor Council against this renowned anti-labour corporation. As a compromise embarrassed civic officials agreed to annex into the city a large chunk of Barton Township, which included the Deering site, and to assess any industry locating in this district at the current township rate (approximately one-third of the city rate) for the next 15 years – a deal probably worth more than $50,000. Shortly afterward Deering became part of the new US agricultural implement merger, International Harvester.[23]

The Hamilton elite did not wait for such firms to come calling. Early in the new century, Hobson and other city businessmen helped the municipal government with a major booster campaign to advertise the advantages of locating in the city – a campaign paralleled in countless North American cities in this period.[24] Business interests in the city began producing lavish brochures and magazines, publications that eventually became known as the *Made-In-Hamilton Quarterly*. Early in 1909 a large group of manufacturers, merchants, and local politicians also created a new promotional organization, the Greater Hamilton Association, in an apparent effort to make building up the city's industrial potential a movement with wide popular support.[25] That year a Hamilton *Spectator* journalist, William Muliss, became the city's full-time industrial commissioner, assigned to carry on this promotional work, and over the next two decades he and his successors coaxed growing numbers of national and transnational corporations to locate branch factories in Hamilton.[26]

The local business community liked to turn factory production into popular culture by inviting the public into exhibitions of industrial goods. In this case, the Greater Hamilton Exposition was held at the city's short-lived Maple Leaf amusement park. (HPL)

Not surprisingly, the trickle of branch plants soon became a flood, reaching nearly 100 by 1920. One of the most important was the massive expansion of Westinghouse's Hamilton operations in 1904 in order to manufacture a wider range of the corporation's electrical products. Westinghouse was to be Hamilton's largest single employer throughout the half-century before 1940.[27]

This American penetration of Hamilton's economic life followed an interesting pattern. With the important exception of International Harvester, the American firms tended to produce goods requiring technical competence that was weak or non-existent in Canada. Corporations such as Westinghouse expanded into Canada, as they were doing in Britain and Europe, on the basis of their unique industrial strengths. In Hamilton they tended to fill gaps in the industrial structure rather than to take over or compete directly with Canadian industry. In any case, given the boosterism and community aggrandizement involved in the bonusing of US branch plants in the years down to World War One, little concern was expressed for the wider impact on the Canadian economy. The aim seems to have been primarily to strengthen each city in its competitive struggle for survival with larger centres, especially Toronto. Each large branch plant made that survival more possible. In city council debates over the Deering bonus, supporters of the corporation emphasized that its production would not compete with the local farm-equipment producer, Sawyer-Massey, without ever mentioning Massey-Harris in Toronto. Hamilton capitalists seemed to be setting the pace for other community businessmen in allying themselves with US capital as a strategy for industrial growth.[28]

Paradoxically, inviting in the Americans made sense to otherwise protectionist businessmen in Hamilton (and other Southern Ontario centres).[29] More firms, covering more industrial sectors, would broaden the possibilities for new Canadian investment in related industries. They would bring in more workers to purchase the products of Canadian industry (which was generally strongest in the consumer-goods industries) and would provide a market for the iron and steel industry, which had been quickly recognized as the underpinning of the city's success. Moreover, Hamilton capitalists may have hoped in time to "Canadianize" the control of some of these companies, as they had done with the local rolling mills and the screw, tack, and blast-furnace companies.[30] Whatever the explanation, two of the city's industrial giants,

International Harvester and the Steel Company of Canada, nestled side by side on the Hamilton waterfront, symbolizing the collaboration of local and foreign capital that generated the industrial growth of the period.

By the 1920s there were still many enterprises based in Hamilton and locally controlled. They were not all moribund remnants of an earlier age. Many were relatively new companies that had benefited from the opportunities opened up by the new investment of so much domestic and foreign capital. Some found a lucrative niche producing specialty products or ancillary industrial services within the growing iron and steel complex.[31] Some of the small metalworking firms even did jobbing work for the bigger companies, including Westinghouse. Other manufacturers, notably the clothing manufacturer Coppley, Noyes, and Randall and the Imperial Cotton Company, carved out spots for themselves in the clothing and textile sectors. Hamilton also became one of the country's leading centres for the production of knit goods.[32] For some of these smaller firms, the newly intensified competition was painful, and the companies in stove and knit-good production eventually sought stability in the late-19th-century solution of industry associations. In general, however, these firms differed from their predecessors. They were most often joint-stock companies, not the enterprises of individual entrepreneurs or private partnerships. They also operated in much larger national and continental markets and co-existed with the Hamilton branches of corporate empires with headquarters far from the city. The economic life of the city had passed from a locally based to a national and continental framework. Industrial growth that had once depended almost completely on local initiative now had to fit the imperatives of the larger world of a more expansive capitalism.

Capitalist willpower alone, however, could not guarantee success when the larger structures of Canadian capitalism were unreceptive. Indeed, the new national economy of the early 20th century was chronically unstable. Hamilton's industrialists (and their workers) would soon discover the exhilaration and panic of the city's roller-coaster ride of peaks and troughs. Between the 1890s and 1920s Hamilton unquestionably looked like a boomtown, with thousands of new jobs opening up in factories and on construction sites, but that growth came in fits and starts. The swings of the business cycle brought severe downturns in 1907–9, 1913–15, 1920–26, and for most of the decade after 1929.[33]

The cycles of expansion and contraction fit into the larger national and international patterns of financing, investment, production, and overproduction. Canadian manufacturers, especially the Hamilton men, were operating on a particularly fragile, uncertain base. At various times, groups of manufacturers, such as the city's stove foundrymen, the Steel Company, and the textile firms, wailed loudly about the destructive competition they faced in the new wider markets, and especially about the US practice of "dumping" excess goods on the Canadian market at cutthroat prices.[34]

Still more serious problems were built into the structure of the fragile new national economy. Like most Canadian manufacturers, Hamilton's industries produced for an expanding domestic market, including the great new population of Prairie farmers who were responsible for the country's leading export, wheat. Hamilton's commerce and industry were particularly attuned to the needs of the Western farmer. Grain production in Canada was extremely unstable, however, responding to the vagaries of the weather and the volatile international market. Farmers frequently lacked the income

to buy manufactured products. In 1922 Hobson urged the people of Hamilton to "pray that the farmers may have better crops next year."[35] Prayer did not prevent the city from suffering through nearly 20 years of severe depression in the first four decades of the 20th century.

By 1930 Hamilton, then, had changed from a city of smallish factories run by local capitalists to a manufacturing centre dominated by huge plants owned by large corporations, both national and transnational, which commanded much larger pools of capital, organized far larger sites and networks of production, and reached much larger markets. In place of the diversified production of the late 19th century was a new concentration on iron and steel production and, to a lesser extent, textile manufacturing. Holding the levers of power was a transformed capitalist elite – sober, confident, increasingly aloof, powerful, and unified by shared interests in promoting the economic well-being of their firms and by the desire to maintain their social hegemony.

Bigwigs

Robert Hobson and his business associates were a vigorous, ambitious, tightly knit group. While the men maintained a remarkable unity of purpose and activity, their ranks nonetheless contained visible clusters and strata. The most powerful and illustrious fraction of the Hamilton elite had its roots in the dynamic entrepreneurship of the late 19th century, but it now commanded superior economic resources. The great wholesale merchants who had once been at the pinnacle of local society – men like Hobson's father-in-law, A.T. Wood – had been eclipsed by those with their feet solidly in both finance and industry. They increasingly operated through proliferating directorships in larger corporate units; they participated in a wider sphere that went beyond Hamilton alone. These local "captains of industry," who wielded the most clout in shaping the process of industrial growth in the city, were being drawn into an emerging national capitalist class, which by the 1920s occupied the commanding heights of the new, more integrated Canadian economy.[36]

A striking characteristic of these big capitalists was overlapping memberships on the boards of directors of several of the city's large enterprises. One group centred in the iron and steel industry moved in the last years before the war into control of several other Hamilton companies, notably Sawyer-Massey and Tuckett Tobacco.[37] A second group controlled Dominion Power and extended into the textile sector.[38] Plenty of crossovers existed, particularly in financial institutions such as the Bank of Hamilton and the Hamilton Provident and Loan Society, and by World War One the directorships of the two groups were converging even more.[39] An extremely important link was William J. Southam, publisher of the city's largest newspaper, the *Spectator*. Southam's many directorships included the Steel Company and Cataract/Dominion Power, and his newspaper promoted and defended local business interests.[40]

These corporate magnates were becoming less tied to one industry alone, and many were being drawn into larger webs of corporate power centred in Toronto or Montreal. Hobson, for example, was vice-president of Canada Steamship Lines and a director of the Canadian Locomotive Company (in Kingston), Toronto General Trusts, General Accident Insurance, North Star Oil and Refining (Winnipeg), Canadian Northern Railway, and, after 1924, the Bank of Commerce,[41] while Dominion Power's John M. Gibson was a director of the Bank of Commerce, Canada Life Assurance, Toronto General Trusts, and Dominion Telegraph.[42] By the 1920s these and other Hamilton capitalists were moving in the highest circles of the Canadian corporate elite. They also held office in the leading national business organizations. Hobson was president of the Canadian Manufacturers' Association (CMA) in 1908 and joined the executive of the Canadian Reconstruction Association in 1918.[43]

This coalescence of a Canadian *haute bourgeoisie* was one of the most important changes in Hamilton's economic life before 1940. A few of the city's most prominent businessmen were gradually losing their strong community orientation and assuming the mantle of national statesmen of industry. The shift in their commitment was evident in 1915, when a well-substantiated rumour floated through the city that the Royal Bank was about to absorb the Bank of Hamilton. The city's Board of Control "vigorously and unanimously" opposed the merger as a threat to Hamilton's prosperity and independence. A protest meeting drew out several municipal politicians, small businessmen, and a few labour leaders to register public indignation at the move. Hobson, however, rose in the meeting to defend the big national banks. He insisted, "It is in the public's interest that the amalgamation should go through." Although the deal fell apart, the new loyalties of the city's corporate magnates had been laid bare for all to see.[44] The same attitude probably helps to explain the absence of these men from local politics by World War One, in contrast to the marked civic activism of Hamilton's leading businessmen in earlier decades.[45]

A second recognizable fragment of the local capitalist class consisted of the managers of the major local branch plants. For the most part, these men did not figure prominently in the ruling circles of Hamilton industry and commerce because they ranked only as middle-range executives who simply conducted their factories according to policies laid down in the head offices of the US corporations. A few, however, were integrated into the upper reaches of the local elite and participated prominently in the public life of the city. In particular, the general managers of the city's two largest American firms, International Harvester and Canadian Westinghouse, could not be ignored. Paul J. Myler, Westinghouse's US-born vice-president and general manager, was an intimate of the most powerful capitalists in the city and held directorships in several major Canadian financial and industrial corporations.[46]

The third and by far largest group of Hamilton capitalists included the numerous industrialists in control of smaller local factories. These included the likes of foundrymen John Milne and John Tilden and wire-goods manufacturer S.O. Greening, all of whom had built up substantial enterprises well before the turn of the century, as well as the crowd of newcomers who set up metalworking, clothing, or textile businesses after 1900.[47] In contrast to their corporate big brothers, these smaller-scale capitalists retained a commitment to the Hamilton community as their base of operations and took a keener interest in its local social life and political development. From this large pool of entrepreneurial and managerial talent came most of the capitalists who entered political life in Hamilton.

Despite these gradations of power and status among Hamilton capitalists (with plenty of room for conflict or disagreement), an essential unity of purpose, a will to work together to expand, diversify, and enhance the profit-making potential of Hamilton's business life, held sway. Quiet evenings in the Hamilton Club or private discussions in various corporate boardrooms were no doubt the regular channels for mutual support, but there were also formal public institutions in which the city's industrial magnates assembled to pursue their common goals. The oldest was the Board of Trade, originally founded in 1845 and moribund in the early years of the 20th century before being thoroughly revitalized in 1911 (and then transformed into a Chamber of Commerce in 1920). This rebirth was actually part of a wave of new energy exhibited by local capitalists as the clouds of the 1907–9 depression began to lift. The creation of the Greater Hamilton Association in 1909 was followed a year later by the launching of the Hamilton branch of the Canadian Manufacturers' Association, with Hobson as its first chairman, Arthur F. Hatch of Canada Steel Goods as vice-chairman, and W.R. Dunn of International Harvester as treasurer. By the outbreak of World War One, nearly 200 local firms sent representatives to the CMA's monthly meetings to discuss questions of the tariff, technical education, transportation and energy problems, and a variety of labour-related issues including workers' compensation and the wages of civic employees. These organizations did more than draw local businessmen together behind closed doors. They helped promote Hamilton's advantages to outside firms and lobbied governments on a wide range of issues. They also worked at building popular support for their enterprises and the products manufactured there. The Board of Trade began organizing an annual Industrial Day for manufacturers to open their doors to visitors and put together a gala week of events in August 1913 to celebrate Hamilton's centennial. They strove to make sure that the factory (and its owners) remained at the centre of public consciousness.[48]

The business life of Hamilton was peopled with men, but the women in these upper-class families often took a keen interest in the marketplace. Thanks to a series of married women's property laws passed in Ontario in the second half of the 19th century, women had more control over their own property and exercised a fair

J.M. Gibson and J.S. Hendrie were prominent members of Hamilton's social elite who, while maintaining active business careers, entered provincial politics and became cabinet ministers: Gibson as a Liberal, Hendrie as a Conservative. Each was eventually rewarded with an appointment as lieutenant-governor.

(HPL)

directors of numerous social institutions – the hospitals and charities, social-welfare agencies such as the Children's Aid Society, Babies Dispensary Guild, and Canadian Patriotic Fund (CPF), youth groups such as the Young Men's Christian Association (YMCA) and Boy Scouts, the Rotary and Kiwanis clubs, and much, much more. In a similar way, they provided leadership for the city's two pre-war regiments of part-time soldiers – the militia. Indeed, military paraphernalia provided many leading men in this class with symbols of their power and status, lending a decidedly British and Tory cast to upper-class life in the city. John Gibson, John S. Hendrie, and Col. S.C. Mewburn were particularly prominent in the Canadian military, and World War One swept up even more of the local capitalists into military fervour.

Their wives and daughters were even more active in the creation and administration of voluntary organizations for charity, child welfare, and public morality. The desire to cast their mothering functions over wider social spheres led these women onto the boards of the Young Women's Christian Association (YWCA), Hamilton Health Association, Playgrounds Association, and Baby Welfare Association, among others. They also took special responsibility for nurturing the new institutions of "high" culture, including the symphony orchestra, Elgar Choir, and Hamilton Art Gallery (opened in 1914), often in the face of indifference from business and civic leaders (despite the ongoing efforts of these women, the small, poorly housed art gallery was known as one of the worst in the country by the 1930s). The Imperial Order Daughters of the Empire (IODE), founded in 1900, also gave large numbers of upper-class women the space to promote a wider political vision of British imperial fervour. Not only did the Order promote imperial consciousness in local schools with

amount of independence in their investments, which typically included real estate, banks, mortgages, and some industrial stocks. Sometimes their husbands managed this capital, but not always, and many single and widowed women made investment decisions on their own. In the early 20th century, widows generally faced fewer constraints on the use of their inheritances than they had experienced in the past.[49]

The power of the city's industrialists also extended beyond the economic sphere to all three levels of the state. Perhaps even more importantly, men like Hobson undertook a kind of stewardship role to help regulate the city's social life through their memberships on boards of regular donations of flags and cadet equipment, but also, immediately after its formation, it organized a large exhibition of Canadian manufacturing. In addition it spearheaded a major project to combat tuberculosis. The umbrella group for all of this elite female activity was the Local Council of Women, founded in 1893.[50]

The men of this new economic elite were mostly born in the 1850s and 1860s. They generally had no more than public high-school education and, while rarely rising from rags to riches, most often had not been born into great wealth.[51] Yet by the turn of the century their business success was allowing them to create more distance from less-well-off, subordinate groups in the city. They left behind the mid-19th-century notion that they should guarantee social cohesion by maintaining close contact with other classes, residentially and socially.[52] Instead they struck a posture of aloof paternalism, and in their private lives wrapped themselves in a new cocoon of social exclusiveness. There they cultivated a refinement of taste and civility of manners that were woven into a new class culture and performed in conscious opposition to "coarser" popular cultures.[53]

On the way home from his east-end office, Robert Hobson probably stopped off at the private Hamilton Club for drinks and chats with the city's other male corporate leaders. Like several Hamilton businessmen, he also held memberships in private men's clubs in Montreal, Ottawa, and Toronto for his sojourns in those cities. He headed back to his home in the neighbourhood of mansions in the southwest corner of the city, amidst the sylvan serenity of the lower slopes of Hamilton Mountain. There he could find an oasis of domestic opulence in huge rooms stuffed with ornate furniture, exotic bric-a-brac, large statuary, potted plants, crystal chandeliers, heavy drapes, and thick carpets.

Home of the Steel Company's Robert Hobson and his family. (HM, 1909-10, 43)

The men of Hamilton's ruling class enhanced their social leadership symbolically by donning the uniforms of military officers to lead pre-war militia exercises and wartime activities, usually far from the trenches. Here Col. J.M. Gibson (centre) visits Camp Valcartier in 1918. (HPL)

Like their counterparts in many parts of the Western world in this period, these families were turning away from earlier bourgeois prudery and asceticism towards more conspicuous displays of self-indulgent luxury. Hobson's wife and daughter presided over this lavish household (and its servants) and orchestrated the intricate social life that sustained the networks of kinship, friendship, and intimacy within the elite. The women of these households sustained rituals of formal sociability among bourgeois Hamiltonians through "at-homes," dinners, musicales, and balls.[54] Many children in such families were packed off to the city's expensive private schools – notably the Wesleyan Ladies'

The Hamilton Club was an exclusive space in the city for elite men to relax and network. (HPL , Bailey Collection)

The Hamilton Yacht Club, photographed here around 1914, provided summertime recreation for the wealthy of Hamilton. (CTA, Fonds 1244, Item 9012)

College (dating back to 1861) and the new High-field School for Boys, organized in 1901 with the active support of John Hendrie and John Gibson – or to such out-of-town institutions as the Upper Canada or Ridley colleges. "Growing up was a wonderful experience," a daughter of one of these households later recalled. "Going to Miss Walton's private school here, to Europe for finishing, then coming out. A huge reception in the afternoon, with friends of the older generation pouring [drinks]. At night a ball."[55]

Outside their homes, members of the elite participated in a class-segregated public sphere of cultural venues for theatre or music, which were restricted by the high price of admission and regulated by strict standards of propriety and gentility far removed from plebeian life, whether rough or respectable.[56] On Sunday mornings Hobson led his family to their pew in the elegant Central Presbyterian Church, no doubt nodding to many of his neighbours and business associates, almost all of whom chose this church or the Anglicans' Christ Church Cathedral for their weekly worship.[57] Humbler folk might be present at these events in theatres and churches, but they were kept at a distance in the cheap seats and galleries. Perhaps the Hobsons would later display their exalted respectability by joining other elite families in a promenade by carriage (or later by automobile) through the city's premier public park, Dundurn, undertaking a ritual of bourgeois sociability and providing a spectacle of social hierarchy that the hoi polloi could watch in respectful awe (until the practice died out in the interwar period).[58]

Generally, however, Hobson left his wife and daughter behind in his leisure time and went off to socialize with other upper-class men. Like virtually all of them, he was a Mason in the prestigious Scottish Rite. In the face of more sedentary managerial work lives, men like Hobson also turned with a passion to sports to prove their manliness. They joined the private clubs for each sport that had been appearing in Hamilton since the 1890s. There Hobson met men of his own social circle to golf, curl, sail a yacht, race horses, fish, or enjoy the outdoors.[59] For their part, women like Hobson's wife and daughter organized their own genteel social life. With servants to handle most domestic labour (the Hobsons had three in 1911),[60] these women had the time to open their own homes for special events or to travel to more public places in the city for special gatherings. For literary and cultural pleasures they turned to new organizations like the Wentworth Historical Society or the Women's Canadian Club, or they might have

In the southwest corner of the city, mansions sprouted to house Hamilton's upper class. This one, known as "Wesanford," was the family home of Senator W.E. Sanford, the city's leading clothing manufacturer.

(HPL; Head of the Lake Historical Society)

helped organize concerts of the Elgar Choir or the Ladies' String Orchestra. Those with an artistic flare might spend long hours in the Hamilton Art School or the sketch clubs of the Women's Art Association, and then display their work at the association's annual exhibitions. Far more often, however, socializing with women of their class was a by-product of their church and philanthropic activities, such as the high-society card parties set up by IODE branches to raise funds for the fight against tuberculosis.[61]

Many of these women developed life-long commitments to particular projects, and in the process displayed remarkable administrative and political acumen. Adelaide (Hunter) Hoodless, wife of a furniture manufacturer, was the driving force behind the launch of the local (and national) YWCA in the 1890s and the campaign for "domestic science" in the schools at the turn of the century. Sara (Galbraith) Calder, wife of a clothing manufacturer and a keen amateur artist, led the Women's Art Association for 20

years after its founding in 1894, and played a major role in getting the city's art gallery established in a permanent home in 1914. Elizabeth (Orr) Lyle, wife of the minister at the Central Presbyterian Church, threw herself into the anti-tuberculosis campaign through the Hamilton Health Association, while Marion (Stinson) Crerar, wife of a corporate lawyer, also vaulted into prominence through her leadership of the IODE. In the 1920s Annie (Cascaden) Carpenter,

The Wesleyan Ladies' College was a private school for upper-class girls. (HPL, Bailey Collection)

Mary Hawkins was one of the numerous women of Hamilton's upper class who ran private charities. Her many activities included the founding of Canada's first birth-control clinic. (HPL, Bailey Collection)

A new dominant social class thus took shape – a local version of Canada's bourgeoisie.[63] More than merely a visible group with common economic interests, it was a self-confident, ambitious, increasingly powerful social sector, highly conscious of its distinct status. It actively intervened economically, culturally, and politically to shape the city in ways that suited its needs. It was a class engaged in making itself.

Caught in the Middle

Civic officials and business leaders regularly made the factory, with its humming machinery, belching smoke, and happy workers the central symbol of Hamilton life. Yet, as a cultural metaphor, a factory can convey a misleading impression of a local class structure. As in other regions of capitalist society, Hamilton's population sorted itself into more than just the two most obvious classes of corporate industrialists and wage-earners. There had always been groups in the middle who were not caught up directly in those relations of production, even though they had to adapt to them in various ways. Since the mid-19th century an urban middle class had been an important component of local society,[64] but, as with other classes, its complexion was changing.

A core feature of middle-class people everywhere was their relative independence.[65] They were self-employed or, if female, children, disabled, or elderly, relied on the income of self-employed males in their family. They employed few, if any, workers, other than family members and perhaps a servant. They embodied both capital and labour. That group had once included a considerable range of small-scale businessmen, mostly male artisans and shopkeepers of either gender, who amassed relatively little wealth but maintained a degree of respectable comfort (often including a servant in the

another prominent lawyer's wife, took over the presidency of the Local Council of Women and, after years of activism in the Women's Liberal Association, ran (unsuccessfully) for the Ontario legislature in 1926. In the same interwar period, Mary (Chambers) Hawkins led the professionalization of social work in the city through new community agencies, including the country's first birth control clinic in 1932. The list of such women could go on and on.[62]

household). They developed a collective sense of their distinctiveness as a social group and their distance from both the "decadent" upper classes and the "disreputable" lower classes. This was the recruiting ground for self-improvers, evangelical Protestants, and temperance supporters. By the turn of the century, small-scale businessmen survived, but the scale of industrial development was leaving little room for the self-employed artisan beyond such figures as building contractors, tailors, shoe repairmen, or auto mechanics (a few women might be dressmakers or milliners).[66]

Retailing faced much slower incursions by corporate enterprises, and shopkeepers, both male and female, proliferated as the bulk of a large, diffuse "lower" middle class ("petite bourgeoisie"), who were modest property-holders, often spread out along streets through working-class neighbourhoods. They did not easily coalesce with other, more prosperous elements of the middle class, nor were they always welcome in such circles. Not only were they less well off and probably had less schooling, but after the turn of the century they became more ethnically diverse. While they might ape the lifestyle of the more genteel middle class, they could be construed as "the wrong kind of people." Their allegiances and daily associations might be more commonly with the working people around them – sitting together in the same lodge meetings or church pews, for example. Indeed, they might move back and forth between wage-earning and self-employment, especially in hard times, or help to get their adult sons into proletarian jobs. They were a fluid, profoundly ambivalent group, whose political allegiances could sometimes lean leftward.[67]

The more exalted elements of the older middling groups had always been the traditional professions – lawyers, doctors, and clergymen – who by the late 19th century were building their version of independence and respectability based not simply on their economic independence and considerable affluence, but on specific expertise gained through formal college training and self-government through professional societies. More occupations, including dentists, pharmacists, and architects, adopted the same mantle of authority. They were joined at the turn of the century by new groups of salaried professionals who earned high incomes and would play a significant role in the new workplace regime of the Second Industrial Revolution that the new corporations set in motion. They were notably engineers, accountants, and chemists, whose numbers multiplied by leaps and bounds.[68] Until the early 20th century, women emerging from middle-class families had extremely limited access to professional status other than through teaching, but by the 1920s many more of them were gaining a university training with expectations of better jobs before marriage. Some women in nursing, social work, and journalism had new professional aspirations, though, like teachers, they still rarely succeeded in the ways that their male counterparts did. Once married, female professionals left behind their occupational identities for domestic responsibilities.[69]

All these professional male and female groups had high levels of civic consciousness and developed their own maps of social problems, and their own solutions. They often mobilized to get action from the state and business – new management systems in factories, new approaches to poverty, new programs of public health, or new agendas for child care. Hamilton, for example, heard the voices of such outspoken advocates as James Roberts, the medical officer of health after 1905, and L.W. Gill, an electrical engineer and educational expert recruited to run the new

Hamilton Technical School in 1922.[70] These men and women had a strong sense of strict personal and public morality and were the main propagators of discourses to promote the disciplined body and mind throughout society. They were joiners, and appeared in the ranks of many voluntary organizations, from churches to moral-reform societies to public-health groups. They tended to be the "thinkers" in bourgeois Hamilton. They were more prone to wider reflection on social issues and remained the movers and shakers behind the local Canadian Club and the Hamilton Association for the Advancement of Literature, Science, and Art, whose lectures ranged from biology to, by World War One, psychology and social work, and contributed to a modest public intellectual culture.[71] McMaster University's decision to move from Toronto to Hamilton in 1930 finally brought academic content to these discussions. Middle-class professionals also had a keen sense of their entitlement as citizens and the importance of the state for regulating society. Yet most were not radical critics of the liberal-capitalist order. Instead they tried to contribute to its smoother functioning and collaborated willingly with members of the corporate elite on matters of common concern. Indeed, business organization and practices often provided the inspiration for the more "scientific," "efficient" programs and policies that middle-class professionals developed.[72]

Newcomers to the class structure made up a third element within the middling group. They were the new middle managers hired in growing numbers to handle the complexities of internal administration within the new corporations and, to a lesser extent, within the civil service at all three levels of government. Some of these men (there were virtually no women) had worked their way up the corporate job ladder and left behind more humble roots. Others had

undergone professional training – most commonly engineering or accounting – but their professional loyalties weakened inside the corporate bureaucracies in which they worked, and their devotion to the interests of their employers became paramount. Many of them began to participate in such wider industry associations as the National Electric Light Association or American Iron and Steel Institute, where common problems of corporate administration could be addressed.[73] They were also drawn to the new male service clubs that emerged after World War One (the Lions and Kinsmen, for example). As salaried employees they had compromised their independence, but they were well paid and exercised considerable autonomous power over workers and resources in particular departments – indeed, within their particular industrial bailiwicks they assumed a large part of the authority of the old-style entrepreneur. The ambitious, competitive climb up the corporate hierarchy allowed for a new expression of middle-class masculinity.[74] They stood apart from the expanding ranks of supposedly less responsible clerical workers, large numbers of them women, who handled the routine details of corporate administration. As a result, middle managers developed a strong sense of difference from the rest of the workforce, in both blue and white collars, that brought them into closer association with other well-heeled middle-class people.[75]

Hamilton's middle class in the early 20th century, then, might be seen as two loose clusterings of people whose livelihoods rested on different forms of non-manual labour, a "lower" group in shopkeeping and more menial clerical work (including large numbers of women) and an "upper" group with a considerable material stake in the system.[76] The members of the upper group were self-consciously and earnestly upright, self-disciplined, respectable, and intolerant of disorder in public or private life. Typically they had spent more years in school than had the average Hamiltonian, and associated their formal education with both expertise and refinement of taste. In Hamilton, they were the intellectuals. They were also almost invariably white and Anglo-Canadian and measured others outside those exclusive ranks against their own cultural yardstick. Some of the more affluent among them moved comfortably in the same clubs and churches as did the city's economic elite, and virtually all identified strongly with the main dynamics of the industrial-capitalist order. They had counterparts in cities across the continent, but their numbers were somewhat smaller in a city so narrowly focused on factory production.[77]

The Common Good

Everyone living in Hamilton at the turn of the 20th century fell within the orbit of a liberal state, which was responsible for handling matters that were presumed to be shared in common. Authority within the state was somewhat fragmented, with elected legislative bodies at the municipal, provincial, and federal levels, powerful executive leaders (cabinets at the provincial and federal levels, a board of control in the city), a growing array of appointed administrative and regulatory boards, a slowly expanding bureaucracy of civil servants, and the various courts, which both interpreted and made law.

Aside from the tight control of the executive over the legislatures through disciplined political parties, these components of the state could operate relatively autonomously of each other, and certainly rarely took direct instructions from the private economic and social elite. Yet, in their distinctive activities, they shared a broad consensus about what the state should do in a liberal-capitalist order. Whether in new pieces of legislation, regulatory orders, or judicial decisions, state actors were committed to three central political tenets: individual equality, personal liberty, and, above all, the sanctity of private property. State policy and action evolved through the early 20th century within this central framework.[78]

Hamilton's elite seemed comfortable with this conception of state and society. They wanted no interference with their private projects of capital accumulation, and indeed expected protection against any interference with those activities. Their mantra was that the market of supply and demand would "naturally" regulate all economic and social questions. They much preferred co-operation outside the state to any legal intervention to deal with economic and social issues. They expected to be able to manage many public issues through private, voluntary effort and capitalist paternalism, and to sidestep meddling by politicians or public officials. Over the decades, again and again, they would mobilize individual initiative and private resources to deal with such critical matters as public health, child neglect, industrial unrest, and unemployment. Yet they also had a good sense of how the state could help them – providing policies and programs to encourage investment and stimulate capital accumulation (tariffs to keep out competition, immigration programs to stock the labour market, and municipal bonusing to bring in more industry were shining examples), guaranteeing public order and private moral regulation through effective policing and police-court proceedings, and, overall, setting an enforceable legal framework for class relations within the city and across the continent.

In a political system that enfranchised thousands of citizen voters, Hamilton's corporate leaders could not simply dictate state policy directly, but some of the elite stepped right in to make sure that government responded to their needs in appropriate ways. Beyond lobbying through bodies like the Canadian Manufacturers' Association or the Chamber of Commerce, and probably more informally through their networks of social clubs, many participated actively in political parties, and in some cases got elected to public office. Manufacturers such as George Tuckett, John Hendrie, J.I. McLaren, George Lees, and George C. Coppley occupied the mayor's chair for important periods of municipal growth. Others dotted the city council, Board of Control, and other boards and committees. By the early 1930s one student of Hamilton industry argued that the city was "unique because manufacturers are strongly represented in city administration."[79]

In the provincial legislature, Gibson and later Hendrie represented the interests of Hamilton capital. Each also became lieutenant-governor after service in Liberal and Conservative cabinets respectively, for which each also won a knighthood.

At the national level corporate lawyer and financier Samuel Barker, manufacturer T.J. Stewart, and lawyer-industrialist S.C. Mewburn filled seats in Parliament. Mewburn was also the minister of militia for three years in the wartime Union government. George Lynch-Staunton, a local corporate lawyer, was appointed to the Senate. The Conservative Party was the political vehicle for the great majority of Hamilton's capitalists, and even committed Liberals like Hobson eventually switched their allegiance. Hobson became a close confidant of the federal cabinet under Prime Minister Robert Borden and especially of Finance Minister Thomas White, who later joined the Steel Company's board of directors. The voice of private capital was never far from the highest circles of state administration.[80] They did not always need to be so

centrally involved. Most politicians and public officials embraced the sense that the city's fortunes rested on the economic health of its factories and regularly trumpeted Hamilton's business success. They willingly devoted public resources to sustain them – backing publicly owned hydroelectricity, harbour improvements, tax incentives, technical schools, and much more.

Businessmen were nonetheless suspicious of too much democracy, and their collective organizations championed new institutions that shifted decision-making away from popular forums to boards of appointed "experts," usually men like themselves – a technical school board, a parks board, a hydro-electric board, and a tariff board. They also touted the value of "efficiency" within political processes – a slippery concept that highlighted science and technical competence, but most often indicated an effort to transpose into the public sphere such corporate administrative practices as authoritarian hierarchy, strict discipline, and cost-cutting.[81]

The courts were a somewhat different matter. Certainly men with backgrounds in corporate law found their way onto the bench. But they based their rulings less on private self-interest than on well-entrenched legal traditions that privileged individual property rights and struck down any menacing collective activity, including unions, strikes, and boycotts. At the turn of the century, businesses turned to the courts for a new tool, the injunction, to restrain working-class militancy, and defended their economic interests through civil suits against unions for damages. But in the local police court, where most workers confronted the legal system, the city's long-serving police magistrate, George Jelfs, did not need any special prodding to convict idle workers for vagrancy, inebriated men for drunkenness and disorder, precocious women for prostitution, footloose boys for juvenile delinquency, or petty pilferers for criminal theft. The law was not only a discursive force that justified the existing power structure and social relations of the liberal-capitalist order. It was also a drastic tool for directly controlling the behaviour of subordinate classes. Its enforcement rested on a growing, more professional police force and a set of specialized penal institutions ranging from the city jail to specific provincial reformatories for boys, girls, and women, to harshly administered penitentiaries. The rule of law nonetheless had a wide base of popular support.[82]

The edges of state authority remained blurry, and the power to regulate the minds and bodies of the Hamilton population often flowed through agencies organized outside the state, though frequently legally sanctioned and supported financially by government grants – for example, the Children's Aid Society, well-baby clinics, playgrounds movement, and Big Brothers. The social and political processes at work in this way vastly extended the reach of disciplinary regulation. This was a zone of close collaboration between upper- and middle-class activists in promoting such new programs.

Public-private co-operation reached a peak when Canada entered the Great War of 1914–18. At the outset, the federal government relied heavily on non-governmental activity to find recruits for the Canadian Expeditionary Force, look after their families, help the wounded, mobilize munitions production, and generally build pro-war morale. Hobson was prominent in that work. Eventually the state took over war administration much more directly and set to work a food controller and other economic regulators, introduced compulsory military conscription, outlawed alcohol production and consumption, and banned "loafing." In a significant departure from peacetime practice, the state used intense emotional appeals to promote selfless commitment to a single national cause. The state of the 1920s, however, shed all such collectivist inclinations and returned to its conventional liberal framework.[83]

So, despite the close connections between private capital and public officialdom, the state in Hamilton (and Canada more generally) was not simply a creature of corporate manipulation. The notion of citizenship meant that other social groups could mobilize for particular kinds of state intervention. Indeed, an activist middle class expected to make some headway here, and in the early 20th century was actually quite successful in launching many new social programs, from public health to prohibition. More threatening were the new efforts by the local labour movement to get state action on their concerns, most of which failed. More generally, party politics created plenty of emotionally intense rivalry and controversy over public policy. Nothing was certain in politics, and popular pressures could destabilize bourgeois goals. Businessmen regularly expressed frustration with excessive democracy, especially within municipal government, where before the war they promoted a powerful Board of Control, to be elected in a city-wide vote, to weaken city council, which was established in 1910, and (unsuccessfully) a more business-like administrator to be known as a "city manager."[84] Throughout the period the state thus remained an arena of conflict over the range and content of its activities.

Hobson's Hamilton

In early-20th-century Hamilton, new factories sprung up in whole new neighbourhoods. Older businesses quietly shut their doors. Most workers now found jobs in plants working with iron and steel or making textiles. Their employers were typically large corporate enterprises with more distant, impersonal directors, who had pulled themselves and their families apart into cocoons of social exclusiveness, but nonetheless extended a controlling influence over most social institutions in the city. In managing the social consequences of such a capitalist order, the economic elite worked with the more respectable middle classes and kept a close eye on state activity to ensure that it facilitated and did not threaten the smooth functioning of the liberal-capitalist order.

The reconstitution of capitalist practices over a half-century was remarkable enough, but it was the factory owners' ability to construct the health of their own private, profit-making enterprises as the paramount public good that was perhaps their greatest social accomplishment. Again and again, citizens were encouraged to rally around the factory as the cultural essence of the city. When a socialist ran for mayor in 1902 and piled up a respectable vote, the victorious candidate, the Conservative industrialist Hendrie, angrily denounced his opponent's campaign: "Capitalists looking for a place to locate a manufacturing concern will avoid a socialistic city every time."[85] Election campaigns saw the Conservatives raising similar fears of industrial devastation if the tariff were lowered. But more positively, civic culture in the city continuously celebrated this new manufacturing complex as the wellspring of prosperity and its owners as industrial statesmen. Special exhibitions kept factories and their goods in the public eye. The cities' newspapers, especially the *Spectator*, regularly cast factory development in glowing terms. Local businessmen had their own publicity organs as well. Indeed, the rhetoric that exalted the factory and subordinated everything else to its nurturing became the most powerful hegemonic discourse in Hamilton's public life.

Hobson and his capitalist associates thus created a new set of material and cultural structures within which the city's working people were expected to adapt and conform. Workers lived, worked, and socialized in the shadow of smokestacks that, for them, primarily symbolized jobs and wages. Many no doubt respected the industrialists whose companies hired them. But most had their own ideas about what mattered and how to make this new industrial system meet their needs.

3

In 1913 Methodist and Presbyterian social surveyors found 23 Bulgarians living in this Hamilton boarding house and sharing only 13 beds in shifts. (UCCA)

Studholme's People

AT 245 BOLD STREET, a few blocks west of the centre of Hamilton and about the same distance south of the old Ontario Works of the Steel Company of Canada, sits a small, semi-detached house on a narrow lot. In the early years of the 20th century a family of five was living there, headed by an aging foundry worker, Allan Studholme, and his wife Priscilla. Every day neighbours along the street passed their door on the way to work in the city's factories and construction sites or to haggle with grocers at the corner. It was a modest, unassuming neighbourhood of working people.[1]

Late on the night of 4 December 1906 Studholme, at age 60, returned to Bold Street as a

Allan Studholme. (HPL)

hero. He had just won an upset victory as an independent labour candidate in a provincial by-election for the East Hamilton seat. Within a year he would be representing the new Independent Labor Party (ILP). For the next 13 years, until his death in 1919, he travelled to Toronto every winter to rise in the Ontario legislature and lash out at government indifference to the kind of people who lived along Bold Street. As the province's only working-class parliamentarian during these years, the "Little Stove-Mounter," as he was often known, believed that he spoke for all the many men and women who depended on wages from Robert Hobson and his fellow capitalists for the survival of themselves and their unwaged family members.

As they moved into (and out of) jobs, households, and neighbourhoods, thousands of individuals and families – Studholme's people – gave working-class Hamilton a new overall shape and complexion. They did so within the constraints set by capitalist industry and real-estate conditions, state regulation, and deeply ingrained class and ethnic prejudices. Indeed, it was the dynamic tension between workers acting on their desires and aspirations for particular ways of life and the obstacles and opportunities in

Hamilton that produced key elements in their distinctive working-class experience.

The Rising Tide

Between 1901 and 1931 Hamilton's population tripled in size to over 150,000.[2] Some of the increase resulted from the city's annexation of adjacent rural land on which many newcomers had set up households. Part of the growth could no doubt also be traced to the city's buoyant birth rate, which lasted into the 1920s. Yet the explanation for the massive population growth lies less in a spectacular baby boom than in a huge influx of outsiders.[3] Many of them were established Canadians: throughout the period the Canadian-born in Hamilton, mostly from Ontario, remained the majority, although their proportion of the local population would slip from 74 to 61 per cent between 1901 and 1931.[4]

What brought so many people to the city? Many visitors thought the setting was ideal. In 1893 Lady Ishbel Aberdeen, the wife of Canada's governor-general, stood on Hamilton Mountain and pointed her Kodak camera across the orderly rows of houses and factories below. She waxed lyrical about the little city's charming natural setting at the foot of the Niagara Escarpment: "It is a place which photographs do not do justice to."[5] Yet, on the whole, it was not Hamilton's aesthetic virtues that convinced people to make their homes there. For most newcomers and long-time residents alike, the city's main attraction can be summed up in a more prosaic word: jobs. In the half-century after 1890, the new investment pouring into Hamilton's industries created a demand for thousands of new workers. They came out of established Hamilton households, travelled in from the Ontario countryside, and, in large numbers, found their way to the city from far outside the country. Many passed through quickly, and many stayed for only a few years before departing. But eventually large numbers settled in to make lives for themselves.

Hamilton's leading industries in this new industrial age called for a particular mix of skills and occupational experience. In Hamilton, factories provided most of the working-class jobs, and, unlike larger cities such as Montreal, Toronto, or Winnipeg, transportation facilities made a relatively minor demand on the local labour market. As in other cities, the dramatic and rapid pre-war expansion swelled the ranks of building tradesmen, yet it was factories that absorbed half of the local workforce in 1911 and took in three out of five workers 30 years later. By 1930 Hamilton was recognized as the country's third-largest manufacturing centre. Of all cities it was the most heavily dependent on manufacturing industries.[6]

Over that same period the range of factory jobs narrowed. Iron and steel production and metalworking employed less than a quarter of manufacturing workers in 1901, but half in 1921. Work in most consumer-goods industries stagnated or declined, but textiles, especially the production of knit goods, expanded to become the second-largest category of employment. By 1931 textile workers officially made up 15 per cent of the factory workforce and in reality probably over 20 per cent.[7]

Finding the required workers was a challenge for the major growth industries. Some potential employees were ready and waiting. After a half-century of industrialization, the city had a seasoned, settled workforce, especially in some branches of metalworking and textiles. The economic depression of the early 1890s may have prompted many local workers to push on, but by the early 20th century some of the new corporations locating in Hamilton were impressed with the quality of the existing pool of labour.

Several had major foundries in their operations and must have recognized the large reservoir of reliable expertise and competence built up in the city's many foundries in the late 19th century.[8]

Still, the need for workers outstripped the local wage-earning population. Some companies, notably Hamilton Steel and Iron, International Harvester, and Canadian Westinghouse, imported specialized help in start-up phases.[9] Others, like the textile companies, simply wanted more experienced help than they could find in town on a regular basis and therefore had to recruit them specifically.[10] Some undoubtedly made use of private employment agencies overseas, including one operated by the Canadian Manufacturers' Association in London, England. That office raised the hackles of the Canadian labour movement by sending out workers at the specific request of employers in 1907–8 and 1912–13. The CMA's Hamilton branch was a leading voice in 1912 in pushing the association towards a solution to the "considerable shortage of labor during the past year."[11] Federal immigration policy put limits on these efforts because immigration agents were supposed to promote only domestic servants and agricultural labourers, and an Alien Labour Act was intended to block recruitment of non-Canadian labour. But, in the confines of a CMA meeting, manufacturers admitted to finding the government, "in really serious cases, ready to make things as easy for employers as possible" with "a disposition to administer the Act with reasonable latitude."[12] In any case, under pressure from the large railway companies, mine owners, and lumber barons, federal officials were allowing many more industrial recruits to come in after 1907.[13]

Most firms wanted to be able to meet all their needs for skilled and unskilled labour more quickly in a well-stocked local labour market. They benefited from the steady migration of young people from the Ontario countryside, where new concerns about rural depopulation were rampant.[14] To advertise opportunities in Canada and, where possible, the kinds of jobs waiting for immigrant workers in Hamilton, they also relied on federal immigration officials, philanthropic societies (such as the Salvation Army), and steamship company agents scattered through Britain and Western Europe. "Why, agents are going all over England holding lectures with limelight views of Canadian industries, urging English mechanics and workmen to emigrate to Canada at once," one newcomer told a Hamilton labour leader in 1904. "At one lecture I saw the International Harvester works of Hamilton thrown on canvass with its numerous buildings, and the Westinghouse industries of the same city, we were told that a thousand men were wanted in Hamilton at once, so I came." Another English immigrant who arrived in Hamilton that year later recalled: "You'd never believe the propaganda. You get a certain amount of soap literature today, but it is nothing to what was handed out about Canada." A decade later, volunteer relief officers were appalled to find how many British immigrants in distress were "sent here on all sorts of misrepresentation."[15]

Eventually these methods were reinforced by the reports that immigrants sent home and by the active intervention in some ethnic communities of labour agents (known as *padroni* among the Italians). Chain migrations then took off and drew into the city large numbers of people from the same regions in Britain and Continental Europe – Armenians from Keghi and Italians from Abruzzi and Sicily (especially the mining town of Racalmuto), for example – or from their scattered settlements in Canada and the United States. "Every day," the Hamilton *Herald* reported in 1912, "the foreigner with not a word of English comes into the [east-end police] station and shoves over the dirty note with an address scribbled on it and is directed to his new home." An ethnic intermediary might also help a newcomer find a job. In 1916 an Italian migrant working in Smith Falls, northeast of Kingston, got word that the Hamilton foundries were hiring, and made the long trip to that city. Checking into a boarding house run by a man from the same region back home, he started work immediately at the Dominion Foundries and Steel. As much as this "commerce of migration" was well organized, it was based on thousands of individual decisions, not on large collective emigration projects. It could be chaotic and confusing.[16]

Not all of the thousands of newcomers stepping down from the train in Hamilton in the early 20th century made a smooth transition into a new life. Many found themselves stranded on arrival, without immediate accommodation or friends or relatives to help. "The foreigners are looked after far better than the people from the British Isles," the local immigration officer observed in 1913. British immigrants often huddled in large family groups in the train stations while the husband/father tramped the streets in search of scarce housing. Stepping off the same trains as well were large numbers of single women who had migrated from Ontario farms or British cities to find work as domestics or factory workers. In the station, all of these disoriented newcomers could expect help from the immigration officer, a Traveller's Aid worker, or a representative of an ethnic charity like St. George's Benevolent Society or the British Welcome League. For a few years the increasingly derelict old Custom House on the edge of the north end became a temporary shelter for some homeless arrivals. In 1913 the voluntary British Welcome League opened another place of refuge.[17]

The non-Canadian newcomers to Hamilton were part of the great human migration that was dispersing millions of Europeans across Europe, Australia, and North and South America. In 1901 a mere 1,540 people in the city had immigrated over the previous decade, but the immigrant tide rose steadily after the turn of the century, cresting at unprecedented and, eventually, controversial levels in the five years before the war. The gates were closed during the war and postwar depression, but reopened for a few years in the second half of the 1920s before again shutting tight during the 1930s.[18]

By far the largest immigrant group arrived from the British Isles. The British-born population of Hamilton increased by nearly 30,000 over the first three decades of the century, reaching almost 30 per cent of the total population in the 1920s. In contrast to the 19th century, few newcomers came from Ireland. Most arrived from England, though in the 1920s half of the 10,000 new arrivals from Britain were Scots. The statistics do not tell us from which regions of the United Kingdom these people hailed, but a writer in the locally published *Labor News* suggested in 1914 that Lancashire and Yorkshire were sending the largest number, and the organization of a Lancashire Football Club in the city would tend to support him. The "Old Country" men did not necessarily find the transition to work in Hamilton plants easy because their experience "at home" had lagged behind: British industries were not keeping pace with the industrial transformation underway in North America in the early 20th century. By the 1920s major employers in the city were demanding a year's experience in a Canadian or US plant before hiring a British workman.[19]

The other large group of new immigrants in Hamilton had travelled from the more unfamiliar regions of Southern and Eastern Europe (including Western Asia), although identifying which Europeans arrived and determining precise figures for many of the Eastern European national groups who lived in Hamilton after 1900 has become an elaborate game of guesswork. Census-takers asked for "racial origin" and "nativity," and, according to later demographers, "racial origin" was open to a bewildering variety of interpretations when the question was put to interviewees on their doorsteps.[20] The language barrier no doubt also contributed to inaccuracies. In 1911 the *Herald* reported that the Ottawa census bureau was sending its enumerators back to get the information on "origins of the people" that their limited language skills had prevented them from getting the first time around.[21] "Nativity" meant country of birth, but, before World War One, many nationalities in Eastern Europe that would later find self-expression in nation-states of their own remained hidden in the multicultural empires of Russia, Germany, and Austria-Hungary.[22] Much of this highly transient population may well have eluded the census net in any case.[23]

At the turn of the century, Hamilton's few residents of European origin were lost in a huge Anglo-Celtic sea. Only 3,000 people counted in 1901 were born outside the British Empire, and a mere 265 residents had arrived from Southern or Eastern Europe, most of whom were small-scale retailers. This ethnic mix was typical in most of Southern Ontario, but it stood in marked contrast to the many large US cities, where a new wave of immigration had started 20 years earlier.[24] Over the next three decades Continental Europeans in Hamilton became a much larger, more visible element in the local population. During the 1920s Canada became the preferred target for many of these ethnic groups as the United States tightened its restrictions on immigrants from abroad. By 1931 the European-born "foreigners" in the city had risen to over 8 per cent of the total population, though they made up a much larger percentage of the adult

New immigrants from Southern and Eastern Europe found their job prospects limited to heavier, less skilled, poorly paid jobs. Here a labourer does road work in 1907.

(LSL, LS475)

census – the residue of a great flood simply passing through this and many other Canadian and US cities in the early 20th century.[27] Initially, men often came alone in search of work, never intending to stay. The pattern was most striking among the European newcomers. With the exception of the Jews, who generally came in family groups to escape oppression and persecution in Russia and Austria-Hungary, and later the Armenians, who were fleeing similar treatment,[28] Hamilton's new European immigrants were predominantly lone male migrants looking for short-term, unskilled jobs, and most often intending to return home.[29] These men lived cheaply, saved every penny possible to send home to their families, and eventually left the city. Even among those whose trans-Atlantic migration was more permanent, such as many Ukrainians, Hamilton might only be a stop before they amassed the cash to go off to begin farming in Western Canada. In the words of a Ukrainian who arrived in 1907, "I came for the money – that was all."[30]

Most were from rural families attempting to cope with the impact of capitalist agriculture. Often they had already worked part of their time as sharecroppers, agricultural labourers, or industrial workers. Typically they were not the poorest from their villages – the poorest could never afford the cost of travel – but rather were lower-to-middling peasants and skilled artisans. Driven by worsening underemployment, overpopulation, and agricultural depression, many of the men in Italy's Mezzogiorno, southeast Poland, and similar agricultural regions of Southern and Eastern Europe had begun a process of seasonal migration to earn cash that might help to better their families' situation.[31] Once in North America, they travelled widely in search of work. One Italian who arrived in Canada at age 15 and eventually settled as a shopkeeper in Hamilton recalled his wide-ranging trek:

workforce, reaching what was probably a peak of 22 per cent in 1918. Italians, Poles, "Russians" (many of them most likely Ukrainians and Belarusians), and Jews initially stood out as the most numerous among the new Europeans. By the 1920s large numbers of other Slavic groups, especially Hungarians, Ukrainians, Yugoslavians, Czechs, and Slovaks, and a growing group of Armenians, had also arrived. At the end of the 1930s, some 24,000 residents (in a total population of 166,000) claimed Southern and Eastern European ancestry; nearly half of those people had been born in Europe. The Italians had become the largest non-English-speaking group, followed closely by the Poles.[25]

Over the same decades a much smaller number of Chinese immigrants also arrived in Hamilton. From only 30 in 1901, their numbers grew to 162 in 1911 and nearly 400 in 1931. They were controversial newcomers, but numerically they made up only a tiny proportion of the local population and generally did not find work in the city's factories.[26]

These statistics register those who came to stay or who happened to be in town at the time of the

I never knew nobody. I land Montreal. I work, and stay three months. Then I got to Toronto and I stay a year. Then I go to Whitby. Then back to Toronto. Then I come over to Hamilton, and I work in the steel plant for six months. I just went to the steel plant and got it. From there I went to Calgary for the threshing. I stayed in a caboose and I worked in the threshing.[32]

On this side of the Atlantic the seasonal cycles were often extended into longer sojourns, especially if unemployment, accident, or ill health had eaten up the labourers' savings. These workers were nonetheless always on the move, looking for quick earnings. "A great many of the Italians in Hamilton have left the city in search of work wherever it can be found," reported Hamilton's first Italian priest, Giovanni Bonomi, in the midst of the 1908 depression. "A segment of the population is still unemployed and another is about to return to Italy ... only a few families remain." The local Presbyterians abandoned their missionary efforts amongst the city's Armenians in 1909 when they discovered that three-quarters of the newcomers had departed. Late in 1913 the *Herald* reported that 2,000 of the city's European immigrants had booked passage to their homelands and predicted that "full three quarters of those leaving will be back again."[33]

World War One cut off return trips across the Atlantic, but by 1919 large numbers in the Hamilton "foreign colony" wasted no time in heading home. "Sojourning" picked up again in the second half of the 1920s and then stopped abruptly in 1930 with new immigration restrictions that would last until the late 1940s. By 1931 nearly two in every five of Hamilton's "foreigners" had arrived in Canada only in the previous ten years. The 1930s, however, would be a period of settling down.[34]

Trekking so far and wide through North America's industrial centres and rubbing shoulders with some unforgettable workmates must have led to remarkably rich experiences. In 1912 the *Herald* discovered that Manuel Pardinas Serato, the Spanish anarchist who had just assassinated the prime minister of Spain, had spent 15 months in Hamilton in 1908–9 working at the steel plant, before heading off to Latin America. The element of transiency provided a certain anonymity in the factory: when asked about the Serato case, the Steel Company officials admitted that "they could not tell whether such a man had ever worked there or not, as frequently foreigners' names are misspelled and more often they were known by numbers rather than names." The same year no one could discover the name of an Italian who was killed by a falling steel beam in an east-end plant. The Hamilton *Times* commented: "He was timed by number, paid by number and was lost in the great plant like one of the numbered pieces of machinery."[35]

The British and Anglo-Canadians had similar though less highly publicized migratory patterns. British workingmen with families seemed to come and go with remarkable frequency. In 1912 the *Herald* learned from the city's steamship agents that 700 British people were leaving for Christmas at home and expected back in the spring. Prolonged strikes and depressions also regularly sent such families packing.[36] Many Ontario workers moved back and forth across the border into the industrial states below the Great Lakes, especially Michigan and New York, frequently connecting with kin in other industrial centres. A 1916 royal commission heard testimony from a few of the hundreds of footloose single machinists, known in their trade as "boomers," who had heard of the labour needs of the munitions plants and hit the road for Hamilton "just for a change" and "just to see" the city.[37] In 1925 the US consul in Hamilton announced that 30 to 50 people were applying for visas every day. "Young men, mechanics mostly," the *Spectator* reported, "were crossing the line in search of work, and sending for their families a week or so later." The superintendent of the local Ontario Employment Office noted two years later, "A large number of men have returned from the United States." Hamilton, he said, was always a "stopping-off place for transient workers proceeding from Canada to the United States or from the States to Canada."[38]

Most neighbourhoods got used to so many people coming and going. In household after household, occupants came and went with startling regularity. For example, in a sample of streets in north-end and west-central neighbourhoods, between two and four out of every ten households had apparently left the city over each decade. In 1910 a third of those neighbourhoods' household heads listed in the city directory in 1900 had left town. A decade later roughly a quarter of the 1910 group had disappeared. On three east-end blocks, the proportion of the 1920 household heads with no directory listing in 1930 ranged between one-fifth and one-third. In one block this transiency declined in the 1930s, but on three others a quarter of household heads vanished over the decade; in another, three out of ten were gone, and in still another nearly four out of ten.[39] Tenants were far more mobile than owners. In 1941 census-takers found that tenants had lived in their homes on average for less than five years, while owners had stayed put on average for more than 14 years.[40]

Eventually, more and more of the "birds of passage" decided to stay. After a period of sojourning, a man might send for his wife and children and set up a new household. In 1912 the *Herald* highlighted the example of Paul Gravetz, a Polish migrant. After three years of work in an east-end factory, Gravetz brought over his wife and family to run a boarding house and soon after built his own house. Transiency and sojourning became less sensible during the prolonged years of economic depression in the city's industries between the wars. Decades later, interviews of those who stayed in Hamilton sometimes also evoked memories of a strong desire to turn their backs on harsh conditions in the homeland. In some of the European immigrant groups, the 1920s saw a marked increase in the number of women, notably among the Italians, where women had reached 42 per cent by 1931 and 44 percent a decade later. These people were coming to stay.[41]

Overall, then, the much larger workforce that came and went (and perhaps returned again) in early-20th-century Hamilton had important new hues in its complexion – notably, less occupational diversity and much more ethnic heterogeneity. With such a large percentage of new, mobile migrants, the working class in Hamilton did not face the industrial transformation of the period as a settled population with a common heritage and a shared local experience. Instead, workers arrived in waves from parts of the world in different states of industrial development. Although the great majority of them had nonetheless been born and raised in an industrial society, they brought into an already established working-class community diverse experiences, values, and attitudes towards work in capitalist industry and life in industrial communities.

Setting Up House

Industrialists opened up the job possibilities, but for the most part they left their wage-earners to sort out their own living arrangements, whether temporary or permanent. In contrast to today, workers rarely lived alone. Virtually all the residents of working-class Hamilton were clustered in nuclear groups centred around one or two parents. Before World War Two, the typical working-class household was a family home, but, in practice, "families" took many forms. By 1931 one in five family households was headed by a lone individual, most often a woman who was widowed, abandoned, divorced, or unmarried.[42] Then too, as the birth rate declined, all family groups included steadily fewer children. Households also often included more than parents and their offspring. Children might grow up with a relative unable to live alone as a result of illness, disability, or old age.[43] Families might be encouraged to make room for one or more unrelated boarders. In some immigrant households the sojourning boarders might be so numerous that they overwhelmed the family housing them (in a few cases, renters simply "batched" together without a landlady for short periods). At the same time the occupants were usually still connected to a settled family household back home, with whom they communicated and to which they returned intermittently. In these ways, for many years before their womenfolk began to arrive in significant numbers, newcomers sometimes established surrogate families.[44] As well, not everyone married, and unmarried adults generally lived with their own kin or attached themselves to others as boarders (even those trying to escape their own families had to rely on another family household for room and board).[45]

All these diverse processes of household formation in an expanding city soon put pressure on a rapidly changing housing industry straining to keep up with new demands.[46] Like most smaller cities in Canada, Hamilton at the close of the 19th century had none of the tenements and apartments that predominated in New York, Berlin, Paris, and Glasgow, nor the duplexes and triplexes so common in Montreal, Chicago, and Boston. It had little of the row or "terraced"

housing so common in most British and many US cities.[47] Still, after a half-century of industrialization, Hamilton had an extensive stock of working-class housing available by the 1890s, though it varied a good deal in quality. The building of the Toronto, Hamilton, and Buffalo Railway in 1895 ate up some of that accommodation by cutting a swath of destruction through the heart of the colourful old Irish working-class neighbourhood of Corktown. Nevertheless, at the turn of the century the federal census-takers found a roughly even balance of families and available housing in the city, which means that most working-class families must have had a whole house to themselves at that time.[48] Indeed, small single-family dwellings would remain more or less the norm in working-class housing until at least World War Two.

Whether simply leaving their parents' household or arriving in the city as adults, workers expected to rent their homes, at least initially. The available houses could be one of a small number of styles ranging from the "cottage" to the "bungalow," with four to six rooms, one or two storeys, and either frame or, more often, brick exteriors. Occasionally the house was part of a row, or semi-detached, but by 1931 three-quarters of Hamilton's houses were detached. Workers' houses were commonly situated on small, rectangular lots that in Hamilton averaged 25 to 30 feet by 100 feet.[49]

As much larger numbers of newcomers flocked in over the early years of the century, and new building did not keep pace, housing shortages rapidly became more acute. The available accommodation was too limited and rents spiralled upward.[50] In 1904 reports began to circulate that whole families in Hamilton were sharing a single room, and that two or three families were occupying the same house. The next spring the *Spectator*'s editor suggested that "the cheap houses in this city have doubled their population." By 1911 the census-takers recorded a surplus of 554 families over available dwellings. Doubling-up had a long history among urban industrial workers, but the proportions were evidently disturbing to community leaders. The next year, James Roberts, the crusading local medical officer of health, worried that overcrowding was sowing the "germs of the slum" in the settled parts of the city. His inspection of 263 family households that year brought to light numerous examples of severely cramped accommodation in subdivided houses, basements, attics, and outbuildings. The cleanup campaign that Roberts and his staff launched probably made even less space available for housing. "There is not a vacant house to be obtained in the city of Hamilton today," the *Herald* reported in June 1913. A public-health nurse told the press that spring that "it was not an uncommon thing to find a family of from five to seven people living in one small room."[51]

The pre-war depression forced many workers to leave the city, and by February 1915 the Hamilton correspondent of the *Labour Gazette*, the monthly publication of the federal Department of Labour, could report many empty houses, some of which were being offered as temporary accommodation for the unemployed. But the quickening of the economic pulse during the war brought new reports of housing shortages. Munitions workers flocking into the city found less space available because some families formerly sharing a house were taking advantage of wartime prosperity to indulge in the luxury of a home of their own. In a familiar vein, the assessment commissioner noted in 1918 that doubling up had created a "congested condition among the artisan and labouring class."[52]

Despite a new burst of building activity in 1919–20, this new housing crisis lasted well into the postwar period. By 1919 some returned soldiers and their families were reported to be living in tents on vacant land, and some workers were moving to the fringes of the city, where, according to various reports, they settled in deplorably "congested conditions" in the east end and "slum" conditions in shacks and converted boathouses along the marshy western end of the bay. A public health department survey in 1920 found only 62 vacant houses in Hamilton, almost all of them in the European immigrant neighbourhoods. Roberts warned that "practically no houses worthy of occupation are available for the needs of people with slender incomes, in any part of the city." A Town Planning Board report sounded a similar warning in 1922, and the Central Bureau of Family Welfare was still raising these concerns with the Board of Control at the end of the decade. The housing "famine" was a relentless fact of life in working-class Hamilton.[53]

The reorganization of household space to take in extra families or individuals remained common over the decades, especially at the peaks of the business cycles, when inflowing job-seekers were looking for immediate shelter, and during economic hard times, when families tried to economize by living in less space or by taking in others to share the cost. By the end of World War One, many Hamilton houses had been more or less permanently divided to create what were now commonly called "flats."[54] In 1919 the Ontario Housing Committee recommended that working-class houses should have no more than six rooms because any more would simply be rented out – an unacceptable violation of family privacy in the eyes of the committee.[55] According to the census-takers, "doubling-up" reached a peak in 1921, when nearly one in ten city households contained more than one family.[56]

The thousands of newcomers who came alone needed temporary accommodation as lodgers in a family household. Many Hamilton householders seized the opportunity to boost the family income by renting out rooms to unattached men and women. The older working-class north end had "hardly a house" without "one or more boarders and roomers," the *Spectator* reported in 1906. Throughout other city neighbourhoods, "Ring the first door bell you see, and if that is not a boarding house, likely the next one is." The same year the local YWCA estimated that about 5,000 women were boarding in the city, not counting live-in domestic servants. The association itself ran a boarding house for young working women and could never meet the demand.[57] Male boarders were far more numerous.[58]

Boarding houses were particularly important in the European immigrant neighbourhoods, where so many newcomers were single male sojourners. The lifestyle of these immigrants in the city reflected their transiency. In the first decade of the century, a group of men sometimes shared makeshift quarters in hastily constructed shacks on undeveloped land as primitive as any found in logging and construction camps. More commonly, a husband and wife from one ethnic group would open a boarding house crowded with as many beds as possible – in attics, basements, and all spare rooms – and rent out space in these barrack-like conditions to their fellow countrymen. In 1904 a reporter found a loft over a shed in the east end with "no less than eighteen beds, ranging along the wall like the steerage accommodation of an ocean liner," each rented at ten cents a night without board. The next year local health officials visited the rough-hewn shacks that the new immigrant workers had constructed on the property of the Hamilton Steel and Iron Company in the east end. They found,

according to the *Spectator*, that men slept on "benches as many as five or six in a single small area." In 1906 another reporter visited a large, ten-room house on Hughson Street with 75 Italian boarders. Each of the occupants had a space three feet by six feet marked in chalk on the floor around his bed. Roberts's 1912 report had similar examples, but a detailed study of a block of immigrant housing in the east end by Methodist and Presbyterian investigators the next year was even more striking. In 17 eight-room houses occupied by Italians, Bulgarians, Poles, Romanians, and Macedonians, they found 232 men, 19 women, and 12 children, and discovered that 213 of the men were single, either boarding or "batching." Roberts's staff attacked these conditions by taking landlords to court.[59]

Just how cramped this lifestyle could be was revealed to a census-taker who arrived at dinnertime in June 1911. He recorded the relevant information for 11 men, who were eating their dinner and afterwards departed for the night shift. "No sooner had they left the house than no less than a dozen foreigners marched in, ate from the same table and the same dishes, and then retired to bed, having just finished their labors," he explained to the press. "That seems to be the way in most of the foreign boarding houses – the beds never grow cold."[60]

Despite the shock and dismay of such middle-class investigators and visitors, Hamilton's overcrowding did not reach the scale of some other North American cities with large immigrant populations. After a tour of the city's congested housing areas in 1910, a Toronto mission worker proclaimed Hamilton "about the freest city in Ontario from slum conditions." The next year the census enumerators, paradoxically, found these households "more or less deplorable," yet surprising in their "degree of neatness." Even the fastidious medical officer

Roberts had to admit that there was considerable improvement as more of them settled in. "The average foreigner, particularly the Italian, has been done a great injustice by most people," he argued in 1919. "While a great many of the foreigners are anything but clean, the majority are particular in their habits."[61]

By the interwar period the rough, frontier-like overcrowding had declined as the percentage of European-immigrant families setting up their own households steadily increased, but boarding houses persisted. By 1931 census-takers still counted some 12,000 lodgers in the city, and one in five households had one or more under their roofs. The lodgers were spread evenly between owned and rented households. Even after sojourning wound down in the 1930s, the still large surplus of men in immigrant neighbourhoods prolonged the need for boarding accommodation. By that point, "boarders" were more often becoming "roomers," with less direct contact with the families in their households.[62]

Families sharing household space were seeking mutual advantage – on one side, extra income, and, on the other, affordable accommodation. A fine balance of daily tolerance and respect had to be maintained in these situations, but family life could easily be disrupted by angry disputes over overdue rent, property damage, misuse of space, or undue familiarity with family members. Domestic bliss required tactful negotiation.[63]

Building Homes

With so many new workers, the construction industry initially could not, or would not, produce enough houses. In a 1907 survey of Hamilton's "housing famine" the *Canadian Architect and Builder* reported, "Builders are doing little to remedy the trouble as yet." Making an initial effort to overcome the inadequacies of the market,

a few firms – Westinghouse, International Harvester, F.W. Bird, and later Firestone – arranged for houses to be built for some of their employees. Most of these dwellings did not become the kind of long-term rental accommodation found in single-industry textile or mining towns; instead they were soon sold to the companies' workers. This kind of company housing was ultimately only a short-term solution, scarcely making a dent in the local housing problem.[64]

For several years Hamilton businessmen worried that the housing crisis was driving away workers and leading to higher wage demands; and in spring 1912, responding to a request from the local branch of the Canadian Manufacturers' Association, the mayor called a public meeting on the "housing question." At that gathering, a new broad-based Housing Committee was mandated to investigate solutions. With the enthusiastic endorsement of the Hamilton Trades and Labor Council, the committee set out to organize a so-called "co-operative" housing project to be developed by private businessmen on the model of the Toronto Housing Company – the so-called "philanthropy and five per cent" solution (that is, charity with a profit). But more than a year and a half of discussion and planning brought no action, perhaps because local real-estate interests were unenthusiastic, and certainly because the crisis passed when the local economy slumped severely late in 1913 and many workers left the city.[65]

Yet another initiative came at the end of the war, as working-class protest, veteran discontent, and general public indignation at the extent of the housing crisis in many industrial centres across the country prompted the federal government to make public funds available for the construction of working-class dwellings through the provincial governments. The state never did build houses for workers in Hamilton before World War Two, but in 1918 the Ontario government released $2 million of this money to local municipalities to promote private construction of working-class housing at a low interest rate. In the following year Hamilton's city council established a Housing Commission to handle local applications. The poorly publicized program eventually assisted in the construction of 123 houses in Hamilton built privately by or for their owners, mostly in the east end. Once again, this program was a drop in a growing bucket. Not until the late 1930s would federal funding begin to trickle back in to help the housing shortage, this time under the National Housing Act of 1938.[66] None of these special projects ever came close to meeting the apparently insatiable demand for houses in the city.

In the end, private enterprise was left to cope with the escalating demand. By the turn of the century, the housing industry was undergoing some important changes. Probably most important was the emergence of an aggressive new real-estate sector. In 19th-century Hamilton, as elsewhere, house-building had been a highly decentralized process; for the most part, artisans in the construction trades had contracted to custom-build for small-scale landowners who had wanted their lots developed. By the turn of the century, a new specialized business organization had appeared to handle the subdivision and marketing of residential property on a grander scale – the real-estate firm. By 1913 Hamilton had 42 of these enterprises, their large advertisements spilling across the pages of the city's newspapers each week. Their most important contribution was to develop and promote new working-class suburbs, made possible by the expanding network of electric street-railways. Between 1906 and 1915, developers registered 192 surveys, often with upwards of 100 small lots laid out in a simple

(HH, 4 March 1911, 9)

grid pattern, mostly on former farmlands at the edge of the city. Some two-thirds of the surveys were platted in the second half of that decade in the largest expansion of residential space in Hamilton until after World War Two. Some of the suburban subdivisions extended south and west of the city, but most stretched eastward along the plain below Hamilton Mountain, in close proximity to the new east-end factory district, a large area annexed in five steps between 1902 and 1912 and expanded further after the war. After 1909 the first subdivisions also began to appear on the Mountain. With such endearing names as Homeside, Avondale, Kenilworth, Melrose, and Brightside, most of these new suburbs were advertised as being ideal living spots for the workers of the nearby factories. Subtle distinctions in price and locale appealed both to the families headed by skilled men and to those headed by less-skilled workers of limited means. The suburbs in the northeast, closest to the harbour and the large new factories, such as Brightside, required residents to cope with excessive noise, soot, foul smells, and toxic air. As a result they drew more of the poorly paid European immigrants.[67]

The real-estate developers brought a whole new promotional style to the industry, including, according to a local official in 1911, "the most flaring newspaper headlines," brass-band concerts with free lunches, and "other methods to induce the more thrifty type of wage earner to vie with his fellow worker in his eagerness to become a landed proprietor." Land prices quickly shot up in response to the heavy demand for the new lots. Some workers may have been making a choice to move out of inner cities to "healthier" suburbs. The houses in Union Park, for example, were far to the east of the new factory district. But far more workers were pushed out to the edge of town by the shortage of rental accommodation near their factory jobs. A recent English immigrant used this logic in a 1907 discussion with a *Herald* reporter. He had been evicted four times in one year as houses were sold out from under him and his family. "I have got to buy a house now if I want to live in one," he explained, as he signed on to buy an International Harvester house. "There are absolutely no houses in this district to rent for more than a monthly term." Some five years later the *Herald* reported that many people were still facing the same pressure.[68] Evidently many working-class families were keenly interested in becoming homeowners for compelling, practical reasons.[69]

Financing these homes was getting easier. In the 19th century workers often had great difficulty cobbling together the large down payment and meeting the stringent mortgaging requirements. But in the early 20th century they found loan and insurance companies or, far more commonly, private lenders ready to provide mortgages. By 1907 a worker could buy a house for $1,500 to $1,700 by putting $200 down and

paying $16 a month for five and a half years at 5.5 per cent interest. Some 17 years later, $300 down and $18 a month would still get a small "bungal-ette." Alternatively workers could simply buy lots in the new suburbs for $75 to $200 "on the instalment plan," which, by 1909, typically required only $10 down and $5 a week, but could be as low as $5 down and $1 to $4 a week. With careful budgeting, many working-class families could eventually make the leap to suburban home ownership.[70]

In the late 19th century only a small minority of the city's wage-earning families were able to buy their own homes, and throughout the years from the 1890s to the 1930s a majority of those families continued to rent. In 1891 and 1901 only one-third of the city's household heads as a whole were homeowners. In 1911 that figure jumped to one-half, where it remained for the next 30 years. Western Canadian home-owner-ship figures ran much higher, but, by North American standards, 50 per cent was a relatively high figure. Local civic boosters liked to trumpet this condition as a clear sign of prosperity.[71] Yet the families of blue-collar workers, especially the less-skilled, were far more likely to be renters than were the families of white-collar workers, professionals, or businessmen. Workers under the age of 45 were also much more likely to be renters. For most working-class households, home-owning became possible only later in life, and only a thin majority of workers could probably expect to reach that goal by their fifties or sixties.[72] Finally, the really remarkable growth in working-class home ownership in Hamilton was concentrated in the new suburbs. On land annexed after 1902, 51 per cent of residents owned their homes in 1911 and a remarkable 72 per cent in 1921.[73]

The construction of the houses remained less corporatized than were the land sales. Some of the land developers were also builders, but the process of house-building in these new working-class suburbs remained small-scale. Speculative contractors probably built most of the houses for sale or rent, in batches as small as a short row or as large as whole blocks. At the same time, with the increasing availability of standardized, factory-made building products, workingmen themselves were often able to invest "sweat equity" by building their own new homes, perhaps with help from kin and friends.[74]

Would-be home-builders could obtain pattern books to provide basic guidelines (by 1907 the public library was stocking a wide range of these publications), and the newspapers regularly published plans. A few bought the build-your-own kits available through department stores. A Hamilton firm, Halliday Homes, was a major producer of these prefabricated houses. Alf Ready, a Westinghouse worker, later recalled buying a tiny one, which he assembled on rented land near the waterfront and occupied with his wife and young son in the early 1930s. But most workers probably used whatever skills and imagination they could muster on their own. "Neighbours gladly helped each other to gather materials and erect homes, humble though they were in those days," the *Spectator* recalled in 1923. "They bought the lots in the cheapest sections possible and built the first unit of their homes thereon. That first unit was usually the kitchen, and from that portion gradually grew and expanded the finished home." A developer later recalled how the first settlers in the Crown Point suburb (near what became Ottawa Street), "mostly Old Country people, would get a few planks from a lumber yard and have their family drag them out there. Then they would work . . .until midnight putting up the eight by ten shack which was to be their home. Usually there were no windows, and the building was tar paper covered." Sometimes, as the city's chief sanitary inspector noted, the expansion beyond one room was halted because either the owner was "satisfied with the single room arrangement, or he is not in such a financial position as would warrant him to proceed with the completion of his home." Many more were expanded and rebuilt as family finances permitted.[75]

The owner-built houses made for a jumble of primitive architectural styles and irregular streetscapes that offended middle-class sensibilities. Engineer and town planner A.G. Dalzell found such dwellings "peculiar in plan," because they were "built in instalments without a well conceived plan from the start, and so to anyone except the actual builder have little appeal, and are hard to sell." In one east-end suburb known as "Dufftown," located beyond the city limits in Barton Township, a delegation complained to the township council in 1919 that houses were "built in the backyards of other dwellings, three and four houses built on lots originally intended by the surveyors for one, and most unsanitary conditions are prevailing." Public health officials generally found these owner-built, suburban dwellings "a menace to the moral and physical health of the community." A public-health nurse described a one-room house that served a man, a woman, and their three children:

> In this one room there were two beds, a cook stove, table chairs and other necessary furniture, and even the usual quarter ton of coal supply, stored in a box in one corner. In this cramped and stuffy room these five people lived, ate and slept, and the space between beds, stove and table was so narrow that I could not pass between them without lifting my hand grip above the level of the furniture.[76]

Hamilton's working-class suburbanites were, then, urban pioneers. A sympathetic visitor to a "shacktown" in 1909 found the houses "rude and some of them rickety; some only half-built and most of them shells; newspapers on the walls and scarcely even mats on the new floors; three in a bed very often, and no cots or cradles for the children." Living conditions could remain primitive for some time, since so much of the early development was unregulated and chaotic and the development of water mains, sewers, roads, sidewalks, and street-railway lines often lagged behind the house-building. For example, the first east-end suburb, Union Park, opened far out beyond the city limits in 1900, but had no municipal services until after the area was annexed in 1909 and no street-railway service until 1912–13. By that point local newspapers were running regular reports of East Hamilton residents mired in mud and waiting impatiently for overcrowded streetcars to arrive. In these circumstances, working-class residents often had to band together and petition the city for services. Given that such improvements had to be paid for through higher municipal property taxes on individual properties, poorer residents sometimes petitioned against the services. By World War One, many of the developers were offering serviced lots. A large percentage of working-class homeowners in East Hamilton, must have suffered through the inconvenience and discomfort of this early suburban development, a phase that lasted into the 1920s on the eastern edge of the city.[77]

Working-class suburbia remained largely unregulated until the enactment of Hamilton's new, more rigorous municipal building code in May 1914 (which did not cover those suburbs that spilled over into the neighbouring rural townships). The small number of workers in the east end who made use of the postwar state housing funds to build their own houses also had to meet stricter regulations about planning and standards. Reflecting on this working-class pattern of house construction, Dalzell argued in 1928, "In no other part of the Empire is so much home building undertaken by the owners themselves, or aided by unskilled workers, as in Canada." This process of urban homesteading on the edge of the city certainly made it possible for many more working-class families with limited savings, including relatively recent immigrants, to own their own homes.[78]

Households in working-class Hamilton, then, took shape within the constraints of the city's particular real-estate markets. On balance, a shelter industry based on private enterprise had not served Hamilton workers especially well. At any one time, a solid majority of working-class families wanted space to rent – indeed, virtually all would have been renters for some part of their lives – both because many were uncertain about staying permanently in the city and because most could not afford the nest egg for a down payment. Yet there was seldom enough affordable housing to rent in Hamilton after the turn of the century. The results were extremely high rents, serious overcrowding in many cases, and, paradoxically, pressure on many workers to head out to the new suburbs to buy or build their own homes.[79]

Hamilton's housing conditions improved somewhat after World War One, as the housing industry recovered from the shock of so many new arrivals, and the rugged pioneering phase of suburban development eventually passed. By the interwar period, most of the housing stock in working-class Hamilton was solid and substantial, especially once municipal regulation got some teeth. Basic water, sewage, gas, and electrical services were eventually available in almost all neighbourhoods.[80] The houses were small and close together, but urban density remained low compared to larger metropolitan cities. Overall, the quality of housing was thus at least modestly better than it had been for many workers in 19th-century Hamilton, and no doubt immensely better than the housing that many recent immigrants had left behind in industrial Britain or rural Europe.[81]

Serious problems lingered. A substantial minority of working-class families could not enjoy the luxury of having a full house to themselves. Living on limited incomes, they "doubled up" with other families, and thus made do with crowded accommodations ill designed for their needs. These people were not just recent immigrants waiting to find their feet on the ladder to home ownership. They were also, more commonly, a broad range of working-class families simply trying to cope with the poverty generated by unemployment, illness, injury, or, death. The 192 randomly chosen "unsanitary dwellings" visited by two health department officials in 1938 were largely occupied by tenants on relief or "in the near-relief category." The residents had to cope with poor plumbing, leaking roofs, crumbling plaster, defective stairs, and other forms of deterioration as well as infestations of insects and rats. Researchers Michael J. Doucet and John Weaver estimate that, by extension, this kind of housing may have amounted to nearly one Hamilton household in ten (and clearly a higher proportion in working-class neighbourhoods).[82] Some three years later federal census-takers identified one in six of the city's dwellings as being "in need of external repairs" (one in five among tenants).[83]

The real-estate industry's image of rose-covered cottages was also seriously marred by the industrial pollution from the belching smokestacks of east-end factories that hung over the many working-class neighbourhoods huddled below. It would be a major struggle for most families in working-class Hamilton to make a household into the "home" that could satisfy their many needs and aspirations.

Neighbourhoods

In theory workers could set up their households wherever they chose, but in practice their choices were limited by many economic, environmental, and cultural constraints. The homes of Hamilton's working-class residents were not spread evenly over the whole city. They were clustered in specific neighbourhoods that soon contained a full range of community organizations, institutions, and services to sustain distinctive working-class ways of life.

Many new householders most likely located themselves near kin and friends, and this was especially true of new arrivals in the city who might need this neighbourhood support. But those choices fell within larger patterns. Certainly people had to move into accommodation that fell within the means of their individual or family incomes, and working-class families could not afford large spacious homes in more affluent neighbourhoods. In a city where even by the 1930s few workers owned cars, male breadwinners also had to be reasonably close to their workplaces, either by foot or, as the city expanded, on the much maligned street-railway lines. That need was in part what drew so many of them to the east-end suburbs near the large new industries. Scholars now distinguish between "industrial" suburbs, which grew up close to factories, and "residential" suburbs, which appeared somewhat more independently of industry, although workers typically commuted to industrial jobs. Hamilton had both, and many working-class families had to get used to the clatter of machinery and the smells and soot drifting into their open windows from nearby factories.[84]

This grocery store and boarding house served "Russian" immigrants in 1913. (UCCA)

The combination of working-class need and bourgeois exclusiveness had already created a north-south divide in Hamilton by the end of the 19th century. Businessmen and professionals clustered on the higher ground to the south, and real-estate advertisers played to that preference. In a 1919 appeal to middle-class buyers in a Mount Hamilton subdivision a real-estate firm asked: "Can you imagine anything more delightful than a spot with neat, progressive people all around you, splendid clear atmosphere, far from stockyards, stenches and factory fumes?"[85]

At the turn of the century, workers' homes were concentrated in the centre and north near the factories and the port. The most distinctively working-class neighbourhood was the north end, a lively, rough-edged area close to the harbour.[86] As the population mushroomed after the turn of the century and the city sprawled eastward, the north end and the east end, and especially the northeast, became preponderantly working-class districts, with only a sprinkling of non-working-class residents. The city council's Ward Eight in particular contained such a population. Here were clustered many neighbourhoods

in which blue-collar workers headed 70 to 75 per cent of the households.[87] At their centres emerged new strips of shops and other commercial services to satisfy a family's needs. As a worker reported from the east end in 1914, "Churches have been built for the moral welfare of the people; halls here and there for the several fraternal orders who have organized branches, and thriving moving picture shows operating for the amusement of the horny-handed, hard-working man, his wife and family."[88]

These neighbourhoods were far from homogeneous. The more impoverished families clustered in cheaper, poorer quality housing, while a few blocks away substantial, better maintained housing with clean lace curtains on the parlour windows signified the more secure, probably skilled jobs of the families' wage-earners. More important distinctions developed along ethnic lines. In the 19th century Hamilton had witnessed the emergence of a distinct ethnic neighbourhood – the Irish working-class enclave known as Corktown – but as the city expanded after 1890 it was obliterated. The newcomers from Continental Europe also clustered together in households and on streets where fellow countrymen could speak their languages, help them find jobs, feed them their accustomed foods, and allow them to relax and socialize in familiar ways. As sojourners they had little interest in integrating into Anglo-Canadian ways of life, and, as their numbers grew, shopkeepers and other small-scale businessmen within each ethnic group began to provide all the services that these newcomers would need within specific neighbourhoods.

Whatever their preference for familiar customs, the new immigrants were also blocked from moving into certain neighbourhoods. Landlords or their agents often refused to rent to the new European population, and property owners avoided selling houses to "foreigners." Newly developed suburban areas also had restrictive covenants on the housing, which pre-screened would-be residents by banning industrial activities and constraining the kind and value of housing that could be erected. "No shacks allowed," one ad announced. "Each house must cost at least $2,000." Some of the covenants were blunter. "None of the lands described ... shall be used, occupied by or let or sold to Negroes, Asiatics, Bulgarians, Austrians, Russians, Serbs, Romanians, Turks, Armenians, whether British subjects or not, or foreign-born Italians, Greeks, or Jews," stipulated the covenant for the new west-end suburb of Westdale. One Italian immigrant later remembered that even in the interwar period, "Italians were not allowed to move into the area south of King Street, even St Pat's. I remember signs that were up warning Blacks, Chinese, and Italians not to move into the area." Another newcomer faced discrimination when he tried to buy a house outside the neighbourhood near the Steel Company. Since most of these new arrivals were wage-earners and their families, this explicit racism reinforced class biases. Space in the city for affordable working-class housing was thus limited as these restrictive covenants spread over more class-conscious neighbourhoods.[89]

English-speaking workers quickly distanced themselves. A Polish woman who arrived in 1908 remembered the English-speaking workers moving out as the "foreigners" moved into their neighbourhoods. "On North Sherman avenue, which is the main thoroughfare in the foreign district," a journalist noted in 1912, "there are only two or three English families to leaven the lump." Despite the housing shortage at the end of World War One, the *Herald* reported, Anglo-Canadian workers would not move into the houses vacated by hundreds of departing

European sojourners because "thousands of them are still in the districts and they are not regarded as desirable neighbours."[90]

Two separate multilingual neighbourhoods grew up as the city's so-called "foreign colony." Both were near the heaviest industries in the northeast and northwest sectors of Hamilton, especially the Steel Company's plants. In the northwest end, ethnic settlement spread along the streets in the vicinity of Barton and James streets, while at the eastern end of Barton Street a large enclave of Europeans centred around Sherman Avenue. The city's Italian population was split between these two sites, each with a different cluster of regional sojourners: Sicilians (especially those from the town of Racalmuto) and other southerners in the larger westend "colony," and Abruzzesi and other central and northeastern Italians in the east end. A few households clustered together, and occasionally a whole street, might take on a specific ethnic flavour, but generally the immigrant quarter was too small to allow for complete segregation by nationality. Italian or Polish households stood cheek by jowl with Bulgarian or Hungarian houses.

By 1913 a visitor to these neighbourhoods could stroll up streets lined with grocery stores, butcher shops, barber shops, steamship agents, and restaurants with predominantly European immigrant clientele. He might also have seen local Italians reading the latest edition of *L'Italia di Hamilton*, a newspaper published in the city between 1912 and 1914. Street life in these neighbourhoods was exotic and colourful, and English newspaper readers in the city received regular reports of raucous celebrations of weddings or christenings, at which alcoholic refreshments flowed freely, and of bloody street fights with knives flashing angrily. A boy growing up in the north end later remembered that, when you reached a street of Italians, "You knew when you were there ... they were on both sides, all sitting on their lawns, talking or singing."[91]

Ethnic identity was an equally powerful force in shaping some English-speaking working-class neighbourhoods as well, especially in east Hamilton. Recent English immigrants congregated in sufficient numbers in the east end to stamp their neighbourhoods with a particular flavour. Hamilton's Canadian-born residents regularly acknowledged what they heard as thick, sometimes only semi-intelligible accents – by dubbing the speakers as "Chirpers," and one of their earliest suburbs, Crown Point, "Chirperville." The English wore slightly different clothes, patronized shops that sold "Old Country" newspapers or the food expected on English working-class tables, and organized their favourite activities, such as soccer and cricket (rather than baseball). They also supported each other through crises as other immigrant groups were learning to do. English immigrants interviewed years later remembered how Anglo-Canadians made them aware of their differences. One resented how "When we were walking down the sidewalk, they'd step over and say 'yessir.' And we'd have to walk around." Another, however, believed this kind of harassment, also experienced on the job and in the schoolyards, made the newcomers "a little more self-conscious and a little more bull-headed and determined." As important as this sense of difference was for the residents of the new east-end suburbs, they were still within the dominant ethnic fold and were never subjected to the kinds of discrimination that the European newcomers faced. One English immigrant explained that he became Canadian as soon as he got rid of his English clothes and bought two Canadian suits.[92]

Like other industrial centres Hamilton was, then, residentially segregated into neighbourhoods with distinctive class and ethnic identities.

Alongside the home and the paid workplace, the streets of these neighbourhoods and the institutions that grew up on them – stores, theatres, churches, schools, fraternal societies, unions – provided another crucial arena of class formation. Neighbours in these working-class communities kept a careful distance from each other, and there may have been less communal space and fewer chances for casual interaction between the privatized households than in some urban areas on the other side of the Atlantic. Yet the streets of these neighbourhoods were lively, gregarious spaces that contrasted with the more sedate, withdrawn atmosphere of middle- and upper-class avenues. They could also be sites of nasty confrontations over wayward children, excessive noise, or disputed fence lines that could see men fighting or women screaming and pulling each other's hair, all of which might extend into the police court. Neighbours might also "snitch" on each other to welfare agencies.[93]

Many neighbours nonetheless never hesitated to help each other through family crises such as illness, pregnancy, or death. In particular, married women from working-class households met in the streets and the shops and over back fences and built their networks of mutual support and communication (sometimes, no doubt, as petty gossip). The men also learned quickly to co-operate in demanding better services for their neighbourhoods, and predominantly working-class "improvement societies" sprang up in the north and east ends in the years before World War One.

Eventually the sense of common identities and the habits of helping out would take deep root as a politically independent class-consciousness. These neighbourhoods were too new to be able to invoke any long-standing histories or traditions, but new mythologies about the common struggles to get established and to survive in this often rugged urban environment soon became the basis for pride and confrontation. Suburbs, then, did not automatically mean a "middle-class" way of life, as so many commentators have assumed since World War Two.[94]

Studholme's People

The social geography of working-class Hamilton was a complex interplay of agency and structure. Workers came as individuals and families to find waged work and tried to carve out for themselves useful and comfortable domestic spaces. Many did not linger for long, but by the 1920s a settling down process was under way, even among the European newcomers. Generally some rough strategizing about family fortunes was involved, whether the whole family relocated to Hamilton or most members remained behind on a farm in rural Canada or Europe. But families had to make these choices within severe constraints. Industrialists wanted only specific kinds of workers – coal miners or silk weavers need not apply. The level and regularity of wages determined what kind of housing workers could afford, and the suburban location of so many factories focused much of the new housing development for wage-earners and their families. Real-estate developers, builders, and landlords also made available only a certain range of choices in working-class accommodation, much of it shockingly expensive.

The relentless monotony of the grid pattern and the dominance of the single-family house spread out working-class families in regular formation and relative isolation from each other, rather than piling them together in close quarters. Municipal officials further shaped the available options with their eventually tighter regulation of public health and building standards, and class and ethnic prejudices channelled workers away from certain neighbourhoods and into others. Still, in the process of highly structured decision-making, Hamilton's workers made choices that brought them together in common patterns of association and support. Allan Studholme could thus feel confident that he was speaking for men and women who lived a life apart.

PART II

Keeping the Wolf from the Door

4

(SLS, LS533)

Labouring for Love

IN THE SPRING OF 1916 a flurry of controversy erupted over a new experiment: the tinkering with time known as "daylight saving." It was an issue that would surface regularly for several years to come. Turning the hands of the clock ahead an hour to catch an extra hour of daylight was intended as a new form of war-induced industrial efficiency, but it was deeply unpopular in working-class Hamilton. In angry letters spilling out onto the pages of the *Spectator*, working people decried the disruptions to their daily routines. A central theme in the agitation from both men and women who joined the debate was that housewives would suffer severely.[1]

Given that workers in Hamilton rarely dragged the private world of their family households into public debates, the issue turned an unusual light onto these domestic spaces, and the controversy especially highlighted key features of women's domestic labour in working-class Hamilton in the early 20th century. The debates emphasized a housewife's typical need to co-ordinate her work schedules with the rhythms set by the factory whistle. Her day began before the sun rose. She got up at 5:30 a.m. to make breakfast and fill lunch buckets for her husband and any other wage-earners in the house, including boarders. She took care to see that her husband was properly rested and replenished so he could go out and earn the wages that the family needed for its well-being.

"I didn't mind for myself, getting up at half past four all last summer in order to have a decent breakfast for my husband, but I did mind terribly for him," wrote one woman, who signed herself "Fair Play." "He is no longer a young man, and it is no more than the truth to say 'daylight-saving' made a nervous wreck of him last summer." Women also wrote in to remind readers that they had to mesh these outside demands with the inside needs of the household, especially looking after the children. Daylight saving, they argued, seriously disrupted children's bedtimes. "It is impossible to get them to sleep at a reasonable hour, because of the heat and noise. We cannot all live in large, cool houses with spacious grounds." The letters revealed the strain that "overwrought mothers" could experience in coping with "fractious children." One insisted, "A nursing mother needs her rest as much as a workingman if the babies are to grow up healthy."[2]

Women's contributions to the daylight-savings debate not only emphasized their nurturing activities within working-class households – the work of reproduction or, in popular parlance, the "labour of love" – but also brought to light the difficult physical and emotional demands of those roles. Adapting to the clock being moved forward or back was by no means the only challenge faced by working-class housewives in this period. Hampered by limited incomes and labour-intensive domestic tasks, they struggled with persistent epidemic diseases, workplace (and military) injuries, and aging or disabled kin. They confronted a growing barrage of public criticism of the ways in which they did their domestic work – an onslaught that was now emanating from an increasingly harmonious chorus of bourgeois women, professional "experts," commercial advertisers, and state bureaucrats.

Hamilton's working-class housewives did their best to negotiate their way through all of these changing expectations while continuing to provide the material and emotional sustenance that they believed their families needed. Many took great pride in running their households effectively, and thus felt able to exercise some power within their families and earn respect within their neighbourhoods. At the same time as they went through the daylight-savings controversy, some of the more political among them began to demand new public policies that would address their own sense of what they needed. One way or another, their private, normally unacknowledged domestic labour was becoming deeply politicized.[3]

The Bonds of Matrimony

The core understanding of the working-class household was the marriage contract, a complex interplay of law, custom, and emotion that created a division of labour, a hierarchy of power, and a set of definite expectations. The couple was certainly constrained by Canada's strict legal regime, which defined marriage as a fundamental relationship in the social order. That regime buttressed patriarchal dominance and, with a newly codified Criminal Code in 1892, laid down harsh penalties for anyone who strayed from the rigid moral conventions of heterosexual monogamy. Virtually every day local courts ruled on transgressions, punishing bigamists, adulterers, rapists, prostitutes, abortionists, sodomites, and sundry others. The law also made it extremely difficult to end a marriage. In Ontario before 1930 every divorce required a specific act of the national Parliament.[4]

Beyond the law, churches sanctified marriage with intense ritual and relentlessly preached commitment and conformity. More informally, kin and community passed on their diverse, sometimes unconventional expectations of the married couple, often based in deep-rooted histories that had transpired far from Hamilton – in working-class neighbourhoods of Lancashire or Glasgow, peasant villages in Sicily or Galicia, or farmlands in rural Ontario. Within those ever-present confines, working-class spouses had to work out the basics of their married lives on their own. When the Canadian Patriotic Fund, established to aid soldiers and their dependants, lifted the veil on the lives of soldiers' families during World War One, it found many couples acting as though they were married without having undergone the legal and religious formalities.[5]

Despite the romantic imagery surrounding marriage, young people usually took stock of their economic prospects before tying the knot. Hamilton couples jumped into wedlock in greatest numbers when the economy was booming and held back when it slumped.[6] Despite these fluctuations, proportionally more adults were getting married in Hamilton by the 1930s,[7] and, while data is scarce, it seems that the age at marriage was falling slightly, at least for women. A unique 1941 census report revealed that by 1920 considerably more women were marrying before age 25. But although a new cultural preference was emerging to make marriage an act of youthful and perhaps eroticized companionship, the union still had to be co-ordinated with the requirements of economic need.[8]

Every morning six days a week, a wife hoped to be able to hand her husband his well-stocked lunch bucket and send him off into the dawn to earn wages, confident for the moment that he was living up to his part of the marriage deal. As she closed the door behind him, she had no doubts about what was expected of her in return. She was his money-manager, his domestic servant, his children's caregiver, and his emotional support and faithful sexual partner. He was the provider; she was the domestic manager and nurturer. Unlike her husband, she rarely got payment for her work beyond emotional satisfaction. Her domestic tasks were tied up in relations of love, not terms of employment. A woman could derive self-esteem and considerable pride from successfully keeping up her end of the bargain, or experience frustration and guilt from failure. While this appeared to be a companionate arrangement of complementary roles, it was in essence a relationship that assumed and reproduced male dominance and female subservience. Working-class housewives knew their place, but also their entitlements within their marriage. They were prepared to defend themselves, their children, and the marriage itself against their husbands' shortcomings and abuse.[9]

Men generally knew what they wanted from their wives. Through the veil of careful privacy that working-class couples seemed to cast over their sexual behaviour inside marriage, the couple's sexual demands are the hardest to assess. Whatever mutual sexual attraction they had before the wedding, the married couple's sexual intimacy must have been severely constrained by their long hours of separation each working day, the tendency to spend their leisure time with members of the same sex, the exhaustion each brought to the marriage bed after demanding days – in both cases – of physical

Every week some working-class wives brought serious private problems in their marriages to be resolved in a formal, public courtroom. Newspaper reporters jotted down every detail for publication the next day. (HPL)

labour, and the lack of privacy in their cramped dwellings once children arrived and boarders settled in. Deep affection between husband and wife undoubtedly existed, and it may well have become a stronger ideal in the interwar period, when marriage was discussed more often as intimate partnership and companionship.[10]

Whatever the loving feelings, a man expected exclusive possession of his wife's body, and any whiff of infidelity could raise his jealous ire – legitimately so, according to local police magistrate George Jelfs, who declared in 1920, "A husband can run after her as much as he likes if he wants to find out what she is doing."[11] On a regular basis in most households, a man was probably more concerned that his wife could make ends meet and keep an orderly household. Marriage was always a highly practical project.[12] Indeed, if a wife disappeared or was unable to fill her part of the bargain, a female child or other relative almost invariably stepped in to pick up the slack – like the ten-year-old girl that health department visitors found running one household in 1923.[13]

Matters in the domestic sphere might often work relatively smoothly, but they nonetheless left plenty of room for disagreement and bitter conflict.[14] Beyond difficulties rooted in individual personalities, either partner might become upset if the other failed to keep up his or her end of the marriage deal. The relentless insecurities of the working-class family household made sustaining each end of the bargain a regular challenge. Money problems were by far the most common source of tension, particularly because husbands and wives might have competing priorities over expenditures – usually a husband's personal indulgence versus family needs. Plenty of women no doubt avoided direct confrontations over these issues, but many a wife might be outraged if her husband did not consistently bring home the bacon, especially if she believed that wages were being squandered on alcohol. "She's a very fine woman when there's a pile of money on the table. She's very nice and gentle then," one man insisted in 1920. "But [not] when the money's gone."[15]

After prolonged verbal battles, some wives had recourse to the police court to compel their spouses to provide for them. At those moments a husband might prove to be equally irate at his wife's deficiencies as a housekeeper, especially her failure to have meals ready for him,[16] or at her nagging about his shortcomings, which could challenge his status in the household. In justifying himself, he appealed to what he thought was widely understood about marriage relationships. "No woman will walk over me," one man blustered in a 1910 court case. "I'm reasonable, but they can't get away with any tongue lashings with me." Several years later another complained, "She thinks she is boss. She thinks she can fight. A fellow can't take that all the time." A husband could also be outraged if he detected any sexual improprieties – perhaps his wife was staying out of the house too long or showing excessive friendliness towards a boarder. "Our lives are not safe with him," a wife reported in 1910. "He is jealous of every boarder that comes into the house." In 1930 one husband complained that his wife "was bootlegging and setting out with other men at a ghastly hour of the morning."[17]

In this relationship husbands clearly held the dominant position. Within working-class communities on both sides of the Atlantic and more formally in the courts, husbands enjoyed a long-standing "right" to "correct" their wives as part of their legitimate masculine authority within the household. As late as 1930 Hamilton's police magistrate could still proclaim in his courtroom: "It wasn't so long ago that men could administer corporal punishment to their wives if the occasion demanded and I'm not so sure it was a bad idea."[18]

Many women apparently suffered in silence in the face of abuse within their marriages. Some fought back with their own verbal and even physical responses. Some tried to shut out the abusive husband temporarily or permanently. Some turned for informal help to clergymen or police constables on the neighbourhood beat. Some left the family household and sought shelter with their parents, eventually perhaps abandoning hope that living with their spouses was possible.[19] And some found their way to the office of Jelfs, who, during his 36 years as the city's sole police magistrate, evidently functioned as an informal marriage counsellor and helped women decide whether to charge their husbands with non-support, assault, criminal threatening, or perhaps drunkenness. "Wife vs. Husband is a serio-comic continuous performance at the King William street police court," the *Spectator*'s court reporter quipped in 1910, "and few days go by in a week that some wife does not complain to the court of her husband's conduct."[20] The scene had not much changed 20 years later.

In his long career as police magistrate, George Jelfs presided over innumerable cases of domestic abuse and neglect in working-class households. He often advised women in such cases privately in his office. (HPL)

Despite their prominence in the daily press, court cases over wife abuse never involved more than a tiny handful of the city's wives (all of them working class; women of the middle and upper classes would never air their marital problems in public). Their outcome is nonetheless revealing. In the eyes of police magistrates, husbands could indeed cross a line into "unnatural" or "intolerable" cruelty, and gradually from the 1870s onward the law provided stiffer penalties for excessive wife abuse. In 1897 Ontario legislation empowered a magistrate to grant a separation agreement to a wife who had left her husband as a result of "repeated assaults or other acts of cruelty," and in 1909 an amendment to the federal Criminal Code allowed magistrates to order a whipping for excessive brutality to a wife. Increasingly, extraordinarily violent husbands could ignite judicial harshness.

Most likely aware of the widespread publicity that such cases got through the police-court columns of the three local newspapers, Jelfs and his successor, Henry A. Burbidge, made examples of a few particularly abusive men. Some were sent to jail, and in a dramatic instance in 1910 one also received ten lashes – the first whipping of a wife-beater that anyone could remember.[21] "Any man who kicks his wife deserves the lash," Jelfs declared three months later, though at the wife's request he limited the sentence to three months in jail. Burbidge was still meting out corporal punishment and stiff jail sentences in such cases 20 years later. He was particularly keen to discipline violent husbands in European immigrant households, announcing, "We've got to teach these people they can't manhandle women."[22] The exact impact of these highly publicized penalties for wife abuse in the early 20th century remains obscure, but many husbands surely recognized that punching, kicking, biting, or otherwise assaulting their wives had lost much of its customary legitimacy.

In particular, no doubt thanks in large measure to the persistent agitations of the Woman's Christian Temperance Union (WCTU), drunkenness became an increasingly inadequate excuse for attacking a wife – "No man can hit a woman when he is drunk," Burbidge declared in 1930 – and women frequently convinced the magistrates to put their husbands on the so-called "Indian List" of men whom local saloon keepers and liquor-store owners were not supposed to serve. Many women insisted on a legal separation and maintenance order that would protect them from their husbands' brutality while guaranteeing them a small income (although the enforcement of men's legal obligation was usually weak).[23]

A wife's reputation for respectability had to be completely untarnished. Any indication of a woman's drunkenness or philandering could undermine her case. "You know when a woman has a husband who is the least bit jealous and she does not try to help him she is doing a great wrong, and I have no sympathy for her," Jelfs told a woman in a non-support case in 1910. Later that year he was even harder on a woman

who he discovered was living common-law with her abusive spouse. "This is what comes of leading an improper life," he declared. "You must leave the house. I'll give you until Wednesday." He similarly dismissed another case of a woman who had separated from her husband: "Failing to live with her husband would have created trouble enough between them quickly enough." On other occasions, according to reports, he stressed that "too many women anger men into striking them and then leave and want support to live separate" and indicated that "if he had his way every woman who broke the marriage vows would be sentenced to imprisonment for ten years."[24] The magistrates also gave less support to wives who had failed to fulfil their matrimonial responsibilities. "Some wives do not look after their husbands and do not make home pleasant enough to induce the men to be good," Jelfs argued in 1910. In 1930 Burbidge dismissed a case with a lecture to the abused wife, noting that she "would have gotten a more sympathetic hearing if she had got rid of his mother-in-law and performed her duties as a wife."[25]

Most often a woman ended up heading home with the abuser, clinging to flimsy "guarantees" that his violent temper would not flare up again. In roughly one case out of seven of the 113 located in the *Spectator* police-court columns in 1900, 1910, 1920, and 1930, a man had to lay out money in the form of sureties to keep the peace. In roughly one case out of fourteen a fine was imposed (with jail as an alternative). One in ten cases resulted in a suspended sentence, sometimes when a wife begged that her husband not be sent to jail. Close to half of all the cases were dismissed. A quarter of the dismissals resulted when the wife failed to show up for the trial or refused to press charges once her husband was in the prisoner's box. Sometimes she had asked for him to be arrested only to curb his drunkenness and was now content to take him home sober and contrite. Some women may have lacked evidence to support the assault charges, feared a still worse life without a breadwinner, or were concerned for the future of their children or the family's respectability. Many were certainly trying to use the courts to salvage a rocky marriage. Most often, however, the magistrate decided that the evidence was unconvincing or that domestic bliss could return if he gave a man a stern lecture and a warning of dire consequences should his behaviour continue.

Jelfs, preferring to help couples reconcile, regularly sent them home to "settle their differences." The details of these cases are sketchy, but in hindsight it would appear that the magistrate's judgment about possible reconciliation was often misplaced. In 1900, for example, a wife told the court that her husband had struck her repeatedly and even bitten her arm; the man was sent home on a suspended sentence for a week "to square himself with his wife." Ten years later a woman claimed that her husband, a heavy drinker, came home one night, beat her "something fierce," and, when she fled, smashed all the furniture and dishes in the house. Jelfs simply dismissed the case and urged the woman to report any further drunkenness so that he could put the man on the Indian List. In 1920 he dismissed an assault case in which money had been a central source of conflict: "What you people need is a little more consideration and sympathy with one another. The trouble with married people is that they flare up at one another instead of keeping back and reasoning a little." He also explained, "I generally leave [punishment] in a way to the wife. If a woman demands harsh treatment I conclude that the husband is, perhaps more blameless than the wife." He insisted on the power of publicity to bring husbands into line, advising women "to have the charge heard

in open court, for few men wish the public to know they are charged with such an offence, and will effect a settlement or reconciliation first." Partly thanks to his resistance, Hamilton would not have a separate family court until 1930, when his successor started hearing "domestic relations" cases more quietly and informally on a specific weekday afternoon. A more independent family court was created six years later, although the police magistrate still presided (as he did over the local juvenile court).[26]

The police court thus remained an uncertain and unreliable remedy for neglected or abused wives. The increasing intolerance of excessive brutality was counterbalanced by the magistrates' willingness to send women back into potentially dangerous situations and their moralistic judgments about proper wifely comportment that held the women to higher standards than the men.

A wife in working-class Hamilton could expect that the love that was supposed to bind her to her husband could be fraught with anxiety and tension, that he might be insensitive or even brutal, that some help could be expected from the legal system, but that most often she had to work out her own survival strategies based on some mixture of meek compliance, persistent nagging, bold confrontation and bluster, or retreat and separation. Ultimately, in most working-class households, husband and wife must have negotiated a more or less workable partnership – what one British writer in the period called "a kind of dogged comradeship."[27]

Keeping House

Each morning, with breakfast over and her husband out the door and on his way to his job, a working-class housewife would head for the stove, the wash tub, the sewing machine, or the mop and pail – while also, if necessary, keeping

Eliza Fowler, a Hamilton moulder's wife, carrying firewood around 1910. (SLS, LS509)

First World War, most houses had running water (cold, not hot), and inside toilets connected to sewers had replaced privies, though bathtubs remained a luxury.[29] Still, out in the new working-class suburbs there could be lengthy delays in hooking up water pipes, and everywhere families doubling up in households might also find awkward water connections in upper storeys or attics. Many houses had gas for lighting, but electricity remained a novelty in the early years of the century. The local private-power conglomerate, Dominion Power, showed little interest in accommodating a domestic market that was not expected to be as profitable as the industrial sector. Part of the appeal of the campaign for publicly owned electrical power facilities after 1906 was the possibility of making cheap power available to working-class families. By the 1920s most households were wired for electricity. Initially, few of these electrified households plugged in more than electric lamps because most of the electrical appliances flooding onto the market by the 1920s were prohibitively expensive.[30]

Until well into the interwar period, cooking food in most working-class homes was still done on cast-iron stoves that had to be stoked with coal or wood, emptied of ashes, and regularly "blacked." Controlling the heat of these stoves for cooking or baking required great skill. The first electric and gas stoves remained beyond the budgets of most working-class families until the 1930s. The use of electric stoves among the wired homes of the province's urban domestic customers increased steadily during the 1930s (to 30 per cent in 1938, along with 18 per cent of homes using hot plates), thanks no doubt to aggressive promotion by the local Hydro Shop. Just as many homes must have acquired gas stoves; in 1941 federal census-takers reported that 99 per cent of Hamilton households used either gas or

an eye on the children and helping out any other adults in the house. Her daily work, more than simply menial tasks, represented acts of caring and nurturing – unquestionably, in her eyes, expressions of love. If she were lucky, at least one more older child, or maybe more, would be around to help through the day, but as time passed the tighter enforcement of school attendance laws and an increase in the school-leaving age often left her alone with the toddlers, the disabled, and the elderly. Some husbands might help out if they were out of work or when they got home from the job, but most took care to avoid any housework that would threaten gender conventions or (as in the case of hanging out the laundry) their own masculine status in the community.[28]

The workspace of a working-class Hamilton housewife was small – seldom more than six rooms and sometimes fewer – and the tools and facilities available to her required heavy physical exertion. The housewife of the 1890s would nonetheless notice some changes in her granddaughter's kitchen of the 1930s. By the

In 1908 housewives still liked to hunt for bargains in Hamilton's central open-air market. As the city spread further east the market became less accessible for many working-class families.

(CTA, Fonds 1244, Item 9011)

electricity for cooking. By that point too, many seemed to be buying the cheap toasters that had come onto the market. The new cooking technologies of the 1930s and later would undoubtedly bring the biggest changes in Hamilton housewives' domestic work processes.[31]

Mechanical appliances for refrigerating food also proved popular as prices began to come down somewhat in the 1930s, but far fewer families could afford them. By 1941 half the city's households had a gas or electric refrigerator, but 39 per cent of homes still had ice boxes and 11 per cent no refrigeration at all. (Among tenants, only 45 per cent had a gas or electric refrigerator; 43 per cent had ice boxes; and 12 per cent had no refrigeration.) In the east end, an old-timer recalled, ice was delivered twice a week in the 1930s.[32] Housewives improvised with snow and ice in the cooler weather, but otherwise expected to have to use quickly whatever was growing in the backyard or to shop frequently for perishables.

Much of the family's food was prepared from scratch, as in the late 19th century, but proportionally more pre-processed foods, such as bakery bread and canned goods, found their way into workers' kitchens after the turn of the century, some of them heavily promoted through advertising. Tight budgets and labour-intensive housework probably kept meals plain and simple.[33] As the city expanded, the city's central market was no longer within easy reach for the many shoppers. Housewives relied instead on nearby corner grocery stores or the many vendors who drove through their neighbourhoods selling milk, bread, tea and coffee, and other commodities. Working-class households rarely had telephones that might have allowed for ordering groceries, and few had cars for transporting them (in any case men controlled these vehicles).[34]

Making the family clothing had also long been part of women's work at home. By the turn of the century, workingmen were accustomed to

Door-to-door delivery of all kinds of goods became more common. (SLS, LS47)

Maintaining the cast-iron kitchen stove was a heavy job for housewives. (CIHM, 84009)

RALSTON'S MATCHLESS STOVE POLISH

In the old days

stove polishing was a task always dreaded.

¶ This polish has removed the drudgery and made the task easy and pleasurable.

Gives a high and lasting polish. TRY IT.

Some housewives turned to cheap commercial laundries to lighten the burden of washing clothes. (HS, 1 June 1925, 18)

Wet Wash 5c per lb.

Regent 1442-1443 City LAUNDRY

buying most of their garments ready-made. But housewives continued to make clothes for themselves and their children well into the interwar period, when the first mass-market dresses and underwear became more affordable. Penny-pinching would nonetheless keep them at their sewing machines, mending worn clothing or remodelling items for younger children.[35] As housewives turned more regularly to the market for products they had once made in their homes, advertisers stepped forward to help them make decisions about quality and price.[36] In the end decreased home production and greater reliance on the market for the family's needs meant even more penny-pinching and efforts to stretch the dollar.

Meanwhile, the grime that fell from the stacks of the many new factories made the fight against dirt relentless.[37] Cleaning was probably the most exhausting work that a housewife faced each week, and in this regard little would change over the years. For many working-class housewives the new and relatively expensive vacuum cleaner never displaced the brooms, mops, brushes, and buckets of soapy water. According to the Hydro-Electric Power Commission, only one in five urban households across Ontario that had hooked up to electricity had a vacuum cleaner in the 1920s, and only one in three by the end of the 1930s. About half the households in Hamilton had these appliances in 1941 (and less than two out of every five tenants). Eliminating the boiling and hard scrubbing of laundry on a washboard with an electric washing machine was equally unlikely in the 1920s, but prices fell somewhat in the 1930s and by 1938 half of Hydro's domestic customers had installed a machine, probably including a small minority of working-class households. The biggest breakthrough was the electric iron, a cheap appliance that replaced the heavy old cast-iron device, which had to be heated on the stove. The new irons were found in four out of five Ontario homes with electricity by the early 1920s and in virtually all by the end of the 1930s.[38]

Still, advanced technology does not by itself dictate the standards of housework, and most women struggled to maintain some degree of what they understood to be respectability – particularly cleanliness and order.[39] Some household changes brought new pressures on those self-imposed standards. An indoor bathroom was another room to clean, for example, and sending children to school every day meant more washing, ironing, and mending to be able to dress them appropriately.[40]

A housewife's work could also be increased by the pressure to maintain appropriate standards as set by outsiders. In 1893, on the assumption that inadequate housekeeping caused poverty, drunkenness, and sundry other social problems, the local Young Women's Christian Association (YWCA), led by the tireless Adelaide Hoodless, the wife of a local manufacturer, began running small cooking and sewing classes in the north end to teach working-class girls proper housewifery. In 1904 Hoodless convinced the Hamilton school board to introduce "domestic science" into the local elementary school curriculum to teach "the value of pure air, proper food, systematic management, economy, care of children, domestic and civil sanitation and the prevention of disease."[41]

Henceforth Hamilton's housewives could expect their young adolescent daughters to arrive home each week with suggestions about how to do household tasks more "scientifically." At least one housewife in working-class Hamilton remained unconvinced. She informed readers of the *Spectator* in 1904 that she thought this teaching was unnecessary – and insulting – twaddle. She resented a school trustee's insinuation that

Adelaide Hoodless, wife of a Hamilton manufacturer, was a tireless campaigner for programs to teach girls more "scientific" household skills. (HPL)

The patent-medicine companies that produced Dr. Chase's Nerve Food and Lydia E. Pinkham's Vegetable Compound used advertising images that spoke directly to the daily experience of hard physical labour and emotional stress for working-class women.

(*HS*, 25 March 1907, 11; 20 March 1907, 24; 13 Oct. 1917, 23)

Young Hamilton women in an early domestic science class. (HPL)

"poor food badly cooked is what causes drunkenness among the working class," and attacked domestic science as a "fad": "The best cooks today are those who cook as their mothers did, and I would advise anyone to have one good cook book in the house; it is a great help." Another woman told a reporter three years later that "children could be better taught at home by their mothers in a practical way." She told the story of a girl in a local household science class who found the curriculum contradicting what her mother had taught her and made a better cake than her classmates by using her mother's technique. Children of new immigrant families also carried home recipes for food that would never appear on the family's table (porridge or rice pudding, for example). Not for the first time did Hamilton's working-class housewives find their children's schooling used against them.[42]

The message of "scientific" approaches to housework reached housewives in other ways. More and more of the cookbooks supplied free by food-processing companies contained detailed recipes that abandoned loose rule-of-thumb measurements in favour of scientific precision. The 1905 *Blue Ribbon Cook Book*, distributed by a manufacturer of coffee, tea, and various baking ingredients, warned housewives, "Recipes are written accurately by experts after they have been tried several times, so it is better to follow them exactly. Nine out of ten mishaps, or failures, are due almost entirely to a lack of mixing, or change of the recipe, or from failure to observe the proper heat."[43] Some two decades later the federal government's Division of Child Welfare brought together the key notions of scientific housewifery in a free booklet, *How to Manage Housework in Canada*, borrowing heavily from a widely read US book, Christine Frederick's *Scientific Management in the Home*.[44]

Gradually, too, advertisers in the city's daily newspapers reshaped their messages to suggest that housekeepers should meet their obligations to families by buying products that promised "scientific" results. In 1901, for example, Royal Baking Powder was promoted simply as being "indispensable to the preparation of the finest cake, hot-breads, rolls and muffins," but three decades later Magic Baking Powder ads were including precise recipes from the company's cookbook, along with the warning "not to deviate in any way" from the instructions. In the interwar period, the Ontario Hydro-Electric Commission and its Hamilton distributor entered the fray through compelling advertising suggesting that the acquisition of electrical household appliances was essential to proper housekeeping. In general, housewives of the 1930s were bombarded with conceptions of transformed household workspaces, reorganized according to "scientific" principles and well stocked with new appliances. Most Hamilton housewives must have wondered how they could ever afford such renovations and technological investments.[45]

Housework in working-class Hamilton, then, evolved unevenly between the 1890s and 1930s. New stoves and packaged foods made meal preparation somewhat easier in the interwar period, but overall domestic labour remained a series of physically demanding tasks with tools that were only beginning to change by the 1930s, and then generally only in a minority of households.[46] After 1920 housewives had electrical lighting, but it was not until well into the 1930s that large numbers had electrical stoves. Far fewer had fridges or washing machines, fewer still vacuum cleaners. The households of newer European immigrants and people of colour, where the breadwinner's wages were invariably lower, probably lagged furthest behind. For many women arriving from peasant villages in Europe, running a household in Hamilton in their own time-honoured fashion must have presented new challenges and difficulties.[47] Certainly, in working-class households new tools to lighten women's domestic labours were not always a high priority (by 1941 95 per cent of Hamilton households had a radio, evidently a more highly valued investment in leisure).[48] In any case, by the 1930s for working-class housewives – and whatever easing of their daily burden had started to become possible – the demanding expectations of "scientific" housework invariably meant more work for mother.

Raising Kids

Women's workdays were filled with child care in addition to the other many domestic tasks, and in the early 20th century working-class mothers also faced increased pressure to adjust their parenting practices – which only added new stress to the workload of child-rearing. Making and nurturing babies filled many years of a younger woman's life, and mothers with large families could be worn out by middle age.

Women had limited ability to control the size of their families, and husbands typically showed little interest in that issue. Young working-class women often entered marriage with little knowledge of sex and reproduction; their mothers rarely discussed the subject. According to the nurse who worked in the city's small birth-control clinic, which opened in 1932, preventing pregnancy for most couples involved douching or getting the husbands' co-operation in coitus interruptus or abstinence. Until the 1920s, medical practitioners complicated efforts at contraception by giving faulty information about the "safe" periods for women who followed the rhythm method. The Criminal Code had made all artificial birth-control devices illegal, and doctors and public-health nurses refused to discuss them (other than in the birth-control centre, which mostly supplied diaphragms and contraceptive jelly). Catholic doctors were particularly negative. Many working-class men suspected that such devices were a middle-class plot to limit working-class fecundity. In any case, even though condoms and vaginal suppositories were being sold under the counter in drug stores by the 1930s, they were too expensive for most working-class wives.[49]

These women were at the centre of the new birth-control clinic's vision in the 1930s, and, despite the fiery threats of the local Catholic bishop and the need for a doctor's referral (when many families could not afford a doctor's care), by 1939 some 2,000 mothers had nervously made their way to the weekly clinic, where the $3 fee for the devices provided was ultimately waived in half the cases. Only those who were married and had already had at least two children were served, and many women harboured lingering doubts about what the clinic offered. In 1937 the clinic's nurse was assigned to knock on doors to encourage more working-class women to attend; she met with polite resistance from most.[50]

The law was even less intolerant of abortions, but a few doctors were apparently willing to terminate a pregnancy, and some women were prepared to try dangerous self-induced procedures. Some tried old herbal potions or one of the patent medicines with abortifacient reputations. The Hamilton Medical Society was concerned enough about the extent of "criminal abortions" in 1907 to call a special meeting, which included several local clergymen, and three decades later federal and provincial studies concluded that between one in five and one in seven pregnancies were still being terminated. Popular assumptions that abortions were acceptable as long as the fetus had not quickened in the womb (in the fourth or fifth month) may have made these decisions easier.[51]

By whatever means, working-class women in Hamilton seemed to be trying to have fewer children, and during economic slumps they clearly succeeded. By 1940 the number of children born to Hamilton families (as elsewhere in Canada) had gone down.[52] In the 1920s and 1930s more than four out of five families among the whole population had a maximum of two children.[53] Working-class families tended to be larger than average, especially in the new immigrant neighbourhoods, but in all cases were getting smaller after 1920.[54]

Preparing for a new arrival involved worrying about new costs (the doctor's bill, new clothing and bedding, additional food), arranging nursing help during a mother's convalescence (a week to ten days), and finding short-term care for any other children. Soon, however, mothers had to return to their regular work around the house with the additional responsibility of a new infant to care for. As the family grew, so too did the time and effort devoted to raising the children.

Feeding and health care were crucial, but mothers also had moral control over working-class households. They were primarily responsible for teaching and enforcing proper behaviour among their children, with only occasional intervention by fathers. Part of a family's respectability in a neighbourhood rested on a mother's ability to control her youngsters. Long before the end of the 19th century mothers had felt the blast of religious instruction on how to instil moral fibre, with the help of the various churches. Since the 1850s most had also been willing to turn over their children to middle-class teachers in the public or separate school systems, though the demands of the family economy had regularly pulled the offspring out of the classroom.[55] The 1890s, however, saw the beginning of a series of new initiatives to intervene in working-class childhood and impinge on a mother's care of her offspring.

Working-class parents doubtless had a story or an aphorism for every occasion to teach their children right from wrong,[56] but, with fathers gone so long each day and mothers weighed down with domestic drudgery, they seemed ready to hand over their youngsters to others for more regular instruction in morality, discipline, and practical academic skills. Young children found themselves led off first to a local Sunday school and then to the neighbourhood elementary school (either public or separate). There they were expected to learn how to behave properly and to pick up basic literacy and numeracy. In this process they came under the supervision and tutelage of others with agendas that could be quite different from those of their parents.

Middle-class teachers, virtually all of them women, took charge[57] and tried to use the rigid provincial curriculum and the authority to maintain strict order and discipline to mould the workers' children into obedient, respectful, self-controlled children. They closely regulated the energetic young bodies in rigidly structured classrooms, insisted on rote learning from standardized textbooks, maintained constant oversight of personal hygiene, and administered stern lessons in "respect for religion and the principles of Christian morality, and the highest regard for truth, justice, love of country, humanity, benevolence, sobriety, industry, frugality, purity, temperance and all other virtues" (as an 1896 law required). "Some teachers," an elderly Hamilton woman later recalled, "felt they were kind of missionaries."[58]

Schooling got more intense in the 1890s and early 1900s, when child labour was restricted by law, year-round elementary schooling became compulsory, and truancy was monitored more closely. In the process, mothers lost some control over the socialization of their young children, as other women from a different class background drilled into them the expectations of orderly behaviour and moral restraint on a daily basis and used corporal punishment to instil fearful obedience. New features of the curriculum implicitly challenged working-class mothering. "The school must be the agent through which the homes of the next generation will be influenced," Hoodless said as she launched her campaign to teach scientific housewifery. The Woman's Christian Temperance Union was just as triumphant when in 1893 it got "scientific temperance" introduced into the Ontario school system as a compulsory subject. Military training for boys, inaugurated in senior classes of the elementary schools just before the war, sought to instil order and discipline among their sons. A Penny Bank was also set up in 1908 to teach habits of thrift and deter frivolous expenditures on the pleasures of the street, on the apparent assumption that parents could not be trusted to teach such behaviour. Generally working-class parents nonetheless seemed to defer to the teachers' authority and call for their children's obedience. "Our parents insisted that we respect them," one woman from a working-class family recalled. Good mothering now included efforts to ensure that the children performed adequately in the state schooling system.[59]

As children grew older, they found more time outside their mothers' direct supervision to organize their own games and activities in backyards, streets, and other public spaces. Some also took to the street to help the family economy (or themselves) by selling, scavenging, or begging. Sometimes, especially when mothers were trying to manage without a spouse, the children's behaviour ran up against laws prohibiting street rowdiness, truancy, petty theft, and sundry other offences. In the last half of the 19th century the police magistrate might send such youngsters to jail or, in response to growing concerns about the need for special treatment, to the new

The Children's Aid Society's Inspector Hunter was legally empowered to remove children from homes in which parents were considered to be neglectful.

(OSNDCR, 1910, 74)

Victoria Industrial School at Mimico, which was designed to reform wayward children.[60]

Since at least the 1870s, moral reformers had been trying to modify the behaviour of these children by coaxing them into such organizations as Sunday schools and Bands of Hope. Such charitable institutions as the local Orphan Asylum or the Girls' Home had also been engaged in "rescue work" through housing the children of the poor, but, by the 1890s, there was a growing reaction against putting children into institutions, rather than using the corrective powers of actual family settings.[61] In 1893 the Ontario government passed new legislation for dealing with these "neglected and dependent" children. It authorized the creation of local privately run Children's Aid Societies (CAS), which were empowered to apply for custody of such children and to place them in foster homes. Hamilton's own Society appeared early the next year, and a part-time officer watched the streets for such loosely disciplined children (until 1910 he doubled as the city's truant officer). He could institute police-court proceedings to snatch children from their parents (until 1913 they were temporarily placed in local charitable institutions, and after that date in the new CAS shelter),

but far more often he simply gave parents stern warnings to control their offspring. An officer of the St. Vincent de Paul Society did the same with Catholic families.[62]

Before the war the CAS had an upper-class "ladies' committee," whose members might also knock at the doors of working-class households when they suspected neglect was taking place on the inside. In fact, the number of wards supervised by the Society was always tiny alongside those whose families were simply "encouraged and helped to make a fresh start in life and to do their duty to their little ones." By the 1920s the Society's inspector and a female social worker were handling some 1,000 children a year, a number that climbed to nearly 1,700 in 1931 (the number of social workers would soon rise to 12). "In a great many cases," the CAS inspector reported in 1923, "complaints are received that parents are neglecting their children, bootlegging or mothers are living immoral lives." If a visit to the household did not seem to bring the desired results, spying would follow. "To secure sufficient evidence against suspected parties," the inspector explained, "night watching and shadowing were necessary." A daughter might be swept off to the CAS shelter until the parents improved their home, or charges might be laid. By that point the local Rotary Club was supplementing the inspector's wages to allow him to become an informal probation officer with children facing charges in court. The club also set up the city's first Big Brother organization to provide volunteers to work with boys in such circumstances (a Big Sisters organization followed soon after). When the city finally authorized the creation of a juvenile court in 1923 (16 years after federal enabling legislation had been passed), the CAS and volunteer Big Brothers and Big Sisters were formally integrated into the new probation system to watch over the youths and their families. The CAS was thus a new agency armed with increasing state authority that stood as a regular, increasingly visible threat to working-class mothers who had difficulty controlling their youngsters.[63]

Workers' children did not have to have brushes with the law to attract the child-savers' attention. In 1909 a group of upper-class citizens were disturbed enough by the uncontrolled playfulness of the children in working-class neighbourhoods to found the Hamilton Playgrounds Association to provide a well-equipped, supervised space for pre-adolescent youngsters during the summer months. By 1918 there were four of these privately sponsored recreational facilities, and 17 by 1931 when the city took them over.[64] Close supervision by trained staff was crucial, and children were never allowed to play on their own. In fact, the play space was closed and locked up after hours. "By keeping them off the street, they are kept out of trouble, out of the police court, and out of our reformatories," the *Times* suggested, "and in the supervised grounds they are taught to be lovers of law and order, and fair play all round, and more than that, good and respectful manners towards each other and to their elders."[65] Beyond the swings and teeter-totters, the structured play was segregated by sex, and much of the boys' time was spent in energetic games and sports while the girls spent more time in handicraft and sewing classes and other domestic instruction. Often a gramophone belted out "Rule Britannia" and other patriotic songs while the children played. At various points, physicians were brought in to talk to mothers and children about matters such as health care and obedience to parents.[66]

Despite the overt structure of firm discipline (a child could be sent home to wash his face or expelled from a playground for swearing, for example), hundreds of children up to about age 12 flocked into these play spaces every year. Indeed, the staff regularly reported that mothers dropped off tots while they did their shopping. Sometimes, if the women had to be out of the house earning money, they sent the youngest with older siblings to stay for the day. At one west-end playground, four out of ten children showing up in the summer of 1913 were "foreign," probably from the densely packed households of the new immigrant neighbourhood taking shape around the Steel Company's rolling mills. Parents were not encouraged to linger with their children, and had no role in the Association's recreational program other than as spectators at special performances. Publicly the Playgrounds Association's officers lauded the improved manners and habits of the children who attended regularly, but behind the scenes the staff admitted to sometimes reaching their limits in curbing childish rambunctiousness (well into the 1920s supervisors also complained about the quality of some of the staff). Whatever mothers thought about the efforts to correct their children's behaviour and teach them "obedience, self control, self sacrifice, kindness and courtesy," they could appreciate the resulting free day care off dangerous streets.[67] The problem was that few children, especially boys, would stay in these programs into their early adolescent years, when the street-corner gang became a more powerful alternative attraction.

School teachers, playground supervisors, truant officers, child-protection officials, probation officers – the network of professionals concerned with instilling greater discipline within working-class children grew slowly before the war, replacing the individual volunteers from upper-class households, and became more solidly entrenched after 1920. By that point, much like the social workers within charities who scrutinized working-class family economies, and like the health-care workers who hectored working-class housewives, more of these people were trained professionals applying an expertise to what they perceived as problems of bad child-rearing in working-class homes. In schools and playgrounds they took children out of the reach of parents, but the officials who were lined up to tackle juvenile delinquency confronted the youngsters in their own homes. In most cases they had the power of the state behind them. Mothers undoubtedly greeted them with ambivalence – welcoming their help with problem sons and daughters, but resenting the blaming and insensitivity to the economic insecurities of working-class life.

Feeling Poorly

Cooking, cleaning, and caution (in the form of watchfulness): for working-class mothers, these were the touchstones, the crucial ways in which they tried to keep their families safe and healthy. Yet limited household income, cramped or awkward living space, and the relentless pollution of the natural environment by the city's factories and sewage system could compromise those efforts.[68] So too could disease and injury. When family members became sick and disabled, running a household would require integrating into daily routines the unpredictable, sometimes long-term care of the weakened bodies, and working-class wives and mothers shouldered the major responsibility for this work. Over the decades the demand for home-based health care declined scarcely at all.

The women's own health was most often an issue during pregnancies. The chances were good that working-class wives faced their first childbirths with minimal knowledge of what to expect; parents rarely discussed the subject with their children and schools provided little direct information. Most women, it seems, consulted

a doctor only in the final stages of pregnancy.[69] Complications in childbirth were common. Each year before 1920 an average of 5 per cent of pregnancies in Hamilton resulted in stillbirths, peaking at 8 per cent in 1919 and declining only to an annual average of 3.5 per cent in the interwar period.[70] Giving birth also remained remarkably dangerous for mothers themselves, especially those with other complications resulting from poor health, malnutrition, or exhaustion from domestic chores. Hamilton's statistics on maternal mortality over the half-century before World War Two reveal no pattern of significant decline – roughly 6 deaths per 1,000 live births. Indeed, down to the late 1930s, among women of childbearing age only tuberculosis was more common than childbirth as a cause of death. The striking dimensions of the problem prompted Hamilton's Local Council of Women to stage a huge, well-attended pageant entitled "Drama on Motherhood" in 1930 to highlight the issue of maternal deaths and to invoke "Progress, Science and Humanity" to "fight for mothers."[71] Becoming a mother could clearly blend surging excitement with deep undercurrents of anxiety and fear.

Pregnancies did not necessarily produce long-lived children. Before World War One, the number of newborns who died in their first year ran close to one in five, a figure that tapered off gradually after that point, reaching an average annual rate in the 1930s of about one in 20.[72] The leading causes of these deaths were gastrointestinal illnesses that induced vomiting and diarrhea.[73] The children who survived were susceptible to a considerable range of diseases, some merely briefly upsetting, others potentially deadly. A mother would have dreaded the news that her child had diphtheria, measles, scarlet fever, or whooping cough, all of which spread through the city's households regularly in the early 20th century and hit youngsters particularly hard. Between 1905 and 1914, for example, more than 1,200 cases of diphtheria were reported, resulting in 116 deaths – nearly one in ten. These cases appeared preponderantly in working-class neighbourhoods.[74] In the same ten-year period, nearly 5,700 cases of measles were tallied up, including major outbreaks roughly every two years (a pattern that would continue right through to the 1930s). Although only 46 deaths resulted directly, all too often measles developed more life-threatening complications, especially pneumonia (still one in four or five cases in 1930), for which the wonder-drug antibiotics had not yet been invented.[75] In the decade before 1914 doctors also reported 45 deaths from 1,766 cases of scarlet fever and 316 deaths from 1,377 cases of whooping cough – nearly one in four. By 1934 medical researchers were predicting that whooping cough would "soon be causing as many deaths as diphtheria, scarlet fever, and measles combined."[76] Infants were particularly hard hit by these four diseases. A 1932 study noted that the illnesses still caused more than a third of all deaths in Ontario in the one-to-fourteen age bracket.[77] Then too, in 1910 the city had been hit with its first serious incidence of poliomyelitis, which killed 10 of the 98 infected that year, and returned periodically.[78]

With the exception of diphtheria, the number of reported cases of these virulent childhood diseases did not decline much over the period, and epidemics flared up unpredictably. The available statistics undoubtedly underestimate their impact. Public-health officials always assumed that the level of reporting was low because mild cases might be treated without medical intervention and symptoms could be easily misdiagnosed.[79]

Mothers also had to worry about other diseases that could strike any member of the family. The great plagues of the 19th century were receding, but some were persistent. Smallpox, though it was no longer the looming threat to health in the city that it had once been, erupted in minor epidemics in 1901 and 1912.[80] Far more devastating was the outbreak of influenza in the winter of 1918–19 and then again a year later. Up to that point it had struck often but left few deaths, although complications could lead to potentially fatal pneumonia. In this postwar pandemic, however, more than 12,000 people got sick in Hamilton, and 600 died between 1918 and 1920. Young adults between 20 and 50 were particularly vulnerable, as were industrial wage-earners, according to the leading North American insurance companies. Ward Eight's east-end working-class population was hit particularly hard. The disease returned to many households in the interwar period, taking nearly another 600 lives in the city between 1921 and 1940.[81]

By that period, chronic "wasting" diseases were gradually displacing contagious diseases as the leading killers of adults in the city. Tuberculosis was classified as contagious, but, unlike other diseases in that category, did not spread in epidemics. At the turn of the century it had struck particularly hard in working-class families, and it continued to be a major cause of death well into the interwar period.[82] By that point, however, heart disease and cancer had emerged as more serious ailments, disproportionately so within the wage-earning population.[83] Like tuberculosis, both could be fatal, but generally not before lengthy confinement to bed, which would require the wife's regular nursing care.

Housewives also often had to provide health care for disabled husbands and other adults in their homes. The city's high rate of industrial accidents required many women to nurse injured wage-earners through their recovery and, often, to help them cope with permanent disabilities.

Every year between 1915 and 1940 some 1,700 wage-earners in Wentworth County (in which Hamilton was located) came home with injuries that had required medical attention, and almost 1,500 more were temporarily disabled. Over the same period a total of more than 4,200 workers were permanently disabled through industrial accidents. Hundreds more men returned from the trenches after World War One in a similar condition.[84]

Other adults in working-class households might also require longer-term care. Census-takers counted 1,888 adult dependants in 1921 and 1,550 in 1931. Some of these people might have been mentally challenged – for many working-class families the local "lunatic asylum" was too costly. More often these extra dependants would be elderly relatives needing a degree of regular attention and care (more than half in 1931 were over 44).[85] The proportion of those aged 65 and over rose from 3.4 per cent of Hamilton's population in 1891 to 5.3 in 1931,[86] and they were becoming more vulnerable and dependent.[87] By the end of the 19th century, provincial funding priorities had directed most tax dollars into institutional care rather than providing outdoor relief that might have allowed the indigent elderly to stay in their own homes. Still, over the following decades the city's two old-age homes – the House of Refuge and the Home for Aged Women – remained tiny charitable institutions with places for fewer than a hundred inmates. When those facilities were needed, they would most likely be full. They also remained cold, unpleasant surroundings and were avoided as much as possible as a place to spend the final years of life.[88]

Amid the relentless rhythm of preparing meals, cleaning, and watching over children, then, Hamilton's working-class housewives had to juggle their own pregnancies and the unpredictable health-care needs of family members. In many households, particularly in the new European immigrant neighbourhoods, such responsibilities extended to the boarders who lived under the same roof and had no other family in the city to care for them. Most often, women had to handle all this domestic nursing on their own, relying for common ailments on time-worn remedies, which were probably regularly shared among kin or women in a neighbourhood (or consulted at the back of most cookbooks). Ads in the city's daily newspapers also kept women abreast of the health claims of sundry patent medicines. Even the voice of middle-class femininity, *Chatelaine*, reminded readers in 1932: "Every woman should know what remedies to use in the treatment of slight ailments – little matters for which a physician would not be consulted but which, if neglected, may lead to grave disorders."[89]

Getting Help

When health issues became too daunting, especially during childbirth, housewives looked outside the home for help. Sprinkled through working-class Hamilton were a variety of health-care providers who offered advice or familiar herbal remedies for various ailments. In the early 1920s, for example, an Italian "barber-doctor" arrived in town with a special book of cures and remedies. Many newcomers from the other side of the Atlantic would have been familiar with midwives as significant health practitioners, and while a few midwives may have worked quietly in the city,[90] the profession was illegal in Ontario. Here the only specialists who could set up shop legally were doctors, who had held a monopoly on health care under provincial law since the 1860s. They had not always enjoyed widespread popularity, but the status of the general practitioner in cities like Hamilton was generally secure by the turn of the century.

The doctors to whom working-class families turned for health care were mostly generalists with a smattering of knowledge about the treatment of injuries and the diagnosis and handling of diseases. Increasingly after the 1880s, they had begun practice with a degree from a university medical school and more and more often staked their claim to professional competence on a standardized, scientifically rigorous knowledge of the body and its ailments. Their most important claim to new therapeutic expertise rested on the science of bacteriology (the so-called "germ" theory of disease), which took hold among medical practitioners at the close of the 19th century.[91] In reality, general practice proved to be far from scientifically predictable, and well into the early 20th century many physicians admitted that their training still prepared them poorly for many of the cases they confronted in households or at their offices. They had done too little clinical work in childbirth or surgery, in particular, and had virtually no experience in preventive medicine or psychology (despite the regular demands on them to counsel patients on nervous disorders or to judge their mental health). They did a lot of learning on the job, and, for all the talk of science, the practice of medicine remained something of an art in human relations.

For working-class women it was a fact of life that doctors were almost always white males who assumed that the male body was the norm and the female body was problematic. The most common occasion for such women to need a doctor's care for themselves – pregnancy – lost much of its status as a natural process and was steadily reconstructed in medical literature as a condition fraught with uncertainty and pathologized as yet another kind of disease, requiring direct medical intervention. In the absence of legally recognized midwives, many women were still leery of male medical care, as Dr. Elizabeth

Advertisements for patent medicines in local newspapers at the turn of the century offered cures for almost any ailment, even tuberculosis.

(*HS*, 18 March 1899, 2)

Bagshaw, one of Hamilton's first female doctors, discovered when she began practising in the city in 1906. By the 1920s she was still signing more birth certificates than any other city doctor (especially among recent European immigrants, who had been accustomed to midwifery back home). The city had a handful of other female physicians in the early decades of the century, and they saw only women and children. Otherwise, engaging a doctor for family health care was to enter a terrain of class, gender, and ethnic condescension.[92]

Moreover, while doctors were now much better able to identify diseases than were their predecessors, before the arrival of sulpha drugs in the late 1930s medical science could offer few cures for serious ailments. Physicians concentrated instead on symptoms. Patients regularly got common-sense advice about isolation or bed rest and if necessary were prescribed a drug to dull the suffering. A working-class mother may have breathed easier when the ailment had a name, and she might have had a better idea of what to do with a seriously sick or disabled family member. But, aside from delivering a baby,

At the close of the 19th century the Hamilton City Hospital was a charitable institution intended to help only those so poor that they could not pay for their own health care.

(HPL , Bailey Collection)

resetting a bone, or cutting out an appendix or an unwanted growth, a doctor's intervention seldom changed the health conditions of a patient fundamentally, and most often the mother still had to do the caregiving herself.[93] In any case, physicians became less accessible over the years. In 1911 there was one doctor for every 683 residents, in 1931 only one for every 774, and in 1941 one for every 836; and growing numbers of these were specialists, not general practitioners.[94]

Sometimes working-class mothers could not manage all the nursing care themselves, and that was especially true during their own pregnancies. Neighbours often helped each other out, and the "ladies' auxiliaries" of churches, unions, and fraternal societies dropped in occasionally.[95] Evangelical missions of various kinds, including the Order of the King's Daughters, also paid visits to the sick. A few of the Protestant churches, notably the Methodists, sent in young middle-class women, dressed in special uniforms and known as "deaconesses," who were trained to perform this work without salary.[96] It was this tradition that inspired the National Council of Women to begin plans for a new Victorian Order of Home Helpers in 1897, under the active sponsorship of Lady Ishbel Aberdeen. Some three decades later

four Red Cross "Visiting Housekeepers" would be sent into Hamilton households.[97]

Some neighbourhood women without professional nursing training could also be hired for a small fee. In the 1890s a "nurse" was still a fluid term for any woman, trained or otherwise, who helped the sick. As late as 1924 the *Canadian Nurse* regretted that "every community has more than its quota of so-called 'practical nurses.'"[98] These health-care helpers operated independently, establishing their own relationship with those needing care and applying whatever skills they had to offer with minimal supervision.

By the turn of the century the health-care workers graduating from the City Hospital's new Training School of Nursing (opened in 1890) and other nursing schools across the country were a different breed. The trained nurse offered a more detached, "professional" service made possible by a rigorous three-year apprenticeship. "The care of the patient is turned over entirely to her," one nurse explained to the *Spectator* in 1907. The nurse had to use "firmness, combined with tact, to keep the distracted family from disturbing the patient." She was no longer an independent caregiver, but rather worked as an extension of doctors' authority into the home. "Hand in hand she must work with the physician," the Hamilton nurse said. "As she looks to him for orders and advice, he, in turn, depends upon her to watch his patient closely during the long hours, and quickly notifies him of any change."[99]

It was the need for nursing assistance among lower-income families that had at least in part inspired the advent of the Victorian Order of Home Helpers. But doctors' organizations looked in horror at the potential independence of such health-care workers from medical authority and insisted that the new order recruit only properly trained nurses. The renamed Victorian Order of Nurses (VON) was thus safely integrated into the doctor-controlled patriarchal health-care hierarchy.[100] Initially the new organization was intended to make available specially trained nurses to geographically isolated households, but in Hamilton, as in several other Canadian cities, upper-class women quickly concluded that many working-class households could benefit as well. Hoodless, the treasurer of the national VON, helped to organize a meeting through the Local Council of Women early in 1899 to start a Hamilton branch. One nurse was set to work that summer, a second was added in 1904, a third in 1906, and a fourth in 1912. They visited only cases recommended by doctors and were therefore less accessible to those who could not afford medical attention. The VON forbade them from treating contagious diseases.[101]

A surviving logbook covering a few months in 1904 gives a brief window on the VON's Hamilton clientele. One in six of those who could be traced in the city directory were widows, and two-thirds of the households visited were headed by manual workers, most of them skilled. By 1908 the nurses' annual caseload had reached 491, with two-thirds of the cases involving pregnant mothers. The Order said it was handling one-fifth of the births in the city in the pre-war years. Its impact on working-class Hamilton, though difficult to determine, was probably growing. In 1911 the Order took on a new role in providing home visits to Metropolitan Life's policy-holders who were acutely sick, a large proportion of whom were wage-earners and their families. Some three years later that group was expanded to include mothers and their newborns.[102]

In working-class families, health care was most often home care, no matter who was providing it. Doctors regularly visited patients in their homes, and two Hamilton doctors who started their practices in the 1930s remembered delivering babies and removing tonsils on kitchen tables. One recalled, "The grandmother usually came in and helped."[103]

Working people were a lot more reluctant to head to a hospital. Indeed, at the turn of the century a housewife would rarely let anyone in her family go near either of the two major hospitals – the larger, municipally owned and operated City Hospital (renamed Hamilton General in 1919) or the privately funded St. Joseph's, opened in 1890. The relationship was partly because, like all other 19th-century hospitals in Canada, the City Hospital had long catered only to those who could not afford to pay doctors' fees, especially the chronically ill. "Many people look upon the hospital as a last resort for the needy people and think that it is something of a disgrace to seek admission to one," the *Spectator* reported. The hospital was run as a parsimonious charity, and to be admitted a sick person required not only a doctor's signature, but also investigation by the municipal relief officer and then approval from the city council's Hospital Committee (starting in 1912 St. Joseph's also qualified for city support for charity cases).

In the 1890s men from blue-collar occupations made up a large proportion of the City Hospital "inmates," as they were called, probably mostly those without kin to look after them. Few children were admitted, and only a tiny handful of destitute women risked their lives by entering the cramped maternity wing (the local press reported a maternal death rate of one in fourteen in 1891). Seriously ill patients were mostly housed in large public wards with between eight and fifteen beds, which remained so seriously overcrowded and dirty that a judicial investigation was launched in 1913. Judge Colin Snider found them "almost up to the shade of being criminal," with "poor equipment and the wards so overcrowded with patients that it seems practically impossible to keep them at all times

Before the 1920s only a tiny minority of babies were, like these, born in Hamilton hospitals. (*SLS, LS8*)

in a sanitary condition."[104] The two equally over-crowded isolation wards for scarlet fever and diphtheria regularly overflowed into tents on the hospital grounds. As late as 1927 the Hamilton General's medical superintendent, W.F. Langrill, admitted, "Nothing had been done to provide for public ward medical and surgical cases. Conditions in this respect were the same as four decades ago." No mother would want to drop any of her family into such conditions unless there was no alternative.[105]

New hospital policies at the turn of the century put up another, different kind of bar to working-class access. Whole new wings were built to service a richer clientele, and the two institutions' new antiseptic practices, techno-logical sophistication, and more professional nursing staff proved attractive to people who were able and willing to pay $8 to $10 a week for more lavish private rooms.[106] Many working-class families would not submit themselves to the rigorous screening necessary to become charity cases and could not afford the much higher fees for the newer hospital space (after 1905, to be paid in advance).[107] Yet another option known as "semi-private" care attracted some families with steadier, better paid bread-winners. Langrill argued that these lower-cost facilities helped to avoid "pauperizing a large class

of citizens who would otherwise be forced into the public wards." The number of semi-private beds remained limited, and the debts accumu-lated could be crippling, but by 1918 the real growth in patient use of the City Hospital was unquestionably in semi-private care, which took in more than half of the 6,317 patients admitted that year (compared with 11.5 per cent in private care and 38 per cent in the public wards).[108]

The fragility of working-class incomes could undermine the semi-private option, and after 1929 the prolonged and especially severe eco-nomic slump shifted the proportion of "indi-gents" cared for in the public wards dramatically upward. In the interwar period, some patients were also paying a small fee for their care in public wards ($12.25 per week in the mid-1930s). Indeed, in 1938 Hamilton had a much higher per-centage of self-pay public patients than did any other large Ontario city – 38 per cent (compared to only 22 per cent in Toronto and 11 per cent in Ottawa and London) – and roughly the same as the proportion of fully funded indigents (private and semi-private combined had slumped below 17 per cent).[109]

After World War One working-class Hamil-ton appears to have turned to the city's hospitals in considerably larger numbers. In 1920 Hamil-ton General and St. Joseph's together had 11,500 patients, in 1930 15,500, and in 1938 more than 19,000.[110] These numbers partly reflect the grad-ual expansion of space in these institutions, and partly the prolonged periods of economic in-security that forced families to turn to the public wards. But they also suggest that the reputation of poor care in those wards was probably fading. The most striking change came in the doctors' success in insisting on delivering babies in one of the two major hospitals.

Home birth was the norm before the war, though various kinds of "maternity boarding houses" (licensed under 1897 provincial legislation) or charitable facilities for unwed mothers existed as cheaper alternatives for a handful of pregnant women.[111] In either case, doctors were almost invariably present. Although a small maternity cottage, set apart from the rest of the City Hospital's operations, had finally opened in 1892, hospitals still handled few pregnancies at the turn of the century – only 4.6 per cent of Hamilton births in 1901 – and most of those were desperately poor, often unwed mothers. As hospital facilities improved and new maternity services were made available to the higher-paying patients (at the City Hospital in 1907 and St. Joseph's in 1912), the proportion of hospital births slowly grew – 9 per cent by the outbreak of World War One and 24 per cent by 1920 – although the facilities for public-ward patients remained, in the opinion of the provincial inspector, "a place entirely unfit." The number of beds made available to maternity cases nonetheless remained extremely limited, until St. Joseph's opened its new maternity hospital in 1924 and Hamilton General added one on the Mountain in 1932. The trend accelerated during the interwar period, though in 1930 still slightly more than half of the city's babies were born outside hospitals. The costs and the lingering uncertainty about medical practitioners most likely meant that working-class mothers made up a large proportion of those still giving birth at home. At the same time, the huge number of public-ward patients in the 1930s undoubtedly included many women who could not afford doctors' fees. By 1939 a dramatic shift had certainly taken place, given that three out of four births were now taking place in the two main hospitals.[112]

What is more remarkable is that hospitalization did not reduce the risk of mothers dying during pregnancy. In Ontario hospitals, 5.3 mothers died out of every 1,000 live births,

compared to only 2.3 who had their babies at home. In 1930 19 of the 21 deaths in Hamilton ascribed to "puerperal causes" occurred in hospitals (in which only half of the city's births took place that year). Moreover, in every 1,000 live births, 8.2 Ontario mothers died when doctors were involved, but only 2.3 when there was no medical interference. In 1925 one Hamilton doctor blamed his colleagues' practices of intervention: "With little excuse men every day are rupturing the membranes too soon, forcibly dilating the cervix, applying forceps and doing version [turning the fetus in the womb]. All of these procedures potentially infect the uterus by conveying infection from below upwards." Elsewhere this kind of operation was denounced as "meddlesome midwifery."[113]

Beyond a doctor's office and a hospital ward, working-class wives and mothers could also turn to a new health-care institution and clinic that specialized in care for the leading killer of adult workers, tuberculosis. Although communicable, tuberculosis attacked only certain people in certain parts of the population, particularly the poor. Hamilton's wealthiest citizens were evidently edgy about the "white plague" lurking in the city, and in 1905 an enthusiastic coalition of businessmen, professionals, and club women put together the Hamilton Health Association, Ontario's first local tuberculosis society, to construct and operate a sanatorium on the Mountain, with crucial ongoing help from the elite women of the local Imperial Order Daughters of the Empire.[114] There patients got lots of good food, plenty of exposure to fresh air and sunshine, rest, light exercise, and, ultimately most important, instruction in how to change their personal habits to build up resistance to the disease and prevent its spread to others, especially at home. The "San," as it was soon known, had 118 patients in 1908 and 201 in 1914 (130 adults

At the Hamilton Health Association's Sanatorium, plenty of rest time in fresh air was the main treatment given to patients with tuberculosis. (HPL)

and 71 children). By 1919 more than 1,500 patients had passed through the institution since its opening.[115]

In 1908, to reach more workers, Dr. J.H. Holbrook also expanded the small existing tuberculosis clinic at the City Hospital, with its staff nurse, into a more substantial outpatient "dispensary" situated in a downtown working-class neighbourhood as a specialized clinic and educational centre with a nurse to do follow-up visits to workers' homes. By 1919 more than 1,500 patients were under the dispensary's gaze. Reports on the increasingly heavy traffic through this clinic's door suggest that people in the area had a keen interest in finding out what help was available, although the clinic's staff managed to examine only a minority of the visitors.[116]

The Public's Health

When family members were in dire need, anxious wives and mothers set out to find help from doctors and nurses. But some of those same health-care practitioners came knocking without an invitation. Soon after the turn of the century a multi-pronged movement of public-health activists, sponsored by both municipal

institutions and private agencies, emerged to confront what they perceived to be threats to the general health of the community. They beat a path to the doors of working-class households, and there applied their own new definitions of problems to be solved.

In the city's own health department, a turning point came with the appointment in 1905 of the aggressive, headstrong young doctor James Roberts, who brought to the office of medical officer of health a commitment to the emerging principles of sanitary reform based on microbiology that public-health movements in Britain, Europe, and the United States had begun to implement.[117] Hamilton's housewives might have first felt the impact of Roberts's crusading zeal in the decade before the war through his crackdown on overcrowded housing, attacks on water pollution (including a war on backyard privies), and efforts to guarantee purer milk.[118] But more often Hamiltonians were made aware of the department's battles against communicable diseases. Thanks to germ theory, public-health staff shifted their focus from the physical environment (and sanitation) to the individual carrier of disease. The state of medical science allowed practitioners to

Dr. J.H. Holbrook and staff at the city's tubercular clinic in 1919. (AO, I0005272)

immunize against only two diseases, smallpox and diphtheria. In the pre-war period, compulsory vaccination against smallpox, started in the 1880s, struggled on against popular resistance and lingering medical ignorance.[119] As for diphtheria, a new toxoid, produced at the Connaught Laboratories in Toronto, was first administered free to thousands of Hamilton children in 1922, prompting an astonishingly quick reduction in deaths from the disease. For all other contagious diseases, public-health officials could offer neither inoculation nor cure. Even diagnosis was often difficult until the city's health department finally got a laboratory to test for possible infections in 1910.[120]

After identifying contagious illnesses, the health department staff most commonly ordered the sick to be isolated in their homes, quarantined behind special placards tacked to their front doors. Yet Roberts distrusted the housewife's nursing care. "When the focus of the infection remains in the home," he wrote of typhoid outbreaks, "isolation and nursing facilities are inadequate, contact and fly infection little understood and their seriousness disregarded." With scarlet fever and diphtheria, patients were whisked off to overcrowded isolation wings in the City Hospital, but there was no such space for patients with other contagious diseases.[121]

Otherwise, Roberts aimed simply to promote personal hygiene by having the city's population examined by doctors and public-health nurses. In 1907 for the first time the city's working-class youngsters arrived home with notes for their parents about their alleged health defects. The school board had authorized Roberts to undertake medical inspections of elementary school children. He lost control of this program to the school trustees the next year,[122] but kept arguing for such work by his department. "What we want is a staff that can go out and visit homes and educate the people," he argued in 1917. His pleas fell on deaf ears at city hall, however, in contrast to more positive responses to the same question coming from civic officials in Toronto, Winnipeg, and Vancouver.[123] When the influenza epidemic hit in 1918, Roberts had to recruit a temporary staff of trained nurses to oversee 200 female volunteers (dubbed the "Sisters of Service") to work in the homes of the sick.[124]

That epidemic broke down the solid wall of civic parsimony,[125] and by the early 1920s the

Fundraising for the Babies' Dispensary Guild.

(*HH*, 20 June 1912, 6)

At this 1912 Babies' Dispensary Guild clinic, working-class mothers not only got milk for their infants but also instructions on proper mothering. (*CN*, July 1912, 357)

Department of Health in Hamilton was running a substantial downtown Health Centre with a large staff and extensive outreach programs of inspections, clinics, and school and home visitations. Yet public health in Hamilton, as elsewhere in North America, was never allowed to develop into state-run medical care. Right down to the 1930s, municipal funding was limited, and private charities ran many of the programs. The medical profession, moreover, resisted any effort to undermine private practice. Public-health offices thus always operated to a great extent as a referral service for the city's self-employed doctors.[126]

The health department was not alone in raising public-health issues. In the decade before World War One, a rising chorus of voices

in Hamilton from outside working-class households expressed concern that too many babies were dying in the city. The great majority of the deaths came from gastrointestinal ailments that could be traced to poor-quality milk. A lot seemed to be at stake here. In the words of one of the city's activist physicians, infant mortality damaged "not only the happiness of the home but the welfare of the nation and the future of the race."[127] When the summer of 1908 proved to be particularly hard on infants, the Hamilton Medical Society sponsored a Milk Commission and convinced the VON to take responsibility for supplying clean milk at cost (or, in a tiny number of cases, for free) to the mothers of infants during the summers of 1909 and 1910 – an initiative also launched in several other Canadian cities (and other parts of the Europeanized world) in this pre-war period. Mothers got their babies weighed first and received both advice on the appropriate formula (if the much preferred breast-feeding was not possible) and free literature on proper home care. One nurse also followed up with home visits to dispense "advice and instruction" on infant care.[128]

The project's organizers claimed immediate success in lowering infant mortality, but, in fact, they had only limited contact with working-class households. Mothers brought only 253 babies to the five milk dispensaries in 1910. When the milk project's sponsors reorganized themselves the next year into a year-round, medically controlled well-baby charity, known as the Babies' Dispensary Guild of Hamilton, the numbers participating continued to be low.[129]

The Guild expanded considerably after the war, and was still the main place for mothers on limited incomes to take their newborns.[130] By that point, too, they had another option. In 1921 the municipal health department began running its own child-welfare clinics with virtually

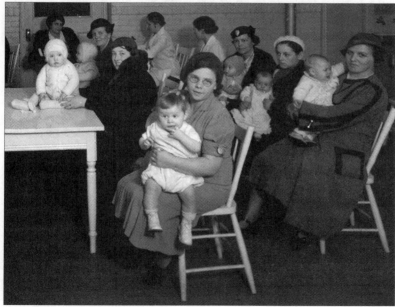

Mothers who showed up at the city's well-baby clinic were often most interested in having their infants weighed.
(AO, I0005274; HPL, Bailey Collection)

the same program of weighing babies and instructing mothers. For the first time, health department nurses also now visited the homes of all newborn infants after their registration to leave a "baby book" and invite mothers to attend a well-baby clinic. At other times, nurses visiting homes to check on communicable diseases also took the opportunity to lecture on child care.[131]

A doctor examines a pregnant woman at a public-health clinic.
(AO, I0005275)

Mothers with school-age children also found nurses, sent by the Board of Education, knocking at their doors. The first school nurse began work in 1908 – the first in Canada – and four years later two more were added (the separate school board also had one). By 1914 over 9,000 students in 18 public schools were under regular surveillance. The nurses visited each of the lower grades once a month. They undertook to teach better personal hygiene – such as how to blow your nose or brush your teeth properly – but spent most of their time examining individual students, ostensibly looking for communicable diseases. They would send infected children home or to the City Hospital or the San. But they devoted far more attention to identifying children's personal health defects and pushing parents to correct them. The problems spotted ran from general uncleanliness to poor eyesight to lice to bad teeth (which fully 90 per cent of the children were shown to have after the first full dental inspections in 1910).[132]

Many mothers trying to juggle tight budgets must have grumbled about notes sent home urging them to take their children straight to a doctor or dentist, and many too must have greeted with mixed emotions the nurses who decided to follow up specific cases with a home visit. The new immigrant population got special attention. "With the foreign population," Roberts reported, "pediculosis [lice] and personal uncleanliness is difficult to eradicate and requires constant attention." In reality, most mothers were probably spared these moments of embarrassment and criticism because before the war the nurses had far too little time to drop in on more than their small quota of 25 homes per week.[133]

The number of reported inspections and home visitations shot up after the school board hired its first full-time school medical officer, Dr. J.E. Davey, in 1922. By the end of the decade Davey was working with eleven nurses and five part-time medical officers, four of them female physicians. He started a new program in 1923 to weigh and measure children and to enrol those showing "malnourishment or under-nourishment" in special nutritional classes. They got half a pint of milk a day, and, as Davey explained, their parents were brought in to learn how to "supervise their habits of diet, rest, exercise, sleep, etc."[134]

Children in school were also facing closer scrutiny of their mental health. Since the turn of the century, the slippery new term "feeble-mindedness" had been used with increasing frequency to label those who might later be called mentally retarded or challenged. Commentators invariably set this newly constructed mental-health issue in the framework of "eugenics," which assumed the hereditary transmission of mental "defects," linked this form of mental illness with diverse social problems (including poverty, crime, alcoholism, and prostitution), and aimed to prevent procreation among the "feeble-minded" and "mentally defective." Such work became known as "mental hygiene."[135]

In the 19th century a Hamilton family struggling with mental illness or handicaps might have turned to the local lunatic asylum, which had opened in the 1870s and accommodated more than 1,200 inmates by the early 20th century, a substantial minority of whom were working class.[136] But that care was beyond the means of most families, and in any case, in treatment of the newly defined feeble-minded, patients were directed elsewhere. The new approach particularly targeted school children who could be identified as "backward" and hived off into special auxiliary classes with dead-end programs aimed at smoothing their transition into "productive" low-skill jobs (or into special institutions, as yet not created). Hamilton established such a class in 1910, and by 1929 some 212 children were in auxiliary classes in ten city elementary schools, now screened out by IQ tests. In 1930–31 these classes were consolidated into separate boys' and girls' Handicraft Schools.[137]

The problem was that the criteria for mental deficiency were vague (the terms "moron," "imbecile," and "idiot" floated loosely), and slid easily into judgments of "moral weakness." The search for causes led to a scattergun attack on the prevailing living conditions of workers – poor nutrition, wage-earning mothers, sexual immorality, illegitimacy, alcoholism, and the genetic transmission of a propensity to all this behaviour. Various kinds of anti-social conduct could invoke the label. As the country's leading expert, Helen MacMurchy, proclaimed, "Mental defectives are those who cannot make or help to make a home."[138] In 1925 the school board's medical director explained, "Men who had a deep knowledge of child psychology were brought here and general tests were conducted," but there was no resident expertise to assess children's "mental coefficient" (which was a highly questionable concept in any case). In 1934 the school board was still complaining that it lacked "competent, trained examiners" able to assess "children who are mentally retarded and others presenting deviations from the normal in their social adjustment."[139]

Within the rigid schooling programs of the period, failure to perform and conform in various ways could isolate children as "abnormal." In 1924 an outraged father threatened to take the school board to court for classifying his son as "subnormal" and relegating him to an auxiliary class, where he spent his time shovelling snow and cinders. According to school officials, the boy had demonstrated his feeble-mindedness when he "refused to work for the teacher, had run out of school, and ... in the presence of two teachers, had spanked one of the girls." The definition could be highly elastic: in 1929 (when Hamilton still did not have a full-time psychiatrist in its medical community), the medical director of the National Committee on Mental Health told a local audience that *half* the city's school children were mentally defective. He noted that mental hygienists were interested in what he called the "dull normals," who did not engage well with the academic curriculum and dropped out early.[140]

An emphasis on failure to adjust and conform could easily be extended to juvenile delinquency, and invariably discussion of the feeble-minded in the city drew evidence from the institutions that dealt with wayward children and youth, who were typically from working-class families. For girls and young women, a diagnosis of mental defectiveness often hinged on evidence of sexual precociousness and illegitimate offspring. Immigrants in allegedly inferior ethnic groups also faced particularly fierce criticism within mental-hygiene writings. As a result, children who were unusually shy, nervous, inarticulate, inattentive, wilful, or (in late-20th-century parlance) hyperactive, who had such disabilities as speech defects, or who were unfamiliar or uncomfortable with the Anglo-Celtic, middle-class cultural patterns taught to them could find themselves identified as feeble-minded and channelled into auxiliary classes. Boys with behaviour problems must have been targeted more often because there were two and a half times more of them among the 350 to 400 children in the Handicraft Schools each year in the 1930s. The eugenicist flavour of the mental-hygiene movement that highlighted inherited biological traits shifted

in the interwar period towards a more environmental perspective, but, for a working-class mother with an "abnormal" child, little changed in the loose diagnoses.[141]

These kinds of judgments were not popular in working-class Hamilton, and, not surprisingly, a local doctor told the province's royal commissioner on feeble-mindedness in 1919 that "examination of children was frowned upon by parents and the work was greatly retarded by them."[142] More generally, Hamilton's working-class mothers and their families viewed all the public-health campaigns with uneasiness and a determination to keep a distance.

A Healthier Hamilton?

The impact of all these public-health measures on working-class health in early-20th-century Hamilton was ambiguous and undoubtedly less momentous than Roberts or Davey and their staffs liked to boast about.[143] To be sure, both the general and infant mortality rates did decline between the turn of the century and the 1930s, and especially after 1914. Better sanitation and cleaner water certainly helped to wipe out the 19th-century scourge of typhoid epidemics. Drug therapies eventually cut out smallpox and diphtheria. Contagious diseases that had caused one in five deaths at the turn of the century resulted in less than one in twenty by the 1930s.[144]

Cleaning up water and milk supplies also undoubtedly reduced the risk of infant illness and death from gastrointestinal ailments (though suddenly in 1925 infant deaths from infectious diarrhoea jumped to epidemic proportions), and infant mortality did drop remarkably in the 30 years after 1910.[145] These statistics are somewhat misleading because an unknown (but significant) number of parents neglected to register their children's births in the early years.[146] The long-term trend could nonetheless lead mothers to begin to expect that far more of their newborns would survive (although at the same time public-health officials rarely dwelled on how the rate of stillbirths remained high, suggesting that many pregnancies continued to be complicated and many would-be mothers were none too healthy).[147]

Combatting almost all other communicable diseases, however, involved nothing more than diagnosis and isolation as the diseases ran their course. Some illnesses appeared to be uncontrollable. In the wake of a serious measles epidemic in 1909–10, in which 2,300 cases had been reported and 18 patients had died, Roberts noted how little could be done: "The measures used for the control of other communicable diseases have practically no effect in checking epidemics of measles." He gave the same warning in 1930.[148] Similarly, medical researchers reported in 1934 that mortality rates from whooping cough over 50 years showed "no evidence of any sustained decline" and that "there is no evidence ... that the efforts directed at its control have been at all successful."[149]

The devastating waves of influenza in 1918–20 were a shocking reminder of the limitations of scientific medicine. Despite doctors' recommendations of everything from cloth masks to oxygen to enemas to alcohol, there were no cures or effective preventive measures for the disease. The usual techniques of isolating the sick, recommending bed rest and plenty of fresh air, and, this time, also banning public meetings, school classes, church services, and theatrical shows and restricting retail (but not factory) operations did not stop the spread of the disease (though the incidence did seem to decline somewhat under these prohibitions). Home remedies and patent medicines took a new lease on life as credible alternatives.[150]

The highly publicized fight against tuberculosis had just as limited results. Holbrook admitted in 1913, with no apparent irony: "Our ideas with regard to treatment are still somewhat unsettled." Indeed, the San's therapy practices drew little at all from medicinal science, and the basic formula of food, sun, and, above all, rest was never fundamentally varied. Tuberculosis gradually hit fewer people in the city not because a cure had been found but more likely because identifying and isolating those with the disease inhibited wider infection. The number of cases and deaths reported in the city tapered off somewhat after the war, but took no precipitous plunge. As Holbrook regularly complained, many sufferers waited until the disease was advanced before appealing for this help, and "very few advanced cases can recover completely."[151]

For many years accommodation in the San was in fairly primitive "huts" because no one was expected to settle in for longer than three or four months. How many patients were cured in that time is difficult to determine. At the San, after ten years of operation, one-third of the 963 patients treated had died of tuberculosis, and another 13.5 per cent were either still in the institution or "at home but not able to work."[152] In 1919 only one in three was counted as "apparently cured." In 1936 some patients at the San staged a protest over the process of ejecting "arrested" patients too quickly and turning them over to their "overburdened relatives" and expecting them "to make a living in competition with healthy men and women." They noted that 90 per cent were disabled to some degree and had "no chance for rehabilitation." The concerns apparently fell on deaf ears.[153]

Holbrook's program was, first and foremost, a form of moral education to encourage temperance, discipline, and self-reliance after release from the institutions. He believed that "the

By the 1910s many more nurses were criss-crossing working-class Hamilton. (HPL)

whole Sanatorium life is in a sense a schooling for adults and children alike," and that within the institution a key lesson was "to learn to be obedient to authority" until "obedience becomes an instinct and the authority becomes that of his own reason." This was a process of rehabilitation, not cure, and follow-up work might be necessary to ensure compliance with what had been taught. Medically prescribed behaviour had to triumph over "the interference of friends and family," since "a home is not a hospital" and "one's anxious relatives do not make the best nurses under such conditions." The theory and practice of tuberculosis control, then, put the weight of responsibility (and blame) on individuals and their personal behaviour and on the standards of cleanliness and order in their family household.[154]

Ultimately, prevention seemed limited to the probably reasonably effective attack on overcrowding in houses and the isolation of infected people (especially important for airborne infections), and to stern lectures on proper housekeeping, which relied on the direct intervention of nurses into working-class housewifery.[155] In the end, moreover, public-health officials remained unhelpful with the increasingly potent chronic diseases, and particularly with the leading killers of adults by the 1920s, heart disease and cancer.[156] The contribution that air pollution from the city's belching factory smokestacks and coal-fired stoves and furnaces might have made to those diseases was rarely acknowledged because clean air was never a priority in the city's public-health programs. Indeed, occupational health remained a marginal, undeveloped field of medical inquiry.[157]

The funding crunch that hit the municipal government in the 1930s curbed the work of the public-health agencies, which had only just begun to expand in the postwar decade. Several nurses were laid off. Once again it was clear, as it had been so often over the previous half-century, that the Canadian state was not prepared to fund comprehensive health care for its working-class population.

Overall, measured by death rates, the standards of health in the city actually deteriorated considerably in the first decade of the 20th century, as deaths per 1,000 persons climbed to 20 in 1910, and then, from World War One onward, settled into a relatively constant level of 10 to 12 over the next three decades.[158] From 1911 to 1916 insured male wage-earners (the more economically secure workers) aged 25 to 34 across North America had a 36 per cent higher death rate than did men in the general population. The rate for men aged 35 to 44 was 58 per cent higher. By the 1930s the gap had narrowed, but had not closed completely.[159]

Blaming Mother

For the working-class housewife, medical attention was a mixed blessing. It could bring much needed help, but also led to another problem. A central thrust of public-health campaigns was mother-blaming. Spokespersons and practitioners regularly demeaned a woman's own health-care practices and chastised her for her failings. Ultimately they did little to lighten the burden of work in her own household.

The leading doctors of the city's public-health efforts regularly blasted the state of workers' households and the wives' domestic practices. "It is the ignorant mother (I mean ignorant of the value of scientific feeding, and that comprises a large number of mothers of the poorer classes) whom we are endeavouring to teach," a Babies' Dispensary Guild doctor explained. As late as 1928 Roberts was still attributing high infant death rates to "poverty, ignorance, and inherited unfitness for motherhood."[160]

Working-class housewives also found themselves heavily implicated in anti-tuberculosis campaigns. The treatment actually increased the pressure on them by discouraging their spouses from returning to regular wage-earning and by turning a spotlight on the inadequacies of their housekeeping. By taking or sending a family member to the TB dispensary, a housewife might unleash a storm of criticism on her own head. More and more often by World War One, anti-tuberculosis specialists denounced not environment factors but "ignorance." As Holbrook told a nurses' convention in 1912, it was "a social disease predisposed to by incorrect living." A year later he revealed his limited understanding of working-class family economies when he declared, "Poverty is the cause of tuberculosis, and ignorance, alcohol, and tuberculosis are the greatest causes of poverty." His nurse argued that a family living in crowded housing on meagre earnings from both father and mother should be "admonished" to give a "pale, delicate looking" child "extra care, plenty of nourishing food and an abundant supply of fresh air."[161]

The growing numbers of public-health nurses were the shock troops in the assault on working-class housewives. By 1920 nurses working for various agencies were criss-crossing Hamilton and visiting hundreds of working-class households. When she entered these homes, a nurse's gaze went far beyond the specific mandate of the agency she worked for. "She has to teach that household practically a new standard of living," Holbrook insisted. The overarching goal was to instil "Intelligent Motherhood."[162] The health-care workers operated on the shared assumption that health problems within the families they saw were the direct result of mothers' "ignorance" about child-rearing.

At the Babies' Dispensary Guild, needy mothers got not just clean high-grade milk but also a grilling from a doctor about their child-care practices and specific recommendations for changes. With help from upper-class volunteers, staff nurses explained and demonstrated the doctor's instructions for food preparation and made follow-up visits to the mothers' homes, sometimes as often as every two days, where they took on the role of social workers. "By her instructions in regard to cleanliness in preparation of the child's food and in the general care of the child," a clinic doctor explained, "she gives the mother an added incentive to raise the standard of living in the household."[163]

Alongside her instructions on feeding, the Guild's visiting nurse "incidentally" undertook "a complete social investigation of the conditions of the family and others living in the house, the number of rooms, the rent paid, the church attended, other dispensaries and charitable organizations visited by the members of the family, etc." She developed carefully annotated files on all clients. The staff hoped to stay in touch with each child for three years. If necessary, the nurse could call in the health department or the Guild's upper-class Women's Board, which handled the relief work for indigent mothers. These volunteers also tried to encourage housewives' self-sufficiency by gathering them together in sewing classes, punctuated with "short talks and demonstrations" by the nurses on "the Care of the Baby, Personal Hygiene, Ventilation, etc."[164]

Still, despite their expressions of condescending judgment, Hamilton's public-health nurses had remarkably little to say about the allegedly improper practices of the working-class mothers they visited and instructed. Sporadic advice to nursing mothers to avoid "salads, pickles and spicy foods" and tea, coffee, and alcoholic beverages suggests a certain consternation with working-class eating habits, and the VON's warnings against giving babies "bananas, candy, popcorn sugar or anything else but milk" must have reflected misgivings about what they saw in those households.[165] They also criticized the exhibition of too much physical contact with children. "If children were let alone and allowed to have their cry out, instead of being tossed and petted and hushed, they would be far better for it," the VON advised. Intergenerational advice was also disparaged. "One stumbling block is the grandmother," said a Babies' Dispensary Guild doctor.[166] Nor did they make any effort to support or enhance the well-established networks of mutual help in working-class neighbourhoods. Instead, they saw all of them as untrustworthy. Indeed, these health practitioners took for granted that there was no value whatsoever in folk wisdom and practices. "Old ideas regarding personal habits of life are not easily shaken off," Nurse C.H. Jarvis complained.[167] Rather, they argued that they had to teach a new science of mothering, boasting of its "efficiency." In reality, the message was not fundamentally scientific, in that the medical science lying behind these confident assertions was seldom laid out for housewives clearly and intelligibly. Rather, it was a "gospel" – a set of rigid tenets to be taught didactically and to be learned and obeyed uncritically. They applauded mothers who conformed deferentially.[168]

Nurses and their medical supervisors also rarely acknowledged the experiences of working-class life that would undermine their recommendations for "providing the most suitable surroundings in the home."[169] Seldom was any great sensitivity shown to the difficulties of meshing rigid child-care schedules with the movements of wage-earners in the household set by the factory whistle. Feeding a baby whenever it cried or letting it sleep as long as possible might have been ways of avoiding conflict with exhausted husbands, for example. Nor, more importantly, did nurses foreground uncertain family income or full-scale poverty as significant problems to be confronted in raising the living standards of working people.[170] Nor, for that matter, did they recognize the difficulties and frustrations that mothers faced when forced to deal with charitable agencies; the tiny handful of women who got milk or other items for free were screened through the same net of suspicion and constraint that motivated charity work in the city. A household with no single-purpose bathtub and no hot running water, with soot from coal-fired stoves and nearby factory smokestacks settling over them every day, and with limited changes of clothing for children – this place might have trouble meeting rigid standards of cleanliness. Limited money for food and no refrigeration could frustrate the nurses' expectations for feeding. The desperate mother who was compelled to go out to work for wages was castigated for neglecting her children. Letting an infant sleep with anyone else was denounced, even though working-class households often lacked the space and the extra beds to do otherwise. The public-health workers' fixation on fresh air turned easily to condemnation of overcrowding rather than a recognition of the high price of housing that prompted such cramped living. Indeed, nurses were ready to bring in sanitary inspectors and their legal power to break up such households. "Neglect and ignorance are, therefore, more important than poverty as causative factors in the cause of infant illness and death," the editor of the *Public Health Journal* insisted in 1915. "Intelligent motherhood alone can give the infant that which neither wealth nor state nor yet science can offer with equal benefit to mother or child."[171]

Hamilton's public-health nurses regularly made judgments about how well a mother could cope with limited resources, and they judged her with all the suspicion of a charity worker. "It is the variableness in the skill of the home-keeper that makes it hard to decide whether financial help with the milk should be given," the Babies' Dispensary Guild's head nurse Helen Smith argued in 1918. "Neither home conditions or amount of income decides the real need of help.

The problem is to investigate closely enough to know whether help will tend to promote gradually independence, or develop a state of accepted pauperism." In 1920 the Health Association's nurse, C.H. Jarvis, wrote, "Although poverty may to a large extent be responsible for conditions that predispose to tuberculosis, the lack of intelligence and education in the raising and feeding of children does more." Nurse Jarvis attributed "adverse conditions" mostly to "the lack of the all important instinct for cleanliness and order."[172]

Education therefore predominated in this health-care program. According to Jarvis, the visiting nurse had to step in with self-proclaimed "sympathy and understanding to pass along any knowledge gained." The nurse also had to have "an ever-present watchfulness, teaching the Gospel of caution, cleanliness, sunshine, fresh air and cheerfulness to those who are sick, and to those who are well, proper feeding of children, proper rest and work, play for the growing boys and girls." These nurses brought to working-class households a keen sense of their own scientifically based expertise, learned in formal training in their nursing programs, which included both their ability to identify diseases and monitor symptoms and their preferred methods of treatment. When they warned about the importance of breast-feeding, pure milk, and antisepsis in the home, they undoubtedly had some rigorous scientific analysis to call upon. But much of the "teaching" that they undertook in their clinics and at kitchen tables in working-class Hamilton was based much more on moral judgments about the connections between cleanliness, orderliness, moral purity, and good health. In 1911, for example, the Guild's Helen Smith included "cleanliness," "exactness," and "regularity" as the key principles of infant care that she tried to instil.[173]

GREATER HAMILTON
BABY WEEK
JUNE 19 - 25

"Come Let's Save the Kiddies"

"This Week Is Ours"

BETTER BABIES
BETTER MOTHERS
BETTER CITY

Starting in 1915, annual baby weeks showcased the best practices of "scientific" motherhood.
(*HH*, 21 June 1915, 1)

Personal exhortations over the kitchen table were backed up by a widening educational campaign to drive home the message of scientific motherhood. In June 1915, as school was winding down for the year, mothers faced a new barrage of instruction. In church, on what they were told was "Baby Sabbath," they heard special sermons. All week merchants shoved leaflets into their shopping bags, and the three daily newspapers ran big stories on child care. Then their children arrived home from school with booklets containing "practical information for the mother." It was "Baby Week" – the first in the country – sponsored by a new Baby Welfare Association of Greater Hamilton, a common front of all the city's charitable agencies working with children brought together by the Babies' Dispensary Guild.[174] A few working-class mothers may have taken up the invitation to visit the homes, orphanages, shelters, and playgrounds that had thrown their doors open to the public. Many more probably took their children to a huge picnic at Dundurn Park to get free ice cream and candies and enjoy band concerts, fireworks, and other colourful amusements. Baby Week

became an annual event for educating mothers (and the public more generally) in approved infant-care methods. The next year the educational emphasis was stepped up with movies, shown to hundreds of school children, and thinly attended lectures for parents. How many mothers (or future mothers) actually picked up new ideas about child-rearing is open to question. The organizers' efforts to provide earnest instruction tended to be eclipsed by the circus-like features of each year's program. But the movement certainly got a high profile and enhanced credibility, and perhaps the seeds had been planted in the interwar generation of new mothers.[175]

Public-health nurses also distributed free literature on child care to Hamilton mothers, and after 1920 had access to a large volume of new Canadian publications.[176] Even mothers who received none of this didactic literature found similar messages in the pages of the newspapers, in both advice columns and advertisements for child-care products, and by the 1930s on daytime radio. It may well have been that the widening distribution of these ideas of scientific motherhood, seeping into daily advertisements for countless household products, did more to shape them into the new "common sense" and create more receptiveness in the face-to-face meetings with visiting nurses.[177]

Perhaps some mothers did lack domestic skills or maternal motivation, and could no doubt pick up valuable tips about child care from these nurses. But ultimately the arrogance of the message left little room for dialogue or for building on existing knowledge and practices in working-class communities.

The Bill of Health

Doctors and nurses had thus staked a claim to superior knowledge about how to deal with the sick and disabled in working-class Hamilton.

Some went further and demanded changes in working-class lifestyles in the name of a generally healthier city. For their part, working-class housewives and their families appear to have viewed the city's professional health-care providers with a mixture of reverential respect and wary suspicion. They undoubtedly consulted doctors when absolutely necessary, but medical practitioners often complained that the city's patients waited too long before getting in touch. They may have been the caregivers of last resort.[178] Perhaps the general reluctance to approach doctors was rooted in shame, as the medical community blamed household practices for infant mortality and such deadly illnesses as tuberculosis and cancer.[179] Workers certainly held back out of concern about the drain on family budgets and out of an apparent reluctance to completely accept the authority of the professionals in their family health care.

In an age before public-health insurance, turning to doctors and nurses was an option that many working-class families could not afford. In 1902 the Hamilton Medical Society set a sliding scale of fees based on the income of patients, but $1 for a simple home visit, $10 to fix a broken leg, or anywhere from $5 to $25 for minor operations could cut deeply into family budgets during a time when, before the war, even skilled workers might be earning no more than $2 a day.[180] One angry Hamilton labour leader told the Royal Commission on Industrial Relations in 1919 that "there does not seem to be any limit to the prices the medical profession will set upon its services," and cited a next-door neighbour who earned only $25 a week but had run up a doctor bill of $850 for an operation and convalescent care.[181] A year later the Medical Society's decision to hike its fees to $3 a visit brought an outcry from the local Trades and Labor Council. One Council leader argued, "Some doctors are sucking

the life out of the workingman," while another claimed, "Many workingmen were enslaved in debt, owing to heavy doctor bills, when illness occurred in their family." The Mount Hamilton Women's Independent Labor Party appealed to other branches of the Independent Labor Party for concerted action against the increase.[182] This was a time when medical fees were actually rising much more slowly than the general cost of living, but, over the decade before World War One and then even more dramatically after 1916, the soaring costs of food and rent often left little money for health care, unless the situation got extremely serious.

Wage-earners who could afford to belong to benevolent societies usually had their medical bills covered, though, according to one prominent local doctor, the service under these plans, often provided by young medical men for a fixed annual fee, could be "abominable." Some also joined company-run medical plans.[183] Others agreed to pay their medical debts in instalments, and doctors often grumbled about unpaid bills. Some doctors were willing to waive fees in desperate cases, but their practices depended on most patients paying. The impact of unemployment on medical care became unmistakably clear when a Canadian Medical Association survey of Hamilton doctors discovered that their incomes had declined 36.5 per cent in the depths of economic depression between 1929 and 1933. A third of patients could not afford to pay anything, and another third could afford only half the full fee. At that point, in the face of massive unemployment, the city used provincial enabling legislation to introduce a program of medical relief for those unemployed and receiving relief.[184]

Those in serious poverty had the option of making use of the City Hospital's out-patient clinic, initially known as a "dispensary," where they had access to the hospital's in-house medical staff and pharmaceutical services. Like those who stayed in the hospital as charity cases, these patients had to be means-tested by the city relief officer. At the turn of the century some 3,000 people a year lined up for hours in corridors to get access to this service. As with most other agencies dealing with the poor, some doctors regularly complained that too many people who could afford to pay private medical fees were showing up. A new wing for these patients was nonetheless opened in 1924, and five years later the Outdoor Department was still handling nearly 2,500 patients a year. By 1933, in the depths of the depression, that number had tripled and in 1939 reached more than 33,000.[185]

Even the San expected resident tuberculosis patients to pay fees unless they were supported as means-tested charity cases. Late in 1906 the Hamilton Trades and Labor Council complained that the prohibitive rate of $7 to $8 per week contradicted the mayor's promise that "poor people would be housed at very reasonable rates." The Council called the new institution "a rather aristocratic establishment" and wanted it made "accessible to the workingman."[186] A residential facility also cost a workingman his foregone wages, which most working-class families could ill afford to do without.

Nurses were also prohibitively expensive. Their rate of at least $10 a week in the 1890s (a week's pay for many workingmen) placed them far beyond the reach of working-class households. By 1907, when there were 40 to 50 such practitioners at work in Hamilton, their rate had reached $18 a week, or $21 if they were handling contagious diseases.[187] The sponsors of the Victorian Order of Nurses recognized that those fees were not affordable for workers, but they too charged a sliding scale of fees – from 5 to 50 cents per visit – though VON did provide care for

free in dire circumstances, on approval of the society women on its House Committee. Paying patients would always outnumber those who got the service for free.[188]

Public-health staff also regularly ran up against wage-earners' insistence that ill health should not keep them home from work. Placarding and quarantining of patients with contagious diseases might, therefore, be unpopular. In 1900 police had to escort home two brothers working in local factories when they refused to honour the quarantine for smallpox imposed on their family household. Some nine years later Roberts complained that "quarantines were being broken all over the city," and in 1915 he said that parents were engaging in "concealment and deception." The issue arose most forcefully during the influenza epidemic, when many workers argued that they could not afford to stay home.[189]

Hamilton's Independent Labor Party raised the issue of socialized health care through health insurance at the end of World War One, but until the doctors' incomes collapsed in the 1930s the medical profession remained largely indifferent to the issue, and provincial governments made no significant moves in that direction. By 1937 private medical insurance plans covered only 700 people across the whole country.[190]

As the financial managers for their families, then, working-class housewives might hold back from taking a sick child or husband off to a doctor's office. Meanwhile they were continually receiving unsolicited help and advice from the public-health agencies – and the public-health nurses liked to lace their published reports with claims about the mothers' gushing gratitude. However self-promotional such statements could be, many poor women must no doubt have welcomed reliable, cheap sources of milk and useful advice about the health of their infants. A letter to the press from "A Grateful Mother" conveyed those feelings.[191] The stress that a crying baby could add to a working-class household must have led to more than one mother to seek help, as in this case:

> I thought I would come and see if you could help me with my baby. He cries all the time. You see we only have a couple of rooms in another person's house, and she told me yesterday that we would have to get out if we couldn't keep the baby quiet; she couldn't stand it any longer, and then my husband got cross last night, too. He says that if he has to go to work every day he must have some sleep. I didn't think he could get so cross with the baby.[192]

As a young nurse at the Babies' Dispensary Guild no doubt correctly suggested, "Many have no intimate friends in the city, [and] it means much to them to have some one come to talk to them."[193]

Yet more negative comments surfaced as well.[194] Roberts grumbled that "some parents unfortunately are found, too ignorant, or too lazy, or with too little inclination or even too resentful to follow the advice given." Many a working-class mother must have questioned the credibility of an unmarried, middle-class woman, standing on her doorstep with a patronizing tone and a critical look. "Not infrequently the parents are prejudiced against the nurse before they ever see her, for they conceive the idea that she is interfering with their authority over their children," a Canadian manual for school nursing acknowledged. "Some will receive her cordially, while others will pour a tirade of abuse upon her unlucky head." In 1928 a Hamilton woman was reported to have told a nurse, "I don't need any guild, or new-fangled notions; my mother had ten, and if she can't tell me about them your clinic can't." Others may have bristled at any condescension from the middle- and upper-class volunteers who regularly helped out at the specialized clinics.[195]

In fact, for many years only a small minority of mothers used any well-baby clinics. In 1920 the Guild handled only 15 per cent of the city's new babies, and by 1930 still fewer than a quarter. Admittedly, this agency was intended only "for those whose purses would not warrant the attention of a general practitioner, not for those who can afford to pay," but, by the end of the 1920s, nearly two-thirds of newborn infants were never brought to the city health department's clinics either.[196] Moreover, during the 1920s, three-quarters of mothers did not bring their babies to the Guild clinics until they were more than a month old, which suggests that they might have been looking for help with specific problems rather than general instruction. In the same decade the Guild staff reported that between a fifth and a third of those brought in were "discontinued for non-attendance," which indicates a clear rejection of ongoing supervision. Many mothers seemed willing to drop in for advice, but, as one health department nurse reported, "A large number of mothers bring their babies for the sole purpose of having them weighed." Perhaps, too, interest in the work of the clinics declined after the first birth; juggling the child care of older toddlers with trips to the clinic might be impossible. The health-care workers' repeated concern about poor teeth suggests that tight budgets made visits to the dentist impossible, and the free clinics for children occasionally provoked concern that dentists were pulling out too many teeth.[197] Reports on the need for "care, tact, and discretion," along with patience and persistence, in handling mothers mired in "prejudice and traditional methods," indicates a certain resistance to the nurses' pushing and prodding, especially among new immigrants from Continental Europe. As in

Canadian Communists found a limited place for the housewife in working-class struggles.

(*Worker*, 21 Feb. 1931, 3)

the hospitals, however, the deepening depression of the early 1930s brought a flood of new cases looking for free help.[198]

Most likely, as in Ontario more generally, Hamilton's working-class mothers typically took from the new programs what worked for them practically and financially and rejected the rest. The often urgent need for help had to be balanced against the discomforts and indignities of inspection and surveillance. Practical advice about preparing for pregnancy or the rigidity of the recommended child-care regime would have often run against the grain of often more indulgent working-class practice and might have seemed irrelevant to the much more pressing worries about how to keep children fed and healthy. Mothers who lacked money for medicine or surgery (not available at the well-baby clinics), or even an icebox to prevent milk from going sour, might well have resented the emphasis on education. They had been handed an increased responsibility for health care but did not have the resources necessary to meet the heightened expectations.[199]

The wives and mothers who bore the responsibilities for their families' health had good reason, then, to wonder about just how helpful doctors and nurses could be. The housewife-cum-family financial manager often found the cost of medical services in doctors' offices, hospitals, or tuberculosis sanatorium crippling for household budgets. Only the most desperately poor could qualify for subsidized care through a dispensary or public ward of a hospital, and access to those overcrowded, often inferior facilities required completing the demeaning means tests of the city relief department. Moreover, for most of the serious ailments that she was trying to cope with, the medical community offered no effective cures. Long hours of bedside nursing was still the essence of health care.[200] Indeed, the remedies proposed – including the much more militant quarantining of contagious cases – tended to require even more work on her part. By World War One the medical authorities were too often constructing health-care problems as the result of a mother's inadequacies or failings as a housekeeper and caregiver. As medical discourse increasingly connected proper child care with the stability and efficiency of the "nation," help turned into blame.[201]

The Politics of Motherhood

In the half-century before World War Two, then, working-class women in Hamilton, as in other industrial centres, found their work as caregivers scarcely less onerous. Indeed, the role arguably generated more anxiety in their lives. Their protection from abusive husbands had not grown substantially. The tools and facilities available in their households had not released them from much hard physical labour, and tougher enforcement of school attendance had taken away the daily help of adolescent daughters. The work and worry of nursing sick or disabled family members had not relented given that so many of the new health-care institutions were unaffordable or limited. Women also faced pressures to adapt their child-rearing practices to the new standards set by pushy doctors, nurses, teachers, home economists, recreation workers, and social workers. In public-health propaganda and on the pages of daily newspapers, they confronted a rising chorus of blame for their alleged inadequacies. Yet it seemed that, wherever possible, these housewives took advantage of what was made available to them. Throughout the barrage of new pressures to adapt to new, externally imposed standards for "scientific" mothering, they seemed to assess innovations in the light of their own working-class standards of good mothering. And there is no reason to believe that they all lost any pride in their abilities to protect and nurture their families.[202]

In some ways they could arguably take some comfort from the politicization of motherhood since the 1890s, which had opened up important issues in their daily lives, even if the framing of problems and solutions did not always ease their burdens or address their central concerns. Professional "experts," particularly doctors, and bourgeois women's organizations created the politics of motherhood in this period by mobilizing people and resources to establish private agencies (notably the Children's Aid Society, Playgrounds Association, Hamilton Health Association, VON, and the Babies' Dispensary Guild) and establishing niches within the state where necessary (schooling and some public health programming, for example). The male professionals shaped these campaigns to put themselves in control wherever possible. The maternalism of the WCTU, Local Council of Women, YWCA, VON, IODE, or the Guild was a more complex mix of the patronizing condescension of upper-class ladies and emerging middle-class professionals and the female solidarities of shared concern to ennoble mothering and to expand its social relevance

into nation-building and "racial renewal." All of these projects made the conduct of life in working-class households the main issue, but never the family economy, which working-class housewives knew was crucial to the protection and nurturing of their families. Hamilton lacked anything approaching the cross-class feminist approaches of Britain's Fabian Women's Group or the Women's Cooperative Guild, in which middle-class women tried to speak with and for working-class housewives.[203]

Their menfolk rarely took up their cause. The male activists in the industrial and political wings of the workers' movements might occasionally evoke working-class mothers as symbolic heroines of proletarian mutual support,[204] but on the whole they showed minimal interest in the politics of motherhood and contributed little to debates about public policy in this area. The Trades and Labor Council, Independent Labor Party, and the newspapers that supported them simply insisted that the way to sustain healthy families was to pay the breadwinner good wages and otherwise tipped their caps to the work of the bourgeois women's organizations.[205]

Yet the so-called "maternal feminism" got a new twist in 1917 when a group of wives of local labour leaders formed a distinctly working-class voice of maternalist politics, the Women's Independent Labor Party, which eventually had four branches in the city. Besides speaking out against food profiteering and the high cost of living, the discussions revealed a marked concern about the health and education of their children. In 1919 and 1921 they convinced the main ILP organization to put a female candidate on the party slate for the school board because "women understand children and their educational needs far better than men." In one meeting a speaker proclaimed, "In the home women acted as dressmakers, chief cooks and bottle washers, and were of high economic value to the state." They were also a moving force behind the extension of such politics to the provincial stage through the creation of the United Women's Educational Federation of Ontario in 1920. Its program included free state-funded maternity care, nationalization of the medical profession, and milk and hot meals for undernourished school children. A smaller Communist-inspired Women's Labor League carried on this agitation in the 1920s and early 1930s.[206]

Despite their enthusiasm, the working-class women's groups remained marginal in postwar politics. They declined in the 1920s along with the rest of the workers' revolt that had erupted at the end of World War One, and their program of better health care and educational policies to benefit themselves and their families failed to materialize over these years. In 1940 as in 1890, they could justifiably say that the labours of love they carried out for the families were still never done.

5

Bringing Home the Bacon

It's Saturday, Lord, and he's just got his pay –
Make daddy come home with his wages.
To squander his pay he cannot afford;
We want it for rent and for fire and for board;
Hurry right out and find him, O Lord,
And send him straight home with his wages.
— Richard Kernighan

KNOWN LOCALLY AS "THE KHAN," Richard Kernighan was Hamilton's most popular poet at the turn of the 20th century. He knew how to tug at heart strings. His maudlin image of a child on her knees in prayer appeared at the end of a poem entitled "When Daddy Comes Home with His Wages." In previous stanzas he had portrayed the whole family waiting anxiously for the father's return. The rent would be paid, the baby would have a new dress, there would be "tomatoes an' peaches an' meat" on the table, and the family could have an outing to the beach or the Mountain. But, if father did not show up with wages in hand, the family faced "sorrow and woe." There would be a shortage of potatoes and meat, the children would be fearfully quiet, and mother would look "frightened and nervous and ill." So daddy had better come straight home.[1]

Working-class families in Hamilton, as in most of the rest of the industrialized world, expected the wages of the male head of the household, usually the husband and father, to provide the bulk of their incomes. Labour leaders regularly argued that an adult man's wages ought to be enough to support the whole family – what they liked to call a "living wage" and what is now known as a "family wage." Employers generally agreed with that notion – disagreements were usually over how much was enough – and in hard times many gave preference to married men. When it was organizing depression relief work, the city explicitly discriminated against single men. All the city's private charitable and relief organizations shared the assumption that a working-class family should be supported by a male breadwinner, or some male kin. That approach was the bedrock of social order.[2]

Labour leaders justified the family wage above all as a crucial defence of their families against poverty and suffering.[3] Male wage-earners, whether employed or unemployed, repeatedly justified their demands as necessary for their families. As a jobless man asked in 1914, "What are we going to do to get an honest crust of bread for our wives and children?"[4] Yet workingmen also used this important breadwinner role as a major prop for a masculine identity that gave them both privileges within the family and rights in the labour market and public life – what has appropriately been called "economic citizenship" – rights and privileges generally denied to the women in their households. Arguing for a decent family wage helped to restrict women to service to their men through unpaid labour at home or to waged labour at much lower rates than those received by men. Female wage-earners could only be seen as supplementary income-generators on a relatively short-term basis, not as independent breadwinners. Similarly, few questioned the low wages for sojourning labourers because of an assumption that transient workers did not have to provide for their families, who were looking after themselves back home in the European rural villages. Theirs was not "white" labour. The family wage was thus contained within a potent ideology about social justice, gender roles, and white Anglo-Canadian male entitlement.[5]

The ideological claims of the male breadwinner were balanced by the ideological constraints on possibilities for a woman. The independence and self-sufficiency that were believed to flow from a workingman's right to work for wages were at the core of his identity as a man and a citizen, but his wife had only one legitimate sphere in which she could nurture a respected identity: the home, where her unpaid labour was assumed to be merely sustaining male efforts in the labour market and won her none of the same larger entitlements of economic citizenship. A single woman was assumed to be simply en route to marriage and family. If she entered the labour market, she found her employment prospects and earning capacity sharply limited by informal employment practices and workingmen's exclusiveness, even when laws were passed to protect her in the paid workplace. She may even have found her wage an embarrassing mark of family poverty rather than a symbol of dignity and respect. She could make no claim to a "right" to work as her menfolk did. Hardly anyone thought this was unfair.[6]

This "gendered imagination" was highly unstable.[7] Many working-class families in Hamilton, especially those headed by less-skilled workers, found that the concept of the family wage remained more an ideal than a reality. In practice, most working-class housewives knew that to keep the family economy afloat they had to "do their bit" to bring in extra income or, at least, to manage the family's limited resources with skill and care. In early-20th-century Hamilton, the pressures on women to do so were shifting and intensifying, especially because male wages were becoming increasingly insecure. Yet they won no larger social and economic rewards for those efforts. The patriarchal family survived as the central cultural icon of working-class culture.

Working and Not Working

An adult male man in working-class Hamilton was expected to follow a two-act cultural script. First, as a young bachelor, he worked full-time and contributed most of his wages to help his family, with whom he was usually still living. Then, by marrying, he moved out and became the primary supporter of a family household of his own.

Some men found this script difficult to follow. Before marriage, some migrated far from their family households to find work – Hamilton had hundreds of such men at different points in the early 20th century – and, although boarding in another family's household and still sending home money to their parents, they spent much of their after-work time with other bachelors, many of them just as transient. They could enjoy some personal freedom in these circumstances, but, if the economy slumped, they might find themselves lining up at soup kitchens and spending nights in a Salvation Army hostel or even in the city jail. Some men (roughly one in ten in the interwar period) never married and, in a few cases, eventually spent the last years of their lives in the city's dreary old folks home. Just how many of these men lived outside a family orbit, or how much the bonds of family remained strong in spite of distance (European newcomers certainly kept close touch with relatives back home) is difficult to say. In any case the great majority of adult males in Hamilton followed the conventional script and, with sometimes wavering commitment, accepted the responsibility of breadwinning for their wives and children.[8]

To ensure that they could earn enough to support their families, workingmen wanted jobs that were well-paying and steady. In practice they had to apply for employment that matched their training and experience. A minority expected a substantial wage appropriate to their skills, while much larger numbers of semi-skilled or unskilled workers took what they could get. The difference between skilled and less-skilled employment went beyond wage rates to job security, though few occupations were completely secure. The picture was further complicated by the growing tendency to put semi-skilled workers on piecework, which might mean a thick pay packet when the economy was booming.

The male labour markets functioned extremely informally throughout most of the years from 1890 to 1940. A boy often got his first and subsequent jobs when his father, brother, uncle, or neighbour put in a good word for him with a foreman, who before 1920, even in the largest companies, did almost all the hiring for his department. Even after 1920, when the larger firms began to set up employment offices to screen applicants, foremen were regularly consulted about new recruits. One man hired in 1936 at Stelco, where his father was a foreman, recalled: "The Anglo-Saxons were there as brothers or cousins. I was kept on, even though others with years of experience were being laid off, because I was Bill Martin's son." A recent immigrant might follow a similar route through personal connections, or follow up a lead provided by one of the men in his boarding house, tavern, or church. Some of the skilled unionists still expected that their craft unions could direct them to new jobs (sometimes in other cities), but they were a distinct minority. Far more men simply trudged around to companies that they had somehow heard might need their labour power. Only in times of labour shortages did most employers resort to the help-wanted section of local newspapers. In economically gloomier times, a job listing would send a crowd scampering off to apply. If an opening was posted outside the *Spectator* office, as an unemployed man wrote in 1923, "It would be very amusing, if it was not so tragic, to see the poor devils beating it up the street after the job."[9]

A few men were recruited abroad through private agencies to work for a specific employer in the city, and a number of firms brought in groups of workmen when they opened a Hamilton plant. Unless they arrived as strikebreakers, the men were usually only the most skilled. A few private employment agents in Hamilton handled particular kinds of labour, especially unskilled European migrants.[10] A provincial government employment office first appeared in 1907 to offer a free service, in an early attempt to rationalize local hiring and job-hunting practices, but it never handled more than 200 to 300 workers a year and remained largely irrelevant.[11] The difficulties of mobilizing industrial labour in the unusual full-employment conditions of World War One and then of resettling thousands of returning soldiers brought a huge expansion of this state effort. A much larger, better staffed provincial employment office opened in January 1917 and funnelled greater numbers of both male and female wage-earners into jobs. After the war that service was integrated into a national network of employment offices, but in the early 1920s the federal government cut funding for these centres and restricted the scope of their operations. They thus handled only a limited number of job-seekers.[12]

For most of the five decades, then, a male wage-earner had to look to his own devices to find work. The search often entailed joining small bands of job-seekers at the back doors of factories. "People used to wander into the factory grounds off the street, and ask the first boss-like person they saw for a job," a retiring Proctor and Gamble worker recalled about the 1920s. "I have travelled the streets of Hamilton looking for work so much," a discouraged worker wrote in 1923, "that I have got to know the color of pretty nearly every house and factory in the city." This sense of frustration and demoralization might well have been the reality behind the social workers' pathology of the listless, lazy, irresponsible breadwinner.[13] Finding and keeping a job required not only determination but also attention to personal dynamics inside the workplace. After World War One, the largest companies eventually developed internal labour markets, and tried wherever possible to fill jobs from within. Men therefore learned to curry favour to ensure promotion when more lucrative positions opened up, and to gain job security when production slumped. One Westinghouse worker remembered that holding onto the brass disc stamped with a worker's employment number, to be hung by the time clock, was a visible symbol of continuing employment.[14]

For workers, gainful employment proved to be highly irregular.[15] Hamilton's wage-earners told the census-takers in the relatively prosperous year of 1911 that they had sustained an average of nearly ten weeks of unemployment during the preceding year. Even in the new wartime boom 30 years later, they experienced an average of over seven weeks of joblessness a year.[16] Why were so many weeks of work lost even in good times? In 1941 census-takers discovered that 40 per cent of male unemployment in Hamilton resulted from illness or accidents to workers that left them unable to work. The most days lost at the Steel Company by the end of the 1930s resulted from gastrointestinal problems, sometimes peptic ulcers, which, according to a company doctor, resulted from shift work and "the very nature of the work, with its intense heat, gas, and dust, [which] predisposes to the

Outdoor construction work, such as laying a highway from Hamilton to Toronto in 1911, offered uncertain jobs. It was easily disrupted by the weather and stopped in the winter.

(CTA, Fonds 1244, Item 110A)

occurrence of disorders of digestion." Infectious diseases could also lay employees up for several weeks. Chronic illnesses – tuberculosis, cancer, and heart disease in particular – could slow them down and eventually incapacitate them permanently. Some of these conditions were work-related diseases that could be expected to shorten the wage-earning days (and the lives) of most workers in that occupation. Moulders, for example, developed severe respiratory problems. Labourers and construction workers were susceptible to rheumatism and pneumonia. Serious injuries on the job were also common and could require lengthy recuperation. They could leave a worker disabled to some degree for life. World War One also left many more partially disabled men on the streets of Hamilton. Older men were more susceptible to illness and thus more prone to being out of work.[17]

Many jobs had some form of seasonality built into them. Most noticeably, the climate brought

most outdoor work, especially construction and shipping, to a halt in wet weather and during much of the period between early December and late March. Building tradesmen and labourers of all types felt the impact of this climatic seasonality most severely, but intense heat waves in Hamilton's summers also shut down some foundries, rolling mills, and other fiery metal-manufacturing plants.[18] Most of the fluctuation in employment, however, was due to industry routines or management decisions. Even the best employed factory workers had to sit out two or more unpaid weeks each year while their employers took inventory and repaired machinery.[19] In the early part of the century many workers also faced seasonal demands for the products they made – clothing, shoes, beer, stoves, farm machinery, and other consumer goods – which led to layoffs or "short time" (reduced hours per week) between buying seasons. In the stove foundries and the tobacco plants, the period of

Bringing Home the Bacon **105**

idleness could last several weeks in mid-winter.[20] Regular seasonality probably became a less common characteristic of factory employment as the city's industrial base shifted towards the production of machinery and other producer goods (although the buyers of such machinery as elevators or harvesters would still have been most likely to make their purchases in the warmer seasons). Yet a less predictable slump in demand for specific products could hit other plants as well, resulting in layoffs. At the end of the 1930s, a social worker reported that the greatest cause of poverty in the east end was "the short time or seasonal employment of so many industries."[21]

Hamilton's leading industries, especially metalworking firms, appear to have been particularly prone to shutdown. Unemployment among workers in those factories was much higher than average in the pre-war depression and again in the 1920s and 1930s, when Hamilton's employment levels lagged well behind Toronto's, the province's, and the country's as a whole, except in 1928–29 and 1937. Manufacturing employment always fell below general employment levels, and employment in iron and steel work remained much lower still.[22] Few factory workers in Hamilton would have escaped at least some period of unemployment each year, although the time off undoubtedly varied in length from year to year.

Far more devastating were the slumps in the business cycle that pushed thousands onto the streets at the same time to live without any wages for weeks or even months at a time. Many factory workers also faced short time during economic downturns, when wage-earning continued but at much lower levels. Like other industrial centres in Canada, Hamilton faced major depressions of increasing intensity after the turn of the century, broken by no more than four or five boom years at a stretch.

Indeed, the path of that economic roller-coaster indicates that Canada's industrial economy fell into increasingly deep, prolonged depressions. The first, in 1904, was little more than a pause in the turn-of-the-century prosperity, in which the most disturbing development was the decision of the city's biggest new employer, International Harvester, to lay off several hundred workmen. By the following spring, the pace had quickened again and jobs were plentiful.[23] Early in the winter of 1907–8, however, local firms slowed down much more than usual as a result of the much discussed "financial stringency." By mid-winter several corporate employers, including Westinghouse, International Harvester, Hamilton Bridge, and the Hamilton Steel and Iron Company, had reduced their staffs drastically and put the rest on short time. Many other firms simply shut down. The summer saw little improvement, and it was not until the spring of 1909 that production began to pick up to pre-depression levels. Before long men were earning overtime wages.[24]

Only four years later, the city's industries entered a much more severe depression that would last well into 1915. In March 1913 International Harvester announced a shortened workweek, and by mid-summer the customary two-week stock-taking in many plants was being stretched out to a month or more. The Steel Company had slashed its staff from 2,500 to 1,500 and Westinghouse from 3,250 to 1,600. Construction was at a complete standstill. Finding other jobs was further complicated because 1913 was the high-water mark for immigration into the country, and more than 12,000 newcomers had arrived in this city of nearly 100,000 during the previous year (inevitably, many of the unemployed blamed this heavy immigration for their problems). The following winter the number of men registered for city relief work reached 2,100, and probably twice that number could not find any work. Surveying the city woodyard, where the unemployed found temporary work, the editor of *Labor News* saw men in April 1914 "whom he had known for 20 years – moulders, laborers, and men of other trades – who had been ratepayers of Hamilton for very many years, and they would not have been there had they not been in dire need of work."[25]

At that juncture the economic gloom deepened, as the Steel Company, perilously close to bankruptcy, announced the closing of its blast furnaces. It was no longer able to sell its pig iron to the many Canadian foundries that had closed down. That summer all the city's plants either shut down or cut back production so that wage-earners had no more than two or three days of work per week. The winter of 1914–15 consequently became the most severe in living memory for Hamilton's unemployed, whose personal resources were now exhausted. The local *Labour Gazette* correspondent reflected that conditions had "never been so bad here before as during the present winter." Despite new war orders for many factories, more workers were still on short time in June 1915 than in the previous summer, and International Harvester only reopened in July, with a reduced workforce.[26] It was against this background of high unemployment that so many men signed up for military service in the first year of the war.

The next three years brought as full employment as had ever been known – and a level that would not be seen again until World War Two. The signing of the Armistice in November 1918 abruptly ended the heady wartime prosperity, and hundreds of workers were laid off that winter to join the large numbers of returning soldiers looking for work.[27] Over the next two years Hamilton manufacturers attempted to keep their factories humming. But in the winter of 1920–21,

facing excess productive capacity, high labour costs, and unsold stock, they began to shut down their plants, limit production, cut wages, and lay off workers. The signal of real trouble came when International Harvester announced a three-month closing in April 1921. During that year the army of the jobless grew to unprecedented proportions, and in the next year public relief was flowing out to 23,700 persons – close to a quarter of the population. The Department of Labour's new monthly surveys of employment levels in industry revealed that, despite a slight recovery in the summer of 1923, substantial improvement was not evident until 1925, and the number of jobs reported in January 1920 was not reached again until September 1926.[28] The new burst of business activity in the second half of the 1920s then ended abruptly in 1929 with the onset of a deep, prolonged slump that would last with only minor relief for a decade.

The federal census-takers found shockingly severe joblessness among Hamilton workers in 1931. Nearly a quarter of male wage-earners over the age of 20 were out of work on 1 June 1931. Half the entire male workforce had been out of work at some point in the previous year (including 55 per cent of factory workers, nearly 64 per cent of machinists, 76 per cent of labourers, and 80 per cent of moulders and core-makers). Among those men, the average number of weeks lost was just under 26 (nearly 24 weeks in manufacturing). The seven-tenths of the male workers giving "No Job" as their explanation averaged over 31 weeks without work, and the one-quarter on temporary layoff averaged nearly 17 weeks. The numbers no doubt increased as the depression deepened over the two years after the census. Trade unionists – normally better employed than the average worker – reported an increase from only 3.5 per cent unemployment in July 1929 to 25 per cent in the same month in 1931.

Companies reported employment levels in the city in the first half of 1932 that were one-third lower than at the peak in 1929. Once again, by February 1933 nearly one-quarter of the city's families were on relief. A modest revival occurred after 1934, but a new dip followed in 1938.[29]

Woven into these annual and cyclical unemployment patterns were the rhythms of the life cycle for individual workers. Young single men with less work experience and less call on the consciences of employers, politicians, and charitable agencies were often the first to be sacked in any trimming of staff. Adult male wage-earners in the age bracket when they were most likely to be heads of families, from 25 to 50, were the least likely to be laid off in good times, though obviously many were. The census snapshots of unemployment in 1911, 1921, 1931, and 1941 reveal that, as male wage-earners passed into their twenties, their average period of idleness each year got shorter, until they reached their forties and fifties, when it began to increase again. Their problems clearly mounted as they approached old age. Only tiny numbers had any kind of private or government pension. Unable to continue in physically demanding jobs, they might find themselves permanently unemployed, or competing for lighter unskilled work, perhaps as a janitor or night watchman. In the prosperous year of 1911, census-takers found 35 per cent of those over 65 unemployed, and in the depressed times of 1921 and 1931 the percentage rose to 39 and 49. Old age thus brought lower wages and more idleness, but rarely the comforts of "retirement."[30]

In the half-century before World War Two, then, Hamilton's working-class families had to cope with periodic economic depressions that became deeper and longer each time they hit. The jobs of the chief breadwinners either disappeared or became part-time and uncertain.

These crises came on top of the regular, shorter bouts of enforced idleness that many male wage-earners faced each year, and on top of any sickness or industrial injuries that might prevent workers from earning their regular wages. The insecurity of their position contrasted sharply with the experience of white-collar workers, who often had something closer to year-round employment.[31] For older wage-earners no longer able to work or shunned by employers, unemployment could become permanent. For any workingman, being without a job could trigger great anxiety. In 1916 the 50-year-old treasurer of the local painters' union committed suicide after being "out of work and despondent for some time" – a stark example of the crisis of masculinity that social workers had begun to identify among some unemployed men by the 1930s.[32]

Many if not most workers lived close enough to the edge of poverty that losing a job was disastrous, especially if they had large families.[33] Whether chief breadwinners for their families or single sojourners, most able-bodied men did try to find some other source of income when their wage-earning stopped. Hanging around the streets without a job could get workers arrested for vagrancy. As union organizers discovered in trying to maintain strikes among unskilled or semi-skilled wage-earners, few workers had savings to draw on; they could not wait long before trying to find another source of income.

Some of the luckier workers had a meagre measure of insurance against the loss of wages, usually through a contributory benefit fund run by a craft union, fraternal society, or company benefit society. If so they might receive small weekly sums in times of sickness or injury (and occasionally idleness), and sometimes a tiny old-age pension. The family might receive a lump sum if the wage-earner died. In 1913 only 14 of Hamilton's 31 union locals, totalling only 1,800 members, paid benefits. The three or four dollars a week that these funds provided were never intended to be more than a modest supplement to a family income and certainly could not alone sustain a family through a crisis. Fraternal societies had few unskilled members (only 29 labourers and helpers out of nearly 3,000 members in five Hamilton lodges of Masons and Odd Fellows). Across the country, before the 1930s, only about 30 per cent of Canadian working-class males joined such lodges. Even among those who did, prolonged unemployment might force men to miss insurance payments and thus lose coverage.[34]

Some men anticipated the seasonality of their work and tried to mesh the seasonal cycles of different industries in the city or elsewhere. For example, until the 1920s the most common way for unskilled labourers to earn wages in January and February was to cut ice in the harbour for the various firms that controlled the ice houses. A few with the right political connections could also look forward to shovelling snow off city streets. Workers without jobs also often looked for work on nearby Ontario farms or headed west at the end of August for the annual "Harvest Excursion" to Prairie wheatfields.[35] But the local competition could be intense. Late in the winter of 1902 the *Labour Gazette* correspondent noted, "The longshoremen complain of many of the skilled crafts seeking employment in their slack seasons on the dock, etc., thereby depriving men who have no other means of support of a situation, and having a tendency to lower wages." In January 1911 a "skilled tradesman" reported jostling with "all sorts and conditions of men" for ice-cutting work. By the 1930s workers with the necessary skills competed for jobs as truck or taxi drivers. Non-Anglo-Canadian newcomers might find many of these off-season jobs closed to them.[36]

Every winter unemployed men looked for work cutting ice on the harbour. By the 1920s water pollution had forced the end of the ice harvest. (HPL)

Often, finding a new job meant leaving the city permanently. This was especially true for the more transient workers who had flocked in during the intervening booms and were often the first to be let go in a slump.[37] For some English machinists, Italian peasant-labourers, and many other sojourners, travelling to Hamilton in the first place had been an attempt to overcome economic hardship back home. They would keep looking elsewhere or head back. A man might set off on his own to scout the prospects (a few despondent men might even use this separation to abandon their families permanently).[38] Or whole families might depart together. In 1914 Hamilton's mayor saw many people leaving the city and remarked "that many of the old country immigrants had sold

Some men found work in the winter shovelling show from the streets.

(HPL , Bailey Collection)

their furniture to send their families back home, and that these men now desired a job to make enough to go back themselves." City authorities actually encouraged single men to leave by denying them relief. The first wave of enlistments in the Canadian Expeditionary Force in 1914–15 was to a great extent a solution to the widespread unemployment of the previous year, especially among younger British-born men. The same pattern of out-migration occurred again in the early 1920s. Some 300,000 people were estimated to have left the country in the first half of the decade. Losing a job certainly did not necessarily mean sitting on a doorstep and waiting to be rehired.[39]

The Pay Packet

Through all these challenges, breadwinners were expected to lay their wages on the kitchen table each week to sustain their families. Exactly what workers carried home in their pay packets in early-20th-century Hamilton remains unclear.[40] The available figures suggest that wage rates for all workers rose steadily up to 1913, fell

slightly during the pre-war depression, and then took a great leap upward during the war before falling back somewhat to a new equilibrium in the interwar period. Wage cuts were common during economic slumps, most noticeably in the early 1920s.[41] For all occupations, including salaried white-collar workers, the census-takers who asked the workers themselves determined that the average weekly earnings in Hamilton rose from $14.48 in 1911 to $25.30 in 1921, $26.35 in 1931, and $27.51 in 1941. Skilled blue-collar workers were invariably able to get more than the less-skilled did, but the war economy pulled up the less-skilled average proportionately much further than it did that of the skilled. The relative gap between the earnings for the highest- and lowest-paid had narrowed somewhat by the 1920s.[42]

The real take-home pay of the thousands of semi-skilled pieceworkers must remain something of a mystery.[43] In boom times, especially the last three years of World War One, overtime could become quite common for many workers.[44] But more often wage-earning got interrupted by unemployment, whether through illness, injury, or layoffs (or quitting). If workers could not find work for three months, they might have to stretch 40 weeks' earnings over 52.[45] Taking these interruptions in wage-earning into consideration brings all the male breadwinner's actual weekly earnings down considerably from the more widely quoted averages. In the reasonably good year of 1911, the average weekly earnings in Hamilton reported to the census dropped from $14.48 to only $11.90 when the average unemployment was taken into consideration.[46] The impact of unemployment was quite uneven, however, as textile, printing, and transportation workers had much smaller gaps between weekly averages and actual earnings. The hardest hit were not necessarily the least skilled, but rather those in the most vulnerable industries. Overall, Hamilton's uncertain economy was hard on its workers.[47]

The amount a man presented to his family each week was not necessarily all that his employer had paid him. Men reserved the right to hold back some portion for their own needs and pleasures, and the law agreed. "Husbands are not obliged to hand over their wages to their wives," Police Magistrate George Jelfs ruled in 1916. "If they provide shelter and clothing and food, that's all. The women folk get all that's coming to them when the hubbies do that." That sum could be negotiated, or decided arbitrarily. In some cases, men simply handed over a fixed housekeeping allowance. There was no universal standard of how much a man could keep for himself, and many wives probably had no idea how much their husbands took off the top each week. Many men held onto enough for streetcar fare, tobacco, alcohol, sporting events, gambling, or other small pleasures.[48]

One masculine indulgence that seemed to flourish in every working-class neighbourhood

Gambling was a popular pastime for men that could drain family resources.

(Head of the Lake Historical Society, *Hamilton*, 21)

was gambling. For workingmen and their families, the seemingly irrational twists of fate that hit them with unemployment, accidents, sickness, or, at the other extreme, boom-time wages must have encouraged a strong faith in luck. A game of craps behind a garage, a few hands of poker, or a small bet on a cockfight or horse race could be part male sporting activity (which might require some skill to win) and part persistent hope in the possibility of a small jackpot to take home (although some men simply spent such winnings on a barrel of booze for friends). Betting on pool games was also common. One man recalled that in the 1930s his father "would take twenty-five cents if we had it in the house and go down to the pool room and come home with four or five dollars because he was a good player. And that was gravy. That was big time gravy." More often the gambler came away empty-handed, but generally, unless obsessively driven, he had probably not wagered enough to seriously undermine his family's fortunes. Many men also dropped small sums into the various lotteries and sweepstakes that were springing up after World War One (one of which, run by the otherwise radical One Big Union, was the largest weekly lottery in Canada).[49]

The decline of alcohol consumption during the various depressions suggests that many men curbed their personal spending in hard times. Indeed, the lack of pocket money could be a major embarrassment that eroded their masculine pride.[50] Others no doubt followed the temperance movement's script and, no matter the economic climate, drank up much of their wages or gambled them away before their families saw any money. The Khan's little girl praying that her father not squander too much on the way home highlighted this fundamental male privilege.

Some men may have been temperamentally unable to hold down a job, or too thoroughly worn down and demoralized to be able to look for work. Returned soldiers were often reported to be suffering from this blockage. Some simply gave up and abandoned their families. Charity workers had a standard litany of complaints about ne'er-do-well husbands who refused to work or support their families. New laws tried to snap errant husbands and fathers into line.[51] Almost every week throughout the period, the police magistrate heard cases of non-support filed by disgruntled wives whose patience had evaporated after weeks or months of neglect. Although he did not always do so, the magistrate could issue a court order requiring a husband to give his wife a small fixed sum each week (a mere $3 in 1900, $5 in 1910, and somewhere between $5 and $10 in the interwar period). Or, to make domestic finances worse, he could send the offending husband to jail for up to six months. In such situations, some women dropped their charges in panic, or the magistrate might just as often send the couple home to reconcile their differences or scold the woman for her bad behaviour.[52]

Overall, these neglectful husbands could not have been a major proportion of the married men in working-class Hamilton. Most men felt the economic pressure and had a sense of masculine pride in bringing home the bacon for their families. There was always the lingering worry that they were not earning enough. This fear was more than a matter of simple accounting. Committed breadwinners argued that they wanted to bring home a "fair" or "living" wage, by which they meant enough to support their whole families without their wives or children having to work, and enough to keep their households within a "decent," respectable standard of living. The approach represented a fluid, highly controversial notion that pitted them not only against capitalists but also against anyone willing to work for lower wages – women, children, new immigrants, or scabs.[53]

Adding to the Pot

Whether or not they were out of work, many workingmen had other projects outside regular wage-earning to help support their families. The proceeds were always supplementary to wages, but could be vital to enhancing the living standards of their households.

Many used their own labour to make non-monetary contributions. Some caught fish along the marshy shores of the bay to feed to their families or to sell, though those waters became steadily more polluted with sewage and industrial waste. In the late 19th century, fishing practices also came under tighter state regulations to conserve fish for sport fishermen, and unlicensed spearing or netting of fish could bring down a fine on a worker's head. Hundreds of ice-fishing huts nonetheless appeared on the bay each winter. Some men might go hunting in the fall, if the ducks along the bay were not driven away by industrial development or protected by conservationists.[54] More commonly men raised chickens or pigeons or tilled their backyards to plant vegetables for family consumption. These home gardens were common throughout the city, and they expanded when the cost of living soared during World War One and again during the depression of the 1930s. They most often remained men's work. People living upstairs in rented rooms would most likely have no access to yards. Indeed, when garden plots were made available to hundreds of the unemployed in the early 1930s, the organizers found that they had to provide tools, "as in the majority of cases the workers have no equipment."[55]

Some wage-earning men tried to establish a small measure of security by using savings to speculate in building lots or to buy and rent out an extra house, generally to other workers. Only a small percentage of the better-paid workers could afford to sink precious income into property, however. One study found that only 19 to 31 per cent of the rental units surveyed were owned by skilled workers between the 1890s and 1930s, and generally less than 3 per cent were owned by labourers. In any case, that was a risky approach – a house might sit empty or require expensive repairs, and in times of general depression the flow of rents from tenants might stop.[56]

Sometimes men looked for some form of self-employment to tide them over or to take them out of the cycle of economic uncertainty of wage-earning permanently. Often this was only a continuation of the moonlighting that they had undertaken from time to time while employed. Scattered stories have survived to indicate a pattern that may have been woven into many lives, though it certainly never applied to a large proportion of workers. The old 19th-century pattern of shifting into full-fledged entrepreneurship in the mainstream of industrial production was generally rare in the new age of corporate capitalism. A group of Hamilton moulders did manage

Ice-fishing inside a hut on the harbour in the 1890s.
(HPL, Bailey Collection)

A few chickens in the backyard could always help to keep household expenses down.
(Head of the Lake Historical Society, *Hamilton*, 255)

to start up a successful foundry in 1910 during a prolonged strike, but more often individual men took up small-scale contracting in the few trades in which craft skills survived, especially in construction. Men might also try their hand at peddling or shopkeeping, particularly as the city's rapid suburbanization made trips to the central Hamilton Market extremely difficult. When Eric Jamieson, a Scottish immigrant who arrived in Hamilton in 1905, found his wages as a shingler too low and began, first, small-scale

Some workers supplemented their wages by bootlegging. A few were able to turn their success in the underground economy into great success – most notably Rocco Perri, a former labourer, who is shown here distraught at the 1930 funeral of his wife, who had been gunned down by a competitor. (HPL)

hawking and then moved up to a grocery store, he was following a familiar path in the city (and elsewhere). In 1905 the *Canadian Grocer* was convinced that former wage-earners had started up nearly half the small retail stores in the country. Among Ontario retailers, the proportion was probably even higher. Tiny, backstreet shops run out of small households in working-class neighbourhoods proliferated after the turn of the century.[57]

For many of these working-class families, opening a front-parlour grocery store on a shoe-string was a direct response to unemployment and economic depression rather than being a purposeful drive to get out of the working class. Indeed, it was not unusual for the same man to continue wage-earning while shopkeeping, with the help of his family. In Hamilton's European immigrant communities, many shopkeepers had recent roots in wage-earning. As a 1931 survey revealed, Jewish workers seemed particularly likely to make this occupational shift as the city's garment industry dwindled in size. Many

of these tiny enterprises failed, of course, and gave workers little real hope of upward mobility. By the 1920s, breaking into retailing was getting much more difficult as shopkeeping practices were modernized, chain stores proliferated, and wholesalers' terms of credit tightened. The percentage of shopkeepers from blue-collar working-class backgrounds steadily declined after 1920 and particularly in the later 1930s.[58]

Some retailing was in defiance of the law. As the first European-immigrant enclaves took shape in the city before World War One, the police regularly pounced on unlicensed liquor sales in immigrant households. Opportunities of this sort expanded after prohibition arrived in 1916. Every week in the 1920s, bootleggers were dragged into the Hamilton police court after police or special provincial "spotters" had uncovered their illicit operations.[59] "Just about every family that I knew during prohibition was involved with bootlegging," one Italian-Canadian man later remembered. "They had to do it if they wanted to stay alive. Back then there was no work and there was no unemployment insurance." Another recalled: "The money that Italian men brought home from work was not enough.... They would make 10–15 barrels of wine and sell it to the English down the street in order to make extra money.... The police knew about this. They were the biggest buyers." The most successful Hamilton bootlegger was the infamous Rocco Perri, a former labourer and shopkeeper. Bootlegging, however, was not a uniquely Italian occupation. It flourished in other ethnic communities as well, including among Anglo-Canadians.[60]

Did unemployment also prompt more men to steal as a form of survival? At a public meeting to discuss the city's unemployment crisis in 1914, Sheriff James T. Middleton announced his belief that "many arrests had been made for stealing which would never have happened if the men had had opportunities for work." At another meeting an unemployed worker declared, melodramatically, "that if he could not sell his labor, which was all he had to sell to supply his wife and four children with food, he would be forced to take what he needed." Six years later a man charged with breaking and entering pleaded, "I couldn't get employment. I had no money; I could get no eats."[61] Crime statistics suggest that the theft rate did rise slowly after the 1890s and took a sharper turn upward in 1913 in the context of severe unemployment and the growth of a much larger transient population. But police vigilance fluctuated enough to make it hard to make an easy link between economic deprivation and property crime. Notably, the 1930s saw no major increase in arrests for theft. Still, by the middle of that decade, citizens continued to report huge numbers of petty thefts, mostly from their homes.[62]

The pilfering of cash, clothing, food, bicycles, and other goods probably fit into a variety of patterns that included children's scavenging, wilful vengeance, and juvenile adventures. Some people evidently attempted to make a living from burglary and armed robbery (and thus provided the stereotypes for crime novels, gangster movies, and sensationalized newspaper stories), but more working-class men (and no doubt women) may have taken up stealing just to survive, perhaps snatching small items that could be resold. One young man who confessed to house-breaking in 1925 told the police magistrate that he robbed "because he wanted money on which to get married." His accomplice claimed he "just wanted something to spend, owing to the fact that he was out of work." Most theft supplemented meagre incomes at the expense of other residents, sometimes neighbours. We can never know how many were tempted by the opportunities offered by an open kitchen window, a string of sausage on a counter, a purse hanging loosely from an arm, a bicycle left unattended, or a pile of lumber or copper pipe in a yard. We can safely assume, however, that theft never played a central role in the economic strategizing of most working-class families.[63]

More commonly, when depressions hit the city, large numbers of men organized themselves to demand that the city provide work. The speeches at their meetings rang with the injured pride of breadwinners and single men, both of whom felt they were entitled to work for wages. Their street meetings and marches helped to overcome their isolation and rekindled the male camaraderie of the workplace (in 1914 the group that met frequently, marched about, and lounged about city hall was dubbed the "Cigarette Brigade"). Generally they were successful each time in getting the city to organize some municipal make-work projects to provide a day or two a week for unemployed, generally married male residents.[64]

Clearly, the range of income-earning possibilities for male wage-earners could vary tremendously, especially those growing numbers who were not closely connected to the older crafts. The experience of one man is suggestive, though not necessarily typical. Charles Emery arrived in Hamilton in 1904 at age 14 with his father, a one-time farm hand turned steamfitter whom International Harvester brought in from Chicago. After a short spell at that company, the boy moved through a series of labouring jobs before beginning small-scale contracting in construction around 1910. In the pre-war depression his family moved back to farming near Ingersoll, but in 1915 Emery again got a job at International Harvester. By the 1920s he was back on building sites, moving in and out of contracting until the 1930s, when he landed a job as a technical-school instructor. From one angle this was an upwardly mobile worker intent on making it out of the working class. But from another he was responding promptly to shifting economic pressures and opportunities to make a modest income and never really moved out of a blue-collar milieu. It would certainly be misleading to call him a "penny capitalist." He acted as if he was aware of the collective interests of his fellow wage-earners, by getting himself blacklisted at International Harvester in 1907 for involvement in a strike and later winning election to the company's Industrial Council at the end of the war. What his life highlights above all is the uncertainty of opportunities and challenges that made breadwinning a relentlessly unstable base on which to build a family economy.[65]

Doing Her Bit

Clichés abound in public debate. So it was not surprising that a man styling himself "Lover of Justice" would include in his letter to the press early in 1919 the hoary platitude that "A woman's place is in the home." He was responding to a suggestion from a soldier's wife that women should be allowed to stay at work until their husbands were resettled. "If this kind of thing continues," he argued, "woman will soon lose her place in the world of home-making and become a mere machine in the office and factory of to-day."[66] No other notion about feminine behaviour was more all-pervasive in the discourses of early-20th-century Canada than that of "separate spheres" for men and men. Despite the extension of the right to vote and hold public office to women towards the end of World War One and the new laws that reduced men's freedom to be irresponsible, this commitment to distinct social roles for males and females was never seriously breached in Hamilton at any point between the 1890s and 1930s.

Workingmen and their unions never questioned this division of labour. "We do not want conditions in Hamilton, where mothers, daughters and children have to go out to earn a living," labour leader Samuel Landers told a gathering of garment workers in 1910. The Trades and Labor Congress of Canada, whose 1899 platform of principles formed the basis of many labour campaigns before World War One, called for the abolition of female labour "in all branches of industrial life." That clause was finally amended in 1914 to call for equal pay for men and women – a formula aimed at discouraging employers from hiring women in preference to men. Indeed women who arrived on the shop floor were usually seen as a potential threat to masculine status and male wages – a fear that became more real when employers used them to cheapen labour costs, as in the city's munitions plants after 1916, the tobacco plants in 1918, and the restaurant of the Royal Connaught Hotel in 1922. Eventually, when women workers rose up in militancy, some union leaders grudgingly admitted that, if they were working for wages, they should be organized. But few unionists ever abandoned the assumption that women ought to be at home. In 1929 Hamilton's Walter Rollo – an earnest, Scottish-born, one-time broom-maker, former Labor school trustee, and West Hamilton's MLA and labour minister in the Farmer-Labour government – was still proclaiming his belief that working mothers were shirking their maternal duties and calling for a law to prevent the employment of women with small children.[67]

This was a model of social order that sank its deepest roots in middle- and upper-class families. The women of Hamilton's working-class households were actually at home for intensely practical, as well as ideological, reasons – after all, managing a working-class household remained a physically demanding, time-consuming job that allowed little room for cultivating the gentility and fragility of bourgeois ideals. Many working-class husbands thought of their wives as working partners rather than fragile objects on a pedestal. As Allan Studholme argued in the Ontario legislature in 1912, "No man can get on this floor tonight, and say that woman is not his equal." But for working-class women the notion of separate spheres was more prescriptive than descriptive. Home and work were not as rigidly separate as the bourgeois model might suggest. Women could not rely on their husbands, fathers, and brothers for all the family income, and they had to do their bit to help make ends meet, both before and after marriage.[68]

Although a majority of young women worked for wages at some point before settling down with a husband, for most working-class women marriage was supposed to mark the end of regular wage-earning. In most cases it did. In 1927 a Communist organizer included in her list of "obstacles to be combatted" the argument that "women do not take wage earning seriously. To them it is only a temporary necessity, a means of living just before getting married and after, just to meet a temporary difficulty."[69] The census data through to 1941 show only a small (but intriguing, and little-studied) minority of adult women in the paid workforce in Hamilton beyond the marrying age of 24 – roughly one in four aged 25 to 34 and one in seven aged 35 to 44 by the 1920s.[70] The great majority of women without men to support them – single, widowed, or divorced – had wage-earning jobs.[71]

The apparent inevitability of marriage rested not only on the limited job prospects and low wages that left women dependent on men for their survival, but also powerful cultural pressures. Workingmen preferred to have their wives at home, but this gendered division of labour was not simply a decision imposed inside the family circle. Employers were reluctant to hire married women, believing that the women's domestic responsibilities could both interfere with efficient performance on the job and threaten the stability of the households from which they drew their workforce. Many refused to keep married women on; in the 1920s and 1930s getting married might still lead to getting fired. Later in their lives two women described how they had kept their marriages secret for over a year, until their pregnancies gave them away (one was threatened with blackmail by a foreman who found out). Another woman told how she wore gloves to hide her wedding ring when she applied for a job in a radio factory in the 1930s.[72]

This patriarchal prejudice temporarily lifted only during World War One, when labour shortages prompted government officials, charity workers, and industrial employers to encourage married women, especially soldiers' wives, to take up wage labour. A third of those applying to the provincial government's Employment Bureau for munitions work in 1917 were married, and nearly half were over 30. An Ontario government official reported, "Hamilton had the largest number of applications of women over 40 years of age." Even the Canadian Patriotic Fund, which provided financial assistance to soldiers' wives, raised no objections to married women seeking this kind of extra income.[73] This more flexible attitude did not survive the war. In times of economic distress (notably the postwar slump and the 1930s), public debate could rage against married women holding down jobs while their husbands worked or while single women needed work. The letters to the editor columns bristled with complaints that married women should quit and let either single women or returned men have their jobs. Even the Mount Hamilton Women's Independent Labor Party sent a deputation around to theatre owners in 1921 asking them not to hire wives while single women were unemployed.[74]

Wage-earning women felt their vulnerability especially sharply whenever the economy took a serious tumble. Local unemployment relief measures were set up for male breadwinners, and were never designed to include women. Early in 1921 a member of the city's Board of Control made clear that unless women looking for work turned to the jobs in domestic service offered to them (which many had apparently been rejecting), they would get no help. The same attitudes prevailed during the 1930s. During that decade labour publications such as the *Canadian Congress Journal* published denunciations of working women, and even women's organizations like the Local Council of Women and YWCA had no sympathy for wage-earning wives.[75]

For working-class housewives, leaving the home to find paid work might be frowned upon, but, in many ways, marriage opened a new phase in a working-class woman's ability to contribute income to her family's coffers. A wife could help her family reach key goals, such as buying a new house, supporting a child through more schooling, or paying off a large medical bill. She could contribute to its survival in the face of a family financial crisis. In the early 20th century a wife, compared to her grandmother of half a century earlier, generally had fewer options for generating income, but her income could still be quite important for her family. Most women who found ways to "do their bit" worked in their own homes. Faced with a family crisis, some would have to leave the house and, in the process, work out an awkward, probably painful balance between wage-earning and domestic responsibilities. Rarely could married women set aside their predetermined role as domestic managers and caregivers for their families.[76]

The most common way for these women to make money was to take in boarders, and that is why many households in working-class Hamilton opened their doors to single sojourners. The most widely discussed cases at the time were the overpopulated European households, in which beds for as many extra bodies as possible were often squeezed into every available space. More commonly, families took in only one or two boarders. Of course, welcoming outsiders was only possible in households with room to spare (and room was often made by bunching up children together).[77]

Sharing household space might be a family decision, but housewives did the bulk of the work involved in looking after single boarders (though not the whole families who rented part of the house; that was a different way to make extra money that left the tenants to look after their own upkeep). Older children might help out, though by the 1920s they were much more likely to be in school. By the interwar period there was a growing trend towards "rooming," that is, getting only a room without board.[78] The extra cash that boarders brought into the household had to be balanced against the complex negotiations and possible tensions in the family's most intimate spaces. Any number of unreasonable demands for domestic service might arise. Children had to be kept quiet so as not to disturb the boarder. Drunks might have to be managed, and sexual advances deflected (or accepted, with additional complications). Being a landlady was unquestionably demanding work.[79]

During the same period women were finding fewer opportunities to produce commercial goods at home. Before 1900 the city's major clothing manufacturers had encouraged some women to take in sewing (although Hamilton's garment manufacturers relied largely on small subcontracting shops, in contrast to Montreal or Toronto). But in the decade before World War One, the leading firms moved most of their production inside factories, and home-sewing disappeared as a significant money-making option for married women. Few manufacturers of any kind had much work for women to do in their homes. The more skilled would still sew for neighbours and relatives – wedding dresses and the like – but could no longer expect any role in the mainstream of mass production. The Woman's Christian Temperance Union, YWCA, and Babies' Dispensary Guild ran small needlework classes to help a few women develop sewing skills, though probably mainly for family use. A social worker in 1930 stumbled onto another common home craft when she saw a card advertising "Sox for Sale." Knitting machines were widely marketed to working-class housewives for this purpose. Before World War One another charity ran a "Women's Exchange" through which housewives could sell the products of their household labour. Among women receiving mothers' allowances in Ontario in 1922, one in eight of those making additional money did sewing and knitting at home.[80] Women could also take in laundry from more affluent households, but they faced stiff competition from commercial laundries.

Otherwise, working-class housewives who wanted to generate at least a small income at home provided various services for their working-class neighbours. They might run small groceries. A visitor to a "shacktown" in 1909 dropped into the shop of a bricklayer-turned-grocer who had "stocked in a few things for his wife to sell when he was away bricklaying." In some cases (as in that shacktown grocery), if the business prospered, these women might find themselves pushed aside by their husbands, who took control full-time. Even if they were widows, they might face sexist discrimination

from wholesalers, and most women ran only shoestring shops. The 1931 census listed 249 women as being engaged in some kind of retailing, just over half of them running food stores (60 groceries and 47 confectioneries). Another 100 ran various service enterprises, with 58 of the ventures described as "beauty salons." Some women who cut hair never hung out a shingle and simply worked in the family kitchen. Other services might also be offered less formally and publicly for female neighbours who needed help with their domestic labour. Some women took in laundry. Others minded neighbourhood children whose mothers had to go out to work or were ill or giving birth. In the 1920s a remarkable number of women took up bootlegging booze (and thus might find themselves before the police magistrate facing a stiff fine).[81]

Working-class housewives were always looking for ways of bringing in extra income while they kept up their domestic responsibilities at home. Going out to work was another matter. The wife of a better-paid workingman bruised his masculine pride if she took paid work outside the home. Only a severe crisis that deprived the family of the husband's income would send a married woman out in search of wages. Invariably these were domestic tasks performed for others, rather than jobs in the mainstream of industry. The limited range of possibilities was summed up in a list of jobs that soldiers' wives told the Canadian Patriotic Fund they could take up in 1916: "assistance in the care of children, housework by the day, cook for hotel or club, washing by the day, office cleaning, housekeeper to elderly couple, ironing [and] sewing at home, companion or governess or embroidery work." This is more or less the same range of work that Mothers' Allowance Commission investigators found single mothers taking up to support their families in the 1920s. Charring was by far the most common job.[82]

Many of these married women had children, and they either needed work that they could take the youngsters along to, or else reliable babysitting at home while they were out. "The mother with one or two children to accompany her and desiring a position as housekeeper is ... difficult to place," the Ontario government Employment Bureau reported in 1919.[83] Neighbours and relatives could help with child care. So too could the city's only day nursery, founded in 1896 by a local branch of the Woman's Christian Temperance Union. The organization saw itself as "assisting the poor to make a livelihood, and doing away with the pauperizing system that is such a menace to society." Its house initially cared for 40 children daily at a fee of five cents a day, but eventually hundreds were left there for a few days every year. During 1904, for example, the nursery minded over 2,200 children, and by the mid-1920s the number came to 5,000 to 6,000 every year. A small number stayed at the WCTU day and night while their mothers were in hospital. In keeping with the WCTU's central concerns, this "creche" was actually a kind of centre for working-class women without adequate family support. Coffee and cake were available when the mothers dropped off their children. An employment service helped them find jobs.[84]

As the city stretched eastward, the centrally located WCTU nursery was too far away from the thousands of east-end households. In 1928 social workers finally prodded the Local Council of Women into starting up an East End Creche. It opened with space for only 36 children, and in 1936 handled only 79 from 48 families, with an average daily attendance of 13. A daily charge of 81 cents per child probably deterred many mothers.[85] Far more youngsters were no doubt left with older sisters or brothers, neighbours, or relatives throughout the period. If a mother had to work full-time in a factory she might opt to board her children with relatives or in an orphanage until she had saved enough to re-establish the family household.[86]

With their husbands facing regular seasonal layoffs, some women had to be out looking for wages at one or another point every year. "Many East Hamilton laborers were out of employment during the greater part of last winter," the *Herald* reported in 1913, "and in some instances wives of men had to work to make ends meet."[87] Others had the unexpected mantle of chief breadwinner thrust on them by the illness, injury, death, or disappearance of their husbands. In 1931 one household in seven was headed by a woman without a husband.[88] It was the severe depressions that descended on all Hamilton industry in the early 20th century, however, that brought out the largest numbers of women trying to earn a small sum to help the family survive while their husbands were out of work. In September 1914 the *Labour Gazette*'s Hamilton correspondent reported that the normally insatiable demand for domestic servants had been silenced because "many married women whose husbands were without work are themselves working as domestics." The Salvation Army ran a free labour bureau for such women, but had far more applicants than jobs. When a restaurant owner advertised for a woman to do half a day's cleaning, "over 40 begged to be given the work to do." That year the WCTU day nursery had to cope with more than 5,000 children. By 1919 the wives of unemployed veterans were similarly pounding the pavement in search of such work. "The casual branch of the work is, without doubt, the busiest," the director of the Employment Bureau's women's department reported in 1923. She added, "The general trend of labour conditions can be followed by the rise and fall of numbers of applicants applying for this class of work." She was pleased that the Bureau could help the more than 5,000 women who got casual placements that year to earn "a daily wage, a ready means of support for themselves and their families, which tides them over times of stress." By that point domestic service was undergoing a change away from live-in servants that made this kind of work possible for married women, but mistresses were gradually cutting down the amount of help they wanted. "While there were more orders they were for shorter time, some being for only a few hours where most jobs used to be for the day," the Employment Bureau observed in 1926. As the Bureau staff reported five years later, layoffs in other industries could also bring factory or office workers into competition with housewives for these jobs.[89]

After World War One the pressure for married women to take up wage-earning increased, partly as a result of the increased schooling and declining earning power of the adolescents in the household, and partly because of the prolonged layoffs that male breadwinners lived through in so much of the interwar period. Perhaps, too, the wage-earning experience of married women during World War One had raised young women's expectations and softened up some of the ideological resistance. In September 1919 a *Spectator* reporter certainly thought he was seeing something new in "the increasing number of young married women who are holding down jobs" – of women claiming that it took "two pay envelopes, instead of one, to make ends meet." He also found some of these working wives unashamed to admit that "domesticity, with its routine and its sacrifices, is repugnant to them." They preferred "business life to that of homemaking" – a development, he thought, that "must surely give the thoughtful economist pause!"[90]

Even the Ontario Minimum Wage Board noted a few years later, "Women do not now

Most "working girls" quit paid work when they married, but by the 1920s more women, like this seamstress at Hamilton's Membery Mattress factory, were continuing to work after marriage.

always quit their jobs when they get married." The Board estimated in 1926 that across the province married women made up about 33 per cent of the females working in hotels, restaurants, and laundries, and 10 to 20 per cent in all other occupations. Its annual statistics, based on detailed wage tables from the province's employers, certainly confirmed the trend in Hamilton. In the two largest categories of women's industrial work, the proportion of married women under age 50 in textiles rose from under 15 per cent to nearly 20 between 1924 and 1930, while in the clothing industry the rate began at over 20 per cent and climbed up to 33 per cent by 1931. "Doubtless ... some wives have gone to work when their husband's jobs failed," the Board argued in 1930. "The women's trades, on the whole, suffer less than the men's in times of depression." Census-takers also recorded a slow, but steady rise in the percentage of older, presumably married women in the paid workforce. Small wonder that the debates about married women's waged labour got so intense in the depression of the 1930s.[91]

The income that married women could bring into their households in working-class Hamilton is extremely difficult to quantify. Federal statisticians considered wives' wages to be so insignificant that they omitted them from the tables on wage-earners' family income in the 1911 and 1921 censuses. In 1931 women's reported earnings amounted to less than 1 per cent of total family income in Hamilton. Much more money undoubtedly went unreported because so much was arranged informally and left no records. Many husbands who were gone from their homes for ten or more hours a day might not even have been fully aware of their wives' casual income. In any case, it could never have averaged much more than a few dollars a week, and even full-time wage-earning outside the home could provide no more than half a male wage, generally too little to survive for long. After 1872 in Ontario a woman had legal control over her own earnings, but the law still assumed that she was dependent on a male breadwinner. She owed him her labour as a condition of marriage, and was in no way an equal economic partner with him.[92] Far more important than earning anything was the married woman's responsibility for managing all the family's money.

Still, the women in Hamilton's working-class households clearly made important, often crucial, contributions to their families' economic welfare. In the process they moved back and forth across the boundary of public and private – in and out of the paid labour market and through various channels of what we would now call the "underground economy" of part-time work and neighbourhood barter. In the process they implicitly challenged any notion that their sphere was strictly limited to the household. As labour organizer Mary McNab wrote in 1921, the debate about women's right to vote and fill public office ignored the ways in which working women were already busy outside the home: "It has not been recorded yet where the soul of man has been filled with anguish at the sight of a poor woman scrubbing the floors of a public building."[93]

A Family Economy

For a married couple in working-class Hamilton, then, the regular flow of the husband's wages was the key element in the family's survival. Yet it was so uncertain. Would his boss keep him regularly employed most of the year? Could he find other work during layoffs in the ever deeper economic slumps? Would he be stuck in bed indefinitely with a serious injury or chronic illness, or the infirmities of old age? Were there other opportunities for making some money on the side? Could his wife keep him focused on these responsibilities, or might she lose him to his drinking buddies in a saloon, or even find him simply gone one day without a trace?

When he was working, could she cut corners and stretch his wages enough? If necessary, could she handle a boarder or two, or perhaps take in some laundry? Could she get work outside the home when her husband could not, or would not, provide, and, if so, could she find some child care? Should they give up on Hamilton and head off to look for more secure wages elsewhere?

The room to manoeuvre was constantly constrained by skill levels, gender expectations, and ethnic identities. Small wonder that so many working people expected regular help from their children.

6

Boys in the school-
yard at Hess Street
Public School.
(Oliphant, *Hess Street School*)

School Bells and Factory Whistles

"AS A WORKINGMAN, I PROTEST. I think this is an injustice." In a 1916 letter to the *Spectator* a man signing himself "Indignant" took exception to an idea being put forward by the Hamilton Board of Education to raise the age for leaving school from 14 to 15. He could not afford to keep his six children in school for that extra year, he explained. Children needed to be workers, not drains on their family resources. "Restrictions of this sort," he insisted, "will certainly encourage race-suicide among the poorer classes, who won't be able to afford children."[1]

For Hamilton's working-class families, maintaining household economies was a delicate balancing act. On one side they had their needs at home, on the other the constellation of opportunities and constraints created by local labour markets and schooling regulations.[2] By the early 1920s they were facing new challenges that threatened to deprive them of the wages of young adolescent workers. The nosedive of the business cycle and the continuing changes in the labour processes that reduced the need for juvenile labour were bad enough, but the state also made new moves. New minimum-wage rates for women established by 1920 provincial legislation prompted some employers to begin dispensing with their youngest female help in favour of more mature, efficient workers. Far more important was the growing competition for teenagers' time from the city's school system.

The war years saw two important new initiatives in secondary education that would have major consequences for working-class families after 1920 – the large-scale expansion of a new stream of schooling eventually known as "vocational education" and the raising of the legal age for leaving school. These were distinct projects, but they came to be closely related. Families in working-class Hamilton had to find ways to adapt.

School Days

By the close of the 19th century, a childhood in Hamilton had come to involve considerable time in a schoolroom. The opening of the publicly supported Central School in 1853 and the Roman Catholic separate-school system in 1856 had launched a new era in mass institutionalization of children. By 1871 the great majority of children between the ages of 5 and 12 were enrolled in city schools. At that point they often did not show up every day, but daily attendance increased. Some 20 years later, three-quarters of public-school students were in a classroom for more than 100 days a year, and well over half were there more than 150 days.[3] That year, when asked to explain why 12 per cent of those aged 7 to 13 had not attended for 100 days, Hamilton's teachers reported that only one in six had left to work for wages (a roughly equivalent number could not be traced).[4] Most parents of all social classes had evidently chosen to keep their younger children in school more or less regularly.

A growing thicket of provincial legislation was making it harder for parents to do otherwise. The Ontario Factories Act, which came into force in 1886, had outlawed the employment of boys under 12 and girls under 14 in factories, and

nine years later the age for boys was raised to 14. That act and parallel legislation governing work in shops also limited the hours per day and per week that young workers could be employed. The 1893 provincial Children's Protection Act also put tighter restrictions on children working in such "street trades" as selling newspapers and in amusement places, and authorized local Children's Aid Societies to intervene when parents were not controlling such children.[5]

Undoubtedly the weak provisions for inspection or prosecution in these acts severely limited their effectiveness in eliminating child labour.[6] In 1891, however, the state pressure on parents increased when the provincial government made full-time school attendance compulsory for children up to age 14 and empowered municipalities to appoint truant officers to keep the youngsters in the classroom. In Hamilton the local truant officer was expected to follow up reports from teachers who were not satisfied with explanations for students' absences. The officer eventually got regular weekly reports on absentees from the principals of all the city's public and separate schools.[7] Thereafter the Department of Education's figures for both public and separate schools showed more students attending classes each day and for more days each year. Early in 1901 the truant officer reported 860 children under age 14 not attending school – one in seven (and probably much higher among the older ones) – while only 25 exemptions were granted that year for children to work. A few months later the federal census-takers found 92 per cent of the school population attending for more than seven months in the year. These statisticians also continued to report a decline in wage-earning children under 15 – from 335 in 1911, to 239 in 1921, to 8 in 1931, then rising slightly to 46 in 1941. These figures were undoubtedly low – misrepresenting the age of young workers

Boys working at the Greening Wire Company at the turn of the century. (SLS)

had a long history in Canada – but the trend was evident.[8]

Working-class parents evidently believed that their young children needed and deserved a basic education. The local school board did not always make that choice easy for them. Despite repeated petitions by the local Trades and Labor Council and efforts by the Independent Labor Party's school-board trustees during World War One, students had to pay for their own school books, and school fees of 10 to 12 cents a month per child prevailed until 1919, in contrast to students in Toronto, Ottawa, and London. As a Council delegation argued in 1907, "While the amount might not seem to be much to members of the board it meant a good deal to the working classes where the large families were found." Those in desperate need could apply to the Board to have their fees waived, but, as the Council argued, "That looked too much like beggary and the other children in the schools would soon know of it and point their fingers at the poor ones."[9]

There was often also a serious shortage of classroom space. The tight-fisted Board of Education pursued a cautious building program that resulted in overflowing classrooms. For intervals before and after World War One, overcrowding in the public schools of the city's fastest-growing neighbourhoods, particularly in the heavily working-class east end, resulted in half-day schedules to accommodate all the school-aged children.[10] The anger of working-class parents that erupted when the frequent overcrowding threatened the quality of their children's schooling points to the depth of their commitment to a basic education for their children. In 1913 a public-health nurse warned the school trustees that she had encountered considerable hostility to the half-time schooling on her visits to workers' homes. She warned, "The feeling of dissatisfaction is so strong that something should be done in haste to avert open objection."[11]

A decade later the complaints got louder. In September 1922 a small delegation of women from the east end marched angrily into a Board of Education meeting to protest the continuation of half-time schooling for their children.

According to the *Herald*, Mrs. Burtick, the group's spokesperson, "complained bitterly" that at age ten some children could not spell words of more than one syllable. "I scrubbed floors last year to pay my taxes, and I demand that my children be educated as they should be," she declared. Her wrath continued to spill out over the expensive frills in schools that did not provide more classroom space. "I'll tell you what you've done. You've built auditoriums for entertainments that we poor people, who pay the money you spend, cannot go to. Cut out entertainment auditoriums and give us schools," she demanded. Before departing, the delegation suggested temporarily cancelling kindergarten classes so that older students could attend school more regularly.[12]

In many working-class families, the move into more or less full-time work, paid or unpaid, was determined by family need rather than legislation. Since the city had only one truant officer and no centralized record-keeping in the school system before the 1920s, it was not that difficult to quietly circumvent the school-attendance law. Some parents needed daughters to help out at home. One mother of an eight-year-old girl pleaded that "she needed the girl's help," while a father explained that "he had to keep his little girl home to mind the baby, as his wife was out of the city." Another father who had been ill said that "his wife had to go out and work, and the children were kept home to do the housework."[13] In the early 20th century, moreover, some local employers evidently had no qualms about hiring underage child workers. In 1902 a 10-year-old girl got a job in a local textile mill, as did a 12-year-old just off the boat from England eight years later.[14]

It was most likely children close to the legal school-leaving age who kept the truant officer busy. In 1905 he told the *Spectator*, "For some years past the tendency has been for parents in the working classes to take their children out of the public schools before they reach the school age limit ... the boys particularly being taken from school before they have passed the entrance examinations and put to work."[15] In 1903 he had sent 350 notices to such parents. By 1910 he was delivering twice that number, and he must have had trouble keeping up with the mushrooming population in the years before World War One. A few dozen of these parents appeared before the magistrate each year before 1914, though only a tiny handful were ever convicted. Like one father in 1910, many no doubt "could not get the boy to attend school." On the eve of World War One, more than 1,500 students were still reported as "not attending school," an administrative category for suspicious absences. The wartime economic boom drew more children out of the classroom into the workforce, as truancy notices sent to parents jumped by more than 50 per cent, from 769 in 1913 to 1,271 in 1916.[16] A major textile firm was convicted of illegally employing child labour in 1916, as were tobacco, clothing, and soap manufacturers two years later.[17] By 1920 the truant officer was still investigating 1,625 cases a year and issuing warning notices to 705 parents. He (and the officer working for the separate-school board) claimed that many of these were children of immigrant households.[18]

Despite this regular slippage, after the turn of the century most children under 14 were under the daily custodial care of school teachers. Work might still take precedence over school if an individual family needed the extra income from children under 14, and some unruly children might continue to escape the control of parents and school officials, but in the early 20th century these tendencies were becoming exceptions to the general pattern of keeping young children in school on a regular basis.

First Jobs

From a relatively early age, children in Hamilton's working-class families were expected to help make ends meet. Girls most commonly had to help out around the house, but boys started to take responsibility for earning some income, either to contribute to the family coffers or to pay for their own small pleasures (one boy worked part-time to pay his ten-cent-a-month school fee). From time to time boys could earn pennies for doing odd jobs for individuals or other families. In the summer they might pick berries or even work briefly in local canning factories. Some took on the more demanding year-round part-time jobs of delivering groceries, selling newspapers, shining shoes, or setting up pins in bowling alleys. Many were sent out to scavenge for coal or firewood (or in a few desperate situations, to beg).[19]

At some stage working-class children were expected to leave school behind and start contributing full-time to household needs. Back in the 1860s and 1870s, as jobs had opened up in the first wave of industrialization, teenagers from working-class households, especially boys, had been increasingly likely to move into wage labour after age 12 and thereby contribute to the family income. By the early 20th century the only change was the roughly two-year delay before starting work at age 14 as required by the province's 1891 legislation. "As soon as you got the rudiments of schooling, it was up to you to start working," one man raised in a Hamilton working-class family recalled. "I was getting to the age where I would be expected to work and everybody had to bring home their share of the bacon, no matter what family they belonged to," another explained. "If you could afford more or less it made no difference. You had at a certain age to go off and earn your living." In 1911 children's earnings comprised a third of the average yearly income of Hamilton families reported to census-takers. In white-collar occupations and several skilled trades, the share was much smaller, but, among skilled metalworkers, moulders still relied on their children for a third of their families' earnings and machinists for a fifth, while the children of labourers contributed 44 per cent. Apparently, only regular employment at good craftworkers' wages allowed a working-class family in early-20th-century Hamilton to come close to relying completely on one breadwinner.[20]

In contrast to young workers a century later, these young workers typically turned all their earnings over to their mothers to help cover general family needs, though clearly there was plenty of room for negotiation and conflict over spending money.[21] Their role was not only to bring in money when their father could not work, but also to help cover part of a down payment on a house or help with other large expenditures that the father's income alone did not allow. Interviews with elderly Hamilton residents in the 1970s found many whose families had "all chipped in" to buy a house. "We started to work very early," one English immigrant recalled. "So that's how we got it."[22]

Precisely how many teenage boys and girls were working for wages in Hamilton (or any other Canadian city) in the early 20th century is difficult to determine.[23] The 1911 census, the first to provide detailed occupational information by age, lumped together all full-time workers between the ages of 15 and 24. The more subtly detailed 1921 report reveals a pattern in which full-time employment among Hamilton's adolescents was increasingly common after the age of 14. Even in that economically depressed year, 44 per cent of 15-year-old boys were working full-time, 68 per cent of 16-year-olds, and 77 per cent of 17-year-olds; the comparable figures for girls were 37, 56, and 64 per cent. These rates, especially among girls, were well above the provincial average and above the rates of all other Canadian cities with populations over 30,000.[24]

Boys and girls had different roles in contributing to communal finances. Working-class girls and young women beyond the age of compulsory schooling moved between two worlds of work. Most were expected to help out at home. "In those days, there were a lot of girls stayed home ... helping mother," one woman remembered. "If there was more than one, one nearly always stayed home." Some never left the domestic sphere, even sacrificing marriage prospects to spend their lives as unwaged, dependent caregivers. "We saw that happen so often when I was young, where the unmarried daughter was sort of left in a bad spot," another woman recalled. "But it seemed to be sort of taken for granted. There seemed to be in every family an unmarried aunt who was available to come and that kind of thing."[25] If mothers disappeared, young girls could find themselves with heavy adult domestic responsibilities for their families' economic security. In 1908 "The Khan" penned some touching lines about "Her Father's Dinner Pail":

How serious is her gentle face,
    How wise her woman's way;
For she has taken her mother's place,
    Who died the other day.
She 'tends the baby that was left
    And stills its feeble wail,
Except when she must go abroad
    With father's dinner pail.

She mends the children's dresses;
    Her little brothers three
They lisp their prayer at bed-time
    All clustered around her knee.

Each morning she prepares a lunch
    For father without fail.

The last stanza praises her "true and faithful heart" and "fearlessness," but such sentimentality obscured the agonizing burden of this work on young shoulders.[26] A young woman wrote to the press in 1913 with a stronger tone of despair:

I work as hard as I can, I and my sister. We try to be the men of the house, because my father cannot work at a hard job; his health will not let him. My father gives me $20 a month – that is what he makes – and all that goes to pay for house and stove, which we are getting by payments. I made last week, and the week before, both together, $12. My young sister makes $4 a week. I have no mother and my sister has to stay home to keep house. Tell me how that keeps four? I have not had a new winter dress for three years. I cannot get one, because our money is gone before we get it.... I am not the worst. I think myself lucky compared with some of my poor neighbours who are going to ruin. Help us, please.[27]

At any one time a slight majority of Hamilton girls and women in their late teens and early twenties left their homes each day as wage-earning "working girls."[28] Many of those not counted in the workforce at a specific moment would probably have worked for wages at some point in the eight to ten years between school and marriage. The youngest were usually in the textile mills. By their early twenties they got access to more responsible jobs, such as running sewing or knitting machines.

Almost all still found jobs in female ghettoes that were extensions of women's work in the home or allegedly involved specifically female

Young women stemming tobacco leaves at Tuckett Tobacco.
(SLS, LS15)

attributes, even inside "heavy" industry.[29] In early-20th-century Hamilton, seven out of every ten female wage-earners in manufacturing punched the clock in clothing and textile factories, three out of four by the end of the period. During these years textiles replaced clothing as the chief employer. Within the textile mills and garment factories, women made up between three-fifths and two-thirds of the workforce throughout the period. Almost all other working girls in factories toiled in small pockets of less than 100 workers, spread over a variety of industries, such as the McPherson shoe company, Tuckett Tobacco Company, or Proctor and Gamble. A few hundred had jobs in metalworking plants, running machines to make nails and screws at Canada Screw, lacquering brass castings at the Chadwick brass foundry, making small cores in the International Harvester foundry, or winding coils for electric motors at Westinghouse. Girls' alleged special qualities of nimbleness and dexterity with fine, detailed work got them these jobs. "Delicate work it is, to be sure, for a man with big fingers would be practically unable to lift the delicate sand figure from the half of the mould and place it on the plate alongside," a *Spectator* reporter explained after a tour of the Harvester foundry in 1907. "But the girls, with deft fingers, can do this delicate piece of lifting without hesitation, and, after they get into the way of it, seldom break a core."[30]

The wartime "dilution" of machinists' work brought a few hundred more women into a traditionally male preserve, but not as direct replacements for men. The director of the Imperial Munitions Board's Labour Department explained that dilution meant "spreading over either a greater time or a greater number of machines, the available men, and under charge of these men, placing women in their midst." In

Like these women working on knitting machines at Mercury Mills in 1928, female wage-earners often found jobs running light machinery. (SLS)

Women workers packing olives at the McLaren's factory. (SLS , LS516)

the end many of the munitions jobs that women ended up in had been redefined to make new "diluted" categories of "women's work" – repetitive, less-skilled tasks on specialized machinery. The local machinists' business agent, Richard Riley, believed not only that the women were "being exploited by the manufacturers," but also that they threatened male wages.[31] Equally striking was the employers' foot-dragging reluctance to breach the walls of gender segregation, largely because mixing the sexes on the shop floor would require major innovations to provide services and amenities for the "gentler sex," as well as compliance with the Ontario factory legislation, dating back to the 1880s, forbidding overtime for women.[32]

"We met opposition from every shop superintendent," the chairman of the Imperial Munitions Board, Joseph Flavelle, wrote in 1917. "The manufacturer hesitated at the outlay necessary to accommodate women operators, and generally what has been accomplished was achieved with considerable difficulty." The women disappeared from the machine shops immediately after the Armistice.[33]

There were many other forms of "women's work." Roughly one female worker in six or eight continued to work in trade, mainly retail sales, throughout the period. But the category of personal service that had absorbed so many girls and young women for so many decades dropped off steadily (except for a brief resurgence in the deep depression of the early 1930s). The small size of the middle class in the city meant that fewer households wanted to hire this kind of worker, but in the early 20th century Hamilton's young women were also just as scornful of the work as their counterparts throughout urban Canada.[34] "There's a whole lot of women who think a servant ain't worth her salt if she can't watch the potatoes, scrubs the floors, do the ironing, mind the front door, look after the butcher's boy, do the dusting, and come when she calls, all at the same time," one maid wrote in 1905. "When ladies begin to treat their maids more like human beings and less like machines, that will be the first step towards solving the domestic problem," a housemaid signing herself "Thistle" wrote to the *Herald* in 1913. "A girl's much freer in a factory," another told a *Spectator* reporter six years later, after quitting her job as a servant. "She has her own evenings; she isn't looked down on so much, and treated as if she belonged to another kind of being than the mistress. She doesn't have to wear a cap and apron,

At the turn of the century domestic servants made up the largest number of women earning wages, but their proportion in the female workforce dropped steadily thereafter. (HPL)

and be called by her last name – or her first, if she doesn't want to." Women presiding over upper- and middle-class households became increasingly desperate for "help."[35]

Female employment patterns showed other shifts. The proportion of wage-earners working in factories began to drop in the interwar period, thanks in part to the long years of economic depression and the decline of older, labour-intensive industries, notably the city's garment factories, that had once employed many more women.[36] But two other job opportunities were slowly opening up to absorb some single working-class women – nursing and clerical work. The first had begun seriously in the city in 1890 when the Hamilton General Hospital opened its own school of nursing, and by the 1920s nurses were struggling to establish a sense of professional standards and identity that slowly raised their status.[37] The second field of work was

accessible only to women who had learned clerical skills, either in high school or at one of the city's private business schools, and perhaps had picked up the social graces necessary for office work among white-collared managers. World War One opened up far more female clerical jobs for the first time, but in the interwar period Hamilton girls and women got access to this work slowly, as public-sector and industrial employers continued to prefer male clerks. Clerical workers made up one in five female wage-earners between the wars and generally earned far more than other working girls did.[38]

In many cases, the new recruits for nursing and clerical positions were middle-class daughters with the necessary schooling and polish as well as the desire for good pay. Indeed, for these women, office work and nursing, along with teaching, became the main occupational outlets. In contrast, a *Spectator* reporter concluded from

Many women found working as a servant too demanding.
(*HS*, 25 Feb. 1905, 11)

his interviews with wage-earning women in 1919 that "many intelligent, wholesome and sensible girls" had been held back from a nursing career by "a question of social standing."[39] For the better clerical jobs, parents had to be willing to cover the costs of their daughters' prolonged schooling and thus forego her earnings. This was a luxury that only the families of better-paid, more regularly employed skilled workers could afford. They typically relied much less heavily on their children's contributions to the household economy. Yet less-well-paid, low-end office work did not require as much training, and girls from blue-collar households flocked into the city's private business schools and high-school commercial courses in the 1920s and 1930s, suggesting that this was an increasingly attractive option.[40]

Working-class parents knew that boys had more job opportunities open to them in the city than did their sisters, and that employers generally paid boys more than girls as they aged. Boys were found spread out through many more occupations and industries. They could run the streets as messengers, ride the wagons and trucks with teamsters, tote and fetch as labourers, and begin the slow climb up occupational ladders that could lead from helper to semi-skilled

worker or, in a few cases, from apprentice to craftworker, especially in the metalworking shops that employed machinists, blacksmiths, and the like. Factory jobs were most important among boys aged 15 to 17 (36 per cent), followed by labouring (28 per cent). All adolescent workers earned less than adults did, but boys could normally expect to find much better-paying jobs than girls could.[41]

In each of the census years between 1911 and 1941, the average weekly earnings of female workers in Hamilton were only half that of the average male workers, and many earned even less (a difference that was perpetuated for the few who qualified for the new workers' compensation program after 1914). The difference had little to do with the scarcity of their skills in the labour market – textile knitters often had to be imported, for example, but never earned anything close to comparably skilled men. The issue was simply that they were female and had to accept a "woman's wage."[42] Typically the average female wage-earner in Hamilton suffered less unemployment than did a male, especially in the 1930s, probably because, on the whole, the manufacturing industries in which the women worked were less unstable than the male-dominated metalworking industries.

Well before World War One, Canadian women's organizations had started agitating for some state action to deal with the low wages of wage-earning women. Their rationale was not equity between men and women, but the need to protect the allegedly frail, vulnerable bodies and maternal capabilities of young working women, just as the provisions of the much older factory and shop acts had done in regulating hours of work. The labour movement had dragged its heels for many years, preferring to demand a decent family wage for male breadwinners, but eventually added its support for minimum-wage legislation during the postwar labour revolt. Business was also pushed to agree, as the price for keeping the state out of any further labour-market regulation and, to some extent, as a measure for more "efficient" management. All of these groups came to accept the premise that women wage-earners could not contract for their labour power as supposedly freely as men did and therefore needed special legal status to protect them.[43]

In 1920 Ontario's Farmer-Labour government enacted a new minimum-wage law for women in selected industries. The board appointed to administer it, which included women, held hearings with businessmen and labour representatives and proceeded to set separate wage rates for each industry, rather than a flat rate for all female employees. It also calculated women's needs on the assumption that they were single and sparingly self-supporting, not breadwinners for a family. The wage levels tapered up from those for the young and inexperienced to the more seasoned worker (in retail, for example, from $8 to $12 a week). In virtually all cases, it merely confirmed the existing wage levels in these industries. Various administrative loopholes and weak inspection also gave employers plenty of room to juggle their books and pay many women less. Some of the least well paid, typically the youngest, were simply let go. For those who remained the new legislation probably meant work intensification because employers who were denied the possibility of cutting wages wanted to ensure that they got the most out of their workforces. In the end the law had done nothing to improve the earning potential of female wage-earners. The gendered inequities of the workplace payroll were merely reinforced and, in fact, given legal sanction.[44]

By World War One working-class families had already begun to discover that local labour markets for their young sons and daughters were changing. The numerous light manufacturing industries that had hired so many adolescent workers at the turn of the century were disappearing, eclipsed by metalworking plants that demanded the heavy labour of more mature adult males. Moreover, work processes and employment practices in many factories were undergoing major changes as employers eliminated opportunities for apprenticeships, mechanized much of the fetching and carrying work formerly done by young workers, and recruited from a new pool of cheap, unskilled labour – the city's new male European immigrants.[45]

Yet factory jobs for teenage boys and girls had by no means disappeared; two out of three workers aged 15 to 17 still earned their wages in factories in 1921. The percentage of wage-earners' children working had not dropped, but, probably because of the depression, which hit them much harder than adults,[46] their proportion of family income had fallen to only 15 per cent. Again, variations existed depending on the insecurities of the father's job. Tailors, blacksmiths, and moulders still relied on their wage-earning offspring for roughly a quarter of the family earnings. Labourers relied on the young for a fifth of family earnings, and weavers, riveters, and machinists about a sixth, while printers and clerical workers got a mere 6 and 8 per cent from their children respectively.[47] Perhaps the explanation for this continued use of juvenile waged labour lies – at least in comparison to the United States – in the relatively slower arrival of Canada's Second Industrial Revolution and the relatively smaller numbers of European immigrants available, especially for the textile industries.[48]

High School

This pattern of wage-earning clearly left little room for a high-school education. In 1901 only

663 of the city's 5,500 young people aged 15 to 19 were enrolled in the Hamilton Collegiate Institute, the city's only academic high school until 1924, and only 56 more in the "Fifth-Book" classes (later Grades 9 and 10) offered by the separate-school board within their primary-school buildings (a separate Catholic high school did not open until 1928).[49] The public Board of Education certainly never did provide classroom space for many young people in this age group before the 1920s. The Collegiate Institute was stretched to the limit when its enrolment climbed up to over 1,000 in the five years before World War One, and presumably the 100-odd students in the Catholic system created similar problems in this period. The census figures published at ten-year intervals give an impression of steady growth in the high-school population, but the statistics published annually by the provincial Department of Education and monthly by the local Board of Education reveal a much more complex pattern of attendance at the Hamilton Collegiate Institute.[50]

Few working-class parents in Hamilton, it seems, saw secondary schooling as a valid avenue for their children's upward mobility. The Hamilton Collegiate Institute (and the separate-school classes) had a narrowly academic curriculum that was intended to prepare students for university or professional training, especially teaching, but offered no direct preparation for work on the shop floor in the city's factories or other work sites.[51] The tiny proportion of working-class teenagers who passed the difficult entrance examination and arrived at the Collegiate's door indicates how few of Hamilton's working-class families aspired to push their children into a professional world. The Department of Education's crude breakdown of the occupations of students' fathers reveals that the school always had a substantial minority of young people from families headed by skilled workers, but the great majority of students came from what the educators described as commercial, agricultural, and professional backgrounds.[52] "If you went to school after you were fourteen," recalled a former student at Hess Street Public School, "your old man was either a banker or a brewer or he owned a store or was quite wealthy."[53] On average, in each of the 30 years before 1920 only one in four of the city's academic high-school students came from homes with fathers working at a trade.[54] During these first two decades of the 20th century, then, the percentage of Hamilton adolescents at school still dropped off sharply at the end of elementary school. Within the Hamilton Collegiate Institute itself, few students completed the six-year program; generally about half were found in the Lower School (the equivalent of what would become Grades 9 and 10).[55]

Other patterns of attendance point to how working-class families viewed the secondary-school system. Many commentators then and now assume that prosperity encourages parents to keep their children in school.[56] In early-20th-century Hamilton precisely the opposite happened. In general, young people left the Collegiate if a more pressing need arose for their work or wages, and they returned when the job opportunities in the waged economy dried up.[57] Annual high-school enrolment declined absolutely both at the turn of the century and just before the war, in close parallel with new bursts of economic activity, better job prospects for young teenagers, and rising costs of rent, food, and other necessities.[58] The severe 1913–15 depression then pushed many young workers out of work and back into classrooms. Working-class enrolment jumped by nearly two-thirds during that period. This pattern of movement in and out of high school must have been primarily a working-class experience because in each boom period most of the students who left the Collegiate were from working-class families. The contrast with other occupational groups was most striking in the four years of steady working-class withdrawal from the high school before the 1913 depression set in, when the number of students from professional families held steady and those with fathers in "commerce" increased by over 30 per cent.[59]

The local high-school inspector's monthly attendance reports – without specifying which students were coming and going – reveal a familiar variation of adjusting to the rhythms of the local economy in times of boom and slump. In prosperous years annual enrolment peaked in the late fall, as students apparently dribbled in after the annual seasonal layoff of less-skilled workers; enrolment declined abruptly in May and June when the hiring of adolescent labour presumably picked up again. For example, between September 1904 and June 1905 one in four students had left; and the figures for September 1911 to June 1912 showed one in six. In gloomier times the enrolment fluctuated much less. In 1908 the high school lost less than 7 per cent of its students, and in the economically troubled spring of 1914 less than 6 per cent had gone. Not only did high-school students stop attending as regularly in the spring, but considerable numbers disappeared briefly in December, probably to work in the Christmas retail boom.[60]

According to Department of Education annual statistical returns, between one-third and two-fifths of enrolled high-school students were absent on an average day before 1920, in contrast to the level of around 75 per cent average daily attendance in the elementary schools.[61] Probably the labour of these teenagers was needed from time to time at home or in the workforce (though the students might also have been drawn into

youthful street cultures). Such irregularity must have affected academic performance: by the early 1920s a school board committee found that more than two-fifths of the 3,500 students aged 14 and 15 were still in the city's elementary schools.[62]

During the wartime boom after 1915, high-school enrolment tumbled again. By 1917 the Collegiate had a third fewer students than it did in 1915, and 41 per cent fewer working-class youths. Students with working-class fathers accounted for roughly half the decline in enrolment over that period. The high-school inspector reported with relief that the recent problem of overcrowding in the Collegiate classrooms had evaporated. Attendance also dropped off much more drastically each spring in the later years of the war. By 1918 Catholic secondary-school enrolment had similarly plummeted to 61 students, a mere one-fifth of the depression-related peak.[63]

Along with the increase in wage-earning among children under 14 (including the child-labour convictions), these trends indicate that the old family economy that drew on the labour of all family members was apparently still alive and well in working-class households. As the cost of living in the city soared after 1917 and labour shortages continued in local industries, families were evidently mobilizing the earning capacities of their children to the fullest. The end of the war brought no quick return to the classroom. Academic high-school enrolment remained at pre-1908 levels until 1922. Indeed, federal census officials noted after their survey of the city in June 1921 that Hamilton had a far lower percentage of school attendance among 15-to-18-year-olds than did any of the other 14 largest cities in Canada.[64]

Why did this old working-class household economy survive so long, and why did so few working-class parents choose to push their

Classes at the Hamilton Technical School in metalworking, printing, and motor mechanics. (HPL)

children into secondary education? And why was this pattern so much more marked in Hamilton than in other Canadian cities? It would be difficult to argue that these parents were abnormally greedy for their children's wages or had an unusually low interest in schooling. After all, they

did send their teenagers to school when they had little chance of earning wages or helping out at home. The answer seems to lie instead not only in the continuing availability of teenage jobs but also in the chronic insecurity of income within the city's working-class households. Given that Hamilton's preponderant iron and steel production was among the most vulnerable to deep and prolonged unemployment in the Canadian manufacturing sector, and since the male heads of household who worked in these metalworking industries could not always bring home a reliable family wage and their wives seldom took on waged work, their teenage children were expected to help. Swinging between inflation and unemployment, Hamilton's wage-earning families struggled to stay afloat.

Training for Work

Meanwhile, the local school system was attempting to entice students to stay in school, ostensibly to enhance their job prospects. Hamilton was a pioneer in establishing new streams of secondary schooling known as commercial and technical education. Commercial classes in a new three-year program began quietly in 1905 and were soon attracting roughly 400 to 500 students, although here too enrolment rose and fell with the business cycle, dropping to a low of 180 in 1918.[65] Technical education was designed primarily for boys and had far more publicity. Despite all the hoopla that greeted the city's first Technical and Art School in 1909, however, it failed to capture the imagination of many working-class families before the war. School officials complained regularly about low enrolments, and by 1915–16 only 40 students were enrolled full-time in the Hamilton technical school day courses, with 100 more part-time and 480 at night – hardly a major breakthrough into the ranks of the city's wage-earning teenagers.[66]

Hamilton's workers left no record of the reasons for their indifference, but, besides the usual conflict between the classroom and the need for juvenile wages in the household economy, it seems likely that the school's program appeared to be too abstracted from the real world of work and the familiar opportunities for getting ahead that lay in experience and social relations on the shop floor, not in a classroom.[67] In 1916 the Board's Industrial Technical Committee finally realized "that they had never been able to induce the public to appreciate the class of education given at the technical school." The Board thus hired an energetic new principal, G.L. Sprague, who quickly revitalized and expanded the school's programs.[68]

Sprague hoped to tap into the aspirations for upward mobility that he evidently believed existed in working-class households. His school, he wrote in 1918, would "hold the door of opportunity open for our boys and girls to give them preparation for their life work." It would provide training for the many workers who thanks to "economic necessity or lack of information" were not properly prepared for a vocation. In that way they could "increase their efficiency and better their lot in life."[69]

Although by 1920 the city had a substantial alternative stream of secondary-school education that evidently appealed to many young male workers and their parents,[70] the response to the new programs was limited in some notable ways. The total enrolment of full-time students had reached only 203 by 1920 – a substantial increase over pre-war levels but still a small percentage of the city's thousands of teenagers. The combined full-time enrolment in public academic and technical high schools in 1921 was only 1,139, just slightly higher than the pre-war peak at the Collegiate Institute. With the addition of the 279 separate-school students

At the Hamilton Technical Institute girls only got classes in domestic skills such as sewing. (HPL)

and 332 commercial students, the city's secondary-school system still absorbed fewer than one in five of Hamilton's youth aged 15 to 19.[71] As in the past, moreover, it was the children of more skilled, better-paid workers who appeared on the rolls. Tradesmen sent by far the largest number of students to the daytime classes.[72]

Full-time high-school education of any sort was still out of the question for most working-class families. Almost all the technical students had opted for the short courses that led quickly to the labour market, where Sprague made great efforts to find them positions as apprentices. Only a tiny handful hitched their stars to the four-year, university-bound program. The full-time classes also offered little to girls, who numbered no more than a hundred until a new wing known as the School of Domestic Science and Art was opened in 1923. A few female graduates found jobs as "apprentices" in millinery shops, but for most girls the school's programs were mainly intended to help them "to prepare themselves for the important vocation of making a home beautiful."[73] Not only did school officials believe, in their patriarchal fashion, that women should not be employed outside the family household, but they probably also realized how few wage-earning jobs available to women required the extensive preparation anticipated in industrial education.[74]

Far more impressive were the vastly increased enrolments in night classes. Male and female wage-earners of all ages and occupations signed up for courses that they evidently believed would improve their chances of a promotion or a better job. In the economically depressed winter of 1920–21, young men flocked into the classes of the Hamilton Technical and Art School to hone their skills for a better chance in the local labour market.[75] As with the many students enrolled in commercial courses, a new generation was learning to connect its material aspirations to formal classroom training. In contrast to the full-time day classes, this kind of occupational upgrading did not have to disrupt the household economy. Above all, what had been created in Hamilton's technical school was a large, popular adult-education program.

More Schooling

The domestic arrangements of Hamilton's workers faced a far more disruptive challenge when the provincial government decided in 1919 to raise the school-leaving age from 14 to 16. In contrast to the locally based development of technical education, this initiative emanated from the provincial Department of Education. For more than a decade, key figures in the department's staff had been following the debate carried out on both sides of the Atlantic, but especially in the United States, on the alleged growing crisis of male adolescence that required the intervention of educators.[76] Particularly troubling these officials was the army of working-class boys dropping out of school at age 14, apparently ill prepared for the labour market. Educators believed that, as the range of jobs available to boys aged 14 to 16 dwindled, especially the apprenticeships tied to skilled crafts, these young workers were drifting aimlessly in low-wage, "dead-end" jobs. The educators worried about the precarious fragility of adolescent boys in the "most critical years of life" and their need for careful guidance in the transition to the adult work world. The Hamilton Technical and Art School's Principal Sprague was a local voice of this concern about adolescent boys:

> These children are poorly prepared for their life's work. When labor conditions are normal they earn but a pittance in the kind of work open to them. They enter factories, messenger and delivery service and domestic service. Very few obtain jobs which offer room for advancement to positions of skill in industry or business. They drift about from one job to another, usually holding two or three jobs in a year. What is the result? After a few years of this shifting process, these children find themselves without a trade or anything approaching the mastery of any particular vocation in life. They land mostly in the unskilled labor class.[77]

The educators actually had only a slight understanding of how youth labour markets worked, or even of how limited the old apprenticeship systems had been for drawing boys into men's work. In their eyes, the problem lay not in the shrinking market for young labour power, but in the young worker's failure to prepare himself adequately for a job. Not surprisingly among professionals whose own training had involved prolonged schooling, their solution for working-class boys was to combine vocational education and a higher school-leaving age. Ontario's director of industrial and technical education, F.W. Merchant, kept up a steady campaign to win support for such changes. He was convinced that existing night-time courses could not meet the problem because, as he noted in 1914, it was older men, not adolescent boys, who were flocking to evening classes in the technical schools. "They drop out of school and wander about for several years before they apply for admission to an evening school," he wrote. Like other educators, when it came to young adolescents he had more faith in the efficacy of compulsory daytime industrial classes, which would be part-time and integrated with wage-earning work.[78]

The Conservative government's Adolescent School Attendance Act, introduced in April 1919, provided for the extension of full-time, rather than part-time, schooling largely because it addressed another set of concerns. The education minister who rose in the legislature to justify the new legislation was Henry J. Cody, an Anglican clergyman, university professor, and recent recruit to the Tory cabinet. With broad interests in the political culture of his age, Cody was disturbed at the widespread evidence of disaffection from the existing social and economic order at the end of the war and saw a role for the school system as a powerful moral force, much as Egerton Ryerson had envisioned for the first public schools 70 years earlier. Cody saw this measure for keeping youngsters in school for two more years as part of a program to better prepare youngsters for "effective citizenship," by which he meant appropriate moral and occupational training for an evolving industrial-capitalist society within the British Empire. "No State is safe if only some of its social units are educated," he told the legislature. A few years later, at the official opening of a new high school in Hamilton, Conservative premier Howard Ferguson would similarly defend the legislation as "tending to inculcate a sense of responsible citizenship." Keeping adolescents in school for two extra years, then, was a political project as much as a technocratic adjustment of the relationship between school and the labour market.[79]

The new legislation was to take effect in January 1921. Besides raising the legal age for quitting school, it also contained the often-discussed option of part-time, day-time schooling (at least 400 hours per year, or roughly eight hours a week) for 14- to 15-year-olds who applied for and received special permits. These youths had to convince school attendance officers that their families needed their income and that employers were ready to hire them. Some of their part-time classes also had to be vocational. (The legislation contained similar provisions for youths aged 16 and 17, but these were later withdrawn under a shower of protest from Hamilton's city council, Chamber of Commerce, and other business-minded groups across the province.) To ensure that students actually ended up in the classrooms, parallel legislation required school boards to appoint school attendance officers to replace the old truant officers and designated a provincial attendance officer to oversee the enforcement process.[80]

In Hamilton the new legislation was not greeted with universal enthusiasm, and the local school administration was slow to respond.[81] The school trustees grumbled about the costs and in 1922 considered joining the fight against the act that the city of Chatham had begun. Only in January 1923 were the special part-time classes put in motion in a separate department at the technical school. By the end of that year a special committee investigating the implementation of the act in Hamilton could still conclude, "There seemed to be a leakage of Adolescents, 14–16, from all the schools."[82]

Initially, part of the problem was that there were too few classrooms. The two existing high schools – one academic and one technical – were already trying to cope with the familiar problem of jobless teenagers flocking into their classrooms in response to the devastating depression of the early 1920s. There was little space for any others pushed into these institutions by the new legislation. The Board of Education was thus forced reluctantly into a massive building program over the next decade. The technical school was expanded and renamed the Hamilton Technical Institute; by 1925 it was handling more than 1,200 full-time students. As the enrolment at the Hamilton Collegiate Institute similarly climbed to 1,300 in 1923 and 1924, the Board agreed to build a second academic high school to serve the east end, and Delta Collegiate Institute opened in 1924. In the same year provision was made for more vocational education for girls when both collegiates began offering commercial programs for the first time. In 1928 the more than 900 students in these programs (700 of them female) were transferred from their various locations in the elementary schools to distinct wings in the three high schools (and one elementary school) and organized as a single administrative unit known as the High School of Commerce. That school moved into its own new building in 1932. Finally, a fifth high school was opened in 1931 in the new west-end, middle-class suburb of Westdale. This was the city's first composite school – bringing the three distinct streams of academic, technical, and commercial together under the same roof. By the mid-1930s the combined enrolment of the city's five public high schools had climbed to over 5,500, nearly five times the 1921 total. In addition, after 1928 the new Cathedral High School welcomed close to 400 Catholic students, nearly 50 per cent more than in 1920.[83]

Beyond the new buildings and vastly increased student numbers was the qualitative change in technical education. The new term "vocational" suggested a shift in emphasis from adult education, which had been so popular at the end of the war, to adolescent schooling. Provision for evening classes was restricted,

and, after a brief resurgence at the end of the 1920s, they were finally cancelled by a budget-trimming Board of Education in 1933. A year later the special classes for part-time students under the Adolescent School Attendance Act were also scrapped.[84]

A visitor entering the technical or commercial schools would find the halls filled with teenagers and their activities organized on the same principles as the academic high schools. They had cafeterias, student councils, school bands, choirs, and cadet corps. The whole post-secondary system had become an overt streaming mechanism for the city's adolescents. Each of the three programs intended to feed students into hierarchically structured labour markets and, implicitly, into distinct class positions.[85]

Let Well Enough Alone

Hamilton's working-class parents greeted this new effort to push their adolescent children into the classroom with mixed emotions. The craft unionists in the Trades and Labor Council had often endorsed legislation to reduce the exploitation of young workers and increase their chances for formal education, and in the legislature Allan Studholme had championed such a measure for years.[86] But many of the people who supported this approach were not as reliant on the wages of young family members as were the bulk of the city's workers. Some of those who needed their youngsters' income much more expressed their disgruntlement in letters to the local press. One wrote in 1916 that parents had a right to "start to reap a little benefit" when their children reached age 14. The writer believed that the school board chairman, who had spoken in favour of the higher age, "would change his tone" if "he was earning ten dollars a week and [had] a home to keep up." Another worker, the father of six children, all under the age of nine, complained that it was "very hard to raise them and clothe them till they are fourteen years, and as they get older they eat more, and need more clothes as they get a little more particular around fourteen years, and before the first one is able to leave school it will be costing me 60 cents a month in school fees." A mother backed him up a few days later. "Education is a fine thing," she wrote, "but it does not fill the stomach." Some two years later a working-class father signing himself "Let Well Enough Alone" defended the notion of the household economy that had been operating in the city for decades. In the face of the high cost of living, he argued, a housewife could not make ends meet on her husband's wages alone, "and a boy of 14 years with a fair education can work and help the home a little and attend technical school at night to complete his education." He also worried that a boy kept in school until age 16 would disdain the traditions of mutuality and hard work that kept workers' families going: "A boy going to school till 16 years gets such high notions into his head that he wants to have more of the good time he has had at school, and don't [sic] tackle work then as he should, and if anything is said to him he is off from under the parental roof, and that is the thanks you get for giving him the good education."[87] Such sentiments resonated particularly strongly in the European immigrant community, where adolescent children, many of them born in Canada, were becoming more numerous by the interwar period.[88]

After five years of administering the Act, the new school attendance officer, Walter Rollo, said he believed that "the average parent is desirous of keeping his children at school as long as he can afford to do so and a large number do so when conditions would warrant the exemption of the eldest child." Yet he had also met parents "who apply for exemption as soon as their children reach the age of 14 years whether their circumstances warrant the same or not."[89] This quiet, stubborn determination to hold onto their teenagers' wage-earning power was probably the most common form of resistance to the extended period of adolescent schooling once it was entrenched in law.

Inevitably, this shift in requirements for school attendance shook up family economies in working-class households. In the first year under the new legislation, most of the 900 or so teenagers who applied got an exemption, which meant that those who had already left school were not compelled to return. But Rollo was soon rejecting many more applications and within five years had cut their number in half.[90] He also visited employers of adolescents to get their compliance and found that most were choosing older workers: "When there is a surplus of labour, employers prefer to employ those who are over school age." The *Canadian Textile Journal* had already discovered that part-time schooling was unpopular with the city's largest employers of juvenile factory labour, the textile companies. "There is a tendency," the *Journal* reported, "to eliminate the younger help and employ those who are exempt from the continuation schooling as the half day weekly away from the mills breaks into production." Others noted the same trend. "Many of the factories are not taking girls," the Big Sisters' Association discovered. The Ontario Minimum Wage Board reported a drastic decline in the employment of girls under 18 in Hamilton's textile factories, from 28 per cent of their workforce in 1922 to 16.5 by 1925, 9.5 by 1930, and 2.1 by 1933 (a modest increase in the proportion of this juvenile labour occurred in the later 1930s). The local employers' unwillingness to employ adolescents enrolled in part-time day classes prompted the Board of Education in 1925 to allow students to take

Large numbers of young women learned office work in Hamilton's commercial courses. (*Three Roads to a Vocation*)

evening classes instead when their wages were clearly necessary for their families. By the early 1930s, the range of jobs for youths had narrowed such that 70 per cent of male permit-holders had to find work as messengers. Youths were also now monitored through a more highly centralized registry of enrolment to eliminate truancy.[91]

From the mid-1920s onward, then, working-class parents in Hamilton began to lose the contribution of their younger adolescent children as full-time secondary wage-earners. Between 1921 and 1930 the enrolment of children from blue-collar families in the city's public academic high schools rose from 373 to 719 (peaking at 990 in 1927), while the number of full-time technical students from the same kinds of households soared from 206 to over 1,400. The enrolment of commercial students from similar backgrounds reached 440 at the end of the decade.[92] During the late 1920s and early 1930s (when the relevant Department of Education statistics stopped appearing), the percentage of high-school students whose fathers worked in a trade or labouring occupation increased in the academic schools to between 30 and 45 per cent, and in the vocational courses hovered between 50 and 66 per cent. The substantial increase in the participation of labourers' children was particularly striking.

By the early 1930s, two-thirds of the families of tradesmen and labourers with youngsters of high-school age were opting to place them in the new vocational courses.

For the most part, with scarcely any full-time work available for their younger teenagers, working-class families had little choice but to send them to high school. Few employers had jobs for young adolescents at the best of times, and many of those jobs disappeared in the prolonged interwar slump that was broken only for a few years in the late 1920s, and much more briefly in 1937.[93] It was undoubtedly the grim economic conditions, more than any other single factor, that conditioned the city's working-class families to the new reality of extended schooling for their older children. The relatively lower cost of living in the city in the 1920s and 1930s also probably put less pressure on families than in boom periods. Not surprisingly, then, census-takers found in 1931 that younger adolescents were less regular contributors to the family coffers. Only 65 of the city's 2,600 15-year-olds were reported to be gainfully employed, and only a third of the nearly 6,000 of those aged 16 and 17 had jobs. Overall, in the families headed by male wage-earners, the percentage of children living at home who were in school rose from 36 per cent in 1921 to 44 per cent in 1931, while the proportion aged 15 and over living at home and earning wages dropped from 78 to 59 per cent. In Hamilton the wages of family members other than husbands and wives amounted to only an average of 8 per cent of family earnings, half their contributions of a decade earlier (and a quarter of that in 1911).[94] In this context, there was a perceptible change in the place of children in the family economy; and the sharp drop of the birthrate in the 1930s reflected an awareness that children were more likely to be dependants than producers of family income.

At the same time, despite their efforts to adapt, in many ways Hamilton families clung to old, familiar survival strategies. When the local economy picked up sufficiently after 1926 and demanded more labour, high-school enrolment dropped slightly, prompting the technical education committee of the local branch of the Canadian Manufacturers' Association to blame "the improved business conditions in Hamilton, which has [sic] resulted in a greater demand for young workers."[95] More indicative of the continuing need for teenagers' wages was the 50 per cent increase in applications for exemptions from the school-attendance legislation that would permit full-time work – from 608 in 1925 to 937 in 1929 – at a time when the Department of Education counted only 2,253 students of this age in Hamilton's public secondary schools.[96] Equally striking were the 2,800 absentee notices that the attendance officer issued in 1929 to permit-holders who had missed their part-time classes. When the economy collapsed in the early 1930s, Rollo was convinced "that there are hundreds of girls and boys attending school at this time because there are no positions available." He noted that "just as soon" as jobs opened up, there would "be an increased demand for permits."[97] Indeed, a slight improvement in local employment opportunities in 1937 and 1940 saw applications for these permits climb to over 1,100 – more than triple the number of the early 1930s.

Nor is it clear that Hamilton's working-class families had given up all hope that their adolescent children could contribute wages to the family budget and had accepted the idea of long-term high-school training for them instead. The census never bothered to record part-time teenage labour after school and during vacations in these years, but, as federal labour department staff concluded in 1930, there was most likely a substantial amount of it. Census figures for that year reveal that 17 per cent of retail jobs in Hamilton were part-time. For female shop workers the figure was 22 per cent. In the various food-retailing stores, the proportion was much higher – 30 per cent of all jobs and over half of all female jobs. Chain stores were particularly eager to use part-time labour to avoid minimum-wage laws. According to evidence from the Royal Commission on Price Spreads, two-thirds of clerks in the Metropolitan department stores were part-time, and William Carroll's grocery chain hired 91 girls under 18 on Saturdays and 59 boys on weekdays after school. In 1932 a special study of the "street trades" for the Hamilton Children's Aid Society was alarmed at the levels of after-school work for children. Many people who grew up in Hamilton's working-class households in the interwar period later described their relentless search for part-time jobs – shovelling snow, weeding gardens, picking fruit and vegetables, carrying bags and parcels for shoppers, collecting pop bottles – often with the same entrepreneurial shrewdness that their parents showed in trying to find extra income. They were earning less than children had in previous decades, but they were still making small contributions to the family coffers (as well as to their own supply of spending money).[98]

Marking Time

These youths and their parents also showed little interest in prolonging this new phase of schooling past the new legal age for leaving. In 1928 the Hamilton Technical Institute's principal, L.W. Gill, admitted that "the great majority" of boys in the vocational schools left at age 16. Some seven years later a special committee of Hamilton's school trustees, officials, and high-school principals also concluded that a "large number" of high-school students "leave at about the age of 16 for economic reasons without having completed any course of study. Many of these constitute a group of students who are merely marking time and are more or less indifferent to a course of study that leads to any definite goal."[99]

The academic stream still held onto proportionally more students, but had nonetheless lost roughly a third by the third year and more than half by the fourth. The situation was much more dramatic in the more popular vocational streams. An increasing majority of students opted for technical and commercial courses – their numbers rose from just over half of all the city's high-school students in Form One in 1933 to two-thirds by 1940 – but few of them stayed to complete their courses. The dropout rates in these two streams were consistently and substantially larger than were those in academic courses. The vast majority of technical students were in the three-year course (fewer than 5 per cent continued past Form Three), but nearly half left after Form One and more than two-thirds by the end of Form Two. In the three-year commercial course, about a third left after the first year and just under two-thirds by the end of the second. Perhaps even more striking were the local school officials' statistics on average monthly attendance.[100] In a pattern quite different from the Hamilton Collegiate Institute, technical-student attendance dropped away quickly whenever job prospects improved slightly. Most noticeably, enrolment in the Hamilton Technical School, which started from around 1,600 to 1,700 each September in the mid-1930s, had fallen by about a quarter each spring, and average daily attendance by about a third. Despite the creation of a Vocational Guidance Council in Hamilton in 1932 and a guidance committee in each school to help connect schooling and later employment, what would one day become known as "credentialism" for better jobs remained weak.[101]

For the great majority of Hamilton students and their families, these figures suggest anything but enthusiasm for the new high-school regime. Equally important, they suggest the complete failure of the educators' grand visions for vocational schooling. The 3,000 to 4,000 workers who enrolled in evening classes in the late 1920s and early 1930s revealed the considerable working-class interest in the alternative of part-time technical training after work, but that option was snuffed out in 1933.

For many students, dropping out of vocational courses reflected their frustration with schooling in general. "The majority of boys, when they reach the age of 13 or 14, begin to get restless under the restraint of the classroom," Principal Gill concluded in 1928. "They have little interest in school work and look upon the school as a kind of prison." Yet they had a practical reason as well. Staying in school did not guarantee a more skilled job. Gill admitted this limitation: "Our aim is to give that boy a general education and a good character, to develop his judgment, reasoning powers and manual skill and to give him the fundamentals of some kind of industrial work." Specific, job-related training could be useless in any case: "If [at age 16, when most drop out] they cannot quickly find a job in the particular line of work along which they have received training at school, they will seize the first opportunity to earn some money. The result is that in many cases the special training is of no value to them." In 1930 the girls in the High School of Commerce even walked out on strike because they were being forced to endure longer hours in the classroom than were students at other high schools in the city.[102]

Employers had their own misgivings. In 1922 *Canadian Machinery* reported a feeling among machinery manufacturers that "the youth from the technical school cannot always content himself with the position available to him when he emerges from the shell of instruction to make his first scratch upon an industrial pay-roll." One Hamilton factory owner, F. Ford-Smith, admitted that technical education "increases a boy's fund of knowledge and improves his usefulness," but he still preferred to have his apprentices start at age 15 or 16 to get "the fire of experience and wisely directed discipline." Others preferred to do their own on-the-job training. Principal Gill abandoned plans for an industrial-chemistry class when the city's chemical firms bluntly told him that they did not need highly skilled graduates from his school: "Special skill and knowledge are unnecessary for their purpose." Likewise, textile employers made it clear that "they did not want the beginner given any prior instruction at all. They preferred to train their own help along their own lines."[103] Employers' doubts about the school's role in job-training were evident in the tiny enrolments in the apprenticeship programs arranged between the technical school and several local corporations. Most Hamilton firms seemed to prefer to train their own workers.

Extensive schooling would not make much difference for most jobs in Hamilton. The scattered evidence drawn from interviews with retired Hamilton workers points to the much greater importance of family or neighbourhood contacts in finding work – contacts that often came through the patronage networks of the lower-level supervisors in the city's plants.[104] The help-wanted columns in the city's newspapers offered a few job openings in the 1930s, but the *Spectator*'s listings on the last Saturday of each month in 1930 indicate that only five of the 243 ads for male jobs included "education" as a necessary qualification for applicants; none of those five ads were for industrial positions (two in sales, two for apprentice druggists, and one

unspecified). Of the 257 ads for female labour, only one clerical position asked for educational background. For the skilled manual and white-collar jobs, it was far more common to demand experience and references. In 1940, a much more economically buoyant year, newspaper listings disclose that 14 of the 326 positions advertised for male workers – including 4 for skilled industrial work – required applicants to state their education. The single ad that mentioned technical education caught the ambiguities of the period in asking for a "Young man for electric service with practical or Technical school training." Only one of the 259 ads for women mentioned education explicitly as a requirement for application.[105] The major exception was commercial education, in which boys and girls learned some skills, such as typing or shorthand, that could make them more employable; help-wanted ads sometimes requested this background (the number of boys in these courses nearly quadrupled from 98 in 1933 to 368 in 1938). On the whole, the promise of vocationalism had not been delivered, at least for working-class boys.

The picture was somewhat more complex for girls.[106] They had never featured prominently in the project to create a stream of technical education. Indeed, from the beginning they had been segregated into courses aimed explicitly at making them skilled homemakers, not wage-earners. By the mid-1920s the girls in the technical program had been excluded from the Industrial stream and confined to a department soon known as Practical Arts. A few courses offered marketable skills in dress-making, millinery, laundry, home-nursing, power-operating, sales work, and dietetics, but none of these led to major employment opportunities. Small wonder, then, that no more than a fifth of the city's female high-school students could be found in these courses in the 1930s,

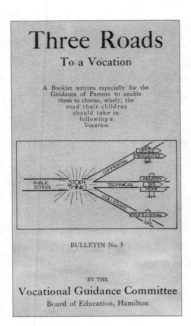

Three Roads

To a Vocation

A Booklet written especially for the Guidance of Parents to enable them to choose, wisely, the road their children should take in following a Vocation

BULLETIN No. 5

BY THE

Vocational Guidance Committee
Board of Education, Hamilton

A Hamilton Board of Education pamphlet was blunt about the streaming of students into schooling that led to particular class-based occupations. (HPL)

and that between one-half and two-thirds of them generally left after the first year.[107] The commercial courses proved much more popular, for the simple reason that they provided useful skills for wage-earning in the city. Between 1931 and 1940 the numbers of girls in these courses nearly doubled to 1,100 – comprising more than a third of female enrolment. While most of these girls did not complete the three or four years necessary to get a diploma, they probably picked up a smattering of office skills, especially typing, that could help them find clerical work. Yet the most popular courses by far remained the academic courses in the collegiates, which absorbed just under half of the high-school girls through most of the 1930s. By the end of that decade females had moved into a slight majority over males in these schools. Perhaps the academic program gave young women some of the polish necessary to succeed in the particular jobs that awaited them – as secretaries or salespersons, for example.[108]

Evidently the scarcity of jobs in the 1930s kept more students in the classroom, but this was due more to the lack of an alternative than to a new commitment to upward mobility through the school system. Even in 1931, when the public and Catholic boards of education reported fewer than 5,000 enrolled in high schools, census statistics show that more than 3,000 of the 14,000 Hamiltonians aged 15 to 19 were neither at school nor at work. They were probably helping out at home or simply biding their time (nearly 900 of those aged 14 to 19 indicated they had never had a job but were looking for one). The preference for work over school was once again clear by 1941, as the city was swept up into a war economy. Census-takers found that the percentage of adolescents aged 15 to 19 in the paid workforce had risen to just over half, up from 29 per cent a decade earlier.[109]

Hamilton's working-class teenagers generally did not enter a vastly longer period of formal schooling in the interwar period. Although the technical and commercial courses proved most popular, they fell far short of the educators' earlier dreams. They did not capture the students' interest and do not appear to have provided the credentials for much upward mobility or even for better entry-level positions in the local factories, since the great majority of these students left school at age 16 without completing any formal high-school program. Even the Workmen's Compensation Board and the Mothers' Allowance Commission took for granted that 16 was the threshold of full-time work and cut widows' pensions when their children reached that age. Most Hamilton teenagers seemed to remain in school not out of a greater enthusiasm for formal schooling and a new commitment to credentialism, but rather because the state compelled them to and because they had few other options.[110] In most cases, the beginning of the work experience – and the regular contribution to the family economy – were simply delayed for two years. In the period as a whole, high-school days thus remained a relatively limited phase in a working-class adolescence in Hamilton. With two-thirds of working-class students in the vocational programs, the high school was nonetheless an important device for institutional streaming that reminded working-class youngsters of their origins and ultimate destiny in the capitalist economy.

The Kids' Money

After 1920, then, the family economies of working-class Hamilton felt the full blast of state intervention. Young family members were wrenched out of full-time wage labour and held for at least two additional years in new educational institutions that gave them minimal vocational training. Families inevitably felt the pinch of these changes, especially as men's employment was so insecure in the interwar period. Most teenagers no doubt still did what they could to find part-time work, and left school as soon after their sixteenth birthdays as possible to start contributing full-time wages to the collective family pot. But their years of wage-earning before marriage had been shortened, and it was wives and mothers who inevitably felt more pressure to take up the slack.

7

Corner grocery stores were a great advantage to working-class households because they were not only close but also offered credit. (SLS, LS685)

Spending the Hard-Earned Bucks

A MOULDER PUNCHED THE CLOCK at the foundry and trudged wearily home. On the doorstep he met his teenage son, also returning from his day of labouring in a nearby factory. They were greeted in the hallway by a young daughter with a baby in her arms. Everyone headed for the kitchen, where three more children were playing or helping their mother prepare dinner. The youngsters watched wide-eyed as the man and boy dropped their wage packets on the table. The mother shifted her pot of stew off the heat and reached for a cracked cup on the shelf where she had earlier dropped the rent from the boarder. She sat down at the table, cleared some space among the vegetable peelings, and, with an uneasy look on her face, began counting out money into small piles.

With endless variations this scene was re-enacted every payday as the central ritual of family economics in working-class Hamilton. That woman's calculations could bring relief or anxiety for the little group of people nearby, who were bound together not only by blood and sentiment but also by mutual obligation and trust to stick together for their collective survival and comfort. Such a melodramatic narrative had a powerful impact on the collective imagination of the city's working people.

Yet things could also go radically wrong. The family's deeply etched expectations became the standard against which to measure the father who stopped at a saloon on payday, the son who kept too much of his pay for his own pleasure, or the children who preferred running up and down the streets with their friends to helping out at home. Many voices, from unionists to social workers to prohibitionists, invoked the central theme of mutual responsibility in the story.

By the interwar period another narrative was also in place. In this version the working-man parked his car by the curb. Getting out and lighting a cigarette, he strolled up to the front door of a snug brick bungalow. As he took off his coat in the hallway, his teenage son wandered in from the dining room with his electricity textbook in hand, happy to take a break from studying for his technical school's final exams. In the kitchen the two of them found the smiling mother unpacking a shopping basket brimming with brand-name goods. She promised dinner as soon as she could warm up the canned pork and beans on the electric stove. In the living room two children refused to be distracted from the exciting radio drama they were listening to, and another girl was absorbed in the fashion photos in a department store catalogue. "Let's see what movie's on up the street tonight," Dad suggested as an appropriate payday celebration.

This second rendition of working-class life ignores the household budget and highlights the consumer products of the interwar period that promised to bring ease and pleasure to the family. In practice this payday scenario may have

been much less common in Hamilton's working-class households. Yet, in one form or another, it beamed out of much of the public discourse about workers' lives, and has been prominent in much historical writing.[1] It may have acted as an inspiration for many workers' dreams for themselves and their families, as well as a potential measure of failure. It certainly turns our attention to where the money went and what was behind the decision to spend scarce dollars in particular ways. Working-class families had to survive, but they hoped for more – not least some dignity and respectability, and possibly some fun. Families were not homogeneous, however, and individual family members responded to the tug of consumerism differently depending on gender and age. The males and the unmarried adult wage-earning children were the most susceptible.

Ultimately the two narratives of constraint and desire co-existed, sustained by the contradictory experiences of ongoing economic insecurity and relentless stimulus to buy. The advent of both mass production and mass merchandising of consumer goods was a new social and cultural force in the early 20th century. But the good life was not ensured. Spending on these new products might seem spontaneous and impulsive to critical outsiders, but generally required careful budgeting, self-denial, and complex negotiation within the power relations of the family. If at times we lose sight of the weary woman counting out pennies, we should remember that her management of those meagre funds, often at the expense of her own needs and aspirations, could be as important to fulfilling the family's dreams as were the wages earned in the city's factories.[2]

The Logic of Spending

All too often writers then and now have assumed that the key question in working-class consumer patterns was whether wages (and other rivulets of income) were sufficient to cover costs. Did "real" wages keep pace with the rising cost of living? As important as it is to examine workers' earnings and their relationship to household expenses, the question of spending requires more than a mathematical calculation. Just as important is what workers spent their money on and why. Spending was a highly discretionary act that reflected a family's aspirations and values as well their apparent "needs."

Unquestionably the top priorities in a working-class family budget were the elements of basic subsistence – food, shelter, and fuel (both for cooking and, for at least half the year, warmth). Food alone regularly absorbed more than half the family income.[3] Yet appropriate standards for any of these expenditures were not fixed or uniform across all households. Family size, the age of parents and children, and a mother's ingenuity at substituting home-made goods for commercial products could alter what was spent. Cultural background could also shape the food a family chose to eat – Yorkshire pudding among the English, kobasa sausage on Polish tables, polenta in Italian homes, or matzah ball soup among Jews, for example – and the determination to cling to traditional foods could be an act of stubborn persistence in an otherwise tumultuous world. Serving a Sunday roast or Christmas turkey was a special performance meant to impress or celebrate family and kin, rather than merely satisfying a need to survive.[4] Similarly, clothing was about more than keeping warm, and the choice of housing (and house furnishings) involved more than the cost of the items.

Lifestyle preferences would depend at least partly on cultural influences but also, more generally, on working-class notions of respectability, a much used but often poorly understood concept in writing about workers. The most simple-minded approach has been to assume that workers simply aped middle-class tastes, in a kind of cultural trickle-down. More sensitive readings have recognized that workers had no delusions that they could become middle class so easily. Emulation had its limits. In the words of one British writer, respectability arose "more from a concern not to drop down, not to succumb to the environment, than from an anxiety to go up." Certainly such workers shared some hegemonic bourgeois values, but they appropriated from upper classes mainly what made sense to them and then infused it with meaning suitable for their own material context. That could mean a democratic insistence that workers had a right to enjoy certain pleasures and comforts as fully as their betters, but, as several writers have noted, working-class respectability also put much more emphasis than the middle class did on manual labour, mutual aid, and collective self-help in achieving those goals. What workers aspired to was some respect for creating independence, order, propriety, and comfort in their lives in the face of the cruel unpredictability of the economic order.[5]

Respectability was more an ideal and an aspiration than a fixed reality, a set of norms against which behaviour (and its consequences) could be judged. As a British historian points out, it was "always a process, a dialogue with oneself and with one's fellows, never a fixed position." Earning respect required a performance for an appreciative audience – indeed several different audiences, including relatives, immediate neighbours, workmates, employers, middle-class investigators (such as clergymen, social workers, or nurses), and others. For each audience somewhat distinct respectable roles would have to be played out, but the acts had some consistency. They included some elements of a code of values and behaviour – notably, responsible breadwinning and orderly housekeeping – as well as a display of some markers of material success – the house and its furnishings, good food, decent clothing, schooling for children, church, lodge, or union memberships – as badges of triumph over potential poverty, which allowed workingmen and workingwomen to hold their heads a little higher than did those living a more "disreputable" existence. Working-class respectability was not necessarily conservative in a political sense – there was a long continuum between Tory and socialist variants – but it could sometimes provoke status battles within neighbourhood gossip networks, and was certainly suffused with a gender ideology that highlighted the patriarchal family and its rigid division of labour and hierarchy of power, and a notion of racial order that privileged white, Anglo-Canadian workers.[6]

The underpinning of respectability was a steady income large enough to permit self-sufficiency and a measure of economic security. Some relative freedom from the fear of poverty could be built on a regular, well-paying job, the good health of the breadwinner, the pooling of all family members' wage packets, and reasonably cheap, reliable housing. Workers' search for security could obviously be threatened by either widespread unemployment or rapidly rising retail prices, especially rents.

Spending in general was women's work.[7] A husband probably bought his own clothing and covered his personal needs, and certainly had a major say in the big-ticket purchases. But his wife controlled most of the other buying. She did the daily and weekly shopping, paid the bills, and negotiated for credit. Her consumer decisions were not completely unfettered, however. She obviously had to stay within the limits of her household budget, but she was also regularly exhorted to apply some moral standards to her shopping. Local businessmen urged her to support local industry by giving preference to products made in Hamilton or Canada. Racists urged her to avoid Chinese businesses. Governments during World War One called on her to ration scarce food (notably on "meatless" days). Craft unionists in the local Union Label League reminded her to buy products from unionized workplaces, rather than cheap non-union goods that undermined the good wages of union men. Public-health investigators pushed her towards certain "healthy" products, notably milk for children, and away from others, especially the spicier products in European immigrant diets. Increasingly, moreover, advertisers wove moralistic messages into their promotional copy. They suggested that a married woman's obligations to run an orderly, healthy, respectable household required buying particular products, from baby soap to breakfast cereal.[8]

Wives and mothers also had to bow to the demands of some family members for the right to spend money on themselves. When husbands kept back some part of their wages for drinks, tobacco, tickets to ball games, and sundry other personal choices, these purchases became expressions of the masculine identities they cultivated with other men. As part of the highly commercialized world of peer-group socializing and courtship, young, unmarried men and women in the family circle could also show independence in buying their own clothing (sometimes needed for work, but more often for leisure) and in using some of their earnings for outings to movies, dance halls, or amusement parks.

A housewife also had to work around the regular disruptions in the flow of earnings. The uncertainties of wages resulting from seasonality, abrupt swings in the business cycles, and unexpected personal calamities made the long-term planning of working-class budgets painfully difficult. As one woman remembered, "When you couldn't buy anything, you did without."[9] It was not surprising that in special moments of greater economic security families might splurge on some simple pleasures that scarcity otherwise denied. The return of full employment at unprecedented wages during World War One was one such moment. The Canadian Patriotic Fund's local officials worried that merchants were "giving extensive credit to dependents for goods that can hardly be considered necessities," and for the rest of the war pressured the soldiers' wives under their care to avoid such loose spending and to put their surplus earnings in the bank. The press soon joined the chorus. In 1917 the *Herald*'s editor quoted at length from a letter penned by a charity worker "whose business takes her much among the factory workers." The worker claimed to find in east-end homes "expensive talking machines" (gramophones) and "pianos, player-pianos, and expensive toys." She said that one workingman's wife had spent $6.95 on a Christmas turkey, and that another laid out $7 for a doll. Such shoppers, she insisted, were "throwing money away on luxuries," without thought of savings. "They have been poor and now that they are rich they are determined to have the worth of their money. They live from hand to mouth, and whether they have $10 a week or $10 a day, seem bound, some of them at any rate, perhaps most of them, to spend it."[10]

While these hostile reports are not reliable documents on working-class consumption, they highlight two issues that popped up regularly in contemporary discussions of workers' spending patterns. First were the allegedly spendthrift habits of the working class. Many commentators from outside the working class had little faith in the ability of these families to put aside money for future use. Community leaders handling charity and relief regularly blamed workers' poverty on a lack of frugality. In the initial, hard winter of the pre-war depression, Mayor John Allan, a former construction worker turned contractor, sniped: "Everyone of them squandered some money recklessly during the year. There is some that could have saved." The moralistic prescription was typically to spend less and save more. Some middle-class reformers thought habits of thrift had to be inculcated into workers at an early age. The local YWCA organized a penny savings plan for the youngsters in its North End branch classes at the turn of the century, and the Board of Education introduced the program in the city's elementary schools in 1908. After the war, the Eaton Knitting Company also set up a savings bank for its largely female workforce.[11]

The uncertainties of employment and wages meant that many families found it hard to save, but, still, many did nonetheless. Within a few years after Mayor Allan's jibes, thousands of wage-earners were putting their money into war bonds.[12] Moreover, each week large numbers of local workers carefully set aside a small contribution for insurance policies. As in the late 19th century, many of these policies were handled by fraternal societies, which a good number of Hamilton men joined. as both male social clubs and providers of some combination of health and death benefits, including the Odd Fellows (the largest), Knights of Pythias, Maccabees, Foresters, and Ancient Order of United Workmen, and ethnic societies such as the Irish Protestant Benevolent Society, First Hungarian Sick Benefit Society, or Sons of Italy. Membership in the Anglo-Canadian orders slid rapidly downward after 1920, however.[13] Since the turn of the century they had been challenged by a few large, private insurance companies, notably

Metropolitan Life, which offered new "industrial" insurance plans to urban workers. Local agents visited working-class homes each week to collect a few pennies for policies, often for women and children, that in most cases covered only the costs of a respectable funeral for the deceased. Insurance plans seem to have been more popular than savings accounts. They were an investment in the respectability of a proper public display at the time of death.[14]

Most working-class children would have learned more about saving at the family kitchen table than they did in classrooms. There is considerable evidence that many of their mothers were able to stretch their modest budgets enough each week to build up small surpluses for major expenditures. Well before World War One, many household products could be bought for a few dollars each week on the instalment plan: a stove, icebox, electric iron, dining table, gramophone, radio, and much more (and the same products could be repossessed if payments stopped).[15] With mortgages available for buying land or a finished home, many families took advantage of the opportunity, especially out in Hamilton's working-class suburbs. The east-end clergyman who muttered about profligate spending in 1917 also admitted that many women had built up "substantial bank accounts" and that middle-aged men who made good wages working in munitions plants had mostly been thrifty: "Many have paid off the mortgages on their homes, while others have invested in war bonds." Much spending, then, was deliberate, cautious, and far from impulsive.[16]

The second issue raised by the wartime critics clearly related to what the hard-earned money was spent on. Decades later, some writers cast an equally scornful gaze on working-class consumption as seemingly mindless responses to manipulative corporate advertising (an

(*HS*, 22 April 1920, 17; 9 April 1920, 19)

acquisitiveness sometimes labelled "commodity fetishism").[17] But that perspective has given way to a more sensitive analysis that sees the buyer engaged by consumerist blandishments, but also more actively and self-consciously involved in the process. There is no denying that ever stronger incentives to consume a wide range of mass-produced goods were penetrating working-class Hamilton in the early 20th century. By World War One, many manufacturers were bypassing wholesalers and undertaking much more direct, national marketing of brand-name goods to replace the barrels of no-name products sold in corner stores. At almost any point between the turn of the century and the late 1930s, eye-catching advertisements spilled

Merchants offered easy payment terms for household items, especially those intended for the working-class housewife. (*HS*, 4 May 1917, 12; 26 October 1917, 15)

across the pages of local newspapers inviting people to express themselves by buying things. In the interwar period the ads were not only more numerous and visually more engaging, but also qualitatively different, as the emphasis shifted from the product to the positive attributes that the consumer would take on by purchasing the item (so-called "scare ads," such as Listerine's infamous warnings about halitosis, reminded readers of what social disasters could result from not buying the product). In the 1930s similar messages blared out of the radios that were appearing in so many households.

Through forms of moral parables, these ads appealed to the consumer's yearnings and aspirations and offered a daily vision of the healthy, happy, respectable "good life" that buying more goods could provide.[18]

How much did workers respond to the discourses of spending?[19] Labour leaders had certainly long fought for the right of workers to consume – for enough purchasing power to establish decent living standards. In the words of Southern Ontario's leading labour paper, the *Industrial Banner*, "The twentieth century workingman wants more of the good things in life." The stimulus of advertising doubtless brought new notions of the "good things." "They may have Victrolas and something like that in their house, which perhaps they did not have a few years ago, but in any case they are not getting more than they deserve," the machinists' business agent, Richard Riley, argued before the Royal Commission on Industrial Relations in 1919. "They are every year desiring a better standard of living, and they are becoming every year more determined to get it."[20]

To what extent advertising was able to tap into this desire cannot be measured. Certainly, a few ads made direct appeals to working people *as* workers. They presented visual images of manual labour or labour-intensive housework; they addressed workers as sensible decision-makers about their needs. A Tip Top Tailor clothing ad assured union men that its coats were union-made. A C.C.M. bicycle ad not only promised savings of time and money, but also appealed to a workingman's mechanical expertise to judge "skilled workmanship." An ad for Kitchen's overalls appealed to the pride and dignity of men who wanted durable work clothes that would be "The Business Suit of the Workingman." Dr. Chase's Nerve Food was promoted as a remedy for working women's "nervous troubles" and fatigue. Both Frye's Cocoa and O'Keefe's Ale promised similar relief for workingmen.[21]

Yet far more ads featured much more affluent people in higher-class settings. These ads might have encouraged working-class fantasies of sharing upper-class lustre through purchases of a particular soap or chocolate,[22] but it is equally possible that they were aimed at middle-class consumers and resonated little among working-class shoppers. In any case, as US advertisers knew, a majority of working-class families probably lacked the resources to buy much of anything beyond the basics. After all, underemployment in Hamilton was chronic through the years between the world wars, and spending in the 1930s dropped off drastically. Some working people later recalled little difference between the two interwar decades. According to one, "We didn't have anything like music, sports, or movies to give up."[23]

Moreover, even when it was possible, buying a mass-produced product did not lead in a straightforward fashion to any unifying mass consciousness. The goods that workers could afford to buy got their meaning from the ways in which they met the particular concerns and aspirations arising from their daily lives. The patterns of their consumption were distinctive, as advertisers well understood. "Consumerism" is, moreover, a slippery term, often mixing indiscriminately the commodification of certain basic needs (bakery bread, canned fruit, laundry soap, or an electric washing machine, for example) and the promotion of more whimsical spending on non-essentials (flashy clothes, soft drinks, chewing gum, or movie tickets). This important distinction in working-class spending habits dated back decades, as workingmen had diverted family funds into such luxuries as beer and tobacco. In the early 20th century, as mass production and mass merchandising

(*HS*, 20 November 1920, 18; 1 April 1920, 23)

brought more products within reach, working-class consumers seemed to want to spend to some extent on both basics and non-essentials. Members of these families were certainly buying more, but usually made careful choices about their purchases that middle-class clergymen and social workers might not have understood (or approved of).[24]

Among working people, consumption of more than the daily basics of subsistence actually fell into two distinct patterns. One involved the young, single people within a family. When they were bringing home better wages, they could

(*HS*, 20 April 1920, 6)

take personal delight in buying consumer items, such as new clothing, to help enrich their world of amusement outside the house, items that their parents would probably never think of purchasing. According to the wartime comments of the east-end clergyman, one young woman, a former domestic, used her earnings from munitions work for "an elaborate wardrobe to show off her earnings, including several expensive dresses" and for a down payment on a fur coat. Others, he stated, had "little else to show for their earnings but luxuries." A female munitions worker had to return her new player piano when she lost her job and could not keep up her payments. Men were no better, the minister argued. "Silk shirts at $6 a throw, silk socks at one buck per pair, long-vamped Havana brown oxfords, at $10 and $12, are all said to have been factors in the drainage process of their bank rolls."[25]

If consumerist impulses and a concern for fashion were emerging anywhere in working-class Hamilton, it was among these young people, who, even with their meagre earnings, also filled up the dance halls, amusement parks, and the vaudeville and movie shows. Young women had far less to spend in these ways and relied on their male companions to pay for many amusements; while young men focused much of their spending on such homosocial activities as public drinking and professional sports. Young women and men did not simply merge into a larger, cross-class world of mass culture, but rather used these new commercialized pleasures to augment working-class youth cultures and socializing rituals. These were, indeed, junior versions of the search for some measure of respectability and fun within economically pinched lives.

A completely different pattern entailed shopping for the whole family. Unquestionably housewives felt the siren call of Campbell, Heinz, Quaker Oats, or Proctor and Gamble. Mass-produced, standardized food, cleaning products, and other household goods became more affordable and time-saving in the early 20th century. Most items simply replaced preparation from scratch, and few could be called luxuries. Convincing housewives to buy these goods was certainly a model of hard-sell advertising, which in working-class neighbourhoods often involved premiums to encourage brand-buying.[26] Other family-oriented spending happened more infrequently. Appliances intended to make a wife's housework easier – in particular, electric stoves, refrigerators, washing machines, or vacuum cleaners – came slowly, and often must have been a low priority in husbands' reckoning. A majority of the city's households still did not have these products in 1941. Similarly, most likely only a minority of families were able to afford to advance the respectability (and leisure-time fun) of their households with pianos or gramophones, or even to marshal the whole family for an occasional summer picnic or visit to a movie house. Only the radio managed to penetrate most households, and not until the

1930s. When such purchases were made they had to be affordable but also reliable and durable. Once again, the consumerist choices made at these moments arose from and were adapted to familiar working-class lifestyle preferences. Many such customers, particularly immigrants, preferred to shop in stores where they were known, and where they could buy by instalment, not in the city's handful of department stores, which were more lavish, fixed-price, cash-only emporiums designed much more for the specific tastes of middle-class shoppers. Some better-off, Anglo-Canadian workers nonetheless must have taken advantage of bargain days in those stores, as they did at Eaton's stores across the country.[27]

Family transportation was a somewhat different issue. For generations Hamilton had been a walking city, but the sprawling suburban developments brought a greater reliance on street cars. More privatized transportation also gradually emerged. Bicycles that had been generally too expensive for workers at the turn of the century came down in price and were a common way of getting to work when the roads were passable.[28] The bigger change was the arrival of a more affordable automobile, largely after World War One (before that they had been the fancy toys of elite men, like the founders of the Hamilton Automobile Club).[29] Passenger-car registrations in Hamilton rose from under 7,000 in 1920 to almost 25,000 in 1939. More affluent households might have more than one vehicle. The census-takers of 1941 found that only two households in five in the city actually had a car. The proportion of car ownerships among working-class families was undoubtedly considerably lower. Photographs of International Harvester's parking lot in the late 1930s show at least as much space set aside for the men's bicycles as for automobiles.[30] A 1937–38 national survey determined that the residents of Canada's major cities

(*HS*, 13 December 1929, 41; 14 August 1914, 18)

had paid an average of $473 for their cars ($350 in Toronto); so the purchases were not decisions taken easily, and the instalment payments would certainly have required decent, regular wages. Cars were thus far more common among middle-class families. Yet the two-fifths of families who had them in 1941 must have included many

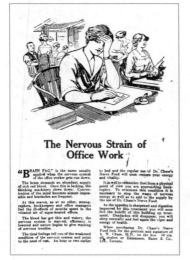

Buying a car became a decision wrapped in profound cultural meaning, but its significance before World War Two was ambiguous. Since husbands invariably controlled the family car, vehicle ownership quickly became associated with their masculine identities – the independent male in control of a powerful, speedy machine that symbolized some kind of liberation from the constraints and pressures of daily life; the skilled handyman who could keep it in good running order; and the good provider who could boost his family's status by loading them up for an outing to the beach. Many a family photo album had snapshots of a man with his foot proudly on the running board of his car. While still under the family roof, a son no doubt hoped to get access to this new symbol of virility to enhance his own leisure-time fun and courtship activities (others might simply "borrow" a car for a joyride).[32] Yet a large gap must have existed between the sleek, powerful images in mass advertising and the older, shabbier, used models that were more typically affordable for working people in the 1930s. Nor does it seem likely that tight family budgets could indulge male fantasies without the purchases being immensely practical as well. For Hamilton's workers, a car was probably mainly a sensible solution to covering long distances to get to work, especially from the peripheral suburbs, where streetcar service might be inadequate or unreliable. It might also have opened up more recreational possibilities, but these would have been far from the motoring holidays of the 1950s, because before World War Two most wage-earners still worked five and a half or six days a week and had no paid vacations. In any case, the cost of gas and oil, along with maintenance and repairs, would have curtailed long trips for families on tight budgets. The new bus services were probably more affordable for special outings.[33]

headed by wage-earners who had taken advantage of the huge growth in the used-car market, where by the mid-1930s older vehicles could sometimes be picked up for well under $100. One Westinghouse worker got a 1924 Chevrolet in the mid-1930s for $13.[31]

Spending in working-class Hamilton, then, was a complex process shaped by both basic material needs and cultural and ethical concerns and practices. Unquestionably, workers were presented with tantalizing visions of a life filled with many more commercial products, and no doubt a small proportion of them with more disposable income reached out and bought some of those items. Yet despite the seeming inevitability of the huge post–World War Two expansion in consumer spending and its appearance as early as the 1920s, most working-class incomes in the interwar period simply remained too low for such indulgence, preventing a total breakthrough into a new kind of consumer consciousness. Members of these families could only cautiously edge into new consumer spending. Drawn by the commercial allure that promised to amplify their individual or collective respectability, they necessarily continued to calculate the practical needs of their households and their own lives. In doing so they took up distinctively working-class modes of spending shaped by custom, hope, and economic insecurity.

Getting By

Given the uncertainties of employment in early 20th-century Hamilton, spending had to be prudent. Restraint in buying might keep the family afloat through hard times. But even during economic booms a family's cautious aspirations and careful household accounting could be seriously thrown off track by soaring retail prices. During the second decade of the century, all households faced sharply upward pressures in the cost of basic necessities. These pressures always occurred during times of full employment and in the face of rising expectations that regular wages would bring better living standards. Plenty of ink was spilled over the high cost of living during the decade spanning World War One, and

No One Refuses Chiclets !

FOR the man who spends hours in the workshop under the strain of whirring machinery—the Chiclet habit is a good habit. Especially when a man can't use tobacco to relieve the tension. A Chiclet refreshes and stimulates, shortens the hours, makes the work seem lighter. To the man on night-shift, Chiclets are a god-send.

Get a packet while you're waiting for the car in the morning, when you buy smokes, or when you go out at lunch-hour.

Almost every store sells Chiclets, ten for 5c. And there's a family-size packet, just the thing for week-ends—25c.

—an Adams product, particularly prepared

ADAMS Chiclets CANDY COATED GUM

Canadian Chewing Gum Co., Limited, Toronto, Winnipeg, Vancouver.

(HS, 29 September 1919, 8; 20 October 1919, 4)

as blame came to be laid at the door of "profiteering," working-class protest heated up.

Government officials, recognizing the significant impact of the cost of living on labour relations, undertook investigations to determine its severity. In 1914 the federal Department of Labour pulled together statistics on price inflation for a Board of Inquiry into the Cost of Living. Its figures for Hamilton indicated that the cost of a weekly food budget for a family of five had jumped from $4.88 in 1900 to $7.50 in 1913 – that is, by 54 per cent – and rents on a six-room dwelling in a working-class neighbourhood had climbed by between 67 and 80 per cent over the same period. Rising housing costs were emerging as the *bête noire* of household economies. British newcomers would have found these increases far greater than they had been experiencing back home, but the figures were comparable to what US workers faced in the same years.[34]

In 1910 the department had begun publishing monthly lists of prices for regular expenditures in a working-class household, based on reports sent in by its local correspondents. Some five years later it added a weekly budget for a working-class family of five, adapted from an account prepared by the US Bureau of Labor Statistics in 1901.[35] This official attempt to peg workers' living costs had numerous problems, not least that the monthly figures were gathered by untrained, part-time statisticians, usually local craft unionists, who had their own view of acceptable living standards. The department's shopping basket was also undoubtedly much fuller than many working-class families could afford, and it would be misleading to say that it revealed a "poverty line" because many families could probably get by, for example, without the large quantities of meat included. Shelter costs similarly assumed that a family would have a whole house to themselves, which was not always possible. In 1921, one-third of Hamilton's tenants told the census-takers that they paid less than the $20 monthly minimum that the local correspondent said it cost to rent a six-room house without an indoor toilet in the city; and one-half said they paid less than the $25 that he reported was needed for a house with indoor facilities.[36] The department's budget could also not take account of changing spending habits in the face of price shifts and altered family circumstances – for example, buying cheaper cuts of meat or moving into smaller quarters in hard times.[37]

Yet, with all these limitations in mind, the budget provides a rough sense of the changing retail cost of basic items for a family of five. The details of the labour department's weekly budget in Hamilton between 1910 and 1940 follow a pattern familiar in studies of Montreal, Toronto, Winnipeg, and Vancouver.[38] Prices rose steadily after 1910, with only a slight decline in the depression year of 1914, and soared between 1917 and 1920, when they reached a peak at more than

twice the 1910 level. In the early 1920s prices, especially for food, came down in another serious depression and then remained fairly stable for the remainder of the decade, before plunging again in the 1930s. The statistics indicate that for heat, light, rent, and a well-stocked larder, a family needed $12 in 1911, nearly $20 in 1921, and just under $17 a decade later.[39]

In December 1913, in a effort to move beyond the limitations of these government statistics, W.E. Gilroy, at the time Hamilton's most pro-labour clergyman, published a working-class family budget that scaled down some of the costs and incorporated other expenditures. Allowing only 47 cents a day for bread, milk, butter, and meat, he calculated that those four food items, along with rent and fuel, totalled almost $9 a week (compared to $12 for the Department of Labour budget, which included much more food). He estimated the cost of clothing and household furnishings at roughly 50 cents a week each, and insurance, church fees and amusements, and streetcar fare at about 30 cents each. The total came to almost $11 a week, with no allowance made for school fees, doctor bills (which could be staggering unless a patient was poor enough to qualify for free care at the City Hospital Outdoor Department), elder care, or funerals.[40]

Would 50 cents a week ($26 a year) really cover clothing and household furnishings? Garnet W. Wickson, a factory worker at Westinghouse and later at the Otis-Fensom Elevator Company, kept a detailed account of all his expenditures in Hamilton (and a few months in Toronto) from 1911 to 1915. His annual clothing bill for 1912 totalled $45.40, for 1913 $57.75, and for 1914 $67.25. As a bachelor, he was probably a bit more of a dandy than was the average married workingman (buying more collars, ties, and garters, for example), and each year he made one major purchase – a suit, an overcoat, or a raincoat – that could be expected to last several years. But mostly he bought underwear, shirts, socks, shoes, overalls, and other basic clothing that would have to be replaced more often. Those items cost him much more than the roughly $13 allowed for clothing alone in the Gilroy budget. A husband with a family would probably try to get by with less, but his needs for proper clothing at work and in public generally would be a regular drain on any working-class family budget.[41]

Similarly, a decade later Ontario's Minimum Wage Board constructed a cost-of-living budget for a single wage-earning woman. It estimated that 20 per cent of her income went to clothing (roughly $86 in 1914 currency). This amount was again probably much more than the expenditure of a married woman, who would not have to dress up for work, but it did contain a careful list of essential items that a housewife required (dresses, underwear, and coats in particular). A survey of newspaper advertisements at five-year intervals between 1890 and 1940 indicates that the cost of cheap boots, overalls, wool suits, and coats followed the general trend of the family-budget data, notably showing a sharp spike after 1915.[42]

For families, after food, fuel, and rent the most pressing need was clothing.[43] The thrifty housewife no doubt watched closely for bargains in special sales events. Yet clothing was generally one of the most flexible categories of family spending, and the life of increasingly shabby garments might have to be stretched indefinitely. Where necessary, women and children also made do with homemade garments, patch-ups, makeovers, and hand-me-downs to avoid cash purchases. Some families simply could not adequately clothe their children. In the 1920s the school board had to start a charity to supply children who stayed home from school because of a lack of adequate footwear. In the 1930s families on relief had to accept identical mass-produced clothing that could be easily recognized on the street.[44]

As for furniture and necessary household items, at a bare minimum a family needed a cooking stove (usually a cast-iron model), one or more beds, a table and chairs, a lamp or two, and crockery, kitchenware, and bedding.[45] As soon as possible the household might add a dresser, sideboard, and stuffed sofa and such refinements as curtains and carpets. As income rose or stabilized, new purchases might include an icebox, a Hoosier kitchen cabinet, perhaps even a gramophone or piano. Some of the available furniture and appliances could cost more than a man's weekly wages. A stove was around $20 in 1910 and over $50 by 1930. A dining-room suite could cost $30 in 1905 and three times that much in 1930. At critical moments – marriage or recent immigration to the city – a whole household had to be furnished from scratch (newlyweds probably got help from their families, but new immigrants would not be so lucky). Many people must have bought used furniture. The new gas and electrical appliances of the interwar period proved too costly for many working-class families in the city – washing machines at $25 and up, stoves at $30 to $80, and refrigerators at well over $100. Such major expenditures were only possible with either some careful saving in advance or generous credit terms. Many families undoubtedly had to set aside at least a dollar a week for each of the costlier items they acquired – considerably more than Gilroy estimated.[46]

The central point of controversy about consumption in the period was whether wages were keeping pace with price inflation. The published federal census statistics recorded at ten-year intervals what wage-earners claimed to have earned in the previous 12 months. Although these figures show a sharp shift towards greater reliance on the wages of the male head of the household (as family contribution declined from a third to a twelfth), the average total family income would seem to have been more than enough to cover the Department of Labour's shopping basket or Gilroy's longer list of purchases, although by 1931 the department's budget would have eaten up all but $4 of the average family's total weekly take-home pay.[47]

Averages are suggestive, but misleading. They include thousands of well-paid, regularly employed professionals and white-collar workers, whose annual salaries were far larger than blue-collar wages.[48] Even among manual workers, a huge variation existed in the amounts actually counted out on kitchen tables each week, depending on occupation, ethnicity, the demographic structure of the household, the health of the chief breadwinner, the fortunes of the particular industries where the wage-earners worked, the extent of unionization, and the general state of the local economy. The uncertainty of employment, especially between the wars, led to major fluctuations in income. Moreover, as in other industrial towns and cities, each working-class family in Hamilton had its own particular mix of resources for making ends meet. If the male breadwinner was skilled and regularly employed, the family could expect more economic security, allowing it to keep children in school longer, buy more clothing, purchase a house, pay church, lodge, or union dues, enjoy more outings, and put aside some savings. In 1921 the families of bricklayers, plumbers, electricians, printers, and, above all, railway running-trades workers were more likely to be enjoying such possibilities, but they made up only a small portion of the labour force, and there were not many other such well-placed occupational groups.

The income gap between skilled and unskilled was already eroding through technological and managerial innovations, and was thus seldom great enough to create a well-entrenched "labour aristocracy."

A basic reliance on low or irregular wages undoubtedly cut off certain spending possibilities. Medical Officer of Health James Roberts saw the constraints of working-class budgets in 1906:

> Let me tell you that the weekly incomes of the bread winners, even when augmented by additions from an older boy or girl, are not sufficient in a large percentage of cases to stand any avoidable strain, especially in these strenuous times, when working folk pay high rents for houses in poor repair, and have to depend on heavy coal bills to keep them tolerably habitable.[49]

In 1929 a National Steel Car worker explained how budgeting in his household worked on $20 a week:

> We get credit at the grocers and pay off a little each week. By the end of the winter we are in debt for coal and food but during the summer, food is cheaper and no coal is needed, so sometimes we get clear, but last year one of my kids died and the funeral cost $50 and with small kids there are always other bills, so we are always owing some.[50]

A number of people in working-class Hamilton merely eked out an existence on the fringes of the labour market, living hand to mouth, highly dependent on charity to survive. Fatherless households could end up in this state for long stretches. Young, transient, unskilled men who were penniless and out of work could also find themselves with no family household to sustain them. They risked police hostility as they begged, stole, or merely hung about in streets and parks waiting for some new opportunity to come their way.

For housewives, managing the family budget was challenging enough when earnings stopped coming in, but it could be equally difficult when a dollar began to buy so much less at the grocer's. The two leaps in the cost of living between 1910 and 1920, especially during the four years after 1916, provoked intense public discussion and widespread working-class resentment against alleged profiteering. In both cases explosions of anger came from people who had been doing better in a booming economy and felt cheated by inflationary prices. In 1913 a Tory workingman on the city's Board of Control, C.G. Bird, thundered that "it was a shame the way people were being robbed on the market for their foodstuffs." He vowed to investigate. At several points over the next few years the local Trades and Labor Council passed angry resolutions calling on governments to control prices, just as other labour organizations across the country were doing. Late in 1915 the Council challenged local bakers to lower the price of bread or face the prospect of a new co-operative bakery to provide cheaper goods. A year later it called on the city to open a municipal bakery and investigated bringing in carloads of potatoes to be sold at cost, a move it finally convinced city council to undertake in 1920. By that point, in the face of escalating fuel costs, the city had already bought coal in bulk to be sold to consumers.[51]

Demands for the "conscription of wealth" started to echo through the public arena. When the federal government appointed a food controller in 1917, his report on excess profits brought a new flurry of outrage. The Trades and Labor Council called for the firing of the Imperial Munitions Board chairman, Sir Joseph Flavelle, a corporate pork-packer (and demanded the stripping of his knighthood). The elusive "profiteer" became a central figure in a prevailing demonology fuelling the emergence of more dynamic independent labour politics. In 1919, under this kind of public pressure, city council set up a Fair Prices Committee to review consumer prices, and the short-lived federal Board of Commerce prosecuted a few local grocers for "making excess profits."[52]

Meanwhile, a group of defiant workers had founded a retail co-operative to avoid the clutches of "profiteering" stores. The Canadian Co-operative Concern opened in 1906 and within four years was one of the largest in the country, providing a large range of goods to some 2,000 members. But the store was sold in 1910 to a private concern, which turned it into a department store. A year later plans were laid for a new project based on the British Rochdale system. The venture promised workers that it would "increase the spending value of their wages and protect them against monopoly." In 1914 a store known as the Industrial Co-operative Society of Hamilton opened at a major intersection in the east end. By spring 1919 it had 179 members engaged in a modest but symbolically important search for alternatives to commercial retailing. In the early 1930s a newly established co-operative dairy had some 5,000 customers.[53]

The politics of spending was thus a powerful force within the workers' revolt at the end of the war. After 1920, however, the deflationary pressures of a sluggish economy in the interwar period kept these concerns from reigniting as bitterly.[54]

Stretching the Dollars
A housewife's financial wizardry could be crucial in getting the family through tight periods or in saving for major purchases such as a house.

As household manager, she bore a huge weight of responsibility for the living standards and respectability of the family. In the Italian community, this resourcefulness was known as *arrangiarsi*.[55] She had to learn to stretch the dollar with daily hunts for bargains or by haggling with the grocer or butcher. She produced as much as possible in the household, as frugally as possible, to avoid using precious cash, especially for food and clothing. When her husband's wages shrank for any reason she had to rack her brain for new ways to economize. Alf Ready, the future president of the first industrial union at Westinghouse, remembered how, during a week of little work in the early 1930s, his wife burst into tears when she discovered that the company had deducted 95 cents for sick benefits after she had carefully calculated how to use every penny of the $2.40 he had earned. If the family had no option but to apply for relief during a serious slump, a wife would have to cope with far less income and tight restrictions on what she could buy.[56]

The variables that a wife and mother could juggle shifted after 1920. In the lengthening cycles of economic depression the male breadwinner's wages were increasingly less certain – and especially when employers imposed wage cuts. Opportunities for small-scale self-employment shrank, especially in retailing. With the rise of the school-leaving age and the decline of youth employment, the family's young adolescents could contribute less. The housewife herself was more often having to bring in increased income.

Female ingenuity came to the fore in a 1923 exchange of letters in the *Spectator*. A woman signing herself "Mrs. Slim" wrote asking readers for advice on "how to keep a house going on $16 a week." She was feeling pressure at home: "When I complain my husband says there are lots more only getting 30 cents an hour who have bigger families than we have – and we have three children." A chirpy letter two days later from "One Who Has Solved This Problem" offered helpful suggestions:

1. Let off part of the house for, say, half of the amount per month now being paid on the house. This will partly solve the rent, and the coal problem, because her tenant will buy coal to heat her portion.

2. As far as food is concerned, if great care is exercised in its selection, I believe she will find it possible to economize quite a lot in this direction. Stale bread is known to go much farther than new, and, while it is not perhaps so appetizing, it is satisfying. Soup made from meat cuttings, which can be bought very cheaply of some butchers, provides quite a pleasant meal. Oleomargerine can be used as a substitute for butter, and the entire family taught that plain food similar to the foregoing, in conjunction with rolled oats, barley meal, rice, etc., is capable of sustaining life equally with some of the other fancy foods.

As regards clothes, I would advise her to watch for bankrupt sales. In this way suits can be bought quite cheap, and as a last resort would call her attention to the number of second-hand clothes stores in the city.

Mrs. Slim's husband might have been no more pleased with this advice than was another letter writer, who wanted to know "how many men who do manual labor for ten hours daily want to live on this diet" or to "go around rigged up in somebody else's hand-me-downs."[57]

Moving the family into cheaper accommodation, especially "doubling up" in another family household, was another option.[58] When desperate, women might find some object of value in their households that could be turned into cash at one of the city's two pawn shops or the much more numerous second-hand stores.[59] In the 1930s some mothers were also still sending their children scavenging for coal or cast-off food. One man who grew up in the north end remembered coal trucks deliberately speeding up as they rounded a particular street corner to send coal scattering over the roadside. He and his sister then shovelled it into buckets and trundled it home. A woman recalled haunting the market near closing time to get leftover fruits, vegetables, and even a pig's head.[60]

The optimistic letter writer neglected to mention an equally common practice: delaying payment of debts, including holding back money owed to doctors or landlords – and landlords in particular were often inclined to wait for payment for extended periods, recognizing how difficult it might be to find new tenants in hard times.[61] Even more important, securing credit at the local shops was central to a housewife's strategizing. In 1907 a milkman in the east end complained that the credit system encouraged customers to think "that we can wait for six or eight months – it doesn't matter." The system was crucial in times of mass unemployment. "The grocers of Hamilton have over a hundred thousand dollars owing to them by the citizens in general," a spokesman for the local Retail Grocers' Association told a civic gathering in 1914, adding that the grocers "had done far more to relieve the situation than the city ever had." In 1931 the Toronto office of the Bradstreet Company of Canada reported that credit in Hamilton had shot up by 25 to 40 per cent since 1928–29, and a few years later a city controller stated that "the small grocers were the real relief department of the city." For a time the possibility of working out these financial arrangements with a familiar face in a neighbourhood store limited the

impact of more impersonal, cash-only chain and department stores. Unfortunately for working-class housewives, however, the trend in retailing by the 1920s and 1930s was gradually away from informal, long-term credit towards cash payments, as price-cutting chain stores increasingly set the pace of city retailing. In 1930 the city directory listed 57 branches of Hamilton's leading retail chain (the country's first), William Carroll's, as well as 24 Dominion, 10 A and P, and 6 Loblaws stores – totalling a quarter of all grocery stores in the city. Most of these chain stores were strung out along the busiest thoroughfares in the east end. Still, the depression was hard on these new retailers, and by 1940 11 Carroll's and 15 Dominion branches had disappeared as impoverished shoppers evidently avoided their cash and carry policies.[62]

Women in working-class neighbourhoods also depended on each other for help. Neighbours and kin borrowed and bartered goods and services informally, though within well-understood conventions about obligations to reciprocate. "We were very close with our neighbours," one woman later recalled. "If they were in trouble they'd come to mother." Another had a similar story about her mother: "If anyone died, she'd go and help lay them out. Anybody was sick, she'd go and help them. Jobs like that – if they wanted. Same with a child coming, and the doctor was not available. She could help." An Armenian-Canadian woman later recalled such mutual support as being central to neighbourhood life: "There was no competitive living. Like if you wanted something, needed something, the other would help. It was sort of a you-help-me, I'll-help-you. Like this is why I think we all survived." That pattern of co-operation may well explain the apparent success of a potato boycott declared in the spring of 1920 by the local federation of women's auxiliaries to veterans' organizations, as a tactic to combat the high price of this basic foodstuff. The next month the Mount Hamilton Women's Labor Party similarly resolved to fight the high cost of bread by baking their own.[63]

When family wage-earners were regularly employed and reasonably well paid, a working-class housewife could take pride in her financial juggling to cover all the family's living costs and build up a small surplus to meet regular payments on a house or furniture. Those with fewer or less secure resources might maintain their dignity simply by avoiding both big debts at the grocer's or trips to a second-hand shop. But not all women were so fortunate, and inevitably some had more trouble wielding the tools of household management under stress. Investigators from charities and social agencies often found weary, dispirited women on the doorsteps of shabby, overcrowded households, wearing on their faces and revealing through obviously tired limbs the strain of their struggles to make ends meet and thus feed, clothe, and shelter their families.[64]

Home Sweet Home

The most inflationary cost in the weekly budget was housing. In 1931 tenants spent on average a quarter of their incomes on rent.[65] With a new real-estate industry promoting home ownership, growing numbers of Hamilton's working-class families made the ambitious decision to buy (or build) houses of their own. While homes were not mass-produced on the same scale as canned goods or cars, contractors did throw up rows of identical houses, and companies marketed cheap build-your-own housing kits that apparently sold well. Brash advertising for new housing possibilities blared out of the daily press.

Civic boosters, industrialists, and government housing experts loudly applauded the home-owning trend, arguing that it was a steadying, stabilizing, even conservationist force in working-class communities. As the *Hamilton Manufacturer* confidently proclaimed in 1913, "The opportunity to buy homes on the easiest terms, cheap rents, the abundance of seasonable foodstuffs at reasonable prices are elements which contribute to the contented condition of the labouring man." A contented worker would also serve his employer better as a more productive, efficient worker. "It is a recognized fact," two local town planners argued a decade later, "that where a man owns his own home, he has a stake in the community in which he lives, and is therefore a more responsible citizen, and a greater asset." Civic planner Thomas Adams told a Hamilton audience in 1919, "We are not going to have a sober people if we do not give them counter attractions for the public house and its evils." An ad in *Industrial Canada* suggested the goal was to "Kill Bolshevism by Erecting Houses." Workers would have a bigger stake in the capitalist system and dissolve their separate identities into a broader middle-class-dominated culture of consumerist domesticity. With a mortgage to pay, the argument ran, a "responsible" citizen would be less likely to take the risk of striking or otherwise confronting his employer. The Steel Company's vice-president, H.H. Champ, argued in 1928 that home ownership also discouraged labour turnover. The Ontario government's Housing Act of 1918 was aimed at diffusing such social unrest, and, symbolically, in 1919, at a moment of considerable class tension, the Hamilton Real Estate Board staged a Better Homes Exhibit in the Hamilton Armouries "to educate the average renter into the method and means of ownership."[66]

From a more pessimistic perspective, Friedrich Engels had similarly predicted that home ownership would "stifle all revolutionary spirit" by "chaining the workers by this property to the factory in which they work" – or, in the coy words of a team of recent American scholars, "lawns for pawns."[67] This line of thinking extended into the late 20th century, when social scientists tried to document some of the claims that home ownership meant social and political conservatism, especially in Reagan's America or Thatcher's Britain (although the issue is often blurred with others, such as racism). Unfortunately, too much of this long-standing discourse on home ownership reflects a limited understanding of what a residence meant to working-class families and why so many were willing to scrimp and save with enormous sacrifices to get one of their own long before governments and promoters had begun to prod them into buying.[68]

A "home" does not have a universal significance. Buying one could have varied meanings for different social groups. The ideal middle-class family home was far from the world of business. It was a retreat, a "haven in a heartless world," and the embodiment of the cultural refinement, personal decorum, and moral rigour central to bourgeois values. The space within the household was also organized to create functionally specialized rooms – especially a dining room separate from the kitchen – and to maximize individual privacy for family members. Increasingly, too, in the early 20th century, the middle-class home was expected to be the embodiment of efficiency and order, reflected in new spacial arrangements, technology, and furnishings. These were the ideals that public-health nurses and social workers carried with them on their increasingly frequent visits to working-class households. These conditions were also embodied in the kind of philanthropic housing project under discussion in Hamilton just before World War One (which in the end never materialized) and in the small postwar government housing

program, in which applicants had to conform to specific models and state officials monitored all deviations; and they beamed out of newspaper and magazine discussions of working-class home ownership throughout the period.[69]

Workers generally had different and complex needs when they set up their own homes. First and foremost, their households played a central economic role in their family lives. A home was more than simply a place for wage-earners to eat and rest their weary bones; it was an organizing station in which the waged and unwaged carried out a gendered division of labour to ensure their mutual survival. It was the site of important functions in the family economy: from the handing over of wages earned outside to be stretched into enough consumer goods for the whole household, to production of food or clothing for household consumption, to cash-earning activities such as laundry or hairdressing. Working-class households were hives of self-help, producing, building, maintaining, and repairing for family use. Arranging a household that reflected these needs was therefore a matter of practical concern – proximity to factories or the street-railway line, for example, or the availability of a garden plot for growing vegetables for the household and space for a chicken coop. An easier access to "nature" had less to do with aesthetics than with the productive possibilities therein. Hamilton's new real-estate developers played to these concerns in their advertising. In 1910 a promoter of the new east-end Brightside subdivision emphasized "the fine quality of the soil," which was "suitable for growing vegetables and is in itself a big consideration to the thrifty workingman, as he may on a comparatively small piece of ground, purchased at low cost, raise his year's supply of staple vegetables without much trouble and less expense." Another developer boasted that his lots were "deep, and there is room for a stable and garden. Fruit trees are on many lots." Still another declared, "The fine sandy soil is ideal for the keeping of poultry, raising vegetables and the like." A working-class family could also use its house to generate income by making room for paying boarders or tenants, and, indeed, between 20 and 30 per cent of families headed by skilled and semi-skilled wage-earners followed that practice in the decades from 1890 to 1940. In doing this they might well have sacrificed the privacy of individual family members – a great concern to middle-class reformers – in the interest of family finances, including paying for the house itself.[70]

Owning a house, moreover, related to immediate and longer-range needs within the family economy. Typical mortgage payments of $5 a month could be much cheaper than rents, especially in the periods of intense housing shortages, and, then too, many of the new workers' homes on the suburban edges of the city were constructed by their owners (and relatives and friends), who used their "sweat equity" to save building costs. Families often spent several years in crowded "shacks" that were slowly expanded to add more rooms. No middle-class family would have lived that way. Once paid off, the house also gave workers a buffer against the uncertainties, whether unemployment or old age, of the waged labour market. Buying a house – usually in the later life of the male head of a working-class household and the peak years of family income – was intended to ensure a measure of economic security for the elderly or retired (whether or not it was to be sold to produce a cash nest egg). It may also have been part of a working-class strategy of inheritance, allowing parents to pass on a small legacy of real estate to their children. Still, only slightly over half of Hamilton's older skilled and semi-skilled workers and far fewer labourers managed

to get homes in their own names in this period, though the dream must have remained alive as a cherished goal among many more working-class families. The economic functions of the working-class household were thus centrally important, in marked contrast to middle-class homes, where the split between paid work and domestic space was usually much sharper.[71]

Even so, household formation was much more than a matter of dollars and cents. The word "home" also embodied a range of central values and aspirations. Working-class families were particularly concerned with the economic and social independence that their own home seemed to promise. The demand for independence from the indignities of tenancy, a prominent theme in the late-19th-century labour reform movements, was an implicitly radical challenge to the increasingly dependent status of those relying on wages for their survival. In 1912, when Allan Studholme praised the new business-community project for working-class housing, he indicated that he would "prefer a proposition by which the workingman would secure his home instead of becoming a perpetual tenant."[72] Newcomers from non-Anglo-Celtic backgrounds were just as eager to shed the long-standing indignities of tenancy rooted in feudal social relations. By the 1920s and 1930s a third of Polish households in Hamilton were owner-occupied, as were half of those of Italian families, who had surpassed the level of Anglo-Celtic home ownership by 1936.[73] This widespread desire for freedom from subordination would become a central theme in many aspects of the lives of Hamilton workers.[74]

Independence was also tied closely to respectability. As an International Harvester worker argued in 1919, "If he is any kind of citizen, if he has any responsibility about him, if he aspires to pass as a good and praiseworthy citizen of Canada, he wants to live in a house where he can have some common decency for himself and his children."[75] For working-class men that inclination meant putting down deeper roots in the urban community, obtaining a bigger stake in political decision-making, and gaining a greater sense of entitlement. Until 1917, voters' lists were generated from the city's assessment rolls of taxable property. Moreover, before property restrictions were removed in 1921, as Hamilton's Independent Labor Party discovered when it began nominating candidates, it was only substantial homeowners who could qualify to run for municipal office. Subtle distinctions undoubtedly crept into working-class communities between those who could afford this limited degree of respectability and those who were restricted to rental accommodation, probably reinforcing distinctions already experienced between the more and less skilled in the paid workforce. Yet the question of home ownership does not appear to have led to a fundamental split in working-class communities.[76] Rather than being expressly conservative, the working-class homeowners of Hamilton's east end showed themselves repeatedly after 1906 to be sufficiently politically independent and consistently class-conscious to send Independent Labor candidates to the legislature and eventually to city council – a pattern found in many other Canadian working-class suburbs before World War Two.[77]

Respectability shone through in other ways. A house was a highly public possession. Home ownership provided the opportunity for a sense of modest dignity – working-class families could pour their energies and imaginations into additions, renovations, fences, gardens, and such embellishments as flowery wallpaper and stuffed furniture. Wherever possible in their small households, families set aside a front room as a little-used parlour for special occasions, where they might sometimes display such highly prized objects as a piano or a gramophone. When James Sullivan retired as president of the local Trades and Labor Council in 1915, his grateful colleagues presented him with symbols of this kind of respectability – a china cabinet and collection of cut glassware. All of this stood as a working-class badge of victory over the forces of economic insecurity that could drag a family down. It did not mean simply emulating middle-class emblems of respectability, despite some superficial similarities. In households of their own, workers could display their distinctive stylistic preferences, with some debts to the middle-class taste that was being intrusively promoted among working-class mothers, but they paid much more heed to a more complex blend of affordability, comfort, usefulness, and rural and ethnic traditions. This aspect of respectability owed a great deal to the house-proud working-class housewife, whose standards of order and cleanliness helped to give a family its status on the street.[78]

Workers in Hamilton further defined their respectability by how they used their household space and by its relationship to the outside world. Where overcrowding did not prevent it, there was a sharper differentiation of interior space, including the parlour, dining room, and more separate bedrooms, though the willingness to "double up" and take in lodgers suggests that individual privacy was far less important than it was in middle-class households. The working-class house also faced the public in different ways, which were already evident in British housing by the end of the 19th century. In contrast to some earlier, more primitive forms of working-class housing in which households might share water and privies or even common entranceways and courtyards, working-class families in Hamilton, as in similar settings on both sides of the

Atlantic in the late 19th and early 20th centuries, made their homes private spaces closed off from the street. They were households in which little formal socializing took place on a regular basis. Years later, many interviewees described what was in essence "an established code of neighbourly behaviour." One woman summed it up: "In the neighbourhood . . . no one would come in and visit. Talk to them outside, and if there was a death there, we all tried to go to the funeral. We were close in that way, but not to the extent of visiting." Yet families lived close together on narrow lots, and strong bonds of neighbourliness sustained them. The ubiquitous verandah probably played a mediating role between the privacy of the home and the gregarious sociability of the streets – a place, particularly important for women, outside the house yet still attached to it, where some quiet household activities could be carried on and where neighbours could be greeted and welcomed informally.[79]

In the value system of most working-class families, maintaining an independent household was also part of carving out space for the warmth and creativity that was increasingly denied in the paid workplace. A working-class version of the "cult of domesticity" put the wife and mother at the centre of the family's emotional solace and nurturing – even though in practice this could prove an impossibly oppressive role to play. Architecturally the central place assigned to the kitchen (and, increasingly, the dining room) in the working-class home symbolized the so-called labour of love that women poured into their domestic work and that other members of the working-class family must have recognized as being crucial for their well-being. For the husband/father, the household could also be an expressive outlet for various handicrafts, from gardening to carpentry, that workdays in a factory might deny. A working-class home was

in part a place of refuge, emotional sustenance, and creative expression.[80]

In working-class Hamilton, then, owning your own home was not a simple goal. Developers' advertising tried to package the intricate mix of material, social, and emotional concerns in their pre–World War One promotion of new suburban lots. The garden and the park were often central images,[81] but, like so many contemporary middle-class commentators, developers tended to miss the ways in which workers made choices about household arrangements that were much more hard-nosed and practical – aimed at their survival in an industrial capitalist society – and that did not necessarily imply a retreat into the kind of bucolic privacy that was the hallmark of middle-class domesticity. Nor did these promoters admit how far beyond the reach of most families a home of their own actually was.

Cautious Consumers

In the early decades of the 20th century, then, working people found that meeting their needs and aspirations meant steadily spending more of the hard-earned dollars that came into their households. Before 1920 these expenditures were driven in part by retail price inflation on essential goods and services, especially housing and food – the much debated "high cost of living." But, within those external pressures, families and individuals made decisions about what to buy that reflected their search for economic security, respectability, comfort, and, whenever possible, fun, while depending mostly on wages for survival.

Most often wives and mothers did this spending on behalf of the whole family, but in limited ways husbands and older sons and daughters got to make some personal consumer choices. Soon after the turn of the century, advertisers began trying to convince the city's workers to satisfy their yearnings by purchasing new mass-produced products – from canned goods to ready-made clothing to gramophones to suburban bungalows – and the companies offered payment-by-instalment plans to make it all possible. After 1920 those voices got more insistent and more sophisticated in suggesting how particular products could help fulfil the dreams of working-class family members. Happiness could be achieved through spending, not saving.

This new cultural force was unquestionably a powerful element in working-class life. The urge to participate must have been compelling. In some ways, workers drew from this glittering marketplace what could enhance their display of respectability – a young woman's flamboyant hat, a workingman's Sunday suit, or a gramophone for the parlour. But most consumer choices reflected not simply blind adherence to well-packaged consumerist messages, but cautious, sober calculations. Working-class consumption, especially for such big-ticket items as houses or automobiles, was much more practical than whimsical, and required carefully setting aside small sums for weekly payments over long stretches of time. Moreover, the products purchased were put to use within the daily rhythms of distinctly proletarian lives – a sewing machine for making children's clothing, a flashy hat or snappy suit for neighbourhood courtship rituals, a radio for cheap family entertainment, a car for lower-cost transportation to work, and, above all, a house as a base for generating income and limiting reliance on the commercial market for family needs. All such careful spending would, it was hoped, add a good deal to the security and respectability of the family and its individual members.

Before 1940, in Canadian cities such as Hamilton, economic uncertainty always put a severe brake on any kind of spending. Wages in the more prosperous times of the first two decades of the century regularly fell behind the soaring cost of living, but in the interwar period faltering employment kept most working-class families well outside the consumerist experiences being promoted by more aggressive advertising. While some were buying washing machines, gramophones, houses, and cars, most were not. Without steady income, instalment payments were impossible. In the post-1920 period, the tension between commercially hyped aspirations and economic scarcity became particularly poignant. The most common form of consumerism among workers probably involved cheaper goods for personal pleasure – such as special clothing, chewing gum, cigarettes, beauty aids, or tickets to vaudeville and movie shows – and it was young, unmarried people, rather than married couples, who entered this consumerist space most often. Yet when wages dried up even simple male pleasures like a beer after work might have to be sacrificed. Well-ingrained habits of thrift and fatalism about unpredictable calamities in personal and family fortunes were still more compelling within working-class Hamilton than were spendthrift cultures of consumption.

In the end the workers' ability to buy new goods was most likely only small compensation for their relative powerlessness in workplaces or public life, especially after 1920. Workers were not necessarily straightforwardly convinced by the messages of the advertising industry and subject to the satisfaction promised in the marketeers' ads. Rather than it being a case of consumer-consciousness replacing class-consciousness, then, both could co-exist as class experience shaped consumer choices. Certainly some products brought pleasure and comfort – makeup for women, beer for men, or radios for whole families, for example – but they gained their meaning in the specifically working-class contexts in which they were used, in distinctive patterns based on age, gender, and ethnicity. The spending of money cannot be isolated from the complex set of daily practices developed by people who relied primarily on income from wage-earning for their survival.

8

The Hamilton police distributed Christmas relief baskets to the poor. (HPL)

The Last Resort

LATE IN OCTOBER 1910 a journalist witnessed a couple being hauled before Hamilton's police magistrate on a charge of "false pretenses." Assuming that her husband would be starting a construction job the next day, the wife had signed a promissory note to get $9 worth of groceries. But her husband's foot was too sore to allow him to work, the couple could not pay, and the grocer wanted his money. The *Spectator*'s court reporter was moved by the "pathetic sight" of the couple, "evidently being the victims of poverty, yet having all the marks of honest people."

Some 11 years later a city councillor spotted similar despair. A man returned home after a fruitless day of tramping all over the city to look for work to support his sick and pregnant wife and his children. They had run up debts for groceries and rent. Some of their furniture had already been repossessed. The children were eating plain porridge. With winter setting in, the man looked into the future, as the councillor observed, "without hope and with a bitter spirit."

In 1924 the mother of five children, one of them an infant, was likewise gloomy. Her husband had gone to jail for theft three months earlier. Her landlord had just evicted the family, after refusing to let her take in boarders. She had sold her kitchen cabinet and was about to lose her stove because she was unable to keep up payments. Her 14-year-old son wanted to find a job, but lacked the right clothing. Neighbours were impressed with "the spirit that is prompting the mother to the last to hold her family together."[1]

What could a family do when wages dried up, savings evaporated, and the corner grocer cut off credit? The answer depended on whether the family had anyone capable of filling the shoes of the male breadwinner, or whether the able-bodied husband was simply unable to find work.[2] In the absence of a wage-earning husband, a desperate wife and mother could turn to the city's many voluntary charities, some with long histories. In many cases she would find herself dealing with the women from other social classes who organized and administered this help. They might sympathize with her domestic hardships but had their own firm notions about the causes and cures of such suffering. A few government programs appeared after 1914 with similar principles and practices, but it was the private initiatives outside the state that remained far more important for poor women right down to World War Two.

Unemployed men generally wanted nothing to do with charity. Most philanthropic societies ignored them anyway. Such men were more likely to turn in frustration to the municipal government to provide some kind of work for wages, which they preferred to see as their right as citizens. If unemployment continued, such distinctions between the categories of helpless dependant and jobless wage-earner could get blurred in the administration of relief.

Never were these desperate men and women allowed to forget how far they had wandered from the prevailing ideal of self-sufficiency: a patriarchal family was to be sustained by wages earned in the labour market. Across a full half-century the forms of assistance available to Hamilton's working-class families in crisis underwent certain changes, but the philosophies and policies sustaining welfare provision stayed remarkably consistent.

Reaching Out

Families facing crises such as illness, unemployment, or the death of either the male breadwinner or the housewife eventually had to reach outside their own households for support. Typically they turned first to kin and neighbours, who most often offered their own labour – taking in children, perhaps, or cooking meals or otherwise helping out around the house.

"When someone was down on their luck, either because they lost their job or if they got ill, neighbours would help out," one woman later explained. "If you needed a loan, people of the community would always come together and lend you as much as they could." In 1936 men in one plant took up a collection to help out a fellow worker who had staggering medical and funeral bills for his wife and children. The elderly were likely to get particular attention from the community. People who grew up in working-class Hamilton later recalled this neighbourliness all around them. Only fleeting glimpses remain of this kind of mutual support. In 1911, for example, a one-armed painter, his wife, and eight small children suddenly became homeless when their house burned down. Men who worked with the man – 15 carpenters, a bricklayer, and a number of plasterers – promptly volunteered to build the family a new house; they completed it in one day that spring. The same year the local sheriff complained that he could do nothing for the wife and four children of "an undoubted brute of a husband" because "her friends and neighbors were supporting them." In 1919 an east-end charity worker described to a government inquiry how neighbours had held a concert to raise money for a woman who had lost her husband and all her children except a newborn infant in the influenza epidemic. The same year a small veterans' organization sold tickets for a draw to help the family of an unemployed and disabled returned soldier. In 1923 a *Herald* reporter visited the "slum" home of an east-end family and found that the mother of six youngsters lay ill in bed and "some neighbors were cooking something for the invalid, whose husband has been in hospital for the past four months." In 1930 another social worker found a desperate woman cooking potatoes, the only food in the house, given to her by a neighbour.[3]

Still, relatives and neighbours could usually help out only for short spells or in limited ways. Many families and single people, especially recent immigrants, might not get much help from this direction in any case.[4] They eventually had to turn to more formally organized forms of economic assistance. When men were bedridden with prolonged sickness or injury, a substantial minority of them might be able to get a little help from the fraternal societies, company benefit plans, or unions that they belonged to, as a charity-free return on their investment in collective self-help (although those benefits would always be far less than a regular wage).[5] Otherwise they or their wives could approach a bewildering variety of private and public agencies. Which ones they chose or were directed to depended in part on their religion and ethnicity or, in some cases, their age, marital status, or special disability. Over the decades Hamilton's working people found their way to four different sorts of agencies of charitable relief: private charities, the city relief department, live-in charitable institutions, and, beginning during World War One, a few state-sponsored welfare programs.

Working-class families without the regular income of a male breadwinner – especially widows and the elderly, but also recent immigrants – were most likely to use the social networks of their neighbourhoods to get help from churches or ethnically based societies (which were often closely linked). They might not actually make the first move – a clergyman or neighbour could discover the family's problem and provide the link. The white Anglo-Canadians and recent British immigrants could turn to one or more of several well-established societies.[6] European newcomers also found fraternal societies among their fellow countrymen in the city. Christian churches might help out as well, whether directly through the clergyman or through the intervention of a local Ladies' Aid. The Order of the King's Daughters and Methodist deaconesses were particularly active, and the non-denominational Woman's Christian Temperance Union had ongoing programs to help impoverished mothers.[7]

Impoverished families could also get help from programs that had no religious or ethnic basis. A few groups of working-class women organized to help suffering families. Among them were a group of wives of unionists in the north end, an organization known as Maple Leaf Women's Own in the east end, and the Social Relief Auxiliary associated with the east-end police station.[8] After World War One, veterans' organizations also helped their members cope with hardship. A small number of much more specialized charities also appeared in the interwar period to assist families with specific problems. The Women's Auxiliary of the Hamilton General Hospital provided medical supplies and material relief to the sick and injured, while the Women's Auxiliary of the Blind Institute helped the sightless. The Samaritan Club targeted families coping with tuberculosis in their households.

In the 19th century Hamilton's House of Refuge had been a general poorhouse run by the city, but by the turn of the century it was taking in only the elderly poor with no means of support and no one to look after them. (HPL)

The Board of Education also provided clothing and shoes for small numbers of impoverished children, and, for growing numbers, free pints of milk.[9]

A small amount of relief from the local government was also woven into this patchwork. Ontario had no poor-law legislation that required the state to look after the indigent, but, as in many other municipalities, Hamilton's city council maintained a small program of "outdoor relief" (that is, handouts to people living in their own homes), administered by a full-time relief officer, a position held from 1898 to 1934 by John H. McMenemy. These funds were meagre and intended only to fill in when the private charities fell short, particularly with newcomers stranded in the city without relatives, friends, or neighbours. The aid was also generally seen as help through the winter that should end in the spring, and, like the private charities, it was aimed only at exceptional cases of disability, decrepitude, or temporary dislocation.[10]

The charity provided by both private and public agencies could be cash, but was more often orders for groceries, fuel, or clothing, or the actual items themselves. At Christmas special baskets of food were prepared and delivered

to those in need. The St. George's Benevolent Society delivered 200 food baskets in 1910 to help 907 people and 350 in the more difficult winter of 1913 for 1,803 souls. The flow of this particular charity was probably typical, peaking in the depression years of 1907–9, 1913–14, and the early 1920s. The Society also helped men find jobs, provided free medical care for the sick or injured, took care of funerals, and arranged trips home for widows of Englishmen.[11]

All of these efforts were aimed at keeping the family intact, but, if that appeared no longer economically possible, individual family members could be handed over to one of the several special institutions run by private charities or the city. By the close of the 19th century these places were mainly orphanages and old-age homes. They allowed individuals who qualified to move in, though often they provided outdoor relief to others. The various "homes" ran on a combination of private fund-raising, residents' fees, and provincial and municipal grants (and were thus subject to provincial inspection). Usually a parent in distress or a near-relative made the decision to place a family member there, though a charitable society, the city's relief officer, or the Children's Aid Society might be involved in proposing and overseeing the process.[12]

With children, the death or disappearance of a parent might trigger such a move. Walter Rollo, labour leader and politician (and for a time school attendance officer), told an enquiry in 1919: "About the first thing that enters the mother's mind is that she will have to put those children in a Home."[13] Fathers might break up their families if their wives died. Europeans (especially Catholics accustomed to such institutions back home) seemed more ready to take this step. An Infants' Home official stated in 1919, "We have not found that the foreigner has any idea of stigma being attached to putting his child into other people's care. We find our sturdy immigrants from Scotland and England don't take their children except in case of necessity."[14]

For most of the period between the 1890s and the 1930s, children in dire or difficult circumstances who could not live with relatives were placed in one of the city's five or six orphanages, two of them infants' homes. Some stayed until school-leaving age; others were adopted or indentured as "apprentices" on farms. Only a small proportion of these youngsters had actually lost both parents, and most stayed no more than a few years, often no more than a few months. Many were reclaimed by parents once the family had regained a minimum of economic stability or when the child reached the wage-earning age of 14. The corresponding secretary of the Girls' Home complained about "parents forcibly removing children from the homes where they had been placed, and the unwarranted interference of relatives who take not the slightest interest in their welfare until they are old enough to be of use to them." The orphanage administrators might disrupt these family strategies with their own agendas for "child-saving," but they nonetheless expected parents or relatives to pay board for their children if at all possible.[15]

By the close of the 19th century most general poorhouses in Ontario were narrowing their clientele to the elderly. The city's House of Refuge made that shift, and the Ladies' Benevolent Society wound down its orphans' asylum and outdoor relief work to concentrate on looking after resident elderly women.[16] In Hamilton those who could no longer maintain themselves and had no family able or willing to support them in their own households might find their way to one of three old-age homes: the municipally run House of Refuge (renamed Home for the Aged and Infirm in 1919), the private-charity Aged Women's Home, or the

The Boys' Home and Girls' Home were orphanages run by private charities. (HPL)

small Anglican-sponsored St. Peter's Infirmary. Provincial government policy in the late 19th century had cut back on outdoor relief for the elderly in favour of these institutions. Most of the residents in these Hamilton institutions seem to have been single, and a majority were men, who were apparently less able to look after their own domestic needs than were women. Wherever possible, they had to pay board, and the Aged Women's Home in particular charged a hefty admission fee ($200 in 1912). A small number of people stayed in these homes only for short periods before finding a place with kin. The average stay in the House of Refuge was only about 250 days a year. By the turn of the century, the government was determined to reduce

The Salvation Army opened the Metropole as a hostel for single men; ten cents got a bed for the night. (HPL)

expenditures on institutional care for the elderly and push responsibility back onto their families, and in 1921 added a Parents' Maintenance Act to the statute book to better enforce that notion (though it was rarely used). Some elderly men and women found their way into the Hamilton jail for the winter, typically as vagrants; they left in the spring and got readmitted in the fall. After the turn of the century, these people were gradually weeded out of the local jail population. The House of Refuge also made such comings and goings much more difficult.[17]

In general Hamilton's working people found these live-in charitable institutions far less important in the relief of distress after the turn of the century than had earlier been the case. Almost all of the facilities were located in the older parts of the city – the downtown and north end – and were thus not accessible to the thousands of east-end working-class suburbanites. The space available in them for "inmates" also never kept

pace with the massive increase in the working-class population after 1900. By the 1930s all the orphanages except St. Mary's Orphan Asylum were allowing their inmate population to dwindle, as child welfare shifted decisively away from institutional solutions.[18] Their relevance to most working-class families as temporary or long-term boarding services for children thus steadily declined. Similarly, the old-age homes, which had a total of 244 inmates in 1900, could handle no more than 30 or 40 more by the mid-1920s, and built up long waiting lists.[19] All these "refuges" and "homes" nonetheless continued to eat up a huge proportion of municipal funds directed to supporting the poor, even though they were becoming steadily less useful to working-class families.[20] The remaining private charities thus faced ever greater pressure to cope with the demands of the swelling population.

Single men alone in the city and unable to afford proper lodging had to rely on charitable

The Hamilton police distributed relief to the poor. (HPL)

hostels, especially the Salvation Army's Metropole hostel and the Central Police Station. Well into the 1930s a couple of hundred men might bed down each night in such places during winter months, but were sent packing in warm weather. "Most of the men were local laborers, who possessed no settled home," the Salvation Army told a reporter in 1921. "Outsiders were not encouraged to patronize the place." Those identified by local police as "idlers," "loafers," or "tramps" were told to leave the city. Otherwise they would face prosecution for vagrancy.[21]

The State Steps In

Hamilton's serendipitous mixture of private charity and public relief was typical of cities across the country before World War Two, providing the basic framework for supporting working-class families and individuals through their economic crises.[22] The only major addition was the insertion of a small number of state programs to deal with families of specifically disadvantaged groups – those disabled on the

job or in the war, widowed mothers, and the elderly. In each case the state undertook the unfamiliar role of administering pensions to working people systematically and on the basis of right. The new programs incorporated most of the philosophy and administrative practices of the existing private welfare network, but divided those practices into two distinct streams: one intended to bolster the disabled male wage-earner, the other to support dependants of absent male breadwinners, especially mothers.[23]

The first of these new programs came into force on 1 January 1915, under the Ontario Workmen's Compensation Act, after several years of debate between business organizations and the Ontario labour movement – a dialogue among men about men, in which women played virtually no part. This legislation disrupted the old common-law right of a family to sue a company for damages if a breadwinner was injured or died. Juries in these cases had begun to show considerable sympathy to the bereaved family, as in the case of the deceased Joseph Graham, an International Harvester employee killed on the job in 1903. His family got $1,500 from their court action. The new act pre-empted most of these suits, but guaranteed a fixed rate of compensation in cases of either death or permanent disability. The program was in essence an insurance plan. Disabled workers or families of workers killed on the job now submitted their claims to a Workmen's Compensation Board (WCB), which determined the level of support to be paid in each case out of a fund created from employers' contributions. One of the three board members was to be a labour representative. Most significant for working-class families was the central philosophy of the program: as industrial workers, workingmen (and a few working women) and their families were entitled to this money by right, not as charity. Compensation was based on allegedly scientific criteria related to the man's occupational skills, not a means test. Business had eventually agreed to this system as more stable, "scientifically" efficient, and bureaucratically predictable. In a similar fashion, the federal government created a pension plan, administered by a Board of Pension Commissioners, for men disabled during military service and families of those killed during World War One.[24]

These were the only new state initiatives based on the social entitlement of men unable to work for wages and the only ones that used "social insurance" as their organizing principle.[25] Both workers' compensation and veterans' pension programs shared the commitment to families unable to survive without a male breadwinner. That same commitment also conditioned two other new programs – mothers' allowances and old-age pensions – but the clientele and the methods of those new projects were substantially different. Mothers' allowance had its roots in the care of families of men

serving overseas during World War One. Soon after the outbreak of the war, Hamilton's leading businessmen set up a local branch of a national voluntary organization, the Canadian Patriotic Fund, which undertook to raise money through private subscription to assist enlisted men's families. Robert Hobson chaired the finance committee. Those in need of extra money, on top of the men's pay and the "separation allowance" paid to all soldiers' and sailors' dependants, could apply to the local fund for financial support. Its Relief Committee would "determine the amount necessary to enable a typical family to maintain a decent scale of living in their community" and award the appropriate subsidy where it deemed appropriate. By the end of 1918 the Hamilton committee had handed over $2 million to some 5,000 families, including more than 15,000 individuals, though the largest number receiving the aid at any one time was never more than half that number. Undoubtedly the great majority of these were from working-class families – people who lacked the savings or other income to survive on soldiers' meagre pay of $1.10 a day. The local fund's officials also arranged for cheap coal when prices soared after 1916 and helped soldiers' dependants who faced a variety of problems with landlords, mortgage holders, hospitals, and state bureaucracies. Eventually the fund's staff also had to handle family crises when a mother died or became incapacitated or, in the eyes of the administrators, showed morally questionable behaviour.[26]

From the beginning the fund's officers and administrators made loud public statements about the recipients' right to this support in return for the military service of their menfolk. "The fund is not a charity," a promotional article declared early in 1915. "Formerly her husband or son was the breadwinner, to-day the Patriotic Fund simply takes this place and the pay envelope comes in regularly just the same." Towards the end of the war, the Relief Committee patted itself on the back for avoiding "the objectionable features of organized Charity which has as its basis often an 'existence' and not the 'decent living' which the fund desires dependents of enlisted men to have." A letter to the press from a disgruntled applicant signing herself "A British Soldier's Wife" suggests how deeply this distinction was rooted. "We have done our duty and our husbands are doing theirs, but we want our rights, and we want them straight way," she wrote. "We do not want charity; most of us are too British to accept it; but we want our husbands to go away knowing that their families are getting what has been promised them right away."[27]

Initially the fund had also accepted responsibility for helping to find work for returned soldiers, who were usually wounded, but early in 1916 a Soldiers' Aid Commission took over this responsibility. This body saw its role primarily as facilitating the reintegration of the veterans into the city's social and economic life rather than handing out any kind of financial help. In 1918, however, the commission's chief administrator finally convinced the board of the need for a relief fund to be made available in the form of loans. In the two years after the Armistice, the work of the Canadian Patriotic Fund and the Soldiers' Aid Commission increasingly tended to overlap. Both had nonetheless enormously expanded public expectations of the state's responsibility to help working-class families in need. Although they were officially non-governmental organizations, they were so closely attached to the national war effort and to the treatment of soldiers' families that the distinction was undoubtedly lost on the public by the end of the war.[28]

The idea that motherhood could be a public service was an important ideological legacy of the war period. At a more practical level, so too was the discovery of the desperate need in many working-class families – a need so great that the existing charities and relief programs were unable to cope with it adequately. Out of this experience came an intense national debate about "mothers' pensions," which was fundamentally different from the discussions that had led to workers' compensation legislation a few years earlier. This time the leading voices were upper-class women and a number of male supporters, generally people who had experience in charity work. One of the hearings that the provincial government held on this issue took place in Hamilton in February 1919. The first person to present himself was W.H. Lovering, the secretary and chief administrator of the Canadian Patriotic Fund and an activist in Catholic charity and the Children's Aid Society. He was followed by a parade of charity workers and labour leaders who consistently supported the idea that mothers who were living without the benefit of husbands' wages, especially mothers widowed and deserted, had a right to state support as agents of the government in "maintaining the children in the home in the way the State demanded." The central concern here was the children, not the women themselves. Payments were for mothering, not independent breadwinning.[29]

Numerous women's, social-welfare, professional, and labour groups aired the same sentiments across the province (and across the country), and in 1920 the Ontario government carried through with mothers' allowances legislation. Like the law establishing Children's Aid Societies three decades earlier, this program aimed at keeping children in a home environment rather than in an orphanage. A single mother in distress was now to be "an employee of the state, receiving remuneration for services rendered in the proper care of her children."

According to Walter Rollo, these children could then "be properly cared for, educated and grow up to be useful citizens and to prevent the children on account of lack of home training from drifting into police courts, jails, houses of correction and penitentiaries."[30]

Many single mothers in distress could expect no help from this new program; in the first year a quarter of the 3,500 applications across the province were rejected. Generally, only widows with more than one child (and at least one child below the school-leaving age or permanently incapacitated) who did not have more than $350 in liquid assets or a house worth more than $2,500 could apply for assistance. A woman with a husband in an asylum (but not a penitentiary) or a permanently disabled spouse could also be considered (women with tubercular husbands soon became a growing part of the program). Widows with only one child (a number nearly equal to all those with more than one) were ineligible, on the assumption that the offspring could easily be absorbed into another family household as a domestic or dependent kin. Early in the life of the program, Hamilton labour leaders were unable to convince the government to extend the program to mothers with only one child. Only in 1935 – well after other provinces – did the new Liberal government at Queen's Park finally relent.

Suspicions about the moral soundness of unmarried, deserted, and divorced mothers also blocked those categories from applying (although after 1921 wives whose husbands had been absent for at least five years were included, as were, in 1935, those abandoned for more than three years). Instead, the province passed two new laws in 1922 to put more pressure on errant fathers to support their families: the Children of Unmarried Parents Act and the Deserted Wives and Children's Maintenance Act. Mothers also

had to be British subjects, by birth or naturalization, and resident in Canada for at least three years, in Ontario for two years, and in her municipality one year before application. Many impoverished newcomers were thus excluded from the program. Not surprisingly, only 101 Hamilton widows qualified for an allowance in 1921, 197 in 1926, and 297 in 1930. In the following year census-takers counted more than 3,500 widowed, divorced, unmarried, and abandoned women with children in Hamilton.[31]

In 1927 the state took another step to support working-class dependants, this time the elderly. Publicly supported old-age pensions had been on the agenda of numerous labour and social-reform groups since just before World War One, and got widespread endorsement immediately after the war. They had already been introduced in some form in other industrialized countries (excluding the United States) and were recommended by a parliamentary committee in 1924. But it took a political crisis in the House of Commons to get them incorporated into legislation. In 1926 Winnipeg Labour MPs J.S. Woodsworth and A.A. Heaps agreed to support the Mackenzie King government in return for pension legislation, which was passed the next year. The new act required provincial co-operation, and an extremely reluctant Ontario government did not opt in until 1929.[32]

The new legislation, assuming that, even if currently unemployed, the younger generation still had primary responsibility for looking after their aging mothers and fathers, made pensions available only to those without any family support. Applicants had to be at least 70 years old, British subjects, and residents of Canada for at least 20 consecutive years and Ontario for 5. They also had to be clearly destitute (they were not allowed to have an income of more than $125 a year above their pensions). By 1940 only 6 per cent of new old-age pension recipients in Hamilton were "foreign born," compared to close to 10 per cent in the total population. Residents of old-age homes were not permitted to apply.[33]

Even so, by 1931 some 1,900 Hamiltonians – nearly two out of five over the age of 69 – had got over all these hurdles, a sign that points to the level of need among the city's elderly. A year later tight-fisted provincial officials were pushing many people off the pension rolls in an effort to compel more children of applicants to support their parents. Like workers' compensation, veterans' pensions, and mothers' allowances, another state program that had begun with a flourish of rhetoric about entitlement had quickly devolved into a form of state-sponsored, heavily restricted charity.

Through No Fault of Their Own

All of these efforts – the private and public outdoor relief, the institutional houses and homes, and the new government programs – were designed only to assist unemployable people from families in which no male breadwinner could provide for his dependants. What was to be done when large numbers of able-bodied men could not find work because local employers had simply laid them off?

When, in the slack winter months, seasonal unemployment hit some workers, especially unskilled labourers, the city's relief officer doled out small sums in return for hard labour on various city projects, organized out of a "labour bureau." Workers who were some combination of single, unskilled, and transient made up the bulk of these relief recipients. The numbers of these wintertime cases swelled whenever the economy slumped, and those spells only got longer in the early 20th century, particularly between the world wars.[34] These were unemployed wage-earners who normally never went near a relief office, and typically delayed as long as possible before seeking aid. The largest numbers had young families (and therefore no secondary wage-earners) or had arrived in the city relatively recently. Private charities could not handle the extra demand and turned to the municipality to deal with this new category of need. As each economic crisis deepened, embittered wage-earners also demanded that the state take on extra responsibility for helping the unemployed.[35]

The depressions of the 1890s and 1907–9 brought many workers to the city relief office's door, but it was the 1913–15 slump that first forced the city council to open a much bigger relief fund and arrange for several special public works projects. The interwar depressions were even more challenging. Governments at all three levels eventually surmised that they were facing a crisis on a scale not seen since the 19th century, a crisis for which private charity would never suffice. In the early 1920s and again in the early 1930s, the federal government agreed for the first time to enter cost-sharing programs with the Ontario government and cities such as Hamilton to help pay local relief costs (Hamilton businessmen and politicians took the lead in pushing for this increased government involvement). In each of these three worsening slumps, the city distributed relief but also organized temporary jobs during the winter months for the able-bodied unemployed – breaking stones, cutting wood, or digging roads and sewers in three-days shifts (much to the chagrin of the city engineer, who preferred more "efficient" labour). The scale of the crisis was evident by 1931, when the city distributed almost $700,000 in relief, compared to only $44,000 in 1929. Private charities doled out only one-seventh of that figure. After 1932 works projects were less important than direct relief. But relief payments continued to climb to the spring of 1933, when 8,500 families were on the "dole" – some 25 per cent of the city's population, a proportion comparable to the hard winters of 1914–15 and 1921–22. Only in the 1930s, when the average length of time on relief continued to rise, did government officials at any level begin to view these economic crises as anything more than a temporary calamity that would soon disappear.[36]

By the outbreak of World War Two, the one other state welfare program that could have assisted workers who were jobless through no fault of their own remained a non-starter – unemployment insurance. The idea was to create a fund from which unemployed wage-earners could draw relief. Britain and other European countries had implemented versions of such programs before World War One, and the Ontario Commission on Unemployment gave the idea its first public endorsement in its 1916 report. The labour movement and other social-reform groups were also agitating for some unemployment-insurance program by the end of the war. The idea got support in 1919 from the federal Royal Commission on Industrial Relations, Liberal Party of Canada, and International Labour Conference in Washington. The political momentum for such a program died with the defeat of the postwar workers' revolt, and only the mass unemployment of the 1930s brought it back onto the political agenda. By the middle of that decade, workers' movements in Canada had put unemployment insurance back at the centre of their political demands, and even leading businessmen were advocating some form of the plan to stave off financial crises for the state. In a surprise move Prime Minister R.B. Bennett included it in his New Deal package of reforms in 1935. His legislation quickly passed through Parliament, but the courts struck it down as being outside

federal jurisdiction. Mackenzie King's new Liberal government tested the waters of provincial consent in 1938 with a new bill, but found too much opposition in the provincial capitals. The final enactment of an unemployment insurance plan in 1940 owed much to fears about postwar unemployment. For the previous half-century, then, Hamilton's unemployed wage-earners and their families were never able to benefit from the kind of state program that had been in place in Britain since 1909.[37]

Only the Deserving

Members of working-class families who approached charitable and relief agencies in Hamilton in the half-century before World War Two soon discovered that they would have to jump a number of hurdles before getting any material assistance. If they were newcomers to the city, and especially if they were single men or not Anglo-Canadian, they might face pressure to leave so that local residents could get more attention. Those living in the new suburbs just beyond the boundaries of the city would have to turn to financially cautious township councils for help. In all cases, their motives in applying for aid were suspect from the start.

Throughout the whole period, applicants to both private charities and state-sponsored programs faced an abiding mistrust of whether they were really "deserving." Charity workers were relentlessly suspicious of dishonesty and "pauperism" – of people, that is, who resorted to living off charity rather than seeking to maintain themselves through wage labour. In 1892 the president of the Ladies' Benevolent Society warned against "the success of imposters, owing to the carelessness of the benevolent," and applicants who "are encouraged in their evil ways, becoming worse and worse." This central precept of 19th-century charity died hard in Hamilton.

"To adopt a policy of giving relief to all who ask for it would be to put a premium on shiftlessness and invite an epidemic of malingering," the *Spectator*'s editor declared in 1926. A few years later an unemployed steelworker lined up all night for city relief, only to be confronted with open allegations and insults. "Why the hell ain't you working?" the staff wanted to know.[38]

Even the new social-assistance programs of the World War One period and later, based on the publicly proclaimed "right" of the recipient to support, were relentless in their search for the "undeserving." The Canadian Patriotic Fund went so far as to write to all clergymen in the city asking them to watch the relief recipients for any transgressions and then to encourage neighbours to report "any cases in which the fund may possibly seem to be abused." The Relief Committee was subsequently inundated with anonymous reports, most of which proved to be erroneous. "Guard the Fund, Do Not Pauperize, Do Not Patronise," the committee told its staff. As soon as a physically fit soldier was discharged he was expected to take up his responsibilities as breadwinner, and his family's allowance was cut off immediately.[39] Applicants for the new mothers' allowance and old-age pensions were rigorously scrutinized to determine their eligibility. They had to provide exhaustive information on family finances, and their homes were examined for frills such as cars or radios. The staff of the workers' compensation and veterans' pension boards also advised vigilance against "malingering," while the Mothers' Allowance Commission set a full-time medical officer to work in 1931 to try to weed out cases in which seriously incapacitated husbands could do some kind of wage-earning work.[40]

What did these people mean by "deserving" cases? Normally the charities and relief programs assumed that their main clientele lacked a male breadwinner to provide income and did not have the ability to maintain themselves – the widowed, sick, injured, young, and elderly in particular. Even drawing precise lines around this group could often perplex Hamilton's various relief administrators because they wanted irrefutable proof that the people they were helping had no other personal assets or willing relatives. They spent a lot of their time assessing marginal cases. Their criteria in judging applicants were also overtly moral. Especially with women, they wanted to be assured about sexual propriety, good housekeeping habits, industriousness, and deferential and co-operative behaviour, conditions that coincided with mothers' allowance legislation that barred unmarried, deserted, and divorced mothers on moral grounds. Common-law widows got nothing from the Workmen's Compensation Board either, and other widows could be cut off if their morality was thrown into question or if they failed to keep their households "in a manner which the Board deems satisfactory." Snitching by neighbours was again encouraged and could be the basis of rejection.[41]

Not surprisingly, few of these charity and relief administrators were ever comfortable with providing help to able-bodied unemployed men. The hardy old assumption that the unemployed breadwinner was responsible for his own joblessness lingered on after the turn of the century even when the cause was patently beyond that worker's control. Increasingly that notion had to co-exist, awkwardly and uncomfortably, with the recognition that labour markets were impersonal and highly unstable in this boom and bust economy. Several times in the decade before World War One, for example, the St. George's Benevolent Society complained about the large number of British immigrants who found themselves stranded on arrival in the city because unscrupulous immigration and labour agents back home had misled them about the real prospects of work in Hamilton or other Canadian cities. These societies were even more perplexed by the masses of unemployed – newcomers and long-time residents alike – needing relief during major business downturns. At those moments, like the unemployed themselves, the organizations turned to the local government for action. At that point, proving eligibility for relief could be an uphill battle. By the 1930s the city's welfare commissioner was insisting that unemployed homeowners had to mortgage their houses and live off the loans before they could expect help from the city.[42]

Welfare administrators also worried about how recipients of charity or relief might knock at the doors of more than one agency to get hand-outs – the slippery slope to "pauperism." They proposed closer co-operation among charities to prevent too much support for the same families, but in this regard they made only limited progress at best. Before World War One, each of the many societies, institutions, and agencies normally undertook its own fund-raising canvass of the city. They handled their own clienteles with little reference to what other societies or institutions might be doing. From time to time they communicated with each other about specific cases – a society attempting to get a child into an orphanage, an aged person into a home, a sick or injured person into the hospital, or simply trying to find some agency to take an individual. Sometimes the city relief officer was also involved in assessing individual need for some of the charities.

In many cities of Britain and North America, debate raged over how to overcome this lack of co-ordination, and the most commonly discussed solution was the establishment of a charity organization society, which would pull together local relief efforts and impose consistent standards.[43] In Hamilton efforts to co-operate were sporadic and short-lived before the 1920s. Only when the great economic depressions of the period strained their resources to the limit did local charities start to co-operate, usually with the help of the city relief department. In 1891–93 and again in 1908–9 they created an organization known as the Associated Charities to administer a common relief fund for the much larger numbers in need. In both cases the effort at co-ordination lapsed when fuller employment returned, and not until the serious crisis of the 1913–15 slump was it renewed.[44]

At that point a "Confidential Exchange" was first established in the civic relief department. Then the major charities and the city merged their relief work into a new Hamilton United Relief Association in the fall of 1914. Hobson acted as chair at the founding meeting. The association undertook joint fundraising and distributed groceries and necessities to a few thousand men in return for short stints on civic works projects or stone-breaking and wood-cutting. Marion Crerar, a veteran of many charitable boards in the city and convenor of the new organization's auxiliary of "lady visitors," agreed to participate only on the assurance that "a complete loose leaf and index system was being installed whereby the committee knew that people could not duplicate orders given them." She was relieved that "Hamilton has at last arrived at a stage where charity will be handled systematically." She said she knew of cases "where people simply lived on charity. The whole family lived at ease while the eldest daughter played the piano at her leisure." The association shut down in May 1915 as the war economy gradually absorbed the jobless.[45] But the city and the charities had to open a similar, even larger relief operation late in 1921. Once again, a Citizens' Relief Committee emerged to work with the city's relief department.[46]

By that point both the mayor (clothing manufacturer George Coppley) and the local Chamber of Commerce were anxious to develop a program run by prominent citizens outside the municipal government.[47] Their concern meshed with growing interest among female voluntary charity workers, led by the upper-class Mary Hawkins, to co-ordinate their activities more effectively. The local medical society was also promoting such an effort. The Chamber of Commerce therefore organized a series of discussions with these groups, all of whom were troubled by the inefficiency of the existing fragmented system and the need for "businesslike benevolence." Businessmen in particular hoped that this approach could stave off any further drains on government treasuries and demands for state intervention to support the poor. They consulted "experts in relief, charitable, general welfare, psychiatric and sanitary work." The model they chose was common in many cities across North America in which business and the new profession of social work were looking to new methods of dealing with the poor. Both groups shared a desire to get the poor off charity and relief – the businessmen because they disliked the cost and the threat to industrial discipline, and the social workers because they believed in teaching self-reliance as the fundamental solution to poverty.

In 1923 the Chamber of Commerce was able to play midwife at the birth of the new non-governmental Central Bureau of Social Agencies, organized to bring a more rigorous, "scientific," and "efficient" approach to charity and relief work (renamed the Central Bureau of Family Welfare in 1929 and the Family Service Bureau in 1935). Taking up a familiar refrain, the bureau's first president, businessman R.L. Smith, stated that it would weed out a growing "mendicant class" who were "gradually becoming habitual seekers for aid [and] could move

about from one organization to another." There were plans for "a complete survey of the city" so that "all those who are either permanently or temporarily in need of assistance, can be charted and systematically and scientifically dealt with." By 1926 the bureau had developed central files on over 4,000 families from 76 charitable and social-welfare agencies, including health-care groups, churches, schools and youth workers.[48]

The bureau evidently had trouble getting full co-operation from many organizations, including the city relief department, and in 1927 it shed its co-ordinating functions to concentrate on family casework. Once again, the Chamber of Commerce intervened that year to oversee the birth of two new co-ordinating organizations: on the one hand, the Council of Social Agencies, which took over the central card index of charity clients (renamed the Social Service Exchange) and ran educational programs for member agencies on social-work practice; and, on the other, the Hamilton Community Fund, the business-dominated fundraiser for all participating charitable societies and institutions (later renamed the Community Chest). A single executive secretary served both organizations. Only 18 agencies participated in the Community Fund, but the Council of Social Agencies was soon patting itself on the back for preventing 703 families from getting more than one Christmas basket. Clergymen in particular seemed reticent to register their parishioners' names in the central files, and the city's relief officer insisted that the council should not get the names of citizens getting handouts from the city because they were receiving help as a right, not as charity.

The rising tide of needy families after 1929 also made co-ordination difficult. Sociologist Harry Cassidy, who surveyed Hamilton's relief activities in the winter of 1930–31, found the city's own relief program still co-existing with the work of more than 20 distinct organizations. A provincial investigator who submitted a report on the city's relief work was disgusted. Various agencies had their own investigators, and apparently there was "no material harmony or co-ordination among any of them." The investigator concluded that "instead of co-ordination rivalry exists." When the Ottawa-based Canadian Welfare Council was asked to survey Hamilton's social-welfare activities in 1937, it found little commitment to or co-operation with the local Council of Social Agencies. Only 14 of the 43 members (including by that time the city relief department) made regular use of the Social Service Exchange. Clearly the Council of Social Agencies had not fundamentally transformed charity and relief practice in the city.[49]

At the end of the 1930s, then, a working-class family in distress would have found a jumble of charity and relief agencies with only slightly more regular interaction than a similar family would have encountered in the 1890s. Aside from the city itself, almost all the groups that provided material help still ran their own shows and had only limited contact with each other.[50] As a result, working-class families tended to reach out through the familiar personal networks of neighbourhood, ethnicity, and religion, though many more had come to rely on help from state relief.

Charity and relief workers continued to see the challenge facing them as one of keeping the access to relief from degenerating into "pauperism" among the "undeserving."[51] The only major change over a half-century was a post–World War One preference for the word "dependence" over pauperism. Ultimately, the persistent hegemonic discourse of mistrust that still predominated in relief activities in the 1920s and 1930s helped to deflect more critical analyses of the growing problem of unemployment in the city.

Investigation

The mistrust of impoverished workers led directly to a second constant feature of welfare work – surveillance of their daily lives. All applicants were rigorously investigated and, in most cases, regulated through frequent visits to their homes. From the 1890s through to the 1930s, all private charity cases, applicants for city relief, or would-be inmates of a charitable institution had a designated "visitor" sitting at their kitchen tables asking probing questions and casting a critical eye around the household before any material help arrived. This took place even during interwar unemployment crises when the numbers soared into the thousands.[52]

Initially, two traditions of visiting co-existed in the city's charitable work. The ethnic charities and some of the churches used only men – usually prominent businessmen and professionals – to enter the workers' homes and assess their needs. The city's relief officer was also a man throughout the whole period, and the municipal committee that oversaw the House of Refuge was likewise all made up of men. To get into the city's Home for the Aged and Infirm, a person had to be investigated by the relief officer and perhaps even the medical officer of health and a special subcommittee of the city's property and licence committee. In each of the major unemployment crises, the city's relief work eventually involved some kind of investigation before relief was provided.[53]

Most other charities and the later state programs drew on the well-established practice of sending out "visiting ladies." Around the turn of the century these were invariably the wives (and occasionally the daughters) of the city's leading businessmen and professionals, people who carried into working-class households both a sympathy for their fellow females and a squeamish discomfort and patronizing concern to implant bourgeois habits and values.[54] By the 1890s, for example, the Ladies' Benevolent Society had a well-developed network of ward visitors who reported to the board regularly on the deserving and undeserving applicants and then dispensed the relief.[55] An exception to this general pattern may have been the women of the Ladies' Aid groups in some working-class neighbourhoods. These women were more often themselves members of working-class families living a few streets away, and they therefore crossed no great social divide in their visits to the sick and needy.[56] But, in the overall range of institutional charities, working-class charity workers were far outnumbered by those from the upper and middle classes.

All these men and women were unpaid volunteers with no particular training or consistent standards to apply. An entry in the minutes of the board of the Ladies' Benevolent Society in 1899 highlighted how subjective their assessments of applicants could be. One visitor recommended that a recently widowed woman give up her children to the Children's Aid Society because she "was not the most suitable person (in her opinion) to have the care of them" and should be pushed into wage labour. Another visitor, challenging that judgment, insisted that the woman was "a hardworking industrious woman, and most anxious to keep her children with her, promising to send the little girl to school regularly." There is no record of how this debate was resolved. Clearly, aid for families like this one hinged on casual, flexible, and highly moralistic criteria. In the case of the House of Refuge, the direct involvement of city aldermen in the assessment process meant that political influence and patronage could easily come into play. This amateurism was nonetheless cherished as fulfilling the Christian ideal of "personal service."

In the words of a city clergyman, addressing a meeting of charity workers in 1911, "What men and women often require in this life is oftentimes the hand-grasp, or a sympathetic word, the moral support of human fellowship." More fundamentally, the upper-class men and women who administered the great majority of the relief were concerned about extending a bond between social classes through their philanthropy.[57]

Professionalism was slow to emerge in Hamilton's charity work. In the early 20th century the Protestant church deaconesses visited the poor to provide both spiritual and material help.[58] Otherwise, for most of the years between the 1890s and World War One, Relief Officer McMenemy was the only full-time investigator of charity cases, and private societies and institutions sometimes relied on him for reports. By 1911 he had at least one female assistant. Some three years later so few full-time relief workers were available for the emergency relief program to sniff out any "professional mendicants" that the city had to use inspectors from the Board of Health.[59]

The new social-welfare demands of wartime society expanded the pool of full-time investigators. When the Canadian Patriotic Fund wanted more contact with the soldiers' wives whom it was supporting, it followed in the old tradition by calling on experienced upper-class visitors, at first businessmen like George Coppley of the St. George's Benevolent Society and then several upper-class women. The Soldiers' Aid Commission enlisted A.W. Kaye, who had extensive experience in handling relief cases during the prewar depression. Both organizations also took a new step by hiring a small number of full-time female visitors. The CPF staff were responsible for the initial judgment on the family's particular needs for support, for regular checkups on changed circumstances (including working children, illnesses, and any accusations of mis-behaviour lodged against the recipients), and in general "conditions of health, home, thrift, conduct, [and] education." During 1918 alone, CPF visitors knocked on the doors of more than 6,000 homes in working-class Hamilton, while visitors from the Soldiers' Aid Commission crossed over 3,000 thresholds in each of the next two years. These women nonetheless continued to work with committees of upper-class men and women.[60] Lovering, chair of the CPF's Relief Committee, told a government inquiry in 1919 that "the trained social worker would need the vision, imagination and big heartedness of the volunteer worker." Crerar, another experienced "visiting lady," similarly argued that upper-class women like herself should have their long experience recognized in any welfare programs.[61]

Male wage-earners took a slightly different position. Most of them rarely confronted this world of charity administration, whether because they were ineligible or because they dreaded the dishonour of admitting their failure as breadwinners. The better-paid, more regularly employed men knew little of the suffering, humiliation, and negotiation faced by impoverished women. As Rollo admitted in 1919, "I don't know that the Trades and Labor Council could give any direct evidence as to the need, as they do not come in direct contact with it in the way that women of the City of Hamilton would do, who have given a great deal of their time and money in trying to relieve cases of distress." The Council simply made small annual donations to select charities.[62]

A few did nonetheless use the occasion of hearings on mothers' allowances in 1919 to argue publicly for a different approach to helping. Rollo wanted the staff of any new program to be people with "a knowledge of the conditions of the average workingman and family." A.

Griffiths, speaking for the Independent Labor Party, insisted:

> There should be a representative from the same class as the widows who would have to receive the pensions ... preferably a mother who has been recognized in the locality as being a mother. We have all met those people whom the locality always recognize as being "motherly." Those are the people who can do the best work and instruct.

Griffiths also argued against aggressive interventionism in the new program: "It seems to me that it would be making it a charity, if we were going to hand it out and say, 'You should do so and so with it.'" While he acknowledged the "splendid work" done by women workers in Hamilton, he added, "Sometimes there have been busybodies who went around and the mother finally told them to keep out."[63]

After the war unpaid volunteers still ran many charitable activities, including the local mothers' allowance and old-age pension boards. But increasingly on their doorsteps poor women faced full-time, middle-class, female investigators in place of volunteers. The visitors were recruited for the postwar municipal relief work and for the investigative work of the new mothers' allowance program and, much later, for old-age pension administration.[64] Gradually they also appeared in private social agencies. Some of these were Hamilton's first welfare workers trained in the emerging profession of social work, but most were not. Public-health nursing or education were more common backgrounds for the women selected as investigators in mothers' allowance programs in the 1920s and civic relief work in the 1930s, for example. The mothers' allowance program was more enmeshed in the Ontario Conservative Party's patronage networks than in the new forums of social work. Yet these visitors were part of larger bureaucratic systems whose procedures they had to follow, and whose rules they had to enforce. With a crippling caseload and limited resources, the investigators nonetheless turned regularly to the older charitable agencies for help.[65]

The driving wedge of the social-work profession was the Central Bureau of Social Agencies. One of the bureau's prime concerns was to establish "family case work" by properly trained experts as the key approach to handling the poor. That meant a heavy dose of psychology in assessing families, along with the cool detachment of professional "objectivity." The bureau began with two experienced social workers brought in from Toronto, assisted by some "special volunteer workers" to investigate "doubtful cases." In 1926 it opened an east-end office under the supervision of an experienced social worker from Akron, Ohio. A trained caseworker was available to work with any charitable agency that could use her help with their clients. By 1930 five caseworkers were roaming the city, and an East End Welfare Club was bringing together nurses and social workers from factories, schools, and social agencies for biweekly noon-hour meetings "to discuss common needs and problems." A few voluntary agencies also began hiring graduates of social-work programs.[66]

Investigation of family circumstances permitted a social worker to plan what she believed was an appropriate strategy for the family's recovery and work with the relevant organizations to bring about the family's self-sufficiency (rather than dispensing any charity themselves). This process inevitably involved constant supervision. According to the bureau's president, the social worker would use "observation and interviews" to determine "the real cause of their trouble," and work out with the family "the best

method of pulling themselves out of the hole and keeping out." This work required "a good deal of hard, patient work, the interviewing of many people and the handling of the everlasting problem with intelligence, sympathy and firmness." In the words of a local journalist, a Family Welfare visitor was "something of a detective, a lawyer, a doctor, a diplomat, a spiritual adviser, a loving sister, and a tender-hearted mother."[67]

These visitations were probably more consistent and systematic than those made by the old-style volunteers, and the new professionals carried a much greater conviction that their approach would actually eradicate poverty, rather than just apply short-term band-aids. Professional confidence, bordering on arrogance, presented this work as rational and scientific, based on sound principles rather than ad-hoc amateurism. The parallels with "scientific" management or "scientific" mothering were clear, not least to their business supporters. Yet, in many ways, not so much had changed since the 1890s. Back then, the visiting ladies tried to act "not as almsgivers, but as sympathetic friends, leaving the giving of required help to other agencies," wherever possible providing "much useful information on domestic management." For those in need of an income to tide their families through a crisis, however, there may have been an important difference in the new casework of the professionalizing social workers: they did not believe in giving much material aid. "Relief itself has no moral qualities," argued M.S. Thompson, executive secretary of the Central Bureau of Social Agencies in 1925, as she proudly cited instances "where families had been put back on their feet again without the actual giving out of relief." In 1927 a bureau speaker "looked forward to the day when there would be less bread and coal and clothing purchased, and more stress placed on education and encouragement." The president of the St. George's Benevolent Society had undoubtedly been right when predicting in 1909 that the arrival of more professional, scientific approaches to charity would mean that "the Relief given out by an unsentimental, coldly calculating machine would be far less than it is now. Better to make a few mistakes than kill the kind impulses aroused by a national [ethnic] sentiment."[68]

Still, the shift to professionals did not sweep aside all amateurism. Old and new practices co-existed throughout the interwar period, much to the chagrin of social workers. In 1932 a provincial relief inspector was dismayed to discover that Hamilton's relief administration was under the control of a left-wing Labor controller, Sam Lawrence, who trusted "too much to the honesty of the people they are dealing with and to some of the neighbours reporting certain matters to the relief office," without fixed relief rates or home investigation (though neighbours were interviewed). Indeed, with the size of the unemployment crisis, even the five social workers at the Central Bureau of Family Welfare "found it well nigh impossible to give the time and personal service necessary to preserve the family morale and give the understanding sympathy and encouragement which would tend to lessen the burden."[69]

The 1930s nonetheless saw major changes. In 1932 Hamilton created a new public welfare board, changed the name of the relief department to the Public Welfare Department, and replaced the word "relief" with "assistance." Some two years later a dramatically new system of administering this program began. Families no longer showed up at a central depot to face a battery of questions and then leave with vouchers for groceries, fuel, or rent. Now a family was visited at home every ten days by one of forty-two full-time municipal relief investigators, half of

them women, to determine its eligibility. These visitors observed "the daily life of each family, their mental or physical condition, and the general environment of the home," and recorded the details in a central registry. The welfare workers were ostensibly "able to correct many undesirable conditions developing in the home through unemployment and bad environment," referring particularly bad cases to the relevant social agencies. They also lectured housewives on how to shop economically enough to live on the relief allowance. Within three months they had driven some 6,000 recipients in 1,200 families off the rolls, and found 2,000 households in which children's income had not been reported. "Well, boys," Welfare Commissioner A.P. Kappelle told a group of unemployed men in 1936, "to tell you the truth, I have a dirty job."[70]

Professionally trained social workers were nonetheless still concerned that so many full-time welfare workers, including the city's many new investigators, had no social-work credentials. In 1937 the Canadian Welfare Council criticized the lack of professional social-work standards in so many of the charitable agencies and institutions that it surveyed in Hamilton. Surveillance of working-class households in crisis in this city was more intense and regular, but professionalism among the investigators still had only a toehold before World War Two.[71]

Correcting Bad Habits

Not surprisingly, then, any Hamilton workers who turned to these agencies or programs for financial help at any point between the 1890s and the 1930s could expect to have to put up with a third central feature of welfare administration that never fundamentally changed: an effort to make them alter their behaviour. In the 1890s the Ladies' Benevolent Society aimed "not only to relieve want but to prevent it, by helping the poor to help themselves," and virtually all relief administrators thereafter insisted on using the process of giving charity as an educational experience to promote self-help and self-discipline. It was certainly significant that the leading secular organization to which many Hamilton charity workers belonged up to World War One was appropriately known as the Canadian Conference on Charities and Correction and included officers of prisons and other penal institutions as well as the societies and institutions inclined to charitable work.[72]

Recipients of material help got the unmistakable lesson that looking for charity outside their families would bring little comfort. Relief administrators also continued to believe in the power of physical labour to teach recipients that they would get nothing without hard work. Within the charitable "homes," manual labour was part of the daily regime. Residents of the Girls' Home were taught needlework and other domestic skills that they were expected to apply in the institution and presumably in their future work as domestics or mothers. Male residents of the House of Refuge had to cut wood, sweep the streets, and perform other tasks around the building, even if they paid board. Right through to the 1930s, unemployed male breadwinners had to show a willingness to put in time on city make-work projects before getting their food, clothing, and fuel.[73]

The unpleasantness of life inside charitable institutions was also supposed to educate both inmates and those outside about the importance of self-sufficiency. The old-age homes, especially the Home for the Aged and Infirm, had a reputation for stern discipline and management that made clear that there would be no easy ride through the golden years. Residents were subject to strict rules, could not leave without permission, and, under Ontario law, even lost their right to vote. Speakers in a Trades and Labor Council discussion of old-age pensions in 1912 noted "many cases where elderly people endured great privation rather than enter a public institution," a reluctance that interviewees in the 1970s remembered well. A city alderman must have recognized this stigma when in 1929 he barred a newspaper from photographing a 95-year-old resident of the city-run old-age home on the grounds that the man should not have to suffer the embarrassment of being publicly identified. Similarly, like the mothers' allowance program, city relief in the 1930s required applicants to sacrifice luxuries, especially radios, car licences, and liquor permits.[74]

Yet teaching impoverished workers better habits was considered a highly important task. Charity workers had been trying to do so for decades, but the new social-work professionals staked the credibility of their expertise on their claims to know how best to intervene in workers' lives to nudge and prod them into individual self-sufficiency. They talked about more social and "environmental" causes of poverty – including unavoidable unemployment and bad housing – but still laced their analysis with the moralism of the preceding century, now more often expressed in the new language of eugenics and psychology. In 1929 the Central Bureau of Family Welfare said that the causes of nearly two out of five of its client families' problems were economic (principally unemployment), but also still listed "bad housekeeping," "infelicity," "intemperance," "begging tendency," "character defects," and "immorality" as contributing factors. According to a bureau speaker, it was "the social worker's duty to put virtue into them to stiffen their backs – to build out of weakness a new source of strength." The bureau's executive secretary cited "re-education, the changing of habits, and the development of personality and character" as "the service which social case-workers should render."[75]

Almost invariably this intervention by any kind of welfare worker assumed that workers could simply not sort out their own problems. The Canadian Patriotic Fund's Relief Committee was explicit that its staff were "in the position of 'Big Brothers' to the families of those men who are 'Out There' and are to take the position of the former head of household." In a celebratory publication released after the war, the local Hamilton branch cited a handful of cases that suggested the importance of their work with soldiers' families. In one instance a woman developed some unspecified but clearly unacceptable relationship with "an undesirable boarder, separated from his wife." The CPF's staff brought in the Children's Aid Society, which unsuccessfully attempted to get custody of her children. The Fund then punished her by cutting her off their payroll and forcing her to work for wages and to make her own arrangements for child care. In another case, the CPF's visitor decided that a soldier's wife was "a bad manager, handicapped by deafness," who let her 11-year-old daughter do too much of the shopping. Her allowance from the Fund was therefore administered for her. A third woman took in a young female boarder "with an unenviable reputation," who brought "undesirable characters" to the house, apparently upsetting some neighbours. When the wife dug in her heels against the visitor's demand that she get rid of her boarder, the Children's Aid Society was brought in to scoop up her two small boys, and steady badgering got her to promise to get a job and "remove herself from her companions." In each case the story concluded with the return of order, stability, and acceptable morality as a result of the Fund's intervention. What the chronicler failed to add was that the women's independence of action was never a serious consideration.[76]

The mothers' allowance program was equally explicit about the state standing in for the absent husband and intervening on behalf of his children. It gave the full-time investigators wide latitude to manage their clients' lives. The Hamilton office's visitor, E.M. Storms, made frequent return trips to help a mother "work out a suitable plan under which the home may be maintained" and to supervise her behaviour. Moral renewal was Storms's central concern, interpreted through the lens of bourgeois preoccupations with maternalism, order, and cleanliness in housekeeping. Each year she and the other provincial investigators provided glowing reports of reunited families, healthier, better-mannered children, more regular school attendance, improved housing, and tidier homes, often sprinkled with quotations from "grateful" mothers.[77]

They also revealed that they were prepared to coerce and manipulate some women. They negotiated behind their backs with teachers, truant officers, and Big Brother workers to guarantee a child's school attendance. They reported "children wrongly kept at home, or exemption papers [under the Adolescent School Attendance Act] secured by falsifying age or misrepresentation of the need in the home." Investigators wielded the threat to withdraw the allowance against the "unfit" mothers who resisted suggestions to deal with "poor standards in the home." More often they simply lectured their clients on how to change their ways, sometimes on visits every day. "Often the allowance has to be administered to insure the family deriving the proper benefit from it, particularly where the mother is of low mentality," the Mothers' Allowance Commission noted in 1923. A year later it concluded, "Mothers who have been indifferent housekeepers and home makers, through the efforts of the

Investigator and the local Board, become thrifty, cleanly and painstaking." The men from the Hamilton Kiwanis Club who became "Kiwanis Daddies" could also be relied upon "to visit the boy in his home and offer suggestions as to the improvement of conditions." This kind of scrutiny was particularly hard on the small minority of European-born immigrants and non-whites who qualified. Humble compliance in response to these interventions was highly praised, but often the exchanges between mothers and investigators must have been stark confrontations between "rough" and "respectable." Any woman who lost her allowance as "not a fit and proper person" was promptly reported to the Children's Aid Society and other social agencies for further intervention. The official propaganda for the program insisted that a mothers' allowance cheque was not charity, but many women could be forgiven for seeing little difference between the invasiveness of the program and that of other Hamilton charities.[78]

The Central Bureau of Family Welfare boasted in the local press about its aggressive interventions into working-class life, with each case delivering a short parable about the good results of its pushing and badgering. In one, a social worker dug into the health record of a man who allegedly "hated hard work" and determined that the man had been pampered in his childhood because of a heart condition. Attributing the subject's weakness to pure laziness, the social worker asked the man's foreman to give him a "strict warning." She then appeared on his doorstep in the morning to check up on him. When she learned he was still in bed, she sent word up "that it would be wise for him to get dressed and report at the mill at noon." She waited downstairs until he left for work and then got his foreman's promise to report any absenteeism. A social worker told another man who

was reported to have lost his job as a result of a fiery temper "that help could not be continued unless he made an honest effort to do the right thing and that lying in bed in the morning would not bring him work." This warning was followed with a threat to drag him before the magistrate for non-support of his family. "The constant proddings had effect, and after three weeks he started at a new job." In these and several other stories, the impoverished workers had rarely asked the women to enter their lives; generally, the bureau became aware of their plight through reports from neighbours, teachers, employers, or other agencies. And the cases were not a matter of brief encounters: "It often takes years in one particular family for its advice and guidance and assistance to reap their reward in improved living conditions, sounder domestic economy, and happier family arrangements."[79]

In the eyes of the charities and their investigators and visitors, material salvation was seen as an individual or at most a family project. Late-19th-century charity workers may have seen personal moral failing behind much poverty, but the new social workers had little more than a smattering of new psychological language to make the same case. As the head social worker at the Central Bureau of Social Agencies argued in 1926, "Poverty is frequently the sign of a complexity of physical, mental and moral handicaps with which heritage and environment have saddled the individual." She continued: "The bureau feels strongly that the development of individuality must be the motive of all its work among families. Relieve a family of personal responsibility and you prepare them for pauperism, beggary, and criminality. Develop a sense of responsibility and you encourage self-respect and self-support."[80]

None of these programs encouraged low-income working-class families to work together

The Dale
Community Centre.
(SLS, LS744)

to solve any of their problems. Only in 1935 did a crack appear in this stern consensus when some social workers began to work with the Dale Community Centre, a small idealistic project of collective self-help started by a handful of unemployed men and women. They got support from the Family Service Bureau for a wide range of programs that soon resembled a settlement house without the patronizing control of middle-class outsiders. The social workers there defined their professional activity as more advisory "group work." "It is not enough that we try therapy on maladjusted individuals," one of them wrote in 1937. "We must help to guide them when the dynamic has been found which galvanizes them into action." This shift in direction represented a significant departure from decades of practice among Hamilton's poor and unemployed.[81]

Less Is Better

When the moment finally came for an actual handout, Hamilton workers would have been conscious of the mistrustful, manipulative, and patronizing intentions of relief administrators. What families in crisis desperately needed was

money. Many charities provided only groceries, clothing, or fuel, or paid a landlord directly, rather than trust the family with cash. In times of serious depression, the city bought clothing in bulk. Retired workers later recalled how many children arrived at school wearing identical shoes or sweaters.[82] But, more important, not one of the public and private programs was willing to provide enough to actually sustain a family. The idea was that those getting aid would still have an incentive to work for the rest of the income they needed or would learn to economize more effectively. As the city's relief officer admitted in 1897, "No organization in Hamilton gave enough relief to prevent the pinch of poverty and the pang of cold."[83]

Right through to the 1930s, all welfare programs stuck to the 19th-century assumption that payments should be less than the earnings of the lowest-paid labourers (a practice springing from the "less eligibility" principle in the English Poor Law legislation of 1834). Handouts to individual families were therefore small.[84] The city's relief program of the early 1920s gave two dollars' worth of goods twice a week for each family and three days' work every two weeks. In 1923 that provision allowed one unemployed man to earn only $10.80 (the average male wage in the city was more than twice that). "I am no shirker, or kicker, either," that man wrote. "But if anyone can tell me how to keep a family, pay rent, light, etc., on that money, they must certainly be money wizards." Sociologist Harry Cassidy agreed a decade later that relief payments did not come close to meeting the basic needs of a working-class family in Ontario. In the 1930s the city's relief department nonetheless reduced its payments in the spring and summer months to encourage the unemployed to take up gardening.[85]

The Canadian Patriotic Fund trumpeted its much more generous level of support, but in practice it too tried to keep the income flowing out to soldiers' wives and mothers as low as possible. In 1915 maximum support for wives and children was capped at $30 a month, and support for childless wives fell to a maximum of $5, with a promise of further cuts in summer months. A few months later the Relief Committee congratulated itself on the "very considerable saving to the fund" that these changes had brought about, In fact, in May 1916 the average payment in Hamilton was only $20. A woman signing herself "Soldier's Wife" wrote to the press in the following year to voice what must have been an increasingly common complaint about such stinginess in the face of the rapidly rising cost of living: "Would it be too generous to allow soldiers' wives a larger check monthly, so as to make it possible to save a little, or are they always to be treated as incapable? There is one thing certain, many are living a life of shame, and the question may be asked why."[86]

The new state welfare programs also handed out inadequate amounts. Workers' compensation payments were never intended to compensate fully for lost wages, and the program was premised on getting workers back into the labour market in one form or another as quickly as possible. For a worker to be eligible for more than medical expenses, a disability had to last more than a week. The worker could then get compensation until a doctor declared him "fit to work" – a controversial decision in many cases in which workers did not feel ready to return to full-time wage-earning. The WCB could also award pensions for permanent disabilities. If it decided that a man's injury would reduce his earning capacity permanently by less than 10 per cent, he got a single lump sum (each body part had a fixed value). Otherwise the Board awarded a pension based on debatable assumptions about the percentage of earnings lost as a result of particular disabilities. The Board dealt with injuries to the body as a result of accidents but hardly any debilitating diseases.[87] Initially the monthly WCB payments were not to exceed 55 per cent of the dead or disabled worker's previous earnings; in 1920 the proportion was raised to two-thirds. As a WCB survey discovered in 1921, three out of five of the permanently disabled pensioners actually had to find some kind of job or, in a small number of cases, had set up small businesses on their own. Only a quarter were classified as "unemployed." This was a program aimed explicitly at male breadwinners. The many women workers in domestic service, retail sales, and clerical work were automatically excluded from the program. In any case, injured female workers were assumed to be able to rely on their families for support; they made up little more than 1 per cent of the claimants in the 1920s.[88]

Income from state programs for married women was never based on their husbands' earnings. The state was clearly not prepared to pay a breadwinner's income to a fatherless family. To begin with, the workers' compensation pension for the widow of a man killed on the job was only $20 a month and $5 for each child under age 16, to a maximum of $40; in 1920 the figures doubled to $40 and $10 (after that point the total was not to exceed two-thirds of the dead man's normal earnings). As a result, a quarter of the province's female pensioners could not maintain their own households, and a quarter of the same group had to find other income.[89]

The monthly cheques from the Mothers' Allowance Commission were also far from adequate to cover basic living costs. In theory, recipients with two children in an urban area such as Hamilton could get up to $40 a month and $5 more for each additional child under age 16, to a maximum of $55 – lower than other provincial rates and lower than the Canadian Patriotic Fund and workers' compensation rates. In practice, during the first decade of the program the average monthly payment in Hamilton ranged between only $36 and $39, when an average female wage was nearly $12 a week and men's roughly $25.[90] From the beginning, the provincial Mothers' Allowance Commission was explicit that its payments were "insufficient to maintain the family and can only be regarded as supplementary to the mother's own earnings or other source of income." As a commission investigator argued in 1924, "Were the allowance made to cover the full maintenance it would create wastefulness and probably laziness." Its staff actively discouraged work outside the home, but helped mothers find part-time, home-based work, such as taking in boarders, dressmaking, or washing other people's clothes, all poorly paid. Like the relief department, they also urged backyard gardening as a means for the family to provide food for itself. Often, the Commission nonetheless had to admit, "The allowance and the mother's earnings are insufficient to maintain the family without extra help from other relief agencies during emergencies, such as sickness in the family." Older children were expected to contribute to the family, and their earnings were deducted from the allowance (*potential* earnings from these family members, whether or not they were actually employed, could render a mother ineligible). Payments were apparently intended to cover only the children's maintenance, not the mother's; and all payments stopped when the last child reached age 16. A mother was then suddenly left with no income in her middle age, when generating her own earnings would be extremely difficult. Many no doubt ended up turning to private charity or city relief.[91]

By age 70 both women and men might well apply for an old-age pension. This program offered up to $20 a month, but in 1931 the first pensioners in Hamilton got on average only $18.27 – a sum nowhere near enough to maintain themselves (though probably welcome nonetheless). Over the next four years between a quarter and half of those who qualified got less than a full pension. Yet another means-tested state welfare program would leave recipients to look elsewhere for more financial help.[92]

All these private and public programs were heavily biased against European newcomers to the city and single people generally. Europeans found most private charities organized to cater to specific ethnic or broadly Anglo-Canadian clients. The new state programs required British citizenship and lengthy residence in the country. In the worst depressions, immigrants lined up with other citizens for municipal handouts, sometimes causing critical comment (in the long, hard winter of 1914–15 the city restricted jobs on relief projects to men born in the British Empire). Otherwise they had to rely on the charitable resources of the Catholic Church and their own ethnic neighbourhoods. The Jewish community was undoubtedly the best organized, and by the late 1920s had its own Council of Jewish Agencies. Other new ethnic groups created their own benefit societies, such as the Sons of Italy.[93]

Single, able-bodied, transient men found few charity and relief programs interested in helping them. In times of economic depression, their ranks were swollen by those who drifted into town in the hopes of finding work or relief. They were doubly damned as outsiders and as rootless men without families to care for them. In 1914 the Hamilton *Times* published a colourful tale about the plight of one man who was found unconscious in a ditch on the edge of the city in the first winter of the pre-war depression. The farmer who found him took him in and offered him some work for the winter. This slice of Victorian melodrama was far from typical, however. Before World War One such workers could find a bed for the night in shelters runs by the Salvation Army or more informally by the local police department (where over 1,000 men and women bedded down during 1912, nearly 1,600 in 1921, and 5,500 in 1926); or they could obtain a ticket from a clergyman for accommodation in one of the city's privately run "flophouses." The newcomers were the most likely customers at the soup kitchens set up during particularly bad patches of unemployment. As non-residents they felt the loud public scorn about their eligibility for any relief. In 1914 young single men were threatened with arrest for vagrancy if they refused to accept work on farms. In the early 1920s and 1930s the city left most of them to Salvation Army, Grand Army of United Veterans, or Red Cross hostels, but after 1930 pressured them to relocate to one of the provincial highway-construction camps or the federal government's new work camps in Northern Ontario. European immigrants in similar straits were regularly deported to their homelands.[94]

Single unemployed women could expect even less help from charitable agencies. They were almost never treated as full-time wage-earners, still less chief breadwinners. Officials assumed that if they had no jobs and no income, their families should look after them. Charity or relief should come to them through their fathers or brothers. The city's relief projects in the major depressions of the period never provided directly for women, and thus ignored the substantial numbers who would have been the major support for their families (especially for their aging parents). Prime Minister Bennett's unemployment insurance scheme would have provided them with much lower benefits than those received by males. Small numbers completely on their own would seek shelter in the police department's hostel. In 1930 the Local Council of Women organized a small relief fund and temporary lodging for them, while pressuring them to take up domestic service, as did the YWCA. But until they reached old age, no other programs existed to help them.[95]

Navigating the Welfare System

Faced with the patronizing, interventionist philosophies and methods of relief administration in Hamilton, many workers understandably saw these programs as a last resort to be avoided if at all possible.[96] Those who accepted help responded with their own mixtures of gratitude, resentment, mistrust, and calculation. Many may indeed have welcomed help in coping with overwhelming odds. Yet many were more calculating. By the turn of the century, working people were accustomed to using orphanages and old-folks homes as short-term accommodation for family members before bringing them back into the family fold when the family's fortunes improved. Single men used the city jail as a seasonal refuge. But after 1900 these ways of using the charity system were in sharp decline. If we were to take the comments of charity and relief officials and social workers at face value, we would have to conclude that many workers were much more duplicitous, choosing to live off charity whether or not they needed it – "a charitably disposed population," in the words of the Central Bureau's R.L. Smith.[97] The more scrupulous visitations and investigations of the 1920s claimed to find considerable evidence of these practices, although, with no actual case records available, the claims are difficult to weigh. It is not hard to believe that a small number of people with no other resources, especially the disabled and elderly, had to live off charity more or less permanently – though, as a result of the meagre amounts handed out by any one relief agency, it seems that they would have been forced to look to more than one agency, or seek help in other forms. Still, the social workers' own published evidence indicates that even though all agencies deliberately provided less aid than applicants needed, the great majority of recipients – from 66 to 80 per cent in the 1920s – had not approached more than one charitable source.[98] Most of those helped were undoubtedly women trying to hold together a family without the income of a male breadwinner. Many of these may well have sought aid from the less professional groups – perhaps the St. Vincent de Paul or St. Andrew's societies – but, wherever the influence of professional social work was felt, these women probably got less material help and more vigilant supervision of their households.

While some women no doubt appreciated the visitors' help in coping with their troubles, the stories told by social workers suggest that the agencies' meddling also met with resistance and caused irritation. Women raised in working-class households might simply not believe that women visitors from other class backgrounds, often unmarried, had much practical advice to offer them. There may have been a great incentive to "cheat" or at least to try to get around invasive busybodies who were demanding lifestyle changes. It is not hard to imagine the class tensions that were played out on doorsteps between working-class women and middle-class visitors.

Unemployed male wage-earners wanted none of that outside meddling. Labour leaders repeatedly distinguished between state programs based on the right of citizenship and the principles of private charity. Claims to entitlement echo through the unemployed agitations that erupted in the worst depressions. In those situations the unemployed themselves insisted on differentiating themselves from the more usual unemployable recipients of charity. "We do not ask for charity," a "laboring man" wrote to the press in 1914. "It is work we want." Such men demanded that the city provide jobs through public works projects and eventually, in the interwar period, looked to other levels of government for an unemployment insurance program.[99] In part, of course, they were distancing themselves as adult men from the overwhelmingly female, juvenile, and elderly clientele of the charities. But they were also arguing for a principle – that the state had an obligation to help and to treat recipients of that help equitably and respectfully. The Chamber of Commerce's initiative in the early 1920s to create a more professional, privately run social-welfare system was a direct challenge to that perspective and an alternative response to the dislocation of economic depression and demobilization after World War One. The city's relief department held out against this new approach for some time, refusing through the 1920s to turn names in its files over to the social workers at the Central Bureau of Social Agencies; and the city's initial relief program in the early 1930s was administered without the army of invasive investigators that descended on working-class Hamilton in 1934.

In contrast to the individualism of charity, relief, and social-work programs, Hamilton workers were also prepared to use collective organization both to fight specific battles for survival and to pressure the state to support its citizens. Often the male bonding of young male transients was a source of strength, resistance, and no doubt inventiveness in the face of official scorn. They shared information about good prospects for handouts – a clergyman complained in 1907 that all the transient unemployed men who arrived at his door to ask for support sang sad songs after hearing on the lodging-house grapevine that he was susceptible to sentimentality. In 1914 the unemployed assembled in mass meetings and visited the Board of Control to demand civic works projects with a minimum wage of 20 cents an hour. One group of relief workers staged a brief strike in October 1914 to demand cash instead of groceries and other goods (they were quickly replaced). In the early 1920s and early 1930s demonstrations and marches also erupted, this time under left-wing leadership. The actions made civic authorities more aware of the resentments of the unemployed, but did not fundamentally alter the shape of relief administration in Hamilton.[100]

More of the Same

By the 1930s, then, working-class families in need of financial aid were encountering a "relief community" in which much had changed but much had also survived from 19th-century charity. There was undoubtedly greater need, brought on by the demographic changes of shattered families and aging elders and by the worsening underemployment and joblessness. Help was also limited as the charitable houses and homes languished, and the private societies were overwhelmed. By that point, the state had stepped in, but not with the kinds of universal programs that would emerge during and following World War Two. Indeed, Hamilton's middle and upper classes had put far more effort into finding other solutions for poverty outside the state, including following a more "scientific" approach to welfare administration through the new social-work profession. In the absence of a strong labour movement, workers had not been able to sustain a discourse of universal rights in the public discussion of welfare, as their counterparts in Britain, Australia, New Zealand, and parts of Western Europe had done.[101]

Workers thus still had to find their way around a chaotic patchwork of agencies and programs that could by no stretch of the imagination be called a welfare state, and that was only partly within the orbit of the new social-work profession. The fragmentation was not necessarily a problem for workers in need. While it could no doubt be frustrating and confusing for the widow with a young child or the wife of a tubercular husband, the failure to co-ordinate all the "helping hands" in the city probably spared those women from the stern, persistent, intrusive planning of their lives by the professional social workers of the more centralized welfare regime and their business supporters, consolidated in the Central Bureau of Family Welfare. Poverty-stricken families may well have found that the charities that clung to their older philanthropic voluntarism put up fewer obstacles to getting the food, clothing, and other resources that they so desperately needed to survive.

Yet all workers could not work the welfare system equally. What had congealed by the 1930s was a two-tiered system of social assistance administered jointly by public and private institutions. In one policy stream were the unemployable dependants, mostly women and children without male providers, who got charity doled out as parsimoniously as it had been since the early days of the English Poor Laws. Small numbers of these unfortunates – permanently disabled men, widowed mothers, and the elderly – had access to new state programs, but whether private or public, the administration of these programs assumed the subordination of women and other dependants within the patriarchal family. The programs never made any effort to raise the women's incomes to anything comparable to that of workingmen. This fundamentally patriarchal view of the family meant that women, the most common applicants for charity, could never expect to find that any of the material help available to them through private or public agencies would allow them any real independence.

In the other stream were the able-bodied male breadwinners who were unemployed through no fault of their own and who appealed for help on the basis of right, not charity. Programs for them typically aimed to restore some part of their wage-earning capacity. Injured workers, both industrial and military, got some compensation for lost wages through new state programs, but most commonly help for the unemployed took the form of relief work for paltry wages. A few got help every winter, but thousands of men swallowed their pride in the depths of the increasingly severe economic slumps to ask for help at the city relief office. There was never enough to go around, and their ability to be breadwinners invariably collapsed.

None of the new public welfare programs strayed far from the ideology and methodology of existing charity practice. Most workers were kept away by both the narrow terms of eligibility and the embarrassing social stigma that never left them. Even the injured breadwinners who got workers' compensation or veterans' disability pensions on the basis of their rights as breadwinners faced suspicion and minimal support. Ultimately, in a liberal-capitalist society a family was still expected to look after its own, and all welfare programs were premised on the assumption that unwaged family members should be supported by a family wage brought home by the male breadwinner and, where necessary, supplemented by the pay packets of wage-earning children.

In 1935 as in 1895, workers in Hamilton could expect financial help only if that family economy no longer worked. Even then, public and private welfare administration was coloured by a persistent spirit of mistrust, interventionism, and tight-fisted restraint. The surveillance of working-class households intensified, along with the stigma of the "dole." To prevent families from relying solely on charity and relief and to encourage independence and self-reliance, those in positions of authority kept material aid deliberately below a level adequate to support a family. Such a strategy might have some chance of success when the economy was booming, but made no sense in the context of mass layoffs and reduced work hours.

PART III

Punching the Clock

9

At the close of
the 19th century
these wire weavers
at Greening Wire
proudly displayed the
tools of their trade.
(SLS, LS482)

Hold the Fort

Every time they shove in their ticket they do
so with a grudge in every move, and there
is often far more ginger put into a vigorous
smash on the clock lever than in any other
operation that takes place in the shop hours.
— *Canadian Machinery*, 1920

THE CROWDS OF WAGE-EARNERS trudging
through Hamilton's streets at the crack of dawn
clutching lunch buckets and handbags began

to break up as separate streams of them turned
through the gates of the city's big new companies.[1] As a symbol of the mental and physical adjustment they were about to make when they
crossed the threshold of these enterprises, each
worker had to punch a time clock. They then
stepped inside the harsh new industrial world of
the Second Industrial Revolution.

The new workplace regime of the 1920s
symbolized by the time clock did not emerge
overnight. Getting there involved overcoming
the deeply rooted routines and customs that
governed work in Hamilton factories at the turn
of the century. By the 1890s a half-century of industrial capitalism had brought the city's industries a long way from the artisanal workshops

The moulders at Dominion Foundries and Steel worked by hand, with little mechanical equipment. (LAC, PA-24525)

of the early 19th century. Belching smokestacks throughout the factory district testified to the widespread use of steam engines; the clatter of machinery could be heard through many factory windows. Yet as local factory owners tried to increase their output to meet the challenge of the new turn-of-the-century economic boom, they soon discovered the limitations of that first phase of industrialization. For, despite the steam engines and the new machines, most owners still relied to a great extent on their workers' manual labour, skilled and unskilled, which could be inflexible, unpredictable, and unreliable.

As Hamilton's industrialists eagerly welcomed the return of economic prosperity at the turn of the century, they found their opportunities for increased profits hampered by their limited control over the production processes in their plants. Expansion of output within such a system of production meant hiring more workers, both skilled and unskilled, and workers were getting more difficult to find and consequently more expensive. As the surplus of skilled workers dried up and competition increased for the unskilled, employers lost the upper hand in the labour market. To overcome the obstacles to achieving faster, cheaper, and higher-volume production, the industrialists had to confront deeply entrenched patterns of solidarity within working-class Hamilton, where, in harmony with the popular labour song, workers were determined to "Hold the Fort." The opening salvos of that confrontation came as early as the first decade of the 20th century.[2]

The Weight of the Past

In the 1890s, like its English namesake, this Canadian "Birmingham" was not a cluster of massive factories. The largest, the Tuckett Tobacco plant, had around 600 workers, while

In the local mass-production garment industry, the tailor's traditional labour was broken down into specialized tasks, but the cutters, such as these at Grafton's in nearby Dundas, were nonetheless highly valued for their manual skills. (HPL)

the Ontario Rolling Mills employed some 500. Far more workplaces retained the older shape of the enlarged workshop, which rarely had payrolls exceeding 200 names. The largest employer in the city was the Sanford clothing firm, but its garment workers were distributed through many small subcontracting shops near the centre of the city. As in Birmingham, it was the metal trades in particular that operated in smaller-scale operations.[3]

A peek through factory windows at the turn of the century would have revealed remarkable diversity in the forms of production. In the first wave of industrialization, the general thrust had been to subdivide and mechanize the skills of the artisan wherever possible, but the results were quite uneven. High levels of skill survived in many workplaces. In many cases the first industrialists had been able to do no more than draw together highly skilled men under one roof to continue to practise their pre-industrial crafts. Tuckett Tobacco had dozens of skilled cigar-makers. The local glass companies relied on seasoned glass-blowers. The broom factory had skilled men producing brooms and brushes by hand. Until the mid-1890s printers set the type in the city's print shops manually. Construction work was also a bastion of highly prized craft skills.[4]

Nowhere was the incompleteness of the First Industrial Revolution more evident than in the city's several foundries, where hundreds of moulders still followed the ancient craft that they liked to trace back to the biblical figure Tubalcain. From their skilled hands came metal castings as diverse as stoves, machinery casing, and ornamental iron and brass work. Technological change had almost completely bypassed the foundry, which remained down to the end of the 19th century a classic "manufactory" of highly

Until 1918 cigar-makers at Tuckett Tobacco rolled cigars by hand.
(SLS, LS120)

foundries, with "a single job sometimes entailing days of careful labor, and the work being given a finish in which the maker took pride."[5]

In other Hamilton plants, where machinery had been used to transform formerly manual work processes, new skills had appeared. The local textile mills and the boot and shoe factory embodied some of the most impressive attempts to replace craft practices by subdividing skills, hiring new, non-artisanal workforces, and introducing complex machinery. But new demands for skill had emerged, notably mule-spinning in the textile mills and cutting and lasting in the shoe plant. In the city's production of men's ready-made clothing, the new division of labour made cutting the cloth a specialized but highly skilled manual job, while sewing-machine operators still needed care and precision. Similarly, in the Ontario Rolling Mills, huge steam-powered rolls replaced the muscle power of the blacksmith, but, in the new organization of production, tending the puddling or bushelling furnaces to melt the iron and manipulating the hot iron through the heating and rolling processes were highly skilled jobs that required plenty of strength and independent discretion. So too did the work of the furnace-keepers and blowers at the new Hamilton Blast Furnace works. The city's newspapers were also discovering that the mechanization of typesetting with the new lino-type machines had not eliminated the need for skilled printers; it had simply created new skill requirements for machine operation.[6]

The machinists – the men who built the many machines that were rolled out of Hamilton shops and factories – were probably the most important new group of skilled workers to emerge out of the First Industrial Revolution in Hamilton. By 1900 their craft was little more than a century old, but it had evolved considerably. When the peripatetic Royal Commission

skilled craftworkers gathered in one employer's shop. A turn-of-the-century article in *Iron Age* emphasized that the craft was "learned almost entirely by the sense of feeling, a sense that cannot be transferred to paper. It is something that must be acquired by actual practice." This sense was what craftsmen liked to call the "mystery" of their trade. With a few tools and the necessary knowledge under his cap, the moulder prepared the moulds to receive the molten iron or brass. A mould began with a pattern, usually wood, in the shape of the finished casting, which was imbedded in sand. Preparing and ramming the sand (that is, pounding it firmly with iron-shod poles) required great care and precision so that when the pattern was drawn out a perfect mould remained to hold the molten metal. If a cast product was to have a hollow space, the moulder inserted a core, a lump of specially prepared sand that had been carefully shaped and baked hard at the core-maker's bench (originally moulders had made their own cores, but gradually a distinct division of labour emerged). Once cool the casting was shaken out of the sand and cleaned, to be ready for any finishing processes. The size of the objects to be cast ranged so widely that the moulder might work at a bench or prepare his moulds in great stretches of sand on the foundry floor. "The jobs he undertook were varied in the extreme," recalled one observer of Canadian

In 1906 the Hamilton Steel and Iron Company still relied on the manual skill of these men in its rolling mills (formerly the Ontario Rolling Mills). (SLS)

on the Relations of Labour and Capital opened its hearings in Hamilton early in 1888, an elderly machinist named William Collins appeared. A retired artisan with British training, Collins described himself as "a general workman." He said, "I learned the whole art or mystery of mechanics – that is, so far as human skill, I suppose could accomplish it, either wood, iron, brass, blacksmithing, or anything; I am one of the old school." He was, in fact, a relic of that period in the late 18th and early 19th centuries when a millwright, as he was then known, was a highly valued mechanic whose skills and ingenuity in the construction of machinery made possible the innovations of the Industrial Revolution in Britain. By mid-century, however, the typical British machine-builder was less in the Collins mould and more often a skilled operator of metalworking machinery. With new steam-powered equipment, especially lathes and planers, the craft had entered a new, technically more sophisticated phase, in which an engineer or machinist used a mechanized cutting tool to shape metal objects – anything from machinery parts

to gun barrels – usually in manufacturing firms or railway shops. The tools of the trade might be any number of simple lathes, drills, planers, shapers, or slotters, as well as various devices for careful measurement of the cut.[7]

While William Collins might have regretted that mechanization had been "detrimental to the interest of the employé" because it "reduced the labour required," individual manual skill did not disappear. Most machine-shop work still required the careful, trained hands of the craftworker; machine tools simply facilitated precision.[8] Another Hamilton machinist emphasized before the same royal commission in 1888 that running his planer demanded expertise: "There is no man who can run a machine properly after three years apprenticeship. I served my time seven years at Whitworth's, of Manchester, the finest shop in the world, and I found I had something else to learn." Employers also recognized that the indispensable skills of these craftworkers gave them a functional autonomy on the shop floor. According to a 1903 article in *Canadian Engineer*:

If a certain piece of work was to be done, a drawing showing the essential dimensions accompanied the stock which went to the machinist, who followed his own way in (a) setting the work; (b) selecting the cutting tool and grinding it as he knew best; (c) choosing the running speed; (d) determining the cut; (e) and adjusting the feed.

The writer complained that the completion of the work was "(1) limited by his intelligence; (2) restricted by his experience; [and] (3) governed by his inclination." Not surprisingly, these workers were confident that "the industrial world depended for its success largely on the skill and technical knowledge of the machinist."[9]

Hamilton's late-19th-century industry also relied heavily on the hands and muscles of the unskilled. Seldom were there machines for fetching, lifting, carrying, or loading and unloading. Often in factories children or teenagers performed these tasks to assist the adult workers. The royal commissioners heard plenty of testimony about these youngsters in 1888, and their faces were still beaming out of group portraits of Hamilton workers in the 1890s.[10] For the heavier work, however, employers hired brawny men. Outdoor construction work, like the digging of the Toronto, Hamilton, and Buffalo Railway tunnel in 1895, absorbed many pick and shovel brigades.[11] So too did the various factories and workshops. At the new iron works, for example, labourers still shovelled coal, iron ore, and other material out of railway cars or ships' holds, loaded them in huge wheelbarrows, and trundled them up to and into the blast furnace. The only mechanical help they got was an elevator up the side of the furnace. Others lugged the pig iron out of the casting house after it had cooled. A retired executive of the Ontario Rolling Mills later recalled: "In the industries of that day almost no labor-saving machinery was used. All the lifting was done directly by hand labor. . . . Even cranes, derricks, tackle and all the various simple labour-saving devices were rarely used in any factories at that time."[12] As production took off, labourers could be in short supply, and thus extract higher wages from frustrated employers.[13]

The production systems in use in Hamilton's factories and workshops by the 1890s, then, were an uneven mixture of mechanical and human resources in which skilled and unskilled manual labour was still essential. The consequences for control over the pace and rhythms of production were profound. Most manufacturers in Hamilton wanted as much direct control as possible over the labour power they had purchased from their workers, and often used foremen and incentives such as fines or piecework to goad them to work harder and faster.[14] Yet many of the employers had learned, often reluctantly, that they had to leave much shop-floor decision-making to the more skilled men and the work groups they headed. Even the unskilled could occasionally exert some control over their work routines. In 1910 an efficiency drive in the city's waterworks department brought to light long-standing practices of this sort. The city engineer told the press in shocked tones that "the men have been accustomed to electing their own foreman" and "one man would do the digging while the other three would do nothing but smoke their pipes, taking turn and turn about."[15]

In the late 19th century, employers regularly challenged this kind of informal power in the workplace, but their craftworkers frequently tried to buttress it with union organization. Their craft unions developed elaborate constitutions that stipulated all rules and procedures covering recruitment into the trade through apprenticeship, wages or piece rates, hours of work, and daily workload. The moulders' "set," for example, was a regulation of output established by the local union in an effort to prevent reductions in piece rates and to maintain a humane pace of work.[16] Craft organizations in the city had seen better days by the early 1890s, however, as unemployment, employer hostility, and conflicts within the local and international labour movements had sapped these unions of their vitality. The cotton companies provoked their weavers into a lengthy, bitter, but ultimately fruitless strike in 1890, and two years later the leading foundrymen drove the moulders' union out of their shops. Membership fell away and locals dissolved. By 1894 unions were too weak to mount a parade to celebrate the country's first official Labour Day.[17]

The return of prosperity at the end of the decade provided a basis for a new wave of union organizing among the city's skilled workers. Once again wage-earners responded to the call of an American labour movement. This time it was a new group of international craft unions that had emerged out of the debacle of the Knights of Labor and rallied under the banner of the American Federation of Labor (AFL) in the United States. By the late 1890s the AFL's tough-minded president, a cigar-maker named Samuel Gompers, was concerned that Canadian workers might become low-wage competitors with American craft unionists and pumped some money into organizing north of the border. As in the past, Hamilton's extensive industrial base and its proximity to the US border made it a major centre of international unionism in the country. In the summer of 1900, John Flett, a Hamilton carpenter who had just begun his long career as the AFL's chief organizer in Canada, reported to headquarters that he was holding nightly organizational meetings in his hometown. He sent back glowing reports of his success in helping to launch new local unions. In April 1904 the

In 1900 the American Federation of Labor hired Hamilton carpenter and union leader John Flett as its first full-time organizer in Canada. He reported immediate success in helping many union locals get started in Hamilton. (SLS, LS613)

federal Department of Labour listed 59 unions in the city.[18]

With few exceptions, this was a movement of skilled, male, white, English-speaking wage-earners. The men who were swept up in this unionizing upsurge could be grouped under four rough headings. The first and most persistent group consisted of the skilled workers of the building trades – bricklayers and masons, carpenters, plumbers, lathers, plasterers, painters, sheet-metal workers, and electricians.[19] The manufacturing industries harboured a second, varied group of craftworkers. In the century's first decade they were either highly skilled men earning their wages in "manufactories" in which industrial capitalism had not yet transformed their handicraft skills into subdivided, mechanized factory jobs – cigar-makers, broom-makers, custom tailors, leather workers, bakers, glass blowers, and moulders, for example – or the new skilled groups, such as cutters in the footwear and clothing industries.[20] A third, much less stable grouping consisted of a variety of service workers who largely drew their strength from a predominantly working-class clientele – barbers, bartenders, musicians, stage employees, waiters, retail clerks, teamsters, letter carriers,

Hamilton's building-trades workers put on a good display of their manual skills during the city's centennial celebrations in 1913 by building a house in a day. (HPL)

and firemen. Finally, the ranks of organized labour included several categories of men in the transportation industries, from the local street-railwaymen to a handful in each of the more exclusive railway running trades. These workers kept their distance from the rest of the labour movement.[21]

By no means did all of these groups of unionized workers have what by any objective standard could be considered precious skills. Stove-mounters, for example, simply assembled the parts of cast-iron stoves, and street-railwaymen certainly needed limited training for their jobs. But the ideology of the craft union movement permitted and encouraged such groups to organize around their occupational identities. "Our aim and object is to put our craft on a higher plane," a local street-railwayman wrote in 1902. They nevertheless had to respect the jurisdictional boundaries of the established craft bodies – a subject of endless contention within the AFL. Most of the men whose representatives gathered every two weeks for Trades and Labor Council meetings in the upstairs rooms of Labor Hall on John Street had learned a highly valued manual skill that was in ready demand in Hamilton. A broom-maker like Walter Rollo, a cigar-maker like James Sullivan, a leather worker like William Berry, a barber like Harry Halford, or a printer like Philip Obermeyer each knew the intricate techniques of their respective trades, which they were anxious to protect through the collective organization of their fellow craftworkers.[22]

In the industrialized world craft unionism came in many forms, and the AFL leaders who reached north to recruit Canadian members had developed a unique anti-statist brand shaped by battles with anti-union corporations and the US courts. Although unions had not been legally blocked from engaging in voluntary collective bargaining, they had found the courts increasingly more interested in protecting employers' common-law property rights in situations of industrial conflict. Judges nodded sympathetically when employers sued unions for damage to their businesses caused by picket lines, boycotts, and sympathy strikes, and granted them a new legal tool to fight workers' collective action – the injunction. The AFL also brought across the border a disillusionment about labour legislation after the US courts struck down most new labour-standards laws, such as those enforcing shorter hours of work, as violations of constitutional rights to individual liberty. In the context of all these legal assaults, the US craft union leaders to whom so many more Canadian workers were looking for guidance had rethought their strategies and tactics. They veered sharply away from broader campaigns for legislative reforms or any other reliance on the state and concentrated on what has been called "liberal voluntarism" – a form of private ordering of relations between employees and their bosses, worked out on their own without direct state involvement in the content of their deal. Unions, AFL leaders believed, should rely only on the collective self-help of their members to guarantee job control and workplace justice.[23]

Craft unionism was thus changing in important ways at the turn of the century. The individual international unions emphasized much more "businesslike," administratively competent procedures. Each levied high membership dues to build up substantial treasuries and strike funds, and centralized much more power in the hands of full-time salaried officials at international headquarters. A staff of roving professional organizers also regularly took charge of local negotiations with employers. In Hamilton virtually every strike by craftworkers was preceded by negotiating efforts orchestrated by international officers. Besides Flett, Hamilton's contributions to this small army of what were often called "walking delegates" included Sam

Landers, Canadian vice-president of the United Garment Workers, Eddie O'Dell of the Boot and Shoe Workers, and Hugh Robinson of the Journeymen Tailors. Eventually, by World War One, a few individual unions in Hamilton would begin to appoint their own local organizers, known as "business agents," who, sometimes on a part-time basis, were responsible for overseeing the practice of the craft and finding work in the union-approved shops for new arrivals in the city. In addition, most crafts created province-wide or district organizations, often with a full-time organizer, to co-ordinate the affairs of the particular craftworkers in the region.[24]

The new craft union movement also placed growing emphasis on negotiating formal contracts, or "trade agreements," with individual employers or, where possible, with groups of employers within one industry. In return for written guarantees of terms and conditions of employment, unions agreed to avoid strikes or other disruptions of work. In the United States the bituminous coal miners pioneered these contracts, and by the early years of the first decade moulders, machinists, printers, and potters had evolved formal industry-wide collective bargaining arrangements. In Hamilton, as in various other Southern Ontario towns and cities, craftworkers undertook to win these new contractual agreements to guarantee the status and customary practices of their trades. In the burst of turn-of-the-century prosperity, many of Hamilton's new unions convinced their employers to accept stable collective bargaining relationships and signed some kind of contracts. The building trades were probably the most successful in formalizing bargaining between each craft union and the respective builders' organization.[25]

In stove moulding, a model existed in the United States in the Stove Founders' Defense Association, originally a militantly anti-union organization, which had begun annual national conferences with the International Molders' Union to develop common practices and regular arbitration procedures for all member stove shops. In an industry dispersed through hundreds of small-scale firms, foundrymen hoped to reduce cutthroat competition by standardizing labour practices and wage rates. Canadian foundries were not covered by these agreements, but local unions attempted to apply in Canadian towns and cities the criteria worked out with the association. In 1902 the International Molders' Canadian vice-president set out to establish this kind of collective bargaining in the Ontario stove industry. By concentrating on Hamilton, he won an agreement for a 5 per cent wage increase with the city's stove founders, "whose decision it was recognized would determine the policy of the rest of Ontario." The organizer thanked John Tilden of Hamilton's Gurney-Tilden Company profusely for his role in bringing the Ontario employers into line. Evidently the manufacturers saw this strategy as a means of allying their skilled workers with them against the destructive competition that might threaten the future of the industry.[26] No formal procedures similar to the American defence association emerged at first, but the two sides held annual local conferences to adjust differences. In 1905 the union refined its province-wide bargaining machinery by forming an Ontario Conference Board drawn from 16 towns and cities; and it elected Hamilton's John Carson as its first president. The board met annually thereafter to clarify the terms to be presented to the foundrymen. In the face of this more co-ordinated approach by the unions, along with more threatening competition from US industry during a bad depression, stove foundrymen launched the Dominion Iron Founders' Defense Association in 1908, with Tilden as its first president.[27]

Along the lake in Toronto, employers were firing up a vigorous open-shop campaign to drive out unions.[28] In contrast, most Hamilton employers responded to the tight labour market at the turn of the century by entering into regular negotiation with the unions in their enterprises. The agreements they reached sometimes required local unions to show the teeth of militancy, but virtually all of the approximately 20 strikes in Hamilton involving craftworkers between 1901 and 1904 were small and settled amicably.

The hallmark of this new approach to industrial relations was the contract. In 1903 John Flett, by then president of the Trades and Labor Congress of Canada, warned delegates to the annual convention about the sanctity of contracts: "To be successful there must be organization with discipline in order to enforce a due observance of these agreements, and all contracts religiously lived up to." Some three years later the president of the garment workers' union warned Ontario members of "the urgent necessity and obligation of our people keeping their agreements and contracts." Similarly in 1911 the printer Philip Obermeyer, who contributed a weekly labour column to the *Herald*, blustered: "It is nothing short of arrant nonsense to talk 'general strike' while union men are working under agreements with employers. Unionists cannot afford to break contracts, even under the most irritating circumstances."[29]

As a stepping stone to such agreements, labour leaders placed great emphasis on voluntary conciliation and arbitration – what the *Industrial Banner* called "the corner stone of organized labour." In 1903 the Hamilton Trades and Labor Council convinced the local Board of Trade to appoint members to a joint conciliation board. The model of the National Civic Federation in the United States was in the mind of at

HAMILTON UNION LABEL LEAGUE

THIS space will in future be devoted to Union Label matters in the interest of the unions affiliated with the above League, which meets at Labor Hall the 1st and 3rd Thursday in each month.
W. COOPER, 120 Kent Street, Secretary.

CIGAR MAKERS' BLUE LABEL—The Pioneer of them all.

BARBERS' SHOP CARD

TOBACCO WORKER'S LABEL

STAGE EMPLOYEES' EMBLEM

PRINTING PRESSMENS' LABEL

Bartenders' Union Button

The union label became a central tool for many of Hamilton's craft unions.

(*LN*, 12 Feb. 1912, 3)

least one local manufacturer, who hoped that "the idea of the proposed board would work up a civic federation." It does not seem to have survived past the early months of 1905, however. At least one union nonetheless built arbitration into its agreements. "In our contracts we have a clause making strikes impossible, and calling for arbitration," the garment workers' Landers explained in 1910. State officials like the young William Lyon Mackenzie King were beginning to craft state programs to encourage this kind

of "responsible" unionism by offering mediation and conciliation services to help the parties reach an agreement.[30]

Equally impressive was the campaign for the union label launched in Hamilton in the late 1890s. During that decade, more and more craft unions turned to this method of enlisting the patronage of working-class consumers for goods produced by unionized workers, originally pioneered 20 years earlier in the United States. The quiet consultation in company offices, rather than the threat of industrial militancy, that was involved in winning union recognition in this way must have fit the increasing sense of respectable, responsible unionism among many local craft union leaders. In the words of one Hamilton unionist, "It supercedes the strike, the lockout and the destructive boycotts; it is the outward manifestation of harmony between employer and workman, binding both parties to maintain their friendly relations and the continued approval and patronage of a discriminating public." Several manufacturers of consumer goods decided to enter this kind of partnership with their unionized workers. In almost all cases, these were firms that ran relatively labour-intensive production processes, and operated in highly competitive markets. They evidently hoped that agreements with their workers' unions would help to stabilize the costs of production and promote the sale of their products.[31]

Hamilton quickly became a national leader in the promotion of union labels. In 1898 the Sanford clothing company announced an agreement with the local United Garment Workers to put the union label on the firm's ready-made products, and shortly afterward the Journeymen Tailors' Union convinced all merchant tailors to adopt the label on their custom work. Both the city and the street-railway company required the label on any uniforms they purchased. Some two years later the McPherson shoe company became the first footwear firm in Canada to attach a union label, and the bakers' union convinced many local bakeshops to put its label on their bread. The handful of skilled broom-makers at the Walter Woods firm had their label accepted in 1903 (by the end of World War One this was the only local of this tiny union in the country). Printers and stove moulders had similar success. Working-class patronage also allowed unionization of virtually all the barber shops, theatres,

bars, and the city's small breweries. Most significantly, the cigar-makers' and tobacco workers' unions helped the Tuckett company build a national reputation as Canada's only producer of union-label tobacco products. The label in each case symbolized union recognition and collective bargaining relationships, which in most cases lasted until the end of World War One.[32]

To keep up labour's end of the bargain, the unionists undertook to encourage workers to buy the goods they produced. A Union Label League co-ordinated all this advertising in Hamilton at the turn of the century, and, after a moribund period, was prodded back to life in 1910 by the AFL's new Union Label Department. It published a monthly bulletin for a short time, exhibited a special AFL movie on union labels in 1911, and continued its efforts to encourage local merchants to stock union-made merchandise on into the 1920s, with dwindling success. In 1913 Hamilton had one of only three label leagues left in Canada. Over the years local labour leaders also lent support to the efforts of labour parliamentarians like Ralph Smith to wring from Parliament legislation allowing unions to register their labels legally – a measure that was not finally enacted until 1927.[33]

No fundamentally different objectives lay behind all these new departures. They simply represented new strategies by craftworkers to solidify more formally the workplace power and independence that they had struggled to assert throughout the late 19th century. But the new procedures of craft unionism did make a difference. Particularly as a result of the trend towards bureaucratization, they placed much higher value on caution and sobriety and were more resistant to spontaneity in industrial conflict. The advantage to be gained from this formal and orderly process was allegedly the security of wage rates and work practices guaranteed by the contractual arrangements. Decades later, scholars would begin to call these practices "workplace contractualism" and "industrial legality."[34]

A Community in Solidarity

Working-class Hamilton posed a larger problem for the city's industrialists than simply the stubbornness of particular craftworkers and their unions. In the first decade of the century workers revived the kind of community solidarity that had blossomed so richly in the 1870s and 1880s. The men at the head of the labour movement organized across occupational lines to promote the common interests of wage-earners and, to some extent at least, their families. In 1906, when one of the largest new corporate employers antagonized both its employees and the broader public, the spirit of working-class solidarity erupted on streets across the city. Men and women were prepared to stand together publicly in common cause.

At first blush, craft unionists in early-20th-century Hamilton might seem to have been simply trying to protect the narrow interests of the more skilled, better-paid male wage-earners. Certainly the boundaries around craft unions were more carefully guarded than ever before, and there was no welcome mat for most of the unskilled at the door of the house of labour, especially after 1901 when the AFL passed its famous Scranton Declaration that organization by craft was the only legitimate form of unionism.[35] Yet this was a cultural as well as an economistic stance. As in the 19th century, craftworkers placed a high value on the self-reliant, independent man of principle who stood by his craft organization. Appeals to non-unionists were usually exhortations to individual conscience and a sense of "manhood."[36] In 1914 the Labor News described "a sort of unwritten law in the Hamilton Trades and Labor Council not to waste much time in giving aid to any class of wage earners who were persistent in refusing to aid themselves ... and who will not recognize the principle of self help and unite and maintain an organization."[37] The craftworkers' moral criteria for the independent, self-disciplined character of a good worker apparently blinded them to the concrete difficulties faced by the unskilled in organizing on the job – low wages, recurrent unemployment, and an often chronically overstocked labour market.

Craft identity was also deeply masculine – these were self-consciously crafts*men* – combining the male wage-earner's pride in his manual skill and his responsibility for taking home a family wage. This definition of unionists' "manhood" had little room for women. In the few unionized industries in which women worked, most of them remained unorganized or, like the local garment and shoe workers, were hived off into their own tiny locals. There their vulnerability as low-wage workers and limited sojourn in the paid workforce (or in one workplace) undermined their effectiveness. If the male workers took the initiative in industrial action, women nonetheless generally supported them, as in two successful strikes in 1903 and 1906.[38]

Male unionists preferred to see the problem as rooted in their femininity. The short-lived efforts to hold together a female tailors' union in 1897 prompted "Hank" to blame the "barriers of reserve and false dignity" and "the natural timidity among women to enter into organizations of this nature." The international showed little sensitivity to the problem; a turn of the century study of the union concluded, "In the determination of the general policy of the union the women have had little, if any, influence." Union leader Landers liked to refer to the home as women's "natural sphere" and decried how business had drawn women out of that sphere, how in some trades they even outnumbered men. In most of the pre-war years, women remained peripheral to the garment union's organization in Hamilton, as they were to almost all other unions in the city. The first (and only) women to appear at a Trades and Labor Council meeting before World War One – representatives of the female workers at McPherson's shoe company – were a cause for surprised comment.[39]

Yet, in a halting and ambivalent fashion, this new craft union movement in Hamilton brought more than occupational exclusivism. Craft union leaders encouraged co-operation and solidarity among unionists wherever possible and tried to provide leadership on a wider range of issues. The local labour movement had a long history of co-operation across occupational lines dating back to the first "trades assembly" in 1864. Unionized wage-earners had also coalesced into the militant Nine-Hour League in 1872 and then made Hamilton one of the Canadian bastions of the more open, flexible Knights of Labor in the 1880s. It was in that decade that large numbers of Hamilton workers participated in a significant shift away from their attachments to various kinds of industrial paternalism to more independent expressions of class identity. Union locals had blossomed. Local assemblies of the Knights had sprung up. Tough-minded strikes had proliferated. A weekly labour newspaper "spread the light" of labour reform. Rallies, parades, and picnics drew together thousands of wage-earners and their families. A distinct labour message was carried into the first (largely unsuccessful) independent electoral campaigns. The decline of that expansive movement and the rise of more narrowly focused craft unions did not wipe out these patterns of class-based solidarity. Some local craft unionists helped new groups to organize – the builders' labourers, for example, and the less-skilled street-railwaymen.[40]

Since 1888 local unions had also been co-operating in the Hamilton Trades and Labor Council to pursue common working-class interests, particularly in relation to the municipal government. Lobbying efforts had brought notable guarantees for unionized workers. In 1897 the city council was persuaded to become one of the first in the country to require union labels on all city printing, police and firemen's clothing, and city horseshoes. It also legislated a requirement of fair-wage clauses in city contracts. The craftworkers were also prepared to campaign for measures to maintain decent working conditions for all workers, skilled and unskilled. One issue of direct concern to the less-skilled was contracting out municipal construction projects. The craft union movement aggressively promoted the direct hiring of labourers, the so-called "day-labour system," to protect these workers from exploitation by unscrupulous private contractors. The business press may have believed that "men working for the Government will not exert themselves as they are required and compelled to do when they work for an individual," but, when a debate erupted over the issue in 1900, the Trades and Labor Council went head to head with some of the city's biggest contractors, notably M.A. Pigott, to counter such arguments. In essence, the Council argued that contract labour was a "sweating" system that allowed employers to underpay their workers and rake off tidy profits. "Municipal construction by day labour with the [City] Engineer as inspector will mean better work and better wages, and no doubt less swearing at the men," wrote Landers, as Trades and Labor Council president. After considerable debate, the city council voted virtually unanimously to use the day-labour plan and in 1905 also ended a contract for providing asphalt for road construction in favour of a city asphalt plant. Not until the early 1920s did the contract system return in full force.[41] It was a similar concern with decent working conditions that prompted a major labour campaign to block any city bonus to the Deering Harvester Company for locating in Hamilton. Then too, the craft unionists would be prepared to challenge the political hegemony of the Tories and Liberals.

After the turn of the century craft unionists in two specific industrial sectors also created new bodies to co-ordinate their common interests – the Building Trades Council in 1903 and the Metal Trades Council in 1910. These bodies reported to the respective departments of the American Federation of Labor, which made sure that their activities in no way threatened the independence of each of the component unions. Co-operation was usually limited to helping with organizing and trying to get employers to hire unionists in all skilled jobs.[42]

In the first decade of the century, then, Hamilton's craft unionists had rebuilt a solid base in local industry and promoted new practices of collective defence – through stronger continental organizations and codification of workplace relations into formal agreements with their bosses. They had also re-established their status as the voice of the working-class community, at least the respectable, male element within it. Each fall at the turn of the century, they mobilized a strong showing of their collective strength, determination, and cultural creativity in a dramatic Labour Day parade, where they kicked up dust in the street showing off their respectability, the great value of their manual skills, and their occupational solidarities.[43]

Open Shops

Spectators at the Labour Day parade in September 1900 got a hint that all was not so rosy for local unions. A prison stood atop a dramatic float

Since the 1880s Hamilton unions had been putting on an annual display of pride and respectability on Labour Day.
(HS, 4 Sept. 1897, 8)

emblazoned with the words "Lots of Law, But Little Justice." It had been hammered together by the local metal polishers' union, which, two weeks earlier, in the midst of a strike, had found nine of its leaders and members summoned to court by the Hamilton Brass Company on criminal charges of "watching and besetting" the company's premises – that is, successfully talking strikebreakers into quitting. The men were subsequently convicted and fined partly on the strength of a recent high-profile case involving striking moulders at Massey-Harris in Brantford a few months earlier, a case that signalled how Southern Ontario industrialists, led by Toronto's metalworking firms and following the example of their US counterparts, were developing a more belligerent opposition to unions in their midst, turning to the courts for the same legal weapons against unionism – notably the injunction – that US jurists had provided 20 years before.[44] Hamilton would soon feel the heat of this emerging open-shop campaign.

The city's Crown attorney in the metal polishers' prosecution emphasized that this would be a precedent-setting case in emerging local industrial relations, but, then again, for the next few years most Hamilton employers did not seem much interested in building on this incident of rabid anti-unionism, especially the turn to the courts. In 1903, however, Cirus Birge, head of the local Ontario Tack Company, used his presidential address to the Canadian Manufacturers' Association to raise the "labor question" and to suggest that "the events of the past year have developed a condition which, unless satisfactorily solved, threatens the very foundations of business stability and the happiness of thousands of homes." That year the association's Parliamentary Committee argued that unions had never made "such determined, and in many cases unreasonable, efforts to secure for labor the domination of Canadian factories, and to wrest from the employer his inherent rights, to control the policy of his business and manage it, as he thinks best." A special committee on labour brought forward a stridently anti-union Declaration of Principles, which included the right of employers "to be unmolested and unhampered in the management of their business in determining the amount and quality of their product, and in the use of any methods or systems of factory management which are just and equitable." Hamilton's union leaders must have sensed a shift under way, since the same month they sponsored a resolution at the annual convention of the Trades and Labor Congress of Canada denouncing employers' increasing resort to the courts.[45]

Indeed, the tide was turning. The largest new corporate employers in the city had been setting the pace by stamping out any incipient unionizing efforts in their midst. There seems to have been a determination to insulate the new east-end factory district from the union influence that had spread over the older, downtown industrial areas. Robert Hobson's Hamilton Steel and Iron Company broke two strikes in 1900 and 1901 involving the rolling-mill hands imported from the United States to start up the new plant. The new workers were members of the Amalgamated Association of Iron, Steel, and Tin Workers and were insisting on the union wage scale. In 1902 that company's blast-furnace workers struck for a wage increase and reached out for community support with a lengthy, polite, carefully argued statement in the press. Rumours circulated that the strikers would like to abolish the 12-hour day in the plant and were taking the first step towards unionization. The company undermined their strike by importing a trainload of Italian labourers from Buffalo.[46]

The steel company's neighbours in the east-end factory district were taking a similar stand. Although the local machinists' union claimed to have a good working relationship with Westinghouse in 1903, George Westinghouse, president of both the Canadian and US companies, engaged in a much publicized exchange with AFL president Gompers that year over the question of unionizing his staff, making it quite clear that this was one corporation that would tolerate no workers' organizations in its plants. The Westinghouse management in Hamilton never wavered from that position.[47] Similarly, International Harvester's predecessor companies in the United States had built up such an anti-labour record, dating from the mid-1880s, that the Hamilton labour movement had mounted a vigorous and ultimately successful campaign to prevent the city fathers from granting the Deering Harvester Company a bonus to locate in the city. Then in 1904 the corporation provoked a walkout of its 70 unionized machinists by demanding that each man operate two machines and firing those who protested. The machinists' union had first confronted the two-machine issue across the continent in the 1890s and made clear that the acceptable norms of the trade as embodied in the union constitution forbade this heavier workload. The controversy became muddier as increasingly complex machinery appeared in the shops, but opposition persisted nonetheless. At the new Harvester plant this was "the last straw" for the machinists, who had been "dissatisfied at other things for a considerable period." The *Spectator* concluded that the dispute would "determine which is to have the whip hand, the company or the union." The corporation's slack production schedule for that summer gave it the advantage, and after more than two months the men agreed to return to work on the company's terms.[48] The next year the anti-union spirit spread to the large Sawyer-Massey agricultural implement company, which drove out the moulders' union, and in the fall of 1906 the Canadian Iron Foundry Company and the Grand Trunk shops did the same.[49]

All of these disputes paled alongside the confrontation that blew up in the fall of 1906 with one of the city's most powerful employers, the Cataract Power Company, owner of the Hamilton Street Railway. Here was the battle between corporate arrogance and working-class organization that highlighted the larger issues at stake and the depth of solidarity that could be summoned up in working-class Hamilton. To make their business pay, the company, like its counterparts in other cities, had always striven to keep wages low, hours long, discipline tight, and their workers non-union. In 1892 the workers' discontent with new work routines in the wake of electrification of its lines that summer boiled over. The street-railway company had sternly refused to deal with a fledgling union, and broke the short-lived strike by firing its leadership.[50]

Street-railway workers provided a vital service in a city sprawling outward across former farmland.
(HPL, Head of the Lake Society Collection)

The turning point in workplace relations on the street-railway came in 1899. That year Cataract Power absorbed the street-railway into its growing utilities empire. The change in managerial style was evident immediately. An employee described the new manager, C.K. Green, as "a very reserved and painstaking man." He was "full of business from his feet up," the worker said. "To say we are getting more like New York every day is putting it mild," he explained. "We now have to make out our own time when we have finished our day's run, on slips supplied by the company. Each and every man has a badge, such badge to be worn when on duty on the left breast of his coat." Earlier that year, however, in the wake of a tumultuous street-railway strike in London, 15 street-railwaymen had met secretly in the middle of the night, fearful of company spies, and, with the guidance of Philip Obermeyer, had signed the application for a charter to launch Division 107 of the Amalgamated Association of Street and Electric Railway Employees of America. Membership quickly expanded to include all employees, and within a month the company recognized the union. Less than a year later the first contract was signed, raising wages, reducing hours from 72 to 60 per week, and establishing a grievance system. Although the collective bargaining would have rocky moments that lurched to the brink of strikes, these agreements were renewed regularly until the summer of 1906.[51]

At that point the union demanded a wage increase and shorter hours, and inclusion of the poorly paid employees of the two new, rapidly expanding suburban radial railways owned by Cataract, whose workers had just joined the union. The company initially refused, but eventually agreed to three separate agreements, with the terms to be settled by arbitration. The arbitrators, one of whom was Allan Studholme, produced a compromise on 6 October that the union agreed to accept despite its weaker terms for the workers on the suburban lines. But the company delayed implementing the settlement for nearly a month and began to offer employees higher wages if they abandoned the union. The recently organized men in the car shops and on one suburban line complied (neither group had benefited from the arbitration award), while union supporters on that line were fired and replaced. The manager then informed the union that he had no intention of implementing the arbitrated agreement. Exasperated at this arrogant contempt for their union and its collective bargaining procedures, the men voted unanimously to walk out on 4 November, once again demanding the higher wages being denied by the arbitrators. Local officers pledged non-violence and sent for Fred Fay, the Amalgamated's international organizer, to provide direction during the strike.[52]

Cataract could expect little support from the people of Hamilton. The street-railway had always operated under terms set by the city council, which included rents for the city treasury, guaranteed working conditions for employees,[53] and cheap tickets for wage-earners to facilitate their commuting to and from work, especially in the emerging east-end factory district. But deteriorating service in the early 1900s had provoked public outrage. In 1904 the city council had to take the company to court to get them to stop restricting the sale of its "workmen's" tickets,[54] and two years later the council laid a much wider set of concerns before the new Ontario Railway and Municipal Board, charging that the whole street-railway system was "in a state of collapse." The aging cars were noisy and dirty, and the rails worn out. The road was so uneven and poorly ballasted that the street pavement could not be kept in repair. Service in several lines was alleged to be inadequate. All indications were that the company was trying to squeeze more profit out of this mass-transit system while investing as little as possible in renewal and upgrading of equipment. Privately John M. Gibson, Cataract's president, had complained to Premier James P. Whitney that the city's terms were too stringent to be able to pay dividends to shareholders and that democratic accountability to city council was an unacceptable burden. As negotiations with the union deteriorated in August 1906, the mayor suspected that "the company was holding out to force the hand of the city council in order to obtain concessions that could not be got any other way."[55]

The corporation had thus put itself on a collision course with both its workers and the whole community. Not surprisingly, it anticipated the kind of trouble that had exploded in street-railway strikes in other cities, most recently a few months earlier in Winnipeg, where crowds of union supporters had confronted company vehicles. Already, in 1902, a former Hamilton motorman who had worked as a scab during a Toronto street-railway strike had been harassed when he returned to Hamilton. "Some of the citizens gave him a reception one night of stale eggs and old cabbage," according to the union secretary. Now, as negotiations with the union stalemated late in August 1906, the company conjured up what the *Spectator* called "visions of riots and wrecked cars" and formally asked the city council and the police "to see that full protection was given in case there should be any opposition to the running of cars with non-union men." In a vain attempt to discredit the union, the company claimed that it had learned that "some of the men, anticipating a strike, have been collecting a quantity of aged eggs and other unsavory stuff to hurl at the heads of anyone who attempts to take a car out of the barns." The *Spectator* dismissed all this fear-mongering as "a bluff."[56]

Public sympathy was solidly on the side of the workers as the strike unfolded two months later. "The day is gone when soulless corporations can defy public opinion and common decency," the *Industrial Banner* announced. "And now is the time when every citizen of Hamilton should avail himself or herself of the opportunity to get even for the past." Even the Conservative *Spectator*, normally no friend of labour, admitted the strikers had "the backing of public opinion." The company had "foolishly made it a point to fight the 'union,' and in various ways it has forfeited its right to consideration by an impartial public." In particular, "inasmuch as the company has, of late, exhibited no particular desire to give the people the best street car service it could, the people will be slow to accept the company's excuse for not avoiding the strike."[57]

The people were not slow to show active support for the strikers. As always in street-railway strikes of the period, citizens pinned ribbons declaring "We Walk" on their chests, and refused to ride any streetcars that the company tried to run over the next four weeks. A prominent retailer (and one-time streetcar conductor),

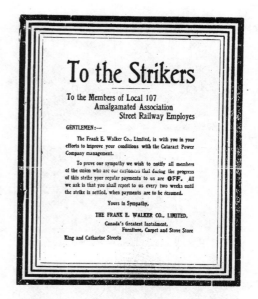

The street-railway workers' strike drew support from many Hamiltonians, including this merchant who was prepared to suspend payments on household goods purchased from him. (*HS*, 6 Nov. 1906, 7)

Frank E. Walker, donated $100 to the strike fund and suspended instalment payments owing to him during the strike. Other merchants offered free goods or special discounts to strikers, and two doctors promised free medical services. Cash donations rolled in from all sides. Letters and poems poured into the city's newspapers in support of the strikers. At large public meetings held in Hamilton, Dundas, and Burlington, local labour leaders and politicians denounced Cataract and praised the patience of the strikers and the justice of their cause. Twice the Trades and Labor Council organized parades through the downtown streets to put the solidarity of local unions on display. On two Sundays during the strike, the street-railwaymen also paraded to local churches, where sympathetic clergymen preached sermons to comfort and encourage them.[58]

During the 1906 street-railway strike, crowds of supporters attacked streetcars driven by strikebreakers, the offices of the Hamilton Street Railway Company, and the boarding houses where strikebreakers were billeted.

(HPL; SLS, LS646, LS676)

On the streets the union's struggle ignited the deep-seated anger of thousands of citizens for Cataract's arrogance and contempt for the population in general. For almost two weeks, the only vehicles the company sent out of its barns were cars for the suburban lines, whose employees had abandoned the union just before the strike (but were now gradually joining the strikers). Every day, crowds loudly jeered at the scabs and attacked the streetcars with stones, bottles, eggs, and other missiles aimed at smashing windows. "The popular idea that all cars running during strike time should be battered by citizens was

exemplified at the Radial station this morning, when the Dundas car pulled out," a *Spectator* reporter noted on the third day of the strike. "A lady standing near was highly indignant that the car should be allowed to go on its way unmolested. 'Just to think,' she exclaimed disgustedly, 'there were so many men standing there, and not one of them threw a stone.'"[59] Crowds also pelted the company offices and the boarding house where the company was housing its imported strikebreakers and private police. Obstacles of various kinds appeared on streetcar tracks. A stick of dynamite was discovered on one track, and another blew a hole in the roof of a company shed. Shots were occasionally exchanged with the scabs riding the cars. Most of these attacks took place after dark, and, until the end of the third week, the mayor managed to convince the company to stop running any cars in the evening. Company officials were also bombarded with anonymous letters threatening their lives.[60]

The union uncomfortably distanced itself from all this "rough" behaviour, and the press attributed it to "a rabble of boys and toughs." Young men and boys no doubt played a prominent role, but the roving crowds seemed to be a cross-section of working-class Hamilton. One report noted that trouble ensued "when the employees of the large factories were let loose," and those arrested came from a wide variety of occupations.[61] Nor was this merely a burst of masculine energy. After one particularly vigorous crowd action, two observers estimated that a third of the crowd were women and young girls, "many of them without escorts," including "four women with baby buggies containing infants." Another observer complained, "The papers decry the fact that the police struck women and children, but in the same lines they do not say that the men who hurled the bricks were in hiding up the lanes and the stones and bricks were being brought back to them by their wives, sisters, mothers or children."[62] These working people were not engaged in blind or random acts of violence, as the terms "mob" and "riot," typically used by voices most interested in public order, might suggest. Their targets were carefully chosen – the streetcars, the company offices, the scabs – and their behaviour had a disciplined, ritualistic familiarity evident in other street-railway strikes of the period. In essence they were drawing on a repertoire of age-old tactics of direct action and performance in the streets to confront a modern corporation that had affronted the whole community as well as its employees. Their actions revealed a profound concern that what the company was doing was illegitimate, and that it had violated well-understood community values about business in the community – that is, a popular "moral economy," as one famous historian would later name it.[63]

The union and the company remained far apart on the issues of the strike. The company, declaring that the strikers had quit, replaced them with both local recruits and professional strikebreakers with experience in recent battles, in Winnipeg among other places. One reporter described the replacements as some of "the hardest specimens of manhood." Indeed, "I have seen a number of hard-looking citizens," a visiting moulders' leader commented, "but this bunch beats anything I have seen in a long time."[64] The company also imported Pinkerton detectives from Chicago to ride the cars as private police. The unionists refused to turn in their hats, badges, and punches, and insisted on their right to return to their jobs when the dispute was over. Within a few days, moreover, the workers on one suburban line and in the repair shops joined the strike.

Mayor S.D. Biggar strove in vain to bring the two sides together. On 12 November the national employers' association, the Canadian Street Railway Association, called an emergency meeting in Toronto and announced its moral and financial support for the company – the only public sympathy for the company expressed from any quarter. The same day the company declared that no settlement was possible. It put its first cars back onto city streets, and, fully aware that such a move would provoke crowd resistance, demanded that the mayor call in the militia to protect its property.[65] This was more an assertion of managerial prerogative than an attempt to bring back transportation service because it was clear that the only passengers on the scab-driven cars were the private police armed with axe handles and pistols. "We are going to fight, and we are going to fight that union to a finish, even if it takes two or twenty years," manager Green announced on 14 November. "Our cars will be operated by non-union men and will never again be operated by these union men."[66]

The mayor repeatedly rejected the military option, and turned instead to the Ontario Municipal and Railway Board, which had coincidentally just arrived to open hearings on the city's complaints against the street-railway company. When the board brushed aside his suggestion that it take over the streetcar service (privately Premier Whitney would suggest the same move a week later), the mayor spent the next week trying to use the board as a mediating force.[67] The union was deeply suspicious of the board's anti-labour bias as a result of its intervention into the recent street-railway strike in London, and the company resisted any concessions. When these mediation efforts failed, the mayor held the company back from starting its full service while he tried to bring about a settlement personally. In the end, the two sides simply continued their war of words in lengthy press statements.

On Friday 23 November, the company finally threw down the gauntlet by running streetcars after dark, when crowd attacks were most likely. Thousands of citizens converged on the downtown streets to attack these vehicles, the company offices, and the scabs' new boarding house with the usual hail of stones. The police were overwhelmed. "WILD MOB WAS IN COMPLETE CONTROL," screamed the *Spectator*'s banner headline the next day. Late on the night of the riot, 100 soldiers of Canada's regular army arrived from Toronto. Another 50 came from London the next day. On Saturday night, as the same crowd activity was taking shape, the sheriff read the Riot Act and the city police immediately began clearing the streets, indiscriminately swinging their wooden batons at any men or women who were too slow in getting out of their path. Mounted soldiers armed with swords and soldiers on foot with fixed bayonets also swept people before them. Many people were seriously injured in this brutal assault. The next day the sheriff ordered union organizer Fay to leave the city, without charging him with any crime.[68]

The city immediately erupted in outrage, especially against the police activity. City aldermen, newspaper editorials, letters to the editor, and street-corner commentary criticized the unrestrained violence involved in dispersing the crowds. One man who had watched the scene from an upper window denounced the police as "a lot of Russian soldiers" and "hoodlums." Even the head of the professional strikebreakers admitted he had never seen such a police reaction. Small crowds heckled the soldiers as well, and merchants refused to sell provisions to them, or found their teamsters unwilling to deliver to them. By this point too stories were spreading about the strikebreakers' drunkenness on the cars and their wilful damage of company property and store windows.[69]

The street-railway company was evidently unnerved by the intensity of this popular response to its strategy of inciting repression to break the strike. The mayor was able to draw it back into talks aimed at settlement. The union's international president, W.D. Mahon, arrived to handle the workers' side of the negotiations. After several days of arguing over details, the company and the union agreed to an unconditional arbitration by the Railway and Municipal Board on 30 November. A strike that the international union would describe as "one of the most bitterly contested and stubborn strikes marking the history of our Association" had finally ended. The next morning, unionists drove the battered streetcars onto the streets (two were manned by non-unionists, but, when no one would ride in them, the crews quit). A week later the board decided that the company had to recognize the union on all three lines and respect the union's grievance system. A mutually acceptable schedule that somewhat reduced hours and respected seniority was put in place. But no wage increases were granted beyond those of the October arbitration, and none could be expected over the lifetime of the three-year contract.[70]

The union had some cause to claim a victory. In a fitting epilogue to this remarkable month, Studholme won the East Hamilton by-election for Labor on 4 December, and a month later a slate of Labor candidates was swept into city hall. More broadly, the remarkable dispute caught a lot of public attention across Canada, and the federal minister of labour cited it in introducing his new Industrial Disputes Investigation Act early in 1907.[71]

The street-railway strike of November 1906 burned an indelible mark in the public memory of the city.[72] It would be invoked in public debate for years to come. More immediately, it provided different lessons for wage-earners and for capitalists. For Studholme's people, it became an exhilarating inspiration. The following spring, a local paper worried that a "Labour War" had broken out as strikes erupted among largely unorganized unskilled workers in numerous workplaces – builders' labourers, steelworkers, sewer-pipe-makers, railway construction labourers, and the city's own labourers – as well as among unionized plumbers, painters, carpenters, and teamsters. In a familiar pattern, Hamiltonians refused to give the scab teamsters at the large Hendrie Cartage Company directions through the city or provide them with supplies.[73]

It was nonetheless becoming harder to sustain a movement built on wide community support. As the city's production shifted increasingly towards heavy industry that had no direct relationship with local consumers, a strategy based on substantial pressure on employers from working-class consumers could do little or nothing for the thousands of men and women in the large new primary steel, metalworking, and textile mills. Aside from the building trades,[74] much of the craft union movement was rooted in sectors of the local economy that were declining or stagnating, and by World War One few of its members would be found in the large new plants that then dominated industrial life in the city. In 1911, for example, the executive of the Trades and Labor Council consisted of two musicians, two barbers, a bartender, a broom-maker, a retail clerk, a plumber, two garment workers, and a foundry pattern-maker.[75] Increasingly craft unionists were watching industrial life in the city from the sidelines.

For the corporate capitalists of Hobson's Hamilton, the street-railway strike hammered home a more sobering lesson about constraints on their strategies for capital accumulation. A Montreal businessman had summed up the problem during one of the municipal and railway board hearings: "Too much unionism was allowed."[76] Since the late 1890s a resurgent craft union movement had re-established itself in a large number of the city's workplaces, impinged on city politics, and mobilized widespread support from working-class neighbourhoods, whether in appeals to buy union-made products or in the more direct action of a strike. A large number of employers had agreed to sit down and talk directly with these new unions. Now they had second thoughts.

Some leading employers had already decided to have neither truck nor trade with unions and insisted on an "open shop" – notably Hamilton Steel and Iron, International Harvester, and Westinghouse. The serious depression that began in 1907 prompted many more employers in Hamilton to take a permanent, vigorously anti-union turn. The most publicized move came in the winter of 1908–9, when the members of the Dominion Iron Founders' Defense Association turned on the stove moulders in what the *Industrial Banner* called "a manifest attempt to use the business depression as a lever to smash the labor organizations and put them out of business." In Hamilton the foundrymen's demand for a 20 per cent wage cut provoked the union into a long, bitter, and ultimately unsuccessful strike. Imported strikebreakers helped to ensure that the four stove foundries would have no unions to deal with for the next decade.[77]

Other unions were losing their hold as well. Lyons Tailoring, one of the only local firms still using the garment workers' label, had declared an open shop by 1910, and the next year the only firm in Ontario still using the label was Grafton's in neighbouring Dundas. That year a foreman at Thornton and Douglas was reported to be firing workers found with union cards in their pockets.[78] As president of the new Hamilton branch of the Canadian Manufacturers' Association, Hobson set the new tone of the city's employers in 1910 when he rebuffed the efforts of the Trades and Labor Council to initiate discussions between the two organizations.[79]

These industrialists had more on their minds than simply bloody-minded arrogance. They wanted what decades later capitalists would call "flexibility" – freedom from the restraints on their power to initiate workplace changes that unions wanted to negotiate and from community intervention into their decision-making processes. Besides complaining about low-wage competition, for example, the stove founders also registered their concern that union moulders "unduly restricted" production and thus used the strike as the moment to mechanize part of their production.[80] The Second Industrial Revolution that the city's industrialists were beginning to set in motion was a top-down project, and, in contrast to the opening years of the century, negotiating with a well-organized, class-conscious workforce was no longer part of managerial common sense in Hamilton.

10

As this 1906 photo of Westinghouse foremen suggests, the company encouraged its front-line supervisors to identify with the company's senior management. The vice-president and general manager, Paul J. Myler, is seated in the middle of the front row.

(MUA, Westinghouse Fonds, Box 43, File 2)

The Whip Hand

IN THE SUMMER OF 1904 a *Spectator* reporter wanted his readers to understand what was really on International Harvester's mind in the bitter confrontation with its machinists that had just flared up. Drawing on the popular imagery of driving horses, he suggested that it was an issue of who would have "the whip hand." It was an old-fashioned but apt phrase for an emerging attitude in front offices across the city. In the decade before World War One, more and more of Hamilton's factory managers believed that

their production systems left too much control informally in workers' hands.

As the manager of a local foundry declared, "When employes start in to dictate how a business shall be run it is time for the management to take a hand." To realize the profit-making potential of their plants, owners and managers had decided that they needed to curtail the independent capacities of their employees and get more work out of their labour power at lower costs. If there was a crystallizing moment of these individual anxieties into a more widely shared determination, it might have been at a luncheon in January 1905, when many manufacturers showed up to hear P.W. Ellis, a Toronto industrialist, deliver an address on "Factory Costs." That event certainly coincided with the decisions of many local businessmen to stop co-operating with unions, and with an eagerness for new methods to tighten their grip on the labour processes in their plants.[1]

They were not all starting from the same place in their search for solutions. Firms with long histories in the city had to confront the weight of the past directly, while many corporate newcomers had already tussled with the problem in the United States and were hoping to start up in Hamilton with a freer hand. The east-end factory district that was starting to absorb such a large percentage of the city's workforce was indeed a brand new industrial complex, unburdened by the shackles of local tradition. Newness, however, was not necessarily enough, because much depended on the markets for each firm's product. Specialty work or sporadic demand for the company's goods permitted only small-scale batch production and limited technological or organizational innovation in work processes. But steady sales of identical products allowed a shift to the new techniques of "mass production."[2]

To describe the capitalist responses to these diverse situations as a common strategy would be to give them more vision and coherence than they generally had. Industrialists and their top managers were practical men looking for ways of getting more profits out of their factories, and in their search for managerial solutions they selected from a range of options according to their particular needs. They were nonetheless aware that they were part of a general ferment in the corporate-capitalist world. Many of them no doubt poured over articles on management practices in the business and trade journals and discussed them in the meetings of their various business organizations. Some consulted self-styled "experts." The outcome in each case was not the same, but most managerial solutions

began to share a common philosophy and to fall within recognizable patterns. Eventually these individual efforts to organize more productive labour processes merged into a generalized managerial offensive that gave the Second Industrial Revolution its distinctive character.

Skill by Any Other Name

Even without their unions, skilled workers posed difficult problems for Hamilton's employers. Simply put, they were scarce, expensive, and obstructionist. The Canadian Manufacturers' Association co-ordinated efforts to import more of them, but ultimately the workers' role in production had to change if employers wanted more output from their plants. Some, like International Harvester's machinists and the spinners and weavers in the three cotton mills, could be pushed to handle more machines at the same time. In a few cases new machinery was found to substitute directly for skilled hands, but not often.[3] More commonly, skilled work had to be further subdivided, with the jobs assigned to lower-paid, less-skilled workers (often known in this period as "handymen"), and wherever possible mechanized. Few crafts still alive in the 1890s escaped these attacks after the turn of the century, but, as the city shifted so decisively to iron and steel work in the early 20th century, it was the many skilled men in the metal trades, especially the moulders and machinists, who faced the most severe crisis. Before 1900 they were probably employees of different firms, but in the new century they more frequently worked in separate departments of the same larger corporations.

Foundry workers felt the impact of these changes. Wherever there was repetitive work on standardized products, moulders' tasks were narrowed and specialized. By the 1890s, for example, few stove-plate moulders made

Pouring a casting at
Dofasco in the 1930s.
(SLS, LS443)

the castings for an entire stove. International Harvester also used less-skilled European immigrants in gangs to perform each step in moulding large numbers of parts for its farm machinery. The corporation also hired women to work as core-makers. A reporter who visited their work room in 1907 found that "the girls were working apparently for dear life." Both immigrants and female labourers came to their jobs without any well-established notions of what constituted a "fair day's work" in the foundry, and both groups tended to leave the workforce quickly.[4]

To make this kind of subdivision of the moulder's tasks really effective required new technology – in this case, the moulding machine. Actually, there was no one single machine, but rather a range of machinery for ramming sand into the moulds and lifting out the patterns.[5] A 1908 article in *Canadian Machinery* described the advantages of these new devices over the foibles of human producers:

The molding machine is purely and simply a mechanical molder and differing from its human competitor can work the whole twenty-four hours without stopping, knows no distinctions between Sundays, holidays and any ordinary day, requires as its only lubricant a little oil, being in fact abstinent in all other matters, has no near relatives dying at awkward moments, has no athletic propensities, belongs to no labor organization, knows nothing about limitation of output, never thinks of wasting its owner's time in conversation with its fellow machine. War, rumors of war and baseball scores, have no interest for it and its only ambition in life is to do the best possible work in the greatest possible quantity.[6]

Still, the machine did not run itself, and an additional advantage was the speed that could be demanded of the operator to turn out more castings per day. An Ontario factory inspector found that the men who operated the new machines had "to go lively, as the machines are generally speeded up to the limit." At International Harvester, "They had to work like Trojans to keep up," reported the local union president, James W. Ripley, in 1910. "No ordinary mechanic could work that way, because he could not stand the pace.... The foreigners were rugged men, but even they did not last long." An American economist also noted, "The molding-machine operator became himself a mere machine, with none of the variety to his work which characterized the skilled handworker."[7]

Canadian trade journals, passionate promoters of the new equipment, criticized Canadian foundrymen for their backwardness. The editor of *Canadian Engineer* argued in 1906 that the new technology would "revolutionize the foundry business." He stated, "A simple power machine, operated by one laborer, another shovelling sand, and one to carry out the flask, can turn out one mould per minute or on a union rule of seven hours moulding, pouring 140 moulds per man; being twice as much as a union moulder can do by hand."[8] Hamilton's foundries were at the forefront of change. The two biggest, International Harvester and Canadian Westinghouse, were North American pioneers in the field. Henry Pridmore, a leading manufacturer of moulding machines, had begun his experiments in 1886 in the McCormick Harvester works in Chicago (a component of the Harvester merger), where the company introduced the new machinery in a successful attempt to drive out the local moulders' union. A company executive later boasted: "Their great foundries and their novel molding machinery were the admiration of the iron world." Not surprisingly, then, a visitor to the new Hamilton plant's foundry in 1904 spotted moulding machines in each moulder's stall.[9] The Canadian Westinghouse plant was similarly in the vanguard of managerial innovation. Its foundry superintendent, David Reid, was reputedly "one of the most prominent foundrymen of America." As part of his extensive US experience, Reid had managed a foundry in which he had been responsible for a restructuring of the work process, using moulding machines and "dividing labor, whereby the molder practised the art of molding and nothing else," with the result that "the melt was increased from 12 or 15 tons daily to between 50 and 60 tons."[10]

Mechanization in other Hamilton foundries proceeded quickly. At least six that produced machinery installed the new devices between 1908 and 1913,[11] and the stove foundrymen opened the subject in their tense negotiations with the local moulders' union early in 1909. The *Spectator* reported, "If they cannot secure the co-operation of the molders in trying them out, they will have to use other labor." Within a few weeks the strike-bound Gurney-Tilden Company introduced its first mechanical devices, run by Italian labourers. By May these scab moulders had themselves walked out on strike and joined the union.[12]

Mechanization did not sweep relentlessly over the whole foundry industry. In 1916 a committee on foundry methods established by the National Foundrymen's Association reported that not more than 25 per cent of its North American membership had taken advantage of the available mechanical appliances. But it was in the larger foundries, especially those that dominated the industrial landscape, that innovation was most advanced. By the 1920s most of the city's foundries had introduced a wide range of mechanical devices. "Twenty years ago an unskilled man in the foundry would not have been permitted to handle even a slick, being only allowed to assist in the ramming of big jobs perhaps, lifting or similar work," *Canadian Foundryman* gloated in 1928. "Now unskilled labor can step into an up-to-date foundry and within a few days perform a task equal to that of the skilled molder, due to present day equipment."[13]

Along with new technology, foundry owners turned to science as a new ally in their efforts to win more control over the traditional craft skills in their plants. They were able to turn to the growing ranks of industrial chemists, who promised more precise, scientific monitoring of production than the older rule-of-thumb empiricism of the craftworker could deliver. Their impact on industrial life emerged more slowly. The first detailed reports on the big new plants in the city before the war never mentioned any laboratories, but the war stirred up interest in more centralized industrial research, especially after the creation of the Honorary Advisory Council on Industrial and Scientific Research (later renamed the National Research Council)

in 1916, of which the Steel Company's Robert Hobson was a member.[14] By the 1920s journalists were describing laboratories in the International Harvester and Westinghouse plants, where industrial chemists were responsible for regular testing of foundry products. These new professionals were expected to bring their employers more predictability and uniformity. In the process they chipped away more of the power and control of the skilled worker on the shop floor.[15]

During the same years machine shops went through a similar, perhaps even more dramatic, evolution. One breakthrough had been the turret lathe, a machine mounted with a cluster of tools that could be applied to a piece of work in a sequence of operations with no need for that worker to adjust the material in the lathe – although until these processes were automated, the workman's skill was still required. The other great innovation had been the milling machine, a device with a set of rotating cutting tools for planing, curving, or otherwise shaping the metal, which required less individual skill in the hands of the operator. By the turn of the century, machine-shop tools were becoming increasingly complex and specialized, with more automation in their operation and calling for less physical effort and skill to control them. In using these tools, workers were able to turn out high-quality work more quickly.[16] The industry took another technological leap after 1906 with the introduction of a new "high-speed" steel for cutting tools, which allowed cutting speeds to be increased enormously and the rates of production to be pushed up 50 to 400 per cent. A Canadian business journalist stated in 1910 that all the "radical changes" in recent machine-tool practice had resulted from the use of high-speed steel.[17] As in the foundries, the most remarkable changes came wherever the demand for one product allowed for repetitive, high-volume production.

Canadian machining work moved less towards automatic machinery than to creating narrowly trained handymen who could do no more than one specialized task. "Young men come into the factory and soon acquire the necessary skill to become proficient drill press operators or milling machine operators," a survey of the Canadian industry noted in 1913. "They are able to earn fairly good wages in a shorter space of time than if they served the necessary term of apprenticeship to become competent all-round machinists." The trend was clear in Hamilton from the turn of the century. In 1900 the local machinists' union called for "a legal apprenticeship to limit the number of boys and incompetent men employed at low wages in the shops." At that point, the city's machine shops had specialized work for toolmakers, lathe hands, planer and shaper hands, vise hands and fitters, and drill hands, each with a different scale of wages. By 1908 specialization was so widespread that, surveying the sad state of unionism among Hamilton machinists, the union's Canadian vice-president concluded that the local lodge would "have to turn its attention soon to organizing the specialists' class before undertaking any important move in the machine trade."[18]

World War One accelerated this trend. Almost every metalworking plant in the city converted its production to filling large munitions contracts for Allied governments, mostly for shells. Many thus got their first taste of mass production of identical products. In the face of a severe labour shortage, these firms began to subdivide labour more extensively, using workers with no machining experience to operate simple single-purpose equipment that made only one of the series of cuts required on the shell steel, a process that became known as "dilution." By the end of the war, nine-tenths of the country's shell plants were using this specialized machinery.[19]

These simplified procedures made it easier to introduce unskilled women workers into the shell-making shops, and towards the end of 1916 the Imperial Munitions Board's Labour Department began to recruit them. In one munitions plant the use of female labour prompted a subdivision of the shell machining into "twenty-five separate handlings." The advantage of such a new workforce over the artisanal sensibilities of the skilled machinist was soon evident. A business journalist reported that the new workers of both sexes were more reliable than the all-round craftworkers, who generally found "the repetition style of single operation ... too monotonous." Using this new labour on specialized equipment made possible an unprecedented speed-up. In the fall of 1915 one shrapnel shell factory reported an increase in its daily output of from 800 to 2,700, and in 1917 another went from 700–800 shells to 5,000, without expanding its floor space appreciably. Small wonder that contemporaries were talking about a "revolution" in the machine shop.[20]

This was more than a wartime diversion. "Modern manufacturing methods have broken down standards in the machinist trades," Technical School principal Sprague observed in 1921. "The rank and file of men operating machines in what is known as the metal trades are merely machine tenders, operators, and specialists, according to the mastery they possess in producing on some particular machine.[21] In 1924 the editor of *Canadian Machinery* contrasted the new world of the machine shop with a time 20 years earlier when "an unskilled man was not allowed to handle a file, being only permitted to chip burrs off castings, hand the fitter his tools, hold the work in place, or sweep the floors; now the unskilled have jobs in the machine shop, such as drilling, drill sharpening, lathe work, etc. and are slowly ousting skilled men from the field."[22]

Brawn and Elbow Grease

Craftsmen were not the only workers feeling the winds of change in Hamilton's factories after the turn of the century. Employers also turned their attention to the work world of the unskilled. They brought together what they thought could overcome the unpredictability and unruly independence of the labourers in their workforce – the new immigrant and the machine.

First, they began to dip into new pools of labour that they hoped would be plentiful and malleable. Over the first decade of the 20th century, when several of the city's biggest employers in heavy industry began to recruit large numbers of Southern and Eastern European migrant labourers, what they often did was turn to new supplies of those workers that were appearing on construction sites. Italians first arrived in large numbers in excavation work on the Toronto, Hamilton, and Buffalo Railway in 1895, and had come to dominate this work by 1909, when the *Labour Gazette*'s local correspondent reported that "very few English-speaking labourers secured employment on the railway work." Most excavating contractors in the city came to prefer "foreign" labour, and one of the city's biggest general contracting firms, the Cooper construction company, employed only Italians by World War One.[23] Hamilton's manufacturers did not rely on construction contractors to do all the recruiting, however – as exemplified by the Hamilton Steel and Iron Company when it undercut the 1902 strike of its largely Anglo-Canadian blast-furnace labourers by bringing in Italians from Buffalo. The quarters of those newcomers on the company grounds became the core of the new east-end European immigrant community.[24]

Meanwhile, International Harvester was preparing to introduce a new workforce with a similarly diverse ethnic mix. The Chicago agricultural-implement firms that came together into International Harvester had pioneered the practice of hiring European labourers, especially Poles, for the new subdivided jobs in that industry.[25] During the 1902 referendum campaign for bonusing the corporation, the Hamilton Trades and Labor Council denounced the firm's use of "the cheapest of foreign labor" in Chicago, which was "housed on the grounds of the company" and "more closely guarded than the county jail." While a company agent quickly denied any intention to "import cheap labor," many immigrants, especially Poles, were brought from Chicago to work in the new plant. In 1904 a *Spectator* reporter who had just returned from watching the firm's 1,300 employees at work remarked that they were "more varied in nationality than those of almost any other concern in Canada," and three years later an inspector at the plant estimated that "over half of the employees of the Harvester works are foreigners, either Polocks, Italians, or some other peculiar nationality."[26]

With these many Europeans finding their way to Hamilton, the city's manufacturers could simply send word back through relatives or the local ethnic labour agents that they had jobs for more of their fellow countrymen. "Each nationality has one or more citizens who keep their eyes open in the interest of their people," a Hamilton workingman noted in 1914, "and a very striking instance of this may be noted from the fact that one will often see a gang of Italians or Poles, etc., being led around to the various factories by one of their interpreters to help them 'land a job.'"[27] By 1918 a local government official believed that these Europeans did "practically the whole of the heavy and laborious work" in the city's iron, steel, and metalworking plants. That same year the national registration of eligible male workers

The unskilled work of cleaning castings at Dofasco in the 1930s. (SLS, LS372)

found that in Hamilton more than one-fifth of them were Continental Europeans (though that proportion had dropped to one-ninth of the adult male workforce by 1921). A few years later *Canadian Foundryman*'s editor could claim that Europeans operated most of the country's moulding machines.[28]

In popular discourse, the merging of certain jobs and ethnic stereotypes quickly became naturalized and universal. In 1907 a foreman at International Harvester said that the "foreigners" were getting jobs that "a white man would not care to do," just as a *Spectator* reporter claimed the same year that in the steel plant, "Few Canadian-born youths take kindly to the rough nature of the work."[29] In 1916 Clifton W. Sherman, president and general manager of the Dominion Steel Castings Company, explained that his firm, like so many others, chose these European newcomers "because the work is of

such a hot and laborious character that an English-speaking man will not do it." He compared this development to section work in railroading, which "has changed from the hands of Irishmen to the Slav, and is now done entirely by the Italians."[30] These opinions ignored how British workingmen were clearly willing to handle such heavy work back home in the United Kingdom. Unions argued that the city's ethnic specialization resulted from poor wages and working conditions in these jobs.

The advantages of this new unskilled labour force were compelling for local industrialists. Living a thrifty lifestyle for short spells in crowded boarding houses, the newcomers were willing to work for lower wages than were Anglo-Canadians. In 1919 the Steel Company's H.H. Champ countered arguments about deporting the "aliens" by emphasizing their cheapness: "If we expect returned soldiers to do the rough, rugged work, many of us would be out of business because we could not produce at anything like low enough cost."[31] As transients with no deep attachment to their jobs and limited experience in factories, they might also be used flexibly in a changing workplace. As "foreigners," these men were also cut off from other workers by a deep cultural gulf. The *Herald* summed up these advantages bluntly in 1910 in the wake of a strike at the steel plant:

> The fact that almost all of the steel and iron workers are foreign and single men who have no real place in the life of the city, who know nothing about our civic and national affairs, and who are here only for the money they make and will be away when they have saved a sufficiency, and whose standard of living is below that of the average English-speaking workman, makes the public comparatively indifferent to their claims. Thus the great manufacturing corporations serve a double purpose when they import cheap labor from continental Europe. They get work done at a cost less than the cost of getting it done by English-speaking workmen; and they prevent the enlistment of public opinion on the side of the workers when troubles arise with their foreign employees.[32]

The managerial agenda for unskilled work involved more than changing the language spoken by the musclemen. It also involved mechanizing the simple tasks of lifting, carrying, loading, and unloading. Corporate managers wanted to eliminate any bottlenecks in production resulting from human frailty or stubborn resistance – and in the process to speed up production. The cheap new electrical power flowing along Cataract Power lines into most local factories after 1898 made it much easier to replace the labourer, his wheelbarrow and shovel, and the stable of work horses. One of the most important innovations was the electric travelling crane, a large, mobile apparatus that could be driven along the length of the workshop just below the ceiling. It was capable of lifting and carrying loads in excess of 50 tons.[33] New transportation systems were also installed inside the factories to haul raw materials and finished goods. Railway sidings were often extended inside the buildings to bring the stock closer to the workbenches. Raw materials were frequently drawn up on high trestles in hopper cars and dropped into convenient bins for storage, without manual handling. Inside the plants smaller tracks allowed heavy loads to be driven between departments on a powered vehicle. The Westinghouse plant, for instance, had a narrow-gauge electric railway running throughout its buildings and yards. By 1930 the "electric lift truck" requiring no rails had arrived. Increasingly complex conveyor systems also appeared soon after the turn of the century. In the trend-setting Harvester and Westinghouse plants, electrically driven conveyor belts whisked material such as coke to the furnaces. Wartime munitions work brought similar changes to many more plants.[34]

The city's leading steel plant provided a particularly good example of the mechanization of unskilled labour. A huge crane known as a "travelling bridge" was used for unloading raw materials. In place of the dozens of labourers and their wheelbarrows feeding the blast furnace and carting away the hardened pig iron, the company installed new equipment in 1907 for moving raw materials from storage and depositing them in the top of the blast furnaces and for handling the finished iron. A driver in a small, electrically powered car carried the raw materials from bins behind the furnaces over to an inclined lifting device known as a "skip hoist,"

At the Steel Company of Canada, molten steel was drained from open-hearth furnaces into a giant "ladle," whose operator later emptied its contents into moulds to create ingots.
(LAC, PA-24646)

which raised and dumped it into the top of the furnace. At the front of the furnace, operators of huge electric travelling cranes caught much of the molten iron in ladles, from which it could be used immediately in the open-hearth steel-making process, rather than being allowed to harden and then having to be broken apart. For the pig iron that was to be sold to foundries or stored for future use, the company replaced the ironworkers' "brawn and elbow grease" in hammering the pigs apart by introducing an electric crane and a mechanical "pig breaker." After 1920 a conveyor belt of metal moulds known as a "pig-casting machine" replaced the manual methods of handling the pig iron. In the open-hearth department the driver of an "electric charging machine" thrust the raw materials into the furnaces, and cranemen carried away the steel that spilled out into their ladles to be drained into ingot moulds. Cranes again brought the glowing

iron to the rolling mills, where a few men stood in nests of levers to guide the blocks of iron along electrically driven roller tables and through the huge rolls. *Canadian Foundryman* was especially impressed with the Steel Company's new rolling mills, which opened in 1913: "Modern rolling mills are really automatic machines on a large scale, one machine sometimes covering an acre or more of ground, and operated by a few men almost entirely without hard muscular labor." Wire rods, the journal noted, were rolled "by the pure continuous process, and the steel is not touched by hand from the time the billets leave the stock pile until the coiled rods are taken from the bundle conveyor."[35] Labourers had certainly not disappeared from the steel plant – frequent spills, mishaps, and maintenance kept them busy – but the new technology had drastically reduced the need for an unskilled labour force and diminished considerably the pacing of production according to the rhythms of human exertion.[36]

Employers liked this machinery because of its "labour-saving" quality. *Canadian Foundryman* explained how a travelling crane could "do the work of thirty men in a fraction of the time – unloading cars and placing the material at any point within a radius of fifty feet," and a visitor to the new International Harvester plant in 1904 remarked, "Automatic carrying devices are used wherever possible, in order to keep the parts of the finished machines moving more rapidly than would be possible with human motive power." Similarly a visitor to the National Steel Car plant a decade later marvelled at the labour saved by the portable riveters and electric hoists that lifted the frames of the cars. Lifting, hauling, and carrying by human labour had been "reduced to a minimum."[37]

Such devices also eliminated the snags in production brought about by the unpredictable behaviour of labourers. The timing and justification for all this mechanization point to the industrialists' concern for more predictability and productivity. "When labour is scarce and wages are high," a Canadian business journalist suggested, "the need for labor-saving equipment is brought to the attention of executives most forceably." Labour shortages, such as those that appeared briefly at the turn of the century, in the 1911–13 period, and during the war, often provided the impetus.[38] With these short-term advantages in the labour market, the unskilled men could disrupt work schedules by refusing to lug and heave under a hot, summer sun or inside a smoky foundry. "In replacing men on jobs of this character, cranes solve a vexing labor problem," a business journalist explained. "Workmen find it bad enough to be forced to handle frozen pig and scrap iron in winter, but when the summer heat comes beating down the men

become inefficient and discontented. Many of them leave." Perhaps most important, the machines connected the various stages of production and put more pressure on all workers to keep up with the flow.[39]

Unskilled work, then, had been significantly changed. Large parts of it had been labelled "non-white" and filled with cheaper labour from Southern and Eastern Europe; and much more of it had been turned over to operators of powerful new machines, which carried more and ran faster than human muscle power would allow.

The Front Office

Crushing unions, breaking down skills, recruiting a new workforce, and mechanizing unskilled work: all of these practices would not by themselves have created a whole new factory regime without the new rapidly expanding ideology and systems of a more professional, centralized management. Before the turn of the century Hamilton's manufacturing firms were most often run by their owners with the help of a small band of male clerks and shop-floor supervisors, mostly foremen. In early-20th-century Hamilton, managing a factory came to mean placing much more emphasis on centralized planning and co-ordination from the front office, handled by a much larger white-collar managerial staff. Industrialists moved cautiously in abandoning the 19th-century practices of relatively decentralized, ad-hoc decision-making, and adopted the new managerial systems only once they could see higher productivity and profits. For most local firms that conversion took place in the decade before World War One.

The railways had devised the first new complex managerial systems decades before Canadian manufacturers took the subject to heart.[40] By the close of the 19th century, two groups of self-styled "experts" had begun to press for similarly fundamental changes in factory administration. On the one side, the men in charge of the books, the accountants, were arguing for more "system" and orderliness in keeping track of costs within the burgeoning corporations. On the other, the engineers, especially the mechanical and electrical engineers, were experimenting with new techniques and organization of production. Both groups, if not factory owners themselves, were filling jobs that were once part of the entrepreneur's own work – running the office and overseeing the shop. Now they were struggling to win acceptance as professionals, with new university-level training programs, accreditation and licensing procedures, and professional associations. Both groups identified closely with the owners of the firms, and in many cases moved into top-level managerial positions. But as the opportunities for self-employment in this kind of work diminished, they discovered that they had to convince corporate executives of the value of their new professional solutions to the problems of corporate administration. Many used their supervisory positions to experiment and to win support from owners. The most articulate spread the word in the pages of the trade and business press. The most ambitious offered their services as consultants.[41]

The remedies of these "experts" were similar in applying "scientific" principles and methods to practical industrial problems and in promising higher profits through orderly procedures and tighter management control of production – what has come to be known as "systematic management." They found their first and most sympathetic response in the United States, but firms of such experts also began to appear in Canada in the early 20th century to provide special management services, often with a particular industrial focus, such as foundries.[42] At the same time Canadian business journalists began

to popularize these new concepts of factory administration with a steady stream of theoretical articles and case studies of specific management problems and experiments.[43]

There was no single blueprint for reorganizing factory administration, but, in general, the accountants argued for more careful monitoring of costs, while the engineers pushed for more centralized planning and co-ordination. The two emphases were soon submerged within a single coherent managerial ideology that promoted the new cult of efficiency. More rigid cost accounting would ostensibly close up so-called "profit leaks" by providing a more accurate measure of actual production costs and isolating areas in the entire manufacturing operation where costs needed reducing. "Broadly speaking," an accountant explained in *Industrial Canada* in 1906, "factory economy means the production of your output for less money." A costing system would "induce economy by the elimination of waste and . . . by intensifying production."[44]

The most direct, and most loathed, tool of the cost accountant was the time clock, which workers in the larger firms in Hamilton and elsewhere began punching soon after the turn of the century.[45] Management also introduced new methods to be used during the working day. The most elaborate schemes had each product being assigned a card or loose-leaf sheet that contained written instructions for each step of production and on which workers recorded the material used and labour time consumed. Each worker would also have his own card to keep track of his time and daily tasks. The manager could expect the "system" to tell him "the efficiency of every man and every machine per labour hour and machine hour," and inform him of "all delays and the reasons for the failure to arrive at the maximum."[46] Foremen were under new pressure to keep this flow of recorded data moving smoothly and to answer for any productivity problems that might appear. The engineers liked these procedures, but grafted on their own package of reforms in shop-floor management, which included more centralized scheduling, routing, job design, work incentives, and overall planning. Foremen and skilled workers would now be expected to carry out instructions about how work was to be done, rather than making these decisions themselves in the decentralized ways of the 19th century.

These managerial reforms got a boost in 1911 when the hearings of the United States Commission on Interstate Commerce gave wide publicity to the sophisticated management schemes developed by Frederick W. Taylor and his school of "scientific management." The Canadian business press promptly endorsed what has come to be known as Taylorism, even though it soon came under heavy attack from the US labour movement and sympathetic congressional investigators.[47] Taylor drew on the experimentation of others, but added the crucial new ingredient of using stop watches to calculate "scientific" norms for the speed of work. With this data, managerial staff could not only monitor production, but also speed it up with explicit orders from the front office. Taylor's contribution to the emerging authoritarian, bureaucratic mode of factory administration was the patina of indisputable "scientific" truth and objectivity that he claimed for a process that was blatantly biased towards increasing the factory owner's profit-making potential by cutting labour costs. Indeed, these new managerial propagandists redefined the word "efficiency" as a more socially conscious synonym for profitability through centralized power.[48]

Just how extensively Hamilton's industrialists adopted the newest managerial practices or consulted these new efficiency engineers is difficult to determine. A well-attended lecture on "Factory Costs" by the CMA's P.W. Ellis in 1905 probably ignited some interest. Some of the corporate newcomers, however, needed no convincing. The city's large US-owned operations brought the results of years of managerial experimentation with them and were frequently cited as models of organizational sophistication. The experiments continued inside the city's biggest plant, as two strikes at Canadian Westinghouse in February 1913 – against "a change in the method of giving out work and the consequent adjustment in the piece work prices" in the metre assembly department, and against the use of time clocks to keep closer track of work in the punch department – suggest.[49] Business journals extolled even smaller Canadian-owned firms in Hamilton, such as the London Machine Tool Company and the Ford-Smith Machine Company, as innovative leaders in management work.[50] A "Hamilton Mechanic" said in 1912 that "various of the larger firms of this city have employed speed men – that is men who are supposed to time up a machine to its utmost." In his first report as the machinists' local business agent in 1913, Richard Riley noted the spread of the new ideas: "Mr. Taylor's system of scientific shop management is in use in some shops here. In one case, two cuts in piecework have taken place recently. A great many of the men don't know what they are getting until they get their pay envelope." The threat loomed so menacingly that when a local contractor proposed using construction workers to build a house in one day during the city's centennial celebrations, the Hamilton Trades and Labor Council denounced such an attempt "to introduce a speeding up system in the building trade."[51]

To transplant the new concepts and practices of accounting and engineering into local factories, several firms brought in professionally trained managers from the United States. For example, W.M. Currie had graduated from the University of Toronto's engineering program in 1903, worked briefly at the Westinghouse plant in Pittsburgh and the US Steel plant in Homestead, Pa., before arriving in Hamilton in 1910 as vice-president and managing director of Burlington Steel. Other firms regularly filled positions in middle and upper management with US recruits.[52] Local workers began linking the new authoritarianism of the efficiency movement to the US citizenship of these imported managers. In 1916 a worker writing to the *Spectator* lamented, "A few Americans come over here and try to make slaves out of Canadians." A few months later another signing himself "A Victim" wrote a scathing critique of the "numerous foremen and superintendents procured in the United States, who are nothing more than taskmasters and cent-savers." Those people, he said, "are brought here with the express purpose of promoting 'efficiency' of the kind that has recently been the cause of so many strikes and labor troubles over the border." He warned that "Britishers" would defend "liberty and justice and refuse to bow our heads to such foreign tyrants."[53]

The war economy stimulated greater interest in efficient management, especially with the Imperial Munitions Board's centralized co-ordination of war production, and in its wake the new systems reached new sectors of industry. In 1920 International Harvester introduced more formal scientific management through a new, widely discussed Planning Department.[54] The same year the local YMCA launched a course on "Modern Production Methods," run by the Business Training Corporation of New York, for foremen and supervisory personnel from the city's factories. Local supervisors heard lectures on "Team leadership, handling men, organization, equipment, production records, and the

principles of management." The second round of these classes alone had 75 men and women from nine factories in the city, according to the *Spectator*.[55] One graduate from the course, A.F. Knight, superintendent of the Imperial Cotton Company, organized monthly Modern Production classes for his own staff and then oversaw major reorganization of the plant, with the help of a Boston firm of efficiency experts, and the creation of a permanent cost department.[56] Towards the end of the 1920s both the Canadian Cottons and Hamilton Cotton companies hired US consultants to plan similar changes in their work processes, and in the early 1930s Mercury Mills invited in experts in the Bedeaux system of scientific management.[57] Meanwhile, the Hamilton Chamber of Commerce had contributed to the broader development of a corporate culture in the city with a Business Training Course for younger managerial staff from the cities' firms, consisting of guest speakers appearing twice a month to address various business practices.[58]

Centralizing factory administration shook up the front offices themselves. Many more managers and supervisors were needed to monitor and direct the production process, as were growing numbers of clerical workers to handle the swelling flood of paperwork. By 1921 the supervisory staff in Hamilton's firms accounted for 5.4 per cent of the workforce and by 1931, 7.3 per cent. In manufacturing, the percentages were even higher: one managerial-supervisory official was in place for every 10 factory workers in 1921 and for every 12 in 1931.[59] Clerical labour also expanded, from 6.5 per cent of the city's workforce in 1911 to 8.6 per cent in 1931. This too was a work world that was undergoing subdivision and specialization of labour and mechanization of numerous tasks, with telephones, typewriters, Dictaphones, adding machines, and data processors. Typists or adding-machine operators, it

By 1909 the Greening Wire Company office incorporated both female labour and new machinery. (SLS, LS567)

was argued, required the same "nimble fingers" that allegedly made women valuable core-makers and coil winders. Many women found jobs at much lower wages performing the supposedly simplest, least responsible tasks, especially stenography, typing, and, starting in 1916 during the wartime labour shortage, some bookkeeping. The supply of such trained women had increased after 1905, when Hamilton's public school system had begun to enrol a few hundred young women in Commercial classes every year, as did the few privately run business colleges.[60]

The centrally planned factory began to look strikingly different. Work in a well-managed enterprise flowed smoothly, with each stage of production well integrated with the others. On a tour through the new Westinghouse plant in 1905, a *Herald* reporter was struck by

> the manner in which everything is planned out so that everything that is being made makes a direct progression through the

works. Economy is seen everywhere. The raw materials are delivered to the spot where they will be used.... And the machines are situated so that each piece passes right down the line to where the parts are assembled and put together for testing and shipping. Nothing is handled twice.... Everything works like clock-work, and all are truly "parts of one stupendous whole."

A visitor to the new National Steel Car plant in 1913 similarly noticed "the smoothness with which everything moves ... the process is continuous." He watched the men building railway cars along what was becoming known as an assembly line: "The cars are always on the move, and always in the process of construction."[61] Factory buildings had to be specially designed for this kind of integrated production system. In contrast to the tall, multi-storey industrial structures of the late-19th century, the new model was typically long and low, with high ceilings

Assembly-line production in the steel-erection department at National Steel Car around 1918.
(LAC, PA-24624)

for overhead cranes and conveyor systems and large windows for maximum lighting. New firms of specialized architects began to advertise their services for designing factory buildings along the most efficient lines.[62]

All of these changes in managerial practice that were gathered up in the folds of the banner of efficiency in the early 20th century – the anti-unionism, mechanization and subdivision of labour, new recruitment and training procedures, centralization and bureaucratization of decision-making – really amounted to a struggle for power. Like their counterparts throughout North America, Hamilton's manufacturers wanted more control over the production processes they owned in order to turn out more products at less cost. For these men, the factory system that had evolved by the turn of the century had allowed the workers within the labour process too much independence in setting the

pace and rhythms of work. The managerial offensive was, in essence, an effort to control more effectively the labour power of Hamilton's workers so that these men and women would work harder, faster, and without complaint. It combined two previously separate options – the intensification of existing work practices and the subdivision and mechanization of labour. By drawing together so many distinct work processes in the same factory, by linking them up with mechanical devices, and by co-ordinating and closely monitoring the whole system from the front office, industrialists not only transformed the work but also managed to speed it up.

Thinking and Doing

Hamilton's industrialists hoped that their managerial innovations would decisively diminish their reliance on skilled and unskilled manual labour. They wanted a workforce that was pliable and easy to replace. Later writers suggested that they succeeded in "homogenizing" the workforce.[63] In reality, as employers soon discovered, they got a far more complex occupational structure that provided new managerial headaches. Owners and managers soon recognized that they could not proceed from any simple strategic plan, but had to adapt to and learn from the unexpected consequences of their new plans, and particularly from how the workers they recruited contributed their own practices to the evolving labour processes.

Despite triumphant claims in the business press, skill had not been driven out of Hamilton's factories. Nor were the skilled workers who remained simply a shrinking residue of past practices. They still had two important roles in production. First, many firms kept substantial numbers of skilled tradesmen to set up, maintain, and repair their equipment. These workers included toolmakers, millwrights, electricians, pipefitters, and stationary engineers.[64] Second, many firms still needed skilled men in the mainstream of the production process.

In the foundries and machine shops an important part of the work process often still required the craftsworker's careful hands and sound judgment. While mass production of parts for farm equipment might allow International Harvester to break down a moulder's skills using new production methods, local machinery manufacturers with less repetitive work – and in particular those shops doing jobbing work for other firms – still needed the well-rounded craftworker who could prepare enormous castings for hydro-electric generators or any number of other diverse products. The Otis-Fensom Elevator Company, for example, insisted that "good mechanics and the old system of hand molding seem preferable."[65] Similarly, some machine-shop work, especially of

the less specialized kind, continued to be done on machinery that required the craftworker's touch. Even the use of automatically controlled machines increased the need for skilled supervision and for skilled men to construct and repair the equipment. The skilled group included the emerging elite of the machinists' trade, the toolmakers, who prepared the jigs and dies for use on machines handled by the less-skilled. The battle to eliminate skill from the machine shop would continue on into the late 20th century.[66]

If they could not root out this continuing need for craft skill, employers hoped to be able to narrow and circumscribe it as much as possible. A moulder's work could be rigidly confined to the specific tasks requiring his expertise, while other repetitive or purely physical labour was parcelled out to less-skilled workers. "At present," *Canadian Foundryman* noted in 1923, "the proportion of skilled mechanics to the number employed in any foundry is much less than it was twenty years ago and will probably continue to decrease."[67]

Just before World War One the federal Royal Commission on Technical Education heard officials from several local corporations admit that they used many skilled men, and by the 1920s the situation had not changed completely. In some of the larger firms a handful of blacksmiths, boilermakers, or polishers might still be needed for some specialized metalworking. Indeed, skilled metal-trades workers appear to have made up a steady proportion – roughly 7 per cent – of the male workforce from 1911 to 1931, and their numbers actually increased to nearly 9 per cent in 1941.[68]

Even more important, some of the new, revamped production processes had an inherent need for the experienced eye and careful hand of a skilled worker. Cutting the expensive cloth in local men's clothing factories was such a job. In

Men working in the Steel Company's sheet mill had to be skilled at handling and judging the quality of the steel. (SLS, LS 422)

Skilled steelworkers tested the quality of the steel in the furnace. (SLS, LS362)

Firestone's new factory the tire builders were a proudly skilled group who put the tires together by hand. The glass moulders in the Dominion Glass plant enjoyed similar respect for their skills. In the Steel Company's blast furnace and open-hearth departments, skilled men had to judge when the molten iron or steel was ready and when to adjust the brew with the appropriate chemicals. Limitations on the market for the corporation's finished steel products also left many rolling-mill hands working on batch production in more labour-intensive processes that

required considerable skill within their work groups.[69] Still, the tendency to concentrate their efforts, strip away auxiliary tasks, and mechanize wherever possible meant that the labour power of the skilled probably contributed less to the overall costs of production.

Once they had destroyed the craft unions and their apprenticeship systems, employers nonetheless faced a problem in finding the skilled workers they still needed. They also began to worry about finding front-line supervisors with well-rounded knowledge of work processes. In its brief to the Royal Commission on Technical Education in 1911 the Canadian Manufacturers' Association even bemoaned the decline of the apprenticeship system. For the most part employers hoped to be able to continue recruiting skilled help from the ranks of British and US immigrants, using the specialized services of private immigration agencies where necessary and possible. A few, like Westinghouse, International Harvester, and Ford-Smith Machine, organized their own apprenticeship programs supervised by managers, but by 1926 that system involved only 105 young men in Hamilton, including 17 toolmakers, 18 machinists, 6 moulders, and 12 pattern-makers – scarcely enough to meet local needs.[70]

For some manufacturers, Sprague's technical school was part of the answer. After several years of agitation, businessmen convinced the local Board of Education to open the Hamilton Technical and Art School in 1909 as a more reliable training institution for skilled workers than the old craft apprenticeships. In his *Herald* labour column Obermeyer suggested cynically in 1910 that local industrialists saw technical education simply as "a source of supply of skilled labor without the bother of training it." From the beginning, local manufacturers dominated the school's administrative committee, and the local CMA branch's Technical Education Committee kept a close watch on the school's work and awarded prizes for proficiency. Not only were no trade unionists appointed to the school's governing committee, but also, as Studholme argued in 1910, the city's craft unionists, "who were as skilled and as capable of teaching as any of the teachers they had in the school," were being systematically ignored. Many of the teachers were supervisory staff from Hamilton factories, and in 1911 Principal J.G. Witton told the local manufacturers' association that he would add "any department with the necessary equipment, that was demanded or required by any Industrial Concern in the city."[71]

When Sprague arrived at the technical school in 1916 he came with an extensive background in "efficiency engineering" and made new efforts to integrate the larger firms' in-plant training programs more closely with the school's curriculum. By 1918 more than 20 Hamilton firms were requiring their apprentices to attend the school half a day per week, to learn pattern-making, machine- and tool-making, electrical work, drafting, or printing. That year the local manufacturers' association praised this arrangement as "the most encouraging work of the kind on the continent." After Ontario's new Adolescent School Attendance Act of 1919 raised the legal age for leaving school and permitted 14-to-16-year-olds to attend school part-time, enrolment in the Technical and Art School suddenly shot up – from 620 evening students in 1915–16 to 4,730 by 1921–22. A Guidance Officer appointed in 1924 to co-ordinate the needs of local industry with student tastes was instructed to make an "industrial survey" to ascertain the demand for different occupations, advise students and their parents on the most suitable line of work to prepare for, and maintain links with local employers to find the boys jobs after graduation. By

Skilled manual labour remained important in Firestone's tire production. (SLS, LS379)

the end of the 1920s Principal L.W. Gill could convincingly boast that the school was "virtually a special department of industry."[72]

Overall, then, while Hamilton's industrialists had tackled the constricting role of craftworkers in production by subdividing and mechanizing their tasks wherever possible, stripping away many auxiliary tasks from those who could not be replaced and promoting new publicly funded training programs, they had not succeeded in eliminating all skilled work from production. They had simply changed the status of the skilled worker from the kingpin of production to a valuable member of a more complex production team.

Nor had the unskilled labourer disappeared from Hamilton's early-20th-century work world. In 1931 well more than 10,000 male workers – one in five – convinced the census-takers that they were labourers, despite the clear instructions to these officials to find another label wherever possible.[73] But their proportion of the total male workforce was unquestionably dropping – from 27 per cent of the male workforce in 1911 to only 13 per cent in 1941[74] – and both the youngest and the oldest were being eliminated. Child labour had dwindled to insignificance by the 1920s – much of the fetching and carrying work of child labourers was being mechanized – and the new provincial legislation that raised the school-leaving age to 16 was pulling young adolescents out of the paid workforce. Several of the light industries, such as knitting or food-processing, still offered simple, unskilled packaging jobs, now generally done by young women.[75]

At the same time older men were being displaced in Hamilton industry. In 1914, for example, the city engineer announced that to get the most for its money the city would have to dispense with the services of several old men. Later that month, the *Herald* published a letter from an "Old Veteran," aged 60, who said that no one would hire him. The 1921 census officials saw this process as a widespread trend: "The speeding up processes, the simplification of the various steps in fabrication and the breaking up of old handicrafts, often substituting for the skill acquired in the course of years the training of a few weeks, tend to accentuate the advantages inherent in the energy, dexterity, and versatility of youth." An older man thus had a "less certain" job security, and it was "more difficult than a few years ago" to get a position. The aging AFL organizer John Flett told the Royal Commission on Industrial Relations in 1919 about common advertisements for "Vigorous men . . . from 18 to 45 years of age, none others need apply." He regretted that employers were "throwing men on the industrial scrap heap at 45 years of age." By the 1920s older men were regularly hunting for jobs as caretakers or janitors.[76] The worsening plight of the elderly worker probably contributed to the labour movement's new concern with old-age pensions by World War One.

Despite this narrowing of possibilities based on age, labourers were still not one undifferentiated mass. Ethnicity created major new dividing lines among them. Although European immigrants still made up a huge percentage of those who lifted and heaved and swung a shovel, labouring jobs on the city payroll were not for these newcomers.[77] Westinghouse, the city's largest private-sector employer, also generally refused to hire Continental European immigrants. Labourers in Hamilton in the early 20th century worked within a distinctly segregated hierarchy of unskilled positions that left the dirtiest, hottest, most disagreeable, and worst-paid jobs for the European immigrants.

Unquestionably the most important new occupational trend was the emergence of thousands of machine operators, who were soon known as the "semi-skilled." Hamilton's employers liked to argue that most of these workers required little training and exercised no significant skill. In 1913, for example, a Westinghouse official explained that striking metre-assemblers had been easy to replace because they did not need "knowledge of any trade, any young man being able to pick up the work satisfactorily with ordinary intelligence and two or three weeks practice." Similarly in 1916 the Steel Company's Hobson reported that a body of strikers in his firm's munitions department "have no trade and are purely operators which we have created out of the ranks of our common labour." The same year the firm hired a Russian immigrant to learn wire-drawing work and expected that he would be fully trained within a month. In an address to the American Iron and Steel Institute in 1919, Hobson proudly announced that in four and a half years of operating the Steel Company's new electrically driven blooming mill, less than an hour and a half had been necessary for "breaking in new men to operate the motor for the mill." Social scientists have often agreed with these judgments.[78]

Yet to call all these men and women merely unskilled "machine tenders" would be misleading. The equipment they operated varied widely, but few of the machines were completely automatic. The operators had to set them in motion and guide or oversee their movements to some degree. Frequently that meant using a machine to complete a simple task over and over again and as quickly as possible – preparing a small mould in a moulding machine, making a simple cut on an artillery shell, drilling a hole in a harvester part, sewing one seam on a man's coat, or looping the toes on a stocking. These jobs had responsibility, but little variety. To maintain the pace expected of them, the operatives had to be quick, strong, deft, and attentive to detail. They had to know their machines and their raw materials thoroughly and had to watch for problems that could lead to waste or scrap.

Sometimes machine operation could involve a great deal of judgment in quality control or in directing the motion of the equipment.[79] The best example was the craneman, who had to have a keen eye and sound judgment in guiding the massive new electrical devices safely and effectively through the plants. Most workers and their bosses saw this as a highly skilled job. Other machines required similar skill. In the local steel plant, puddlers may have been displaced, but the superintendent of the open-hearth department assured a parliamentary committee in 1910 that for the new steel-making process he could not "go and round up the skilled men and pick them up on the street corner. Take our melters, rollers and first helpers, they are skilled men and the next man to one of these cannot take his place ... the same with the men at the ladles."[80] A few months later the president of the Greening Wire Company could brag to the Royal Commission on Technical Education that new wire-weaving equipment had eliminated 75 skilled men, but he admitted how difficult it was to get "skilled workmen" to operate the new machines.[81] Despite more than a century

Many women working in factories were semi-skilled machine operators like these working at Mercury Mills in 1928. (HPL)

of mechanization, subdivision of labour, and recruitment of cheaper female labour to replace artisanal workers in the textile industry, the manager of Canadian Cottons could still describe the experienced female spinners in the Hamilton plant in 1929 as "skilled." Moreover, especially in continuous-process work like steel-making, the integration of such tasks as handling cranes required judgment in co-ordinating and the ability to adjust and correct the flow of production – what has been called "diagnostic" skills.[82] The technical competence demanded in this kind of machine operation thus made the dividing line between semi-skilled and skilled work in Hamilton factories extremely fuzzy and ever-changing.

What semi-skilled workers had was "experience." Learning how to use the new technology efficiently seldom involved a formal training process; employees learned how to perform the necessary tasks while they were on the job, often while doing less responsible work nearby in the same plant. But workers gained a special knack for the job that combined dexterity and familiarity with the machinery and the raw materials. These qualities translated into more productive labour for their employers, but the skills required to operate many of the machines could not be picked up instantly by newly hired workers. A Westinghouse employee later described how he started in 1910 at a simple job and the next year "learnt coil winding. I managed very well, and advanced to a qualified winder."[83] The corporations recognized that process of training and tended to fill such positions from within the firm wherever possible, or to scoop up workers from other plants, where they had also learned their skills on the job. Many Hamilton companies had to import experienced machine operators from outside the city or the country. Hamilton Steel and Iron brought in several American workmen to handle the more complex machinery in its new open-hearth steel department in 1900, as the Steel Company did for its sheet-metal mill in 1918. In 1901 Imperial Cotton brought many "skilled cotton workers" from Yarmouth, N.S., in order to begin production in Hamilton, and other local textile companies occasionally had to send off for help.[84] The Greening company got experienced wire workers from the United States.[85] National Steel Car also wanted to import experienced car builders for its start-up phase in 1912–13 (presumably from New Jersey, where the US investors already had a car plant), but when federal immigration officials balked, the corporation had to spend precious time using local workers for the "conversion of raw labor into skilled labor . . . instead of working at full capacity in turning out cars." As a result, according to *Canadian Machinery*, "The desired state of efficiency was not obtained so quickly as it otherwise might have been."[86] The corporations tried to hold onto their seasoned help, of course, particularly when depressions struck. In 1908–9 and again in 1913–14, in order to hold together an "efficient organization," Westinghouse cut back on hours rather than lay off large numbers of workers who might leave the city. It would do the same in the 1930s.[87]

The semi-skilled workers themselves recognized that they were more than unskilled labourers in disguise. In 1919 a worker from International Harvester told the Royal Commission on Industrial Relations that he did a "skilled laborer's work." He said, "I am what you would classify as a handy-man; I get a little machinist work and a little of other kinds of work, and therefore my remuneration comes far higher than the ordinary laborer who cannot do that." An important reason for the pay differential was that this man, like so many other semi-skilled workers, was on piecework. World War One saw the numbers of such workers expand enormously. By 1923 the commissioner of the anti-union Canadian Founders' and Metal Trades Association was complaining that the war economy had "tended to lessen the supply of unskilled labor through unusual opportunities afforded this class of workers to become specialists." The result, he said, was that "we now have a surplus of these specialty workers, who cannot be used in jobs requiring a high degree of skill and experience without a definite course of instruction and training, and, who having risen above the ranks of unskilled labor, are reluctant to return to such tasks permanently."[88] Machine operators inside the new factory regime would continue to challenge their employers' narrow definitions of "skill" in their struggles to win respect and proper compensation for their valuable role in the new production processes.

Probably the most important divide among the semi-skilled was along gender lines. For the most part, men and women did different jobs with different machines in separate industries or departments. Many of the women in the factories nonetheless operated machines, most often as part of a fragmented work process. In both the cotton and knitting mills, they ran the largely automatic spinning and knitting machinery. In the men's clothing plants, most worked on sewing machines in narrowly specialized jobs as pocket operators, lining-makers, sleeve-makers, lapel and collar operators, buttonhole-makers, and many others, never completing a garment from beginning to end. Many sewing-machine operators also found similar work in the knitting mills, stitching up the knit cloth into finished underwear.[89] Running these machines required a certain skill – a man off the street would probably not have got the hang of it quickly – but women faced a double disadvantage in getting those skills recognized: the labour market was glutted with girls who had learned sewing at home or in the new domestic science classes in schools; and, even more significantly, all women's work was assumed to be inferior to men's. Still, on several occasions the employers would find the women working in their factories nonetheless asserting a spirited independence and feisty militancy.

Inside the front office itself, the picture was also blurred. There too the white-collar workforce had undergone unexpected twists. In the first place the feminization of clerical work was far from universal. Whether as a result of a shortage of female labour or, more likely, a reluctance to break through traditional definitions of gender roles, many Hamilton employers still maintained a strong preference for men until near the end of the period. Only 42 per cent of office workers were women in 1911, and still only 46 per cent in 1941. The city's manufacturers were much slower to make this transition than were employers in service, trade, or finance. In 1921 only three office workers out of eight in the Hamilton factory offices were women, and only one in four in firms that worked with iron and steel (comparable figures for 1931 or 1941 are not available). This pattern undoubtedly reflects a concern to keep women away from workplaces filled with men, since proportionally more women worked in industrial offices where women were heavily involved in production – closer to half in 1921. Women also got access to specific jobs in all these offices. By 1931 virtually all stenographers and typists were women, as were six out of ten bookkeepers and cashiers. But men still made up nearly four-fifths of the office clerks.[90]

Then too, machines had not completely shaken up the offices. Many office workers undoubtedly used typewriters and adding machines as part of their daily routines, but, since the city lacked any substantial financial or administrative complex that would be handling large quantities of similar data, the work experience of these offices may have been less factory-like for most workers. In 1931 census-takers found only 24 workers (16 of them women) who described themselves as "office appliance operators," and a decade later only 68 (59 of them women).[91] Most clerical work in Hamilton thus became stratified and specialized in the opening decades of the 20th century, but it probably remained more varied and less routine than it would have been in a city with a different economic structure.

Yet another twist within the white-collar workforce was that the male professionals who had been recruited to help solve production problems – accountants, engineers, chemists – had an elitist view of their relationship to production workers, but a bristling independence about their own professional competence. By the end of the war, their concern about their status and prestige within industrial life had revitalized their professional associations and brought a new emphasis on improving salaries and controlling the labour supply of these technicians. The Hamilton branch of the Engineering Institute of Canada grew quickly to 125 members in 1920 and 171 two years later. The leading lights of the branch were top-level executives in firms such as Westinghouse and Hamilton Bridge. They identified strongly with the goals and methods of their corporate employers (in 1921 Hobson was made honorary chairman), but they were asserting an independent interest within the corporate hierarchy that they were anxious to protect. The branch met regularly after the war not only to discuss scientific and technical questions related to the profession but also to support the parent organization's efforts to get the legal right to license professional engineers (new legislation in 1922 gave them only the right to register). But the engineers' prickly pride kept the issues of improved status and income alive for years to come. Meanwhile, in 1919, some of Hamilton's militant technicians in the lower echelons of the profession had set about organizing a local of the more trade-union-oriented International Federation of Technical Engineers, Architects, and Draftsmen, although their efforts apparently proved abortive. Evidently, the new male professionals in the city's occupational structure could pose a new, independent, and unexpected challenge to the corporations to meet their special needs for enhanced status and lucrative salaries.[92]

"Deskilling" and "homogenization," then, are not adequate terms for capturing the complex outcome of the workplace transformations that took place between the 1890s and the 1930s. The occupational structure found in Hamilton factories unquestionably had a new shape. In many local industries in the late 19th century, the pattern among manual workers reflected a clear gap between craftsmen who produced and labourers or helpers who assisted – between "trades" and "labour," as the labour movement had encapsulated the difference. Now there was most often a narrower range of skill spread over an increasingly complex hierarchy of semi-skilled jobs, shading over into the small number of unquestionably skilled production jobs at the top. Within that hierarchy the workforce still spanned a wide variety of occupational differences based on skill, ethnicity, and gender and reinforced through distinct labour markets. Skilled tradesmen and labourers came from larger pools of labour outside individual firms, while skilled and semi-skilled production workers tended to be promoted up the firm's internal job ladders. Women and European immigrants did not have access to the full range of these occupational hierarchies and tended to work in narrowly circumscribed job ghettoes. Equally important, a great divide had opened up in the workforce with the expansion of the front office, to which some of the conceptual activity formerly done on the shop floor had been transferred. Within the new white-collar workforce, there were also new divisions along lines of gender and educational background. The corporations, in short, had not reduced their factory personnel to a homogenized mass.

Moreover, although relatively few workers could still call upon the full range of independence and shop-floor discretion of the old-time craftsman or the cultural and ideological patina of craftsmanship, a considerable proportion of the employees were still expected to exercise independent judgment on the job. Sometimes this role amounted to what we would unquestionably call skill, while in other cases it added up to the responsibility for keeping the machinery running smoothly and productively. Despite Taylor's theorizing, it had not been possible to completely separate conception from execution in the labour process. In general, what had changed was not so much the technical content of the job as the process of skill formation and definition; that is, most factory workers now learned their skills on the job under managerial supervision (rather than through craft union apprenticeships). They were promoted up from the ranks into more skilled jobs and were unlikely to be able to carry their specialized skills to new employers. Skill or discretion was also now exercised within spatially integrated workplaces inside large, bureaucratically administered corporations, not in the somewhat less overwhelming atmosphere of the late-19th-century workshop. Yet these groups of workers retained pockets of strategic power in the production process that could potentially spell trouble for their employers. Their knowledge of the labour process would allow them to conspire quietly to subvert managerial goals, or more aggressively to disrupt production.[93]

Workers shared common workplace experiences by the 1920s not because all their jobs had been reduced to roughly the same low level, but because so many of them worked for a small handful of employers in closely regulated production processes. They were divided from each other not simply by gender and ethnicity, but also by a much deeper dependence on their individual corporate employers for better jobs and economic security and a vulnerability to replacement by ambitious workers below them on the job ladder.[94] This relationship was the key to the new corporate control over the labour process in Hamilton industry. Paradoxically, once workers began to settle into these jobs, each corporation also became more vulnerable to concerted pressure from such a well-integrated workforce.

The Human Touch

If the new factory regime in Hamilton still needed most workers to use their brains during their hours on the job, how could employers keep their employees' thoughts narrowly focused on turning out as many products as quickly and carefully as possible? Most of the new technology did not by itself provide the discipline to make workers work hard and fast or reliably and responsibly. Human intervention would therefore be needed to get the maximum out of all the costly new technology and the labour power that the corporations had purchased. In the prewar years, the predominant view of what made workers work was a simple-minded notion of goading and prodding through greed and fear. Only once Hamilton workers had begun to resist the terms of their employment on a large scale, towards the end of World War One, did a new concept of "personnel management" begin to take shape – although it never did displace the older incentives.

The carrot that Hamilton managers dangled before the vast majority of factory workers in the early 20th century was higher earnings through piecework. Almost every factory had a good portion of its hands working by the ton or by the piece, and many more workers encountered the system during the war, when virtually all munitions workers were on some kind of incentive wage. In 1916 a Hamilton employer of over 1,000 munitions workers insisted, "There is no industrial system which brings out individual value so well as the piece system." A contributor to the machinists' *Bulletin* was less sanguine. "The lust for gain has defeated all reason, and with little or no obstruction in the path of the producer it develops into the survival of the fittest," he wrote. "The contract or piece system has received an impetus that a hundred years of oration on its evils will not eliminate."[95]

This kind of carrot could become a stick, however, when piece rates were cut to push workers to produce more for the same wages. Many workers developed the collective discipline to keep the daily workload within reason – "soldiering," as disgusted managers called it – and as a result some manufacturers experimented with the "premium bonus" plan, rewarding individual workers by paying extra when they completed a task in less than the established time. With this scheme employers could tempt workers with the promise of higher earnings and get increased output without the controversial practice of cutting piece rates. The whole work group did not suffer, and one worker could reap the personal reward in a fatter pay cheque. Some steelworkers and machinists in Hamilton had this system of wage payment by World War One. "On the straight salary basis, ambitious, hardworking employes have no advantage over the shirker," Hobson explained during a strike of his company's shell-makers in 1916. "On the bonus basis the men who are willing to render faithful service make satisfactory wages." Dominion Sheet Metal even tapped into family negotiations over working-class household budgets by giving employees their tonnage bonus payments in separate envelopes. That way the men could hold the extra money back from their wives and enjoy it "as something entirely their own."[96]

Most of the new managerial theorists had such a primitive notion of working-class psychology that they assumed workers could be easily manipulated by incentive wages. Yet the carrot was seldom enough. To push the workers harder – to "drive" them, in the terminology of the period – was the responsibility of the front-line supervisors – the foremen and superintendents. These were usually men (and occasionally, in the female job ghettoes, women) who had been promoted from the ranks, who generally knew the work processes in their departments thoroughly, and who wielded effective power to keep their workers in line. As one worker at International Harvester explained, "The foreman was a little god, a little kaiser in his own department; nobody dared to brook his authority.... Let anyone in his department incur his displeasure, it was either to suffer a life of misery or get out." These officials felt the tightening constraints of closer scrutiny and planning from the front office, but on a daily basis they were generally left to run their departmental fiefs according to their own inclinations, provided they maintained or increased output. Verbal abuse of workers seemed to be common. According to one worker at Canadian Iron Foundries, the foreman "swears at us as though we were slaves yet we dare not protest." Generally it was the personal rapport that a supervisor developed with his or her workers – whether gruff bullying or gentler paternalism – that brought results in productivity and disciplined obedience to managerial authority.[97]

Yet the system was more than a matter of managerial style. These officials held their workers' economic well-being in their hands with their power to hire, fire, promote, and, often, set individual wage rates. "The foreman was the man who sized up the workingman," Westinghouse's assistant works manager explained in 1910. He also kept ambitious or security-conscious workers in line through his control of promotion up the firm's job ladders – a fundamentally different process from the craft unionists' system of apprenticeship. A federal labour department official trying to get a statement after a spontaneous strike at Hamilton Cotton in 1929 was struck by the climate of fear in such a situation. The workers, he said, "absolutely refused to sign anything that would incriminate them, as they are young men and young women who have been in the employ of this company since they quit school and have never worked at anything else." They were "afraid of losing their jobs."[98]

Not all supervisors exercised this power despotically. The newspapers often reported the presentation of Christmas gifts to foremen from groups of presumably grateful workers, and occasionally a strike would erupt to defend a foreman who was being disciplined or fired.[99] But the system was ripe for favouritism and petty tyranny, especially where workers were particularly vulnerable. On the eve of the war, a leading US engineering magazine claimed that almost every factory worker paid "some sort of tribute" to his foreman, typically in the form of "money or service," though sometimes "the tribute is of a nature which cannot be mentioned in an open paper." Hiring by foremen "very often leads to the building up of racial and other cliques in a department that will cause trouble later," a Canadian business journalist noted in 1920. "This is inevitable, as the only source of labour supply that is open to a foreman is through his relatives and friends and the friends of the men in his gang." Workers in the foremen's lodge or church congregation or with the right family connections would have a special advantage, but others might have to pay for their jobs. In 1907 International Harvester discovered that the sub-foremen, or "straw bosses," who supervised smaller groups of immigrant workers were exacting a weekly tribute. Similar practices were unearthed at the Hamilton Steel and Iron Company in 1910. In both cases the companies made great shows of rooting out the extortionists, but in the 1920s and 1930s European workers were still facing demands for money, liquor, and sometimes even the sexual favours of their wives, to keep their jobs. At National Steel Car, workers claimed in 1929 that getting a job could cost them $25. For women workers this despotism could include sexual harassment.[100]

At the end of World War One, as working-class anger and militancy boiled over across

In its employees' magazine *The Fabricator*, Mercury Mills liked to celebrate how parents had got jobs in the plant for their children. (SLS, LS54)

the country, some corporate managers began to admit that this system of shop-floor despotism created ill will in their plants. International Harvester was, at that time, among the first of a small number of Hamilton firms to set up central employment offices, with substantial powers to screen new recruits, although even there foremen retained the final say. "The man applies at the Employment Manager's office for work, and he is asked a series of questions – the kind of work he performs, and that sort of thing," a Harvester official explained in 1919, "and if he is a skilled laborer as a rule we will take him into the foreman of the department and he will ask him some questions, and if he sizes him up all right, he hires him." At the same point a Steel

Company official admitted that his firm had seen a good deal of "trouble" involving "workmen and foremen." He announced his company's interest in training "a better class, a higher class of foremen ... as to what was fair between employer and employee and to produce the best results." This was also undoubtedly a large part of the rationale for the YMCA's Modern Production Classes after the war.[101]

Interviews with retired workers who held jobs in Hamilton plants in the 1920s and 1930s suggest that this interest in reformed foremanship expired quickly, and the older authoritarianism continued to flourish. Indeed, backing that tendency, the city's two largest US-owned firms, International Harvester and Westinghouse, belonged to a secretive organization called the Special Conference Committee, formed in 1919. It was made up of leading executives in the ten largest US corporations, and its principles of industrial management included shoring up the independent power of foremen over personnel matters.[102] Somewhat smaller and less bureaucratized firms in the city had never doubted the wisdom of that arrangement. Factory administration in Hamilton would continue to rely on the direct pressure of front-line supervisors until the consolidation of industrial unionism in the 1940s.[103]

Meanwhile, less coercive approaches were also adopted. Several companies had a tradition dating back to the 1880s of company picnics, banquets, Christmas turkeys, and the like, which encouraged a specific company's workers to bask in the paternalist generosity of the entrepreneur who employed them. A factory owner such as George Tuckett, the tobacco magnate, became a larger-than-life figure in the theatre surrounding these acts of industrial benevolence, while others struck a much more plebeian posture as men among men – people who rose from the ranks but still shared their subordinates' shop-floor skills. Industrial paternalism rewarded loyalty and deference, but also heightened workers' expectations of a boss's material and moral responsibilities to them.[104]

In the early 20th century the executives of large new corporations recast these practices to draw workers into loyalty to a corporate "family," even though the men at the top rarely knew or even met the hundreds of workers on their payrolls. They also recast the language framing what they liked to call "welfare work" to replace the old image of the patriarch and his dependants with one of partnership and co-operation. Rather than just an act of individual paternalists, welfarism became a movement within the business community, actively promoted by the business press. It was one of a range of responses to the pressing problems of labour management and to the larger public debates about the corporation in society and political pressures for social reform. It was no mere coincidence that Hamilton manufacturers began experimenting with so-called welfare work at the same point that they were appearing before government inquiries to oppose the eight-hour day and overly generous workers' compensation.[105]

Before World War One only a handful of Hamilton companies edged far onto this new managerial terrain. A few set up club-like recreation rooms with reading material and pool tables, or helped their men form benefit societies for sickness and death.[106] Many more entered men's baseball or soccer teams into city-wide competitions to link company loyalty to these bursts of masculine energy. International Harvester undoubtedly had the most extensive corporate-welfare programs. In 1908, in all its plants across North America, the corporation introduced a benefit society for the sick and injured, nursing services, and an Industrial

Accident Department to provide compensation "with a view," according to a company executive, "to anticipating any legislation that might be enacted in this country." In Hamilton the company also started an athletic association to arrange track meets, boxing matches, band concerts, team sports, banquets for individual departments, and the annual company picnic. The association collapsed during the war, but was revived with new energy in the spring of 1919 as the Harvester Athletic Club, and within a year had 1,364 members. It was reputedly the biggest sporting organization in the city. In contrast, before the war, the city's biggest employer, Westinghouse, held off starting up anything more than picnics and sports teams.[107]

The pre-war experiments paled alongside the highly publicized burst of corporate largesse right after the war. Unlike their counterparts in the United States, Canadian businesses had not felt any push from government agencies, but in the wartime economy managers were forced to adapt and to learn from workers' behaviour. A new sense of urgency arose in the face of two new developments: the labour militancy and radicalism that erupted in working-class communities across the Western world; and a tendency for workers to individually take advantage of labour scarcity by thumbing their noses at workplace discipline. Like many other industrialists, A.O. Dawson, president of Canadian Cottons, saw both forms of worker behaviour as a threat. He worried that "one of the gravest dangers" was the influence on their employees of "ultra-radical leaders, who are continuously, persistently and aggressively preaching socialist doctrines," but he also criticized the new independence of the "floating" or "drifting" workers, whose full employment at wartime wages had lifted the fear of poverty. He claimed that higher wages during and after the war had caused production to fall

Before World War One International Harvester had the most extensive recreational program for its employees. Here the 1913 bowling champions pose for the camera. (HPL)

off by more than a third: "Many of our people frankly admitted that they did not need to work as continuously as formerly and hence took a day off whenever they felt like it." Workers' energies and commitment needed to be more focused on the firm employing them.[108]

Company welfare programs fell into three categories. The first promised an improved work experience by bringing in plant nurses and doctors and extensive safety and first-aid programs. At the Steel Company, for example, supervisors appointed departmental safety committees to involve reliable workers in promoting more careful, attentive work habits. The second offered a much richer leisure-time program of cafeterias and reading rooms, expanded athletic and recreational activities, and new company magazines – at International Harvester, the Steel

Westinghouse sponsored a championship soccer team.

(MUA, Box 48, File 14a)

Company, the Armour meat-packing plant, Imperial Cotton, Proctor and Gamble, and Hoover. These programs touched all workers, but the third group of measures aimed more narrowly at the male breadwinner's concerns about long-term economic security by offering not only more benefit societies, but also old-age pensions, profit-sharing, and group insurance plans (first made legally possible in 1919). Typically, only long-service employees would be eligible (for pensions, 20 years at International Harvester and 25 at the Steel Company), and only at the discretion of supervisors. Any kind of misbehaviour, from strikes to drunkenness, could cancel a worker's entitlement to these benefits. In a similar fashion, Westinghouse reached out in April 1919 to workers with at least 15 years of continuous employment and invited them to join a new Veteran Employees' Association. It would hold annual picnics and banquets right through the interwar period, but more importantly all members were entitled to two weeks' paid vacation each year, during a time when scarcely any wage-earners had this annual break. Out of 2,400 employees, the association started with about 100 members (including both blue- and white-collar workers) and grew to about 200 in 1922, 400 in 1929, and 500 in 1935. All these measures sidestepped the central concerns of the labour movement – wages and hours – and put more emphasis on linking enhanced productivity and long-term financial benefits for stable, contented workers.[109]

Women workers got particular attention in this new wave of welfarism. The new paternalism was distinctly patriarchal in its content and impact on these predominantly young, single wage-earners. In 1918 the Otis-Fensom Elevator Company became the first workplace in the city to hire a staff member to handle the particular problems of female munitions workers – "to see that the girls are properly housed and cared for, to organize clubs among them and to generally improve their condition." Several more Hamilton firms employing women quickly followed suit.[110] It was good public relations to be showing special concern for the "gentler sex," but the appeal to the workers themselves was more compelling. Most of the extensive programs aimed at women emphasized short-term satisfaction on the job, in hopes of curbing an astonishingly high rate of labour turnover rather than of providing the longer-term economic security offered to men through pension or insurance plans. The emphasis, then, was on more pleasant lunchrooms and off-the-job fun.

Company teams remained popular in the interwar period.
(Courtesy of Ken Paul)

Under the direction of its full-time "welfare secretary," Imperial Cotton undertook one of the most ambitious programs. It sent a tea wagon through the plant twice a day, organized noon-hour sing-songs, sports, social gatherings, and even vacation plans, and provided a small library. The company also published an 18-to-24-page quarterly magazine, the *Fabricator*, which was full of news about the company, with contributions from workers in the plant, health advice, gossip, and snapshots of employees. Imperial Cotton workers could also borrow money for the purchase of a house and pay for their dental bills in instalments through the company. As the family photographs in the company magazine suggest, all of this paternalism complemented a long-standing policy of hiring the sons and daughters of employees. The Hamilton YWCA supplemented these corporate activities by hiring its first "industrial secretary" in 1921 to develop similar programs for wage-earning women, especially in the city's east end. Welfarism in these plants clearly reinforced the

male dominance of the workplaces and the assumed vulnerability of the "working girls," and was based on the assumption that their destiny was elsewhere, in the family household. The companies also tried to build public confidence that these young workers were being well looked after without the need for any more protective legislation.[111]

Nothing in these welfarist measures diminished management power in the workplace in the slightest, but perhaps the most widely discussed innovation appeared to do just that. In 1919, as part of a new program throughout its many plants across North America (which included new benefit measures), International Harvester launched an Industrial Council in its two Hamilton factories as an alternative form of "industrial democracy" to trade unionism. The model was a "works council" originally developed by Canada's Mackenzie King as an industrial-relations consultant for the Rockefellers. King was consulted in the drafting of the Harvester plan. Starting that spring, eight elected worker

In 1919, in the midst of widespread working-class unrest, Westinghouse launched a Veteran Employees' Association to strengthen the loyalty of long-service employees. (MUA, Box 13, Item 1a)

representatives sat down with eight management appointees each month to deliberate over issues arising within the plant. The Industrial Council "guarantees to every employee the right to present any suggestion, request, or complaint and to have it promptly considered and fairly decided," a company brochure promised. Implementation of Council decisions was left to the discretion of senior management, who were free to ignore its recommendations (there was a never-used provision for arbitration of any disagreements). In practice, worker representatives on the Council, along with a network of elected departmental "deputies," became ombudsmen for worker grievances, many of which got handled informally by foremen and superintendents.[112] Although the much smaller Armour meat-packing plant had a similar, but less well-publicized works council, the Harvester experiment caught the spotlight.[113]

This new burst of welfarism, then, was directly linked to Hamilton employers' concerns about productivity in their plants. "Welfare work produces efficiency," the *Canadian Textile Journal* proclaimed in 1916. "Better conditions in the mill mean more work per machine." Steel Company executive F.H. Whitton avoided any old-fashioned sentimentality when he bluntly informed the Royal Commission on Industrial Relations in 1919 that these measures did not represent "philanthropy" towards workers but were intended "to give them a direct interest in the business, and promote continuity of effort and permanence of employment" because "continuous and contented service is an asset to any company."[114] In contrast to earlier industrial paternalism, the welfare programs were tightly linked to the development of more systematic "personnel" policy. By 1918 five leading local firms had their first full-time Employment Managers with their own small departments to administer the mushrooming welfare programs. "The Industries are beginning to see that to hold their place in the labour market, some one person fully acquainted with the needs of both plant and men must have complete control," a local government official noted. For the first time, some firms were taking the same interest

By the end of World War One several companies had provided their female employees with special programs and services, such as Bell Telephone's cafeteria. (SLS, LS733)

in "systematizing" personnel recruitment and stability that they had already begun to show in reorganizing production processes – a trend that meshed well with Principal Sprague's designs for the local technical school.[115]

All this new-style corporate paternalism was primarily an ideological offensive. Hamilton's industrialists, like employers throughout the country, wanted to help restore the public faith in corporate hegemony in Canadian society by showing concern for workers' economic security and safety and for the delicate femininity and dependency of the factory "girls." They also wanted to win back a disaffected working class, which was altogether too interested in unions and radical politics and too little inclined to submit to the pre-war standards of workplace discipline. In short, they wanted to establish the new welfarism as a reformist alternative to radicalism, unionism, or such state intervention as old-age pensions, shorter hours, or minimum-wage legislation. As the head of International Harvester's new Department of Public Relations explained in 1919, corporations would face "a very heavy and hampering harness of government restrictions" unless "industry itself, by its conduct from now on, vindicates the right to go free, and affirmatively proves to the public that there is no need of the straight-jacket."[116]

Nonetheless, welfarism proved to be the other side of the coin of the union-busting that was also underway after the war. Occasionally the connection was overt, such as Armour's decision to sign a contract with its works council to undermine a strike of its workers in 1920. The same year the Banwell-Hoxie wire fence company was pleased to report that higher bonuses earned in a ten-hour day had deflected the call of "agitators" to strike for an eight-hour day.[117] Once the workers' postwar spirit of resistance had been broken, welfarism could help to draw them back into older patterns of deference and loyalism. It urged workers to limit the focus of their solidarity to the place where they worked, rather than expressing solidarity with similar workers across the country or the continent (or the world). It could also play on fears generated by the long postwar crisis of unemployment stretching, in Hamilton, from late 1920 to mid-1926. Welfarism helped to habituate workers to the idea that the new corporate factory regime was "normal."

Still, the ultimate impact of these programs is difficult to gauge. It was probably quite uneven between firms and within each workplace. International Harvester may have been the most successful, but even there the record was mixed. The company's social programs were popular: in June 1916, when the city was being convulsed by a huge machinists' strike, some 1,200 Harvester employees attended the annual company picnic, and the firm claimed that 8,000 men, women, and children turned out in 1919 and 1920.[118] Its Industrial Council also seemed to capture some interest. In March 1919, 89 per cent of the firm's local workforce voted to accept the Council (admittedly with only two days' notice of the vote), and at least one tough old socialist, John Alexander, was willing to take a seat on it. According to a carpenter who had taken short-term work in the plant, "the men themselves seem to think that it should be given a fair trial, if they could bring their views and have them settled in a satisfactory way." The structure of the plan did not make that easy. From his editorial chair at the *Labor News*, F.J. (Fred) Flatman thought that "it might be made to function as a real live forward movement," but only if the workers had an organization behind them. Otherwise, he expected this would be a "soviet of cats and mice." Several unionists who spoke to the Royal Commission on Industrial Relations in May repeated that scepticism. Although unions certainly never found much support inside the plant, two of the first eight employee representatives on the Industrial Council were unionists, and a year later new elections pushed the number up to six. Yet the plan left no space for them to make formal demands on behalf of their organizations.

Meetings of their constituents were not a formal part of the Council's constitution and had to be squeezed into the half-hour lunch break. The company's many European immigrant workers watched all this with indifference in any case because they were excluded from participation in the Industrial Council.[119]

At least some of the Anglo-Canadian workers were nonetheless ready to take up the rhetoric of industrial democracy and negotiate with corporate benevolence over some concerns of their own. Without a union, the unorganized thought this approach was "the best they could do under the circumstances." Before the second meeting of the Industrial Council, the worker representatives unanimously asked for an eight-hour day and a minimum wage of $5 a day. Harvester's superintendent then called them in for a heart-to-heart talk about the state of the company's business and the impossibility of meeting such a request. The workers sheepishly withdrew their petition. According to one of those Council representatives, "That did not satisfy many of the men." When two delegates from the Hamilton Trades and Labor Council met with about 30 Harvester employees soon after these events, they found that the workers saw the Industrial Council "largely as a joke" and "dismissed it as something that was not producing any results." Another Harvester worker told the royal commissioners: "It has not made any difference to the wages scheme so, therefore, the ordinary man does not take much interest in it unless he wanted some privileges granted to him." A year later the employee representatives tried to tackle the wages issue again, and got the two sides on the Council to do their own investigations of the high cost of living. Management used its power over implementation to bury the issue and redirected concerns about price inflation into gardening projects on company plots and worker backyards, along with calls to join the benefit plan.[120]

The company's new plan did nonetheless open up opportunities for workers on less controversial issues. In the royal commission's hearings, the machinists' business agent, Richard Riley, had observed that the company was trying to deflect attention away from the "big grievances," but "they are told that if they have some little grievance in the shop they can take it up and get it adjusted." Indeed, the company's superintendent indicated that there had been "perhaps hundreds of cases in the last few months that have been taken up through the proper channels." Over the next couple of years the company's workers evidently did try to use the new grievance process as an often successful means of getting better working conditions – more heat in cold weather, better washroom facilities and drinking water, safer covers on machines, less dangerous floor surfaces, and much more. During 1920 they also got to vote in referenda on which Easter holiday to take and which schedule of hours should prevail during the summer.[121]

They remained highly susceptible to appeals to company loyalty, however. The employee representatives took their corporate responsibilities seriously, and hectored workers who took off extra days after Christmas or stopped work before the whistle, contrary to decisions of the Industrial Council. Early in 1920 the Council and its *Bulletin* also became useful tools for winning acceptance of the firm's new scientific-management procedures. "Some had a wrong impression of Job Analysis and I set them right," one worker representative reported. The socialist John Alexander even joined the new Planning Department. A year later, despite disgruntlement at not being forewarned, and after a look at the company books, Council members

also issued a statement endorsing wage cuts. *Canadian Machinery* was impressed that "the Harvester people have won the confidence of the men to an unusual degree." Even the radical Armenians who dominated Harvesters' malleable iron foundry and were ineligible for participation in the Industrial Council were grateful enough for the firm's industrial paternalism not to rock the boat much in the interwar period.[122]

At most other plants, welfarism was less expansive and probably had a more limited impact. Workers seemed to pick and choose from the programs in line with their own needs, not always from dewy-eyed corporate loyalty. Indeed, over time, the existence of such amenities as lunchrooms, first-aid stations, and playing fields encouraged a greater sense of entitlement than gratitude – these were what workers now believed they deserved. The sports teams continued to draw crowds looking for excitement after work. Noon-hour games also proved popular, much to the consternation of some managers who found them highly disruptive.[123] A few workers agreed to contribute to company magazines such as Imperial Cotton's *Fabricator*, notably the radical Janet Inman (although other contributors may well have been supervisory personnel). Male wage-earners seemed to prefer the more contractually defined programs oriented towards self-help rather than anything that hinted at charity. The mutual-benefit societies were generally popular where they existed: the Steel Company's two societies had 2,600 members by 1915, for example, and in 1920 three-quarters of International Harvester's workers belonged to its Employees' Benefit Association. Group insurance was similarly valued, though only five firms offered it by the mid-1920s. Much smaller numbers took advantage of stock options or profit-sharing (offered by only six companies), and pension plans would touch even fewer. In 1923 a group of garment workers actually struck against their employer's pressure to buy stock in the firm.[124]

The companies' greater interest in long-range economic security (tied to long service to the company) and their resistance to raising wages missed the central preoccupation of the male breadwinner – the weekly wage packet. The enthusiasts for welfarism thus ultimately remained a small minority of the workforce – the more stable, Anglo-Canadian, male, probably more skilled elements – and were probably workers who had settled into their jobs and identified strongly with their firms. By 1935 the Steel Company was saying that it had 450 employees with at least 25 years of service. Perhaps those workers were able to collapse their pride in their skills into corporate loyalty and pride in the firm's products. Certainly corporations like the Steel Company could count on a considerable minority of these long-service employees to reject unions by the 1940s.[125] In essence the spectrum of workers most likely ran from faithful loyalism through calculated sycophancy and cynicism to smouldering resentment. Most hard-headed workers realized that the programs offered seldom touched on the real problems of the relationship – low wages, long hours, and arbitrary supervision. Welfarism did not keep resistance from boiling up again briefly in the late 1920s and early 1930s.

Indeed, relatively few workers were actually touched by the company welfarism and even for them the experience tended to last only for a short period of time. It was principally the large US-owned corporations that introduced the new measures, most often as part of continent-wide plans. Outside the Steel Company, thousands of workers in the city's largest Canadian-owned metalworking factories – Sawyer-Massey, National Steel Car, Hamilton Bridge, and Dofasco,

among others – felt few of the effects of this new paternalism until the late 1930s. Moreover, in most cases the plans were aimed at only part of the workforce, often excluding European immigrants. Hamilton industrialists showed no interest in assimilating these workers through Canadianization programs to match the Americanization ventures under way in the United States.[126] A final telling comment on the usefulness of these measures is that in the mid-1920s, once the crisis of the labour revolt had passed, some firms quietly abandoned company magazines and other boosterish paraphernalia. Perhaps the role of welfarism as an antidote to unionism made it now expendable, or perhaps it had not worked as the great stabilizer of labour relations that managers had hoped for.[127]

The human touch that was brought to bear in Hamilton plants in the early 20th century, then, was predominantly authoritarian. The managerial bureaucracy had been expanded in some plants to include full-time staff to handle a few of the workers' social needs, generally as part of a process of trying to stabilize and regularize workers' employment patterns, especially reducing labour turnover. But these new officials had little independent authority in the plants, and their programs remained marginal activities that did little to change workers' daily experience on the job. They never displaced the fundamentally repressive orientation of the "drive system," which regained its potency and credibility among industrialists in the 1920s once high unemployment levels had rekindled workers' fears of poverty. Corporate welfare thus had only a limited role in shaping and disciplining the new workforce assembled in the city.[128] Over the long term, wage-incentive systems and the power left to front-line supervisors to keep workers in line provided the crucial cement for the new factory regime.

Factory administration in Hamilton, therefore, incorporated two divergent tendencies: bureaucracy at the top and petty despotism at the bottom. There could be serious friction between the two sets of corporate officials involved. Foremen who had risen through the ranks often distrusted the college boys in the front office, while professionally trained managers might tear their hair in frustration at the crusty empiricism of the shop-floor supervisors. Yet in most cases their mutual respect and tolerance created a dynamic managerial synthesis that had produced an accountable, flexible system for running the plants by the 1920s.[129]

Bodies on the Line

Hamilton's factory managers used increasingly diverse techniques to tug at the hearts and minds of their workers, but those methods were all intended to get the working-class bodies in motion, whether in pure muscular exertion or, more often, as reliable, fast-moving extensions of the machines being operated. Art-nouveau designers liked to feature an idealized version of such a body in the city's promotional literature, but, as the pace cranked up and the risks to the body proliferated, the reality of daily work inside the city's factories could be a good deal less noble and heroic.

Throughout most of the years from the 1890s to the 1920s, Hamilton workers were expected to present themselves at the factory gate by 7 a.m., Monday to Saturday. If they were looking for work, they milled about with others who hoped to be taken on by a foreman or employment manager. The regular workers took careful note of this pool of unemployed labour and hurried inside. In the early years of the new century they signed in or punched the time clock as they entered the plant, but by the 1920s they were heading straight for their departments to punch in because their bosses were less willing to pay for travelling (or dawdling) time inside the plant.[130] Women and men generally headed to separate departments. Walking through the plant, they might recognize few familiar faces – the firm typically had hundreds of employees, and so many came and went every week. Probably they got to know only the workmates in their own department (though they might also have relatives or friends working somewhere in the plant). They certainly would not know the corporate magnates who owned the place and passed through only on ceremonial visits. Even the top managerial staff were generally distant figures who descended to the shop floor only to consult with the foremen and superintendents; they rarely got their hands dirty.[131]

In the steel plant and a few other large factories, the morning-shift workers replaced a weary night shift, but, except during the war,[132] relatively few firms ran around the clock. After punching in, some of the workers, especially the least skilled, then waited for the foremen's instructions. Because of the high labour turnover, several new workers were also invariably hanging about waiting to be trained each day. Most of the others proceeded immediately to their regular work stations, perhaps clutching a batch of orders or specifications, with a clear understanding of how much they were expected to produce that day and how fast. And so began the long, tedious, high-pressure, and dangerous working day.

As the complex production processes in these plants were set in motion each morning, most workers were submerged in a deafening clatter. The hot, thick, unhealthy air was full of cotton particles in the textile plants and smoke and dust in the foundries, machine shops, and other metalworking plants. The newer plants were better lighted and ventilated, but the amenities could still be spartan. Since few factories had cloakrooms or lunchrooms before 1920, most workers could also expect to hang their coats and eat their lunches amid the dirt and odours of their work sites. In 1919 a worker in a plant with 2,000 to 3,000 hands complained in a letter to the *Spectator* that the only drinking fountain was "the tin cup fastened to the wall, where hundreds of men slop over and drink out of the one cup day after day all the year round." Some two years later another cited a local plant "where the only means of washing the hands to get the mid-day lunch is a bucket, if one can be found, and where the lavatories are not fit for animals." Surviving photographs from Hamilton's factories before 1940 occasionally reveal the workers' brave efforts to humanize their workspaces with pin-ups or calendars, but they also show the harsh glaring light bulbs and the general drabness. Few employees would be able to escape this oppressive atmosphere before they had put in nine or ten hours, except on Saturday, when most could leave at noon. In some departments of the steel plant the shifts were 12 hours long, 7 days a week, until 1930.[133]

The actual work routines of their jobs and the demands on their bodies could vary considerably. Skilled maintenance men had considerable flexibility in their work and freedom to move around. Teams of skilled workers in the steel plant were largely left alone to run the blast or open-hearth furnaces or to turn billets into sheet metal.[134] Moulders at Westinghouse or Dofasco preparing massive moulds for generator parts probably enjoyed much the same kind of independence. In many plants, men hopped aboard some kind of vehicle that they would be driving for the next nine to ten hours. These were responsible jobs that required attentiveness and a certain amount of skill, but that were also under the watchful eye of the foreman.

Labourers probably moved around from task to task, indoors and out, constantly badgered by foremen and "straw bosses." Far more workers – handymen in the machine shops, riveters in the railway-car plant, sewing-machine operators in the clothing and knitting factories, and many more – switched on some type of stationery machinery and began a day of mind-numbing tedium and regular harassment by supervisors.

As the day wore on, all these workers of whatever skill would feel the relentless pressure to keep up. Little time outside of lunch breaks opened up for discussing ball games or boyfriends with workmates. Raw materials or parts were shunting steadily in from other parts of the plant, and finished pieces moved on quickly. The foreman blustered and threatened if the flow of production slowed down. Most workers were also keeping mental track of their piecework earnings, cursing any delays in delivery or malfunctioning of machines. Small wonder that by the 1920s researchers were beginning to identify "industrial fatigue" as a new problem in factory work.[135]

Small wonder too that so many workers were injured on the job. For a quarter-century before World War One, Ontario's factory inspectors published grisly annual lists of all accidents reported to them under the Factories Act, that is, those requiring more than six days off work. The reporting was uneven, though it appears that the larger corporations were the most co-operative. Although the sketchy descriptions of the accidents make detailed analysis difficult, certain patterns nonetheless stand out. The number of serious injuries in Hamilton rose faster than the increase in the workforce, noticeably after the creation of the Hamilton Iron and Steel Company in 1899 and then much more dramatically after the opening of International Harvester in 1903. Between 1890 and 1902 the annual toll of workplace accidents in Hamilton was an average of 17, but by 1911 it was 10 times that number and by 1914, 24 times – a total of over 400; and more were fatal – six in 1909, and an average of four a year for the next seven years (when this reporting stopped).[136]

Some workplaces in the pre-war period were much more dangerous than others. Machine operators in the textile plants were most likely to catch their limbs in the gears while trying to clean or repair them, no doubt in a hasty effort to avoid shutting down their machines. In some woodworking and metalworking firms – particularly Norton Manufacturing (later American Can), which used a lot of young workers to make tin cans – the machine operators seem to have hurt themselves on the machinery after succumbing to the mind-numbing repetition of their mechanized tasks. The most astonishing figures, however, came from some of the big new corporations. The pattern in these plants suggests the human carnage that could result from the first phases of speeded-up mass-production work. In 1904 International Harvester reported to the Ontario factory inspectors that 150 of its roughly 1,700 employees – 1 in 11 – had suffered injuries requiring at least a week off work. Similarly high tolls were recorded when the Steel Company expanded its operations in 1907 and 1912, when National Steel Car opened in 1913, and when several plants began munitions work in 1915. In that new wartime boom more than 1,000 workers suffered serious injuries. Almost half of those incidents occurred at the Steel Company's plants.

As surviving photographs reveal, companies provided their workers with virtually no protective gear; so it is not surprising that splashes of molten metal seared their flesh, steel chips hit their eyes, iron castings slipped off piles and crushed their hands or feet, and fast-moving machines grabbed their fingers. "In a plant this size where work is carried through with great rapidity," a *Canadian Machinery* reporter calmly noted after touring the National Steel Car plant in 1913, "there is always some one getting their fingers jammed or sustaining other minor injuries."[137] The long list of injuries (including one death) at the Steel Company's plant in 1916 made grim reading: "Toe and nail bruised; billet fell on foot"; "Severed finger; caught in chain"; "Hand cut and bruised; loading buggy, bar rolled back"; "Back injured; while unloading wire off truck, one bundle fell"; "Right eye cut; shearing scrap in open hearth scrap yard, sliver of same lodged in forehead"; "Leg burned near thigh; bar coming from roughing rolls turned round"; "Finger smashed, foot cut and body bruised; blooms fell off pile and knocked him down" – on and on through blunt vignettes of 488 bodies paying the price for their inexperience in a munitions plant and their boss's relentless speed-up of production. Hardly any of these accounts read as reports on worker negligence. One in five of those accidents – nearly all hand injuries – resulted from operating machinery or equipment. But nearly half involved something heavy or sharp falling on or hitting the body, most often the feet.[138]

The 1916 report of the new Workmen's Compensation Board connected the "heavy increase in claims" to how workers had been "speeded up to a higher notch of productivity." The Board proceeded to publish startling new statistics on workplace accidents (this time, those that required more than two days off work). In the wartime boom between 1916 and 1920, Wentworth County, where Hamilton was by far the dominant industrial centre, had 70 workers killed on the job and 1,334 permanently disabled, in addition to the 15,111 temporarily laid up by their injuries. Industrial casualties peaked again when production picked up briefly in 1923 and more decisively in the late 1920s, when the WCB recorded annual highs of 28 deaths and 308 permanent disabilities.[139]

The most dangerous plants were also those with high proportions of inexperienced, transient workers, often with limited English-language skills. The Ontario factory inspectorate was sufficiently concerned about injuries to "foreigners" that they published translations of warning signs in six different languages in 1914. National Steel Car had safety posters in three. The descriptions of the accidents give the impression of men who were bewildered and caught off guard in an unfamiliar environment, who were probably being pushed to work harder and faster, or who were sent into unsafe work situations without proper precautions because their supervisors implicitly assumed they were easily replaceable labour. International Harvester's chief safety inspector announced in 1920 that "75% of our accidents occurred to the new man." As the Steel Company's Hobson once admitted, company doctors typically made light of workplace injuries. A quarter-century later, a family physician in the city's Italian community believed that many Italian workers were encouraged not to report their injuries out of fear of losing their jobs, and that the company's doctor was equally dismissive of injuries.[140]

The same Italian-Canadian physician was also struck by the lung disease from which so many of his patients were suffering. In 1920 the federal government created a Committee on Industrial Fatigue under the Honorary Advisory Council for Scientific and Industrial Research, which hoped "to make the knowledge and experience of Medical Science, as it bears on industrial health and efficiency, available to all industry." But the Committee collapsed for lack of interest. As the Ontario Medical Association's Committee on Industrial Medicine reported in 1926, most doctors knew little about industrial health hazards and showed little interest in getting better informed, even though cancer had become an increasingly common cause of death. Textile workers continued to contract "brown lung," and foundry workers breathed in such heavy doses of silica dust thrown around by the new machinery that silicosis remained a serious, largely unrecognized disease among them.[141]

In the late 1880s, in response to union demands, the Ontario government had first sent out a handful of inspectors to investigate and report on safety standards and injuries in the province's factories and to enforce the Factories Act. In 1907 the number of inspectors was doubled to ten for the whole province, including two women to cover female employment. Their annual reports occasionally contained critical commentaries on the impact of speed-up and other trends in factory work experience in general (rather than in individual workplaces). But these officials most often saw their work as educational rather than punitive, and rarely prosecuted any negligent employers. As the soaring accident rate before the war made clear, it is unlikely that they were able to make factories significantly safer workplaces.[142]

At the turn of the century employers were under little legal pressure to reduce on-the-job risks. For decades the courts had been left to determine liability for injuries and, using the Common Law, had assumed that a worker chose to accept the risks when he took a job and that, by a "fellow-servant rule," other workmates were involved in "contributory negligence" that let the employer off the hook An 1886 Ontario act weakened that rule, but still required injured workers or their families to launch civil suits against employers for compensation. By the turn of the century, the few who went to court were winning more cases (though by no means all of them), especially where juries heard their stories. Industrialists began to find this "nuisance of litigation" annoyingly unpredictable.[143]

In 1910, as the rates of injuries climbed, the Ontario government again responded to labour pressure and employer concerns about civil suits and appointed Sir William Meredith as a one-man commission to investigate and report on employers' liability to compensate injured workers. His recommendations were translated into the new legislation of 1914 that set a Workmen's Compensation Board to work the next year doling out small payments to cover serious injuries and deaths.

Since the funds for this program came exclusively from employers, factory owners quickly saw the need for safety programs in their plants to try to minimize accidents and thus the costs to the compensation fund. As the *Labor News* suggested, "Under the law as it now stands, it is going to be a costly proposition to kill or maim a worker." An Ontario Safety League and separate associations in specific industries emerged immediately, each with its own staff of inspectors, to promote interest in more safety devices on machinery and Shop Safety Committees to educate workers. The Hamilton branch of the Canadian Manufacturers' Association also held special lectures to promote local accident prevention. "Safety First" campaigns blossomed everywhere "to teach the careless to be careful," especially after World War One as part of the new wave of welfarism. Indeed, reducing accidents was soon folded into the concerns with industrial efficiency. As an International Harvester safety inspector told a Hamilton audience, "Business men are awakening to an intelligent realization of the fact that to preserve the life and limb of their employees and to conserve the human equipment of their plants pays in dollars

and cents and is, therefore, a part of good business organization."[144]

The impact of safety first programs was uncertain. In 1913 National Steel Car could claim that it was "one of the safest car building plants in operation" after installing protective equipment and instructing workmen. Yet that year 99 workers – roughly 1 in 10 – suffered injuries severe enough to lose at least a week of work.[145] By the 1920s the Workmen's Compensation Board was concluding that the safety programs had made a difference to the kinds of injuries. "Less than one-quarter of all accidents now are caused by Machinery," it noted. "A far greater number result from handling, striking against, or being struck by, objects or material." Under pressures to produce at top speed, working safely in any factory generally came from experience with particular plants and their machinery. Accidents tended to decline when the economy slumped and labour turnover declined, and to rise again as new recruits arrived along with renewed pressure to crank up productivity. Certainly the Board's figures show a falling off of accidents in the early 1920s as industry tumbled into a severe depression, with a sharp increase again in the economic boom at the end of the decade. Some 2,000 injured workers were nonetheless being patched up every year.[146]

Industrialists made heavy demands on the bodies of the men and women they hired. Wherever possible, they attempted to restrain the free movement of the body, to focus it narrowly on the specific exertions needed, and to turn up the pressure to work faster. In these circumstances many bodies broke down, through exhaustion, stress, injury, and disease.

The New Factory Regime

In the decade before World War One, then, Hamilton's industrialists had decided to confront what they had come to see as the apparently intractable "labour question" in their plants. They drove out any unions among their workers that obstructed the path to high productivity and profits, but they also looked for more "systematic" solutions. In part, that search meant finding new versions of the earliest innovations of the First Industrial Revolution – dividing up skilled tasks, mechanizing as many as possible, and hiring less well-trained, less expensive workers from new pools of labour. Manual workers of all kinds, from moulders to common labourers, felt the impact of these changes. Much of the mechanization went beyond individual jobs to integrate labour processes and eliminate delays and bottlenecks. What this Second Industrial Revolution added, in fact, was a greater emphasis on tighter control from the top. A much expanded staff of white-collar professionals and clerical workers was put to work co-ordinating and closely monitoring the jobs undertaken out on the factory floor. A new ideology of managerial expertise in guaranteeing efficiency cast a gloss of scientific credibility over the more centralized, bureaucratic, and authoritarian practices of this rapidly evolving industrial system. For workers the most immediate results were speed-up and enhanced danger.

By the 1920s factories consequently looked and were run much differently. Yet, in practice, they did not work according to the simple flow charts of the new managerial theory. In most plants, "efficient" production still relied on the manual know-how of many still-important skilled workers and on the experience of the vastly increased numbers of semi-skilled machine operators. Management policies thus had to acknowledge the "human factor," first with incentive wages and tough foremen to stimulate output and then, as workers both voted with their feet and turned to new unions during and

after World War One, with welfare programs intended to make them feel good about their jobs and to discourage both labour turnover and unionization.

Implementing a Second Industrial Revolution, then, was a much more complex process of trial and error, innovation and adaptation, and managerial re-education in the face of workers' behaviour. A new workplace regime had been put in place with harsh, authoritarian, and dangerous elements, but with plenty of volatility and unpredictability. A good deal of that uncertainty came from the persistent effort of the workers themselves to assert their own priorities of decency and fairness.

11

Within Hamilton's craft-union movement, the printers were among the most successful in winning at the bargaining table. Their 1913 parade float, crowned with their union label, proudly proclaimed their eight-hour-day victory.
(HPL, Bailey Collection)

Standing Up to the Boss

A STRIKERS' PICKET LINE could be a lonely place. Swept by winter winds or baking under summer heat, the space in front of the plant gate was remote from the familiar routines of the normal workday or the warm comforts of the family kitchen. It could also be scary. Standing up to the boss so belligerently meant losing wages in the short term and possibly even your job if no settlement was achieved. Often picketers had to watch other workers – sometimes escorted by private security guards or police – skulk by to take their jobs inside the plant. Strikers might respond with a cry of "scab," a pitched stone, or a swinging fist. Any of those actions could land them in police court.

Yet getting to the moment of walking out on strike, and maintaining the momentum, just as often brought an exhilarating sense of shared possibilities, especially when the actions involved hundreds of workers from the same large plant. Picket lines could even be fun, punctuated by shouting, cursing, laughing, singing, and playful jostling. They were certainly sites of eye-catching spectacles, with picket signs waving above the heads of strikers calling out for justice.

Workers turned to each other in anger, resentment, determination, and hope. Through endless discussions and debates they reaffirmed their commitment to stand together, often in spite of threats from blustering foremen. They wanted things to be different on the job. They wanted their solidarity to be a permanent bulwark of workers' rights. Winning could open new horizons for working-class power and industrial democracy beyond the workplace, as the great street-railway strike of 1906 revealed; but losing could decisively shut down that confidence and permanently weaken larger challenges to workers' subordination.[1]

Strikers and unionists in Hamilton were defying the logic of the new factory regime that had taken shape in the opening decades of the 20th century. It was, as we've seen, a system that required a high degree of working-class compliance for its success. Not only did workers, like other citizens, have to accept the legitimacy of the new consolidated corporate power to shape the destiny of the city, but they also had to cooperate in workplace strategies that owners and managers had developed for increasing productivity and raising profits. To a great extent they did comply, though not without active managerial intervention, without prodding and coaxing. At many points industrial paternalism must have just "made sense," at least until some provocation sparked outrage and resistance. Some workers, however, never abandoned their own individual and collective sense of what was acceptable in the terms and conditions of their employment. Under the right circumstances, some of them were ready to challenge the managerial agenda.

To take such a step, wage-earners had to be able to mobilize resources that would give them an edge in industrial confrontations.[2] A booming economy reduced the threat of unemployment and poverty. A robust tradition of workplace customs provided the ethical high ground and perhaps a repertoire of tactics. A familiar cultural reservoir allowed workers to proclaim the superiority of their skill, ethnicity, or gender. Social networks of mutual support off the job helped in building workplace solidarity. Inspiration from other strikers, nearby or far away in similar factories, might also set off "strike waves," and Hamilton would experience three of these (in 1910–14, 1916–21, and 1929–36); they

learned from each other.[3] Less often, a political advantage (occurring, for instance, in wartime) might enable workers to appeal to a sense of fairness and entitlement. Lacking these kinds of resources could hold them back from standing up to their bosses. Organizing a union and using it to advance their interests was certainly a faint hope during economic slumps and always an uphill battle among less-skilled, more vulnerable workers. Compared to building tradesmen or coal miners, factory workers were particularly vulnerable. They were locked into regimes of close, authoritarian supervision and often lacked transferable skills. Highly dependent on the internal job ladders of individual firms, they were enmeshed in a dynamic system of industrial paternalism.[4]

The Canadian state in this period did not prove to be much of a resource for encouraging or sustaining the collective struggles of wage-earners. No labour legislation was in place to give unionists any of the legal rights they would gain after World War Two. Both the tiny, ineffective Ontario Bureau of Labour and the later Ontario Department of Labour (formed in 1920) were more interested in monitoring minimal employment standards (especially through factory inspection) and promoting labour-market efficiency through employment offices. The much larger federal Department of Labour was keenly interested in promoting industrial peace through state-sponsored conciliation, but, aside from a brief period during World War One, the factories that dominated local employment fell outside the bounds of the main piece of federal labour legislation, the Industrial Disputes Investigation Act. Wage-earners in Hamilton met the state primarily in the form of policemen pushing back their picket lines or magistrates passing unsympathetic judgments on their behaviour as strikers.[5]

Wage-earners also required some consensus about the best kind of organization to create or join and the most promising strategy to follow. Here Hamilton's workers found plenty to disagree about. Over the decades from 1890 to 1940 they were presented with two opposing strategies: either to act on the narrow interests of one occupational group or to rally around a wider collective identity as workers. The political complexions of the workers' movements that reached out to wage-earners could also be contentious. The activists who debated these options were parts of what one historian calls a "militant minority," who played leadership roles in shaping the forms of resistance and the discourses sustaining them, and who often became the sparkplugs of militancy.[6] Generally the tendency from the early years of the century to the mid-1930s was to find common cause among more diverse workmates, though not without plenty of tension and fragmenting tendencies. Small clusters of workmates remained crucial to mobilizing these larger struggles.

Collective action around workplace issues, then, was risky, courageous, and more often than not unsuccessful. Soon after the turn of the century, it became clear that few employers were willing to sit down and talk, especially when a militant union was involved, and a large number of the strikes that unfolded in the city resulted from employers' refusal to negotiate. Whatever the strategy, the power of local industrialists to inhibit unionization and squelch it when it appeared was never broken before 1940.

Can't Stand It No More

Strikes were far from the most frequent display of frustration or outrage. Many workers simply walked away from unacceptable work. "Floating" between jobs – or "labour turnover," as the new labour relations experts called it – was as common in Hamilton as elsewhere whenever jobs were plentiful and the threat of poverty was weak. In 1907 the Hamilton *Times* described "a large roving element in the labor market" that was disturbing employers. These workers comprised "a considerable element of a floating nature, composed in part of foreigners and in part of young men from the country, who come to the city as soon as the fall work is over and expect to go back when spring plowing begins." Most were "none too anxious to take steady jobs," preferring "to put in a week here and a week or two there, moving from place to place and earning only enough to keep them over the winter and enable them to have a pretty good time." The manufacturers did not like them because "men coming and going upset organization in the shops and have an unsettling effect upon the regular hands."[7]

This journalist, and the industrialists he interviewed, misjudged how much this hopping in and out of the labour market might actually be a rational strategy of sojourning to earn quick cash for family economies. But they did capture how these young men refused to be drawn into the web of the new factory regime and spontaneously rejected unacceptable employment by "floating" between jobs – no doubt as part of the youthful masculine culture in which they participated. The Ontario Commission on Unemployment found that women were no less footloose. Its 1915 report deplored the large "floating population" among female workers, "those who earn no trade, but drift from one to another, staying at each a few months." The proportion of such drifters, the Commission noted, "increases with the size of the factory and the subdivision of the work."[8]

This drifting in and out of factories was widely discussed across North America, as various large firms discovered that the number

Forging shells at Dofasco during World War One.
(LAC, Mikan No. 3371038)

passing through could be many times the number needed to staff their plants.[9] This behaviour was far and away the most common response of the unskilled to the speed-ups and more rigid supervision of the new corporate-capitalist work world. Whether European peasants or Anglo-Canadian labourers, they voted with their feet in large numbers to reject the harshness of it all. But skilled men were apparently just as mobile because in 1910 the Hamilton branch of the Canadian Manufacturers' Association held a special meeting to discuss stricter guidelines on hiring practices among its membership to curb the jumping between jobs (and bidding up of wages) that had become a corporate headache. A year later the Trades and Labor Council heard complaints about how employers were collectively forcing workers to wait two weeks after leaving one job before being allowed to take another.[10] Companies began to insist on adequate notice for quitting, and the police magistrate was willing to support them.[11]

Not all workers floated. Among those who settled into a job for any length of time could be found the nucleus for collective resistance – the work group. Here in individual workshops and departments of factories, workmates developed their own collectively understood routines for carrying out shop-floor tasks. They did so under their foreman's stern gaze, but with their own interpretation of how fast to work, how much to produce, and how to protect each other from supervisors' wrath, among other tactics.[12] These were practices that craft unionists had hoped to protect in their formal agreements with employers. More broadly they were also the forms of "soldiering" that Taylor had attempted to root out with his model of scientific management. An investigator nonetheless still found them alive and well across US industry in 1930, and four decades later a Hamilton machinist reported that these unofficial co-operative practices still thrived among workers on the shop floor among some of the city's biggest employers.[13]

In early 20th-century Hamilton the persistence and stubbornness of work groups most often became evident when managers abruptly altered some part of the factory regime, including workload, piece rates, and front-line supervision. Numerous strikes in Hamilton in the two decades before World War One were spontaneous actions by small groups of workmates against such management initiatives.[14] Several were flare-ups over piece rates.[15] Others were efforts to defend discharged workmates.[16] Sometimes the issue was work time or safety on the job.[17] Often actions were triggered by disruptive managerial innovations.[18] Each work group was united by a combination of occupation, gender, and ethnicity. Many managers refused to categorize these "troubles" as strikes,[19] and they sometimes went unreported to the federal Department of Labour and were scarcely noted in the daily press. But they certainly disrupted the managerial agenda and in many cases accomplished their modest goals of rolling back the source of their complaints. These small explosions of informal militancy, many years later dubbed "wildcat" strikes, were a shrewdly used, reasonably effective form of shop-floor bargaining.[20]

In the half-decade before World War One these groups began to coalesce into much larger struggles in the heart of the new mass-production industries. Often, because many of them did not have permanent organizations and clearly identifiable leaders, they left no record of their own concerns, and reporting of the events in newspapers and government files remained opaque. But broad patterns can be discerned. In the decade before World War One, as the craft union movement in Hamilton crumbled, three groups of workers confronted the emerging work world of corporate capital's Second Industrial Revolution in distinctive ways: craftworkers tried to put their issues forward once again;

new immigrants shed their docility; and "working girls" made militancy out of their femininity. The strikes they led disrupted production in many plants and captured public attention, especially in spring 1907 and in 1910, 1912, and 1913. But by the outbreak of the war the workers had little to show for their efforts.

Craftworkers wanted to revive their unions as the bulwark of their dignity, pride, power, and social status, in a way comparable to the city's building-trade workers, who still provided a vibrant example of craft union organizing and bargaining, in which the major unions (bricklayers, carpenters, electricians, painters, and plumbers) all kept renewing agreements with the city's contractors.[21] Each craft group in a factory wanted its own agreement with management setting out the conditions of employment. In the decade before the war this narrow approach to organizing was under attack across North America by more radical ideas of uniting all workers in one workplace in the same union. In response to the dual threat of hostile employers and militant industrial unionists, the American Federation of Labor reconceived the boundaries of craft unionism. In 1911 it endorsed a major new declaration allowing one union's jurisdiction to extend beyond a single occupational group to a whole industry, including semi-skilled handymen and specialists. In practice this new direction would mean separate locals of different occupational groups in one workplace rather than a single, all-inclusive union local.[22] It remained to be seen how widely craft unionists would actually spread their mantle.

In 1912–13 both the moulders' and machinists' unions launched new organizing drives. The moulders made no headway in the stove foundries after their humiliating defeat in 1909, but they did sign up members in 11 large plants that made machinery. They established the nine-hour day and won wage increases in eight of the largest companies.[23] For the first (and only) time, the moulders also set a fixed rate for machine operators in the foundry – in effect, to extend the union's extensive work regulations to cover work on the machines. But three firms, including Westinghouse, refused to concede control of production to the union. The ensuing Westinghouse strike severely disrupted production, costing the company alone some $100,000, but it collapsed in the depression that began in the second half of the year. The union's hold in the other plants soon dissolved as well, as unemployment sapped militancy.[24]

The machinists were split between two frequently antagonistic unions – the British-based Amalgamated Society of Engineers (ASE), dating back to 1851 and regularly renewed by new British immigrants, and the International Association of Machinists (IAM), successor to a number of earlier North American unionizing experiments, which organized Hamilton Lodge 414 in 1897 (reorganized in 1902).[25] According to the IAM's business agent, the two groups were "continually fighting among themselves as to who is responsible for their rotten working conditions." Indeed, given that their craft was vulnerable to further subdivision, mechanization, and invasion by less-skilled non-unionists – who after 1893 were eligible to join in separate units, but seldom did anywhere in North America – the Hamilton locals stagnated.[26] A province-wide organizing campaign early in 1912 generated a spurt of local activity, including weekly mass meetings and home visits, but the machinists' business agent Richard Riley admitted that "in the majority of shops in this city the machinists have not dared to admit they belonged to the I.A. of M., and employers did as they pleased with them." On a spring day in 1913, Riley and an IAM organizer stood watching Westinghouse's 3,300 workers file out at noon hour. The two unionists soberly agreed that it would be "quite a job to organize them."[27]

Neither of the two major groups of metalworking craftworkers, then, had been able to deflect the major trends of managerial innovation in the pre-war period. Although a Metal Trades Council had been organized in 1910, both unions initially found reasons to stay out. Yet perhaps the lessons of their failed organizing drives were sobering, because one day in May 1914 delegates to the Metal Trades Council from the moulders, machinists, and metal polishers sat around Labor Hall discussing the novel idea of amalgamating all metalworking crafts. The deepening depression curtailed such musing, and the Council expired that year before the project got much airing.[28]

The less-skilled found little help in these circles of old-time craft expertise. In contrast to the vigorous "general" unionism in Britain at this time, the space available to the unskilled within the North American craft union movement was extremely limited. The AFL allowed for the creation of so-called "federal labour unions" as local holding tanks for those that did not fit into any identifiable trade, but forbade those bodies to form a national or international organization to promote their own interests. Other than the short-lived 1902 blast-furnace workers' local, Hamilton had no such organization before the war.[29] The ideological alternative was all-inclusive industrial unionism, espoused in its most revolutionary form by the new Industrial Workers of the World (IWW) – popularly known as the Wobblies – founded in Chicago in 1905. In 1908 local socialists launched a branch of the IWW in Hamilton, but it quickly withered and died. A Wobbly organizer passed through the city in spring 1914 hoping to arouse the unemployed, but the visit had no lasting impact.[30]

Less-skilled workers in pre-war Hamilton therefore met the challenge of the changing workplace by drawing on other loyalties. In fall 1913, for example, the Royal Guardian Society, a fraternal society made up largely of labourers, and the East Hamilton Progressive Association, a recently formed workingmen's club in the east-end working-class suburbs, became the defenders of labourers fighting the G.M. Guest Company for higher wages on excavation work.[31] Among some recent immigrants, ethnicity was the cement of their solidarity and militancy in the new mass-production factories. Most of them came from peasant backgrounds, where protest against exploitative landowners might have had deep roots. Some had learned styles of militancy in their treks through workplaces around the continent. Others had imbibed radical ideologies preached by new socialist movements at home or in North America.[32] Certainly they showed an understanding of labour solidarity in their new jobs. Groups of immigrant workers staged several determined strikes in Hamilton in spring 1907, and two years later a group of Italian labourers refused to take the places of striking dock workers. As the *Herald* noted a few years later, these workers "have no union but they have modern ideas."[33]

The most electrifying example of this militancy among the unskilled came in April 1910, a moment of seasonal labour shortage when more than 1,000 immigrant labourers, mostly Italians, with a sprinkling of Poles and Hungarians, shut down both the east-end and west-end plants of the Hamilton Steel and Iron Company. They wanted wage increases from 15 cents to a scale of 17, 18, and 20 cents, and after two days got promises from Robert Hobson, then the company's vice-president and general manager, to collect information on wage rates in the Buffalo steel industry and to fire two foremen who

had been accused of extorting money from immigrant labourers for the privilege of getting work in their gang. Some ten days later the firm announced an elaborate new wage scale with increases of 5 to 10 per cent. The strike had built on ethnic solidarity, and the company blamed the walkout on the "foreign agitators, so-called interpreters who do not work themselves." According to the *Spectator*, "No union exists among the foreigners except union of brotherhood, and they realize that the union does not include English-speaking employees of the steel works, for so far as can be learned no attempts were made to get them to strike." Within their own neighbourhoods, according to the *Herald*, "little groups of foreigners were assembled, apparently discussing the situation, but directly a Britisher hove in sight not a word was heard until he had passed out of hearing distance."[34]

In this short-lived burst of militancy – the most serious disruption of the company's production in the whole half-century before a monumental steel strike in 1946 – this new element in the Hamilton labour force had effectively challenged, though not eliminated, the large corporation's authoritarian, low-wage policies. The workers involved had no permanent organization, but the newly formed Steel Company of Canada faced minor confrontations with its immigrant labourers almost every spring for a decade after 1907, including action involving 500 workers in 1912.[35] This was not the docile workforce that the company must have imagined when it first imported Italians to break the 1902 blast-furnace workers' strike.

Early in 1914 National Steel Car faced a similar strike, although this time the "foreigners" involved apparently achieved some solidarity with Anglo-Canadian workers. In the wake of a recent piece-rate cut, most of the company's 700 workers walked out. After two weeks they

In the 1913 labour parade for the city's centennial, rather than marching in the streets with the men, the women who worked at McPherson's boot and shoe factory were symbolically confined to a wagon – providing a clear indication of their alleged fragility and marginality to wage labour in the eyes of male unionists. (SLS, LS300)

returned to work with a small concession from the company that left many men dissatisfied enough to strike again shortly after. They were promptly replaced.[36] These episodes of mass mobilization did not follow the customary routines of craft unionism. Disciplined mass pickets to stop production and bring management around were much more important than simply withdrawing skill. Organizational savvy no doubt came in large part from the wealth of experience that migrant labourers were carrying with them between jobs across North America. Immediate outside support came not from organized labour, but from the city's ethnic networks, including some radicals in those communities. Ethnicity, then, could be a divisive force, but also a resource binding together workers with common occupational experiences.

As for women, or "working girls," until the immediate pre-war period they had played no significant role in organized labour in the city since the 1880s. Strikes had generally been male affairs, though from time to time women wage-earners had used the informal tactics of shop-floor bargaining to win concessions. It was only in the half-decade before the war that large numbers of them participated in workplace struggles that united the whole, female-dominated workforce in one plant or industrial sector and displayed a new tough-minded brand of working-class femininity.

The main spotlight was on the local clothing factories.[37] The upsurge in the Hamilton clothing industry in 1913 paralleled – and was no doubt inspired by – the ferment and action taking place throughout North American garment districts over the previous four years. Workers in Chicago, New York, Montreal, Toronto, and other major cities frequently ignored the cautious warnings of the union leadership and engaged in militant mass strikes.[38] In the winter of 1912–13 a United Garment Workers' organizer found the Hamilton workers unusually eager to sign up, and three new locals, each representing pressers, cutters, and tailors, soon boasted swelling memberships, including many women. By the early spring of 1913 the workshops seethed with a restlessness to confront the manufacturers, despite efforts by the harassed international union leadership to contain them.[39]

On 15 April, before negotiations with the manufacturers had broken off, the Hamilton workshops erupted. Some 2,000 pressers and tailors walked out on strike; two days later the cutters were laid off and refused to return to work while the strike was on. The entire ready-made men's clothing industry in the city was shut down. Only a few of the tailors were union members, reported an organizer from Toronto, "but they succeeded in pulling out all the workers, a large proportion of which are girls." The tailoresses made up roughly half the strikers, and 985 women signed union cards in the first few days of the strike. Ethnic tensions between Jews and Gentiles seem to have been submerged, and for two weeks the garment workers' solidarity held firm, as their numbers grew to nearly 3,000.[40]

Initially the press depicted female picketers as frivolous and flighty. A roving reporter encountered a group of them outside their headquarters: "'I was never on strike before!' cried one good-looking woman as she shoved into a crowd of girl friends in John Street. 'Gee! but it's lots of fun, isn't it?'"[41] The women workers were actually determined strikers, who maintained their picket lines for the full two weeks of the dispute. Here in Hamilton as in so many other garment districts in the 1909–13 period, the "rising of the women" flowed out of a new female activism percolating through the ranks of the industry's working girls, especially among the many Jewish women in these jobs. This feistier form of working-class femininity blossomed among women who were concentrated inside the city's larger clothing factories rather than being scattered through contract shops.

In this 1913 struggle the women shaped an independent role with their own leaders (who were never named in the press) and with advice from two female organizers from the international union, who must have carried news and experience from the front lines of many other women's struggles. Female activists held separate meetings for women strikers, organized a concert to raise funds for the strikers, and sent their own spokeswomen to the general strike committee. They also used this strike to highlight the special conditions they faced as wage-earners. They brought to the front pages of the city newspapers the hardship of surviving on their low wages, typically no more than $5 a week (less than half of most men's wages in the clothing shops) in a time of rising costs of living. Their independence required the male leaders to reaffirm their commitment publicly and to deny they had made a separate agreement with the employers. The women also pushed union leaders to make a case for more humane treatment for women in the workplace, and notably raised the issue of sexual harassment by a foreman. A union organizer described the complaint as "not uncommon." Although there is no evidence that the phrase was used, this was the same fight for "bread and roses" waged by tens of thousands of women in the same period.[42]

The local women may also have found inspiration in the radical Jewish culture that was taking root in Hamilton. The socialist Workmen's Circle assisted the strikers, and a speaker addressing them emphasized how the revolutionary experiences of Jewish workers in Russia and Poland had taught them to resist oppression. Class, gender, and ethnicity combined to powerfully reinforce the determination of these wage-earning women.

The international union leadership was uncomfortable with this new mass unionism. The United Garment Workers' Union had always been dominated by the concerns of the skilled cutters, trimmers, and pressers, all of them men, who, in classic craft union fashion, kept apart in their own union locals. They used the union-label strategy to avoid such huge confrontations, and they had openly expressed their patriarchal concerns that women did not belong in the paid workforce.[43] During the strike, union spokesmen put particular emphasis on the endangered morality of the female workers, rather than on any rights to proper compensation for their work.[44] The leaders' masculine identity

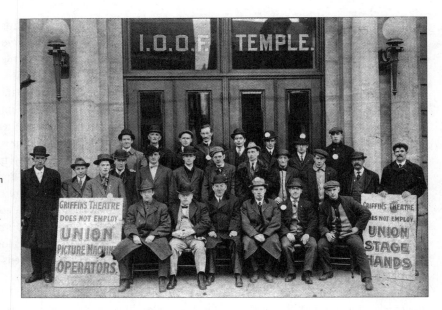

By May 1915 this strike of workers against four Hamilton theatres, including Griffin's, symbolized the decline of unionism among workers who served working-class customers, which had been so vibrant a decade earlier. (HPL)

was deeply rooted in their established skill and breadwinning roles.

When the union's US organizer, Victor Altman, arrived in town, he moved quickly to contain the struggle and shut down the possibilities evident in the women's activism. With some difficulty he convinced the manufacturers to let a settlement committee of workers and bosses hammer out an agreement and sent the strikers back to their jobs on 28 April. A week later they learned that the committee had agreed to the wage scale in existence in Toronto, which would amount to merely what the manufacturers had offered before the strike. More insulting to the women was that workers earning over $10 a week would get an additional $1, while those earning less would get only 50 cents. The wage gap between men and women in the industry thus got even wider. The better-paid men had made good use of the women's militancy to improve their own positions.[45]

The settlement was not popular and, for the local garment workers, not least the women

workers, it confirmed a long-standing dissatisfaction with the United Garment Workers. As the pre-war depression settled in and the local union's membership began to evaporate, Altman added insult to injury by loudly and publicly citing the reasonableness of the manufacturers and denouncing the local clothing workers' militancy. "The whole trouble with you is that you have no idea how to better your working conditions," he blustered. "You are hungry for a strike at all times and I sincerely hope that you will go out some time and stay out until you are licked to a stand still, and return to your jobs with your heads down and humiliated with yourselves." The United Garment Workers' locals in the city quietly died, never to be effectively revived again. Manufacturers generally proceeded to ignore the union, and a blacklist against prominent unionists was soon in force.[46]

The pre-war militancy, then, had pushed the practices of standing up to the boss in new directions and swept up workers from many more occupational groups. Yet the defeat of the moulders, machinists, car-workers, and clothing workers just before the war revealed the huge obstacles that had to be overcome as hostile employers stared down vulnerable, isolated strikers. The resurgent militancy had not created new, ongoing structures of solidarity to build on the fragile, fleeting breakthroughs. The Hamilton Trades and Labor Council still claimed to speak for all workers, but, as battles developed outside the confines of cautious AFL-style unionism, its officers stood back and watched, primly lectured strikers on the need for more orderly unionism, or quietly expressed a wish that "foreigners" and "working girls" would leave the labour market. Such a naive, moralistic misreading of the vulnerability of the less-skilled simply blamed the victims.

At the turn of the century, the Council's leaders had refused to help start a union at Hamilton Bridge during a strike because, in their eyes, it was "not regarded as good policy to begin organization when a strike had been entered on," and that remained their position for years to come. After completely ignoring the National Steel Car strike in his paper, *Labor News* editor Sam Landers sniped at a critic: "We considered it wise to pay attention to those who desire to better their conditions through organization." Another local labour leader admonished workers to show "a little patience" and spend some time getting acquainted with "their duties and responsibilities as union men" before throwing up picket lines. He called the city's clothing workers "good strikers and bad unionists." In 1914 the most that the Council did to consolidate the militancy among female wage-earners was to subscribe to five copies of *Life and Labor*, the magazine of the Women's Trade Union League in the United States. The publication was to be distributed to women's organizations in the city and thus "create more interest in the cause of the female toilers."[47]

War on the Home Front

Periods of industrial conflict in early-20th-century Hamilton regularly collapsed into great troughs of depression. Severe unemployment invariably pushed many wage-earners out of the city to look for work. Many more hunkered down anxiously trying to hold on to any job or curry favour to get one. Paying union dues became too costly for the family budget, and agitating for better working conditions too risky for job prospects. Confidence in the potential of collective working-class action disintegrated. The depression of 1913–15 was the worst the city had seen in 20 years. Unions already battered in pre-war conflicts saw their memberships drain away and their locals collapse. Most of those with business agents let them go.[48] Yet within two years, the wartime boom had brought back the material basis for organizing – poverty no longer loomed as a real threat to constrain militancy – and the conditions of wartime mobilization and administration soon gave workers a common set of grievances.

Before long, the war economy shifted the balance of class forces in local labour markets. By 1916 employers were facing growing labour shortages, despite the arrival of numerous workers from outside points looking for jobs. Working-class households in the city wasted no time in taking advantage of this economic boom by sending out all of the family's available wage-earners, even pulling teenage children out of high school. Bigger pay packets meant relief from the economic insecurity they had so recently experienced. Yet the new-found prosperity was soon threatened in many working-class households by the retail price inflation that began a dizzying ascent in 1917. In most cases wages did not keep pace. Here was a family-based issue that irked the working-class housewife as much as it did her wage-earning husband. The widespread suspicion that some kind of "profiteering" lay behind this problem contributed to resentments. Equally galling were reports that local companies were profiting handsomely from wartime contracts, but refusing to grant wage increases. "Since they are making fat profits out of the dire needs of the government," a machinist argued, "we workers should at least receive our share, a living wage."[49]

The war added to these long-standing issues in working-class Hamilton the extra dimension of national mobilization by the federal government and widespread disillusionment with its performance. Initially Hamilton workers seemed to share, to some degree at least, the national enthusiasm for the war effort. Wage-earners and their families began to fear, however, that, despite the rhetoric of democracy and sacrifice, the state remained insensitive to their concerns. Not only did the government seem reluctant to tackle severe retail price inflation and profiteering, but it tied wage-earners' hands in confronting their own employers by restraining strikes through the imposition of the Industrial Disputes Investigation Act on all war work in the spring of 1915.[50]

The growing state intervention into daily life to curb working-class behaviour, from prohibition to national registration of manpower, gradually turned the sense of patriotic national purpose sour. In 1918 Mark Irish, the Imperial Munitions Board's director of labour, reported, "All the enthusiasm and all the idea that munitions are vitally essential had gone out of the minds of the workpeople." He noted, "Today they take the War, and the work related to it, as they take the sunrise – an incident of the day." That summer the government's own security advisor, Montreal lawyer C.H. Cahan, reported that workers' discontent grew out of

"the weakening of the moral purpose of the people to prosecute the war to a successful end," a deepening awareness of "the bloody sacrifices and irritating burdens entailed by carrying on the war," and "the growing belief that the Union government is failing to deal effectively with the financial, industrial, and economic problems growing out of the war." In contrast to the usual battles in single occupations or industries, these war-related concerns became widely shared working-class grievances.[51]

Early in 1916 a National Steel Car executive wrote to Joseph Flavelle at the Imperial Munitions Board to express his concern about the "strong disposition" among munitions workers "to either cause agitation or work at low efficiency."[52] He was not alone in recognizing that working-class Hamilton was adapting to the war economy in its own ways. Initially the combination of labour-market strength and emerging resentment did not translate into a reborn labour movement. Instead, wage-earners who had not enlisted revived time-worn means of using tighter labour markets to their advantage. They risked a cockier manner and thumbed their noses at foremen's efforts to get them to work harder. They took afternoons off work to enjoy a ball game or a movie, or even move to another job where the boss might be willing to pay still higher wages. In August 1916 the *Spectator* reported that the many semi-skilled shell workers would "leave their work on the slightest pretext ... and in one case a factory here usually employing 1,500 men had 2,300 men in three months ask to be paid off. In their places 2,100 were taken on, and it will require 200 more men to bring the staff up to its full strength." The paper also told of a factory in which production had to be held up when a number of men decided to head for the race track. A few months later an official at the government employment bureau complained about "the unpatriotic action of some women munitions workers, receiving high wages, who occasionally take a holiday for two or three days, leaving their machines idle and hindering production."[53]

The problem, it seemed, was one of money coming all too easily. The Steel Company's F.H. Whitton discovered that workers were spurning hard labour in favour of "a soft job at high wages": "Out of the 14 men who were at the factory applying for positions yesterday not one could be induced to go to work at unloading freight cars." A National Steel Car official likewise bemoaned the difficulty of getting his men "to average 9 hours a day. It is not a question of too little money with them, but the trouble is they have too much. The surplus amount allows them to take a great deal more time off than they ordinarily would." The Canadian Cottons' president later recalled that production fell by about 37 per cent.[54]

That trend in general was a national phenomenon. By the summer of 1918 the Imperial Munitions Board's Mark Irish was reporting to Flavelle about "a shrinkage in production per human unit of about thirty per cent." By the end of the war, according to a government study, "Turnover was universally high, many employers stating that 30 per cent of their staff was floating. Absence was also abnormal, amounting to 5 per cent per day and often running as high as 10 per cent."[55] In many ways this evidence of the impact of fuller employment at higher wages on workplace discipline was at least as important a concern for factory managers as the threat of unionization. This kind of behaviour prompted the Borden government to pass the famous Anti-Loafing Law in spring 1918, requiring all men to be at work. The same phenomenon generated widespread concern about labour turnover in postwar Canada – to the extent that

many of the new welfare capitalist schemes were aimed overtly at altering the footloose habits of workers to make them more stable, reliable, and productive.[56]

At the same time, as in the past, many wage-earners did try to settle their grievances collectively, most often as spontaneous outbursts over specific issues in one department of a plant.[57] Unions generally did not play any role in these confrontations, but in two key industries of the wartime economy, munitions and clothing, they emerged in 1916 to galvanize the sense of injustice taking root among increasing numbers of the city's wage-earners.

Not surprisingly, Hamilton's machinists were among the first to respond to the new workplace conditions. Before the end of 1916 Riley was reporting full employment among his union members, mostly in the booming munitions plants. The machinists' value to the industrial life of the city, and of the country, reached new heights. So too did their discontent with their working conditions, particularly around the steps that factory managers were taking to alter their work processes and recruitment practices. With the blessing of the Imperial Munitions Board, metalworking firms began "diluting" the skilled labour in their shell factories by subdividing the work into narrower, more specialized tasks and hiring less-skilled workers, not only Anglo-Canadian men from other occupations looking for good pay, but also European immigrant labourers, even those designated as "enemy aliens," and, from early in 1917, women. The pace of work was cranked up to new heights.

The most skilled machinists were not displaced, but rather shifted into important set-up and tool-making work, which enhanced their importance and their ability to disrupt production. Yet all was not well. The world as these skilled metalworkers had known it was changing fast, along with certainties about their Anglo-Canadian, masculine, and craft identities. Their uneasiness took concrete shape around the shift in relative earnings in wartime production. Thanks to the long hours at piecework and the general speed-up, many of the new, less-skilled workers were soon taking home enormous pay packets. According to *Canadian Machinery*, "after a few days of preliminary training" these newcomers to the machine shop "were receiving three, four and even five times what they earned before, while the mechanics and toolmakers about the shop who told these men what to do and set the machines in order that they could serve, were forced to work at less than half the wage."[58] A local organizer told a meeting of Hamilton machinists that "it was not to the credit of skilled machinists who had to spend years of apprenticeship and large sums of money for proper tools, to be working almost for laborers' wages and long hours."[59] Press reports on the European immigrants' hefty earnings added fuel to these fires, and Anglo-Canadian workers were quick to complain that "as soon as Canadians and Britishers quit their jobs to enlist foreigners step in to fill their places and draw fat salaries."[60] In a similar vein, the machinists' business agent was concerned that the use of women in the munitions factories was "the cause of reducing the wages of the men shell operators."[61]

The local branches of the International Association of Machinists and Amalgamated Society of Engineers lost no time in organizing regular mass meetings to sign up hundreds of disgruntled machinists. The efforts of national union leaders in Ottawa to get the Imperial Munitions Board to insert fair-wage clauses into munitions contracts failed in the winter of 1915–16, and on 1 April 1916 the IAM circulated to all the city's metal shops a new schedule of wages, hours, and working conditions for machinists. That intervention became a blueprint for reimposing a rigid union policing of working procedures and reasserting the craftworker's control inside the city's machine shops.[62]

Hamilton's metal-trades employers were predictably alarmed at this resurrection of craft unionism in their midst. Individual skirmishes with union organizers gave way to a united front after the local branch of the Canadian Manufacturers' Association struck a special committee early in April to co-ordinate a response.[63] As employer hostility stiffened and a showdown seemed imminent, the federal government appointed a three-man Royal Commission to investigate munitions workers' grievances in Hamilton and Toronto. The Commission's hearings held in the first few days of May gave the machinists the public forum they wanted to carry on their arguments with their bosses. Riley ushered in a parade of worker witnesses and was allowed to cross-examine the company officials who appeared. The testimony was reported in full in Hamilton newspapers.[64] The hearings often turned into extended debates over the nature of work in the city's machine shops, including conflicting views on a worker's productivity in a nine-hour day. All the resentment against the previous decades' changes in their workplace experience surfaced in the munitions workers' testimony.[65]

It quickly became clear that while most workers wanted higher wages to meet the rising cost of living, the union demand for a nine-hour day captured the crux of their discontent. According to a *Herald* reporter, the evidence presented in the hearings showed "that the machines are run at a higher speed than they were in times of peace, and that the consequent strain on [the workers'] constitutions was too great to permit them to work ten hours a day." The employers nonetheless continued their resistance to a shorter working day, correctly fearing a precedent for postwar industry, and rejected the Royal Commission's final recommendation in favour of the nine-hour principle.[66]

On 9 June the combatants gathered their strength. In one hall, a mass meeting of machinists called for a strike within a week. In another, quieter venue, 38 of the city's leading firms gave birth to the Employers' Association of Hamilton, which then announced in a series of strident newspaper advertisements that its purpose was "to see that there shall be no improper restriction of output, and that no conditions shall arise to prevent any workman from earning a wage proportionate to his productive capacity." Wrapping themselves in the Union Jack, they appealed to workers' patriotism to shelve narrow personal concerns during wartime. On 12 June, after several weeks of frantic lobbying by federal and municipal officials to head off the inevitable explosion, between 1,500 and 2,000 machinists and unskilled munitions workers walked out of more than 30 plants, shutting down the city's entire munitions industry and demanding implementation of the Royal Commission's recommendations. According to the *Spectator*, the strike was "a contest of the open shop against the one operated under union regulations ... [and] each is fighting for what it regards as principle."[67]

Waging a wartime strike proved difficult. Along with the Employers' Association's strident anti-union ads came the intervention of the federal wartime censor, who ordered newspapers to stop reporting on the dispute to prevent the militancy from spreading elsewhere. Except for the *Industrial Banner*, all had complied by the third day, including the *Labor News*. Deprived of all publicity and the possibility of appealing for public support, the machinists held on for nearly a month. But the strike had floundered by the end of the summer, in the face of demoralization,

renewed rivalry between the IAM and the ASE, and the departure of 300 to 400 strikers to look for work elsewhere.[68] Never again were the Hamilton machinists able to mount such a challenge. While several firms in the city eventually did concede the shorter working day before the end of the war, those moves were in each case a gesture to pacify their workers without conceding any power to the craftworkers' union.[69]

Meanwhile, the other major group of wage-earners galvanized by war production, the clothing workers, were going through a parallel, if less cataclysmic, process. In April 1916, at the same moment that the machinists' militancy was beginning to boil over, a new era in the Hamilton clothing industry opened with a mass meeting of workers sponsored by the fledgling Amalgamated Clothing Workers of America. Some two years earlier the militants from New York and Chicago had stormed out of the United Garment Workers' convention to found this new union dedicated to full-fledged industrial unionism, instead of the old divisions into locals based on skill and task.[70] In August 1916 the new Hamilton local won a three-week strike against the Davis Brothers clothing firms, whom the workers charged with introducing a version of the piecework system. The strike settlement gave the workers a handsome package, including shorter hours, a wage increase, and a collective bargaining system with union recognition.[71] By the following spring the Amalgamated Clothing Workers had managed to win a more informal agreement covering 600 employees, who got wage increases and a reduction of hours from 49 to 48 (and gradually by 1919 to 44). An energetic young worker from nearby Dundas, Mary McNab, became the union's business agent in Hamilton.[72] For the next two years, however, the larger firms refused to recognize the union formally and preferred to announce changes in employment conditions unilaterally to diffuse support for the new organization. After a promising start, therefore, Hamilton's clothing workers lagged well behind other North American garment centres in their collective-bargaining impact on the city's industry.[73]

In the last year of the war, more Hamilton wage-earners began to show a lot more interest in unions as their sights shifted from wartime problems to what postwar society would have to offer. Workers in many occupations began to pull together more permanent organizations. Older crafts revived, and new groups sent for union charters – retail clerks in March 1918, textile workers in May, blacksmiths in June, civic labourers in July, and, most ominously, policemen in September.[74] In contrast to some Canadian factory towns and cities, their employers were mostly none too enthusiastic about this resurgence, and quickly dug in their heels to prevent any breakthroughs that might be consolidated after the war.[75]

First, in 1918 the city's foundrymen went head to head with the revived moulders' union in a month-long strike of 250 to 300 men from eight firms for a hefty wage increase.[76] Then the city engineer announced that he was "directly and positively opposed" to a civic employees' union, though he was unable to deter those workers from sustaining one.[77] In a similar spirit, Tuckett Tobacco and the other local tobacco companies turned on the cigar-makers' and tobacco workers' unions with whom they had dealt amicably for 20 years in Hamilton, London, and Montreal (and whose union labels had guaranteed them working-class markets). They aggressively forced the workers out on strike and recruited less-skilled strikebreakers, including young women to work on new cigar-making machinery. The unions were permanently broken.[78] The local textile workers faced a similar fate. A new local of the United Textile Workers appeared in mid-1918 and was soon leading a strike in defence of a fired union officer (a widow and mother) at Hamilton Cotton. A federal board of conciliation produced a majority report in favour of the workers' position, but the company ignored the recommendations. Collective bargaining thus remained a will-o'-the-wisp in the local textile plants, and the union withered away.[79]

In the European immigrant community, socialists inspired by the Russian Revolution were also trying to rally their workmates in heavy industry. In contrast to the English-speaking workers, they faced active repression by the Canadian state. In June 1918 A.F. Sherwood, chief commissioner of the Dominion Police, reported to the minister of justice that the immigrant branches of the Social Democratic Party did not exist "for any sinister purpose, but rather for the improvement of their conditions as workers and toward the securing of better pay." He explained that the Dominion Police had interned enemy aliens "to deter these from becoming agitators or connecting themselves with organizations that may prove troublesome." Through the Imperial Munitions Board he had arranged with manufacturers "to place investigators in any plant in order to be in constant touch with any movement that promises trouble." The Steel Company had its own paid spies on the shop floor to keep it abreast of potential trouble. Whether or not as part of this intelligence work, the Hamilton police began to respond to calls from that company to arrest immigrant agitators in its workforce. When one case involving two Russians came up in the police court on 1 August 1918, the magistrate ruled that "When these men become agitators and start to stir up trouble and create disturbances they must disappear." In late September the local police chief was pleased to get the additional powers conferred by a federal order-in-council banning radical immigrant organizations and their newspapers. That month a Ukrainian worker was arrested for sedition for presenting a demand for higher wages from a large group at the Steel Company.[80]

In the second half of the war, then, Hamilton's wage-earners had turned to unions in growing numbers as vehicles for their deepening sense of injustice. They were part of a new working-class ferment across North America (and elsewhere) that saw thousands of workers flooding into unions and striking against intransigent bosses.[81] In other cities they scored significant breakthroughs, but, by the end of the war, Hamilton's powerful corporate employers had made sure that unions had few victories to build on after the war. Particularly noteworthy was the absence of unions in the biggest plants. Despite the widening and deepening militancy, the overall pattern was one of containment and defeat.

People's Minds Are Inflamed

A potent stew of bitter resentments and restless searching for a better "reconstructed world" was nonetheless brewing in many parts of working-class Hamilton. The restraining power of wartime patriotism had evaporated well before the Armistice, and more and more attention was directed to postwar conditions. Many families hoped to hold onto the better standard of living that fuller employment and higher wages had brought, and were scandalized at the rapid retail price inflation that was still eating into their incomes (and would peak in 1920). As war-related work wound down and unemployment rose steeply through the first half of 1919, they were equally worried about holding onto jobs. Some recovery occurred over the next year and a half, but, through the lurching uncertainties and instability of the postwar era, wage-earners and their families looked anxiously into the future and grasped at ways to build more collective economic security into their lives.[82]

Many wage-earners, especially the men, began to look for new levers of working-class power in the workplace to allow them to negotiate terms and conditions of employment that had so often been dictated to them in the past through elitist, authoritarian, and paternalistic practices. The federal government's failure to protect their rights to collective bargaining and the draconian measures in October 1918 to ban strikes and repress dissident organizations had even the normally cautious Trades and Labor Council up in arms.[83]

With unrest rampant far beyond working-class Hamilton, the city's workers could look for inspiration and ideas from the worker insurgency exploding throughout the industrialized world. New manifestos of working-class rights were being unfurled – from the Russian Soviets to the revitalized British Labour Party to the Paris peace conference – and a spirit of hope for a new social order was becoming infectious. Seldom had workers ever been able to command such attention. Middle-class intellectuals of all stripes turned their worried gaze on "the labour problem,"[84] and political officials and businessmen made it a top priority. World leaders sitting down to put together a new international order, well aware that they had to respond to this rising proletarian challenge, launched the new International Labour Organization to try to absorb some of the agitation and deflect interest in more radical alternatives (like the Communist International).[85] A wide-ranging debate was underway about the meaning of "industrial democracy," pitting priorities of efficiency and order against democratic participation through workers' collective organization.[86]

Numerous commentators in Hamilton noted the new mood among workers. Early in 1919 a letter to the *Spectator* from a worker "in one of the largest factories in this city" – signing himself "Anti-Humbug" – argued that "the workingmen are far from satisfied":

> They have been working at high pitch and in exciting times since the war started. They have invested in Victory Bonds, subscribed liberally to the Red Cross, Patriotic Fund, and every other fund that came along ... and what are they getting for it? Well, they know, and they are getting it rubbed in, too, so that between the O.[ntario] T.[emperance] A.[ct], the high cost of living, reduction in wages and, in some cases, unemployment, there is a spirit of unrest and dissatisfaction prevailing, and they are simply waiting for something to happen, and when the last straw comes that breaks the camel's back, well, that something is going to happen.

Another letter writer had attended a public talk by federal labour minister Gideon Robertson in February 1919 and described the "class antagonism" that had welled up in the packed meeting: "Largely the resentment was directed against employers of labor, manufacturers, companies, etc., by their present or would-be employees." A week later the *Spectator*'s editorial writer remarked on "the suspicion which exists in the minds of workers with regard to the capitalist class" and which "is made abundantly evident in every meeting where labor questions are discussed." The Royal Commission on Industrial Relations heard similar warnings in May. "You see, people's minds are inflamed," one union witness explained. A handyman at International Harvester tried to impress upon the commissioners how receptive workers in that plant were to the revolutionary literature circulating among them: "These men that have unrest in their minds, they talk among themselves, and they haven't the means of finding expression, they are grabbing hold of this thing – it is something new for them, and it is surprising to me the quantity that is being handed round from hand to hand." Commentators worriedly labelled this phenomenon as "labour unrest."[87]

What did Hamilton's workers want? The machinists' business agent Riley told the Commission, "Although a great many workers have not given the matter much thought, they are beginning to think that there must be a change in the present competitive system ... they see they had made absolutely no progress in the last 50 or 60 years, that we still have unemployed, low wages, long hours." Alex Boyd, a blacksmith, said that workers had "a new vision" – "they seem to want a higher standard of living entirely."[88] By the early months of 1919 one demand had emerged in every union meeting and at every bargaining table to encapsulate these loose, unfocused aspirations for a better life – the eight-hour day. The city's own civic labourers were prepared to strike over the issue in May, and won. Indeed, even the International Harvester workers wanted to bring the issue to the first meetings of the company's new Industrial Council. Most of the building trades already worked the shorter day, but now insisted on the 44-hour week. The city's major clothing manufacturers introduced the shorter workweek voluntarily.[89]

In part, as machinists had argued in 1916, shorter hours would respond to the speed-up that workers were experiencing on the job. A moulder raised the unfairness of such intensified work: "A workingman appreciates life just as much as anyone else does and he should not be expected to slave so that others could have comfort." Yet, as they had for half a century, workers still saw time away from work as a major social reform that opened up more possibilities for their personal fulfilment and social and civic engagement. As the *Labor News* put it:

> It would give greater opportunity for social and educational development.
> It would raise the standard of living upon which the prosperity depends.
> It would help the taxpayer by putting the tramp to work.
> It would promote an independent spirit, which is lacking in overworked people.

Shorter hours became a right of citizenship. Negotiating such a reform employer-by-employer eventually gave way to demands for an eight-hour law, which would be central to the discussions of the National Industrial Conference in Ottawa in September 1919 and then in the new International Labour Organization. Locally the eight-hour day would be a prominent plank in the platform of the buoyant Independent Labor Party.[90]

With the evidently strong yearning for some kind of "new vision," a climactic confrontation on the industrial front seemed inevitable. Yet that moment did not come in the spring of 1919, when dramatic labour actions were staged in many other Canadian cities at the same time – the famous Winnipeg General Strike, the numerous sympathy strikes across Western Canada, the less successful, short-lived general strike movements in Toronto and Montreal, and the great victories in the Eastern coal and steel industries, among many others. Hamilton had reached an all-time high of 72 union locals, but only a few of them were in a position to press their demands.[91] Indeed, when Hamilton's moulders struck in May 1919 for an eight-hour day, they walked the picket lines alone in what would become a painfully prolonged defeat. No sympathy strikes developed across occupational divisions in the metal trades. As *Labor News* editor Walter Rollo reminded his readers that spring, there were "thousands of handy men, specialists, grinders, helpers and laborers working in the big East End plants with no organization at all." For most of them, that situation would continue to hold true for many years to come.[92]

The pace and rhythms of union organizing varied across the country,[93] and in Hamilton the new momentum was not felt until the fall of 1919, when organizers reached into several new sectors – labourers, steelworkers, packing-house workers, and textile workers, in particular. This task ultimately amounted to only a modest growth of the unionized sector, and most of the biggest factories remained untouched. For most of the new unions, moreover, an Armageddon came that spring and summer in a wave of strikes.[94] The packing-house workers' union suffered a humiliating defeat at the two local plants in April. A dramatic confrontation between the Steel Company and its 98 steam and operating engineers tied up many departments in the company plants and brought a union threat to pull out all the city's engineers, but the company called the union's bluff and no sympathy strike materialized. Imported strikebreakers were housed on company property and protected by the Thiel Detective Agency. Late in May Labour Minister Gideon Robertson brokered a face-saving settlement between the union leaders and Hobson, now president, that sent most of the engineers back to work with little to show for their efforts and a shattered union in the steel mills.[95]

Meanwhile Hobson was facing a potentially bigger challenge. During the annual convention of the Trades and Labor Congress of Canada held in Hamilton in September 1919, some Canadian members of the Amalgamated Association of Iron, Steel, and Tin Workers from other cities played midwife to a new Hamilton lodge of the organization – the last to be formed among all the steelmaking centres in the country. Membership slowly expanded to nearly 1,300 in mid-1920, and the lodge was able to hire a business agent.[96] From the beginning the Amalgamated's Lodge No. 7 was formally committed to an all-inclusive industrial unionism, and in spring 1920 the international vice-president, Ernest Curtis, settled in Hamilton to lead a steady effort to win over more of the nearly 7,000 workers in several plants who were thought to be eligible.[97]

The union was slow to tackle the ethnic divisions in the workforce. It took many months after the lodge was founded before the Amalgamated sent in organizers who spoke European languages, one of whom eventually reported success in signing up "the foreign element" by fall 1920. No doubt the small knots of ethnic radicals in postwar Hamilton were an important catalyst as well because that organizer found the "Soviet idea" was "rampant" among them. Yet all the local executive officers were Anglo-Canadian, and the lodge's weekly meetings and "smokers" – all-male social evenings with speeches, card games, cigars, and refreshments – closely resembled the gatherings of fraternal societies and craft unions. The gatherings, with elaborate rituals and ceremonies, were probably not the warmly familiar cultural events for the Europeans that they were for their Anglo-Canadian workmates. It was soon clear that the most enthusiastic recruits to the new union were the more-skilled men in the city's steel plants, particularly those in the Steel Company's new sheet-metal mill, one of the last holdouts of greater manual-skill requirements. Most of them had been imported recently from the United States and sustained among themselves a vigorous shop-floor solidarity.[98]

Despite its "industrial" flavour, the odour of AFL craft traditions hung over the new organization. The Amalgamated membership offered no more than moral support when the Steel Company's operating engineers struck in spring 1920.[99] Moreover, as in other steelmaking centres, the local Amalgamated lodge itself was divided up along occupational lines that summer, apparently to protect its old core membership among skilled rolling-mill men. Isolated from those skilled men, the less-skilled were left with weaker bargaining clout with their employer.[100]

In any case, neither the Steel Company nor any of the other smaller steel-processing firms ever sat down to negotiate with any of the Amalgamated lodges. At a moment when the huge, countrywide US steel strike of 1919 was still fresh in the public's minds, Hobson's uncompromising open-shop message to the striking stationary engineers in May 1920 was no doubt intended for the larger audience of all the corporation's workers: "This company has always run an open shop and therefore was not prepared to make an agreement with the union."[101] Although the sheet-mill workers were in a strong enough bargaining position with the company to win a 7.5 per cent increase in the sliding scale of wages towards the end of 1920, the company had begun to lay off workers by that point, as the economy slid into depression. Early in 1921 the union was powerless to resist a 20 per cent wage cut. One by one, the locals collapsed.[102]

The other hot spot in 1920 was the city's construction sites. Almost all the local building trades unions had solid bargaining relations with contractors in their respective sectors, and through 1919 had consolidated wage gains and reductions in hours. Their common front, the revived Building Trades Council, claimed to speak for 2,500 workers in 13 unions by spring 1920, when its part-time business agent, the English-born stonecutter Sam Lawrence (and future alderman, controller, and mayor), presented the contractors with a "blanket wage agreement" covering all workers. They hoped to equalize the terms and conditions of employment across the trades and to establish an industrial council of employer and union representatives to handle disputes. Their bosses were now organized as a branch of the national Canadian Building and Construction Industries and, led by the tough-minded corporate contractor Joseph Pigott, refused to consider such a dramatic departure in bargaining. Despite angry mass meetings of tradesmen ready for a general strike, the employers got the Building Trades Council to withdraw the blanket agreement in favour of individual trade negotiations, without a closed shop, and the right to use the new Industrial Council as a voluntary conciliation body for any disputes referred to it. This was the city's only experiment with a body modelled on the so-called Whitley councils in Britain, which attempted to bring industrial peace by having unions and employers at the same table. When the new and unrecognized building labourers' union applied, however, the employers refused both to discuss its case and then to allow the Industrial Council to convene when strikes of sheet-metal workers, bricklayers, electricians, and plumbers erupted at the beginning of May.[103]

Even though the national contractors' association was moving ahead on the formation of a National Joint Conference Board, Pigott declared in July that Hamilton's new council was "practically a dead issue," especially after building labourers struck that month for union recognition and higher wages. They eventually returned to work on condition that the Industrial Council would take up their concerns, but the employers stonewalled until the onset of depression the following winter undermined the union. Then in spring 1921 the bosses used the Industrial Council to turn the tables and, like their counterparts across the country, demanded wage reductions. A local labour leader decried this move as "a reflex of the continent-wide campaign to smash organized labor." In response, the Building Trades Council called a general strike of all its affiliated unions on work sites where the wage cuts were being imposed. More than 1,000 tradesmen walked out, and after nearly three months agreed to a federally sponsored board of conciliation to settle the dispute. The outcome simply confirmed the wage cuts and undercut the unions' strength in the city.[104]

The spring of 1921 saw a similar crisis for two other unions that had established regular collective bargaining with their bosses. After languishing for some time, the Amalgamated Clothing Workers had rebounded in fall 1919. The union, representing virtually all clothing workers in the city, signed a collective agreement with all of the clothing manufacturers in Hamilton and Dundas in April 1920, guaranteeing a 40-hour week, substantial wage increases, and the closed shop.[105] The employers had evidently decided to join the rest of the men's clothing industry in North America in welcoming the Amalgamated and its collective-bargaining structures, including a system of arbitration boards, as a means of stabilizing labour costs in the industry and minimizing costly competition – just as Hamilton's stove foundrymen had done in embracing the moulders' union 20 years earlier. The international union offered the additional enticement of promising to increase productivity as a boost to the industry.[106]

The union prioritized women workers in this new regime to an unprecedented extent. It insisted that the women would have to be organized before any demands would be presented, and then, while apparently never challenging

By the time the Allan Studholme Memorial Labor Temple opened in 1923 to house union offices and meetings, the local labour movement had suffered serious defeats.

(SLS, LS677)

the sexual division of labour in the industry, made an effort to narrow the enormous wage differential between men and women through proportionately larger wage increases for female workers. Several women also filled the roles of business agent and executive members.[107]

In 1920, however, the clothing industry was caught in the grip of depression. Hamilton was particularly hard hit, and by September many of the city's clothing workers were working only two days a week. The manufacturers wasted no time in demanding a rollback of the recent wage hikes. The union promised to increase output if the existing wage rate was preserved and eventually proposed a smaller wage cut. But the companies rejected such offers. They were equally insensitive to union concerns that work be distributed evenly among all workers. The union's local officers believed that some manufacturers "were making attempts to undermine the integrity of the union."[108] On 22 February 1921, 1,100 clothing workers, 70 per cent of them women, walked out in the face of all six employers' refusal to discuss the matter further or to use arbitration

procedures. With three firms shut down for lack of work, the union could not have confronted worse conditions for what the *Spectator* called "a life and death struggle for the organization." On 10 March the workers faced the humiliating defeat of calling off their strike and agreeing to accept the wage cuts. The next month all the city's clothing manufacturers declared open shops. A year later workers complained that "an unreasonable increase in production is demanded and the old employees have been harshly treated."[109]

One more bastion of labour strength and respectability was under siege at the same time. Local craft unionists were galled to see that the venerable printers' union had to resort to a strike in 1921 to get implementation of the 8-hour day and 44-hour week that they had negotiated. This was part of a wider confrontation pitting the International Typographical Union against publishers throughout Central Canada led by the open-shop employers' association, the United Typothetae. Their struggle dragged on for three years before the union admitted defeat.[110]

The hopes of a new vision in the air in 1919 were thus thoroughly dashed within two years. The employers' unanimous and successful move to cut wages and Mayor George Coppley's related initiative to eliminate the fair-wage clause from city contracts in 1921 signalled the final defeat. Labor MLA George G. Halcrow had bluntly nailed these moves late in 1920 as "a premeditated effort on the part of capital to squeeze back the workers into what they call pre-war times." A month later one voice on the side of capital had a similar message. The issue was more than "the readjustment of wage rates," wrote the editor of *Canadian Foundryman*. Workers had to "agree to remove the restrictions upon output which have been a crying evil in the period now drawing to a close."[111]

A Revolt or a Handshake?

Hamilton's wage-earners had risen to the challenge of postwar reconstruction much as workers had done across the country. But the story here was distinctive in many ways. The remarkable power and hostility of Hamilton industrialists, spearheaded by the Steel Company,[112] had beaten back unionizing efforts more thoroughly than in most other industrial towns and cities and, with the help of the Employers' Association of Hamilton, kept the open-shop banner flying over almost all factories.[113] The decisive defeat of the 1916 munitions strike in particular effectively undermined the strategic role that militant metalworkers played elsewhere in North America, Britain, and Western Europe as leaven in the workers' revolt; many of the sparkplugs of militancy in that strike were probably blacklisted and left the city.[114] Industrialists attempted to soften the blow of their anti-unionism with an outpouring of welfarism and a new posture of high-minded citizenship. But they also watched, no doubt with deep satisfaction, as the local labour movement plunged into a civil war that further sapped the energies of the local "workers' revolt."

Hamilton's craft unions had watched the rising militancy with some trepidation. They had a long-standing reputation as one of the staunchest bastions of support for the "Gompersist" craft unionism of the American Federation of Labor, especially the concerns for strict jurisdictional boundaries within the labour movement and for industrial legality in relations with employers. Before the war, Hamilton unionists had also been tireless red-baiters.[115] As the war progressed, these men could stomach an alliance with socialists on the political front, but in workplace strategizing they feared that the reds were too adventurous and disrespectful of their craft jurisdictions. They refused to consider new industrial strategies or the use of industrial weapons like a general strike for more political purposes.[116] It was fitting that the Trades and Labor Congress of Canada should choose Hamilton for the 1919 convention that would see the wary craft unionists decisively defeat the left-wing, industrial unionist forces.[117] So in Hamilton the campaign for militant industrial unionism as the alternative to cautious craft unionism came largely from outside the mainstream and polarized the local labour movement more sharply than it did in most other centres in Central Canada. For craft union leaders, the *bête noire* was the charismatic metalworker Fred Flatman.

Flatman was the key propagandist and organizer for a new kind of workers' movement, which would eventually take on the label of the One Big Union. The remarkably talented, British-born, socialist blacksmith arrived in the city around 1910 and worked at the Dominion Steel Castings Company. After a brief term in 1912 as president of a new Hamilton blacksmiths' local,[118] Flatman left behind mainstream craft unionism and joined the Amalgamated Society of Engineers, quickly rising to a leadership position as district organizer. As a "dual union" in the IAM's jurisdiction, the "Mals" remained a pariah in the North American house of labour and were therefore barred from the local Trades and Labor Council. Perhaps as a result of Flatman's influence, the local ASE became the rallying point in the city for amalgamation of the metal trades unions and for industrial unionism.[119]

By 1918 Flatman was clearly inspired and energized by a deepening class consciousness and spirit of resistance that he believed was emerging far and wide among workers. He undertook to give it voice and focus in Hamilton. That year he took over editorial control of the *Labor News*, the city's six-year-old labour paper, which had passed out of conservative hands when its founder, Sam Landers, enlisted for overseas service. That fall the paper began drawing its readers' attention to the rise of new industrial movements in the English-speaking world, notably the One Big Union in Australia.[120] On 21 March 1919 an editorial endorsed the action of the Western labour conference at Calgary in holding a referendum on secession from the North American craft union movement. Favourable reportage on OBU organizational activity, and generally on the more militant and socialist manifestations of the labour revolt around the world in the spring of 1919, continued until local labour leaders staged a palace coup to oust Flatman from the editor's chair. On 9 May the name of Rollo, broom-maker and secretary of the Trades and Labor Council, suddenly appeared on the masthead as editor, and a front-page article defended AFL-style craft unionism.[121]

Flatman and his socialist comrades promptly regrouped and on 22 May published the first issue of a second weekly Hamilton labour paper under the title of *New Democracy*, in which they continued their political and industrial propaganda. Flatman's rousing weekly editorials resonated with new organizing efforts in the city. In February a new organization of unskilled workers, known as the General Workers' Union, No.1, was born, with Flatman as president and a motto that "an injury to one of our class is an injury to all." It quickly became the recruiting and propaganda body for industrial unionism. "Every worker of brain and brawn is eligible for membership, whether he now be a union or non-union person," a labour paper explained. "Those who are members of existing unions pay the same dues, but are pledged to keep aloft the 'fiery cross' of industrialism in their own craft unions."[122]

When the Royal Commission on Industrial Relations arrived in Hamilton in May 1919, several witnesses commented on the growth of industrial unionist sentiment favourable to the OBU. Henry George (Harry) Fester, Independent Labor Party leader and former cigar-maker at the Tuckett plant, warned that the new General Workers' Union was bent on "extreme measures," and that they were mostly "common labour, unskilled labour mainly ... employed in the big factories throughout this City." An International Harvester worker had heard that it had a hundred members, "all men that have no trade."[123]

Up to this point the General Workers' Union had not affiliated with the Western movement. On 22 April Flatman had written to express interest in joining, but the OBU founding conference would not be held until 4 June. An autonomous general workers' movement was emerging in a few Ontario cities, but a conference of these groups in Toronto at the end of May failed to unite them.[124] In contrast to their Western comrades, but like those of Atlantic Canada, most of the left in Ontario had decided that staying inside the mainstream labour movement was strategically more sensible. The Hamilton radicals nonetheless stuck to their independent path. In mid-July the General Workers' Union formally transformed itself into a unit of the OBU, and later in the summer made plans to split off two new units for metal trades and textile workers. A few weeks later nearly 500 people turned out to hear OBU Eastern organizer Joe Knight. By September the *Spectator* had heard that the OBU was winning recruits among the civic labourers and "the foreign element."[125]

The local craft union movement was shaken.[126] The Hamilton Trades and Labor Council had unanimously rejected the idea of the One Big Union in May, and Rollo relentlessly attacked it in the *Labor News*. But words were not enough.[127] In June the Council belatedly announced a campaign to "organize all the unorganized workers," since there seemed to be "a feeling for organization throughout the entire city."[128] The craft union answer was to find places for various groups of workers in existing organizations within the house of labour, often dividing up the workers in one factory into several different organizations. In September an organizer from the Laborers' and Hod Carriers' International Union arrived to recruit "foreign laborers," and the metal-trades unions held a joint meeting to attempt to organize the National Steel Car workers, an effort that bore no fruit. They also spearheaded the organization of the ill-fated steel, packing-house, and textile unions.[129]

These cautious men could take heart from how the local OBU itself was floundering. Membership in the three local units remained low, and the organization failed to coax any more unions to switch their allegiance. Moreover, although Flatman had agreed to expand *New Democracy*'s circulation from 1,100 to 6,500 in an effort to reach a wider Eastern Canadian readership as the eastern voice of the OBU, he edited his last issue on 23 October. A month later the paper re-emerged under the more conservative editorial hand of Harry Fester. Probably blacklisted, Flatman left the city to work in Niagara Falls, and a local RCMP secret agent reported that after Flatman's departure the local radicals "lacked a man with the qualities of leadership." The OBU lingered on into 1920 in Hamilton, holding a series of increasingly sectarian meetings, but it never did make the breakthrough into mass membership. Eventually in 1921 the organization was quietly dissolved, and most of its leadership gravitated towards the new Communist movement.[130]

By 1920 Harry Fester, the editor of one of the two local labour weeklies, *New Democracy*, was actively promoting a spirit of collaboration with employers. (ND, 16 Dec. 1920, 1)

Meanwhile, while "dishing the reds," the city's leading craft union leaders had been reaching out in a different direction. Central to their notion of industrial legality was their desire to be taken seriously as responsible figures in a formally structured dialogue with employers. They also had an abiding commitment to the kinds of cross-class community co-operation inherent in the union label, the wartime recruiting league (which the Council supported), and the tariff. Not surprisingly, then, in February 1919 they approached the local branch of the Canadian Manufacturers' Association to propose a joint conference, and participated eagerly in a dinner and a series of meetings with industrialist H.L. Frost and a handful of the city's leading capitalists. "The get-together scheme had been in the minds of labor men for months," one local labour leader told a *Herald* reporter. In 1920, as the Trades and Labor Council curtly rejected any idea of a general strike in support of the jailed labour leaders in Winnipeg, labour leaders made overtures to local businessmen to establish regular dialogue and agreed to accept a seat on the newly organized Chamber of Commerce. When several council delegates protested that "one of the objects of the reorganization was to fight labor organizations," the moderate majority argued: "The trade union movement had always been committed to a policy of co-operation, and ... to repudiate a friendly offer when made with sincerity of purpose was equivalent to a renunciation of the principles upon which the union labor movement was founded." When local firms began laying off thousands of workers in 1921, the key labour figure in this policy of collaboration, Fester, urged caution "rather than aggravate the situation by useless criticism and agitation."[131]

In postwar Hamilton, then, the local labour movement had quickly polarized into two hostile camps: craft unionist versus industrial unionist, right versus left. The potential middle ground that had been taken up in some other Canadian cities was abandoned in the hostile battles for leadership of the city's wage-earners. The combination of the unbridled power of the corporations and the deep division in the labour movement thus left wage-earners in Hamilton highly vulnerable to the debilitating impact of mass unemployment and corporate counter-attacks after 1920. A second major wave of militancy had crested and broken.

Fighting Speed-Ups

"Hamilton is a very depressing city," a Communist organizer concluded after a brief visit in 1928. "The Trades Council meets, but no other activity is apparent. No organization work is carried on among the thousands of unskilled and semi-skilled workers." A few months later another was equally blunt: "When workers were questioned as to their conditions and wages, it became obvious what a paradise Hamilton is for

the employers of this continent." The city was "almost completely unorganized and the workers in the large plants are as a result completely at the mercy of the bosses."[132]

That frustration reflected the hard realities for organized labour in Hamilton by the end of the 1920s. Strikes were rare. Craft unions held on only in the nooks and crannies outside major corporations, places where their skills were still valued. Industrial paternalism had been solidly implanted as the alternative to collective bargaining.[133] Yet three forces converging at that point were about to convulse industrial relations in several plants – efficiency experts, angry work groups, and Communists. Over the next decade new industrial unions arose from these confrontations, most often under radical leadership, but none would sustain much vitality before World War Two.

In the decade starting in 1929 the combination of growing competition, slumping demand, and a moribund labour movement prompted several of Hamilton's leading manufacturing companies to substantially reorganize their workplaces. Efficiency experts arrived at Canadian Cottons in 1929 and Mercury Mills in 1932. New equipment and restructured work processes arrived at National Steel Car in 1929, the Steel Company in 1935, and Dominion Glass in 1936. In all cases piece rates suffered, some workers were laid off, and the workload for individual workers increased. At Canadian Cottons, spinners were stripped of cleaning responsibilities but found the number of "sides" they had to handle increased from 6 to 20 or more. At National Steel Car, daily production was pushed up from 25 to 30 cars a day. At Hamilton Cotton Company in 1932 the working day was extended. At Mercury Mills workers had to tend more machines and complete tasks in a shorter time. At Stelco the workforce was drastically reduced,

The women photographed at Mercury Mills in 1928 waged a month-long strike in 1933.
(SLS, LS19)

and the rollers and heaters soon found themselves working harder for less money.[134]

All of these companies expected their vulnerable workers to accept the speed-ups, but in each case resistance arose quickly from informal work groups that refused to comply and then spread swiftly throughout the plants. The city thus saw seven major strikes between 1929 and 1935, each involving hundreds of workers and sometimes lasting weeks. On 29 January 1929 two women at Canadian Cottons refused to accept the increased workload. They stopped work to discuss the issue with other spinners and were consequently fired. The next morning the other women in that department refused to report for work. The strike spread quickly through the plant until all 750 workers (600 of them women) were out and the company had to close the mill that night.[135] A few months later, at National Steel Car, over 400 riveters from the Steel Erection Department walked off the job in protest, stating that their earnings had been reduced by 40 to 50 per cent.

They were soon joined by workers from other departments, and, thanks to the assembly-line production system, were able to bring production to a halt. In 1930 160 Mercury Mills workers refused to sign anti-union "yellow-dog" contracts and tied up a third of the plant's production for four days. Late in 1932 Hamilton Cotton workers marched out for two days against a longer working day. At Mercury Mills, 50 men and 50 women in the boarding and finishing departments stopped work for seven hours in December 1932 as a protest against the men with the stop watches, and then six months later a walkout of about 100 workers in the full-fashioned knitting room quickly spread to other departments until all 750 workers were out. On 24 June the plant closed completely. At the Steel Company, a small spontaneous strike in 1935 by one work group brought higher wages, but the company would have nothing to do with the set of demands that all 300 sheet-mill workers presented a few days later. The men promptly walked out.[136]

Headquarters of the steelworkers' union during its 1935 strike. (SLS, LS637)

Stelco strikers in 1935. (SLS, LS195)

In each case the workers had no experience in running a strike. In 1929 the Canadian Cottons workers got help from the Hamilton Trades and Labor Council to form a new branch of the United Textile Workers, and in 1930 the strikers at Mercury Mills set up a local of the same union. Both bodies were short-lived.[137] But elsewhere a handful of Communist militants provided leadership and helped to form new industrial unions and to shape the strikers' bargaining agendas. Canada's Communists had just entered a new stage in their party's strategizing about unions. Through the 1920s they had followed the lead of the Communist International in attempting to organize inside the mainstream labour movement; they had worked through a propaganda body known as the Trade Union Educational League to promote industrial unionism through the amalgamation of crafts. But they made little headway before they were pushed out by red-baiting union leaders.[138] The Communists then participated with considerable interest in the creation of the new All-Canadian Congress of Labour, which put much more emphasis on industrial, rather than craft, unionism. But, by the end of the decade, party members were making a strategic shift away from trying to stiffen the militancy of existing unions towards organizing tougher ones of their own. At the end of 1929 Communist militants across the country took the momentous step of organizing, under their own leadership, a separate national union central known as the Workers' Unity League (WUL), which spun off a number of industrial unions. In a meeting in October 1931, Hamilton's WUL activists decided to focus their efforts on unions for iron and steel and textile workers.[139]

The columns of the Communists' paper, the *Worker*, filled up with investigations of working conditions in many industrial cities. Articles appeared on working life inside several of Hamilton's leading plants, typically emphasizing the tyranny and repression that guaranteed workers' compliance and low wages. In Hamilton Communist activists were scattered through several factories, and leafleting went on at plant gates, but their impact remained limited.[140] As the spontaneous strikes erupted, however, their organizational experience and determination gave them considerable prominence in the struggles. Although they had only three members at National Steel Car before the 1929 strike, the Communists stepped into the leadership, with help from such seasoned organizers as Harvey Murphy, fresh from a similar fight at General Motors' Oshawa plant. They were convinced that this strike could be the inspirational rallying point of working-class resistance.

Dominion Glass blowers smiled for the camera in 1933, but three years later began a long, bitter strike. (SLS, LS361)

"To unorganized, exploited workers, especially those in the heavy industries, the winning of this strike will be a signal for further strikes against low wages and unbearable conditions," they proclaimed. Through the party's national network of members and sympathizers, they organized a Strikers Relief Committee to help sustain the workers, whose meagre savings would not allow them to weather a long strike. They distributed some $3,000 in relief, gathered from all across the country.[141] Some four years later the Communist newspaper stated that the strikers at Mercury Mills were following the lead of the Workers' Unity League group in the plant, and in 1935 a new Communist-led Steel and Metal Workers' Industrial Union was publishing its own *Stelco News* (though an independent Steel Workers' Union among the sheet-mill workers actually led the sheet-mill strike).[142]

Spontaneous protests thus evolved into more disciplined labour organizations that maintained mass pickets and held regular mass meetings, demonstrations, and social events to maintain worker solidarity. They also formulated more far-reaching demands that moved beyond the immediate issue to highlight long-standing grievances. At Canadian Cottons, the union not only wanted a return to the old system of machine operation and reinstatement of all workers who had lost their jobs under the new efficiency scheme, but also a ban on cleaning machinery while in motion, a grievance committee, and a 25 per cent wage increase in all departments. The new National Steel Car Workers' Industrial Union issued a list of bold demands that went far beyond the original effort to resist a wage cut: a minimum wage of $40 a week, time and a half for overtime, an eight-hour day, abolition of piecework, improved safety measures, dining-room facilities, and better heating in the plant. In 1930 the Mercury Mills workers wanted the company to withdraw its "yellow-dog" contracts and not to discriminate against the strikers, but also to reverse wage cuts of 20 to 30 per cent, withdraw the bonus system, recognize their new union, and accept a grievance committee. In 1933 the 750 strikers at the same plant demanded an end to the Bedeaux system, a restoration of the old wage scale, and no discrimination against any strikers; they also took the occasion to call for a 50-hour workweek and a permanent grievance committee.[143]

Communist leadership also complicated the strikes. A smokescreen of red-baiting sometimes obscured the substantive demands and ate away at community support. Although Labour Controller Sam Lawrence argued that a man had "as much right to be a Communist as he has to be a Conservative," the presence of reds in the union executive at National Steel Car quickly overshadowed all other issues. The company used the leaders' politics as a pretext to avoid bargaining, and the city newspapers denounced the new "red" unionism. The city council refused to let the union hold a tag day to raise funds. "We should stamp out this communist menace as we would a diphtheria epidemic," thundered Mayor W. Burton, who was threatening to suppress Communist open-air meetings in the city as well. The Hamilton Trades and Labor Council similarly withheld support, and, soon after the strike began, the Independent Labor Party representatives on city council joined a secret meeting of the police commissioners and officials of the Steel Company, Hamilton Bridge, International Harvester, and National Steel Car to discuss "curbing the activities of the strikers, or Reds, as they are termed, as this labor trouble might spread to other factories." The city's industrial managers were evidently anxious. Similarly, during the 1933 Mercury Mills strike, the city's Industrial Commissioner (a former manufacturer) conducted his own investigation, which ended up repeating management's charge about a "Red Element" in the mill. Once again, the Trades and Labor Council refused to help these strikers because they were not within the fold of the mainstream labour movement. Lawrence was the lone voice of support. "This Bedeaux system is a bonus system, and bonus systems have always been a curse," he insisted. "The business of speeding everything up to the limits is one of the greatest faults in industry today."[144]

None of the plant managers was prepared to negotiate or accept any mediation in any case. In the words of a Canadian Cottons official, "We certainly cannot pass over to them our authority." Most firms reopened their plants as soon as possible with skeletal production, imported a few strikebreakers where possible, reached out to strikers with letters, ads, or foremen's visits to their homes, and then simply waited until poverty brought the strikers drifting back to work.[145] In the face of such hostility, the strikers showed courage and remarkable persistence – going out for eight weeks at Canadian Cottons, six at National Steel Car, and four at Mercury Mills.[146] But sustaining these strikes taxed the meagre resources of the unskilled and semi-skilled workers. A group of Canadian Cottons strikers told the *Worker* that they had boarded their children with friends because they could not provide food or fuel. At National Steel Car, the collapse of strike relief payments brought the action to an abrupt end. The city relief officer made sure that Mercury Mills strikers' families would not be eligible for the dole.[147]

In none of these battles could the workers claim victories.[148] The corporate management policies that had initially sparked their outrage stayed in place. Their new industrial unions quickly withered and died, and key leaders were blacklisted or quietly fired.[149] By 1935 both companies and unions were drawing lessons from these disputes. On 3 June Steel Company president Ross McMaster announced an Employee Representation Plan with a works council like the one at International Harvester. Meanwhile the sheet-mill workers' union learned the lesson of its isolation and in September began an organizing campaign to recruit workers across the plant into a broad-based industrial union. The Communists disbanded their separate union to support this effort.[150]

Their new inspiration was the Committee for Industrial Organizations (CIO), founded that year within the AFL to recruit the unorganized in mass-production industries (it was renamed the Congress of Industrial Organization in 1937). A new slate of officers sympathetic to this new movement won control of the local Trades and Labor Council early in 1936. Taking a new strategic turn towards building a "popular front" against fascism, the Communists quietly shut down the rest of the Workers' Unity League and poured their energy and enthusiasm into the CIO. In 1936 the fledgling industry-wide steelworkers' union in Hamilton merged into the CIO's US-based Steel Workers' Organizing Committee (SWOC). Those at the Steel Company became Local 1005, and, by 1941, would win a majority of employee seats on the works council. Until then, industrial unionism had been deflected and remained marginal in the city. At Dofasco, some judicious firings of union militants and the firm's new profit-sharing plan, introduced in 1937 as the centrepiece of a wave of new welfarism, undercut the new SWOC Local 1004 in that plant and established the "Dofasco Way" as a permanent alternative to unionization.[151] The open shop remained the cornerstone of employment policy in the city.[15]

By the late 1930s, then, several of Hamilton's leading corporate employers had lived through bitter confrontations with their employees. A decade earlier they had felt confident of their untrammelled hegemony over an apparently compliant workforce, and thus about boldly cranking up work intensity without any worry of resistance. They had misread their workers, as

Sam Lawrence, former stonecutter and CCF member in the Ontario legislature from 1934 to 1937, was an active supporter of the new CIO-style industrial unionism. (SLS, LS311)

the series of bitter strikes revealed, and the patterns of resistance that had repeatedly bubbled up must have reminded their neighbours, as well as their bosses, that standing up to the boss was still possible, if risky. Ultimately, however, this third wave of militancy was not successful in getting workers' demands met, for familiar reasons. The power of Hamilton's factory owners and managers over their vulnerable workers and their determination to keep their plants union-free once again proved overwhelming and decisive. Complicating the resistance that workers tried to mount was the lack of support from Anglo-Canadian male unionists, who were not only still deeply suspicious of European immigrants at National Steel Car and of wage-earning women in the textile mills, but also uncomfortable with industrial unions and ready to join the red-baiting chorus against Communist strike leaders. Until the mid-1930s the reds were also too shrill and sectarian in their efforts to unify

CIO-style industrial unionism prompted Hamilton companies to bring in many new welfare measnures, including Dofasco's famous profit-sharing plan. Here the first cheques were being handed out in 1938. (SLS, LS434)

these distinct struggles into a broader working-class battle against speed-ups (and capitalism). The collapse of each of the huge dramatic confrontations must have left a legacy of demoralization and a return of fear about losing jobs in the depths of a depression.

Clenched Fists and Iron Heels

Among Hamilton's wage-earners, then, life on the job could involve sharp conflict. Repeatedly, workers who found themselves inside the new labour processes of corporate capitalism and swept along by a Second Industrial Revolution decided that they had had enough, and, with clenched fists, took a stand against their bosses. Within the evolving power dynamics of local industry, their efforts were decidedly political as they struggled to reduce the arbitrary authoritarianism of their employers' managerial

policies and implant some version of industrial democracy.[153]

The pattern of industrial conflict in the city does not suggest that working people were rising up angry always and everywhere. Militancy exploded episodically, depending on the conditions of the labour market and the cost of living, the provocations of managerial practices, and the inspiration of diverse forms of labour leadership – in other words, on organizational capacity. People in specific workplaces could also draw on the courage and audacity of other militant workers in Hamilton or elsewhere across the continent. Three distinct waves of militancy resulted – 1910–14, 1916–21, and 1929–36 – each with its own particular dynamics.

The city's wage-earners tended to mobilize narrowly on the basis of work groups within their particular occupation, which frequently incorporated distinct gendered and ethnic identities. The most successful groups were those with a well-respected craft skill, people who revived the local craft union movement in a burst of organizational energy at the turn of the century. But outside the building and printing trades organized workers were beaten back and denied any significant bargaining power in local industries. By World War One, some of the unions were trying to expand their membership base to incorporate less-skilled workers – cutters and pressers reaching out to female tailors, moulders to moulding-machine operators, machinists to specialists, and, by the end of the war, rolling-mill men to labourers. Still, outside the garment workers, their commitment to a broader-based unionism was never convincing. They retreated quickly to their core membership and, as in the case of the iron workers in 1920, segmented other workers into weak, ultimately moribund locals. As the collective voice of these skilled workers, the Hamilton Trades and Labor

Council remained a bastion of exclusivism and caution. After 1920 these unionists would never again feature prominently in local militancy. Right through to the end of the 1930s, they resisted broader forms of unionization and attacked the radicals who led them.[154]

Other groups of wage-earners, especially the mushrooming numbers of semi-skilled workers in local factories, had no such consistent pattern of organizing. Rather, they more often staged spontaneous battles for better wages or against some arbitrary action by their bosses. Typically these began among a small group in one department. Sometimes those limited battles spread quickly across the plant and shut the place down. If the strike lasted, those involved often made an effort to form a union, especially in the interwar period. Generally the only options presented were North America's radical variants of unionism – the IWW, OBU, and Communist formations (with the Amalgamated Clothing Workers the only major exception). Invariably, managers fought these organizing efforts tooth and nail, denouncing "outside agitators" and ultimately crushing the strikes and the unions behind them. Even during the countrywide workers' revolt at the end of World War One, the managerial counteroffensive kept unions out of most of the major factories in the city. Occasionally that strategy meant calling in the support of the police and anti-union and anti-red legal discourses, but, compared to other industrial centres, state repression was not central. More often it was a process of simply intimidating strikers to bring them to heel. In mass-production plants, where so many workers found jobs, then, Hamilton remained an open-shop heaven.

Compared to some other wage-earners, including the local construction tradesmen,[155] factory workers generally had a particularly dismal record. While they were not stripped of all discretion and expertise in the labour process, they were left highly vulnerable by their narrowly focused skill or experience, the constraints of job ladders within individual firms, and the tyrannical powers of front-line supervisors. Compared to their counterparts in Britain, where far more employers had been compelled to accept unions as a part of industrial management in their relatively smaller-scale enterprises, factory workers across North America faced a consistent, belligerent anti-unionism from their corporate bosses. In Hamilton, as in so many other factory towns, militancy was risky.[156]

Hamilton workers therefore were not able to develop long-lived organizations rooted in production to sustain and enhance a distinctive collective identity as wage-earners. The dramatic moments of militancy, such as the 1906 streetrailway strike, the 1913 clothing workers' strike, the 1916 machinists' strike, or the 1929 National Steel Car strike, were fleeting. Instead, their workplace confrontations tended to reinforce the divisions among them along lines of occupation, gender, and ethnicity. Larger identities at work remained limited to the individual firm, as industrial paternalism reigned supreme. It was nonetheless clear by the interwar period that maintaining the allegiance of workers in textiles, steel, or other industries could be an unpredictably rough road for local managers.

PART IV

The Ties
That Bind

12

George Bearman, a British immigrant to Hamilton in 1911, worked as a street-railwayman. A keen amateur photographer, he used his camera to preserve this scene of working-class domesticity in his own dining room.
(Head of the Lake Historical Society, *Hamilton*, 244)

The Family Circle

AT THE TURN OF THE 20TH CENTURY the photograph was still a precious working-class artifact. Few families could afford a camera, and photos on working-class mantles were most often taken in commercial studios on such momentous occasions as weddings. George Bearman, a motorman on the Hamilton Street Railway, was exceptional in his fascination with amateur photography, and his photo of himself with his wife and child was rare in the city. Yet he was only at the cutting edge of picture-taking in working-class Hamilton, as Kodak's simple Brownie box cameras gradually became more affordable and more widely used in the opening decades of the century. Bearman's early picture of his family, most likely taken in their parlour or dining room, also anticipated the tone of so much family photography to follow. Some working people began to give pride of place to albums of snapshots, all of them conveying a powerful sense of how much they valued their home life. Whatever the reality of tension or conflict, the photos invariably commemorated the family experiences in settings of warm intimacy, strong attachments, and fun.[1]

One of the great shifts in social organization during the First Industrial Revolution of the mid-19th century was the separation of most income-generating work from the household and the creation of a more private space apart from public life – the "home."[2] Setting up and maintaining that shared domestic space was the

Like the family of Albert J. Libke, a German-born labourer in the local rolling mills, some working people scraped together the money for a formal studio portrait to display the solid respectability of the patriarchal family circle. (HPL)

central project of a marriage and a key marker of independence and self-reliance among working people. Although almost everyone was born and raised in some kind of family home, some adults had little interest in creating one of their own – the confirmed bachelors and the celibate clergy, for example – or else had great difficulty making one work. The hobos who flopped in the Salvation Army hostel or tried to dun a housewife on her front steps might have spent large parts of their adult lives far from scenes of domestic bliss. Other working people saw their idealized family life crumble as a breadwinner or housewife disappeared, which meant they had to soldier on as lone parents. The great majority nonetheless seemed to find the image of the family home a powerful cultural force. Even unattached bachelors and spinsters often lived in family homes.

On the surface a house in working-class Hamilton at the turn of the century could seem a fragmented place through which people simply passed on different daily and weekly schedules. Family members spent many hours apart every day. Fathers, older children, and boarders were off somewhere in the outside world earning wages, while pre-adolescent children spent growing amounts of time in school. Mothers left for shorter spells on shopping expeditions, and younger children were out with their friends in the streets. Yet everyone came home to sleep under the same roof, and family members tended to spend significant amounts of time together every evening and in some cases on

Saturday afternoons. Generally they were also there every Sunday and on the rare one-day holidays sprinkled across the calendar.

On these occasions family members of all generations shared not only common space and common activities, but also a deeply rooted sense of the home as a refuge of comfort, peace, and emotional security. When family members came together at scattered moments each day and week, they re-created the powerful sense of intimacy, belonging, and connectedness that made working-class family life more than an economic convenience. It was the bedrock of their lives. Given how many people continued to be tenants rather than owners, with a propensity to move often, the family circle was not necessarily connected to a specific place (even though the aspiration to own a house was alive and well). Through the repetitive, ritualistic qualities of much of the time spent together, the family circle used memory as a powerfully cohesive force. This was what they so regularly evoked when they referred to "family" or captured the moment in a snapshot.[3]

Ethnic variations were certainly in place,[4] but essentially the patterns were strikingly similar. When families did not work this way (when coping with abject poverty, lone parenthood, chronic drunkenness, or repeated brutality, for example), they and the others roundabout well understood the standard against which their failure was measured. The image of the family circle did not have to conform to the realities of life actually lived together. As ideology, that image operated as a kind of ordering and discipline that ideally reined in dissolute fathers (or mothers), delinquent sons, and sexually precocious daughters. It could also be used by breadwinners in confrontations with employers and workers' political organizations in building their movements.[5] From outside, politicians, clergy,

Stonecutter and labour leader Sam Lawrence poses for the camera surrounded by his family. (SLS, LS712)

social workers, and businessmen might claim that a secure home would guarantee working-class conformity and contentment.

Despite the family's limited space, restricted income, and personal tensions based to a considerable extent on unequal power and authority within the household, the mother's work was crucial in the attempt to make the family circle a nest of warmth and happiness for everyone. In reality and in memory, "mother" was the mythical symbol of home. Yet the experience of family time differed considerably depending on sex and age. A husband typically saw the home in symbolic terms as the embodiment of his patriarchal status. He came into this domestic arena as part of his after-work leisure time, expecting to rest and relax (and, in some cases, might choose to leave it behind and seek all-male company elsewhere). Children who invariably had domestic tasks to perform after school also expected to be able to use family time for relaxation and play. A wife had no such clear break and saw family time as another part of the nurturing work that required considerable exertion and imagination to please everyone. She was not simply a housekeeper but also a "homemaker." To the extent that women were able to enjoy leisure time, they still had to combine those moments with various domestic tasks in the familiar day-long pattern of work that was "never done." Girls and boys would adapt in their own ways to these gender expectations. The choices made had a rough consistency across families, especially the high value placed on emotional intensity, colour, and theatricality.

Working-class families were certainly not left alone to make their own choices about leisure-time activities. They encountered various forms of disciplinary regulation aimed at their use of time and space. On one side, they were cajoled to exercise restraint, especially on the Sabbath. On the other, they were encouraged to extend the family circle into new commercial spaces, from such outside venues as amusement parks or movie theatres to the new home-based medium of radio. All of these new spaces invited participation in their particular constructions of family. In the end the collective life of the family circle was a complex negotiation of private aspirations and public expectations and opportunities.

At least a few moments of family life reflected a certain togetherness: the inward-looking time spent in the household; the special weekly time slot of Sunday; and the much rarer shared outings to various spots around the city. These moments of togetherness reveal not only how the workers' private worlds changed in early-20th-century Hamilton, but also how much remained the same.

No Place Like Home

Each day, week, and year, the family circle had its own set of rituals for gathering together around the household hearth and dining table. The pinnacle in a predominantly Christian city was the festive season running between Christmas and New Year's. Well before the end of the 19th century, the late December holiday period had been redefined as the most important annual festival of Christian family solidarity. In place of the public revelries that had once marked the holiday, families and their kin were encouraged to turn inward, to gather around a Christmas tree, under which were gifts for children, and to enjoy each other's company in the consumption of good food and drink. Donald Garvie, a member of a Hamilton working-class family, remembered it as "the one time in the winter that the parlour was opened." Gift-giving was limited in working-class families like his. "We would each have a stocking filled with an apple, an orange and good hard Christmas candy," he recalled. "Sometimes we would receive a present wrapped in tissue paper." For him, the big family dinner was the "important part" of Christmas. Indeed, that was the time that local charities considered so important that they filled their seasonal Christmas baskets with the necessary ingredients for a good dinner, including a large bird for roasting.[6] In some neighbourhoods other European traditions brought similar celebrations on saints' days or other important dates on the calendar. In March 1910, for example, all the city's Hungarians "and several other citizens of other nationalities" stayed off work for "jubilant" Easter festivities. Some ten years later International Harvester still had large numbers of its "foreign" workers taking extended breaks at Christmas and Easter. Saints' days could also bring people together. "We would rent dance halls and have parties," one Italian-Canadian man recalled about the Italian *festa*. "We would eat and dance and drink all day long. It was great."[7]

Special moments in the life cycle could bring family and kin together as well. In some communities, christenings, bar mitzvahs, and weddings were small, relatively quiet affairs, but one Italian-Canadian remembered that baptisms were day-long events and wedding celebrations lasted two days. The police grumbled that christenings in the pre-war "foreign colony" were simply excuses for heavy drinking.[8] In all neighbourhoods, funerals generally drew many kin and friends for the rituals of death, and families invested precious savings in insurance funds to see that family members of any age would have a proper, respectable funeral.[9] More regular, less elaborate moments of family sociability occurred as well. Sunday dinners were weekly events in many households. One workingman recalled: "Every Sunday was pretty near like Christmas, my mother was such a great cook."[10]

In more relaxed, informal ways, weekday evenings also brought most working-class families together. The daily interval between dinner and bedtime attracted few investigators or commentators and remained largely out of public view. Yet for a few weeks in 1907, Hamiltonians got glimpses of what working-class families were up to on a weeknight. That spring, from mid-March to late May, everyone in Hamilton was watching for the "Spec. Man" to arrive on their doorsteps. As a promotional gimmick, the *Spectator* – the self-styled "Great Family Journal" – sent out a reporter six nights a week for eight weeks to knock on doors across the city between 7:00 and 8:30 in the evening – the daily interval between dinner and bedtime. If the householder had a copy of that day's paper, the visitor asked to go inside where he would give away one of four envelopes containing a coupon worth up to $5 for goods in city stores. Every night the paper published the names of the winners, a long account of the reporter's experiences on the streets and in the four households he entered, plus his reflections on life in the rapidly changing city. The composite picture that emerged from the series is patchy and sometimes opaque, but revealing nonetheless.

Over those weeks the Spec. Man entered 192 homes in all parts of the city, except the most posh neighbourhoods of the southwest. In the great majority of cases, the households were headed by blue-collar wage-earners, but they were also a particular slice of working-class Hamilton.[11] The Spec. Man went to a specific neighbourhood each night and could choose the houses he tried at random, but he usually picked those with lights on in the front room and avoided seedier dwellings, including the sprinkling of new European immigrant boarding houses. In his reports he made no mention of approaching people of colour. The vast majority were respectable, white, English-speaking households with well-employed breadwinners (the local economy was booming that spring), many of them relatively recent immigrants from Britain. Aside from noting the presence of boarders in several places, he mentioned the tendency to overcrowding only once, when he found two families sharing a small cottage. His stories gave no hint of real poverty – in only one case was a wife working during her husband's illness, and in another a widow was working full-time in the Fearman meat-packing plant – nor was there any tendency to judge, as charity workers invariably did.[12] The articles conveyed images of cozy, amicable domestic relations. They stood as a stark contrast to the police-court columns elsewhere in the paper, where wives regularly accused husbands of abuse and neglect, or child-welfare officers presented allegations of poor parenting.

Once inside, the Spec. Man was usually more interested in conversing with the head of the household about his job, the street-car service, local political issues, or sports (no doubt standard men's talk) than in quizzing wives about making ends meet or coping with their domestic toil. Although his observations were casual and in no way systematic, the Spec. Man nonetheless included many details about the evening routines that he had interrupted. He thus offered rare glimpses into what went on in these homes on a typical evening at a point of significant transition in the city's economic and social life.

The reporter was sometimes invited into a front parlour, but he found most of those formal spaces in darkness, or lit up only to catch his eye. In contrast to middle-class families, working people saved their parlours for special occasions.[13] In a few cases he was ushered into the kitchen, but more often he was welcomed into the dining room, where family members were usually gathered.[14] This was a space that had emerged relatively recently in working-class housing in North America. Like its equivalent in middle-class homes, it was intended to draw together household members for the one common meal of the day around a large, solid table.[15] In early March, when the series began, the Spec. Man found many people lingering in the warmth of the dining-room's fireplace or stove, since few houses would have had central heating until well after World War One. After dark, most family members clustered in the glow of coal-oil lamps. A housewife would have been under regular pressure to furnish and decorate this room to make it cozy and functional for the rest of the family. Only in the hotter summer months would the centre of domestic gravity probably shift to the ubiquitous front verandah.[16]

The Spec. Man typically found several people at home. The wife and mother was almost always there to answer the door and welcome him in, as gatekeeper to the domestic terrain where she worked. If she was out, it was usually because she was shopping or helping a sick neighbour. In the nine out of ten households that reportedly had a husband living there, the visitor found the man home two-thirds of the time.[17] Several husbands were off working night shifts or putting in overtime in one of the local factories, especially International Harvester and Canadian Westinghouse.[18] In many cases a husband's absence went unexplained. He might have been at a lodge or union meeting or treating his friends at a neighbourhood saloon, but no wife said so.[19] Saturday nights seemed to be understood as a man's night out, if he wanted it.[20] Yet, however often married workingmen sought refuge from their families in the company of other adult men, most of them apparently spent a good deal of after-work time within the family circle.[21] Around them flowed children, though the older ones took advantage of the warmer spring evenings to spill out onto the streets. A grandmother or grandfather (apparently widows or widowers) occasionally sauntered in to meet the visiting stranger. So too did any boarders found at home – indeed, they often seemed to be relaxing in the same room as the family.[22] The households without a husband under the roof invariably had unmarried adult children, male and female, living with their mothers. In a sprinkling of places, a cat or dog shared the space.

The households seemed mostly to turn inward on themselves. Certainly, except for children, the Spec. Man found few people gathering in the street to socialize. He concluded that the depth of the mud in so many streets discouraged "across the road neighborly visiting." Yet in several instances he did find neighbours or non-resident kin inside a house chatting over tea.[23] Their presence seemed to be a matter of a casual dropping in, rather than formal entertaining. Years later elderly Hamiltonians explained that, in their youth in this period, socializing between neighbours was rare.[24] Presumably, then, the visitors that the Spec. Man encountered were close friends.[25] On a few occasions, he stumbled into an adult prayer meeting in progress in a house, or parents absent at some kind of religious service.[26]

Although the dining-room (or kitchen) hearth provided a focal point, the rituals of the evening after dinner seemed loose and relaxed and allowed family members to pursue separate activities in and around the house. For many family members, recreation was interspersed with work. The reporter frequently found the wife and mother "ruddy-faced and elbow sleeved from a hot kitchen" because he had interrupted her sewing, ironing, making marmalade, nursing a sick child or husband, putting the children to bed, or launching into the annual spring cleaning. He encountered a number of women who were trying to control a tired, crying child and were undoubtedly aware that the bawling would upset the weary wage-earners in the household.[27] Rarely did he find any woman sitting reading the paper (though several did say they looked at the paper some time during the day).[28] A mother was either in and out of the family circle in the dining room or dodging bodies moving around the kitchen. Meanwhile, men were either resting after their day's labour, with the *Spectator* spread across the table (perhaps keeping an eye on younger children at the same time) or, in many cases, working around the house – painting and otherwise sprucing up the place, or, by May, working on the garden.[29] Only at some point long after the Spec. Man had departed, and children, kin, and boarders had gone to bed, could the husband and wife expect to find any moments together alone, at which point exhaustion might simply send them to bed as well.

The evening certainly seemed to be children's time. Older daughters might be washing supper dishes or minding a baby carriage, and the odd son was helping his father with repairs or yard work. One was looking after his own brood of chickens.[30] But most younger children seemed to be simply having fun within the family fold. The dining room (or kitchen) was their playroom. In one labourer's home, the Spec. Man noted that the dining-room floor was "littered with trains, dolls, and various other child's playthings," but, otherwise, a rag doll in the hands of a policeman's daughter and a bag of marbles clutched by a foundry shipper's child were the only other references to toys, which were probably luxuries for many on limited incomes.[31] Some children were evidently allowed to head out to the street, where they were playing marbles under a lamp post or skipping rope on the corner. By the end of April the reporter was suggesting that the children of the southwest of the city were "monopolizing the streets."[32] Yet the deep mud and inky blackness of so many streets with no lights kept many youngsters indoors until the warmer, lighter evenings of the early summer. Older children and teenagers were not always home, and the silence about their whereabouts suggests that it was not always easy to keep them in the family fold at night.[33]

The Spec. Man's ramblings and ruminations thus provide a small, and rare, window into the working-class households of the early 20th century. Decades later elderly workers in Hamilton would remember that many of the features of family life that the reporter stumbled upon in 1907 were still in place in the interwar period. Young Donald Garvie, the son of a leather worker, grew up in a house with no central heating or electricity. He rarely entered the parlour and saw the kitchen as a "utilitarian" space for cooking on an enormous coal stove. But he remembered parents and siblings converging on the dining room, which had its big, ornate coal stove. "We would do our homework at the end of the table near the stove as the other end of the room was usually cold," he wrote. He also explained what must also have been true in 1907: bedrooms were cold, sparsely furnished, and thus never seen as fit places for the children to retreat to, other than to sleep. In any case, bedrooms were often shared with others. Elderly Hamiltonians had similar memories many years later. Under such conditions, it was hard to create more specialized, private space on the middle-class model.[34]

Selling Family Fun

Families evidently made their own fun on a weekday evening, much of it probably simple conversation and storytelling, but the Spec. Man himself represented the driving wedge of a new commercialism that was targeting the family household. His employer produced and marketed a form of mass-produced culture that had begun to penetrate the home and shape its meaning.

The *Spectator*, a major business owned by the local Southam family, was the flagship of the biggest newspaper empire to emerge in the country in this period. Like its two smaller local competitors, the *Herald* and the *Times*, the paper had become a one-cent evening paper in the 1890s (two cents after 1920). Its rich array of current news included detailed local reporting and wire stories of international events, offered up in a livelier, more popular style than its 19th-century predecessors. It also packed in specialized features on business, unions, sports, religion, theatre, travel, fashion, housekeeping, and recreation and amusement. Sensationalist news items about crime, violence, war, or natural catastrophes became entertainment themselves. "What is a newspaper published for if not to produce sensations," the *Herald* had once argued. The Spec. Man noted that in many households the paper was well read and passed from hand to hand.[35]

By the 1920s a typical Saturday paper was more like a weekly magazine, often running to some 40 pages and full of eye-catching drawings and photos. Over the years, colourful local columnists such as Joseph Tinsley ("Jaques") in the *Herald* and Richard Butler in the *Spectator*, together with a number of syndicated columnists, nestled alongside less newsy items, such as serialized fiction, biographical profiles, photo spreads, comic strips, recipes, classifieds, letters to the editor, and numerous other features geared to leisure-time consumption. Some of this material could be useful for people in dealing with everyday challenges (job ads, dress patterns, retail bargains, or excursion notices, for example), but the overall impact was more entertaining than educational. Since the turn of the century the Saturday edition had been consciously pitched at a broad family readership, with an overall message of domestic harmony and contentment. Like the weekday papers, it also overflowed with advertisements, many of which were the most powerful visual features. Indeed, the daily press was far and away the most important vehicle for Canadian advertisers and the most immediate promoter of more and more goods for home enjoyment and of commercialized fun available outside the home – theatre, sports, excursions, and much more. Although the content of the *Spectator* and its competitors was fragmented, the overall message reassured readers that the world around them worked as well as it could, and page after page attempted to whet their appetites for more commodities from the commercial marketplace. Working people evidently extracted what they found useful, affordable, and stimulating to the imagination.[36]

The Spec. Man also came across another important source of commercialization in working-class Hamilton, and something that would become even more prominent by the interwar period: household music. In 1907 he reported that a few families had pianos (one had an organ, a cheaper instrument), and that women or children were busy practising. This instrument had special meaning beyond the melodic sound it could make. Both as a piece of ornate furniture and as a tool for a particular kind of cultural finishing for girls, a piano had since the mid-19th century been identified with middle-class status-seeking or pretensions to respectability. It had also been associated with women's cultivation of a domestic haven for their families. Piano music, played by female fingers, was supposed to be a balm for worldly troubles and a stimulus to moral uplift. Beyond such performances, family intimacy was strengthened in those memorable moments when everyone gathered around the piano to sing popular songs or religious hymns together. Husbands would want to stay home, and children would be protected from the evils of the street. Under a banner headline – "Stifling Your Home?" – a local piano retailer asked in 1917, "Would you like the responsibility to rest on you for driving your family out of their home for every entertainment they want?"[37] In reality these instruments may have made possible family performances or singsongs, but probably only on special occasions (the Spec. Man reported none) because in working-class homes the bulky "uprights" commonly sat amongst the most respectable furniture in the little-used front parlour. Gathering around the piano was thus one of the more occasional rituals of family solidarity.[38]

How widespread was such a ritual in working-class Hamilton? The Canadian piano industry was expanding rapidly in the early 20th century and, by applying mass-production techniques, was turning out cheaper lines of its products. Ads appeared in the newspapers every week, sometimes with encouragement for consumers to buy on time, and, according to one householder, piano salesmen knocked on doors regularly. The

WAGES INCREASED

Wages are being increased in almost every line of work, and a very small portion of your monthly increase will pay the instalments on a High Grade, Moderate Priced Piano at

Hamilton's No-Interest Piano House
267 KING STREET EAST.

See that your order is placed with us during the month of May and you will get a handsome Duet Bench, worth $12.00, absolutely free.

We make liberal allowances for instruments taken in exchange and also make the terms on balance to suit your convenience. We save you at the least $60.80 interest on the piano. Open evenings except on Wednesday. Phone 2241.

Wartime prosperity made purchasing a piano more possible. (LN, 1918)

sales pitch got intense during World War One, as fuller employment brought somewhat more disposable income.[39] At a minimum of $100, a piano remained a purchase well beyond the means of most working-class families, although instalment buying might have made it possible for those with regular incomes, especially if they dipped into the second-hand market.[40]

The reporter said he had heard many more pianos on his walk through the working-class north end. Some of these people may have felt that having piano music drifting out their windows would enhance their status on the block, but so few visitors ever entered their parlours to admire the instrument itself that it seems reasonable to argue that in many working-class homes piano-playing was more likely a joyful, well-loved lubricant of family sociability (and a skill to carry beyond the household to church, lodge, or union meetings).[41] Other instruments no doubt also sat within reach of the family circle in this period – many workingmen played horns in brass bands, and the fiddle and accordion were popular among the newer European immigrants – yet, unlike the piano, these were usually played by men.[42]

Owning a piano could lead to other purchases. Canadian publishers had a long history

Home Joys

If you or some other member of your household do not play some instrument, your home must be dull indeed, unless you have a

Columbia Graphophone

It is the greatest entertainer and unlimited fun maker in the world. It plays, sings, recites and otherwise imitates every sound of your voice and instrument. You can dance to its well measured music and sing to its accompaniment, for it gives true tone and perfect time.

No Reason To Be Without One

When you can pay a small sum and have one of these matchless instruments sent at once to your Home. Afterwards you make small weekly or monthy payments.

Come in and see, hear and examine our great collection of Columbia Graphophones.

Columbia Phonograph Co Gen'l
119 King Street East

Advertisements for phonographs began to appear regularly in the decade before World War One.

(*HS*, 10 Nov. 1906, 18)

of printing song and instructional books and sheets of "serious" music. But a flood of more popular published music was also rushing across the US border. Since the 1890s the cluster of New York firms known as Tin Pan Alley had been mass-producing sheet music for thousands of tunes. Canadian composers and publishers soon imitated the US style, and, every Saturday before the war, keen musicians could clip a sheet of such music from the *Spectator*.[43] Some pieces were simply old favourites, but many more were fresh off the pens of a stable of composers employed in the song factories of the Alley. The publishers aimed to create hits that everyone would want to sing and play at home or in some other leisure-time setting, like a lodge meeting. To enhance sales, music publishers also turned the covers of their sheet music into works of art that would look attractive on display in a family parlour. The music's popularity was remarkable – in the first decade of the century, some 100 songs sold more than a million copies of sheet music.[44]

This was the new urban folk music. The melodies probably captured hearts more than the lyrics did. The words were simple, and their messages conventional and repetitively

formulaic – nostalgic longing, romance, humour, patriotism. It was participatory music, with simple, repeated choruses that encouraged listeners to join in, and a liveliness conducive to body movement. After setting many tunes to waltz and march rhythms, Tin Pan Alley became the medium for spreading far and wide a popular new form of syncopated music known as "ragtime," composed for both piano and singing (such as the 1902 hit "Bill Bailey, Won't You Please Come Home"), which stimulated numerous new dance styles. With the publication of Irving Berlin's best-selling "Alexander's Ragtime Band" in 1911, ragtime triumphed over all other styles of popular music. Hamilton pianist and band leader Charles E. Wellinger had a number of popular ragtime hits, notably in 1914 "That Captivating Rag." Just before the war, a new brand of African-American music began to appear in print (notably "St. Louis Blues" in 1914), and by the 1920s the industry was vigorously promoting the more unconventional sounds of jazz. Whether or not a family owned a piano, the chances were good that they would absorb much of this new popular music.[45]

Since the turn of the century, aggressive businessmen had also been offering families a different way to hear their favourite music – through a machine. One version was the player piano (or pianola), which, starting around 1906, allowed listeners to hear professional performances in their own homes by running perforated paper rolls through machinery that set the piano keys in motion. At a cost of at least $600 (or $500 used), the novelty would have been affordable only rarely for a working-class family.[46] In any case, player pianos faced stiff competition from a new, entirely different device called a phonograph or gramophone. This machine, produced cheaply by large US manufacturers (mainly Edison, Victor, and Columbia), played pre-recorded wax cylinders or discs, and, like the piano, was available through local music stores on the instalment plan. Some were housed in large, elegant cabinets, but businesses also promoted small portable versions for use at home or out of doors.[47]

Advertising for this new device promised what one company called "Home Joys." The Hamilton branch of Columbia Phonograph Co. promised that its Graphophone machine was "the greatest entertainer and unlimited fun maker in the world," allowing families to listen or sing along and dance. Before World War One, few working-class families could afford to buy many recordings at 25 to 50 cents apiece (the Spec. Man did not comment on any in his 1907 home visits)[48] – and $1 by the 1920s – and, since in any case the sound quality of the two-to-four-minute performances was variable, the "talking machines" no doubt remained something of a novelty in the cluttered parlours of a small minority of households. Even there they were probably reserved for only occasional use. During the wartime boom, however, one Hamilton social worker was worried that far too many families were taking advantage of higher earnings to invest in this version of home entertainment. In that decade, Hamilton music stores were selling some phonographs for as little as $20, payable in small instalments. By the interwar period, as costs came down, many more households (though probably still a decided minority) must have had them.[49]

Families expected to listen, dance, or sing along with music they had heard in the street, the church, the theatre, or their own parlours. Tin Pan Alley funnelled a flood of its popular tunes through the recording industry, and immigrant groups snatched up recordings of their favourite homeland melodies.[50] In this case, then, the mass culture that entered the working-class

Families gathered around the radio to enjoy programs, but often dispersed if the broadcast was not to their individual tastes. (SLS, LS722)

home turned out to be a packaging of familiar strains within the family circle. Since listening to recorded music was not yet the individualized experience it would be decades later, playing a particular record became an act of sharing and remembering among family members and, more broadly, among wider communities of listeners with similar musical tastes. Industry sources indicated that wives and mothers played a major role in buying and playing records for family enjoyment. Thus, without having to learn musical skills, women could still use music in their efforts to make the home a haven of peace and happiness.[51]

Tuning In

In the late 1920s the commercial invasion of the family home took a huge leap forward when the arrival of radio quickly eclipsed the phonograph and the piano in the home entertainment market.[52] Until the mid-1920s "wireless" receivers were technically complex novelties for dedicated hobbyists, invariably men and boys (the building of and fiddling with crystal sets carried on older artisan traditions and anticipated tinkering with cars). Usually the devices had no speakers to allow for group listening (though

Advertisements for
radios in 1930 high-
lighted the popularity
of Amos 'n' Andy.
(*HS*, 7 Nov. 1930, 18)

special events such as election returns or major
sports events were occasionally broadcast to
large crowds in public places). Then, towards
the end of the decade, as the equipment became
easier to use and listen to, manufacturers (such
as the local Westinghouse plant) started referring to a radio as a "musical instrument" and
placing it inside fancy wooden cabinets with
loudspeakers for use in the family parlour. The
machine had been re-gendered as an element of
the domestic realm organized by women. The
price quickly soared beyond the easy reach of
working-class families, but after 1929 smaller,
cheaper radios came onto the market. When
federal census-takers knocked on doors in
Hamilton in 1931, they caught the crest of a consumerist wave that saw the proportion of households with a radio reach nearly three out of five.
Doubtless that group included many working-
class families who had scraped together a down
payment and somehow paid the monthly instalments. Many more who could not afford to buy
probably gravitated to households that had the
new machines to hear favourite programs. The
census ten years later reported more than nine
out of ten households in the city had a radio (by
comparison, at the same point, fewer than half
had a telephone and even fewer had a car or a

refrigerator). A radio had apparently become a
household necessity.[53]

Radio could make economic sense for working people in an economic depression, since,
unlike other forms of entertainment, listening
in cost nothing beyond the expense of replacing
tubes and an annual licence fee of $1 in the 1920s
and $2 after 1932 (a fee that frequently went un-
paid). Yet the willingness of so many families to
make this purchase in the face of the severe unemployment of the 1930s was based at least as
much on the quality of programming available.
Hamilton's first radio station, CKOC, was owned
by a local radio equipment retailer, Wentworth
Radio Supply. The station had gone on the air
in 1922 (a year of radio mania across the continent), and five years later was joined by CHML.
Neither of these stations had much broadcasting strength, and they were on the air only a few
hours a day.[54] But radio sets could pick up many
more stations outside the city with stronger signals, and listeners regularly tuned in to the fuller,
slicker offerings of powerful US broadcasters.
By the late 1920s, moreover, many US stations
had been tied together through huge national
networks run by NBC and CBS, which broadcast
standardized programming for all affiliated stations at the same time (much of it produced by
advertising agencies for specific commercial
sponsors – *The Fleischmann Hour* and *The Lux
Radio Theatre*, for example).[55]

Hamilton's families thus had access to the
same corporate-sponsored programming that
beamed into millions of other households
across North America. The US shows apparently got huge audiences in the city. In November 1930, local radio retailers filled a whole page
in the *Spectator* with ads urging readers to buy
a radio so that they could hear the wildly popular US comedy series *Amos 'n' Andy*, launched a
year earlier. CHML simply went off the air for 15

minutes six nights a week when that program came on a Buffalo station. "When the big network shows in the U.S. began, our audiences went away," a former announcer explained. The radio program listings published regularly in Hamilton newspapers in the 1930s were packed with US network offerings.[56] Never before had so much mass-produced culture entered so directly and easily into the family circle.

What did they listen to? Initially, radio programming was a cross between a newspaper and a phonograph, though the immediacy of live broadcasts made a considerable difference (after 1925 the use of recordings was severely curtailed by government regulators). Despite considerable discussion about the potential of radio for education and cultural uplift, it provided mostly entertainment. Programming was dotted with short news reports, sports broadcasts, church services, occasional lectures on health or housekeeping, public-service notices, and, at election time, political speeches. It thus brought lots of information and many issues of public debate into the home.[57] Yet musical concerts filled up more air time than anything else (making up two-thirds of US network programming time in the mid-1930s). Indeed, far more than the piano or the phonograph, radio made music central to daily household life, including the family's evening hours. Cautious radio programmers initially concentrated on light classical pieces, but soon gave more air time to popular sentimental tunes, old favourites, and, more controversially, various versions of jazz. Much of the music played on radio stations was locally produced. "We broadcast all the orchestras playing at local hotels like the Royal Connaught and the Alexandra Ballroom," one former announcer at CHML recalled. "We also did all kinds of small groups from around town." Future MP Ellen Fairclough, a clerical worker at the time,

remembered playing a musical duet with her sister on CHML, and school choirs got air play. Music also fit nicely into the variety show, an increasingly popular format produced in both the United States and Canada.[58]

In the late 1920s and early 1930s a heavy borrowing from theatre, vaudeville, and popular fiction also regularly brought mysteries, dramas, and, above all, comedies onto the airwaves, with almost all of the programs produced in the United States.[59] After music, comedy always rated highest, though men also liked sports. In 1929 *Amos 'n' Andy* pioneered the format of network-wide programs that families regularly gathered to listen to at fixed times. Other programming had a specifically Canadian appeal, like the opening of Parliament, the King's Christmas Day message, or the weekly *Hockey Night in Canada*. Since the most popular programs were invariably sponsored by major corporations, listeners also got a steady diet of commercials, mostly for such small household goods as Pepsodent, Palmolive, Jell-O, or Imperial Oil. The content here would have been familiar because powerful visual advertising had already caught the audience's eye on street-corner billboards and on virtually every page of local newspapers, but the voice of the radio announcer brought the sponsor's pitch much more directly and, perhaps, more persuasively into the home. Radio thus conveyed into the family circle many features of the public sphere – the concert hall, vaudeville theatre, sports field, political rally, retail store – but with a remarkable intimacy familiar to the family home. For working-class housewives, who no doubt listened to the radio more than anyone else in the household, the result was an unprecedented infusion of the public into the domestic domain.[60]

According to surveys on both sides of the Atlantic, people at the lower end of the social scale tuned in far more often than the rich. When surveyors put on their crude lenses for class, they also found a decided (and distinctive) preference for comedy, popular music, and sports among lower socio-economic groups in cities.[61] Undoubtedly listening in Hamilton followed a pattern identified in US surveys, which showed families in 85 per cent of households listening together in the evening (the emerging tendency for affluent families to individualize radio listening by buying more receivers would have been beyond the reach of Hamilton's working people).[62] Listeners had to adapt to a clock-bound punctuality to catch their favourite programs, but, by the same token, radio programmers also had to build their schedules around the typical rhythms of family life, with the family dinner as a crucial daily transition period. *Amos 'n' Andy* came on at 7 p.m., for example.

Like so much of the new mass culture, the radio audience was fragmented to some extent by age and gender – daytime soap operas for housewives, dance music for young adults, special late-afternoon shows (like *Little Orphan Annie*) for children, hockey or the "fights" for men – but, more often, especially in the evening slot that years later would become known as "prime time," programs were aimed at an undifferentiated audience of listeners who could all enjoy Jack Benny's jokes, the Shadow's sly sleuthing, or, with more Canadian content, *The Happy Gang*'s musical lineup. One man remembers that after the weekly bath, "We'd go listen to the hockey game on the radio and have an apple. We did that every Saturday night for years when we were kids."[63] Radio retailers promoted a carefully constructed image of the whole family gathered around a set each evening, rapturously absorbed in the sounds spilling out into their homes, and programmers worked hard to turn the medium into a welcome visitor in the family circle.

An intimate solo by a crooner like Rudy Vallée, a gruff monologue from a storytelling private detective, a "fireside chat" by Prime Minister R.B. Bennett (mimicking the US president), or an announcer's earnest promotion of the merits of a hand soap were all efforts to use this new medium effectively. As it turned out, "listening in" was akin to eavesdropping, and fit long-standing oral modes of working-class communication at home and elsewhere. The message delivered on radio was overall comforting and reassuring. In that sense, it played well in a domestic setting that was ideally supposed to be just that for members of the household.[64] Still, Hamilton apparently had no programs in any other language than English before 1940,[65] which means that the resonance of what was available would have been much weaker in households in which English was not the first language. The programming may well have divided first- and second-generation family members.

For the most part, though, with radio thus welcomed into the family circle, it added entertainment, information, and propaganda to an evening together that the Spec. Man certainly had not found a quarter-century earlier, and it allowed diverse voices into the family home – voices that tried to integrate the household into various larger "imagined communities" – motherhood, youth, athletics, Christianity, the nation, and more. For brief moments each week, when millions of listeners were tuned in to the same show, the line between "private" and "public" was certainly blurred.[66]

Had the Spec. Man returned to knock on doors in the 1930s, he would most likely have been astonished at the pride of place given to new technology in the heart of the family circle around which members gathered in an evening. Yet the essential patterns of working-class home life that he had stepped into in 1907 had not changed fundamentally. Among those who could afford them, phonographs and radios had not "privatized" family life. Long before their arrival, working-class families had made a habit of converging on a common space (the kitchen, dining room, or parlour) at a regular time each day (from dinner to bedtime) to enjoy the simple pleasures of informal human interaction and shared activities. The new technologies reinforced existing routines and the values sustaining them, rather than replacing them with new practices. However much family members squabbled among themselves, and however much they integrated mass-produced culture into this setting, they still accepted the loosely ritualized domestic routines of an evening at home as essential ingredients of the pleasure, love, and respect that, at some level, they believed should bind them together.

Keeping the Sabbath

In many ways Sunday was similar to weeknights. But it was also significantly different. To be sure, if a father or older brothers worked at one of the steel plants or on the railroad, or if a sister was a live-in servant in a richer household, a child would not see much more of them than on any other day. But, otherwise, members of the household who were normally out of the house all week, especially the father and any male boarders, were more likely to be home on Sunday. Indeed, other family members might well have spent the early hours of Sunday morning tiptoeing around to avoid disturbing their sleep.

Eventually a child would learn that, by law and custom, all schools, stores, offices, banks, saloons, theatres, sporting events, and most factories had to shut down for the day out of respect for the Christian Sabbath.[67] Sunday was special, set apart from regular work routines as the only day for rest, relaxation, reflection, and recreation. Of course, children would see no such relief for their mothers because families still had to be fed and the sick nursed, and bringing a family together on Sundays around a big meal required special planning and extra work. A girl herself usually felt the same pressure to pitch in as on any other day.

Yet in many working-class households, Sunday was nonetheless a day of special activities that could draw family members together in various ways, often outside the home. Whenever they set off together as a group, family members attempted to project pride and respectability in appearance and deportment. They were as well dressed as their limited wardrobes allowed, and children's behaviour, especially that of the girls, was watched over carefully. What they could actually do together on this day of rest, however, remained controversial.

The peel of church bells in every neighbourhood reminded householders of one possible family outing. Only a tiny handful of Hamilton residents told the census-takers every ten years that they were non-believers. At the turn of the century, seven out of ten said they were Anglicans, Methodists, or Presbyterians, in roughly even proportions with a slight edge to the Methodists. Of other denominations, only the Catholics came close, at roughly one in six. Over the next two decades the growing wave of British immigrants pushed the proportion of Anglicans and Presbyterians considerably higher, until together they totalled more than half of the population by 1921. The Anglicans alone were close to a third. Some four years later almost all the local Presbyterian congregations voted against entering the new United Church of Canada,[68] which brought together Methodists, Presbyterians, and Congregationalists across the country, and to which more than one in five Hamilton people adhered by the 1930s. Meanwhile the arrival of many more Continental European immigrants brought the proportion of Catholics in the city's population up slightly, to nearly one in five by the 1930s. By that point the more ritualist Catholics and Anglicans made up a decided majority of the city's population (and probably of working-class Hamilton). The hold of the more evangelical churches had declined since the turn of the century.[69]

Working people from many parts of the city were certainly among those slipping into church pews on Sunday mornings (and at other times of the week). They made up a significant minority in several of the large downtown Protestant congregations with socially mixed memberships, though less so in such grand churches as Central Presbyterian or Christ Church Cathedral, where most of the industrial, commercial, and professional elite of the city gathered.[70] In several other congregations, workers predominated. In the 1880s a local "citadel" of the Salvation Army had emerged as a new voice of working-class evangelical Protestantism with its own distinctive forms of worship. In 1892, moreover, a substantial dissident group in Hamilton, headed by the charismatic P.W. Philpott, broke away from the Army over issues of democracy and equity and created the Christian Workers' Church, which eventually opened the Gospel Tabernacle as a flourishing rallying point for working-class premillennial evangelicalism.[71]

The mainstream churches also had congregations made up overwhelmingly of workers. Notable among these were the "mission" churches in solidly working-class neighbourhoods, within easy walking distance of workers' homes. Sponsored by older, bourgeois congregations, these efforts had begun in the late 19th century in the north end and then, after the turn of the century, extended into the muddy new suburbs pushing eastward into the new factory district. The first meeting places in the east end were usually minimal – in some cases, large tents or an old park pavilion – but solid, if modest, church buildings soon appeared, often as the result of plenty of volunteer labour from the congregations.[72]

These new congregations soon shed the blanket of upper-class paternalism and flexed their independence as thoroughly working-class institutions with a distinct proletarian flavour.[73] Along with fraternal lodges, ethnic societies, and unions, they became important examples of collective, worker-controlled, voluntary organizing in their own communities, with links to larger networks beyond the neighbourhood and the city. In these churches workers made up a clear majority of the local governing committees, choirs, Bible classes, and affiliated groups for women, men, and children. Skilled workingmen provided slightly more of the leadership than did semi-skilled and unskilled members, but in the early 20th century that gap narrowed (no doubt a reflection of a narrowing range within the local workforce). Even the handful of self-employed men who took on leadership roles in congregations were usually no more exalted than local grocers, butchers, and other shopkeepers.[74] Children would no doubt recognize familiar people from their own neighbourhood climbing the steps of the local church each week. Recent immigrants might hear familiar dialects among the fellow parishioners who made the churches an important part of their community-building in the city – whether the Irish at St. Lawrence, the Italians at St. Anthony's, the Poles at St. Stanislas, the English at St. Luke's Anglican or Barton St. Methodist, or the Scots at St. David's Presbyterian. The African Methodist Episcopal Church was particularly important for the city's black workers.[75]

Despite their energetic fundraising projects, women had no role in the churches' main decision-making. A young girl must have noticed, as she glanced around on a Sunday morning, that the pews held more females than males. She might have sensed that, for women like her mother, churchgoing offered a rare opportunity not only to get out of the house and socialize in a respectable setting, but also to express the deep piety that working-class women often relied on for comfort, reassurance, and hope for themselves and their families. Her older brothers, like other young bachelors, were seldom there. Although more married than single men tended to go to church, fathers attended less often than the mothers and unmarried daughters, or simply sent their wives alone. In contrast to the practices of many men in the small local Jewish community, husbands in many Catholic and Protestant families usually let their wives take responsibility for the spiritual well-being of the family and often limited their participation to Christmas, Easter, or other special celebrations, which in the European immigrant communities included the festivals of patrons saints, such as the *festa* of the Madonna del Monte. Women might also see their church attendance as a kind of mutual insurance, because the visitations and small handouts that the women gave each other could help to pull their families through illness or financial crises. Churchgoing, children would learn, was a particularly female experience and responsibility.[76]

To enter a church on a Sunday morning was to rediscover a unique space in the neighbourhood. Although less awe-inspiring than the majestic downtown church buildings, the relatively simple architecture of the working-class churches – a reflection of the modest incomes of the worshippers – was certainly grander than most anything else on nearby streets, and almost always included a large meeting hall built alongside for Sunday school and popular weeknight religious, social, and recreational programs.[77] Taking her seat in the hushed, reverent calm of the assembled crowd on a Sunday, a little girl must have been impressed with the theatrical qualities of the place and its furnishings, especially in the more elaborately decorated Catholic and Anglican churches, with their particular combinations of statues, stain glass, painted murals, ornate altars, and flickering candle light,[78] but even in the more spartan Protestant meeting places, where women like her mother in the Ladies' Aid might have contributed warm touches such as flowers or a fancy cloth for the Communion table. A modest organ bathed the scene in soft music. The clergyman appeared in the high pulpit in some kind of flowing robe and led the congregation through various dramatically powerful rituals, which, from time to time, included Communion, baptisms, or, in some churches, confirmation ceremonies. Choirs and soloists, perhaps also in robes, added sonorous depth to the performance.

Most churchgoers would doubtless have been caught up in the emotional intensity of the weekly services because, as elsewhere, Hamilton's proletarian worshippers typically gravitated either to the elaborate ritualism of high-church Anglican and Catholic practices or to the evangelical Protestant "old-time religion" of plain-spoken, fire-and-brimstone preaching, fervent praying, and lusty collective singing, rather than to the more restrained, more intellectually inclined practices of middle- and upper-class Protestant churches (including the local voices of the Social Gospel). The messages delivered were different: unlike the less individualist thrust of the High Anglican and Catholic sermons, the revivalist message promised the equality of all souls and the power of self-renewal through conversion and faith.[79]

Many children growing up in working-class Hamilton, then, would have expected to

The Barton St. Methodist Church used this preaching wagon for outdoor revival meetings. (HPL)

head off on Sunday mornings (or evenings, since there were sometimes three services a day) in their best clothes, hand in hand with their mothers and sometimes their fathers, to experience the weekly renewal of their faith and to make a public statement about the family's respectability.[80] Still, many would not. It is impossible to determine what percentage of working people were churchgoers in the early 20th century, but, throughout the city, just as in so many other industrial centres, clergymen agonized repeatedly about the relatively small numbers of working-class worshippers who settled into the pews of their churches. Regular churchgoing was most likely a minority experience. Out of 1,162 people who declared themselves as Anglicans within the north end's St. Luke's parish in 1901, for example, the "communicants" (those able to take Communion) totalled no more than 200, a mere 17 per cent, along with 225 in its Sunday school.[81] This example reflects the broad pattern of Anglicanism in the city because each year over the next three decades local parishes reported to their headquarters "church populations" vastly larger than their "actual communicants." Methodists too, despite their sterner expectations of regular attendance, reported membership numbers well below their totals in the federal census. Italian Catholic parishioners had similarly weak attendance patterns.[82]

There were certainly strong deterrents. Dressing a family for the occasion could be costly when family budgets were tight, and regular contributions to the upkeep of a church could be beyond the means of many economically strapped families, or at least less attractive than other spending possibilities.[83] Yet when workingmen explained their non-attendance, they focused more on how unwelcome they felt within institutions seemingly attuned to the wealthy and powerful. One north-end lad (who later became a clergyman) remembered showing up at the elitist Centenary Methodist in his best suit, only to be sent dismissively to the back gallery by an usher wearing kid gloves and carrying a silk hat.[84] Workingmen also resented the indifference of the churches and their clergy towards such basic labour issues as higher wages, shorter hours, and union rights. More politically independent, radical, and unionized men in particular tore shreds off the preachers of "Churchianity." Some, like the ILP's Studholme, dropped in on the Sunday-evening services of the city's few pro-labour clergymen, especially W.E. Gilroy at First Congregational and Banks Nelson at Knox Presbyterian. Many more apparently stayed away. By the 1930s they had the option of listening to church services on the radio.[85]

Children might sense their parents' spirituality nonetheless. Without ever taking them near a church, the parents might regularly invoke the Ten Commandments or other Biblical parables as lessons for life. In many families the spiritual mingled with the magical to create currents of popular religious belief that worried about inescapably cruel fate and divine intervention and, in the case of Italian, Armenian, and other

Like these Roma- nians, most Hamilton workers turned to their churches for major rituals of life, including funerals. (AO, I0050076)

immigrant families, encouraged the wearing of charms to ward off the "evil eye." In most Catholic households, a simple crucifix or other religious image hung on the wall, and in the homes of European newcomers, women often maintained small shrines with lighted candles. Daily devotions might be more important than weekly treks to mass.[86] The children in a family might also hear their fathers, like other men in the local labour movement, remind them that Jesus was a humble carpenter who identified with the poor and downtrodden, and that his message of love and brotherhood was a powerful thread in workers' struggles for social justice.[87] Or they might hear about the revival meetings held from time to time on a Sunday evening or outside factory gates at lunchtime during the week, at which many men like their fathers experienced a deeply moving renewal of their faith (though seldom changing their churchgoing patterns). Like the Presbyterians' north-end City Mission (later St. David's), Barton St. Methodist even kept a decorated wagon and portable organ for that kind of open-air, revivalist preaching in the east

end. Other congregations borrowed the wagon from time to time.[88]

Even those who did not attend weekly religious services regularly or observe any religious rituals in the home had their marriages consecrated, their deceased blessed, and their children baptized by clergymen, either at church or in their homes.[89] Many working-class parents also seemed to believe that their young offspring needed a good grounding in Christian morality and sent them off to the care of mostly female Sunday-school teachers in all the Protestant churches or the priest in a Catholic church. Thousands of children trooped into the city's Sunday-school halls each year, even in working-class neighbourhoods.[90] Indeed, the new spinoff mission churches in those areas often prioritized Sunday schools in their recruitment and building programs.[91] By the late 1930s a survey of elementary-school students aged eight to fourteen in two north-end wards revealed that nearly nine out ten went to Sunday school or church. Clearly, whether their parents saw this as convenient day care on a Sunday morning or an important spiritual indoctrination for youngsters, a large number of working-class children in many parts of the city passed through the moral training grounds of the Sunday-school classroom and absorbed elemental notions of the wages of sin and the beauty of universal love. The Sunday-school curriculum of the early 20th century put increasing emphasis on personal morality – kindness, honesty, purity, and fairness – as well as spirituality.[92]

Saintly Repose

Whether or not some or all family members went to church on Sunday, many hours of the day were left over for other activities. Sunday was a primary battleground over how to spend leisure time in a sober, religiously sanctioned fashion. Forces of moral authority, centred in the city's churches and backed by law, struggled to curb various expressions of popular culture and recreation, particularly as they appeared in working-class Hamilton.

The family's midday meal, perhaps featuring a big roast in Anglo-Celtic households, was most often an important weekly event,[93] but after that what? The range of possibilities was much smaller than on most weekdays, thanks to decades of agitation by evangelical Protestants, who believed that all labour and commercial transactions should cease and that the day should be enjoyed sedately at home in reading the Bible and other religious literature, praying, and quietly reflecting. The goal was well-disciplined "rest," not self-indulgent "idleness" or sensuous "pleasure," a message drilled into the children who had attended Sunday school that morning.[94]

Sabbatarians had been part of a widening cultural juggernaut that aimed at criminalizing the public activities of the street and forcing social life into the narrow confines of the private family household. They had been responsible for the first provincial Lord's Day Act back in 1845 (a parallel move to the first mid-century efforts to ban alcohol consumption through legislation). They had also relentlessly pressured the local police to get the Act enforced,[95] and had generally succeeded in curtailing most public activities on Sunday, particularly commercial amusements. The widespread assumption that this day of rest should be a quiet time prompted at least some of the city's working-class parents to forbid their children from playing outside on Sundays. "In those days if your parents were like mine," an elderly man recalled of his boyhood in the north end in the 1930s, "you were supposed to dress up and sit like an idiot." By that point, if so inclined, such children could at least listen to the radio's musical programs. Some families, notably in the Italian community, spent a few hours on the front porch with kin, perhaps watching a *bocce* game in the yard.[96]

Cracks had appeared in this moralistic facade at the close of the 19th century. Many forms of public transportation continued to operate, especially railways, steamboats, and, most controversially, streetcars.[97] Workers in Hamilton (as elsewhere) took advantage of the trolleys and boats to get out of their small houses on Sundays and enjoy outdoor recreational pleasures on the edges of the city. In the warmer months, mothers might occasionally bundle up a lunch for a picnic in a city park or for a trip down to the waterfront on the bay or out to the cooler breezes of the beach. Some working-class families might have been able to afford the occasional longer day-excursions on a train or steamboat, but the fares would have been prohibitive for most. As one man recalled, "It was a special treat if we went."[98]

Presbyterian and Methodist clergymen watched these developments with horror, worried that the looser "American" or (worse

Despite the Lord's Day Act, steamers continued to run on Sundays. (HPL)

yet) wide-open "Continental" Sunday would take hold. At Hamilton's Erskine Presbyterian Church, John G. Shearer, a key figure in the Ontario branch of the Lord's Day Alliance and after 1900 the Alliance's national secretary, saw Sunday cars as the "forerunner of a great deal of Sunday business, Sunday concerts, spectacular exhibitions and desecration by open pleasuring." The local Woman's Christian Temperance Union deplored "the decided increase of Sunday traffic in our city, especially to the Beach and Grimsby Park." Anglicans and Catholics generally saw less to complain about. Indeed, according to the Catholic *Register*, "limited car service" might actually improve Sunday morality: "There is more tendency to drink and immorality when people are crowded together in miserable rooms in cities than when breathing the fresh air of suburban districts."[99] The evangelical clergy, spearheaded by the Presbyterians, nonetheless soldiered on in their interdenominational Sabbatarian alliance. In 1895 they convinced the provincial government to take the Hamilton Street Railway to court for violating the Lord's Day Act, but eight years later, in a landmark decision, the Judicial Committee of the Privy Council threw out the case on the grounds that the provinces had invaded federal jurisdiction by trying to curb this form of "criminal" behaviour. Undaunted, the national Lord's Day Alliance cobbled together a fragile new coalition, including the Trades and Labor Congress of Canada, around the common goal of a day's rest,[100] and in 1906 managed to convince Sir Wilfrid Laurier to introduce a new Lord's Day Act. After lengthy, bitter debate and a stream of compromising amendments, it came into force on 1 March 1907.[101]

The Act changed little in the existing pattern of working-class Sunday pleasures. Some men would still have to head off to work as usual, thanks to the exemptions for companies with continuous operations like the Hamilton Steel and Iron Company, and young women

The Family Circle **325**

In the interwar period buses provided intercity transportation for outings. (CTA, Fonds 16, Series 71, Item 6146)

working as servants got no help from the legis-lation.[102] Recreational activities that required an entrance fee – concerts, sports, vaudeville shows, movies, amusement parks – had to shut down for the day, but few of these had been operating on Sundays in any case. The Hamil-ton branch of the Lord's Day Alliance (like other branches) continued to act as a vigilante force, with members roaming the city on Sundays to find any Sabbath violators. They pushed the police to stop sales of Sunday newspapers, ice cream, and tobacco with some well-publicized convictions, and late in 1907 turned on movie-house operators. The nativist streak in Alliance propaganda shone through, as many of those charged were "foreigners" – a Jewish newspaper agent, several Greek ice-cream vendors, and Chi-nese gamblers, for example. Heavy coercion was generally unnecessary because most small shop-keepers seemed ready to conform.[103] A Rational Sunday League began agitating for access to tasteful musical concerts and cultural facilities, but, despite support from the *Herald*, made no headway. Even the local libraries, the museum in Dundurn Park, and children's playgrounds remained closed.[104] What did eventually revive were the steamer excursions. When an Irish family moved into Hamilton's north end in 1912, they found "absolute bedlam" among the

Sunday crowds boarding streetcars heading for the ferry docks, where it seemed "half of Ham-ilton" was jostling for space on the steamers. In the interwar period the steamer and radial-car excursions gave way to bus trips or car rides, where affordable.[105]

Sundays, then, had only limited offerings for family fun. An angry letter to the press in 1911 must have caught the resentments of many in working-class Hamilton. The writer noted the absurdity of fining someone for "purchasing a dish of ice cream on a hot Sunday." Why could a man "hire a rig, which entails labor on the livery stable employee," he asked, but not "handle a fishing rod"? He thought "listening on a Sunday to a good band in Dundurn park, discoursing sacred music, would do more good than sitting in a hot church listening to some of the talk that, if one does go, one has to listen to." He called for "more in the spirit of brotherly kindness, espe-cially to thousands of men and women who are engaged in work six days a week."[106]

The war compelled some loosening of the tight constraints. After all, fighting did not stop on Sundays, nor did munitions production in many cases. Recruiting rallies, sometimes with movies, often took place on Sunday night, and benefit concerts raised funds for the Canadian Patriotic Fund. Sabbatarians were on the defen-sive, but they had little cause for concern be-cause the lid was tightened down again after the war. In 1919 Water Rollo called on the Independ-ent Labor Party to protest a city property com-mittee resolution banning the sale of ice cream on Sundays. "Goodness knows, that's about the only pleasure a workingman has on Sundays," he argued (without success). Throughout the interwar period, commercial amusements, notably sports and theatres, still had to close, and a shopkeeper could still be fined for selling tobacco, camera film, or candy on Sundays. For

Many working-class children went to Sunday school and had the chance to enjoy picnics like this one organized by the Barton St. Baptist Church in 1919. (HPL)

most families, getting out of the house on Sundays continued to mean picnic excursions.[107]

Sunday in Hamilton, then, was a weekly reminder of how families should order their leisure time, of what was appropriate and beyond the pale. As a day of strictly regimented behaviour, it became a moral bastion from which broader assaults on popular culture and recreation could be launched, with highly variable success.

Going Out

If Sundays were constrained, small wonder that working-class Hamilton looked forward to the other moments on the calendar when most waged labour stopped and family outings became possible: Saturday afternoons and public holidays. Those were the times on which they sometimes ventured out to occupy more public space in the city and experience a widening range of cultural options.

After decades of six-day, 60-hour workweeks, a Saturday afternoon off work was a new departure for wage-earners. Unions had been demanding it since 1872, and after the turn of the century

employers gradually conceded it. In 1910 all the leading manufacturers (except the large cotton companies and the Steel Company) claimed to be working their staffs only five hours on Saturday. Many men (and women) certainly continued to work right through that day, but a new weekly block of "free" time was opening up for growing numbers of wage-earners. Many weeks men no doubt used the time for such routine domestic work as gardening or household maintenance. Some no doubt unwound in a barroom. All spectator sports invariably had well-attended Saturday-afternoon games, which suggests that many men, married and unmarried, also spent time in the stands cheering on their favourite athletes rather than staying home with their families. Yet the local poet Richard Kernighan undoubtedly conveyed many family members' high expectations for a "Sweet Saturday Afternoon," when, occasionally at least, all of them left their houses together.[108]

Everyone also looked forward to the four great one-day holidays in the warmer seasons: Victoria Day in May, Dominion Day in July, the

Hamilton's beach on Lake Ontario drew many families. (HPL)

generic Civic Holiday in August, and Labour Day, the new early-September holiday enacted by Parliament in 1894.[109] Some European immigrant communities, too, often also had their ethno-religious festivals. Since few wage-earners in Hamilton (or anywhere else in Canada) got paid vacations before World War Two,[110] these special holidays became their only brief moments for less inhibited pleasure. They were times in which the family circle might extend out into the city.[111]

Craft unionists had led the fight for such public pleasure, setting a tone of entitlement and respectability in the working-class celebration of Saturday afternoon and public holidays.[112] On these occasions a working-class mother sometimes packed up a picnic lunch and marshalled the family to leave the house for an outing.[113] Expectations could run high as everyone looked forward to happy, liminal, hopefully memorable experiences outside the rhythms and stresses of factory, household, and school, which could continue to circulate in family storytelling (or photo albums) long afterward.[114]

Families might carry their picnic baskets into larger excursions – often numbering hundreds of participants – sponsored by employers, churches, fraternal societies, unions, ethnic organizations, and political parties, among other groups. On such outings family members often burned off energy in vigorous games and contests and boisterous sociability. A child might compete for prizes in special races for girls or boys. Married women, fat men, and other groups had their own races. People could play in or watch informal baseball, lacrosse, or soccer matches between teams of picnickers. Sponsors of these events hoped to harness family aspirations for recreation with other institutional loyalties.[115]

Labour picnics had a long history in working-class Hamilton, and since the mid-1880s local labour leaders (like their counterparts across the continent) had struggled to create a specific annual workers' holiday that combined the usual pleasures of a public holiday with a celebration of labour's strength and accomplishments. By the time the federal government finally legalized Labour Day, the city's craftworkers had established a more-or-less annual pattern of local programming to hold public attention on "labour's day," with street parades, speeches, and recreational activities in a park afterward. After 1906, however, the waning power of unions in Hamilton was reflected in the Trades and Labor Council's decision to limit organized Labour Day events to picnics, games, races, raffles, and baby shows in a city park. The parade was not revived before World War Two.[116] Public ceremonies of any kind became less common on all summertime holidays as families generally voted with their feet for more privatized recreation. The general weakness of the local labour movement over so much of the first four decades of the 20th century meant that family outings merged into many different loyalties and associational patterns, not all of them explicitly working-class.[117]

Space for all this recreation became an issue. Holidayers tended to head for city parks, private parks that charged admission, the large city cemetery, or the nearby countryside,[118] but by World War One green play space was disappearing. In

Families were encouraged to join outings organized by unions, churches, fraternal societies, and companies, such as this one held for Dofasco workers. (SLS, LS743)

part this problem reflected the city's remarkably fast expansion, as new factories and residential suburbs gobbled up huge tracts of land and filled in the waterfront for industrial uses.[119] By the war much of the shoreline of the most important play space in the area, Burlington Bay (later renamed Hamilton Harbour), was monopolized by private industry and also seriously polluted with industrial waste from factories and effluent from the many new sewer connections. After 1920 the water in many parts of the bay was not safe for swimming (even ice-cutting in the winter had to be stopped).[120] Yet inadequate recreational space also resulted from contentious political disputes over land use. In particular, working people tended to find the city government slow to put resources into public parks that fit their needs.

Before the 1890s the city had set aside little space for public parks.[121] Only in 1899 did it take a major leap into green-space development with the purchase of a 40-acre, privately run site in the west end, Dundurn Park, described as "the only pleasure grounds within the city limits."[122] Other land was gradually set aside, but often lay undeveloped for years. North-end residents in particular regularly complained about the neglect of their waterfront park site (eventually known as Eastwood), which was little more than a landfill dump in the early part of the century.[123] The burgeoning east end was also comparatively neglected until 1917, when the first of two new parks finally opened (Gage and Scott, together totalling only 85 acres).[124]

The waterfront became another striking instance of indifference to working-class leisure. At Hamilton Beach on the far side of the bay, affluent citizens had been allowed to monopolize much of the land at the close of the 19th century, building gracious summer residences and a large clubhouse for their exclusive Royal Hamilton Yacht Club, in what the *Spectator* referred to as "a little aristocratic village all by themselves."

Hamilton's public parks, such as Gore Park, pictured here, were organized to ensure quiet, genteel behaviour.

(HPL, Bailey Collection)

They dug in their heels against the development of a more extensive public beach and swimming facilities. The appointed commission that governed the beach (as an alternative to direct control by Hamilton's city council) resisted the creation of a public park until 1909. Eventually the city also opened Lansdowne Park on the immediate waterfront in 1916 and four years later Wabasso Park (renamed La Salle in 1926) on the north side of the bay. Wabasso became a waterfront destination for working-class families who could afford the steamer fare. The pollution of the bay quickly made these spots less attractive, and by 1922 the city's medical officer of health, James Roberts, had proclaimed that Lansdowne's waterfront was "not fit for animals to bathe in."[125]

Green spaces were controversial for other reasons as well. The civic officials who presided over the slow park development initially had a particular notion of how the designated areas should be used. Upper-class families expected to be able to appreciate nature from the safety and comfort of carriages or, later, automobiles as they drove through the parks, and got park authorities to maintain roads and paths for their use. For other residents, in the words of the *Times*, parks were "breathing and resting places." The experience was intended to restrain and discipline visitors' bodies. All expressive, playful behaviour had to be controlled, preferably by parents and if necessary by police. In the Gore, working people had to accustom themselves to promenading properly along straight, formal paths and sitting primly on benches to contemplate the ornamental gardens and elegant fountain in the shadow of imposing statues of Sir John A. Macdonald and Queen Victoria (and, after 1923, a cenotaph to the war dead). One speaker at a Trades and Labor Council meeting grumbled bitterly about the "Keep Off the Grass Signs." The iron fencing around the park was locked from 8 p.m. to 7 a.m.[126]

Large parts of Dundurn Park fit that pattern when it opened in 1900. The liquor permit allowing beer at baseball games was scrapped. Organizations booking space for special events were restricted to strictly designated spots, and a bell even sounded to announce closing time. Within two weeks after the park's opening, two boys were in police court for "misbehaving themselves and going where they had no right to be." The parks board regularly sponsored band concerts to add to the genteel tone, but denied many other groups use of the space. A small museum and zoo were intended to be wholesome, educational recreation for the masses. In a similar vein, after its opening in 1919, Gage Park became a horticultural showcase with an indoor conservatory rather than a recreational site. At the Beach, the park that opened after 1909 had a wooden promenade for strolling and small pagodas for sedate contemplation of the water, but no picnic or athletic grounds, refreshment stands, or commercial amusements. For those who ventured into the water anywhere around the city, a by-law required that the body be covered from neck to knee joints with a woolen or cotton bathing suit.[127]

The small amusement parks in the Hamilton area, such as this one at Wabasso Park, drew some families with a little money to spend on cheap fun, but many workers could not afford such an outing. (HPL)

Although, at the turn of the century, the parks board arranged for "swimming baths" on the north-end waterfront and some outdoor skating rinks in the coldest winter months, few parks had sports fields. In a symbolic act, the parks board decided in March 1900 that the existing fenced-in baseball diamond in Dundurn Park was "not immediately required for Park purposes" and leased it back to the former private operator.[128] This move would not have bothered wealthy men, who had facilities for their preferred amateur sports in private clubs devoted to cricket, golf, tennis, or sailing, but workingmen wanted space to play baseball, soccer, and other games and to watch sporting events, often professional or semi-professional.[129] Before World War One many of those spectator sports took place in the privately owned Britannia Park, which was sold for a housing development during the war.[130]

By 1920, when a by-law for better park funding was on the municipal ballot, the working-class preference was clear to the editor of a city labour newspaper: "The citizens of East Hamilton have been clamoring for many years for decent sporting grounds, where soccer matches, baseball and other games could be played under conditions that would be attractive alike to spectator and player." Over the next decade athletic facilities were finally developed more extensively in Scott, Eastwood, and Victoria parks. In contrast, safe, affordable swimming facilities for working-class families were shrinking by the 1920s, as the immediate bay-front spots were closed off and the cross-the-bay options required expensive transportation by boat. In 1924 the parks board chairman admitted, "It is a shame that a city located as Hamilton is has no park except Wabasso with water adjoining. Victoria is the only park with a wading pool, and with the exception of the Gore, not a single park which can boast even a fountain."[131]

Pay for Play

Free recreation space, then, fell far short of working-class families' needs, and what existed might well have inhibited exuberant fun on their outings. Small wonder that wherever they rambled in a holiday mood, they regularly turned to new commercial spaces. For families socializing together, what was important about these

THEY'RE OFF TO THE GREAT BARNUM AND BAILEY CIRCUS

Travelling circuses were always popular. (*HH*, 18 June 1913, 13)

sites of commercial pleasure was that the possibilities stood apart from the well-established venues of public male sporting culture – saloons, poolrooms, race tracks, and boxing rings, for instance. Local entrepreneurs and capitalists with much more wide-ranging business empires – "showmen," in the apt phrase of one scholar[132] – were packaging colourful attractions to delight both sexes and all ages.

At the turn of the century, businesses still shut down and thousands of people lined the sidewalks to watch the arrival of the large, exotic circus companies or "Wild West" shows that paraded into the city each summer and pitched their tents for one or two days on the east-end field set aside for them. Entering this contained space, visitors found multidimensional performances that combined animals, acrobats, clowns, strongmen, freaks, and sundry other novelties into a world of fantasy and wonder far different from what the public parks board offered.[133]

The impact of these travelling shows steadily diminished, however, as other, more permanent commercial diversions appeared in and around the city, particularly amusement parks. The inspiration for this brand-new form of cheap urban entertainment was the complex of attractions on Coney Island in New York, particularly the world-famous Luna Park, which brought together fantasy and fun in the form of Ferris wheels, roller coasters, and other thrilling mechanized rides that subjected the body to dizzying turns and jolts, along with various games, vaudeville shows, band concerts, and unusual sensory experiences, like funhouses, in a storybook ambience of anti-modern "Orientalism." The loud, exuberant, colourful atmosphere of these spaces encouraged visitors to shed their inhibitions and share a collective carnival-like spirit of emotional release and revelry within a highly structured and standardized form of play – a truly urban, industrial-capitalist creation. Hamilton workers, it seems, got only a pale copy of that experience in the small amusement parks out at the end of local radial lines – the Beach, the Mountain, Wabasso Park, and Grimsby – where facilities were limited. The only attempt to open something more ambitious, the heavily promoted Maple Leaf Park in the east end, died after only one season in 1909.[134]

Perhaps the limited pocketbooks of the city's working-class families undermined any initiative on the scale of Toronto's Canadian National Exhibition or the Calgary Stampede. Yet the small amusement parks were cheap enough that, on special occasions, children might feel they could beg for the pennies for a ride on a merry-go-round or Ferris wheel or for a cheap treat from a refreshment stand. For most working-class families, though, such special occasions would be rare.[135]

Sometimes in the cooler seasons, if the funds were available, a family outing in working-class Hamilton might include a visit to a local theatre, but seldom before about 1907.[136] Up to that point theatrical offerings were either too expensive for most workers or geared almost exclusively to male audiences. By the close of the 19th century theatres across North America had divided into distinctive "high" and "low" cultural forms. Upper-class audiences had gravitated away from the more popular venues to lavish theatrical spaces that charged higher admission prices and offered more "refined" performances and more restrained audiences.[137] The opening of the beautifully furnished Grand Opera House in 1880 fit that pattern. With nearly 1,200 seats, it was the city's main home of "legitimate" theatre in which amateur performers and travelling companies of professionals staged numerous plays and musicals each season. Admission prices that started at 50 cents seldom fell within the reach of working-class spectators, though occasionally a seat on the hard wooden benches in the gallery could go for as little as 15 to 25 cents. A separate entrance to this level kept the riff-raff from disturbing the bourgeois theatregoers in the plush velvet seats below.[138]

By the turn of the century more affordable forms of popular theatre had also taken hold. One version was the minstrel show, which Hamilton audiences had been enjoying since well back in the 19th century. Another was the dime museum, which offered small displays of scientific oddities and other unusual sights, along with variety shows of regularly changing novelty acts.[139] The larger downtown Star Theatre caught the most public attention. Originally opened as the People's Theatre and rechristened in 1892, it was a 900-seat, exclusively male enclave that featured a small band out on the street to attract patrons. It had a reputation for earthy, off-colour music and comedy on stage. It often highlighted burlesque acts featuring scantily clad women in titillating poses. Performers on the Star's stage reached out across heavy clouds of tobacco smoke to particularly rowdy audiences, especially the young men and boys in the ten-cent gallery seats.[140]

The variety shows in such theatres borrowed heavily from the carnivalesque traditions of

At the turn of the century the Star Theatre sent its house band outside to drum up customers for its earthy vaudeville shows. Typically only men and boys filled the seats. (HPL)

The large new Savoy Theatre replaced the Star and offered vaudeville programs to attract women and children as well as men. The upper balcony, often called "the gods," still nonetheless attracted noisy young men and boys. (HPL)

circuses, minstrel shows, dime museums, and concert saloons (no longer legal under Ontario law). By the turn of the century they were increasingly integrated into "circuits" controlled by powerful US booking agencies. Hamilton audiences thus got to see comedians, singers, musicians, dancers, jugglers, contortionists, acrobats, magicians, trained animals, and more, performing non-stop all day long in constantly changing 15-to-20-minute acts. Among these entertainers were a growing number of "stars" whose reputations spanned the continent and whose photographs began appearing in the local newspapers alongside glowing commentary. By the 1890s this new form of theatre had

The elegant new Loew's Theatre, opened in 1918, offered vaudeville and movies, but at higher prices than did local neighbourhood theatres. (HPL)

been labelled "vaudeville," and by the first decade of the new century it was rapidly becoming big business.[141]

To expand the potential audience, the trend in the North American vaudeville business was to tame the rougher elements and to present packaged performances that were more acceptable to middle-class audiences and to women and children.[142] In 1902 a new manager began to reorient the Star's programming to "Polite Vaudeville," and in 1906 he convinced the owners to tear down the building and put up in its place the elegant, 1,500-seat Savoy Theatre. He promised "strictly first-class family vaudeville theatre, catering for the patronage of men, women and children who enjoy bright, clever, wholesome entertainment."[143] Less than a year later the large US-based Keith chain launched what the local press called a "vaudeville war" by building Bennett's Theatre (renamed the Temple in 1910), with seating for over 1,600. It too promised "high-class" vaudeville.[144] More large downtown theatres opened – the Lyric and Griffin's in 1913, the lavish 2,900-seat Loew's in

1918 (which featured a ten-piece orchestra and a huge organ), and the sumptuous 3,500-seat Pantages in 1921, all part of large North American theatre chains.[145]

Vaudeville was certainly popular. According to a *Herald* writer who had examined the theatre managers' books, 200,000 people visited the Savoy and 150,000 packed into Bennett's in the last four months of 1907.[146] Obviously many people went back more than once because those figures amounted to two or three times the city's population. How many of those spectators were working people is difficult to determine. "Bigtime" vaudeville in the large theatres never tried to democratize its seating. Just as in legitimate theatre, working people would rarely be found in the high-priced boxes or orchestra seats in the Savoy, Temple, or Lyric, which before the war usually cost 75 and 50 cents each and attracted the new middle-class patrons.[147] Indeed, a 1918 manual on theatre management urged that "persons of questionable repute" should not be seated next to "those of high social standing" and that "individuals who are likely to smell 'garlicky' or be poorly dressed were to be particularly discouraged."[148] Workers climbed up to the 10-cent seats in the gallery or upper balcony. So the same show in the same hall might be seen by significantly different audiences. Across North America pre-war surveys of vaudeville audiences concluded that white-collar workers were the most common new patrons. Men still predominated (though less so than in the past), and few poor workers ever attended.[149] It seems likely that in Hamilton only small numbers of better-off working-class families (or single men and their female companions) could afford an outing to the large downtown theatres. In 1912, in the face of Protestant ministers' agitation against a new theatre's licence application, the Hamilton Trades and Labor Council loudly decried the "lack of popular priced wholesome theatrical amusement in the city to meet the demand of wage earners and their families."[150]

Well before that point, vaudeville acts were facing a new challenger: motion pictures. As in other parts of the Western world, movies had arrived in Hamilton in 1896 as crowd-pleasing novelties, each lasting only a few minutes. The films were technically and artistically unsophisticated, and silent, though usually accompanied by live music and perhaps a lecturer to provide commentary.[151] Vaudeville houses were soon including them as light closing numbers for their shows.[152] Hamilton residents with a few cents to spare could also watch programs of movies alone in short-run special exhibitions. The first major US producers, especially Vitograph, regularly booked Association Hall for a program of films documenting great events like Queen Victoria's Diamond Jubilee of 1897, episodes of the South African War and other military manoeuvres, and even major prize fights, as well as travelogues, "trick" films, sensational or comic scenes from daily life, and titillating glimpses of

women. By 1905 the films were more often short narrative dramas, adventures, and comedies, many of them merely vaudeville acts on film – all for as little as 10 cents for the cheapest seats.[153] In 1907 a major shift occurred in the Hamilton theatre world when at least six small store-front movie parlours, known elsewhere as "nickelodeons," opened in the downtown area and, for only 5 cents, allowed visitors to watch short films in individual viewing machines or on small screens.[154] At half the price of even the cheapest theatre seats, these places quickly became sites of working-class play.[155]

The sea-change in popular amusement that the movies brought became more evident as the nickelodeons and other small-scale exhibitors gradually shifted to more conventional theatre seating with a screen and some modest elegance in decor. Some of these small movie houses were in the downtown area, within easy reach of the north end, and after 1910 east-end working-class neighbourhoods were served by several more.[156] The pricing policies for admission created distinct ranks of movie theatres that evolved into so-called "first-run" houses downtown, charging at least 25 cents for evening shows (and higher prices for balcony and box seats), and "second-run" neighbourhood theatres charging 10 or 15 cents for all seats.[157]

Patrons could enjoy a full evening's entertainment with a continuous program of the latest films, which changed several times a week. "Come when you like and stay as long as you like," was one theatre's slogan. Along with a pianist, a singer (usually local talent) was often hired to perform "illustrated songs" and to lead sing-alongs between films. In the following decade audiences began seeing not only the usual series of short items, but also full-length multi-reel features that told a fictional story, with familiar subject matter drawn from melodrama, vaudeville, dime novels, and, above all, comedy. These places often added live vaudeville acts to make a kind of hybrid theatre, though movies remained the main attraction on the bill.[158]

A full-scale alternative form of theatrical entertainment had thus sprung up alongside the large downtown vaudeville houses, and its popularity mushroomed.[159] By the 1920s "big-time" vaudeville had survived but was in retreat, even in the huge new "palaces," whose flashy newspaper advertising gave bigger billing to their feature films.[160] "Talkies" were the final death knell, and by the 1930s movies had completely triumphed over live performances. In that process the highly centralized, US-dominated motion-picture industry had packaged its movies to be seen in the elegance of the old vaudeville houses.[161]

Theatregoing had thus become a new experience in Hamilton. In a sense, the new high-class vaudeville and then the first-run movie houses had reunited the socially divided theatre of the late 19th century, when bourgeois elites and proletarian men had gone their separate ways; now classes, genders, and ethnic groups were reunited. To pull off this cultural coup, theatre owners had created new spaces to vie with other grand civic architecture and undertaken to impose on both performers and audiences the standards of restraint and bourgeois decorum of the upper-class theatre. The opening of the Savoy and Bennett's in 1907 had tongues wagging in Hamilton about the new respectability of vaudeville.[162] Patrons entered ornately decorated spaces with marble foyers, tasteful sculpture and murals, gleaming brass railings, and plush seats and draperies. Uniformed ushers guided them to their seats. In 1912 the Lyric offered a special "ladies' retiring room" and a "nursery for infants in arms with a trained governess in attendance."[163]

Performances were guaranteed to be "kept free from anything tinged with coarseness," so that women, children, and whole families could attend without encountering any threats to prevailing standards of decency. Encouraging the presence of women was supposed to guarantee a higher tone and a distinct curb on the excesses of homosocial theatre behaviour.[164] New rules on program content helped too. "Every performance will be strictly censored before being presented," the Bennett Theatre's management insisted, "and only a clean entertainment of an instructive and educative order will be permitted." The US-based Keith company, which owned Griffith's and, through the United Booking Office, controlled the flow of acts into virtually all big-time North American vaudeville theatres, warned performers to avoid "all vulgarity and suggestiveness in words, action and costume" and to cut out "all vulgar, double-meaning and profane words and songs." Performers could be fired for using such words as "liar, slob, son-of-a-gun, devil, sucker, damn and all other words unfit for the ears of ladies and children" or for referring to "questionable streets, resorts, localities, and bar-rooms." Theatre managers had to submit regular reports on particular acts, which could get any rebels blacklisted. Small wonder that the Keith vaudeville empire was nicknamed "the Sunday School Circuit." In a similar vein, after the war, the manager of the new Hamilton branch of Loew's theatre chain posted notices behind stage against "vulgarity and indecorous conduct," and every Monday afternoon reviewed new acts to excise any "objectionable features." To forestall more restrictive censorship (which was cropping up all over North America) and to shore up the respectability of movie-going, US movie producers developed their own agencies of self-regulation. When the Pantages Theatre opened in 1921,

Mayor Coppley had good reason to predict that it would provide "clean, wholesome entertainment here, and raise the standard of amusement as well as give pleasure."[165]

State intervention backed up this voluntary regime.[166] Theatres had long been regulated informally by the local police under licensing legislation, and, although in 1907 a school trustee denounced nickelodeons as "resorts of rottenness and corruption, defiling the minds of the young and threatening the morals of the nation," the police chief found nothing worth acting on, until in 1910 he brought five movie houses to police court for depicting criminal acts in defiance of provincial legislation. The magistrate's decision in this case was forestalled by news that the provincial government was planning to intervene. The next spring, new legislation forbade children under 15 from attending movies without adult accompaniment and established a provincial board of film censors, which for decades after regularly banned many movies and ordered cuts in many more.[167] For moral crusaders the issue was not only what appeared on the screen, but also what allegedly might go on in such darkened spaces with men, women, and children mixing freely. Between 1911 and 1914, delegations waving petitions regularly showed up at Hamilton city hall to argue against licensing new movie theatres. They usually failed.[168] Cleaning up won out over outright prohibition, and movie houses became steadily more respectable. In prim, middle-class circles, discussions of movies shifted to how to use them effectively for social reform.[169]

By World War One, then, attendance at some kind of theatrical show had become a much more common part of working-class life. Any workers who entered these exotic cultural spaces could revel in the apparent luxury and elegant respectability that they seemed to embody. "A theatre should represent to the less favored of its patrons, something finer and more desirable than their ordinary surroundings," a managers' manual advised.[170] Most working people on tight budgets would have avoided the downtown "palaces" and patronized the less grand five-and-ten-cent "picture shows" closer to home, which sometimes held amateur nights and gave away cheap gifts.[171] In 1910 the *Herald* defended these places: "They supply entertainment, amusement and often-times instruction to thousands of workers who cannot afford to patronize the higher-priced theatres."[172] Some four years later, in the midst of the pre-war depression, an alderman was less positive. "Too many people are spending their money visiting moving picture shows," he said. A flurry of letters to the editor fought back. "My wife and myself had the temerity this past week to visit a local 'movie,' and came away feeling we had been instructed as well as entertained," one man wrote. The same year a writer in the *Labor News* noted that the "thriving moving picture shows" in the east end provided amusement for "the horny-handed, hard-working man, his wife and family" and linked them with new churches and fraternal-society halls as signs of community-building in the new working-class suburbs.[173] Much as in those churches and halls, the seats in a neighbourhood movie house would have been filled primarily with working people, probably including some of the new European immigrants clustered in boarding houses on nearby streets, who, with limited English-language skills, could appreciate the silent films.[174] Full employment in wartime no doubt stimulated even more frequent movie-going in these neighbourhoods.[175] By the interwar period movies had become the kind of hugely popular public amusement that radios were becoming at home.

Within the family, the experience often tended to split along lines of age and gender, as mothers and children in particular families may have had different attendance patterns from those of young men or women with their peers or in courting couples.[176] But there was a growing recognition that sometimes working-class families attended movies together. Some commentators saw motion pictures as a new way of holding together the family circle. "A workingman can take his wife and children to a cheap theatre of an evening; and when he does he is pretty sure to go home with them," the *Herald*'s editor suggested in 1910. "When he goes out alone in the evening for a little recreation or amusement, he may not return home betimes or in a desirable condition physically, mentally or financially." Some two decades later the president of the Ontario Woman's Christian Temperance Union made a similar point. Prohibition, which shut down Ontario saloons from 1916 to 1934, unquestionably curtailed one form of alternative evening outing for fathers.[177] Certainly theatre managers had pitched this new commercial entertainment as a morally sound, respectable form of family recreation.

Like Sundays, then, Saturday afternoons and public holidays not only became occasions for rest and recreation, but were also symbolic times of family solidarity and respectability. The poorest families no doubt enjoyed far fewer of these special days than did those whose wage-earners were bringing in regular, well-filled pay packets (indeed, some charities featured outings for poor children, and sometimes their mothers, who would otherwise have none). Small wonder that free band concerts and street parades remained so popular.[178] Yet reports on the huge crowds that surged into the city's public play spaces on their days off suggest that large numbers of working people made the most of the holiday, and that, although they had a new range of options for their outings, the simple pleasures of

the day – strolling, picnicking, swimming, lazing about – remained most everyone's aspiration.

The Business of Pleasure

In the half-century before World War Two, working-class families were coaxed with increasing intensity and sophistication to embrace a variety of cheap, mass-produced cultural products that promised to enhance the moments they chose to spend together. They were encouraged to buy sheet music or records, listen to the radio, and round up the children and take them out to enjoy the thrills of an amusement park or a movie. Family time should involve buying some pleasure, the message suggested. In the process, we are often told, working-class authenticity gave way to prepackaged moments of carefully controlled fun: riding a mechanized roller coaster on a predetermined track, learning a musical vocabulary from mass-produced songs, listening passively to pre-recorded music, absorbing the slick messages of radio advertisers, or watching in spellbound silence as carefully controlled images flickered on a movie screen. Should we therefore assume that we are witnessing a process of passive cultural co-option into technologically predetermined, sanitized, predominantly bourgeois standards that operated as purely manipulative "escapism" and smothered any independent working-class identity, or at least drained it of its vitality?[179] Not by a long shot.

Consumerism, first of all, could indeed entice individual members of a working-class family to behave in different ways,[180] but for whole families money for commercial pleasures was severely limited. Expenditures on pianos or gramophones were no doubt impossible for a majority of families, and family excursions that involved much cash outlay, especially on transportation, would certainly be occasional at best in most

The Ukrainian Social Democrats had an active Drama Circle that performed for their community.
(AO, I0050072)

households. Only the odd outing to the movies and, by the 1930s, a shared moment around the radio more regularly drew in large numbers of families.[181]

Then too, whether by necessity or choice, working-class parents and their children found ways of having fun without spending much money. They still seemed to spend far more free time together in simple pleasures – kitchen-table storytelling, front-porch socializing, street-corner gossiping, or simply strolling through parks. Groups within their neighbourhoods regularly organized non-commercial activities to draw in family members as participants and spectators – church choirs, lodge picnics, social-ist lectures, band concerts, ethnic theatre, and amateur sports, among many others. For a hard core of labour activists, these activities reflected more than economy – they were a matter of sus-taining independent cultures of learning and critical thinking, from Labour Day picnics to the Workers' Education Association to Hungarian socialist plays.

When they did engage with mass culture, working-class consumers did not necessarily sim-ply take what they were offered without engaging

in a process of negotiation over what they were to receive. There is certainly evidence of their selectiveness and scepticism. When Victor rec-ords tried to sell classical music as a "civilizing" influence on the masses, proletarian music lovers largely ignored those pieces in favour of old fa-vourites (including music to recall memories of immigrant homelands), zippy new ragtime tunes, or more transgressive jazz.[182] As research-ers in the 1930s discovered, radio audiences were also selective and could be critical or dismissive of what they heard (radio programmers cons-equently paid close attention to letters from listeners and audience surveys to adapt plots, characters, and settings). As radio quickly lost its status as a novelty, listeners might not always have been listening as they engaged in other ac-tivities or conversations around the house, even if (as was common) the set was on all day or all evening. Moreover, while whole families might converge on the radio for 15 to 30 minutes to hear *Amos 'n' Andy* or *Jack Benny*, it was unlikely that they would all agree on a whole evening's listen-ing, and, if they did not like, say, orchestral music or dramas, one or more of them might well head off to another activity, as they had done years

Audiences in Hamilton's theatres could often see slices of working-class life, such as this 1907 performance of *A Night in the Slums*. (HH, 25 May 1907, 10)

before. On the home front, the overall impact of the mass culture could be light.[183]

Working people also absorbed mass culture through a frequently collective, participatory process. Radio did not produce reverential individual silence. As they sat together listening, working-class people wove the broadcast voices into their own family dialogues, commenting on and discussing what they heard.[184] Similarly, working people evidently saw local theatres as friendly neighbourhood centres for socializing and relaxing together. The audiences in those spaces often made their tastes known collectively. Unlike legitimate theatre, all vaudeville performances continued to involve direct dialogue between artist and audience; performers crafted their acts to the mood of the crowd they faced on a specific occasion. In that fluid performative creativity, as the audience was engaged in helping to shape the show, rigid managerial expectations could sometimes slide away and the "respectable" could slide easily into the "rough," especially in smaller neighbourhood theatres.[185] Audiences often gave a lukewarm reception to the stars of legitimate stage ostensibly

brought in to clean up the shows, and local managers still paid close attention to such preferences in booking acts. Managers' reports on vaudeville acts made clear that the occupants of the cheapest seats, the young working-class "gallery gods" who stamped and whistled, cheered and hooted, demanded encores, sang along, and otherwise forced the performers to adapt to their expectations, were often still the main arbiters of a successful performance and could make or break an act.[186] Theatre managers had their own uniformed bouncers ("ushers") and tried to get police assistance to help constrain this exuberance,[187] but the proletarian elements in vaudeville audiences continued to be noisy and demanding.[188]

Movie audiences were not much less rowdy, especially in the smaller neighbourhood theatres, where the mixture of live performances and film items on the bill made for what one film historian has called "a theatre experience, not a film experience."[189] Thanks to the continuous performances, audience members arrived and left at their own convenience, not by a manager's fixed schedule. The cheap tickets and democratic seating arrangements encouraged comfortable informality and independence. Although they could not connect directly with film actors, movie audiences expressed themselves volubly in the silent-film era and regularly engaged with the interspersed vaudeville performers and the theatre's pianist, who provided the live musical accompaniment and animated the singalongs. Rather than sitting quietly watching the flickering images on the screen, they too sometimes made plenty of noise (especially during the numerous shorts that were on every program), chatted loudly, and moved around the theatre to socialize with friends. One critic suggested in 1913 that movies had "emancipated the gallery" to enjoy the entertainment without "odium and ridicule." Even after the arrival of talkies, when audience noise levels seem to have declined, theatre managers across North America reported that their patrons were applauding performances they liked or booing unpopular characters (including politicians in newsreels). The east-end Playhouse Theatre (locally known as the "Garlic Opera" thanks to the European ethnicities of its clientele) was still erupting this way in the 1940s. As an American historian insists, working people responded to mass culture partly through the "'contagion' of other people's reactions – their laughter, rumblings, anger, movements, shouts, ecstasies."[190]

Moreover, mass culture ultimately caught the imagination of working people only if it was able to touch the pulse of joys and heartaches in their daily lives. Workers processed the media messages and, in the words of another historian, gave them meaning through the lens of their "historically conditioned prejudices, fantasies, inhibitions, ideologies, archetypes," and their own lived experience.[191] Mass culture therefore had to be informal, unpretentious, and somehow familiar. Tin Pan Alley's music ignored the new high-brow culture of the upper-class concert hall, and, in a much more populist vein, produced songs with simple language laced with popular slang and dialect. Similarly vaudeville, film, and radio comedians spoke the language of the street (albeit cleansed of most overt obscenity and vulgarity) and presented such familiar stock characters as the tramp, the "rube," or the pompous gentleman.

Much of the subject matter addressed in mass culture was also drawn from the familiar world of "ordinary" people, most often meaning urban working-class and immigrant experience (though film producers in particular expanded the scope of their subjects to appeal to more middle-class patrons). However much

the new breed of theatre managers wanted to imitate the ambience of bourgeois high culture, they were trying to build a mass audience and not merely another cultural space for the upper and middle classes. They put on the vaudeville stage the familiar elements of popular variety theatre – the comedians, singers, acrobats, and others, who almost invariably had working-class backgrounds, often in immigrant communities in large US cities,[192] and who remained socially marginal as they trekked about North America, even after they had won star status. Their stage success continued to be built to a great extent on their ability to communicate with proletarian audiences.[193] Many vaudeville stars moved over into movies and then radio and continued their hugely popular trademark styles of performance.

Early moviemakers also set countless stories in the daily context of urban working-class life. When they tried to project a universal experience, the scenario was frequently drawn from workers' lives. Charlie Chaplin's famous screen character, the little tramp, was probably the most famous example. To be sure, by the 1920s countless movie plots unfolded in exotic, lavish settings, but many also dealt with workers in complex relationships with the rich. Certainly the working-class world continued to reappear in comedies and in the wave of gangster movies that arrived in the early 1930s. In that decade too, "working girls" could see themselves in the strong-willed, ambitious screen roles of actresses such as Joan Crawford and Jean Arthur, often as "gold-diggers" flaunting the pretensions of the rich.[194]

At the same time, although some works certainly dealt with large moral dilemmas, mass-cultural products seldom evoked grand narratives of class conflict. Sometimes, as in the case of the early films of D.W. Griffiths, which were produced at Biograph before World War

One, the new medium presented stirring critiques of sweatshops or child labour. Some workers' film groups also produced intensely political stories of the conflict between capital and labour. Their movies managed to circulate through the more independent distribution channels, but had been marginalized by the 1920s.[195]

More often, in songs, stage and movie performances, or radio broadcasts, workers typically got small, often ironic vignettes on coping with familiar challenges of daily life outside the waged workplace – courtship, marriage, death, aging – and particular constructions of the social dynamics within those situations. Mass culture's strongest appeal to working people seemed to cluster around two poles: sentimentality and humour, tears and laughter. Sentimentality saturated almost everything. Tin Pan Alley (and its Canadian imitators) churned out thousands of sad ballads (known as "tearjerkers") that yearned for home, mother, or a lost sweetheart (starting with the hugely successful 1892 hit "After the Ball"), as well as light romantic tunes proclaiming current love (such as "Down by the Old Mill Stream" or "Let Me Call You Sweetheart," both released in 1910), sometimes with a whiff of sexual longing (as in "Shine On, Harvest Moon," 1908). Many pieces invoked the comforts of home, marriage, and motherhood as the essential core of life (the 1912 Irish ballad "Mother Machree" or the 1917 ditty "For Me and My Gal," for example).[196] Recorded music took up similar themes. In responses to a 1921 Edison Company survey, US record listeners expressed strong preferences for old "parlour songs" (known in the industry as "hearth-and-home" pieces), which they said unlocked powerful nostalgia for happy family times or departed relatives every time they were played.[197]

In all forms of storytelling within mass culture, melodrama cropped up regularly, and through the decades to 1940 almost all stories told on stage, screen, or radio, no matter the subject matter – all the popular costume dramas, westerns, social-problem stories, and comedies – dissolved into sentimentally happy (or morally reassuring) endings.[198] Radio in particular raised the emotional temperature to new heights in its popular soap operas of the 1930s. Gender relations were thus mostly reduced to bromides of conventionality.

Ethnic and racial prejudices were also reconfirmed regularly. Minstrelsy contributed a heavy legacy of blackface performance to all the new media. Tin Pan Alley churned out large numbers of so-called "coon songs," comic pieces that highlighted black incompetence and inferiority. In Hamilton as elsewhere, white performers in blackface were hits as "darkies" in stage, screen, and radio performances, peaking with *Amos 'n' Andy* in the 1930s, which presented blacks as the innocent fools that they had been in popular amusements for decades. Stock figures with Irish, Jewish, or German accents also littered the landscape of mass culture and perpetuated deep-seated, unflattering stereotypes. Tub-thumping patriotism in songs or verbal patter could also project a more hard-edged racism. As audiences embraced these elements in mass culture, they reinforced hierarchies of power and privilege in their society.[199]

Yet comedy could also be more subversive. Vaudeville performers used slapstick comedy and humorous acrobatics to defy genteel conventions – "a combination of outrageous distortion, noisy satire, and mad humor, adding up to an insanely imaginative entertainment," according to an early historian of vaudeville. In a kind of comic realism, they did hilarious sketches, monologues, and powerfully evocative songs with a cynical edge about the ups and downs of working-class marriages (including mothers-in-law). They made fun of pretentious bosses, policemen, clergymen, doctors, shop-keepers, landladies, and other troublesome figures that working people faced every day. Among British music-hall performers, this kind of awareness was called "knowingness," a resilient set of perceptive popular discourses distinct from the preachy language of respectability.[200]

Many well-known performers put all this comedy on records for home listening. Many also carried their zany antics into movie studios, notably at Mack Sennett's Keystone Studios. As a result the manic, transgressive behaviour of Charlie Chaplin, Ben Turpin, Fatty Arbuckle, Buster Keaton, Laurel and Hardy, and many more filled innumerable short and feature films that appeared on virtually every movie house's playbill. In the hard times of the 1930s, radio audiences could also take heart from similar performers who freely mocked themselves (and their sidekicks) for their own inadequacies and generated laughter in a democratic spirit. The comedians' quick wisecracking repartee not only poked fun at authority or incompetence, but also gave voice to some of the bitterness and resentment of working-class listeners who were struggling through the depression. Various characters (Andy from the famous twosome, Eddie Cantor on *The Chase and Sanborn Hour*, Jack Benny's butler Rochester, the bumbling Fibber McGee and his wife Molly, among many others) used their verbal agility to demonstrate a spirited resilience and an ability to survive in the face of adversity. Many housewives must have found the heroines of daytime soaps like the long-running *Ma Perkins* equally inspiring.[201]

In lusty, exuberant songs and suggestive sketches, some irreverent performers also flouted prim bourgeois standards of decency and morality. Men could acknowledge their sexual attractions or their philandering, and women could also proclaim an active sexuality. Some Tin Pan Alley songs celebrated male flight from domesticity (the 1909 hit "I Love My Wife, But Oh, You Kid!") or female gold-digging (the sad 1900 song "A Bird in a Gilded Cage") or sensuality (the highly suggestive 1909 number "Do Your Duty, Doctor," or the 1920 show-tune "I'm Just Wild about Harry").[202] The rebellious undercurrent was nonetheless tightly contained; nothing was allowed to upset the apple cart of social relations or the political status quo. Studio and network production codes made sure that the content of movies and radio programs was tailored to offend no established tastes or moral scruples, and that for the most part the material conveyed inoffensive messages about social hierarchies of class, gender, and race/ethnicity.

What did all this add up to? In the early 20th century moral reformers and cultural commentators regularly denounced popular music, amusement parks, vaudeville shows, movies, and radio programs as crass, trivial, empty, and downright dangerous. Socialists and labour leaders could be just as dismissive. Years later many writers would similarly label it all as mindless escapism that distracted working people from any critical appreciation of social realities. The standard of comparison is (and was) usually some more refined intellectually and politically engaging cultural activity. Certainly the disruptive potential of mass culture for power relations in society was curtailed and tamed, and various forms of sexist and racist oppression went largely unchallenged. But it would be too much to argue that the influence of these amusements alone limited workers' visionary horizons. Such a perspective will not help us much in understanding their appeal or ultimate impact.

To be sure, mass culture could console people facing difficult lives, but not simply by getting them to forget. Rather, what gave a ragtime song, a Mary Pickford movie, or an Eddie Cantor radio show its power was the particular construction that it placed for working people on familiar situations in real life. Audiences willingly suspended their disbelief in succumbing to tears and laughter. As familiar as the imaginary situations might be, people did not expect to encounter straightforward documentary analysis of their working-class misery. Yet, after watching or listening to larger-than-life performers with a common touch, who spoke their language and handled everyday dilemmas, and, in the end, seeing good triumph over evil, they could come away feeling a bit better about themselves – reassured that there could be some hope for ultimate happiness in the struggle for survival. That result did not automatically translate into either quiescence in the face of exploitation and oppression or fiery resistance, but simply into an ability to face with a bit more determination and resilience the countless small battles of daily existence in a capitalist, patriarchal, and racist society. In an oddly similar way this is also roughly what churchgoing gave to pious working people. Arguably, then, working-class families used commercialized amusements to reinforce older patterns of making the family circle a supportive, comforting niche.[203]

At the same time, importantly, these experiences were not simply individual ones, because working people spontaneously shared their reactions to mass culture and made them collective responses, whether at the dining-room table or in a theatre balcony. What can never be denied is how widely some of the products of mass culture spread through working-class communities, so that across the continent – and in some cases, on both sides of the Atlantic – certain performers became household names and their musical or acting trademarks entered into daily discourse. The result could be an opening up of shared cultural awareness. Producers of ethnic musical recordings could help to bring together fragmented immigrant groups into more coherent "Italianness" or "Polishness," alongside the Britishness of many newcomers from the United Kingdom. On a larger scale, elements of mass culture could also link these disparate groups. However much young white workers laughed at *Amos 'n' Andy*, they also embraced the new music inspired and played by Louis Armstrong, Bessie Smith, and other black musicians, including a few artists in Hamilton.[204]

In the same way mass culture gave all workers, regardless of ethnicity or race, common cultural reference points. In a city with so many working-class households in which English was not the first language, the ubiquitous radios, with their completely English-language programming, must have been central to this process of cultural convergence. These shared elements of mass culture became part of a new repertoire for surviving in, and sometimes confronting, the world around them.[205] In 1914, for example, *Labor News* turned one of the city's first newspaper comic strips, *Mutt and Jeff*, into a campaign broadside in Studholme's third election campaign as an ILP candidate. Three decades later striking workers coined new words for a popular song to denounce a female alderman who was unsympathetic to their cause, promising to "Hang Nora Frances by the Sour Apple Tree."[206]

Mass culture, then, gave Hamilton's working people a blinkered, oversimplified, often offensive, but also comforting and reassuring view of their world and its social relations. But it was not simply imposed on unsuspecting working-class families. It was shaped in part by what cultural entrepreneurs thought workers wanted, and it was incorporated into working-class life in particular ways that turned it into new versions of popular culture. It had an uneven impact on those families (depending on income, gender, ethnicity, or age); it was appropriated selectively and adapted to familiar rhythms within working-class daily life; and it made itself felt within working-class consciousness in subtle ways that added up to more than mere passive escapism. It certainly limited expressions of overt dissent or unconventional behaviour, but it also allowed working people space to construct its meaning for their own lives.

Making Family Time

Getting together within the family circle was far from the only way that Hamilton's working people built bonds of community. In many working-class families, poverty, abuse, or personal tensions made family time little to look forward to. But within most working-class households a regular, partly ritualized set of socializing practices occurred in daily, weekly, and more infrequent moments. They were practices that wives and mothers worked hard to fashion – sprucing up, eating well, singing, playing games, promenading, and more, depending on the occasion. The family circle turned inward for collective comfort, pleasure, and fun, but also reached out into the city. At least a few times a year, especially in the warmer months, many families put on their best clothes and headed out to various places to enjoy what their small households could seldom provide and to merge into public, family-oriented activities.

Many groups and institutions encouraged these families to integrate themselves into the programs they had established – church services, union or lodge picnics, circuses and amusement parks, movie shows, radio programs – and, as more of them did, they came to share a much broader cultural vocabulary that came, on one hand, from religion and moral earnestness

and, on the other, from popular songs, movies, and radio. Early-20th-century moral reformers polarized these options with attacks on popular amusements, and workers attached to evangelical Protestant churches probably avoided many of them. Public policy reinforced the evangelical critique, particularly by shutting down Sundays, constraining behaviour in streets and public parks, and censoring movies. The corporate owners of the amusement industries voluntarily tamed their offerings in similar responses to moralistic attacks. Yet, especially among the growing numbers of Anglicans, Catholics, Orthodox Christians, and Jews, whose faith was generally less intolerant of commercial pleasures, many working people in Hamilton were happy to take what worked for their families from what cultural entrepreneurs offered and to consider those small pleasures perfectly respectable. In the post-1920 interwar period, those highlights included the phonograph, the radio, the picture show, and for some the photograph.

The choices that these families made within the limitations of moral regulation and low incomes had a distinctly proletarian flavour. They wanted to spend leisure time in spaces and cultural contexts that connected with the larger rhythms of their lives and that respected their rights to self-expression, from working-class churches to neighbourhood movie theatres to radio shows heard at the family dinner table. They looked for alternatives to the drab confines of their homes and jobs – alternatives that could give them inspiration and renewed energy for the daily struggle of survival, whether in the expansiveness of nature on picnics, in the colour, spectacle, and emotional power of church services or commercial amusements, or in the imagined realms of radio.

This was not simply "privatization" or a "culture of consolation."[207] It was a range of active responses to lives based on wage labour. The workers' right to those pleasures was a backbone to many demands raised by labour leaders in the period. In 1906 the *Industrial Banner* responded to the campaign to suppress drinking by invoking that vision of the family circle that had been percolating up since the Nine-Hours campaign of the early 1870s:

> The best substitute for the saloon is the home, and a better one cannot be proposed. The trade union aims to make the home beautiful and attractive through improving the environment of the toiling masses, by shortening the work-day and obtaining a wage that will enable the husband and father to clothe his wife and children decently, have pictures on the wall, carpets on the floor and music in the home.[208]

In such moments, the pleasures of the family circle could certainly be political.

13

A Bell Telephone operator and her friends enjoy a summer outing together before World War One.
(SLS, LS704, LS705)

One of the Girls

THEY STREAMED OUT of the knitting and cotton mills. They crowded into streetcars. They lined up to get into the movie theatres. They wiggled and twisted wildly across dance floors. They frolicked on beaches. They made their way more soberly up church steps. They strolled sedately through streets and parks. No one in Hamilton could miss the ever-larger numbers of young "working girls" out and about in the public spaces of the city in the early 20th century. Over the half-century before World War Two they got bolder and more assertive, and their public behaviour often provoked controversy.[1]

The distinctively working-class femininity they were expressing was a product of the longer span in their life cycle, which started as girls at home, moved through schooling and other forms of supervision, and typically ended in marriage and motherhood. The patriarchal framework of their domestic and public experience set the limits of most possibilities in their lives, including their apparently more carefree young adulthood. But between the 1890s and 1930s working-class women in Hamilton pushed back repeatedly at the frontiers of their oppression and in many ways recast their place in the city.

Becoming a Girl

On any morning in the early 20th century, small girls woke early to face the particular demands placed on them as young females in working-class households. As infants or toddlers they might be alternately ignored or coddled indulgently,[2] but from an early age they tended to have mothers who assigned them household tasks – sweeping, scrubbing, washing dishes, fetching, and, above all, child-minding while their mothers cooked or did the laundry. The older girls in the family often had to babysit even when they were outside playing on the street. The staff of the city's new children's playgrounds noticed how many girls arrived in charge of younger brothers and sisters.[3]

All of the children in a working-class family had to pitch in, but, in contrast to her brothers' responsibilities, a girl's work was more than just helping her mother; it was training for what would presumably be her life's work – looking after her own family household. Her mother was the ever-present role model. By the time they were eight or ten, girls generally had different tasks than their brothers did and were far less likely to look for part-time work outside the household. Indeed, in 1910 the local Children's Aid Society announced that it would clamp down on any girls selling newspapers in the streets. A girl might nonetheless head out with her siblings to scavenge for coal on the railway tracks or cast-off food in the market. More important, she could expect to be called in from a game of hopscotch or skipping with other girls on the block whenever her mother needed her, while boys at the same age were beginning to get more time to themselves and more freedom to roam.[4]

Starting at age six, girls got away for several hours each weekday to attend school, but they usually had to fill much of their time before and after the school bells rang with household labour. It was not uncommon to be kept home from school if mothers needed help. When one nine-year-old girl just off the boat from England in 1908 had a miserable first day in the classroom, her father told her that, as the eldest of seven children, she should not waste her time in school when her pregnant mother needed her. She never went back. This kind of absenteeism never caused school officials the same degree of outrage as the truancy of more irresponsible boys, who, if not working illegally for wages, were usually just footloose in the street. Another ten-year-old girl who stayed home for months with a pregnant mother got a visit from the city's truant officer, but once he discovered what she was doing the official never returned. The parents of such girls rarely appeared in police court. After 1921, when the school-leaving age rose to 16, the school-attendance officer regularly granted a small number of "home permits" to allow girls under that age to stay home, largely "through sickness of the mother who at times cannot be left alone." Evidently this kind of backup domestic labour was legally tolerable and, indeed, good preparation for becoming a wife and mother, which would require personal sacrifice for the good of the family.[5]

Most girls stayed in school. As a co-educational experience – with girls sitting side by side with boys in the classroom – school could have opened up a wider range of possibilities for girls. After all, this was a public arena in which notions of a feminine identity came from outside the working-class family home. In practice, school time simply reinforced what parents were teaching about the connection between domesticity and femininity, along with an extra measure of concern about morality and propriety. Girls got gender lessons at every turn. Girls and boys entered the school building through separate entrances. They had separate cloakrooms and washrooms, and at recess they played in separate school yards, where the girls were fenced off from the rowdier boys and skipped

Working-class girls learned household tasks at an early age. (HPL)

rope or played distinctively female games. Seated at their desks, immersed in their readers, girls found stories about the daring adventures of heroic males alongside others that reminded them of their inevitable future of domesticity and devoted motherhood.[6] The Physiology and Temperance classes launched across Ontario in 1893 (rejigged as Physiology and Hygiene in 1906) helped girls to think of their bodies as frail structures that needed protection for child-bearing and confronted them with images of female modesty and moral restraint. From the early years of the century girls in the public (but not the Catholic separate) elementary schools also got gendered instruction in the weekly Domestic Science class while boys were immersed in Manual Training. During the war the school board provided yarn for the girls to knit into socks for soldiers.[7]

In their regular Physical Culture classes, girls mostly did formal calisthenics, swung around dumbbells and Indian clubs, and, by World War One, learned folk dancing, while the boys marched about, engaging in more vigorous military drills. After 1909 when the Strathcona Trust provided massive funding for military training and drills in the schools, both girls and boys did plenty of marching, but their athletic programs remained distinct. According to the school board's drill instructor, the boys did "military drill, physical drill and rifle shooting," while girls had "physical training exercises and games." After the war girls were allowed to play competitive sports, provided the activities involved no body contact or otherwise did not encourage "manliness" (basketball, baseball, swimming, and track and field were acceptable). Directly and indirectly schools presented a powerful hegemonic version of femininity, although the learning rarely touched on the physically and emotionally demanding expectations that females would experience in working-class households.[8]

After 1920, when the school-leaving age was pushed up to 16 and many more girls (and boys) entered the new vocational streams of high-school education, any girls who were funnelled into the auxiliary classes for the "feeble-minded" studied "sewing, power-operating, laundering and similar subjects."[9] Large numbers of the new conscripts to high-school training did not complete the courses, but by lingering in school into their mid-teens they poured some of their adolescent energies into the schools' formally structured recreational activities and into the informal associational life among their classmates.

After school, when not working at home, girls could be found playing on their own, for the most part with other girls. Although perhaps loyal to particular circles of friends, they did not form distinct gangs, as did their brothers (at least contemporary commentators rarely labelled groupings as such).[10] Before they reached puberty, they seldom raised the level of concern about disruptive, disorderly behaviour that the "Boy Problem" generated. A few might pursue an independent life on the streets that could prompt parents, a policeman, or the Children's Aid Society to try to rein them in, but hardly any young girls ended up in police court.[11] There were nonetheless plenty of fears about potential moral dangers. Parents sternly warned a girl about avoiding potentially compromising situations that threatened physical harm or, more importantly, sexual impropriety, which could damage her reputation and that of her family. Improper behaviour among girls was almost always defined as sexual precociousness.[12]

Various external agencies also tried to corral girls into structured activities in their play time that would reinforce the school's messages about female domesticity and moral purity. Sunday schools were probably the most pervasive of these institutions.[13] Otherwise the nondenominational (but consistently Protestant) Woman's Christian Temperance Union ranked as the leading provider of evangelical programming for proletarian youngsters in the early 1890s. Its clubs known as Bands of Hope drew in some 4,000 boys and girls aged roughly 7 to 14 in 1895, and its sewing and cooking schools attracted nearly 500 girls. "Our work is a preventative one," wrote one leader. "Teach girls to work and you reduce by half the temptation to a life of sin." But the membership tapered off rapidly, and the domestic programs had all been abandoned by the early years of the century. The public schools had taken up some of this work in any case.[14]

Around the same time the local YWCA ran a similar program, which was smaller but lasted longer. In 1893 Adelaide Hoodless convinced the Y to rent rooms in the old Custom House on the edge of the north end to teach local working-class girls the key skills of "domestic science," and it was not long before Hoodless laid out her more ambitious plans for an expanded public-school curriculum that included this training. But the North End Branch of the Y soldiered on with limited support from the main branch downtown. Some 40 to 60 girls showed up on Saturday afternoons to sew and sing hymns, but they probably brought much of their street play indoors because a convener later admitted that it was often "almost impossible to get the children to work." The branch was quietly closed in 1917.[15]

Meanwhile, two more substantial projects to reach out to Hamilton's working-class girls had taken off. During the summer months of 1909 supervised playgrounds began to operate in a few working-class neighbourhoods. According to one reporter, the staff members offered no organized sports for girls who showed up. Instead they kept the girls busy with such games as "tag, London bridge, running and walking races, spelling matches, etc." Each week they also got singing, folk dancing, and sewing lessons (leading to prizes for the best work) to help them "make clothing for themselves and for other members of the family." Only at the end of the season did they get a chance to burn off energy in a set of girls-only competitive races. The older girls were also given responsibility for looking after the youngest tots who were left by busy mothers. In all activities, including picnic outings, they were segregated from the boys under a separate female supervisor. By the end of the war roughly a hundred girls might be found on each of the four playgrounds every day through the summer.[16]

Then, in 1912, the YWCA responded to prewar fears about endangered femininity by starting up a local Girl Guide company for ages 11 to 16 (Hamilton had no younger Brownies or older Rangers before the 1920s), three years after the launching of the international Guide movement in Britain. A second company appeared two years later. The Guides ran on a paramilitary model, with uniforms, drill, and proficiency badges that mimicked the Boy Scouts, but the goal of the movement was to make girls morally upright and skilled in domestic tasks, all in aid of building a stronger, healthier "race" atop the sprawling British Empire. Like its predecessors, the Guides aimed, according to one of its pamphlets, "to make girls better housekeepers, more capable in womanly arts from cooking, washing and sick-nursing to the training and management of children." The girls were also assumed to be learning skills in community service – "home nursing, hygiene, first aid to the injured and many simple useful things." In practice the Guide program provided an additional, potentially contradictory outlet for robust outdoor activities – hiking, energetic games, and camping – in the company of teenage friends outside the family household. In the early years

the girls broadened their skill-building efforts by improvising from Lord Baden-Powell's *Scouting for Boys* to learn to tie knots, do signals, study nature, and master handicrafts. Overall, however, the Guide program was confined to wholesome, carefully supervised fun to distract girls from the morally risky activities of the street and commercial amusements. A Guide should not become anything like the "flapper" of the 1920s. This sphere of activity was not a merely temporary diversion, but long-term training in devoted patriotic motherhood and maternalist citizenship.[17]

By 1915 the Hamilton Guides had reached a peak of nearly 300 members, but wartime employment and volunteer work undercut their appeal. Membership slipped to only 44 in 1920. By that point the national YWCA had rethought its program for younger girls and had given its support to a new, less militaristic church-based organization known as Canadian Girls in Training (CGIT), aimed primarily at middle-class high-school girls. Some two years later an independent council outside the Y took over Guide organizations in the city. An organizational revival brought several more companies into existence over the next decade, most of them affiliated with Anglican churches (annual church parades often ended up at the Anglican cathedral). The organization nonetheless remained marginal: in 1931 – a year when federal census-takers counted nearly 14,000 girls of ages 10 to 19 in the city – the Guides' Hamilton Division (including the neighbouring towns of Winona and Dundas) could boast only 379 Guides spread through 18 companies, 106 Brownies (of ages 8 to 11) in five packs, and one Ranger company of 20 girls (of ages 16 and over).[18]

Few of these, it seems, were working-class girls. The leaders of the international movement imagined that Guides would "raise the slum girl from the gutter," but in Hamilton such a girl generally stayed away. Before the war, an effort to interest north-end girls bore no fruit, and an eager group in the working-class suburb of Crown Point never coalesced into a permanent organization. In the 1920s there were three Guide companies attached to religious and social-uplift projects among working people – St. Luke's Anglican Church in the north end, the East-End YWCA, and the Presbyterian settlement house, Neighbourhood House, also in the east. But the membership of these groups was never large. The cost of participating could be a significant deterrent – a uniform costing $5 in 1912 would certainly be beyond most girls' reach, as were the camp fees in the 1920s of $5 to $7. The uncertainty of family incomes in working-class Hamilton between the wars left little room for such expenditures.[19]

Guide programming could deter them as well. Prim Y staff members and what a local newspaper called "ladies of position" supervised them every week, and, with the venerable Lily Hendrie in the chair as virtually perpetual president, a committee of upper-class ladies watched carefully over their activities (the Dominion Council was similarly dominated by such elite women). Some girls might have appreciated the ennobling imperialist message presented to them in publications such as the first handbook, *How Guides Can Help to Build up the Empire*, or speeches at annual parades like the words of a clergyman at the Anglican cathedral assuring the assembled Guides that "the future of the Empire" and "the great responsibility of the welfare of the British race" rested on their shoulders. Clearly young women from other ethnic and racial groups might not feel so welcome. Class and racial awareness (and resentment) probably bristled among the working girls who had any experience with the organization.[20]

For many working girls the Anglican respect for hierarchy and deference in this quasi-military organization must have run too strongly against the grain of the rest of their more free-spirited recreational lives. Certainly the failure to attract girls over 16 into the Rangers would signal that they had competing domestic commitments or preferred other commercial amusements. Even the younger teenagers who joined managed to bring their adolescent rambunctiousness into their weekly meetings, with only limited resistance from their middle-class leaders. A log book kept by Guides at the working-class East End Y in the mid-1930s, which was written up by a different Guide each week and read aloud a week later, reported girls showing up without uniforms, complaints of bad behaviour during parades, and endemic raucous conversations during the intervals when they met separately in their own patrols and were supposed to be learning Morse code, handicrafts, or whatever. (In one case in 1933 the Daffodil Patrol devilishly belted out a loud rendition of "You've Got to Be a Football Hero.") These girls certainly performed the usual rituals of the meeting and seemed to enjoy the outdoor activities and the indoor "campfire" with storytelling and singing. Yet, in important ways, they shaped Guide meetings to meet their own needs and used them to enhance the social life of the schoolyard and street.[21]

A few blocks away a number of girls from Ukrainian families regularly found their way to another youth-oriented program, but with a sharply different political content. At the Ukrainian Labour Temple, they participated in a Children's School, where, along with boys, they got instruction in the Ukrainian language, read stories and wrote their own, sang and learned to play the mandolin, watched and performed plays, and imbibed a heavy dose of

In 1924 the Ukrainian Labour Temple was running an educational program for children. (AO, I0050071)

Marxism-Leninism. Girls were also hived off to learn handicrafts.[22]

For working-class girls, then, childhood was full of heavy responsibility and frequent reminders of behavioural boundaries. Parents, teachers, and various youth workers instructed them relentlessly that they had inevitable futures as mothers, and worried about their vulnerability. Yet the messages were mixed. They grew up in a home setting in which their mothers generally gave their children a powerful lesson in the highly valued strength, resourcefulness, and indispensability that girls could expect to exercise themselves one day in their own homes. In the public activities they passed through, they encountered more adult women, most of them middle class – teachers, Sunday-school leaders, nurses, playground supervisors, youth workers – who provided examples of various kinds of female authority. In their playtime they also found street-corner friendships that evolved with some distance from the household. These were all components of complex female identities that they would carry forward into their adolescent years and early adulthood.

Working Girls

Girls from working-class families approaching adolescence were not easy to recruit into after-school programs in large part because their responsibilities at home kept them too busy. Moreover, by the girls' mid-teens, many families expected them to move into full-time jobs, generally while continuing to help out at home to some degree; and, indeed, a majority of girls were working full-time by age 16 or 17, even into the interwar period. Over much of the next eight to ten years in their lives, before they married and began housekeeping on their own, these "working girls" stayed in paid labour as long as they were not needed on a full-time basis at home. After the turn of the century, they were far less likely than in the past to find isolating jobs as servants in more affluent households. They moved in large numbers into the many new jobs in factories, shops, and offices,

Like these young women at Proctor and Gamble, working girls developed close bonds on the job. (SLS, LS22)

where they wound up in work groups made up overwhelmingly of other young, single women like themselves.

Almost nothing in their engagement with specific labour processes gave them the basis on which to build a gender identity rooted in wage-earning. Some took pride in the skills they exercised – at a sewing or knitting machine or a typewriter, for example – but rarely did managers acknowledge them. Most did simple, numbingly repetitive, enervating work on light machinery or in packing departments. Like virtually all working-class wage-earners, they had to rely on the strength and dexterity of their young bodies in their work – from good eyesight to strong backs to their often-noticed "nimble fingers." The justification for all this, which most women no doubt accepted, was that they had no future in the paid workplace and were destined for unpaid work in their own family households. That was also the excuse for the paltry wages they were paid, still far below a male's earnings. As they punched the time clock at the end of the day, they also stepped out into a terrain on which their public behaviour was rigorously scrutinized for its potential violations of appropriate feminine decorum. All of these conditions deprived young women of the independence that their male counterparts were developing at the same age.

Yet, within these constraints, some opportunities did arise. As a greater number of them shunned jobs in domestic service, they worked more fixed hours with more clearly defined free time, and their status as wage-earners within their families often earned them the right to spend some of that leisure time and some small part of their earnings outside the home. Many working-class women later looked back on this phase of their lives as a time of greater freedom and fun. Domestic burdens might lighten up somewhat for some, especially if another sister was staying home. That sense of entitlement could vary between different ethnic groups – young Jewish women seemed to have a particularly strong leverage within their culture, Italians somewhat less so – but most working-class daughters preferred to gain some distance from the small domestic spaces and close supervision of the family circle.[23] For some, plunging into a social life beyond the home was a form of rebellion against the constraints of domesticity and, in certain cases, against abusive relationships with parents.[24] By World War One, moreover, hundreds who had apparently migrated to the city on their own in search of work were living in boarding houses far from the direct oversight of parents (although landladies invariably kept an eye on them, and moral reformers watched them anxiously). Still, most young working women seemed to recognize that their attachment and commitment to their families were paramount – this was particularly though not exclusively so for those in the European immigrant households, and few made a complete break.[25] Those who were able to keep a small part of their wages for their own use had some time and income for enjoying a few pleasures of their own. In contrast to most of their middle-class counterparts, they turned the streets and other public sites into spaces for private socializing.[26]

A Bell Telephone operator and her friends at the beach.
(SLS, LS705)

Many working girls drifted between jobs in search of more satisfying or better-paid work,[27] but everywhere they tended to develop the close bonds with workmates that, for instance, percolated up onto the picket lines of strikes like that of the city's garment workers in 1913 or textile workers in 1929 and 1933. To some extent these relationships were a coping strategy in the face of degrading work situations. Like many other wage-earners, they co-operated on the job to help each other out. They told stories, joked and teased each other, sang songs, discussed novels, and chatted and gossiped intimately.[28] They had a lot in common – most of them were single, and they ranged in age from the mid-teens to mid-twenties. As a result of the informal recruitment processes, it was not unusual to have sisters or friends from the neighbourhood working nearby.[29] Knowing that in most cases their futures lay in domestic labour as wives and mothers, they shared a fascination with romance and courtship. When corporate employers began to design recreational programs for their female workers towards the end of World War One, they tried to build on these workplace practices of sociability.

In many cases the workplace friendships overflowed into lively fun off the job.[30] As investigators in many cities at the time and several writers more recently have noted, the feminine cultural practices they cultivated proclaimed a sense of entitlement, dignity, and pride that differed considerably from what men developed on the job. They turned away from the harshness and indignities of their wage-earning experiences and focused on leisure time in the present, particularly on aspirations to be well dressed and attractive, to enjoy some immediate pleasures, and to express their sexuality in the company of men. In the only novel written by a Hamilton author about working women in this period, Mabel Burkholders's *The Course of Impatience Carningham*, the young heroine tells an upper-class questioner that she wants what one recent historian argues was every working girl's aspiration – to become "a beautiful lady."[31] These young women turned modest consumerism to their own ends and tried to shape their feminine identities as "ladies" through cheap goods and amusements purchased for pleasure. They were more active agents than passive victims. They made fullest use of the limited consumerist resources available to them to fashion an agenda of public possibilities – in short, to dream.[32] In the process their young bodies became the main vehicle for expressing femininities that were distinctively working class, and that in many ways pushed at the boundaries of prescribed gender expectations.

Looking attractive, and especially dressing well, were central. Before World War One, investigators into working girls' lives across the continent repeatedly found them willing to forego other essentials – streetcar fare and even occasionally lunch – to be able to buy fancy dresses, elegant high-heeled shoes, and above all, flamboyant hats, which feature prominently in photographs of young women in the pre-war period and caused great consternation within theatre audiences. In the interwar period their head gear became simpler but still essential.[33] Escaping from the family cycle of hand-me-downs must have been an important assertion of independence.[34] Their clothing tastes ran to the flashy, gaudy, and outlandish, in stark contrast to the more restrained middle-class dress standards. As a result, in the perceptive words of one historian, "They staged a carnivalesque inversion that undermined middle-class efforts to control the definition of 'lady.'"[35] Such styles probably also challenged the conventions of mothers from peasant backgrounds in Southern and Eastern Europe as their daughters tried to adapt to North American standards.[36] Here was the most visible way in which working girls could assert that they had not been ground down by wage labour – and this was especially so when they wore the prized clothing to work.

Nothing upset clergymen and moralistic commentators more than did working girls' fascination with "finery."[37] Even Sam Landers, the prim (teetotaling) editor of *Labor News* and a former garment workers' organizer, had the gall to suggest in 1912 that "more girls go astray as a result of vanity and pride in desiring costly clothes, jewelry, etc., that an honest livelihood cannot afford." Staking a claim to social entitlement on the basis of allegedly "frivolous" female consumer practices was far outside the framework of mainstream labour-movement thinking, and indeed threatened the carefully constructed imagery of the family home tended by a virtuous wife that unionists were using in their public postulations. The "rising of the women" in Hamilton's clothing industry in 1913 revealed how they could indeed base their militancy on quite different concepts of femininity. In any case, the charges of wild spending were generally exaggerated. Despite the clothing industry's new output of cheaper, mass-produced garments, young working-class women must have found that their limited incomes allowed few plunges into much extravagant consumerism. Shopping for clothing could be a popular outing, but many women made or altered their own clothes or had their mothers make them. In contrast to their middle-class counterparts, they could rarely afford to indulge in the emerging culture of department stores, which was so overtly aimed at female consumers from the middle class. By whatever means, however, working girls unquestionably struggled to dress in a way that would put on a fine display.[38]

In the decade before the war the debate about the styles of this "finery" heated up. Critics thought that much of it was too provocative and "immodest." By the end of the war the controversies were focusing on shortened skirts, plunging necklines, "georgette waists," "peek-a-boo blouses," bobbed hair, and the growing use of cosmetics to enhance a young woman's features.[39] In 1921 the police admitted that they had no intention of following an Alabama precedent of forcibly scrubbing off the makeup on the faces of young women in the streets, but a year later so many adolescent school girls were applying "powder and paint" that a major conference of youth workers was convened to discuss whether this constituted "dirt" that, by law, a girl could be ordered to wash off. Tolerance triumphed, and over the next few years the "flapper" style of short skirts and short hair similarly took hold.[40] When in 1924 a female evangelist denounced the local YWCA for allowing girls to wear "dresses up to their knees," a young woman had the confidence to rise in the gallery and defend the organization and its young members. Tighter, one-piece bathing suits that exposed more flesh also appeared on Hamilton beaches in the 1920s, and, by the end of the decade, beauty contests had emerged to legitimize these trends. By that point young working women could also look to the movies for models of flamboyant self-presentation as a strategy for social success.[41]

Looking good was a public performance, not a private act. Girls and young women were staking a larger claim to being allowed to enjoy themselves in the public spaces outside their own households. For many, starting in early adolescence, that meant boldly promenading along the streets together in the evening. In the decade before World War One, the police and the Children's Aid Society inspector announced crackdowns on what appeared to be a new practice among young girls (dubbed "linewalkers") of "spending a couple of hours every night on the principal streets." "The practice has become so common as to be conspicuous on the downtown streets and other public places," a reporter noted in 1911. "The YWCA and the Salvation Army officials are agreed," another paper reported a year later, "that the street walking habit amongst the young girls of Hamilton is very bad and has gotten beyond all bounds." A by-law forbade youngsters under 16 from being on the streets unaccompanied after 9 p.m., and the police were prepared to deliver these late-night offenders home to their parents. Girls found out and about too often could soon be labelled "incorrigible" and brought into police court (though few were). But the police never seemed to have been able to stamp out the practice, and some linewalkers were far from submissive. The *Spectator* reported in 1910 that "many of the female sex who have been asked to move . . . have most indignantly refused to be 'bossed' by a man." A *Times* columnist noted, "The toney stare, the indignant look, the muttered words of rebellion and the sarcastic shrug of the shoulders must be aggravating." By the early 1920s many of these girls in the street were also spotted lighting up cigarettes (probably a little later than boys were seen doing the same thing). In his call for restraint, a Baptist clergyman managed to itemize the spirit of independence evident in the streets of Hamilton: "Don't run the streets; don't cultivate a racy style; don't despise your home; don't read salacious literature; don't be too quick to pick up company; don't forget to confide in mother; if away from home don't forget to write; don't be in a rush to marry."[42]

Young girls set out on these promenades to enjoy each other's company, but the real point of "walking the line" was to meet and flirt with boys or men – to "mash" them, in the street vernacular. Men and boys lounging on street corners regularly engaged in suggestive repartee with the passing crowds of females (and sometimes even physically assaulted them). These wandering clusters of young women may have given each other not only some protection but also the courage and skills necessary to negotiate their encounters with males in public places.[43]

The week-long centennial carnival sponsored by the city in August 1913 showcased this increasingly controversial "sparking" in the street. Crowds took over whole downtown streets in various modes of merry-making. "Hundreds of girls who invariably walk the streets with chins tilted disdainfully at angles not conducive to spine restfulness, laughed gaily when tickled under the chins by gay Lotharios – and thought nothing of it," the *Spectator* reported. The male aggressors were using small feather dusters known as "ticklers." Many girls fought back with showers of confetti and ticklers of their own. Clusters of them stood on street corners "gently tapping the male folk as they passed by." An alderman grumpily suggested that some of them should be spanked. Newspaper reporters saw women wearing buttons and ribbons with such provocative slogans as "No Introduction Needed," "See Me Alone," I Have My Eyes on You," "Single, but Willing to Be Married," and "Kiss Me – I'm a Bear." Some who thought that certain men had gone too far punched, slapped, or kicked them, or walloped them with an umbrella. But, on the whole, these interactions appear to have been tolerant and good-natured. On the last night of these "riotous frivolities," in true carnival spirit, an impromptu parade of cross-dressed men and women entertained the crowds. "Yes," said the *Times*, "Mabel, Katie and Vera were Willies, Jims and Johns last night." At the end of the week the *Spectator* concluded that the young people were pleased: "With the removal of irksome restrictions and the supplying of extraordinary channels from the ebullition of their exuberant spirits, their joy was admittedly unconfined." It was this kind of behaviour that prompted the police magistrate to muse a few years later that "the girls do most of the courting nowadays."[44]

Space for Us

The venues for this heterosexual sparking expanded beyond the street corner, especially for girls reaching their later teens. With commercialized sites of more respectable pleasure proliferating after the turn of the century – notably, amusement parks, train and steamship excursions, and vaudeville and movie houses – the owners consciously reached out to women with their elegant decor and morally sound programming. Indeed, the presence of women was supposed to be a guarantee of respectability, although vaudeville-house managers noticed plenty of female interest in the scantily clad bodies of male acrobats or strong men. Women appeared in particularly large numbers in movie houses, which were cheap and relatively safe. Working girls often arrived together in the early evening, or a bit later on the arm of a beau. "We'd go to the show for five cents, get popcorn, and later a bag of chips wrapped in newsprint," one woman remembered. "If you got uptown early enough and had the money, you could take in two features in one night, and many young people did," other old-timers recalled. All of these new amusements sites were free from parental supervision and allowed young women a considerable degree of intimacy with men.[45]

Other commercial spaces, notably skating rinks and dance halls, appealed specifically to young adult courtship. Ice skating had a long history in a city with sub-zero winters and a large frozen harbour. Several indoor rinks were also opened to attract paying customers over a longer stretch of the cooler months. Roller skating first took hold in the 1880s, but by the first decade of the next century the city's three roller rinks were attracting thousands of patrons every year.[46] The owners of these large venues for ice and roller skating provided live bands and organized special events – novelty acts, skating competitions, and "fancy-dress" or "rube" carnivals – which became spectacles to be viewed from the balcony. In February 1907, for example, the Alexandra roller rink announced: "Ladies and gentlemen skating in couples on Thursday Evening. Two very handsome prizes." A month later the Armory rink advertised an "Irish Carnival," with eight prizes for "the best Irish characters, original and comical." The cost of this skating was 35 to 40 cents, with a special rate of 25 cents for "ladies." Watching from the balcony cost 15 cents. Prices began to drop as competition from other amusements increased, especially vaudeville and movies. By the 1920s women skaters regularly paid a quarter. Once the skaters were inside, the lyrics in local ragtime composer Charles E. Wellinger's song "Come with Me for a Roller Skate" advised a man to "Put your arm round her waist" and "Twixt the turns whisper sweet words of love!"[47]

Public dancing was probably the fastest-growing and most controversial activity among the youth of working-class Hamilton before World War One. People here and in most other towns and cities had been dancing for generations, usually as part of kin or community celebrations, such as weddings, civic holidays, lodge socials, or union-sponsored balls.[48] But something new emerged in the early 20th century – a commercialized space for unchaperoned young people to gather and practise much more sexually provocative dance steps. These spaces included dance pavilions at such summertime resorts as Grimsby Beach. In 1906, when the city's licensing laws were overhauled, the licence inspector reported no dance halls within the city limits. Some three years later there was one, and in 1912 only two, but the following year he collected fees from seven and in 1914 ten. A decade later there were nineteen. A few of these were "cabarets" connected to hotels (in Canada dancing had long been banned in drinking establishments), and at least one, located in the east end and run by a woman who had worked as a court interpreter, seemed to be aimed at the European immigrant community.[49]

A dance craze had exploded in every major city across North America in the decade before the war, as thousands of young people learned

Hamilton's Charles E. Wellinger wrote sheet music to celebrate the romanticism of roller skating, which was hugely popular among courting couples.
(www.ragtimepiano.ca)

to do the so-called "animal dances" – the turkey trot, the bunny hug, the grizzly bear, and so on – along with the sensual tango, the more restrained fox trot, and eventually the Charleston, all to the beat of the new ragtime music. When Hamilton staged its centennial celebration in 1913, the downtown streets filled up every night with young dancers showing off their skills at these new steps, and the *Herald* reported that it was becoming "quite popular at all band concerts" for young couples to start dancing behind the bandstand.[50] In 1917 the city saw its first jazz performers, imported from New York, and soon this new music was animating many dances. By the 1920s a working girl could get into a dance hall for a quarter, though higher prices at some venues signalled a more socially exclusive clientele.[51]

This so-called "tough" dancing involved close body contact, a fast pace, and various shakes and shimmies that hinted strongly at sexual intercourse. No other popular amusement gave young women such an open outlet for sexual expression. As a pastime devoted to a dramatic, expressive use of the body, this kind of dancing was at the outer edge of respectability for young women, and, at least until the 1920s, the commercial dance hall attracted mainly working-class youth. Typically young women arrived with female friends and used the setting to find a companion of the opposite sex for the evening (once they were going steady, couples, it seems, were less likely to frequent a dance hall). Here was where a young woman's flamboyant "finery" could pay off, and where she could hone her skills at flirtation and "mashing." Indeed, this was a site where, in defiance of parental expectations and middle-class or ethnic norms, a young working-class woman could exercise an unusual degree of control over her interactions with men, rejecting or changing partners, perhaps outclassing them with her dancing skills, or choosing to dance with other women instead. On the darkened sidelines she might enjoy hugs and kisses with an attractive beau, but later on leave with her girlfriends.[52]

Not surprisingly, the dance hall was quickly constructed as roughly the female equivalent of the most morally suspect male-dominated space, the saloon. In 1913 a telephone operator was fired for dancing the tango at a company tea party, and the next winter both the Young Men's Hebrew Association and the Hamilton Tigers banned dancing from their social events. Several dance-hall owners called their businesses "dance academies" to try to soften the moral scorn, but, whatever the label, bodies still twisted and gyrated across the polished dance floor in the same ways. So many of the city's young women ignored the prudes and embraced the dance craze that in 1919 the local YWCA decided it had to make a historic break with its past policy and allow mixed dancing (and card-playing) during social evenings. Since "the girls get these amusements outside," the board concluded, it would be better to hold onto them "under proper supervision." The same year Mercury Mills, a large plant filled with working girls, welcomed some 800 young men and women for a dance held in the new addition to its factory. A decade later striking textile workers at Canadian Cottons filled an evening with dancing. Although a new city by-law in 1924 banned girls under 16 from entering dance halls and required women to be accompanied by an escort, working girls had found a new environment within the growing world of commercial amusements for asserting independence and expressing desire.[53]

Shorter hair, layers of makeup, more daring necklines, open smoking, exuberant dancing – for growing numbers of working girls, these abrupt changes in public behaviour had begun by the early 1920s to shape a new working-class femininity. At that point a major change in public policy took some of them one step further away from the prim confines of turn-of-the-century feminine identity. In 1919 voters in a province-wide referendum confirmed that a wartime measure to shut down all retail sales of beverage alcohol, including all saloons, would continue indefinitely into the postwar period. Until the Ontario government retreated to a less draconian liquor-control policy in 1927, social drinking was forced into the shadows, where bootleggers and "blind-pig" operators provided single bottles for home consumption or small private spaces for consumption with others. Before prohibition, women rarely appeared in saloons, but in the 1920s the male dominance of social drinking was under attack. Not only were many of the neighbourhood bootleggers women, but now some young women joined boyfriends or spouses in the unregulated space of the blind pig or at the hotel dance hall with flasks in their pockets. Some of the many new immigrants in the city from England and Scotland might have starting drinking back home, where, before the war and even more so after, women joined in pub life much more regularly than they did on this side of the Atlantic. In 1932 the anti-prohibitionist Moderation League organized an unofficial referendum among factory workers across Southern Ontario on selling beer by the glass, and three Hamilton plants with preponderantly young, female workforces voted 80 per cent in favour.[54]

When in 1934 Ontario legislation permitted the opening of beer parlours (known as "beverage rooms"), women could not be waitresses (or sit behind cash registers, even if they were owners or wives of owners),[55] but in each establishment they were allowed to enter separate beverage rooms for "ladies and escorts." These were roughly the same size as the men-only rooms and in the 1930s filled up during peak periods of drinking each week. Photographic evidence reveals that no particular effort was made to make ladies' beverage rooms more attractive to women – they were just as starkly unadorned and uninviting as the men's side – but the regulations tried to maintain some moral decorum by allowing men to enter only in the company of women. Although women could visit beverage rooms in Ontario with female friends, the administrative regime assumed that, as in the dance halls, they were accompanied by, and under the protection of, men, their "escorts." This was part of a broader pattern of inclusion of women in formerly all-male events. In 1930 the *Spectator* had reported "a goodly attendance of ladies" with male companions at boxing matches in recent years.[56]

Some women were as ready as male drinkers to defend their participation in this world of public drinking as a perfectly respectable activity and to take umbrage at poor service or rude patrons. One wrote to the Liquor Control Board of Ontario to complain about the noisy, disreputable clientele that was being allowed to gather in the Armory Hotel – a crowd that

The reopening of public drinking establishments (known as "beverage rooms") in 1934 included separate spaces for "Ladies and Escorts," such as at this Hamilton hotel. (AO, RG 6-36-8)

allegedly consisted of "shabbily dressed women and of a questionable character." Another complained that the International and Savoy hotels were "so noisy and rowdy they were more like a night club than a respectable beer parlor." A black woman was upset that a waiter at the Terminal Hotel would not serve her because she was "coloured." She wrote: "In sixty-one years living and born here I have never been refused to be waited on and I felt so hurt to think of being insulted.... I am well known and have always been respected."[57]

Many women who frequented these drinking places doubtless enjoyed their alcohol as much as their male mates and friends did, and women were often among the raucous crowds leaving the place at closing time. One man reported, "Some women seem to make a practise of being in these Beverage rooms sometime afternoon and nights looking for fellows to buy them beer." In 1935 one worried wife wrote about the Hotel Mart: "On a Saturday night when they have an orchestra the place is overrun with drunken

After World War One many young women, like these baseball players at Westinghouse around 1920, plunged into active sports. (SLS, LS701)

women and men dancing a drunken orgie [*sic*]." Even young, underage women slipped in, it seems. One of many reports on female minors came from a father concerned about conditions at the Vulcania Hotel: "My girl, at seventeen, and her chums can go in there and have all the beer they want, although their ages are very apparent." When confronted with a similar charge, the owner of the Dog and Gun Hotel stated that such young girls came from the nearby Tuckett Tobacco factory. Some young women were anything but demure: when the owner of the Gurry Hotel refused to serve some "young ladies," they called him "some very unpleasant names" and slapped and kicked him before being thrown out. The inspector occasionally reported on female drunks, like the one who staggered out of the Genesse Hotel one night in 1936 and "lay on the sidewalk in a very drunken condition." Occasionally women were even involved in their own fights. In 1935 a brawl erupted outside the Hotel Mart, in which women were described as drunk, "using filthy hotel staff language," and "screeching, hollering and cursing" along several city streets. Some such women were barred from particular beverage rooms by the owners. In a few

hotels women evidently used the ladies' beverage rooms as a space for offering their services as prostitutes, though this seems to have required the connivance of the hotel staff.[58] Although certainly far from all, or even most, young working-class women entered a beverage room, a public space had opened that enabled the more daring among them to expand the range of more outlandish, transgressive possibilities.

As more and more young working women found new ways of expressing themselves by using their bodies in unconventional ways – from promenading to dancing to getting drunk – many also began to turn to somewhat less controversial activities: sports. Before World War One, almost the only athletic outlet for young adult women, offered mainly by the middle-class YWCA, was some version of the highly structured calisthenics they had learned in school, usually carried out with piano accompaniment.[59] A new generation of girls benefited from the 1913 revisions to the Department of Education guidelines permitting team sports within physical education classes. The first sport to take off among them was basketball, which began at the YWCA in 1908 and became so popular across the city by 1919 that a Hamilton team competed in the finals of the Ontario Ladies Basketball Association. The following year a well-publicized girls' basketball league included teams from several churches, the Oliver Chilled Plow works, and the YWCA itself.[60] When the courts were closed for the summer, many working girls headed out to playing fields to play softball. In 1920 teams from eight large factories and a war veterans' women's auxiliary drew good crowds to local baseball diamonds, and the winning team from Imperial Cotton had its picture prominently displayed on the sports page of the *Spectator*.[61] As non-contact sports, both these games escaped some of the moral outrage about potential dangers to women's re-productive capacity.[62]

Women also began to get involved in their own track and field events. A women's section of the Hamilton Olympic Club (formed in 1926) gave many the chance to practise and make strong showings in international Olympic competitions from 1928 on and in a meet organized alongside the British Empire Games played in Hamilton in 1930.[63] Often these athletic women excelled in several sports. In 1930, for example, Gladys Hand, a local track and softball star, made a good showing in a speed-skating competition. The amateur athletes who played these sports not only had a new outlet for energetic physical activity, but also became acclaimed heroines for much larger numbers of female spectators. Working-class women seemed far less restrained by the physical expressiveness involved, or by the controversies over scanty sports attire, excessive competitiveness, male coaching, and general "masculinizing" influences.[64] In the interwar period, then, a young working woman could incorporate a love of strenuous bodily exertion into an acceptable feminine identity.

Local sport stars like Olympic hurdler Betty Taylor might inspire working girls, but these young women also had a larger reservoir of brazen femininity available to them. The blossoming popular culture that targeted young working women provided a host of female images and role models that reinforced their audacity in pushing the limits of permissible femininity. Alongside bevies of provocative chorus girls, the vaudeville and movie circuits highlighted female stars, often brash, aggressive, stylishly sensual figures, who legitimized women's active presence in the public sphere – women as diverse as Mary Pickford and Theda Bara, and, later, Greta Garbo, Marlene Dietrich, and Mae West. These stars, featured in the local newspapers' theatre columns and advertisements, developed a following of loyal fans. Advertisers took advantage of this public adoration by using stars to promote their soaps or face creams. On stage and screen (and later radio), featured performers often portrayed independent women with courage, biting wit, and active sexual appetites. Sometimes they boldly cross-dressed to play male roles, or put on black-face to sing comical "coon songs" or act out outlandish slapstick comedy. Others won the label of "vamps" for their steamy performances. Still others entered a circus ring, vaudeville stage, or movie set to handle snakes or wild animals, or displayed their scantily clad, well-muscled female bodies in spectacular, gender-bending acrobatic turns. (Sometimes men played these same roles in drag.)[65]

All female performers had to struggle with deep-seated assumptions that such eroticized public spectacles made them little more than prostitutes, but they were able to embrace a new respectability provided by their bosses, who had turned these venues into sites of wholesome family entertainment. These showmen made efforts to contain the women's performances within acceptable bounds of female behaviour and to publicize their good characters and dedication to home and family. But the women's bold, unconventional public lives nonetheless suggested the possibility in the early 20th century of new feminine identities beyond the dominant images of frailty, passivity, and domesticity. Some female entertainers, including circus star Josie DeMott Robinson and movie heroine Mary Pickford, pushed the implications of their public presence still further by actively supporting campaigns to give women the vote. A young woman who summoned up the pluck to jump up onto the stage in some east-Hamilton theatre's amateur night may have secretly yearned for escape to this exciting world of female expressiveness (as fan culture encouraged them to do). Certainly moral reformers worried obsessively about the power of popular amusements to stimulate the social and sexual imagination of girls and young women.[66]

Those anxious moralists could take some comfort from considering how most poorly paid or seasonally employed working girls could afford only limited contact with the new commercial pleasures. Even with male companions, the "girls" might stick to simple pastimes. In 1907 the Spec. Man found many couples simply ambling along on the edge of the city in the evening. "We used to go walking – that was the only entertainment we had," the daughter of a wire-drawer later recalled. In cold weather this couple simply met in the corner grocery store.[67]

Generally, young women looked to their beaus to pay for outings. One man remembered courting his wife through numerous amusements, which he must have paid for: "We'd go to a dance on Saturday night. And in the summer we'd go on the Moonlights [cruises]. We'd go down to Grimsby with two bands on there and stop in Grimsby for an hour. They had games and all that sort of thing."[68]

Relying on men to pay their way could open up major risks for young women. In the intimacy of the dance floor or the darkened movie theatre, men might well demand sexual favours in return, and trading sex for access to commercial entertainment could taint a working girl's reputation and, of course, possibly result in an unwanted pregnancy. Across North America such women were labelled "charity girls" and "occasional" prostitutes. As early as 1891 a local Anglican clergymen told the Ontario Prison Reform Commission: "They are not admitted to society unless they are well dressed; they are not even admitted into church unless they are well dressed. It takes all they can do to earn enough to keep them and they must steal or misconduct themselves for the clothes they wear." A quarter-century later, when a female store clerk was charged with stealing shirtwaists and petticoats from the department store where she worked, she argued that theft was an alternative to immorality. "There are loads of girl clerks in this city who are kept by men," she insisted. "They feel that they are forced to accept that support, but I have not and will not stoop to that sort of thing." Moral reformers assumed that such tendencies led to a quick, slippery slope into full-fledged prostitution, particularly among girls who were tempted by a "soft, easy" life rather than hard work. One front-page newspaper story in 1913 told of a policeman who had encountered a young woman leaving a brothel. The officer said the woman claimed that "she was not receiving enough wages and had to put on some style at work." Since there was never a census of prostitutes, it is impossible to know how many cash-strapped working girls stepped over this line, but for worried moral activists it was the blurring of the boundaries between precocious flirting and serious soliciting that sounded alarm bells.[69]

Of course, many young women avoided all these controversial pleasures and their alleged dangers. Fatigue at the end of a working day and lack of money often held them back. Parents also set limits because they both expected help with domestic labour and worried about the sexual dangers. Some ethnic groups were much more protective of their daughters. Many Southern Italian parents insisted that their daughters had to be chaperoned by brothers, although younger siblings may have escaped this surveillance.[70] An adolescent girl had to negotiate her leisure time away from the family and her curfew, and often found mothers waiting up for her return home on a Saturday night. Landladies in boarding houses could also be watchful. Yet, since she was rarely chaperoned, a young working-class woman probably had more relative freedom to step out than did her middle-class counterpart.[71]

Some young women would not have participated in all this burgeoning popular culture by choice. Perhaps they were uncomfortable with the loose morality associated with public amusements and concerned about their reputations. In many cases, their "escape" from the demands of their lives was into novels. "The fiction shelves are greatly patronized by girls of the working classes," Hamilton's chief librarian stated in 1919. "Many girls who might otherwise be looking for amusement on the streets and in dance halls were provided with plenty of thrills at home by the stories of Robert W. Chambers, Arthur B. Reeves, and other writers of the class that forms an irresistible attraction to most lovers of light fiction." Only a small percentage of the population used the public library, however. In 1920, as the population topped 100,000, fewer than 18,000 people held library cards. Most of its collection was in the main downtown building, and, although the working-class east end got its own small branch in 1908, it was poorly stocked and uninviting. By the 1920s two small outlets in that district served mostly children, and even the new building opened with great fanfare in 1932 had pathetically little on its shelves. It was closed three years later in a civic cost-cutting move, amidst a flurry of protest from unions and workers' political organizations.[72]

Beyond the library were the dime novels. These mass-produced, sometimes serialized, formulaic tales of romance and thrilling adventure, often involving working-class women escaping the clutches of bourgeois or aristocratic fiends, were not the earnest, didactic books focusing on character development that were favoured by

Some young women were not drawn into commercialized fun, and preferred a quiet time at home with a book of romantic fiction. (SLS, LS719)

middle-class readers. Nor did they highlight industrial conflict or political confrontation as men in the labour movement might have expected. Young women could nonetheless find fascinating heroines from their own class – women who demonstrated their resourcefulness, triumphed over adversity, and asserted their own brand of "ladyhood." It is hard to know how widely read this literature became. Probably, as in the US, there was a market for dime novels, which then circulated from hand to hand at lunch breaks on the job, where discussion of plots and characters could be lively.[73]

Looking back from the 1930s, then, single working girls could marvel at how much had changed in working-class Hamilton since the days of their mothers or grandmothers. They had a few more job options and more free time, though no better pay. They were still expected to help out with domestic labour at home. Yet, after work, among their friends, they were able to cultivate a much more expansive recreational life as new socializing rituals and commercial amusements welcomed them. Working girls had begun pushing back constraints on their public behaviour in the decade before World War One, and the partial blurring of gender prescriptions during that war, including most symbolically the granting of the right to vote, had engendered more confidence.[74] By the interwar period they could wear provocative clothing and makeup. They could go to movies and dances. They could smoke, drink, play energetic sports, and do a good deal more without arousing much moral outrage. If she wanted to, a working girl could cultivate defiant, flamboyant ways of displaying and using her body to assert a distinctively working-class femininity. The distance between such behaviour and the more restrained deportment of shyer or more religiously inclined young women – between what had once been designated the "respectable" and the "rough" – had certainly narrowed.

Safer Paths

Outside the family household, in the decade before the war a hue and cry arose in the city (as elsewhere) about how working girls were facing grave moral dangers. Ironically, what happened to these young women after work got far more attention than did their wages or working conditions on the job.[75]

In 1906 a group of moral activists formed a Citizen's League to battle such evils as gambling, drinking, obscenity, and prostitution. Some three years later the group, rechristened the Hamilton branch of the Moral and Social Reform Council of Canada, highlighted the issue of "social purity" and were soon joined by the WCTU, Local Council of Women, YWCA, Ministerial Association, and a new Social Purity League in whipping up a moral panic about the lurking risk of "white slavery." In 1912 the National Committee for the Suppression of the White Slave Traffic also spawned a Hamilton branch. As these moral activists caught sight of so many more young women out and about in the city, they announced that there was "an organized movement to lead young women astray" and that Hamilton was "a centre of the White Slave Traffic." Innocent young girls, they charged, were in danger of unknowing recruitment into prostitution by smooth-talking brothel-keepers. Newcomers to the city arriving on their own were the most vulnerable to being "enticed into a life of shame," and, starting in 1910, the Hamilton YWCA kept a traveller's aid worker at the train station to watch out for the arrival of unaccompanied young women. The campaign overtly aimed to protect "white women" and regularly targeted people of colour, especially Asians, as the culprits. The publicity invariably relied on lurid anecdotes but was almost never sustained by hard evidence that could lead to prosecutions. The Hamilton press nonetheless treated it seriously, and anxieties apparently ran rampant about both the dangers awaiting naive, impressionable girls and the unsavoury situations they were getting themselves into. Evidently, as one scholar argues, "white slavery" became a "symbol or emblem of everything that was dangerous to single women in the new urban environment – and everything that was dangerous *about* such women."[76]

There were parallel campaigns to attack the main sites of working girls' courting pleasures, notably the darkened movie theatre and the cheap dance hall,[77] but the notion of "women adrift" in a dangerous urban environment was fading by World War One. An immoral young woman was increasingly assumed to be the author of her own downfall, and therefore needed to be educated or controlled to curb her independence. A stern resolution passed by the governing body of Hamilton Presbyterians in 1920 denounced "the excessive devotion to pleasure-seeking … manifest in many forms, such as the mania for dancing, the encroachments on the rest and worship of the Lord's Day, [and] the drift toward such motion-pictures and theatres as pander to depraved taste."[78]

A working girl bumped up against various legal structures of regulation that aimed at restraining her behaviour. A bold, sassy young woman might find herself nose to nose with a policeman questioning why she was out at such an hour or what she had been up to. Any whiff of moral impropriety could bring such a woman before the police magistrate. Parents with daughters who fought the constraints of domesticity and liked to escape to the streets also frequently turned to the police and the courts for help in strengthening parental authority. By World War One an allegedly promiscuous working-class girl with repeated offences might also be labelled "feeble-minded" – part of the emerging category of sweeping medical diagnosis to cover sundry forms of anti-social behaviour, based on assumptions about hereditary defects. Too much interest in urban amusements and male companionship could be designated as "sex crazed" and "abnormal" behaviour. As more young women found pleasure in commercialized amusements by the 1920s, fears about out-of-control sexuality among them mounted.

A girl under 16 could be designated a "delinquent" under the 1908 Juvenile Delinquents Act, a term with a fluid definition, which in 1924 was expanded to explicitly include "sexual immorality or any other form of vice." An older working girl could face a vagrancy charge, which for women almost always connoted sexual looseness. A handful might also be jailed for actually selling sexual services as inmates of a bawdy or "disorderly" house. Judging by conviction rates, Hamilton police treated brothels with considerable tolerance until the social-purity agitation that first erupted around 1909 pressured them to crack down on as many as 8 or 10 a year (14 in 1915). That brought a handful of female "inmates" to court each year (almost never accompanied by their male customers), but, meanwhile, far more

sex workers finding customers on the street were swept up as vagrants. Under Ontario legislation passed in 1918, many of those apprehended for any of these crimes were subjected to compulsory tests for venereal diseases.[79]

Every year Hamilton's police magistrate sent a small number of young women (invariably working class) to the Mercer Reformatory in Toronto for open-ended sentences of up to two years less a day. There they were expected to learn to devote themselves to hard work and avoid sexually compromising situations.[80] For the younger offenders, probation became more common once the Juvenile court began functioning in the 1920s. A group of young upper-class women formed a new Big Sisters organization in 1919 to take female delinquents under their wing. Adult volunteers met the girls in court and agreed to watch over and counsel them on a regular basis. During the 1920s Big Sisters focused more on what it called "preventive" work by reaching out to adolescent girls who had been referred to it by teachers or various social-welfare agencies.[81]

Even if these repressive measures actually touched only a tiny number of young women in the city, the demonstration effect must have made many precocious girls aware of what awaited them if their behaviour caught too much attention. They also faced persistent efforts to "educate" them. The WCTU had tried to use its mothers' meetings to urge mothers to undertake careful instruction of their daughters in "purity," but the numbers they attracted were small, and their own members were reluctant to do the instructing.[82] As the extent of venereal disease among soldiers (and their sexual partners) became more widely known during World War One, a local "social hygiene" organization was formed early in 1918. It sponsored a large mass meeting of 2,000 women that spring. The

Church groups, like this choir at the Caroline St. Mission, attracted some young working girls. (HPL)

city's health department soon added a "social hygiene" department with a full-time nurse to monitor and treat cases. Responsible sexual behaviour had become a much more public subject of discussion, even if still couched in grave warnings about immorality. A girl might be handed one of the provincial government's new pamphlets on venereal diseases, which urged, above all, self-control and taking care not to arouse the lust of men.[83]

The moral reformers' best hope, it seems, was to find activities that would divert young women from the lurking dangers of commercial amusements and predatory men. The Big Sisters were far from the first organization to offer alternative recreational activities for working girls. The various churches made consistent efforts to create mid-week programming for young women, including, where possible, those from working-class families. Unmarried women made up a much larger percentage of church members in the city than did their bachelor brothers, and on weeknights they found their way to meetings of groups such as the Girls' Friendly Society in the north-end St. Luke's Anglican, the Sunbeam

Circle at the east-end Calvin Presbyterian, or the Junior Catholic Women's League at the St. Patrick's Girls' Clubhouse. They also joined in with the mixed-gender choirs and Bible classes. Their churches' social programs provided many working girls with their main source of weekly recreation and conviviality, particularly before World War One. Some three-quarters of the single women at Calvin Presbyterian Church, for example, had factory jobs.[84]

Among the non-denominational agencies, the YWCA had the longest, most ambitious track record.[85] From its founding its core clientele consisted of white-collar office and retail workers ("business girls"), most of them from middle-class families. But from time to time in the two decades before World War One, the Y gingerly reached out into the unfamiliar world of what was coming to be known as the "industrial girl." Periodically the Y approached factory managers to take out memberships for all their female employees, sent special invitations to working girls to attend evening social events, and hired an "extension" or "industrial" secretary to visit working-class girls, especially recent immigrants, individually. Evidently few responded, and fewer returned.[86]

If they wouldn't come to the downtown building, perhaps they would be more interested in something closer to their own neighbourhoods. The Y's North End Branch tried to drum up interest in a small lunchroom for local working girls in 1897, and eight years later invited local factory girls to weekly Saturday-night socials and then to short-lived Sunday evening prayer meetings at this satellite branch. Small turnouts quickly killed the projects. Over the next decade the organizers made repeated attempts to pull together a club for wage-earning girls, though the weekly attendance seldom reached as high as 25 before, in September 1917, the faltering branch was quietly shut down.[87] That year the Y shifted its focus eastward, and put a new emphasis on organizing industrial girls into self-governing clubs in a new east-end branch. The girls once again showed limited interest.[88]

Like the Christian churches at the same time, the YWCA wanted to position itself as a mediator of class tensions in postwar Canada. Addressing the recreational needs of working girls more effectively would stave off more menacing social and political projects being discussed and promoted in the period. "Canada is at the crossroads," one local official warned. "It is our work to see that all girls have a chance to develop along the right lines." Y officials were also conscious that the arrival of votes for women since 1916 had raised new challenges for women in the public sphere, and began to refer to their work as training for "citizenship."[89] Yet after conducting a special survey in Hamilton, the head of the national Y's Industrial Department reported in 1920 that the local Y was reaching only "the girls of a better class" and not the estimated 5,300 young women employed in factories. "The churches do not provide any recreational program for these girls,"

she reported, "their enjoyment being practically limited to dance halls and movies." She stressed the need "to compete with these amusements, indirectly raising the standard of enjoyment, and bringing in better influences."[90]

In 1920 the Y decided to invade the east-end factories themselves. With the blessing of plant managers, once a week the Y's staff and volunteers, including some 25 young middle-class women, began visiting working girls in their lunch hours in a few of the largest east-end plants. They entertained the women with musical programs and held sing-songs. Managers at Mercury Mills and the Imperial Cotton Company, in particular, welcomed these visits as enhancements of their own blossoming welfare-capitalist programs. Of the roughly 600 working girls whom the Y said it was in touch with, however, only tiny numbers accepted invitations to weekly social and devotional meetings at the main Y building.[91]

Some two years later the east-end project reopened in a spacious room over a bank under the name of the Blue Triangle Club, which still did not catch fire until the national office loaned its industrial secretary, Berta Hamilton, to study and then run the east-end operation in the city. Hamilton moved quickly to expand the programs and outreach of the Blue Triangle Club. Young women could join specialized clubs to do gymnastics, play basketball, swim, or set off on hikes, practise dancing, acting, or singing, and learn dressmaking, home nursing, basketry, or even lip-reading. Married women started their own club, as did a group of British immigrant domestics. Sunday afternoon sing-songs and thinly attended evening services kept alive the devotional theme. The industrial secretary also worked with social-welfare agencies to get help for girls in financial trouble. An in-house branch of the city's Workers' Educational Association did not get off the ground, but a study group on economics did.[92]

Hamilton stressed the draw of a club for working girls, rather than a straightforward effort to get them to take out Y memberships, especially since so many could not afford the 50-cent fee. Each of the clubs elected a representative to an executive of the Blue Triangle Club. Her vision of the Y program in the east end was unquestionably that of a community centre, and she quickly helped to shepherd into existence a completely new building in the east end. The branch opened in spring 1925 with a live-in staff, and within three years it could report nearly 700 members in classes and clubs. Independent groups were encouraged to hold their meetings in the building as well, and dances drew in good numbers of non-members every Saturday night. The choral, drama, and debating clubs, public lectures, concerts, and plays, lending library, card and dance parties, and other programs in this new Y outpost, mostly run by self-governing clubs, strongly resembled the work of the settlement houses that reached into working-class and immigrant neighbourhoods across North America.[93]

Before the war all these church and interdenominational projects had thought of their work as an evangelical alternative to theatres and dance halls.[94] Typically they had offered working girls heavy doses of earnest singing around a piano, Bible study and prayer, or such didactic activities as guided reading or sewing and cooking classes, organized in an overtly patronizing way. Some young women, especially the churchgoers, might have been temperamentally and morally inclined to such pastimes, but the reluctance of the great majority of working girls to attend regularly after exhausting days on the job was understandable. The YWCA's landmark decision to allow dancing and cards in 1919 signalled

a change in how to confront the new commercialized culture of working girls, as did the new self-governing clubs that followed. Yet the core of the Y's thinking was still that Hamilton's working women were culturally deprived, that their home and neighbourhood environment gave them nothing of value. East-end Y workers argued that, unless "these girls from unattractive homes can come to spend the evening in proper and attractive surroundings," they would be "left to find their pleasure on the street." They seemed particularly uneasy about the family life of European immigrants and not surprisingly drew in few women from these households.[95]

The upper-class board members and middle-class staff were also never completely comfortable with factory work for young women (when the depression left many of them jobless in the 1930s, the Y's answer was to offer classes in domestic science to refashion them into employable servants).[96] Board members and staff assumed that the girls' jobs could endanger their future reproductive capacities and, in the short term, stimulate too much interest in exciting after-work fun. "Girls do not deliberately choose recreation and companionship which will exert a degenerative influence against them physically and morally," a 1924 fundraising appeal argued. "But music, excitement and gayety make a strong appeal to a girl whose daily occupation is colorless." Since "commercial interests" had "seized upon the need of the girl for pleasure and friends," the Y had to offer the recreation she needed with "kindly and understanding supervision, and introducing other wholesome interests into her life."[97] YWCA board members continued to harbour suspicions that these young women should not be expected to look after themselves and resented the independence of first the Blue Triangle Club and then the East End Branch, as well as the development of programs that had not been centrally approved, notably regular Saturday-night dances.[98]

Working girls themselves had mixed feelings about the Y and its programs. Most stayed away. Perhaps they were unable to afford the membership fees,[99] or perhaps they were suspicious of the organization's motives. "Everywhere is the concealed fear that the Association is trying to better the industrial girl," one Y worker wrote in the organization's national magazine, "and the industrial girl does not welcome the betterment."[100] Some evidently did join, particularly to use the swimming pool and the basketball court, or to enjoy the Saturday-night dances (the devotional meetings were never as popular).[101] For them the Y was simply one of a range of cultural resources that they could tap into in their neighbourhoods. The new postwar emphasis on self-government among Y members also gave them scope to speak out more independently.[102] When the cornerstone was laid for the new East End Branch, a working girl from the Blue Triangle Club wrote enthusiastically in a *Spectator* article that she and her friends were finally "being given a chance to express themselves as individuals instead of being regarded [as] just one class, Industrials." She saw them as "the future voters of the city" who "know from first hand their industrial needs, so therefore need to mix socially with other members of their class and discuss from equal positions the tangle and disorder of conditions in industry at the present time."[103]

That writer might have been Janey English, who was emerging as a prominent voice among the Y's east-end members and a symbol of the independent working-class femininity blossoming in that branch of the association. She had migrated to Hamilton from Lancashire, England, in 1923, and, although married, found a job as a weaver at the Hamilton Cotton Company. She joined classes of the Workers' Education Association and the Blue Triangle Club and became what the *Spectator* called "the guide, philosopher, and friend" to a group of "young folks at the very start of their working career" – a group known as the Glad Girls' Club. In 1925 she became the first Canadian chosen to attend an eight-week summer program for working-class women at Bryn Mawr College in the United States. That experience apparently radicalized her to some extent – "the 'Truth' stood out in blazing letters," she later wrote to a friend – and the next winter she participated in special Industrial History classes taught at the East End Y. Yet, although a self-styled "Radical," she remained an active member of the predominantly working-class Laidlaw Presbyterian Church – just the sort of sincerely religious young woman the Y hoped to attract. She worked closely with Berta Hamilton, but, after that official's resignation in 1925, found herself and her fellow members in the east end drawn into what she called a "war" with patronizing staff and board members. Even after she had been elected president of the Blue Triangle Club in 1926, she charged that, although "factory girls were never expected to think by a certain class of people," they "do know what they want and say so."[104]

Out in the same working-class neighbourhoods where the YWCA's new east-end members lived were other women who shared English's energy and enthusiasm for social betterment, but who had hitched their stars to unions rather than to a preponderantly bourgeois women's organization. With more women signing union cards than ever before in the years after 1917, the men who had always assumed that unionists were exclusively male were changing their attitudes and behaviour slowly and reluctantly. Union meetings held in smoke-filled halls at late hours were not welcoming for many working

Mary McNab was Hamilton's most prominent female labour leader at the end of World War One.
(SLS, LS51)

girls, but they showed up in good numbers at union dances, card games, and picnics.[105] The local United Textile Workers and Amalgamated Clothing Workers unions made room for some of them within their executives.

One was Mary McNab, whom the *Industrial Banner* accurately described in 1918 as "one of the coming leaders in the women's labor movement." The year before she had poured the organizational acumen and reformist zeal that she had learned in church and YWCA work into a union organizing campaign for clothing workers, and soon became the new local's business agent. She went on to active roles in the local Independent Labor Party, Ontario Independent Labor Party (of which she was vice-president by 1919), Women's Independent Labor Party, and United Women's Educational Federation of Ontario, often speaking from podiums at election rallies. In 1919 she spoke out against the indifference of organizations such as the National Council of Women. "What do they know

of the working girl?" she asked ("with withering scorn," a journalist noted). "The only ones who can look after such girls' interests are either [drawn] from the girls themselves or those who have at some time or other actually worked with them." She used such arguments to advocate joining the National Council "so that working women might be represented by people of their own class." When she declared in 1921 that "the woman of today has new ideals, new moral conceptions, new methods of action, the justice of which has given her the courage of her convictions," she was describing the new current of working-class feminine identity that was taking hold by the early 1920s.[106]

By that decade, then, growing numbers of young working women were participating in the recreational programs offered to them by churches, women's groups, corporate employers, and unions. Some were undoubtedly more comfortable in these safely supervised environments. Others may have simply taken advantage of facilities not available to them elsewhere in working-class Hamilton to have fun with their friends, especially those who filled the numerous church and company baseball and basketball teams.[107] Yet some, like Janey English and Mary McNab, negotiated a feminine identity that incorporated elements of the earnest, respectable, Christian emphasis of these programs, but gave them a particular working-class meaning. A more confident, class-conscious independence could flourish, however uncomfortably, within institutions that expected deference and conformity to a more circumscribed notion of womanhood. The YWCA's new direction after World War One was a belated attempt to come to terms with the ways in which, by the 1920s, young working-class women in Hamilton were fashioning a new range of cultural and gender identities.

A Married Gal

However exciting her life as a single wage-earner might be, a girl in working-class Hamilton had known from far back in her childhood that her destiny was to be a wife and mother. She had practised the household skills she would need, including child-minding. She had found paid work in jobs described as extensions of her domestic work. She had faced the tightly locked doors on other options that low wages and job segregation had thrown up, and had probably had enough of the mindless monotony of so many of her job possibilities. With her young girlfriends, she had revelled in a fantasy life of romance and gradually reached out to the young teenage boys who teased and wooed her.[108] Some never got hitched, by choice or ill luck, but most young women did.

Courtship was not necessarily a straight path to a permanent relationship inside wedlock, especially since most Hamilton women did not marry until a few years into their twenties, but the goal was clear. Marriage became a Rubicon that compelled many women to forsake the more freewheeling associational life they had built up at work and in the neighbourhood movie theatres and dance halls. It severely limited their time and resources for reaching outside the family household for leisure and pleasure. Yet, as they aged, many married women made a new social life with other women inside a variety of organizational frameworks, and, to an increasing extent, with their husbands in new companionate activities. Like the experience of single women, the range of possibilities for married working-class women was shifting and changing.

If dating young men was initially a ticket to enjoying amusements that might otherwise be unaffordable, eventually some long-term attraction or mutual understanding would hold a couple

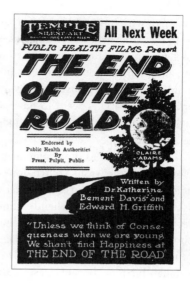

Public-health officials provided women with educational material on sexuality, but its message was moralistic, emphasizing above all abstinence before marriage.
(*HS*, 14 April 1920, 12)

together, and a man would promise to marry his young partner. "She just took it for granted that we would marry because we'd gone out together for so long," one workingman recalled. The moment did not necessarily signal that a good nest egg had been put aside for starting up a new household, but was more often based on a man's job prospects, the family's ability to cope without their children's incomes, and perhaps a frustration with living with parents.[109]

By World War One, mainstream popular culture had begun to cast youthful romanticism in an increasingly erotic light, and the commitment to marriage could be a threshold to premarital sexual experimentation, which, despite relentless condemnation by moral authorities, seemed to be acceptable to many working-class women if they were confident that marriage would follow. Certainly it was common for a single pregnant woman who was abandoned by her partner to charge that he had broken that promise by refusing to "do right by her." More often, after a couple had spent a long period of time together far outside family circles, the young woman's boyfriend would eventually be introduced to the family while all of them were sitting together primly on the front porch or in the parlour, and eventually at the dinner table. This was the mark of a serious relationship. Many working-class parents seem to have allowed daughters considerable latitude in choosing a mate, but the prospects could face strong hostility – for being raised in the wrong neighbourhood or going to the wrong church, for example. Some fathers still insisted on the ritual of a suitor asking for the daughter's hand. Ethnic cohesion could be crucial for parents, as in Italian households, where 80 per cent of marriages in Hamilton between 1921 and 1945 involved two people of Italian birth or descent. Despite the mounting consumerist pressures in the interwar period to make a wedding itself more elaborate, it was most often small and simple, and a honeymoon may have been a luxury for most working-class couples.[110]

For women in working-class Hamilton, marriage brought an end to both the blocks of "free time" after punching the clock and the limited financial independence they had enjoyed. Outside the textile industry, bosses invariably forced women to quit their jobs as soon as they married.[111] Their lives then turned decisively inward on their new households as they took up domestic routines. They would quickly discover that they generally could spare little time to get out of the house for any kind of recreational activity, other than family outings. The concept of "leisure" had no meaning in lives of endless domestic work, which was not broken into the rigid periods of time experienced by wage-earners or school children. Moments of informal socializing were more likely to occur over the back fence, across the counter in the corner grocery store, or on the steps of the church on Sunday morning. Nonetheless, many women seemed to find their way to some kind of organized gathering outside their homes on a regular basis, probably no more than once or twice a week.

Sometimes this outing would be to engage in collective projects, like canning or knitting, or simply to enjoy the company of other women. "We used to meet every week at different houses to play cards," one Armenian woman recalled. "And along with the cards was gossip and stories, jokes and complaints." Most of the more formally organized groups were in one way or another "ladies' auxiliaries" for larger organizations to which they were connected. The most common were the Ladies' Aid groups in Protestant churches or sodalities in Catholic parishes. Working-class women such as those at Calvin Presbyterian Church met each week to combine their pious devotion and domestic skills. They sewed, baked, and marshalled other skills to raise funds for the beautification of their church or for aid to the sick and the poor. In this more public, collective expression of their domesticity, they might have been able to assert some control over church expenditures.[112]

Other women found a similar outlet in the lodges set up exclusively for women related to male members: the Lady Maccabees, the Odd Fellows' Daughters of Rebekah, the Pythian Sisters, the Masons' Order of the Eastern Star, the Daughters and Maids of England (associated with the Sons of England), the Ladies' Orange Benevolent Association, or, by the interwar period, the Daughters of Italy. One woman remembered her mother's outing to Eastern Star meetings one afternoon a week as her only social outlet. Another recalled that in the interwar period she and her friends joined more than one lodge (she belonged to five herself).[113] At the end of World War One women connected to returned soldiers similarly set up several auxiliaries alongside the veterans' organizations, where, as in the lodges, they had programs for themselves, prepared refreshments for joint evenings with their menfolk, and did some charitable work.[114]

In contrast, Hamilton's union locals had virtually no auxiliaries before the war. When prodded by the Women's International Union Label League in 1910, the Hamilton Trades and Labor Council decided simply to "place the matter of Womens Uxeleries [sic] before the different Locals to see what can be done along that line." Evidently nothing was done. Even the local Union Label League, which was intended to motivate working-class women shoppers, was an exclusively male organization.[115]

The most important new women's adjunct to the labour movement emerged in April 1917, when the local Independent Labor Party decided that the recent granting of the vote to women in Ontario required organization among its female supporters.[116] Up to that point, suffragism had been a weak force in the city. The WCTU's repeated calls for votes for women as a force for moral cleansing of public life had largely fallen on deaf ears in upper-class circles.[117] The Local Council of Women, presided over by the wives of the city's leading businessmen, had been slow to adopt the suffrage plank of the National Council, and no middle-class suffrage organization ever appeared in the city. Indeed, Clementina Fessenden, the widow of an Anglican clergyman and a prominent club woman within the city's upper classes, had peppered local newspapers with a steady barrage of anti-suffrage letters.[118]

The strongest public support had come from working-class circles. The Hamilton Trades and Labor Council nominally endorsed the cause in its platform of principles, and in 1910 sponsored a speech by Mrs. Philip Snowden, a British suffragist, apparently an unsuccessful effort to help kick-start a local suffrage organization.

Allan Studholme, as Labor's spokesperson in the Ontario Legislature, championed bills to give women the vote in each session between 1910 and 1914. The Herald picked up a rumour in 1913 that a suffragette group "affiliated with the militant organizations of England" might be formed in the east end, but no such organization ever appeared. A year later the new east-end workingmen's club, the East Hamilton Progressive Association, voted down a suffrage resolution. "The women would not know what to do with the vote; they are too innocent," one speaker argued. He added, with a hint of class awareness: "The few who want it are only seeking notoriety. They don't want the poor working girls to vote, but only the rich property owners."[119]

The new ILP initiative in 1917 was therefore a historic turning point. Any Labourist menfolk who had imagined a meek auxiliary to make tea and sandwiches and dutifully follow their husbands to the polls were soon put in their place. The women, who were largely wives of local labour leaders, insisted on a completely separate organization known as the Women's Independent Labor Party (eventually with branches in the city centre, in the east and west ends, and on the Mountain). The first president, Annie Cassaday, the wife of a carpenter and Trades and Labor Council president, brought long experience in the Maccabees and Catholic women's groups. The ILP men initially arrived at the women's biweekly meeting to teach them how to "use the franchise wisely," but the women took hold of their own party. In a familiar pattern, they staged social evenings for mixing with the men, and occasionally provided "socks and comfort" for soldiers or support for a charity. But they also set up their own discussions of social, economic, and political questions, believing, as the Labor News editor phrased it, that "the future of the working

By 1939 the Ukrainian Labour Temple Association in Hamilton had a large women's section.
(AO, F1405-50-21-158)

classes very much depended upon the amount of working class political knowledge its women possessed."[120]

In contrast to middle-class feminist organizations that tended to collapse after the vote was granted, these women saw the need for using their political rights to raise issues in the political arena that would address the problems of women workers, both paid and unpaid. As Cassaday told the Ontario ILP convention, they were "organizing the working women of the city, and they would make their ballots count in electing representatives who could do no injustice to the men and women of the working class." They brought in guest speakers, including the local progressive Presbyterian clergyman Banks Nelson and the well-known feminists Flora MacDonald Denison and Rose Henderson, and gave speeches of their own – Cassaday on "Greater Food Production" and a Mrs. Petrie on "Citizenship," for example. Arguing that "women understood children and their educational needs far better than men," they insisted on their rights to be candidates in local elections in 1919 and 1921, though they restricted

their nominations to the Board of Education and were never successful. At the height of the ILP's strength in 1919, the Women's ILP membership probably reached a few hundred, but the group's public influence was undoubtedly much greater.[121]

In the early 1920s, as the Women's ILP went into decline, a new more radical group appeared – the Women's Labor League, one of a handful of groups that formed alongside the emergent Communist movement. Its agenda was similar to the Women's ILP, but more wide-ranging in the issues it raised and the solutions it discussed. Although its small membership remained diverse, it was drawn into the orbit of the Women's Department of the Communist Party of Canada, and in 1924 joined a Federation of Women's Labor Leagues, led by the Communist Florence Custance. From 1926 to 1929 members benefited from a hard-hitting monthly magazine, the *Woman Worker*, which, in contrast to most women's magazines of the period, took up questions of both wage-earning and domestic labour, including the touchy issue of birth control. The party's interest in the so-called "Woman Question," especially the concerns of housewives, was limited and short-lived, however, and by the end of the 1920s it submerged these issues in the campaigns for revolutionary industrial unions, which included largely single wage-earning women. Only in the unemployed struggles of the early 1930s did the local Women's Labor League take on new life in addressing issues of household and family. Throughout the League's history, its members seem to have been primarily Anglo-Canadian, but after 1922 a small parallel group (with only 11 Hamilton members in 1926) operated within the Ukrainian Labour Temple as a Women's Section. They had access to their own national magazine, *Robitnytsia (Working Woman)*, where, if they could read, they would find class-conscious and maternalist articles on similar themes to those in the *Woman Worker*, along with Ukrainian poetry, drama, and fiction that promoted an ethnic identity. These women wove together their faith in revolutionary politics, their commitment to their families' well-being, their attachment to their ethnic culture, and their pride as women, in opposition to the male prejudice that one writer called "porcupinism."[122]

One of the spark plugs of this wave of working-class feminism was the irrepressible Janet Inman (née Jeffrey), who had arrived from Glasgow with her husband in 1912. While raising two children, she had continued to work in local textile mills. After helping to launch the Women's ILP, she became president of the Mount Hamilton branch and an executive member of the provincial women's federation. In 1921 she carried the ILP banner into the Ward Eight school-board elections, but lost. She concluded that her defeat had resulted from "the fact that I came out rather radically in favor of grants for scholarships, conveyances to take kiddies to and from school, and swimming pools in the

Janet Inman.
(*LN*, 23 Dec. 1921, 4)

schools." Her party connections nonetheless got her an appointment to the first Minimum Wage Board for the Hamilton area from the new Farmer-Labour government (a position she would hold until 1935). A leading light in the local Theosophist Society, she wrote letters and articles on many issues for the daily press and local labour papers, as well as the Imperial Cotton Company's *Fabricator*. In an apparently brief flirtation with the new (Communist) Workers' Party in 1922, she lectured on "the shortcomings of the suffragist movement, instancing Mrs [Emmeline] Pankhurst and others of her kind who, after making a great noise about votes for women, now had retired and were pretty respectable lecturers for morality." Continuing her agitation in the local Women's Labor League and East Hamilton ILP in the mid-1920s, she served on the executive of the Ontario section of the Canadian Labor Party and was later active in the Co-operative Commonwealth Federation (CCF). Undoubtedly, the many cultural shifts in constructing respectable womanhood within working-class Hamilton, including the new access to citizenship rights, had opened up new possibilities for women with such talents and energy.[123]

Working-class housewives could find other social outlets. Since the turn of the century, non-proletarian reformist organizations like the WCTU and YWCA had sponsored "mothers' meetings" to provide social time for such women, during which moral and practical lessons on child care or sewing could be passed on over tea, cake, and prayers. With their mandate of "reaching the poor, the needy, the discouraged and erring ones," the Methodist deaconesses had done the same. In all cases, however, these occasions had the familiar odour of charity, and never drew many participants.[124] Far more appealing were newer commercial outlets that lured in housewives. In the decade before the war, many mothers flocked into matinee performances of the new nickelodeons and small neighbourhood movie theatres to relax briefly on shopping trips. A visitor to a local theatre in 1914 reported finding an audience "composed principally of women, many with sad, tired faces, a few with children." A month later, in the face of efforts to prevent the opening of one such east-end theatre, an angry self-styled "Working Woman" wrote to the *Herald* to assure readers that, when her children asked if they could still go to movies, she would answer: "We will, with the grace of God and your father's coppers."[125]

By the 1930s movie-house operators were panicking at the stampede of working-class women to an entirely new social activity – bingo, sometimes known by its British name "housie-housie." Voluntary organizations of all kinds – veterans' groups, fraternal societies, and more – ran these games. In 1934 the local CCF ran bingo all day during its annual picnic. Some three years later Ontario's attorney general said that some 25,000 players were converging on bingo halls in Hamilton each week.

The vast majority were women. Here they could spend a pleasant evening in a safe space with female friends and neighbours, while probably convincing themselves that, as they gambled for prizes or (less commonly) money, they still had their family's best interests at heart. The city council told the provincial government in 1937 that "women were making a practice of getting most of their groceries that way." Other prizes included kitchenware. Any cash winnings they carried home would most likely be theirs to spend without negotiations with their husbands. Gambling was generally a disreputable, illegal activity, but the charities and Catholic churches that organized these games cast an air of respectability over the bingo tables.[126]

Whether sitting through lodge or church-group meetings, slipping into a movie matinee, or hovering nervously over bingo cards, married working-class women who ventured into the public sphere largely chose the company of other housewives – while husbands also tended to gather in same-sex groups. Yet, from at least World War One, married couples also found time to go out together without a trail of children in a family outing. In most churches, lodges, unions, veterans' groups, and other such membership organizations, women took the lead in organizing occasional get-togethers between men's and women's branches for banquets or strawberry socials. By 1920 a new pattern of regular companionate outings was clearly taking shape. Many of the same groups held dances and card parties. Euchre and whist had fought their way out of the shadows of evangelical scorn and become extremely popular activities, often advertised in the daily press and featuring well-publicized competitions with prizes.[127] The moviegoing of the social life before marriage might also be occasionally revived. Perhaps most remarkably, married couples began to drink together. After the 1919 referendum on continuing prohibition into peacetime, the *Spectator* expressed surprise at the extent of the "wet" vote, especially in the heavily British working-class neighbourhoods of the east end. "The old-countrymen and their women folk flocked to the polls in Ward 8, intent upon voting a little Blighty atmosphere into the land of their adoption," the paper noted. "The arid spell had not been popular with them, accustomed as they had been to the evening schooner of 'awf and awf.'" So "Erb and the missus decided to do a bit of legislating on their own."[128]

During the prohibition years up to 1927 and then during the seven-year interval when alcohol could be purchased only at government liquor stores for consumption at home, husband and wife were more likely to share the contents of a bottle than they were in the pre-war days of male-dominated saloons. After 1934, when the new regime of beverage rooms opened up a specific space for women in the ladies and escorts sections, many of the couples who used those spaces were married. One woman later remembered how the north end's Modjeska Hotel became "a very popular place" in the neighbourhood: "It was the kind of place you could go into and not be afraid because you knew everybody ... just a neighbourhood place. You'd see, any one of your neighbours on Hughson Street would be there." Another woman even explained to government officials that, although she did not drink beer, she came with her husband and bought his drinks for him at the east-end Jockey Club Hotel. In the licensed clubs (run by veterans and ethnic organizations) the men had to apply to hold special "ladies' nights," but, elsewhere, some hotel owners welcomed into their banquet rooms more informally organized clubs, usually claiming some charitable goal and made up of groups

of married couples looking for a respectable social gathering around sandwiches, beer, and a cribbage board. Like the rest of the clientele of Hamilton's beverage rooms, they were preponderantly working-class.[129]

By the 1930s, then, while a housewife could normally expect to find little time for leisure in her demanding days of labour at home, she did sometimes find social outlets outside her household, first in the auxiliary organizations of churches and lodges and then increasingly in more commercialized public spaces, from theatres to beer parlours. What did not change much was the patriarchal framework within which these activities were still contained. Her outings with women friends were mostly constructed as auxiliary to men's socializing; her visits to movie matinees had to fit into shopping expeditions; her bingo nights were justified as acts of responsibility to her family; and on her nights out with her husband she had to accept his dominant role as escort and protector. For most housewives in working-class Hamilton, all of these occasions were only brief moments in the routine of relentless labour. Within these boundaries, a married women could find some diversion and fun, but, like her grandmother, she still lacked the independence and resources for real leisure.

A New Womanhood

As in so many other aspects of life in working-class Hamilton, the experience of girlhood and womanhood over the half-century before World War Two was a complex blend of continuity and change. In the 1930s as much as in the 1890s, a girl still evolved into a woman knowing that the household and domestic responsibilities would be the core of her life. Her still-limited job prospects and income continued to reinforce her economic dependence. She was still subject in various ways to regulation by legal and social institutions.

Yet what is equally striking is how young working girls and married gals found ways to assert some spunky independence. In choosing to avoid work as domestic servants, they gave themselves more space for leisure in the public sphere, and, both then and after marriage, many took full advantage of the new commercial outlets for recreation. Indeed, they used their limited power as consumers to shape their highly performative public behaviour. Some also turned to voluntary institutions that had adapted their programming to their needs, notably the churches and the East End YWCA. What emerged was a new continuum of respectability that allowed large numbers of working-class women to participate in public activities to the degree that they were comfortable and could still be "ladies." By 1920 far more of them thus found ways of expressing a more assertive femininity through their own combinations of flamboyant clothing, makeup, bobbed hair, dancing, moviegoing, sports, smoking, drinking, and sexual experimentation, alongside church work, union participation, or the rites of citizenship in political activity. There could still be a wide gap between the women who were primarily oriented to their churches and those who patronized beer parlours, but the gap between them seems to have narrowed over the period. In the process these women shaped versions of distinctive working-class femininity that they knew, and regularly declared through their patterns of socializing, were not identical to those of their middle-class counterparts.

14

Street-car workers after a baseball game. (SLS, LS491)

Boys Will Be Boys

"MEN ARE BUT BOYS GROWN UP."

So began a reporter's wry account of the "carefree abandon" and "carnival spirit" that he had seen among working-class men and boys the night before at the 1913 centennial festivities. Many heads would have nodded in agreement that so many elements of a workingman's boyhood shone through in his adult behaviour. Lots of those full-grown men still referred to themselves as "boys." Workingmen in Hamilton writing to a local newspaper to discuss alcoholic consumption, for example, signed themselves "One of the Boys" or "A Bunch of Working Boys." Boyhood infused manhood.[1]

A boy in working-class Hamilton did not become a man in some kind of universal, timeless, or testosterone-driven way. His masculinity was not a mere expression of his biological makeup, but emerged from complex social and cultural processes. It was shaped in part by the expectations, behavioural practices, and various institutional arrangements (schools, law courts, the military, and much more) that defined manhood broadly in Canadian society and justified men's patriarchal dominance over women and children. Scholars like to call that the "hegemonic" masculinity of an era. But working-class males also grounded their masculine identities in the specific dynamics of their own households, neighbourhoods, and workplaces. They worked them out amid the particular demands of economic scarcity, subordination, and, in some cases, ethnic and racial discrimination. Distinctively working-class forms of masculine identity thus took shape. These features were not fixed and static, but were regularly destabilized, negotiated, and renewed in the face of many new challenges in the early 20th century.[2]

Workingmen liked to stake a claim to their masculine privilege based on their responsibility to bring home the bacon. Yet, long before an individual workingman donned the mantle of breadwinner and head of family, he learned and practised, as boy and bachelor, how to be "masculine" at home, in the schoolroom, on the street corner, at work, and on various pleasure sites. Indeed, the layering of experience through this life cycle produced deep contradictions and ambiguities.[3] A man's body, too, proved crucial for expressing his masculinity, often in deliberately performative ways.[4] Working-class male bodies were the source of claims to class pride within demeaning wage labour, to gender superiority over allegedly weaker women, and, in an age of imperialist excess, to racial triumph over the "lesser breeds." In contrast to the expectations of women's bodies, male bodies had to be developed to meet the social demands put on them (in what came to be called "body-reflexive practices").[5] Bodies became both the clear measure of achievement (successful wage-earner, athlete, lover, happy drunk) and the visible sign of failure (weakness, malnutrition, dismemberment, disease, degenerate drunkenness, death). Workingmen literally wore themselves out in pursuit of their masculinity.

Many adult men in Hamilton after 1900 had not grown up in the city, but the thousands who came from towns and cities in the British Isles before World War One and during the 1920s had broadly similar experiences of growing up working-class and male. Those who migrated from the Canadian countryside and the much smaller number from peasant communities in Continental Europe also learned similar ways of being male, though, among those from Europe, the structure of local agriculture, the weaker role of state schooling, and a large place for the Catholic Church made a considerable difference.[6]

Lessons for Life

Before he took up a full-time wage-earning job, a boy in working-class Hamilton learned what it meant to be male at home, in school, and on the street. At home he might frequently hear homilies from his parents on what was expected of him, or get stern lectures on his failure to measure up (decades later, interviewees would remember their working-class parents as strict disciplinarians), but he probably picked up much more simply by watching and doing. He grew up within a family in which his father must have seemed a somewhat shadowy, distant figure who disappeared from the household for more than ten hours a day, six days a week – a father who nevertheless got special care and concern from his mother upon returning home each evening. His father was granted the right to rest from his labours in the evenings and on days off and might also take off one or more nights a week to meet up with other men – in a lodge or union meeting, sports field, ethnic club, political rally, or saloon. Men interviewed years later remembered relatively little emotional interaction with their working-class fathers. "We were afraid of dad, and we'd go to mother for consolation," one recalled – though he added, "We had just undying respect for him."[7]

A boy noticed early on that, like most of the other mothers in the neighbourhood, his mum (beyond her regular trips up the street to corner stores and perhaps to church on Sunday) never seemed to stop working and did not participate much in the wider world through which his father roamed. She was a crucial figure of nurture and admonition in his life, but he could not have missed how fundamentally dependent the whole family was on his father's regular breadwinning. The boy saw his mother's relief when his father handed over his pay packet; her worries if he had not brought home enough to pay all the bills; her anxiety if he was injured, seriously ill, or laid off; or her anger and resentment if he squandered any of his earnings on his personal pleasures, like excessive drinking. In many households, especially among recent European immigrants, a boy saw how the male boarders who lived with his family enjoyed similar status. Indeed, boys might bond closely with the younger men who boarded with them.[8]

At some point the boy might have seen a drunken man in the neighbourhood abusing his family or heard about a wife taking her ne'er-do-well husband to court for non-support. Fathers could be petty tyrants in their own homes, expecting their wives and children to accommodate their every whim. In any of the lengthening stretches of unemployment and underemployment, the boy might also have faced the unpredictable moodiness brought on by his father's wounded pride at having to let his wife look for some waged work or apply for relief. Being a man, the boy saw, meant shouldering a huge obligation to look after a family. But it also meant reaping clear privileges and respect not available in the same forms to females, as well as the right to exercise more power and authority in the household.

He would also learn early in his childhood that working-class family members were all expected to contribute to the family's collective upkeep, but that males and females did different work. He saw his mother juggling a set of demanding domestic tasks. He saw his sisters recruited to assume more and more of this work (or even to do it all if mother was sick or had died). At a young age he might have helped his mother around the house, but there probably came a point in his boyhood when he was not expected to do laundry or cook meals.[9] Once he could be trusted, he was sent regularly on errands in the

Boys learned that working-class husbands and fathers had important responsibilities around the household. (AO, 10050067)

neighbourhood, making his first independent forays into life beyond the household. If the family was in difficult straits, he might go out on foraging expeditions, with sisters, for firewood or coal.[10] This gendering of household labour could be skewed if a family had no girls, or if they were still tiny. One or more of the boys might have to continue helping mother (or replace her if she were sick or absent).[11]

In a still sharper sexual division of labour, a boy was almost certainly expected to help his father with odd bits of work around the house, including gardening. Being a worker, he saw, meant hard physical labour for everyone, but being a man meant leaving most of the domestic tasks to the females in the family and concentrating on the "men's work" around the household and in the paid workforce. To be a man was in large part not to be a girl or a woman. The slow process of extracting himself from household tasks and his mother's supervision probably extended into his teens and could no doubt be conflict-ridden (the number and age of sisters and his place in the birth order could be crucial).[12] He must also have been steadily more aware that all this manual labour at home, as well as the work he was expected (like his father) to take up one day, required developing strength and dexterity. A working-class man had to rely heavily on his body.

Like their sisters, the working-class boys of the early 20th century usually had considerable religious and secular instruction outside the household. Many shuffled off to Sunday school each week, and at age six virtually all made their way into elementary school classrooms. Typically boys left the church at an early age, partly no doubt recognizing that more women than men were churchgoers. Indeed, withdrawing from church activity became part of the gendered division of labour that they were learning, in this case reflecting the mother's special responsibility for nurturing the spiritual health of the family.[13]

Similarly, they were more likely to quit school earlier than were their sisters. During their eight to ten years in school, working-class boys were forcefully presented with the exemplary hegemonic masculinity that they were expected to embrace. They sat in the same classrooms with girls, usually under the direction of a female teacher, but then their academic program divided them by gender for special manual training classes and physical education in the form of military drill. The school curriculum through the years and the annual Empire Day celebrations each spring also encouraged boys to identify strongly with the glories of the British Empire. In 1912 the local school board gave more boys the opportunity to connect even more closely with these imperialist adventures when it extended the military cadet program into the senior elementary schools. Boys 12 and over got uniforms and rifles. Military training remained in the school curriculum until 1933 as, in the words of an instructor, "the breeding box of unselfishness and sacrifice, words, which joined together, mean true loyalty."[14]

Not all boys were completely swept up in the nationalist fervour of this jingoistic hoopla. One man later recalled parading with the cadets in the early 1920s as "one of the best things about school," while another militantly refused to salute the Union Jack during a Royal visit.[15] Some working-class parents must have given their children a more sceptical view of imperialism and militarism. Certainly the Canadian labour movement in the pre-war period was critical. In February 1907, for example, the *Industrial Banner* argued that military training in schools would lead to "the system of destruction of human life and property." Some five years later the *Labor News* insisted on "an immediate protest from working class rate-payers" when the school drill instructor made a pitch to the local school board: "What we need is more 'readin,' 'ritin,' and 'ritmetic' and leave the 'shooting off' to the bellicose warriors."[16]

Even so, for the boys the lessons of imperial adventure that saturated their spellers and readers and the rituals of Anglo-Celtic hegemony that the schools staged certainly fired their imaginations and helped to shape their identities as white males. The actors at the centre of imperial triumphs were all men – soldiers, sailors, hunters, explorers – and their highly performative, often violent acts of courage, duty, and self-sacrifice were presented as models of sterling manhood. These figures cut a swath along colonial frontiers on which there were no women but plenty of inferior "races" to be subdued. To varying degrees, then, Hamilton's Anglo-Canadian boys learned an aggressive virility and a sharper sense of gendered and racial superiority that could seep into their after-school play and frame not only their consciousness of Empire, but also their attitudes to the small local African-Canadian and Chinese populations and their responses to the newly arrived immigrants from Southern and Eastern Europe.[17] Although the children of those European newcomers were almost invariably sent to Catholic separate schools and were thus segregated from Anglo-Canadian children, they got the same curriculum and same lessons in racialized gender-building. It must have been harder, however, for them to identify as closely with the British imperial world.[18]

Other lessons were less inspiring. Working-class boys found little in the curriculum that resonated with their home lives. Their school readers sometimes spoke to them about poverty, for example, but made it seem inevitable, acceptable, even ennobling, and certainly insurmountable, except through individual self-improvement and nose-to-the-grindstone hard work. Most of the academic content of their schooling placed far more value on mental than manual work and on the development of white-collar careers. The teaching was too abstracted from the experience of their families to have much relevance.[19] Above all, the rote learning and strict classroom discipline taught conformity and obedience. Boys learned how to follow orders and to behave in an orderly fashion, respect property, exhibit good manners, and maintain personal hygiene.[20] Teachers inflicted severe corporal punishment on rowdy or disobedient boys to drive home the behavioural norms.[21] The schools seemed to want boys to accept that working-class manhood meant deference to authority and expertise and to the superiority of book-based knowledge over practical know-how learned through daily experience. Small wonder that when the school bell rang, boys were happy to escape to the life of the streets.

Into the Streets

In 1889 a *Spectator* reporter made his way up an alley near the railway station in the north end of Hamilton. He came to a shed, which he quickly confirmed was the "club room" of a gang of boys in their mid-teens. Some 47 years later the executive director of Hamilton's Big Brothers Association found his way to a similar shack, where a handful of boys aged 11 to 12 were spending their time.[22]

Between those dates, journalists, police constables, judges, and child-savers of many varieties regularly commented on the existence of gangs of boys ranging in age from nine or ten through to their late teens or early twenties and thus spanning the years of schooling and full-time wage labour.[23] They were variously dubbed "wayward," "rowdy," "rough," and "tough," and, in their worst forms, "ruffians" and "hoodlums" (though rarely "street arabs," the 19th-century label, or "hooligans," the term used in Britain by the early 20th century).

A gang was simply a cluster of boys or adolescents, usually close to the same age, who separated themselves from the direct oversight of parents, teachers, employers, or police. Some had more or less fixed memberships, probably (though not necessarily) a charismatic leader, and perhaps a name for themselves (some called themselves "clubs"). Others hung out together for no more than an evening or two. "Being in a gang created comradery among the children," a Hamilton man who grew up in the north end later recalled. "It was what we had to do to survive." In these gangs, boys developed patterns of behaviour among themselves and in relation

Working-class boys in Hamilton tended to form small gangs for mischievous fun and adventure.
(HPL; AO, 10019649)

working-class neighbourhood – what a local Congregationalist minister called "the supremacy of the 'gang passion.'"[24]

Their games encouraged a relentless competitiveness (and probably perpetual insecurity) – from craps, to informal team sports that brought respect for physical strength and athletic prowess, to elaborate make-believe fantasies (military warfare, cops-and-robbers chases, or Wild-West confrontations) acted out with simple makeshift toy weapons. Other activities involved challenges to budding masculine honour that could only be met in fist fights, which always drew a crowd. Gangs regularly challenged each other over turf or reputation, but also confronted property owners, shopkeepers, policemen, and others over the limits of acceptable urban behaviour.[25]

Struggles over space were never-ending. Gangs regularly appropriated street corners as their rallying points. There, among themselves, they might engage in roughhouse jostling and horseplay, shoot craps, concoct adventures involving any nearby street activity, or simply stand around talking. It was here that so many boys got their nicknames – "Rats, Bossy, Streetcar Joe, Six

to structures of authority that provided excitement and added strong streaks of solidarity and defiance to their emerging manhood. Invariably this practice involved using their young bodies boldly and aggressively in highly performative, transgressive ways. While most likely not all boys joined some kind of gang, the high visibility of the groups must have been a constant pole of attraction and inspiration in every

Bits, The Ham, Slob, Clutch, Stinky Lou," and so on.[26] On this informal public stage they also played to larger audiences of other people who used the streets. With cigarettes dangling from their lips, they struck defiant poses, shouted, bragged, practised profanities, insulted passers-by, and resisted police efforts to move them on.[27] Gangs seldom stood still for long. They might head off along sidewalks in cocky, four-abreast formation, or ramble through public parks, vacant lots, or empty fields. They might go down to the waterfront to enjoy the water (or ice) of Hamilton's harbour.[28] As new urban development appropriated this natural play space and the new city parks prohibited boyish rowdiness, they defiantly invaded private backyards, railway tracks, and industrial lands, inciting the wrath of property owners and night watchmen.[29]

An abandoned house, a shuttered boathouse, an unlocked warehouse, or a crude shed constructed by gang members themselves as a clubhouse could become a hideaway for more secretive activities, especially smoking, gambling, and occasionally drinking.[30] Some boys also broke into schools and churches and damaged the furnishings in apparent defiance of the moral authority of these institutions.[31] When the boys were in their early teens, some of their gangs moved indoors into poolrooms and cigar stores.[32] They scraped together the pennies for cheap seats in nickelodeons or vaudeville theaters, where they hooted, applauded, whistled, and jeered at the performances.[33] Moral reformers were probably at least partly right to conclude that the slapstick comedians, gunslinging cowboys, and sneering gangsters were models of bravado and defiance in the games that took place out in the streets.[34]

Wherever the youth went, petty pilfering seems to have been common (if not universal) and intended for the boys' own consumption, not family coffers. Some theft was for immediate enjoyment – snatching bread set out to cool behind a bakery, stealing apples from an orchard, or more boldly snatching fruit from stands in front of stores or in the central market. Sometimes boys broke into shops to get tobacco, food, or candy. Other thefts evolved out of the boys' endless scavenging for small objects to be sold quickly for cash either to other boys or to the city's numerous second-hand junk shops. They used the money to buy cigarettes, to pay off gambling debts, or to enjoy such hedonistic pleasures as pork pies, fruitcakes, or ice cream – luxuries that their families probably could rarely afford. The occasional thefts of bicycles, wagons, and, after World War One, automobiles for joy-rides reflected a similar yearning for pleasures denied them by limited family incomes. Only a few of these boys seem to have turned occasional pilfering into more systematic theft, which for decades remained by far the most common charge laid in court against boys under age 16.[35]

Group solidarity also emboldened many youngsters to engage in taunts and physical assaults with stones or snowballs (or frozen horse droppings). Their targets might be other gangs or specific individuals (such as an elderly black man), and sometimes property, including passing trains, streetlights, and store windows. Much of this vandalism could appear to be aimlessly destructive, but some assaults were escalations of verbal battles with proprietors who challenged them or tried to stop their play.[36] Gangs also played pranks of various kinds (such as greasing streetcar tracks or setting piles of leaves on fire) and disrupted such sedate public events as outdoor band concerts.[37]

Sometimes all this boyish exuberance and mischief expanded beyond the street corners or empty lots of a single neighbourhood. Once a year on Halloween, in particular, working-class boys enjoyed remarkable tolerance from the law and the public for a full night of city-wide riotous revelry and outrageous pranks – "the annual saturnalia of questionable fun," as the *Spectator* dubbed it. With blackened faces and sometimes outlandish costumes, gangs paraded brashly through the city's streets each year and more surreptitiously left a trail of mayhem – fences pulled down, gates removed, outhouses overturned (a declining prank as bathrooms moved indoors), ash barrels upended, porch furniture hung in trees, lampposts moved, steps and shutters torn off houses, houses splattered with eggs, wooden sidewalks torn up, barricades thrown across streets, wagons and cars spirited away, tires deflated, fire alarms rung, signs removed or relocated (a "For Sale" sign once appeared on the front of First Methodist Church and, another time, on the Prince of Wales School). During the whole week before Halloween in 1919, boys used peashooters to harass cars and pedestrians throughout the city. Over the next decade the festivities came to include joyriding in stolen automobiles. By that point heavy police surveillance (often involving the entire police force stationed on street corners) had curbed much of the mischief. The evening revelries turned more towards huge costume parades on the main city streets (Charlie Chaplin and other movie stars were popular figures by the early 1920s) and youthful demands that passers-by, merchants, and household residents "shell out" candy, nuts, or coins. The event nonetheless remained a festival of rowdiness that faced little constraint and rarely brought arrests. In 1929 a *Spectator* editorial mentioned that "small boys rank it next to Christmas in importance," and "they have parental permission to do a lot of things they are licked for doing the other 364 days in the year." A workingman later recalled that in the interwar period, "We divided the evening between calling at doors for handouts and later creating a little 'hell.'"[38]

This ancient spirit of "misrule" could erupt at other times as well.[39] Indeed, from time to time the aggressively transgressive challenges to public order, propriety, and property of the gang life of working-class boys became the cutting edge of larger crowd activities across the city, both celebratory and confrontational. After every provincial and federal election before the First World War, for example, crowds thronged the streets to celebrate, usually forming a large, raucous, informal procession. Boys' exuberance punctuated these events with a cacophony of horns, kazoos, cowbells, and their own high-pitched voices. Annual celebrations such as the 24 May holiday also saw boys causing havoc with firecrackers and other forms of rowdiness.[40]

Hamilton's special summer carnivals, held in 1889, 1903, and 1913 (the last in honour of the city's centennial), brought out this riotous revelry every night for several days. A Toronto reporter caught the end of the 1903 festivities, as "crowds took the invitation to turn the town upside down in real earnest." He wrote, "In the middle of the road youths gathered and raced up and down, dragging trees and rolling barrels with them, singing and shouting. When their throats gave out they gathered pans and barrels and thumped them to add to the Babel of fish-horns, squawkers, and a score of other noise-producing instruments." Along with the adults, they tossed confetti, pestered total strangers under the chin with small feather "ticklers," and deafened people with their horns.[41] The same nighttime "riotous frivolity" erupted throughout the downtown area ten years later, as thousands of people surged and danced through the streets each night until well after midnight, shouting, blowing horns, ringing cowbells, and breaking every boundary of acceptable social deportment. Boys and men alike accosted others (especially young women) with confetti, talcum powder, and "ticklers." A reporter noted, "The erstwhile very proper lady from a mansion on the mountain side would submit without a murmur to being tickled under the chin by a feather duster in the hands of the butcher's boy or the iron moulder's helper." Everyday street-corner lounging turned more aggressive as men running the gamut through large crowds of youths and young men had to doff their hats or have them knocked off with sticks.[42]

Such crowd exuberance took a more serious turn during the tumultuous street-railway strike of 1906. According to a *Spectator* reporter, on the first night, "The streets, for the size of the crowd and cheering and hooting, closely resembled an election night." The paper's editorial writer laid the blame on "irresponsible young toughs who seek to create disturbances simply for the sake of the 'fun' of doing it." He was at least partly wrong because many adults joined in the crowd vengeance on the hated street-railway company. Yet boys and youths did emerge regularly as daring instigators, bringing into play their familiar forms of aggression and subversion. On the second night of the strike, the paper estimated that "three thousand people, mostly boys, paraded the streets." Over the next few days one 15-year-old tried to set a streetcar on fire, some youths ignited a flammable liquid to scare the horse of a mounted police officer, and many shouted insults at strikebreakers and pitched stones through streetcar windows. On a number of occasions a crowd surged around a policeman to save a boy from arrest. The *Spectator* saw it all as a "high carnival of riot, disorder, and destruction."[43] Crowd violence was almost always directed at specific company property, but in two cases boys extended the attacks in directions that might suggest some animosity towards particular local firms. One night, following a massive labour parade, six large windows were smashed at the Eagle Knitting plant, where many adolescents had jobs. Several days later, on the night of the most violent confrontations, some 50 boys broke several plate-glass windows at the city's leading department store, Stanley Mills, after workers there had been discharged for wearing "We Walk" ribbons.[44]

Gangs apparently included no girls (though some might hang around the edges), and in various ways these boys turned a misogynist gaze on females. Some boys may have engaged in sexual play with each other or with older males.[45] Certainly many showed little interest in girls. Young women often complained about being mocked, ridiculed, and even assaulted in public spaces. Sometimes these attacks extended to young couples, whose public courting might prompt loud laughter, profanities, or the tossing of projectiles. Around these gangs of adolescent boys hung a collective ambivalence (or even resistance) to heterosexual courtship and bonding. In the summer of 1900 a young man who was out for an evening stroll with his girlfriend encountered a group of youths who "stood at the corner laughing and jeering and making remarks offensive to the young couple." When the young man protested, "The boys began to throw stones and mud." He chased them away but a few nights later "they were again annoyed by the boys." The man ended up in court for breaking one of their noses. During the summer carnivals the boys got even bolder. One night during the 1913 centennial celebrations, "Several hundred ruffians walked up King and James streets, and every young lady that they passed was mauled about and their escorts came in for a lot of abuse." A few years later a man reported that in Dundurn Park a gang of ten youths in their late teens staged a wrestling match in front of him and his "lady friend" and assaulted them with "the most awful language" for their own "great amusement." By the 1930s teenage boys in Hollywood movies were regularly displaying this same contempt for heterosexual bonding.[46]

Working-class boys and teens, then, flexed their public bravado as a form of resistance to oppression. They expressed a determination to establish a sense of self-worth in the face of the indignities of economic scarcity and the many-sided efforts to subordinate, tame, and silence them. They hurled insults, swung fists, and undertook pranks and vandalism as statements of independence and power. They were risk-takers, pushing the limits of tolerance and edging into various forms of rebellion. These were not private, individualized acts. Rather, they were staged in a context in which their behaviour would have the support and approval of others, mostly their peers, whose judgment could affirm their identity as working-class males.[47] Some boys no doubt stayed on the margins of such bold performances, perhaps too closely tied down to family responsibilities. Or perhaps some were more bookish, or simply shy, timid, or less aggressive. Certainly no public space existed for more effeminate "sissies" or "pansies."[48] The tough boys ruled the streets.

What galled the city's leading figures was the remarkable independence of these boys. At the turn of the century, authorities still generally responded with repression.[49] With help from the new truant officer, the police attempted to send rowdy youth home or to school, and, when necessary, pulled them into police court, where they would face a tongue-lashing from the magistrate and the public humiliation of a report in the local newspapers' court columns (as well as possible fines or incarceration).[50] Most working-class parents wanted their children to avoid trouble with

the law, and the most streetwise boys seemed to come from families in which parental control was loosest. Occasionally, parents asked the magistrate to declare their son "incorrigible" and to send him to the Victoria Industrial School at Mimico (30 miles away, near Toronto).[51] After 1894 the new local Children's Aid Society could intervene independently. Some 30 years later about 250 boys a year were passing through juvenile court, where they might be handed over to the Big Brothers for parole supervision. More informally, school principals, store managers, welfare officials, individual policemen, and parents turned over to the Big Brothers boys who "because of their delinquencies and anti-social behavior, presented problems to the community," and by the late 1930s the association was handling more than 500 boys a year.[52]

Meanwhile, in the decade before World War One, local businessmen, professionals, and their wives had founded numerous organizations with programs addressed at what they called the "Boy Problem."[53] These new youth workers drew into their discursive arsenal the claims of the influential US psychologist G. Stanley Hall that "adolescence" was an especially difficult and potentially dangerous phase in a boy's psychological development. Rather than relying on the coercive power of the law, they wanted to distract boys from the thrill of the streets and prevent the drift into juvenile delinquency. In contrast to previous child-savers, they focused on the body more than the mind and looked for ways to deflect boyish exuberance into safer channels with more direct adult supervision. In the process they attempted to nurture a new form of more responsible manhood. Hall insisted that boys innately passed through a phase of "savagery," which, if harnessed constructively, could turn them into the middle-class ideal of "real boys" – strong, fit, courageous, and not "sissified."[54]

Youth workers reached out to try to tame boys' independent behaviour. The Boy Scouts, a small number of whom are shown here in 1913, attracted few recruits until the 1920s. (HPL)

The Christian churches, worried that most older boys were dropping out of the Sunday schools, encouraged local congregations to create boys clubs with vigorous mid-week recreational programs that harnessed the "gang instinct."[55] "Athletics are taught, and innocent and healthful recreation encouraged," a 1905 press report on St. Luke's Anglican Boys' Club said. "The boxing gloves are donned now and again, and the youngsters are taught to fight their way through the world." Even in working-class congregations, some boys joined the churches' baseball or basketball teams.[56] The Young Men's Christian Association also overcame some of its reluctance to work with boys, rather than just young men, and launched a small east-end branch in 1907 and a short-lived Newsboys' Club.[57]

The new supervised playgrounds similarly tried to tame working-class boys. According to later accounts, the first president of the playgrounds' association had overheard some boys in the street who were re-enacting a murder recently committed in Hamilton. "Their dramatic actions were so perfect and so horrifying that [she] determined to put all her energy and ability to getting proper places for children to play." The playground programs channelled the boys' exuberance into vigorous, carefully supervised track and field events and baseball and basketball games. The staff insisted on "absolute obedience" and curbed "all swearing, bullying, abuse of apparatus, selfish monopolization of equipment, lying, smoking and such undesirable practices." Within a few years the organizers confidently proclaimed that they were eroding working-class boys' street culture: "There is no doubt that the grounds are rapidly doing away with the corner gangs. All day, boys who would otherwise be members of these are in the grounds, playing every game imaginable; at night they are too tired to stand around the streets smoking cigarettes and concocting devilment."[58]

In 1910 Hamilton also got its first Boy Scout troop, aimed at boys aged 12 through 18.[59] In contrast to the narrowly militaristic cadet training in local schools,[60] this new paramilitary youth movement promised to use closely supervised, rigorous physical training in the outdoors, combined with community service, to make the boys "loyal, helpful, friendly, courteous, kind, obedient, cheerful, thrifty, and clean" – in short, to build "character." While avoiding any evangelical appeals to moral rigour, the Scout leaders attempted, in essence, to distract adolescents by prolonging the adventurous play of their boyhood (symbolized by wearing shorts). The troop mimicked the basic gang structure in its small patrols headed by senior boys. "This gang spirit was not curbed, it was developed, but along service lines," a local newspaper said. A leading businessman in the city praised the organization for "keeping the boys off the streets at night and giving them healthy training."[61]

The impact of all these interventions into working-class boys' street life was limited before 1920. Truancy work was spotty, and the local police court still had no special provisions for young lawbreakers. The city of 100,000 had only four playgrounds and, like the volunteers in Sunday schools and Boy Scouts, the youth workers there had trouble holding onto older boys. The Scouts had collapsed by 1914, without drawing in many non-Anglo or working-class boys (the first Scout commissioner was the principal of the city's elite boys' college, and the uniforms – potential sources of ridicule on the street – cost a boy a whopping $5, both of which must have deterred participation).[62] The YMCA's programs of physical exercise, business education, and evangelical fellowship also reached primarily a white-collar, middle-class clientele, and the east-end branch never attracted many boys before closing its doors in 1918.[63] The churches also drew in only limited numbers, and many of those may have simply moved their neighbourhood associational networks indoors to make better use of the sports facilities.[64] Before the 1920s there were hardly any trained youth workers with claims to expertise on the "boy problem" in any of these organizations in Hamilton.

Moreover, "misrule" now sometimes included small-scale guerrilla warfare with the new institutions established to tame these boys. Residents near the new playgrounds, for example, regularly complained about noise and commotion when older boys clambered inside the grounds after hours to enjoy the space without adult oversight. According to one petition submitted to the school board in 1911, "Young men and girls had made the place a rendezvous after play hours, and had indulged in disgusting behaviour and bad language." Similar complaints erupted in the 1920s, when the police magistrate vowed to clamp down on the "noisy conduct and horseplay" on these sites. Equipment was also often damaged or stolen late at night or in off-seasons when the grounds were not in use. The Soldiers' Aid Commission's secretary also reported his "considerable annoyance" with Boy Scouts meeting in the same building. Their behaviour included reducing the place to darkness and tearing off window coverings. Their only leader was "a boy about 15 who needs controlling more than any one," according to the frustrated official, who complained to city hall repeatedly. Meanwhile, the separate schools had to disband the interschool Catholic Hockey League when it "got so unruly that it became an embarrassment to the school board."[65]

After 1920, however, middle-class adults intervened much more extensively into the street life of working-class boys. The new school attendance law backed up by more rigorous enforcement kept youth in their classrooms regularly until age 16 (and beyond) and discouraged employers from hiring them. The new juvenile court and its parole system also kicked in to handle problem cases more effectively. Probably far more important was the new invasion into boys' playtime. The number of city playgrounds grew quickly from 4 to 17, and in 1931 the city finally took them over. A Catholic Athletic Club was formed in 1920 to integrate recreational programs in all parishes. The Kiwanis and Kinsmen clubs, formed in 1915 and 1920 respectively, made recreation for "underprivileged" boys their primary service work, while the *Spectator* sponsored a Fresh Air Fund to send such children to summer camp.[66]

Meanwhile, the Provincial Commissioner for Boy Scouts reported a "complete reorganization" in 1920, and, with help from the Chamber of Commerce and the Rotary and Kiwanis clubs, Hamilton's Scout membership (and their younger brothers, the Cubs, first authorized in 1916) climbed quickly from 150 in 1921 to over 1,600 in 1930. By the end of the 1930s the Scouts and Cubs had enrolled 2,000 as churches across the city set up troops as part of their social programs. More working-class boys undoubtedly joined, but, in a city with some 15,000 males of ages 8 to 18 by 1941, most boys evidently still steered clear of any serious commitment to Scouting. The Big Brothers also expanded its outreach to boys who had no contact with the courts, and made recreation programs the predominant thrust of its work. By the 1930s the organization was running 22 basketball teams, 30 hockey teams, a baseball league of 60 teams, and a self-governing East End Boys' Club of some 150 members.[67]

In 1919 the Mount Hamilton branch of the Great War Veterans Association also started a "juvenile branch," which provided boxing lessons for boys. The East End branch of the Independent Labor Party had a youth wing in the 1920s, which reconstituted itself as the Marxian Youth Group in the early 1930s and organized a baseball team, dances, and debating forums. The Communists had their Young Pioneers with a special newspaper for youth, the *Young Worker*, and the radical Ukrainians nurtured their young people with special programs in their Labour Temple.[68]

Perhaps the main long-term result of all these initiatives was to direct much more boyish energy and aggression into organized sport. Yet boys could participate in such weekly events and keep their older street-life activities intact. Some may have simply moved their neighbourhood associational patterns indoors to make better use of the sports facilities. That was how the son of a brewery worker with a paper route later remembered his eager response to the *Spectator*'s sponsorship of his YMCA membership in the early 1920s.[69] Others no doubt kept their distance. One boy's response to his encounter with the playgrounds program in the 1920s was probably common: "After two days, I had had enough. They called this recreation and to me it was only school transposed to an outside setting and no more interesting than what went on inside.... With my friends, I took off for more interesting pursuits in our tree house."[70] Many Scouts also passed through local troops quickly without staying long.[71] For such boys the street corner doubtless remained a regular training ground for the long-familiar pattern of independence, defiance, and subversion of working-class boyhood. That behaviour continued to be splashed across the silver screen in Hal Roach's ever-popular *Our Gang/Little Rascals* films of the 1920s and 1930s.[72]

Throughout the first four decades of the century, then, boys in working-class Hamilton continued to celebrate personal freedom and group solidarity and picked up important, often apparently contradictory attitudes and behaviours – intense loyalty, aggressive display, personal toughness, competitiveness, the importance of peer recognition through performance, and the disowning of any "feminine" tendencies. These patterns of association were more fenced in by new youth programs, but not fundamentally undermined. Middle-class boys might share some of the exuberant playfulness, but their world of play in this period was bounded more strictly by bourgeois conventions about appropriate behaviour and flowed more regularly into the supervised realm of formal boys' organizations. Boys of the middle class also generally had less incentive to rebel against systems of authority over which they would eventually be taking control. In contrast, working-class boys struggled to make their fun with limited resources and a deepening recognition of their long-term subordination. Unlike their middle-class counterparts, who made no significant contribution to their family's upkeep, they were constantly aware that street life had to be balanced against a deeply rooted obligation to contribute to their family economies.[73]

Manly Work

Long before they reached their teens, boys in working-class families were encouraged to start earning money part-time. Newsboys were the most visible of the young wage-earners in the more freewheeling "street trades" and the most likely to be truants from school and active participants in street culture. In 1910 they were even bold enough to stage a one-day strike against the *Spectator* and *Herald*.[74]

A boy's first jobs after leaving school may not have appeared to be very different from his earlier part-time work because they were likely to be insecure and broken by periods of unemployment. Employers in the 1920s turned decisively away from hiring younger adolescents, both in conformity with the new legal school-leaving age of 16 and because of their accumulating frustrations with trying to manage young wage-earners. According to a school attendance officer, youth were "for the most part, unsteady, wasteful, and often unreliable." They were "highly emotional and, in a sense, irresponsible" and "likely to develop an exaggerated sense of their own rights." He maintained that "in a modern, intricate and specialized system of production, employers are finding them unprofitable."[75] Bouts of joblessness might have generated tensions with parents (especially if they resulted from simple disgust with ten-hour days of stern discipline) but would also have allowed even more time for enjoying the companionship of old friends on street corners (in the 1920s and 1930s, despite the new school-leaving age, a lot of young men remained at loose ends). The more rebellious doubtless fought back, trying to preserve a degree of personal autonomy (some of them might well have ended up in the hands of the Children's Aid Society or in court), but most boys found themselves torn between a deeply ingrained sense of responsibility to the mutuality of the working-class family and the unfettered excitement of the street life with their friends – a personal dilemma that would plague some of them for years to come.[76]

Becoming a full-time wage-earner was a major turning point in a boy's life. Like his father, he was now part of a man's world beyond the household. Yet for working-class youth the world of wage labour could be deeply contradictory. On one hand, he had come to expect that he had finally made it – that productive work would now give him independence and respect as a full-fledged man; that his earnings would help both himself and his family and guarantee his power within the domestic sphere and beyond. Henceforth he would insist on his "right" to work. On the other hand, he found himself in a setting that immersed him in potentially hazardous dirt and smoke, that subjected his body to muscle strain, mental stress, and the ever-present danger of accidents, and that demanded subservience to rigid authority that constantly intimidated and demeaned him.[77]

In the early 20th century many young workers were entering workplaces that had rapidly changing work routines. Many well-established trades, especially in the city's all-important metalworking plants, were under attack, and even the new skills created within mass-production factories were only grudgingly recognized by corporate managers. Almost none of the trades had an active apprenticeship program after 1900, and, although a few large corporations tried to reinvent the practice through the local technical school after 1910, the programs involved only a tiny handful of boys. Pride in skill was harder to build in a new environment of cost-cutting front-office managers, roving efficiency experts, and bullying foremen. Proportionally, many more men were expected to learn to operate specialized machinery quickly and effectively under much closer, more rigid supervision that assumed such workers should be given no more responsibility or autonomy than wayward children. Layered onto these sensitivities about skill and discipline were new concerns about ethnicity and race. White Anglo-Celtic skilled men watched nervously as their employers recruited newcomers from Southern and Eastern Europe to cheapen their labour costs, speed up production, and otherwise disrupt what English-speaking workers understood to be the norms of their workplaces. For their part, the European newcomers eagerly took the new jobs that were available to them in mass-production plants and resented the exclusionary practices they faced.[78]

Young workingmen clearly faced a continuing struggle to buttress the beleaguered basis of their masculinity in the workplace. Much of that experience was mediated by relations with their workmates. Many of the jobs for teenagers were labelled "boys' work" by factory managers. The work differed from their previous stints as newsboys or messengers principally in that they were now part of a labour process closely controlled by adult men and supervised by male foremen. At the turn of the century the jobs still tended to be clustered in particular departments of a local tobacco plant, glass factory, brass works, or cotton mill, but by the 1920s they were more thinly scattered through a company's workforce. Companies nonetheless still paid a "boys' rate" of wages.[79] Without any impressive rite of passage, lads began their "adult" employment days working as labourers or helpers. Their fellow workers sometimes subjected them to demeaning initiation rituals – sending the boy in the machine shop to find a "left-handed monkey wrench," ordering the young electrical worker to fetch "a pint of amps," or pelting the new textile worker with yarn – to underscore the youngsters' subordinate status.[80]

Gradually a boy learned the routines and expectations of the particular occupation he was settling into, and the ways in which the men around him constructed a particular masculine pride in the skills or strength demanded of that job. This was a process worked out only among men and boys because, unless he started his employment in one of the textile, tobacco, or food-processing plants, he would encounter no women or girls on the job. He soon came to appreciate the different kinds of masculine behaviour demanded in different workplaces – the

Often group photos of workers in one factory revealed the close bonds that workers shared on the shop floor. This shot was taken at Hamilton Steel and Iron in 1906.
(SLS, LS361, LS382)

steady hand, quick eye, and meticulous care of the typographer, the intense exertion and subtle know-how of the moulder, the muscular strength and keen eye of the rolling-mill hand, or the labourer's reservoir of stamina to lift, heave, and tote for hours on end. Doing each job well and winning the respect of the others in his work group engendered many variants of working-class masculinity.[81]

A boy thus learned that a man grounded his masculinity in his contributions to the upkeep of a family, but also in his ability to feel pride in his skills and respect from his workmates. Gathering around their lunch buckets, the men formed small, tight-knit work groups on the shop floor. Their time together during the working day led to regular sociability and reliable companionship, often with boyish playfulness and practical jokes and mutual support and collusion in the face of management authority. The bonds created might carry over into after-work fun. At the same time these informal social relations on the shop floor could also be competitive, especially as recruitment for the semi-skilled jobs played out in the company's internal labour markets; and, for various reasons, might explode into the same kind of angry quarrels or fisticuffs that the feistier young men displayed

in their "free time" outside the plant.[82] In many ways the shop-floor relations among male wage-earners of all ages strongly resembled the street life of boys.

The male solidarity on the shop floor could also provide the energy and organizational base for spontaneous strikes or long-term efforts to create unions. Leadership most often came from older, married men, who shaped much of the official rhetoric of their organizations around the demands of breadwinners. But unions also drew in earnest, determined young men who carried the toughness of the shop-floor (and street) culture into militancy and learned to express the bonds of solidarity as "brotherhood."[83] The penchant among adult workingmen at all ages to defend their manhood in the workplace – which usually meant self-respect, determination, and a refusal to be pushed around – was an echo of boyhood cockiness. In many ways the men carried over the narrow, local focus of the neighbourhood street gang and the occupational work group, rarely including the new immigrant workers in their union-building projects and making little space for women – they often argued passionately against the employment of married women.

Breadwinner-unionism spoke for few younger workers because the working-class youth who had begun wage-earning in their mid-teens did not rush into marriage. Only a tiny percentage married before age 20, and most of them waited until their mid- to late-twenties.[84] Undoubtedly this delay in tying the knot was based primarily on expectations that it would take that long to be in a position to set up an independent household and support a wife and young family, not least because a young man's parents still needed his wages. As a result, young men in Hamilton (as in most other Canadian cities) commonly went through up to ten years of wage-earning before marrying. That decade in most working-class men's lives began with a few years of transition (symbolized in many cases by continuing to wear the short pants of lingering boyhood), but, in their late teens and early twenties, wage-earning youths were part of a more distinct adult bachelorhood.

This period of early adulthood in the lives of most Hamilton workingmen generally evolved within some continuing relationship with the young man's family. It coincided with a phase in the young worker's life when his earnings rose quickly to near full adult levels, and it included his emergence into full citizenship (providing, once again, that he was Canadian-born, a British subject, or naturalized). During the early 20th century almost no one lived alone – the "bachelor apartment" of the late 20th century was unknown. Most single men did not move out of their parents' home, and most of them, too, were still expected to contribute to the family coffers. Indeed, these were the salad days for such families, as the total family income climbed to a peak in its overall life cycle (especially if more than one offspring were bringing home good wages). Those earnings could be substantial, especially as the young man entered his early twenties. Like their fathers, they could take pride in being providers for their parents and siblings. In some households a young workingman might even do better than his father if the older man's trade was being eroded by industrial transformations or if dad suffered from frailties or disabilities that hindered his wage-earning capacities. How much of this income a young man turned over to his family and how much he got to keep was a subject of ongoing negotiation and inevitable conflict. Reaching the status of full citizenship at age 21 may have reinforced a young man's sense of his rights to greater autonomy. To be sure, his family obligations increased if anything

happened to his father's ability to bring home the bacon. Yet, although parents still apparently expected to get most of his wages, they must have conceded him more spending money as a guarantee that he would not leave home completely.[85]

Whether as a part of family strategizing, a form of resistance to family obligations, a search for adventure, or simply frustration with local employment prospects, some young men took off on their own to look for work or better wages somewhere else in North America – perhaps for a season on the "Harvest Excursion" to the wheatfields of the Prairies, perhaps further afield for longer spells. Many people from elsewhere washed up in Hamilton on such a quest and boarded with other families, in some cases in larger boarding houses (especially in the growing European immigrant community). Most of them probably never completely cut themselves off from their families, and sent home at least some of their wages.[86] These young transient workers were the most likely to have coins jingling in their pockets, though even those living at home probably had enough spending money to allow for a few personal indulgences. Their sisters did not have as much mobility or financial independence.

Young wage-earners in early-20th-century Hamilton, then, entered capitalist workplaces with new labour processes and new labour markets. Those starting work before 1920, especially during the wartime boom, might have found possibilities for moving into new semi-skilled jobs that took advantage of their adaptability and youthful energy. They probably set the pace of freewheeling bachelorhood in working-class Hamilton. But, aside from the short-lived economic upturn of 1926–29, most of the interwar years brought prolonged underemployment and joblessness for large numbers of younger men. Some youth stayed a bit longer in the

Working-class bachelor culture could evidently include some gender-bending. Here a group of Westinghouse workers perform for the annual picnic of the company's Veteran Employees' Association in the 1920s.
(MUA, Westinghouse Fonds, Box 13, Item 1b)

new technical schools, some simply huddled together in parks, and some were sent off to camps for the single unemployed in Northern Ontario.[87] For many, a significant prop for their masculine identity – a job – remained shaky.

Having Fun

Life could nonetheless be good. In the first four decades of the 20th century many young men in working-class Hamilton enjoyed a lengthy space within their life cycles in which their responsibilities to family households were diminishing, their workplace identities were solidifying, and their disposable incomes were rising. While they remained under their parents' roof or in a cheap boarding house, their living expenses were limited. This material reality gave them the opportunity – and the privilege – to participate in a vibrant leisure-time culture of young bachelorhood. That culture had its roots in the pre-industrial world of artisans and resource-industry workers, but over the 19th century had been expanding to include more men drawn into full-time wage-earning within industrial capitalism.[88]

Certainly, a young man's ability to frolic in the special masculine realm within working-class communities faced severe limits – including small, unstable incomes and long hours at physically exhausting work. Some, like the steelworkers, had to endure shift work. Others continued to work on Saturday afternoons and, at best, had only their evenings, Sundays, and public holidays to enjoy their bachelorhoods. Moral reformers succeeded in constraining Sunday activities and regulating many leisure pursuits. Young men had to snatch often brief moments of pleasure whenever they could.

In form and content, the most popular activities that young male wage-earners flocked to in their free time were extensions of the familiar forms of play from the street life of their youth. The "gang spirit" carried over into the sports teams that confronted each other on playing fields. Baseball had long been the universal favourite sport in Hamilton, and factory workers regularly used their lunch hours to play pickup games on the streets or in empty lots. Countless young men put together amateur baseball teams that played challenge matches after work or on public holidays and, on other occasions, in leagues organized by their employers, unions, and churches.[89] By 1910 the arrival of so many new British immigrants had also made soccer a major sport in the city, especially in the east end.[90] Some men were good enough join the professional and semi-professional baseball, soccer, football, and hockey teams that came and went in the early part of the century, and represented Hamilton in regional or national leagues (the lines between amateur and semi-professional were still fluid well into the interwar period). Both amateur and professional games drew large crowds of boisterous men and boys (along with a few women). Young men could also keep in touch with local and continental contests, such as the World Series, through the sports pages of the daily press and, by the late 1920s, radio broadcasts.[91]

The dramatic confrontations between contending teams could symbolize fundamental antagonisms in the spectators' lives – "between good and evil, between the privileged and the underprivileged, between the local and the foreign," as an anthropologist suggests.[92] From the sidelines, men identified so closely and emotionally with the players that they occasionally surged onto the field to interrupt the play or challenge the officials' rulings.[93] Everything about crowd behaviour at spectator sports reflected celebrations of boyish behaviour, albeit more structured and, perhaps, more respectable. The stars of these events emerged as paragons of a working-class manliness that valued bodily strength, aggressive competitiveness, and gang-like teamwork. By the 1920s, commercialized team sports had become mass entertainment.

In working-class Hamilton, young men also still liked watching other men pummel each other in a boxing ring – a fascination not always shared by the police, who intervened frequently to uphold the 1881 federal ban on prize fights.

Some young men, like these in the Boggs foundry at the turn of the century, enjoyed the rituals of fraternal societies. (HPL, Bailey Collection)

After years of viewing or joining in street fights, men might appreciate the muscled, half-naked pugilists who competed in amateur union bouts or prize fights as minor heroes of remarkable strength, athletic prowess, and courage, who defended their honour with dramatically ritualized violence and swaggering braggadocio. All this contrasted with the more restrained, "gentlemanly" boxing encouraged by the likes of the YMCA by the turn of the century. Entrepreneurial promoters increasingly packaged boxing matches as carefully controlled (sometimes corrupt) spectacles for mass consumption. In Hamilton the events were often under the official sponsorship of non-commercial groups, including veterans' and labour organizations.[94]

Like many other spectator sports, including the city's more elite horse racing, these events also widened young workers' opportunities for gambling, which was increasingly well organized in the early 20th century through illicit bookmakers and, later, more respectable "pools" run by newspapers (the *Herald* launched a pool on "Old Country" soccer in 1914). "All the boys can be found down at the Jockey club these days," the steelworkers' union paper reported in 1921. Among the young men of working-class Hamilton, betting on games and races co-existed with apparently widespread, clandestine crap-shooting, often undertaken in public spaces. "Gambling with dice on the streets and in sheltered spots around the City was much in evidence during the year," the local Police Department reported in 1912, "and the Police found great difficulty in securing convictions because of the precautions taken by those engaged in the games" (except among the city's small Chinese population, who were regularly targeted in police crackdowns). Between 1907 and 1912 nearly two-thirds of those caught gambling were under age 30. The *Spectator* tried to explain the "seductive mysteries" of the game: "For those who have learned to roll 'hot sevens' and 'elevens' there is a kind of glamour about it that leads them to run all kinds of risks for the pleasures of rolling the bones." Men were still playing in the north end's Eastwood Park in the 1930s.[95]

Young men often organized themselves into independent social and sporting clubs – the Holycats, Owls, and Pals in the north end, for example – with hangouts in which they could enjoy the homosocial company of their peers outside any moral or commercial supervision, and occasionally entertain women.[96] Companies, unions, churches, ethnic organizations, and other groups tried to harness those energies to their own projects. The two leading soccer teams in the city before the war, for example, were sponsored by Westinghouse and the Independent Labor Party.[97] Agencies of moral reform, in particular, both churches and the YMCA, never relented in trying to redirect this young maleness into a more restrained, overtly Christian form of "muscular" masculinity. Like many other local churches, for example, First Congregational Church installed a billiards table and a rifle gallery and organized a basketball club, while Calvin Presbyterian had a Men's League that sponsored sporting events, lectures and debates, picnics and banquets, and sundry other amusements. Barton St. Methodist ran similar programs. Our Lady of All Souls Catholic Church had bowling and baseball teams. Church leagues flourished in several sports. Yet these efforts had limited appeal to the young blue-collar worker, especially in the predominantly working-class churches. Calvin Presbyterian's Men's League collapsed during the war, and efforts to revive it drew in only 40 to 50 men before its final demise in mid-1925. Laidlaw Presbyterian's Men's Brotherhood had a similarly precarious existence, as did the Brotherhood of St. Andrews at St. Luke's Anglican. The small numbers who participated in this earnest social and recreational life were a distinct minority among their peers.[98]

The part-time militia – Canada's "citizen army" – also reached out to the city's young men. Local regiments offered an attractive uniform, the chance to parade in public processions, perhaps as part of a popular regimental band, and two weeks at camp every summer. Before the war the city's militia regiments drew in only select elements of the local male population – primarily white, Anglo-Celtic (especially British-born), Protestant clerical workers with some affinity for the Conservative Party, it seemed – and the troops' role in curbing strikes in some communities doubtless made them unattractive to many workingmen.[99]

The declaration of war in 1914 changed the appeal of military life. Recruiters tried to catch some of the flavour of masculine social life by pitching an image of soldiering as an extension of manly sportsmanship – "Don a uniform and take part in THE GAME," one ad proclaimed – and contrasting the sickly stay-at-home clerk with the healthy, muscled soldier. For much more complex reasons (including an escape from the ranks of the unemployed in 1914–15), the Canadian Expeditionary Force soaked up thousands of young, unmarried men from Hamilton. Their experience, if they survived the trenches, became a fusion of the hegemonic ideologies of imperial masculinity and the plebeian comradeship of the enlisted men they trained and fought with. The desperate struggles to avoid being killed and the bitter resentments at poor food and equipment, rats and lice, officers' incompetence, and politicians' corruption, punctuated by the horrors of forays into "No Man's Land," forged intense bonds of loyalty among enlisted men at the Front and an occasional willingness to resist or subvert military authority. Behind the lines, they smoked, drank, gambled, and womanized together. They played baseball and other sports and attended music-hall-style concerts and variety shows, where the humour was regularly risqué and anti-authoritarian. Back in Canada, after demobilization, many of them displayed, in the form of wounds or missing limbs, the visible price that their bodies had paid for imperial valour. Many more tried to keep the spirit of boyish comradeship alive in a variety of veterans' organizations. In addition to lobbying for their interests, the groups opened clubhouses and sponsored numerous social and cultural events. Some veterans hung out more informally in small, disconsolate groups in old haunts. For most able-bodied workingmen from their late teens through their mid-thirties during the 1910s (and for many more who did not serve), the war experience of homosocial life and expressiveness through the body sharpened the edges of a working-class masculinity based in prolonged bachelorhood.[100]

Both before and after the war, much of the time that working-class bachelors spent together lacked formal structure but continued the public rituals of boyhood. The street-corner loungers who so irritated police and passers-by were often young male wage-earners. Fights could sometimes erupt in the streets in response to challenges or insults, such as one young man's declaration: "I hear you've been telling a lot of lies about me."[101] The young men now had more money to spend than they had as boys, and some of the "hanging out" took place in poolrooms or the cheap seats of vaudeville and movie theatres.[102] Eventually, at the end of their teens, the men would move into saloons.[103]

Public drinking had been at the centre of bachelor life in cities like Hamilton for generations.[104] By the turn of the century it took place in saloons attached to hotels. State regulation shortened the hours of operation (7 p.m. was the closing time on Saturday evenings), restricted the neighbourhoods in which barrooms could be located, and gradually reduced the number of facilities in the city (from 75 in the 1890s to 55 in 1915). But thousands of workers crowded in each week, especially after work on Saturday, to enjoy the conviviality of shared drinks.[105] The connection between these watering holes and wage-earning could be close. Since many wage-earners from the same neighbourhood or factory clustered in particular saloons, the barrooms were places to pick up news about jobs, buy a foreman a drink, or simply discuss work and its discontents. Probably more important, they were a transition zone between increasingly intense working hours and relaxation at home. The moments spent sharing a drink with workmates or neighbours allowed for the sociability that time on the job in a capitalist workplace usually severely constrained.[106]

These so-called "workingmen's clubs" nourished a boyish freedom from control – the

Informally and out of the public eye, drinking remained a form of male bonding, celebrated here in a comic pose.

(HPL, Bailey Collection)

emotionalism, spontaneity, and irresponsibility that boys enjoyed. Beneath pictures of scantily clad women and scenes of sporting activities, discussions might range over exclusively male activities such as hunting and fishing, sports, politics, or, inevitably, relations with women. Conversations sprinkled with "lewd and profane" language horrified prim Protestant investigators in 1913. In these places, men could smoke, spit, swear, whistle, sing, fart, tell off-colour jokes, laugh loudly and shout, ridicule women, and generally ignore the civilizing constraints of domesticity. A certain cockiness shows through in the surviving photographs of bodies arched back against the bar, one hand wrapped around a drink, the other on the hip, one foot on the brass rail. Here a man could simply be "one of the boys."

Broadly speaking, consuming alcohol allowed workingmen gathered in saloons to play out two different forms of behaviour. One was the boisterous, competitive, potentially violent version that erupted with heavy drinking. This was unquestionably a performance with familiar scripts for the benefit of fellow drinkers,[107] and seems to have been associated with more free-spirited bachelors (both young and old) and

sometimes with the seasonally unemployed. These men often roamed between hotel barrooms on a Saturday night or a public holiday, extending the stage for their loud performances onto the street. In their drunkenness they might brag expansively, insult or offend others, and easily take offence – expressing racist comments about blacks, confronting a strikebreaker, or defending the honour of their womenfolk or their own reputations. Some drunks stood accused of petty theft or more destructive behaviour, including smashing windows. Nor were fights uncommon. A few young men attacked their parents violently. Sometimes, if men became too obstreperous or pugnacious, they earned a trip to police court and, usually, a stiff fine.

Most often, the drunks were single men. Some two-thirds of the just over 1,000 tipplers who faced the police magistrate on charges of public drunkenness (and, in some cases, "disorderliness") in a 12-month period in 1909–10 were bachelors or widowers. In the spring of 1910 the magistrate, not surprisingly, slapped stiffer fines on the rising tide of bachelor drunks. Although the many young men who flocked into Hamilton in the decade before the war were prominent in their ranks, those under age 30 comprised only a third of the unmarried drunks. In that 1909–10 period more than 400 bachelors and widowers in their thirties, forties, and fifties still made heavy drinking in the city's saloons such a central part of their leisure time that they ended up in police court.[108]

Not all drinkers were drunks. In 1913 Methodist and Presbyterian investigators reported spotting only 217 intoxicated men on a Saturday-evening "census" of Hamilton's saloons – a mere 12 per cent of the 1,775 drinkers they tallied up in the last hour before closing. Since these prudish teetotallers would no doubt have been inclined to exaggerate, this is a remarkably low total – far

Under Ontario's post-prohibition regulations these men in the Cecil Hotel's beverage room had to remain seated while drinking. (AO, RG 6-36-8)

less than temperance-movement rhetoric would have prepared the public to expect. Most men apparently restrained their consumption, and went home no more than a bit tipsy, although the boundaries between bachelor-driven expressiveness and more restrained sociability must have been as fluid as the beverages and as unstable as their blood-alcohol levels, especially at more celebratory moments on the calendar. Yet, in the mock-elegant setting of the barroom, with its gleaming mahogany and giant mirrors, most young workingmen could construct their socializing patterns there as being perfectly respectable. Informally and collectively, the men were taming their time and space apart with "the boys" in order to preserve such an important realm of autonomous working-class masculine expression.

That spirit lay behind the Canadian labour movement's campaign to roll back the prohibition of alcoholic beverages immediately after World War One.[109] The position was a historic

shift away from the local labour movement's severe caution about expressing any opinion on alcohol consumption because numerous workingmen, including the prominent Allan Studholme and Sam Landers, did not approve of drinking. Despite massive petition campaigns and demonstrations for the return of full-strength beer (in which some Hamilton labour leaders played prominent roles), public drinking in Ontario remained shut down from 1916 to 1934.[110] In that long interlude of repression, social drinking continued in the shadows – in the bootlegger's "blind pig" or in private homes.[111] Many young men learned to carry a flask of their favourite liquor. Overall, consumption of alcohol probably declined somewhat in this period, more because of the high cost of bootleg liquor and the deep depression that ran through so much of the interwar period than because of the legal prohibition. Ultimately more important, shutting down the saloon eliminated the setting for performing the familiar texts of swaggering

Real Beer!
At Less Than 5c. a Pint

Are you disappointed in 4.4%?

You can brew the kind of Beer you used to get—in your own home, from RITE-GOOD Malt Extract and Hops—a healthful, refreshing beverage, with all the strength, full flavor and body of the finest old-time brews.

And Look at the Economy

Do you know that from a package of RITE-GOOD costing $1.75, you can brew 50 pints of real beer? The same number of bottles of 4.4% costs about $7.50.

Try a package to-day and be convinced that it is real beer, strong and wholesome, for less than five cents a pint. Satisfaction is guaranteed if the simple directions in each package are followed.

$1.00 package makes 25 pints.
$1.75 package makes 50 pints of strong beer.
$2.00 package makes 50 pints of Stout and Porter.

E. B. Nettelfield & Co.
35 Colborne Street, Toronto
or
The St. Lawrence Preserving Co., Regd.
Quebec, P.Q.

Recipe book and the necessary crown corks are supplied with each package

During prohibition, making beer (but not spirits) for home consumption was still legal. (HS, 13 June 1925, 16)

masculine bravado, and public drunkenness was more harshly punished.

Alcoholic beverages went back on sale in government-controlled liquor stores and brewers' warehouses in 1927. In Hamilton after 1934, when legal public drinking returned to Ontario, the Liquor Control Board of Ontario (LCBO) licensed 53 "beverage rooms" attached to hotels (in other provinces they were known as "beer parlours") and 15 private clubs (10 of them run by veterans' organizations). These new drinking establishments operated within rigid LCBO regulations intended to curb the more expressive forms of pre-prohibition drinking culture. As part of the rigorously administered standards of moral architecture, the centrepiece of earlier drinking – the long, gleaming bar – had been banished. All patrons had to be seated and could not move around with their drinks. Nor could they eat any food, play any games, sing, or watch any entertainment. The atmosphere was, in the words of an Ontario poet, "shabby genteel."

The workers who flocked into these drab, unadorned drinking places, and who formed the overwhelming majority of the clientele, nonetheless pushed the limits of this new regulatory regime and re-created many of the associational patterns of the old-time saloons. In particular, the many serious drunks still seemed to be the froth on a much larger sea of moderation among working-class drinkers. Frequent joblessness certainly cut into young workers' abilities to afford such pleasures.[112]

Inevitably considerable numbers of young men avoided all of these public sites of expressive bachelor culture. Some no doubt consciously spurned the moral laxness of this mode of relaxing and turned to more "wholesome" activities in church programs, perhaps the Sunday-afternoon men's meetings (so-called "Pleasant Sunday Afternoons") at the First Congregational or Knox Presbyterian churches or in the Catholic Church's Holy Name Society.[113] Some took evening courses at the new Hamilton Technical Institute, until the classes were gradually wound down in favour of adolescent education.[114] The library also offered reading material for more bookish men.[115] Young men in skilled trades could find an occupational and class culture in union and left-wing halls, including serious meetings, stirring speeches and lectures, and engaging reading material. The small Hamilton branch of the Workers' Educational Association that started up in 1920 gave some of these workers the chance to engage in more academic study.[116] Many more young men found new counterattractions in commercially run leisure sites. Here, however, they were more likely to be moving beyond the homosocial and looking to spend time with women.

Settling Down

The transition from a wholly male associational experience to a life involving females must have been awkward for young workers. However it happened, somehow most young men began to reach out across the social gulf and, at some stage, to spend time with girls as "dates" and potential sexual partners and, eventually, as spouses.

After boys left school, regular contact with girls (other than sisters) became less common. Most young wage-earners were unlikely to see females at work, and, even in plants that employed women and girls, the opposite sex generally had completely different jobs in distinct departments. Men might have struck up acquaintanceships with working girls walking to and from work,[117] but they would have had to run the gamut of the misogynist catcalls and jeering at young heterosexual couples that other boys and young bachelors bellowed out on the streets. In contrast to middle-class practices, working-class courtship was a largely public process.[118] While the streets provided some highly ritualized contact between groups of young men and the young women who were plunging more boldly into the city's public recreational life, more respectable, though also public, settings also existed for striking up relationships with young women, including church-sponsored religious and recreational activities.[119]

Undoubtedly, though, it was in the commercialized leisure spots that young working-class men could most easily meet members of the opposite sex. Generally they could afford the small admission charges to dance halls, roller-skating or ice-skating rinks, ball parks, cruise boats, amusement parks, and vaudeville and movie theatres. In an extension of street flirtations, they might visit these sites with male friends and pick up female companions, or they might invite a young woman to join them on such an outing.[120] In the 1920s the more adventurous might take their dates to one of the city's many small blind pigs or invite them to share a flask while out dancing or skating. After 1934 many young couples visited the new beverage rooms set up for "ladies and escorts." Boisterous, bachelor-driven patterns of male socializing thus came to co-exist cheek by jowl with companionate, heterosexual leisure.[121]

By that point the practices of dating were reflected in and reflective of the romanticized images of heterosexual coupling beaming out of movie screens.[122] There, and in the sophisticated advertising splayed across newspapers, magazines, and billboards, young men saw representations of masculine ideals in dress and comportment. Most of those images did not draw on working-class experience, but they did appeal to the performative dimension of their public lives. Some working-class bachelors no doubt indulged in buying products to look the part, but probably more young men borrowed skills for successful behaviour from Hollywood stars and honed them for performance on their heterosexual outings.[123]

Many bachelors also engaged in sex with women, and perhaps with men: the existing police-court records for 1905–11 list 12 men arrested for "gross indecency," the legal phrase for male same-sex activity, but in this period as a whole the city did not develop the visible homosexual communities of metropolitan centres such as New York or Toronto.[124] However limited their actual sexual knowledge,[125] young men tended to act out an understanding of their own sexuality that assumed they were driven by almost uncontrollable, "natural" lustful passions different from the tendencies of females (who were expected to set the limits), that aggression might be necessary (as in other social relationships), and that they had a right to be the dominant partner.[126]

If they reached adulthood before the 1920s, men would have faced stern hegemonic discourses that encouraged them to exercise self-control, preferably abstinence, but after World War One the frequent films and lectures on venereal disease organized by public-health authorities made sexuality a much more public issue with somewhat less moralism and more medical science.[127]

Hollywood movies also regularly legitimated more expressive sexual lifestyles. Some men simply sought out the few downtown brothels, a practice that became much more visible when so many soldiers arrived back from the trenches of World War One infected with venereal diseases.[128] Alternatively, they might look for quiet spaces to be alone with their dates, such as wooded parks,[129] or find somewhere to go in the jumble of boathouses and shacks along the north-end waterfront. Perhaps, by the 1920s and 1930s, they might take their dates out in automobiles, if they could afford one or perhaps borrow one. They might have expected some sexual favours in return for treating their girlfriends to a dance or a movie.[130] Eventually, "going steady" might well assume some degree of regular consensual sex between partners, on the assumption that marriage would follow.[131]

Some young men assumed that they had a right to bypass such negotiations and simply forced themselves on their sexual partners in what could amount to rape. If they constructed their prey as "bad" or "loose," they might have no qualms about using physical violence to get sex.[132] It was not always easy to draw the line between persistent pressure on a woman to have sex and outright sexual assault, as many court cases revealed (virtually all of them involving working-class males),[133] and many men apparently expected their partners to set the limits.

In 1920 a couple of 17-year-old males met two young women of the same age at a carnival and paired off as they left the grounds. One led his companion on a stroll into Woodlands Park. She later reported that his conversation was "respectable," but that he suddenly grabbed her, threw her to the ground, and covered her mouth with his hand. She escaped his clutches, ran home, and called the police. In the courtroom the young man "quietly admitted his offense" and "said that he had no wrong intentions previously, but 'something got in his head.'" When he found the girl resisting he let her go. Some six years later a man turned reciprocal embraces with a woman he had met at a skating pond into assault, arguing, in essence, that she had led him on. The same year another man on a skating outing raped a woman in what the Crown lawyer and the judge later called "a sudden impulse of passion."[134]

All these practices of male working-class sexual pleasure outside marriage flew in the face of hegemonic bourgeois conventions about sexuality (and the draconian Criminal Code of Canada), but they nonetheless became a training ground for the patriarchal power relations involved in intimacy with women throughout their adult lives.

Dating did not necessarily mean completely abandoning "the boys," though obviously it cut into time spent in all-male company. Homosocial spaces and practices must have remained a reference point for (and perhaps a refuge from) the new relationships with women. A significant minority of men seemed to prefer to linger in this bachelor world, avoiding long-term heterosexual commitment (sustained in popular culture by the lone cowboy, the unattached gangster, the hard-boiled private detective, or such confirmed bachelors as the comedy team of Laurel and Hardy). In later life, many of these men ended up in the city's home for the aged.[135]

Many more men grew tired of the loneliness and insecurities of bachelor ways.[136] At some point in their mid-twenties the great majority of young workingmen made a decision to marry, thus reaching another Rubicon in their lives. Setting up a new household and starting a family brought serious breadwinning responsibilities and expectations that a man would turn his back on the excesses of bachelorhood. In practice, over their married lives working-class men fell somewhere along a continuum of behaviour. At one extreme, if they had not already done so, they withdrew completely from the rowdiness and carousing of young adulthood and, as well as dutifully turning over their wages to their wives, stayed home in their leisure time and took their families on excursions to local parks or beaches on special occasions. They might also be open to a more companionate social life with their wives, as the spread of card parties attested. They were more likely to be convinced to attend church regularly, especially since the main Christian churches had been putting so much effort into giving their faith a more robust "manly" cast.[137]

The already stern legal regime that buttressed a man's breadwinning responsibilities got even tougher through new legislation in the early 1920s to nail a man down to his children and his parents.[138] At the other extreme, a man who remained restless and unwilling to accept the domestic constraints of being a husband and father might have a life punctuated with frequent drunkenness, gambling, absenteeism from work, philandering, or violent behaviour. Some fell into seriously debilitating heavy drinking. In 1909–10 a third of the court cases touching on that issue involved married men.

All too often, irresponsible husbands created havoc with family finances and sometimes attacked their wives and children. Every week, after all, women brought abusive husbands to police court on charges of assault or non-support. A good proportion of these cases involved ongoing

Some married men sacrificed their family's needs for the old pleasures of bachelorhood, especially excessive drinking. (SLS, LS 716)

marital strife or separation. For some time her husband had been "drinking too heavily and abusing her," one wife told the magistrate in 1910, "but last night he had beaten her something fierce." When she fled, "he wreaked his vengeance on the furniture and dishes destroying nearly everything in the house." Smashing furniture and crockery seemed to be a ritual act of violence against the demands of domesticity in a number of these cases. Many such offenders were put on the so-called "Indian List" of people to whom alcohol could not be sold, a list circulated to retailers and saloon-keepers (but which was apparently ineffective in preventing renewed drunkenness). Some men simply deserted their families.[139]

Between the extremes of home-bodies and drunkards, many married working-class men maintained a middle ground that included taking the occasional opportunity to enjoy the all-male camaraderie of their bachelor haunts.

A weekly stop at a saloon or bootlegger's blind pig or an afternoon in a ball park might be enough. Less frequent all-male hunting and fishing expeditions might become rituals of the rougher masculinity as well. Many of these men might also participate in the apparently more sedate homosocial culture of fraternal-society lodge meetings, which remained the most common form of exclusively male socializing right through the decades (though their membership was declining by the interwar period). Those secret conclaves involved passwords, oaths, elaborate regalia, and solemn rituals staged within exotically decorated meeting halls. They also provided educational lectures, light entertainment, and occasionally banquets, picnics, or parades to church, along with pleasant moments of simple, sedate male fellowship over a cigar, without the restraints of female company or the malodorous morality of saloons.[140] Smaller numbers of men found similar respectable company in unions or veterans' organizations, though, in some cases, these too could slide into more easygoing gatherings, as in the case of the Central ILP, which reputedly ended its all-male meetings in the 1920s over a keg of beer, or most of the veterans' social programs, which included alcohol wherever possible.[141]

All this participation in homosocial activities undoubtedly required potentially difficult negotiation with spouses, although many men probably expected their wives and children to accept without question their decisions about how to use their own leisure time and the money needed to support it. To use terms common in working-class Britain at the time, a "good" husband was a man who used a small part of his pocket money to share a few glasses of beer at the end of the working week and headed home with most of his wages intact, while a "bad" husband ignored the needs of his family and indulged himself in

the saloon culture that he had come to enjoy before marriage.[142] Some key elements in bachelor-based gender identities, then, carried over into the life phase of family-based breadwinning.

Working-Class Manhood

Growing up male in working-class Hamilton, then, involved a layering of experiences that produced distinctive class-based gender identities. The evolving processes included relationships with other men as well as with women, with forces of capitalist power and the legal regime, and with hegemonic conceptions of ethnic and racial identities. Certainly through family dynamics, schooling and youth programs, and labour-market structures, a boy learned the privileges of his gender superiority over the females in his life and sharply differentiated himself from them. But early on he also ran up against the structures of class subordination – in particular the economic scarcity that limited everything from his choice of play space to his job prospects to his adult recreational options; and the authority figures who controlled and contained his behaviour, from parents to teachers to policemen to bosses.

Within these confines, a boy and his young male friends developed a cluster of often contradictory masculine practices that defined them as emergent workingmen. In contrast to middle-class men (who turned to muscle-building as compensation for their non-manual work),[143] young male wage-earners took pride in using their bodies to express themselves in virtually all parts of their lives – applying muscular strength on the job, coping with the heat and grime of the workplace, suffering crippling injury or illness (at any age, but especially in middle and old age), eating for nourishment (often on limited income), drinking for pleasure (and to get drunk), playing demanding sports, performing sexually, fighting with and violently assaulting others, and swaggering, shouting, whistling, singing, swearing, belching, and farting – all generally undertaken as some kind of exuberant performance in a public setting. In boyhood, adolescence, and bachelorhood, moreover, they participated to varying degrees in collective practices of class and gender solidarity and of defiance of authority and bourgeois morality. Working-class boys learned to be loud, lewd, and cocky. Much of that behaviour was dismissed with a shrug in the essentialist phrase "boys will be boys."

To be sure, tamer versions of this masculine identity also made their appearance – perhaps boys who stayed in school a bit longer, liked to read or play a musical instrument more than throw stones at neighbours' cats, embraced religion more fervently, avoided the poolroom and the saloon, took up trades that demanded sober concentration, deferentially accepted the authority of foremen, or later emerged as activists in the local labour movement. Beyond differences of individual personality or family culture, this kind of divergence undoubtedly rested in large part on the material resources that a particular working-class family could muster as the boy was growing up – the greater the scarcity, the less likely a boy would be to aspire to such modest respectability, particularly if he belonged to a systematically disadvantaged ethnic or racial group.

Yet all boys and men in working-class Hamilton shared to some degree the profoundly contradictory tendencies between self-indulgent irresponsibility and deeply ingrained commitments to collective solidarity owed to family and workmates. In the end, working-class men constructed their masculine identities largely as survival mechanisms. They enjoyed the privileges of being men and used them to create their own cultural oases, but, aside from the few who were quickly targeted as "incorrigible" boys, chronic drunks, or vagrants, they still had to pitch in to help sustain their families, and they still punched the clock in a capitalist workplace each day.

A lot of these practices dated back to the first encounters with industrial capitalism. But the half-century before World War Two saw significant changes in the lives of working-class males that had brought about a perceptible reconstruction of their gender identities by the 1920s and 1930s. Boys came under closer and more prolonged surveillance and regulation in regular, compulsory schooling and a profusion of new youth organizations and institutions, which must have curbed their autonomy in the streets to at least some extent. At the same time, prolonged schooling and then deepening underemployment undermined their ability to take pride in contributing wages to their families' coffers (and earning some spending money of their own). The disruptive forces of the Second Industrial Revolution gave them new opportunities in semi-skilled work, but demanded a much intensified pace under more bureaucratic and authoritarian management and created new risks of debilitating accident or disease. They were encouraged to identify their masculine practices with imperialist projects, notably the biggest European war in a century, but the military Armageddon that so many of them were caught up in left large numbers physically and psychologically wounded. The independent recreational life that they expected to enjoy as they reached adulthood was undermined by the moral-reform victories that culminated in the complete closure of the bachelors' neighbourhood social centre, the saloon. Meanwhile, the young women in their communities confronted them with a new independence and assertiveness in the public sphere.

Working-class males responded to all these challenges and renegotiated their identities in a variety of ways. In their boyhoods they carried their exuberance and peer-group commitments indoors into the new recreational programs offered to them, but, for far more of their free time, they renewed the older street culture. When they got jobs, their male work-group solidarities provided an important current of resistance to the new workplace regime that helped both to spark strikes and unionizing efforts and to protect their limited occupational privileges against women or other ethnic groups. Once they were earning wages, they turned to cheap consumerist pleasures – drinking, ball games, boxing matches, movies – to fill up more of their free time, but, as the moral reformers closed in on their leisure pursuits, they tamed their rough pleasures and, with the onset of prohibition, argued for the respectability of their drinking and sporting customs. Within the local labour movement, the earnest teetotallers had been succeeded by 1920 by men who were prepared to campaign publicly for beer-drinking and to organize boxing matches or petty gambling.[144]

While they maintained plenty of male-only spaces, men tended to welcome women into their social lives, even to the extent of integrating them into a new companionate public drinking culture, but maintained their dominance as "escorts" for their female companions. The essential power dynamics of patriarchy had not been dissolved, but the forms through which they operated had been reshaped. Workingmen in Hamilton, as elsewhere, continued to struggle with their dual experience as dominators and dominated.

15

For many newcomers from Southern and Eastern Europe, the Catholic Church was an important resource for nurturing ethnic identities. Here the Italians parishioners of St. Anthony of Padua parade on the feast day of their patron saint. (SLS, LS710)

Our Kind

IN THE SUMMER OF 1912 a Hamilton *Herald* reporter took his readers on one of the city's first journalistic tours of the new "foreign section" in the east end. Although a lot of writers engaged in fear-mongering about the "strangers within our gates" in this pre-war period, the tone of this reporter's front-page story was optimistic: the newcomers would be easily assimilated. "Hamilton is a melting pot, where the people of the world come, and in the course of time become good Canadians," he predicted.[1]

That journalist turned out to be a poor prognosticator. Certainly the immigrants from non-Anglo-Celtic backgrounds who chose to stay would continue to learn to adapt to their unfamiliar circumstances in Hamilton. But in the early decades of the 20th century, distinct ethnic identities got stronger, not weaker. While labour markets and real-estate patterns kept ethnic and racialized groups apart, so too did the conscious efforts of community leaders to kindle ethnic solidarities. The residents of working-class Hamilton were thus regularly summoned to rally 'round different flags, and often to view each other with suspicion and resentment. By the interwar years, common experiences were eroding some of these sharp lines of demarcation, but they never disappeared before World War Two.

Rule Britannia

A man, or later a woman, in early-20th-century Hamilton who wanted to participate in public life could not claim to be a *citizen* of Canada.

Hamilton's civic leaders organized a huge celebration of Queen Victoria's Diamond Jubilee in 1897 to promote the glories of the British Empire and British "race."

in Western Europe between 1914 and 1918. In this regard the authorities got support from a growing array of voluntary organizations dedicated to deepening that ethno-cultural commitment to what has been called "popular imperialism."[2]

Queen Victoria's Diamond Jubilee in 1897 provided the occasion to launch this new jingoistic version of British ethnicity. A full day of festivities began with a huge parade that presented a pageant of social integration – children from both public and separate schools, municipal office-holders, militiamen, unionists, aboriginal peoples, fraternal lodge brothers, and members of national benevolent societies representing England, Scotland, and Ireland.[3] That summer the prominent upper-class and superpatriotic activist Clementina Fessenden began to agitate for an annual spectacle of imperial fervour on the last school day before the 24 May holiday for the Queen's Birthday (after the monarch's death in 1901, renamed Victoria Day). Fessenden convinced the Hamilton Board of Education and later the provincial minister of education to inaugurate Empire Day in all Ontario schools as an occasion for stories, plays, patriotic songs, cadet-marching, and stirring speeches about the glories of the Empire.[4]

The public schools assumed a central role in inculcating love of the monarch, his empire, British ethnicity, and the Protestant faith. The school day opened with "God Save the King," and at other times students might be expected to recite the lines of "Rule Britannia" by heart. Their readers brimmed with the superpatriotic poetry of Kipling, Henley, Tennyson, and others, alongside essays on British military might. History texts extolled the unrivalled accomplishments of British institutions. Geography lessons drove home the superiority of the British "race" over all others. "Wherever British control has been exercised," one textbook proclaimed, "the

Rather he or she was a *subject* of the British Crown. Repeatedly Canadians were reminded that the fountainhead of their political culture was a monarch residing in Britain, whose empire extended across the globe, within which Canada was a subordinate "dominion." Participation in such an empire was seen as far more than being simply a colony; it was to be part of a larger, more awe-inspiring "British world." Such was the "imagined community" for Anglo-Canadians born in Canada or in Britain (or one of its other white-settler dominions). It was also an overriding ethno-cultural identity. Indeed, the alleged superiority of the British "race" was a key element in the cement of imperial sentiment within an empire incorporating a huge diversity of ethnic and racial groups, and it served as a justification for subordinating those groups, including those found within Canada's borders. A civilizing mission towards those allegedly degraded cultures became a unifying force among the widely scattered British. Starting in the late 1890s, the Canadian state staged many public rituals to rally Canadians around British imperial identity, including the massive military effort

benefits of civilization have been experienced."
The separate-school system used the same provincially approved texts and delivered the same
message, although tying it to Catholicism.[5]

For all age groups, the military remained
central to local rituals of popular imperialism.
Before World War One, Hamilton supported
two part-time militia regiments, the Thirteenth
Regiment and the kilted Ninety-First Canadian
Highlanders (formed by Scottish Canadians in
1903). Both were sustained by the organizational
energies of local businessmen, who raised funds,
donned the uniforms of colonels, and led the
troops. The regiments' bands were regular features of many public events, and their periodic
parades, featuring brilliant uniforms, horses,
artillery, and martial music, and their dramatically staged manoeuvres provided both popular
entertainment for big crowds and a visible symbolism of British power across the globe. In 1905,
for example, after 1,100 soldiers had marched
through packed streets in the first-ever combined parade of both regiments, some 20,000
people (close to a third of the city's population)
showed up in Dundurn Park for a huge outdoor
religious service.[6] School boys were encouraged
to join such spectacles as junior soldiers in the
school cadet brigades.

Twice in this period soldiers recruited in
Hamilton shouldered rifles to kill and be killed
in real wars in support of the Empire. Both
times, the flames of imperialist fervour burned
brightly on the home front. The first time was the
British intervention in South Africa from 1899 to
1902. Only a handful of local men served there,
but the events of 1 March 1900 revealed the remarkable degree of popular enthusiasm for that
military campaign. Early that morning news
arrived that, after four months, British troops
had finally broken through Boer lines to relieve
the British garrison in the town of Ladysmith.

UNITY OF THE EMPIRE.

Grand Patriotic Concert

TO BE HELD IN

THE ARMORY

Tuesday, January 9th, 1900

Given by the joint Fraternal Societies
of Hamilton, in aid of the fund ♪ ♪
being raised by the Lord Mayor of
London for the benefit of the Widows, Orphans, and Families dependent upon the Soldiers and Sailors
of the Queen who may fall in the
War in South Africa.

Programme—Price 5 Cts.

McPherson & Drope, Printers.

Britain's war in
South Africa brought
an outpouring of
imperial sentiment.
(CIHM No. 36331)

Like newspapers in the rest of the Empire, the
Hamilton press had kept the crisis in the public
eye for weeks, and the news of victory struck a
chord across the city. A rising din of bells, factory whistles, rifle shots, fireworks, and sundry
noisemakers started at dawn and continued for
hours, as thousands of people poured out into
the streets shouting, singing, and waving flags,
oblivious to the huge snow drifts and frigid tem-
peratures. Flags and bunting were strung up
everywhere, including a large stock seized from
city hall by a crowd of 500 (led by two women).
School children were assembled for quick inspirational speeches and a few patriotic songs
and then dismissed to join the outdoor festivities. During the afternoon, factory and shop
workers were similarly released to the streets.
Thousands formed a spontaneous parade by
falling in behind the Sons of England Band and

Hamilton contributed many recruits to the Canadian Expeditionary Force in World War One. The promise of immediate wages appealed to many local workers who had been facing severe unemployment since 1913. (HPL)

singing along with its imperialist music. Other mini-parades took off throughout the downtown area all day. A *Spectator* reporter saw the "poor man with his five-cent flag and the rich man with his expensive show of loyalty." In the evening the Thirteenth Regiment and its band headed up another huge impromptu procession of sleighs and rigs and assorted marchers bearing torches. Firework displays illuminated the ubiquitous Union Jack, "that glorious old flag," as the *Spectator* said, "that has waved in triumph over so many lands in the cause of truth and righteousness." Alcohol flowed freely, until most saloon-keepers shut down early. While other celebrations of British military accomplishments in South Africa took place in the coming year, none matched this spontaneous explosion

of patriotic merrymaking, which, in Hamilton lore, would become known as "Ladysmith Day." In form it resembled the familiar rituals of election night revelry and other informal celebrations, and shared the "feel-good" liminality of those occasions. A week later a local Christian socialist wrote in disillusionment, "The war craze is going from bad to worse and it is almost impossible to do any active work."[7]

The next declaration of war had a far more profound, prolonged impact. As a component of the Empire with little independence in foreign affairs, Canada was automatically involved when Britain declared war on Germany, Austria-Hungary, and their allies in August 1914. In the early days of that month, huge crowds gathered outside the *Spectator* office to watch for reports projected onto a large outdoor screen, cheering the king and booing the kaiser. When news of Britain's declaration of war flashed up on 4 August (Civic Holiday), the crowds broke into deafening cheers and choruses of "God Save the King" and "Rule Britannia," as they did at a massive gathering in Dundurn Park and at a local theatre. In the press, local poets poured out invocations to "sound the loud call" to defend the motherland and hearken to "the call of the blood." Over the next few days, attention shifted to military recruitment. In a scene of "wildest enthusiasm," thousands of Hamilton residents crowded into the armouries to watch volunteers enlist, while bands played and soldiers drilled. A "great cheering mob" followed a military band through the downtown streets. Thousands also turned out for a military parade, and then for the send-off from the train station of the first local contingents for the new Canadian Expeditionary Force (CEF). Newspaper editorials trumpeted their honour and courage. Clergy used their Sunday sermons to wish them Godspeed. Similar pro-war celebrations of British-Canadian identity

Like these Bell Telephone employees, Hamilton workers often joined public campaigns to promote the war effort.
(HPL)

and militarist masculinity took place across the country that month, in what has been called the "Festival of August'"[8]

The journalistic jingoism did not relent for some time, supported by a state-supported propaganda campaign that kept Canadians believing in the romantic myth of duty, valour, and noble service and that screened out the horrors of the battlefields. Recruitment continued, particularly among the British-born. By the end of 1915 some 5,000 Hamilton men had signed up. Yet well before that point, enlistment was flagging, and in July 1915 a group of prominent businessmen and politicians set up the Hamilton Recruiting League, the country's first voluntary committee to encourage men to enlist. These community leaders (and their women's auxiliary) plastered walls and shop windows with signs. They sponsored outdoor recruitment rallies, showed war movies, staged patriotic concerts, addressed crowds at sporting events, inserted messages into pay envelopes, and even brought in the pro-war British suffragette

Emmeline Pankhurst to speak. As the League's secretary later claimed, a man "could not walk ten yards or read for ten minutes without some startling reminder that he had a duty to his empire." Sometimes that pressure amounted to harassing apparent "shirkers" in the streets. This relentless campaign played heavily on themes of obligation to empire and pride in British cultural superiority over the bloodthirsty Germans and their illiberal culture. The many clergymen involved in recruiting rallies gave religious sanction to these appeals.[9]

During 1916 and 1917, Hamilton's League was also at the forefront of national agitation for compulsory registration of manpower resources and then military conscription. Meanwhile the Canadian Patriotic Fund had been established to help soldiers' wives, and late in 1916 the League also spun off another voluntary organization, the Soldiers' Aid Commission, to help returned soldiers find work and get re-established. At home popular enthusiasm waned somewhat as the casualties mounted (and opportunities for

T.H. & B. workers joined too. (HPL)

lucrative employment in war production proliferated). A much-trumpeted parade of 8,000 soldiers in March 1916 elicited no cheering from onlookers. Yet war-bond sales boomed, as did contributions to the Patriotic Fund. By the end of the war some 11,000 Hamilton men had responded to the call – one of the highest rates of recruitment in the country. Some 2,000 local men were killed – a much higher mortality rate than the national average of one in ten.[10]

Labour leaders had come onside early. In a gesture of social integration, the Recruiting League had invited them to participate, and they jumped right in. Any pre-war hesitations about militarism vanished in July 1915, as the *Labor News* proclaimed this military effort "a war for humanity" and the Hamilton Trades and Labor Council announced its concern that "the Empire is at war and the future prosperity of the Dominion is also at stake." During late 1915 and early 1916 Allan Studholme and other labour luminaries attended meetings of the Recruiting League and spoke at rallies. This was their first

opportunity in years to sit down and discuss important issues with major local industrialists, and they took full advantage of the opportunity. They offered to help prevent work stoppages in munitions plants by bringing both parties together to settle their differences and tried to use the League's meetings to raise questions about wartime employment, including munitions wages and job guarantees for those who enlisted and for returned men. But they made little headway. As one local industrialist explained, manufacturers "had no wish to use the League as a medium for discussion of troubles existing between Capital and Labor."[11]

Initially the labour men had hesitations about any compulsion in recruitment, and fought hard against a Recruiting League resolution in February 1916 calling for conscription. Later that year, however, like others in the Central Canadian labour leadership, they supported national registration and, the next year, full-scale conscription, though adding their own twist. "I don't believe in the conscription of men without the conscription of wealth," Studholme told the press. "Conscript everything." Far more jingoistic was Sam Landers, who from the war's outset used his paper, the *Labor News*, to promote recruitment and the war effort more generally, without qualification. He threw himself into Recruiting League activities, speaking frequently at rallies and denouncing any labour leaders who opposed conscription. Late in 1916 his loud weekly outbursts came to an end when he enlisted as a private, with a warm commendation from his elite colleagues in the League. His newspaper soon passed into other, more radical hands, and over the following year the centre of this kind of pro-war agitation would shift to new groups of returned soldiers.[12]

There was no point before 1939 when the Canadian state mobilized more support for the Empire, or when the language of British imperialism and racial superiority was stronger, than during these war years. Despite the chief press censor's best efforts to keep the grisly details of war news out of Canadian households, disillusionment and resentment had begun to surface by 1917, when strikes, union organizing, and a renewed labour party signalled the emergence of a distinctive working-class wartime agenda. Borden's national Union government nonetheless pulled out all the stops in an emotion-charged election campaign in December 1917, in which loyalty to the Empire was the central theme. Less than a year later it was all over. This time the loudest, longest celebrations in the streets of Hamilton came at the news of an armistice, first in response to false news on 7 November 1918 and then again four days later.[13]

Hamilton labour leaders continued to rally around the flag. At a 1919 union convention in the United States, Harry Halford, a stalwart of the Trades and Labor Council and the Independent Labor Party, vigorously defended the Union

The Flag That Never Fails

(*LN*, 25 Dec. 1919, 1)

Jack against charges that it symbolized oppression. "The Canadian delegates are proud of the British flag," he roared. Several months later the local labour movement was deeply troubled that the American Federation of Labor had expressed support for Irish republicanism. The Hamilton steelworkers' union fired off a resolution of protest against these "efforts to disrupt the British Empire."[14]

Yet the tone of hegemonic Anglo-Canadian discourses shifted considerably after the war. Empires had been discredited, and new nation-states were proliferating internationally and finding recognition within a new League of Nations. Canada's distinguished war record and forthright participation in the peace conferences afterward gave new impetus to a construction of nationality that was shifting the centre of gravity from the motherland to the Dominion itself, still within a wider British commonwealth. The ambitious program of events and performances staged for the 60th anniversary of Confederation in 1927, for example, was a nationally co-ordinated project that attempted

The Sons of England Benevolent Society was one of the popular Hamilton organizations celebrating British ethnicity. (HPL)

to build a deeper attachment to the Canadian nation-state, a true "national feeling." Symbolically, on the first day of the Diamond Jubilee celebrations, Hamilton's mayor ordered the Union Jack taken off the city-hall flagpole and replaced with the Canadian Ensign. At a special military tattoo that day the massed bands led the audience in singing "O Canada" and "The Maple Leaf Forever" before striking up "Rule Britannia." In a poem that filled a full-page Eaton's ad, the renowned Canadian poet Charles G.D. Roberts declared, "Canadian am I in blood and bone!" But what defined "Canada"? Rather than evoking the call of the blood, a special edition of the *Spectator* presented the "British Empire Story" in a full-page spread that discussed trade possibilities for Canada. The paper's editorial also emphasized the country's material development. In the same vein, the huge Dominion Day parade was dominated by lavish floats sponsored by the city's leading industries. Late in 1918 East Hamilton's MP, cabinet member S.C. Mewburn, had made a remarkably frank connection between Canada's military intervention into Russia that

winter and the goal of "economic advantage." He argued, "They say that trade follows the flag, and I am satisfied that when the Russian people are offered the opportunity of dealing with the citizens of this country, their decision will be favorably affected by the action which we are taking now."[15]

Yet there was another focus, too. A huge historical pageant staged during that week in 1927, like similar performances across the country, presented symbolic moments in the pre-industrial, colonial past, and then, after Confederation, included only one historical event that could rally citizens – World War One. Indeed, it was the military that put on the biggest shows over the several days of festivities and helped Hamilton audiences remember the recent heroic struggle to defend British civilization. The Anglo-Canadian soldier had become the most compelling national symbol. Small wonder that the Chamber of Commerce, among other local groups, poured its energy and resources into reviving the paramilitary Scouts and Guides in the 1920s. In the rest of the interwar

Members of the Loyal Orange Order, like this group photographed in 1922, promoted the "racial" superiority of the British, particularly their Protestant faith. (HPL)

period, a common Canadianness was elusive, but, however much it embodied more focus on the Dominion than the Empire as the "imagined community," it certainly assumed the cultural dominance of English-speaking, British ethnicity. Ongoing debates about immigration made clear that the Canadian population should continue to have that ethnic cast.[16]

Popular imperialism had a base outside the formal structures of the state as well. In 1900 the most prominent women of Hamilton's upper class formed the first of several local branches of the Imperial Order Daughters of the Empire primarily to promote a mass base for imperial sentiment. They showered local schools with Union Jacks, patriotic literature, and rifles and prizes for cadet corps.[17] A decade later local elites also played central roles in organizing those units of imperialist youth, the Boy Scouts and Girl Guides, who were paraded for special events. Their leaders hoped to shape young minds to appreciate the superiority of the British and the triumphant march of their civilization across the globe (with only limited results).[18] Protestant clergymen, particularly in Anglican parishes, also regularly used their pulpits to convey this message to their congregations. Other prominent voices arose from the St. George's Benevolent Society and its smaller, parallel

organizations, the St. Andrews and Irish Protestant Benevolent societies. "Britishness" allowed space for these distinctive representations of Englishness, Irishness, and Scottishness within the imperial culture – a Burns Night among the Scots, for example – but each group nonetheless joined in public affirmations of a common British identity.

This British racial triumphalism typically also incorporated a belief in the superiority of Protestant Christianity, and no organization was more militant in asserting that claim than was the Loyal Orange Order. This country-wide organization had its roots in the religious battles of Ireland, but, despite the survival of King William on his white horse in Orange parades, it had a more broadly Anglo-Canadian membership by the end of the 19th century, and a solid majority was working-class. Orangemen in Hamilton, as elsewhere, gathered in ritualized weekly lodge meetings, often in their own modest hall, to celebrate both the personal liberty symbolized by the "Open Bible" and the importance of the imperial connection. Although Ontario was the Canadian stronghold of the order, Hamilton's 11 lodges attracted proportionally fewer members before World War One than did their counterparts in Toronto (which had some 15,000 members in 76 lodges by 1914). But, after 1920,

Orange enthusiasts set up many more lodges, and staged large annual celebrations.[19]

Britishness, then, was the "official" ethnicity of the early 20th century. It provided the basis for citizenship and many more social entitlements. It was louder, more self-congratulatory, and more demanding than ever. It provided an imaginative realm that allowed Anglo-Canadians, including workers, to revel in fantasies of accomplishment and superiority. It evolved in an ongoing dynamic with other allegedly inferior cultural identities at home and abroad. And it was profoundly intolerant.

Waving the Union Jack could nonetheless send mixed messages. Rather than simply deferring to monarchist elitism, labour leaders liked to hail the democratic elements of British "civilization" and the social and political entitlements that they thought it gave a workingman. "The English workman is the cause of more labor troubles than any other nationality," a Steel Company manager grumbled in 1912. Britishness was a contested identity.[20]

Others

The much-revered British Empire actually had many racial hues. Britain had colonized a huge diversity of indigenous peoples around the world, and for decades had been evolving policies of governance that struggled to deal with that ethno-cultural diversity. Far from advocating any modern notion of liberal multiculturalism, British colonial authorities had relied for the most part on a combination of repressive and assimilative measures to impose British supremacy.

Even white-settler dominions like Canada posed challenges, and white anglophones moved forcefully in the late 19th and early 20th centuries to curb the rights of ethnic and racial minorities. Aboriginal peoples were confined to reserves and subjected to programs of cultural annihilation. The French-Canadian population outside Quebec faced new measures to eliminate language and educational rights in the West and Ontario. Inside Quebec, a vigorous movement of francophone Catholic nationalism counterpoised its own aggressive ethnic identity.[21]

Moreover, when new patterns of immigration and labour recruitment brought together large numbers of people who spoke neither English nor French and were not even necessarily "white," state policies and voluntary initiatives had to be developed in tandem to control these people and where possible to transform them into acceptable British subjects. Immigration policy became a subject of intense debate as efforts increased to exclude allegedly unassimilable peoples, especially those of colour. Across Canada in the early 20th century, fears about the erosion of racial supremacy (often dubbed "race suicide") were rife. "The immense virility of the Anglo-Saxon race like the sturdy oak may resist the encroachments of the canker worm for generations," James Russell, superintendent of the Hamilton Asylum for the Insane, stated in 1908, "but unless purged and purified of disease it will at last crumble and decay."[22]

Anglo-Canadians and migrants from the British Isles were certainly not the only residents of the city. Hamilton had small communities of First Nations people, blacks, and Chinese, and rapidly growing numbers of Southern and Eastern Europeans. Popular imperialism became a lens through which to view and deal with these "Others." So too were significant elements in North American popular culture that had emerged out of US experience with slavery and mass immigration. Anglo-Canadians of all social classes quickly began to apply familiar cultural constructs about particular racial and ethnic groups and their neighbourhoods that long predated their arrival in the city – notably the ideas of a "Chinatown" and a "foreign colony" – which had as much to do with their own identities as with the newcomers' behaviour and lifestyles.[23]

Canadian writers and public speakers who discussed the idea of race at the close of the 19th century drew on prevailing theories that ranked various groups in a complex hierarchy, at the top of which sat the Anglo-Saxons. These distinctions rested on allegedly scientific analysis that went far beyond physical or anatomical differences and attributed to each "race" specific inborn moral characteristics – ingenuity, industry, sensuality, laziness, proneness to violence, for example – which, it was argued, were transmitted biologically and shaped whole cultures. A 1909 Ontario school geography text, for example, characterized Italians as universally "impetuous, quick-tempered, and sometimes easy-going."[24]

This "racial" grid was also overlaid with a broader differentiation based on colour – whiteness at the top and various shades of darkness below. Far more than skin colour, inclusion within "whiteness" required attributes of independence and self-discipline, and other evidence of supposed civilization (everything from cleanliness to Protestantism) that made a people capable of self-governance. Some groups near the bottom of this racial scale were assumed to be inherently incapable of attaining these features of white identity. Others in the middle had a more indeterminate status. Not until the 1930s were the first questions raised about biological explanations of cultural difference, and even then only tentatively.[25] These were not merely ideas or ideologies about social difference; they were deeply imbedded in public policies and popular practices, in the social structure and social relations of early-20th-century Canadian society.

In the emerging cultural mix within working-class Hamilton, colour was the sharpest line of demarcation. The three most visible minorities were aboriginal, black, and Chinese, none of which amounted to more than a few hundred people in Hamilton. They were constructed in popular discourses as the most degraded human groups and faced the most severe discriminatory laws and practices. Canada's Indian Act had defined First Nations people as legal children with few civil rights – notably no freedom of movement or right to vote – and had imposed such strict controls on their behaviour as a ban on drinking alcohol. Newspaper reports of their occasional appearances in police court took for granted the "primitive," child-like qualities of an inferior people, and ongoing government policies tried to stifle all indigenous cultural forms among the First Nations and to teach "white" behaviour. For the most part, aboriginal peoples were seen as marginal and destined to obliteration. The Six Nations reserve was nonetheless not far from Hamilton, and may have been the source of rising numbers of aboriginal peoples turning up on the census rolls. Presumably these were men and women who found unskilled jobs in the city. Some Six Nations men got a glowing reputation as skilled high-steel riggers.[26]

African Canadians in Hamilton faced comparable stereotyping as an inferior group, but their status was different in important ways. Not only were they much more visible, but they were also framed by two distinct (and somewhat contradictory) historic experiences – on the one hand, slavery in the United States, where many of Hamilton's blacks traced their descent before their forefathers' arrival on the Underground Railroad, and, on the other, the more recent colonization of Africa within the expanding British Empire. Imperialist rhetoric made full use of racist imagery to refer to the conquered

Popular culture was saturated with the racist imagery of African Americans from the US South, mostly based on the traditions of minstrel shows. Whites put on blackface and performed outlandish versions of black behaviour in music, on stage, on radio, and even in this Victory Loan parade in 1918. (HPL)

Al Jolson was America's most famous blackface performer. Hamiltonians bought his records and watched his movies. (HS, 19 July 1930, 4)

and making reference to "Chicken Dinners and Watermelon Feeds" in their headlines.

The lives of African Canadians were constrained by discrimination in a job market that kept them in labouring or low-level service work (men in personal service in hotels or on railways; women in cleaning) and by segregation in housing, partly through restrictive land-sale covenants that were legal in Ontario until 1950, and more commonly through informal refusals to rent or sell to blacks. In the first years of World War One, recruiters rejected African-Canadian men who wanted to enlist in the Canadian Expeditionary Force. Blacks were also segregated into separate branches of many popular organizations – the "coloured" lodges of fraternal societies, the Royal Mary "coloured" union of the WCTU, and a separate congregation of black Baptists. A bill introduced into the Ontario legislature in 1933 by Argue Martin, Conservative member for West Hamilton, called for an end to signs that barred any group from entering public spaces. It was defeated, and as late as the 1940s local hotel-keepers were still allowed to refuse to serve African Canadians in their beverage rooms, theatre owners to bar their access to movies, and dance-hall owners to shut them out. Small wonder that their own African Methodist Episcopal Church became a refuge and a focus of black community life in the city.[28]

Yet, despite their small numbers (under 400 through most of the period), a much more pervasive construction of African-Canadian inferiority ran throughout popular culture, one that represented them simultaneously as dim-witted and indolent, shrewd and wily, outlandish and libidinous. Much earlier, in the 19th century, these attributes had been incorporated into the remarkably popular form of comic entertainment, the minstrel show, to which white working-class men had flocked in fascination.

population of the African continent,[27] but the blacks with whom most workers in Hamilton interacted were mostly a settled population well integrated into the social and cultural life of the city and immersed in the complex legacy of North American slavery. Indeed, the daily press coverage of blacks in the local police court liked to remind readers of the connection of these people with Southern US history, exaggerating the dialect in their published testimony

Here, as several writers have argued, these workingmen identified with the white actors wearing blackface, whose black stage characters could be outrageous and provocative in expressing the frustrations and yearnings of workers on both sides of any colour line. As one scholar points out, "white working-class longings, fantasies, and dreams" were projected onto "supposedly oversexed, lazy, and naive Black characters."[29] Not only did those shows live on well into the 20th century, performed by churches, veterans' groups, and even by a Hamilton Italian club in the 1930s, but the legacy of minstrelsy also moved over into amateur theatre, public processions (like the 1919 Victory Loan parade), vaudeville acts, "coon songs," radio programs (*Amos 'n' Andy*), and movies (notably in the performances of the Jewish actor Al Jolson).[30] The burgeoning popularity of black music – first ragtime, then jazz – involved a somewhat similar, though more respectful appropriation of black culture.

Racist attitudes did not stop the Hamilton letter carriers from electing George Morton as the treasurer of their local union in 1918.

(Federated Association of Letter Carriers, *Convention Souvenir* [Hamilton 1918])

This kind of treatment of a visible minority mixed condescension with grudging appreciation (to be sure, based on gross distortions) and suggested that blacks had a well-understood, generally non-threatening place within working-class Hamilton. In contrast to the huge migration of African Americans to the US urban north, few blacks were allowed through Canada's immigration gates. The exceptions were small groups of women destined to be domestic servants, and over the years their numbers in Hamilton declined as a proportion of the local population.[31] As long as they stuck to their segregated jobs and social spaces, they posed no apparent menace. A 1904 strike of tobacco workers against the importation of African-American workers stands out as an isolated event in the city's history, and it was settled by getting the workers to join the local union. Hamilton's experience with race relations was thus considerably different from that in such nearby US industrial centres as Buffalo and Cleveland.[32]

There could be skirmishes on the boundaries of tolerance, however, if blacks stepped over any lines to challenge white supremacy. Across North America, whites watched in dismay as the flamboyant Jack Johnson defeated Canadian Tommy Burns for a world boxing championship in 1908.[33] But much closer to home, an incident in Hamilton in spring 1920 revealed the depth of concern about black male sexuality. An African-Canadian man, Robert Boyd, was charged with having "carnal knowledge" of a 14-year-old white girl, who claimed he had climbed through her window and assaulted her. The girl subsequently gave birth to a "coloured" child, which soon died. The magistrate, finding the testimony to be suspicious, noted that a black man actually lived in the same house and questioned why the girl had said nothing about the incident until after the baby was born. He dismissed the case. The girl's father loudly cursed the magistrate, and the mother furiously tried to attack Boyd with a chair, screaming "a nigger can do anything in Hamilton."

The case aroused immediate outrage in the city. The Local Council of Women, Women Citizens' League, and city clergymen promised to investigate. The Independent Labor Party heard a tearful presentation by the girl's father, a veteran of the South African war, and, along with the women's groups, decided to write to the attorney general to intervene. Labour leader Halford declared: "A crime has been committed in which a child and a full-grown negro were involved. Was the city of Hamilton going to stand idly by and see this crime go unpunished? If that were the case, then no man's daughter was safe any longer on the city streets." Veterans organizations were similarly irate, and a meeting of the Discharged Soldiers' and Sailors' Federation a few days later set up a committee to investigate. The president of the local Coloured People's Society insisted that in the interest of fairness there should be more balanced discussion of the case. In the end the magistrate refused to buckle to a polite inquiry from the attorney general or to public pressure. The controversy died, but not before plenty of public innuendo about menacing black sexuality.[34]

There were parallels, but also sharp differences, in how the tiny local Chinese population was viewed and dealt with. Throughout the Europeanized world, their racial inferiority had been constructed in the context of imperialist domination of China in the late 19th century. When they migrated in large numbers to the west coast of North America, they found jobs only in the least attractive, least well-paid occupations, and were characterized as an alien group that could never be assimilated. In Hamilton, as in many eastern

cities, Chinese immigrants worked almost exclusively in the service sector, mainly in laundries and restaurants, where they competed with few whites.[35] Yet they were nonetheless construed as a threat because of their allegedly degraded way of life – on one hand, their crowded, "filthy," bachelor-dominated boarding houses and their strict frugality, which contrasted starkly with the family economies of white working-class households, and on the other, their penchant for gambling, smoking opium, and allegedly lusting after white women.[36]

In 1885 federal legislation had first restricted their access to the Canadian labour market with a $50 head tax, which was hiked to $100 in 1900 and $500 three years later. In 1923 a new Chinese Immigration Act effectively closed the door to future immigration. For those already inside the country, predominantly men, a 1914 Ontario law forbade Chinese employers to employ white women, and Hamilton's police kept Chinese restaurants and laundries under close watch. A municipal by-law also restricted the location of Chinese laundries to the immediate precincts of the city's minuscule Chinatown.[37]

When the machinists' Richard Riley protested to his landlord in 1913 that he would "not occupy an office in the same building with Chinks," he was expressing widespread sentiments in the local labour movement, which dated back at least 30 years.[38] The number of Chinese had increased substantially since the turn of the century, but their arrival was a mere trickle alongside the huge wave of British and European newcomers.[39]

The Trades and Labor Council nonetheless expressed alarm about the potential for a "flood" and passed resolutions against these "very undesirable" Asian immigrants. The labour press also kept up a steady flow of hyperbolic warnings. In 1912 the *Industrial Banner* urged Ontario workers to back the struggles of British Columbia's workingmen against "the inferior yellow races of the Orient," and the *Labor News* warned about the moral dangers facing the city's young women from Chinese men. The same paper published ongoing critiques of the city's Chinese laundries. "Some of those Chink joints are in a horrible condition and should be closed up," ILP alderman Halford proclaimed in 1916 after visiting them with a city-hall committee. A year later the city's press suggested that, to meet the wartime labour shortage, the Steel Company and some other employers were recruiting Chinese workers. Even the newly radicalized *Labor News* succumbed to the racializing panic with a warning of "a deliberate plan" that would "use the war conditions as an excuse to allow the flood gates to be opened at the behest of the big industries to practically swamp the Dominion by the unrestricted importation of 100,000 Chinese." This "army of cheap workers" would be "prepared to labor and live upon a scale of wages that would mean starvation to the average workingman or working woman in Canada." The paper concluded, "Canada must be saved from a Chinese invasion and its working class from designed servitude and degradation." By 1920 a less radical *New Democracy* was still supporting campaigns to exclude the Chinese from Canada. At the annual meeting of the Trades and Labor Congress of Canada two years later, a Hamilton delegate deplored how Orientals had been "allowed to enter the country and destroy this standard [of living]."[40]

The much larger numbers of Southern and Eastern Europeans who started to arrive in the city in the decade before World War One raised comparable levels of racial anxiety among white Hamiltonians. Like the Chinese, but on a much larger scale, their lifestyles in the city were frequently construed as threats to Anglo-Canadian

In 1931 Italian workers like this one were still most often labourers.
(AO, 10050065)

society and working-class life in particular. Not yet brought under the broader umbrella of the Caucasian race (a term that did not come into wider use until the 1930s), Italians, Poles, Russians, and other Europeans had an uncertain status as "whites" in the early 20th century, not simply because of their darker complexions, but more because of their deficiencies in individual and collective behaviour (including their professed Catholicism), which seemed to put them outside the circle of white civilization.[41]

Indeed, while everyone in Hamilton was aware of the large African-American presence in the United States, the marginality of the city's small black population may have heightened the tendency to see an Italian or Polish peasant-labourer as the local equivalent. By World War One the terms "foreigner" and "white" became widely used opposites. As an Italian immigrant lamented in 1919, "I am not what you people call a white man." A couple of veterans leaders went so far as to state in the provincial election that year that one candidate was "one of the whitest men they had met," and a steelworker urged union members to "come to the next meeting; show us that you are a white man."[42]

Some middle-class voices argued that, in contrast to the Chinese, these newcomers could be assimilated over the long run. Others wanted various kinds of segregation, restriction, and, if necessary, full-scale exclusion. The effect would be the same because the goal was to impose an Anglo-Canadian identity.[43] Assimilation involved coercive policing measures, but relatively little effort was directed to the more positive processes of integration in Hamilton before 1920, other than some small church missions and marginal English-language classes. As they did in several large Canadian cities, the leading Protestant churches each sponsored missions for specific ethnic groups. In 1909 the Presbyterians started working with Italians in the west end, and in 1910 the Methodists began to do the same with those in the east. Some four years later the Presbyterians also brought in a Hungarian-speaking missionary to minister to his fellow countrymen in a north-end church (which closed less than two years later). By the war the Anglicans also had a small short-lived west-end mission directed at the local Jews, and the Baptists opened one for Russian-born Ukrainians and Belarusians. At various points over the next decade the Presbyterians dithered over starting up missions with Bulgarians, Ukrainians, and Chinese, but nothing materialized. In 1926 they set up a Hungarian mission and took the formerly Methodist Italian mission under their wing.

The primary goal of all these efforts was to convert the newcomers to a Protestant faith, but the clergy and their lay helpers also set up social and cultural programs that tapped into ethnic particularities, such as non-Catholic Italian celebrations of Garibaldi's birthday, while teaching middle-class Anglo-Canadian values and practices. They also offered such practical help as negotiating with doctors or courts, finding a job or unemployment relief, or learning English. The results were minimal. The men were generally too transient and the Catholic priest too hostile. Before the war, Ernest Taylor, the Methodist missionary to Hamilton's Italians, could report only 30 to 40 at religious services, with few conversions. Only ten men went to his English classes in 1912–13. Attendance at kindergarten and mothers' meetings started two years later and had reached only 28 in each case by 1920. Well into the interwar period, Italian men had a calculating approach to the missions – the Italians might call it *furberia* – taking advantage of English classes and, even more, of the job placements with major employers that the clergy managed to deliver. Many missionaries to such immigrants were disappointed with the limited results by that point. The Methodists nonetheless bravely broadened their efforts to reach more ethnic groups in an All Peoples' Mission, while the Presbyterians opened Neighbourhood House in 1927 as part of their small chain of settlement houses across the country. A group of elite women also funded the hiring of a kindergarten teacher and social worker to work with "foreign children" and others at the various missions.[44]

These missions were burdened with unflattering assessments of the "foreign" flocks they were addressing. They operated from an assumption of superiority over these ignorant, unclean, "uncivilized" people. "Our objective on behalf of European foreigners should be to assist in making them English-speaking Christian citizens who are clean, educated, and loyal to the Dominion and to Greater Britain," the Methodist Missionary Society maintained in 1910. Meanwhile, many European newcomers must have found such attention mildly amusing or offensively patronizing, as an east-end Italian grocer pointed out in a letter to the press in 1911. The "conversions," he wrote, were simply occasions when a few young men, fond of "music and pleasure," enjoyed cake, cocoa, and the company of the missionary's young female helpers. In fact, he insisted, Italians in Hamilton "resist and despise all efforts to lure them away from the old Faith." They were already well cared for by "trusted guides," and did not need the services of "defamers and interlopers."[45]

Beyond these church-based efforts at assimilation, the city's politicians, businessmen, and professionals showed little interest in Canadianization of the new immigrants before the war. In 1908 the Italians' new priest, Father Giovanni Bonomi, convinced the separate-school board to start English-language classes for the newcomers with financial help from the local St. Vincent de Paul Society. The same year a Jewish rabbi, Jacob S. Menkin, got the hesitant public-school trustees to grant him a modest subsidy and permission to start evening English-language classes (initially held in the derelict north-end Custom House and then in one or more of the elementary schools). After some interruption the city council agreed in 1914 to provide half the funds to reopen the classes. By 1917 there were only 77 on the roll in two classes in the public system. But, before 1920, the school board seemed content to let the churches, the East End YWCA, and a new Cosmopolitan Mission handle the bulk of this language training.[46]

In the aftermath of the war and amidst debates about reconstruction, discussion of Canadianization heated up.[47] A *Spectator* editorial, comparing Hamilton to other large cities, concluded, "Very little in the nature of true service work has been instituted or carried on with reference to the stranger within the city gates." Drawn from "every dirty corner of rotten Europe," these people had clustered in their own densely packed neighbourhoods where, living "like animals," they "were taught nothing about Canadian laws or Canadian modes of living." Small wonder, the editor argued, that the "foreign section" had become "festering sores breeding poison – crime and murder in the worst degree." Early in 1920 P.W. Philpott, a leading evangelical clergyman who had been helping with the instruction of Armenians, made a strong pitch to the school board. The "problem of the foreigner," he stated, would become a "menace" because the newcomers were "densely ignorant to our morals and standards of citizenship." They were, he said, falling under the influence of "Reds" who taught "blood and fire." In the absence of proper citizenship training, he insisted, "the only place of tuition for the foreigner has been the police court." The Board of Education was not moved to change its existing policy, however, and simply allowed the small, volunteer-run program offered in school buildings to continue. Philpott then turned to the new Chamber of Commerce, which established a Canadianization Committee in 1921. In contrast to the work of such US industrialists as Henry Ford, Hamilton's capitalists showed no interest in investing their own money in such programs, but the Chamber's pressure got the school board, the city's Board of Control, and the provincial Department of Education to agree to three-way funding of evening English classes for immigrants in the new technical school starting in 1922. For the first time substantial public funds were being made available for "Canadianizing" the immigrants. By 1929 a provincial official was declaring that the city's 600 "foreign" students enrolled in three language classes were the largest such group anywhere in the province. Some two years later budget cuts brought these opportunities to an end when all night-school classes were cancelled.[48]

As more of the European newcomers settled down in the city, their children were also targeted for acculturation into Canadian ways. The bulk of them were enrolled in the city's Roman Catholic separate-school system, where they were often segregated from the Anglo-Canadians. Girls of Italian origin in the west end were enrolled in separate classes in either Sacred Heart or Holy Angels schools until Grade 6 and were then merged into the English classes at St. Mary's School. For boys in the east end, one whole floor of St. Ann's School was set aside for Italian and Slavic children and given the name St. Stanislaus School. It had its own staff and segregated playground, and its students were not integrated into St. Ann's until 1931. "We didn't think it was right," one Italian-Canadian recalled about this schooling in the 1920s. "You never mixed too much with the English kids until you went into St Mary's." The Irish-Catholic control of these schools, and the predominantly Irish-Canadian teachers, nonetheless made them sites of strong assimilationist pressure. Indeed, years later many Italian-Canadians who had passed through these schools remembered St. Patrick's Day as a major event in their school experience.[49]

Ultimately, relatively few of the many European sojourners made contact with assimilationist projects during their short stays in Hamilton, and even most of those who did settle down in the city kept their distance. Married women in particular had at best only fleeting contact with the English-speaking forces of acculturation. It was the children of the immigrant neighbourhoods who were most likely to move regularly between the old and new worlds.[50]

Drawing the Line

Many European newcomers nonetheless met the harder edge of Anglo-Canadian efforts to change their lifestyles. Significantly, the 1912 *Herald* story that reported on the city's new "foreign section" saw two forces of assimilation – the school and the police. Health officials harassed newcomers about their overcrowded boarding houses, and, from well before World War One, the local police targeted them for violation of liquor laws.[51] Attacks also came from outside the state. While many of Hamilton's leading employers welcomed the new immigrants into their factories, questions had been raised more broadly in the city's civil society about these "foreigners" since the earliest days of their arrival.

Anglo-Canadian workers had particular concerns, and many responded with suspicion and often outright hostility. Their anxieties rested on deeper and more complex constructions of a threat rather than mere economic competition for jobs. In part they connected the role that they believed these newcomers played in local industry in helping to degrade their work and living standards, but those issues fit into a larger cultural construction of Britishness within a capitalist political economy. Their critiques took something not only from the pervasive bourgeois notions of racial and ethnic hierarchies, an emotional pride in their British identity, and the hideous stereotypes of other races that saturated popular media, but also from their understanding of the history of working-class struggles and from their own lived experience in working-class Hamilton and elsewhere.

Like journalists and other middle-class speakers, Anglo-Canadian workers frequently maintained that Southern and Eastern Europeans were not "white" and that their particular behaviour was "in their blood." In the emerging factory regime of the early 20th century, Anglo-Canadian workers came to expect an ethnic hierarchy in their workplaces – that they would have privileged access to skilled and semi-skilled jobs, while rough, poorly paid labouring work would be relegated to the European newcomers. These less desirable jobs came to be seen as "not fit work" for white English-speaking workmen, who by World War One were assiduously avoiding them.[52] Especially in the metalworking industries, new British immigrants expected to be able to walk right into better jobs and to keep their distance from the "Dagos" and "Hunkies." Implicitly they saw the ethnic hierarchy operating as a caste system of fixed positions for the various racial and ethnic groups. The city's largest employer, Canadian Westinghouse, reinforced that sense of privilege by giving preference to Anglo-Celtic workers for all jobs in its huge metalworking plant.[53] The problem for these men was that other capitalist managers regularly destabilized such understandings by finding ways to employ European immigrants in previously "white" positions, sometimes during periods when Anglo-Canadian workers faced serious unemployment. With little influence over immigration policy, these wage-earners stood their ground in sporadic workplace battles.[54] Flashes of conflict developed whenever the ethnic boundaries were redrawn, most dramatically in the radically altered labour market of the wartime economy.

By the end of the 19th century, American experience had already prepared many Anglo-Canadian workers for the role of European immigrants in cheapening the value of labour in the production process by taking jobs at lower than acceptable rates, sometimes as strikebreakers. Their arrival in Hamilton followed this pattern closely enough to confirm Anglo-Canadian workers' fears. They saw them as cheap labour in the big new plants of the Hamilton Steel and Iron Company and International Harvester and as scabs in strikes of steelworkers in 1902, longshoremen in 1904, and moulders in 1909.[55] For these English-speaking workers the arrival of the European immigrant on the shop floor signalled an effort to degrade their work.[56] Their hostility to the "foreigners" was therefore intimately linked to their resistance to trends in modern industry that threatened their job control, their wage rates, and their employment itself.

"In nine cases out of ten the foreigner who cannot speak a word of English is employed by railways and big corporations," the *Industrial Banner* complained in 1905. "Hundreds of Russians, Jews, Italians, and other foreigners, drawn from the lowest classes in their country, have easily secured jobs this winter as soon as they landed, while intelligent Canadian workmen have been unemployed." In the same year a working-class veteran of the South African war wrote to the *Spectator* to argue that the low wages offered for cutting ice in the harbour that winter were a result of unfair competition: "If less foreigners were employed in our beautiful city, then British subjects would have a far better chance." In the depths of the pre-war depression, local Anglo-Canadian workers complained that the Guest Company, which was constructing a new Hydro conduit system, hired only "foreigners." According to the *Times*, "They would prefer seeing English-speaking people given the chance of working on this job rather than those who spend the greater portions of their earnings in the countries of Southern Europe." These arguments were still being heard in the interwar period. In a letter to the editor, a working-class housewife said that the "foreigners" were getting "the choice of the best-paid jobs in nearly all the factories in the city" while Canadian and British-born men like her husband and son remained jobless.[57]

For articulate craft unionists, the issue was about defending a whole working-class culture of mutuality and solidarity. The *Industrial Banner* argued that workmen who had built labour movements into their national culture had helped to create "a high type of civilization":

> The countries where trade unionism is strong stand highest in the scale of civilization and those where organization is lacking stand way down at the bottom of the list. It is trade unionism that has made Great Britain and the United States what they are today.... It is intelligent labor that always counts; ignorant workers never make a nation great.

Unionism improved workers' terms of employment. It also taught them "independence and self-respect; it has developed their intelligence and taught them that they have a right to share in the benefits of an advancing civilization. Trade unionism marks the boundary between liberty and slavery." In contrast, the immigrant from less "civilized" cultures had no aspirations. "He is an animal and has not learned the power and benefit of organization and co-operation." In their struggles with their employers, Canadian workingmen had to resist being "degraded to the level of the pauper laborer of Europe." In commenting on the Russian revolution of 1905, the same paper drew a stark comparison with European autocracy: "What the Russian workman is today we would be were it not for the self-sacrifice of noble-hearted union men and women who braved death and the dungeon for attaining of the liberties we now enjoy." Workingmen's masculinity was also on the line: "The modern industrial system leaves citizenship, manhood and the home out of the calculation." A few years later, in the depths of the pre-war depression, the same paper warned: "It is slave versus free labor that is in the balance. Whether Canada shall be a country for her own people or for a slave race that shall cringe and fawn at the master's glance."[58]

To attack the new immigration, then, was to assert a working-class notion of citizenship. Fears about the impact of the new European workers wove a conviction that they would drag down the living standard of the whole working class into an argument that the national culture of the English-speaking world, which such workingmen believed they had helped to create, was at risk. Seeing immigrants in Hamilton's "foreign colony" crowded into boarding houses in a spare, frugal lifestyle, and reading regular newspaper accounts of the newcomers' apparent fascination with knives and fighting no doubt confirmed the Anglo-Canadian workers' worst suspicions.[59] Goaded by the *Spectator* about his stand on tariff protection, Studholme snapped back: "What protection have the wage-earners from that low class of foreigners that the Spectator tells us were for a time in the Deering [International Harvester] houses?" Several years later ILP alderman George Halcrow argued that it was "little short of criminal the way many of the foreigners live in this city." For many of these men, then, ethnocentrism was not simply blind jingoism. It also represented a concern with defending hard-won working-class living standards. "I don't object to the aliens coming to this country, because they have as much right here as we have," Studholme insisted in 1913. "But when he does come here he should play the game, and not try to live here as he would in the old land."[60]

In various ways Hamilton's Anglo-Canadian wage-earners tried to police the caste-like rigidity of the labour market. Some craft unions formally excluded the new immigrants from their unions, and, indeed, they extended no hand of solidarity when the steelworkers or car-workers walked out on strike in the years before World War One. Scattered incidents of anti-alien agitation by rank-and-file workers also came to light in the pre-war years. Non-union moulders struck in 1909 when Italians arrived in the Bowes-Jamieson foundry. Some three years later the Steel Company's Canada Works (formerly the Canada Screw Company) precipitated an unsuccessful strike by its wire-drawers when the firm put two Poles to work in the shop. The next year a "foreigner" hired by Westinghouse to work in the core-making department was beaten up at quitting time by two core-makers. When the pair was fired for the assault, their fellow workers marched out in sympathy. A few weeks later Anglo-Canadian workers attending an East Hamilton Progressive Association meeting complained that the new National Steel Car Company was giving preference to "foreigners" and urged that the city slap a discriminatory poll tax on them. The president of the Trades and Labor Congress of Canada also intervened on behalf of Canadian machinists to get immigration officials to block the importation of workers from Chicago to work in that Hamilton plant. The depression of 1913–15 brought much of this resentment to the surface with new intensity. When E.N. Compton, the federal labour department's Fair Wage Officer, passed through Hamilton early in 1914, he heard repeated complaints from local labour leaders about the role of the immigrants in aggravating the unemployment situation. Small wonder, then, that the ILP's declaration of principles promised to "fight for the maintenance of a clean Canada by the exclusion of Chinese and all other Asiatics and all objectionable aliens."[61]

State policies during World War One helped to intensify the anti-alien spirit. The federal government required that "enemy aliens" from Germany, Austria-Hungary, Bulgaria, or Turkey register at a police station each week, and, after November 1916, that they obtain a travelling certificate to be presented to police on leaving or entering the city. Some might be interned, though only a handful in Hamilton actually were. The 1917 Wartime Elections Act also took the vote away from enemy aliens who had become naturalized citizens since 1902. The country's Chief Press Censor also clamped down on foreign-language newspapers, and in September 1918 an order-in-council outlawed ten languages in print or public meetings.[62]

At the same time the jingoistic celebration of Britishness and intolerance of ethnic minorities, particularly French Canadians, who were far less enthusiastic about the war, provided a context for interpreting the rapidly changing circumstances of European immigrants. While initially they had faced severe unemployment, these newcomers found themselves much in demand as the wartime economy took off. Unable to return to Europe, the immigrants continued to roam the continent working at the usual variety of jobs. But with the wartime labour shortage, they found they could work as long as they wanted and at higher wages than ever before. Sergeant William Hawkins, who kept the Hamilton police register of enemy aliens, reported a great influx, especially citizens of Austria-Hungary (mostly Ukrainians and Bulgarians). "The fact that Hamilton industries cannot keep pace with the demands for their output has gone broadcast," he told a reporter. "This and the additional circumstances that wages here in both factories and munitions plants are the highest in the Dominion are the magnets that draw the sons of Hapsburg to this thriving place." During 1916 the number registered in Hawkins's book increased by 2,730. They had become, said the *Herald*, "a floating population that keeps in constant circulation to those cities and town where labor is scarce and wages good." A short-lived (and poorly reported) strike of 700 shell workers at the Steel Company in February 1916 included "about six nationalities." In

September of that year, International Harvester went so far as to bring 130 Poles from the Lakehead to meet its labour requirements (though several left after finding out that prohibition had arrived in Hamilton).[63]

Many of the immigrants were recruited into the city's booming munitions industry, giving them access to mechanized work that had often been closed to them in the past. Before long, reports were circulating about the inflated earnings of these new "plutocrats of Hamilton." They were also reputedly developing a greater material immunity from punishment for breaking the law. In the police court, "the spot-cash wealth of the foreigners" allowed them to pay fines immediately. By mid-1917 the police were concerned about a new "arrogant and impertinent" spirit among the "foreigners."[64] Resentment against the success of the immigrant population was particularly strong among the returned soldiers, some of whom began to complain that the "aliens" were being hired in preference to the veterans. "If a returned soldier is not worth consideration before a foreigner," one private demanded to know, "why, then, should young men volunteer?" Mayor Charles Booker agreed, urging that enemy aliens be fired from munitions plants. No manufacturers shared this view.[65]

The advent of conscription in fall 1917 raised new cries of outrage against the European immigrant population at large – that is, beyond merely the citizens of enemy countries. On 11 September the local street-railwaymen's union called for "conscription of the foreign element in some way so that they may be included in those who help to win the war." A few days later the moulders' union sent a strongly worded letter to the Borden government in Ottawa, revealing the excessive anxiety of many Anglo-Canadian workers. Many European newcomers, it argued, "whether or not with the Entente Allies," were looking forward to conscription as an opportunity to snatch up "the cream of the jobs" and were boasting that "Canada's womanhood – married or single – [would] be accessible for their depraved exploitation." A growing hysteria prevailed in the city about the alleged lawlessness of the immigrants, "so much so," scoffed the *Times*, "that women and girls are well nigh scared out of their wits, and men and women have been writing to the press calling for protection." The local branch of the Great War Veterans' Association (GWVA) called on the government "to safeguard the women and children of the city of Hamilton from the brutal attacks of the foreign element," and Police Magistrate George Jelfs announced that any enemy aliens brought before him on charges of violating the liquor legislation or assaulting women would be interned. A worker at the American Can Company began canvassing his fellow workers to co-sponsor a mass meeting to deal with the insults that the European single male immigrants were allegedly delivering to Hamilton's women. The voice of the deputy police chief insisting that there had been no actual complaints about improper acts by the immigrants was drowned in this chorus of anti-alien hysteria.[66]

In the December 1917 federal election, General S.C. Mewburn, a prominent industrialist and the Unionist candidate in East Hamilton, raised the issue of conscription of the "aliens" in his campaign, and in the early months of 1918 agitation continued for some scheme to conscript the immigrants into the war effort. The GWVA proposal to draft enemy aliens to work at the same wages as Canadian soldiers was endorsed at a mass meeting of 2,000 people on 3 March, and became the model for other such protests elsewhere and for the Great War Veterans' Ontario convention in the spring. The Hamilton Trades and Labor Council's Harry Fester joined the chorus of critics at the meeting, and two weeks later a union delegate demanded that the Council take action against the "alien menace," which included "murders, hold-ups, fighting in restaurants and other lawlessness by the foreign element." As Fester put it, "So dangerous was the situation that policemen positively refused to patrol their beats singly. They were just going about in teams in the foreign section." By the end of the month the Council had endorsed the GWVA position.[67]

One police officer muttered, "The only way to deal with those people is to sit on them, and sit hard."[68] In early April 1918 the federal government did just that with an order-in-council prohibiting idleness, the so-called Anti-Loafing Law, which required all males of ages 16 to 60 to find gainful employment or risk $100 fines or six months in jail. The new law targeted the immigrants, and, two weeks later, the police chief announced that most of the offenders caught under the act were in fact "foreigners." At the same time the city council instituted a "statute labour tax" of $5 applied to men of age 21 to 60 who were not otherwise taxed by the municipality. As an alternative to the poll tax that some other Ontario cities had imposed, this new tax was unabashedly aimed at the immigrants who had been earning high wages without facing any taxation.[69]

As the war ended and munitions work wound down, a new flurry of concern erupted about immigrants hanging on to jobs that most Anglo-Canadian workers in Hamilton thought properly belonged to "white" wage-earners. Again they feared that hiring "foreigners" would mean the permanent cheapening of labour. Early in December two returned soldiers stormed into Mayor Booker's office to complain that a large east-end industrial firm had fired them and replaced them with "Austrians" at lower wages. A

month later a Dofasco worker lodged a similar complaint. At a time when Hamilton's workers were becoming increasingly edgy about their employers' attempts to reduce the high wartime wage rates, keeping out the aliens became a determined battle cry. The Europeans themselves sensed an impending crisis. "Quite a number of people here in Hamilton hate us Italians worse than they do a German," one Italian resident wrote to the press. A committee of Ukrainians warned that they were "passing through very serious moments – moments in which we are not sure of our lives. From day to day we are expecting riots such as took place in Winnipeg, which may pass throughout the Dominion and hurt us mercilessly."[70]

Once again the GWVA spearheaded the attack, with its rapidly growing membership of discharged soldiers, many of them now unemployed workers. Amidst renewed press sensationalism about attacks on women, rising crime rates, unhealthy slums, and dangerous radicalism – "the respectable people of the city should demand a clearing out of the scum which has always been a menace to the people of our land," the *Spectator* cried in January 1919 – the GWVA began to rally public opinion behind a demand to deport all aliens. On 9 February a boisterous crowd of some 10,000, in which "returned soldiers and workingmen seemed to predominate," packed the Lyric Theatre and two additional overflow sites to back the Association's resolution calling for the deportation of "enemy aliens and other undesirables." Speakers included the mayor and representatives of the Board of Trade, Canadian Club, and Hamilton Trades and Labor Council. The Council's participation was complicated by internal disagreement and a degree of sympathy for the honest, patriotic immigrants in the city, but there was a consensus to support the veterans' initiative. "They were our people, of our own flesh and blood," one delegate argued. "Whilst this alien brood had been living on the fat of the land and in solid security, our men were sent to the slaughter at a dollar and ten cents a day." The Council's resolution differed from that of the veterans in calling only for deportation of "enemy aliens" who had proven themselves "disloyal" or "dangerous" and of all aliens convicted of criminal offences. But, at the mass meeting, Fester, as labour's spokesman, gave the Council's message a sharper edge, indicating that "the great bulk of opinion" in the labour movement supported the GWVA position. "Time after time we adjured the government to be careful as to the class of men who they were permitting to enter the country," he declared. "But the government paid no heed. They were the representatives of certain interests and class who desired to obtain cheap labor, and lots of it! (Hear, Hear!)" The ambiguity of the labour position was reflected in a small meeting of 50 workingmen convened at Calvary Methodist Church just before the mass meeting. "With two or three exceptions," the *Spectator* reported, "the views expressed were for discriminate and moderate treatment of the question." But the men were unanimous that ex-soldiers and British workingmen should not be idle while Europeans worked, and that "foreigners" convicted of a crime should be deported.[71]

When a GWVA delegation carried its resolution to Ottawa, the Borden government agreed to apply a provision of the War Measures Act that would allow a Hamilton judge, in a specially convened court, to order internment. Since the last months of the war, when the state's fears had shifted to growing radicalism, the anti-alien agitation had been laced with anti-Bolshevik sentiment. In the following month several radicals in the local immigrant community were dragged before Judge Colin Snider and ordered interned. Meanwhile, Hamilton manufacturers began to discriminate against Europeans in their hiring policies, with International Harvester even barring them from participation in its new Industrial Council. In July federal immigration policy closed the door to any further influx from Eastern Europe and allowed for easier deportation of immigrant radicals.[72]

The immigrants themselves were eager to leave. A meeting of Ukrainians denied that they had been disloyal and appealed to get the borders reopened quickly to allow them to head home. A police spy reported that steamship agents were being thronged by immigrants seeking tickets back to their homelands. By September the city's assessment commissioner estimated that more than 5,000 "foreigners" had left the city. "A visit to the north-end districts of the city where the aliens are wont to congregate reveals the phenomenon . . . of house after house standing empty," the *Spectator* noted. The paper looked forward optimistically to the immigration of British workers "in order to build up a sound, vigorous nation, infused with uniform sentiment, comprehending, and proud of, the constitutional position which has been won by their fathers before them" (that is, free of any ethnic Bolshevist taint).[73]

The efforts to replace European immigrants with Anglo-Canadian labour did not move smoothly or fundamentally disrupt the ethnic hierarchies of Hamilton's factories. "White" workers frequently refused to accept the heavy, dirty labouring jobs that Italians or Poles had filled. "One order for 35 men for the Bay street rolling mills of the Steel Company of Canada could not be wholly filled, as a number of the British speaking men at the [provincial employment] bureau refused to do the work," the *Spectator* reported in February 1919. "Consequently a number of foreigners were sent." Foremen and straw bosses were often not keen to hire them in any case. As a labour spy reported to the Steel Company that month, many immigrants were patiently waiting to be rehired once the Anglo-Canadian aversion to this work had become clear.[74]

Hamilton's fulminations about immigration and ethnicity were part of a countrywide debate about the "foreigners," which had resulted in severe restrictions on European (and Asian) immigration. Yet the anticipated flood from the British Isles was never large enough, and in 1925 the Canadian government reopened the gates to Continental Europeans. As Hamilton's "foreign" population swelled noticeably in the 1920s, the now-familiar pattern of resentment against the newcomers revived with its old vigour. In the 1929 strike at the National Steel Car plant, which involved predominantly European immigrants, the union felt compelled to issue a leaflet urging English workers to abandon their hostility to the "foreigners." The call was in vain.[75]

The most ominous note sounded at that juncture was a march of 1,000 members of the Ku Klux Klan through the city streets in the midst of the strike – a parade that, according to the Toronto *Star*, brought several hundred new members into the organization. The Klan had begun its second life in the American South quietly in 1915 in the wake of D.W. Griffith's blockbuster film *Birth of a Nation*, and five years later exploded into a mass organization with large membership in many large US cities. It retained plenty of racist hatred towards people of colour, but its driving passion was now anti-Catholicism. The first Klan crosses had been lit on Hamilton Mountain in 1923, probably as an extension of the wave of organizing that hit Buffalo and western New York State that year, and late in 1924 a Klan organizer was arrested in the city for carrying a gun. The next year a local newspaper reported that the Women's Canadian

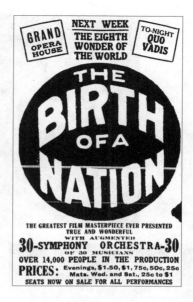

Although priced beyond the reach of most working people, the notoriously racist movie *Birth of a Nation* played to sellout crowds in Hamilton in 1915. Across North America, it helped to revive the Ku Klux Klan.
(*HS*, 16 Oct. 1915, 20)

Ku Klux Klan, with a thousand members and branches in several cities, was headquartered in Hamilton. Fiery crosses continued to appear sporadically over the next several years.[76]

In 1930 Klansmen caught public attention by travelling from Hamilton to nearby Oakville to threaten a man of colour for living with a white woman. The order defended its action as protection of "the Anglo-Saxon people against the ever-increasing menace arising from communism, bolshevism, Reds and Orientals, and the peril of race impurity." The leaders of this brazen demonstration of vigilante justice were later identified in the press as "prominent Hamilton business men." Of the four men arrested for that action, one was none other than the Protestant missionary to local Italians, Ernest Taylor. One of the four vanished, and only one was convicted – a Hamilton chiropractor (he got a $50 fine, later bumped up to three months in jail on appeal). Anglo-Canadian workingmen may have been marching with him (no membership records have surfaced), but studies in urban

The Ku Klux Klan arrived in Hamilton in the mid-1920s. The organization included a women's branch. As part of its agitation against immigrants and people of colour, the KKK burned fiery crosses and paraded through the streets, as in this event around 1930. (HPL)

areas across the United States suggest that, although many white, Protestant, blue-collar wage-earners might have joined, Klan members tended to be disproportionately drawn from lower-middle-class white-collar occupations. The message they delivered through their fiery ceremonies and hooded theatrics may nonetheless have added fuel to Anglo-Canadian workers' resentments towards so-called foreigners in Hamilton.[77]

The Klan never did become a mass organization in Ontario, and seems to have declined after all the publicity over the Oakville incident. But it is likely that this failure reflected the strength of the much older Orange Order, which set up several new lodges in Hamilton in the 1920s with an overwhelmingly working-class leadership. It

seems that the order got new life from the post-war agitations about "foreigners" and the associated "Red Scare." In the face of the "Bolshevik menace," Orangemen preached loyalty more loudly than ever. They avoided hoods or burning crosses, but their fundamental tenet was British ascendancy and anti-Catholicism, a parallel that the Order's journal, the *Orange Sentinel*, liked to note. They also made their hall available to Klan organizers.[78]

Hamilton's Anglo-Canadian workers, then, were far from comfortable with the city's new ethnic rainbow. Their disdain for the newcomers seemed to erupt into confrontations only when the caste-like occupational hierarchy was disrupted and the immigrants got access to "white" jobs. But the gulf between ethnic and racial groups in the city remained deep and wide.

Birds of a Feather

Ethnic groups lived lives apart in Hamilton at least partly by choice. Although discriminatory hiring processes and real-estate practices played a pivotal role in creating walls between them, and anti-alien agitation deepened those divides, newcomers tended to prefer each others' company in any case. A Lancashire textile worker,

Romanian workers had their own fraternal society in Hamilton.
(AO, 0050075)

a Glaswegian carpenter, an Italian construction worker, an Armenian foundry worker, or a Polish labourer: they all generally preferred to live close to others who spoke their dialect or language and near to familiar services and institutions to meet their daily needs for sustenance and companionship – labour agencies, banks, boarding houses, grocery stores, cafés, and bookstores. As sojourning turned to settlement, their wives also built a sense of community as they shopped and made friends along the streets. In those informal neighbourhood settings, the newcomers carved out specific ethnic enclaves in the city, places that distinguished them from other groups. Ethnicity thus came to have a clear spatial dimension.[79]

At the same time they were also encouraged to take part in organized activities to celebrate their cultural identities, which linked homelands and widely dispersed settlements. Hamilton was a patchwork of distinct diasporas. The city saw a proliferation of groups dedicated to binding their fellow countrymen together for mutual support and good times, particularly mutual-benefit societies, churches,

and radical political organizations. The main voices within these initiatives were either small-scale shopkeepers, professionals, and other self-employed men whose business enterprises were the stable element in their communities around which a project of identity formation could coalesce, or else radicalized workers and intellectuals who promoted both ethnic and working-class solidarities.

In early 20th-century Hamilton the benefit society became the most common secular organization for drawing together people of the same ethnic background. It was sometimes the creation of workers themselves, as it had been among better-paid English-speaking workers on both sides of the Atlantic since the 18th century, but by the late 19th century it was more often a cross-class institution. Through a pooling of members' contributions, such a society provided financial assistance to the sick and to a member's family for funeral expenses. It also offered a measure of conviviality for the membership (including well-attended funerals) and sometimes undertook to organize public celebrations.

Within Hamilton's Anglo-Canadian population, each of the major British groups had such a society with a substantial working-class membership before the turn of the century. The largest of them was the Sons of England (and the parallel Daughters and Maids of England), with six branches and its own meeting hall by 1910.[80]

Among many peasant-labourers from Continental Europe, such formal organizations were slower to take hold. They were less common in the countryside back home than in the cities, and, as transients, the men relied on more informal patterns of socializing among others from the same village or region who shared their boarding houses or drank with them in cafés or saloons on the corner.[81] As broader associational patterns developed among them, those local identities might remain far stronger than any attachment to a nation-state.[82] Not surprisingly given their patterns of chain migration and mutual aid, Italians in particular socialized through regional networks and institutions, and the two geographically separated clusters of them in the east and west ends of Hamilton remained culturally distant as well. At least two annual celebrations emerged to preserve distinct parochial loyalties – the feast of St. Anthony, which started in 1910 in the east, and the *festa* of the Madonna del Monte, a narrowly Racalmutese tradition, which began in 1913 in the west.[83]

The benefit society was nonetheless a familiar old-world organization, especially among artisans and shopkeepers.[84] Many may have been simply private arrangements among small groups of fellow countrymen who lived together – such as the *landsmanshaften* among the Jews.[85] But each of the larger immigrant groups in the city also eventually spawned substantial, more public mutual-benefit societies. Since such organizations were hard to sustain among sojourning male workers who might be in the city no more than a few months at a time, it was, not surprisingly, the Jews who were the most active because they more often came from a settled urban background and largely arrived in Canada as permanent immigrants with families.[86]

Organizations within the more transitory communities appeared more slowly, and they tended to be the projects of more settled community leaders trying to construct a new, broader ethnicity and a secure place for it in Canadian society. The First Hungarian Sick Benefit Society, founded in 1907, seems to have been the earliest among the organizations of European newcomers to the city. Apparently founded by migrant workers with socialist and labour-movement experience in Hungary and the United States, the Society had a membership that by the 1920s included mostly skilled and unskilled workers, along with a sprinkling of the shopkeeping elite. Late in that decade, it affiliated with the Communist-led Workers' Society.[87] In the local Italian community it was the established *prominenti* who organized the first Italian society, the Prima Societa Italiana, in 1910, to provide sick, disability, and death benefits. It soon had some 90 members, most of them settled immigrants. Some five years later, in the tradition of *campanilismo*, the more narrowly based Sons of Racalmuto Benefit Society emerged to serve only migrants from that town, a sign of growing settlement among this group.[88] Meanwhile, starting in 1912, the city's Poles formed similar groups, as did the Croats in the 1920s.[89]

While membership in each of these societies probably included only a fraction of the new immigrant population,[90] they did give many European labourers in the city a modicum of insurance against misfortune, a familiar cultural niche for recreation and entertainment, and, for some, experience in organizing men and administering funds. As the elites within each community took control of them, they also took on much larger cultural roles in drawing together fellow countrymen.

Aside from the mutual-benefit societies, the most important collective cultural resource of the Hamilton "foreign colony" was probably the Catholic Church.[91] Like the Irish who had preceded them at the bottom of the occupational structure, European immigrants found that their religious heritage set them apart from the large Protestant majority in Hamilton society.[92] By the early 20th century, however, the Catholic Church was dominated by an Irish-Canadian hierarchy that showed scant sympathy with the newer immigrants' particular national and regional adaptations of the faith. Tensions emerged over the saints to be venerated in feasts and celebrations and the exalted importance of the Virgin Mary in rituals, as well as the mixture of popular traditions and superstitions that were so often a large part of the popular Catholicism of European peasants,[93] but the local church leadership eventually recognized the need for a fresh approach to the new European immigrants arriving in Hamilton, especially since the Protestants were stepping in with their own missionaries to the newcomers. In 1908 the bishop summoned from Boston Giovanni Bonomi, a 26-year-old Scalabrini priest trained in Italy to work with overseas Italians. Bonomi would serve Hamilton's Italians for the next 45 years. He began special services for Italians in a small chapel adjacent to St. Mary's Cathedral in the west end and held open-air services in the east until 1910 when a temporary chapel was opened in St. Ann's School. In 1911 Thomas Tarasiuk was brought from Chicago to serve the city's Polish Catholics. The two ethnic groups did not rely on ecclesiastical sponsorship alone. "We had to make our own church because of the discrimination against the Italian people," one man later insisted. In 1911 a meeting of 300 Poles agreed to give one day's pay a month for the construction of a Polish-language church, while a group of Italians began work on a house of worship for their countrymen. On Easter Sunday 1912 the bishop dedicated the Italian church, St. Anthony of Padua, in the presence of hundreds of fervent worshippers, and blessed the as-yet incomplete Polish church, St. Stanislaus.[94]

In addition to whatever spiritual succour and material relief the Catholic Church could provide for these newcomers, the separate ethnic parishes became an organizing focus for cultural survival. In the Italian communities in particular, St. Anthony's and Our Lady of All Souls' (opened in the west end in 1923) helped to pull together the fragmented Italian community, moving them out of their intense familistic and regional loyalties. According to the local press, the entire Italian population would turn out for each of the colourful ceremonies in honour of St. Anthony and of the Madonna del Monte, which by itself was drawing over 30,000 participants, Italians and non-Italians alike, by 1931.[95]

The intense parochialism that typified the Southern and Eastern European peasant gradually eroded, though it by no means disappeared. In part, the relatively small size of each of these ethnic groups in Hamilton encouraged all fellow countrymen to associate together. The English-Canadian tendency to lump them together into single national groups was also a homogenizing and integrating force. But encouraging a stronger identification with a nation than with a kin network or hometown (*campanile* among Italians) was also a project of the elites within each European immigrant community. These men generally ran the commercial services that provided cohesion, enjoyed high status in their neighbourhoods, and regularly undertook to speak for their communities as intermediaries with Hamilton institutions and to promote integration.[96]

One important role was court interpreter, helping men brought before the police magistrate to defend themselves. An early example of this functionary, Budimir Protich, also ran an employment agency and was frequently consulted by the immigrants on a wide range of matters.[97] In subsequent years the provincial government bestowed civil honours on at least two prominent members of the "foreign colony" in Hamilton by making them justices of the peace – Leopoldo P. Scarrone, a well-established Italian merchant and steamship agent, and Anthony A. Yarosh, a Polish court interpreter and real-estate agent. These intermediaries, along with the rest of the immigrant communities' petty-bourgeois leadership – *prominenti* such as grocers Salvatore Sanzone and Antonio Spicuzza, clothing contractor F. Di Nunzio, or, by the 1920s, the city's first Italian physician, Vincent Agro – worked to encourage an identification with ethnicity and a nation-state back home. Alongside the benefit societies, they launched recreational outlets such as the Italians' east-end Marconi Club and the Dopolavoro Society, founded in 1917 and 1935 respectively. An Italian man recalled that in the interwar period the leader of one of these clubs "could sway the entire club to vote in the way he wished."[98]

Public events were important occasions to cultivate such solidarities. The community leaders behind the Prima Societa Italiana became leading sponsors of annual St. Anthony's Day celebrations and helped to organize the Italian Red Cross Society fundraising drive. In addition to the church festivals, there was a large parade during the city's centennial week celebrations in 1913, and great public celebrations of the unification of Italy, such as the one in Britannia Park a month later, which featured an Italian band, speeches, sports events, and fireworks for the more than 1,300 men and women who turned out. A new Italian newspaper, *L'Italia di Hamilton*, no doubt boosted these events during its short life from 1912 to 1914 (no copies have survived). World War One intensified this unifying trend among the Italians. In the first week after war was declared, L.P. Scarrone and Dr. Louis Aldrighetti, the Italian newspaper editor, organized a public proclamation of loyalty to Canada and the British Empire, a mass meeting to promote the creation of an Italian corps to join the Canadian Expeditionary Force, and an enthusiastic parade. When news reached the city in May 1915 that Italy had joined the Allies, a large spontaneous procession of automobiles waving British and Italian flags brought cheers of "Long Live Italy!" from hundreds of Italians as it passed through the streets. A week later the community turned out for a celebration commemorating the death of the Italian hero Giuseppe Garibaldi. The entertainment at this event included two boys wearing suits composed of flags of the Allies doing a recitation on the Italian flag, and ended with "Garibaldi's Hymn" and "God Save the King" in Italian.[99]

Other ethnic groups had a similar experience. Recruitment for a Polish army and a new fervour for an independent Poland helped to unite the city's Polish community. Some 700 Jews attended a meeting to promote the civil rights of Jews in the warring countries and the establishment of an independent homeland in Palestine. By 1918 recruitment was underway for a Jewish military force to fight in Palestine, part of a broader Canadian initiative. "We want our land and we want to fight for it," Jacob Romer, secretary of the United Hebrew School, told the press. Even the tiny Greek population in the city was reported to be alive with new nationalist fervour. In the face of rising anti-immigrant

The Jewish Workmen's Circle, founded in 1909, was one of the earliest socialist societies among European immigrants. Members posed here on their 30th anniversary. (SLS, LS604)

sentiment, organizations of Italians, Poles, and Ukrainians issued statements defending their war records and devotion to the Allied cause.[100]

The postwar breakup of old empires saw a new age of self-conscious nationalism and state-building in Europe, which brought into existence such new countries as Poland and Czechoslovakia. Some European groups thus had their first chance to connect ethnicity with citizenship back home. Others, such as the Italians and Russians, had more powerful new governments. These developments fed the trend towards ethnic cohesion in the 1920s, particularly among the two largest groups, the Italians and the Poles, both of which contributed large, colourful floats to the Diamond Jubilee parade in 1927. The Italians' stunning float showcased the role of the great men of Italian history in art, exploration, music, and science. Both the Italian and Polish governments actively encouraged nationalist identification with a strong homeland and ruled that these immigrants were to be overseas subjects, not emigrants. Mussolini's fascist government supported the building of an Italian hall, Casa d'Italia, in 1935, which became the home of all the major organizations of the community, including the local branch of the Italian Fascist Party, and the scene of flourishing cultural activities, including concerts and dances. By that point, the city's smaller Hungarian and Croatian communities were also getting political help from back home. In practice, the scattered parts of these European diasporas were being encouraged to dissolve their older parochial, peasant identities in a broader national citizenship linked to trans-Atlantic homelands.[101]

The ethnic elites did not always manage to corral fellow countrymen into these projects. Undoubtedly the older parochialism continued to co-exist with the new ethnic nationalism, especially among immigrant women, who had generally arrived later and participated much less in local public life (beyond church) than did their menfolk. Many of these European newcomers, moreover, must have brought with them an age-old peasant distrust of the state in their homelands, which had so often seemed far more oppressive than inspiring or ennobling.[102]

In some cases local organizations rallied members of a particular ethnic group around

Ukrainians in Hamilton formed a branch of the Social Democratic Party, photographed here in 1916.
(AO, I0050070)

programs of political radicalism. Such groups were formed among the Armenians, Jews, Ukrainians, Russians, Hungarians, Poles, and, by the 1930s, Yugoslavians and Lithuanians. Some of these people had been radicalized in their homelands, but many joined such organizations in the new context of wage-earning and sojourning.[103] In most cases these groups cultivated a strong sense of national oppression along with their socialist or communist commitments. They drew together diverse members of their migrant countrymen and moved beyond narrow regional identities to promote both political liberation and social transformation back home (and in Canada). In 1905, for example, the Armenian Revolutionary Federation (or Dashnaks) undertook fundraising to support victims of a massacre earlier that year, and five years later petitioned the federal government to help free Armenian prisoners in Russia. In 1924 Ukrainian radicals held countrywide protests

against the repression of "ten million Ukrainian peasants and workers" inside Poland and Romania. Such groups also set up social and cultural centres – from an Armenian library and reading room to a Russian bookstore to a Hungarian theatre to the Ukrainian Labour Temple – in which people in their communities could meet for discussions, hear lectures, watch plays and concerts, or simply relax over cards and coffee. Often the local branches were linked to other Canadian groups through some kind of federation, and the radical ethnic press kept them informed of political developments in Canada and overseas – notably Winnipeg's Ukrainian *Robochy Narod* and the Hungarian *Kanadai Magyar Munkas* (Canadian Hungarian Worker), which began publication in Hamilton in 1929. Their radical programs reinforced the migrant workers' new proletarian identities in North America, and some people attached themselves to the mainstream socialist and Communist movements led by Anglo-Canadians. They often locked horns with more conservative nationalists within their communities, including the clergy. In January 1917, for example, Hamilton's Ukrainian Social Democrats proclaimed 7 January, the Ukrainian Christmas, to be the "Nativity of Socialism," and, on doorsteps in their neighbourhoods, sang "socialist carols" set to traditional melodies.[104]

Working-class Hamiltonians, then, had plenty of opportunity to join organizations based on ethnic and racial identities, and many apparently did. The membership of these groups was often heavily proletarian, and many of the "middle-class" men who tended to take on leadership roles were not widely separated in social status from wage-earners (and rarely employed many workers themselves), especially the shopkeepers and small businessmen of various kinds. For many male wage-earners, these groups undoubtedly filled up some of the social space occupied elsewhere by strong, viable unions or workers' parties, which were so weak or short-lived in Hamilton. The organizations encouraged workers to find their self-esteem in the larger glories of broad national groups – whether British, Italian, or Polish – and to identify with the transnational diasporic communities that linked homeland and settlement. Peaceful coexistence among such groups, however, was difficult, as each proclaimed the glories of particular cultures and traditions. Among the non-Anglo-Canadians an early version of "hyphenated Canadianism" was emerging, in which commitment to the Canadian nation-state (including naturalization) and a non-British identity could be intertwined comfortably. In the process they could become undeniably "white."[105]

Living Together

There was probably no time in Canadian history when a city like Hamilton was more awash in vigorous, chest-thumping ethnic identities than in the early 20th century. Anglo-Canadian imperialist patriotism reached peak intensity, and other nationalities responded in kind (eventually, in some cases, with help from their home governments). These were not simply competing cultures. They were consciously constructed ideologies, propagated by the elites in each group and consolidated in separate cultural institutions, which grew out of and reinforced hierarchies of power and privilege, subordination and exclusion. Wage-earners often accepted these versions of reality, though perhaps adapting and interpreting them in their own ways. Hamilton's ethnic and racial groups viewed each other through lenses of contempt and resentment – the prickly Scottish moulder as much as the proud Sicilian labourer. "A deep distrust of 'Anglo-Saxons' existed among many foreign-born peoples," the young radical Peter Hunter discovered in the early 1930s, "and it took time for us to be accepted."[106]

Surprisingly, remarkably little head-on confrontation occurred, at least until the Anglo-Canadians detected a rupture in the caste-like segmentation of local labour markets. The arrival of so many new European sojourners (along with a much smaller influx of Chinese) in the decade before World War One – and their role in the emerging mass-production industries – triggered misgivings and mutterings, but it was the unusual employment conditions of the war economy that brought these worries to a boiling point. By 1919 exclusion had become the new politics of ethnic relations. European newcomers hunkered down to avoid the heat, and thousands quietly left the city (and the country) right after the war as the widening attacks on "foreigners" became entangled in anti-communism. On through the interwar period, Orangemen, veterans, and other ultra-British patriots (including

Klansmen) kept that bigotry alive. An Italian immigrant later remembered that in the 1930s "the Anglos ... were always giving me a hard time ... always discriminating against you." Another recalled, "The English looked down on anything non-English." Still another had memories of being beaten up for being Italian and Catholic.[107]

Yet the story of ethnic relations in working-class Hamilton in the early 20th century was not quite so black and white. After the horrors of World War One the British Empire lost some of its lustre, and the rituals and rhetoric of hegemonic national identity made a perceptible shift to Canada itself. The racialization of ethnicity was also sliding slowly away from biology towards a more cultural definition of difference (though people of colour saw no such change). Moreover, as the *Herald* had overly optimistically predicted in its 1912 front-page article about the city's new "foreign" element, newcomers did adapt through living and working there. Their ethnic communities served both as a "staging ground" for engaging with the wider community and as a retreat from it.[108]

By the same interwar period, as sojourning declined, more stable groups of second-generation immigrants had begun to fashion identities that combined their parents' old-world customs with elements absorbed from their English-language schooling and daily street life (especially in the east end, where European ethnic groups interacted regularly), and their exposure to the mass culture of popular music, movies, comics, and sports. The so-called Garlic Opera in the east end (the Playhouse Theatre) was a lively example of how ethnicities could survive in the midst of new mass-cultural conditions.[109] By the 1930s the gulf between this hyphenated Canadianism and the hegemonic British allegiance was arguably somewhat narrower than what had existed before 1920, and workers in the

city may have begun to share more in common – although cultural convergence would long remain limited by the still robust forms of active, systemic discrimination against non-Anglo-Celts and people of colour.

Ethnic hostilities rarely just fade away by themselves. People have to intervene to argue and agitate for that kind of change. Well before the 1920s voices in working-class Hamilton were actively promoting greater co-operation across ethnic lines. The Catholic Church certainly used its separate-school system in that way, and a handful of Protestant settlement workers tried to allow some cultural pluralism (although their tolerance of European folk cultures may have been simply a step along a road to the assimilation they ultimately expected).[110] Labour too had tried – with the city's unionized clothing workers making perhaps the greatest strides in bridging ethnicities, in an industry with large numbers of Jewish workers, at the end of World War One. In 1919, too, as an odd counterpoint to the bellowing about enemy aliens, the larger Hamilton craft union movement reached out to help Italian construction labourers create a union of their own and the next year brought multilingual organizers to rally immigrant steelworkers into the new Amalgamated Association of Iron, Steel, and Tin Workers.

These hesitant, defensive moves paled alongside what was happening in some US mass-production industries[111] and had more to do with how the real voices of ethnic inclusion were on the radical left. In the wake of the Russian Revolution of 1917 local socialist groups with distinct ethnic memberships collaborated in public organizing.[112] The radical unionist Fred Flatman reached out to the "foreigners" in building the city's branches of the One Big Union. The emerging Communist movement brought together people of varied ethnic backgrounds, always showcasing Ukrainian or Jewish performers at annual May Day festivities and in 1927 including two Chinese speakers, while at the same time working to contain (or completely submerge) ethnic identities within overtly class-conscious politics. In the late 1930s the new Steel Workers' Organizing Committee would similarly reach out to Slavic workers in the local mills.[113] Still, the consistent attacks from employers and the state made these more integrative unions and political organizations a much less influential force within working-class Hamilton than were similar efforts in parts of Europe and North America.

Race and ethnicity, then, were fluid, relational, and changing, not hard, fixed categories of identity. Within working-class Hamilton, they were above all evolving discourses that gave workers a perspective on their place within the new industrial pecking order in the city and mobilized them around a set of loyalties. Concretely, that also meant drawing them into separate ethnic institutions and social practices for comfort, consolation, and mutual support. After work they simply went their separate ways. Their lives within their family circles and neighbourhoods did not bring them into contact with the "Other." Ethnic and racial identities thus pulled workers apart, and allowed those in more privileged positions in the local socio-economic hierarchy to cultivate an air of superiority. Yet that did not necessarily lessen their sense of being workers. Ethnicity and class worked together in what one historian calls a "segmented class formation."[114]

Indeed, aggrieved Anglo-Canadian wage-earners could turn on their employers in class-conscious wrath for employing new ethnic or racial groups, and European sojourners could angrily confront their exploitative straw bosses or attend socialist lectures on a different kind of future for workers. In the end, neither the skilled British machinist nor the Polish labourer could forget that in order to survive, unlike many of their ethnic leaders, he needed to punch a time clock at the crack of dawn every morning.

16

Conservative propaganda in 1911.

(HS, 20 Sept. 1911, 1)

True Blue

"FUTURE STUDENTS OF HISTORY will stand amazed and almost incredulous when they read that the workers who lived in the opening years of the 20th century allowed themselves to be oppressed and exploited by an idle class whom it was possible for them to outvote at any time fifty to one."[1]

This 1905 lament in the *Industrial Banner* posed a problem that would perplex social scientists, theoreticians, and, occasionally, historians throughout the century: the coexistence of liberal democracy with the inequities of a class society. Why did the working-class majority not make greater use of its power at the ballot box to reshape industrial society according to its own needs? Why did these voters defer to wealthier, more powerful men in shaping political possibilities? Why was it, in the words of a proletarian poet, that "united they sweat but divided they vote"?[2]

"Deference" is a slippery term. It connotes respect for and obedience to authority, often as the underside of "paternalism." But it is more than simply an attitude. As a set of behavioural patterns and practices, it is a particular response to some kind of subordination and dependence within a structure of hegemonic power (including the possibility of coercion); and it can take many ritualized forms, ranging from deeply rooted loyalty to calculating obsequiousness to a posture of grudging compliance. Much of the ritual may be scripted by those in authority, but deference almost always involves some agency by deferential subjects in negotiating their needs (for protection from harm, or material rewards, for instance). Mutuality has to exist in the relationship.[3]

The implicit coerciveness never did disappear, and it made it difficult for workers to pose their own political alternatives. Relying on wages for the survival of themselves and their families entailed severe constraints, whether fear of unemployment and poverty, outright intimidation by bosses, or simply sheer fatigue after long hours of work. Their "consent" to the rule of their betters was grounded in the daily reality of this essential dependence and necessary deference, from which there would most often appear to be no escape. Individually and collectively they had difficulty finding the time and resources for political independence. Not surprisingly, by the early years of the century growing numbers of workers were not even bothering to vote.

Yet a depoliticized compliance could never be taken for granted, and indeed was not necessarily desirable. Political mobilization of working-class voters was often necessary for specific public-policy initiatives. More broadly, the discourses and practices of politics could be important to building and maintaining social cohesion in a rapidly changing society. At the turn of the century, two major political parties competed to integrate workers into their political projects – the Liberals (or "Grits") and the Conservatives (or "Tories"). The Tories quickly triumphed as the "natural party of government" at all three levels of government in Hamilton, though they soon had to confront a new political challenge in the form of the local Independent Labor Party. In a city with such a large proletarian population, the Conservative hegemony required not only integrating a loyal band of working-class activists for the cause, but also pitching a message that convinced larger numbers of working-class voters to put their trust in the Tories and their political vision.

To understand that process is to appreciate how the political complexion of working-class voters can never simply be read from their class position or overt material interests. Their participation had to be mobilized and shaped by political organizations using political discourses that connected with the immediate and the personal and gave meaning to workers' daily lives in their workplaces, households, and neighbourhoods. This was far from a simple one-way flow from party to people. In this case the message that the Tories delivered had to be responsive to working-class concerns and aspirations. It had to be able to turn the Tory worldview into a widely shared "common sense." As a result, in constructing a politics of deference the Conservatives made a respectable place for the Tory workingman under their wide blue banner.[4]

At the Ballot Box

"The ballot is worth its weight in gold," Allan Studholme reminded an ILP gathering in 1916, "so value the gem within labor's grasp."[5] The little stove-mounter's enthusiasm for the democratic franchise echoed a century of working-class agitation for access to parliamentary voting in the British political system. Yet in a city like Hamilton that statement could sound hollow in the real world of electoral politics, where constraints and manipulative practices so often undermined the theory of representative democracy. Many voters must have viewed the formal political process with considerably more scepticism than did Hamilton's leading labour parliamentarian.

Countless numbers of workers were effectively disenfranchised by discriminatory electoral processes. As of 1898, when the provinces took over responsibility for who could vote federally, all of Ontario's Canadian-born and naturalized male citizens over age 21 could vote, without any of the property restrictions that had previously existed. "Things have changed," one prominent Liberal asserted that year. "The crowd are in it as never before."[6] Yet for many of Hamilton's workers voting was still hedged with restrictions. Women were barred before 1917; none of the thousands of workers under 21 were eligible; and few of the growing numbers of Asian and European immigrants had the vote (in the 1917 federal election, even those born in enemy countries but naturalized since 1902 were disenfranchised). An electoral system biased in favour of adult Anglo-Canadian males also favoured the more stable, prosperous citizens of the community. The residency requirements – of 12 months in the province, three months in the same municipality, and one month in the actual constituency – were hardest on the highly mobile working class, notably the younger, unmarried, and less-skilled sections of the population who travelled widely to find work.[7]

Moreover, before 1917 the system of recording eligible voters for federal and provincial elections avoided doing a new enumeration for each election. The *Spectator* quite properly called the system "cumbrous, intricate and stupid." Lists of voters were prepared from city assessment rolls, and workers left off the lists had to find time in a working day to appear before registration boards during a short interval before the elections (ten hours a day for six days) to ensure that their names were added. Liberal and Conservative party workers devoted a considerable time to marshalling their supporters before the registrars. "The Elections are more often won in settling the voters' lists than at the polls," a provincial Conservative leader had once written.[8] The rapid growth of Hamilton's population during these years doubtless left many newcomers unregistered.[9] Door-to-door enumeration of voters for each election began only in 1917, but even then anyone missed had to go to the court of revision well before voting day.[10] At the same time the demarcation of electoral boundaries could dilute the working-class vote substantially. In a glaring pattern of gerrymandering, the large new residential area east of Sherman Avenue, which had been annexed to the city from Barton Township in 1903, remained a pocket of the predominantly rural riding of Wentworth that grew to 18,000 voters out of 38,000 by 1921.[11] A similarly skewed arrangement put part of the city's west end in the new, mainly rural riding of Hamilton-Wentworth in the 1930s.[12]

Before 1920, getting to the polls in the hours from 9 a.m. to 5 p.m. set aside for voting ("banking hours," one disgruntled workingman called them) also posed problems. Most shops and factories kept their employees on the job 10 to 12 hours a day and would not have shut down before the polls closed. The electoral law required employers to provide two hours off work at lunch to facilitate voting, but, as the distance between home and work grew in the rapidly expanding city, more and more workers must have hesitated to travel back to their own neighbourhoods in order to vote, even with the party rigs and autos waiting for them outside the plant gates. After years of criticism, the closing hours in the interwar period gradually moved slightly later – to 6 p.m. in 1921, 7 p.m. in 1926, and 8 p.m. in 1934.[13]

To get into an electoral race as a candidate, a Hamilton worker would have faced even more formidable obstacles. A woman was ineligible until 1919 (when the Ontario government finally brought in legislation to allow women to stand in provincial and municipal elections),[14] but even a workingman interested in running for a municipal seat had to meet stiff property qualifications: $1,000 freehold or $2,000 leasehold. Before World War One, several would-be candidates were disqualified. As late as 1919 an ILP leader in Barton Township was complaining that because of limited property holdings, "We were only able, out of a comparatively large membership, to place two candidates in the field."[15] This bar to workers' participation in municipal politics was profoundly important because most candidates for provincial or federal office in the mainstream parties worked their way through city council first, developing political experience and establishing a reputation with the city's voters.[16] Denied access to this training ground, workers had a harder time making the breakthrough into higher offices. In 1914 the Hamilton Trades and Labor Council launched a province-wide campaign to have property qualifications abolished, but it was not until 1920, in the first year of the Farmer-Labour administration at Queen's Park, that this restriction was finally removed.[17]

The most important deterrents to working-class entry into local politics usually hinged on the workers' meagre financial resources. Federal candidates had to post a $200 deposit – a third to a half of most male workers' annual wages in the pre-war period – which was forfeited if the candidate failed to garner half as many votes as the winner.[18] Campaigning to win support for election was similarly expensive. Printing flyers and posters, renting halls, buying newspaper advertisements, and otherwise making one's name known to the electors required substantial funds, which were difficult to assemble in working-class neighbourhoods, as the advocates of independent labour politics discovered. For any aspirant to public office, successful electioneering would

(*HS*, 15 Oct. 1904, 4)

also require time off work and a substantial loss of wages.

The political dice, therefore, were loaded against Hamilton's workers.[19] In addition the political game had its seamy side. In the opening years of the 20th century political organizers used plenty of tricks to manipulate the voting process for the benefit of their parties – techniques the *Spectator* coyly dubbed "human device" election methods. By this point electoral corruption was a well-developed art in Canada, and Hamilton was no stranger to such illegal practices as buying votes and impersonating voters. Studholme may have believed that a vote was as valuable as gold, but he was not endorsing the scarcely veiled practice of exchanging one's vote for hard cash or liquor. The standard bribe in the years before World War One appears to have been two dollars. Principal G.M. Grant of Queen's University was horrified at the flagrant corruption evident in the 1898 provincial election in Kingston, Toronto, London, and Hamilton. "A seedy-looking lot loafed round the booths . . . waiting to get their two dollars apiece before entering," he wrote. "Hundreds got what they waited for." On election day ten years later the *Spectator* noted that on the streets, "Many a man thought more of getting a $2 bill for his vote than he did of deciding the great issues which affect the country."[20]

Both parties delighted in accusing the other of "opening the barr'l" to supporters. Until 1906 provincial voters cast numbered ballots, which allowed the bribers to check that their money had been well spent.[21] The Conservative *Spectator* repeatedly accused the Liberals of "attempting to steal the two Hamilton seats by the money method," and the scandals involving systematic bribery that plagued George Ross's Liberal organization across the province indicated that there was no doubt more than a kernel of truth in the charges. But the Conservatives were just as free with these inducements to supporters. In 1908 a defeated Liberal candidate confessed his amazement at the Tories' "unlimited use of Money Liquor and other nefarious schemes. Their organization in that respect was perfect." Some three years later the liberal *Herald* similarly claimed that "agents of the Conservative party are busily engaged in placing bribe-money 'where it will do the most good.'"[22]

Charges concerning efforts being made to impersonate voters also flew across the political arena. Early in the century both parties warned electors about their opponents' gangs of "pluggers and personators," who would register votes for the many Hamiltonians known to be unlikely to vote – a large number in the days of low voter turnouts. The party that controlled the appointment of assessors to prepare the voters' lists and election officials to watch over the polls often bent electoral rules to assist its candidates. Before the war the city's aldermen controlled the appointment of deputy returning officers. The

Herald decried this system, which, it said, "enabled corrupt public representatives to get on the list deputy returning officers who are subservient to them." In 1908 a minor scandal emerged to highlight the flaws in such an arrangement when a polling clerk offered to sell a batch of ballots to a Liberal organizer. Unfortunately, as the ILP discovered in 1914, the idea of contesting allegedly unfair election practices faced a strong deterrent in the form of a $1,000 fee.[23]

Hamilton businessman and Liberal provincial cabinet minister John M. Gibson was once quoted as saying that the extension of the franchise had created the "low political morality of the electorate." He suggested that manhood suffrage may have been a mistake.[24] Such anti-democratic remarks clearly shifted the blame away from the political machines that organized the "grafters and personators." In the face of rising criticism of such practices (including from the Hamilton Board of Trade), the Conservative government of Sir James P. Whitney brought in tighter legislative controls, and the worst excesses of corruption seemed to be on the wane by November 1914, when Tory candidate John Allan said he had instructed his campaigners that "there was to be no buying votes, or anything of that kind." He attributed his Labor opponent's remarkably high vote to the action of "a whole lot of disappointed men who didn't get $2 each, and who went and voted for [Walter] Rollo just before the polls closed."[25] By the interwar period charges of such blatant corruption had subsided.

Yet another factor inhibiting working-class access to the political process was the "progressive" reform of hiving off important areas of public policy into the jurisdiction of new appointive boards and commissions. These bodies operated independently of democratic control and more according to the needs and principles of efficiently managed business life. In national politics the Board of Railway Commissioners set the pattern.[26] In the pre-war years the same kind of approach to politics brought a Railway and Municipal Board and a Hydro-Electric Commission into the Ontario provincial administration. In a similar vein, Hamilton manufacturers joined the campaign for a permanent "scientific" tariff commission to remove the question of tariff protection from public debate.[27]

At the municipal level a wide range of appointed committees and boards concerned with civic affairs were removed from direct democratic control. A 1913 booklet published by the city boasted that the bodies empowered to administer schools, parks, libraries, hospitals, cemeteries, electric power, and the harbour were "practically independent Boards, in full control of their departments, so far as their management and expenditures are concerned." Among these, only the school board and the Hydro-Electric Commission were elected. Even the appointed Technical Education Committee had virtually complete freedom to direct the affairs of the new technical school. The same spirit of reducing popular access to important areas of public decision-making animated the city's few, unsuccessful campaigners for commission government in city hall.[28]

The local labour movement watched these shifts with growing concern. In January 1913 the Hamilton Trades and Labor Council passed a resolution of regret that with the retirement of Alf Wilkes from the school board the last surviving nominee of organized labour on a city board had disappeared. "Some years ago," the *Industrial Banner* reported, "nominees of the Trades Council were appointed on several of the civic bodies, such as the Parks Board, Library Board, Cemetery Board, Art School, and Board of Education." Some five years later the ILP's municipal

program contended, "Entirely too much power is vested in local public boards. The result of this evil has been to cause stagnation in the local civic administration."[29]

The political process therefore did not offer easy access for Hamilton's workers. They were hampered by formal and informal restrictions on their ability to participate, confronted with shabby electoral practices that debased the franchise, and increasingly aware that important areas of decision-making had moved beyond popular control. Many workers in the city, seeing nothing in such a political system for themselves, cynically accepted the liquor and the two-dollar bill or, more commonly, simply did not bother to vote. In 1912 Canada's old Liberal warhorse, Sir Richard Cartwright, suggested in his *Reminiscences* that theoretically "the people should come out of their own accord; practically, they have to be driven or spurred up." A Hamilton socialist lamented in the same period, "It seems hard to convince them that Socialists would not follow in the well beaten path of the capitalist grafters."[30]

The proportion of Hamilton's electorate that went to the polls dropped steadily after the turn of the century, with municipal politics arousing the least interest. Between 1901 and 1903, for example, the votes cast for mayor never exceeded 8,000, while census-takers found close to 15,000 men over the age of 20 in 1901. In 1913, after a doubling of the city's population, the total vote was still less than 14,000. In 1921 the mayoralty vote totalled only 18,000, while the adult population of the city had climbed to over 70,000.[31] In federal and provincial elections the decline in voter participation before the war was camouflaged by the suspect registration system, which made the percentage of eligible voters casting ballots seem fairly high, especially in federal elections.[32] But the extremely modest increase in the actual number of federal votes cast – from 12,000 in 1896 to a high of 15,000 in 1911 – contrasted sharply with the huge population growth. The absolute number of voters in provincial elections actually declined by 700 between 1898 and 1911. More and more eligible voters were either being excluded from the voters' lists or simply ignoring elections. In a city with such a substantial working-class majority, a large proportion of those missing out must have been workers.[33]

While the cynicism that led to this abstention from politics flowed initially from the constraints and abuses, political attitudes among the growing number of working-class voters who spurned the ballot box were undoubtedly influenced by new daily-life experiences, especially increasing industrial conflict. The *Industrial Banner* may have been right in 1905 when it pointed out that many workers saw "really nothing" for themselves in an election. "It will make very little difference which party is returned to power," the paper argued. "Both are run by the corporations and in the interests of the corporations." Election returns suggest that 1906 was clearly a turning point towards lower participation rates over the long term. In the sour atmosphere following the street-railway strike of that year, a large number of East Hamilton workers expressed their contempt for local politicians by staying home. The turnout dropped to 48.5 per cent, and a local Tory official reported to Premier Whitney, "You could not get them out. They were sore and sullen."[34]

The decade after World War One witnessed the most striking decline, although the new system of enumeration revealed a pattern that had been emerging before the war. A large increase in voters in the 1919 provincial election reflected, in part, the inclusion of women for the first time and a brief resurgence of interest in electoral politics that propelled the ILP into office. Still, in 1923 10,000 fewer votes were cast, and in 1929, at the end of a decade that would see the city's adult population reach 98,000, the total provincial vote came only to 32,000. With the exception of the 1926 provincial election, the turnout for federal and provincial elections in the 1920s hovered at or below 50 per cent of enumerated voters.[35]

In the midst of the 1919 election campaign the *Spectator* scoffed at the many men and women who had not bothered to add their names to the voters' lists. That failure proved, the paper believed, "that there are still in the community citizens to whom the franchise means little or nothing.... The rebuffs encountered by the enumerators show plainly enough how very far off yet are some of our citizens from a due realization of their civic responsibilities." A few months later, after the ILP mayoralty candidate had gone down to defeat, a local labour paper bemoaned "the general apathy of the local electorate, there being not more than 40 per cent of the total vote polled."[36] Although thousands of workers shared Studholme's spirit of responsible citizenship, throughout much of this period a huge proportion of Hamilton workers – probably a majority – never believed in the ballot box's relevance and ignored the whole process. A good deal of the Independent Labor Party's success in 1919 rested on its ability to mobilize the abstainers.[37]

Among those who did vote, the pattern between the 1890s and the 1930s fell into four phases.[38] The first saw a powerful Conservative assault on Liberal strength at the turn of the century. Hamilton had been a Liberal town in the mid-1890s: a Grit majority ruled the city council, and the party held all the provincial and federal seats. But in 1898 the Conservatives took both seats in the provincial election and then swept the federal ridings in 1900. One of these seats slipped away in 1904, but the Conservatives nailed it down permanently in 1908, after which time neither federal seat would leave Tory hands until 1931. These victories anticipated the Conservatives' assumption of power in Ontario in 1905 and federally in 1911. Municipally the party made its lunge for control in the 1901 election, with the prominent manufacturer John Hendrie assuming the major's chair at the head of a 16-man Conservative caucus. Except for a short interval in 1911–12, and again at the peak of Labor strength in 1919–21, the Tories maintained their city-council majority.[39]

The Liberal Party had been shattered. Not until 1934 would it win back any provincial seats. Until then it would not attract more than a third of the votes cast in federal and provincial elections, and in the decade after 1917 its totals slipped well below one-fifth. Indeed, in provincial politics the Liberals did not even nominate candidates in East Hamilton in 1911, 1914, 1919, and 1934. By the outbreak of World War One, in a pattern that had begun to look like the realignment of politics underway in Britain in the early 20th century, it was the new Independent Labor Party that was providing the real electoral alternative to the Tories. Indeed, the second phase of political life in Hamilton was marked by the ILP's increasingly effective challenge to the Conservative hegemony over local politics. After its upset victory in 1906 the ILP held the East Hamilton seat in the provincial legislature for the next 17 years, expanding its municipal representation during the war and adding the West Hamilton seat in 1919.

In the early 1920s the Tories launched a third phase by crushing Labor and regaining their unrivalled control of the state machinery in Hamilton. In the elections of that decade, in which sometimes scarcely more than two registered voters in five went to the polls, Conservative candidates often carried off more than 70 per cent of the vote. By 1930 the *Spectator* could justifiably have reprinted its proud claim from 1903: "The Tories are still on top in Hamilton."[40] The Depression eroded that control, however, and in a fourth phase that ran through the 1930s both Labor and the Liberals rebounded.

For most of three decades in the early 20th century, then, the Conservative Party and its vision of politics and society were dominant in Hamilton, as in so much of urban Ontario in the same period. That triumph rested on an astute manipulation of an electoral system in which voter abstention could be assumed to be large. But it also required an articulation of an ideological alternative to the once-dominant Liberal perspective on public life. That shift required a type of masterful statecraft that rallied voters of all classes around the Tory vision.

The Collapse of Lib-Labism

The ILP's east-end stalwart Sam Lawrence liked to recount how two objects had adorned the parlour walls in the home of his father, a stonecutter: the emblem of the stonecutters' union and a portrait of British prime minister William Ewart Gladstone.[41] Many 19th-century British craftworkers had clung to a liberalism that, in the words of a British historian, "stood for justice and fairness, dignity and respectability, independence and reform." Into the great Victorian coalition that became known as the Liberal Party, headed by the venerable Gladstone, had flowed most of the impulse to reform the British political system – expanding the franchise, installing the secret ballot, abolishing all aristocratic and religious privilege, extending state education, and generally promoting a more egalitarian political society. It was never an easy alliance, but many British workingmen, newly enfranchised in 1867, found an ideological home in the Radical wing of the party.[42]

Similarly, by the time Wilfrid Laurier finally knit together a coherent national Liberal Party in Canada in the 1890s, there was a recognized place for Canadian workingmen within the alliance of francophones, farmers, Catholics, and corporate capitalists that assumed power in Ottawa in 1896.[43] Appeasing the radical workingman was not simply an outgrowth of the pluralist traditions of Liberal doctrine; by the close of the 19th century it was also a recognition that independent-minded craftsworkers were beginning to create their own political organizations outside the Liberal fold. Faced with the crisis of holding together increasingly divergent class interests, the Liberals could not abandon their reformist heritage without threatening their working-class base. Left-wing Liberals more attached to the democratic and reformist principles of liberalism would agree with working-class Liberals like Hamilton's Edward Williams, a locomotive engineer and prominent labour activist, that the new Laurier administration had a particular responsibility to workingmen. It was "essential that the Government should concede many radical conditions that were denied the Trade Unionists by their predecessors," Williams warned one of Hamilton's Liberal MPs. "The life of the Liberal Party depends very much upon marked radical changes of a Social Labor character."[44] Beginning in the 1880s the Liberals had learned the necessity of showing sympathy for the labour movement's demands, but they had also discovered the need for carefully nurturing alliances with independent labour organizations to keep them loosely within the fold of mainstream Liberalism.

In the 1870s many skilled workers had been repelled by the anti-labour posture of the giant of Central Canadian Liberalism, George Brown, but in subsequent years, especially in the heyday of the Knights of Labor, both Ontario premier Oliver Mowat and the national Liberal leader, Edward Blake, had assiduously cultivated the support of organized craftworkers with sympathetic rhetoric and new factory legislation. In Hamilton politics Gibson had won accolades for his prominent role in introducing labour measures in the Ontario legislature.[45] The next burst of interest in labour legislation came in the late 1890s. At the local level the Liberal administration in city hall responded promptly to labour pressure for union labels and fair-wage clauses for city work. Nationally, the Liberals' concern with the labour movement quickened on the eve of the 1900 federal election in the context of surging craft union organization and increasing industrial conflict. The chief architect of these new measures, Postmaster General Sir William Mulock, convinced the Laurier government to pass a Conciliation Act, to appoint a fair-wages officer and an alien-labour officer (Hamilton's Edward Williams), and to establish a Department of Labour, with a string of Liberal-leaning trade unionists as local correspondents across the country, including garment worker Sam Landers in Hamilton. The young, university-trained civil servant Mackenzie King was to supervise. In September of 1900 both Laurier and Mulock addressed the delegates to the annual convention of the Trades and Labor Congress of Canada to assure these workingmen that the Liberal government would embrace their cause.[46]

King became a key figure in attempting to expand the Liberal legislative program, and, borrowing from the policies of American Progressivism and the "New Liberalism" of Winston Churchill and Lloyd George in Britain, he eventually, in 1919, swung the party behind a broad platform of social reform. In Ontario his ally was Newton Wesley Rowell, who brought his Methodist fervour and reforming zeal to the leadership of the provincial party in 1911, and, with help from King as the Ontario party president, enunciated such measures of social legislation as a moderate version of the single tax, a limited eight-hour-day bill, and a new Department of Health to handle industrial diseases. By 1914 King was praising Rowell for his work in rebuilding the Ontario party: "You have laid a solid moral foundation for constructive and progressive reform in the nature of social service."[47] This brand of Liberalism also found expression in several of the livelier popular newspapers of the period, the so-called "people's press." Like the better-known and more flamboyant Toronto *Star*, the Hamilton *Herald* pursued independent-minded liberal journalism, with a slightly more cautious tone than its Toronto counterpart. It was edited by Joseph Lewis and published by the Harris family, who were known as "life-long Reformers." With a wide working-class readership, the paper regularly supported issues raised by the local labour movement, including Studholme's electoral campaigns, and initiated the first weekly labour column in the city, written first by Landers and later by Philip Obermeyer.[48]

Liberal legislation to meet the demands of organized labour had not completely forestalled any working-class interest in independent labour politics. During the 1880s the buoyant Canadian labour movement had launched several independent initiatives, including the Hamilton Labor Political Association. The Liberal Party's most astute strategists sought either to bring these working-class candidates within a Liberal-Labour framework – that is, into a loose affiliation with the party – or to work out mutual non-aggression pacts in electoral campaigns that could lead to eventual absorption of the labourites or perhaps a coalition for legislative purposes.[49]

Hamilton's experiments with this "Lib-Lab" collaboration were more modest in the early 20th century. The boldest manoeuvre came in 1908. King had decided to run in Berlin (now Kitchener) for a seat in the federal House of Commons that year, and prominent Liberals urged him to seek the East Hamilton nomination. He rejected the offer after some consideration but urged the local party officers not to nominate a candidate. Instead, he undertook to ensure the ILP's nomination of Landers, who had more than once worked for the Liberals. "Landers is a Liberal ... in fact a very conspicuous one," King wrote, citing the Hamiltonian's role as *Labour Gazette* correspondent. "I feel quite sure that if in the House of Commons he would be a help to our side." With the *Herald*'s endorsement, King visited Hamilton, dined with the Studholme family – who respected him immensely – and "talked most frankly about the whole situation." He left the city with the impression that, in return for a clear run in Hamilton against the Tories, the ILP leaders would be willing to support him in Berlin. He also got a pledge from Landers to support the Liberals in Parliament. "We must make the alliance and carry it through," he insisted. Unfortunately for King, the Hamilton Liberals backed out of the deal for reasons that remain unclear. Despite Laurier's personal intervention, they nominated James Eastwood, publisher of the Liberal *Times*. Landers ran a poor third and lost his deposit.[50]

For the next federal election, in 1911, the Hamilton Liberals decided to seize upon the Lib-Lab option under their own banner. The nomination went to John Peebles, a jeweller and one-time activist in the Knights of Labor, former ILP alderman, and good friend of Studholme's. There seems to have been some confusion in the ranks of the local Liberals about what commitments were made, but an unidentified "prominent member of the Liberal executive" later told the *Spectator* that the party expected Studholme to "take his coat off and work for Mr. Peebles," who had been the stove-mounter's agent in previous provincial elections. That support did not materialize. In fact, Studholme advised Peebles to withdraw. Peebles thus ran as an overtly Liberal-Labour candidate, without any formal ILP support, and was thoroughly trounced at the polls. Hamilton, therefore, was not to have the Lib-Lab parliamentarian comparable to the figures who had emerged in the West and in Quebec. In provincial elections in 1911 and 1914, the Grits decided not to run against the ILP in East Hamilton. Whatever understanding they may have worked out behind the scenes, it was a thoroughly independent labour campaign that once again left the Liberals in political limbo.[51]

This alliance strategy, born out of a concern with crumbling Liberal support among urban working-class voters, was promoted by the Liberal Party's left wing and never greeted with enthusiasm by the whole party. The Hamilton Liberal Association was as dubious as any. At its head stood corporate magnates, wealthy merchants, and corporate lawyers, notably Gibson, president of Dominion Power – people who were uncomfortable with King's proposed saw-off with the ILP in 1908 and by 1919 were not prepared to pursue formal or informal alliances with Labor. At a pathetic Liberal gathering before the 1919 provincial election, a party stalwart regretted the party's abandonment of East Hamilton to the ILP and raised the spectre of class politics. The man reportedly believed that "labor was attempting to dominate the governments" and declared that he was "strongly opposed to class legislation by labor, temperance or farmer classes." The party's nominee in West Hamilton was left far behind on election day.[52]

A brand of Liberalism that permitted autonomy for working-class organization was out of step with the main trends of the new corporate age in Canada, in which control of economic life was centred in smaller circles of financiers and industrialists and in which similar centralization of control was under way in most workplaces. Lib-Labism was the increasingly anachronistic creation of an earlier age in Canadian industrial development, a time when skilled craftworkers and their organizations enjoyed more power and respect. Moreover, the Liberals' working-class base in industrial Ontario was cutting itself adrift. Disgusted with the big-business orientation of the Laurier and Ross governments, more and more figures within the labour leadership were becoming supporters of independent working-class political action. In this context the local Liberal leadership turned away from alliance politics, preferring to vie directly with the Tories on the hustings for the workers' votes. In that contest they were abjectly unsuccessful.

The Politics of Deference

Late in the evening of 21 September 1911, Hamilton's Tories took to the streets. With the votes in the federal election counted, they massed for the traditional torchlight parade. Behind a raucous marching band came "thousands of yelling, frenzied, triumphant Conservatives – young, old, the well dressed men from their offices and the artizan from the machine shop." In the dewy eyes of the *Spectator* reporter, this "strange but imposing array" symbolized the organic unity of class interests that had been created under the Conservative banner. Some two months later a working-class critic of Toryism preferred to see the party as an agglomeration of "capitalists, millionaires, monopolists, big bugs and ignorant toady workingmen." From either perspective, Hamilton's Conservatives had clearly built an impressive alliance of social groups around a common political vision that blended appeals to material self-interest with more high-minded principle.[53]

In their defence of private property and individual rights, Canada's Conservatives fell solidly within the framework of small-l liberalism, but, like their British cousins, they nonetheless differentiated themselves sharply from capital-L Liberals. They were less inclined to intellectual theories and driven more by attitudes, emotions, and impulses, often in response to Liberal positions. As conservative philosopher George Grant would later write, "Loyalties rather than principles are the mark of the conservative." Less charitably, Governor General Lord Grey once called the Tories "the stupid party."[54] Nonetheless the Conservatives' political views showed considerable ideological coherence. On the whole the Conservatives were highly suspicious of social and political democracy. With the monarchy a central political symbol, they trumpeted tradition in the face of change and defended unequal power and privilege, alongside loyalism and duty. Generally they preferred the bonds of paternalism and deference to the more individualistic, evangelically inspired drive for self-discipline within bourgeois circles. They liked to speak of the national good rather than individual interests. Social cohesion was more important than individual expression. On Canada's political landscape, they were the loudest defenders of Anglo-Celtic "racial" superiority and the glories of the British Empire. Privilege was thus both cultural and economic.

Conservatism in Hamilton, as in the rest of Canada, did not rest on any significant lingering attachment to a landed aristocracy, but it did attempt to preserve a traditional sense of social order dominated by the powerful new elites of industrial-capitalist society. Social leaders drew their right to respect and deference largely from their success in the world of business. In the late 19th century, Sir John A. Macdonald's Conservative Party had staked out a development strategy that spoke for such men, and enhanced their opportunities for capital accumulation under a National Policy. Early-20th-century Conservative leaders, notably Ontario premier Whitney and Prime Minister Borden, believed that the successful businessmen were "experts" who should be left to formulate party platforms and state policy with minimal input from the masses. Hamilton's Tories thus spoke for Queen (and later King), Empire, and Factory, or in the words of a 1900 campaign war cry: "One Policy, One Country, One Empire, One Flag."[55]

The Conservative Party became a crucial vehicle for drawing together a cross-class alliance of social groups prepared to accept such a vision of social relations in an industrial city. At a major Tory rally in Hamilton in 1911, 30 men took seats on the stage. The most exalted figures included nine prominent manufacturers and seven leading wholesale and retail merchants. Rubbing elbows with these luminaries were a handful of contractors, two shopkeepers, a dentist, a designer, a salesman, and two foremen from the city's factories. This last tiny group of ward-heelers, along with two of the small-scale contractors, comprised the only working-class presence on the platform.[56]

All these groups, from the merchants and shopkeepers through the builders, identified their material prosperity with the fortunes of the Conservative Party. In a city in which manufacturing bulked so large, that prosperity was tuned to the hum of factory production. Not surprisingly, therefore, the key men in the party leadership were the industrialists – men such as John Milne, head of a local stove foundry and party president through most of the pre-war period;

J. Orr Callahan, Steel Company executive; W.B. Champ, managing director of the Hamilton Bridge Company; A.F. Hatch, president of Canada Steel Goods; George Coppley, the clothing manufacturer; J.W. Lamoreaux of the Tuckett Tobacco Company; and J.S. Hendrie of Hamilton Bridge and a string of other firms. These captains of industry looked to the Conservative Party to protect their investments, and the Tory respect for privilege and hierarchy must have reassured them as officers of large corporate enterprises and heads of household living a lavish and exclusive life apart from the mass of the local population. The party's appeal to social integration in the face of disruptive social change and rippling class conflict could help to bridge that yawning social gap. In a political system allowing mass popular participation and in a city with a largely working-class electorate, the Hamilton Tories had to construct an organization and make an appeal that would win the hearts of wage-earners.

Retaining a following of working-class Tories was a complex process. The party had no interest in co-operating with any independent organization of interests or classes – the experiment with the Workingmen's Liberal Conservative Union of Canada organized in 1878 was not revived[57] – and in the early 20th century Hamilton Tories always viewed the ILP as a foe to be crushed, not a potential ally. Nor did the party put much effort into promoting individual workingmen into legislative prominence (beyond a few east-end seats on city council). Winning the hearts of individual workers required balancing two contradictory forces. On the one hand, Hamilton's Tory industrialists expected a deference from workers towards their betters, a passive acceptance of leadership and control of the governing process and the political agenda by men of property, leaving little or no room for intervention from

those "ignorant toady" rank-and-file Tories. On the other hand, cementing support for the party in the city required shaping the Tory message to directly address working-class concerns and aspirations. The result was a political program framed in loosely populist rhetoric that emphasized the preservation of jobs, attacked soulless monopolistic corporations, and defended the lifestyle and cultural heritage of the British-Canadian workingman. The city's manufacturers thereby succeeded in inhibiting (though ultimately not preventing) class polarization in the political arena and in assuming political leadership over the same employees that some of them might be battling on the shop floor.

The working-class Tory thus became a regular fixture of Hamilton politics – a deferential figure whose political beliefs and behaviour combined varying doses of respect, fear, resignation, and calculating opportunism.[58] Certain qualities of this man could be traced back to the "Church and King" crowds of 18th-century England,[59] but his prominence in the early 20th century reflected major shifts taking place in industrial capitalist society. As industry moved into larger, more powerful economic units and as workers lost more and more control over the small decisions of daily life, especially on the job, Toryism had a growing constituency of workers with an increased feeling of powerlessness. The new factory loomed large in the city's politics. But that was not because employers dictated the voting patterns of their employees (some probably tried to do so, but the large-scale abstention from voting indicates the weakness of direct coercion), but because the 10 or 12 hours a day spent in the new factory environment had a wider impact on the worldview of the workers within its walls. In contrast to the more independent status of skilled craftworkers, for large numbers of Hamilton workers deference was tied to dependence in their working lives – that is, in the words of a US historian, "the necessary pose of the powerless."[60]

Increasingly in the early 20th century, Hamilton's wage-earners were having to learn a new subordination to authoritarian, centralized management. They were also highly susceptible to emotional appeals that played on their ever-present insecurities about their livelihood. Many of these workers were apparently willing to line up behind the men who provided the main thing of value left in their work experience: the ability to earn their wages. Voting Tory, therefore, involved the same mixture of deference and self-interest that was motivating so many of the city's factory workers to accept the wage-incentive schemes and new work routines introduced by their autocratic managers in a refashioned form of industrial paternalism. Work and politics were never far apart in Hamilton. The phenomenon of the working-class Tory, then, did not reflect simply a set of attitudes among certain workers but also a set of power relations between classes in this factory town.

Defending the Factory

Hamilton's Tory magnates had to cultivate that relationship. Unlike the Liberals, they did not produce a string of legislative reforms reflecting the interests of wage-earners. Their single step in this direction was the Ontario's Workmen's Compensation Act of 1914, which, although an important measure of state support for the incapacitated breadwinner, was in large part an attempted solution to the rising civil litigation over workplace injuries that were plaguing industrialists.[61]

Beyond doubt, the single most important rallying cry to working-class voters was a defence of the industries that they worked in. The tariff was central. Hamilton's manufacturers knew that their prosperity depended on tariff protection to keep cheaper goods out of the domestic market. While both Conservatives and Liberals had endorsed such an industrial development strategy by the 1890s, a nagging uneasiness remained among most industrialists that the Liberals could not be trusted in a time of increasing international competition. A local Tory manufacturer worried in 1900 that the Liberals were "pledged to remove the protection duties piecemeal. They have already hurt some Canadian industries, and I do not know but that mine will be the next."[62] For most of these men the Conservative Party remained the bedrock of protectionist sentiment guaranteeing a basis for Canadian industrial growth.

The Tories had to convince workers in the city that their best interests lay in an alliance with their bosses in defence of the very existence of the city's industries. They had to turn a dry issue of fiscal policy into an emotion-charged touchstone. Actually, this appeal had a long, distinguished life in Hamilton, dating from the mid-19th-century polemics of businessman Isaac Buchanan and reaching full flower in Southern Ontario with the Conservatives' National Policy campaign of 1878.[63]

The "producer ideology" that they had articulated extolled the importance and worth of the craftworker, but it survived into the 20th century in a new, diluted form. Craft skills were no longer as vital to production as they had been in the first phase of industrialization, and few industrialists would now address their employees as "producers." But workers were nonetheless encouraged to recognize that their economic survival depended on an alliance with the manufacturers and their party, the Conservatives. The local Tories continued to make the tariff the central issue of virtually every federal election campaign after 1890, shrilly pushing aside all other concerns (until the mass unemployment of the 1930s compelled more attention). Their protectionist salvos were aimed directly at the economic insecurity of Hamilton workers. Depending on the circumstances of the campaign, they either blamed inadequate tariff protection for the sad plight of the city's wage-earners or terrorized the workers with dire warnings of mass unemployment and industrial stagnation.

Five federal election campaigns – 1908, 1921, 1925, 1930, and 1935 – were fought in the context of economic depression, and on each occasion the Conservatives preached protectionist sermons on the iniquity of the Liberals' commercial policy. In 1908, in a typical speech to a north-end meeting, West Hamilton's new Conservative candidate, Mayor T.J. Stewart, promised that, with higher tariffs, "The factories already located here would soon be working full time again ... and the location in Hamilton and other Canadian cities of many new factories would give employment to hundreds and thousands and make good times again." The ILP's unsuccessful candidate that year, Landers, confided to King that the tariff issue had no doubt been the key to his defeat.[64] Similarly in 1925, after five years of depression among the city's industries, the Conservatives, training their guns on King's Liberal administration and its modest tariff adjustments, caused all the local Liberal and Labor candidates to lose their deposits. The Tories' West Hamilton candidate told his nominating convention that the party was "fighting for the thousands of workers in those plants, who are confronted with the ugly alternative of walking the streets, hungry and in distress, or leaving this country and taking up their abode in the United States." Likewise in 1930, the East Hamilton Tory candidate insisted, "Men and women who work with their hands would have work now with a proper tariff in force, when manufacturers would then be able to pay higher wages to their employees." In a rare gesture to female voters, the Tories distributed a pamphlet, "To the Mothers of Canada," reminding women that the hopes for their children lay in the opportunities created by tariff protection.[65]

The tariff issue was probably most important in the emotion-charged federal campaigns of 1911 and 1921, when powerful agricultural interests across the country were agitating for lower tariff rates on manufactured goods. In 1911 the dreaded possibility of free trade reared up in the form of a proposed reciprocity agreement in natural products between Canada and the United States. When Laurier went to the electorate that year to get support for the agreement, the Hamilton Conservatives, like their contemporaries throughout Southern Ontario, turned the issue into an impassioned crusade to save both Canadian industry and national integrity. The *Spectator* identified the candidates simply as "Anti-Reciprocity" and "Reciprocity," and indeed normal political partisanship dissolved, as Liberal manufacturers like the Steel Company's Hobson joined the strident protest of the Canadian business community against reciprocity. Hobson was an executive member of the Canadian Home Market Association, the front organization of the Canadian Manufacturers' Association, which was pouring its energy and resources into the Conservative campaign. He spoke against the threat at a major rally in Hamilton early in 1911.[66]

The protectionists' rhetoric reached out to the city's workingmen with unmatched fervour. The day before the election the *Spectator* framed a statement on its front page itemizing the horrors that would befall the city should a Reciprocity candidate be elected:

He will vote for a reduction in the staff of many large Hamilton plants.

He will vote for the immediate crippling of many Hamilton industries.

He will vote for frightening every other Hamilton industry with a threat of early "free trade"; and so preventing its expansion, the investment of more capital and the employment of more men.

He will vote for glutting our labour market with all these men thrown out of work, so reducing pay all round and starving the purse upon which our merchants depend for their custom.

He will vote for rows of empty houses, "bread lines" this winter at the doors of our charities . . . and "hard times" all round.

One Conservative candidate struck a symbolic note for the alliance of manufacturer and worker by using a foreman from the Union Drawn Steel plant to second his nomination. The man wove his Toryism into his masculinity by declaring that by voting for reciprocity he would be "a traitor to his employer, who depended upon protection," and "a traitor to his family, who depended upon the money he could earn from the manufacturer."[67]

Across the political battlefield stood the forlorn figure of Peebles, the Liberal-Labour candidate. He insisted, correctly, that Laurier's agreement covered no manufactured products and promised to oppose any threat to their protection. He also attempted to fight back with an alternative perspective that emphasized cheaper food, a theme that had run through working-class liberalism since the British Anti-Corn Law League agitation of the 1840s. "Any man who taxes food commits a crime," Peebles insisted. But Hamilton's voters were clearly not swayed by this brand of Radical Liberalism, and cast their ballots for the Conservatives. The largest manufacturing firms closed down in mid-afternoon to make certain that their hands could easily get to the polls. Peebles lost his deposit in a two-man race.[68]

Significantly, the Hamilton labour movement took no public role in this campaign; its membership was evidently too divided. The ILP nominated no candidates for the two Hamilton seats and prominent local labour leaders kept out of sight. Since the spring Studholme had been defending free trade, but he astutely refused to make public statements in the contest between Liberals and Conservatives. The Trades and Labor Council announced that it had no official position in the controversy. Yet, to perpetuate the confusion in labour's ranks, Hiram Dickout, an independent candidate put up in West Hamilton by the railway brotherhoods, with no connection to the ILP, included attacks on reciprocity in his ill-starred campaign. In a similar vein, Harry G. Fester, the local cigar-maker who later became prominent in the ILP, wrote to the press that reciprocity would "spell ruin" and should be voted down. At a point, therefore, when a class-based party had begun to take shape, the Tories' tariff issue drove a wedge into the fragile working-class unity and placed the Conservatives at the pinnacle of local politics.[69]

A new challenge to the national tariff structure emerged ten years later in the form of an aggressive farmers' movement making an independent foray into national politics on a low-tariff platform.[70] Since the national Liberal Party had also made gestures towards tariff reductions in its elaborate 1919 platform, in an evident bid to

(*HS*, 19 July 1930, 17)

woo the independent-minded farmer, the Conservatives could once more declare their party the natural defender of the country's industrial interests, both manufacturer and worker. They attempted to carry on the old-party alliance of the wartime Union government by dubbing themselves the "National Liberal and Conservative Party." In Hamilton the new name made some sense because most prominent Liberals had slipped their moorings and lined up with the Tories.[71]

Once again this united-front approach stressed the threat to workers' jobs posed by the low-tariff forces. "Free trade and tariff reduction would close or cripple the 700 industries in this city and district and rob their armies of employees of work," the Conservatives charged, and they attacked the credibility of the other local

candidates, who had all scrambled to present themselves as protectionists too. In the midst of an economic slump they warned, "A vote for them will encourage them to remove the protection from the industry which gives you your job and thus close it up and throw you out on the street." This kind of appeal was supported by numerous statements from local manufacturers pointing out the dire consequences for their workers if the tariff were lowered.[72] Despite strong showings by the two ILP candidates, the Conservatives won the election handily.

Throughout the decades, then, the Conservative Party successfully kept the tariff and its benefits to local industry, and particularly to the Hamilton working class, at the forefront of public debate in federal elections. By turning defence of the tariff into a great public crusade, the Tories endowed mundane commercial policy with apocalyptic qualities. Most important, the tariff was an issue that the Conservatives could use to ally workers and their bosses against a common enemy, the free-trader and his political outlet, the Liberal Party, and to prevent the crystallization of class-based issues in national politics.[73]

The Hamilton Conservatives' defence of local factory jobs also had a provincial dimension, which allowed them to enhance still further the notion of an industrial alliance of manufacturers and workers. In the cut and thrust of pre-war Ontario politics, a party led and supported by prominent corporate capitalists managed to cast itself as a quasi-populist champion of the rights of the people against the corporations. In Hamilton, as in the rest of Southern Ontario, Conservative politicians became the foremost critics of the province's new private-utility empires. Manufacturers had their own interests in launching these attacks, namely, the need for access to cheap hydro-electric power, but the campaigns created a much larger popular movement that tapped deep-seated resentment in the working-class community against the new corporate giants.[74]

In February 1902, when the Liberal Ross government moved to renew the private power agreements at Niagara Falls, the provincial Conservative Party first called for public ownership of hydro-electric facilities – "to have the Government at the switch and not the corporations," according to one Tory MLA – and scored political points with mild assaults on the corporations during the provincial election campaign that year.[75] A movement for "public power" was simultaneously gathering steam among manufacturers and municipal politicians in southwestern Ontario, including some prominent Hamilton men. By 1906 it had grown to the proportions of a people's crusade led by Adam Beck, the flamboyant minister-without-portfolio in Whitney's new Conservative government.[76] Conservative leadership of the prolonged local campaigns to win voters' support for public power involved building a cross-class alliance against the corporations, whose monopoly control of vital utilities could allegedly threaten industrial development. This battle was more complicated in Hamilton than in most other southwestern Ontario cities because not all of the city's Tories supported public power.[77] The *Spectator* undoubtedly opposed the movement because of the corporate connections of its publisher, William Southam, who was a director of the large, Hamilton-based Cataract Power Company. Many local manufacturers with Tory leanings also held back their public support, no doubt sharing the *Spectator*'s opinion that the existing supplier of power was quite adequate to their needs (and, almost certainly, worrying about the principle of public ownership). Indeed, not until Dominion Power was sold to Ontario Hydro in 1930 did most Hamilton companies switch their contracts to the Hydro-Electric Commission.[78] Yet, despite this reticence in some Tory circles, there can be no denying that Beck and other members of the Conservative government were the leading spokesmen for public power, and that several Hamilton Tories were at the forefront of the local campaign. Moreover, especially in Hamilton, the Liberals had trouble escaping the taint of being the party of the corporations.

Once the Tories came to power at Queen's Park in 1905, Whitney announced his party's commitment: "The waterpowers of Niagara should be free as air, and . . . shall not in the future be made the sport and prey of capitalists, and shall not be treated as anything else but a valuable asset of the people of Ontario."[79] In 1906 Hendrie, as the West Hamilton MLA and minister-without-portfolio, accepted an appointment to the government's new Hydro-Electric Commission, which Beck chaired. Hendrie spoke at all the public-power rallies in the city over the next five years.[80] Moreover, in the rough and tumble controversy that raged through the city council over the power question, Tory mayor Stewart championed the rights of "the people," to the point of refusing to sign a contract with Dominion Power in 1908 until he was threatened with court action. Some two months later he rode his popularity into a federal election and won the West Hamilton seat back from the Liberals. In the municipal battlefield, party ranks did not always hold firm, but the bulk of the leadership in the fight came from acknowledged Conservatives.[81] In contrast, Gibson, the city's leading Liberal and head of Cataract Power (renamed Dominion Power in 1907), was a vigorous opponent of public ownership. The *Times*, the daily voice of local Liberalism, defended the Cataract Power interests consistently, and in 1911 the more independent *Herald* reported that the local Liberal leadership had insisted to their following "that it was their duty to oppose Hydro-Electric policy for party reasons."[82]

The working class had good reason to respond favourably to the public-power campaign. Workers had accumulated plenty of bitter experience with the city's own variant of the private-power behemoth. Not only were Cataract's domestic power rates extremely high, but the chronically poor service of the corporation's Hamilton Street Railway Company had built up years of resentment. The monumental 1906 strike at the street railway stiffened workers' antipathy to the local corporation. The firm's highhandedness and intransigence towards its motormen and conductors solidified its reputation as a cold, heartless, grasping corporation, prompting one worker-poet to write: "They care not for the citizens/ Nor the city's rights;/ To make enormous dividends/ Is always their delight." With public opinion running strongly against the company, especially when troops arrived to suppress crowds of strike supporters, working-class voters would over the following decade frequently be reminded of the connections between that strike and the utilities corporation that was resisting public ownership.[83]

The strike could not have happened at a worse time for the Liberals and their friends among private utilities interests. A month after the men returned to work, Hamilton's voters went to the polls, along with ratepayers in 18 other Ontario municipalities, to express for the first time their attitudes to Beck's public-power program, and they endorsed the scheme solidly. In the same vote the Liberal candidate for mayor was soundly defeated as "a creature of the Cataract company."[84] The ensuing battles to win final approval of a public-power contract in Hamilton stretched through three more plebiscites – in 1908, 1909, and 1911 – and included a municipal election campaign in 1911 in which

Cataract (now Dominion) Power was the central issue. The Hamilton labour movement was enthusiastic and provided strong public support, including the occasional platform speaker. In July 1911 the Trades and Labor Council voted to supply 20 workers to help on polling day. The same day Studholme told an outdoor rally of workers in the city that the "Hydro-Electric Commission power and its municipal ownership was the salvation of the workingman," and urged workers "to vote for what they knew was at least fair to their interests, not in favor of a company that had always shown itself ready to milk them for their last copper." In the end it was the most solidly working-class wards of the city that carried the 1909 and 1911 referenda on the power question. During the next decade Beck continued to garner steady support from Hamilton workers for the extension of the publicly owned electricity empire into hydro radial railway lines between Southern Ontario cities. In December 1916, on the eve of a referendum on the radial plan, Studholme reminded the members of the Trades and Labor Council: "The very same interests were out to kill Hydro radials that sought to do [the same] for the now successful Hydro-Electric proposition when it was before the people."[85]

Clearly the Conservatives had added more cement to a cross-class alliance that united workers and industrialists against a common enemy, this time the financial barons who controlled the private-utilities services of the region. The progress and prosperity of industry demanded cheap power, and workers deserved it for their homes; once again the Tories could present themselves as the people's tribunes. The commitment of many Conservative manufacturers in Hamilton to this cause may have been weaker than was their faith in the tariff, but the Conservative Party did become the vehicle for implementing public ownership, and in the public eye Tories like Stewart and Hendrie were in the front ranks of the agitation. Conservative candidates were still highlighting Ontario Hydro as one of their signal achievements as late as the 1934 election.[86]

The Hamilton Tories did not have such freedom to manoeuvre because of the absence of any alternative to the left.[87] Not only had they witnessed a popular radicalism of the street erupt into violent rage against the city's most visible capitalist corporation; they had also watched in dismay as this anti-corporate spirit pushed public ownership of all utilities to the forefront of Studholme's successful campaign in December 1906. What the public-power Conservatives were able to do was to co-opt the rhetoric of protest and harness it to their own ends. As Whitney told a correspondent, "It is indeed a ghastly joke to charge the Ontario Government with being socialistic, etc., when it is the bulwark by means of which such influences may be shattered." Similarly, from the other side of the political spectrum, a worker from Devon wrote in a 1911 diatribe against Hamilton's Toryism, "Strange to say, when I came to Hamilton nearly two years ago from the old country, I was told by my friends that, having been a Radical at home, I should have to be a Tory here."[88]

The Glorious Empire

The Conservatives' electoral success did not rest simply on appeals to material self-interest. It also had a powerful cultural dimension. The party presented itself as the foremost defender of all things British and as a hypersensitive critic of any threats to Anglo-Canadian culture and the imperial connection. The city's Tories relentlessly exhorted pride in the glories of Anglo-Celtic Protestant civilization and the worldwide empire that sustained it. All classes,

they believed, should rise above petty self-interest and unite beneath the Union Jack. This brand of imperialist nationalism no doubt touched a need among some workers for a kind of pride and dignity that was otherwise increasingly hard to find in their daily lives. Many others may have warmed to this jingoistic fervour out of a deepening anxiety about the impact of so many new "foreigners" working alongside them on the shop floor. Whatever the extent of this appeal, the Tories never let an opportunity pass to urge the city's Anglo-Canadian workers to celebrate and defend their cultural heritage.[89]

Through all its campaigns, the Conservative Party staked its claim to be the most uncompromising defender of the British-Canadian population. In the years just before the war the *Spectator*, unlike its major competitor, the *Herald*, cultivated the recent British immigrant with extensive weekly news coverage of events in the British Isles – a device that the *Labor News* was quick to appropriate after its inception in 1912. In typical fashion, in 1911 the *Spectator* leapt to the defence of British pauper immigrants against Studholme's charges that the Salvation Army was flooding the Canadian labour market. In the 1911 federal campaign, party workers distributed a pamphlet entitled *An Appeal to the British Born* that explicitly targeted "Old Country" immigrants.[90]

In a city filling up with thousands of British immigrants, the Tories liked to assume the role of watchdog for the interests of the British connection, especially against alleged French-Canadian perfidy.[91] The 1911 federal election allowed the local Tories to wrap themselves in the Union Jack and to denounce the Laurier Liberals as traitors to the imperial connection. During that campaign, the local Conservatives' token spokesman for the workingman insisted that "reciprocity was the thin edge of the wedge

WHAT POLITICS DOES

REGISTRATION BOOTH

Labor Champion Dynes Registers the Chinamen in Large Numbers to Elect Grit Representatives to Parliament.

The Tories charged the Liberals with threatening Anglo-Canadian control by pandering to unpopular minorities, especially the Chinese. (*HS*, 21 Oct. 1904, 1)

which would ultimately separate Canada from the old country, both commercially and nationally." Similarly, in 1917, as the party took the lead in a Union government movement and in Hamilton rode roughshod over any Liberal obstructions, it emphasized the pressing need to defend the motherland – "This Is Not an Election. It is a Battle with the Hun," said one advertisement – and attacked on an openly racist basis the Laurier Liberals who had not joined the coalition.[92] "Quebec Must Not Rule All Canada," announced a huge newspaper advertisement a few days before the election. More than a decade later, R.B. Bennett led the Conservatives back to power in Ottawa by melding the protectionist plank with imperial fervour and promising to promote "Canada First, Then the Empire."[93]

In defending the British heritage within Canada, the Conservatives had a long-standing reputation for outright nativist bigotry. Despite the efforts of some party leaders to mute these sentiments, prominent party men and loyal newspapers could be relied upon to vent their spleens against perceived dangers to Anglo-Canadian Protestant culture.[94] The Tories' close relations with the stridently anti-Catholic Orange Order kept that belligerent Protestantism alive in the city. A new militancy emerged in 1911 when the ebullient Tory backbencher and future premier Howard Ferguson launched his legislative attack on French-language instruction in the province, which over the next five years grew into the celebrated Regulation 17 controversy over bilingual schools. By May 1916 the *Spectator*'s editor was fuelling this francophobia with a call for a constitutional amendment to make English the only official language.[95]

Non-British "foreigners" were also greeted with suspicion. At various points before World War One, the *Spectator* accused the Liberals of marshalling the votes of the city's much maligned Jewish, Chinese, and Italian immigrants.[96] The Conservatives also used election campaigns to fan working-class fears about such newcomers. The *Spectator* often denounced the immigrants that the federal government was funnelling into Western Canadian homesteads as "the scum of creation" and "the scourings of the world."[97] A major campaign rally in 1908 featured the attorney general in British Columbia's Conservative government, who described the alleged dangers of Asian immigration and blamed the Laurier Liberals for bringing in these undesirable competitors with British-Canadian workers. "What was the peril of the laboring classes in British Columbia," he argued, "now might, in the near future, be the peril of the workingmen in Ontario if the Laurier policy was allowed to prevail." In West Hamilton the Conservatives' Stewart made the presence of undesirable immigrants a major issue in this depression-year campaign, and the *Spectator* published a pre-election reminder that a vote for the Tories was "a vote for the protection of Canadian labor in every part of the Dominion."[98] The 1917 federal election also saw the Conservatives in Unionist clothes fanning local working-class resentments against "aliens" benefiting from the war economy. Even the pro-tariff rhetoric of the Tories' campaigns warned about competition from "the products of Cheap European Labor."[99] Tory imperialism also became an emotion-charged response to the surge of labourism and Bolshevism after World War One. "We are British and intend to remain so," a Conservative candidate proclaimed in 1934, "and we will not stand for any Russian tactics brought here under the guise of the C.C.F. [Co-operative Commonwealth Federation] or any other group."[100]

The Conservatives, then, were the party of jingoistic bigotry. In contrast, the Liberals, with their deep roots in francophone Quebec, showed far greater restraint on this terrain and in Hamilton attempted to develop closer links with the European immigrant community, notably in the face of the fierce anti-alien agitation at the end of the war.[101] The message of this feature of Toryism was similar to those involved in promotion of the tariff and public power in that it was once again laced not only with fear-mongering, but also with the defence of privilege – in this case, Anglo-Canadian whiteness. It also encouraged the burying of class interests in favour of unity across the community and opened up the possibility of identifying powerfully and confidently with the nation and the empire. Leading the war effort from 1914 to 1918, first as Conservatives and then as Unionists, gave the Tories this powerful tool of hegemony with which to bring all Anglo-Canadians, regardless of class, together under the Union Jack. Arthur Meighen and Bennett, as federal Conservative leaders, continued to be "ready aye ready" for a commitment to the empire in the interwar period.

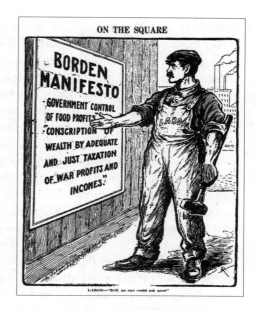

By the 1917 election the Conservatives realized they had to adapt their usual message to meet workers' wartime concerns. (*HS*, 12 Dec. 1917, 11)

Leave Us Alone

The Conservatives played a leading role on another pivotal cultural battlefield in the early 20th century – the controversy over alcohol consumption. After decades of arguing for state action to shut off all sales of booze, prohibitionists were able to use the unusual wartime political consensus to win province-wide prohibition under the 1916 Ontario Temperance Act, which was then extended into the postwar period after a referendum in 1919. The "dry" spell ended eight years later.[102] Cutting off the flow of booze was the leading edge of a broad moral-reform movement, which by the early 20th century was targeting primarily the rougher forms of male working-class leisure – drinking, gambling, and prostitution, in particular.

Workingmen were divided on whether booze was a bad thing. The good number of teetotallers sprinkled throughout the craft unions' ranks worried about the impact of drink on family economies and on working-class independence and respectability. Yet a substantial body of Hamilton's workingmen believed strongly that they had a right to a drink, and, when given the chance, voted against tighter controls on alcohol consumption. Local by-law votes to reduce the number of licences in 1911, 1913, and 1915 were all defeated, with the biggest "wet" majorities in the working-class wards. Even those who had their doubts about drinking preferred moral suasion to state coercion, and many workingmen viewed as "class legislation" any attack on their social gathering spots, while the rich man's private club was not at issue. The Hamilton Trades and Labor Council protested in 1915 that "throughout the Province there are a large number of clubs organized and maintained by and for the benefit of wealthy citizens that are allowed to sell any kind and all kinds of liquors without any restrictions whatever." The Council nonetheless remained deeply divided. In 1916 it devoted hours of discussion to the question of prohibition, and, over the heated protests of the cigarmakers, bartenders, brewery workers, boot and shoe workers, glass-blowers, carpenters, and a few of the metal-trades workers, voted 35 to 23 to maintain its long-standing position of neutrality. Labour thus had no clear voice in public discussions of booze before the war.[103]

The issue thus became a partisan contest between the Liberals and the Conservatives. With its deep roots in rural Ontario, where anti-booze sentiment was strong, the Liberal Party had long had close connections to the temperance cause and in 1911, under the provincial leadership of N.W. Rowell, took up the issue of prohibition with a new passion. In 1913 Rowell tried to win the provincial election on a no-nonsense "banish-the-bar" platform. In Hamilton's municipal politics Rowell's counterpart was T.S. Morris, president of the Hamilton Temperance Federation, grand councillor of the Royal Templars of Temperance, and a member of the local Liberal executive. While Morris retained a seat on city council for many years, largely owing to his support for a variety of progressive issues, the Liberals rallied no significant momentum for their prohibition platform in the city. In the 1914 campaign they were too weak to mount a candidate against Studholme in East Hamilton and in West Hamilton ran a distant second to Hendrie.[104]

Most Tories were temperamentally opposed to restrictions on earthy popular pleasures. Indeed, some had a vested interest in the kind of working-class leisure that prim moralists were attacking, notably horse-racing, brewing and distilling, and vaudeville. For most Tory leaders, however, it was less a question of investment than of inclination. In marked contrast to the vigilance that so many 19th-century employers exercised over their workers' lifestyles, Hamilton's Tory industrialists showed far less fervour for personal salvation through reform. As E.A. Dalley, a Hamilton manufacturer and local Conservative Party executive member, told Premier Whitney in 1906: "This playing to the temperance people and the ministers and all the goody goody roosters who are posing as superior beings in this country don't go with the people as a rule." An event sponsored by the Hamilton Conservative Association one Saturday afternoon in summer 1910 symbolized the Tory style. In contrast to the whiff of Methodist prudery that increasingly hung over the Liberals, the Conservatives opened up the Jockey Club grounds to several thousand people for a "monster picnic" that featured the favoured pleasures of so many workingmen – sports and beer:

> Baseball, refreshments and athletic games were indulged in, and, needless to say, the refreshments proved the greatest attraction for a large number. Before the gates opened hundreds had gathered to make sure of getting a good look in and by the time the sports commenced 6000 people were in attendance. The barroom under the grand stand was immediately crammed, and the large majority were unable to get near it.
>
> Those who managed to get there first had the preferred stock and they hung on until the froth on the last keg had disappeared.[105]

The rising level of adherents to the city's less evangelical Anglican churches was a widening base for such politics.

The Conservatives contributed a few men to the prohibition cause – Mayor George Lees and Controller W.H. Cooper, for example – but the official position of the party and the general orientation of most of the leadership were less moralistic and more tolerant of working-class lifestyles. On assuming office in 1905, Whitney had expressed satisfaction with the existing legislation to regulate the liquor trade and was opposed to prohibition. Hendrie had made the same declaration in his campaign that year.[106] Only under the growing pressure of the prohibition forces did the Whitney government suggest in 1912 that it would consider legislation to abolish the practice of treating (never actually introduced). The hotel owners and liquor interests in Hamilton were well-entrenched parts of the Tory machine, and, as the battle lines were drawn in the various referendum campaigns, prominent Conservatives and the *Spectator* helped to organize against the temperance forces – most often through front-committees, from the Rate-Payers' Association of 1911 to the Personal Liberty League of 1913.[107]

Only under the unusual pressures of war, and after bitter debate inside the Conservative caucus, did the Tories under their new leader, William Hearst, move to close the bars and liquor stores and then, in 1919, to hold a plebiscite on extending the dry regime beyond the war period. That step led to a new configuration of political forces in Hamilton, with both Labor and Conservative voices being raised against a rapidly weakening temperance movement (and its Liberal supporters). Full-fledged prohibition so upset male wage-earners that a major campaign sprang up among unionists across the country to bring back beer-drinking. In 1918 the local Trades and Labor Council broke its silence, and Harry Halford and Harry Fester led 350 local workers to join a 5,000-man march on Queen's Park to demand stronger beer.[108] The Hamilton vote in the provincial referendum solidly supported the sale of alcohol and the reopening of hotels, especially at the polls in the British working-class neighbourhoods of the east end. Labour's ability to make any legislative headway, however, was compromised after the 1919 provincial election by its participation in a coalition government with the United Farmers of Ontario, who were committed to a rigorous crackdown on bootlegging.[109]

The local Conservatives showed little enthusiasm for their premier's dry politics, and several stepped into leadership roles in the new anti-prohibition Citizens' Liberty League in 1919 and then the Moderation League, formed to fight subsequent plebiscites in 1921 and 1924. The Conservatives under Ferguson quickly became the outspoken champions of looser liquor legislation. He led his party to victory in 1923 and held the promised referendum to reconsider prohibition later that year. He proceeded to make slightly stronger beer available, although the so-called "Fergie's Foam" was a none too palatable product for many workers. The 1926 provincial election was fought over the single issue of "John Barleycorn." The floundering Liberals split, and the "dries" ran candidates under the banner of the Hamilton Prohibition Union. The Labor candidates tried to avoid the issue. Voter turnout jumped to nearly two-thirds, the highest of the decade, as Hamilton's workers trooped to the polls to return the Tories' wet candidates with unprecedented majorities. According to the Communist press, "The two worst enemies of the working class have scored a complete triumph, Toryism and Booze." The next year, the victorious Ferguson administration proceeded to establish the government-controlled liquor outlets that it had promised, and alcoholic beverages became available once more (though only in carry-home bottles). Some seven years later Ontario legalized the public drinking of beer and wine in the new "beverage rooms."[110]

The Conservatives thus consolidated a reputation among men in working-class Hamilton as the voice of "personal liberty." The political controversy over booze brought into focus the Tories' odd mixture of paternalism and libertarianism. Here was an important instance of reciprocity in the relationship of political deference. With a touch of paternalist condescension, the Tory magnates declared their support for the workingmen's suspicion of state intervention to "improve" their lives and their right to recreational freedom – to be left alone – which was, of course, a male privilege within the working-class family.[111]

Oiling the Machine

However the Tories framed their message, years of Canadian political experience had taught them a lesson: that a permanent political organization was necessary to maintain party workers in each of the city's neighbourhoods, an organization that would actively promote the party's interests and dispense dollops of the party's largesse – examples of "the smooth talking, paid ward-heeler or corruptionist" that so disgusted one ILP metal-polisher in Hamilton. The Hamilton Conservative Association was in most ways a political machine in the classic North American mould. It managed to knit together a network of party workers and thus stimulated both the paternalistic and the more opportunistic, sycophantic elements in the politics of deference.[112]

Presiding over the local Conservative Association was an executive of prominent Hamilton men who, with considerable autonomy from provincial and national organizations, managed the party in the city. Above all, these men raked in large sums of money for the party's war chest and dispensed campaign funds and political favours. Closely allied with them were the publisher and editors of the *Spectator*, the most important link between the party and Hamilton households. Below the executive level operated a string of ward committees, each with a chairman and secretary – the "ward-heelers" – who canvassed their neighbourhoods for votes and cultivated their political turf between campaigns.[113] The machine was most visible in the weeks before an election, when it would work over the voters' lists, distribute leaflets, tack up posters, coax voters to attend the party's mass rallies, quietly dispense cash or liquor for votes, and marshal fleets of buggies and cars to convey voters to the polls. Before the war these rank-and-file members enjoyed the party's moment of glory in the traditional election-night procession through the city streets – a practice that had largely ended by the 1920s.

To maintain the allegiance of these campaign workers and, ideally, to attract new recruits, the party cultivated an active social life throughout the year. Nothing appeared in Canada on the scale of the British Conservatives' nationwide Primrose League, which gave that party a remarkable mass base (including many women, in contrast to Canada),[114] but their Hamilton cousins made similar efforts. Local ward committees were kept alive with inter-ward sports and euchre contests. Mammoth city-wide events, such as the "monster picnic," could also draw together the faithful and their friends.[115] Since well before the turn of the century the local Conservative Club had also offered a program of banquets, picnics, steamer excursions, dances, amateur concerts, and smokers, despite seemingly drawing its membership from the more affluent circles of the party.[116] The Twentieth Century Club, organized in the west end in 1900, had a similar clientele, although it must have attracted some working-class bachelors because in 1910 the city police chief called the place "a regular nuisance," where "the riff-raff made the place their rendezvous and when any officer was seen they ran inside, presumably to play pool." By 1914 the club had over 500 members.[117] That year, as independent workingmen's clubs and a lively Social Democratic organization were flourishing in the new east-end suburbs, the Conservative Party undertook to plant its banner solidly in the east by organizing the East Hamilton Conservative Association. Within two weeks the new club had 120 members. It promptly organized card parties, dances, a soccer team, and a brass band for outdoor concerts. At the end of that depression year the club even undertook to host a party in which it could "act as Santa Claus for poor children in the east end."[118] The party occasionally used these clubs for a minor program of internal education for its workers, with speakers to discuss the main political issues of the day and to exalt the Conservatives' glorious history.[119] The Tories, like the Liberals, also attempted to penetrate the world

of workingmen's fraternal societies, especially the closely allied Loyal Orange Lodge. Ward-heelers would use the lodge meeting discussions as natural forums to win over supporters.[120] Women were largely ignored until after they got the vote in 1917. The Tories finally organized their first women's auxiliary in 1919.[121]

All these social activities were evidently important to the Conservatives' fortunes – at least their opponents thought so. In 1925, at a dispirited meeting of Hamilton Liberals, one defeated candidate suggested copying the Conservative Association's methods: "Socials and frequent gatherings seemed to solve the problem nicely."[122] Yet the most important oil in the Tory party machinery was patronage, the well-developed practice of rewarding party supporters with material favours. Despite the avowed desire of their national leader, Borden, for cleaner government, the Hamilton Conservatives seemed quite content to solidify their support with liberal use of the "pork barr'l." The party nourished plenty of opportunism in its rank and file. "If you wanted a job, say in the post office, you would get it through the clubs," a woman whose father was active in the Conservative Party later recalled. "My father would have thirty or forty people asking him for jobs." "You can go into any city in Canada and size up the young fellows who are prominent in work for the party," the *Industrial Banner* noted in 1906, "and in nearly every instance they have the bait of a Government job before them. Young men openly state that they are out for the stuff and they won't work unless they get it." A decade later Tory alderman Alf Wright – "Boss" Wright to his opponents – bluntly admitted to a party gathering, "We are in politics essentially for three things, influence, honor, and money."[123]

Supplying the emoluments to party supporters required firm control of as much of the state apparatus as possible. Although their municipal programs seldom had clearly defined differences, the two major parties recognized that control of city council was essential for patronage purposes. In January 1901 a *Spectator* editorial decried the manner in which the Liberal majority on the city council had cornered all committee chairmanships for itself, "and fixed it so that the whole patronage of the council was controlled by the Grit council." In 1902 the *Spectator* charged again: "The provincial election is coming on this year, and the Grit machine desires to keep every Tory out of the council that it may be used for provincial election purposes by the machine." The validity of these charges and countercharges became clear a decade later when the *Herald*, which scorned this style of politics, reported on a meeting of provincial Liberals. The paper said that speakers at the meeting had argued that "the way back to power is through patronage, and they advocated the policy of 'capturing' the municipal councils and using the civil patronage for the benefit of the Liberal Party."[124]

In addition to control of the machinery for voter registration, the spoils of municipal office could include jobs for labourers on the city streets or, for the ward-heelers, in city hall departments; construction and maintenance contracts for schools and other public buildings; and contracts for provisioning the municipally controlled institutions such as the house of refuge and the jail. Provisions for other government departments and institutions, such as the militia, could be lucrative as well.[125] By 1911, when the Conservatives finally won control of the state apparatus at all three levels, the patronage booty was substantial.

For the most illustrious Tories the rewards could be a senatorship or a lieutenant-governorship, as in the case of George Lynch-Staunton and John S. Hendrie respectively. But workingmen who devoted their energies to party work might also eventually find their reward in a local government position or on a Conservative slate for election to city council. The city's Conservative Association controlled all of these opportunities.[126] The *Herald* deplored the whole system and kept its readership informed of Tory handouts, especially jobs in the post office and customs department. The *Industrial Banner* attacked patronage with more passion. It reported in 1915 that a man interested in a position in the post office "was told he would first have to join the Conservative party before he could expect any consideration." These kinds of positions were all a matter of intensely local relationships controlled in the city.[127]

The Tory machine thus fulfilled important functions. For the party leadership it provided the crucial day-to-day links with Hamilton residents that mere platform rhetoric could never sustain. Throughout the city Conservative politicians and their retinue of ward-heelers could provide countless small services for workers, from hiring them on government work to helping to untangling the red tape associated with an increasingly bureaucratic urban society. The machine also served party purposes admirably at election time by mobilizing a small army of canvassers, poll clerks, scrutineers, drivers, and sundry other campaign workers necessary for the stunning Conservative victories.

At the same time, party work also brought a modicum of "influence, honor, and money" for scores of men and women who humbly followed the orders of their political bosses. Serving the Tory machine was not unlike currying a foreman's favour in order to get a better job in a factory or to get a son or daughter hired, or joining the fraternal lodge or church congregation of a factory superintendent, or any number of other individualistic strategies for social mobility within a hierarchical social system of highly unequal power relations. More independent workingmen denounced this behaviour as "toadyism," but, however deferential, it was certainly calculating and opportunistic. The party had to deliver the goods to hold onto this active membership.

The Tory Workingman

Toryism in early-20th-century Hamilton was thus a remarkably successful force. The Conservative Party became the political home of the city's leading businessmen and professionals – of people who had unquestioned material interests in its political priorities and who sustained its war chests. But it was much more than simply a convenient vehicle for cynical men of property. As articulated by party leaders and press, Toryism was an emotional rallying cry that could reach beyond the affluent streets of the southwest into households across the city, including many parts of working-class Hamilton.

It was a politics of fear – fear of unemployment, "foreigners," meddling prudes, Bolsheviks – but also a politics of pride and respectability. It wrapped the Union Jack around narrow economic protectionism and private privilege, promising that, within this great dominion of the British Empire, workingmen could enjoy the prosperity, personal liberties, and cultural superiority of British civilization. As an embattled Liberal candidate explained in 1925, "The propaganda used by the Tories of to-day is as old as history, displaying patriotism and disguising ambition – display the old flag and harpoon the old land, blue ruin for Canada, blue ruin for Britain."[128]

The Tory appeal resonated with a mass of workers whose unifying experience was increasingly that of corporate capitalist industry – especially the large, rigidly supervised speeded-up factory – and who were rapidly losing the self-respect and satisfaction that flows from independent control over daily on-the-job decisions. They lived under the shadow of anticipated unemployment, increasing competition for jobs, escalating living costs, and other threats to their standards of living. For many workers – though by no means all – Toryism had its attractions.

Toryism spoke for tradition. Implicitly, through its internal practices and its public postures, it encouraged workers to respect a social hierarchy with a king as its most visible symbol, to defer to their social betters, and to put their trust and loyalty in men of property, much as they did in the evolving systems of industrial paternalism and welfare capitalism in the city's factories. It thus spoke for privilege within industrial capitalist society. Indeed, for some men it encouraged the same kind of opportunism and sycophancy that could be found almost any day on the shop floor. But Toryism also extended the defence of privilege much more broadly to include all white, male, Anglo-Canadian factory workers who wanted to hold onto their jobs, their "racial" superiority, and their masculine identity, both as breadwinners for their families and as "one of the boys." It respected the patriarchal right of the workingman to enjoy the few private pleasures left to him, especially his pint of beer. Indeed, even after women got the vote, its pitch was almost exclusively to men and their masculine self-esteem.[129] The appeal was therefore not merely a materialist message to a particular stratum of economically advantaged workers (though the party made little room for Hamilton's less-skilled, less-well-paid ethnic and racial minorities), but rather to a broad spectrum of male Anglo-Canadian workers. In a variety of ways it offered these men a measure of respectability.

Although Toryism, like all systems of deference, was rooted in an unequal relationship between classes, it was also a system of subordination with some reciprocity (after all, the much revered British king was a constitutionally restrained monarch, not an unfettered autocrat).[130] A working-class Tory could feel that he got something in return for his submission to a highly elitist political and social leadership. It was this dynamic that produced Ontario's special brand of Tory populism, a political force capable of bridging class differences and absorbing many of the strains of workers' inchoate anger and protest.

Conservative election campaigns were part organizational chicanery, part articulation of ideas, and part theatre. Rallies were staged to provide maximum entertainment value and to convey the most dramatic effect. The thundering rhetoric was often overblown and melodramatic, casting issues in stark light and inciting passionate resentments and surging loyalties. Carnivalesque victory parades gave more scope to these intense emotions. Workers were encouraged to embrace Toryism as deeply and habitually as they would their religion. This public emotionalism contrasted with the prim bourgeois evangelism, so strongly identified with Liberalism, that dated well back into the 19th century – the compelling urge to promote self-improvement and extend moral discipline over the private lives of the working class. Instead, the stability of the Tory brand of politics relied to a considerable extent on the perpetuation of working-class insecurity, dependence, and relative powerlessness and passivity.

Here was the chink in the party's armour. The Tories won elections, but they had not necessarily won over a majority of the working class. The 1902 provincial election provides a glimpse of the superficial support for Tory electioneering. In that campaign a large crowd of some 2,000 spectators gathered to hear speeches by socialist candidates, who were promptly arrested by the police. After milling about for a while, a large part of the crowd trooped over to a half-empty hall where a Tory rally was in progress.[131] Politics was evidently as much entertainment as commitment.

In the decade before the war, aside from the momentous 1911 federal election, the total Conservative vote in the city in provincial and federal elections hovered at only 5,000 to 6,000, at a time when the total population was soaring. Some workingmen were no doubt blocked from voting, while many others cynically simply did not bother to show up at the polls. That electoral abstention reflected the same feeling of lack of efficacy, but could, in altered circumstances, turn in the direction of protest. A growing restlessness also existed in the pre-war decade based on a sense that the rewards on the underside of Toryism were not enough. Increasingly another voice was resonating in working-class Hamilton: the voice of the craftworker, who was attempting to rally all wage-earners to an independent political strategy that rejected deference and addressed workers' own problems directly. By World War One the craftworkers' party had the Tories on the run.

17

The East Hamilton Progressive Association band, photographed on parade as part of the city's centennial celebrations in 1913.
(SLS, LS686)

The Classes and the Masses

"WHAT ABOUT THE CLASS I REPRESENT, the most important class in the province?"

Allan Studholme was on his feet once again in the 1911 session of the Ontario legislature, lambasting the government for ignoring workers' interests. The speech was typical in its bristling class-consciousness as he demanded action to address working-class concerns. In these rhetorical flourishes, the aging foundry worker was speaking from a particular ideological space.

For a good while Studholme was the most prominent spokesperson in Hamilton for a politics of class framed by a version of working-class liberalism that we now call labourism – one that, as Studholme put it in 1914, pitted "the masses against the classes."[1] The political movement he belonged to was the most sustained effort in early-20th-century Hamilton to promote unity through common class experience. Indeed, on the eve of World War One the *Industrial Banner* described the political organization that got Studholme (and eventually several others) elected, the Hamilton Independent Labor Party, as "the best class-conscious organization in Ontario."[2]

At the turn of the 20th century labourism was part of a current with a distinctive sense of what citizens should demand of the state. It was a tendency in working-class politics that had a long history running back through more than a century of popular struggles throughout the English-speaking world. Within this liberal view of politics the state was limited and mostly played only a supplementary and subordinate role to voluntarism in civil society, where associations and institutions of citizens were expected to work out their own relationships, especially through the collective self-help of unionism. A deep sense of community obligation and responsibility set this strand of politics somewhat apart from the political individualism and respect for property of the middle and upper classes, but a faith in a citizen's liberty – the rights of the "free-born Englishman," in its British version – was shared ideological ground. New state policies might be needed to eradicate obstacles to democratic expression (full, universal voting rights without property qualifications, for example), equal opportunity (free public schooling), or breadwinning in properly ordered labour markets (abolition of prison labour, curbs on excessive immigration, or shorter hours of work). But otherwise, after being in hostile hands for generations, the state – especially its disciplining and policing capacity – was an object of suspicion that should be constrained, not hugely expanded.[3]

Alongside this voluntarism ran a wholly different current with an equally long pedigree. This current, which one British historian calls "Jacobinism,"[4] looked to the state to intervene much more aggressively to shape working-class experience and sustain a fuller expectation of citizenship rights. At the turn of the century it generally came with the label of socialism, and far more working-class leaders in Britain and North America rejected that radical perspective. Yet in the opening decades of the new century those leaders often began to promote legislative measures to improve working-class living standards and support the public interest. By the end of World War One they were looking to those possibilities – from mothers' allowances to publicly owned railways and utilities – with a lot more interest than ever before. Most nonetheless still had a constrained view of the public sector and never fully abandoned their uneasiness about a pushy, interventionist state. That would be the story of the Hamilton ILP.

The ILP spoke for a class, but its social base was fairly narrow. Its leadership and active membership came mostly from skilled union men, mainly white, male, and Anglo-Canadian, and its ideology and practices reflected the particular worldview of that slice of working-class Hamilton. As a result two distinct processes were required to bring this political current to life in the city. First, the craftworkers had to be detached from traditional party allegiances, especially from the Liberal Party; second, the adherents of labourism had to harness broader support in the working class to their new political vehicle. The first step was well under way by the early years of the century, but the second was taken much more slowly, advancing only as industrial conflict intensified, living standards deteriorated somewhat, and the promises of mainstream politics proved hollow. By the end of World War One, masses of Hamilton workers had finally bought the message.

The success of labourist politics was thus highly dependent on the health and strength of the local labour movement. Craft unionists brought both strengths and ambivalences to the task of political leadership. The man who plied a valuable skill in Hamilton's industrial life was no man's slave. His functional autonomy in the work process and the workplace traditions that he nourished to control that process gave him far more power and room to manoeuvre than the growing numbers of semi-skilled machine tenders around him had. Central to the craftworkers' outlook on the world was a gritty spirit of independence and determination to resist subordination. In addition to such libertarian principles, the craftworkers infused working-class politics in the city with the traditions of solidarity developed in their union experience, and they contributed valuable organizational skills. Their pride in their manual skills easily expanded into class-conscious assertions of the dignity and worth of all wage-earners.

Yet these men had their limits – being, as they were, less than enthusiastic about women or ethnic minorities in their work world and making limited space for those people in their new party. Moreover, as in their shop-floor politics, the craftworkers would contribute a strong dose of cautious restraint and political moderation to the independent politics of the working class.

Thus politicized craftworkers carried Hamilton's workers to a climactic moment in the fall of 1919, and then failed to meet the challenge of postwar politics. The ILP's collapse in the early 1920s was above all the result of a powerful anti-labour assault, but the party's weak response and its inability to hold onto its large working-class following stemmed, in part at least, from inherent weaknesses in the political style and ideology of labourism.

Paths Not Taken

Labourism was not the first version of independent working-class politics to appear at the turn of the century. At that point, a rich diversity of radical ideas was percolating through working-class Hamilton. Small organizations of critical thinkers were meeting, debating, and reaching out to larger audiences. Eventually, two distinct currents of this political ferment crystallized to promote their own versions of socialism. Although each captured some attention, neither won a large following, and through most of the pre-war period socialists would remain, in the words of a labour journalist, "howling and wandering in the wilderness."[5]

In Hamilton in the late 1890s, as in other Canadian cities at this time, several small societies and clubs met regularly to discuss social reform. A Single Tax Association, with roots running back into the 1880s and reorganized in 1898, promoted Henry George's panacea. Members of a small national socialist organization calling itself the Canadian Co-operative Commonwealth filed into a hall each week to thrash out the principles and practice of establishing utopian socialist colonies. In 1897 C.E. Whitcombe, rector of St. Matthew's Anglican Church, turned his church's basement over to a new East End Workingmen's Club, and became the club's president. Such an organization, Whitcombe believed, would allow workers "to discuss state politics, fiscal questions, municipal politics and questions affecting labor, employment and wages." Taking up his exhortations "to 'agitate' and educate the public," the club lobbied the city fathers in the winter of 1897–98 for shorter hours for workers at the city's sewage disposal plant and for works projects to relieve unemployment. In January 1898 Whitcombe helped to spawn a West End Workingmen's Club in the Church of St. John the Evangelist. Alongside these groups flourished an active, reform-minded temperance movement, centred in the Royal Templars of Temperance. Its journal the *Templar* was published in Hamilton under the editorship of the ardent reformer W.W. Buchanan.[6]

Some of the members of the small Hamilton Trades and Labor Council could be found in these reform organizations, and the Council still reflected the ethical Labour Reform politics of the Knights of Labor era of a decade earlier.[7] In the critical, anti-capitalist vein of the Knights' rhetoric, the Council's founding "Declaration of Principles," republished in its 1897 Labour Day souvenir, looked forward to a system of "productive and distributive co-operation and the self-employment of labor, as only complete independence can be obtained when the laborer is no longer dependent on other individuals for the right to work."[8] Inspired by the new Industrial Brotherhood movement led by London's

Joseph Marks, editor of the fledgling *Industrial Banner* (which soon had a Hamilton edition), the Council decided that "a universal organization of labor is a necessity of social progress and safety" and should be based on "all social reform organizations" in the city. In 1898, in step with a similar move in Toronto, the Council sponsored a meeting of representatives from all of the interested organizations, along with several individuals. Whitcombe took the chair.[9]

Delegates to this new Social Reform Union agreed on a mixed agenda of reforms, and a subsequent declaration of principles proclaimed, "The supreme object of government should be the protection of man, not property, and the promotion of the welfare of all the people."[10] The founding meeting adjourned with hopes of creating a "national movement," but such optimism was evidently misplaced because the organization appears to have disappeared by the end of the year.

Much of the same political sentiment, however, flowed into the new Canadian Socialist League, which had a Hamilton local by 1900 and took its lead from *Citizen and Country*, a newspaper published in Toronto by the energetic radical journalist George Wrigley. The paper's Hamilton correspondent, Comrade Alberta H. Secord, conveyed the Christian Socialist tone that had characterized many of these radicals of the 1890s when she wrote in 1900 about her enthusiasm for "The Socialism of the Lord's Prayer." A Hamilton representative was elected to the first executive of the regional Ontario Socialist League in 1901, but the city's branch did not make much of a dent in local political discourses. Its surviving members eventually drifted towards the more ideologically rigorous Socialist Party of Canada, formed in 1905.[11]

In Hamilton's radical politics, the Socialist League was being elbowed aside at the turn of the century by a much more stridently Marxist variant of socialism. As it did across much of North America, Marxism had first appeared among the city's workers through the Socialist Labor Party (SLP). A small branch was active in Hamilton by the late 1890s. Initially the party was fully welcomed in the city's Labour Reform circles,[12] but the split in the US parent organization in 1899 brought a more caustic tone into the Hamilton comrades' rhetoric, who took their cues from the party's brilliant American leader Daniel De Leon. They built on the evolutionary theories of capitalist development that infused the left in this period, and contemptuously rejected the value of ameliorative political reforms and union bargaining over wages. They believed that a socialist party's task was simply to educate otherwise misinformed workers and implant a revolutionary socialist analysis, in anticipation of capitalism's ultimate, inevitable collapse.[13]

The role of unions in workers' emancipation thus became the great divide in North American labour politics. Since 1894 the AFL leadership had been beating back demands for an independent labour or socialist party in favour of a non-statist reliance on voluntarist collective bargaining (though numerous state and local labour bodies had nonetheless plunged into politics).[14] A virtually unbridgeable rift developed between local socialists and the mainstream labour movement as the socialists repeatedly denounced AFL-style craft unionism and its local leaders, invariably dubbed "labor fakirs" or "frauds." An old cigarmaker who exchanged blows with an SLP orator in 1901 was not the only unionist whose hackles were raised by the weekly harangues from the socialist soapbox in the Market Square. A few years later a one-time supporter, the local AFL organizer John Flett, angrily objected to being "maligned by these men who call themselves

Socialists and who shout their doctrines at us from every soap-box on the street corner." The uncompromising arrogance of the socialist attacks, "that assumption of superior and advanced intellectuality that repels instead of attracts," also provoked a stern lecture from the *Industrial Banner*.[15]

For most of the period before World War One, Hamilton's tiny band of Marxists was contemptuous of what trade unionists thought of them and concentrated instead on their educational campaigns. Between 1900 and 1902 their colourful soapbox oratory hammered home the message that the "interests of the working class and the capitalist are diametrically opposed," and appeared to make a considerable impact. In an age when Saturday evening drew large crowds of shoppers to the city's renowned downtown outdoor market, a speaker holding forth from the back of a wagon or perched on a wooden crate provided a popular form of entertainment – socialist education through flamboyant performance. In mid-September 1901, at the end of a week of journalistic hand-wringing about the anarchist who had just assassinated US president William McKinley, the police nervously moved in to arrest four socialist speakers for obstructing the street. The original audience of some 1,000 quickly grew to a crowd of nearly 10,000, and many of them tried to prevent the police from suppressing free speech with a hail of "large stones, rotten eggs, rotten apples, and other missiles." After fines (and suspended sentences), the socialists were chastened for a while, but the next spring the police swooped down again.[16]

The occasion was a provincial election campaign. By that point the SLP had run in a string of local elections. Their two aldermanic candidates made a small but respectable showing in 1900, as did the SLP mayoralty candidate,

William Barrett, a painter, ran as a socialist candidate for mayor in 1902 and got a third of the vote.
(HPL, Hamilton and District Labor Council, *30th Anniversary Complimentary Souvenir*)

master painter William Barrett, a year later. In 1902 Barrett denied Mayor John S. Hendrie his traditional acclamation to a second term by running as his only opponent. This time the socialist candidate astounded the pundits by rolling up 1,742 votes, a third of Hendrie's total.[17] The momentum carried into the spring provincial election campaign, when two of the party's most energetic young speakers, Robert Rodehouse, an ironworks labourer, and Lockhart Gordon, a machinist, announced their candidacies for the Hamilton seats in the provincial election. They used the ensuing campaign both to denounce capitalism – and manufacturers like Hendrie, now the Tory candidate – and to defend free speech. Their election meetings drew audiences of 600 to 700, and, when the socialists attempted to hold yet another meeting, in Gore Park, the police marched through the nearly 2,000 spectators and arrested the two candidates for obstructing the street. Released on a promise to avoid further outdoor rallies, the socialist pair managed to win only 375 and 195 votes in each of the east and west ridings (7 and 4 per cent of the votes cast respectively). Their court cases dragged on into December, when a jury finally acquitted them.[18]

Whether intimidated by the police harassment or demoralized by its poor electoral showings, the SLP went into decline and within a year had no public face in the city. Many members regrouped inside the new Socialist Party of Canada late in 1905, but had no greater impact politically. Their relentless contempt for unions and strikes remained decisive in undercutting a potentially larger audience for their ideas. No equivalent of Britain's socialist Independent Labour Party appeared to promote closer links with unions.[19]

Socialism, then, remained a weak force in Hamilton in the first decade of the century. The narrative of socialists' activities in the city does not suggest that they failed simply because workers rejected collectivist principles, but more crucially because, in contrast to most other industrialized countries, socialists and unionized wage-earners across North America had built up insurmountable walls of antagonism and mutual recrimination. Moreover, not only did the socialists promote an apparently unpopular brand of politics, but, compared to other large cities, in Hamilton the soil for socialist recruits was thin. The city's small Anglo-Canadian middle class did not produce as many committed social critics as larger metropolitan centres did, and, although the new pre-war immigration brought in a few radicals among the Jews, Armenians, and Ukrainians, the more numerous groups of newcomers, the Italians and Poles, included no visible socialists. Ideologically and demographically, Hamilton's socialists had deep problems.[20]

The Labourist Turn

The divide between socialism and unionism left the craft unionists to work out their own form of working-class politics. Like others in this period, in Canada as well as in Britain and the United States,[21] they did so in step with the tempo of aggressive union organizing and accelerating industrial conflict in the early 20th century. Unlike national US labour leaders, such as Gompers, who repeatedly steered the AFL away from forming a separate labour party, many more of Hamilton's labour men seemed committed to following that independent road in politics.

At the turn of the 20th century, craft unions and the cross-occupational federations to which they belonged had developed a regular practice of lobbying for specific legislative action. The national Trades and Labor Congress met with the federal cabinet each year, and the Congress's Ontario Executive Committee did the same with the provincial government. In both cases labour leaders presented a list of issues to be addressed. Locally the Hamilton Trades and Labor Council had a more informal process of passing resolutions on everything from school fees to voter registration, which were passed on to city council. These were the polite "cap-in-hand" rituals scoffed at by socialists.

The cut and thrust of labour relations across Canada at the dawn of the new century undermined the unionists' faith in lobbying. Although Hamilton's many new craft unions initially faced less of the union-bashing that was hitting several other towns and cities, the city's labour leaders were just as angry about it. In the annual conventions of the Trades and Labor Congress and, after 1903, in the meetings of the Labor Educational Association of Ontario (a loose provincial federation of labour), they joined in such expressions of outrage as a 1903 Congress resolution arguing that the recent legislative campaign by "corporations and manufacturers" was "designed to destroy the usefulness of labor organizations" and enhance corporate "aggrandizement," while legislation for "the welfare of the producing masses" was ignored. A year later Flett argued that unions had been "treated shamefully by all parliaments." He could find not "one piece of legislation passed in the interests of labor this year, though there have been hundreds of bills put through for the capitalists." He ridiculed the established practice of appearing before governments "with our hats in our hands" and humbly "begging for this and praying for that, while the big corporationist could walk in at the door and get what he wanted." It was time for "a new tack" – "get into politics for ourselves in earnest."[22]

Many craft unionists in Hamilton were thus being cut adrift from traditional political practices and allegiances and resolving to go it alone. In 1899 they had mounted a vigorous campaign that helped to defeat mayoralty candidate John Tilden, an anti-labour foundryman who had won his notoriety in a bitter moulders' strike seven years earlier. In 1901 a small meeting of unionists endorsed three labour candidates for alderman. Only one, Michael Basquill, was successful, and he quickly slid into the Liberal caucus on city council.[23] In fall 1903, following impassioned discussions at the Trades and Labor Congress meeting, Hamilton's leading trade unionists undertook a more concerted effort.[24] In October representatives from all the city's unions met to give birth to the Workingmen's Political Association, the first political party of Hamilton craftworkers since the 1880s. For 50 cents any Hamilton worker could join. Aside from Whitcombe, all the executive officers were union leaders active in the local labour movement.[25]

With the hope of holding the balance of power on city council, the Association nominated four candidates for the approaching municipal contest: two moulders, a bartender, and a custom tailor (who later withdrew because of inadequate property qualifications). Their platform incorporated many of the basic elements that would recur in labourist politics for the next 20 years. They championed the wage-earner with an attack on the city's use of contract labour. They decried the bonusing of factories as an act of unacceptable privilege in the marketplace. They attacked monopolies, notably the street-railway service, and called for "municipal ownership of all public franchises." They proposed a more democratic political system through the introduction of the initiative and referendum. Only Thomas Church, a moulder, won a council seat, however, and he soon followed Basquill's path, this time into the Tory camp.[26]

The Workingmen's Political Association continued an active life after the election. It maintained club rooms in which political discussions regularly took place, and in July 1904 sponsored an evening cruise on the lake for some 400 people. The next winter the organization once again named four contenders for municipal office, but Church, with his name on the Tory slate as well, was again the only successful candidate. The craftworkers' party, it seemed, had not been able to crack the old-party affiliations of that small percentage of Hamilton workers who bothered to vote in municipal elections. A month later the well-oiled Conservative machine trampled all opposition in the provincial campaign that finally brought Whitney's party to power. The Workingmen's Political Association quietly disappeared, and no independent labour candidates offered themselves to the electors in January 1906.[27]

Breakthrough

A national labour convention later in 1906 rekindled local enthusiasm. In the fall, fired up by fresh news of the recent successes of the Labour Representation Committee in Britain, the

(*HS*, 28 Nov. 1906, 12)

election of Congress president Alphonse Verville to the House of Commons, and the American Federation of Labor's new (and short-lived) commitment to independent political ventures, the Trades and Labour Congress delegates decided, after hours of debate, to launch a Canadian Labor Party. During the convention Hamilton's representatives received word that the sitting Conservative member for East Hamilton in the provincial legislature had died. They immediately resolved to contest the seat for labour, and in mid-November the Hamilton Trades and Labor Council sponsored a mass meeting of "all wage earners and independent voters" to choose a candidate. Some 100 trade unionists turned out to nominate Studholme, the 60-year-old stove-mounter from the Burrow, Stewart, and Milne foundry.[28]

The Hamilton Conservatives were certainly not in fine fettle for an election. On top of serious internal friction within their local organization, they had great difficulty finding a suitable candidate for the East Hamilton fight. Foundryman John Milne, oddly enough Studholme's employer, was the favourite, but he wavered and finally withdrew. Ultimately a wealthy lawyer, J.J. Scott, reluctantly agreed to run. The dominant party in local politics was momentarily caught off guard.[29]

Meanwhile, ten days after Studholme's nomination the local Liberal organization decided

not to put up a candidate, resolving "that the interests of the Liberal and Labor parties in the present contest are identical." During the four-week campaign the *Spectator* repeatedly decried the alleged collusion to unite against the Conservative candidate. Studholme, the paper claimed, was "simply another of the long list of Liberal candidates put up as Labor candidates at the instance of the Liberal machine, to draw votes from unsuspecting Conservative workingmen." Yet despite open support from the Liberal *Times* and the more independent but Liberal-leaning *Herald* and the undoubted assistance of Liberal campaign workers, there is no evidence of any secret deals between Liberals and labourites.[30]

Charles I. Aitchison, a printer at the *Herald*, headed up a broad-based labour organization that used door-to-door canvassing by ward committees and nightly open-air meetings or indoor rallies. Studholme's platform was simply the Congress's declaration of principles first passed at the 1898 convention and adopted as the new Canadian Labor Party platform in September 1906. But on the stump he spent most of his time attacking the provincial government, especially its recent contract for prison labour in the city at three cents an hour, in "direct competition with free labor," and its decision to remove the Normal School from the city.[31]

Yet the crucial factor was beyond any doubt the tumultuous street-railway strike that exploded into violence on the city streets during the election campaign. The Tories found that their usual appeal for cross-class unity at the polls was shattered by the most dramatic incident of class conflict in the city's history. The *Spectator* admitted that it was labour's "psychological moment." As angry crowds of up to 10,000 faced the sabres and clubs of soldiers and policemen, labour canvassers and supporters not surprisingly "did not hesitate to use the old bogie of capital against labor" and to denounce Scott as "a bloated capitalist and a lawyer in the pay of certain monopolies, including even the hated Cataract Power company." A local Conservative leader admitted to Whitney that "the way the city was worked up and the way things stood I believe if the angel Gabriel had been running for member in East Hamilton he would have been defeated by a tramp."[32]

Curiously, on election day Studholme was not able to sweep up all the mass discontent into a huge labour vote. His victory over Scott by 853 votes certainly sent shock waves through the city and beyond. The *Industrial Banner* jubilantly declared, "The East Hamilton election has encouraged organized labor all over Canada and shows what can be accomplished when unionism means business and votes as it talks." Yet, equally significantly, in terms of the evolution of local political allegiances the voter turnout of only 3,859 was the lowest in the city since 1871 – nearly 2,200 less than in 1905. The militant mood of the strike had clearly pried loose large numbers of workers from their old-party ties, leaving them "sore and sullen," but they had not yet committed themselves wholeheartedly to the craftworkers' party.[33]

In the euphoric aftermath of their surprising victory, local labour leaders spent little time contemplating the poor turnout. The immediate priority was carrying this electoral success into the municipal arena, and 12 labour candidates were promptly nominated for aldermanic seats and three for the school board. The *Spectator* noted that they were evenly split between Conservative and Liberal supporters. Every household in Hamilton received a copy of the Trades and Labour Council's new municipal platform, which promised civic ownership of public utilities, "free and compulsory" education, open

decision-making at city hall, protection of public parks from railway developments, investigation into police brutality, publication of assessment rolls, labour representation on all public boards, civic construction by day labour rather than contract labour, and opposition to any concessions to the street railway or the Cataract Power company. On 7 January 1907 five of the labour men won city-council seats.[34]

After a decade of debate and false starts, organized craftworkers had finally broken loose from the powerful hold of the old parties. They had established the legitimacy of an independent voice for the working class in Hamilton politics and had put themselves at the head of a class-based organization that was on its way to replacing the Liberal Party as the "official opposition" in the city. It had taken a major crisis to disrupt the established patterns of integrating the working class into cross-class parties, but, for the next 15 years, politics in Hamilton would never again be quite the same.

Building a Base

The vehicle for this political transformation was the Hamilton Independent Labor Party, which continued during its lifetime to draw its leaders and active membership from skilled workers. In the decade and a half after 1906, the ILP set out to assume the political leadership of the entire Anglo-Canadian working-class in the city. Until 1914 the party's growth was slow and uneven, but, then, over the next five years, it expanded rapidly and began to chalk up electoral successes at the municipal level. Each of these two phases corresponded to important new developments within the life and labour of the working class.[35]

Although the range of its activities would widen as it gathered strength, the Hamilton ILP mainly ran election campaigns. Creating an electioneering machine with limited funds taxed the talents and imagination of these men. After approaching local craft unions for cash donations to cover basic costs, the party usually rented a small storefront for an election headquarters and funnelled most of the rest of its funds into election cards and leaflets. If the money were available and if a proprietor could be found who would agree to rent a hall,[36] a large indoor rally usually climaxed the campaign. Otherwise electioneering most commonly involved open-air meetings outside plant gates at noon hour or on street corners or in public parks in the evening. Most of the speakers for these events were local ILP leaders, but occasionally labour orators from outside the city would speak for Hamilton candidates. The most important difference from the old parties was the volunteer labour involved – there was no money for salaries or honoraria. Sustaining such a skeletal organization could be discouraging. The party machinery had to be rebuilt from scratch for three of the five provincial and federal campaigns waged between 1908 and 1914. The real continuity of labour politics came from a determined group of craftworkers who formed the first executive and revived the party for each new campaign.[37]

Between elections, at various points after 1908, to sustain morale and, if possible, win new recruits, party leaders attempted to cultivate a recreational life modelled on the male socializing of the craft union movement. At intervals they called regular monthly meetings, occasionally in the form of smokers. A small ILP Social Club also opened its doors in downtown Hamilton from time to time to provide after-work recreation for party members. Probably the most inspired venture was the party's decision to advertise itself on the playing fields by organizing an ILP Football (Soccer) Club. The ILP men in their maroon sweaters were soon charging down the gridiron against corporate teams,

including the Westinghouse Football Club, and in 1910 they came within one point of winning a national championship. The team survived in the city's athletic circles on into the 1920s as the ILP's most successful intervention into the popular culture of the Hamilton working class. In contrast to the socialists, party activists put less effort into writing or distributing literature, though they occasionally held educational sessions with speakers such as Studholme discussing "economic and public questions." In a rare effort at mass public education, the party sponsored a huge public meeting in October 1912 featuring British Labour leader Keir Hardie. All these efforts to create a "movement culture" were a tiny drop in that local sea of popular culture, but they doubtless helped to hold together the committed between electoral campaigns.[38]

Getting off to a wobbly start at the end of 1907, the party lost all its city council seats in January 1908, and no ILP candidate would be seen again in municipal contests before a 1912 by-election.[39] The only ILP contender for a federal seat, Landers, lost his deposit in 1908, and in that June's provincial election the Tories turned up the steam. In a four-way contest they reduced Studholme's total vote to 41 per cent and his margin of victory to only 75 votes. In 1911 the Tories hoped to ride out of their anti-free-trade federal campaign into a triumphant defeat of Studholme (and Barrett, the one-time socialist leader, who ran for the ILP in the rural South Wentworth riding, where the new working-class suburb of Crown Point was growing up). But hundreds of new volunteers joined the ILP campaign, and an eloquent British Labour MP, George H. Roberts, who was touring North America, spent the last week of the campaign speaking for the ILP candidates.

Both sides obviously saw this election as a decisive turning point. The campaign took on

TOM JUTTEN—WOW! OUCH! AND I WAS ONLY TRYING TO SIT ON HIM

According to *Labor News*, Conservative candidate Tom Jutten found the ILP's Studholme a formidable opponent in the 1914 provincial election campaign. (*LN*, 26 June 1914, 1)

more than local dimensions when labour organizations across the province began sending in financial contributions and the *Industrial Banner* turned over its pages to the Hamilton ILP's fight. "The crisis is here," the paper announced, "and the workers of Hamilton are putting up a game fight." In the end the little stove-mounter walked away with a solid 689-vote majority and 55 per cent of the 6,363 votes cast. A crowd of thousands of exultant workingmen formed up into "the greatest parade that has been held after a political fight for years." Amidst the hoopla few noticed that Barrett had scraped together only 209 votes in his east-end fight, alongside the Tory victor's 1,496.[40]

In a now familiar pattern, the party had slipped into a "comatose state" by the end of the year and had to be rebuilt by a handful of the party faithful for the June 1914 provincial election. The campaign and Studholme's subsequent election with a 987-vote majority over his sole Conservative opponent revealed that by the summer of 1914 many working-class voters in the eastern half of the city were shifting their allegiance solidly and apparently permanently to independent labour politics.[41]

The smoke of battle had scarcely cleared when the appointment of Hendrie to the lieutenant-governorship necessitated a by-election for his West Hamilton seat in November. With unflagging enthusiasm, the ILP put up Walter Rollo for another two-man race with the Tories. After years of debating their strength in this riding, which included the most exclusive upper-class neighbourhoods in the city, the labourists had finally decided to test it. On election day Rollo shocked the local Tories by coming within 36 votes of victory. As the *Industrial Banner* later noted, "An army of voters who have hitherto supported the Conservative machine must have broke [*sic*] loose and pulled for Rollo." All the celebrating on election night was in the ILP camp.[42]

What had accounted for the solidifying of the party's support over the eight years since the street-railway strike had catapulted Studholme into Queen's Park? Studholme's principled performance as Ontario's only labourist

Walter Rollo, broom-maker, executive member of the Hamilton Trades and Labor Council, and ILP candidate in West Hamilton in 1914.

(HPL, Hamilton and District Labor Council, *30th Anniversary Complimentary Souvenir*)

LABOR MEETINGS

SATURDAY NIGHT—Market square and James street committee rooms.
MONDAY NIGHT — Point Hill. If weather is unfavorable, James street rooms.
TUESDAY NIGHT—Locke st. church, cor. Locke and Melbourne streets.
THE CANDIDATE.

W. R. ROLLO

assisted by other speakers, will address the meetings.
Friends of the Labor Party wishing to volunteer their services as scrutineers for election day are requested to leave their names at 88 King street west as soon as possible.

H. J. HALFORD, Secretary.

(*HS*, 14 Nov. 1914, 16)

himself as the "Labour Party" in the house, and symbolically wore a small black velvet hat during the legislative sessions, reminiscent of Keir Hardie's famous cloth cap and "meant to breathe defiance to all draughts, even those of the most gusty debates." Eventually in 1909 Whitney recognized his special status in the legislature by moving him down from the rear of the chamber to a front-row seat near the speaker's chair.[43]

From that prominent perch, the self-styled "little stove-mounter" challenged government policies on child labour, immigration, employment standards, workers' compensation, housing, cost of living, wartime profiteering, and soldier resettlement. He introduced his own bills for an eight-hour day, a minimum wage, and votes for women (none of which passed). He was an uncompromising opponent of privilege and a champion of democracy and publicly owned utilities, especially Ontario Hydro. He thus brought to his role in the legislature an aggressiveness, vitality, and unparalleled commitment to serving his working-class constituency, all of which helped to keep the flickering torch of labourist politics from going out in Hamilton. The growing affection for him generally in the city provided a continuing momentum that the faltering party organization alone could never have sustained.[44]

The unwavering support of the city's leading voice of left-liberalism, the widely read *Herald*, was also a crucial factor in the ILP's success. Through each of these pre-war campaigns the paper stepped into the role of chief propaganda agent for the party's position. Between elections it gave Studholme's performance in the legislature front-page coverage. Moreover, it was in the post-election euphoria of Studholme's 1911 re-election that Landers, in 1912, launched his long-awaited *Labor News*, the lively weekly labour paper that reached some 5,000 readers. Such

parliamentarian before 1919 was hugely important. The hallmark of his legislative career was his unwillingness to make deals with Liberals or Conservatives or to move into the orbit of one of their caucuses. As he explained to Mackenzie King when the young civil servant asked for support in his own 1908 election campaign, "Labor men have lost all faith in party men and are determined to have their own Class on the floor of the house so as to have some say in making the laws they have to live under." Studholme viewed

Labor News editor Sam Landers oversees the production of his newspaper. (SLS, LS390)

double-barrelled journalistic support must have helped immeasurably to build ILP strength.[45]

Yet more important were new features of working-class life that were giving class-conscious politics a boost. The large numbers of arrivals from the British Isles who were settling in the new east-end suburbs included a "very large percentage of Englishmen from Lancashire and Yorkshire, the counties in England that cast a big Labor vote," said the *Industrial Banner*, and a considerable number of them had been active in labour politics back home. One of these was the Hamilton party's vice-president in 1911, Duncan Shaw, who reputedly had been "prominent in labor circles in England" and brought good speaking and organizing skills. A year later, after the Keir Hardie lecture, several "Old Country I.L.P. boys" presented themselves to join the local cause. The decision to sponsor soccer, the leading sport of the British workingman, rather than the North American favourite, baseball, suggests the British flavour of the party's membership. Lessons from 20 years of British working-class politics thus flowed into the Hamilton movement. Arguably, this influence helped to deepen the divergence between local labour politics and the policies of the AFL that opposed the creation of a distinct labour party.[46]

Furthermore, the new east-end neighbourhoods into which these newcomers were flowing by the thousands in the years just before the war had many rugged frontier qualities – new housing, atrocious roads, few urban services – and the mutual assistance and neighbourly co-operation that became daily experience soon found institutional expression, notably in the Industrial Co-operative Society of Hamilton. More significant politically was the creation of the Ward Eight Improvement Society and the East Hamilton Progressive Association, both residents' associations determined to agitate for better services in the area. The Progressive Association saw itself, in addition, as a workingmen's club "to benefit the residents morally, socially, and physically." It held regular educational meetings with guest speakers and organized club rooms, a marching band, athletic teams, a tobacco shop, and a branch of the "Pleasant Sunday Afternoon" movement for sober Sabbatarian discussions. It also took on an aggressive agitational role on behalf of east-end workers, supporting a 1913 strike of labourers, sponsoring in January 1914 the city's first major meeting to protest high unemployment, and backing candidates for city hall.[47] Thus a community spirit that would distinguish this area of the city for years to come was being forged through the workers' informal solidarities, associational life, and daily struggles in building brand-new neighbourhoods of British working-class immigrants, along with an independent political presence in a part of the city that the major parties were slower to colonize.[48] In time the ILP would find this area – variously known as East Hamilton, "Little England," or simply Ward Eight – a bedrock of support for its candidates.

If the east-enders had their own special reasons for a new spirit of class solidarity, working and living conditions generally in the city in the half decade before the war were pushing many more workers in the same direction. A new sense of instability and insecurity arose among Hamilton's workers in the years after the 1907–9 depression as the labour market was overrun by vast numbers of new immigrants and as the pace of industrial transformation quickened remarkably.

In many of the city's factories, work routines had begun to change abruptly and rapidly – new management schemes at Westinghouse and other plants, new technology in the steel mills, the machine shops, and most of the foundries, new "labour-saving" devices to facilitate general speed-ups, more and more new European immigrant labourers involved in production, all in much bigger, more impersonal factories. Uneasiness, resentment, and sometimes anger were spreading through the ranks of Hamilton wage-earners – with the result being the marked increase in workplace conflict between 1909 and 1914, in which hundreds of moulders, garment workers, textile workers, building tradesmen, and unskilled labourers locked horns with their bosses.

The Tories could indeed draw on some of this insecurity, but growing numbers of workers were linking various leaders of the Conservative Party to the dislocation and degradation of their working lives. In June 1914, reporting on apparent ILP support from the east-end factory district, the notoriously cautious *Labor News* remarked, "The workers realize this is not an organized labor fight, but it is a fight of capital against labor." The editor singled out Milne, president of the local Conservative association:

> Scores of iron moulders, pattern makers, metal polishers, painters, laborers, machinists and handy men, who were former employees of John Milne will vote for Allan Studholme as a protest against "Old John," the opponent of fair wages, sanitary and other living conditions.... The man who is in favor of low wages and long hours is the enemy of the entire working class. Milne says labor has no rights. Hurl it back in his teeth by voting for Studholme.

Many of these workers must have done just that. "The tide of the East Hamilton election yesterday was turned when the factories in the East End let their men out to vote," the *Herald* reported. "The deputy returning officers, in almost every case, report that the Studholme votes were found tight together in the boxes, the last to be put in." Work and politics were clearly not far apart. In November workers heard Rollo cry from a street corner: "The manufacturing class is the class that frames and controls [the] legislature today, and you working-men need look for no alleviation of your present conditions until you supplant this class by electing men who are heart and soul in sympathy with the conditions under which you exist." With vigorously class-conscious rhetoric, the craftworkers' party was reaching out beyond the circles of skilled workmen to an increasingly responsive body of disgruntled workers in Hamilton workplaces.[49]

Moreover, as the severe depression that had begun a year earlier dragged on through 1914, the ILP was striking a responsive chord among many of the unemployed, who resented the "few financial and political juggernauts" who "manipulated and controlled" the means of subsistence. In fall 1914 a letter to the *Herald* from an unemployed worker argued that workers now wanted "radical changes." The letter writer argued: "If it was said of the first election of Allan Studholme that the workers of East Hamilton needed to have their heads cracked by a policeman's club before they would vote for their own interests by putting in a labor man, it may also be said that the club of unemployment and starvation now used should be effective in returning a labor man for West Hamilton." Studholme's cry that "it was the old fight of the masses against the classes" must have struck home.[50]

Towards the New Democracy

By the end of 1914 the Hamilton ILP was linking up with the currents of working-class discontent in the city to produce its most successful showing since 1906. Consolidating itself as what the *Industrial Banner* called "the most effective working class political organization in Canada,"[51] it would build to a pinnacle of strength in 1919. The characteristics of this new phase were a more secure, permanent, and expanding organizational base, the eclipsing of Studholme by a new band of younger labourites, and a series of significant electoral victories.

Efforts were made to end the pattern of slumbering between elections that had characterized the party's pre-war institutional life. Membership cards were once again printed up for sale through factories and workshops, and by the end of the war contests were being held to spur on the recruiting of new members. The social and educational programs were beefed up and maintained on a more or less year-round basis. Regular bimonthly meetings were turned over to discussions of major social questions, such as the ruminations over the causes and cures of unemployment in March 1915. As their representation on city council increased during the war, the labourites used these meetings more often to air the practical problems of wartime working-class life, especially the rising cost of living.[52]

Social life in the party also blossomed. ILP baseball teams hit the diamonds, and the party's soccer team was revived. Its first annual picnic in August 1915 drew some 300 people, and the numbers grew in the following summers. The next winter the party turned to euchre, another perennially favourite pastime among respectable workingmen, and eventually added whist to its repertoire. Men could enjoy smokers and bring their wives to regular dances and ice-cream socials. In 1920 the party even held a carnival and two years later it staged a highly successful professional boxing match, both as fundraising events.[53]

The ILP also eventually spawned new suburban branches – an east-end outpost in 1914, which lasted less than a year but was reborn on the eve of the 1917 election, and by the end of the war, others out in Mount Hamilton, Dundas, West Hamilton, and Homeside. In spring 1917, moreover, the party finally brought women into its fold with the formation of the Women's Independent Labor Party.[54]

With this new organizational base, combined with the swelling treasuries of the city's thriving unions, the ILP made its breakthrough into municipal politics. Beginning in January 1915 the party nominated several members in each municipal election for controller, alderman, school trustee, and even hydro commissioner. Before 1919 only a handful of these men won seats, but the small nucleus of ILP aldermen managed to establish themselves as a vocal, widely respected presence in city politics. Foremost among them was George Halcrow, a modest, thoughtful, tough-minded plumber born and raised in the city. Halcrow was party president when he was elected to city council in 1915.[55]

Moreover, late in 1917, when the Borden administration finally moved to seek a mandate under its new Unionist label, the Hamilton ILP decided to enter the fray. As the Conservatives and Liberals squabbled over whose representative would carry the Unionist banner, the ILP leaders rejected all overtures to join the Union coalition. A new optimism animated the entire labour movement across the province after the founding of the Independent Labor Party of Ontario on Dominion Day 1917, with Rollo once again as president. Halcrow was nominated to run as the party's candidate in East Hamilton and Rollo, now a school trustee, in West Hamilton. Simultaneously a group of ILP supporters in the suburban east end, a large part of which was in the rural Wentworth riding, chose the city's leading socialist, Fred Flatman, as their candidate. In the face of rampant jingoism, the solid second-place spots that Halcrow and Rollo won with 36 and 34 per cent of the vote respectively were far better than the results for other ILP candidates across the country in that election – the others almost universally lost their deposits. In

the Hamilton section of the Wentworth riding Flatman also ran second, though with only 22 per cent of the total votes. The *Industrial Banner*'s Hamilton correspondent reported that the local party emerged from the fight with renewed vigour and hundreds of new members.[56]

By the end of the war the ILP's fortunes were rising on a groundswell of working-class discontent in the city. The party trumpeted the rising resentment against retail price inflation, widely believed to be engineered by "profiteers." In a speech for the 1917 federal campaign, Rollo lambasted Sir Joseph Flavelle and his fellow meatpackers for "exploiting the public – including, to their shame, soldiers' wives and dependents – by making 75 and 80 per cent profit on pork."[57] Several ILP meetings were given over to discussions of profiteering, and a prominent theme of the activities of the ILP aldermen was ferreting out instances of profiteering on fuel or other necessities in Hamilton. Similarly, workers saw their employers making handsome profits while resisting any efforts to organize in their plants. The defeat of the great machinists' strike in 1916 had been followed by other acts of employers' intransigence in 1918 and 1919, and by the winter of 1918–19, moreover, most of the city's industries were threatening massive layoffs and wage cuts, which would gravely threaten workers' improved standards of living.

Much of the workers' anger and frustration was directed at the federal government for "its scandals, profiteers, investigations, sins of omission and commission and mismanagement," as the *Industrial Banner* phrased it, and its glaring insensitivity to the interests of workers and returned soldiers. Although various arms of the state were relentlessly urging workers to commit themselves wholeheartedly to the war effort – with exhortations to enlist, to increase productivity, to buy war bonds, to plant their own gardens, to ration meat and other commodities – many workers recognized that no such constraints were called for when it came to the profit motive of the country's capitalists. "If it is right to conscript flesh and blood, then I say likewise should Canada's whole natural resources and wealth be conscripted," Halcrow insisted before an enthusiastic crowd in the 1917 election. "Also the railways, cold storage, [and] munitions plants should be controlled and operated by the Canadian Government."[58]

What was particularly galling to local trade unionists was the Borden government's attempt to construct a non-partisan Unionist coalition without including labour. The ILP's 1917 election manifesto stressed that the overriding issue was winning the war, but that such a national effort would be possible only with the inclusion, as in Britain and the United States, of "all sections, classes, and parties in the country that have the welfare of this vast Dominion and the greater empire at heart." Labour demanded its place alongside the "big interests." This concern was met, temporarily, early in 1918 when Rollo and other trade unionists were drawn into a consultative framework with Borden's cabinet, but by the fall, when the Union government moved to ban first radical organizations and then strikes, Hamilton's union men were furious. Such measures, combined with the restrictions of the provincial government's prohibition legislation, solidified the image of a repressive, autocratic state and flew in the face of the democratic rhetoric that blanketed the war effort on the home front.[59]

The war was an unusual conjuncture that generalized class conflict beyond the sectional struggles of any single group of workers and focused all workers' attention on common enemies, whether profiteers or arbitrary governments. It also generalized, probably for the first time in Canadian history, class identity on

Thomas O'Heir, a plumber, was elected ILP controller in 1919.
(HPL, Hamilton and District Labor Council, *30th Anniversary Complimentary Souvenir*)

a national scale – a sense that workers across Canada shared the same wartime experiences – and unified Canadian working-class life, which had otherwise tended to follow the independent rhythms of individual communities or, at best, regions. The conduct of this war also saturated daily life with principles of sacrifice, public service, democracy, and justice, which could be turned back on businessmen and politicians who appeared to violate these principles.[60]

Swept along by this widespread unrest, the ILP had begun by the end of the war to shape a program of reconstruction that would maintain the greater economic security enjoyed during the war and fulfil the promise of "the war to save democracy." Echoing US president Wilson, in December 1918 the *Labor News* published the ILP platform for the municipal election as "Fourteen Points of Democracy." The party promised action on a host of issues emphasizing the protection of working-class living standards: housing, hydro-electric policy, fuel distribution, soldier resettlement, fair wages, street-railway service, taxation of property, and school fees. More successfully than ever before, the craftworkers leading the ILP had articulated the concerns of all the city's wage-earners.[61]

On New Year's Day 1919, Hamilton voters swept 9 of the ILP's 11 municipal candidates into office. The two contenders for controller, Halcrow and the barber Harry Halford, ran first and third, and Halcrow's total of 6,500 – more than 1,100 over his nearest opponent – was the largest ever won by a controller in Hamilton. The five aldermanic candidates who won seats all topped their respective polls. These seven men would now comprise one-third of the city council. In the school board race Robert Wright, a returned soldier, knocked out the widely respected manufacturer H.L. Frost, and Gordon Nelson, publisher of the *Labor News*, accomplished the same feat with Tory MP T.J. Stewart on the hydro board. In the wake of this victory the *Herald* suggested that "the elected representation of Labor interests will govern this big city." The *Spectator* accurately gauged the new mood of the time: "Labor is strong, and is determined to protect its privileges, and to see that all the talk about democracy is not going to be merely a 'voice and nothing more.'"[62]

The class polarization evident in the municipal campaign re-emerged in a March plebiscite on Adam Beck's scheme for publicly owned hydro-electric radial railway lines. A new Property Owners' Protective League, widely believed to be a thinly disguised Tory front organization, was formed in February and led the fight against public ownership. The opposition included all three daily newspapers, the entire Hamilton business community, and, most surprisingly, Stewart, the Tories' one-time champion of public power. Public ownership, which was the real issue in the campaign, had always been something of a political football in Hamilton and now, as it became clear that the labourist political movement might be carrying it, propertied interests in the city closed ranks against a fearful future. "It was a fight between classes," the *Spectator* pointed

out, "as witness the majority of 1,423 in ward 8, the stronghold of the toilers, and the rejection of the by-law in ward 2, a somewhat exclusive section." On this basis the by-law was carried.[63]

The year 1919 unquestionably represented the peak of ILP strength in Hamilton (and across the province). While the ILP members of city council won more press attention than ever before, the party's membership soared: a picnic it organized for August drew some 2,500 frolickers, and by Christmas the Central branch alone had over 1,200 card-carrying members. The party set a special committee to work to find a meeting space for a projected membership of more than 3,000, and reported a new interest in joining among "professional men, bank clerks, office men and store clerks." Some activists saw the broadening of the party's social base moving along parallel lines to that of the British Labour Party.[64] The various branches were meeting frequently and sponsoring more social events, educational discussions, and lectures than ever. ILP gatherings were turning into forums for debating and attempting to resolve the practical problems of working-class life in the city, and the ILP's municipal office-holders carried these concerns into their work at city hall. The party's growth and popularity paralleled numerous other working-class initiatives in Hamilton in 1919, including the launching of new industrial unions and demands for the eight-hour day. It was a time of great ferment among workers, and they were evidently prepared to seize on any weapon at their disposal to prevent a return to pre-war poverty and powerlessness. Thousands of them therefore turned to the political vehicle presented to them by the organized craftworkers in the fall of 1919.

The shaky Conservative administration of Sir William Hearst called a provincial election for 20 October. The Tories were suffering from internal tensions over policy and leadership, especially over prohibition and hydro-electric policy, and from the tight collar of Union government in Ottawa, which had curtailed the normal flow of patronage, a vital ingredient for retaining the party's retinue of opportunists.[65] More important, this time there was no way that the Tories could push aside class-based issues in the electoral arena. In Hamilton workers were too determined to assert their own needs, which had too often been submerged in Tory appeals to the national good or the manufacturing interest.

For its part the ILP attempted to court an alliance with the city's veterans' organizations, but in mid-August these negotiations became more complicated when Landers – since well before the war the local labour movement's best-known opportunist and now a recently discharged soldier – announced his entry into the East Hamilton contest as a "Soldier-Labour" candidate. The Tories must have arranged some agreement with Landers because they did not put up a candidate against him. Halcrow and Rollo formed the ILP ticket for the east and west ridings and began a vigorous fight against a Conservative and a Liberal in the west and Landers in the east. This campaign also saw the first ILP efforts to ally with farmers in a common front of "producers" in suburban ridings. W.A. Crockett, reeve of Barton Township and a member of the Mount Hamilton ILP, was chosen for the South Wentworth contest at a joint nominating convention of Labour and United Farmer representatives. In North Wentworth the ILP supported Frank C. Biggs, a Farmer nominee.[66]

In the campaign the two main approaches to wooing Hamilton's voters clashed head on. While parading his long roots in the labour movement, Landers wrapped himself in the Union Jack and boasted of his personal war record, first as an energetic member of the Recruiting League and then as a soldier at the front.

George Halcrow, plumber and ILP leader, was elected city alderman, later controller, and in October 1919 member of the provincial legislature for East Hamilton.

(HPL, Hamilton and District Labor Council, *30th Anniversary Complimentary Souvenir*)

Sam Landers, former garment worker and labour journalist, unexpectedly appeared as a Soldier-Labor candidate in East Hamilton in 1919. He was soundly defeated by the ILP's George Halcrow.

(HPL, Hamilton and District Labor Council, *30th Anniversary Complimentary Souvenir*)

Halcrow, like his running mate, defended the ILP's war record and managed to push the future prosperity and social security of Hamilton workers to the forefront of the campaign. Appeals to "race pride" and patriotism took a back seat to the spirit of class solidarity.

The ILP was now proclaiming a new commitment to a minimal program of social-security measures, notably mothers' allowances and old-age pensions – an emphasis that had been missing from its pre-war rhetoric and that moved it slightly closer to modern social democracy. Yet, as in the past, the concerns of the male breadwinner remained paramount. Strengthening a workingman's power on the job and in the labour market would be the best guarantee of working-class prosperity. Legislation for minimum wages and maximum hours would help,

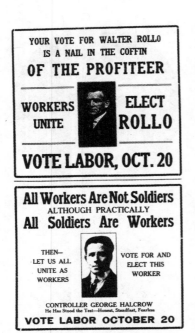

YOUR VOTE FOR WALTER ROLLO
IS A NAIL IN THE COFFIN

OF THE PROFITEER

WORKERS
UNITE

ELECT
ROLLO

VOTE LABOR, OCT. 20

All Workers Are Not Soldiers
ALTHOUGH PRACTICALLY
All Soldiers Are Workers

THEN—
LET US ALL
UNITE AS
WORKERS

VOTE FOR AND
ELECT THIS
WORKER

CONTROLLER GEORGE HALCROW
He Has Stood the Test---Honest, Steadfast, Fearless

VOTE LABOR OCTOBER 20

(*LN*, 10 Oct. 1919, 6)

but steady employment was central. The Ontario ILP's platform, Halcrow argued, promised that "to every person who is able and willing to work, congenial occupation should be provided for that person at a maximum hourly day of eight hours; at a wage that shall ensure to that person and his family adequate food, shelter and clothing, education for his children, protection in old age and adversity, with a reasonable amount of luxuries of this life." ILP sloganeering also once again pinpointed the dramatic rise in the cost of living and the role of profiteering: "Your Vote for Walter Rollo is a Nail in the Coffin of the Profiteer," one advertisement promised. The appeal to a common class interest in opposition to capital rang through the rhetoric. "Capital shall not press a crown of thorns on Labor's brow," proclaimed a *Labor News* editorial. "Capital shall not crucify Labor on a cross of gold." Yet an ILP victory would not overthrow the economic order. A lengthy article in the same paper argued for a shift in capitalist power

relations simply to enhance workers' power on the job: "When the capitalist realizes beyond a doubt that the workingman is in possession of equal legislative rights as himself, then, and only then, will he consider the rights of his employees in actual earnestness."[67]

On election day Hamilton's wage-earners threw their support behind the ILP with unrivalled solidarity. The voter turnout jumped up to 70 per cent, and Halcrow and Rollo each won 60 per cent of the vote in their constituencies. As the *Spectator* bitterly conceded the next day, the most stunning majorities were rolled up in the east-end polls: "In the thoroughly British constituency of ward 8, which sent more volunteers to France, in comparison with population, than any other section in the province, the people have decided that the war is over, that this is another day, and that the labor chariot is the vehicle that is going to transport the masses to the promised land." The paper's sobered editor saw the outcome as "one of the most decisive verdicts ever recorded by any class of Hamilton's population at the polls" and "vivid testimony to the strength of the masses when lined up in a common cause." A few weeks later the two Hamilton ILP MLAs joined nine others from across the province in a Farmer-Labour coalition government, and Rollo became Ontario's first minister of labour in the new cabinet.[68]

It was a climactic moment in Hamilton's working-class history. Building on its pre-war success, the craftworkers' party had won a place for itself at the head of a powerful working-class movement of wartime and postwar protest against the perceived injustices of profiteering, the insensitivity and arbitrariness of existing governments, and the employment practices of the city's industrialists. It was linked to larger provincial and national aspirations, and identified with international developments such as the

Planks of the I.L.P. Platform, II---THE EIGHT-HOUR DAY

THE 8 HOUR DAY.	
DAY	HOUR'S WK
Mon.	8
Tue.	8
Wed.	8
Thurs.	8
Fri.	8
Sat	4
Sun.	0
	44

THE 48 HOUR WEEK	
DAY	HOURS WK (POSSIBLY)
Mon.	9
Tue.	10
Wed.	4
Thurs.	12
Fri	10
Sat.	3
Sun	0
	48

(*IB*, 28 Nov. 1919, 1)

LABOR—"Let's have the eight-hour day, with no chances of exploitation."

British and Australian Labour parties. Evidently the Hamilton workers, like so many other parts of the Canadian working class, had high hopes that they might be standing on the threshold on a new age, the era of what one local radical liked to call the "New Democracy."[69]

Movement on the Left

The Independent Labor Party's remarkable success at galvanizing working-class discontent into a political movement of major proportions rested, in part, on the abilities of several Marxist socialists who had abandoned their long-standing hostility to labourism and joined the party. By 1918 these left-wingers were helping to energize party activity and provide it with valuable intellectual talent. The unity of the left in the city by 1919 played no small part in the ILP's success.[70]

Hamilton's tiny band of socialists had a marginal life in the city by 1910. That spring they had

splintered and drifted away from the Socialist Party of Canada, as part of the general disillusionment in Ontario with the party's Western leadership. A new Karl Marx Club reunited the "Red" fragments in the city (which now included the Jewish Workmen's Circle, formed in 1909), and returned to their patient path of Marxist education. They faced dwindling interest in their open-air meetings on Market Square and their celebrations of the Paris Commune and May Day. Late in 1912 the Hamilton comrades turned their club into a branch of the new Social Democratic Party (SDP), founded a year earlier as the predominant socialist organization in Eastern Canada, but membership remained small.[71]

During 1913 the SDP had a quickening pulse as its centre of gravity and the focus of its activities shifted eastward into the new suburban neighbourhoods filling up with British working-class newcomers, many of whom evidently had socialist sympathies. Members dropped leaflets on doorsteps and held well-attended outdoor meetings throughout the district. Every Saturday night a newsboy flogged *Cotton's Weekly*, the party's national organ. Members also sold literature from socialist publishers, set up a library of socialist classics, and rented a room for their regular meetings, bringing in a series of guest speakers who attracted good crowds. In contrast to the austere didacticism of the preceding decade, the local socialists also began hosting smokers for men and special social evenings to attract women (at least two of whom actually joined). At the end of March 1914, one smoker drew 150 participants, who butted out their last cigars singing a rousing chorus of "The Red Flag." The Social Democrats' sudden growth and apparent popularity in the east end soon had the police chief muttering threats of using the Lord's Day Act to suppress their Sunday meetings (in the end, he left them alone).[72]

That momentum was checked by the new surge of east-end labourism in the 1914 provincial election campaign to re-elect Studholme, whom the Social Democrats decided to support as "an exemplary labor representative" and "a good co-worker for any of our comrades who got elected." The local socialists' sensible course seemed to be "to keep plugging away with our literature distribution and other propaganda, and so lay the solid foundation of a Socialist constituency." The outbreak of war was far more debilitating. As early as September 1914 the *Herald* was shedding its liberal garb and denouncing the SDP's antiwar position, and urging police action against them. By the following summer, as military recruitment in the city began to slump, the Hamilton police were disrupting socialist meetings. The weekly educational forums were eventually resumed but evidently with much more limited success.[73]

By the spring and summer of 1917 the Social Democrats had new sources of inspiration. Not only had the Russian Revolution galvanized the European socialist groups in the city and brought about the creation of an International Socialist Federation, but labourist politics were also taking an important new turn with the relaunching of the Independent Labor Party of Ontario in July. The founding convention sanctioned co-operation with "other bona fide parties which are clearly not capitalistic organizations" and named the Social Democratic Party as a legitimate ally.[74]

The Hamilton Social Democrats began to make unmistakable overtures to mainstream labourites for some kind of working alliance, similar to that developed in Toronto before the war and carried forward in the pages of the *Industrial Banner*. "Now is the time to put our boasted intelligence and ability to a practical use," wrote W.S. Bruton, a local draftsman and SDP activist. "There is a good feeling here between the I.L.P. and the Social Democrats," the *Industrial Banner*'s Hamilton correspondent reported in April 1917. "The time has come when all the progressives in Canada should do as they are doing in Britain – get together and pull on the one string." The chief architect of this new strategy in Hamilton was Flatman, the radical blacksmith and leading proponent of industrial unionism. A self-taught working-class intellectual with a wide knowledge of history, economics, literature, and the socialist classics, Flatman had arrived in Hamilton with a wealth of experience in British Marxist politics under his belt. He had contributed several theoretical articles to *Cotton's Weekly* and developed a reputation as a powerful orator. He worked with a handful of articulate socialists who shared his new enthusiasm for co-operation on the left. In July Flatman wrote in the *Banner*: "Let us drop our sectarian catch words and phrases and get together and understand the principles and the possibilities of mass action."[75]

After spearheading an unsuccessful request from the union he led, the Amalgamated Society of Engineers, to affiliate as a group,[76] Flatman emerged late in 1917 as the ILP candidate in the federal Wentworth riding, which contained most of Ward Eight and several of the growing working-class suburbs beyond the city limits, as well as the town of Dundas. Although his campaign was virtually ignored in the daily press, Flatman and his associates became a whirlwind of activity on the periphery of the city. The defunct East Hamilton ILP was revived and within two weeks several new ILP branches were initiated, all loosely affiliated to a new Wentworth County ILP. "Flatman and his workers in Wentworth certainly deserve credit for the great campaign they are putting up," the Labor News declared on the eve of the election. His defeat in the predominantly rural riding was nonetheless not unexpected.[77]

Flatman's commitment to ILP work was immediately evident in a 28 December article in the Industrial Banner on "The Future of the Independent Labor Party in Canada." In it Flatman laid out a series of practical organizational suggestions, including a campaign fund, an organizational secretary, and a parliamentary correspondent to the Banner "to keep our readers well informed as to the doings of the so-called Union government, giving us, of course, a working class interpretation of all matters discussed." In the tradition of the city's Marxist movement, his main emphasis here, as in so much of his work over the next two years, was on "aggressive educational propaganda," from lectures and study groups to a vigorous labour press, to "combat the propaganda of the capitalistic press."[78] In spring 1918 he snatched up the opportunity to take over, quietly and unofficially,

LABOR RALLY
In support of
F. J. FLATMAN
LABOR'S CANDIDATE
TO-NIGHT
At Phoenix Hall, Kensington Avenue.
Chairman, Miss MacNab, business agent Amalgamated Clothing Workers.
Speakers, H. Fester, Cigar Makers' Union; H. MacKinnon, Iron Moulders' Union, the Candidate and others.
On Monday, Dec. 17, Vote For Labor
Don't be a traitor to your class.

(HS, 15 Dec. 1917, 16)

the editorial direction of the Labor News, which had passed into the hands of Gordon Nelson, a non-Marxist printer and publisher. Officially Flatman was only circulation manager, but the editorials and articles increasingly bore a subtle Marxist stamp that could only have come from his pen.[79] He campaigned ceaselessly within the ILP to build up the paper's circulation, and in December produced unquestionably the most effective propaganda for an ILP municipal campaign – the party had never before used the Labor News as successfully.[80]

Throughout this journalistic work Flatman stressed unity on the left and co-operation among "Socialists, Social Democrats, Socialist Laborites, Trade Unionists, Single Taxers, and Co-operators."[81] At the same time he used every device available to him to tug the ILP leftward and to implant a socialist perspective in his readers. He sprinkled the pages of the paper with reports on working-class militancy and radical movements from around the world, from the newly reconstructed British Labour Party to the Australian and New Zealand labour movements to Russian Bolshevism, and welcomed a growing number of local radicals as regular contributors. Flatman also wrote particularly hopefully about the new Canadian Labor Party, formed in March 1918 – on the 47th anniversary of the Paris Commune, he added – which, unlike the ILP of Ontario, was a federative organization allowing the socialists to affiliate en bloc. The local Social Democrats promptly did so.[82]

Throughout 1918 Flatman and his small core of socialist comrades played crucial roles in the ongoing programs of the suburban ILP branches, especially those in the east end and on the Mountain. In effect, they simply transferred their well-established organizational and educational work to a place inside the confines of the ILP. The SDP maintained a separate existence with its Sunday afternoon lectures and economics classes and, in fact, increased its membership substantially, until a repressive federal order-in-council forced the party to disband in October 1918. In contrast to the less adventurous Central Hamilton ILP branch, the suburban organizations sponsored educational meetings and hosted a steady stream of guest speakers, often drawn from the Ontario Social Democratic stable of orators and writers, such as Toronto's Jimmy Simpson. They also aggressively promoted sales of the *Industrial Banner* and *Labor News*. Also in contrast to the Central Hamilton body, these branches followed the socialist practice of admitting men and women equally to their meetings. In October a series of Flatman's articles on "The Food Profiteer" was published as a pamphlet, and the Mount Hamilton party set out to distribute thousands of copies. Early in 1919 the East Hamilton labourites also started up two study groups on "Sociology, Industrial History, Municipal Science and Political Economy," and later that year organized a weekly Open Forum in a local movie house featuring labourist and socialist speakers. For a few months early in 1920, the Mount Hamilton group even ran a Labour Church.[83]

In these ways the suburban ILP branches were something of a loyal opposition within the Hamilton ILP, a parallel political tendency to the larger, more cautious Central branch. As the dominant voice of this tendency, Flatman had acquired considerable stature in the party. When the West Hamilton and North Barton ILP branches were organized in January 1919, he joined Studholme and other well-known ILP leaders as a platform speaker. He was similarly prominent in the hydro-radial campaign that spring. At the Ontario ILP convention in April he was still urging avoidance of "sectarian catch phrases" and altered his resolution calling for the "common ownership of industry" to "democratic ownership" after objections were raised by Harry Fester. The respect he had accumulated with some party leaders was evident early in May when ILP controller Halcrow nominated him for a seat on a new city housing commission and won a three-to-two vote in Flatman's favour on the Board of Control. The Board's decision, however, was later overturned in a city-council meeting, where the ILP representatives split[84] – a moment coinciding with Flatman's ejection from the editor's chair at the *Labour News* for his support of radical industrial unionism.

As the debate picked up over a postwar strategy for the working class, the alliance between labourism and socialism became increasingly uneasy. As Flatman himself observed, labour was "at the fork of the roads, one way leads to Queensland, and the other to Russia."[85]

Decline and Fall

In the winter of 1919–20 the Hamilton ILP reached a plateau of strength to which it clung for much of the next year before beginning a rapid decline. The party's municipal campaigns of 1920 and 1921 were its most ambitious, featuring Halford and Halcrow as mayoralty candidates at the head of large slates, including their first women to run for the Board of Education. But in each case it was unable to surpass its 1919 city-council strength. By the spring of 1921, moreover, the party organization was deteriorating, and the Central branch could report only 110 paid-up members (down from more than 1,200 late in 1919).[86] Some rallying occurred for the federal election in fall 1921, in which the standard-bearers were Thomas O'Heir, a plumber and ILP controller, and E.J. Etherington, a former Anglican priest who had drifted away from his church. Each won respectable second-place spots, which prompted the *Spectator* to suggest that the party had emerged "with its prestige much increased."[87] But in the 1922 and 1923 municipal elections its city-council representation was slashed,[88] and in the provincial election of June 1923 Halcrow and Rollo went down to crushing defeat at the hands of the Conservatives. "The glory of the I.L.P. is departed," a pro-Tory labour paper gloated that summer, "its prestige is no more."[89] After that date the ILP ran no candidates in provincial or federal elections until 1931. Municipal representation fell to only two aldermanic seats in 1925. The Central and East End ILP branches were the only ones still standing.[90]

What had happened? Why did the craftsmen's party suffer such a rapid decline in the early 1920s after its spectacular successes in the immediate postwar period? The overarching cause was the combined impact of Hamilton employers' open-shop campaigns and the postwar economic crisis – a time when unions of both the craft and industrial varieties were systematically destroyed in strikes or undermined by belligerent management policies. Most of the new

unions collapsed and the membership of the older ones shrank dramatically. For more than five years after 1920, unemployment further weakened workers' power to resist this assault. Pro-labour propaganda diminished as both of the city's labour papers cut back to monthly publication by summer 1921, and their pages were increasingly filled with stale clippings from US labour journals. This collapse of Hamilton's unions was part of a national pattern of defeat,[91] and lay behind Canadian labour's failure to match the British Labour Party's success in permanently replacing the Liberal Party in an essentially two-party system. The financial and organizational base had been cut away, much as it was in the United States, but it had never been as thoroughly established as in Britain (or Australia and New Zealand).

For the ILP, a political movement that relied so heavily on volunteer efforts and union funding, Hamilton workers' defeats and consequent demoralization in the early 1920s were decisive in its decline after 1919. In that context, the old Tory politics of deference made inroads once again, and the emotional 1921 election campaign in defence of the tariff forced many workers to chose between the preservation of their jobs and a less certain labourist alternative of longer-term social security. Many cynically rejected them both by not voting.

The consequences for the ILP were grave. The unity of 1917–19 fractured on the shoals of conflict over an appropriate political approach to coping with the crisis; and Hamilton's brand of labourism began to show its weaknesses and limitations. Its inability to respond decisively and creatively to the challenge facing workers further disillusioned the party's working-class following. The disintegration of the party, therefore, can be seen as a dynamic process of assault from without and decay from within.

Among local labour leaders, Harry Halford, a barber, long-time executive member of the Trades and Labor Council, and an ILP member of city council, was a voice for caution, moderation, and accommodation with politicians and the business community.

(HPL, Hamilton and District Labor Council, *30th Anniversary Complimentary Souvenir*)

The seeds of a right-left split had been germinating since the arrival of the socialists inside the ILP's ranks in 1917. Flatman's nomination as an ILP candidate that year had brought grumbling from "strong union men" about "revolutionary talk and work in the Labor ranks." One of the foremost critics was Fester, a leading propagandist for the single tax. At the 1919 Ontario ILP convention Fester spoke for many of the Hamilton leaders when he leaped to his feet to oppose Flatman's resolution endorsing "common ownership of industry." "Thousands of workers are supporting us rather than the Socialist parties because we are holding aloof from the latter," he contended. "Public ownership of public utilities is all right, but collectivism in general – no." Similar outbursts followed the passage of a collective-ownership resolution two years later. Late in 1921 the Central ILP finally moved to silence such sentiments by barring the East Hamilton and Mount Hamilton branches from helping to choose a federal candidate, on the grounds that too many "Reds" were showing up when those units participated. At the same time the socialist-inspired clause calling for

"Democratic Control of Industry" was dropped from the local party's platform.[92]

These anti-Marxist sentiments got much more intense in mid-1919, when the right-left tensions exploded over the question of an appropriate industrial strategy. It was Winnipeg, not Russia, that forced the split. The craft unionists recoiled in horror at the rise of the One Big Union sentiment because it appeared once again that the socialists wanted to destroy craft unionism. They therefore deposed Flatman as *Labor News* editor and installed Rollo in his place. The split was formalized when Flatman and his radical colleagues brought out *New Democracy*, but then this venture in radical journalism collapsed in the early fall, in the wake of the Hamilton convention of the Trades and Labor Congress of Canada and just at the moment when the ILP leadership was pulling off its greatest triumph in the provincial elections. A revived *New Democracy* appeared a month later with none other than the red-baiting Fester in the editor's chair. At an ILP rally during the municipal election campaign at the end of the year, ILP alderman Thomas O'Heir proudly alluded to a crisis comparable to the Winnipeg General Strike, "which, unknown to the citizens, the city would have faced last summer had it not been for the stabilizing influence of the Labor members of the city council."[93]

The radicals for their part were inspired by the Western Canadian example, and an increasingly sectarian tone crept into their activities as they drew the battle lines with their erstwhile political allies. At first there were no overt breaks with the ILP. In July 1919, for example, *New Democracy* indicated it would support, "wholeheartedly, the candidates of the Canadian Labor Party and the I.L.P. in every campaign which resolves itself into a clear cut contest between real labor interests and the opponents of same." Yet

Flatman's fixation on the revolutionary industrial unionism of the General Workers' Union and then the OBU revealed a workplace-oriented turn in his radicalism, and an impatience with labourism. By the fall he was sneering from his editor's chair that all ILP candidates accepted "the right of capitalists to exploit labour," and, if elected, would "do all in their power to perpetuate the present competitive system." Workers who voted for them should "not expect them to lead you out of the wilderness of toil and exploitation."[94]

The same two streams of labour politics were emerging at this point throughout the western world. During 1920, as the OBU experiment collapsed, small numbers of Hamilton radicals were being drawn towards the new North American Communist movement. The Communists' efforts to redirect union strategies and to organize the unemployed during the 1920s faced steady hostility from established labour leaders in the city. Similar battles emerged in the Ontario Section of the Canadian Labor Party (CLP). Originally organized in 1918 and revived in 1921, the CLP had always differed in structure from the ILP in that individual unions as well as local labour parties and socialist societies could affiliate as organizations. The Communists found that this structure gave them more room to manoeuvre and by 1925 had firm control over the organization. In 1922 Hamilton's Central ILP consequently decided not to renew its affiliation, and less than a year later the Trades and Labour Council pulled out. In 1924 the local Communists nonetheless took the initiative in pulling together a new Labor Representation Political Association modelled on the CLP to co-ordinate working-class political activity in the city. The Trades and Labour Council boycotted it, but the local ILP branches and some 25 individual unions joined, until the aggressive Communist presence prompted them

to withdraw a year later. The Association made a pitiful showing in the federal and provincial elections of 1925 and 1926.[95]

Communism never did pose an effective challenge to labourism in Hamilton, but the anti-Marxist, anti-revolutionary biases of local labour leaders nonetheless stiffened after 1919. Recoiling into the narrow base that was left for them by the open-shop onslaught of the early 1920s, the craft unionists who still manned the declining ILP expended more and more precious energy in red-baiting and denunciations of Communist activity. In their frustration with this labourist attitude, the radicals often indulged in the same sectarianism that had hindered their work before the war. The intransigence and restraint of the ILP leadership had given them good cause, and it is difficult to imagine the preservation of that fragile unity of 1917–19 that both sides had supported in the context of surging working-class confidence and self-consciousness. Once unemployment and employers' belligerence had taken their toll, the absence of that mass support and momentum reduced the urgency for mutual tolerance between the right- and left-wing camps within labour's ranks, and older patterns resurfaced.

Working Men's Liberalism

Left-wingers were not alone in their criticism of Hamilton labourism. The declining support of voters and, even more, the massive boycott of the ballot box that saw a drop of 10,000 voters between 1919 and 1923 indicate that the city's wage-earners were disillusioned with the ILP for its failure to fulfil the "new vision" that had been on the horizon in 1919.[96] The party's poor record related, in the end, to problems rooted in its ideology and practice. In many ways, as the ideology of a movement of working-class protest, it was compromised from the start and, once given access to power, could not meet the challenge of the postwar crisis or the expectations of its newly won following.

Like the British Labour Party and unlike many European socialist parties or even large parts of the Socialist Party of America, Hamilton's craftworker-politicians usually preferred to discuss issues of practical and immediate importance and seldom presented lengthy or lofty statements of their perspectives on the world. The official objective of the Ontario ILP, on whose platform the Hamilton labourites ran after 1917, promised only "to promote the political, economic and social interests of people who live by their labor, mental or manual, as distinguished from those who live by profit upon the labor of others." The platform ended with the simple but ambiguous declaration: "We stand for the industrial freedom of those who toil and the political liberation of those who for so long have been denied justice."[97] It was common to hear ILP candidates promising simply "a square deal" for workers. Consequently any attempt to examine the elusive ideological frame of reference of Hamilton labourism must cut through a thick fog and piece together many scattered fragments from men who often revealed strikingly contradictory tendencies in their thinking.

Labourism as manifested in this one Southern Ontario city was part of a much larger political phenomenon that had spread throughout Canada and other parts of the British Empire.[98] The craftworkers who headed the Hamilton ILP never completely abandoned a 19th-century view of society rooted in Radical liberalism, which had counterposed "a sense of fraternity and obligation to the arbitrariness of individual self-interest," but also saw the root of social problems primarily in "privilege and political inequality."[99] Their outlook reflected their own relative independence as producers who insisted on respect and personal freedom but respected manufacturers as fellow producers. In general they saved their harshest criticisms for the monopolists and "special privilege men" who interfered with productive life and threatened working-class living standards. Throughout its history the Hamilton ILP included the single tax in its platform, a cause dear to Studholme's heart, and Fester, party president by 1920, campaigned tirelessly against "landlordism." The villains whom the party most commonly attacked were Dominion Power, the local gas and coal companies, and the unscrupulous but elusive "profiteer." While ILP leaders might lambaste specific industrialists for their heartlessness, they never questioned the right of those businesses to exist in an idealized society. The only public ownership planks in their platform were aimed at utilities, and, by the end of the war, at banks and undefined "national sources of wealth."[100] Moreover, they vigorously resisted any broadening of the public-ownership strategy to the socialists' vision of a "co-operative commonwealth." This strain in labourist politics reflected an earlier stage of capitalist development that had seen less social distance between entrepreneur and craftsman and that had incorporated a more crucial role for the skilled worker than corporate capitalist industry generally allowed (though the many building tradesmen in the party would still experience more of these older relations of production).

Oddly enough, this artisanal sense of co-partnership with industrial capitalists had been reinforced in the early 20th century due to the fragility of so many of the manufacturing industries in which unionized craft groups worked. In consumer-goods production in particular — stoves, cigars, clothing, shoes, brooms — workers had been thrown into defensive alliances with their employers in both union-label and tariff

THE MAN ON TOP

THE DOMINANT "PARTNER"

The regional labour newspaper
Industrial Banner published this image
at the height of the workers' revolt
in Canada, suggesting the common
plight of workers and their employers.
(*IB*, 9 May 1919, 1)

campaigns. The particularly bumptious, competitive boosterism that characterized Hamilton business and industry in this period also spread into the ranks of organized labour; the *Labor News* under Landers's editorship, for example, often exhorted workers to buy Hamilton-made goods, and a number of labour leaders, including Studholme, joined the public protest against the absorption of the Bank of Hamilton in 1915. Hamilton labourites were thus accustomed, through years of campaigning to defend local industry, to show concern for the general welfare of the economic status quo. A pinch of Tory populism got into the radical pot.[101]

In the uncertain postwar economic climate, Hamilton's business community was delighted to find the ILP taking a keen interest in trying to promote better relations between workers and their bosses and in ensuring the general health of the city's industries. Fester, the former

cigar-maker, was again a key figure here. When he took over *New Democracy* late in 1919, he set out to make the paper a leading mouthpiece for the manufacturers' "Made-in-Canada" movement. His advertising salesmen presented industrialists with a letter from Sir John Willison, on the letterhead of the Canadian Reconstruction Association, endorsing the paper, and large advertising contracts quickly flowed in from major local firms, all the way up to the Steel Company of Canada. In April 1920 Fester turned out a fat "Made in Canada" issue – the first of many – festooned with a huge drawing of capital and labour shaking hands. Buying goods "produced in Canada by Canadian workmen" would "return to us the blessings of a prosperous and happy nation."[102]

The more important question was the tariff. In the postwar period Hamilton's labour leaders showed none of the ambiguity on the issue that had characterized their response to reciprocity in 1911. In August 1919 the Hamilton Trades and Labor Council endorsed the pet scheme of the Canadian Manufacturers' Association, a "permanent scientific tariff commission" in order to remove the issue from politics and "place it on a non-partisan, scientific basis." The following spring the local ILP went on the offensive when its provincial parent body adopted a low-tariff plank. In a lengthy editorial the *Labor News* raised the Tories' favourite argument against lowering tariffs: that the city's industries "would be in a sorry plight under a free trade regime." The Central and East Hamilton branches both attacked the Ontario ILP decision and forced the party to retreat on the issue. In the 1921 federal election campaign both O'Heir and Etherington declared that they were "squarely and unequivocally for protection for our manufacturers."[103]

With their sober sense of responsibility and commitment to preserving industrial life, then, the ILP's craftsmen-politicians found themselves in alliance with the very industrialists against whom Hamilton workers had been expressing their anger in 1919. This did not make them charlatans; most, in fact, were sincere men of principle. The strident class-conscious rhetoric of Studholme's career and of all subsequent ILP campaigns did not, in their minds, contradict the spirit of community consciousness. Rather, the two strains were complementary in an ideology that emphasized full political equality for workers within capitalist society. The workingmen who headed the craftworkers' party regularly mounted the hustings to decry the way in which the working class was excluded from arenas of power in Canadian society. It was not the mere existence of rampant capitalist power that irked these men, but rather the exclusiveness and unchecked tyranny – the "classes versus the masses." Social injustice was primarily political. What they demanded was simply the right for working people to the full promise of liberal democracy, to be able to share power with other social groups, including capital. While the party proposed a small package of reforms to ensure the social security of the working class, representation became an end in itself.[104]

This limited social vision revealed an idealized, liberal view of the state. Parliamentary democracy, the labourists insisted, should allow for full access of all citizens to a neutral state apparatus that could service an undefined common good. To ensure that the interests of the working class were protected, the ILP platform in each provincial and federal election emphasized sweeping aside all unjust restrictions on access to political power – from property qualifications and election deposits to obstacles to full female suffrage – along with introducing some form of proportional representation, and, most important, sending labour representatives to the legislative halls of all three levels of government. To keep the legislators close to the popular will the party proposed systems of referendum, initiative, and recall, and insisted that undemocratic institutions such as the Senate should be abolished or made elective. The rhetoric suggested that parliamentary democracy was the product of popular (and ongoing) struggle against privileged power, but had been subverted by loosely defined "interests." The liberal-democratic state was not viewed as an instrument of hegemony for the working-class majority.

In this sense the creation of an independent political base for workers paralleled the emergence of a more professional, bureaucratic unionism at the turn of the century. Both moves represented attempts by craftworkers to solidify formal, institutionalized niches for workers in a hierarchically stratified, corporate capitalist society. "Labor had just as much right to representation in the City council and governments of the country as had capital," the president of the Workingmen's Political Association had asserted back in 1903, "and only by electing candidates of their own would workingmen get what was coming to them." This theme recurred in ILP rhetoric. "Are not the manufacturers and others of their class represented? Any number of lawyers too? Why not the workers?" an irate worker wrote to the press during the 1911 ILP provincial campaign. Some two years later, in exhorting his fellow moulders to independent political action, James Roberts, a future editor of the *Labor News*, stated that their goal should be "to cultivate and consolidate the whole of the masses when by aggressive but not dominant action labor may have its fair share of what is due to them who are toiling." The Hamilton ILP made the right of workers to participate in a wartime government a central theme of the 1917 federal election campaign. In January 1919, basking in their party's electoral successes at city hall, the new ILP office-holders emphasized to a victory rally that "primarily they intended to legislate for the best interests of the community wholly – not class."[105]

After the electoral gains of January 1919, which gave the party a third of the city-council seats and half of the Board of Control, the ILP repeatedly shied away from flexing its new-found strength. In a highly symbolic moment early that year, as the new city councillors began jockeying for committee chairmanships, the ILP group announced its decision not to contest any of those positions. When a deadlock developed over who would chair the important Works Committee and O'Heir was nominated, Halcrow broke the tie by voting against O'Heir, reasoning that as a workingman his colleague "had not sufficient time to devote to the work." A year later the ILP aldermen pursued a similar course. In

the grim days of the party's decline in 1922, Rollo was still insisting that the party "was not looking for control, but rather fair representation in the City Council."[106]

Tied to labour's view of political economy, the state, and its role as a party was an unflinching commitment to gradualism. "To obtain a perfect state of society when everything shall be changed at a given time, even altho [*sic*] the majority are in favor of it, seems to me impossible," Halcrow wrote in 1916. It was this orientation that prompted Rollo, as minister of labour, repeatedly to urge patience in anticipation of new social legislation from the Farmer-Labour government. "Nobody has any need to get excited because the Ontario government hasn't legislated to date for the eight-hour day and inserted the fair wage clause in government contracts," the *Labor News*, which he helped to edit, insisted in 1922. "Don't let us overlook the fact that Rome wasn't built in a day."[107]

The commitment to gradualist politics was well-established in the labourist tradition, not least because of the long series of small victories that British workingmen had achieved within industrial capitalist society.[108] The social formation in Canada, as in Britain, rarely presented itself as a rigid and stratified monolith that required a sudden cataclysmic overthrow. Yet, for many of Hamilton's workers in the early 1920s, the ILP's caution and commitment to gradualism must have seemed inadequate to the needs of a working-class community under assault by employers and unemployment.

The Burden of Office

With this range of ideological proclivities, the ILP in office increasingly looked like a weak, uncertain alternative in Hamilton politics and government. Party representatives elected to city council in particular had difficulty establishing a

As editor of *New Democracy*, Harry Fester, a former cigar-maker, fought leftists within the ILP and then cut his links with the party and supported the Conservatives.

(HPL, Hamilton and District Labor Council, *30th Anniversary Complimentary Souvenir*)

distinctive political program. Most of their work on council was either routine administration, or agitation for better working conditions for civic employees and unspecific demands for some modest action to deal with rising consumer prices or housing shortages. Like Studholme in the Ontario legislature, they did add a new note to council sessions in that they could be relied upon to express the workingman's critique of measures that came before them. But they rarely introduced substantial reforms of their own that would dramatically improve the conditions of life and work for Hamilton's working class.

In January 1919 Flatman's *Labor News* urged the new ILP aldermen to proceed promptly with a program for municipal ownership of public utilities, with Dominion Power as a major priority. But a month later he was lamenting the aimless drift in the party caucus. "Have the two controllers in particular been placed in their positions and then left entirely to their own resources?" he asked. He urged the party to specify a clear legislative program "that would act as a compass to our public representatives on the various bodies and function as the catholic rallying point for our rapidly growing army of adherents and sympathizers," and stressed

tighter party discipline among the ILP office-holders. His proposal was ignored, and a year later even his adversary on the right, Fester, was concerned. Surveying the disappointing electoral results in January 1920, Fester argued: "If the Labor Party in Hamilton is to maintain its standing in the community, a definite municipal policy will have to be adopted ... at the earliest possible date."[109]

Fester also noted the inevitable result of this lack of political focus: the electorate would make its choice on the basis of the qualities of individual candidates. That could mean long-term popularity for men like Ward-Eight alderman Sam Lawrence, the handsome English stone-cutter. But the party had also drawn in growing numbers of men who hoped to ride to power on the crest of ILP popularity. Chester Walters, an accountant, had joined the party in 1914 and built up a personal following in its ranks before running successfully as an independent candidate for mayor the next winter. By the 1920 municipal election the ILP slate contained a handful of men who seemed to have hopped on the bandwagon – petit-bourgeois figures such as Alfred Hurst, a tobacconist; E.A. Fearnside, a wood dealer; and Charles Brayley, a contractor. Fester worried about "the number of old line politicians that are joining the party."[110]

The real problem became opportunism among ILP leaders whose credentials in the movement had previously been sterling. Gradually after 1920 the Hamilton ILP watched in dismay as some of its representatives drifted out of the party along careerist paths. As early as April 1920, reports were heard that some ILP aldermen were no longer attending the regular Saturday caucuses, and a year and half later the Central ILP considered a resolution that the ILP councillors "be asked to attend at least one meeting of this branch each month." By 1923 the party had to make conferring with the executive at least once a month a condition for being an ILP candidate, and late in the year was lamenting "the absence of our elected representatives from the meetings of this branch."[111] Between 1921 and 1923 alderman Archie Burton, controllers O'Heir and Etherington, and Hydro commissioner Gordon Nelson all resigned or were expelled from the party for their individualistic behaviour in city politics.[112]

By 1923 these renegades had the support of another defector from Labour's ranks, Harry Fester. Early in 1923 Fester, by then a well-paid commissioner on the Ontario Minimum Wage Board, turned his newspaper against the ILP, whom he took to calling "exploiters of labor." In August 1923 he changed the paper's name to the less controversial *Canadian Labor World*, and slowly its editorial policy moved towards support of the Ferguson Conservatives. In the 1926 federal election campaign, Fester appeared on a Tory platform in London, Ontario.[113]

If the party had increasing difficulty convincing municipal voters that it had anything distinctive to offer, the failure of the Farmer-Labour government at Queen's Park to meet the expectations of Hamilton workers, even with Rollo in the cabinet, weakened the ILP irreparably as a political force in the city. The coalition government had been an uneasy arrangement from the beginning, owing to the important divisions between the farmers and workers over key labour movement demands. Only three months after the election Halcrow warned about possible "dissension and disruption" between the "wage-paying members" in the Farmer caucus and the wage-earners in the ILP's ranks over the issues of "minimum wage, pension schemes, and the eight-hour day." He also crossed swords with farmer representatives over ending the prohibition on beer consumption. In July 1921 a Central

ILP meeting erupted with anger against the provincial government for the low wages paid to labourers on government contracts and the failure to implement an unemployment-insurance measure and minimum-wage legislation at a time when the city's manufacturers were slashing wages and laying off thousands. A campaign was subsequently launched to win support for a minimum-wage act. By March 1922 the Hamilton Unemployed Association was loudly denouncing Rollo for "the disgraceful situation of the unemployed in this city."[114]

Halcrow became the mouthpiece for all the frustrations with the cautious, limited legislative program of the Farmer-Labour government. Although chosen to head the ILP caucus in the House, he had not been happy with the coalition from the beginning, and his increasingly vocal criticisms of the government's failure to implement labour measures eventually forced him to cross the house and sit in opposition. His performance, however, was purely an individualistic act of conscience, not a political move to reorient party policy, and Mary McNab, the city's leading female labour leader, angrily denounced him at the Ontario ILP convention for his lack of solidarity with labour. When the Hamilton branch of the party met to choose its standard-bearers for the 1923 provincial campaign, Halcrow announced to a dismayed audience that he could not accept the ILP nomination as long as it required commitment to a Farmer-Labour coalition. He ran in East Hamilton as an independent – "Allan Studholme's Logical Successor," his advertisement proclaimed – without an official ILP opponent. In the end the efforts to construct a "producers' alliance" at Queen's Park had torn the party apart.[115]

As an unrepentant defender of the Farmer-Labour coalition, Rollo could face the West Hamilton electors with only a paltry list of social reforms, including mothers' allowances, minimum wages for women, and revisions of the Workmen's Compensation Act, all enacted in the first session in 1920 and based on work already begun by the previous Hearst administration. With the party organization in disarray and his own record so uninspiring, Rollo, like Halcrow, was doomed to defeat. Ironically the ILP platform, which Rollo had quoted frequently to eager audiences in 1919, had concluded with the phrase "performance is better than promise." By 1923 Hamilton's workers evidently recognized that the party's performance had been abysmal, and the 42.5 per cent of the electorate that bothered to vote overwhelmingly rejected the ILP candidates.[116]

In the end the craftworkers' party crumbled because of its failure to fulfil the promise of the "new vision" that was so pervasive in the working class in 1919. Instead of undertaking a vigorous, imaginative program of social reconstruction that would have seriously attempted to prevent a return to pre-war living standards for working-class families, or at least of resisting the anti-labour assault with some vigour, ILP leaders wallowed in the confusion and caution of a narrowly circumscribed ideology and a gradualist orientation to politics. In a final gasp of exasperation with the ILP leaders he had tried to work with for two years, Flatman had sounded a sour, yet prophetic note amidst the post-election euphoria of October 1919: "A Labor party looking towards the Manchester School of Economics for inspiration is foredoomed to failure. Failure to the point that when the working class have tried them on the political field, when they have been weighed in the balance and found wanting ... they will be thrown into the discard, as other parties have been before."[117]

With no clear municipal program and a willingness to postpone and compromise provincial action – in a context of rising unemployment, falling wages, and union-busting – the party could neither hold onto wayward members nor maintain the electoral support of the working class. In this situation the hope of social transformation inherent in its 1919 electoral success evaporated, and Hamilton's workers turned away from politics once again to seek out older, more limited strategies of survival.

18

(*Worker*, 25 March 1931, 1)

Unassailable Rights

IN JANUARY 1919 A WORKINGMAN sat down to write a long letter to the *Spectator* on the subject of "unemployment and unrest." He closed with a blunt warning:

> When a man has walked many miles, for many days together, and asked for work at endless places, only to be told "nothing doing," and when the landlord and the grocer have to be paid and nothing to pay with, then is the time he lies open to anything going, and sees no comfort in the promise that times will improve.[1]

His was not an isolated voice. He was part of a rising chorus of anxious debate about the future in working-class Hamilton, especially the uncertainties of wage-earning. Those without jobs were indeed listening to "anything going" for answers to their plight.

Across the globe popular agitations of many kinds were widening the boundaries of the public sphere and drawing more participants into vigorous debate about the nature of citizenship in the postwar world.[2] In Hamilton determined unionists and ILP activists renewed their pre-war momentum and took a stand on the contested terrain of what everyone began calling "reconstruction." At the same time the crucible of social crisis after the war produced important new voices, each of which arose as a distinctive response to the unusual circumstances. Among those voices, three in particular – businessmen, veterans, and Communists – emerged to argue their cases publicly and largely from outside the structures of formal electoral politics, each of them seeking to establish a new kind of political agenda. Each would quickly congeal into a permanent movement with its own institutions and ideology. Confronting the postwar crisis provided them all with a script for constructing local events over the next 20 years. Central to each project was a redefinition of citizenship and of the entitlements attached to it.

All of these groups soon found that no issue in interwar Hamilton was more urgent than working-class unemployment. There were those (on the right and the left) who believed that the unemployed themselves might easily bond as a cohesive social movement.[3] The sight of crowds of such men hanging around street corners, huddled on park benches, or angrily pushing their way into relief offices sometimes troubled politicians, policemen, businessmen, or various "respectable" types. Occasionally a group of disgruntled men coalesced into a spontaneous demonstration to demand immediate action from city officials.[4]

Despite common frustrations with local relief policies, joblessness had distinctive patterns – skilled versus unskilled, men versus women, single versus married, young versus old, Anglo-Canadians versus European immigrants – that did not necessarily create the social cement of solidarity. Nor did the lack of employment lead directly to any specific consciousness about social injustice. Dispensers of charity and moral judgment had long been equating a lack of work with personal failure, and many wage-earners must have blamed themselves and looked for private solutions to their dilemmas. Still, as the shorter slumps of 1907–9 and 1913–15 had made clear, major downturns in the business cycle could not be blamed on the workers, and could provoke bitter resentment. So too could the long stretches of unemployment and underemployment in the 1920s and 1930s. Yet none of the diverse responses to these conditions were predictable.

The unemployed did not gel naturally and easily into a coherent political force. Rather, they were exposed to persistent efforts to address them as an amorphous body that required specific kinds of intervention. Businessmen, veterans, and Communists each had their own perspectives on joblessness, based on their larger political projects. They developed particular political discourses and practices to deal with the unemployed in the city; and the relative discomfort of unionists and labourists with the unemployed heightened the importance of these other players. Indeed, the interaction of the three groups would create the specific politics of unemployment through much of the period. Ultimately the shock of mass unemployment in the 1930s pushed past these forces into the formal political arena.

The Call of Service

Local figures at the pinnacles of bourgeois power and authority in Hamilton, like their counterparts throughout the Western world, were deeply troubled by the shockingly new ideas about how postwar society should be reconstructed – ideas that were percolating throughout working-class neighbourhoods at the end of the war. Particularly disturbing were the growing demands for more public regulation through various forms of state intervention – from prohibition to mothers' allowances to old-age pensions to a legislated eight-hour day. "There is on every hand a tendency to exalt the state," wrote the editor of the *Canadian Banker*. "Men appeal to Government to cure every ill, to solve every tangle, to regulate every field of human endeavour."[5]

Some within the Canadian business community had proposed a more aggressive use of the state to guide capitalism, through, for example, the short-lived regulatory Board of Commerce, but that enthusiasm withered quickly after the urgency of war evaporated.[6] Far more people in that community would have been much happier to return to the social dynamics of the pre-war era, when they had been accustomed to exercising relatively unencumbered command over economic, social, and cultural life in the city. The Conservative Party was an important vehicle for focusing attention on the large economic issues of the postwar economy and for rallying resistance to the labourist challenge in the electoral arena, but redirecting public life away from menacing projects and ideologies required a more concerted effort to take charge of civil society. The local elite consequently began to search for ways to rebuild social cohesion through their own leadership and to promote an alternative reconstruction through the familiar channels of private enterprise, voluntarism, individual initiative, and moral probity. In this process of redefining their private interests as public good, local businessmen struck the earnest posture of high-minded statesmen in the cause of "service." In attempting to convince workers and others of the legitimacy of their project, they practised an artful politics of reassurance.

Business got advice and admonition from many sides to rally behind this call to service. On Sunday mornings, seated in the pews of the city's grandest Christian churches, they sometimes

DISPOSSESSING THE GOOSE

Newspaper images regularly depicted radicalism as alien and destructive.
(*HS*, 24 Feb. 1919, 4)

heard lessons from concerned clergy who promoted the new forms of social reconciliation under discussion in the large national denominations of which they were part. During the war church leaders had fused their moral fervour with the international struggle against "kaiserism" and imagined a postwar world of renewed social purpose. Towards the end of the war the national conferences of the leading Protestant churches proclaimed far-reaching agendas of social reform. The most widely discussed was the statement of the Methodist Church, passed at a General Conference that met in Hamilton in fall 1918. It called for "nothing less than a transference of the whole of economic life from a basis of competition and profits to one of co-operation and service." The national interfaith agency, the Social Service Council of Canada, carried this message most aggressively, publishing a new monthly magazine, *Social Welfare*, to spread the word. Even the Catholic press reprinted the similarly visionary program of US bishops in 1919.[7]

These messages sounded radical. Yet listening more carefully, churchgoers might actually have been struck by how this language and the measures associated with it were intended first and foremost to build social cohesion through an understanding of mutual responsibility among contending social groups. The much-discussed desire for "co-operation" rather than "competition" was not an invocation of socialist collectivism, but a call, started well before the war, for an infusion of Christian principles to guide relationships between classes within industrial capitalism. Christianity and its diverse ministers would be the arbiters of harmonious, mutually respectful social relations. Since the turn of the century, some local clergy had delivered that message in their annual Labour Sunday sermons (on the day before Labour Day) and in the midst of major industrial crises.[8]

Yet in 1919, as in the past, the major churches and most of their local clergy made no direct overtures to the Canadian labour movement and, indeed, grew steadily more uncomfortable with the nationwide workers' revolt that was unfolding by 1919. As the Methodists' own national magazine admitted, their national gatherings spoke for "the privileged classes" and included no one from "the underprivileged classes." The most that the local Ministerial Association would do was to offer its services as a mediator of social tensions. With the activist clergyman W.E. Gilroy gone, the outspoken Presbyterian Banks Nelson, who several times in 1918 shocked the city by praising the Bolsheviks and who regularly addressed working people, was largely a voice in the wilderness. Local sermons were more likely to be warnings against radicalism than cries of solidarity with labour. The churches (and such interdenominational

organizations as the YMCA and YWCA) turned instead to leading employers and supported their efforts at corporate welfarism. In 1920 Laidlaw Presbyterian's minister R.M. Dicky, for example, sang the praises of profit-sharing. When the workers' revolt erupted in the Methodists' own publishing house in 1921, the church helped to break the continent-wide printers' strike.[9]

Some businessmen were loud in their protests against the delivering of political advice from churches. The Steel Company's Cyrus Birge argued from the floor of the Methodists' 1918 conference that the political statement about working for "co-operation and service" would simply incite more dissent, and the next month Toronto's S.J. Parsons, past-president of the Canadian Manufacturers' Association, used a talk at Hamilton's Centenary Methodist Church to kick off a campaign against the Methodist pronouncement. When the regional Hamilton Conference considered the statement a few months later (in the immediate wake of the Winnipeg General Strike), the clergy and lay members agreed to a compromise version that condemned both profiteering and strikes. The Presbyterian General Assembly, which also met in Hamilton in summer 1919, reached a similarly cautious position, arguing that both capital and labour were jointly obliged "to serve the people as a whole." Across the country a few radicalized clergymen drifted out of their pulpits to join the political struggle, including Hamilton's E.J. Etherington, an Anglican minister who had resigned his charge in 1917 to take up factory work and who had become an ILP candidate in the federal election of 1921. In practice local clergy were generally far more concerned with the saving of individual souls than with any expansive social programs.[10] Some of the religious rhetoric of "social service" may have rubbed off on Hamilton's business leaders, who were generally faithful churchgoers and often active in lay administration, although they were preponderantly adherents of the more cautious Presbyterian and Anglican churches.

Yet businessmen also had their own secular projects. They beamed a message of co-operation and service at workers, who, they believed, should be concerned about the long-term health of the firms they worked for – from the productivity of particular plants to the market protection guaranteed by tariffs. At the national level, the Canadian Reconstruction Association took up the role of corporate statesman to turn citizens' attention towards the concerns of national "efficiency." Hamilton's capitalists took steps of their own. Early in 1919 wire manufacturer H.L. Frost launched a project known as the "Open Forum" to encourage discussion of postwar problems. He also hosted a series of conferences between prominent labour leaders and leading manufacturers, "with the object of bringing the big employers of labor and employees closer together." After preliminary negotiations, six labour leaders, with no official sanction from their unions or the Independent Labor Party, met on 17 February with seven industrialists – executive officers of Canada Steel Goods, Canadian Westinghouse, Steel Company of Canada, International Harvester, Dominion Foundries and Steel, and Frost Steel and Wire. The statement issued by this group and published in all the city newspapers the next day noted that "the interests of capital and labor are identical and each cannot get along without the other." The manufacturers made a vague concession to labour concerns by agreeing that managers should "give direct personal assistance in adjusting difficulties in their own plant," but this was a far cry from recognizing the right to organize and bargain collectively. The labour representatives nonetheless came away satisfied that "if the manufacturers

Your Cigar and Pipe Will Be Next!

MEMBERS of the Women's Christian Temperance Union did their best to prevent cigarettes being sent to Canadian soldiers in the trenches.

Field secretaries of the Anti-cigarette League have been working all summer organizing a national campaign, to banish all forms of tobacco. It is predicted the movies will be the next to be attacked.

Professional reformers are in the ascendancy—and "the Devil loves nothing better than the intolerance of reformers".

Now is the time to check the spirit of rabid intolerance and interference with personal rights. "Hell is paved with good intentions".

Join with the Citizens' Liberty League in its honest, sincere endeavor to obtain a fair and just solution to Ontario's vexed temperance problem—the repeal of the unsatisfactory Ontario Temperance Act and the enaction of new legislation that will permit the sale of light beer and wine generally and the sale of pure spirituous liquors through Government agencies only.

Vote "YES" to all Four Questions

Mark your ballot with an X. Any other marking will spoil it. Remember, also—every voter must vote on every question or his ballot will be spoiled.

CITIZENS' LIBERTY LEAGUE | Citizens' Liberty League

Several members of the Hamilton elite stepped into the leadership of the campaign to end prohibition. They emphasized personal liberty free of state interference.

(HS, 10 Oct. 1919, 37)

continue to display the same sincerity which obviously actuated them at this meeting, much good must inevitably develop from future conferences where Labor meets Capital man to man." This private meeting led immediately to the creation of an employment committee of two soldiers, two labour men, and two manufacturers, subsequently dubbed the Triangle Committee, to facilitate the re-employment of returned soldiers and unemployed civilians with families. The committee met through the spring and early summer, but apparently could do little more than make public assurances that everything possible was being done. This initiative to promote dialogue with "safe and sane" elements of the labour movement won applause from the Canadian Manufacturers' Association, which recommended it to other communities.[11]

Bourgeois leadership appeared on another, unexpected front in 1919 – the fight against prohibition. After the Conservative government decided to hold a referendum on making permanent the dry regime launched in 1916, in the run-up to the vote in October 1919 a new, broad-based coalition emerged as the Hamilton branch of the province-wide Citizens' Liberty League. It was led by a number of the leading lights of bourgeois Hamilton: industrialist William Hendrie, John's brother, was the honorary president, with A.F. Hatch serving as president, Paul Myler as vice-president, and H.J. Waddie as treasurer – the heads of Canada Steel Goods, Canadian Westinghouse, and Canadian Drawn Steel, respectively. The executive and council were littered with equally prominent lawyers, merchants, and industrialists. The sole labour representative was the ILP's Harry Halford. In subsequent campaigns in the early 1920s, this group re-emerged as the Moderation League.[12]

These men objected to state-sanctioned moral regulation and argued for personal liberty (and in effect male privilege). The bourgeois leaders of the postwar anti-prohibition movement had more on their minds than well-stocked wine cellars and brandy with their cigars after dinner. In the face of widespread bootlegging, the Citizens' Liberty League warned that prohibition "had brought the law into contempt, thus tending to destroy our national life as sober, law-abiding citizens." It argued that prohibition bred "dissatisfaction and discontent among our workers, returned men and a large section of the citizens generally." The choice, it asserted, was between "Compromise and Harmony, or Intolerance and Widespread Resentment." A letter to the *Spectator* was blunt in its criticism of the Ontario Temperance Act: "The issue is sanity versus bolshevism." The writer cited a host of challenges to the rule of law: "Open, flagrant

and continuous violations of the law; corruption of public servants, without whose connivance such violations would not take place; enormous profits obtained by breaking the law; injustice as between rich and poor." All of these conditions would "destroy respect for the law," "undermine confidence in government," and "loosen the very foundation of society." The alternative had to be "well-ordered liberty and the stability of our institutions."[13]

This bourgeois version of anti-prohibition politics was driven, then, both by a deep fear of generalized discontent and resentment and the potential for instability, and by opposition to statist interventionism of all kinds (including the disruption of private enterprise). These elite activists wanted to deflect such concerns into what has been called "social liberalism" – the right to be left alone, to be freed of the incursive social engineers of all stripes, including prohibitionists. Canadians had to reduce their sense of social entitlement and their demands on the state and be encouraged to move in more self-reliant directions. Building a popular coalition that tied together personal liberty and a roll-back of state intervention would help to redirect politics into safer channels. "We call it stabilized democracy, which is the broad highway up the centre of the road of just, ordinary, clean decent Anglo-Saxon living," the president of the provincial Citizens' Liberty League announced in 1920. "On the one hand are the uplifters ... on the other are the Reds."[14]

Short-term projects to stabilize labour relations and to repeal moralistic legislation would not be enough over the long term, and two new initiatives became central to a business-led program of reconstruction. The first was the rapid expansion of so-called service clubs among local businessmen and professionals. The Rotary Club had appeared in Hamilton on a small scale in 1913 and the Kiwanis Club two years later, but both took off after the war, when they were joined by the first Lions, Kinsmen, Optimist, and Gyro clubs. These were convivial groups whose exclusively male members met weekly for jocular, informal lunches and occasionally for dinner dances with wives and girlfriends. Yet, in contrast to the homosocial fraternal societies to which many middle-class men had long belonged, these new bodies had a more restrictive membership base and a high-profile program of public service. Each local branch admitted only one member from each occupation or profession, a man who was presumed to be the most prominent within each category in Hamilton (each club adopted the same structure, but the Rotary Club apparently skimmed off the cream in each case). By 1925 the local Rotary Club had 150 members and the Kiwanis 140. These men were intended to be conduits of efficiency and other good business practice into each sector, though they typically avoided thorny issues of labour relations. More broadly they claimed to be committed, in the words of a Kiwanis speaker, to "social and civic service" to the community, an idealism "practised by means of business-like organizations and by modern business methods." All service clubs required members to adhere to a code of ethics that highlighted fair practices and service to customers or clients. In the Lions Club code, for example, two clauses demanded that members carry out their business practices with a conscience:

> To show my faith in the worthiness of my vocation by industrious application to the end that I may merit a reputation for quality of service.
>
> To seek success and to demand all fair remuneration or profit as my just due, but to accept no profit or success at the price of my own self-respect lost because of unfair advantage taken or because of questionable acts on my part.

Alongside such well-publicized pledges of ethical rigour, these paradigms of good citizenship were also vigorous boosters of civic development. They devoted part of their dues, as well as personal time, to support projects of community service. Usually they directed funds in an unsystematic, piecemeal fashion to institutions run by others, especially those involving working-class children and youth. The Rotarians launched the Big Brothers movement, for example, and the Kiwanians promoted summer camps for similar children. Both supported the revival of the Boy Scouts in the early 1920s. Most also dispensed limited charitable funds to the poor, especially at Christmas. The public lesson was clear: there was no need for state intervention when such public-spirited voluntarism was available.[15]

Here was a new public persona of the businessman – not a selfish individualist, not a greedy capitalist, but a man dedicated to co-operation with other men like himself in promotion of professionalism, efficiency, and public service. In fact, the Rotarians' motto was "Service Above Self." In a period in which private enterprise had been tainted by charges of profiteering from the war effort, the service clubs helped to provide a much-needed gloss on business and its ability to meet social needs without public intrusion through regulation or legislated controls. Moreover, as one Kiwanis leader explained, "There can be no stronger bulwark than the type of citizen which the social service club is producing, against the revolutionary tide."[16]

A similar spirit of capitalist statesmanship animated an even bigger and ultimately more important project. Early in 1920, only months after the ILP had swept the provincial election, joined a new Farmer-Labour government, and then solidified its presence in municipal politics, the city's business leaders began to question their ability to shape public debate. The old Board of Trade seemed to be on its last legs as an effective voice of business, as its membership dwindled and its staff departed. It consequently brought in a team of consultants from the Canadian City Bureau (a branch of the American City Bureau) to assess the best way to proceed. The experts recommended that the Board transform itself into a new organization, to be known as the Chamber of Commerce, modelled on other local bodies being created across North America. The difference would be that the organization would present itself as a community institution that integrated as many sectors of local society as possible in order to work out wide-ranging policy issues. When the Hamilton Chamber of Commerce was indeed launched in the spring, the *Spectator* was enthusiastic. "Professional men are invited to co-operate with business men for the general advancement of the city's interests, not merely material, but spiritual.... It will create a civic conscience, aiming at certain definite objects, and achieving results impossible of attainment under ordinary hit-or-miss methods." The motivation would, once again, be service. "Progressive schemes" would be worked out and brought to fruition more effectively. Board members would thus become "leaders in community thought," a leadership "very badly needed in this city, as we all know only too well." The outcome would be "not merely in the matter of industrial growth, but in the creation and satisfaction of higher social and ethical standards."[17]

Rotary Club members were apparently heavily involved in setting up this new body, and there were other connections to parallel developments in the city's industrial life. The Trades and Labor Council accepted an invitation to join (although one delegate argued that a "watchdog" in the new body "would stand little chance among a pack of wolves"), and a few months later the ILP reached out to the Chamber to create a forum for discussing pressing social issues.[18] But the Chamber was more attuned to the spirit of new experiments in corporate welfarism. Its membership structure allocated a greater number of seats to larger companies, which were encouraged to assign at least one to a worker. According to the body's first president, George Coppley, this kind of inclusiveness would bring "into the service of the community as many persons who have, or ought to have, a share in working out its problems." One official of the organization visited the Industrial Council at International Harvester and "pointed out the value of having the workmen sharing in the work of the new body in order that they may get together with their employers."[19] The Chamber was nonetheless careful to avoid any open entanglement in specific incidents of industrial conflict – notably turning down the Employing Printers' Association's request for support in its battle against the 44-hour week. That caution did not stop the Chamber from lobbying against an Ontario minimum-wage bill for male workers in 1922.[20]

The Chamber of Commerce was thus conceived as a kind of community parliament, controlled by the city's leading businessmen, in which solutions to a variety of problems could be worked out without invoking state power unless absolutely necessary.[21] Coppley's victory in the mayoralty campaign in January 1921 brought a close, sympathetic relationship between the Chamber and city hall (he resigned as president of the Chamber, but continued to attend the meetings of its board of directors). Public forums sponsored by the Chamber discussed "citizenship and community spirit, education, clean-up, public health and hospital extension, harbor development," and more.[22] But practical remedies to the city's problems were hammered out in the weekly meetings of the board of directors. No issue escaped their attention – taxation policies by all three levels of government, the gas supply, road, rail, and port developments, traffic and parking, civic planning, parks and playgrounds, hospitals and public health, foreign trade and the city market, movies and carnivals, city government – often handled by special committees sent off to work with municipal officials or to lobby higher levels of government. Over the next few years the board of directors brokered an arrangement for English classes for adult immigrants, saw to the revival of the Boy Scouts and Girl Guides, and created a Council of Social Agencies and a new Red Cross Society – all efforts to strengthen voluntary programs of regulation. The loose, populist practices of the city council frustrated Chamber directors, who promoted the hiring of a city manager to run a more businesslike administration. Late in 1921 a board committee on Municipal Research proposed steps for shaping the outcome of the next municipal election. Eventually a pamphlet was sent to all electors. The idea of convening a luncheon of city clergymen to give them guidelines for sermons on "citizenship" was dropped because the proposal was "liable to increase the feeling already held by some that the Chamber of Commerce was trying to control public action." Indeed, earlier that year, ILP controller Charlie Aitchison had warned the Trades and Labor Council about the Chamber's broadening influence and urged labour to resist this trend.[23]

The Chamber thus became the capstone in local efforts by business leaders to respond to potentially threatening postwar critiques. With all the fervour of other social movements of the period, they set about to give the process of private capital accumulation and the social hierarchy of power and wealth renewed legitimacy. This goal would be carried out by casting businessmen as socially conscious community leaders and by creating new forums – from industrial councils to informal get-togethers to a major new institution, the Chamber of Commerce – that would perform the continuing role not just of drawing in potential critics but also of finding mechanisms for defusing social conflict and avoiding new activist roles for the state. The unemployment that began to deepen in the city over the winter of 1920–21 would put this new capitalist statesmanship through its stiffest test.

Fit for Heroes

Meanwhile, large numbers of men had arrived back in Hamilton with profoundly different concerns and mobilized a social movement of their own. Some 11,000 Hamilton men served in the Allied cause during World War One. The 9,000 who survived came back in two distinct phases. Before November 1918, returned soldiers were men sent home in astonishingly large numbers with illnesses (notably tuberculosis) or wounds too severe to allow them to return to the front. After that the remainder were demobilized in batches of up to 500 over an extended period lasting until the summer of 1919. The delays on the return trip were agonizing, and in April the *Spectator* interviewed men who had participated in the riots at Kinmel in Wales, where the frustrations of the waiting Canadian troops had exploded into two days of violent confrontations and looting.[24]

Some veterans arrived unexpectedly and found no one waiting for them. More typically soldiers came in mass by train, and, to the disgust of some who had no more patience for military discipline, they were compelled to parade in full gear behind a brass band through streets lined with cheering crowds. After marching to the armouries, they were formally discharged to civilian life. Members of a civic reception committee shook their hands, and their families swept them away. The local newspapers listed all their names and the highlights of their battalions' battle history, and soon after they would all be invited to large banquets in their honour.[25]

Their glory was short-lived. The process of demobilization was intended to be quick, and they were expected to pick up the traces of their old lives as soon as possible. To help the transition, the federal government agreed in December 1918 to provide a one-time-only War Service Gratuity of up to $600, based on the length of their service (the average payment turned out to be only $240). Where possible, their former employers took them back into their old positions. More often, the local government employment office tried to guide them into appropriate work. The disabled could get a meagre pension, but officials in the new Department of Soldiers' Civil Re-establishment preferred to push them into retraining for some kind of remunerative work and self-sufficiency. The local Soldiers' Aid Commission would help all vets with job-hunting and other issues of adjustment, including marriage-counselling.[26]

Many veterans were troubled by what they found back in Canada. Living on a soldier's pay of $1.10 a day, unchanged since 1914, had not allowed them to save much, and the Canadian Patriotic Fund had been anything but generous with their families. The cost of living had soared and made providing for their families difficult. Affordable housing was almost impossible to find. Jobs were not always easy to land for disabled men, and for the psychologically wounded positions were frequently hard to keep – as one writer said, the men were cursed by a "terrible restlessness which possesses us like an evil spirit." Wage rates too often fell below what the veterans thought they deserved. New moral prudery deprived them of their friendly glass of beer. Everywhere they believed they saw evidence of how the "slackers" who had stayed behind had done well, especially those who had worked in munitions. Foremost among those were, once again, the "foreigners," who had visibly done so well in the wartime economy. In contrast, veterans seemed to get little respect in the daily life of the city. They were not getting a "square deal."[27]

A large proportion of these veterans most likely made the transition quietly, if gloomily, and dissolved back into civil society. A good number wanted to stay together. Late in 1916 they began to organize to promote and protect their particular interests in Hamilton and beyond. The focus of local veterans' groups evolved from a heavy emphasis on the concerns of the disabled towards the problems confronting the able-bodied and their families. Their war experiences had left them with a strong sense of justice and entitlement. "We don't want speeches and fancy words. We want fair play for our comrades," a private shouted at a civic reception in April 1918, amid thunderous applause. "We fought for liberty, against the Hun, and when the boys come back, they're going to fight for liberty in Canada."[28]

Unity proved elusive. The returned men drew stark distinctions among themselves: those who had served overseas versus those who had not; those who had actually seen battle versus those who had not; those who had signed up voluntarily versus those who were conscripted; those who had survived from the earliest days of the war (the self-styled "Originals") versus the latecomers; and those who had served in particular regiments. These fragmented military identities were reflected in the numerous separate groups they set up. By far the most important was the Great War Veterans' Association, a national organization founded in April 1917, which brought together a groundswell of local organizing across the country, including a Hamilton group formed the previous December.[29] In September 1918, as its membership soared past 1,000, this local organization split into east and central branches, and the following spring it added others in the west end and on Mount Hamilton. The Great War Veterans co-existed with several smaller groups – the Army and Navy Veterans, the Originals, Veterans of France, Honourably Discharged Soldiers' Association, Grand Army of Canada, and several battalion clubs, each with its own specific qualifications for membership.[30] Rivalries and tensions kept these groups apart, and many veterans steered completely clear of them all.[31]

The veterans certainly had a basis for unity. The overarching concern of all these organizations was to promote "comradeship." Symbolically, early in their existence, members dispensed with military titles and began to call each other "comrade."[32] In part that meant rekindling the special bonds of masculine solidarity that had emerged in the camps and trenches. Each organization set up a clubhouse and ran an active social program of concerts, minstrel shows, smokers, and whist drives for the men, with picnics and dances for their families and girlfriends. They sponsored teams to compete in local sports leagues, and the Great War Veterans had their own band, which performed at numerous events. "One only has to inquire of the wife or mother of the returned man," a journalist explained, to discover that "the only time they see him happy is when he returns home after having spent an evening with soldier friends."[33]

Having fun together was not enough. The first priority of these comrades was to look after each other – just as they had done in the trenches – and the veterans' groups pursued a host of issues that were plaguing returned soldiers. They battled with bureaucrats over better pensions for soldiers' widows and disabled vets, delays in payments of gratuities, and other problems of parsimony and red tape.[34] They demanded that factory owners give preference to veterans in hiring[35] and hounded government officials about placing them in public-service jobs.[36] They pushed the city to make use of senior government funds for new working-class housing and badgered the new housing commission over the slow pace of its work.[37] They also repeatedly demanded action to expel "aliens" who allegedly threatened their job prospects and British institutions more generally, sponsoring large mass meetings in March 1918 and February 1919 to rally public support for their cause.

Yet comradeship had a much larger meaning for these groups than merely having a good time together or protecting their own rights. It was intended to convey what the war had taught soldiers about how the world should work. The editor of the Great War Veterans' magazine, the *Veteran*, argued in its inaugural issue in 1917 that the army created "a real brotherhood between men who have fought together, and taught them to sink the individual aim and purpose in the common cause." It encouraged "the creation of citizens, people imbued with the ideal of the general welfare, who will set aside private schemes and ambitions and work harmoniously with their fellowmen for the highest good of the community." Veterans could

create a widespread and powerful body of opinion, which will demand and insist upon a cleaner and more efficient system of Government, a more intelligent and public spirited attitude toward national affairs, a new type of representative in Parliamentary life, and above all a gradual reorganization of our Canadian community for mutual service and common happiness rather than for individual profits and huge dividends.[38]

As the Great War Veterans' president said at its 1918 convention in Hamilton, "The comradeship of camp and trench is presented to the community as an ideal of what should obtain in all departments of life." This ideal, he argued, "calls us to sink our own personal peculiarities and our personal feelings in the desire for the common good, and the truest welfare of the whole Dominion. Collective humanity instead of individualistic ideas. Co-operation as against competition."[39] Those notions, expressed repeatedly over the next few years, gave the veterans' leaders the sharp edge of moral righteousness in debates about the shape that postwar society should take. By their warrior valour they had proven their commitment to the higher good of liberty and well-being in Canada, and they insisted that Canadians pay attention.

Comradeship was nonetheless an ideological hot potato. For veterans with cautious conservative instincts (and material interests at stake), especially the officers drawn from the Hamilton elite, this could be a rallying cry for sacrifice and loyalty, to submerge narrow demands (such as higher wages or better housing) in a common effort to build social cohesion under their leadership and thus to restore the normal functioning of the capitalist economy and the social relations of pre-war Canada that sustained it. Initially the veterans' executive bodies had former officers sitting cheek by jowl with sergeants and privates, and gave men like Colonel William Hendrie, an industrialist, Lieutenant-Colonel J.E. Davey, a prominent doctor, Charles W. Heming, a transportation magnate, and Major H.A.

Burbidge, a corporate lawyer (and law partner of General S.C. Mewburn, East Hamilton's MP and minister of militia and defence) the space to promote unity and collaboration.[40] Such men became leading voices for rallying around the British flag and defending British culture and institutions against "aliens" and "Bolsheviks." The same voices struggled to restrain demands for militancy on pressing issues (such as the anti-immigrant rioting that erupted in Toronto in 1918) and to keep their organizations out of politics.

Elite figures like William Hendrie saw the veterans' groups as part of the process of managing the social turmoil of reconstruction. It was no accident that he was simultaneously honorary president of the anti-prohibitionist Citizens' Liberty League. If returning soldiers were not quickly satisfied, he wrote late in 1918, "Do the people of this province realize what is likely to happen?" He also worked to keep veterans from straying into the hands of radicals, urging the East Hamilton Great War Veterans to be "most careful" in administering their organization and to focus on "a constructive policy" rather than engage in excessive criticism.[41]

In June 1919, against the backdrop of the final violent climax of the Winnipeg General Strike, the Dominion executive of the Great War Veterans issued a "declaration of principles," immediately forwarded to Prime Minister Borden. The statement led off with a ringing denunciation of "the doctrines of Bolshevism and anarchy" and "the underlying principles of the 'One Big Union,' which expresses itself as being in full accord with the Russian Bolsheviki and the German spartacans." That tendency would result, the writers said, in "the menacing of our institutions of government and the threat of their replacement by soviet rule." The writers promised to "lend active assistance in upholding constitutional authority, the laws of the country and good order," and proposed joint consultative measures and a list of ameliorative reforms "as an antidote to unrest." A member of that executive, William Hendrie, explained to the Hamilton Central Branch that the statement had been drawn up in response to radical resolutions passed at the recent British Columbia Federation of Labor convention. "The Great War Veterans' association," he declared, "upheld law and order, and would do everything possible in order to maintain it."[42]

For many more ex-soldiers, comradeship meant something potentially much more radical – a belief in collectivist social responsibility and a challenge to any vested interests that threatened the common good. To be sure, those threats included "aliens," whose habits and behaviour could be construed as undermining the British identity of the country, and, by extension, Bolsheviks (typically assumed to be alien) whose alleged preference for violent action could subvert Canadian-style parliamentary democracy. But the enemy could also be the profiteer or the insensitive manufacturer. As far back as 1917, the *Veteran*'s editor had argued:

> The old selfish order of civilization with its unrestricted private ownership of the instruments of production and its vaunted freedom of contract, patently failed to make the best use of our country's natural resources and to produce for the generation now living the largest amount of useful commodities and services. Not here only but all the world over it has failed even to secure, as regards a large part of the population, the primary needs of maintenance for themselves and their families in a state of health and efficiency.

At a Hamilton reception, a returned private proclaimed that "the returned man is going to be a power in the land very soon, despite all the capitalists try to do to keep him under." The high cost of living drew complaints from the local Veterans of France about "large interests and profiteers" who compelled "wives, mothers and children of soldiers who fought for country and King ... to exist without the necessities of life." The Great War Veterans' provincial executive similarly pointed to "the suspicion that the workers are being systematically robbed by profiteers."[43]

After the division of the Great War Veterans in Hamilton into two branches, the much more proletarian East Hamilton leadership was more prone to striking an aggressive posture.[44] In contrast to William Hendrie's Central Hamilton Branch, the East Hamilton group expressed outrage in June 1919 at "the methods adopted by the government in connection with the reading of the Riot act and the shooting of returned soldiers and civilians during the Winnipeg labor unrest." They laid the blame for the unrest on profiteers, demanding that the government "take immediate action in punishing all profiteers, as they are a menace to the welfare of the entire country."[45]

In the summer and fall of 1919 this rhetoric reached full blossom in Hamilton, as elsewhere, around a single demand that revealed how enlisted men had moved into the leadership. A proposal from Calgary veterans for lump-sum bonuses or "gratuities" for all returned soldiers ($1,000, $1,500, and $2,000 depending on where they had served) became the talking point in veterans' halls across the country. It captured the vets' resentment against what their East Hamilton president, Albert H. Peart, described as the "the very apparent signs of tremendous prosperity enjoyed by a huge number of those who remained at home during the war." "How many men gave up homes, good homes, too, and now come back to a paltry gratuity?" a worker

For returned soldiers, as for workers, profiteering became a central issue in postwar politics.

(*Veteran*, December 1919, 11)

wrote to the press. "I got $600, and it went on home furniture, not a house, because I'll never own a house. I'm only a common laborer, and it's up to us common laborers to stick and try our hardest for the extra gratuity."[46]

A mass protest meeting in Toronto in September brought another player into the fray – a new group known as the Returned Soldiers' Gratuity League, headed by a charismatic veteran named J. Harry Flynn, whose fiery rhetoric threatened force if necessary. With that inspiration, a mass meeting of some 2,500 veterans was held a few days later in Hamilton on the gratuities issue, where speakers once again focused on profiteers. According to William Jordan, an electrician and president of the East Hamilton Great War Veterans:

> All the labour unrest … and the discontent expressed by former soldiers can be laid at the doors of the profiteers. It is useless to ask the government to prosecute those profiteers, as the government is just as deeply in the mire as all that element. (Cheers.)

We fought to defeat autocracy and replace it with democracy, but the former has grown to enormous proportions during the time we were away.[47]

A week later, another mass meeting of 3,500 Hamilton veterans in Dundurn Park heard Flynn denounce the cautious toadyism of the Great War Veterans and proclaim: "It is idle to say the government cannot force the profiteers, who robbed your women and children, to part with some of their wealth. Sooner or later you will have the opportunity to show that your power is greater than wealth." Soon after, Flynn's organization renamed itself the United Veterans' League and declared overtly political goals. At the end of September a Hamilton branch was formed, and Flynn became a regular visitor to veterans' meetings in the city.[48]

The federal government's intransigence on gratuities had two longer-term results for Hamilton's veterans. First, the various local groups – this time including all the Great War Veterans branches – quickly moved towards a common front to pursue shared goals. The Discharged Soldiers' and Sailors' Federation was launched in November with all local groups participating.[49] This was not an amalgamation, however, and it would prove to be a rocky alliance, especially when Flynn and the United Veterans' League started a house-to-house petition campaign for the gratuity, which the Great War Veterans, alone among veterans' organizations, refused to support. The preference of the flamboyant Flynn for denunciations of the Great War Veterans' leadership and for large outdoor rallies ran against the grain of most other organizations. He added fuel to the fire by announcing at a mass meeting in Hamilton that, if the government did not listen, he would lead a march of 50,000 veterans to Ottawa. The government remained intransigent, and the issue slowly faded from public debate, without any on-to-Ottawa treks.[50] The Discharged Soldiers' and Sailors' Federation struggled on amid all the organizational rivalries, and discussions about complete amalgamation continued to surface, notably after the Grand Army of Canada and the United Veterans' League merged to form the Grand Army of United Veterans in April 1920.[51]

The second new development in the fall of 1919 was the veterans' decisive step towards independent politics. The small Grand Army of Canada had always favoured political action, and at the end of August nominated a candidate, Maurice L. Fitzgerald, to enter the race for the East Hamilton provincial seat in the fall election. In his campaign, a reporter noted, Fitzgerald "denounced the profiteers in strong language and promised to make war on them if elected to the legislature."[52] Another self-styled "soldier-labour" figure – the ambitious, irrepressible Sam Landers – upstaged Fitzgerald with his own high-profile candidacy, under the sponsorship of a short-lived Soldiers' and Sailors' Labor Party (renamed a Political League before the election), the endorsement of all the local Great War Veterans' branches, and apparently the tacit support of the Conservative Party. His stump rhetoric exalted his own war record and tried to turn his leading opponent, ILP candidate George Halcrow, into a slacker who had attacked conscription. "The war is the real issue," Landers declared. In contrast, Halcrow played to popular resentments of the profiteer that were bouncing around public forums that fall. The campaign proved the limited popular support for simple emotional appeals to loyalty and warrior heroism, and Landers suffered a humiliating defeat.[53] Shortly thereafter, the Great War Veterans nonetheless decided by referendum for the first time officially to allow branches to discuss politics.[54]

Since the late summer labour leaders in Hamilton had been trying to develop some kind of political alliance with the local veterans' organizations.[55] Landers's candidacy had derailed that initiative, but, even after his defeat, the vets kept their distance. There was still resentment that labour leaders had allegedly dragged their heels on military conscription and the deportation of "aliens."[56] In the run-up to the January 1920 municipal elections, the new Discharged Soldiers' and Sailors' Federation put together a slate of ten candidates of their own, only two of whom were elected. Across Ontario, veterans' groups had suffered similar defeats, which provoked soul-searching about the narrowness and isolation of their cause.[57]

In Hamilton a few veterans' leaders sensed the need for some kind of understanding with the ILP. Peart, as a prominent member of the Great War Veterans, addressed the party's Central Branch in late January to win support for better widows' and disabled soldiers' pensions. "Most of the privates came from the working classes," he argued, "and for that reason the matter was

Like this group, several veterans' organizations got permission to serve beer in their clubrooms after the return of public drinking in 1934. (AO, RG-36-8)

one which should appeal to branches of the I.L.P. and other workers' associations." Party spokespersons agreed, and in April the provincial ILP convention endorsed the vets' demand for increased gratuities. Yet, as an indication of how difficult such a political alliance would be to build, the Great War Veterans' provincial convention defeated a motion of moral support for labour and legal strikes.[58]

The Grand Army of United Veterans was less negative, and announced a platform with many labour-friendly planks, including heavier income taxes, an eight-hour day, minimum wages, health and unemployment insurance, immigration restrictions, proportional representation, abolition of property qualifications in elections, and economic development to promote employment. It also agreed not to form a separate party, and eventually announced a willingness to support the ILP. In November 1920 the Discharged Soldiers' and Sailors' Federation approached the

ILP about forming a common slate in the upcoming municipal elections. The joint campaign put up twenty-four candidates, but, of the eight who were elected, only one, a school-board trustee, was a veterans' representative.[59]

After that campaign the veterans largely faded from public view. The Soldiers' and Sailors' Federation decided to take no part in the 1921 federal election[60] and turned more attention to staging boxing matches. All the local organizations became primarily social clubs with dwindling memberships (until they got liquor licences for their clubhouses in the 1930s), and then charities supporting poverty-stricken unemployed vets.[61] At the national level the emphasis was on help for the disabled – a small proportion of the returned men. The various groups moved painfully slowly towards some kind of amalgamation. The ultimate consolidation of the Canadian Legion as the new all-inclusive organization in 1925 represented a significant change in leadership that brought senior military officers back into control. The rabble-rousing days of the veterans were over. They took to the street only to parade to church on special occasions or to raise funds by selling paper poppies.[62]

Returned soldiers had thus been a volatile, unpredictable force in Hamilton from 1917 to 1921. They had managed to get sympathy and respect for their war service, and to receive some gestures towards giving them a leg up in the local labour market. Yet, as a movement of protest, they were hampered not only by the cross-class membership of a returning army, in which officers were given deference despite the egalitarianism of comradeship, but also by the splits and rivalries among competing organizations. They also suffered from an ambiguity about whether they were a narrow interest group with a list of grievances or a partner in a broader coalition for social justice. Their wide-ranging critique of how Canadian society had changed in their absence overlapped with other critical forces in postwar reconstruction, notably the labour movement. Yet, besides the caution expressed by many veterans' leaders about any kind of radicalism, many rank-and-file members seemed to be suspicious and resentful of those who had not faced the enemy fire overseas. The decision to collaborate with labour at the end of 1920 came too late, and, like so many others in Hamilton, veterans were soon struggling to cope with a level of mass unemployment not seen since before the war. The public voice of veterans was henceforth reduced largely to imperialist patriotism and intolerance of non-British residents. As unemployment deepened after 1929, however, they would again be heard making claims to privileged access to jobs based on their war records and the issue of employment of "foreigners."[63]

Workers of the World, Unite!

In the year after the war ended yet another extraparliamentary force was at work in the city. The collapse of Russian absolutism in the spring of 1917 and the triumph of the Bolsheviks the following October had reinvigorated the radical left in the city, as elsewhere in Canada, and encouraged its members to emulate the Russian example with a homegrown revolutionary movement. The apparent threat they posed brought the weight of state repression down on them, but, in the shadowy spaces of working-class Hamilton, a relatively small group of revolutionary socialists corresponded with their counterparts in the United States and Europe and debated the way forward. By 1921 these activists had a new reference point: the Communist Party of Canada.

The news of the Russian Revolution brought rejoicing among members of the local Social Democratic Party, then organized into separate Russian, Jewish, Ukrainian, and English branches. In March 1917 they held a boisterous celebration of the downfall of the czar. A May Day meeting the next year, at which leading revolutionaries from all these ethnic groups trumpeted their condemnation of capitalism and lauded Bolshevism, so upset the local Board of Trade that it fired off a resolution to the Borden government demanding suppression of such "seditious and traitorous" propaganda. The mayor simultaneously asked the police to mount a surveillance of the local socialist meetings. More quietly, the Dominion Police placed spies in the immigrant communities, and the Steel Company of Canada hired a detective agency to provide secret reports on radicalism among its workers.[64]

The federal government had been watching such developments with apprehension, and late in September 1918 passed orders-in-council to suppress a number of radical organizations, immigrant newspapers, and meetings in several foreign languages, including Ukrainian and Russian. All parts of the Social Democratic Party were initially included in this edict, and, in this new phase of illegality, the organization proceeded to splinter. Many local members of the English-language section, notably Flatman, continued to collaborate with the labourists in the resurgent Independent Labor Party. But late that fall, across south-central Ontario, Ukrainian Social Democrats, Russian anarchists, and a sprinkling of Anglo-Canadian Marxists began to coalesce into an underground organization that initially called itself a "soviet" and by the spring had adopted as its name the Communist Party of Canada. In an atmosphere of state repression that must have reminded some members of European autocracy, its adherents adopted a politics of insurrection modelled on the Russian Bolsheviks.[65]

Starting in late November 1918, these Canadian Bolsheviks dropped a series of revolutionary pamphlets on thousands of doorsteps throughout working-class neighbourhoods in Hamilton and other Southern Ontario cities. The first pamphlet, "Peace and the Workers," called on workers and soldiers to "overthrow the capitalist government," to "crush the capitalists as they have crushed you since you were born." It asked them to "take over and run all industries for the benefit of the working class," to imprison "capitalist officials" who refused to co-operate, to establish workers' and soldiers' councils, and to imprison all who opposed the rule of the councils. Flatman's distance from this project was evident in a disparaging reference to the document as a "fragmentary essay in anti-capitalist agitation," though most of his sharp invective addressed the hysterical reaction of the pro-capitalist press.[66] The tract produced for May Day 1919 argued: "Either starvation and death, or revolution – these are the only alternatives. The sham of parliamentary action has been destroyed, tinkering with reforms does not help the working class, only the complete overthrow of capitalism can emancipate the workers . . . Revolution!"

The moment did not seem ripe for such politics. At one point, when a red flag was hoisted to draw attention to an auction of military equipment, a group of immigrants marched in expecting a political meeting, but otherwise the leaflets did not spark a revolutionary uprising. Indeed, a Steel Company spy found deep fear and apprehension about deportation in the local immigrant community (the veterans' campaign to have aliens thrown out was peaking at this same moment). Yet, to the disgust of the *Spectator*, no one involved in the distribution of the pamphlets was reported to the police. Two men, Fred Kimlik and Joseph Szabak, were eventually caught in the act of handing out the May Day leaflet, and were charged with sedition. Unlike its Winnipeg counterpart, the local Trades and Labor Council did not spring to the defence of these radicals. Before their trials several months later, the two men eventually jumped bail and disappeared.[67]

The first Communist Party thus collapsed, and supporters of such an insurrectionary project dwindled. In January 1920 the police chief told a federal immigration official, "There are only 13 known Radicals or Bolshevists in Hamilton, all of whom are under constant surveillance of his operatives." Ukrainian and Russian radicals continued to hold joint meetings, maintaining what a spy described as "a sort of reading room and centre for revolutionary reading matter" in the office of an immigrant banker and steamship agent by the name of Rotenberg and sponsoring a revolutionary play, *Strike*, in August 1920. Late that year the radical Ukrainians founded their own labour temple, which was a branch of the national movement centred in Winnipeg. A police spy referred to this little band as "the knot of foreigners who hold meetings in Hamilton," and it was undoubtedly their oratory at the steelworkers' union organizing meetings that prompted the *Spectator* to fulminate against radical meetings held in the east end and led a visiting Montreal organizer to express surprise that "the foreigners are being led along Soviet lines by three Soviet agitators." Nonetheless, a strong fear of arrest and deportation remained among the tiny revolutionary cadre in immigrant neighbourhoods.[68]

Meanwhile, during 1920 the radicals who had been drawn into the city's One Big Union branches were slowly becoming disheartened and exploring political alternatives. The ILP's breakthrough into provincial power had briefly been distracting, but disillusionment quickly set in. A wide-ranging discussion was under way about forming a new kind of party on the Russian model. Some radicals had established contact with the two main Communist groups in the United States that had emerged in September 1919, and each had a faction of supporters in the city by late 1920. Both focused on visiting speakers and public education to win support for Communism. One formed a "Plebs League," which, starting in October 1920, ran weekly classes on Marxist theory in Hamilton under the rubric of the Ontario Labor College. Early the following year that group quietly affiliated with the United Communist Party of America. The other group (with 46 members in Hamilton, most of them apparently European immigrants) took its lead from the Communist Party of America and operated behind the name of "Workers' International Educational Association." To help

(*Worker*, 2 Oct. 1922, 1)

bring together the rival factions across Canada, a representative of the Communist International arrived in April 1921 and, in a secret meeting in a barn near Guelph, helped them to unite in an underground Communist Party of Canada, which affiliated itself with the Communist International in Moscow. A parallel legal organization known as the Workers' Party of Canada was founded in mid-February 1922, and the underground organization gradually faded away.[69]

No Communists from Hamilton were in the Guelph barn, but a few representatives from the city turned up at the organizational conference of the Workers' Party in mid-December 1921 and a few were also probably at the founding convention two months later. A local branch had been established by early January and was soon making its presence felt at unemployed meetings. On 26 February party members led what the *Spectator* called "a good imitation of a European Mayday celebration" as part of a nationally coordinated day of protest against unemployment. In March Tim Buck, who was then a Communist organizer in Toronto, helped two independent groups to merge into a single English-language branch, which included Flatman and others who had worked with the OBU's Hamilton affiliates. But the bulk of the small membership was in

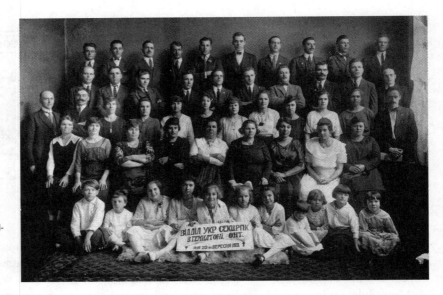

Hamilton's Communists remained a kind of federation of ethnic groups, including radical Ukrainians, photographed here in 1924.

(AO, F1405-50-21-73)

separate ethnic federations affiliated with the party, especially the Ukrainians in the Ukrainian Labor Temple. Each of the federations operated with considerable autonomy. A few years later a local chapter of the Women's Labor League began drawing in a small group of radical women, including the energetic Janet Inman, and in 1926 a branch of the Young Communist League was launched. The party also attracted what would eventually be known as "fellow travellers" who belonged to the more leftish East Hamilton ILP, notably alderman Sam Lawrence, a former long-time Social Democrat.[70]

The Workers' Party (renamed the Communist Party in 1924) had a completely different mode of operation than did its predecessors on the Canadian left, immersing itself in a variety of popular struggles beyond the lecture hall, the soap box, and the ballot box. Communists believed that they had to mobilize workers through determined leadership of these struggles. They got inspiration and confidence from their connection to the international Communist movement and took direction in their

political strategies from the Communist International. With nudging from Moscow, the party moved away from the sharply sectarian spirit of the splits on the left since the war, especially around the One Big Union, to focus on building a united front within mainstream unions and the federated Canadian Labor Party.[71] Communists created among themselves a vibrant, intense culture of radical politics, even though their influence in Hamilton was limited – much more so than in Toronto or Winnipeg – especially after the Trades and Labor Council and most of the ILP refused to have anything more to do with them by 1925. Through much of the 1920s their weekly meetings on the Market Square and their annual May Day events might draw a respectable crowd to hear the Ukrainian children's choir and rousing speeches, frequently by the roving national leadership of the party. Often they focused on international events that the party had prioritized – trade with the Soviet Union, the revolution in China, or the execution of the US radicals Sacco and Vanzetti, for example. But these events were probably no more than pep rallies for the small core of committed activists and lively entertainment for other curious spectators.[72]

Generally those small gatherings had little more reverberation than the pre-war socialists' meetings had most often had. Nor did the work of the loosely affiliated Women's Labor League or the local branch of the Canadian Labor Defence League, despite its claim to having 150 members in four branches by the end of the decade. Starting in 1928 the party also burned bridges with other local radicals as it followed the international Communist turn into a so-called Third Period of intense sectarianism. Like other local labour leaders, their erstwhile ally Sam Lawrence was now denounced as a "labour fakir" and "social fascist," and even the faithful Fred Flatman was driven out for incorrect politics. Yet the Hamilton Communists did not seem to benefit much from this new revolutionary fervour. In 1929, when women in the Canadian Cottons plant struck spontaneously, the editor of the *Worker* scoffed that "the Communists of Hamilton have been sleeping at the switch. Our comrades must criticize their lack of activity and do better the next time." A few months later they did play a central role in the tumultuous strike at National Steel Car, but, again, that event was a resounding failure. Blacklisting and rising unemployment broke the momentum. By 1931 the small branch of Young Pioneers organized only three years earlier had collapsed, and the local party correspondent sent in gloomy reports of weak membership and declining activity. In August of that year the Communist Party was banned under Section 98 of the Criminal Code, and eight of its national leaders were thrown into prison.[73]

Despite all these limitations, a commitment to mass mobilization did bring Hamilton's Communists into regular contact with the large numbers of unemployed men, and they would become key figures in the evolving efforts to construct a politics of the unemployed in the interwar period.

Addressing the Unemployed

Late in 1920 many people began to notice the downward slide of Hamilton's industrial life that was bringing on levels of unemployment not seen since 1914. Through no fault of their own, thousands of workers found themselves without jobs over the next few months, a situation that showed little sign of improvement over the summer of 1921. As in the pre-war depressions, jobless men congregating at the provincial employment bureau, the city relief office, or some relief works project occasionally marched together into city hall seeking immediate attention.[74] But groups of businessmen, veterans, and left-wing radicals intervened to shape distinctive understandings of unemployment and to encourage particular responses that fit the larger visions of their organizations.

The Chamber of Commerce wasted no time in acting to diffuse the disruptive potential of joblessness by placing themselves at the head of a large-scale project of earnest inquiry and calm reassurance. Earlier in 1920, the ILP's Halford and Herb West had approached the Chamber to establish some kind of regular dialogue on major social issues, including unemployment, but little had happened by December. W.H. Cooper, the city's leading construction contractor and former controller, who had been appointed by the Chamber to chair an Industrial Committee to meet with the ILP, now took charge of convening a large, well-publicized "roundtable conference" in the Chamber's auditorium. The meeting brought together city politicians, executives of all the major firms, representatives of organized labour and veterans, and spokespersons for the unemployed. A banker, a manufacturer, and a merchant each got a chance to explain their respective plights, and two Ontario cabinet ministers, including the Hamilton ILP's Walter Rollo, minister of labour, laid out prospects for relief. The upshot was the creation of a "special committee on social service" to conduct a survey aimed at spreading out available employment more equitably. Besides investigating the extent of the need, that group undertook to ask companies to avoid overtime and to reduce time for all employees rather than laying them off. Nothing substantial resulted from these efforts, beyond the creation of an ad-hoc committee on unemployment consisting of Mayor-elect Coppley and Cooper (both from the Chamber) and two city controllers (one of them the ILP's Thomas O'Heir). The numbers of the unemployed continued to rise. Most attention came to be focused on the city's relief handouts and its specific make-work projects, which workingmen typically preferred to charity handouts.[75]

When the dark economic clouds did not lift during 1921, the Chamber began to contemplate taking a leadership role in promoting more effective co-operation among charitable groups. Mayor Coppley liked that approach because "the matter would be taken away from the City Hall." In the fall the Chamber helped to bring together a Citizens' Relief Committee, and in December it geared up to organize a special relief fund, which it then quietly abandoned at the request of the city when the provincial and federal governments agreed to contribute. But the crisis was pushing the Chamber to reconsider the administration of charity and relief, and, with advice from upper-class activist Mary Hawkins, they struck a Committee on Federation of Charities to investigate a "financial organization to co-ordinate the collection of subscriptions for charitable and philanthropic work" and the "formation of a social service council." The outcome, a year later, was the new Central Bureau of Social Agencies. The goal was to strengthen and institutionalize the treatment of unemployment and poverty as individual problems, to be handled more "efficiently" by professionally trained experts, rather than to rely on ad-hoc voluntarism and expensive programs of state relief. Businessmen oversaw fundraising, with help from the service clubs.[76]

Meanwhile the streets had been erupting with protests by the unemployed. Coppley, as Chamber of Commerce president, had announced his strong disapproval of mass meetings of the unemployed because, as he argued, "A very unfavorable impression was thus advertised abroad as to conditions here."[77] But businessmen's displeasure did not stop such rabble-rousing gatherings. Early in December 1920, just when the Chamber was trying to assume leadership of the debate, the veterans were forging their political alliance with the ILP for the municipal election and called the first mass meetings of unemployed men in halls and on Market Square. They attracted several hundred and demanded immediate action from the city's Board of Control to provide work.[78]

By the new year the anger and frustration were palpable in the almost daily meetings. A few voices threw up the familiar scapegoats of "foreign" immigrants and married women, but, although the leaders of the unemployed rejected accusations of Red influence, much of the rhetoric had more than a tinge of radicalism, especially from the acknowledged leader, Edgar Haslam, a returned soldier, who was prone to threats of direct action. Resolutions now demanded "work or bread" and efforts by the government to reopen factories, and condemned the "philanthropic methods of handling this important national problem," which ate away at "a worker's greatest virtue, viz., self-respect." By February the veterans involved were calling themselves the International Soldiers' and Workers' Association and said they had more than 300 members "of both foreign and British extraction." A spontaneous parade through the downtown to look for Mayor Coppley one winter night was only a slightly more dramatic version of the frequent confrontations that His Worship had with crowds of disgruntled men demanding speedier relief.[79]

In February 1920, in line with their long history of harassing left-wing soap-boxers, the Hamilton police moved in on the organizers, whom the leaders of the Trades and Labor Council claimed were former One Big Union supporters. Four leaders of the International Soldiers' and Workers' Association, including Haslam, were arraigned in police court for being officers of an unlawful, seditious society under the recently minted Section 98 of the Criminal Code. A former member, several policemen, and Mayor Coppley testified as to the revolutionary rhetoric and threats of violence to which Haslam in particular was prone. In the end the four were acquitted by a jury, but their two months in jail and prolonged prosecution had broken the momentum of unemployed organizing.[80]

Meanwhile, in the fall of 1921 a group of left-wing labour activists, including Lawrence, convinced several of the city's unions and the Trades and Labor Council to support the creation of a new Hamilton Unemployed Association "to soften the edge of what promises to be a winter of unparalleled economic depression."[81] A few months later the Workers' Party also threw its energies into the Association, and in February and March 1922 got the organization to sponsor two large rallies. The banners, placards, and speeches at both events brimmed with anti-capitalist rhetoric. In February Lawrence urged workers and the unemployed not only to fight for temporary relief but also "to work for the overthrow of the capitalist system, under which the periods of prosperity have been becoming shorter and the periods of depression becoming oftener." William Mariner, a veteran adorned with medals and clearly a Communist, had been among the arrested the previous winter and now denounced the treatment of workers who, unlike their bosses, had fought in the trenches but as single unemployed men were relegated to a hostel in former army barracks: "There is to be a cenotaph for the boys who were killed and the Scott barracks for those who are starving." At both meetings unanimous resolutions called for immediate, effective relief for the jobless and the replacement of private ownership with a socialized economy in a workers' republic.[82]

The success of these events (which had their parallels in several other Canadian cities) encouraged the local Communists to organize a May Day celebration, with another boisterous procession and speeches, under the auspices of the Unemployed Association, Workers' Party, Amalgamated Clothing Workers, and (Jewish) Workmen's Circle. This time the city police intervened to stop the marchers, who were belting out "The Internationale," and attempted to seize their red flag from the 35-year-old Canadian woman, Algava Osborne, who carried it. She "fought fiercely," but, acting on pre-existing orders, the police used their batons aggressively to disperse the marchers and arrested four of them, including Osborne, for violating a city by-law against carrying a red flag without a Union Jack or Canadian Ensign alongside it (they later got $50 fines). At the ensuing meeting on Market Square, speakers including Mariner and Flatman denounced these actions, and the crowd adopted long-winded resolutions demanding "access to the means of production or full maintenance for all." The Workers' Party branch had been through what its newspaper called its "baptism of fire."[83]

The Communists apparently could not sustain that kind of leadership, and no more such dramatic actions followed. The Unemployed Association continued on under left-wing leadership, but seems to have had relatively little impact beyond an educational role in attempting to radicalize the unemployed. In January 1923, after prolonged debate, the Trades and Labor Council pulled out, on the grounds, according to one speaker, that the unemployed group was "a breeding ground for the Workers' Party" and a source of too frequent criticism of the mainstream labour movement. Late in 1924 another Unemployed Council appeared, apparently as an alternative to the Communist-led organization, but in mid-1925 the older Unemployed Association was still holding open-air meetings and attempting to put pressure on city officials. As local industry started to pull out of the economic slump after 1925, it quietly ceased to function. By 1928 the Communist Party's priority had shifted to organizing industrial unions.[84]

The Dirty Thirties

The massive layoffs that began in the winter of 1929–30 brought the issue of unemployment back to the front burner. Once again, veterans, Communists, and businessmen intervened to shape discussion of unemployment and to promote particular action.

The veterans' organizations were quick off the mark to make the public aware of their particular suffering and entitlement to preferential treatment. All the main arguments of the immediate postwar period resurfaced with a new petulance. Early in 1930 a long-time proponent of veterans' rights wrote to the *Spectator* about the "distress" in the city among families of "those who served and suffered that righteousness might obtain in those days and in the years to come." Veterans' leaders, reporting that the relief available from their Poppy Fund was drying up, advertised for more financial help. They set up a special unemployment committee and approached employers about keeping ex-service men on staff or rehiring them (within six weeks they had placed 25 men). "We are men who offered ourselves to the gods of war for the sake of humanity," they wrote to the country's leading politicians. "Our reward has been to be cast upon the heap of industry, some of us begging, pleading, praying for any kind of situation, if it only offers a bare existence, but such are not to be found." In their only gesture to a wider social program, they argued for unemployment insurance. But some familiar themes of narrow exclusiveness arose in this agitation. "I wonder when the government is going to stop so much immigration to this country," one unemployed ex-soldier wrote to the press. "What chance has a Canadian got with so many nationalities coming here?" A speaker at a joint veterans' association meeting also warned that some in their ranks were unfortunately "inclined to adopt the views of the internationale." It was therefore essential to "prevent the spread of such feeling" by getting "the fullest kind of co-operation of industrial heads." Small wonder that in 1933 Hamilton's police commissioners proposed turning to ex-servicemen as special reserves to combat Communist-inspired demonstrations. Veterans thus appealed, once again, to a form of citizenship based on loyalty to king and country and staked their claim to unemployment relief on their status as warrior-breadwinners to whom a grateful nation owed protection.[85]

Such an approach touched only a small part of working-class Hamilton. For the rest, in 1929–30 the city resurrected the makeshift measures of preceding winters to help married (but not single) men with relief handouts, but was soon overwhelmed by the numbers of the unemployed. By the next fall it was clear that more extensive emergency measures were once again necessary. As in the past, the Chamber of Commerce met quietly to discuss the scope of the issue and struck a special Unemployment Committee, again chaired by Coppley, to advise the municipal government and guide its relief policies. A year later three prominent members of the Chamber were appointed to the city's new Welfare Board (which otherwise had only the mayor and the senior controller as members). Meanwhile, the local service clubs also stepped in to provide food and recreation – most notably the Lions Club soup kitchen – in hopes of maintaining morale and discouraging disgruntled protest.[86]

Protest erupted nonetheless. Nationally the Communist Party was turning its attention to unemployed organizing as part of its Third Period of ideological realignment. International and national Communist leaders insisted that in this new economic context workers were radicalizing quickly and were allegedly ready to confront the whole capitalist system as long as they had aggressive Communist leadership. Tactically that meant mobilizing masses in the streets, in defiance of any resistance from state authority. Across the country Communists called public rallies to protest exploitation, war, and then the denial of civil liberties in the face of "savage police terror."[87]

Local comrades were instructed to get unemployed groups on their feet. In December 1929 Hamilton's Communists proclaimed that the city's workers had a "desire for struggle," and helped to pull together a new Unemployed Workers' Association. Within a month the Association had 800 to 900 members, who met

(Worker, 17 Feb. 1934, 3)

almost daily in the old butter market. The following summer the group became a branch of the National Unemployed Workers' Association, an affiliate of the Communist-led union movement, the Workers' Unity League, and it continued to follow the party's centralized policy on the unemployed.[88]

The hard-nosed local organizers, recognizing that they had to tackle concrete issues of relief policy in the city in that first hard winter of the renewed economic slump, began leading delegations to the Board of Control to get the city to provide both work as unemployment relief and better treatment for the single unemployed. They wanted to restore wage-earning power for unemployed men – "work or full maintenance" (at the optimistically high level of $25 a week). But winning any such concessions was not the Communists' first priority, and, once again, as a decade earlier, jobless men were rallied into mass meetings to hear stirring anti-capitalist speeches and to be led on marches from the Market Square to city hall beneath provocative banners – "Defend the Soviet Union," "Join the Communist Party," "We Will Not Starve, We Will Fight," and "Down with Police Terror." This was a politics that tried to appeal to the young, tough, swaggering, street-smart working-class male, whose rough-and-ready street culture regularly involved confrontations with authority in public space. These men were seen as the hard-core shock troops of the repeated street actions that became the trademark Communist tactics. Members of the Young Communist League played an especially prominent role.

The Hamilton police did not look kindly on any of these developments. For them, free speech was as expendable as it had always been. Toronto was setting the pace in breaking up demonstrations and, when possible, disrupting radical unemployed associations by arresting leaders on charges of making seditious utterances or such minor offences as vagrancy or interfering with the police. When the country's police chiefs met in Hamilton in July 1930 the *Spectator* learned that they had discussed confronting "the menace of communism" with "the severest treatment that lies within the scope of law enforcement," using "bludgeons and batons." Hamilton's police had already come out swinging. William Kashtan, district organizer of the Young Communist League, went to jail for three to six months in March 1930, ostensibly on a vagrancy charge but in fact, as police witnesses admitted, to silence his Communistic speeches. The next month the police swept up a visiting Toronto Communist speaker on a charge of sedition and, a few days later, a local Young Communist leader, Saul Cohen, for vagrancy. Cohen's case was thrown out of police court, and cheekily the Communists ran him as their candidate in the federal election that summer (he amassed 357 votes). In November the police attacked a large parade of the unemployed, dispersed the marchers, and arrested eight Communist leaders, including Toronto's Annie Buller, on charges of vagrancy and participation in an "unlawful assembly." The eight, along with two key organizers who were arrested the night before for vagrancy, got jail terms or suspended sentences with an order to stay away from demonstrations.[89]

The party began to rethink its strategy towards the unemployed. In February 1931 it turned to the potentially unifying demand of non-contributory unemployment insurance to be promoted through a massive petition campaign by the Workers' Unity League, a demand with more resonance for the unemployed family man. The leaders of Hamilton's unemployed insisted in their written statements that individuals had "unassailable rights" to the necessities of life, "even though it be at the expense of the more opulent of the citizens," and that governments had a constitutional responsibility for "giving every person the things necessary for their existence." Workers should be enabled to live "in comfort and decency."[90]

The police continued to attack the marches and demonstrations, which drew smaller numbers, and in May local Communists had to expel a former unemployed leader who was exposed as a police agent. In June a correspondent admitted that the Association had "not had any activity since May 1st to speak of."[91] It was in this trough of organizational energy for Communist organizing in many cities that the federal, provincial, and municipal governments developed a concerted plan to outlaw the Communist Party under Section 98 and suppress Communist-inspired activity. Authorities arrested nine leaders from across the country, and all but one of them were convicted and imprisoned in Kingston Penitentiary. The party continued on through its front organizations, including those in Hamilton. But the day of the iconic street-fighting Communist youth had passed.

By the end of 1931 the local Communists were following the party's shift to expand the family focus by organizing united-front neighbourhood

A Communist parade in the early 1930s.

defence groups to confront specific local issues. "The making of contacts, the formulation of immediate relief demands for the unemployed workers and their children, the fight against evictions," the party's paper advised, "should be done by calling neighborhood meetings, to which all workers are invited irrespective of political or union affiliations." The first neighbourhood council started up in Hamilton in October, and the party press said that by the spring of 1932 the city had 40 of these groups, united in a city-wide Central Council. Initially this body co-existed with the local branch of the National Unemployed Workers' Association, but in March that organization changed its name to the National Council of Unemployed Councils. The local Communist correspondent noted that the new slogan of the unemployed was "Out with the Bailiffs!" and that these officials were being thrown out of houses or blocked from entering by supportive neighbours. The Unemployed Workers' Association's Grievance Committee took up individual cases with city officials every day. In contrast to the earlier sloganeering, their placards now read: "For the restoration of the dollar; against soup kitchens; for the payment of light and gas; against coal oil lamps for the unemployed; out with the bailiffs!"[92]

For perhaps the first time, by spring 1932 the Communist-led unemployed movement seemed to be winning what it called "real prestige" among workers. In succeeding months it also created more space for women's activism and a revived role for the local Women's Labor League. On one occasion the league mobilized a demonstration of women to invade the office of the city's relief officer and sat in until they received higher relief payments. On another it organized a protest of widows who had been told they would have to do sewing for their relief payments. The group members quietly converged on the mayor's office and sat down until their demands were met.[93]

In a new burst of coalition-building, local Communists had convened "Conferences for the Repeal of Section 98" involving "sixteen other working-class organizations" and hosted an Eastern Canadian Emergency Conference in February 1932. When party activists planned a Hunger March to Ottawa the next month, local members reported having drawn 4,000 people to an outdoor meeting in the east end to support the marchers, along with a large police contingent. No violence resulted this time, but in April, outside city hall, police dispersed an unemployed demonstration called to protest new cuts in relief payments. A few days later a crowd of 7,000 gathered at Woodlands Park, where members chose a delegation to go to the Board of Control. They marched through the streets to city hall, and this time they were allowed to meet the politicians. The party's message to the unemployed seemed to be taking hold.[94]

By this point the police had clearly decided that the growing political momentum of the demonstrations had to be stopped. They recruited 50 new constables and got permission to swear in the city firefighters as special officers if needed. They issued court summons for eight activists, raided ten homes and three halls, and arrested two Communists leafleting for the upcoming May Day demonstration. The police had not misread the temper of working-class Hamilton that spring. Despite a ban on meeting in Woodlands Park, thousands showed up on 1 May – 10,000 according to the *Spectator*, twice that according to the *Worker* – unquestionably the largest turnout to any protest since the street-railway strike of 1906. The *Spectator* saw "the immense majority" as simply being "curious citizens" who showed up "to watch the police move against the alleged radical element." But police preparations and crowd responses suggest otherwise. A small army of 250 constables and firemen, directed by the police chief and officers of the Ontario Provincial Police and the RCMP, moved in to arrest the leaders as soon as they appeared on the bandstand to speak. The force broke up the demonstration with swinging batons. When police officers moved to stop another speaker on the steps of a neighbouring church, they were overwhelmed by men and women attacking them. The crowds

refused to disperse after an hour and instead surrounded the nearby arena where those arrested were being held. The firefighters turned on their powerful hoses to drive them back. The battle to suppress the demonstration lasted four hours. The memories of this violence were deeply etched decades later. "It was *terrible*. I was *very* upset," a woman told an interviewer. "The people in power were very callous."[95]

Of the 21 people who ended up in jail, most of them, in contrast to many previous confrontations, were Anglo-Canadian. Most would also later be convicted. The "reign of terror" was not over – in the early days of May the police broke up a Canadian Labor Defence League protest meeting against the May Day arrests (again with help from firemen) and made two more arrests. They banned the ILP's Open Forum, closed down a Russian club, and warned hall owners, under the threat of Section 98, not to rent to radicals. The Communists' petition campaign for "free speech" in the city had over 2,000 signatures by midsummer, but the repression had once again effectively shattered local organizing. A local correspondent admitted that Hamilton no longer had an unemployed group "strong enough to put up a real organized fight."[96]

Many people had been politicized in the spring confrontations, and by the end of the summer of 1932 a new Workers' Protective Association was functioning, apparently without Communist tutelage but with the party's support. It sent five women delegates to the Workers' Economic Conference held in Ottawa that summer. A new player was on the scene as well – a small branch of a national organization of radicalized veterans known as the Workers' Ex-Servicemen's League, which participated in some of the ensuing confrontations. That fall the new unemployed association led campaigns for cash relief and restoration of cuts in relief, and against evictions and "forced labour on relief." In late October police moved in on a demonstration called to take these demands to city hall and arrested five instigators. In response the Association staged a week of daily demonstrations until Mayor John Peebles conceded their most important demands.[97]

Meanwhile the Communists were rebuilding the network of neighbourhood councils and a central council alongside (and in co-operation with) the Workers' Protective Association. In March 1933, for example, the east-end Jockey Club Neighbourhood Council used mass pickets to block the eviction of a family. As the sheriff's staff moved the furniture out, the pickets carried them back in. "The agitation was rewarded by the pressure developed and by the individual cases won," one of the young activists would later write. "The shoes or coat won for a child unable to go to school for want of clothing; the bag of coal for a family freezing in mid-winter; the medicine for someone ill; the removal of a welfare official for insulting relief recipients; the interpreter supplied for some damn foreigner."[98]

That spring the unemployed organizations mounted a series of protests against cuts to relief and, unquestionably with Communist inspiration, against alleged war preparations. This time May Day events were organized to support a deputation to city hall, with the representatives chosen the day before at a mass meeting in Woodlands Park. On May Day itself, workers rallying in that park heard speeches before marching to Market Square to join a second rally, where the delegation to the Board of Control reported back. Organizers estimated that 10,000 participated, this time without police harassment.[99]

By the end of May 1933 the Welfare Board's decision to cut married men's relief by 10 to 20 per cent and to reduce the meals provided for

(*Worker*, 21 April 1934, 1)

single men to two per day had triggered a new wave of organizing. A new Single Men's Unemployed Association, affiliated with the Workers' Protective Association, demanded work for wages in cash and sponsored a mass meeting at which several men tore up their work cards, refusing to work without pay. Within a few days at least 50 more had made this defiant gesture. At a mass meeting the following weekend sponsored by the Workers' Protective Association, participants proclaimed a strike of relief workers. Picket lines went up at all work sites, but the police arrived to keep the places open to anyone who chose to work. Arrests on charges of intimidation, obstructing police, "watching and besetting" strikebreakers, and vagrancy soon mounted up. Many men were cut off relief. After three weeks the organizers called an end to what was a collapsing effort. The national secretary of the Workers' Unity League sharply criticized the Hamilton comrades for their eagerness to join the wave of relief strikes across the country and their haste in calling a strike of single workers without adequate preparation.[100]

The Communists' rigid sectarianism started to diminish over the following months, and they attempted to rebuild working relationships with the city's unions and the ILP. Such co-operation would continue into what the Communists called the Popular Front period beginning in 1935. That spring the much-maligned Lawrence and other members of the new Co-operative Commonwealth Federation (CCF) joined Communists at the head of a 4,000-person May Day parade. The next year Lawrence joined a union tour of the Soviet Union and returned with glowing reports.[101]

Meanwhile, others in Hamilton were drawing different conclusions from the tumultuous events of the early 1930s. As they did a decade earlier, local businessmen tried to channel protest into the politically safer terrain of voluntarism. The Chamber of Commerce had not taken a public stand on the many months of police repression, but in 1932 did pressure city councillors to cut expenditures on relief. In April 1933 it took a decisive move towards a potentially more effective way of diffusing dissent and deflecting the unemployed away from both reliance on state relief and radical leadership. The Chamber was concerned that, with the soaring numbers out of work, the political pressure on the city's Welfare Board for higher relief food allowances could not be met (without, of course, dipping deeper into the public purse). Two years earlier the city had begun to request owners of empty lots to turn them over for use as gardens by the unemployed, and a few companies had provided space. Now those on relief were informed that such gardening was compulsory.

The Chamber took charge of a hugely expanded community garden plot project through which more than 5,000 married men on relief were assigned space to grow vegetables for their families and were at the same time exempted from the Welfare Board's new requirement that they work for their relief (what the Communists called "forced labour"). With six or seven large companies looking after about a quarter of these men, a special Chamber committee co-ordinated the whole project with the assistance of a general supervisor paid for by the Steel Company and 14 other supervisors. The committee provided seeds and tools and offered prizes for the best gardens. Great care was taken to select the best seeds and to oversee cultivation "to assure as great a yield as possible." At the end of 1934 the Chamber's committee could report: "The abundant yield of the past two seasons has given these families more than sufficient vegetables for table use during the season and also enabled them to store a considerable quantity for use throughout the winter." Many men with no gardening experience, it was said, became skilled at urban agriculture. Older men who had the hardest time finding work were particularly enthusiastic participants. This program ran until the end of the decade, with more than 5,000 men participating again in 1934, but only half that number by 1937 as more jobs became available.[102]

The businessmen in charge believed that such a project would have the advantage of "keeping up the morale of the men and occupying their spare time." As in the immediate postwar period, the initiative would also cast the businessman in a more favourable light as a provider of community service and demonstrate "that the problem of caring for the unemployed married man is receiving the sympathy and support of those in a position to do so." Late in April 1933 the committee chair, construction magnate H.P. Frid, confidently predicted, "The action which had already been taken would have a very favorable effect on any 1st of May labor agitation which might be considered as already some of those who had been agitators were taking an active interest in the work." He was too optimistic – May Day drew out thousands that year – but, by the end of the second year, the organizers were congratulating themselves that "since the inauguration of the garden scheme in Hamilton there has been no evidence of trouble or discontent among our unemployed." Indeed, the frequent unemployed protests did decline after the middle of 1933 (though the redirection of Communist policy away from unemployed organizing by 1934–35 was probably part of the reason). More strikes of relief workers in October 1934 and January 1935 collapsed quickly, and by early 1936 the mayor could safely promise "sharp reductions to recipients, so that the people will not make a profession of relief." A few months later the city council confidently banned demonstrations on Market Square. The Workers' Protective Association had deteriorated, and efforts by both Communists and CCFers to get a new organization of the unemployed off the ground during 1936 were slow and halting.[103]

The community garden program proved to be a brilliantly conceived process of turning the attention of unemployed breadwinners away from marches and demonstrations towards physical work to sustain their families. Ideologically it also reinvigorated the notion that individual solutions to social problems were preferable to "socialization," which, one Chamber member bemoaned in 1934, was the "constant demand from various classes of society for matters to be undertaken by the State."[104]

Voting for Humanity

To the horror of such men, the crisis of unemployment was transforming electoral politics in Hamilton in the 1930s, as it did across the country. Unemployment became the issue that could not be avoided in public debates and could not easily be solved within civil society.

As the economic depression deepened, the Independent Labor Party began to rebuild. (*HS*, 29 Nov. 1930, 27)

The decade had opened with Bennett leading the federal Conservatives in a successful rout of King's Liberal government and promising a dramatic cure for unemployment through tariff reform to keep out foreign goods.[105] In 1931 a by-election in East Hamilton brought the Tories a stunning defeat, and for the rest of the decade they found their support slipping away. Their social-democratic and liberal opponents were far more successful in shaping a popular politics of renewal and hope.

Labourists were the first beneficiaries of the politicization of unemployment, though not for long. In the 1931 federal by-election, true to their imperialist colours, the Conservatives ran "Empire Bobby" Robinson, a *Spectator* sports writer who had organized the British Empire Games in Hamilton the year before and who pledged himself repeatedly to "Canada first, but Canada within the Empire." The Empire was not the issue, however, as he was thrown on the defensive by the staggering jobless count and the failure of Bennett's year-old promises. His only serious opponent was the ILP's Humphrey Mitchell, an English-born electrical worker, long-time secretary of the Hamilton Trades and Labor Council, and part of the small ILP caucus on city council.[106] In meetings called at Woodlands Park and other familiar sites where unemployed men gathered, the ILP campaign highlighted the need for unemployment insurance and legislated shorter hours to spread around work, along with better old-age pensions and health insurance. Workers should cast "A Vote for Humanity," Mitchell's advertising urged. For the first time the ILP made a specific pitch to "foreign" workers. The Tories' attempt to red-bait the ILP and its supporters fell flat, and Mitchell picked up nearly 60 per cent of the vote. The *Spectator* sadly agreed with Robinson that his defeat could be explained by "the revulsion of feeling caused by disappointed hopes and the general dissatisfaction of the times." Hamilton had its first-ever Labor MP, and Canada had its first east of Manitoba.[107]

Hamilton's labourites had taken a new lease on life, and in 1932 and 1933 they won six seats on city council. Yet trouble was brewing. The old right-left tensions between the Central ILP Branch and the east-end and other suburban branches still simmered, especially after the launching of the Co-operative Commonwealth Federation in 1933. Four local ILP branches joined the area's six CCF clubs in a Regional Council of the new party, and rekindled both educational programs and electoral ambitions. But the ILP's Central Branch voted to stay out, and Mitchell refused to join. With Mitchell on the fringes of the Liberal caucus in Ottawa, that organization resurrected a kind of Lib-Labism that had not been so vigorous since the early years of the century. The split soon extended to city council, where a handful of ILP councillors also kept their distance from the new party. The ILP's ever-popular controller, Lawrence, however, was an enthusiastic CCF supporter.[108]

In the 1934 provincial election the CCF ran candidates in all four local ridings and made minimum wages for all workers and unemployment insurance central campaign issues. Of those candidates, three lost, but Lawrence won handily in East Hamilton (again without Liberal opposition), where his Tory opponent conceded that "the general depression, discontent and dissatisfaction of the working classes" had brought his defeat. For the next three years Lawrence was the CCF's lone voice in the Ontario legislature, where he argued that unemployment could be solved only by the "establishment of a planned, scientific economy and by scrapping the present system." That fall the CCF optimistically ran candidates for controller, alderman, and school trustee, and, in the federal election the next year, put up the eloquent John Mitchell against the incumbent ILPer, Humphrey Mitchell (no relation), who had the scarcely concealed support of the Liberals.[109] In their new enthusiasm for a "popular front," the Communists agreed to support the CCFers. Yet the left fragmented in any case, both through the ongoing tension with the Central ILP and with the appearance of Reconstruction candidates in all three federal ridings – people inspired by the message of the renegade Conservative H.H. Stevens about wealthy Canadians' misuse of power – who walked off with nearly a quarter of the votes. In the municipal contests, the CCF was reduced to one council seat between 1934 and 1936 and only two in 1937 and 1938. All the ILPers were also defeated. In the 1935 federal fight the Conservatives managed, with just over a third of the votes, to squeeze by the multitude of progressive candidates in all three local ridings (despite the vicious heckling of Bennett when he spoke in Hamilton during the campaign).[110]

The left had not just split; it was also being outmanoeuvred by resurgent Liberalism. In the 1934 provincial election the Liberals won three of the four Hamilton ridings as part of their province-wide victory. The revived party under Mitchell Hepburn's leadership had leaned left sufficiently to catch much of the protest vote, promising unemployment insurance and good government in general. By 1937 Hepburn's populist credentials were tarnished by his heavy-handed intervention into the Oshawa autoworkers' strike and his fever-pitch denunciation of the new CIO union organizing in Ontario. But he rode confidently into the election that year, and in Hamilton put up a Liberal against Lawrence. It was a bad moment for Lawrence. Not only did he have to contend with the relentless sniping of the Lib-Labbers, but he was also centrally involved in the vicious battles between the craft unionists and industrial unionists that tore apart the local Trades and Labor Council that year. His campaign for re-election made almost no dent in the press coverage, and he went down to a humiliating defeat, running third behind the victorious Liberal and the defeated Tory.[111]

The federal Liberals used less populist campaign rhetoric, but once back in office in 1935 they began slowly to construct more state-centred programs to handle unemployment. This trajectory owed less to the ever-cautious King, who was primarily interested in cutting government spending and restoring the work ethic among the unemployed, than to the small cadre of social scientists drawn into Liberal policy forums and the federal civil service to help construct a new agenda for liberalism, including a new approach to unemployment. The short-lived National Employment Commission became the first hothouse for these ideas. Rather than focusing on job creation, it emphasized the deficiencies of the unemployed and the need for training programs to make them "employable." Then, late in 1937, its final report picked up the issue that had been a central refrain in popular protest and in all the provincial and federal campaigns over the previous five years – state-sponsored unemployment insurance. Before his defeat in 1935 the arch-Tory Prime Minister Bennett had shocked the country by pushing a measure through Parliament, but in 1937 it bounced back from the highest courts as being constitutionally beyond federal jurisdiction. Pushed by his advisers and by public support from groups like the Hamilton Trades and Labor Council and the Communist Party, King gradually accepted this new federal responsibility and eventually got the provinces onside to allow for the passing of the Unemployment Insurance Act of 1940, despite the active opposition of the Canadian Chamber of Commerce and other business groups. In contrast to earlier Communist demands, this measure required workers to contribute some of their earnings to a central fund. It was thus an enforced savings program for those with jobs, to prepare them for the rainy day of unemployment. It also ignored several occupational groups, including many women, and, in the long tradition of charity administration, to avoid competing with wage labour it kept benefits below the lowest wage rates.[112]

The political hot potato of unemployment thus passed out of the hands of the extraparliamentary forces that had shaped it since 1920 into the bureaucratic channels of liberal technocrats. The thousands of local workers who faced or feared the threat of joblessness had turned their gaze on the politicians of the centre and left, who promised a less demeaning solution than the one still being promoted by businessmen and a less confrontational process of getting there than the method proposed by the Communists. They ultimately got a carefully restricted program of insurance against losing a job, but it was a plan that fit into a new era of citizenship and its entitlements ushered in during World War Two – well beyond anything that working-class Hamilton had known in the previous half-century.

The Lessons of Unemployment

In the two decades between the world wars, then, unemployment became a touchstone for competing groups in civil society, each promoting a distinctive notion of citizenship. In their own ways, businessmen, veterans, and Communists each had some success in shaping responses to unemployment and directing the behaviour of large numbers of the jobless. Each group articulated a different sense of citizens' rights and spoke to the masses of unemployed people in Hamilton in the 1920s and 1930s. They dominated the public debates about how working people should understand their plight.

The Chamber's proclaimed commitment to community service and its dedication to finding new forms of social cohesion that did not rock the boat of liberal industrial capitalism brought its members to the forefront of debates over how to respond to unemployment. Its businesslike efforts to stimulate confidence in the economic system, to lean on municipal governments to maintain order and restraint in the face of depressions, and to put in place programs and practices that encouraged individuals' responsibility for their well-being – from social-work casework to garden plots – all must have had an impact on how at least some jobless men came to understand and respond to their plight. Rely on your own energies and resources, the voice of the city's business community told them. Citizenship meant independent self-reliance, they insisted.

Some of the same businessmen crossed over into the leadership of veterans groups and tried to carry the experience of military service into civilian life. Right after the war, however, the veterans' organizations were too volatile and too full of populist anger to be lulled into quiescent loyalty, and their ideological construction of the needs of Canadian society put them beyond the reach of bourgeois leadership. In the end, most pulled back from any broader alliances and staked a more limited claim for the rights of their own membership on the basis of the noble, valorous service of male warriors to Canada and the Empire, and they disparaged the rights of the "foreign-born" and the radical left. Warriors were super-citizens with special rights and entitlements, they argued.

Some leaders in the ranks of veterans nonetheless carried the agitation beyond those limitations onto a terrain of radicalism where the leading voices were Communists. These "Reds" made the most persistent, determined efforts to rally all the unemployed, including the veterans, hoping to bring them to a radical awareness of capitalist exploitation and a commitment to revolutionary transformation. Workers were citizens who should expect the state to meet their collective needs for social security, they proclaimed, and who should be organized in militant groups to demand (and, they hoped, win) such rights.

The three groups interacted. The Chamber's approach was shaped in part by the agitations of angry veterans and the emergence of new postwar radicalism. The garden plot project would probably never have appeared if Communist militants had not managed to focus so much anger and bitterness on the inadequate relief system. The veterans had an internal tussle between men with more affinity to the Chamber and those who were drawn to the clarity of the radical left. The Communists fought to discredit the integrative paternalism of the business response and what they feared were neo-fascist tendencies in the Legion.

This was not a polite debate about alternative citizenships – it was a series of confrontations in which class power came to play a decisive role. The capitalist statesmanship of the Chamber of Commerce was effectively sustained by the armed force of the state against the more radical and militant organizers of the unemployed. The large numbers of workers who converged on Woodlands Park on May Day 1932 were definitely listening to Communist agitators, and the iron heel that the police brought down on them may have deepened those convictions. When Tim Buck walked onto a stage in Hamilton's Alexander Academy in 1935, after his release from prison, he contrasted his audience of 2,500 with the 200 who had shown up to hear him on his last visit.[113]

Yet when at any point in the interwar period the Communists tried to translate the resentment and gut-level radicalism into votes in a ballot box, they failed miserably. Their main competitors on the left, the ILP and CCF, carried many of the same concerns into their own electoral campaigns, but their mutual hostility in the context of the great North American labour war over CIO-style industrial unionism weakened their attacks and allowed liberals to construct their own new, but more limited, vision of "social" citizenship. By 1940, then, after two decades of agitation and contestation, a workingman could for the first time claim some right to be at least partially protected from the uncertainties of wage labour.[114]

19

(*CLW*, 28 Aug. 1925,1)

Lunch-Bucket Politics

THE LUNCH BUCKET HAS A STORY OF ITS OWN. At the turn of the century most wage-earners carried a cheap, mass-produced pail with internal compartments and a lid. Then the Thermos corporation brought a new lunch container onto the market – the now iconic rectangular box with a humped lid, into which the company's new "vacuum flask" would nicely fit. By the 1930s thousands of workers across the continent had been convinced to make the switch. The typical workers' lunch bucket had a completely new look.[1]

It would be easy to say that the shape of working-class life in cities such as Hamilton went through a similarly dramatic makeover during that same period. Certainly workers confronted many pressures to change their habits between the 1890s and the 1930s. Workplaces grew larger and more authoritarian, the pace of work was cranked up, neighbourhoods swelled with sometimes unfamiliar newcomers, and families were prodded and poked with new social policies. Making ends meet became more difficult, even as new incentives to buy and spend appeared at every turn. In workplaces, households, and neighbourhoods, much was new by World War Two. Yet workers in Hamilton did not let all of these pressures simply sweep them along. Just as their fancy new lunch containers were ultimately still just cheap metal boxes with all of the same multiple meanings for their lives as witnessed over the decades, so too were there important continuities within the disruptive transformation of workers' experience.

Workers were pushed, prodded, tempted, and cajoled to adapt to the new world taking shape around them. Many did, willingly or reluctantly. Many accepted the inevitability of the new social order and their subordination within it. It was just "common sense." Yet important patterns of resistance also came to the fore. In various ways Hamilton's workers doggedly held onto well-established ways of living and found countless ways of avoiding change. As much as possible they made use of familiar coping mechanisms and adapted those strategies to new circumstances. In other ways they challenged the main currents of change, confronting them with new ideas and practices, often selectively appropriating the innovations and adapting them to their own needs. By all these routes, they often found ways of negotiating outcomes that were different from those intended. The core of these coping practices for working people was to maintain some independence – holding onto their ability to make their own decisions based on their own criteria and standards, that is, a minimum

of proletarian democracy – along with a commitment to mutual support and aspirations for dignity, security, and, where possible, pleasure. A persistent realism about what might be possible at any particular moment made those aspirations open-ended and potentially expansive if the threat of poverty receded and alternative political and cultural visions offered new hope. In the process a lot changed, and a lot did not.

In hindsight it seems that 1920 turned out to be a kind of rough dividing line in the experience of working people. Up to that point, practices and relationships in working-class Hamilton tended to follow lines that had been worked out in the First Industrial Revolution of the late 19th century. By about 1905, workers had begun to face sharp new interventions in their households, workplaces, and social networks that threatened their familiar ways of coping. The impact of these new challenges was initially limited, but World War One became a major catalyst. It accelerated both workers' desire for more secure, respectable independence and the assault on that independence. The war legitimized more interventionism into working-class life, and provided the basis for extended programs after the war, when widespread underemployment weakened their room to manoeuvre. In the interwar period after 1920 workers had to remake their lives in many complex ways.

Living Apart

At the turn of the 20th century Hamilton's working people could look back on a half-century of experience in learning how to adapt to a system of wage labour. In the late 19th century Hamilton's industrialists had brought together a rich mix of occupations to turn out a huge variety of products, construct buildings, and provide many services. By the 1890s these wage-earners and their families were a fairly stable population made up mostly of white Anglo-Canadians well attuned to the rhythms and demands of industrial capitalism. In previous decades working people had been confronted with new pressures and constraints that shaped their abilities to survive primarily on wages. Yet in their own version of working-class realism, they had built a way of life that attempted to meet their material needs and at the same time maintain some dignity and independence from bourgeois authority at work, at home, and in their neighbourhoods. As the great wave of labour organizing in the 1880s revealed, this way of life could become the basis of much more expansive aspirations and demands. Despite setbacks, these practices persisted with remarkable determination well into the early 20th century.

Workers' families were the bedrock of daily survival. The unpaid labour of housewives and children sustained the wage-earners who found jobs in the city, and nurtured the next generation of workers. For the most part, working-class women were left alone to run their households and raise their children. Their competence as domestic managers, especially in juggling household budgets, was essential to working-class existence and could be a source of pride. These were family economies based on wages as income, but also, as much as possible, on self-help and self-reliance, including a husband's building and repairing, backyard gardening, and, where possible, hunting and fishing, and a wife's willingness to look after boarders or perhaps offer nursing services in the neighbourhood. More troubling for these housewives was the persistent need for home health care in the face of sometimes deadly contagious diseases and other serious illnesses, injuries, and disabilities. Schooling for their offspring was respected, as enrolment figures in local schools attested, but by early adolescence most youngsters were expected to be helping out at home or bringing home wages.

Weekly spending in all working-class families was usually limited to necessities, and only a housewife's careful budgeting could allow for bigger purchases, whether a stove, a suit, or a house (which relatively few workers owned). The fragile family economies could be abruptly undermined. The disappearance of the husband's wage through unemployment, accident, sickness, death, or desertion could be devastating, no matter what skill level or status in the workforce he had. Before World War One no state programs were in place to deal with such crises. When they could, families invested in various insurance schemes to protect against calamities; otherwise they turned to kin and neighbours for help. Only fatherless households could expect any ongoing charity, which most families avoided at all costs as being too demeaning. Sometimes families in crisis could send their children off to an orphanage or elderly parents to an old-folks home, but these were often short-term strategies for putting the family economy back together. Getting by on their own was a core component in the respectability to which most of these working-class families aspired.

For some, a family economy had no meaning. Fatherless families with no wages flowing in clung to a meagre existence with handouts from tight-fisted charities. Rootless single men far from families and out of work often had no place to turn to other than a hostel or a flophouse. In hard times they might head off to the city's stone yard and a soup kitchen. Unlike the women and children mired in poverty, these men tended to move on.

Jobs brought different challenges. For a family's wage-earners, especially the husband/father, the long working days in local factories and other work sites severely constrained their bodies and their time. The simple industrial paternalism that their bosses or foremen extended over them could be stifling and demeaning, though, for some, the security guaranteed by that relationship helped sustain their family economies. At the turn of the century workers also knew that production processes still relied to a remarkable degree on their manual labour, whether skilled or unskilled, and the know-how that went with it. That had been the basis of strong, informal solidarity within work groups on the shop floor and of their ability to control some of the rhythms of production. It had also enabled a surge of organization among wage-earners in the 1880s, and, after severe setbacks in the union-busting economic doldrums of the early 1890s, a vibrant craft union movement sprang back to life in the city. For a short time after the turn of the century, these unions were able to nail down relatively stable collective-bargaining relationships, symbolized by the union label on many consumer goods, and to pressure many of the city's employers to reduce the working week by a half-day on Saturday. As a sign of the solidarities that had taken root, the city's workers turned a confrontation between unionized street-railway workers and their corporate employer into riotous public battles through the city streets for four weeks in 1906.

In such a large city, the working people typically lived in neighbourhoods full of other workers. They could therefore expect to rub shoulders with others like themselves when they entered a nearby store, church, saloon, or lodge meeting hall. The popular culture that they could afford in these neighbourhoods thus tended to reinforce their class awareness, and furthered their desire for independence to make their own lives. Much of Hamilton workers' free time was lived beyond the household in the public spaces of the city. Boys roamed about in gangs, and, as they grew up, often found their way into informal sports and eventually pool halls, saloons, and perhaps lodge meeting rooms. Girls were generally more constrained by domestic responsibilities and family fears about moral dangers, but nonetheless also enjoyed some fun in the streets. Eventually they might find a recreational as well as spiritual outlet in a local church. Social reform groups reached out to them, but attracted few recruits. Whole families sometimes also ventured out together, perhaps to a Sunday church service or on a holiday picnic in a park. But far more often bachelors and married men headed out on their own to find the informal company of other men. They left their wives, mothers, and sisters struggling with the burdens of domestic labour on their own.

Plenty of this working-class behaviour faced close regulation. The police court was a particularly important site for constraining the excesses of working-class masculinities, from street-fighting to drunkenness to petty pilfering to violent acts of patriarchal authority against spouses and children. For decades moral-reform bodies attempted to actively restrain overly expressive public behaviour – particularly prohibitionists raging against the consumption of booze and Sabbatarians against almost everything that workers liked to do on Sundays. A more stringent Criminal Code passed in 1892 also tightened the moral oversight of personal relationships. To varying degrees workers found ways of carrying out their own versions of courtship or male bonding that slipped under the radar of this bourgeois scorn.

In the city other forces were at work that aimed to pull workers out of their life apart and to encourage them to celebrate identities they shared with other social classes. Many workers bowed their heads in a church pew or cheered at the sight of the Union Jack, but often they made their religion or patriotism fit their own standards and values. In the same way, politics was the most important social cement for some workingmen. Those who could vote, and did, might find echoes of their aspirations in the rhetoric and platforms of the Liberal and Conservative parties. The Tories were particularly adept at shaping a message for a proletarian audience. They used their promises of secure factory jobs in a tariff-protected industrial economy in particular to gradually win control of all three levels of government. Many of the city's leading craft unionists, disillusioned with both parties for their indifference to labour issues, organized a few independent labour campaigns. But by 1905 they had little to show for their efforts. Nor did the city's tiny socialist organizations.

Working-class Hamilton at the turn of the century was far from a completely homogeneous, unified community. The battered wife in court seeking support from a drunken husband exposed the violence simmering beneath the surface of the patriarchal household. Spotting her son among the unruly boys throwing rocks through a window or a daughter flirting with boys under a lamppost reminded a mother about generational tensions and raised her fears for the family's respectability. Neighbours watching members of a printer's family set off in their best outfits for a Dominion Day picnic could see what extra pleasures a skilled worker's regular wages could provide. The poorly paid labourer leaning on his shovel as he watched the moulders filing into a closed union meeting felt the limits of workplace solidarity. The proud machinist who watched an older worker doff his cap as the boss passed through the shop spat in disgust at such acts of deference within industrial paternalism. The labour candidate who ran last in the municipal election saw how deep divergent political allegiances ran in his neighbourhood.

Yet these were all conflicts within a working-class context. They reflected broad patterns of class awareness, but differences about what to do with it. As much as the printer's family, the rebellious drunk or juvenile delinquent wanted relief from the pressures and expectations of life as a worker. The labourer and the machinist shared a cynicism about organizing possibilities, though for different reasons. The labour candidate would probably run again.

The Gathering Storm

Much of that working-class world was destabilized in the decade and a half before 1920. Corporations sent out the first shock waves as they restructured the local economy. Long-standing operations based in consumer-goods production withered away, along with their labour-intensive work processes and their more secure niches for craft unionism, while whole new mass-production plants sprang up to make heavier metal and textile goods. New labour markets emerged that left behind most child labourers, and offered work to many more young women and immigrant labourers. As immigration agents herded thousands of eager new workers into Canada, working-class Hamilton swelled with newcomers looking for jobs, many of them from parts of Southern and Eastern Europe or even China.

The households from which this new workforce emerged each day faced deeply troubling challenges. Retail prices shot up, and wild boom-and-bust business cycles pushed chief breadwinners in and out of work. More frequent workplace injuries undercut the household income, and youngsters found it harder to contribute to the family coffers as full-time wage-earners. Labour markets were disrupted as employers undermined traditional occupational hierarchies on the shop floor and dipped into the new, cheaper pools of immigrant labour. At the same time families in working-class Hamilton encountered rising pressures to buy more consumer goods for their households and to put a little of their precious cash into commercialized fun.

Along with these economic pressures on wage-earning and housekeeping came much more direct interventions to alter workers' habits and behaviour in almost all arenas of working-class life. This was not a tightly co-ordinated project, but plenty of cross-fertilization occurred among the movements that spearheaded these diverse efforts. In some cases the campaigns were purely repressive in the 19th-century mode, relying on harsh legal penalties – arrests for vagrancy and prostitution, blue-Sunday laws, curbs on behaviour in parks, suppression of gambling and prize-fighting, movie censorship, the prohibition of alcohol consumption, clamping down on immigrant boardinghouse life, constraints on picketing, repression of demonstrations, and even the national Anti-Loafing Law of 1918. A much tighter net of legal constraints was thrown up to restrict disruptive or transgressive working-class practices.

Yet more characteristic of this new period were efforts to correct working-class behaviour through closer surveillance and direction, under the banner of "efficiency" and "science." Middle-class professionals most often provided the ideas and blueprints that were then picked up and put into place by private enterprise, independent agencies, and government departments. Perhaps most famously, managerial experts helped industrialists to reorganize production processes in the city's factories. They set out to redesign jobs to eliminate or at least reduce workers' independence on the job and to put control over the pace and process of work more solidly in the front office. They developed elaborate systems of incentives to encourage workers to buy

in – piecework and bonus schemes on one hand, various welfare measures on the other. The war economy gave all these practices a huge boost as the city's factories fired up to produce shells, uniforms, and much more. Industrial paternalism had entered its corporate phase.

The "science" that the new industrial experts claimed for these new programs became something of a touchstone for efforts in other parts of life. Indeed, "scientific" mothering was promoted relentlessly. Child-savers labelled working-class parenting skills inadequate, and designed new institutions – notably the Children's Aid Society, juvenile court, and Big Brothers and Big Sisters – to take charge of the apparently wayward, with new inspectorates to monitor parents. Special programs were designed to handle working-class children deemed to fall within the loose definition of "feeble-minded." Public-health workers targeted all proletarian mothers with radically new approaches to infant care, and those with tubercular husbands with new procedures and expectations. Marketing experts made buying many commercial products into a marker of good housekeeping and responsible motherhood. If families or single mothers were in dire straits, the emerging professionals in the field of social work would intervene to investigate, advise, and supervise.

Working-class youth were also targeted. Educators insisted they should be staying in school longer and taking more vocationally oriented classes. New professionally trained youth workers ran programs in supervised playgrounds or for the YMCA and YWCA, Scouts and Guides, and sundry other religious and secular youth agencies, including the Big Brothers and Big Sisters. The goal was to bring working-class youth under more direct middle-class oversight during their playtime. In the same vein, small numbers of churchmen also decided that the new European immigrants needed to be integrated and assimilated into the new social order through Canadianization projects.

For families in trouble, the old charitable "homes" that were once expected to house the dependent poor, and that many working-class families had learned to use on a short-term basis, were fading into insignificance. Instead, the priority in privately and publicly administered social welfare became direct intervention in the working-class household by full-time "visitors," who could teach new habits, culminating in the use of professionally trained social workers.

The state was not central to this process, but it had certainly helped. Repressive laws to control public and private behaviour proliferated and gave the police magistrate a fuller courtroom each morning. Legislation to enable more intervention and surveillance empowered some voluntary groups of child-savers, and eventually brought much of their energy inside the civil service in special new or expanded departments of education, child welfare, and public health.

Holding On

This vast, interconnected program of social engineering did not quickly find its legs, and although eventually able to make a significant impact after 1920, it was never completely successful. It was not a matter of either total victory or completely effective resistance. Rather, working-class Hamiltonians negotiated their responses through a complex process of compliance, adaptation, and resistance.

The limited outcome came about, first of all, because of the weak response that the new experts got from business and the state. The ideologues and practitioners of social engineering were often battering their heads against a wall of scepticism and parsimony. Tongues were certainly wagging about pioneering experiments before World War One – the Westinghouse time clocks, the technical school, the well-baby clinic, the supervised playgrounds, and the school nurses, for example – but those projects were isolated and made only a tiny dent in working-class life. Local firms continued to rely on the familiar "drive" methods of front-line foremen, and few had embraced scientific management or full-fledged welfarism before the end of World War One. Even in the 1920s, many of the new welfarist measures were quietly abandoned in favour of more old-fashioned methods of workplace rule. Outside the factories, the medical officer of health raged about the unwillingness of the city or the Board of Education to fund public-health work, at least until the devastating influenza epidemic of 1918–20, and much of the city's socialized health care – notably well-baby clinics and tuberculosis care – remained in philanthropic hands into the 1930s. The city also refused to support a juvenile court until the early 1920s, and left a charity to run playgrounds until the 1930s. Right through to the end of that decade, social workers gnashed their teeth in frustration at how little effort Hamilton's charitable agencies put into co-ordinating their efforts and how many charity and relief workers still had no training in their new profession. "Progressivism" certainly did not sweep all before it in early 20th-century Hamilton.

These multiplying interventions into working-class life also proved limited because, wherever they could, workers kept their distance and stood their ground against them, or extracted only the parts that made sense to them. To a great extent they clung to old habits and reactivated familiar practices. Their family economies were particularly resilient. As rents in the city soared, many people crammed boarders or even whole families into their households, or seized the opportunity to buy up small plots of land on the edge of the city and hammer together small homes with their own sweat equity. If the economy was booming (as it did notably during World War One), they pulled their children out of school and sent them to work. Often technical training was left for evening classes somewhat later in life. Even in the interwar period this kind of family strategizing survived to a remarkable degree: most teenagers stayed in school no longer than legally required; family size was reduced; and mothers began to work in the early years of their marriages. In the cramped immigrant boardinghouses, the newcomers defied bourgeois standards of household propriety in their temporary living arrangements and focused on how to sustain their families back home in the peasant villages of Southern and Eastern Europe with the cash they earned during their brief sojourns in Hamilton. They almost completely ignored the evangelical preachers who tried to win them over.

If male wage-earning faltered, the city's workers tried to deploy their own family labour – putting children and mothers to work – with help from kin and neighbours, rather than turning to new social-work agencies. In the face of demands that they change their daily habits, many mothers stayed away from charities and clinics, and, for the same reasons, many youngsters steered clear of playgrounds, Scouts and Guides, and the male and female Ys. In a wave of civil disobedience, gambling continued in city parks, and thirsty drinkers defied prohibition by visiting neighbourhood bootleggers.

These working people exhibited a persistent preference for older, more familiar, more independent ways of living that did not patronize or disparage them. Many eligible working-class voters – perhaps even a majority – rejected the paternalistic discourses of the mainstream parties and simply stayed away from the polls on election days. A similar attitude kept many away from the mainstream churches, and the success of so many working-class churches rested on this quiet spirit of independence. Workers, regularly turning their backs on the blandishments of advertisers, spent their leisure time in inexpensive social settings – family picnics in parks, courting rituals on street corners, quiet drinks with workmates in saloons, blind pigs, and beverage rooms, or more sober discussions in lodge, church, or union meeting halls.

In the realm of waged labour, many workers responded to oppressive new workplace environments by staying off work (if the economy was booming) or moving on, often out of frustration with the stress of the jobs, though perhaps after piling up handsome pay packets at high-pressure piecework. Men and women who were offered their employer's welfarist goodies often turned up their noses at such efforts to create the new "corporate family" as company magazines.

Simply avoiding the forces of disruptive change had its limits. Especially after 1920, maintaining distance was getting more difficult. Children were kept in the clutches of the school system for longer, and youth programs of various kinds embraced them in much larger numbers – more playgrounds, Scout and Guide troops, and Big Brothers' programs, for example. Public-health nurses crossed the doorsteps of many more working-class households. Charities and relief-work projects, especially during the years of severe unemployment in the 1930s, developed greater co-ordination in tracking the poor (although their attempts were still far from complete). Spurred on by wartime munitions production, scientific management got far more space in the city's leading metalworking and textile plants after the war, and speed-up became widespread. Consumerist messages about the good life available through buying the right products on easy credit terms were cranked up to a new intensity.

Taking a Stand

Yet Hamilton's workers did more than try to turn their backs on the new pressures. They pushed back against many of the most troubling changes, adapted them to their own needs, and devised alternatives. Some workers stepped forward with a clear sounding of working-class dilemmas and offered leadership for collective responses.

Those who engaged with interventionist agencies often took the parts of the programs that suited them and shaped the services to fit into their daily lives. Mothers had doctors attend their births, but stayed away from hospitals (until the mass poverty of the 1930s drove them there). They got their babies weighed at well-baby clinics, but dodged the preaching about new feeding by the clock. Working girls played basketball at the Y, but stayed away from religious services. Some workers attended neighbourhood churches, but generally only if the messages and activities met their needs. Immigrants learned to defer to Protestant missionaries if the church figures could put in a word for them at a factory employment office, but paid no attention to the evangelical message.

Corporate welfarism also had unexpected outcomes. Wage-earners focused on measures that promised more economic security and independence, such as benefit plans, or jobs for their children. International Harvester quickly found that its workers wanted to use its celebrated Industrial Council in 1919 to reduce working hours and make the factory safer. Company picnics were probably more important in allowing employees to nourish the bonds of family and workplace comradeship at company expense than they were at promoting company loyalty. Some key features of welfare capitalism evolved from gestures of benevolence into what workers came to see as entitlements.

Consumption also proved to be a complicated matter. By World War One many young, unmarried women had begun using their careful spending to fashion a "ladylike" world of fancy hats, makeup, cigarettes, and outings to dance halls, movies, and eventually even beverage rooms, a world that was distinctively working class in its bold, sassy style. Their brothers did the same in saloons or blind pigs, pool halls, and sporting arenas, and paid for most courtship activities with their dates. At all ages, workers reached out to mass culture selectively. They chose what fit with their values and expectations, and fashioned the new cultural products to fit into working-class courtship, friendship, family time, and other socializing practices. Commercial "showmen" tried to adapt to these attitudes and practices by offering pleasures that working people of different ages, genders, and marital status could get access to cheaply and comfortably – notably in sports arenas, amusement parks, dance halls, roller and ice rinks, and vaudeville and movie theatres.

Meanwhile, on the front lines of the domestic economy, housewives recognized when to grasp new patterns of spending that could make life easier – canned goods and store-bought bread, cheap ready-made clothing, an inexpensive electric iron, a radio for no-cost family entertainment – but they were not about to be easily lured into frivolous expenditures. They stayed at the edges of the consumer economy. They were never willing or, in the interwar period, able to buy much beyond basic needs, and struggled to save enough to withstand the next shockwaves of joblessness and, perhaps, to buy the security of a family home. At different points housewives also turned to co-operative stores, tried boycotts of high-priced goods, and applauded the efforts of labour spokespeople to fight the accursed high cost of living. By 1920 a small number of them were organizing politically to promote and defend the interests of the working-class housewife and mother, first in the Women's Independent Labor Party and then in the Women's Labor League (and its Ukrainian counterpart), which would become active in unemployed agitations in the 1930s.

On the job both male and female wage-earners often mobilized their immediate work groups to resist particularly infuriating management initiatives that disrupted customary workplace practices. Occasionally they appealed to the rest of a factory workforce to shut off their machines and march out on strike, often doing this without the aid of a union. Craftworkers, notably moulders and machinists, were the best placed to take these stands, though they had a painfully limited track record within the Second Industrial Revolution. The gap between "trades" and "labour" had been narrowing and filling in with many new semi-skilled workers. While the city still had many skilled workers, their positions were increasingly enmeshed in more complex occupational hierarchies and subject to the close supervision, speed-up, and, by the interwar period, insecurity of employment that faced the whole workforce. As they became steadily more disillusioned with the emerging corporate-capitalist order, skilled workers were sometimes more ready to find common cause with others in working-class Hamilton and to assume the leadership. They struggled to adapt their craft traditions to the new context, particularly with tighter, more bureaucratized unions, and to articulate an alternative vision to the authoritarian factory regime that was emerging. In limited ways they eventually reached out to the less skilled – until their own interests seemed threatened.

In moments of confidence, especially during and following World War One, larger numbers of workers banded together to demand new institutions and procedures for negotiating over their needs. All-inclusive unions briefly appealed to textile, steel, and packing-house workers, among others, and radical militants promoted the One Big Union as an alternative. For many, the demand for a legislated eight-hour day encapsulated their aspirations. In many ways the remarkable success of the local Independent Labor Party rested on this desire for economic security, independence, and respectability. The craftworkers who led the labourist charge promised reforms to strengthen the capacities of the male breadwinners to provide for their families and to protect those without that kind of support with mothers' allowances and old-age pensions. Above all, they advocated a new, respected status for the working class, symbolized by adequate representation in legislative chambers.

The ILP's cautious, but expanding view of the need for state action got more backbone from the articulate socialists who were working within the party by the end of World War One. Those radicals were also linked to the clusters of Eastern Europeans who drew new inspiration from the Russian Revolution and were soon attempting to imitate the Bolshevik model. By 1921 the new Communist Party drew in many of these seasoned agitators, and for the next two decades became the driving force behind most industrial unionism and efforts to organize the unemployed. Starting in 1929 these radicals were centrally responsible for inspiring angry groups of factory workers to coalesce into militant unions in the midst of bitter strikes. The massive May Day protest of 1932 probably marked the pinnacle of Communist influence in the city.

Labourists, socialists, and communists were the intellectuals within the working class, providing analysis and arguments in their lectures, speeches, and newspaper columns to ignite the city's workers. When local workers' movements had size and momentum, those voices helped to expand public debate about state initiatives to improve working-class lives. A few modest measures owed their appearance to labour agitation – workers' compensation, women's minimum wage, old-age pensions, and, belatedly, unemployment insurance. Yet in the end the impact of the various workers' movements was severely limited. For most workers, taking a stand required resources to sustain the confrontations, especially enough available jobs in the local labour market to be able to avoid the whip of unemployment, victimization, and potential poverty.

The increasingly severe slumps in the business cycle in the early 20th century took the wind out of labour's sails and allowed for forces of authority to push back. Both craft and industrial unions were repeatedly driven out of Hamilton plants by determined employers, who by the interwar period were using spies and blacklists to keep them out. By the 1920s the Tories also managed to overwhelm the appeal of the Independent Labor Party. The police and courts came down hard on radicals who attempted to organize the unemployed in the 1920s and 1930s. In such a context more cautious labour leaders nervously reached out for formal recognition, willingly joining hands with industrialists, clergymen, and politicians to promote local industry, boost the war effort, or develop an ultimately fruitless dialogue about friendly industrial relations, all the while distancing themselves from radicals who rocked the boat.

The fleeting moments of solidarity were vastly outweighed by skilled workers' reluctance to risk their positions of occupational privilege. Deep divisions of status within working-class Hamilton based on skill, gender, and ethnic or racial group persisted and in some ways intensified in new forms. In contrast to most of their neighbours, the relatively small numbers of skilled men with regular, well-paying jobs could probably buy into some important new features of the period – keeping their children in school, purchasing a house (and maybe later a used car), acquiring a piano or a washing machine, joining churches and fraternal societies, taking their families on holiday outings, supporting a union, or running for political office. Their aspirations were probably not so different from the majority of people in working-class Hamilton, but they had greater resources available to realize their dreams; and they were generally reluctant to risk their advantages.

In the 1930s they were still standing in the way of industrial unionism with as much determination as they had at the turn of the century, and still defended the narrow, exclusivist approach of the American Federation of Labor. With only limited exceptions they showed no interest in their oppressed workmates who spoke another language, were held down in the low-wage jobs, and lived in separate neighbourhoods. "Foreigners" were viewed with suspicion and even contempt, and, while Hamilton lacked the deep racial divides between black and white that appeared in such US cities as Buffalo, Cleveland, or Detroit, Anglo-Canadian workers built few links with Southern and Eastern Europeans.

Hamilton ultimately had a bleak history of independent working-class organizing between the 1890s and 1930s. And the disillusionment and cynicism about such possibilities must have hung like a cloud over the city's working-class neighbourhoods. Without strong, deeply rooted class institutions, workers were more susceptible to other ideological constructions of their situations and other loyalties. Many recognized the need to accommodate to the industrial paternalism of workplace regimes controlled by powerful foremen and watchful front-office officials, and fell into patterns of respectful or calculating deference to benefit from the patronage of job security.

In a city with the lines between ethnic and racial groups deeply etched, some workers felt the call of burgeoning ethnic identities and focused their anger on other workers who spoke a different language or had a different skin colour. In an atmosphere of fear about disappearing jobs and immigrant competitors in the labour market, some workers embraced the Tory view of political economy. Some took comfort in the moral rigour of religious piety or the reassuring fantasies of movies and radio. Many no doubt knit together a combination of these different constructions of reality.

In the end an unknowable proportion, but probably a majority, simply developed a sense of realism about what was possible. In the bedrock of their families they tried, as much as possible, to continue struggling to find the security that would allow them to live their distinctive ways of life apart from bourgeois norms.

The Politics of the Lunch Bucket

The story of one city's working class has its moments of heroism, as groups of workers stood up to bosses, politicians, police, and others in an effort to make a substantially better life for themselves. But most often those moments passed, and the strikes, demonstrations, and campaigns had a sadly limited impact. Over the longer term, what stands out is the much quieter heroism of families, neighbours, gangs of friends, and groups of workmates who used every resource available to them to fashion daily lives that would give them a modicum of security and at least a small amount of pleasure – lives

that would lead to a profound sense of personal decency and respectability.

This quest was never an individualistic project – it required the mutual support of family, kin, neighbours, and workmates that was so central to working-class experience. Many people no doubt failed in that effort. The unevenness of personal resources in skill level or ethnic status, the calamities of illness or injury, or the variability of men's commitment to breadwinning or women's abilities to make ends meet could be crucial. But for that army of wage-earners heading into the streets each morning with their lunch buckets in hand, and for the families who depended on and supported those workers, there seemed to be a shared determination to make the best of their seriously constrained circumstances and maybe even to keep alive a flickering hope for a better day.

Abbreviations

ACCDNA	Anglican Church of Canada, Diocese of Niagara Archives (McMaster University)
ACWAP	Amalgamated Clothing Workers of America, *Proceedings*
AF	*American Federationist*
AFL	American Federation of Labor
AFLP	American Federation of Labor, *Proceedings*
AFR	*Annual Financial Review*
AHR	*American Historical Review*
AJ	*Amalgamated Journal*
AMMM	Ambrose McGhee Medical Museum
AO	Archives of Ontario
BBAA	Big Brothers Association Archives
CAC	*Citizen and Country*
CAR	*Canadian Annual Review*
CBICLR	Canada, Board of Inquiry into the Cost of Living, *Report*
CBMH	*Canadian Bulletin of Medical History*
CC	*Census of Canada*
CCCCP	Canadian Conference on Charities and Corrections, *Proceedings*
CCJ	*Canadian Congress Journal*
CCSWP	Canadian Council on Social Work, *Proceedings*
CE	*Canadian Engineer*
CES	*Canadian Ethnic Studies*
CF	*Canadian Foundryman*
CHAAR	Canadian Historical Association, *Annual Report*
CHAHP	Canadian Historical Association, *Historical Papers*
CHR	*Canadian Historical Review*
CIHM	Canadian Institute for Historical Microreproductions
CJF	*Canadian Journal of Fabrics*
CJS	*Canadian Journal of Sociology*
CLW	*Canadian Labor World*
CM	*Canadian Machinery*
CMJ	*Canadian Mining Journal*
CMR	*Canadian Mining Review*
CN	*Canadian Nurse*
CPHJ	*Canadian Public Health Journal*
CRCRLC	Canada, Royal Commission on the Relations of Labour and Capital
CRSA	*Canadian Review of Sociology and Anthropology*
CTJ	*Canadian Textile Journal*
CW	*Cotton's Weekly*
CWRT	*Canadian White Ribbon Tidings*
CYB	*Canada Year Book*
DCB	*Dictionary of Canadian Biography*
DHB	*Dictionary of Hamilton Biography*
GG	Girl Guides of Canada, Escarpment Branch Archives
GW	*Garment Worker*
HBEM	Hamilton, Board of Education, *Minutes*
HBHR	Hamilton, Board of Health, *Annual Report*
HCC	Hamilton Chamber of Commerce
HCCM	Hamilton, City Council, *Minutes*
HH	*Hamilton Herald*
HHAR	Hamilton Health Association, *Annual Report*
HHB	*Hamilton Harvester Bulletin*
HHSA	Hamilton Health Association Archives (McMaster University)
HJ	*Historical Journal*
HPL	Hamilton Public Library, Local History and Archives Department
HS	*Hamilton Spectator*
HSE	*Historical Studies in Education*
HS/SH	*Histoire sociale/Social History*
HT	*Hamilton Times*
HTLC	Hamilton Trades and Labor Council
HWJ	*History Workshop Journal*
HYWCAA	Hamilton Young Women's Christian Association Archives
IAMPC	International Association of Machinists, *Proceedings of the Convention*
IA	*Iron Age*
IB	*Industrial Banner*
IC	*Industrial Canada*
ILP	Independent Labor Party
ILWCH	*International Labor and Working-Class History*
IMJ	*Iron Molders' Journal*
IODEA	IODE, Municipal Chapter Archives
IRSH	*International Review of Social History*
ISC	*Iron and Steel of Canada*
JAH	*Journal of American History*
JCHA	*Journal of the Canadian Historical Association*
JCS	*Journal of Canadian Studies*
JSH	*Journal of Social History*
JUH	*Journal of Urban History*
LAC	Library and Archives Canada (Ottawa)
LCBO	Liquor Control Board of Ontario
LCBOR	Liquor Control Board of Ontario, *Annual Report*
LG	*Labour Gazette*
LH	*Labor History*
LL	*Labor Leader*
L/LT	*Labour/Le Travail*
LN	*Labor News*
LOC	*Labour Organizations in Canada*
MC	*Motorman and Conductor*
MHSO	Multicultural History Society of Ontario Archives

MPSS	Methodist Church of Canada, Department of Temperance and Moral Reform, and Presbyterian Church of Canada, Board of Social Service and Evangelism, *Report of a Preliminary and General Social Survey of Hamilton*
MT	*Monetary Times*
MUA	McMaster University Archives
NC	*New Commonwealth*
ND	*New Democracy*
NTLCCP	National Trades and Labor Congress of Canada, *Proceedings*
OCPR	Ontario, Commissioners Appointed to Enquire into the Prison and Reformatory System of Ontario, *Report*
OCUR	Ontario, Commission on Unemployment, *Report*
ODLR	Ontario, Department of Labour, *Annual Report*
OH	*Ontario History*
OIFR	Ontario, Inspectors of Factories, *Annual Report*
OICHR	Ontario, Inspector of Charities and Hospitals, *Annual Report*
OIPPCR	Ontario, Inspector of Prisons and Public Charities, *Annual Report*
OMACR	Ontario, Mothers' Allowance Commission, *Annual Report*
OMWBR	Ontario, Minimum Wage Board, *Annual Report*
OPBHR	Ontario, Provincial Board of Health, *Annual Report*
ORGR	Ontario, Registrar General, *Annual Report*
OSNDCR	Ontario, Superintendent of Neglected and Dependent Children, *Annual Report*
OTLBR	Ontario, Trades and Labour Branch, *Annual Report*
OWCBR	Ontario, Workmen's Compensation Board, *Annual Report*
PAM	Provincial Archives of Manitoba
PCCA	Presbyterian Church in Canada Archives
PHJ	*Public Health Journal*
RHAF	*Revue d'histoire de l'Amérique française*
RI/IR	*Relations industrielles/Industrial Relations*
SLS	School of Labour Studies, McMaster University
SPE	*Studies in Political Economy*
SW	*Social Welfare*
TFL	Thomas Fisher Rare Books Library, University of Toronto
TLCCP	Trades and Labor Congress of Canada, *Proceedings*
TPL	Toronto Public Libraries, Reference Library
TQ	*Templar Quarterly*
UBC	University of British Columbia Library, Special Collections
UCCA	United Church of Canada Archives (Toronto)
UHR	*Urban History Review*
UTL	University of Toronto Libraries
VCHD	*Vernon's City of Hamilton Directory*
VONA	Victoria Order of Nurses Archives (Hamilton)
VP	Vintage Postcards
WAHC	Workers' Arts and Heritage Centre Collection
WC	John Weaver Collection, Department of History, McMaster University
WG	*Workers' Guard*
WCTU	Woman's Christian Temperance Union
YMCA	Young Men's Christian Association
YWCA	Young Women's Christian Association

Notes

1. Opening the Lunch Bucket

1. See, for example, *HS*, 1 Oct. 1900, 5, where a Conservative candidate insisted that the tariff "always provided a fairly well filled dinner pail for the workingman."

2. *Oxford Dictionary of English Idioms*.

3. See, for example, National Film Board photos of women munitions workers in World War Two in LAC, R1196-14-7-E, Mikan no. 317924, 3197926.

4. By 1920 some employers were catering to this concern by offering cheap lunches in company cafeterias. See, for example, the photo in LAC, R1196-14-7-E, Mikan no. 3371124.

5. Sometimes, if wage-earners lived close to the workplace, children might bring them a hot lunch straight from the family kitchen at noon – a practice that was not common in large cities with long distances between home and work.

6. Proulx, *Pardon My Lunch Bucket*.

7. For generations Canadian historians were generally indifferent to the concept of class in history; see Meeling, "Concept of Social Class." Only in the 1970s did they begin to explore class. See, for example, Kealey, "Labour and Working-Class History." I explore these issues at greater length in Heron, "Harold, Marg, and the Boys."

8. The dominant group has been far from unified and cohesive across time and had to be constructed and reconstructed through different phases of economic development. Certain conflicts of interests had to be handled, for example, between financial and industrial capital, or manufacturing and resource extraction. In more complex, often conflictual processes, members of the upper class have also had to build alliances with relatively autonomous state and cultural elites to create fairly fluid power blocs that constitute the ruling group of particular periods. These blocs, bound together by a common commitment to the defence of private property, public order, the country's moral fibre, and much more, would set the boundaries of what is possible politically. That could involve building consensus around matters as diverse as the value of a high tariff structure (or free trade), the desirability of abolishing child labour, the need to reform divorce legislation, the shape of post-secondary education, or the urgency of environmental policy. For a discussion of this process from the 1920s to the 1940s, see Nerbas, *Dominion of Capital*.

9. Wacquant, "Making Class"; Mills, *White Collar*; Lockwood, *Blackcoated Worker*; Bourdieu, *Distinction*; Blumin, *Emergence of the Middle Class*; Bledstein and Johnston,

eds., *Middling Sorts*; Holman, *Sense of Their Duty*; Burley, *Particular Condition*.

10. Dean, *Governmentality*; Eley and Nield, *Future of Class*, 150–54.

11. Post-structuralist thinkers have often rejected such an approach as crude "reductionism" or "economism." The three most influential books in critiquing materialism were Jones, *Languages of Class*; Scott, *Gender and the Politics of History*; and Joyce, *Visions of the People*. See also Joyce, ed., *Class*; Hall, ed., *Reworking Class*.

12. Heron and Storey, "On the Job in Canada"; Kealey, "Structure of Canadian Working-Class History."

13. One influential theorist labels such "durable, transposable dispositions" as the "habitus" that shaped much behaviour. Bourdieu, *Outline of a Theory of Practice*; and Bourdieu, "What Makes a Social Class?"

14. Thompson, *Making of the English Working Class*, 9–15; Sewell, "How Classes Are Made"; Steinberg, "'Talkin' Class"; Steinberg, "Culturally Speaking"; Canning, *Gender History in Practice*, 72–77, 101–20; Eley and Nield, *Future of Class*. In an effort to break the simplistic assumption that awareness of working-class self-interest leads straightforwardly to collective organization in support of those interests, Ira Katzelson has tried to elaborate a more sophisticated analytical framework of "levels" of awareness, which, however, do not fundamentally abandon the close association of material situation and political expression. Katzneson, "Working-Class Formation: Constructing Cases and Comparisons," in Katznelson and Zolberg, eds., *Working-Class Formation*, 3–41. Even one of the severest critics of postmodern history, Neville Kirk, admits, "Language and systems of discourse play active roles in the creation of aspects of social reality, rather than being mere expressions or reflections of a *totally* given, or pre-existing external reality." Kirk, "History, Language, Ideas, and Post-Modernism," 333.

15. Gramsci, *Prison Notebooks*; Lears, "Concept of Cultural Hegemony"; Constant and Ducharme, eds., *Liberalism and Hegemony*; Anstead, "Fraternalism."

16. Therborn, "Why Some Classes Are More Successful Than Others"; Tilly, *From Mobilization to Revolution*.

17. Frager and Patrias, *Discounted Labour*; Ramirez, *On the Move*.

18. Bailey, "'Will the Real Bill Banks Please Stand Up?'"; Scott, *Domination and the Arts of Resistance*; Butler, *Gender Trouble*.

19. Canning, "Body as Method?"; Baron, "Masculinity, the Embodied Male Body, and the Historian's Gaze."

20. Walsh and High, "Rethinking the Concept of Community."

21. As Richard Ostreicher argues, "What seems possible always limits a sense of what is just." Oestreicher, *Solidarity and Fragmentation*, 67. I use "realism" as a much more

fluid, flexible, and changeable term than John Bodnar's more static concept in "Working-Class Realism." I explore how this sense of realism played out in one working-class family after World War Two in Heron, "Harold, Marg, and the Boys."

22. Heron and Storey, "On the Job in Canada"; Kealey, "Structure of Canadian Working-Class History."

23. Heron, "Factory Workers"; Heron, *Booze*; McKay, "Canada as a Long Liberal Revolution."

24. For example, Braverman, *Labour and Monopoly Capitalism*; Ewen, *Captains of Consciousness*.

25. Samuel, "Workshop of the World"; McKay, "Capital and Labour in the Halifax Baking and Confectionery Industry"; Kealey, *Toronto Workers*; Palmer, *Culture in Conflict*; Bradbury, *Working Families;* Heron, "Factory Workers."

26. Frank, *J.B. McLachlan*, is a superb example.

27. The most influential national study has been E.P. Thompson's *Making of the English Working Class*. For examples of international comparisons, see Kirk, *Labor and Society*; Katznelson and Zolberg, eds., *Working-Class Formation*; Cross, "Labour in Settler-State Democracies"; Marks, *Unions in Politics*; Friedman, *State-Making and Labor Movements*; Halpern and Morris, eds., *American Exceptionalism?*

28. See, for example, Radforth, *Bushworkers and Bosses*; Lowe, *Women in the Administrative Revolution*; Steedman, *Angels of the Workplace*; Heron, *Working in Steel*.

29. The most striking contrast here might be Katz, *People of Hamilton, Canada West*, and Parr, *Gender of Breadwinners*.

2. Hobson's Hamilton

1. See, for example, Belshaw, *Colonization and Community*; Robertson, *Driving Force*.

2. Heron, "Hobson"; Middleton and Landon, *Province of Ontario*, Vol. 3, 61 (quotation).

3. The notion of a "ruling class" does not assume conspiracy. Elites can (and usually do) believe in their own superiority and the necessity of class stratification.

4. Baskerville and Sager, *Unwilling Idlers*.

5. *Hamilton: The Birmingham of Canada*. The booklet was prepared in anticipation of overflowing tourism from the Chicago World's Fair the next year and was probably the first in Hamilton's history to make lavish use of photographs.

6. *Hamilton, Canada: Its History, Commerce, Industries, Resources*.

7. *Hamilton, Canada: Its History, Commerce, Industries, Resources* (quotation at 94–95).

8. *Hamilton, Canada: The City of Opportunity*.

9. During those same decades, federal census-takers had also documented the concentration of production in much larger units and the shift towards specialization in heavy metals and textiles (see Table 10).

10. Weaver, *Hamilton*, 41–92; McCalla, "Decline of Hamilton"; Forster, *Conjunction of Interests*; Bloomfield, "Boards of Trade"; Ward, "Hamilton, Ontario, as a Manufacturing Center"; Roberts, "Changing Patterns"; Storey, "Industrialization in Canada"; Acheson, "Social Origins of Canadian Industrialism"; Katz, *People of Hamilton, Canada West*; Kristofferson, *Craft Capitalism*; Palmer, *Culture in Conflict*. The Bank of Hamilton grew to substantial proportions by the early 20th century, running 145 branches by 1923, half of them in Western Canada. Ames, "Bank of Hamilton."

11. Donald, *Canadian Iron and Steel Industry*; *CE*, July 1895, 74–76; *CMR*, February 1896, 38–39; *MT*, 18 May 1894, 1444; *HS*, 14 Nov. 1895, 8; 31 Dec. 1895, 4; Weaver, *Hamilton*, 80–87; Donald, *Canadian Iron and Steel*, 114; Kilbourn, *Elements Combined*, 48–49. Tom Naylor's statement that "American promoters remained in charge of the Hamilton Iron and Steel Co." is incorrect. *History of Canadian Business*, Vol. 2, 118.

12. *HS*, 31 Dec. 1895, 5. Business and trade journals were making similar forecasts; see, for example, *CE*, December 1895, 214.

13. *Iron Age*, 25 Jan. 1900, 12, listed 19 leading Hamilton businessmen on the board of directors of the Nickel Copper Company. Other less grandiose schemes of local co-operation followed. In 1910 a group of local capitalists regained control of the Sawyer-Massey agricultural implement firm, recapitalized it at $7 million, and expanded enormously the company's production of road-making and agricultural machinery, especially steam tractors. Two years later the Tuckett Tobacco Company was reorganized under local control and similarly expanded to include branches in London and Montreal and a local workforce of 900. *HH*, 15 Jan. 1910, 1; 5 July 1912, 1; *CM*, 6 March 1913, 233; *AFR*, 1916, 329; Denison, *Harvest Triumphant*, 123, 126, 206–7, 240; Phillips, *Agricultural Implement Industry*, 176; *HH*, 15 Jan. 1910, 16; *CM*, 6 March 1913, 233; *LG*, July 1912, 25.

14. The federal government refused to impose export duties on unprocessed nickel and the experimental refining technology proved unsatisfactory. LAC, R10811-0-X-E, Vol. 7, 2456 (J.M. Gibson to Laurier, 27 June 1898); Vol. 68, 21342–45 (Hamilton Board of Trade to Laurier, 9, 27 March 1898); Nelles, *Politics of Development*, 87–102; Main, *Canadian Nickel Industry*, 40–54; Thompson and Beasley, *For Years to Come*, 122–24.

15. Acheson, "Social Origins"; and "Maritimes and 'Empire Canada'"; Epp, "Co-operation among Capitalists"; Bliss, *Living Profit*, 33–54; Weldon, "Consolidations in Canadian Industry"; Traves, *State and Enterprise*, 73–100; Fowke, *National Policy*; Thompson, *Harvests of War*; Mackintosh, *Economic Background*, 40–70; Spelt, *Urban Development*, 150–86; Taylor and Baskerville, *Concise History*, 248–61; Brown and Cook, *Canada*, 1896–1921, 91–94.

16. The earliest was Canadian Coloured Cottons' swallowing up of the Ontario Cotton Company in 1892 (Naylor, *History*, Vol. 2, 170). Others were to follow: Canadian Iron Corporation (later Canada Iron Foundries and then Canron) integrated a Hamilton plant into its 1908 merger (*LG*, January 1909, 757); London Machine Tool Company disappeared into the Canadian Machinery Corporation in 1912 (*HH*, 31 Jan. 1912; 1); Dominion Flint Glass Company entered the new Dominion Glass Company in 1913 (*AFR*, 1928, 442); Canada Steamship Lines absorbed local shipping firms in the same year (*HH*, 10 June 1913, 1); Zimmerman Manufacturing (organized in 1907) merged with Reliance Knitting in 1919, absorbed Harvey Knitting and Hosiers Limited in 1928, and in turn was taken over by York Knitting in 1930. McCullough, *Primary Textile Industry*, 84.

17. Ross and Trigge, *History of the Canadian Bank of Commerce*, Vol. 3, 42–45; Mills, *Cataract Traction*, 3–4; *AFR*, 1928, 811. Other mergers included Imperial Cotton, which became part of a new company known as Cosmos Imperial; Bird and Son, which merged into Building Products Limited in 1926; Standard Underground Cable, which became part of the Canada Wire and Cable Company a year later; and two local bakeries, two breweries, and a vinegar company, which were included in Canada Bread Company in 1919, Canadian Brewing Corporation in 1927, and Canada Vinegars Limited in 1928 respectively. *AFR*, 1928, 252, 417, 507; 1929, 297, 304, 335.

18. Hall, "Electrical Utilities," 101–26; Mills, *Cataract Traction*, 3–4; Cody, "Who Were the Five Johns?"

19. Kilbourn, *Elements Combined*, 56–78. Naylor's suggestion that this merger was "the CPR's . . . effort to consolidate an integrated iron and steel complex of its own" (*History*, Vol. 2, 189) is ludicrous. Not only was control not centred in Montreal, but production in the new corporation was not geared primarily to railway requirements. Wallace Clement repeated this error in his *Canadian Corporate Elite*, 75–77.

20. Wilkins, *Emergence of Multinational Enterprise*.

21. Bliss, "Canadianizing American Business."

22. See, for example, Ward, "Manufacturing Center," 48–49; Donald, *Canadian Iron and Steel*, 114; Roberts, "Manufacturing Activity," 98. Bonusing had stopped by 1920. HCCM, 1920, 132.

23. *HT*, 22 April 1902, 8; 19 May 1902, 8; 20 May 1902, 5; 22 May 1902, 4, 7; 6 June 1902, 8; Ward, "Manufacturing Center," 90–91; Weaver, *Hamilton*, 88–89.

24. In 1904 the city council appointed an industrial committee of prominent local manufacturers, including Hobson, to work with the assessment commissioner in luring new industries. *LG*, June 1904, 1208; Ward, "Manufacturing Center," 53–54. Hamilton's civic boosterism in this period is discussed in Middleton and Walker, "Manufacturers and Industrial Development Policy." For other cities, see Artibise, "In Pursuit of Growth."

25. *HH*, 16 March 1909, 5; *Hamilton, The Manufacturing Metropolis of Canada*, 30–31.

26. HPL, Scrapbooks, Hamilton Industries, n.p. Even popular summer festivals and "old-boy reunions" in 1903 and 1913 were shaped in order to showcase Hamilton's manufacturing advantages and accomplishments. In reviewing the 1913 Industrial Exhibition, C.R. McCullough, editor of the boosterist *Hamilton Manufacturer*, wrote, "A Manufacturers' Week will do the industrial interests of Hamilton more good than any number of 'Old Home Weeks,' 'Carnivals,' and such like concomitants of community conditions of bygone years." See *Hamilton Spectator Carnival Souvenir*; *Hamilton Manufacturer*, 4 (1913), 59. For a history of the Industrial Commissioner's office, see Lonnee, "City of Hamilton's Maitre D' to Industry."

27. Among the other US corporate giants that located in Hamilton, the Otis Elevator Company of New York arrived in 1902 (becoming Otis-Fensom in 1905); F.W. Bird and Company, industrial paper manufacturers from East Walpole, Mass., in 1905; Union Drawn Steel Company of Beaver Falls, Pa., the same year; the Berlin Machine Company of Beloit, Wisc., the world's leading manufacturer of woodworking machinery, in 1906; the American Can Company, taking over the Norton Manufacturing Company, in 1909; the Oliver Chilled Plow Company of South Bend, Ind., in 1910 (absorbed by International Harvester in 1919); the Grasselli Chemical Company of Cleveland in 1911; the Standard Underground Cable Company of Pittsburgh the same year; the Proctor and Gamble Company of Cincinnati in 1914; the Stanley Steel Company of New Britain, Conn., also in 1914; the Norton Company of Worcester, Mass., manufacturer of grinding wheels, in 1919; and the Firestone Tire and Rubber Company the same year. Roberts, "Manufacturing Activity," 91–128; Ward, "Manufacturing Center," 62–63; MUA, Westinghouse Fonds, P.J. Myler Scrapbook; *LG*, April 1905, 1069; August 1906, 133; April 1909, 1059; June 1910, 1371; July 1911, 27; October 1911, 324; August 1914, 169; *CM*, May 1905, 207.

28. Wilkins, *Multinational Enterprise*, 66; *HT*, 29 April 1902, 6. Hamilton capitalists were equally willing to work in partnership with US capital in initiating new enterprises. John M. Gibson, president of Dominion Power, had been active in promoting Canadian Westinghouse as an important link with his electrical utilities empire and sat on its board for many years. Similarly the National Steel Car Company set up in Hamilton in 1913 after Hobson won over some US capitalists to the city's advantages. Gibson became president of the new company, two other local capitalists joined the board of directors, and ten more took out stock in the firm. *AFR*, 1913, 257.

29. Michael Bliss discusses this paradox in "Canadianizing American Business."

30. O.D. Skelton noted in 1913 "the frequency with which the United States interests were bought out by their Canadian associates after a few years' co-operation." Skelton, "General Economic History," 270.

31. These included Frost Steel and Wire, Canada Steel Goods, Canada Wire Goods, Canadian Drawn Steel (later Burlington Steel), Ford-Smith Machines, and Dominion Steel Foundry (later Dominion Foundries and Steel, or Dofasco)

32. The knit goods were produced in the Eagle, Chipman-Holton, Zimmerman, Canadian Knitting, Mercury, Eaton, Porritt and Spencer, and National Hosiery mills.

33. The best regular reports on the peaks and troughs of local economic activity, especially before the war, were published monthly in the *Labour Gazette*. On the business cycles of this period, see Hay, "Early Twentieth Century Business Cycles"; Chambers, "Canadian Business Cycles."

34. See, for example, *HS*, 27 Nov. 1920, 8; LAC, R3735-3-9.

35. *IC*, January 1922, 122.

36. See Piedalue, "Les groupes financiers"; Acheson, "Changing Social Origins"; Nerbas, *Politics of Capital*.

37. Prominent in this group were C.S. Wilcox, Cyrus Birge, and Robert Hobson of the Steel Company of Canada and John S. Hendrie of Hamilton Bridge. *AFR*, 1910, 216; 1913, 311.

38. This group included promoter John Patterson, provincial politician and corporate lawyer John M. Gibson, and textile manufacturer J.R. Moodie. *AFR*, 1902, 232; Morgan, ed., *Canadian Men and Women*, 443, 818, 888.

39. William Gibson, John M.'s father, was president of the Bank of Hamilton and a director of the Hamilton Loan and Provident Society, as well as a director of the Steel Company. (Morgan, *Canadian Men and Women*, 444–45.) By 1914 John Hendrie was president of the bank and Cyrus Birge vice-president; a year later Hobson joined the board. (*AFR*, 1914, 98; 1915, 92.) A.V. Young, a textile manufacturer, and H.S. Ambrose of Tuckett Tobacco also became directors of the bank in the early 1920s (*AFR*, 1923, 114). During the war Hobson and Birge also joined the board of Dominion Power (*AFR*, 1917, 418).

40. Bruce, *News and the Southams*, 30–33; *IC*, October 1905, 218; *HT*, 15 Oct. 1910, 1; *AFR*, 1913, 257.

41. Morgan, *Canadian Men and Women*, 537; Ross and Trigge, *Canadian Bank of Commerce*, Vol. 3, 45; *AFR*, 1920, 567; *HH*, 18 Sept. 1918, 1.

42. Houston, ed., *Directory of Directors in Canada*, 1912, Part 1, 95; *AFR*, 1916, 684.

43. Heron, "Hobson."

44. Nerbas, *Politics of Capital*; *HH*, 19 Aug. 1915, 1, 10; 21 Aug. 1915, 5. The number of Hamilton members of the "big bourgeoisie" should not be exaggerated. In 1917, of the 102 members that Don Nerbas tracked in the *AFR*, Hamilton had only 6; this was the third-largest number after Montreal (47) and Toronto (29). Nerbas, *Dominion of Capital*.

45. Middleton and Walker, "Manufacturers and Industrial Development Policy."

46. *Who's Who in Canada*, 1921, 733; *CM*, 9 April 1914, 363; *AFR*, 1919, 297. The various managers of International Harvester were certainly prominent in class-conscious organizations like the Hamilton branch of the Canadian Manufacturers' Association, but they do not seem to have been as thoroughly integrated into the social life of Hamilton's established elite as Myler was.

47. H.L. Frost brought the Frost Steel and Wire Company into the city from Welland in 1904 (Wingfield, *Hamilton Centennial*, 106). Arthur F. Hatch moved the Canada Steel Goods Company from Leamington in 1905 to manufacture builders' hardware (*CM*, June 1905, 251). Alexander Donald reorganized the Canada Wire Goods Manufacturing Company in 1907 ("Hamilton – The Electric City of Canada," *Magazine of Industry* [Hamilton], Souvenir Edition [December 1910], 59). H.J. Waddie came to the city after a varied career that included a term as a manager of the Clergue enterprises at Sault Ste. Marie and proceeded to organize the Canadian Drawn Steel Company in 1905 (*IC*, March 1905, 499). Percy Ford-Smith arrived from England with extensive experience in machine-shop management and founded the Ford-Smith Machine Company to produce machine tools (*CM*, 22 Feb. 1917, 163). Clifton W. Sherman moved north from the US in 1912, after years of experience in foundry management, to head up the new Dominion Steel Foundry Company (later Dominion Foundries and Steel, or Dofasco) ("Hamilton – Electric City," 14 Sept. 1916, 297). George Coppley co-founded in 1900 the clothing firm of Coppley, Noyes, and Randall; W.A. Holton opened the Chipman-Holton Knitting Company in 1902; Adam Zimmerman, MP, became president of a knitting firm in 1907 ("Hamilton – Electric City," 42, 39, 35). And the Firth Brothers, Norman and John, opened a high-class tailoring enterprise in 1910 and soon had retail outlets across the country (HS, 13 June 1929, 17).

48. *HH*, 14 Jan. 1911, 8; 21 Jan. 1911, 4; 4 May 1911, 6; 20 Jan. 1912, 11; 20 June 1912, 10; 29 June 1912, 2; 20 Aug. 1913, 4; LAC, R3096-0-8-E, 230, Vol. 16.

49. Baskerville, *Silent Revolution?*

50. Wentworth Historical Society, *Proceedings;* Women's Canadian Club, *Proceedings*; Kallman, *History of Music*, 204, 213; MacCuaig, *Women's Art Association*; HPL, Young Women's Christian Association Scrapbook; Playgrounds Scrapbook; Hamilton Health Association Scrapbook; Johnston, *Head of the Lake*, 256; *LN*, 21 May 1915; Hamilton Local Council of Women, *Fifty Years*; Canadian

Patriotic Fund, Hamilton and Wentworth Branch, *Five Years*; Strong-Boag, *Parliament of Women*, 56–130.

51. The following discussion is based on biographical details on 56 Hamilton businessmen who played a commanding role in shaping the new economy of the period from the 1890s to the 1920s. The information was drawn from *DHB* and contemporary biographical sources, principally Morgan, *Canadian Men and Women*; *Who's Who in Canada*; *Canadian Who's Who*; and Charlesworth, ed., *Cyclopaedia of Canadian Biography*.

52. Kristofferson, *Craft Capitalism*.

53. Beckert, *Moneyed Metropolis*; Trachtenberg, *Incorporation of America*, 140–81; Bliss, *Canadian Millionaire*; Westley, *Remembrance of Grandeur*.

54. *Society Blue Book*.

55. *DHB*, Vol. 2, 63–64; Vol. 3, 37; *Hamilton: The Birmingham of Canada*, n.p.; Campbell, *Mountain and a City*, 171 (quotation); Synge, "Family and Community," ch. 6. In 1920 the school was renamed Hillcrest and in 1929 Hillfield.

56. Levine, *Highbrow/Lowbrow*.

57. Of the 56 businessmen studied, 24 were Presbyterians, 19 Anglicans, 11 Methodists, and only 2 Roman Catholics. These are the same proportions that Nerbas found nationally. Nerbas, *Dominion of Capital*, 14. See also Campbell, "Class, Status, and Crisis."

58. Beveridge, "Hamilton's 'Public' Parks," 4–5; Scobey, "Anatomy of the Promenade"; McDonald, "'Holy Retreat' or 'Practical Breathing Spot'?"

59. The most important were the Royal Yacht Club, Hamilton Golf and Country Club, Royal Thistle Curling Club, Hamilton Jockey Club, Caledon Mountain Trout Club, and Tamahaac Club. The yachtsmen had a huge richly appointed clubhouse on the beach strip with its own large ballroom where members could bring their wives to elegant balls. Penny, *One Hundred Years*, 10–11.

60. LAC, Census of Canada, 1911, West Hamilton, Ward 2, Enumeration District 4, p. 36, ll.20–2.

61. Campbell, *Mountain and a City*, 171.

62. DHB, Vol. 2, 71–78, 156–59; Vol. 3, 24–27, 92–93, 161–62; MacCuaig, *Women's Art Association*, 6–12.

63. For a discussion of the usefulness of this term, see Beckert, *Moneyed Metropolis*, 6–7.

64. Kristofferson, *Craft Capitalism*; Holman, *Sense of Their Duty*; Blumin, *Emergence of the Middle Class*.

65. Bledstein, "Introduction," 5. The term "middling classes" began to appear in the first half of the 19th century and got singularized to "middle class" in the second half.

66. In 1913, for example, Morris Silverman, a former garment worker (and one-time treasurer of the Hamilton Trades and Labor Council), started his own tailoring business. *GW*, 3 Oct. 1913, 1.

67. Holman, *Sense of Their Duty*; Blumin, *Emergence of the Middle Class*; Anstead, "Fraternalism"; Mayer, "Lower Middle Class"; Crossick, "Petite Bourgeoisie"; Crossick, ed., *Lower Middle Class*; Crossick and Haupt, *Petite Bourgeoisie*; Monod, *Store Wars*; Cohen, "Obstacles to History?"; Johnston, "Conclusion: Historians and the American Middle Class." In early 20th-century Hamilton some of the people were drawn to the city's Independent Labor Party (see chapter 17).

68. See Table 13.

69. Gidney and Millar, *Professional Gentlemen*; Millard, *Master Spirit of the Age*; Kinnear, *In Subordination*; McPherson, *Bedside Matters*. In 1921 the Certified General Accountants Association voted against admitting women, although it began to relent in the interwar period. Fairclough, *Saturday's Child*, 39. In 1917 Margaret K. Strong, a social worker, led the formation of a Business Women's Club, which drew together middle-class professional women for social and educational activities. *HH*, 7 June 1919, 7; 5 Jan. 1924, 6. Later the Zonta Club would provide this niche for business and professional women. Fairclough, *Saturday's Child*, 48–49.

70. DHB, Vol. 3, 77–78, 175–88.

71. Hamilton Association for the Advancement of Literature, Science, and Art, *100th Anniversary*, 38–39.

72. Comacchio, "Mechanomorphosis."

73. On the National Electric Light Association, see *HH*, 4 March 1912, 1; 4 Dec. 1912, 4; 6 March 1913, 3.

74. Davis, "Corporate Reconstruction."

75. Lowe, "Administrative Revolution"; Lowe, *Women in the Administrative Revolution*; Armstrong and Nelles, *Monopoly's Moment*; Chandler, *Visible Hand*, 381–414; Zunz, *Making America Corporate*, 37–66; Coates and McGuinness, *Only in Canada*. In 1924 the Business Women's Club president, Nettie McGillivray, an accountant and business manager in a local firm, was described by the Hamilton *Herald* as holding "one of the few executive posts occupied by women in Hamilton." *HH*, 5 Jan. 1924, 6.

76. In 1911, according to unpublished census data, Hamilton's 100 managers (not including banks or retail) earned on average $1,510 a year, 35 superintendents earned $1,355, and 200 accountants and bookkeepers earned $1,037, while machinists earned $689, moulders $668, carpenters $652, and labourers $485. Synge, "Family and Community," ch. 6.2.

77. The lack of a civil service complex, any bloc of financial or commercial institutions, any headquarters of national religious or voluntary association, or any college or university (until McMaster University arrived in 1930) left only a tiny group of 1,250 middle-class professionals in 1911, amounting to only 3.3 per cent of the workforce (not including the stenographers, typists, and general office employees that the census bureau lumped under the heading of "professional" in 1911). The percentage of professional income-earners would double by the 1930s,

but the great majority of the gainfully employed remained blue-collar workers (see Table 12).

78. McKay, "Liberal Order Framework."

79. DHB, Vol. 1, 200–1; Vol. 2, 5–9, 63–66,; Vol. 3, 37–38, 66–77, 111–16, 140–45, 199–200; Vol. 4, 176; Ward, "Manufacturing Center," 359 (quotation).

80. Kilbourn, *Elements Combined*, 114.

81. In the 1960s US historians began calling these efforts to reshape the state "corporate liberalism." See Sklar, *Corporate Reconstruction of American Capitalism*.

82. Fudge and Tucker, *Labour before the Law*; Oliver, *"Terror to Evil-Doers"*; Weaver, *Crimes, Constables, and Courts*.

83. Heron and Siemiatycki, "Great War, the State, and Working-Class Canada."

84. In 1919 one city politician promoted a commission government of an elected mayor, an appointed engineer, and an appointed business expert to replace city council. "It is a system of government, I believe, that would get Hamilton's business out of politics," he declared. *HS*, 3 Oct. 1919, 1. The Chamber of Commerce took up this cry a few years later.

85. *HT*, 7 Jan. 1902, 1 (quotation).

3. Studholme's People

1. Census of Canada, 1901, Hamilton (City), Ward 3, C-6, p.1, l. 46 (http://automatedgenealogy.com/census/).

2. Census officials found nearly 53,000 people living in Hamilton in 1901, only some 5,000 more than a decade earlier. Just before World War One the figure reached 100,000, by 1931 152,000, and by 1941 166,000. CC, 1891, Vol. 2, 6; 1901, Vol. 4, 8; 1911, Vol. 1, 22; 1921, Vol. 2, 80; 1931, Vol. 3, 29; 1941, Vol. 3, 65.

3. For the birth rate, see Table 6. For a discussion of the factors behind population growth in the period, see Weaver, *Hamilton*, 93.

4. CC, 1901, Vol. 1, 408; 1931, Vol. 2, 746.

5. *Hamilton: The Birmingham of Canada*, n.p. (quotation). "I had no idea Hamilton was such a beautiful place," a British businessman similarly announced during the 1890 visit of the British Iron and Steel Institute; "beautiful in situation, beautiful in itself," one of his colleagues declared. Henley, *Hamilton 1889–1890*, 98–99.

6. Transportation employed only 2,400 in 1911. Less than 1,000 of those worked for the railways – a proportion that increased only very slightly over the next 20 years and then dropped during the 1930s. Building-trades workers made up 11 per cent of the workforce in 1911, and then dropped back to over 7 per cent in 1921 and 1931. See Table 11; Ward, "Manufacturing Centre," 336.

7. The published census data did not distinguish clearly enough between garment and knitting factory employees. Since the number of clothing factories in the city had declined dramatically by 1931, we can safely assume that most of those in the category "Textile Goods, Garments" worked in knit goods. See Table 17.

8. *Hamilton, Canada: Its History, Commerce, Industries, Resources*, 95–96; Weaver, "Location of Manufacturing Enterprises."

9. Canada, House of Commons, *Journals*, 14 (1909–10), Appendix, Part 3, 162; *HS*, 20 April 1904, 4; LAC, R1176-0-E, 2373; Doucet and Weaver, *Housing the North American City*, 209–10. By 1913 this practice of firms importing their own workers had become more controversial. The new National Steel Car Company faced strong resistance from the Hamilton Trades and Labor Council and eventually the intervention of the federal government to block its efforts to bring in labour. HPL, Hamilton Trades and Labor Council, Minutes, 15 Nov. 1912; LAC, R3096-0-8-E, Vol. 256, 144858–61.

10. See, for example, *CJF*, July 1901, 22; June 1904, 131; *LG*, August 1904, 207; *HS*, 23 Aug. 1983, A7. In 1923 a writer in Imperial Cotton's company magazine suggested where most employees had been recruited: "If Imperialites don't come from Manchester or Yarmouth [N.S.], guess at Oldham is a pretty good rule." *Fabricator*, July 1923, 2. On the general practice of recruiting textile workers for Ontario mills, see Parr, *Gender of Breadwinners*, 16–26.

11. LAC, R3096-0-8-E, Vol. 11, Special Committee on Labour Supply, 8 Oct. 1912; Vol. 30 (British Office Committee), 29; Heron and Palmer, "Through the Prism of the Strike," 452–54; Goutor, *Guarding the Gates*, 123–37.

12. Goutor, *Guarding the Gates*; Atherton, "Department of Labour," 238–93; Avery, *Reluctant Host*, 36–37; LAC, R3096-8-E, Vol. 11, 20 Nov. 1911, 5 (quotation).

13. Avery, "Dangerous Foreigners," 16–38.

14. Hann, *Farmers Confront Industrialism*; Shortt, "Social Change and Political Crisis"; MacDougall, *Rural Life in Canada*; Brookes and Wilson, "'Working Away' from the Farm"; Crerar, "Ties That Bind"; Sylvester, "Rural to Urban Migration."

15. Avery, *"Dangerous Foreigners,"* 6–38; Glynn, "'Exporting Outcast London'"; *Toiler* (Toronto), 25 March 1904 (quotation); Synge, "Immigrant Communities," 39 (quotation); *HH*, 23 Jan. 1914, 1; see also *LG*, July 1904, 54–55; March 1905, 1002; April 1905, 1128; November 1910, 584; January 1911, 811–12; *IMJ*, November 1904, 841; Patrias, *Patriots and Proletarians*, 60–64. Scandal swirled around the overseas agents who got a $5 bonus for directing immigrants to Canada; Petryshyn, "Canadian Immigration and the North Atlantic Trading Company." The Trades and Labor Congress of Canada and other Canadian labour bodies repeatedly charged that working-class immigrants from Britain had been misled about job prospects in Canada; Goutor, *Guarding the Gates*, 103–8.

16. *HH*, 31 Aug. 1912, 5 (quotation); 2 June 1913, 1; *LN*, 30 Oct. 1914, 1; MHSO, ITA-0815–ANO; ITA-0826–CRE; Brandino,

"Italians of Hamilton," 51; Cumbo, "Italians in Hamilton"; Cumbo, *Italian Presence*; Patrias, *Patriots and Proletarians*, 65–66; Kaprielian-Churchill, *Like Our Mountains*, 19, 164–70; Harney, "Commerce of Migration"; Harney, "Padrone and the Immigrant"; Ramirez, *Crossing the 49th Parallel*, 155–65; Sturino, "Italian Emigration"; Zucchi, "Mining, Railway Building, and Street Construction."

17. *HS*, 30 May 1906, 1; 27 June 1907, 1, 12; 20 Nov. 1907, 4; 18 March 1913, 1; 9 May 1913, 1; 31 May 1913, 1; 2 June 1913, 1; 9 June 1913, 10; 4 July 1913, 20; *HH*, 20 May 1911, 18; 13 March 1913, 5 (quotation); 12 June 1913, 4.

18. Thistlethwaite, "Migration from Europe Overseas"; Hoerder and Moch, eds., *European Migrants*; CC, 1901, Vol. 1, 461; Avery, *Reluctant Host*, 82–125.

19. Table 1; *LN*, 30 Oct. 1914, 1; ODLR, 1925, 16. By 1913 three-quarters of British emigrants were choosing to settle in the Empire. Canada got close to half those who left Britain in the pre-war decade, and two out of five in the second half of the 1920s. A majority settled in Ontario. Within that province, the British were also the largest single immigrant group. Reynolds, *British Immigrant*, 26, 42, 43.

20. Ryder, "Interpretation of Origin Statistics."

21. *HH*, 31 Oct. 1911, 6.

22. The number of Poles in the city before the war, for example, is difficult to determine, since Poland did not emerge as an independent nation-state until 1918. Census-takers found 557 Hamilton residents who claimed Polish origins in 1911; yet a year later some 1,200 were present at the dedication of a new Polish Roman Catholic Church, and in 1913 Methodist and Presbyterian investigators estimated the Polish population at between 5,000 and 6,000. Precise figures on other Eastern European ethnic groups are equally difficult to grasp. The 1913 study estimated that there were 1,000 "Russians" in the city, while two years earlier the census had revealed less than 200 people of Russian ethnicity (the larger number were probably Russian-born Poles, Ukrainians, and Belarusans). Similarly, the census reported only 1,442 Italians in Hamilton, but four years later an Italian government official estimated the total at 4,000. The introduction to the relevant volume of the 1921 census includes the following warning: "Owing to changes in national alignments in Europe as a result of the World War, strictly accurate comparisons with pre-war censuses as to the classification of the foreign-born in Canada according to the country of birth are not possible." Tables 1–3 present the published census figures. *HH*, 20 May 1912, 5; Shahrodi, "Early Polish Settlement"; MPSS, 11; Kukushkin, *From Peasants to Labourers*; Zucchi, "Mining, Railway Building, and Street Construction," 8; CC, 1911, Vol. 1, 372; 1921, Vol. 2, xvii (quotation).

23. The 1911 census, for example, was taken in June when many local immigrants might have left for the work camps of the north and west.

24. See Tables 1 and 2. Nearly 2,000 of these were US citizens. The 3,900 Germans were the largest European ethnic group, but this was an old, settled population – less than a fifth of them had been born in Germany. On US immigration, see Bodnar, *Transplanted*.

25. In June 1918 the Canada Registration Board found 22 per cent of men and women over age 15 were "foreigners." *SW*, 1 Nov. 1919; Cumbo, *Italian Presence*; *VCHD*, 1909, 530; CC, 1941, Vol. 3, 362–63, 468–69, 594. Totals and percentage calculations are mine.

26. See Table 1. For anti-Chinese sentiment, see chapter 15 here.

27. Just before World War One, Robert Coats, editor of the Department of Labour's *Labour Gazette* and soon to be Dominion Statistician, pointed out the huge gap between the 1,700,000 immigrants to Canada that the Immigration Branch had counted between 1900 and 1910 and the 950,000-person growth in the population recorded by the census over the same period. OCCUR, 211.

28. Tulchinsky, *Taking Root*; Kurman, "Hamilton Jewish Community," 8–12; Campbell, *History of Beth Jacob Congregation*; HPL, Wilensky, "Report Re the Jewish Community"; Kaprielian-Churchill, *Like Our Mountains*.

29. In 1911 only 29 per cent of the foreign-born Europeans were women – among the Italians only 21 per cent. See Table 2.

30. Cumbo, *Italian Presence*; Kaprielian-Churchill, *Like Our Mountains*, 1–44; Synge, "Immigrant Communities," 42 (quotation); MHSO, ITA-0883–ANO; Martynowych, *Ukrainians*, 109–13, 129–32, Gabaccia, "Women of the Mass Migrations." The general process of return migration to Europe is discussed in Wyman, *Round-Trip to America*. The flow of cash to families back home could be disrupted: one Pole sadly reported that the friend he had entrusted with taking his savings back to his village had disappeared with the money; *HS*, 11 April 1910, 12.

31. MHSO, ITA-09829–GRI; Avery, *"Dangerous Foreigners"*; Ramirez, *On the Move*; Harney, "Men Without Women"; Brandino, "Italians of Hamilton"; Patrias, *Patriots and Proletarians*, 22–30; Kukushkin, *From Peasants to Labourers*, 12–54; Radecki and Heydenkorn, *Member of a Distinguished Family*; Reczyňska, *For Bread and a Better Future*, 11–31; Kaprielian-Churchill, *Like Our Mountains*, 3–44; Martynowych, *Ukrainians*, 3–11; Gabaccia, *Italy's Many Diasporas*, 58–152; Bodnar, *Transplanted*, 1–84; Hoerder, "Introduction to Labor Migration"; Hoerder, "Immigration and the Working Class."

32. Synge, "Immigrant Communities," 42 (quotation); Patrias, *Patriots and Proletarians*, 60–64; Kaprielian-Churchill, *Like Our Mountains*, 29; *HS*, 5 Oct. 1910, 14; Ramirez, *Crossing the 49th Parallel*.

33. Cumbo, "Italians in Hamilton," 35 (quotation); PCCA, 1977–3014, 13 March 1909, 8–9; *HH*, 12 Nov. 1913, 1

(quotation). The ethnic mix of the closest US centre of iron and steel production, Buffalo, N.Y., a little over 100 kilometres away, was so similar to Hamilton's (with a preponderance of Italians and Poles) that there must have been a regular flow of immigrants between these cities. Only in the 1920s did the arrival of thousands of southern-born African Americans give Buffalo a decidedly different racial complexion. Carpenter, *Nationality, Color, and Ethnic Opportunity*, 97–106.

34. In 1941, after ten years of immigration restriction, 92 per cent had arrived in the country before 1931, and 83 per cent of the population had lived in Ontario either their whole lives or for 20 years or more, while less than 3 per cent had arrived in the province in the preceding 5 years. CC, 1931, Vol. 5, 1600; 1941, Vol. 3, 505.

35. *HH*, 18 Nov. 1912, 1; *HT*, 7 May 1912, 1. In 1920 the Frid Construction Company also admitted that it had employee numbers and not names. *HS*, 23 Jan. 1920, 23.

36. *HH*, 12 Dec. 1912, 1; 12 Jan. 1914, 1; 16 Sept. 1914, 4; 4 May 1916, 9; *HS*, 4 May 1916, 8; *HT*, 14 Jan. 1914, 1; 15 April 1914, 1; *LG*, February 1915, 901; LAC, R224-0-4-E, Vol. 1 (Unemployment 1914), Hamilton; ODLR, 1924, 12; *CTJ*, 14 Oct. 1924, 939–40.

37. Roberts, "Toronto Metal Workers," 56–57; Ramirez, *Crossing the 49th Parallel*, 109–12, 130–31; *HH*, 4 May 1916, 13; *HS*, 4 May 1916, 8. As a young machinist recently off the boat from Britain, Sam Scarlett moved from Guelph to Hamilton for a few months in 1904, before taking off to Chicago, California, and many other places. Avery, "British-Born 'Radicals,'" 68.

38. ODLR, 1927, 21 (quotation); 1929, 24; *HS*, 16 Sept. 1925, 5 (quotation). Earlier that year, leaders of the Hamilton Trades and Labor Council voiced strong resentment against a proposed US quota on Canadian southward migration. *HS*, 20 Jan. 1925, 5.

39. The number still in the same homes on all six blocks after ten years, however, had risen to between four and five out of ten by 1940. See Table 4. These patterns had a history. Several historians of 19th-century North American urban history highlighted transiency as a major theme, including Michael Katz in his studies of Hamilton from 1851 to 1871, *People of Hamilton, Canada West*, and (with Michael J. Doucet and Mark J. Stern), *Social Organization of Early Industrial Capitalism.*

40. CC, 1941, Vol. 9, 37.

41. *HH*, 31 Aug. 1912, 5; MHSO, ITA-0826–CRE; ITA-0830–SAL; ITA-09826–FER; ITA-0913–FOU; ITA-0982–PAS; Kaprielian-Churchill, *Like Our Mountains*, 179–200; Reczyńska, *For Bread and a Better Future*, 96–97; Petryshyn, *Peasants in the Promised Land*; Bodnar, *Transplanted*. In 1941 the European-born population in Hamilton was nearly 41 per cent female; the percentage among the Polish born was 43. CC, 1941, Vol. 3, 363.

42. In 1931 three-quarters were women. No comparable statistics on household heads are available before that date. A decade later the single heads of household had dropped to 12 per cent. ORGR, 1896–1941; CC, 1901, Vol. 1, 12–13; 1911, Vol. 1, 322–23; 1921, Vol. 2, 184–85; 1931, Vol. 5, 1282; 1941, Vol. 5, 308; Kalbach and McVey, *Demographic Bases*, 306–42; Beaujot and McQuillan, *Growth and Dualism*, 51–78.

43. Although these people amounted to only 7 per cent of the number of households in 1921 and 4 per cent in 1931, many more families would undoubtedly have sheltered dependants like these at some point in the family life-cycle. ORGR, 1896–1941; CC, 1921, Vol. 3, 57, 72–73; 1931, Vol. 5, 700–1; 1161, 1188–89; 1412–13.

44. Kaprielian-Churchill, *Like Our Mountains*, 65–67; Kukushkin, *From Peasants to Labourers*, 121–25; Harney "Boarding and Belonging."

45. Roughly one man in ten and one woman in eight over age 34 told census-takers they were unmarried in the interwar decades (the published census gives no such breakdown before 1921). In 1931 only 7 per cent of family households consisted of one person, half of whom were over age 55, and in 1941 only 4 per cent. CC, 1921, Vol. 2, 184; 1931, Vol. 3, 136–37; Vol. 5, 1161, 1188; 1941, Vol. 3, 122; Vol. 9, 34. Calculations of proportions are mine.

46. Much of the ensuing discussion owes a debt to the excellent study by Michael J. Doucet and John Weaver, *Housing the North American City*, which uses Hamilton as its major data base.

47. Ames, *City Below the Hill*; Bradbury, *Working Families*; Burnett, *Social History of Housing*; Wright, *Building the Dream*, 58–72, 114–34, 177–92; Daunton, ed., *Housing the Workers*.

48. CC, 1891, Vol. 1, 46–47; Doucet, "Working Class Housing"; Doucet and Weaver, *Housing the North American City*, 20–76; Weaver, *Hamilton*, 99; *HS*, 11 April 1907, 1; 24 April 1907, 7. In 1901 only 89 families had to double up in the 10,802 houses in Hamilton. CC, 1901, Vol. 1, 7; Vol. 4, 349.

49. A 1931 census study found that Hamilton households had on average 5.8 rooms and a relatively high average of 1.41 persons per room (the same as Toronto). Dickey, "Houses of Hamilton," 20; CBICLR, Vol. 1, 486; CC, 1931, Vol. 5, 978; Doucet and Weaver, *Housing the North American City*, 71, 175, 201–42, 388–419; Greenway, *Housing*, 458. The first free-standing apartment building was not built in Hamilton until 1912; the first duplex appeared in 1919. They were predominantly middle-class accommodation. *HS*, 25 July 1912, 1; *HH*, 12 May 1919, 6; 11 April 1921, 1; Braybrook, "First Apartment Dwellers." For a similar pattern of working-class housing, see Zunz, *Changing Face of Inequality*, 156–58. As Richard Dennis notes, the relative absence of apartment buildings reflected in large measure the concerns of civic leaders and social commentators that they might breed urban

problems and must therefore be discouraged; Dennis "Apartment Housing."

50. This "house famine" emerged in urban centres across the country, but initially south-central Ontario seemed to be particularly hard hit. *LG*, October 1904, 367–80.

51. The families visited in Roberts's survey had an average of four rooms, and 113 (43 per cent) were living in three rooms or less. He found that 18 families had only one room. *HH*, 18 April 1912, 12; 25 April 1912, 5; 7 June 1913, 15 (quotation); *HS*, 10 May 1904, 10; 17 June 1904, 10; 15 May 1905, 4 (quotation); 21 May 1907, 1; 12 April 1913, 5 (quotation); *HT*, 28 Oct. 1910, 1; *LG*, October 1904, 371; HPL, Hamilton Board of Trade, Minutes, 16 Oct. 1906, 149; 2 July 1907, 177; CC, 1911, Vol. 1, 532; OPBHR, 1912, 450–52. Roberts's report was reprinted as "Housing Situation, Hamilton." See also HBHR, 1909–10, 21; 1911–12, 20; 1912–13, 25–26.

52. The construction of new houses dropped from 6,200 in 1910–14 (peaking in 1913 at over 1,800 in one year) to only 1,600 between 1915 and 1918. *LG*, February 1915, 902; *HH*, 16 March 1916, 1; 12 April 1916, 1; 28 April 1916, 13; 24 July 1916, 1; 12 Oct. 1916, 1; 24 Nov. 1916, 18; 5 Jan. 1917, 1; 8 Feb. 1917, 3; 22 March 1917, 1; 28 March 1917, 2; 2 May 1918, 5; 21 July 1918; 21 Aug. 1918, 4; 11 April 1921, 8; *HS*, 13 June 1916, 10; *HT*, 12 Oct. 1917, 1; Ontario, Housing Committee, *Report*, 13 (quotation).

53. *HH*, 8 Oct. 1920; 1 (quotation); 7 Aug. 1930; Dickey, "Houses of Hamilton," 21; HPL, Soldiers' Aid Commission, Minutes, March, June, July 1920; *HS*, 16 Sept. 1919, 1; 17 Sept. 1919, 6; 4 Oct. 1919, 5; 12 Nov. 1920, 1; 18 Nov. 1922, 13; 13 Jan. 1930, 7; 9 Oct. 1930, 7; *LN*, 19 Sept. 1919, 1; *SW*, October 1920, 5; OPBHR, 1920, 223; *Annual Reports of the Social Agencies*, 1930, 40, 45; Bouchier and Cruikshank, "War on the Squatters."

54. *LN*, 28 March 1919, 1; Doucet and Weaver, *Housing the North American City*, 340–41, 379–81.

55. Gilliland and Sendbuehler, "To Produce the Highest Type of Manhood and Womanhood"; Harris, "End Justified the Means," 350.

56. The proportion of doubling up was about 8 per cent in 1931 and 7 per cent in 1941. CC, 1931, Vol. 5, 982, 1054; 1941, Vol. 5, 100.

57. *HS*, 27 Oct. 1906, 13 (quotation) (for similar reports, see *HH*, 19 March 1907, 1; 5 April 1907, 1; 16 April 1907, 9). A letter to the press from "A Working Girl" complained that the YWCA's rates were too high for most working women and the "poorer class of working girls ... are compelled to seek a home elsewhere in the city, often in questionable places." The Y's local secretary vigorously denied the charge, but a weekly rate of $2.50 to $4.00 could indeed be difficult for young working women earning $10–12 a week. *HH*, 7 Dec. 1910, 11; 9 Dec. 1910, 13. The Y was also a clearing house of information on accommodation for single women; in 1912 its local secretary indicated that the Y had room for only 107 women, but passed out a list of 20 other boarding houses catering to women; *HS*, 23 May 1912, 7; see also Sebire, *Women's Place*.

58. Baskerville, "Familiar Strangers," 323; CC, 1921, Vol. 1, 340; 1931, Vol. 5, 988–89, 1050, 1054, 1062–63, 1080, 1092, 1103.

59. *HS*, 17 June 1904, 10 (quotation); 18 Oct. 1905, 10 (quotation); 27 Oct. 1906, 13; 20 May 1913, 1; MPSS, 39; Stewart, "Housing of Our Immigrant Workers,"107; *HH*, 7 May 1907, 12; 27 Feb. 1909, 1; 5 June 1911, 1, 12; 31 Aug. 1912, 1, 5; 28 July 1918, 11 (quotation); 9 Nov. 1920, 1; *HT*, 26 Oct. 1910, 11; 21 Dec. 1912, 43; 28 June 1913, 1; 16 May 1914, 1; OPBHR, 1912, 450–51; HBHR, 1909–10, 21; 1911–12, 20; 1912–13, 25–26; 1917–18, 16.

60. *HS*, 10 May 1904, 10; *HH*, 28 June 1911 (quotation); 26 July 1918, 6; 28 Jan. 1919, 12; WAHC, interview with Joyce Yakmalian; MHSO, ITA-0808–CEC; ITA-0883–ANO; ITA-09829–GRI; ITA-0982–PAS; Cumbo, *Italian Presence*; Patrias, *Patriots and Proletarians*, 82–86; Kaprielian-Churchill, *Like Our Mountains*, 66–67. For descriptions of eating arrangements in two Polish boarding houses in Hamilton, see Synge, "Immigrant Communities," 43. The important role of boarding houses in these communities is discussed in Harney, "Boarding and Belonging." Baskerville shows that cultural affinities were already important in determining the accommodation of boarders in 1901; see "Familiar Strangers."

61. *HT*, 3 Jan. 1910, 1 (quotation); 3 May 1910, 1; 27 May 1910, 1; *HH*, 31 May 1911, 4; 5 June 1911, 1, 12; 28 June 1911, 1 (quotation); 1 Jan. 1917, 5; 18 Sept. 1919, 1 (quotation); MPSS, 39.

62. CC, 1931, Vol. 5, 1002–3, 1050. Of those households with lodgers, 69 per cent had only one, 19 per cent had only two, and 6 per cent (421) had four or more. In all, over 28 per cent of households had extra families or single lodgers under their roofs in 1931. The proportion of working-class households that were crowded together in these ways at some point in their life cycle was probably much higher. These figures are only slightly lower than those for Toronto and considerably higher than those for urban Canada generally. Harris, "Flexible House," 35. Harris's calculations from city directories suggest lodging reached a low in 1926–27, but leaped up again over the next six years and again in the later 1930s; Harris, "Flexible House," 41, 44. On the shifting from "boarding" to "rooming," see Harris, "End Justified the Means," 337.

63. For examples of police court cases involving confrontations between landlords and tenants, see *HS*, 14 Feb. 1900, 8; 8 March 1900, 8; 11 April 1900, 8; 10 Jan. 1901, 8; 9 May 1901, 8; 14 June 1910, 12; 14 Nov. 1910, 14; 14 Jan. 1920, 13; 28 Jan. 1920, 13; 8 April 1920, 17; 19 May 1920, 17; 23 Feb. 1925, 5; 24 Jan. 1930, 7; 26 March 1930, 7. See also

Campbell, "Respectable Citizens," 165; Benson, *Household Accounts*, 77–103.

64. By spring 1907 so many International Harvester workers had objected to the high rents in the houses of the company's real-estate subsidiary, the Eastern Building Company, that the firm decided to sell them to "industrious and economical" employees who would not "later prove undesirable employes." *Canadian Architect and Builder*, May 1907, 70 (quotation); *CM*, August 1905, 336; *HS*, 1 Dec. 1906, 24; *LG*, September 1905, 261; September 1907, 271; *Canadian Architect and Builder*, May 1907, 69–70, 83; *HH*, 4 May 1907, 10; 11 May 1907, 21; 30 July 1907, 9; *HT*, 30 Oct. 1919, 14. On company housing, see Crawford, *Building the Workingman's Paradise*.

65. *HS*, 17 Oct. 1906, 7; 21 May 1907, 1; *HH*, 25 April 1912, 5; 23 May 1912, 7; 22 June 1912, 1; 25 June 1912, 1; 8 Aug. 1912, 7; 11 Jan. 1913, 1; 13 June 1913, 11; HTLC, Minutes, 27 June 1912, 172; 28 June 1912, 177; 5 July 1912, 180–81; 2 Aug. 1912, 188; 15 Nov. 1912, 216–17; 17 Oct. 1913, 328; *LN*, 26 July 1912, 1; 2 Aug. 1912, 1; 23 Aug. 1912, 1; 6 Sept. 1912, 4; 20 Sept. 1912, 5; *LG*, May 1912, 1044; August 1912, 143–45; November 1913, 522; LAC, R3096-0-8-E, Vol. 16, File 1911–12, Executive Committee, Minutes, 1, 10 April 1912; File 1912–13, 3 Sept. 1912; File 1913–14, Municipal and Legislation Committee, 4 Nov. 1913; CBICLR, Vol. 1, 485–86. On 16 Sept. 1914 the *Herald* reported that more than 2,500 houses in Hamilton were vacant. For the story of the more active Toronto Housing Company, see Spragge, "Confluence of Interests"; Hurl, "Toronto Housing Company"; Purdy, "'This Is Not a Company; It Is a Cause.'"

66. *HH*, 29 Sept. 1919, 3; Gilliland and Sendbuehler "'To Produce the Highest Type of Manhood and Womanhood'"; Saywell, *Housing Canadians*, 150–89; Bacher, *Keeping to the Marketplace*, 56–62.

67. Doucet and Weaver, *Housing the North American City*; Harris and Senduehler, "Making of a Working-Class Suburb"; McCann, "Suburbs of Desire"; Gardner, "Slow Wave"; Harris and Lewis, "Geography of North American Cities and Suburbs"; Cruikshank and Bouchier, "Blighted Areas and Obnoxious Industries." The emergence of working-class suburbs was far from unique to Hamilton – similar communities were springing up on the edges of industrial centres across North America. See, for example, Holdsworth, "Cottages and Castles"; McCririck and Wynn, "Building 'Self-Respect and Hopefulness'"; Harris, "Working-Class Suburb"; Harris, "Canada's All Right"; Chodo and Harris, "Local Culture of Property"; Hiebert, "Class, Ethnicity, and Residential Structure"; Seager and Fowler, "Burnaby"; Gilliland and Sendbuehler, "'To Produce the Highest Type of Manhood and of Womanhood'"; Harris and Lewis, "Geography of North American Cities and Suburbs," 272–76; Nicolaides, "'Where the Working Man Is Welcomed.'"

68. Bridle, "Shack-Town Christmas"; Harris and Sendbuehler, "Hamilton's East End"; Campbell, *Mountain and a City*, 206; Weaver, *Hamilton*, 102; Doucet and Weaver, *Housing the North American City*, 90–97, 107; *HH*, 4 May 1907, 10 (quotation); 6 April 1912, 1; 18 Nov. 1912, 1; 21 Dec. 1912, 1; 20 June 1913, 9; 13 Jan. 1914, 1; 27 Jan. 1914, 1; 31 Jan. 1914, 1; 7 Sept. 1923, 2; *HS*, 3 April 1907, 1; 29 April 1907, 5; 2 May 1907, 7; 4 May 1907, 1; 11 May 1911, 12; 14 May 1907, 7.

69. Richard Harris's survey of the divergent patterns of working-class home ownership across Canada in 1931 suggests that high rents could push workers into buying their own homes if the prices were cheap enough; he found that, for most families dependent on wages, homes were more affordable in Hamilton than in other large Central and Eastern Canadian cities (though less so than in Western cities). Harris, "Working-Class Home Ownership."

70. Roberts, "Insanitary Areas,"178; *HH*, 4 May 1907, 10; 25 May 1907, 16; 16 April 1909, 2; 23 April 1910, 17; 20 May 1910; 15 Sept. 1910, 10; 9 Dec. 1910, 16; 16 Dec. 1910, 15; 23 May 1911, 14; 12 July 1912, 15; 17 Oct. 1912, 13; 18 Feb. 1924, 23; *HS*, 16 May 1907, 12; 10 Nov. 1911, 10 (for a sample of the hoopla around the sale of lots); Weaver, *Hamilton*, 99, 197; Doucet and Weaver, *Housing the North American City*, 87–97, 243–304; Johnston, *Head of the Lake*, 247–48; Campbell, *Mountain and a City*, 206. In the late 19th century, fewer than three out of ten of Hamilton's housing purchases involved mortgages, and most ran only three to four years. Harris and Sendbuehler found that in Union Park, an early east-end suburb, 96 per cent of mortgages were held by private individuals. Harris and Ragonetti found nine out of ten mortgages in Hamilton were held by individuals before the 1920s, and eight of ten over that decade. Ross reached similar conclusions on Toronto mortgages. Katz, Doucet, and Stern, *Social Organization*, 148–50; Harris and Sendbuehler, "Making of a Working-Class Suburb," 493; Harris and Ragonetti, "Where Credit Is Due," 231; Ross, "Housing Finance."

71. CRCRLC, *Report: Evidence – Ontario*, 736–42; Doucet, "Working Class Housing"; Doucet and Weaver, *Housing the North American City*, 72–76; *HH*, 9 Aug. 1910, 10; *Hamilton Manufacturer*, 1913, n.p.

72. Doucet and Weaver found that from 1891 to 1941 only 32–40 per cent of skilled and semi-skilled workers in a large sample and 16–29 per cent of labourers owned their own homes (except in the 1920s, when levels climbed briefly to 50 and 40 per cent respectively). There was only modest upward movement in these levels and major depressions brought them down, notably the slump of the 1930s (there were also minor panics in 1914, 1921, and 1931 that many working-class householders would lose their homes through default on their mortgages). Both a local health department survey in 1922 and census-takers

in 1931 also found that only four out of ten workers owned their own houses. Katz, Doucet, and Stern, *Social Organization*, 156; *HH*, 4 May 1907, 10; *Globe*, 5 March 1915; 13 March 1915; *IB*, 12 March 1915; 26 Feb. 1915; 26 March 1915; *LN*, 23 Dec. 1921; OPBHR, 1922, 274; Doucet and Weaver, *Housing the North American City*, 310–33. The provincial government passed legislation in 1931 to make foreclosures more difficult. Cassidy, *Unemployment and Relief*, 119.

73. In contrast, home-ownership levels within the older north-end working-class neighbourhoods inside the original city limits lagged behind the overall city rate by the 1920s, rising only from 28 to 36 per cent in the northwestern section and from 35 to 40 per cent in the northeast between 1891 and 1921. Doucet and Weaver, *Housing the North American City*, 310–33; Harris and Sendbuehler, "Making of a Working-Class Suburb"; see also *HS*, 1 June 1936; 25 Oct. 1938. For comparison, see Harris, *Class and Housing Tenure*; Chodo and Harris, "Local Culture of Property"; Harris and Hammett, "Myth of the Promised Land"; Daunton, "Cities of Homes and Cities of Tenements." It is not possible to determine precisely which workers moved to the new suburbs, but the large numbers of recent British immigrants suggest that this process of suburbanization was not simply a movement of former inner-city dwellers outward, as seems to have been the case in some US cities; see, for example, Edel, Sclar, and Luria, *Shaky Palaces*.

74. Harris and Sendbuehler, "Hamilton's East End"; Harris and Sendbuehler, "Making of a Working-Class Suburb"; Weaver, *Hamilton*, 103; Doucet and Weaver, *Housing the North American City*, 108, 201–42; Ennals and Holdsworth, *Homeplace*, 192–231; *Canadian Architect and Builder*, June 1907, 103; Bridle, "Shack-Town Christmas"; *HH*, 25 May 1907, 16; 16 April 1909, 2; 23 June 1913, 9; *HS*, 12 April 1913, 5.

75. *HS*, 16 May 1919, 1; 17 May 1919, 1; 16 Sept. 1919, 1; 17 Sept. 1919, 6; 4 Oct. 1919, 5; 13 April 1921, 6; 10 Aug. 1923, 10; 15 July 1936, n.p.; Roberts, ed., *Organizing Westinghouse*, 6; *LG*, August 1918, 558; *LN*, 19 Sept. 1919, 1; Dickey, "Houses of Hamilton," 20–21; OWAHC, interview with Fred Purser. There is no available data to determine precisely what proportions of these houses in Hamilton's new suburbs were built by contractors and owners. Harris estimates that perhaps two-fifths of all new homes in Toronto before World War One and for a few years after were owner-built, and that some 86 per cent of the owner-builders were blue-collar workers, especially though not exclusively building-trades workers; see Harris, *Growth of Home Ownership*; Harris, "Self-Building in the Urban Housing Market"; Harris, "Self-Building and the Social Geography of Toronto"; Saywell, *Housing Canadians*, 113; Zunz, *Changing Face of Inequality*, 170–76; Daunton,

"Introduction," *Housing the Workers*, 13, 15–16; Nicolaides, "'Where the Working Man Is Welcomed.'"

76. *HS*, 16 Sept. 1919, 12; 12 April 1913, 5 (quotation).

77. *HH*, 11 Dec. 1909, 11; 11 Nov. 1912, 1; 13 Nov. 1912, 1; 18 Nov. 1912, 1; 6 June 1913, 11; 19 June 1913, 1; 27 March 1914, 18; *HS*, 20 March 1907, 1; 27 March 1907, 8; 28 March 1909, 10; 16 April 1907, 1; Harris and Sendbuehler, "Hamilton's East End"; Doucet and Weaver, *Housing the North American City*, 95–96, 99, 107. In 1925 the *Herald* noted the "deplorable condition" of Kenilworth Avenue, which was still unpaved; *HH*, 23 April 1925.

78. Dalzell, *Housing in Canada II*, 25–29 (quotation); *HH*, 4 Oct. 1919, 21; OPBHR, 1920, 223; 1922, 275; Gowans, *Comfortable House*.

79. Confrontations with landlords remained isolated battles with the myriad of individual owners, a good number of them blue-collar workers themselves, and never mushroomed into the large rent strikes that hit cities of tenements like New York or Glasgow. Doucet and Weaver, *Housing the North American City*, 343–87; Daunton, "Introduction," in Daunton, ed., *Housing the Workers*, 21–22.

80. By 1941 over 99 per cent of Hamilton houses had electrical lighting, inside running water, and flush toilets. CC, 1941, Vol. 9, 65, 68, 75.

81. Doucet and Weaver, *Housing the North American City*, 431–45. Hamilton dwellings had an average of 5.8 rooms, roughly comparable with Toronto, Saint John, Ottawa, and London, but higher than Vancouver, Victoria, Winnipeg, Windsor, Montreal, and Halifax. On average each Hamilton dwelling sheltered four people, compared to 5.3 in Quebec City, 4.7 in Halifax, 4.6 in Ottawa, 4.4 in Montreal, 4.1 in Toronto, but only 3.6 in London, 3.5 in Vancouver, and 3.3 in Victoria. CC, 1941, Vol. 9, 168.

82. HPL, "Report of Some Housing Conditions"; Doucet and Weaver, *Housing the North American City*, 462.

83. CC, 1941, Vol. 9, 11.

84. Harris, *Creeping Conformity*. Olivier Zunz makes a useful distinction between "production" suburbs, which grew up in the shadow of Detroit's factories, and "residential" suburbs, which were developed far from industries; see *Changing Face of Inequality*, 354–59. For complaints about noise, see HPL, RG 12, Series A, 7 Nov. 1922, 4 Dec. 1922, 26 April 1928.

85. *HT*, 14 July 1919. For discussion of another more exclusive suburb, see Day, "Creation of a Neighbourhood."

86. Murphy and Murphy, *Tales from the North End*.

87. Doucet and Weaver, *Housing the North American City*, 110–11, 446–56. My own sampling of the residents of six randomly chosen blocks in the west-centre, north, and east ends revealed the preponderance of blue-collar workers, skilled and unskilled, with only a sprinkling of clerical and sales workers and self-employed people (most of them shop-keepers); see Table 15.

88. *HH*, 11 Dec. 1909, 11; *HS*, 16 April 1907, 1; *LN*, 16 Oct. 1914, 1 (quotation).

89. *HH*, 4 May 1907, 10; 6 June 1913, 11; 7 June 1913, 5; 13 Aug. 1913; 14 July 1919, 6; 18 Sept. 1919, 1; MHSO, ITA-6489–BOR (quotation); ITA-0808–CEC; ITA-0882–ANO; Brandino, "Italians," 53; Doucet and Weaver, *Housing the North American City*, 99–102, 122–23 (quotation at 123). In 1924 a YWCA official claimed that in the east end "the foreigners are pushing the English speaking population further south." HYWCAA, Minutes, 19 Feb. 1924. Blacks were also barred from many neighbourhoods. Beattie, *John Christie Holland*, 66. The restrictive covenants were not ruled unconstitutional until after World War Two.

90. *VCHD*, 1905–13; MPSS, 39; Synge, "Immigrant Communities," 40; Foster, "Ethnic Settlement," 27–28, 45; *HH*, 31 Aug. 1912, 1 (quotation); 18 Sept. 1919 (quotation).

91. Holman, "Corktown"; Weaver, *Hamilton*, 32, 60, 99, 175; *HH*, 31 Aug. 1912, 1; Roberts, ed., *Organizing Westinghouse*, 1; MHSO, ITA-0883–ANO; ITA-0815–ANO; ITA-09826–FER; ITA-0809–GRO; ITA-0982–PAS; Cumbo, "Italians in Hamilton"; Cumbo, *Italian Presence*; Patrias, *Patriots and Proletarians*, 76–87; Kaprielian-Churchill, *Like Our Mountains*, 58–64; Shahrodi, "Early Polish Settlement." In 1914 an Italian official visiting Hamilton found numerous Italian retailers: 10 grocers who imported foodstuffs, 22 fruit dealers (other than peddlers), 3 tailors, 6 barbers, 7 butchers, 4 shoemakers, and a cigar factory. Cumbo, *Italian Presence*. For comparable ethnic enclaves see Hiebert, "Class, Ethnicity, and Residential Structure"; Barman, "Neighbourhood and Community."

92. Synge, "Immigrant Communities," 39–40 (quotation); *LN*, 13 Feb. 1914; 16 Oct. 1914; *HH*, 11 Dec. 1909, 11; 11 Nov. 1912, 1; 19 Aug. 1913; 11 Nov. 1922, 5; 13 July 1923, 19; 10 Aug. 1923, 17. The *Herald* also ran a regular column of East Hamilton news in 1913 and 1914. These English settlements were common in other Canadian cities; see McCormack, "Cloth Caps and Jobs," 45–46; McCormack, "Networks among British Immigrants"; Bridle, "Shack-Town Christmas"; Harris, "Canada's All Right"; Barman, "Neighbourhood and Community," 102; Reynolds, *British Immigrant*, 114–32.

93. See, for example, *HS*, 23 March 190, 8; 1 May 1900, 8; 18 Sept. 1900, 8; 8 Oct. 1900, 8; 6 Dec. 1900, 8; 20 May 1901, 8; 28 July 1903, 10; 10 June 1910, 10; 18 July 1910, 10; 21 July 1910, 10; 9 Aug. 1910, 10; 23 Aug. 1910, 10; 1 June 1920; 22 July 1930, 7; 29 Aug. 1930, 7; 20 Oct. 1930, 7. In 1912 Police Magistrate Jelfs declared neighbours' fights "a grave evil" and promised to "do all in his power to suppress them." *HT*, 15 July 1912, 1.

94. Gilliland and Sendbuehler, "To Produce the Highest Type of Manhood and Womanhood"; Synge, "Self-Help and Neighbourliness," 97–104; MHSO, ITA-6990–ROB; Bridle, "Shack-Town Christmas"; Harris, "Residential Segregation and Class Formation"; Harris, *Creeping Conformity*, 74–105.

4. Labouring for Love

1. With pressure from the local business community, Hamilton city council voted to introduce daylight saving on 4 June 1916, but, despite endorsement by the Trades and Labor Council, loud opposition swelled up among workers, many of whom held informal referenda in their workplaces on ending the new scheme. One worker called it "Kaiserism." City councillors soon backed down, and standard time resumed on 13 August. In 1918 the federal government introduced it for one season, but thereafter left the decision to the municipalities. Hamiltonians debated a local measure repeatedly in the interwar period. LAC, R3096-0-8-E, Municipal and Legislative Committee, 20 April 1915; *LN*, 14 May 1915, 1; 11 April 1919, 1; 18 April 1919, 1; 25 April 1919, 1; *HH*, 14 Feb. 1916, 1; 18 May 1916, 1; 25 May 1916, 1; 30 May 1916, 2; 31 May 1916, 5; 3 June 1916, 2; 5 June 1916, 1; 7 June 1916, 1; 9 June 1916, 1, 2; 8 July 1916, 5; 23 July 1916, 5; 25 July 1916, 1–2; 1 Aug. 1916, 2; 29 July 1916, 2; 31 July 1916, 1; 3 Aug. 1916, 1; 5 Aug. 1916, 1; 9 Aug. 1916, 7; 10 Aug. 1916, 1; 11 Aug. 1916, 11, 12; 12 April 1918, 6; 15 April 1918, 1; 6 May 1919, 2; *HS*, 10 June 1916, 7; 13 June 1916, 7; 14 June 1916, 6; 5 July 1916, 1, 15; 16 April 1930, 33; *IB*, 14 July 1916, 4; 11 Aug. 1916, 2; *CLW*, 18 Dec. 1926, 4; HCC, *Annual Report*, 1929–30, 30; 1930–31, 25; 1931–32, 22; 1935, 8.

2. *HS*, 24 Feb. 1919, 6; 2 April 1919, 6; 5 April 1919, 6; 5 April 1919, 6; 5 July 1916, 15; 4 April 1919, 26; see also 22 Feb. 1922, 6; 1 April 1922, 7.

3. Joanna Bourke writes forcefully about the British working-class housewife's sense of accomplishment in her domestic labour in this period; see Bourke, *Working-Class Cultures*, 64–71.

4. Snell, "'The White Life for Two'"; Snell, *In the Shadow of the Law*; Valverde, *Age of Soap, Light, and Water*; Chunn, *From Punishment to Doing Good*; Weaver, "Social Control, Martial Conformity, and Community Entanglement"; Givertz, "Sex and Order." There was a perceptible increase in divorces in the 1930s. In 1941 156 men and 754 women in Hamilton told the census-takers they were divorced, compared to only two men and six women in 1901 and only 53 and 76 in 1931. But these were still only 2 per cent of the heads of households in the city in 1941.

5. Gillis, *For Better, For Worse*; Morton, *Fight or Pay*.

6. The marriage rate in Hamilton took a tumble in the economic gloom of the 1890s, hitting a low in 1895. But it rose sharply in the boom of the early 1900s, peaked in 1907, then declined slightly through the two depression years that followed, before hitting a new high in 1912 (despite a housing shortage and rapid retail price inflation). Marriage rates slowed again through the pre-war

depression and still more during the war itself, when the departure of so many marriageable men for the trenches brought the rate down to a new low. Once the soldiers returned, the rate again bounced back in 1920. During the postwar depression that followed, a steady decline in the marriage rate occurred until 1925, with only a slight rise in the more prosperous years of the late 1920s. Many more couples delayed their marriage plans in the deep depression of the early 1930s, and the rate slumped to the lowest level since the 1890s. It edged slightly upward during the rest of the decade until it jumped up in 1940 as the new war economy gathered steam. See Table 6.

7. In 1941 46.5 per cent were married, compared to only 34 per cent in 1891 and 36 per cent in 1901. This was a national trend. CC, 1891, Vol. 1, 154–55; 1901, Vol. 1, 12–13; 1941, Vol. 3, 122. Calculations of percentages are mine. The Ontario government strengthened its Marriage Act in 1919 and 1921 to require clearer parental consent and to tighten up licensing procedures for marriages, but this made no perceptible impact on marriage patterns in a city like Hamilton. Snell and Abeele, "Regulating Nuptiality."

8. The proportion of Hamilton women marrying before age 25 climbed from 63 per cent in the first decade of the century to 73 per cent in the decade spanning World War One, and levelled off at 72 in the 1920s. Even more striking, the proportion marrying in their teens climbed from 16 to 21 to 26 per cent. CC, 1941, Vol. 3, 732. Similar information on husbands was not published in 1941. Right through to 1941, adult women generally outnumbered adult men in the decennial censuses, with the exception of 1911, when the many transient sojourners and boomers arriving in the great population explosion before World War One pushed up the male total. CC, 1891, Vol. 2, 7–9; 1901, Vol. 4, 10–13; 1921, Vol. 1, 340; Vol. 2, 272–73; 1931, Vol. 2, 157; Vol. 3, 29–30; 1941, Vol. 3, 65–67. The ratio of men to 100 women in Hamilton was 93 in 1891, 99 in 1901, 106 in 1911, 97 in 1921, and 99 in 1931 and 1941. After 1920 the female majority was concentrated in their wage-earning years of 15 to 29, no doubt a reflection of the migration of so many single women to the city to find jobs and the death of so many men in World War One.

9. Denyse Baillargeon explores all these expectations in Montreal working-class marriages in the interwar period in *Making Do*, 47–65. In that same period the national labour magazine, the *Canadian Congress Journal*, ran a women's page, which several times offered advice to women about how to please a husband. *CCJ*, March 1928, 39; August 1928, 40; October 1928, 36–37; January 1929, 38; April 1932, 23.

10. Suzanne Morton has traced these new attitudes in working-class Halifax, but Baillargeon found a more practical orientation among the women she interviewed in Montreal. Morton, "June Bride as the Working-Class Bride"; Baillargeon, *Making Do*, 47–59.

11. *HS*, 4 Sept. 1920, 27.

12. The thousands of new immigrants who arrived from Britain after 1900 would certainly have been raised with this expectation; see Ross, "'Fierce Questions and Taunts'"; Gillis, *For Better, For Worse*; Ayers and Lambertz, "Marriage Relations, Money, and Domestic Violence." In her interviews with women growing up in northwestern England, Elizabeth Roberts discovered "the very practical, unromantic view that most working-class people had of marriage"; see *A Woman's Place*, 81–124. John Gillis added that, between the mid-19th and mid-20th centuries, British working-class husbands and wives relied more on kin, friends, and community for emotional support and personal satisfaction than on each other; *For Better, For Worse*, 231–59. See also Susan Porter Benson's examination of US working-class marriages in the interwar period; *Household Accounts*, 17–18.

13. OPBHR, 1923, 385.

14. Gillis points out how in Britain "domestic dispute was a major theme of music hall comedy at the turn of the century." *For Better, For Worse*, 251.

15. *HS*, 28 Dec. 1920, 15. Ellen Ross argues that in these battles money (and the failure to provide it) was the central point of contention for working-class women; *Love and Toil*, 73.

16. See, for example, *HS*, 7 March 1910, 12; 26 March 1910, 15; 3 Aug. 1910, 12; 11 Nov. 1910, 11; 7 March 1930, 7; 13 March 1930, 7; 28 May 1930, 7; 2 June 1930, 7; 10 Dec. 1930, 7.

17. *HS*, 7 March 1910, 12 (quotation); 24 March 1910, 15; 18 Aug. 1910, 10 (quotation); 11 March 1930, 7 (quotation); *HH*, 7 Feb. 1924. Ross delineates these expectations in the English context in *Love and Toil*, 70–72; see also Stansell, *City of Women*, 77–83.

18. Tomes, "'Torrent of Abuse'"; Ross, "'Fierce Questions and Taunts'"; Gillis, *For Better, For Worse*; Hammerton, *Cruelty and Companionship*, 13–67; Clark, "Domesticity and the Problem of Wifebeating"; Rowbotham, "'Only When Drunk'"; Ayers and Lambertz, "Marriage Relations, Money, and Domestic Violence"; Ross, *Love and Toil*, 84–86; *HS*, 15 Sept. 1930, 7. Annmarie Hughes argues that domestic violence was still common in interwar Scotland, which was a source of many immigrants to Hamilton in the 1920s; see "Representations and Counter-Representations of Domestic Violence."

19. On all these tactics, see, for example, *HS*, 8 March 1900, 8; 30 May 1900, 8; 20 Aug. 1900, 8; 18 Sept. 1900, 8; 28 Dec. 1900, 8; 4 Jan. 1910, 12; 4 Feb. 1910, 15; 11 March 1910, 20; 26 March 1910, 15; 25 May 1910, 14; 7 June 1920, 23; 27 Nov. 1920, 22; Weaver, *Crimes, Constables, and Courts*, 199; Weaver, "Social Control, Martial Conformity, and Community Entanglement."

20. Weaver, *Crimes, Constables, and Courts*, 70; *HS*, 3 Aug. 1910, 12 (quotation).

21. *HS*, 29 June 1910, 14. Later that year, Jelfs sent a Hungarian worker to prison for ten years for slashing his wife with a razor. *HS*, 28 Dec. 1910, 1.

22. *HS*, 22 Sept. 1910, 12 (quotation); 27 March 1930, 7; 4 June 1930, 7; 21 Aug. 1930, 7; 9 Oct. 1930, 7; 22 May 1930, 7 (quotation).

23. *HS*, 15 Sept. 1930, 7 (quotation); Golz, "'If a Man's Wife Does Not Obey Him, What Can He Do?'"; McLean, "'Deserving' Wives and 'Drunken' Husbands"; Weaver, *Crimes, Constables, and Courts*, 74.

24. *HS*, 26 April 1910, 1 (quotation); 24 Oct. 1910, 12 (quotation); 28 May 1920, 22 (quotation); *HH*, 12 Oct. 1918 (quotation); 21 Dec. 1918, 1 (quotation).

25. *HS*, 24 March 1910, 15 (quotation); 2 June 1930, 7 (quotation). "If married women were themselves what they ought to be, loving, forgiving, patient, tactful, forbearing and more tolerant in their conduct towards their husbands, there would be fewer causes for complaint," Jelfs wrote in his 1925 book, *Man's Natural, Moral, and Social Duties* (103–4). "But if a woman is addicted to scolding or nagging, she is largely responsible from this cause alone, for many acts of violence by her husband, for generally as she loses control of her tongue, so he loses control of his temper."

26. *HS*, 16 Jan. 1900, 8 (quotation); 4 May 1910, 14 (quotation); 12 Aug. 1920, 8; Crozier, "Jelfs," 98 (quotation); *HH*, 18 March 1921, 1 (quotation); Golz, "'If a Man's Wife Does Not Obey Him,'" 335–37; McLean, "'Deserving' Wives and 'Drunken' Husbands"; Chunn, *From Punishment to Doing Good*, 87–89, 99, 105.

27. George Sturt, *Change in the Village*, quoted in Malcolmson, *Life and Labour*, 69.

28. See Parr, *Gender of Breadwinners*, 90–91; Benson, *Household Accounts*, 46–49.

29. Synge, "Family and Community," ch. 3.1.

30. Roberts, "Housing Situation, Hamilton," 256; Lucas, "Conflict over Public Power"; Dodd, "Delivering Electrical Technology," 91–94, 163. In 1914 the Ontario Hydro-Electric Power Commission had 65,000 customers across the province; in 1920 194,000; in 1930 433,000; and in 1938 over 500,000. Dodd, "Delivering Electrical Technology," 133. As an indication of the predominance of lighting in electrical usage, advertisements for electric irons in a 1909 cookbook show them being plugged into light sockets; St. Giles Presbyterian Church, Ladies' Aid and Friends, *Choice Recipes*.

31. Dodd, "Delivering Electrical Technology," 163; CC, 1941, Vol. 9, 62.

32. CC, 1941, Vol. 9, 62, 79–80; WAHC, interviews with Mary and Louis Fiori, Lil Seager, Floyd Read. In 1925 the average price of refrigerators in Ontario was $425; by 1936 it was $166. Dodd, "Delivering Electrical Technology," 141. The 1951 census reported that while 98 per cent of Hamilton households had stoves, a quarter still had no refrigerator. CC, 1951, Vol. 3, 99–99.

33. WAHC, interview with Florence Fisher; Cowan, *More Work for Mother*, 71–75; Strasser, *Satisfaction Guaranteed*; Strong-Boag, *New Day Recalled*, 130–33.

34. Murphy, *Tales from the North End*, 219–35; WAHC, interviews, North End Community Meeting, 11 June 1995; interview with Mary and Louis Fiori. Less than half of Hamilton's households had telephones in 1941, and only 38 per cent among tenants; overall, 43 per cent of households had a car, but only 37 per cent of tenants. CC, Vol. 9, 83.

35. Steedman, *Angels of the Workplace*, 41–42; Synge, "Family and Community," ch. 3.1; Strasser, *Never Done*, 125–44.

36. See, for example, ads for Dominion tomato soup, Heinz baked beans, Post bran flakes, Acme Farmers milk, and Sunlight soap; *HS*, 7 April 1920, 10; 16 June 1925, 3; 17 May 1929, 26; 28 July 1931, 17; 2 May 1932, 10.

37. In 1900 an office worker in downtown Hamilton reported in a letter to the editor that "one of those large chimneys vomits forth its clouds of black smoke, and to leave the door or window open subjects my books, papers and furniture to a greasy covering of soot. Mine is not an isolated case; hundreds are up in arms against this nuisance." Ten years later the *Spectator* reported that the local anti-smoke by-law seemed to be useless, since, at the downtown corner of King and James, passers-by were met with "a deluge of particles which float downwards from adjoining high buildings and make pedestrians look as though they have just returned unwashed from Pittsburgh." One can only imagine conditions out in the factory district. *HS*, 24 Jan. 1900, 8; 26 Feb. 1900, 8; 26 April 1910, 1.

38. Dodd, "Delivering Electrical Technology," 163, 197–98; CC, 1941, Vol. 9, 83–84; WAHC, interviews with Mary and Louis Fiori, Florence Fisher; Bowden and Offer, "Technological Revolution That Never Was." The magazine of the Trades and Labor Congress of Canada, the *Canadian Congress Journal*, had a women's page at the end of the 1920s, and its advice on how to carry out basic household tasks still assumed that the laundry would be done without a washing machine; see *CCJ*, June 1929, 39.

39. WAHC, interviews with Fred Purser, Floyd Read; Cumbo, "As the Twig Is Bent," 29–30.

40. Fahrni, "Rhetoric of Order"; Ross, "'Not the Sort That Would Sit on the Doorstep'"; Tomes, *Gospel of Germs*, 190–95; Cowan, *More Work for Mother*.

41. The YWCA's north-end branch, opened in 1893, fell short of Hoodless's expectations. It had 174 girls enrolled in 1901, and soldiered on with dwindling numbers until World War One. Sebire, *Woman's Place*, 76–77; MacDonald, *Adelaide Hoodless* (quotation at 46).

42. *HS*, 13 June 1904, 4 (quotation); 6 April 1907, 1–2 (quotation); Crowley, "Madonnas Before Magdalenes"; Lyle, *Hamilton Local Council of Women*, 9–11; Cumbo, "As the Twig Is Bent," 188–90.

43. Blue Ribbon Limited, *Blue Ribbon Cook Book*; see also Egg-o Baking Powder Company, *Helpful Recipes and Helpful Hints*; Ogilvie Flour Mills Company Limited, *Ogilvie's Book for a Cook*. In 1921 the Borden Company held a recipe contest among Hamilton women "to promote better cooking" through "the concentration of effort and the making available of tested proven recipes." *HS*, 5 May 1921, 11.

44. Dodd, "Advice to Parents," 215; Strasser, *Never Done*, 202–23.

45. *HS*, 26 March 1901, 10; 6 May 1930, 19 (quotations); Dodd, "Women in Advertising," 134–51; Hobbs and Pierson, "'A Kitchen That Wastes No Steps.'"

46. This was the conclusion of Ruth Schwartz Cowan about their counterparts in the US; see *More Work for Mother*, 160–72, 181–90.

47. Frank, "White Working-Class Women." For an example of ethnic differences, see Glenn, *Daughters of the Shtetl*, 68–76.

48. CC, 1941, Vol. 9, 83.

49. Synge, "Family and Community," ch. 3.1; Wild, *Elizabeth Bagshaw*, 40–52; MHSO, ITA-0808-CEC. For the similar attitudes and practices of US and English working-class women, see Dubinsky, *Improper Advances*, 128; Roberts, *Woman's Place*, 86–103; Ross, *Love and Toil*, 97–106; Bourke, *Working-Class Cultures*, 29–40; Hoggart, *Uses of Literacy*, 41–42; Seccombe, *Weathering the Storm*, 157–93.

50. Dodd, "Women's Involvement in the Canadian Birth Control Movement"; Annau, "Eager Eugenicists"; Annau, "Promoting Prophylactics"; McLaren and McLaren, *Bedroom and the State*.

51. AMMM, RG 1, A-A, Hamilton Medical Society, Minutes, 3 Feb. 1907; Phair and Sellers, "Study of Maternal Deaths," 566; Backhouse, "Physicians, Abortions, and the Law"; McLaren and McLaren, *Bedroom and the State*, 32–53; McLaren, "Illegal Operations"; Comacchio, *Nations Are Built of Babies*, 71–72. This pattern of birth control without much use of artificial devices was also evident in Britain; see Brookes, "Women and Reproduction." By the 1930s the Communists were praising the availability of legal abortions in the Soviet Union; *Worker*, 10 Feb. 1934, 2.

52. Hamilton's birthrate generally languished in economic doldrums and revived vigorously in better times. It hit 33 per 1,000 population in 1908 and 28 in 1912, fell off over the next decade of depression and war, and shot up to nearly 31 in 1921. After that point there was a slow, steady decrease through the 1920s and 1930s in what scholars like to call a "fertility decline." See Stern, *Society and Family Strategy*, 7–22. The proportion of the population under age 15 fell from 29, where it had been since the turn of the century, to 27 in 1931 and 22 in 1941.

53. No record exists of the average family size before 1921. In 1921 only one in five families with children had more than three; a decade later the number had fallen to one in six, though among European immigrants the proportions were still much higher – one in four in Polish families and two in five among Italians. CC, 1931, Vol. 5, 1188–89, 1512–13 (calculations are mine).

54. According to a special study in the 1941 census, among those who would have finished their child-bearing, those 65 and over had an average of 3.7 children, while those age 55 to 60 averaged 3.1 and those 44 to 54 only 2.8. But poorer families still had more. Families of wage-earners existing on less than $450 per year had an average of 2.8 children, while those in families with incomes of between $450 and $1,449 (roughly half the total) averaged 2.2 children, and those living on more than $1,450 per year had only two. Ethnicity also made a difference. That year all Italian mothers averaged 3.3 children, Jewish 2.4, Eastern European 2.3, and British, German, and Scandinavian 2.2. Italian women over 65 had produced 5.9, compared to 4.6 among those 45 to 64, while Eastern European women in each of these age groups had given birth to 5.1 and 3.6 and British women 3.4 and 2.7. CC, 1941, Vol. 5, 442–43, 574–75 (calculations of averages are mine). Ross also discovered that working-class mothers in London had considerably larger families than did their middle-class counterparts; see *Love and Toil*, 92–94.

55. Synge, "Family and Community"; Gillis, *For Better, For Worse*, 248; Ross, "'Not the Sort That Would Sit on the Doorstep,'" 48–50; Semple, "Nurture and Admonition"; Cumbo, "Salvation in Indifference," 214; Davey, "Educational Reform and the Working Class."

56. Jane Synge's interviewees remembered their parents' strong desire to instil a sense of obedience, respectful behaviour, and "decency." Synge, "Family and Community," ch. 3.3; also Synge, "Work and Family Support Patterns," 143. Peter Hunter remembered getting sound moral lessons in his left-leaning, Scottish-immigrant family; Hunter, *Which Side Are You On, Boys*, 4–5. Enrico Carlson Cumbo's interviews with Italians in Hamilton revealed the use of folk tales, fables, and proverbs. Cumbo, *Italian Presence*. See also Reynolds, *British Immigrant*, 214.

57. In the 1890s Hamilton's elementary schools had no male teachers, other than principals. By the 1920s the schools still had only 23 men out of 418 total. HBEM, 1895, 30–34; 1900, 27–31; 1920, 36–45.

58. Stamp, *Schools of Ontario*, 39 (quotation); Synge, "Family and Community," ch. 3.3 (quotation).

59. Hoodless, "Social Influence of the Home," 12 (quotation); Stamp, *Schools of Ontario*, 39; *HS*, 17 April 1920, 15; Cumbo, "As the Twig Is Bent," 161; Synge, "Family

and Community" (quotation); Barman, "'Knowledge Is Essential.'"

60. Bennett, "Taming 'Bad Boys'"; Bennett, "Turning 'Bad Boys' into 'Good Citizens'"; Matters, "Boys' Industrial School"; Hogeveen, "'Can't You Be a Man?'"

61. Rooke and Schnell, *Discarding the Asylum*.

62. OSNDCR, 1894–1912; Adam Brown, Speech, CCCCP, 1911, 37–40; *HS*, 23 Jan. 1894, 31 Jan. 1894, 23 Feb. 1894, 30 Jan. 1901, 31 Dec. 1902, 18 Dec. 1903, 29 June 1904, 2 Feb. 1910, 27 Sept. 1910, 25 Nov. 1922 (clippings in HPL, Children's Aid Society Scrapbook); *HS*, 5 Sept. 1903, 11; Benner, 100 *Years for Children*.

63. *HH*, 18 Oct. 1918, 18; 17 Nov. 1920, 7 (quotation); 17 Dec. 1921, 35; 14 Nov. 1924, 6 (quotation); 20 Dec. 1924, 18; *HS*, 23 Jan. 1894; 31 Jan. 1894; 23 Feb. 1893 (clippings in HPL, Children's Aid Society Scrapbook); 14 Dec. 1894, 5; 18 Dec. 1903, 5; 29 June 1904, 4; 8 April 1907, 7; 30 Oct. 1919, 14; 25 Nov. 1922, 1; 14 Nov. 1924, 19 (quotation); 10 Nov. 1927, 25; *HT*, 30 Jan. 1901, 3; 8 Nov. 1911, 10; 2 March 1912, 11; Benner, 100 *Years for Children*.

64. Hamilton Playgrounds Association, *Souvenir Number*. The City of Hamilton took control of the playgrounds in 1931.

65. *HT*, 18 June 1910; 1 March 1911.

66. CCCCP, 1911, 46; *HT*, 4 Aug., 1911, 4.

67. CCCCP, 1911, 46; *HT*, 28 Oct. 1911, 5; 4 July 1914, 11; *HH*, 23 May 1913, 3; 13 July 1916, 12; *HS*, 21 May 1915, 10; HPL, Hamilton Playgrounds, General Report, 1918–25.

68. A Canadian Red Cross researcher noted that nutritional levels declined when families were on relief; see McCready, "Analysis of Weekly Relief Food Orders." See also Dodd, "Advice to Parents," 223–24. On Hamilton's environment, see Cruikshank and Bouchier, "Blighted Areas and Obnoxious Industries."

69. Mitchinson, *Giving Birth*, 129; Ross, *Love and Toil*, 106.

70. See Table 6. Calculations are mine.

71. See Table 6. Between 1901 and 1911, an average of 5.9 women died annually from "puerperal causes" for every 1,000 live births. From 1911 to 1920 the number was 6.6, and in the 1920s and 1930s 6 – more than the 5.5 calculated in contemporary national and provincial studies in the interwar period, and probably an underestimate by as much as 17–27 per cent. In the 1920s Canada's maternal-mortality rate was the worst among 14 countries studied. Phair and Sellers, "Study of Maternal Deaths," 563–79; Mitchinson, *Giving Birth in Canada*, 260–85; Oppenheimer, "Childbirth in Ontario"; Comacchio, *Nations Are Built of Babies*, 70–72, 223, 229–30; Emery, *Facts of Life*, 116–36; McVean, "Pageant of Motherhood." The play was written by the young journalist Nora-Frances Henderson. *DHB*, Vol. 4, 124.

72. See Table 6.

73. HBHR, 1895–1914; Dallyn, "Diarrhoea and Enteritis"; Ross, "Typhoid Fever Mortality."

74. James Roberts, Hamilton's medical officer of health, reported that 45 per cent of diphtheria cases between 1905 and 1910 were "derived from the districts of the city where the industrial classes are centred, where the housing is inferior, the sewer accommodation insufficient, and where overcrowding exists to a greater or lesser extent." Roberts, "Insanitary Areas," 179.

75. AMMM, RG 1, A-A, Hamilton Medical Society, Minutes, 6 June 1900; HBHR, 1909–10, 16; *HS*, 15 May 1905, 10; 7 May 1907, 11; 28 Feb. 1930, 7.

76. McKinnon and Ross, "Whooping Cough," 533.

77. Ross, "Mortality in Ontario."

78. HBHR, 1910, 149. See Table 9.

79. See, for example, HBHR, 1896, 141; 1897, 128; 1902, 165. In 1934 medical researchers estimated that 60–80 per cent of Ontario's population had contracted whooping cough in their lifetimes, probably five to six times as many cases as were actually reported. McKinnon and Ross, "Whooping Cough," 533.

80. HBHR, 1901, 1909, 1912.

81. McGinnis, "Impact of Epidemic Influenza"; Jones, "Searching for the Springs of Health"; Dublin et al., *Mortality Experience of Industrial Policyholders*, 33–38; Chan and Kluge, "Epidemic Spreads," 49. See Table 6.

82. See Table 7. Ontario's Registrar General published a one-time-only occupational breakdown of those who died of tuberculosis in 1898. Of the 87 deaths in Wentworth County (of which Hamilton was a part), 24 were clearly in working-class occupations, 21 were housewives, 21 were children, and only 6 were farmers. ORGR, 1900, 48–50 (totals are mine). See also Dublin, Kopf, and Van Buren, *Mortality Statistics of Insured Wage-Earners and Their Families*, 43–64; Dublin et al., *Mortality Experience of Industrial Policyholders*, 17–28.

83. Dublin, Kopf, and Van Buren, *Mortality Statistics of Insured Wage-Earners and Their Families*, 65–71, 147–72; Dublin et al., *Mortality Experience of Industrial Policyholders*, 44–52, 86–90; Dublin, Kopf, and Van Buren, *Cancer Mortality*; Dublin and Lotka, *Twenty-Five Years of Health Progress*, 163–225, 227–316. In 1910 59 Hamiltonians died of cancer and 72 of heart disease; in 1939 the numbers were 257 and 321 – an increase far greater than local population growth. See Table 7.

84. See Table 26; Morton, *When Your Number's Up*.

85. CC, 1921, Vol. 3, 57; 1931, Vol. 5, 1161; Snell, *Citizen's Wage*, 23–26.

86. This change was partly a statistical result of the decline in the proportion of children under 15, from 28.3 per cent in 1901 to 26.6 in 1931. Among all adults age 30 and over, the percentage of those 65 and over remained constant between these two dates, at just under 11 per cent. CC, 1901, Vol. 4, 8–13; 1931, Vol. 2, 272–73. Totals and calculations are mine.

87. Unemployment among the men in this age group rose from about a third in 1911 to just under a half in 1931, and no more than 6 per cent of the women ever found jobs, even though there were increasingly more females than males among the elderly. CC, 1891, Vol. 2, 9; 1931, Vol. 2, 273. The female portion of this age group rose from 52 to 55.8 per cent over the same 40-year period. As Edgar-André Montigny argues, most of the elderly continued to live in their own households, although regular help from daughters or other kin might nonetheless increase. Montigny, *Foisted Upon the Government?* 25–29.

88. In 1925 one home was bursting at the seams with 140 inmates, apparently because more relatives could not afford to keep them in depressed economic times. *HS*, 6 July 1925, 5; Montigny, "Families, Institutions, and the State," 74–93; Synge, "Work and Family Support Patterns," 140–44. A police court case in 1925 revealed the family tensions that care of the elderly could spark. One sister sued another under the Parents' Maintenance Act for a contribution to their mother's upkeep. The husband of the accused refused to have his mother-in-law in the house. *HS*, 25 Jan. 1925, 5.

89. Lewis, "Goose Grease and Turpentine"; Loeb, "Beating the Flu"; Ross, *Love and Toil*, 176–79; Mitchinson, *Giving Birth*, 30–34 (quotation at 31).

90. Cumbo, *Italian Presence*; Ewen, *Immigrant Women*, 130–35. In 1933 a woman wrote to the Hamilton Academy of Medicine describing herself as "a practical nurse and midwife," trained at the Liverpool Maternity Hospital, and asking for access to maternity nursing work in the city's relief program. The academy turned her down. A man interviewed many years later explained that his mother was a qualified midwife in the interwar period. Just how many women with such training quietly practised their craft in Hamilton in the early 20th century will remain unknown. AMMM, RG 1, A-A, Hamilton Academy of Medicine, Executive Committee, Minutes, 24 March, 17 April 1933; WAHC, interview with Ken Withers; Ross, *Love and Toil*, 114–22.

91. Shortt, "'Before the Age of Miracles'"; Mitchinson, *Giving Birth*, 19–46, 54–57; Gidney and Millar, *Professional Gentlemen*, 362–68; Stott, *Hamilton's Doctors*, 23–33.

92. Wild, *Elizabeth Bagshaw*, 24–25; Stott, *Hamilton's Doctors*, 58–61; Biggs, "Case of the Missing Midwives," 20–35; Mitchinson, *Giving Birth*, 39–40, 45; Comacchio, *Nations Are Built of Babies*, 104–8.

93. Shortt, "'Before the Age of Miracles'"; AMMM, RG 2-G, Fred Bowman, "Autobiography"; Rosenberg, "Framing Disease," 310.

94. CC, 1911, Vol. 6, 314; 1931, Vol. 7, 188; 1941, Vol. 7, 194, 198 (calculations are mine). Indeed, GPs were feeling sufficiently marginalized in Hamilton's rapidly specializing professional community that they created their own

organization in the early 1930s. Stott, *Hamilton's Doctors*, 166–77.

95. Stott, *Hamilton's Doctors*, 200; Synge, "Family and Community," ch. 3.1.

96. The first Methodist deaconess started work out of Centenary Church in 1901, and the next year the church set up a residential home from which a staff of up to nine in the pre-war years set out to visit homes all over the city. Financial support for the deaconesses declined after the war. *HS*, 10 May 1901, 5; Methodist Church, Board of Management of the Toronto Deaconess Home and Training School, *Annual Report*, 1900–20, in UCA, Methodist Church (Canada), Toronto Conference, Deaconess Board of Management, 78.101C, Box 4; Thomas, "Servants of the Church"; Bailey et al., *Presbytery of Hamilton*, 97; Boutilier, "Helpers or Heroines?" 18, 27–30.

97. Boutilier, "Helpers or Heroines?" 17–35; Gibson, *Victorian Order of Nurses for Canada*, 4–10; "Visiting Housekeepers in Hamilton," *SW*, February 1930, 136.

98. *HH*, 21 Sept. 1916, 2; OTLBR, 1917, 13; OMACR, 1921–22, 19; 1922–23, 19–22; Arnup, *Education for Motherhood*, 75 (quotation).

99. *HS*, 31 Aug. 1907, 17; McPherson, *Bedside Matters*.

100. Boutilier, "Helpers or Heroines?"

101. VONA, Minutes, 1899–1914; *HS*, 18 March 1899, 5; 17 May 1900, 5; 10 May 1901, 5; 23 Oct. 1902, 3; 28 Oct. 1903, 6; Gibson, *Victorian Order of Nurses for Canada*; Dalley, *History of the Hamilton Branch of the Victorian Order of Nurses for Canada*.

102. Metropolitan Life's visiting nurse program had begun in New York in 1909 and quickly spread across the continent. The company's agents recommended policyholders who needed the nurses' attention. VONA, Minutes, 1899–1914; Victoria Order of Nurses for Canada, Board of Governors, *Report*, 1908, 35; Hamilton, "Cost of Caring"; Baillargeon, "Care of Mothers and Infants," 164–67; Dublin, *Family of 30 Million*, 2834, 421–41; James, *Metropolitan Life*, 183–87. Starting in 1921, Catholic working-class families also had access to a few nurses from the similar St. Elizabeth Nurses' Association. *HS*, 2 Feb. 1921, 15.

103. AMMM, RG 2-E, AA Numbers Collection, Victor A. Cecilioni, RM Stringer; see also Wild, *Elizabeth Bagshaw*, 25–30.

104. Cortiula, "Social Transformation," 70, 123, 222, 229; Campbell, *Hamilton General Hospital School of Nursing*, 46, 56, 83, 85–90; HPL, RG 13, A, 29 July, 26 Aug., 19 Dec. 1913; *HH*, 10 June 1913, 1 (quotations); *HS*, 29 Dec. 1920, 4; Gagan and Gagan, *For Patients of Moderate Means*, 19, 58–59, 73. On the reluctance of Hamiltonians to use the hospital, see HBHR, 1911–12, 18; also LAC, R1176-0-0-E, 2427.

105. HPL, RG 12, Series A, 19 March 1901; 23 Jan., 6 Feb., 17 March, 20 June 1905; 7 May, 22 Oct. 1906, 24 Jan., 31 March, 25 May, 17 Aug., 22 Sept., 27 Oct. 1908; 22, 26 Feb.,

26 March, 31 Aug. 1909; 25 June 1912; *HS*, 16 July 1927, 15 (Langrill quotation). It is thus not surprising that the two main hospitals handled only 1,800 in-patients in 1900 and 3,700 in 1910 (when the population was climbing to over 90,000). Patients in the public wards stayed longer on average than did paying patients. Ontario, Department of Health, Division of Medical Statistics, *Survey of Public General Hospitals in Ontario*, Part 1, 14.

106. St. Joseph's had reached out to these clients from its inception, and the City Hospital took a decisive step in 1897 when it opened the much more lavish, comfortably furnished Jubilee wing. The next expansion undertaken ten years later (the Queen Alexandra Wing) and a new building opened far out on the Mountain in 1917 were also limited to pricier accommodation. Gagan and Gagan, *For Patients of Moderate Means*, 23–70, 110; Cortiula, "Social Transformation"; Campbell, *Hamilton General Hospital School of Nursing*, 66, 71; *HS*, 19 May 1916, 22; 9 Sept. 1916, 11.

107. HPL, RG 13, Series A, 11 April, 17 Oct. 1905; R1176-0-0-E, 2419. One local doctor claimed that the city relief officer was "very generous" in authorizing subsidized health care, but an International Harvester worker insisted that "the occupancy of a public ward in the Hamilton hospital carried a certain stigma of charity with it," an opinion supported by the Reverend Banks Nelson, based on his years as a pastor in the city. R1176-0-0-E, 2343, 2344, 2446. For a taste of the fixation on getting patients to pay in a Canadian hospital, see Gagan and Gagan, "'Evil Reports' for 'Ignorant Minds'?"

108. HPL, RG 13, Series A, 31 May 1910; Langrill, "Hospital from the Viewpoint of the Medical Superintendent"; HPL, RG 13, Series A, 29 Jan. 1919. At $4.90 a week for regular care and $10.50 for maternity care, semi-private was half the cost for private rooms in 1910. The semi-private rate in 1916 was still $4.90: HPL, RG 13, Series A, 31 May 1910; *HS*, 9 Sept. 1916, 11. No patient records from the City Hospital (Hamilton General) from the early 20th century have survived, but one case that appeared in the board of governors minutes in 1912 may be indicative: a prominent labour leader, E.W. B. O'Dell, an organizer for the Boot and Shoe Workers' Union, petitioned the board for a reduction in his debt to the hospital (which amounted to half the $40.75 he was charged) because his daughter had been bumped into a public ward as a result of a lack of space in semi-private. HPL, RG 13, Series A, 26 Nov. 1912. Significantly, Workmen's Compensation cases were given semi-private care; HPL, RG 13, Series A, 28 Nov. 1928.

109. Ontario, Department of Health, Division of Medical Statistics, *Survey of Public General Hospitals in Ontario*, Part 4, 48. The two Hamilton hospitals showed marked differences: St. Joseph's had just over half of its patients in the self-pay public category, only an eighth in indigent care, and a third in private and semi-private care, while Hamilton General had only a third in the first category, 44 per cent in the second, and only one in seven in the third; Ontario, Department of Health, Division of Medical Statistics, *Survey of Public General Hospitals in Ontario*, Part 4, 49.

110. OICHR, 1895–1930; Ontario, Department of Health, Division of Medical Statistics, *Survey of Public General Hospitals*, Part 2, 21.

111. AMMM, RG 2-G, Babies Dispensary Guild, Scrapbook. In 1930 Medical Officer of Health Roberts was still denouncing maternity boarding houses, which got an annual licence for a mere $1. HPL, RG 12, Series A, 28 Feb., 31 March 1930.

112. Wild, *Elizabeth Bagshaw*, 24, 54–55; Campbell, *Hamilton General Hospital School of Nursing*, 46, 56, 72, 122, 137; *HS*, 23 Sept. 1913, 1 (quotation); 3 Oct. 1913, 1; 31 Dec. 1920, 13; 8 April 1924, 5; 26 Nov. 1925, 25; 16 July 1927, 15; 18 April 1950, 16; HPL, RG 13, Series A, 27 Aug. 1907; OPBHR, 1924–25, 43; OICHR, 1920, 1930, 1939 (calculations are mine). The provincial trends were similarly upward; see Ontario, Department of Health, Division of Medical Statistics, *Survey of Public General Hospitals*, Part 2, 11. In 1933 semi-private maternity care at the Mount Hamilton branch of the Hamilton General cost $14 per week and at St. Joseph's, $16.45; HPL, RG 13, Series A, 30 Oct. 1933.

113. Oppenheimer, "Childbirth in Ontario," 62–67; Mitchinson, *Giving Birth*, 260–85 (quotation at 279); Emery, *Facts of Life*; OIRGR, 1930, 250.

114. A widely publicized address to the annual meeting of the Canadian Conference on Charities and Correction in Hamilton cranked up bourgeois concerns. HHSA, Hamilton Health Association Records, Annual Reports, File: Annual Report, copy made from reports of the Canadian Association for the Prevention of Tuberculosis, 1902–1912 (typescript); AMMM, RG 1, A-A, Hamilton Medical Society, Minutes, 9 Jan., 22 May 1901; 7 June, 8 Oct., 3 Dec. 1902; 24 Feb. 1905; IODEA, Municipal Chapter, Minutes, 23 April, 6 May, 3 June, 9 Sept., 7 Oct., 4 Nov. 1904; 3 Feb., 6 March, 7 April 1905; St. Elizabeth Chapter, Minutes; HBHR, 1904–5, 11; OPBHR, 1901, 95; 1902, 167; 1903, 84; *HS*, 16 March 1904, 3; 4 Oct. 1905, 5; 4 Oct. 1905, 5; 21 Oct. 1905, 8; *LG*, February 1906, 851; Roberts, "Tuberculosis in Hamilton"; Lyle, *Hamilton Local Council of Women*, 13–15; Campbell, *Holbrook of the San*, 65–68; Gray, "Stinson."

115. Meikeljohn, "Anti-Tuberculosis Work"; Holbrook, "Tuberculosis from the Nurse's Standpoint"; Holbrook, "Fight Against Tuberculosis"; Feldberg, *Disease and Class*, 1–124; Rothman, *Living in the Shadow of Death*, 179–225; McCuaig, *Weariness, Fever, and Fret*, 3–31; Tomes, *Gospel of Germs*, 113–34. In 1910 a so-called "Preventorium" was also opened for small numbers of children referred by the school nurse, physicians, or others, who had their own

Chapter 4: Labouring for Love **575**

open-air school on the site. *HT*, 10 May 1911, 11; Holbrook, "First Regular Open Air School"; Campbell, *Holbrook of the San*, 83–94. A considerable expansion took place during the war when large numbers of tubercular soldiers were sent for treatment; Campbell, *Holbrook of the San*, 106–17.

116. *HS*, 12 Dec. 1908, 9; 23 April 1915, 1; 6 May 1922, 3; Meikeljohn, "Anti-Tuberculosis Work in Canada," *CN*, November 1907, 582; Renton, "Dispensary and Work amongst Down-Town Tuberculosis Patients"; HHAR, 1906–18; 1919, 49; 1923, 24; 1929, 16–19; 1930, 13–16; OPBHR, 1920, 223; Feldberg, *Disease and Class*, 98–100, 103–4; McCuaig, *The Weariness, the Fever, and the Fret*, 29–31, 45–47. The work of the tuberculosis nurse is explored in Robbins, "Class Struggles in the Tubercular World." A so-called "Billikin Club" of Hamilton society women (later renamed the Junior Health League and then the Samaritan Club) raised funds to provide milk and eggs for deserving families of the "tubercular downtown poor." These rarely totalled more than 10 to 12 families before the war and about 25 by the 1920s, and the club monitored them each month (in 1929 it hired a full-time social worker). In 1920 the dispensary moved into the basement of the city's new Health Centre and was absorbed into the municipal health department.

117. "The modern theory of infection finds the source of disease in the individual himself, the excretions and emanations of his body," he later explained, "and the transmission of the virus to his fellow human beings by contact, direct or indirect, the well-nigh universal route." Roberts, "Public Health Organization," 241. For Roberts's career in Hamilton, see Gagan, " Roberts."

118. In 1911 the city council was convinced to pass a new by-law requiring more rigorous inspection of sanitary standards in milk production. Under this pressure, the larger dairies began to pasteurize their milk and gradually to sell it in bottles, rather than out of open cans on milk wagons (44 dealers were still providing milk this way in 1913). By the early 1920s virtually all milk was pasteurized and sanitary standards had improved considerably, though only in 1928 did the city finally make pasteurization compulsory. *HS*, 28 March 1901, 8; Ontario, Milk Commission, *Report*, 22; OPBHR, 169; 1903, 84; 1911, 132; 1912, 452; 1922, 256; HBHR, 1905–6, 16; 1912–13, 21; Roberts, "Insanitary Areas"; Roberts, "Queries and Answers," 505; OPBHR, 1898, 90; 1911, 132; 1912, 452; 1914, 236; 1921, 323; 1922, 256–57; 1923, 376–78; *HH*, 27 Aug. 1920, 11; HPL, RG 12, Series A, 27 Dec. 1922, 31 Aug. 1923; Murray, "Extent of Pasteurization," 31.

119. For a useful analysis of public-health programs in Canada, see Cassel, "Public Health in Canada." In 1901 the parents of one child in eight unvaccinated children refused to let their children be vaccinated, and in 1912 the *Spectator*'s editor and the local Board of Health were opposed to vaccination. HPL, RG 12, Series A, 18 Feb., 4 March, 18 March, 1 April, 8 April, 27 May, 3 June 1901; 21 Nov. 1912; 17 Feb. 1914; HBEM, 1900, 14; 14 March 1901, 18–19; 11 April 1901, 44; 27 May 1901, 57; 7 March 1912, 41; *HS*, 27 May 1900, 8; 30 March 1901, 12; 22 April 1912, 6; 19 Nov. 1912, 1; OPBHR, 1901, 93–94; 1920, 166; Bator, "Health Reformers Versus the Common Canadian."

120. OPBHR, 1895, 122; 1897, 128; 1898, 121; 1902, 166; 1915, 129; Roberts, "Campaign against Diphtheria"; Roberts, "Radio Talk"; Lewis, "Prevention of Diphtheria"; Dolman, "Landmarks and Pioneers"; Gryfe, "Taming of Diphtheria"; Braithwaite, Keating, and Vicer, "Problem of Diphtheria"; OPBHR, 1910, 150.

121. OPBHR, 1902, 93; 1903, 82; 1912, 449 (quotation); 1917, 185. During the influenza epidemic, makeshift hospital facilities had to be set up in local military and maternity hospitals and in the east-end Jockey Club Hotel. HPL, RG 12, Series A, 9, 11, 18 Oct. 1918.

122. HDHR, 1906–7, 24–25; HBEM, 3 Jan. 1906, 118; 7 March 1907, 39, 79; 7 Nov. 1907, 103, 105; 5 Dec. 1907, 115–16, 119; *HS*, 8 March 1907, 3.

123. Hamilton's slowness to launch the often-cited public-health programs of a handful of other cities in Canada (Toronto's Health Department, for example, had 37 public-health nurses in the field by 1915) was closer to Montreal's experience and underlines the unevenness of these developments across the country and the dangers of overgeneralizing the impact of public-health reforms in Canada. MacDougall, *Activists and Advocates*, 60–64; Royce, *Eunice Dyke*; Jones, "Searching for the Springs of Health," 32–44; Andrews, "Emergence of Bureaucracy"; Copp, *Anatomy of Poverty*, 88–105.

124. HBHR, 1909–10, 22; 1916–17, 4; 1917–18, 5–7; OPBHR, 1917, 186–87; *HS*, 1 Feb. 1917, 4 (quotation); *HT*, 18 July 1914, 18; 27 Jan. 1915, 6; *HH*, 9 Dec. 1918; Pope, "Essence of Altruism"; see also Starr, *Social Transformation*, 191.

125. Roberts, "Twenty-Three Years," 556; Manning, "1918 Influenza Epidemic."

126. OPBHR, 1920, 219–20; Roberts, "Twenty-Three Years"; see also Starr, *Social Transformation*, 181–97.

127. Gagan, "Disease, Mortality, and Public Health," 126, 169; CCCCP, 1911, 65 (quotation). On the wider background to the clean-milk campaign, see Sutherland, *Children in English-Canadian Society*, 56.

128. AMMM, RG 1, A-A, Hamilton Medical Society, Minutes, 14 June 1905; 23 June, 6 Oct. 1909; 9 Feb. 1910; 11 June 1911; VONA, Minutes, 6 July, 7 Sept. 1909; 18 April – 15 Sept. 1910; 9 May, 19 June 1911; Victoria Order of Nurses for Canada, *Report of the Board of Governors*, 1910, 29–35; 1911, 28; *HS*, 2 Feb. 1911, 4; Mullin, "Child Welfare," 446–48; *CN*, July 1910; Hanna, "Clean Milk for Babies"; Stott, *Hamilton's Doctors*, 104–5; Comacchio, *Nations Are Built*

of Babies, 43–50; Baillargeon, *Un Québec en mal d'enfants*; Lewis, *Politics of Motherhood*; Dyhouse, "Working-Class Mothers and Infant Mortality"; Featherstone, "Infant Ideologies." Throughout the period under study, cow's milk would remain the pinnacle of nutritional perfection in public-health programs; see Ostry, "Early Development of Nutrition Policy."

129. Mullen, "History of the Organization of the Babies' Dispensary Guild"; Cody, "Scope and Function of the Medical Staff"; Mullen, "Child Welfare"; *HH*, 12 May 1911, 1; 13 March 1913, n.p.; *LN*, 21 June 1912, 1; MacMurchy, ed., *Handbook of Child Welfare Work*, 135–36; Bruegernan, "With the Babies' Dispensary."

130. By 1920 it was running 7 clinics and by the end of that decade 14, including one especially for pre-natal care (for women admitted to the Outdoor Department of the Hamilton General) and another for pre-schoolers, all supported by 6 nurses, 14 middle-class volunteers, and up to 15 doctors. AMMM, RG 2-G, Babies' Dispensary Guild, Scrapbook.

131. OPBHR, 1920, 219; 1921, 328–30; 1922, 245–46, 258–60; 1923, 382–87; HDHR, 1923–24, 62–64; 1924–25, 20–21; Roberts, "Twenty-Three Years," 552.

132. HBEM, 1908, 89. Ten years later dentists in the Health Department's dental clinic used the same figure, even though two dental clinics for the free treatment of school children had opened in 1916 (this time under the control of Roberts's Health Department). By 1930 a new survey still found three-quarters in need of dental treatment. Roberts, "Twenty-Three Years," 553; HBEM, 1931, 358.

133. OPBHR, 1911, 150; HBEM, 1909, 86–87, 141; 1910, 108, 122, 134; 1911, 85, 124–25; 1912, 71, 83, 95–98, 108; 1913, 13; *PHJ*, March 1914, 161; HDHR, 1916–17, 8–9; 1923–24, 43–45. The provincial inspector noted in 1913 that the staff was too small and the work too uncoordinated. The next year one of the nurses reported that there was no systematic method of gathering data. *HT*, 15 Feb. 1913; HBEM, September 1914, 148.

134. By November 1924 all pupils in the school system had been examined. For the rest of the decade over 200 children each year were drawn into such classes in about half the elementary schools, and were eligible for half a pint of free milk each day. As the depression of the early 1930s deepened, the number of children receiving free milk climbed steeply to 1,300 by the spring of 1933. HBEM, 1922, 189–91 (quotation); 1923, 9, 116, 248, 272; 1924, 162, 232; 1925, 233, 285; 1926, 241; 1927, 157, 246; 1928, 169, 268; 1929, 278; 1930, 198; 1931, 212, 323, 356; 1932, 141, 166, 200, 381, 384; 1933, 343; 1934, 16, 80, 112, 138; *HS*, 25 April 1929, 14.

135. In 1897 the National Council of Women had set up their own standing committee on feeble-mindedness, chaired by Hamilton's Mrs. Robert Evans, who remained a leading activist on the issue in the city. Eight years later Ontario appointed a crusading female doctor, Helen MacMurchy, to investigate the problem and submit annual reports. Lyle, *Hamilton Local Council of Women*, 20–22; Simmons, *From Asylum to Welfare*, 65–71. In 1916 a group of businessmen, professionals, and upper-class women launched a Hamilton branch of the Provincial Association for the Care of the Feeble-Minded to agitate for special treatment of the "mentally defective," but this initiative, as elsewhere, had limited impact until after the war. In 1922 several of the city's doctors and prominent businessmen formed a new Mental Hygiene Society, which sponsored a small clinic at the Hamilton General (later absorbed by the city Health Department). It also advised school authorities. MacMurchy, *Report on the Feeble-Minded*, 1919, 19; Wills, "Account of the Work for the Feeble-Minded"; Roberts, "Twenty-Three Years," 555; *HH*, 22 Feb. 1919, 10; *HS*, 14 Sept. 1922, 3; 16 April 1927 (clipping in HPL Scrapbook); Stott, *Hamilton's Doctors*, 145–46.

136. The proportion of working-class inmates declined after 1900. In the last quarter of the 19th century nearly three out of five men were skilled or unskilled wage-earners, and almost half the women were servants and domestics. Of the 235 admitted to the Hamilton Hospital for the Insane in 1915, only 40 per cent of those with occupations were working-class; ten years later, the proportion was only 37 per cent. That the institution expected patients' families to pay for their care whenever possible probably discouraged greater use of the facility. Lilley, "'These Walls Around Me'"; Ontario, Inspectors of the Hospitals for the Insane, *Annual Report*, 1915, 33, 36; 1925, ix, xiv; 1930, 15 (calculations are mine).

137. MacMurchy, *Reports on the Feeble-Minded*, 1907–20, especially 1918, 10–15; 1919, 19–20; Wills, "Account of Work for the Feeble-Minded"; HBEM, 1909, 109; 1910, 83; 1917, 132; 1918, 9; 1930, 42; 1934, 277; *HH*, 22 Feb. 1919, 1, 10; *HS*, 14 Sept. 1922, 3; Lyle, *Hamilton Local Council of Women*, 35–36, 39; 41; CCSWP, 1934, 68; Simmons, *From Asylum to Welfare*, 71–109, 119–21; McConnachie, "Science and Ideology"; MacLennan, "Beyond the Asylum"; Richardson, *Century of the Child*.

138. For examples of the slippery definitions, see MacMurchy, *Care of the Feeble-Minded in Ontario*, 1907, 3–4; Hodgins, *Report on the Care and Control of the Mentally Defective and Feeble-Minded*, 46–51 (quotation at 51).

139. *HS*, 5 Aug. 1925, 11. In 1920 a teacher at the local Normal School addressed the Hamilton Teachers' Institute on "Intelligent Tests and Measurements," pointing out that "the more one dealt with mentally deficient children the less reliance one might place upon facial expression." *HH*, 28 Feb. 1920, 5.

140. *HH*, 8 Feb. 1924 (quotation); *HS*, 16 April 1929, 7. In a similar vein, mothers who were being encouraged to visit the

city's new birth-control clinic after 1932 could hardly have missed the strident eugenicist message of its founders and administrators that the poor should not be allowed to continue breeding freely. Annau, "Eager Eugenicists." In 1934 a Hamilton physician, Morris Siegel, also produced a widely read marriage manual, *Constructive Eugenics and Rational Marriage*, which argued against the marriage of the "unfit." McLaren, *Our Own Master Race*, 76.

141. HBEM, 1934, 277; 1932–40 (for reports on Handicraft School enrolment each May; calculation of male-female ratios is mine); Sutherland, *Children in English-Canadian Society*, 71–78; McConnachie, "Science and Ideology"; McLaren, *Our Own Master Race*; Strange, *Toronto's Girl Problem*, 113–15. In Toronto, tests in the early 1920s claimed to find disproportionate numbers of poor and immigrant children among the "defective," and mental-hygiene activists were at the forefront of postwar campaigns for immigration restriction.

142. *HS*, 22 Feb. 1919, 10 (quotation).

143. Rosemary Gagan reaches this conclusion for the pre-war period; see "Disease, Mortality, and Public Health." See also Woods, "Mortality and Sanitary Conditions"; Szreter, "Importance of Social Intervention." For examples of Roberts's self-congratulatory statements, see *HS*, 29 June 1927, 35; 14 Dec. 1935, 37; Roberts, "Twenty-Three Years."

144. Ross, "Typhoid Fever Mortality"; HDHR, 1928–29, 5; Roberts, "Campaign against Diphtheria"; Power, "Hamilton Diphtheria Exhibit." See Tables 7 and 8 for the decline of contagious diseases.

145. HDHR, 1924–25, 22; *HS*, 13 April 1926 (clipping in HPL Scrapbook). Roberts regularly claimed lower rates than those published by the registrar general, undoubtedly to advertise the success of his public-health program. I have used the registrar general's statistics.

146. The problem of under-registration was still serious enough in 1916 that the Baby Welfare Association included a movie on the subject in its Baby Week festivities, and the medical director of an infant-care clinic admitted two years later that "statistics can be of no real value until we get a more complete birth registration." HBHR, 1905–6, 6; 1906–7, 16; 1923–24, 8; CCCCP, 1911, 65; Mullin, "Child Welfare in a Democracy" (quotation); Sutherland, *Children in English-Canadian Society*, 68–69.

147. In 1912 Roberts attempted to brush aside the figures on stillbirths by suggesting: "We have a large incoming population seeking housing, homes and a livelihood under stress and strain, both physical and mental, and often under circumstances altogether uncomfortable." HBHR, 1911–12, 11.

148. HBHR, 14; *HS*, 28 Feb. 1930, 7. One of Roberts's predecessors had made similar comments; see OPBHR, 1901, 84.

149. McKinnon and Ross, "Whooping Cough," 533. The evidence on these intractable health problems leads me to a more pessimistic assessment of health in the interwar period than that of Cynthia Comacchio in *Nations Are Built of Babies*, 35.

150. Lisowka, "Healing and Treatment"; Benn, "Steel City Shutdown"; Penell, "'Relics of Barbarism'"; McGinnis, "Impact of Epidemic Influenza," 454–58; Jones, "Searching for the Springs of Health," 275–76; Andrews, "Epidemic and Public Health," 25–26; Tomkins, "Failure of Expertise"; Loeb, "Beating the Flu."

151. HHAR, 1927, 5. Another local doctor complained, "The promiscuous sale of cough syrup by druggists helped to allow the disease to advance beyond the incipient stage." AMMM, RG 1, A-A, Hamilton Medical Society, Minutes, 24 Feb. 1905. See Table 9 for statistics on deaths from contagious diseases.

152. HHA, *Annual Report*, 1916, 31.

153. *NC*, 7 March 1936, 2.

154. A few patients got weekly doses of the ineffective drug tuberculin. After the war the San added X-ray and laboratory equipment to help diagnosis, as well as dental equipment (because Holbrook believed bad teeth encouraged the development of tuberculosis); it made limited use of pneumothorax surgery in the 1930s to collapse part of the lung. Campbell, *Holbook of the San*, 183–84; Holbrook, "First Regular Open Air School," 144 (quotation); HHAR, 1918, 14 (quotation); 1919, 25; 1920, 24 (where Holbrook admits the impact of "infected teeth" was actually "hard to estimate"); CCCCP, 1911, 83–84 (quotations); Burgar, "Difficulties in Re-Establishing Discharged Sanatorium Patients."

155. In so much of his work, moreover, Roberts was constrained by lack of sufficient resources from a tight-fisted city council – as late as 1927 he was still arguing with the mayor about replacing the rotting floor in the health centre's basement clinic – and, until 1934, by the fragmentation of health-care programs among autonomous agencies, both public and private. *HT*, 17 June 1912, 11; 27 Jan. 1915, 6; *HH*, 1 Feb. 1917, 5; 8 Feb. 1918, 17; 15 Sept. 1920, 1; *HS*, 15 Jan. 1927, 13; HBHR, 1916–17, 4; HPL, RG 12, Series A (Board of Health Minutes), 29 March 1926; Roberts, *Report of the Medical Officer of Health on Amalgamation of Health Service*.

156. In the first decade of the century one death in ten was caused by these two diseases, but by the 1930s they killed one in three (see Table 7). See also Clow, *Negotiating Disease*; Hayter, "Medicalizing Malignancy."

157. An apparently short-lived interest in "smoke nuisances" among public-health workers in the 1920s brought the hasty intervention of the local Chamber of Commerce to ensure that no more than "largely educational and advisory" measures were undertaken, resulting in no significant changes in factory-owners' smoke emission. OPBHR, 1920, 224–25 (quotation at 225); 1921, 320–22; 1922, 265–68; 1923, 391–93.

158. See Table 6.

159. Dublin, Kopf, and Van Buren, *Mortality Statistics of Insured Wage-Earners and Their Families*, 24; Dublin and Lotka, *Twenty-Five Years of Health Progress*, 24–27.

160. Parry, "Keeping Babies Well," 69–70; Roberts, "Twenty-Three Years," 554.

161. Holbrook, "Tuberculosis from the Nurse's Standpoint," 384; HHAR, 1912, 12; 1913, 21.

162. Holbrook, "Tuberculosis from the Nurse's Standpoint," 383 (quotation); *HS*, 19 June 1916 (quotation); OPBHR, 1923, 383–84; see also Dehli, "'Health Scouts' for the State."

163. Mullen, "History"; Mullen, "Child Welfare"; Smith, "Possibilities of Women's Work"; Parry, "Keeping Babies Well."

164. Smith, "Child Welfare" (quotation at 594); AMMM, RG 2-G, Babies' Dispensary Guild.

165. VON, *How to Take Care of Babies*, title page; OPBHR, 1920, 227. English child-welfare workers struggled in vain to discourage working-class mothers from feeding their babies solid food at too young an age; see Ross, *Love and Toil*, 143.

166. Parry, "Keeping Babies Well," 70; Comacchio, *Nations Are Built of Babies*, 53.

167. OPBHR, 1917, 187; see also Renton, "Dispensary and Work amongst Down-Town Tuberculosis Patients," 374, 376; HHAR, 1914, 30.

168. See, for example, *HS*, 21 May 1925, 2; Gleason, "Race, Class, and Health," 104–5; Tomes, *Gospel of Germs*, 183–95. Examples of this approach include VON, *How to Take Care of Babies*; Ontario, Department of Health, *The Baby*.

169. OPBHR, 1922, 243; Dyhouse, "Working-Class Mothers and Infant Mortality," 261.

170. A British doctor also found working-class families resistant to a rigid schedule of feeding that required waking a sleeping baby. Davin, "Imperialism and Motherhood," 35. A public-health nurse sent to Kenora in Northern Ontario in the 1920s faced the same issues of poverty; see Stuart, "Ideology and Experience," 118–21.

171. OPBHR, 1923, 384; *HS*, 12 April 1913, 5; Synge, "Family and Community," ch. 3.1; Comacchio, *Nations Are Built of Babies*, 53 (quotation); Gleason, "Race, Class, and Health," 103–4.

172. HHAR, 1918, 29; 1919, 50; 1920, 47 (quotation); OPBHR, 1922, 260; Comacchio, *Nations Are Made of Babies*, 52.

173. McPherson, *Bedside Matters*, 78–86; Gleason, "Race, Class, and Health," 104–5; Smith, "Keeping Babies Well"; *How to Take Care of Babies during Hot Weather* (copy in AMMM, RG 2-G, Babies' Dispensary Guild); Tomes, *Gospel of Germs*, 16–17, 103; Valverde, *Age of Light, Soap, and Water*; Hoy, *Chasing Dirt*, 87–149; HHAR, 1921, 16 (quotation). For similar moralistic goals, see Smith, "Keeping Babies Well," 74; *HS*, 21 May 1925, 2.

174. These events had already exploded across the US, where there had been 2,000 during 1912. Ewbank and Preston, "Personal Health Behaviour," 127.

175. Walters, "Duty of the City to the Child"; Mullin, "Child Welfare," 454–56; *LN*, 21 May 1915, 1; *HS*, 21–26 June 1915; 19–24 June 1916; 24 Oct. 1921, 19; AMMM, RG 2-G, Babies' Dispensary Guild, Scrapbook; Stott, *Hamilton's Doctors*, 109–12.

176. The Division of Maternal and Child Hygiene within the Ontario Bureau of Child Welfare (established in 1916) spread its booklet *The Care of the Baby* far and wide, while the new federal Division of Child Welfare churned out 15 so-called "Little Blue Books," along with a mass-market manual, *The Canadian Mother's Book*, written by the Division's director, Helen MacMurchy. The new umbrella organization for child-welfare work, Canadian Council on Child Welfare, also founded in 1920 under the leadership of Charlotte Whitton, distributed similar material, including, starting in the late 1920s, a series of "letters" sent directly to many mothers. *HS*, 27 March 1930, 2; Dodd, "Advice to Parents"; Comacchio, *Nations Are Built of Babies*, 92–103, 116–43; Arnup, *Education for Motherhood*, 32–83.

177. Comacchio, *Nations Are Built of Babies*, 184–91.

178. For "caregivers of the last resort," see, for example, Roberts, "Campaign against Diphtheria," 44; HHAR, 1927, 5. In 1930 a woman was taken to court for "failing to obtain medical assistance at the birth of her child, who subsequently died." *HS*, 13 March 1930, 7. Ross notes how often London's working people delayed calling on the doctor for help; *Love and Toil*, 171. As Comacchio argues, delaying a visit to the doctor meant the working-class patient was probably in much worse health than others, and the standards of working-class women's child-rearing practices and home nursing were therefore more likely to be perceived as inadequate. Comacchio, *Nations Are Built of Babies*, 40. Still, according to the chroniclers of north-end history, one doctor was well-known to everyone: "Hardly a family in the area would not be able to recall a broken arm or leg that was mended by the tall, reserved bespectacled doctor, or a child that came into the world under his careful supervision." Murphy and Murphy, *Tales from the North End*, 101.

179. Feldberg, *Disease and Class*; Clow, *Negotiating Disease*; Rothman, *Living in the Shadow of Death*.

180. AMMM, RG 1, A-A, Hamilton Medical Society, Minutes, 5 March, 2 April 1902; RG 2-G, A.E. Walkey, Call Lists, 1908–16; A.P. McKinnon, Call Lists, 1917; William James McNichol, Account Book, 1912–18.

181. LAC, R1176-0-0-E, 2416. See also the testimony of an International Harvester worker, speaking to the commission on behalf of a meeting of unorganized workers, who told of a labourer whose wife's operation for appendicitis cost

him $170–200, so "that man is saddled with a debt that it will take him two or three years probably to pay." LAC, R1176-0-0-E, 2342.

182. *HS*, 1 June 1920, 1; *LL*, 11 June 1920, 1 (quotations), 3.

183. Anstead, "Fraternalism," 128–29; LAC, R1176-0-0-E, 2449–52; "It is impossible to believe that a man getting one dollar a year from 200 patients can give them that amount of service," Dr H. Mullen told the Royal Commission on Industrial Relations in 1919. From time to time the Hamilton Medical Society (and its successor, the Hamilton Academy of Medicine) tried to get its members to agree to abandon what they called "lodge practice," but apparently to no avail. AMMM, RG 1, A-A, Hamilton Medical Society, Minutes, 8 Jan. 1902, 4 Sept. 1911; A-C, Petitions to Stop Lodge Practice, 1936–37; D-E, Box 1, General Practitioners Section, Minutes, 26 Jan. 1938; 11 Jan. 1939; MHSO, ITA-09826-FER; Naylor, *Private Practice, Public Payment*, 14–15, 31–32; Comacchio, *Nations Are Built of Babies*, 200–1. For company-run plans, see Ontario, Inspector of Insurance and Registrar of Friendly Societies, *Report*, 1902, C130; 1915, 132–33, 148–49; R1176-0-0-E, Vol. 3, 2377; Roberts, ed., *Organizing Westinghouse*, 9.

184. Shortt, "'Before the Age of Miracles,'" 135–36; Stott, *Hamilton's Doctors*, 54–55, 171–74, 181; Wild, *Elizabeth Bagshaw*, 25; Murphy and Murphy, *Tales from the North End*, 101; *Canadian Medical Association Journal*, September 1934, Supplement, 51; Wales, "Medical Relief"; Kappele, "Public Relief and Care of the Sick." For similar patterns of inability to pay doctors' fees, in Vancouver, see Andrews, "Medical Attendance."

185. HPL, RG 13, Series A, 19 June, 18 Sept. 1900; 19 March 1901; Campbell, *Hamilton General Hospital School of Nursing*, 64, 114; *HH*, 14 Dec. 1929; 29 July 1933; Gagan and Gagan, *For Patients of Moderate Means*, 59, 80, 111; Davis and Warner, *Dispensaries*; Rosenberg, "Social Class and Medical Care"; Kappele, "Public Relief and Care of the Sick," 154.

186. *HS*, 17 Nov. 1906, 1. In 1918 the daily fee was $1.25. HHAR, 1919, 5. In the first few years patients' fees made up a third of the San's revenue, a figure that had dropped closer to a fifth by the outbreak of the war. The bulk of the other revenue came from the city and provincial government. HHAR, 1908–15.

187. Campbell, *Hamilton General Hospital School of Nursing*, 76–77; *HS*, 31 Aug. 1907, 17; Nieman, "How Can Skilled Nurses Be Secured in the Homes of the Workingman?" McPherson reports that a private-duty nurse's fee of $25 a week was common everywhere in the early 20th century; *Bedside Matters*, 51–52. Census-takers reported a rapid increase in the number of nurses in Hamilton in the period – from 118 in 1911 to 525 in 1921 to 704 in 1931. CC, 1911, Vol. 6, 314; 1921, Vol. 4, 416; 1931, Vol. 7, 188.

188. VONA, Minutes, 1899–1914; *HS*, 18 March 1899, 5; 17 May 1900, 5; 10 May 1901, 5; 23 Oct. 1902, 3; 28 Oct. 1903, 6; Gibson, *Victorian Order of Nurses for Canada*; Dalley, *History of the Hamilton Branch of the Victorian Order of Nurses for Canada*.

189. *HS*, 27 May 1900, 8; HPL, RG 12, Series A, 7 May 1906; *HS*, 27 May 1900, 8; *HH*, 26 Jan. 1909, 1; OPBHR, 1915, 129; see also OPBHR, 1896, 141; 1901, 84; 1903, 82; 1912, 448; 1920, 221. See also Gleason, "Race, Class, and Health," 99; Jones, "Searching for the Springs of Health," 127–28.

190. AMMM, RG 1-C-I, *Bulletin of the Hamilton Medical Society*, December 1929, 3; Jan. 1931, 12–16; March 1931, 8–9; Gagan and Gagan, *For Patients of Moderate Means*, 87; Stott, *Hamilton's Doctors*, 166–77; Bothwell and English, "Pragmatic Physician." In 1921 the ILP staged a debate on the "nationalization" of the medical profession between one of its leaders, Harry Fester, and a prominent Hamilton doctor, J.H. Mullen. *HS*, 9 April 1921, 12.

191. *HS*, 9 Oct. 1911, 6. Ross found similar gratitude in working-class London; *Love and Toil*, 172–74; see also Lewis, *Politics of Motherhood*, 99–101. For voluminous evidence of the same responses, see also Ladd-Taylor, ed., *Raising a Baby the Government Way*.

192. AMMM, RG 2-G, Babies Dispensary Guild, Scrapbook, *HT* clipping (undated). I am nonetheless somewhat more sceptical than Comacchio that public-health nurses found as much growing enthusiasm among mothers as their public reports claimed. These were promotional documents, not objective accounts. Baillargeon interviewed 30 Montreal women who had given birth between the wars and found that, although some lacked anyone to help them after the birth and might appreciate the help of a visiting nurse, many expressed strong reservations about the nursing programs that had been available to them; see Baillargeon, "Care of Mothers and Infants," 170–78.

193. Bruegernan, "With the Babies' Dispensary," 256.

194. It was not only working-class mothers who were circumspect; Hamilton doctors were highly suspicious of the independence of these roaming health-care workers. In the interwar period they expressed "considerable objection" to nursing visits to mothers of newborns and intervened to limit their contact to leaving infant-care literature and recommending consultation with a physician. They also objected to school board's instructions to parents to consult school doctors rather than their own physicians. Comacchio, *Nations Are Built of Babies*, 155; AMMM, RG 1, A-A, Hamilton Academy of Medicine, Executive Committee, Minutes, 17 April 1933. For similar sentiments, see Stuart, "Ideology and Experience."

195. Dehli, "Health Scouts," 250 (quotation); Dyhouse, "Working-Class and Infant Mortality"; Robbins, "Class Struggles," 423–28; Struthers, *School Nurse*, 71

(quotation); *HS*, 4 June 1928, 10. In 1932 a women's column in *Canadian Congress Journal* presented a story of a young mother struggling to impose the prescribed regular routines on her crying infant and an older woman ("who had five children of her own and 'didn't hold' with new-fangled notions") who helped her appreciate how to be more flexible and sympathetic in handling babies. *CCJ*, February 1932, 27. Ross has nicely summarized London mothers' attitudes to baby clinics as "a constantly shifting mixture of gratitude, secretiveness, intimidation, and learning." *Love and Toil*, 215.

196. AMMM, RG 2-G, Babies' Dispensary Guild, Scrapbook; *HH*, 21 May 1925, 2; *HS*, 29 March 1928, 7; 27 March 1930, 31; HDHR, 1927–28; 1928–29, 31. In 1932 the Guild's cut-off line for helping mothers was a weekly family income of $25; *HS*, 10 Nov. 1932, 20. In their optimistic assessment of the impact of these child-rearing instructions in the US, Ewbank and Preston not only have to admit that their adoption can only be inferred since there was no systematic survey of household practices, but also ignore the issue of how many mothers actually got this instruction; "Personal Health Behaviour," 143.

197. *HS*, 28 April 1923, 11; 21 May 1925, 2; 13 April 1926 (clipping in HPL Scrapbook); 24 March 1927, 2; 5 May 1932, 27; OPBHR, 1923, 246 (quotation); 1924, 386; Baillargeon, "Care of Mothers and Infants," 174. On the other hand, British women may have brought over with them the popular superstition that baby-weighing was bad luck. Lewis, *Politics of Motherhood*, 99. For dentistry, see HPL, RG 12, A, 4 June 1918. The case discussed in this meeting involved an irate mother whose child was allegedly slapped for screaming by a dentist who was unnecessarily extracting more teeth in a school clinic than the mother had agreed to.

198. *HS*, 30 March 1933; Smith, "Keeping Babies Well" (quotation); Meikeljohn, "Anti-Tuberculosis Work," 583–84 (quotation); Renton, "Dispensary Work," 374–76; HHAR, 1916, 34; OPBHR, 1917, 187; 1921, 329; 1922, 260; *HS*, 29 March 1928, 7; 2 Nov. 1929, 14. In 1931 the Guild's Head Nurse, Helen Mulme, proclaimed that "we rarely meet with the prejudice so rife a decade ago." *HS*, 24 March 1931 (clipping in HPL Scrapbook). On the other hand, Nancy Tomes has argued that immigrant women sometimes "venerated the childcare advice given by visiting nurses and local physicians" as part of a superior US health knowledge; see *Gospel of Germs*, 192–93.

199. Comacchio, *Nations Are Built of Babies*, 181–212; Robbins, "Class Struggles," 426–28; Tomes, *Gospel of Germs*, 185, 188–95, 204; Ross, *Love and Toil*, 195–21; Lewis, "Working-Class Wife and Mother," 109–15. The absence of case files for any of the agencies for which public-health nurses worked in this period makes it difficult to draw firm conclusions in this regard.

200. Ross describes the loving commitment of London's working-class mothers to the bedside of their sick children in *Love and Toil*, 166–94.

201. Comacchio, *Nations Are Built of Babies*; Davin, "Imperialism and Motherhood"; Sears, "Before the Welfare State."

202. Lewis, "Working-Class Wife and Mother and State Intervention," 108.

203. Koven and Michel, "Womanly Duties"; Reeves, *Round About a Pound a Week*; Ross, "Good and Bad Mothers," 188–91.

204. Ross, "Good and Bad Mothers," 191–92.

205. Rowan, "Child Welfare and the Working-Class Family," 229–30, 237. In September 1921, in the twilight days of Independent Labor Party influence in civic politics, a delegation from the party (George Halcrow and Herb West) argued before the Board of Health that "proper food and shelter was necessary to the workingman to maintain his health standard" and that a minimum wage for men should be established by law "for the proper protection of their health." The party made no other presentation to the board on health issues. HPL, RG 12, A, 27 Sept. 1921.

206. *LN*, 20 April 1917, 1; 14 June 1918, 1; 16 Aug. 1918, 1; 27 Dec. 1918, 1; 11 April 1919, 1; 28 Nov. 1919, 1; 6 Feb. 1920, 1; 13 Feb. 1920, 1; 19 June 1920, 1; 16 July 1920, 1; 13 Aug. 1920, 1; 27 May, 1; 21 Oct. 1920, 1; 16 Dec. 1920, 1; 21 Jan. 1921, 1; 24 Feb. 1922, 1 (quotation); *IB*, 4 May 1917, 1: 6 July 1917, 1; 5 Oct. 1917, 2: *ND*, 27 Nov. 1919, 1; 1 July 1920, 1; 29 July 1920, 1; 27 May 1921, 4; Sangster, *Dreams of Equality*; Naylor, *New Democracy*, 145–54.

5. Bringing Home the Bacon

1. *MMJ*, February 1906. On Kernighan, see *DHB*, Vol. 3, 101–2.

2. Single men had much more trouble getting relief work than married men did; *HT*, 13 Jan. 1914, 10; 20 Jan. 1914, 12; *HH*, 3 March 1922, 1; ODLR, 1922, 31, 34; HCCM, 1921, 19–21; "Report on Unemployment," HCCM, 1930, 89; Archibald, "Distress, Dissent, and Alienation," 17; MacDowell, "Relief Camp Workers."

3. Humphries, "Working Class Family."

4. HYWCAA, Scrapbooks, 1890–1909, undated clipping (c.1914).

5. Kessler-Harris, *Woman's Wage*; Kessler-Harris, *In Pursuit of Equity*; Humphries, "Class Struggle"; May, "Bread before Roses"; May, "Historical Problem of the Family Wage"; Seccombe, "Patriarchy Stabilized"; Seccombe *Weathering the Storm*, 111–24; Glickman, *Living Wage*; Comacchio, "Postscript for Father."

6. Kessler-Harris, *Woman's Wage*; Kessler-Harris, *In Pursuit of Equity*; Lewis, "Dealing with Dependency."

7. The phrase is from Kessler-Harris, *In Pursuit of Equity*, 5–6, a book that has heavily informed this discussion.

8. On the presence of "tramps" in Hamilton before the war, see *HH*, 23 March 1910, 1; 23 April 1910, 1; 6 Feb. 1911, 12; 8 Jan. 1914, 1; 21 Oct. 1914, 1; *HT*, 29 Aug. 1912, 12. See also Phillips, "Poverty, Unemployment, and the Administration of Criminal Law"; Pitsula, "Treatment of Tramps"; Bright, "Loafers Are Not Going to Subsist." The percentage of men over age 34 who were still single was 11 in 1921, 9 in 1931, and 10 in 1941. CC, 1921, Vol, 2, 184–85; 1931, Vol. 3, 136–37; 1941, Vol. 3, 122. A special 1931 census study on housing found only 476 people living alone in Hamilton. Greenway, *Housing*, 558.

9. *HT*, 7 Oct. 1910, 13; *HS*, 12 March 1923, 6 (quotation); Roberts, ed., *Baptism of Union*, 11; WAHC, interviews with Floyd Read, Charles Old, Lil Seager; MHSO, ITA-09826-FER; Storey, "Workers, Unions, and Steel," 208–12, 215–16; Freeman, 1005, 29–31; Reynolds, *British Immigrant*, 167–68; Baskerville and Sager, *Unwilling Idlers*, 79–80. Protestant clergymen sometimes lured Catholic European newcomers with their ability to find them jobs. MHSO, ITA-09829-GRI; ITA-0811-PIS; ITA-0810-SAR; ITA-0884-VIO.

10. By the outbreak of World War One, these private agencies were required to obtain a municipal licence and had to charge set fees of no more than 25 to 75 cents (75 per cent refundable after one week). A hint of exploitative practices always hung over their work, and after the war few survived tighter licensing regulations. *LG*, September 1904, 264; February 1912, 746; May 1914, 1359; March 1915, 1068; May 1916, 1247; *HH*, 31 Jan. 1912, 9; 16 March 1912, 3; 30 April 1912, 1; 8 May 1913, 1; 15 May 1913, 1; 26 Jan. 1914, 1; 9 April 1914, 1; 13 April 1914, 1; *HS*, 20 Nov. 1907, 4; OBLR, 1908, 245; MPSS, 17; *HT*, 21 Sept. 1917, 16; AO, RG 7, II-1, Vol. 2, File: "Private Agencies – No Date"; File: "MacDiarmid, F.G., Minister of Public Works, 1914–19"; Sauter, "Origins of the Employment Service of Canada," 99, 110. In 1917 the Soldiers' Aid Commission started to play an active role in helping returning soldiers find jobs. HPL, Soldiers' Aid Commission, Minutes, 9 Nov. 1917; 30 June 1918; 3 Sept. 1918; 22 Jan. 1919.

11. *LG*, February 1907, 861; March 1907, 1008; OBLR, 1908–15; Sauter, "Origins of the Employment Service of Canada," 100–1.

12. Sauter, "Origins of the Employment Service of Canada," 102–12; Struthers, *No Fault of Their Own*, 12–43. For a clear statement of how Hamilton's labour markets worked at the end of World War One, see AO, RG 7, 2–1, Box 3, File: "Reports – Employment Offices (B-N)." In his study of British immigrants to Montreal in the interwar period, Lloyd Reynolds discovered some dismay among these newcomers that public employment offices played such an insignificant role in Canada and that finding a job was such an informal process. Reynolds, *British Immigrant*, 165.

13. *HS*, 12 March 1923, 6; Social Service Council, Industrial Life Committee, *Men Out of Work*, 26–30.

14. Storey, "Workers, Unions, and Steel"; "Bert Button Looks Back," 15 (quotation); Roberts, ed., *Organizing Westinghouse*, 5 (quotation); Archibald, "Small Expectations and Great Adjustments," 379. Two US scholars have argued that, except for a small core of more skilled workers, most industrial jobs were unstable until after World War One; see Jacoby and Sharma, "Employment Duration."

15. The concept of unemployment itself was new in public discourse at the end of the 19th century. Public awareness was generally still rooted in a view of joblessness as a mark of personal immorality or inadequacy. Ontario's wide-ranging Commission on Unemployment, created in 1915, was really the first public body to recognize how the phenomenon grew out of industrial conditions beyond an individual's control, but the transition in thinking was not even complete by the 1930s. The Canadian state was slow to show much interest. It rarely gathered meaningful statistics on unemployment before 1920, and gathered only partial information thereafter. Nonetheless, glimpses of the prevailing conditions appear in the sporadic, limited reports in publications of the provincial and federal labour departments and the national census bureau.

The 1901 census-takers asked workers about how much unemployment they experienced, but the data was never assembled into published statistics. Only in 1915 did the Ontario Commission on Unemployment attempt the first careful assessment of unemployment that linked employers' reports with the 1911 census data. In 1916 the federal Department of Labour began asking unions to report levels of unemployment among its members, a tiny segment of the labour market, and soon thereafter started requesting employment data from employers. Both of these would be published monthly in the *Labour Gazette* in the interwar period. The director of the Employment Service of Canada could nonetheless tell a parliamentary committee in 1928 that he "would not even hazard a guess" as to the actual number of unemployed in the country. Burnett, *Idle Hands*; Baskerville and Sager, *Unwilling Idlers*, 3–9; Sauter, "Measuring Unemployment" (quotation at 483); Worton, *Dominion Bureau of Statistics*, 30, 90.

16. See Table 23. In their sample of 10 per cent of Hamilton's households in 1901 (a prosperous year), Baskerville and Sager found one-third had lost at least a month of work, and one in seven had experienced at least four months of unemployment. This was a much higher level of unemployment than they discovered in the other five major cities they studied. *Unwilling Idlers*, 86.

17. CC, 1931, Vol. 6, 342; 1941, Vol. 6, 950; Day, "Gastro-Intestinal Diseases," 555 (quotation); Baskerville and Sager, *Unwilling Idlers*, 67–68; Social Service Council of Canada,

Industrial Life Committee, *Man Out of Work*, 15–18; Morton, *When Your Number's Up*. On fatal diseases, see Table 7. On workplace injuries, see Tables 25, 26.

18. Rouse and Burghardt, "Climate, Weather and Society." Building-trades unions reported annual unemployment of anywhere from 5 to 15 weeks in the decade and a half before the war. OBLR, 1900–14; see also *LG*, August 1911, 121. The federal labour department's figures on employment levels that began to appear in the 1920s showed the old pattern of troughs in January and peaks sometime in the summer, until the depression created new, unpredictable points of decline and recovery each year; see *LG*, January 1929, 53–54; January 1933, 64; January 1935, 54; January 1937, 73; January 1939, 66.

19. OBLR, 1900–14; *LG*, August 1913, 133; *CM*, 3 July 1913, 23; *HH*, 19 July 1913, 4; *HS*, 30 March 1907, 14.

20. Baskerville and Sager, *Unwilling Idlers*, 82–85; *HS*, 30 March 1907, 14; 3 April 1907, 3.

21. *HS*, 15 April 1939. In his study of Montreal's interwar employment conditions, Reynolds found the unskilled labour market simply "chaotic ... particularly in seasonal manufacturing and in casual labour." Reynolds, *British Immigrant*, 180.

22. The Ontario Commission on Unemployment surveyed several hundred manufacturers in the province and estimated that in 1914 the unemployment rate among factory workers reached about 14 per cent generally, but 27 per cent among workers making iron and steel products and 19 per cent among those turning out other metal goods. CC, 1931, Vol. 5, 26; OCCUR, 89–100; Jackson, "Cycles of Unemployment"; see Table 24.

23. *LG*, May 1904, 1104–5; June 1904, 1208; July 1904, 33–34; June 1905, 1326.

24. *HS*, 23 March 1908 1; 24 March 1908, 1; 2 June 1908, 1; 26 Nov. 1908, 1; *LG*, November 1907, 516; February 1908, 907, 964; March 1908, 1059; June 1908, 1416; July 1908, 33; August 1908, 133; September 1908, 246; December 1908, 575; January 1909, 740; February 1909, 832; April 1909, 1059; October 1909, 436; November 1909, 553; December 1909, 655.

25. LAC, R224-0-4-E, Vol. 1 (Unemployment 1914), Hamilton; *HH*, 3 March 1913, 1; 19 July 1913, 4; 1 Nov. 1913, 1; 6 Jan. 1914, 4; 12 Jan. 1914, 1; 13 Jan. 1914, 12; 15 Jan. 1914, 4; 19 Jan. 1914, 4; 21 Jan. 1914, 4; 22 Jan. 1914, 1; 27 Jan. 1914, 4; 3 March 1914, 1; 9 March 1914, 1; 16 March 1914, 1; 26 March 1914, 4; 14 April 1914, 1; 15 April 1914, 4; 16 April 1914, 4; *HS*, 16 April 1914, 11; 17 April 1914, 1; 18 April 1914, 15; 20 April 1914, 1; *HT*, 6 Jan. 1914, 1; 8 Jan. 1914, 1; 9 Jan. 1914, 1; 10 Jan. 1914, 1; 13 Jan. 1914, 4, 10; 14 Jan. 1914, 1; 16 Jan. 1914, 1; 14 April 1914, 1; 16 April 1914, 1; *LG*, August 1913, 133; September 1913, 2649; December 1913, 667; February 1914, 1141–42; May 1914, 1268; *LN*, 16 Jan. 1914, 1; 17 Oct. 1914, 1; 24 April 1914, 1 (quotation).

26. *HH*, 17 Sept. 1914, 13; 29 Sept. 1914, 8; 5 Oct. 1914, 1; 8 Oct. 1914, 2, 9; 13 Oct. 1914, 2; 14 Oct. 1914, 2; 3 May 1915, 11; 8 June 1915, 1; 7 July 1915, 1, 2; *HT*, 27 May 1915, 12; *LN*, 9 Oct. 1914, 1; 23 Oct. 1914, 1; 27 Nov. 1914, 3; *LG*, June 1914, 1391; July 1914, 9, 28–29; August 1914, 169; September 1914, 351; October 1914, 442; November 1914, 551–52; December 1914, 658; February 1915, 901–2; March 1915, 1038, 1040; April 1915, 1159–60; May 1915, 1274; June 1915, 1388–89; July 1915, 33; November 1915, 555; OCUR, 89–100; MHSO, ITA-0982-PAS.

27. *LN*, 10 Jan. 1919, 1; *HS*, 8 Jan. 1919, 5; 11 Jan. 1919, 13; 15 Jan. 1919, 15; 31 Jan. 1919, 1; 4 Feb. 1919, 9; 6 Feb. 1919, 15; 7 Feb. 1919, 1; 12 Feb. 1919, 5; 5 March 1919, 17.

28. *HH*, 27 Feb. 1922, 5; 3 March 1922, 1; 4 March 1922, 4; *ND*, 3 Feb. 1922, 1; 7 April 1922, 1; *IC*, January 1922, 121–25; *LG*, 1920–26, especially March 1921, 301–12; January 1926, 62; ODLR, 1921–25; AO, RG 7, XIV-3, Vol. 1 (Associated Agencies, 1920–53), Employment Service Council of Ontario, 1920–23. Cassidy concluded: "During the decade of the nineteen-twenties Canada's percentage of unemployment may have been just as heavy as Britain's, the country that is most commonly considered to rank first among those cursed with unemployment and doles." Cassidy, *Unemployment and Relief*, 19.

29. CC, 1931, *Unemployment among Wage-Earners, Bulletin No. 6; LG*, 1929–40. The worst hit by the depression were the youngest and oldest workers, and within manufacturing those in steel and iron production and metalworking. See also Archibald, "Do Status Differences Among Workers Make a Difference During Economic Crises?"

30. See Table 23; Baskerville and Sager, *Unwilling Idlers*, 114–16; CC, 1931, *Unemployment among Wage-Earners, Bulletin No. 6*, x–xi; Snell, *Citizen's Wage*, 26–35; Graebner, *History of Retirement*; Orloff, *Politics of Pensions*, 101–2.

31. Baskerville and Sager, *Unwilling Idlers*, 92–95. In 1921 male manufacturing workers in Hamilton experienced nearly 7 weeks without work and labourers more than 13, while male clerks lost only 3 weeks. Some 10 years later the contrast was even starker – manufacturing workers and labourers lost 14 weeks and 23 weeks respectively, but clerks only 5 weeks. CC, 1931, Vol. 5, 35, 39.

32. *LN*, 18 Feb. 1916, 2; *HH*, 10 Feb. 1916, 7; Pierson, "Gender and Unemployment Insurance Debates"; Hobbs, "Gender in Crisis"; Campbell, "Respectable Citizens," 95–141.

33. LAC, R244-76-4-E, Vol. 297, File: 3251; Vol. 343, File: 29 (87); Cassidy, *Unemployment and Relief*, 49.

34. Union sick benefits in 1913 ranged from $2.50 a week for machinists to $3.00 for carpenters, tobacco workers, and railway trainmen, $4.00 for pattern-makers and bartenders, $5.00 for cigar-makers, barbers, and boot- and shoemakers, and $5.40 for moulders. MPSS, 16. Company benefit plans became proportionally more important; in 1920 three-quarters of International Harvester's workers

had joined its Employees' Benefit Association, which gave sick men half their weekly wages for up to a year. *HHB*, March 1920, 15; *CM*, 30 Dec. 1920, 599. On other benefit plans, see Emery and Emery, *Young Man's Benefit*; Palmer, "Mutuality," 112; Anstead, "Fraternalism"; Houston and Smyth, *Sash Canada Wore*, 127–34; Stubbs, "Visions of the Common Good," 72–84; Pennefather, *Orange and the Black*, 53; Patrias, *Patriots and Proletarians*, 100–2. The various fraternal societies did not all provide the same range of benefits. For example, the Odd Fellows paid out only sick and funeral benefits, while the Maccabees, Foresters, and Ancient Order of United Workmen provided life insurance and the Masons and Elks only discretionary handouts as needed. Emery and Emery, *Young Man's Benefit*, 11. These authors found that coverage under such plans could be further limited because in the early 20th century the members of the Odd Fellows typically joined in their twenties and left within five years.

35. *LG*, September 1908, 246; *HH*, 19 Sept. 1912, 1; 17 July 1913, 1; 30 Aug. 1913, 3; *HS*, 17 Nov. 1920, 1, 26; LAC, R224-0-4-E, Vol. 1 (Unemployment), Hamilton, 1914–16, Report of William Cooper, 1 July 1914, 16 Aug. 1915; AO, RG 7, 2-1, Box 3, File: "Reports – Employment Offices (B-N)," 6.

36. *HS*, 6 Feb. 1901, 8; 10 March 1909, 7; *LG*, April 1902, 578; *HH*, 28 Jan. 1911, 9; Murphy and Murphy, *Tales from the North End*, 27–29, 67–72; Thompson, "Bringing in the Sheaves"; MacKinnon, "Relief Not Insurance," 63; Harney, "Men Without Women."

37. In 1914 the city's mayor and relief officer estimated that 85–90 per cent of those on relief were recent immigrants. LAC, RG 27, Vol. 1 (Unemployment, 1914), Hamilton, Report of E.N. Compton, 18 Feb. 1914.

38. Most years in the 1930s the police department logbooks had an average of 200 "missing" men. Archibald, "Distress, Dissent, and Alienation," 14. One old-timer said that when Stelco laid off his father in the 1930s, the man "went down to Nova Scotia to look for work in a mill there," but then "just disappeared." Broadfoot, *Ten Lost Years*, 270.

39. *HT*, 15 April 1914, 1 (quotation); 16 April 1914, 1; Morton, *When Your Number's Up*, 50–52; Copp, *Anatomy of Poverty*, 38; for comparison, see Scates, "'Knocking Out a Living,'" 38–39.

40. Historians who have presented confident conclusions about working-class incomes anywhere in Canada in this period have papered over serious deficiencies in the available data: a bias towards skilled workers and an underreporting of the less-skilled; a tendency to average all wages in an industry regardless of skill; and some glaring contradictions in the statistical evidence. It would certainly be a mistake to build elaborate arguments on such a shaky foundation. With care, however, we can extract some impressions of the wages that workingmen in Hamilton could command after the turn of the century.

Both the provincial and federal labour departments started publishing wage statistics soon after the turn of the century. The most thorough work was carried out by a special federal board of inquiry on the cost of living in Canada in 1914 (see CBICLR). But generally this information appeared erratically before World War One and tended to focus on well-paid craftworkers, especially the unionized. Unskilled labourers and the mushrooming numbers of semi-skilled factory workers, often working on piece rates, found little space on these statistical charts. Even after the war the department's statistics on the wages of "common factory labour" were based on no more than a handful of unnamed establishments in each city, without any indication of the number of workers employed. The Canadian data was far less extensive than that of the US Bureau of Labor Statistics in the same period. See Douglas, *Real Wages*, 73–94.

Up to 1911 federal census-takers had aggregated all the wages paid in each industry in the city, which could be divided by the total workforce in that sector to obtain a single income figure for anyone working in it, regardless of occupation or skill. The new Dominion Bureau of Statistics (DBS) did this annually after 1918. This was data provided by employers. After the war, at ten-year intervals, the same department also began publishing in its census reports information on annual average earnings of all workers in particular industries in the city gleaned from what workers revealed to census-takers on their doorsteps (see Table 20). Statistics on average incomes allowed for some occupational comparisons, but obviously could not reveal individual variations. The 1921 and 1931 data were also somewhat misleading since those censuses were taken in the depths of severe depressions.

Moulders who told the provincial Bureau of Labour in 1906 that they could earn $15.90 a week in 1906, for example, were reported in federal statistics as making over $20 a week. Hamilton machinists' hourly rate in 1911 appeared in one federal labour department publication at 27.5 cents an hour and in another as 32.5 cents. This was more than bad reporting; it reflected the different perspectives of the informants (whether unionists or managers) and the difficulty of finding a common rate that spanned many different industrial situations and employment policies. OBLR, 1906, 53; CBICLR, Vol. 1, 593; Canada, Department of Labour, *Wages and Hours of Labour in Canada*, 1901-1920, 13–14 (calculation of weekly wages is mine).

41. This pattern is similar to that found in other studies across North America; Copp, *Anatomy of Poverty*, 30–35; Piva, *Condition of the Working Class*, 27–59; Douglas, *Real Wages*; *IB*, 27 Nov. 1914, 1. For a vigorous defence of cutting wages during depressions, see *IC*, February 1908, 544.

42. Although bricklayers and locomotive engineers could command rates of over $20 a week by the outbreak of

the war, most highly skilled building-trades workers and metalworking craftsmen, especially moulders and machinists, could expect between $15 and $18. A smaller skilled stratum in some consumer goods industries (broom-makers, tailors, garment-cutters, and stove-mounters, for example) earned between $12 and $15 a week. By the time census-takers were knocking on doors in Hamilton to ask about earnings in the year ending June 1921, most of these skilled rates were about $10 higher in most cases and hovered around that level for much of the interwar period, with slight declines in the 1930s. At the other end of the occupational scale, unskilled men in factories probably could expect to earn no more than $9 to $10 for a 60-hour week in pre-war Hamilton. According to federal statistics, the "average manufacturing wage" in the city also stayed below $11 until the war. Common labourers in factories were earning close to $20 a week by 1920–21 and $18 a decade later. The average manufacturing wage also climbed to nearly $20 in 1920, nearly $23 in 1925, and just under $25 by 1930. CBICLR, Vol. 1; Canada, Department of Labour, *Wages and Hours of Labour in Canada*, 1901–1920; 1920–1929; CC, 1921, Vol. 3, 136, 142, 152; 1931, Vol. 5, 4–5, 60, 72; 1941, 14–15, 236–46; Canada, *Postal Census of Manufactures*, 1916; *CYB* (various years).

43. Published payroll data is not available for this period. A search for payrolls turned up nothing at all the major companies in Hamilton until a belated discovery of uncatalogued wage books from Stelco's Ontario Works at LAC as this book's manuscript was virtually complete.

44. In May and June 1907 the *Spectator*'s door-to-door visitors, collectively known as the "Spec. Man," found many men working overtime. *HS*, 21 March 1907, 5; 23 March, 1; 2 April 1907, 7; 11 April 1907, 1; 13 April 1907, 12; 20 April 1907, 7; 22 April 1907, 7; 23 April 1907, 7; 7 May 1907, 11; 8 May 1907, 3.

45. In 1921 federal census staff members compared their data with the information on wage rates produced by the Department of Labour, which appeared "much higher" as a result of a failure to take account of unemployment, and noted "the limited usefulness of hourly rates as an indication in the trend of earnings." CC, 1921, Vol. 3, xxi–xxii.

46. The census staff averaged earnings only over the weeks that were actually worked. Only two publications brought together wage rates and levels of unemployment – the Ontario Bureau of Labour's pre-war lists of union wages and the Dominion Bureau of Statistics census tables. Factoring in unemployment indicates that carpenters' actual wages dropped from $17.60 to $14.79, lathers from $17.50 to $11.80, and tailors from $15 to $13.64. In 1921 the impact of a six-month slump in the business cycle is evident in the drop for moulders from a rate of $26 to earnings of $22, for tobacco workers from $19.38 to $14.47, for weavers from $17.36 to $11.71, and for labourers from $19.77

to $16.12. A decade later, when unemployment had been severe for well more than a year before the census, the difference between rates and earnings was far more striking. Carpenters who could command over $26 a week while working actually had to live on $16.40 (a pattern common to most construction workers); machinists saw a drop from $24.61 to $17.63; moulders went from $22 to $11.50; labourers from $18 to $10. Synge, "Transition from School to Work," 255–56; and Table 20. The calculations of the impact of unemployment are mine.

47. In 1931 a Hamilton family earned on average $1,449 a year (tenants only $1,217) and half fell below $1,289 per year – the second-lowest figures among Canada's 14 largest cities (the lowest were in nearby Brantford). Greenway, *Housing*, 467, 471.

48. *HH*, 6 Oct. 1916, 1; Seccombe, *Weathering the Storm*, 146–55; Benson, "Living on the Margin," 217–20.

49. Murphy and Murphy, *Tales from the North End*, 175–79; WAHC, interviews with Floyd Read (quotation), Ken Withers; Morton, *At Odds*, 49–65; McKibbin, "Working-Class Gambling." A delegation of taxi drivers told the Parks Board in 1924 that craps were played in Gore Park from 5 p.m. until 4 a.m. *HS*, 8 April 1924, 16. One boy earned a quarter on Sunday mornings for watching out for the police while a huge craps game took place in a north-end park. WAHC, interview with Floyd Read.

50. Heron, *Booze*, 86, 122, 265, 284–85; Synge, "Changing Conditions for Women," 82; Davies, *Leisure, Gender, and Poverty*, 30–54; Benson, *Household Accounts*, 22–25; Forestall, "Gendered Terrains," ch. 3. The number of personal liquor permits issued to Ontario residents by the Liquor Control Board dropped from 416,185 in 1929 to 192,894 in 1933. LCBOR, 1929, 1933.

51. See, for example, the comments of the president of St. George's Benevolent Society in 1910; HPL, St. George's Benevolent Society of Hamilton, Minutes, 17 Jan. 1910, 33. In 1910 the city's relief officer announced that he would be more aggressively pursuing men who "go away for the winter and leave their wives in destitute circumstances. It is becoming a habit," he claimed. *HS*, 26 Oct. 1910 14. In 1888 the provincial government had codified its responsibilities in the Maintenance of Deserted Wives Act, and in 1921–22 added three new laws to make sure male heads of household supported dependent children and senior parents – the Parents' Maintenance Act, Children of Unmarried Parents Act, and a revised Deserted Wives and Children's Maintenance Act (although the legislation was not often used). Dymond, *Laws of Ontario Relating to Women and Children*, 36–41, 57–70; Seccombe, "Patriarchy Stabilized"; Griswold *Fatherhood*, 43–51; Ursel, *Private Lives, Public Policy*, 143–45, 341; Snell, "Filial Responsibility Laws"; Chambers, *Misconceptions*. On the US, see Willrich, "Home Slackers."

52. *HS*, 12 Jan. 1900, 8; 29 March 1900, 8; 11 April 1900, 8; 11 June 1900, 8; 22 June 1900, 8; 6 July 1900, 8; 23 July 1900, 8; 18 Aug. 1900, 8 (quotation); 15 Sept. 1900, 8; 20 Dec. 1900, 8; 23 Jan. 1901, 8; 13 Feb. 1901, 8; 4 Jan. 1910, 12; 23 Feb. 1910, 12; 26 April 1910, 1, 6; 21 May 1910, 12; 13 June 1910, 12; 30 June 1910, 14; 16 Aug. 1910, 10; 17 Aug. 1910, 12; 7 Oct. 1910, 13; 20 Oct. 1910, 12; 25 Oct. 1910, 14; 26 Oct. 1910, 14; 4 Nov. 1910, 20; 10 Nov. 1910, 14; 13 Nov. 1910, 12; 14 Nov. 1910, 14; 8 Dec. 1910, 14; 16 March 1920, 17 (quotation); 30 March 1920, 21; 31 March 1920, 27; 8 April 1920, 21; 10 April 1920, 26; 12 April 1920, 27; 15 April 1920, 19; 7 May 1920, 23; 10 May 1920, 22; 27 May 1920, 19; 28 May 1920, 22; 29 May 1920, 16; 17 June 1920, 5; 12 July 1920, 27; 23 July 1920, 27; 28 July 1920, 19; 6 Aug. 1920, 26 (quotation); 23 Sept. 1920, 19; 30 Sept. 1920, 19; 7 Oct. 1920, 23; 19 Oct. 1920, 19; 20 Oct. 1920, 19; 21 Oct. 1920, 19; 27 Nov. 1920, 22; 1 Dec. 1920, 22; 9 Dec. 1920, 19; 7 Jan. 1930, 7; 19 Feb. 1930, 7; 11 April 1930, 7; 22 May 1930, 7; 6 June 1930, 7; 9 June 1930, 7; 12 June 1930, 7; 19 June 1930, 7; 26 June 1930, 7; 7 July 1930, 7; 17 July 1930, 7; 28 July 1930, 7; 8 Aug. 1930, 7; 13 Aug. 1930, 7; 15 Aug. 1930, 7; 18 Aug. 1930, 7; 10 Sept. 1930, 7; 19 Sept. 1920, 7; 22 Sept. 1930, 7; 25 Sept. 1930, 7; 8 Oct. 1930, 7; 10 Oct. 1930, 7; 15 Oct. 1930, 7; 31 Oct. 1930, 7; 5 Nov. 1930, 7; 7 Nov. 1930, 7; 14 Nov. 1930, 7; 18 Nov. 1930, 7; 19 Nov. 1930, 27; 20 Nov. 1930, 7; 25 Nov. 1930, 7.

53. Glickman, *Living Wage*.

54. Bouchier and Cruikshank, "'Sportsmen and Pothunters'"; *HS*, 25 April 1901, 8; *HH*, 13 Feb. 1909; 11 Sept. 1914, 1. The *Herald* reported in 1914: "Duck hunters say that the ducks will be scarce on the bay this year owing to the growth of the city's industrial section all along the south shore, which used to be an ideal spot for the duck hunter." *HH*, 11 Sept. 1914, 1. Six years later some 100 workingmen submitted a petition to the city's Board of Control protesting a proposal to turn the Dundas marsh into a game preserve, complaining that they could not head north for two weeks like upper-class hunters but wanted to "shoot around home." *HS*, 28 Sept. 1920, 15.

55. Murphy and Murphy, *Tales from the North End*, 100, 109; Roberts, ed., *Organizing Westinghouse*, 2; *LN*, 11 May 1917, 1; *HH*, 4 May 1917, 2; 8 May 1917, 1; 6 June 1918, 3; HPL, HCC, Board of Directors, Minutes, 7 Jan. 1935 (quotation). Labour leader Rollo was secretary of the Hamilton Poultry Association, a club of chicken-raisers. *HS*, 10 June 1920, 12. In 1915 a Garden Club was organized as a relief measure to allow the unemployed to cultivate some vacant land within the city. LAC, RG 27, Vol. 1 (Unemployment), Hamilton, 1914–16, Report of William Cooper, 15 Feb. 1915; *LG*, April 1915, 1160. In 1920 International Harvester created a Garden Club among its workers, opened up 200 garden plots on its property, published instructional literature on good gardening, and held gardening contests, though

only 52 of the more than 2,000 employees registered their home gardens. *HHB*, March 1920, 12–13; April 1920, 29–32; June 1920, 6.

56. Doucet and Weaver, *Housing the North American City*, 344–45. Harris and Sendbuehler found that over a third of the speculators in the working-class suburb of Union Park were blue-collar workers; see "Making of Working-Class Suburb," 491.

57. Monod, "Ontario Retailers"; Monod, *Store Wars*; Benson, "Retailing in Hamilton"; Benson, *Entrepreneurism*, 54, 83; Baillargeon, "'If You Had No Money, You Had No Trouble, Did You?'" 253–54; Taschereau, "'Behind the Store.'" In 1919 the *Spectator* noted that some men who enjoyed the eight-hour day were "going into various sidelines of commercial and mechanical activity." *HS*, 26 April 1919, 10. Hunter recalled that, during a bout of unemployment in the 1920s, his father and a brother-in-law started a small bakery at home and delivered baked goods door-to-door. Hunter, *Which Side Are You On, Boys*, 49.

58. In contrast to the experience in other large Central Canadian cities, a 1931 survey of 458 of the 550 male heads of Jewish households found 280 "small tradesmen" and only 87 "skilled mechanics." MHSO, ITA-0883-AN; ITA-0815-ANO; ITA-0830-SAL; ITA-0809-GRO; ITA-0982-PAS; HPL, Wilensky, "Report Re the Jewish Community," 14; Kaprielian-Churchill, *Like Our Mountains*, 75–79, 260–64; Patrias, *Patriots and Proletarians*, 86–87; Shahrodi, "Early Polish Settlement"; Tulchinsky, *Taking Root*, 161–63; Frager, *Sweatshop Strife*, 17–18; Steedman, *Angels of the Workplace*; Bodnar, *Transplanted*, 131–38.

59. See, for example, *HS*, 12 Jan. 1920, 19; 21 Jan. 1920, 4; 2 Feb. 1910, 12; 5 Feb. 1920, 27; 10 Feb. 1920, 16; 25 March 1920, 23; 31 March 1920, 27; 29 April 1920, 21; 21 June 1920, 19; 28 July 1920, 19; 6 Aug. 1920, 26; 12 Aug. 1920, 8; 2 Sept. 1920, 15; 20 Sept. 1920, 15; 25 Sept. 1920, 27; 21 Oct. 1920, 19; 26 Oct. 1920, 17; 7 Nov. 1920, 20; 24 Nov. 1920, 26; 29 Nov. 1920, 8; 9 Dec. 1920, 19; 10 Dec. 1920, 21; 28 Dec. 1920, 1; 3 Jan. 1925, 5; 29 Jan. 1925, 5; 4 Feb. 1925, 5; 18 Jan. 1925, 5; 7 March 1925, 5; 17 March 1925, 5; 19 March 1925, 5; 26 March 1925, 5; 21 April 1925, 5; 23 April 1925, 5; 27 April 1925, 5; 11 May 1925, 5; 13 May 1925, 5; 28 May 1925, 5; 11 June 1925, 5; 30 July 1925, 5; 13 Aug. 1925, 5; 20 Aug. 1925, 5; 25 Aug. 1925, 5; 27 Aug. 1925, 5; 2 Sept. 1925, 5; 4 Sept. 1925, 5; 11 Sept. 1925, 5; 12 Sept. 1925, 5; 16 Sept. 1920, 5; 23 Sept. 1925, 5; 25 Sept. 1925, 5; 2 Oct. 1925, 5.

60. MHSO, ITA-6489-BOR; ITA-0826-CRE; ITA-09826; Dubro and Rowland, *King of the Mob*; Hunt, *Whiskey and Ice*. A study of 271 warrants issued in 1928 to search premises for liquor revealed that 70 per cent of the suspects were blue-collar workers living in preponderantly working-class neighbourhoods, especially the north end. Two out of five were Italian, a quarter English, one-fifth Slavs, and 8 per cent Polish. Avolio, "Hamilton's Social Landscape."

61. *HT*, 13 Jan. 1914, 10 (quotations); *HS*, 13 Jan. 1920, 13 (quotation).

62. Weaver, *Crimes, Constables, and Courts*, 188–262.

63. *HS*, 2 Feb. 1925, 5 (quotations); Huzel, "Incidence of Crime." Pawn shops and second-hand dealers were tightly regulated and closely watched by the police to discourage the fencing of stolen goods. *HS*, 16 March 1907, 13; 21 March 1908, 1; 27 March 1908, 1; 24 Feb. 1920, 6; 17 March 1920, 26; 19 April 1920, 17; 28 April 1920, 21; 15 July 1920, 13; 21 July 1920, 22; HPL, RG 10, Series S, 5 August 1896, 5 Oct. 1897, 11 June 1900, 6 Dec. 1905, 31 Oct. 1911, 6 Dec. 1911.

64. *HT*, 23 Jan. 1914; 16 April 1914; *HH*, 27 Feb. 1922, 5; 3 March 1922, 1.

65. Doucet and Weaver, *Building the North American City*, 209–12. The father of future Conservative MP Ellen Fairclough had a similar pattern of shuffling from contracting to wage-earning after moving to Hamilton in 1904. Fairclough, *Saturday's Child*, 16.

66. *HS*, 17 Feb. 1919, 6. Three years earlier ILP school trustee Rollo had similarly argued that the Board of Education should not employ married female teachers, on the curious assumption that a woman with a working husband could accept lower wages and thereby undercut the earnings of single women. *HS*, 9 June 1916, 16.

67. *HS*, 2 Sept. 1910, 1; LAC, R244-76-4-E, Vol. 308, File: 18 (41); Vol. 328, File: 22 (19); Hobbs and Sangster, eds., *Woman Worker*, 67; Frager, "No Proper Deal"; Frager and Patrias, *Discounted Labour*; Kenneally, *Women and American Trade Unions*.

68. Bradbury, "Home as Workplace"; Roberts, *Woman's Place*, 125–68; Ross, *Love and Toil*; Reeves, *Round About a Pound a Week*; Rice, *Working-Class Wives*; Byington, *Homestead*; Gabaccia, *From the Other Side*, 45–60; *HH*, 27 March 1912, 4 (quotation); 2 April 1913, 13 (quotation). It is impossible to extract from the historical record how many single women in Hamilton were self-supporting, but it cannot have been a large proportion – even those living in boarding houses were no doubt closely tied in to family economies far from the city.

69. Scott, *Female Labour*, 25; OCCUR, 66–67; TFL, Kenney Collection, Box 2 (Communist Party of Canada, Proceedings and National Conventions), 1927, F. Custance, "Our Tasks Among Women," 64 (quotation).

70. See Table 16. In 1967 the *Spectator* interviewed one of these women on her 99th birthday. Frances Telfer had left the Tuckett Tobacco plant in 1940 after 52 years of employment. *HS*, 20 June 1967, 17.

71. The 1921 census reported that 87 per cent of those single, widowed, and divorced women age 25 to 34 and 70 per cent of those age 35 to 49 were employed. CC, 1921, Vol. 4, liii.

72. Synge, "Young Working Class Women," 144; Synge, "Family and Community," ch. 3.6; Bird, "Hamilton Working Women," 132; see also OWAHC, interview with Lil Seager (former Tuckett Tobacco worker).

73. OTLBR, 1917, 12 (quotation); HPL, Canadian Patriotic Fund, Scrapbooks, Vol. 1, 19 May 1916; Vol. 2, 28 Oct. 1915.

74. See, for example, *HS*, 16 Nov. 1920, 18; 20 Nov. 1920, 2; 24 Nov. 1920, 6; 12 Jan. 1921, 6; 5 May 1921, 23; 15 Sept. 1921, 6; *LL*, 4 Feb. 1921, 4; Archibald, "Distress, Dissent, and Alienation," 17. For labour's ongoing critique of married women earning wages, see Tite, "Married Women in Industry."

75. *HS*, 19 Jan. 1921, 1; *Worker*, 20 Feb. 1931, 4; Hobbs, "Rethinking Antifeminism"; Hobbs, "Equality and Difference"; Kessler-Harris, "Gender Ideology."

76. These patterns were still clear in the 1930s; see Archibald, "Distress, Dissent, and Alienation," 13.

77. CC, 1931, Vol. 5, 1002–3, 1050. Four out of five of those who were lodging with renters were in houses in the middle rental range of $16 to $39 a month. CC, 1931, Vol. 5, 1092.

78. Kaprielian-Churchill, *Like Our Mountains*, 256–57; Greenway, *Housing*, 564–65; Davidoff, "Separation of Home and Work?" Among Hungarians in the interwar period, a man who brought over his wife gained an advantage because with a woman "money came into the house." Patrias, *Patriots and Proletarians*, 83.

79. Patrias, *Patriots and Proletarians*, 83–84; *HS*, 5 Feb. 1920, 27; 5 May 1920, 19; 13 May 1920, 17.

80. In 1922 a Mothers' Allowance investigator reported women in her district making plasticine products, women's woolen hats, Christmas tree decorations, artificial flowers, brushes, ice cream, baked goods, dresses, and hats; she also found women carding buttons, hairdressing, clipping wool for a factory, sewing soles on slippers and canvas shoes, shirt-finishing, and making buttonholes. Wright, *Report upon the Sweating System*, 6; King, *Report to the Honourable Postmaster General*, 6, 9, 16–20; OMACR, 1921–22, 19, 29; *HH*, 20 Dec. 1930, n.p.; Strong-Boag, *New Day Recalled*; MHSO, ITA-0815-ANO. According to this last informant, "Italian seamstresses would sew for one another but not publicly. . . . Women were not allowed to engage in any type of business activity." See also OWCBR 1921, 60–61.

81. Bridle, "Shack-Town Christmas"; MHSO , ITA-0982-PAS; CC, 1931, Vol. 10, 614–19; Vol. 11, 284–87; Monod, "Ontario Retailers"; Monod, *Store Wars*; WAHC, interview with Lil Seager; OTLBR, 1917, 13; OMACR, 1922–23, 19–22; Murphy and Murphy, *Tales from the North End*, 106; *HS*, 29 March 1920, 21; 23 April 1920, 31; 22 Nov. 1920, 22; 9 Jan. 1925, 5; 22 Jan. 1925, 5; 2 Feb. 1925, 5; 24 April 1925, 5; 28 April 1925, 5; 26 May 1925, 5; 13 June 1925, 5; 19 June 1925, 5; 24 June 1925, 5; 2 July 1925, 5; 7 July 1925, 5; 11 Aug.

1925, 5; 14 Aug. 1925, 5; 20 Aug. 1925, 5; 25 Aug. 1925, 5. Most of these jobs parallelled those taken in Britain; see Robert, *Woman's Place*, 139–41.

82. *HH*, 21 Sept 1916, 2; 7 Dec. 1918, 15; *HS*, 20 Sept. 1919, 17; OMACR, 1921–22, 19; 1922–23, 19–22.

83. OTLBR, 1919, 22.

84. Lodging was also provided for "homeless young girls until they get employment, and females discharged from the hospital too weak to work," who were soon assigned to looking after the children. "Respectable working girls" could also board in the building. In 1904 1,720 adult women got accommodation for some period and in 1908 1,153. OA, F 885, WCTU, Ontario Convention, *Proceedings*, Report on Evangelical Work, 1897; Report on Juvenile Work, 1899; Report of Corresponding Secretary, 1900–2; Report of Hamilton Day Nursery, 1902, 1904; *CWRT*, 15 July 1908; April 1909; August 1919; August 1921; October 1921; October 1922; *HS*, 12, 17 Oct. 1900, 5; 7 June 1904, 4; 4 Dec. 1906, 6; 3 March 1909, 12; 2 June 1916, 6; 21 June 1916, 12; *HH*, 18 Dec. 1909, 47; 12 Nov. 1914, 5; 1 March 1924, 6. The Hamilton Cotton Company and Chipman-Holton knitting company each made a donation to the YWCA in 1904, which suggests where many of these women were finding work. *HS*, 8 Oct. 1904, 9.

85. *Annual Reports of the Social Agencies, Members of the Hamilton Community Fund*, 1929, 20–30; 1930, 27–28; *HS*, 10 Feb. 1930, 2; Canadian Welfare Council, *Study of the Community Fund*, 58.

86. A charity worker found that a lone mother had to leave her seven children under the care of the oldest "while she went out washing and scrubbing" to pay the rent. *HH*, 6 June 1913, 11. See also AO, RG 7-12-0-21, File: "Mothers' Allowance, Hamilton Enquiry, Thursday February 20, 1919," 44; OMACR, 1920–21, 21–23; 1921–22, 25–26.

87. *HH*, 20 Aug. 1913, 26. For comparable Winnipeg experience, see McCormack, "Networks among British Immigrants," 205.

88. There were 3,546 widows, 1,085 with an "absent" husband, 49 divorcees, and 937 single women. CC, 1931, Vol. 7, 1282.

89. OCUR 59–60; Campbell, *Mountain and a City*, 314; *HH*, 7 Dec. 1918, 15; *HS*, 20 Sept. 1919, 1; ODLR, 1920, 26; 1923, 14, 20 (quotation); 1924, 13; 1925, 16; 1926, 14 (quotation); 1931, 22; 1936, 20; 1940, 13.

90. *HS*, 20 Sept. 1919, 18 (quotation).

91. OMWBR, 1926, 35–36; 1930, 5 (quotation); 1931, 12, 14. As married women's wage-earning became more controversial in the depths of the depression, the Board stopped reporting their proportion in the workforce. The proportion of women age 25 to 34 in the waged labour force rose from a quarter in 1921 to nearly a third in 1941, and among those 35 to 44 the percentage edged up from 15 to 22. Similarly, the share of all female wage-earners made up of women over age 34 climbed from a quarter to a third. This change did not reflect a larger percentage of unmarried women in the local population because the proportions of married and single women in these age groups remained roughly the same. CC, 1911, Vol. 6, 306–7; 1921, Vol. 2, 184–85; Vol. 4, 400–1; 1931, Vol. 3, 136–37; Vol. 7, 180–81; 1941, Vol. 2, 252–53; Vol. 7, 196–97 (percentage calculations are mine). Ellen Fairclough became a working wife in the 1930s when her husband's salary proved inadequate. Fairclough, *Saturday's Child*.

92. CC, 1921, Vol. 3, 468–69; 1931, Vol. 5, 842–43; 1941, Vol. 5, 100–1; May, "'Good Managers'"; Bradbury, *Working Families*, 180; Chambers, *Married Women and Property Law*, 183.

93. Mary MacNab, "Woman's Place in Citizenship," *ND*, 5 Sept. 1921, 2.

6. School Bells and Factory Whistles

1. *HS*, 3 June 1916, 4.

2. These patterns have been explored elsewhere; see Bradbury, *Working Families*; Bose, "Household Resources"; Hareven, *Family Time and Industrial Time*; Benson, *Household Accounts*; Byington, *Homestead*; Reynolds, *British Immigrant*, 190–205.

3. Davey, "Educational Reform and the Working Class"; HBEM, 1892, 35. Calculations of percentages are mine.

4. HBEM, 1891, 9–10. The 1891 census recorded 496 boys and 206 girls under age 16 working in industrial establishments in Hamilton. CC, 1891, Vol. 3, 384. For a survey of the employment patterns of children in 19th-century Ontario factories, see Heron, "Factory Workers," 520–27.

5. Dymond, *Laws of Ontario Relating to Women and Children*, 112–25; Canada, Department of Labour, *Employment of Children and Young Persons*, 106–32; Hurl, "Overcoming the Inevitable"; Tucker, "Making the Workplace 'Safe'"; Jones and Rutman, *In the Children's Aid*.

6. Tucker, *Administering Danger*.

7. ODER, 1891, 62–64; HPL, RG 10, Series S, 6 Aug., 1 Sept., 13 Nov. 1891; 21 May, 2 Aug., 27 Aug., 4 Oct. 1892; 4 March 1893; 22 Jan., 10 May, 4 July, 7 Aug. 1894, HBEM, 1900, 62; 1921, 67–69.

8. *HS*, 28 Sept. 1900, 8; 31 Jan. 1901, 8; 22 Jan. 1902, 8; ODER, 1890–1940; CC, 1901, Vol. 4, 303, 311; 1911, Vol. 6, 307; 1921, Vol. 4, 400; 1931, Vol. 7, 180; 1941, Vol. 7, 190. For the failure of school attendance laws to keep students out of the workforce, see Ontario, Legislative Assembly, *Journals*, 41 (1907), Appendix 1; on misrepresentation of ages, see Heron, "Factory Workers," 522. A federal Department of Labour study in 1930 concluded that the census figures on child labour underestimated the extent of part-time employment; Canada, Department of Labour, *Employment of Children and Young Persons*, 11–14.

9. In 1907, as a serious depression settled over the city, the fee structure was simplified to 10 cents a month for city

residents. In December 1914 fees were waived for the war period but then reimposed two months later by the new Board of Education. Future MP Ellen Fairclough remembered that her family decided in 1914 that they could not afford the 30 cents a month to keep three children in school in Hamilton. *HS*, 8 Dec. 1906, 1; 8 March 1907, 3; 12 Feb. 1915, 1; 9 April 1915, 13; HBEM, 1907, 11, 92, 93; 1909, 10, 20; 1914, 121, 169, 170; 1916, 8, 231, 233; 1917, 7; 1919, 8; *LN*, 11 Dec. 1914, 1; 18 Dec. 1914, 1; *IB*, 26 March 1915, 3; Spalding, *History and Romance of Education*, 30; Fairclough, *Saturday's Child*, 19.

10. *HT*, 2 Nov. 1911, 7; 15 Feb. 1913, 8; *HH*, 6 Sept. 1912, 9; 14 June 1918, 9; *HS*, 9 Sept. 1921, 1; HBEM, 1919, 9, 48; 1922, 55, 164. The school board generally coped with rising enrolment by adding classrooms to existing schools, rather than building many new ones. In 1894 21 schools handled 8,689 students, while in 1919 22 schools squeezed in 16,854. *HH*, 20 Dec. 1919, 16.

11. HBEM, 1913, 115.

12. *HH*, 15 Sept. 1922, 1 (quotations); *HS*, 20 Jan. 1922, 18.

13. *HS*, 3 March 1910, 12; 6 April 1910, 14; 26 April 1910, 36.

14. Synge, "Transition from School to Work," 257; *LG*, February 1902, 443; see also November 1902, 306; *HS*, 3 Oct. 1900, 8.

15. *HS*, 15 May 1905, 10.

16. HBEM, 1900, 62; ODER, 1895–1920; *HS*, 9 Feb. 1910, 12 (see also 11 Jan. 1900, 8; 26 Feb. 1900, 8; 25 April 1900, 8; 16 May 1900, 8; 6 Oct. 1900, 8; 15 Nov. 1900, 8; 10 Dec. 1900, 8; 11 May 1910, 12; 2 June 1910, 12; 22 June 1910, 1; 29 Sept. 1910, 12; 10 Nov. 1910, 14; 27 May 1920, 19); *HT*, 12 Feb. 1913, 5.

17. OTLBR, 1916, 10; 1919, 54; *HH*, 4 July 1918, 1; 5 July 1918, 1. The same year the *Spectator* found an 11–year-old boy at work; *HS*, 3 May 1918. Years later a Proctor and Gamble employee recalled starting work that year at age 12. *Galaxy*, 1975. The percentage of the total Canadian workforce under age 16 rose from 2.1 in 1915 to slightly over 3 per cent in 1917 and 1918 and 2.9 per cent in 1919; *CYB*, 1922–23, 4.

18. HBEM, 1921, 69. The 1921 census statistics on school attendance suggest that immigrants might have had more reason to pull their children out of school than did Canadian-born parents: 93.5 per cent of Canadian-born children age 7 to 14 attended school, as contrasted with 89.5 per cent of British-born and 86.3 per cent of other "foreign born"; CC, 1921, Vol. 2, 742–43.

19. Oliphant, comp., *Hess Street School*, 38; WAHC, interviews with Ed Fisher, Florence Fisher, Fred Purser, Ken Withers; Synge, "Family and Community," ch. 3.6; Murphy and Murphy, *Tales from the North End*, 123–28, 159; Beattie, *John Christie Holland*, 44–46; Hunter, *Which Side Are You On, Boys*, 5; *HH*, 30 March 1911, 1; *HS*, 17 April 1901, 10; 21 Jan. 1902, 8; 11 Aug. 1910, 10; 6 Nov. 1920, 4; 18 Nov. 1920,

9; OSNDRC, 1901, 45; AO, F 885, WCTU, Annual Report, 1922 (for reports on children begging). In 1934 the federal Royal Commission on Price Spreads learned that the city's biggest grocery chain relied on many boys delivering orders after school for $1.50 to 2.50 a week or 5 to 10 cents per order. Canada, Royal Commission on Price Spreads, *Minutes of Evidence*, 1001. In 1925 the police magistrate complained that too many children, especially from "foreign" families, had appeared before him on charges of stealing coal, most often "told to do so by their parents." *HS*, 25 March 1925, 5; see also 23 May 1925, 5.

20. Davey, "Educational Reform and the Working Class"; Synge, "Transition from School to Work," 257, 254–56 (quotations). See Table 22.

21. Synge, "Transition From School to Work," 258–62; Synge, "Young Working Class Women"; Synge, "Changing Conditions for Women"; Ewen, *Immigrant Women*, 106–8. Negotiating spending money was not necessarily easy. In 1929 the Big Sisters reported the difficulties of one girl: "Her father insists on drawing all her money and making himself disagreeable; will not clothe her properly, claiming it is his right to receive and spend it on himself. Nothing we say will alter him. The result is that no employer will keep Ethel." Hamilton Community Fund, *Reports*, 1929, 17.

22. Synge, "Work and Family Support Patterns," 142.

23. On the weaknesses of the census for studying youth employment, see Canada, Department of Labour, *Employment of Children*, 11–14. The decennial censuses are the most thorough sources, but they can be misleading both because in 1921 and 1931 they fell in the depths of economic depressions and because they missed part-time or seasonal jobs

24. Canada, Department of Labour, *Employment of Children*, 27; CC, 1921, Vol. 4, lii.

25. Synge, "Work and Family Support Patterns," 142 (quotation); Synge, "Changing Conditions for Women," 14, 38, 41 (quotation).

26. *MMJ*, November 1908, 990.

27. *HH*, 15 Jan. 1913, 4 (quotation); see also *HH*, 6 June 1913, 11; Strong-Boag, *New Day Recalled*, 17.

28. See Table 16.

29. As with men, recruitment often came through the informal channels of personal connection. A woman who started at the Tuckett Tobacco plant in the 1920s recalled that managers who needed extra hands simply asked their workers if they had sisters looking for jobs. The Imperial Cotton Company similarly prided itself on family recruitment. WAHC, interview with Lil Seager; *Fabricator*, April 1921, 10–11; August 1921, 4. Joan Sangster found similar practices in Peterborough. Sangster, *Earning Respect*, 52.

30. CC, 1911, Vol. 6, 308–12; 1921, Vol. 4, 400–8; 1931, Vol. 7, 180–4; *CM*, August 1906, 292; *HS*, 20 April 1907, 18 (quotation); ODLR, 1920, 25. For a more detailed discussion of

women's jobs in the metal trades see Butler, *Women and the Trades*, 209–29. Census-takers found 242 working in metalworking plants in 1911, 479 in 1921, and 505 in 1931.

31. A special employment bureau for women opened in Hamilton in January 1917 to funnel females into the factories. *HH*, 27 June 1916, 8; 9 Sept. 1916, 11; 23 Sept. 1916, 11; 27 Sept. 1916, 10; 30 Nov. 1916, 4; 4 Dec. 1916; 6 Dec. 1916; 7 Dec. 1916, 3; 14 Dec. 1916; 4 Jan. 1917, 14; 6 Jan. 1917, 7; 8 Jan. 1917, 4; 11 Jan. 1917, 7; 12 Jan. 1917, 2; 16 Jan. 1917, 4; 23 Jan. 1917, 1; 14 Feb. 1917, 1; 1 March 1917; *LG*, September 1916, 1535; *LN*, 12 Jan. 1917; 19 Jan. 1917; 23 Feb. 1917; 26 Feb. 1917; Irish, "'Dilution' of Labor," 717; "Female Labor on 8 in. High Explosive Shell Machining," *CM*, 17, 8 March 1917, 207; OTLBR, 1917–18; LAC, R1449-0-5-E, Vol. 38, File 1915–17; OA, RG 7, II-1, Box 3, File: "Reports – Employment Offices (B-N)," Hamilton, Margaret K. Strong to W.A. Riddell, 13 Dec. 1918; State Historical Society of Wisconsin, American Federation of Labor Papers, Samuel Gompers Files, Series II, A, Box 23, R. Riley to A. Holder, 4 July 1917.

32. *HH*, 9 Sept. 1916, 11; 27 Sept. 1916, 10; LAC, MG 26, H 1(c), Vol. 211, 118736 (A. Boyer to J. Flavelle, 29 March 1916); Bliss, *Canadian Millionaire*, 306.

33. Bliss, *Canadian Millionaire*, 306 (quotation); LAC, MG 39, A, 16, Vol. 38 (Irish, Mark H.), 1915–17, Flavelle to Irish, 10 Nov. 1916; *HH*, 9 Sept. 1916, 11; 23 Sept. 1916, 11; 27 Sept. 1916, 1; 16 Nov. 1916, 14; 30 Nov. 1916, 1; 7 Dec. 1916, 3; 4 Jan. 1917, 4; 6 Jan. 1917, 1, 7; 8 Jan. 1917, 1; 11 Jan. 1917, 7; 12 Jan. 1917; 16 Jan. 1917, 14; 23 Jan. 1917, 1; 14 Feb. 1917, 1; 1 March 1917, 2; 13 June 1917, 2; *LN*, 12 Jan. 1917, 3; 19 Jan. 1917, 1; 23 Feb. 1917, 1; Sangster, "Mobilizing Women," 163–75.

34. In 1911 census-takers found just over 1,000 women who identified themselves as domestic servants, making up almost one in seven female wage-earners; by 1941, despite the doubling of the city's population, the figure was still only about 1,200, comprising only one in 20 women workers. CC, 1911, Vol. 6, 307; 1941, Vol. 6, 246. In 1911 only 24 per cent of gainfully employed women in Hamilton worked in "domestic and personal service," compared to 42 per cent in Vancouver, 39 per cent in Winnipeg and Ottawa, 33 per cent in Montreal, and 27 per cent in Toronto. In 1931 fewer than 12 per cent of Hamilton's working women were domestic servants and in 1941 only 6.5 per cent. For Vancouver the comparable figures were 15 and 14 per cent, for Winnipeg 19 and 17 per cent, for Toronto 13 and 10 per cent, and for Montreal 15 and 16 per cent. CC, 1911, Vol. 6, 250, 262, 276, 286, 296, 306; 1931, Vol. 7; 1941, Vol. 6. Calculations are mine.

35. *HH*, 10 May 1913, 7 (quotation); *HS*, 25 Feb. 1905, 11 (quotation); 20 Sept. 1919, 17 (quotation); 6 May 1920, 27; *LL*, 28 Jan. 1921, 4; Synge, "Changing Conditions for Women," 18; Sebire, *Woman's Place*, 98–106; Heron et al., *All That*

Our Hands Have Done, 57; Reynolds, *British Immigrant*, 48; Barber, *Immigrant Domestic Servants*. On the preference of working women for other than domestic work and upper-class women's difficulty in finding or holding onto them, see *IB*, April 1899, 4; *HH*, 18 April 1911, 1; 16 May 1911, 4; 19 Sept. 1912, 1; 12 June 1916, 4; 20 April 1918, 3; *HS*, 24 Aug. 1910, 12; 14 Jan. 1920, 1; 21 Jan. 1920, 1; 29 Nov. 1920, 8; 15 Nov. 1934 (clipping in HPL Scrapbook); OTLBR, 1917, 21; 1918, 26; 1919, 22; National Council of Women of Canada, *Women of Canada*, 108; Thomson, *Conditions of Female Labour*, 19; Hamilton Local Council of Women, *Fifty Years of Activity*; Roberts, *Honest Womanhood*, 13–16; Leslie, "Domestic Service in Canada."

By World War One the "mistresses" of upper- and middle-class households had come to rely mostly on British immigrants and on greater use of day labour rather than live-in servants. African-Canadian women were also always available in small numbers, since they generally found most other doors to employment closed to them. If the economy slumped, factory workers might turn to domestic work, though, as a local government official noted in 1921, they would "insist on sleeping at home." In the 1930s the YWCA organized classes to better train young women for this work and opened a Home Service Training Centre under a federal youth-training program. But few women were drawn to this belated effort to raise the status of a difficult, unattractive job. OCUR, 168; *HS*, 20 Sept. 1919, 17; 6 May 1920, 27; Barber, "Women Ontario Welcomed"; Shadd, *Journey from Tollgate to Parkway*; Brand, "We Weren't Allowed to Go into Factory Work."

36. See Table 17.

37. McPherson, *Bedside Matters*.

38. See Tables 12 and 17. The 19 women hired into clerical jobs at city hall during the war stayed on. *HH*, 7 April 1919, 1.

39. *HS*, 20 Sept. 1919, 17; Synge, "Changing Conditions for Women," 19–24.

40. Ellen Fairclough was a fairly typical example of the young female worker who moved out of local commercial schooling into clerical work in a series of offices. Fairclough, *Saturday's Child*, 25–35.

41. CC, 1921, Vol. 4, 400–19; 1931, Vol. 7, 180–91; 1941, Vol. 7, 190–201, 796–98, 802–4. In 1911 Hamilton males age 15 to 24 earned $11.27 on average, while females earned $6.73. The later censuses had subtler categories. In 1921 the average weekly wage packet for boys age 15 to 19 was $13.61 and for girls $10.26. In 1931 boys age 16 to 17 were earning $8.86 a week, only slightly higher than the $7.59 earned by girls, but their older brothers age 18 to 19 took home $13.15 compared to the girls' $10.31. CC, 1931, Vol. 5, 20–26.

42. For comparison of male and female earnings, see Tables 20 and 21. A cigar-makers' union leader admitted in 1919

that women were never paid the same as men. RCIRE, Vol. 4, 2403. When 15 blanket weavers at Porritts and Spence struck in 1923, the manager admitted, "We could not replace them," but noted the workers were earning only $18 to $20 a month. LAC, RG 27, Vol. 331, File: 23 (51). In 1919 the *Spectator* reported, "There is no place in Hamilton of any kind where the self-supporting single woman, no matter what her business, can find suitable accommodation of a home variety at a reasonable figure." *HS*, 6 Sept. 1919, 15. Some teenage girls earned little or nothing when they were learning a job; see *HS*, 15 Oct. 1921, 13. "The female wage allowed women to survive," Kessler-Harris notes. "The male wage suggested a contribution to national economic well-being." *Woman's Wage*, 19. On women workers and workers' compensation in this period, see Storey, "From Invisibility to Equality?" 79–87.

43. Tucker, *Administering Danger*; Kessler-Harris, *Woman's Wage*, 33–56; McCallum, "Keeping Women in Their Place"; Kealey, "Women and Labour"; Lee, "Redivision of Labour"; Lehrer, *Origins of Protective Labor Legislation*.

44. OMWBR, 1921–40; *HS*, 5 Oct. 1921, 10; 25 Oct. 1921, 13.

45. See Troen, "Discovery of the Adolescent"; Osterman, "Education and Labor Markets"; Perlman, "After Leaving School." In 1921 census-takers identified only 163 apprentices in factory crafts among the more than 2,000 factory workers under age 18; just over half were in printing and more than a quarter were learning the machinist's trade. CC, 1921, Vol. 4, 400–9 (calculations are mine). These factors may help to explain why in 1921 only 14 per cent of 14-year-old boys and 11 per cent of 14-year-old girls had full-time jobs, even though they were still not forbidden by law from taking full-time employment (the census was taken in June, and Ontario's new legislation that raised the school-leaving age to 16 did not come into effect until September).

46. In 1921 wage-earners under age 20 reported almost nine weeks of unemployment, compared to only six and a half weeks for all ages. CC, 1921, Vol. 3, 128.

47. CC, 1921, Vol. 5, 842–49. Calculations are mine.

48. Arguably, this prolonged use of juvenile labour made Canada a little more like Britain than the US.

49. CC, 1901, Vol. 4, 10; ODER, 1901; Campbell, *Mountain and a City*, 160–61, 225–29. Since the provincial Department of Education's enrolment figures for the separate-school students grouped with those in the elementary grades and never subjected to the same statistical analysis as those at the Hamilton Collegiate Institute, it is not possible to comment on the gender or occupational background of these Catholic secondary students. Moreover, since the Catholic high school was run by the diocese, not the separate school board, no enrolment information appeared in the department's reports. A small number of secular private schools in the city apparently enrolled scores of boys and girls from the city's wealthiest families, but little statistical information is available about them.

50. See Table 31.

51. See Gidney and Millar, *Inventing Secondary Education*.

52. See Table 33.

53. Oliphant, *Hess Street School*, 38.

54. These calculations are based on the statistics reported in ODER, 1890–1920. In 1911 the Board of Education authorized "night matriculation classes" for those working during the day, but weekly enrolment hovered around only 20 students. By 1922 these numbers had risen to 250, but the appeal was predominantly to white-collar workers with their eyes on university; the collegiate principal reported that two-thirds were clerks, teachers, stenographers, and bookkeepers. HBEM, 1912, 58–59; 1920, 268–69; 1923, 14.

55. ODER, 1891–1921 (calculations are mine).In 1916 school officials estimated that eight out of ten children who entered the city's public schools left before reaching high school (*HT*, 31 Aug. 1916). Five years later the census-takers found 78 per cent were enrolled at age 14, but only 47 per cent at age 15, 31 per cent at age 16, 18 per cent at age 17, and 8 per cent at ages 18 to 19. CC, 1921, Vol. 4, lii.

56. A federal labour official writing in 1930 incorrectly assumed that the higher rates of school attendance in 1921 reflected the increased prosperity of the war period when families had decided to keep their children in school; as we will see, he got it backwards. See Canada, Department of Labour, *Employment of Children*, 15.

57. Pamela Barnhouse Walters discovered the same pattern in the US; see "Occupational and Labor Market Effects."

58. In 1899, as the local economy began to lift out of the deep depression of the 1890s, working-class enrolment in the collegiate fell by 30 per cent over the previous year and continued to slide to nearly half by 1901. In 1907, in the face of another serious crisis of unemployment, enrolment climbed again but dropped away swiftly with the return of prosperity after 1909. Between that year and 1913 the enrolment of collegiate students with fathers employed as tradesmen and labourers plummeted by 43 per cent, reaching a low for the post-1890 period of 21 per cent. During that same pre-war interlude of prosperity, the cost of providing food and shelter for a family of five in the city jumped up by nearly 16 per cent. See Table 31.

59. Catholic secondary-school enrolment in Hamilton followed a similar pattern. It peaked first at 121 in 1908, in the depths of the two-year slump, then fell by 19 per cent over the next three years. The lack of jobs in the pre-war depression pushed enrolment up to 282 by 1915. The lack of occupational data for these students' fathers prevents any tracking of the working-class proportions. ODER, 1909–17.

60. Calculations based on average monthly attendance figures reported in HBER, 1890–1920.

61. ODER, 1891–1921. Synge also discovered through her interviews that irregular attendance was common. "Transition from School to Work," 264.

62. HBEM, 1923, 252.

63. HBEM, 1917, 126 (see also *HH*, 27 Jan. 1917, 2); ODER, 1918–19; calculations of attendance based on average monthly attendance figures reported in HBEM, 1915–20.

64. CC, 1921, Vol. 4, lii.

65. See Table 31. Ellen Fairclough remembered that she had to attend a different school for each year of the three-year program. Fairclough, *Saturday's Child*, 20–21. There were also a few private business colleges offering commercial training; *HH*, 1 Aug. 1919, 4.

66. *HH*, 8 Oct. 1910, 1; 14 June 1913, 6; Seath, *Education for Industrial Purposes*, Appendix: J.G. Witton, "Hamilton Technical and Art School," 380–81; LAC, R3096-0-8-E, Vol. 16 (Hamilton Branch Minutes), File: 1911–12, Technical Education Committee, 25 Sept. 1911, 2; HBEM, 1918, 170.

67. Principal Witton reported "a good demand for instruction in those subjects which promise immediate benefit to the pupil ... and very little interest in the academic branches ... whose value, though no less real, is less apparent"; see "Hamilton Technical and Art School," 381. On the recruitment process, see the comments of International Harvester's superintendent in Seath, *Education for Industrial Purposes*, 365; WAHC, interviews with Lil Seager, Charles Olds, Floyd Read; Heron, *Working in Steel*, 74–98.

68. *HH*, 22 June 1916, 6. For a biographical note on Sprague, see *CM*, 13 Jan. 1921, 39.

69. HBEM, 1918, 176.

70. At least half the day students enrolled in the Hamilton Technical and Art School came from households headed by a father in "trades" or "labouring," while those with "commercial" or "professional" fathers comprised less than 14 per cent in 1919. See Table 34.

71. HBEM, 1920; ODER, 1922; CC, 1921, Vol. 2, 80. Calculations are mine.

72. ODER, 1917–21.

73. HBEM, 1920, 174; *Made in Hamilton Quarterly*, June 1923, 2 (quotation).

74. Rury, "Vocationalism for Home and Work," 34–36; Clifford, "'Marry, Stitch, Die or Do Worse.'"

75. *LG*, February 1921, 203. The province's director of industrial and technical education noted in 1918 that a shift was underway in the nationality of night-school students; earlier, 60 to 70 per cent had been British-born, apparently because "night schools had been a recognized part of the educational system in Great Britain for many years," but Canadians were now "acquiring the habit of attending." ODER, 1918, Appendix B ("Report of the Director of Industrial and Technical Education"), 19–20. For all the enthusiasm for night classes, they had extremely high absenteeism and dropout rates; Witton, "Hamilton Technical and Art School," 381; HBEM, 1919, 97; ODER, 1922, 17.

76. See Seath, *Education for Industrial Purposes*; Leake, *Industrial Problems*; Leake, *Vocational Education of Girls and Women*; Douglas, *American Apprenticeship and Industrial Education*. Ontario's director of technical education, F.W. Merchant, also filled his annual reports with references to the latest surveys and reports on youth employment. These discussions typically relied on foreign data and off-the-cuff observations on Canadian experience because apparently no Ontario studies were undertaken before 1919. ODER, 1914–19. All this theorizing about adolescence and work is discussed in Dunn, "Teaching the Meaning of Work"; Troen, "Discovery of the Adolescent," 244–49; Kett, "Adolescence of Vocational Education."

77. *HT*, 31 Aug. 1916.

78. ODER, 1914, 694–702; 1916, 56–63; 1917, 37–39.

79. Stamp, *Schools of Ontario*, 107; *Globe* (Toronto), 16 April 1919; *HH*, 29 Nov. 1924; Masters, *Henry John Cody*. By the end of the war the province's director of technical education was also framing his arguments in the language of "reconstruction" that had gripped public debate. He noted, "The schools are being looked to, on the one hand, for the development of the character of the youth and, on the other, for a training in efficiency," and warned, "If the child's schooling closes at the end of the elementary school period, the chief opportunity for character direction is lost to the school, because the significant aims and purposes of life do not begin to take shape until the youth enters upon the period of adolescence." ODER, 1918, 25–35; see also 1919, 11. A conservative emphasis on the value of vocational education for political order ran through much of the US writing on the subject in the same period; see Kett, "Adolescence of Vocational Education," 85.

80. Stamp, *Schools of Ontario*, 107–9; HPL, HCC, Board of Directors, Minutes, 15 May 1923, 26; *Annual Report*, 1923–24, 16–17.

81. A brief flurry of controversy had already occurred about a higher school-leaving age in 1916, when the Board of Education's Industrial Technical Committee recommended that compulsory attendance up to age 16 be imposed under Ontario's existing local-option legislation (at that point applied by no municipality in the province) as a means of promoting technical education. The Board of Trade and the local branch of the Canadian Manufacturers' Association quickly made their opposition clear. Apparently the city's employers wanted access to better-trained workers but balked at losing their ready supply of young labour in the wartime economy. Despite warm support from the local labour movement, the trustees beat a

hasty retreat, recognizing, in the words of the board chairman, that such action "might seriously affect local manufacturing concerns wherein the labor problem was at the present time a serious question." HBEM, 1916, 26, 108, 128; *HS*, 8 Feb. 1916, 1; 11 Feb. 1916, 1; 9 June 1916, 16; *HH*, 11 Feb. 1916, 15. In 1923 the local Chamber of Commerce's secretary thought "the whole [Adolescent Attendance] act was wrong and every effort should be made to obtain its repeal." HPL, HCC, Board of Directors, Minutes, 15 May 1923, 26.

82. HBEM, 1920, 285; 1922, 223, 229; 1923, 7, 198, 252; *HH*, 14 July 1922, 11. As late as 1925 one school trustee was grumbling, "If all the children go in for a high school education, where are we to get our workmen from? . . . Instead of seeing labourers walking around unemployed, we will see young men with white collars doing the same thing." *HS*, 27 March 1925, 5. Robert Stamp's discussion of the immediate impact of the Adolescent School Attendance Act overlooks this foot-dragging as a factor; see *Ontario Secondary School Program Innovations and Student Retention Rates*, 8–14.

83. ODER, 1920–35; *HS*, 4 Sept. 1928, 15, 21. For an insightful discussion of the merging of commercial classes into the vocational stream, see Goodson and Anstead, *Through the Schoolhouse Door*, 115–43.

84. HBEM, 1933–34. The evening classes were revived in 1939.

85. *HH*, 13 Oct. 1923, 12–13; HBEM, 1920–40; Stamp, "Canadian High Schools," 83–84. On the processes of streaming later in the 20th century, see Curtis, Livingstone, and Smaller, *Stacking the Deck*.

86. See, for example, *Globe*, 11 April 1919; 16 April 1919.

87. *HS*, 8 Feb. 1916, 1; 3 June 1916, 4; 8 June 1916, 12; *HH*, 30 Jan. 1918, 5. In the 1923 provincial election a Conservative candidate called the new act "an unnecessary burden on the average workingman" and promised to move to have it abolished. *HS*, 14 June 1923, 1. Some workers supported the new schooling legislation; see, for example, *HS*, 19 March 1921, 29: "give us more education; the boy will have more time to develop."

88. Cumbo, "As the Twig Is Bent," 4–10, 166–81.

89. HBEM, 1927, 61.

90. See Table 36.

91. OMWBR, 1926, 36; 1933, 15; HBEM, 1925, 202; 1927, 61; 1932, 70; "Apprentice Training at Hamilton, Ont.," *CTJ*, 19 Dec. 1922, 563 (quotation); Hamilton Community Fund, *Report*, 1928, 17 (quotation). The investigators working under the new Mothers' Allowances program also pushed mothers under their supervision to keep their children in school until age 18 and not use the special exemptions. OMACR, 1920–21, 19. Part-time schooling for youths age 14 and 15 was never popular among school officials in Hamilton, and in 1932 the school trustees convinced a provincial convention of their counterparts to petition the

minister of education for either the lowering of the legal school-leaving age to 15 or the granting of full exemptions without part-time classes. *HH*, 18 June 1932.

92. See Tables 34 and 35.

93. *LG*, January 1929, 52–67; January 1939, 66–68; January 1940, 33–36; January 1941, 42–44.

94. CC, 1911, Vol. 6, 306–17; 1921, Vol. 4, 400; 1931, Vol. 3, 29; Vol. 5, 700; Vol. 7, 180. As in the past, variations existed depending on the insecurities of the father's job. Tailors, blacksmiths, and moulders relied on their wage-earning offspring for roughly a quarter of the family earnings, labourers for a fifth, and weavers, riveters, and machinists for about a sixth, while printers and clerical workers got a mere 6.2 and 7.6 per cent from their children respectively. This Canadian experience contrasted sharply with the still-extensive employment of young adolescents in interwar England; see Todd, "Breadwinners and Dependants."

95. LAC, R3096-0-8-E, Vol. 18, File: 1926–30, 26 April 1927, 1.

96. ODER, 1929, 220–25, 318–23. For the exemptions from school-attendance legislation, see Table 36.

97. HBEM, 1932, 70.

98. Canada, Department of Labour, *Employment of Children*; CC, 1931, Vol. 10, 614–15 (calculations are mine); Monod, *Store Wars*; *LG*, February 1933, 113; Canada, Royal Commission on Price Spreads, *Minutes of Evidence*, 1001; Garvie, *Growing Up*, 21–22; WAHC, interviews with Ed Fisher, Fred Purser, Ken Withers. Purser remembered that farmers would drive into the city with trucks to pick up "maybe a hundred kids and women" each day that they needed them. Daily earnings might be anywhere from 15 to 75 cents for the day. Neil Sutherland's study of working-class Vancouver childhood in this period reveals regular part-time youth employment; see "'We Always Had Things to Do.'"

99. Gill, "Specialized Training," 873; "Special Committee Re Revision of Course of Study for the Westdale Secondary School," 11 Sept. 1935, in HBEM, 1935, 255. A rare tabulation of students by age, sex, and grade in June 1929 found one-third fewer 16-year-old boys in academic courses than 15-year-olds; at the same time, 387 boys and 322 girls of age 15 were enrolled in vocational courses but only 108 boys and 122 girls age 16 and only 39 and 55 age 17. ODER, 1929, 220–25, 318–23. Similar patterns emerged from an analysis of the board's annual statistics for 1933–40. See Table 37.

100. This discussion is based on indices of average monthly attendance at the Hamilton Technical School, derived from HBEM, 1927–40.

101. HBEM, 1933–37; ODER, 1931, 2–5; HBEM, 1933, 7; 1934, 59.

102. Gill, "Specialized Training," 874–75 (quotations); *HS*, 2 Oct. 1930, 7. The girls' strike did not last a full day. Donald

Garvie recalled his profound boredom that led to quitting before finishing his printing course; *Growing Up*, 12–13.

103. *CM*, 21 Sept. 1922, 19–20; Williams, "Textile Classes for Hamilton." Another Hamilton businessman wrote to the provincial education minister about office workers: "I think it is better that an office boy should be moulded after he goes into an office because each office has a distinctive system and an 18 year old boy would have to relearn a lot of things and forget a number of others." AO, MU 4989, C-1, Minister of Education Papers, 1918–19, File: 20 ("Suggestions and Criticism on Educational Matters"), 16.

104. Roberts, ed., *Organizing Westinghouse*, 5–6; Roberts, *Baptism of a Union*, 11; Storey, "Workers, Unions, and Steel," 208–12; WAHC, interview with Floyd Read.

105. *HS*, 25 Jan. 1930, 16; 22 Feb. 1930, 18; 29 March 1930, 24; 26 April 1930, 20; 31 May 1930, 18; 28 June 1930, 18; 26 July 1930, 18; 30 Aug. 1930, 16; 27 Sept. 1930, 16; 25 Oct. 1930, 13; 29 Nov. 1930, 18; 27 Dec. 1930, 14; 27 Jan. 1940, 16; 24 Feb. 1940, 18; 30 March 1940, 18; 27 April 1940, 18; 25 May 1940, 16; 29 June 1940, 18; 27 July 1940, 14; 31 Aug. 1940, 16; 28 Sept. 1940, 16; 26 Oct. 1940, 16; 23 Nov. 1940, 18; 28 Dec. 1940, 14.

106. See Table 32.

107. See Table 37.

108. Clifford, "'Marry, Stitch, Die or Do Worse,'" 250–54. Some young women must have tried to enhance their chances of landing a good clerical job: in 1935 the provincial director of technical education reported that many students were transferring to commercial schools as "special" students after a few years in the academic stream. ODER, 1935, 24.

109. CC, 1931, Vol. 6, 1010; 1941, Vol. 7, 190–91. The new surge of youth employment and decline of high-school retention rates were general across the province during the war; see Stamp, *Ontario Secondary School Program Innovations and Student Retention Rates*, 40–52.

110. Cf. Walters, "Occupational and Labor Market Effects." Some boys undoubtedly would have preferred to stay in school. One who quit at the end of the 1930s remembered: "I enjoyed school. I would have loved to go to school. But there was things that was more important at that time. In those days, if you were big enough, old enough, you're able enough, get a job." WAHC, interview with Floyd Read. Another got encouragement from a high-school teacher to continue on to university, but his mother insisted, "No, he's got to go out and work when he's 16. We have no money coming in and he's got to leave school." *HS*, 23 Nov. 1999, D3.

7. Spending the Hard-Earned Bucks

1. Ewen, *Captains of Consciousness*; Ewen and Ewen, *Channels of Desire*; Lears, *Fables of Abundance*; Strasser, *Satisfaction Guaranteed*; Cross, *Time and Money*; Palmer, *Working-Class Experience*, 229–36.

2. Monod, *Store Wars*, 99–148; Calder, *Financing the American Dream*; Cohen, "Class Experience of Mass Production"; Benson, "Living on the Margin"; Strasser, "Gender, Generation, and Consumption."

3. See Tables 22 and 28; also Shergold, *Working-Class Life*, 179–85.

4. Gabaccia, *We Are What We Eat*, 36–63.

5. Hoggart, *Uses of Literacy*, 78 (quotation); Gray, *Labour Aristocracy*; Crossick, *Artisan Elite*; Kirk, *Change, Continuity, and Class*, 111–40; Glickman, *Living Wage*, 61–91.

6. Bailey, "'Will the Real Bill Banks Please Stand Up?'"; Harrison, "Traditions of Respectability" (quotation at 161); Ross, "'Not the Sort That Would Sit on the Doorstep'"; McCalman, "Respectability"; Meacham, *A Life Apart*, 29; Johnson, *Saving and Spending*, 225–27; Fahrni, "Rhetoric of Order"; Anstead, "Fraternalism"; Marks, *Revivals and Roller Rinks*; Sangster, *Earning Respect*; Morton, *Ideal Surroundings*, 32–50; Cohen, "Class Experience of Mass Consumption."

7. According to the Ontario Commission on Unemployment's 1915 report, "Women have the spending of the larger portion of the family income." OCCUR, 65. On the working-class housewife's role as domestic manager in Canada and elsewhere, see also *CCJ*, March 1928, 39; Monod, *Store Wars*, 114–15; Forestall, "Gendered Terrains," ch. 3; Frank, "Miner's Financier"; Benson, *Household Accounts*, 27–33; De Grazia with Furlough, eds., *Sex of Things*; Marchand, *Advertising the American Dream*, 66–69.

8. *Made-in-Hamilton Quarterly*; Glickman, *Living Wage*, 85–91; *HH*, 20 Aug. 1917, 2; Spedden, *Trade Union Label*; Frank, *Purchasing Power*; Frank, "Where Are the Workers"; Gabaccia, *We Are What We Eat*, 131–36.

9. Quoted in Archibald, "Great Expectations and Small Adjustments," 374.

10. *HH*, 11 Jan. 1917, 6 (quotation). A few months later the *Times* carried a similar story on such "extravagances," this time citing an east-end clergyman. *HT*, 24 Aug. 1917, 1. See also HPL, Canadian Patriotic Fund, Scrapbooks, Vol. 2, 5 Nov. 1915, 83. When the Dominion Housefurnishing Company held a sale in 1916, the crowds got so large that they blocked traffic, and the police were called to control them. *HH*, 12 June 1916, 5.

11. Monod, *Store Wars*, 138–39; Sebire, *Woman's Place*, 77; *HS*, 17 April 1920, 15; 22 Oct. 1924, 5; *HH*, 6 Jan. 1914, 4 (quotation). For an extended discussion of these critiques in the US, see Horowitz, *Morality of Spending*.

12. *HH*, 16 Sept. 1916, 6; LAC, R1176-0-0-E, 2287. International Harvester's roughly 2,000 workers invested $30,000. *Harvester World*, January 1919, 8.

13. Palmer, "Mutuality and the Masking/Making of Difference"; Anstead, "Fraternalism," 127–60; Emery and

Emery, *Young Man's Benefit*, 9–18. See Table 4: in 1911, when census-takers first asked Canadians if they had insurance, half of those on the west-central and north-end blocks included in the table indicated that they did. This included roughly half the skilled and semi-skilled but, predictably, only about one in five among labourers. (Calculations are mine.)

14. When Metropolitan Life began selling cheap insurance policies to US workers in 1879, it borrowed the model (and many of the staff) of Britain's Prudential Insurance Company, which also ran a US branch. In 1894 Metropolitan aggressively extended its reach into Canada, opening a Hamilton office, among others, and 30 years later, when it opened a Canadian head office in Ottawa, it was the second-largest life-insurance company in the country, with 1.5 million policyholders, a great majority of them working class. The 1,600 agents hired to collect weekly dues were also typically working-class men, though by the interwar period they were getting special training for their jobs. Over the years the number of lapsed industrial policies was enormous, especially during depressions, though starting in 1892 such policyholders would not forfeit all their payments if they were paid up for five years. Canada's largest insurance company, Sun Life, launched a "Thrift Plan" for wage-earners in 1895 but abandoned it in 1910. James, *Metropolitan Life*, 61, 73–93, 120–25, 176–82, 272; Dublin, *Family of Thirty Million*, 121–43, 279–96; Schull, *Century of the Sun*, 39; Johnson, *Saving and Spending*, 66–69; Chapin, *Standard of Living*, 191. In 1926 only 41 of Imperial Cotton's 260 employees had taken advantage of the savings accounts run by the company. When Harry Cassidy surveyed unemployed married men in the early 1930s, he discovered that two out of five had life insurance, but only 6.5 per cent had bank accounts – a tendency later noted in Britain. *Fabricator*, May 1926, 14; Cassidy, *Unemployment and Relief*, 40; Johnson, *Saving and Spending*, 220–23.

15. Buying on credit had had a long history among workers, especially when it came to groceries, but the well-advertised instalment plans of the early 20th century were new. Furniture in particular could often be purchased for a low down payment of $1 to $5 and then $1 a week. For examples of instalment buying offers (often called "clubs"), see advertisements in *HS*, 21 July 1904, 4; 10 Nov. 1906, 18; 21 Oct. 1910, 4; 3 Nov. 1911, 15; 16 Dec. 1911, 17; 7 May 1915, 4, 18; 4 May 1917, 12; 28 Nov. 1919, 10; 26 Nov. 1920, 19; 17 May 1929, 33. For repossessions, see, for example, *HS*, 7 Dec. 1921, 3; 10 Dec. 1921, 5. In the US, where surveys of consumer habits started much earlier than in Canada, researchers found class differences in instalment buying. First, the lower the income the least likely were people to buy on time. Second, middle-class consumers tended to buy more expensive items by instalment (cars,

electric refrigerators, expensive furniture), while working-class shoppers were more likely to buy less expensive durable goods, such as washing machines, phonographs, or radios. Calder, *Financing the American Dream*, 203–4.

16. *HT*, 24 Aug. 1917, 11 (quotation); Cross, *All-Consuming Century*, 29.

17. Notably Ewen, *Captains of Consciousness*. The issues swirling around consumerism are sensitively dissected in Belisle, "Toward a Canadian Consumer History." For a review of left-wing contempt for working-class consumerism, see Nava, "Consumerism Reconsidered," 158–68.

18. Johnston, *Selling Themselves*; Cross, *All-Consuming Century*; Lears, *Fables of Abundance*.

19. For suggestions that the interwar period saw the rise of mass consumerism among Canadian workers, see Palmer, *Working-Class Experience*; Morton, *Ideal Surroundings*. For similar developments among US workers, see Edsforth, *Class Conflict and Cultural Consensus*.

20. Glickman, *Living Wage*; Heron et al., *All That Our Hands Have Done*, 85 (quotation); RCIRE, Vol. 4, 2282 (quotation).

21. See, for example, *HS*, 14 Aug. 1914, 18; 3 April 1920, 12; 20 April 1920, 6; 22 April 1920, 17; 29 April 1920, 16; 17 July 1920, 21; 20 Nov. 1920, 18; 13 Dec. 1929, 41.

22. Marchand, *Advertising the American Dream*, 194–200.

23. Archibald, "Small Expectations and Great Adjustments," 375 (quotation). A 1934 US study of wage-earners' spending patterns in the 1920s found that more than half of all families spent little on luxuries and were able to save little. Leven, Moulton, and Warburton, *America's Capacity to Consume*, 70–71, 84, 119, 248–49. Historian Roland Marchand found that US advertisers wrote off between one-third and two-thirds of the US population as economically incapable of participating in a "consumers' republic" in the interwar period; *Advertising the American Dream*, 63–66. See also Stricker, "Affluence for Whom?"; Benson, "Living on the Margin."

24. Cohen, "Class Experience of Mass Consumption," 136–37; Strasser, *Satisfaction Guaranteed*, 138–61; Cohen, *Making a New Deal*, 101–20; Nickles, "More Is Better"; Bourdieu, *Distinction*. By World War One some US social surveys had also noted marked differences in the ways in which middle-class and working-class families spent their money; see Horowitz, *Morality of Spending*. Lizabeth Cohen has posed the conceptual dilemma of working-class consumerism suggestively: "Does the purchase of a new car make a factory worker feel like a full-fledged participant in an egalitarian society or merely a working-class person who has managed to buy a new car, one marketed perhaps to his distinctive tastes and financed in a characteristically working-class way, with longer and higher interest payments?" Cohen, "Class Experience of Mass Consumption," 136.

25. *HT*, 24 Aug. 1917, 11.

26. Strasser, *Satisfaction Guaranteed*, especially 163–202; Lears, *Fables of Abundance*; Marchand, *Advertising the American Dream*. For an example of product promotion, see "Heinz Special Baked Beans Week," during which cans of beans were sold at much reduced prices in nearly 50 Hamilton grocery stores. *HS*, 22 April 1920, 12.

27. For descriptions of Hamilton department stores, see *HS*, 19 Jan. 1903, 7; *HH*, 26 Oct. 1910, 9; 14 June 1915, 12; 28 Sept. 1916, 4; 7 March 1917; 6 June 1919, 1; 1 Nov. 1919; 20 Dec. 1919, 25; 20 Oct. 1920; 29 Sept. 1924, 5. See *HS*, 27 May 1925 for a report on a crowd of 5,000 shoppers who showed up for a sale at one Hamilton department store. The development of such stores in Canada is explored in Belisle, "Rise of Mass Retail"; Wright, "Most Prominent Rendezvous"; Monod, *Store Wars*, 116–24. On the working-class insistence on durability, see Parr, "Household Choices." In 1932 Mary Quayle Innis penned a short story about a young working-class mother's visit to a department store purely as a spectator, and all the glories that could be found there. See Belisle, "Rise of Mass Retail," 222–24; Belisle, *Negotiating Paternalism*.

28. Norcliffe, *Ride to Modernity*. In 1920 about 300 of International Harvester's 2,000 employees rode bicycles to work. *HHB*, November 1920, 9.

29. Founded in 1903 (the country's first), the club had as its first president and vice-president industrialists S.O. Greening and J.R. Moodie (who had purchased Canada's first car). Ruffilli, "Car in Canadian Culture," 66–67; *HS*, 1 Aug. 1929, 17. Even in the US cars were initially beyond the pocketbooks of wage-earners. Lendol Calder points out that in 1916 a US worker would have had to put almost half his annual income into the cheapest, a Ford Model T. Calder, *Financing the American Dream*, 186.

30. Davies, "'Reckless Walking'"; Weaver, *Hamilton*, 125, 201; *CC*, 1931, Vol. 10, 614–15; 1941, Vol. 9, 83. The percentage of car owners across Ontario who were identified as "labourers" was only 1 per cent in 1919 and 3.2 per cent in 1922 (after which no such occupational breakdowns were published). Farmers were the largest single category. Ontario, Department of Public Highways, *Annual Reports*, 1919–22 (calculations are mine). Only about 40 International Harvester workers drove to work in 1920. *HHB*, December 1920, 11. At the end of the 1920s automobile registrations in Canada were half the US level per capita, and cars in Canada were considerably more expensive than in the US. Even in the US workers in larger cities were far less likely to own cars. US studies established that registrations could be a misleading indicator, since many wealthier families had more than one, and that no more than a third of wage-earners and "lower-salaried men" owned cars in 1929. James J. Flink also shows that the often-cited claims of Robert and Helen Lynd about working-class car ownership in the 1920s and 1930s in "Middletown" were exaggerated, and that only 45 per cent of chief wage-earners in Pittsburgh in 1934 had one. Traves, *State and Enterprise*, 103; Stricker, "Affluence for Whom?" 30–33; Flink, *Automobile Age*, 129–35.

31. A national study of family spending patterns in 12 Canadian cities (not Hamilton) in 1937–38 found that on average cars were more than four years old when purchased (five in Toronto and London) and more than seven years old at the time of the survey. Half had been manufactured before 1930. Canada, Dominion Bureau of Statistics, *Family Income and Expenditure*, 162–64; Roberts, ed., *Organizing Westinghouse*, 6; For a sample of the large number of *Spectator* ads for used cars, see *HS*, 3 May 1935, 21; 4 May 1935, 21; 10 May 1935, 17; 18 May 1935, 17. Sean O'Connell found a similarly large market in Britain for used cars, which some skilled workers could afford.. O'Connell, *Car in British Society*, 32–37.

32. Flink, *Automobile Age*, 158–87; McShane, *Down the Asphalt Path*, 125–71; O'Connell, *Car in British Society*, 43–76, 102–6.

33. Due, *Intercity Electric Railway Industry*, 52–55, 61–68; Berger, "Car's Impact"; Bottles, "Mass Politics." Some families may have had occasional access to a car for an outing through borrowing from kin, as their counterparts did in Britain. O'Connell, *Car in British Society*, 33–34. Working-class access to summer cottaging would have to wait until after World War Two. Stevens, "Getting Away from It All."

34. CBICLR, Vol. 1, 142, 473, 475; Worton, *Dominion Bureau of Statistics*, 47–57; Liverant, "Promise of a More Abundant Life"; Shergold, *Working-Class Life*, 92, 140–41.

35. Atherton, "Department of Labour"; Worton, *Dominion Bureau of Statistics*, 47–57. In 1921 the census-takers concluded that the average family in Hamilton had 2.34 children. *CC*, 1921, Vol. 3, 124.

36. *LG*, January 1922, 99; *CC*, 1921, Vol. 3, 66–67. Terry Copp's ground-breaking study of working-class living standards in Montreal in this period first made the Department of Labour family budget a misleading "poverty line"; see *Anatomy of Poverty*, 30–43. See also Piva, *Condition of the Working Class*, 27–60. The labour department said explicitly that its budget was "intended to show the changes in the cost of items included, not to show the minimum cost for an average family." As late as the 1950s, Canada's Dominion statistician was still admitting "there are no official statistics regarding minimum living costs in Canada." Quoted in Leadbeater, *Setting Minimum Living Standards*, 4–5.

37. British and US investigations of the cost of living had similar problems; see Shergold, *Working-Class Life*, 111–14.

38. Copp, *Anatomy of Poverty*; Piva, *Condition of the Working Class*; Sutcliffe and Phillips, "Real Wages"; Bartlett, "Real Wages."

39. See Table 28.

40. Turkstra, "Christianity and the Working Class," 213.

41. The account book is in the WAHC Archives.

42. See Table 29. OMWR, 1922, 8–9 (conversion from 1922 to 1914 dollars through http://www.bankofcanada.ca/en/rates/inflation_calc.html).

43. Contemporary British and US studies found that, among working-class families, clothing made up about 12 per cent of weekly expenditures. Shergold, *Working-Class Life*, 196–201.

44. HBEM, 1922–32; MHSO, ITA-0982–PAS; WAHC, interview with Fred Purser.

45. Contemporary British and US studies suggested that furniture absorbed only between 2 and 3 per cent of workers' weekly budgets in the early part of the 20th century. Shergold, *Working-Class Life*, 196–201.

46. *HS*, 12 Oct. 1905, 5; 11 Oct. 1910, 4; 1 May 1930, 3; 2 May 1930, 19; 3 Oct. 1930, 6, 8; 2 May 1935, 3, 15; 3 May 1935, 10, 18; 4 May 1935, 29; 9 May 1935, 3; 10 May 1935, 4; 1 May 1940, 10; 3 May 1940, 15, 17; 7 May 1940, 7; 9 May 1940, 28; 10 May 1940, 21; 13 May 1940, 13; CC, 1941, Vol. 9, 79–84. Again (see chapter 4), more than half of the city's tenant households had no mechanized refrigerator in 1941 and more than three out of five had no vacuum cleaner.

47. In 1911 the average male weekly wage in Hamilton was $13.74, in 1921 just over $22, and in 1931 just under $20. In all three years, that would have been two or three dollars above the Department of Labour budget. But family contributions brought average household income up to over $21 in 1911, over $34 in 1921, and down to under $21 in 1931. Synge, "Transition from School to Work," 254–55; CC, 1921, Vol. 3, 468–69; 1931, Vol. 5, 842–45. See Tables 22 and 28.

48. In 1921 and 1931, for example, census-takers found that Hamilton's engineers had an average annual income of some $2,400 and $2,800, more than twice what machinists and moulders took home. CC, 1931, Vol. 5, 705.

49. HBHR, 1905–6, 10.

50. *Worker*, 16 Nov. 1929.

51. *HH*, 5 Aug. 1913, 1 (quotation); 8 April 1916, 5; 21 Jan. 1918, 1; *LN*, 11 Sept. 1914, 1; 12 Nov. 1915, 1; 19 Nov. 1915, 1; 26 Nov. 1915, 1; 27 Oct. 1916, 1; 11 May 1917, 1; 27 July 1917, 1; 9 Nov. 1917, 1; *IB*, 24 Nov. 1916, 2; *HS*, 20 Nov. 1920, 27; 22 Nov. 1920, 1; 23 Nov. 1920, 1; 29 Nov. 1920, 1.

52. *LN*, 27 July 1917, 1; *HS*, 24 Sept. 1919, 1 (quotation).

53. *LG*, November 1909, 581–82; *HH*, 26 March 1909, 14; 22 Aug. 1910, 9; 23 April 1914, 16; HPL, Hamilton Trades and Labor Council, Minutes, 21 April 1911, 57, 59; 5 May 1911, 62; 20 Oct. 1911, 109; *LN*, 29 May 1912, 3; 5 July 1912, 1 (quotation); 2 Jan. 1914, 8; 26 April 1914, 1; 14 Aug. 1914, 8; 4 Sept. 1914, 8; 11 Dec. 1914, 1; 19 Feb. 1915, 1; 14 May 1915, 1; 7 Dec. 1917, 1; 28 June 1918, 1; 27 Sept. 1918, 1; 4 April 1919, 6; *ND*, 7 Jan. 1920, 1; *NC*, 8 Sept. 1934, 7. A co-op

also opened in Mount Hamilton in 1920. *ND*, 12 Feb. 1920, 1. A group of workers at International Harvester also got up a petition to start a co-op store in the plant, but their Industrial Council representative discouraged them. Harvester Industrial Council, *Bulletin*, February 1920, 13.

54. *HH*, 1 Feb. 1912, 7; 5 Aug. 1913, 1 (quotation); *LN*, 11 Sept. 1914, 1; 12 Nov. 1915, 1; 19 Nov. 1915, 1; 26 Nov. 1915, 1; 27 Oct. 1916, 1; 11 May 1917, 1; 27 July 1917, 1; 9 Nov. 1917, 1; *IB*, 24 Nov. 1916, 2; *HS*, 11 May 1917, 8; 5 Sept. 1917, 6; 18 Sept. 1919, 1; 24 Sept. 1919, 1 (quotation); 20 Nov. 1920, 27; 22 Nov. 1920, 1; 23 Nov. 1920, 1; 29 Nov. 1920, 1; HCCM, 1918, 750–53; Monod, *Store Wars*, 128–37. Retail price inflation sparked an usual form of protest in 1920 – a decision of many white-collar workers in Hamilton and other cities to wear workingmen's overalls to work in protest over the high cost of clothing. *HS*, 20 April 1920, 1.

55. Perin and Sturino, eds., *Arrangiarsi*; Cumbo, "As the Twig Is Bent," 31. One Italian Canadian stated in an interview years later that "most immigrants were more resourceful than the English." MHSO, ITA-09826–FER.

56. Public-health nurses worried about the difficulties of the food budget on a relief allowance; see McCready, "Analysis of Weekly Relief Food Orders"; and "Relief Diets." For Alf Ready, see Roberts, ed., *Organizing Westinghouse*, 5.

57. *HS*, 8, March 1923, 6 (quotation); 10 March 1923, 6; 13 March 1923, 6 (quotation); 14 March 1923, 7. Two years earlier another worker had scoffed at men with too much "false pride" to wear used clothing. *HS*, 4 Oct. 1921, 6. One family kept only one stove running during the winter to save on coal. *IB*, May 1909, 2. For similar examples of domestic inventiveness, see *IB*, 5 Jan. 1917, 7; Archibald, "Distress, Dissent, and Alienation," 14.

58. A 1931 housing survey of 727 of Hamilton's poorest families found that nearly two out of five had gone through "forced moves" in the previous two years. Cassidy, *Unemployment and Relief*, 244.

59. License Inspector, "Report," in HCCM, 1910–30; McAree, *Cabbagetown Store*; Johnson, *Saving and Spending*, 144–92; Tebutt, *Making Ends Meet*; Benson, *Household Accounts*, 126–30, 150–59. In 1930 Hamilton's 51 second-hand stores reported doing more than $400,000 worth of business (.6 per cent of all retail sales in the city). CC, 1931, Vol. 10, 618–19. None of the 20 senior citizens who lived in the north end before World War Two and attended a community meeting in 1995, however, could remember residents of this old working-class area making use of pawnbrokers. WAHC, North End Community interview.

60. WAHC, interviews with Floyd Read, Florence Fisher.

61. *HS*, 15 Dec. 1921, 2; Doucet and Weaver, *Housing the North American City*, 343–87; *Worker*, 24 March 1936, 3 (quotation). In 1914 the *Labor News* carried a touching story of the eviction of an elderly women and her daughter on

Cannon St. E., which was described as "not often seen in Hamilton." *LN*, 8 May 1914, 1. By the 1930s evictions had become more serious; Hunter, *Which Side Are You On, Boys*, 21; *Worker*, 17 Sept. 1935, 3.

62. *HS*, 23 April 1907, 7 (quotation); 28 Oct. 1910, 4; *HT*, 9 Jan. 1914 (clipping in HPL, Times Scrapbooks); 15 Sept. 1914, 7; HPL, Canadian Patriotic Fund, Scrapbooks, Vol. 2, 83 (unidentified clipping, 3 Nov. 1915); Cassidy, *Unemployment and Relief*, 242; Monod, *Store Wars*; Cohen, *Making a New Deal*, 101–20; *VCHD*, 1930, 174–75, 1448–49; 1940, 129, 328–29, 733 (totals are mine). Across Ontario in 1930, two-thirds of retail sales were by independent stores (figures for Hamilton are not available). In Hamilton 899 shops sold food of all kinds, 248 sold apparel, and 75 sold furniture, while there were only three department stores. CC, 1931, Vol. 10, lxxx, 614–16. The challenge of the chain stores came largely after World War One. Hamilton's William Carroll opened his first grocery in 1893 and soon launched his retail grocery chain, which had 6 outlets in 1906, 19 by 1919, and 113 by 1934 (59 of them in Hamilton). By that point the Royal Commission on Price Spreads noted how the firm's sales had been in steady decline as the depression set in. There was much less chain activity outside groceries. Canada, Royal Commission on Price Spreads, *Minutes of Evidence*, 990–1011; Cheasley, *Chain Store Movement*, 57–78; *HS*, 23 Sept. 1920, 19; Monod, *Store Wars*, 124–28; Belisle, *Retail Nation*.

63. Quotations from Synge, "Self-Help and Neighbourliness," 103; WAHC, interview with Joyce Yakmalian. For discussions of these practices elsewhere, see Parr, *Gender of Breadwinners*, 77–95; Ross, "Survival Networks"; Gittins, "Marital Status, Work and Kinship"; Benson, *Household Accounts*, 104–39. Other local women's organizations scurried to take up such co-operative food ventures: the Women's Canadian Club, IODE, and Local Council of Women. *HT*, 20 April 1920, 1; *HS*, 19 April 1920, 1; 20 April 1920, 1; 23 April 1920, 1; *LL*, 7 May 1920, 4.

64. See, for example, *HS*, 3 July 1930, 2. Susan Porter Benson describes how, among US working-class housewives in the interwar period, "feelings of responsibility and tendencies towards self-blame and self-exploitation increased as material possibilities shrank." *Household Accounts*, 29.

65. Those earning $400 to $799 paid 29 per cent of their income for rent. The percentage declined as income rose. Greenway, *Housing*, 483, 485.

66. *HH*, 4 Oct. 1919, 21 (quotation); *Hamilton Manufacturer*, 1913, n.p (quotation); *HS*, 18 Nov. 1922 (quotation); *LG*, July 1928, 749; *IC*, November 1920, 1 (quotation); Doucet and Weaver, *Housing the North American City*, 119. Imperial Cotton and Dominion Sheet Metal both loaned their employees money to buy homes; McCallum, "Corporate Welfarism," 68; AO, RG 7, VII-1, Vol. 8. For an assessment of working-class home ownership that stresses conservatism and convergence with a middle-class lifestyle, see Holdsworth, "House and Home."

67. Engels, *Housing Question*, 35 (quotation); Edel, Sclar, and Luria, *Shaky Palaces*, 169 (quotation).

68. Richard Harris has explored the apparently strong desire for home ownership among Canadian working-class families in "Working Class Home Ownership."

69. Purdy, "This is Not a Company; It Is a Cause"; Delaney, "Garden Suburb"; Gilliland and Sendbuehler, "To Produce the Highest Type of Manhood and of Womanhood"; Strong-Boag, "Keeping House in God's Country," 130–35; Wright, *Moralism and the Model Home*; Wright, *Building the Dream*, 158–76; Motz and Browne, eds., *Making the American Home*; Daunton, "Rows and Tenements," 255–56; Cowan, *More Work for Mother*, 69–101, 151–91.

70. *HH*, 20 May 1910, 13 (quotations); *HS*, 2 Sept. 1911, 9. On housing patterns in a Toronto working-class suburb, see Harris, *Unplanned Suburbs*, 109–40; see also Nicolaides, "'Where the Working Man Is Welcomed.'" "Where people are crowded three, four or more in sleeping apartments with insufficient light and air," MOH Roberts worried in 1912, "can we expect other results than immodesty, a lowering of moral tone and strangulation of ideals?" OPBHR, 1912, 451.

71. *HH*, 20 May, 15 Sept. 1910; Harris, "Home in Working-Class Life"; Doucet and Weaver, *Housing the North American City*, 310–18, 329–32, 344. The economic dimension of middle-class homes worked differently from the working-class pattern of dependence on wage-earning outside the home. Among the lower middle class, shopkeeping families often lived behind or above their stores (see McAree, *Cabbagetown Store*; Taschereau, "'Behind the Store'"); some self-employed professionals such as doctors sometimes had their offices in their homes, though by the end of World War One this mixture of business and domesticity had largely died out among Canadian physicians, who had generally moved their offices outside the household (Short, "General Practice," 132–33).

72. Quoted in Doucet and Weaver, *Housing the North American City*, 198; see also Edel, Sclar, and Luria, *Shaky Palaces*, 266–76. Severe depressions could threaten these working-class homeowners with the loss of their household independence through foreclosure on mortgages, as the mayors and Board of Trade presidents of Ontario municipalities warned the provincial government in 1914. That year the Ontario executive of the Trades and Labor Congress of Canada called on the provincial government to pass emergency legislation to suspend workers' mortgage payments, but the measure introduced early in 1915 was weak. In 1921, in the depths of another slump, the local Trades and Labor Council reiterated the call for a

mortgage moratorium. *CAR*, 1914; *IB*, 26 Feb. 1915, 1; 26 March 1915, 3; *LN*, 23 Dec. 1921, 1.

73. The Eastern Europeans owned 33.3 per cent of their houses in 1926 and 35.3 in 1936; the Italians owned 46.1 per cent in 1926 and 53.9 in 1936; the Anglo-Celtic families owned 48.7 per cent in 1926 and 39.7 per cent in 1936, a decline probably explained by the spread of apartment accommodation among this group. Doucet and Weaver, *Housing the North American City*, 336.

74. For contrasting spacial arrangements in working-class housing, see Dunton, ed., *Housing the Workers*.

75. LAC, R1176-0-0-E, 2350.

76. See, for example, Zunz, *Changing Face of Inequality*.

77. On other cities, see Harris, "'Canada's All Right'"; Schultz, *East York Workers' Association*; Patrias, *Relief Strike*; Seager and Fowler, "Burnaby: The First Fifty Years"; Barman, "Neighbourhood and Community"; for the modern period, see Pratt, "Housing Tenure and Social Cleavages."

78. *IB*, 26 Feb. 1915, 3; Cohen, "Embellishing a Life of Labor"; Burnett, *Social History of Housing*, 171–76.

79. Synge, "Self-Help and Neighbourliness,"103 (quotation); Daunton, "Cities of Homes and Cities of Tenements," 295; Beckham, "American Front Porch"; Gilliland and Sendbuehler, "To Produce the Highest Type of Manhood and of Womanhood."

80. Cohen, "Embellishing a Life of Labor," 334, 343; Gilliland and Sendbuehler, "To Produce the Highest Type of Manhood and of Womanhood"; Doucet and Weaver, *Housing the North American City*, 199; Hoggart, *Uses of Literacy*.

81. Doucet and Weaver, *Housing the North American City*, 174–78.

8. The Last Resort

1. *HS*, 28 Oct. 1910, 4 (quotation); 7 Dec. 1921, 3 (quotation); *HH*, 28 Aug. 1924, 5 (quotation).

2. Nelson, "Origins of the Two-Channel Welfare State"; Gordon, "Social Insurance and Public Assistance." The distinction was recognized in 1930 when Ontario's first Department of Public Welfare was not initially assigned responsibility for relief of the unemployed. Williams, *Decades of Service*, 7.

3. *HH*, 26 April 1911, 1; 10 Sept. 1923, 1 (quotation); 28 Aug. 1924, 5; 5 July 1930, 2; *HS*, 14 May 1919, 14; CCCCP, 1911, 20 (quotation); AO, RG 7-12-0-21, File: Mothers' Allowance, "Mothers' Pension Allowance, Hamilton Enquiry," 31; Synge, "Self-Help and Neighbourliness" (quotation); Archibald, "Distress, Dissent, and Alienation," 14; MHSO, ITA-6990-ROB (quotation); *Clarion*, 27 Oct. 1936, 3; Montigny, *Foisted Upon the Government?* 63–81; Snell, *Citizen's Wage*, 60–67; Reynolds, *British Immigrant*, 136, 215–16. The Canadian Families Project, which studied a sample of the 1901 Canadian census, found a large number of relatives living with kin, an indicator of the level

of support that extended families provided; see Burke, "Transitions in Household and Family Structure," 32–33; Darroch, "Families, Fostering, and Flying the Coop."

4. Recent British immigrants seemed to be least likely to have help from friends and relatives. In 1907 the city relief officer reported that the majority of charity applicants were "English people" and hardly any European "foreigners" had applied. In 1914 the mayor insisted that 90 per cent of those needing relief were "English immigrants and foreigners." In 1921 almost half those receiving relief from the city in Hamilton were from the British Isles. *HS*, 30 May 1906, 1; 20 Nov. 1907, 4 (quotation); *HH*, 27 June 1907, 10; LAC, R244-0-4-E, Vol. 1, Unemployment, 1914: Niagara Falls, Brantford, Hamilton, Toronto, Report of E.N. Compton, 18 Feb. 1914; ODLR, 1921, 32–33, 35.

5. Anstead, "Fraternalism," 127–60; Palmer, "Mutuality."

6. The Ladies' Benevolent Society, St. George's Benevolent Society, Sons of England Benevolent Society, St. Andrew's Society, Irish Protestant Benevolent Society (the charity arm of the Orange Order), St. Vincent de Paul Society, Israelite Benevolent Society, or Salvation Army. HPL, St. George's Benevolent Society of Hamilton, Minutes, 1905–26; *HT*, 10 April 1901, 5; 16 April 1902, 5; 24 April 1902, 5; 16 April 1910, 13; 27 Aug. 1912, 5; *HH*, 24 Dec. 1909, 1; 23 Dec. 1910, 1; 19 Jan. 1911, 1; 2 Sept. 1914, 7; 15 Dec. 1923, 12; 19 July 1924, 17 (St. Vincent de Paul Society); 20 Dec. 1924; *HS*, 21 July 1920; 19 Feb. 1921, 14 (Salvation Army).

7. UCCA, Local History Files, Hamilton Presbytery, File: "Women's Association Local Histories" (1957); PCCA, 1988-4002-3-9 (Calvin Presbyterian Church, Ladies' Aid, Minutes, March 1922–December 1931); HPL, RG 3, Series A , Vol. 1, 21 Nov. 1893, 114; 19 Dec. 1893, 117; Aged Women's Home, Minutes, 11 March 1901, 666–67; 28 March 1901, 669; *HS*, 26 Jan. 1897, 7; 19 Nov. 1901, 5; *HH*, 17 Jan. 1910, 11; 2 Jan. 1914, 1; *HT*, 13 Jan. 1914, 1; Addison, "Life and Culture," 53–54; Smith "Working-Class Anglicans," 139; Draper, "People's Religion," 116; AO, F 885, Hamilton Reports. Some Anglican parishes had Dorcas societies to help the poor; Smith, "Dialectics of Faith," 200–1, 223. In 1930–31 all the local United churches created a special fund of $5,000 to be administered by clergymen and lay persons, and the Philpott Tabernacle distributed food. Cassidy, *Unemployment and Relief*, 226–27.

8. *HH*, 4 March 1911, 2; *HS*, 26 April 1918, 30; *HS*, 4 Dec. 1914, 1; Weaver, "Social Control, Martial Conformity, and Community Entanglement," 121, 124; Weaver, *Crimes, Constables, and Courts*, 137–38. Organized in 1915 as a Baptist church auxiliary, the "Maple Leaves" were "composed for the most part of Lancashire women, and altogether of Old Country women living now in Hamilton." They originally did sewing and knitting for the war effort, and then the roughly 30 young mothers cut their links with

the church, to become a branch of the WCTU. They then formed the "Helping Hand Club," to "assist, inconspicuously, all those with whom it came in touch who were in financial or other distress." Their motto was "Helping Without Hurting." *HH*, 4 Jan. 1924. The IODE took an untypical interest in helping the poor late in the grim winter of 1907–8 and then, more characteristically, set up a Visiting and Relief Committee to help soldiers' wives during World War One; the body continued to operate through the 1920s and 1930s. IODEA, Municipal Chapter, Minutes, 15 Feb., 28 Feb. 1908; HPL, Archives File, IODE, Paardeburg Chapter, Annual Reports, 1915–40.

9. *HS*, 29 Oct. 1920, 7; *Annual Reports of the Social Agencies*, 1929, 52–55, 60–61, 69; 1930, 50–55, 59–61; HBEM, 1922–32; Canadian Welfare Council, *Study of the Community Fund*, 76–84.

10. Splane, *Social Welfare in Ontario*, 79–118; "Annual Report of Relief Officer," in HCCM, 1904, 35–36. In the early 1890s applicants for relief had to apply directly to the mayor. Canada, Royal Commission on the Liquor Traffic, *Minutes of Evidence*, Vol. 4, Part 1: *Province of Ontario*, 186.

11. HPL, St. George's Benevolent Society of Hamilton, Minutes, 1905–26; *HH*, 20 Dec. 1909, 1. The Society spent only $183 in 1910, but nearly $1,300 in 1913 and over $1,400 in 1924.

12. Splane, *Social Welfare in Ontario*, 79–118; Varty, "City and the Ladies." Unwed mothers could find shelter with the Home for the Friendless and Infants Home or the Salvation Army's Rescue Home. *HS*, 29 May 1908, 12; 11 Oct. 1908; 12 Oct. 1908 (clippings in HPL Scrapbook). Abandoned wives used the Infants' Home as well. OA, RG 7-12-0-21, File: Mothers' Allowance, "Mothers' Pension Allowance, Hamilton Enquiry," 11. The indigent poor could also get free treatment from either of the city's two hospitals.

13. RG 7-12-0-21, File: Mothers' Allowance, "Mothers' Pension Allowance, Hamilton Enquiry," 16. See also *HS*, 31 March 1900, 8; *HH*, 28 Aug. 1924, 3.

14. AO, RG 7-12-0-21, File: Mothers' Allowance, "Mothers' Pension Allowance, Hamilton Enquiry," 30.

15. The orphanages were the Boys' Home, Girls' Home, St. Mary's Orphan Asylum (run by the Sisters of St. Joseph), Infant Home, and Hamilton Orphan Asylum. The last of these had been combined with the Aged Women's Home since it was founded by the Ladies' Benevolent Society, but at the turn of the century the institution stopped taking in orphans. By this point the Salvation Army had opened its Rescue Home. OICHR, 1890–1930; HPL, Hamilton Orphan Asylum, Aged Women's Home, and Ladies' Benevolent Society, Minutes, 1890–1920; and *Annual Report*, 1891–1926; *HS*, 7 May 1891, 8; 7 May 1896, 3; 6 May 1897, 7; 5 May 1898, 5; 4 May 1899, 5; 30 Oct. 1906, 9; 2 Jan. 1909, 11; *HH*, 11 Feb. 1910, 2; 25 Nov. 1919, 7; 25 Jan.

1921 (clipping in HPL Scrapbook); 19 May 1923, 15; OA, RG 7-12-0-21, File: Mothers' Allowance, "Mothers' Pension Allowance, Hamilton Enquiry," 17, 25–29; Parr, *Labouring Children*; Bradbury, "Fragmented Family"; Struthers, *Limits of Affluence*, 23. In Hamilton all charitable institutions tried to make residents or their families contribute to board – roughly $4 a month at the turn of the century and the same amount per week by the 1920s. In 1896 the families' contributions to the Girls' Home were considerably larger than the government grant, as they still were 40 years later in sustaining the St. Mary's Orphan Asylum. HPL, RG 3, Series A, Vol. 2, 19 Oct. 1903, 85; 23 Nov. 1903, 86; 6 Aug. 1909, 128; *HS*, 29 June 1922, 4.

16. The Home kept on a handful of orphans until they grew up and doled out small quantities of outdoor relief to the elderly until 1917. Some had been receiving the Society's help for years, and a handful were eventually admitted to the Home.

17. OICHR, 1890–1930; HPL, Aged Women's Home, Minutes, 30 Nov. 1891, 261; Aged Women's Home, *Annual Report*, 1925–26, 8; *HS*, 19 Sept. 1894, 8; 24 Nov. 1920, 15; 29 June 1922, 4; HPL, Aged Women's Home, *Annual Report*, 1891–26; Cummings, "Care of the Destitute Poor," 47; Montigny, *Foisted upon the Government?* 30–31, 82–107; Snell, "Filial Responsibility Laws"; Synge, "Work and Family Support Patterns."

18. In 1900 the five orphanages housed 237 boys and 298 girls, and in 1923 still only 318 boys and 376 girls. OICHR, 1900, 1923; Canadian Welfare Council, *Study of the Community Fund*, 50–56, 71. In 1937 only 258 children remained in institutional care in Hamilton, half of them in St. Mary's Orphanage.

19. HPL, Aged Women's Home, *Annual Report*, 1924–25, 8; 1925–26, 8. In 1929 the city added a wing to its Home for the Aged and Infirm able to accommodate 100 more residents, but this was largely a response to the provincial government's decision to transfer elderly indigents from the local psychiatric hospital; *HS*, 2 April 1929 (clipping in HPL Scrapbook).

20. In 1912 and 1913 outdoor relief (groceries, fuel, and clothing) comprised only 15 per cent of the city's total relief department outlay. The proportion rose to about one-quarter the next year, but returned to roughly pre-war levels during and immediately following World War One. See Table 30.

21. HPL, RG 10, Series A, 1905–28; *HH*, 23 March 1910, 1; 23 April 1910, 1; 6 Feb. 1911, 12; 8 Jan. 1914, 1; 21 Oct. 1914, 1; *HT*, 29 Aug. 1912, 12; *HS*, 19 Feb. 1921, 14 (quotation); 27 Jan. 1930, 7.

22. Mariana Valverde coined the useful phrase "mixed social economy" for this private-state collaboration. Valverde, "Mixed Social Economy"; Marks, "Indigent Committees and Ladies Benevolent Societies"; Maurutto, *Governing*

Charities; Copp, *Anatomy of Poverty*, 106–27; Piva, *Condition of the Working Class*, 73–86.

23. Nelson, "Origins of the Two-Channel Welfare State," develops this perspective.

24. Piva, "Workmen's Compensation Movement"; Campbell, "'Balance Wheel of the Industrial System'"; Nelson, "Origins of the Two-Channel Welfare State," 133–37; Morton, "Resisting the Pension Evil"; "Morton, *When Your Number's Up*, 253–75; Morton and Wright, *Winning the Second Battle*.

25. On the important distinction between social-insurance and public-assistance programs, see Gordon, "Social Insurance and Public Assistance."

26. HPL, Canadian Patriotic Fund, Hamilton and Wentworth Branch, "Report of the Relief Committee, October 1914 to January 1918" (typescript); and Scrapbooks; Canadian Patriotic Fund, Hamilton and Wentworth Branch, *Five Years of Service*; Morton, *Fight or Pay*; Christie, *Engendering the State*, 46–93; Rutherdale, *Hometown Horizons*, 88–118.

27. HPL, Canadian Patriotic Fund, Hamilton and Wentworth Branch, Scrapbooks, Vol. 2, 27 Jan. 1915 (quotation); 18 Oct. 1915 (quotation).

28. *HT*, 27 Jan. 1915, 10; HPL, Canadian Patriotic Fund, Hamilton and Wentworth Branch, Scrapbooks, and "Report of the Relief Committee"; Soldiers' Aid Commission, Minutes; Canadian Patriotic Fund, Hamilton and Wentworth Branch, *Five Years of Service*.

29. AO, RG 7-12-0-21, File: Mothers' Allowance, "Mothers' Pension Allowance, Hamilton Enquiry."

30. Little, "*No Car, No Radio, No Liquor Permit*"; Strong-Boag, "'Wages for Housework'"; Davies, "'Services Rendered'"; OMACR, 1920–21, 64; *HS*, 4 Oct. 1920, 7 (quotation).

31. OMACR, 1920–21, 26, 29; Little, "*No Car, No Radio, No Liquor Permit*"; Struthers, *Limits of Affluence*, 19–49, 99; Ursel, *Private Lives, Public Policy*, 341; CC, 1931, Vol. 5, 1282.

32. Orloff, *Politics of Pensions*, 14.

33. Canada, House of Commons, Special Committee on Old Age Pensions, *Proceedings* (1912); Canada, House of Commons, *Journals*, 61 (1924), Appendix 4; Bryden, *Old Age Pensions*, 61–102; Struthers, *Limits of Affluence*, 50–76; Williams, *Decades of Service*, 8–9; Orloff, *Politics of Pensions*, 14, 240–68; "Aged Women's Home," *Annual Reports of the Social Agencies*, 1929, 39; Ontario, Minister of Public Welfare, *Report*, 1931–40. Ontario's various social-welfare programs were brought together in a new Department of Public Welfare in 1930. Williams, *Decades of Service*.

34. *LG*, December 1900, 146; February 1901, 271; September 1904, 261. In 1897 the city's relief office helped 13,000 people, in 1900 nearly 5,600, in 1903 only 4,000, but more than 13,000 again in 1909. "Annual Report of Relief Officer," in HCCM, 1904, 35–36; 1909, 31.

35. On the swamping of established social-welfare agencies during economic slumps, see, for example, *Annual Reports of the Social Agencies*, 1930.

36. The numbers on relief dropped slowly to 7,400 families in 1934, 6,600 in 1935, 4,800 in 1936, and 4,000 in 1937 as relief administration tightened and the local economy improved somewhat in the mid-1930s. But the number had returned to 4,500 families in 1939. *LG*, December 1900, 146; February 1901, 271; February 1914; September 1914, 351; *HH*, 22 Jan. 1914, 1; 16 April 1914, 1, 4; 11 Sept. 1914, 1; 14 Sept. 1914, 1; *HT*, 14 Jan. 1914, 1; LAC, R224-0-4-E, Vol. 1, Unemployment 1914, File: Hamilton, 1914–16; HCCM, 1913, 893; 1914, 28, 817; 1915, 23, 79; 1921, 19–23, 35, 69–71, 918–19, 923–24, 1100, 1141; 1922, 82–88, 150–55, 230–33, 282–83, 320–22, 344–45, 584; 1923, 30, 137, 227; 1924, 17, 18, 45, 60, 962, 965; HPL, HCC, Board of Directors, Minutes, 22 Dec. 1921, 126; 3 Jan. 1922, 133; Cassidy, *Unemployment and Relief*, 45, 50, 63–64, 166, 234; Weaver, *Hamilton*, 135; Archibald, "Distress, Dissent, and Alienation," 10; McKinnon, "Relief Not Insurance"; Struthers, *No Fault of Their Own*.

37. Struthers, *No Fault of Their Own*; Pal, *State, Class, and Bureaucracy*; Finkel, *Business and Social Reform*; Cuneo, "State, Class and Reserve Labour."

38. HPL, Hamilton Orphan Asylum, Aged Women's Home, and Ladies' Benevolent Society, *Annual Report*, 1891–92, 4 (quotation); St. George's Benevolent Society, Minutes, 14 Jan. 1914, 68; 24 Dec. 1920, 160; *HS*, 29 June 1922 (clipping in HPL Scrapbook); CPF, Scrapbooks, Vol. 1, 20 March, 5, 30 June, 10 Aug., 29 Dec. 1916; OWCBR, 1922, 67; Morton, "Resisting the Pension Evil," 211; Little, "Regulation of Ontario's Single Mothers," 21–25; Storey, "Workers, Unions, and Steel," 167 (quotation).

39. HPL, Canadian Patriotic Fund, Hamilton and Wentworth Branch, Scrapbook, Vol. 1, 20 March 1916 (quotation); "Report of Relief Committee" (quotation); Morton, *Fight or Pay*, 99–103.

40. Little, "*No Car, No Radio, No Liquor Permit*," 96–100; Struthers, *Limits of Affluence*, 62–75.

41. Struthers, *Limits of Affluence*, 34–38; Little, "*No Car, No Radio, No Liquor Permit*," 51–106; *Worker*, 24 March 1936, 3.

42. *HS*, 15 Nov. 1921, 12; 23 Nov. 1921, 1; 28 Nov. 1921, 15; 24 Jan. 1922, 15; 2 Feb. 1922, 1; *Worker*, 3 Dec. 1935, 2. In the early 1920s and after 1932 the federal government agreed to co-fund only direct relief, not relief work projects. The Bennett government had a relief works program in place from 1930 to 1931. Struthers, *No Fault of Their Own*.

43. Katz, *In the Shadow of the Poorhouse*, 58–84; Wills, *Marriage of Convenience* 33–55; Copp, *Anatomy of Poverty*, 114–20.

44. HPL, Aged Women's Home, Minutes, 6 Oct. 1891, 249; 26 Oct. 1891, 253–54; 30 Nov. 1891, 258–59; 13 June 1892, 278; Aged Women's Home, *Report*, 1891–92, 5; 1892–93, 5; *HS*, 26 Oct. 1891, 1; 29 Oct. 1891, 8; 30 Oct. 1891, 1; 5 Nov. 1891, 1; 2 Dec. 1891, 8; 7 Dec. 1891, 1; 5 Sept. 1893, 5. Discussions

of co-ordination continued through 1895 under the auspices of the Local Council of Women. Lyle, *Hamilton Local Council of Women*, 12.

45. *HH*, 13 Dec. 1913, 1; 15 Sept. 1914, 5; 29 Sept. 1914, 8; 5 Oct. 1914, 1; 8 Oct. 1914, 4; 13 Oct. 1914, 2; 14 Oct. 1914, 9; 20 Oct. 1914, 1; 3 May 1915, 3; *HT*, 14 Sept. 1914, 1; 15 Sept. 1914, 7; 23 Oct. 1914; 21 Nov. 1914; 16 Dec. 1914 (clippings in HPL Times Scrapbook); 17 Sept. 1915, 1; *LG*, November 1914, 551–52; December, 658; April 1915, 1159; MHSO, ITA-0982-PAS.

46. *HS*, 30 Sept. 1921, 19; 12 Nov. 1921, 31; 17 Nov. 1921, 16; 16 Dec. 1921, 23; 15 Dec. 1921, 2; 21 March 1922, 14; HCCM, 1921, 35, 645, 1012, 1145; 1922, 282, 283.

47. HPL, HCC, Board of Directors, Minutes, 28 June 1921, 35; 23 Aug. 1921, 60; 6 Sept. 1921, 66; 16 Dec. 1921, 1–4; 20 Dec. 1921, 115. The same concern surfaced again a decade later. HCC, *Annual Report*, 1930–31, 19.

48. In January 1920 a United Community Service League was constituted to work with the city's relief officer. Lyle, *Hamilton Local Council of Women*, 42–43; HPL, HCC, Board of Directors, Minutes, 12 April 1921, 184; 31 May 1921, 27; 14 Feb. 1922, 160; 6 March 1923, 192; 16 May 1923, 23; Committee Re Federation of Charities, Minutes, 13, 27 March, 8, 22 April, 8 May 1922, *Annual Report*, 1925–26, 23; 1926–27, 21–22; *HS*, 12 Jan. 1924, 9; 1 April 1924, 14; 8 Nov. 1924, 5; 10 Jan. 1925, 2; 31 March 1925, 11; 28 April 1926 (clipping in HPL Scrapbook); 31 March 1926, 20; 16 Oct. 1926, 5. On the general growth of community chests in Canada, see Tillotson, *Contributing Citizens*.

49. HPL, HCC, *Annual Report*, 1927–28, 21; 1928–29, 23, 24; 1929–30, 30; 1930–31, 22, 24; 1931–32, 20–22; *HS*, 6 May 1926; 30 March, 1927; 9 Aug. 1927 (clippings in HPL Scrapbook); 5 May 1932, 15 (on the Red Cross's co-ordination of used clothing distribution); *SW*, August 1927, 498; September 1927, 521; November 1927, 43; *Annual Reports of the Social Agencies*, 1929, 5–12; 1930, 5–12; Hamilton Community Chest, *Twenty-Five Years*; Canadian Welfare Council, *Study of the Community Fund*, 5–6 (quotation). In 1934 a social worker in Hamilton's Public Welfare Department deplored the great divide between the private charities and public relief, and the "decided lowering of standards in the family field in the last five years." Canadian Conference on Social Work, *Proceedings*, 1934, 141. The Canadian Welfare Council study echoed the frustrations that social workers were experiencing across the country in the 1930s. Struthers, "Profession in Crisis."

50. Hamilton's poor record of co-ordination and co-operation among charities contrasts with Toronto's experience, and suggests that the larger metropolitan experiences may not have been typical. Wills, *Marriage of Experience*.

51. Suspicions of charity abusers were widespread, and neighbours were often willing to snitch on people they thought

did not deserve support. In 1922 Controller Tom Jutten explained that he was inundated with anonymous letters about alleged cheaters on relief. *HS*, 4 Feb. 1922, 1.

52. *HS*, 26 Oct. 1921, 1. The city relief office also made clear that it would prosecute anyone who misrepresented their financial situation to get relief; see *HS*, 2 Nov. 1921, 14, 18.

53. *HS*, 29 June 1922, 3; *HT*, 15 Sept. 1914, 5.

54. See, for example, *HH*, 19 July 1924, for the St. Vincent de Paul Society. For an insightful discussion of this tension in one charitable society, see Simmons, "'Helping the Poorer Sisters.'"

55. In one such Society deliberation in 1899 it was decided "to give the Crooks family $1 for May – and Mrs Parker (on account of receiving considerable work) was not to receive an allowance this month unless absolutely necessary in which case $1 might be given." HPL, Aged Women's Home, Minutes, 29 May 1899, 573. When the numbers it dealt with rose dramatically, the St. George's Benevolent Society also introduced "a more thorough system of investigation." HPL, St. George's Benevolent Society, Minutes, 18 Jan. 1909, 24; 14 Jan. 1914, 66.

56. For example, the Ladies' Aid of Calvin Presbyterian Church, whose Visiting Committee made a handful of calls on the sick and needy each month. PCCA, 1988-4002-3-9; see also UCA, Local History Files, Hamilton Presbytery, File: Women's Association Local Histories (1957).

57. Father Coty, "Personal Service," CCCCP, 1911, 30.

58. UCA, Methodist Church (Canada), Toronto Conference, Deaconess Board of Management, 78.101C, Box 4, Toronto Deaconess Home and Training School of the Methodist Church, *Annual Reports*, 1900–20.

59. HCCM, 1914, 873; 1918, 210; *HS*, 19 Dec. 1911, 1; *HT*, 14 Jan. 1914, 1; *HH*, 27 Jan. 1914, 4. One of McMenemy's assistants was his daughter Hazel.

60. The Soldiers' Aid Commission committee included the wives of a Steel Company vice-president and a prominent corporate lawyer. *HH*, 9 Oct. 1914, 2; HPL, CPF, Scrapbooks, Vol. 1, "Visitors Report Form"; Vol. 2, 26, 31 Aug., 3 Oct. 1915; CFP, *Five Years of Service*, 21; Morton, *Fight or Pay*, 121–28; HPL, Soldiers' Aid Commission, Minutes, 14 Nov., 5, 12 Dec. 1917; 13 Feb., 13, 15 March, 10 April, 1, 8 May, 30 June, 3 July, 3 Sept., 2 Oct., 13 Nov. 1918; February, 12 March, April, 31 Dec. 1919; 31 Dec. 1920. One of the "visitors" had ten years' experience as a Poor Law investigator in England; the armed forces also had a paid "investigator" in this period; the visitors continued their work into 1921; HPL, Soldiers' Aid Commission, Minutes, 31 Dec. 1918, 13 March 1918, March 1921.

61. RG 7-12-0-21, File: Mothers' Allowance, "Mothers' Pension Allowance, Hamilton Enquiry," 3, 7, 9.

62. RG 7-12-0-21, File: Mothers' Allowance, "Mothers' Pension Allowance, Hamilton Enquiry," 15; *LN*, 9 Oct. 1914.

63. The local board in Hamilton appointed by the Farmer-Labour government under the new provincial mothers' allowance legislation included one strong working-class woman, the colourful ILP activist Janet Inman, but she was overwhelmed by the two businessmen, two upper-class women, and one labour man on the same board. AO, RG 7-12-0-21, File: Mothers' Allowance, "Mothers' Pension Allowance, Hamilton Enquiry," 19, 69, 73–74; *ND*, 7 Oct. 1920, 1.

64. HCCM, 1918, 210; 1919, 598, 602; 1920, 1118; 1921, 1012, 1145; 1922, 444; OMACR, 1920–21, 15–31; Struthers, *Limits of Affluence*, 33, 70–73. The city's Relief Department had five full-time staff in 1928–29, but expanded quickly to 31 by the summer of 1931. Cassidy, *Unemployment and Relief*, 172.

65. Little, "*No Car, No Radio, No Liquor Permit*," 42–50; Struthers, *Limits of Affluence*, 19–49; Kappelle, "City of Hamilton Set-Up"; Kappelle, "'Administrative Set-Up."

66. HCC, *Annual Report*, 1925–26, 23; 1926–27, 21; 1927–28, 21; 1928–29, 23; 1929–30, 30; 1930–31, 22; 1931–32, 20; Hardie, "Inter-Relation"; Chandler, "Agency Autonomy" (quotation at 133); *Annual Reports of the Social Agencies*, 1930, 70 (quotation). The interwar decades saw the birth of social work as a profession in Canada, including the creation of the Canadian Association of Social Workers in 1926. Wills, *Marriage of Convenience*. In 1937 the Canadian Welfare Council found four out of six caseworkers at the Family Service Bureau, one at the Samaritan Club, and eight at the Children's Aid Society with at least some · social-work training. Canadian Welfare Council, *Study of the Community Fund*.

67. *HS*, 31 March 1926, 20 (quotations). A few years later, recognizing the inadequacy of relief allowances for food, Red Cross Visiting Housekeepers saw their role as instructing women "to spend most wisely the amounts received for food," believing that "if the mothers could buy and cook to advantage ... an adequate diet could be obtained from the most meagre allowance." McCready, "Relief Diets," 54, 57.

68. HPL, Hamilton Orphan Asylum, Aged Women's Home, and Ladies' Benevolent Society, *Annual Report*, 1892–93, 5 (quotation); *HS*, 31 March 1925, 11 (quotation); 30 March 1927, 17 (quotation); HPL, St. George's Benevolent Society, Minutebook, 18 Jan. 1909, 30 (quotation).

69. HPL, HCC, *Annual Report*, 1929–30, 30 (quotation). The provincial officer also charged that Lawrence's political ambitions led him to provide too much help to "foreigners." AO, RG 29-135-1-6, "Report of the Unemployment Situation."

70. Kappelle, "City of Hamilton Set-Up" (quotation at 49); Kappelle, "Administrative Set-Up" (quotations at 194, 195); Struthers, *Limits of Affluence*, 89; Weaver, *Hamilton*, 135; *Worker*, 8 June 1936, 3 (quotation). *HS*, 17 Dec. 1932, 16,

describes the previous system of centralized inquisition of relief applicants.

71. Struthers, *Limits of Affluence*, 33; AO, RG 29-135-1-6, "Report of the Unemployment Situation"; Canadian Welfare Council, *Study of the Community Fund*. This was a persistent concern of the emerging social work profession; see Struthers, "'Lord Give Us Men'"; Struthers, "Profession in Crisis."

72. HPL, Hamilton Orphan Asylum, Aged Women's Home, and Ladies' Benevolent Society, *Annual Report*, 1891–92, 5 (quotation). The first circular issued after the founding meeting of the conference was explicit in connecting poverty and criminality through studying "the most efficient as well as the most economic management of the criminal, defective, delinquent and dependent classes" and discussing "the causes of increase and the means for the prevention and diminution of crime, pauperism and insanity among us." CCCCP, 1899, 25.

73. In 1897 the Salvation Army began making single men in their hotel saw wood in return for accommodation. Each winter at the turn of the century, the city's relief officer used his "labour bureau" to assign unemployed men to work projects around the city. *HS*, 8 Oct. 1897, 8; 5 May 1898, 1; 1 March 1901, 10; HCCM, 1921, 20; 1922, 82; by the summer of 1915 city relief was denied to unemployed young men "if in a position to wear a uniform." *HT*, 13 July 1915, 1.

74. *HS*, 17 Oct. 1891, 5; HPL, RG 3, Series A, Vol. 1, 9 Aug. 1894, 156; 28 Aug. 1895, 218; 17 Oct. 1895, 224; MPSS, 44; *HH*, 16 March 1912, 1; Synge, "Work and Family Support Patterns," 140–41; *HS*, 28 May 1929, 5; *Worker*, 24 Oct. 1936, 3; Archibald, "Distress, Dissent, and Alienation," 8, 11, 17; Snell, *Citizen's Wage*, 36–72; Struthers, *Limits of Affluence*, 50–59; Little, "Regulation of Ontario Single Mothers," 17. Mary McKinnon concludes that in Canada relief recipients "were subjected to far more restrictions and humiliations than were the unemployed in Britain." McKinnon, "Relief Not Insurance," 53.

75. *Annual Reports of Social Agencies*, 1929, 41 (quotation); Canadian Welfare Council, *Study of the Community Fund*, 75; *HS*, 12 Jan. 1924, 9 (quotation), 31 March 1926, 20 (quotation).

76. AO, RG 7-12-0-21, File: Mothers' Allowance, "Mothers' Pension Allowance, Hamilton Enquiry," 5 (quotation); HPL, CPF, "Report of Relief Committee," 7; CPF, *Five Years of Service*, 32–33 (quotations). In testimony before a special enquiry on mothers' pensions in 1919, Lovering boasted that he had also intervened to prevent mothers from sending their 14-year-old children out to work rather than keeping them in school. AO, RG 7-12-0-21, File: Mothers' Allowance, "Mothers' Pension Allowance, Hamilton Enquiry," 4.

77. OMACR, 1920–34; Struthers, *Limits of Affluence*, 35–37.

78. The act of cutting mothers off for bad conduct seems to have been relatively rare. In 1921–22 only 8 women across Ontario lost their allowances for "unsatisfactory home conditions," 26 for "immorality," and 14 for "unsatisfactory care of children." OMACR, 1920–21, 19; 1921–22, 10, 22–31; 1926–27, 17–23. Little, "*No Car, No Radio, No Liquor Permit*," 51–106.

79. *HH*, 20 Dec. 1930.

80. *HS*, 31 March 1926, 20.

81. Pettit, "Integration of Case Work and Group Work," 139; Heron et al., *All That Our Hands Have Done*, 137–38. For other less mainstream social-work practice, see Wills, *Marriage of Convenience*, 30; Moffatt, *Poetics of Social Work*, 46–68.

82. AO, RG 29-135-1-6, "Report of the Employment Situation"; MHSO, ITA-0982-PAS; WAHC, interview with Fred Purser.

83. *HS*, 2 Feb. 1897, 8.

84. The Ladies' Benevolent Society dispensed an average of only $2.50 a week (the equivalent of a skilled worker's daily wage) to each of nearly 500 families through the whole of 1896–97; the St. George's Benevolent Society gave out an average of only $10 in 1908, while the same year the city's relief appropriations averaged well less than $2 per family (although they were tailored to specific family needs, without a specific upper limit). HPL, Ladies' Benevolent Society, *Annual Report*, 1896–97, 4; St. George's Benevolent Society, Minutes, 18 Jan. 1909, 18, 24; HCC, Minutes, 16 Dec. 1921, 115; HCCM, 1909, 31; MPSS, 40.

85. *HS*, 12 March 1923; Cassidy, *Unemployment and Relief*, 146–47; Archibald, "Distress, Dissent, and Alienation," 6.

86. HPL, CPF, Hamilton and Wentworth Branch, Scrapbooks, Vol. 1, 9 March 1917; Vol. 2, 17 Sept., 18 Oct. 1915, 76; Lovering, "How Much Should Be Given by the Fund"; *HH*, 14 Oct. 1914, 11; Morton, *Fight or Pay*, 96. In April 1917 the maximum was raised from $20 to $45, and late in 1918 to $50. Morton, *Fight or Pay*, 184.

87. Piva, "Workmen's Compensation Movement"; Roberts, "Studies in the Toronto Labour Movement"; Campbell, "'Balance Wheel of the Industrial System'"; Reasons, *Assault on the Worker*, 160–200; Forestall, "Gendered Terrains," ch. 4.

88. OWCBR, 1914, 1–2, 36–39; 1917, 60–63; 1920, 52–56; 1921, 59–64; Dymond, *Laws of Ontario*, 101–6; Storey, "From Invisibility to Equality?" 83.

89. OWCBR, 1914, 34–39; 1917, 60–63; 1920, 52–56; 1921, 50–64; Forestall, "Gendered Terrains." Other dependants – particularly elderly mothers and fathers – could also be eligible if they could convince the board of their need.

90. OMACR, 1920–30 (calculations are mine); Little, "*No Car, No Radio, No Liquor Permit*," 32–50; Struthers, *Limits of Affluence*, 33–38.

91. OMACR, 1920–21, 10–11, 21, 28; 1921–22, 22–33; 1922–23, 16–22; 1923–24, 14–19; 1924–25, 11–15; *LG*, May 1922, 458; Struther, *Limits of Affluence*, 48–49; Little, "Regulation of Ontario Single Mothers."

92. Ontario, Minister of Public Welfare, *Report*, 1931–35. Calculations are mine.

93. *HT*, 16 April 1914, 1; LAC, R224-0-4-E, Vol. 1, Hamilton, Ontario, 1914–16, 15 Oct. 1915; Canadian Welfare Council, *Study of the Community Fund*, 84–86; MHSO, ITA-09826-FER; Archibald, "Distress, Dissent, and Alienation," 14.

94. *HS*, 9 Dec. 1907, 6; 16 April 1910, 7; 21 Sept. 1912, 7; 14 Oct. 1921, 20; *HH*, 26 March 1914, 1; *HT*, 14 Jan. 1914, 1; MPSS, 49; LAC, R224-0-4-E, Vol. 1 (Unemployment 1914–16), Hamilton; HPL, RG 10, Series A, 1905–28; Weaver, "Social Control, Martial Conformity, and Community Entanglement," 123–24; *HT*, 14 Jan. 1914, 1; *HH*, 9 March 1914, 1; *LN*, 24 April 1914, 1; HCCM, 1922, 584; 1923, 227; 1930, 89; ODLR, 1931, 14–15; 1932, 20–21; McKinnon, "Relief Not Insurance," 52; Cassidy, *Unemployment and Relief*, 98, 105, 157, 203–11, 223; Archibald, "Distress, Dissent, and Alienation," 6; MacDowell, "Relief Camp Workers"; MacDowell, "Canada's 'Gulag'"; Roberts, *Whence They Came*. Hamilton had a one-year residency rule for eligibility for relief. In 1921 non-resident single men were sent to the Grand Army of United Veterans hostel for three nights and then "told to move on." In January 1931 only 107 out of 4,700 relief recipients were single. By the end of that year 355 had been sent north to highway projects. HPL, HCC, Minutes, 16 Dec. 1921, 115; Cassidy, *Unemployment and Relief*, 174, 209; AO, RG 7-12-0-153, "Placement on Northern Development Highway Projects by Districts," 1 Dec. 1931. The city subsidized some of the hostels for single men; AO, RG 29-135-1-6, "Report of the Unemployed Situation."

95. MPSS, 49; Cassidy, *Unemployment and Relief*, 93, 211–12; Pierson, "Gender and the Unemployment Insurance Debates"; Sebire, *Woman's Place*, 97–100; Archibald, "Distress, Dissent, and Alienation," 6. In 1912 49 women were sheltered at the central police station (compared to more than 1,000 men).

96. Many working-class families even spurned the Canadian Patriotic Fund. Morton, *Fight or Pay*, 95.

97. They particularly liked to enumerate how many Christmas baskets devious families might get but for the sharing of information among agencies. See, for example, *HS*, 12 Jan. 1924, 9; 1 April 1924, 13; 10 Jan. 1925, 2; 30 March 1927, 17.

98. *HS*, 30 March 1926, 20; *Annual Reports of Social Agencies*, 1929, 12; 1930, 12.

99. HYWCAA, Scrapbooks, 1890–1909, undated clipping (c.1914); *HT*, 6 Jan. 1914, 1; 8 Jan. 1914, 1; *HH*, 6 Jan. 1914, 4; 30 Oct. 1914, 17; *LN*, 16 Jan. 1914; 24 April 1914; 27 Nov. 1914, 1; *LG*, May 1914, 1268.

100. *LN*, 16 Jan. 1914; 27 Nov. 1914, 1; *HT*, 6, Jan. 1914, 1; 8 Jan. 1914, 5; 9 Jan. 1914, 4; 13 Jan. 1914, 10; 14 Jan. 1914, 1; 21 Jan. 1914, 1; 22 Jan. 1914, 1; 26 Jan. 1914, 1; 14 April 1914, 1; 15 April 1914, 1; *HH*, 15 April 1914, 4; 16 April 1914, 4; 30 Oct. 1914, 17; 27 Feb. 1922; 3 March 1922; *HS*, 9 Dec. 1907, 6; 13 Jan. 1914, 11; 3 March 1914, 14; 16 April 1914, 11; 18 April 1914, 15; 20 April 1914, 1; 7 Jan. 1921, 1; 5 Feb. 1921, 1; 15 April 1921, 5; 31 March 1925, 11; *LG*, November 1924, 915; AO, RG 3, Series 8, Box 168, File: "Unemployment Relief, From Aug.1, 1933 #1," 1933, Argue Martin to G.S. Henry, 23 Oct. 1933; Heron et al., *All That Our Hands Have Done*, 139–40.

101. Cohen and Hanagan, "Politics of Gender."

9. Hold the Fort

1. *CM*, 23 Sept. 1920, 293 (quotation).

2. Phillips Thompson, a leading Canadian radical writer of the 1880s, had penned a version of this song in his *Labor Reform Songster*. A different version appeared among British dock workers and later in the songbook of the Industrial Workers of the World.

3. *Hamilton: The Birmingham of Canada*.

4. Palmer, *Culture in Conflict*, 75–66, 82–83, 189; Kealey, "Work Control, the Labour Process, and Nineteenth-Century Canadian Printers." The decentralized authority on the shop floor was evident as late as 1910, when a cigar-maker at Tuckett's was still allowed to hire a boy to work as his helper. Stove-mounters also still hired their own helpers. *HS*, 3 April 1907, 3; 7 Feb. 1910, 12.

5. Sadlier, "Problem of the Molder" (quotation); Benjamin Brooks, "Molders," reprinted from *Scribner's* in *IMJ*, November 1906, 801–8; Stecker, "Founders, the Molders, and the Molding Machine"; *CF*, May 1928, 39.

6. Willetts, *Workers of the Nation*, Vol. 2, 261–69, 309–14; Lazonick, "Industrial Relations and Technical Change"; Heron, *Working in Steel*, 34–42; Kealey, "Work Control."

7. RCRLCR, 826 (see also Bertram, "Development of the Machine Tool Industry," for similar comments on the skills of John Bertram, an artisanal entrepreneur in nearby Dundas); Rolt, *Tools for the Job*, 122–91; Jeffreys, *Story of the Engineers*, 9–14. These craftworkers were known as engineers in Britain and machinists in North America.

8. RCRCLR, 827–28; Samuel, "Workshop of the World."

9. RCRCLR, 881 (quotation); Lozier, "Variable Motor Speeds and Their Relation to New Shop Methods,"189 (quotation); *HH*, 23 March 1912, 19 (quotation); Roberts, "Toronto Metal Workers," 51–57; Montgomery, *Fall of the House of Labor*, 180–203.

10. See, for example, the cover photograph on Palmer, *Culture in Conflict*, showing the children of the Tuckett Tobacco Company, as well as several photos in the McMaster University Labour Studies Collection. When 30 boys in the riveting shop of Hamilton Bridge, "not many years in their teens," began a strike for higher wages in March 1900, the company's owner, J.S. Hendrie, explained their role in the firm's production. "They received from 80 cents to $1 a day for work that required no skill," he told a reporter, "but the trouble was they wanted men's wages before they were men." *HS*, 30 March 1900, 8.

11. Helm, *In the Shadow of the Giants*; Heron et al., *All That Our Hands Have Done*, 26.

12. *HS*, 10 Feb. 1896, 8; 15 July 1926, 8 (quotation); 31 Dec. 1958, 21; *CMR*, February 1896, 39; *CE*, January 1896, 248–49; *Stelco Flashes*, June 1950, 6; Montgomery, *Fall of the House of Labor*, 58–81.

13. See, for example, *LG*, November 1906, 484; May 1910, 1231; June 1910, 1372; September 190, 305; October 1912, 24; *HS*, 14 April 1910, 12; *HT*, 30 May 1910, 1.

14. Heron, "Factory Workers," 231–45.

15. *HS*, 20 April 1910, 1; *HH*, 15 April 1910, 12. Bryan Palmer was, I think, mistaken to see this behaviour as "unskilled labour's cultivation of traditional craft control mechanisms" (*Culture in Conflict*, 208); it is much more likely a residue of 19th-century labouring practices.

16. Frey and Commons, "Conciliation in the Stove Industry," 177. On the moulders' workplace customs, see Kealey, "'Honest Workingman' and Workers' Control," 40–43.

17. Palmer, *Culture in Conflict*, 125–98; White, "Work, Protest, and Community Power." Hamilton unionists had been celebrating a local version of Labour Day since 1883; Heron and Penfold, *Workers' Festival*, 33.

18. *AF*, June 1900, 175; December 1900, 393; February 1901, 57; June 1901, 209; *LG*, April 1904, 1065–66. On Flett, see Trades and Labor Congress of Canada, *Official Book*, 1901; and Babcock, *Gompers in Canada*, 41–54. In 1901 the Hamilton Trades and Labor Council ruled that only members of international unions could sit in its meetings – a full year before the national Trades and Labor Congress made a similar decision. *HS*, 7 Sept. 1901, 10.

19. See Table 27. For a discussion of the craftworkers of the building trades whose experience paralleled that of their Hamilton counterparts, see Roberts, "Artisans, Aristocrats, and Handymen."

20. Willets, *Workers of the Nation*.

21. The quite distinctive story of the railway unions is chronicled in Tuck, "Canadian Railways and the International Brotherhoods."

22. *MC*, July 1902, 196 (quotation); Taft, *A.F. of L.*, 185–212; Foner, *History of the Labour Movement, III*, 205–14; Montgomery, *Workers' Control in America*, 15–18; Palmer, *Culture in Conflict*, 71–95; Kealey, *Toronto Workers*, 53–97. Street-railway workers got the national Trades and Labor Congress to endorse their call for a 30-day apprenticeship for their work, but no one else listened. Tucker, "Who's Running the Road?" 461.

23. Ansell and Joseph, "Mass Production of Craft Unionism"; Forbath, *Law and the Shaping of the American Labor Movement*; Tomlins, *State and the Unions*, 3–95; Fink, "Labor, Liberty, and the Law." There was a more radical minority within the AFL that was never able to displace cautious "Gompersism." Montgomery, *Fall of the House of Labor*, 257–329.

24. Van Tine, *Making of the Labor Bureaucrat*, 1–84; *LOC*, 1914, 187. A short-lived Building Trades Council was formed in Hamilton in 1901, and provincial organizations appeared among boot and shoe workers the same year, bricklayers in 1903, moulders in 1905, garment workers in 1907, carpenters in 1911, barbers in 1915, machinists in 1918, and plumbers in 1928. *LG*, July 1901, 73–75; January 1919, June 1919, 717; August 1926, 788–89; April 1928, 384–85; *LOC*, 1918–30; *HT*, 1 Aug. 1901, 5; OBLR, 1903, 66; 1907, 144; *LN*, 28 May 1915, 1; Thwaites, "International Association of Machinists," 774.

25. Ramirez, *When Workers Fight*, 3–84. For examples of these agreements involving the city's bricklayers and printers, see *LG*, April 1909, 1128–29; July 1909, 99–100. On the building trades, see, for example, *LG*, May 1904, 1105 (carpenters); March 1905, 955 (bricklayers, painters); June 1913, 1359 (plumbers); *LN*, 10 May 1912, 1 (sheet-metal workers).

26. Frey and Commons, "Conciliation in the Stove Industry"; Stockton, *International Molders' Union*, 120–25; Hilbert, "Trade Union Agreements in the Iron Molders' Union," 229–32. *IMJ*, March 1900, 143; August 1900, 534, June 1902, 385. Similar negotiations took place in 1903; see *HS*, 2 April 1903, 1; 19 May 1903, 1; 20 May 1903, 1; 26 May 1903, 1; 27 May 1903, 1; 28 May 1903, 1. Earlier in 1902 the stove manufacturers had talked their workers out of a 15 per cent wage increase on the basis of outside competition. *LG*, May 1902, 649.

27. HS, 16 Feb. 1909, 7; *IMJ*, March 1906, 148; May 1908, 351. J.H. Barnett of Toronto was appointed the Conference Board's first business agent. Within a few years he had been replaced by W.J. Lucas of Hamilton. John Tilden was succeeded as president of the founders' organization by Stanley Robinson of Hamilton's D. Moore Company. *CF*, October 1910, 18.

28. Piva, *Condition of the Working Class*, 150–52; Heron and Palmer, "Through the Prism of the Strike," 446–52.

29. TLCCP, 1903, 7 (quotation); United Garment Workers of America, *Proceedings*, 1906, 17 (quotation); *HH*, 10 June 1911, 15 (quotation).

30. *IB*, April 1902; HPL, Hamilton Board of Trade, Minutes, 30 Nov. 1903, 65, 67; 25 Jan. 1904, 69; 11 April 1904, 75; *HS*, 5 July 1904, 5; 6 Aug. 1904, 4; *LG*, December 1904, 496; January 1905, 735; April 1905, 1070; *HH*, 18 April 1910, 2 (quotation); Craven, *Impartial Umpire*. The federal Department of Labour and the much more modest Ontario Bureau of Labour were both set up in 1900. Southern Ontario factory workers got far less of their attention than did the transportation and resource industries. Indeed, the much-touted Industrial Disputes Investigation Act passed in 1907 did not apply to manufacturing before World War One.

31. Spedden, *Trade Union Label*; Bogert, "Union Labels," 10 (quotation).

32. *IB*, March 1897, 2; April 1897, 2; March 1908, 4; February 1911, 1; March 1911, 1; 12 April 1918, 4; *AF*, September 1897, 176; April 1898, 42; December 1900, 393; *CJF*, December 1898, 375; *MC*, October 1899, 2; March 1903, 13; *LG*, November 1900, 92; December 1900, 147; February 1901, 271; 2 Sept. 1901, 140; February 1902, 442; December 1918, 1112; April 1927, 378; OBLR, 1901, 124–25; 1902, 149–50; *HS*, 2 Feb. 1897, 5; *HH*, 8 Jan. 1910, 20; 16 May 1910, 6; 17 Dec. 1910, 2; 24 Dec. 1910, 2; *HT*, 3 April 1901, 7; 14 May 1910, 1; 31 May 1910, 4; *Broom Maker*, March 1903, 110; *LN*, 23 Sept. 1920, 1; 25 Feb. 1921, 1, 29 April 1921, 1; *IC*, July 1905, 832; March 1906, 516; LAC, R10811-0-X-E, Vol. 352, 94028 (Hamilton Trades and Labor Council to Laurier, 23 Jan. 1905).

33. HPL, Hamilton Trades and Labor Council, Minutes, 6 Jan. 1911, 32; 19 May 1911, 67; 19 July 1912, 84–85; *Hamilton Labor Directory*, 1911, 31; *HH*, 16 May 1910, 6; *LOC*, 1913, 187; *CLW*, 30 July 1925, 2; *CCJ*, September 1927, 30.

34. Brody, *In Labor's Cause*, 221; Fudge and Tucker, *Labour before the Law*, 1–15.

35. Foner, *History of the Labor Movement*, Vol. III, 200–2.

36. On this ethical strain in craft ideology, see Crossick, "Labour Aristocracy," 317–18; Montgomery, *Workers' Control in America*, 13–14.

37. *LN*, 25 Sept. 1914, 4.

38. The United Garment Workers' token female on the international executive board, Kate Doody, spent a few days in Hamilton in 1897 to stir up the women workers, but with no lasting results. By 1905 the Hamilton local had only 18 women members (out of a female workforce of 1,500). *HS*, 24 March 1899, 6 (quotation); 22 May 1903, 5; 26 May 1903, 1; 27 May 1903, 1; 28 May 1903, 8; 29 May 1903, 1; 30 May 1903, 1; 1 June 1903, 1; 2 June 1903, 1; 24 Feb. 1906, 1; 25 Feb. 1906, 1; 26 Feb. 1906, 1; 27 Feb. 1906, 1; 28 Feb. 1906, 1; 1 March 1906, 1.

39. *IB*, July 1897, 2 (quotation); April 1899, 3; *GW*, April 1899, 16; Willett, *Employment of Women*, 175 (quotation); *LG*, September 1901, 140; May 1903, 844; OBLR, 1905, 35; Frager, *Sweatshop Strife*, 111 (quotation); Steedman, *Angels of the Workplace*, 62–69. In 1901 the only UGWA women's local in Canada was in Manitoba. Willett, *Employment of Women*, 187.

40. Palmer, *Culture in Conflict*.

41. *MT*, 4 May 1894, 1378 (see also *CE*, 27 May 1910, 1); *CAC*, 4 May 1900; *HT*, 31 March 1900, 4; *HS*, 3 April 1900, 8; City

Engineer, *Report*, 1905, 35; 1922–23, 115–16; 1927–28, 17. In 1897–98 John R. Common contributed a lengthy series of articles to the *American Federationist*, "A Comparison of Day Labor and Contract Labor on Municipal Works." He concluded that day labour "protects home labor against outsiders, affords fair wages and reasonable hours, gives employment at those times when employment is scarce, fixes the minimum wages and hours for private contractors, increases the efficiency and raises the character of the workingmen." *AF*, 4 Aug. 1897, 112.

42. The Building Trades Council dissolved in 1912, and the metalworkers let theirs fall apart during the severe pre-war depression. Both would be revived during the war. *LG*, July 1903, 88; June 1904, 1209; August 1914, 169; *HH*, 24 April 1911, 1; 7 Feb. 1914, 7; *LN*, 12 April 1912, 1; 16 Jan. 1914, 8; *IB*, 22 May 1914, 7; *LOC*, 1912, 157; 1914, Helbring, *Departments of the American Federation of Labor.*

43. Heron and Penfold, *Workers' Festival*, 41–79.

44. The codification of the Criminal Code in 1892 had created ambiguity by leaving out the previously explicit qualification that peaceful communication by picketers did not constitute a criminal offence. Employers, however, were turning more often to civil law, where the injunction became the most effective tool, especially in the wake of the 1901 British courts decision in the Taff Vale case. *HS*, 11 Aug. 1900, 8; 18 Aug. 1900, 8; 20 Aug. 1900, 8; 21 Aug. 1900, 8; 22 Aug. 1900, 8; 23 Aug. 1900, 8; 24 Aug. 1900, 8; 4 Sept. 1900, 5; 11 Sept. 1900, 8; 12 Sept. 1900, 5 (quotation); Tucker and Fudge, "Forging Responsible Unionism"; Fudge and Tucker, *Labour before the Law*, 18–34; Heron and Palmer, "Through the Prism of the Strike," 448–49; Piva, *Condition of the Working Class*, 150–52; Roberts, "Toronto Metal Workers," 64–72.

45. *IC*, October 1903, 111 (quotation), 130 (quotation),133–36 (quotation at 134).

46. The company continued to pay the union rate to the rolling-mill men without recognizing the union, which never established a Hamilton lodge before World War One. The Ontario Bureau of Labour listed a Smelter Workers Union (AFL Federal Labour Union No. 9805) in 1903, but it was never heard from again. *CE*, April 1900, 332; *LG*, April 1901, 402; *HS*, 2 April 1900, 1; 3 April 1900, 1; 4 April 1900, 1; 5 April 1900, 1; 30 March 1901, 1; 1 April 1901, 1; *HT*, 2 April 1900, 1; 3 April 1900, 1; 30 March 1901, 1; OBLR, 1903, 100; Heron, "Hamilton Steelworkers," 114. Ironically, the company continued to negotiate with the bricklayers' union, whose work was important around the furnaces. *HS*, 6 Jan. 1904, 1.

47. The local machinists' union had been first organized in 1897 but had to be reorganized in 1902. In 1913 IAM members complained in union meetings that Westinghouse had fired them for their union sympathies. Three years later the firm's general manager, P.J. Myler, circulated to his employees a letter making clear that the company "had always maintained and proposes to continue to maintain an 'open shop,'" and the machinists' union president confirmed that attitude in 1919. *HS*, 8 Oct. 1903, 8; *Pittsburgh Dispatch*, 3 May 1903 (clipping in MUA, Westinghouse Fonds, P.J. Myler Scrapbook); International Association of Machinists Fonds, Minutes, 4 June, 27 Aug. 1913; LAC, R1449-0-5-E, Vol. 2, File 11 (Department of Labour, 1916), P.J. Myler to Flavelle, 5 June 1916; R1176-0-0-E, 2265.

48. HPL, International Harvester Scrapbook, Vol. 1; Ozanne, *Century of Labor-Management Relations*; IAMPC, 1895, XIII; 1900, 78–79; *MMJ*, September 1899, 335; October 1901, 654; October 1903, 619; March 1904, 226; July 1904, 603–4; *HS*, 27 May 1904, 10; 30 May 1904, 1; 3 June 1904, 10 (quotation); 10 June 1904, 1; 14 June 1904, 5; 3 Aug. 1904, 1; 12 Aug. 1904, 8 (quotation); 15 Aug. 1904, 1; *LG*, June 1904, 1209; July 1904, 84; September 1904, 240, 294; Thwaites, "International Association of Machinists," 54. In their local union meetings, the machinists admitted in 1913 that International Harvester "had always been very hard to approach" and "the principle of 'One man, one machine' could not be justified in these days of highly perfected automatics." MUA, International Association of Machinists Fonds, Minutes, 27 Aug., 17 Dec. 1913.

49. *LG*, February 1905, 898–99; April 1905, 1070; May 1905, 1268: June 1905, 1381; September 1906, 299, 301–2; November 1906, 560; January 1907, 791; *HS*, 30 Aug. 1906, 1; 6 Sept. 1906, 1.

50. *HS*, 8 Sept. 1892, 1, 4; 9 Sept. 1892, 1, 4; Ferns, "Theaker"; Mills, *Cataract Traction*, 73–83.

51. *MC*, October 1899, 2; February 1900, 681; April 1900, 712 (quotation); October 1900, 776; November 1900, 796; February 1901, 120; August 1901, 19; September 1901, 31; April 1902, 149–50; March 1903, 13; December 1903, 25; April 1904, 23; May 1904, 22; September 1906, 7–8, 24–25; November 1906, 31–32; *IB*, March 1902, 2; June 1908, 3; 19 Oct. 1917, 4; *CAC*, 6 May 1899, 3; 24 Aug. 1900, 1; *HS*, 25 July 1904, 1; 12 Aug. 1904, 1; 10 Oct. 1904, 10; *LG*, December 1899, 147; September 1901, 140; February 1902, 443; March 1902, 505; April 1902, 578; Ferns, "Theaker"; Jaggard and Cracknell, *75 Years*, n.p. On the unionization of street-railway workers in this period, see Tucker, "Who's Running the Road?"; Palmer "'Give Us the Road.'"

52. *HS*, 15 Aug. 1906, 1; 18 Aug. 1906, 1; 20 Aug. 1906, 1; 21 Aug. 1906, 1; 22 Aug. 1906, 1; 23 Aug. 1906, 1; 24 Aug. 1906, 1; 25 Aug. 1906, 1; 27 Aug. 1906, 1, 4; 28 Aug. 1906, 1; 29 Aug. 1906, 1; 30 Aug. 1906, 1; 31 Aug. 1906, 1; 1 Sept. 1906, 1; 4 Sept. 1906, 1; 5 Sept. 1906, 1; 7 Sept. 1906, 1; 8 Sept. 1906, 1; 12 Sept. 1906, 1; 14 Sept. 1906, 1; 18 Sept. 1906, 1; 29 Sept. 1906, 1; 1 Oct. 1906, 1; 2 Oct. 1906, 1; 6 Oct. 1906, 1; 27 Oct. 1906, 1; 29 Oct. 1906, 12; 31 Oct. 1906,

1; 1 Nov. 1906, 1; 2 Nov. 1906, 1, 2; 3 Nov. 1906, 1; 5 Nov. 1906, 1; *IB*, September 1906, 1, 3; October 1906, 4; November 1906, 1; December 1906, 1; Ferns "Theaker."

53. In 1904, for example, a by-law was passed requiring an enclosed vestibule to protect drivers from the cold in winter months. *MC*, February 1904, 23. In 1906 this protection was incorporated into the new Ontario Railway Act. *MC*, August 1906, 25.

54. *HS*, 25 Oct. 1904, 10; 27 Oct. 1904, 10; 28 Oct. 1904, 3, 10; *LG*, December 1904, 655. The company appealed, and the case had reached the Supreme Court by the end of November 1906. *HS*, 27 Nov. 1906, 1.

55. *HS*, 6 Sept. 1906, 1 (quotation); 27 Aug. 1906, 1 (quotation); AO, F 5-1, J.M. Gibson to Whitney, 24 Jan. 1906.

56. *MC*, August 1902, 212 (quotation); *HS*, 25 Aug. 1906, 4 (quotation). The *Spectator*, a Conservative paper, had little sympathy for the corporate manoeuvres of Cataract president John M. Gibson, the city's leading Liberal. The regional labour press was even more incensed; see *IB*, September 1906, 3.

57. *IB*, November 1906, 1 (quotation); *HS*, 5 Nov. 1906, 6 (quotation).

58. *HS*, 4–12 Nov. 1906.

59. *HS*, 6 Nov. 1906, 4 (quotation).

60. *HS*, 12–24 Nov. 1906.

61. *HS*, 20 Nov. 1906, 1 (quotation); Palmer, *Culture in Conflict*, 215–16.

62. *HS*, 26 Nov. 1906, 3; 27 Nov. 1906, 1 (quotation).

63. On the patterns of crowd activities, see Rudé, *Crowd in History*; Thompson, *Customs in Common*, 185–258 (on moral economy); Tilly, *Politics of Collective Violence*; Tucker, "Who's Running the Road?"

64. *IMJ*, December 1906, 922 (quotation).

65. After the strike was over, *Industrial Canada*, the organ of the Canadian Manufacturers' Association, put this case bluntly: "The company had a franchise to run cars in the city; for this purpose they had invested large capital; they had the cars ready and the men to operate them. Why should they have been prevented from doing business for several weeks? Is a body of disorderly citizens to usurp control of the city?" *IC*, December 1906, 427.

66. *HS*, 14 Nov. 1906,1 (quotation).

67. AO, F 5-1, Whitney to James Leitch, 20 Nov. 1906. The Board was authorized by law to both arbitrate street-railway disputes and to simply investigate and publish findings. Tucker, "Who's Running the Road?" 466.

68. *HS*, 24–25 Nov. 1906.

69. *HS*, 26 Nov. 1906 (quotation at 3).

70. *MC*, December 1906, 16–19, 26–28 (quotation at 15); *LG*, January 1907, 794–98; *HS*, 1 Dec. 1906, 1; *HS*, 5 Dec. 1907, 1; 7 Dec. 1907, 1, 10.

71. Tucker, "Who's Running the Road?" 466. The men serving terms in the Central Prison for charges related to the rioting were all released in March as a result of the lobbying of local Conservative MP Adam Zimmerman. *HS*, 20 March 1907, 1. The strike left the street-railwaymen's union bitterly divided, and a few months later some members withdrew to join a nationalist union, quietly supported by the company, but never attracting many members. In January 1908 the company also fired John Theaker, the union's president. After a federal conciliation hearing on his case, the Liberal government (to which company president Gibson was closely connected) diffused the issue by offering him a job in the local post office, which he accepted. *MC*, April 1907, 27; March 1908, 22–23; *HS*, 27 Dec. 1906, 1; 28 Dec. 1906, 1, 4; 7 Jan. 1907, 1; 9 Jan. 1907, 1; *HH*, 16 Aug. 1907, 1; NTLCCP, 1907, 12, 15; *IB*, May 1907, 1; June 1907, 1; December 1907, 4; February 1908, 3; March 1908, 2; April 1908, 1; May 1908, 3; Ferns, "Theaker."

72. A *Spectator* reporter discovered in April 1907 that the wife of one motorman had stitched together a cushion cover from "We Walk" ribbons, while her husband kept a scab's bludgeon on display. *HS*, 2 April 1907, 7.

73. *LG*, May 1907, 1296, 1299, 1301, 1303; June 1907, 1435, 1437–38, 1440–41; July 1907, 99, 104–6; August 1907, 230; LAC, RG 27, Vol. 294, Files 2854, 2857, 2868, 2876, 2882, 2890, 2922, 2926; *HS*, 8 April 1907, 1; 16 April 1907, 12; 30 April 1907, 5; 24 April 1907, 1; 16 May 1907, 1; 17 May 1907, 1; 18 May 1907, 1; 10 June 1907, 1; *HT*, 8 April 1907, 1; *HH*, 1 May 1907, 1; 3 May 1907, 1; 6 May 1907, 1; 7 May 1907, 1; 8 May 1907, 1; *IB*, May 1907, 4, June 1907, 4.

74. The building trades sustained the new-model craft unionism most successfully in the early 20th century in a regular pattern of collective bargaining with local contractors, although occasionally they had to fight off substantial challenges; in 1907, for example, the plumbers held out against a nasty mood among employers, who alleged "they had been bound down by agreements for the past 5 or 6 years to such an extent that they had woven a net about themselves which prevented them doing anything." An agreement was ultimately signed. LAC, R244-76-4-E, Vol. 294, File 2868; *HS*, 4 May 1907, 1 (quotation); *IB*, June 1907, 4.

75. HPL, HTLC, Minutes, 3 Feb. 1911, 41.

76. *HS*, 13 Nov. 1906, 1.

77. *IB*, April 1909; LAC, RG 27, Vol. 296, File: 1909–3124; *LG*, March 1909, 936–37; April 1910, 1146; May 1909, 1257; *HS*, 15 Feb. 1909, 1; 16 Feb. 1909, 7; 18 Feb. 1909, 1; 19 Feb. 1909, 5; 23 Feb. 1909, 1; 14 Feb. 1909, 1; 25 Feb. 1909, 1, 7; 26 Feb. 1909, 1; 1 March 1909, 1; 22 March 1909, 4; 24 March 1909, 1, 4; 27 March 1909; 13 May 1909, 1; *HH*, 24 Feb. 1909, 1; 26 Feb. 1909, 1; 15 March 1909, 5; 23 March 1909, 1. On the stove founders' growing concerns about US competition in the Canadian market, see LAC, R200-275-4-E, Vol. 4, 232. The *Herald* described the strike as "one of the most stubborn fights ever put up by a union in this city, as rather than give in, the union moulders

left homes and families and went to work in other places. Some even removed their families from the city." Confrontation between union and non-union moulders continued to crop up in bars and on the streets well into 1910. *HH*, 12 April 1910, 1; 5 May 1910, 1 (quotation); 7 June 1910, 12; 5 Aug. 1910, 1; 20 Dec. 1910, 12; *HT*, 14 April 1910, 1; *LG*, June 1910, 1372.

78. UGWA, *Proceedings*, 1910, 284; *HT*, 15 May 1911, 1; *HH*, 20 May 1911, 1; HPL, Hamilton Trades and Labor Council, Minutes, 6 Oct. 1912, 107.

79. *HH*, 8 Jan. 1910, 1.

80. LAC, R244-76-4-E, Vol. 296, File 1909–3124.

10. The Whip Hand

1. *HS*, 15 July 1903, 1 (quotation); 30 Aug. 1904, 1 (quotation); 13 Jan. 1905, 7. Three years earlier, as president of the Canadian Manufacturers' Association, Ellis had denounced "the growing tendency of certain unions to claim privileges relating to the government of businesses which practically mean the handing over of the management by those who have the responsibility to those who have not." *IC*, November 1901, 121. Five months later Hamilton manufacturers heard another address on "Cost Accounting," by Sinclair G. Richardson, which *Industrial Canada* reprinted (July 1905, 843–44) as part of its new series of articles on cost accounting.

2. See, for example, the brief presented to a federal tariff board in 1905 by Hamilton's machine-tool and small-tool manufacturers. LAC, R244-76-4-E, Vol. 4, 305. The term "mass production" first won social-scientific credibility when it appeared in the 1926 edition of *Encyclopaedia Britannica*, at the head of an entry signed by Henry Ford but actually written by an employee. Hounshell, *From the American System to Mass Production*, 1.

3. On International Harvester's machinists, see chapter 9 here; on textile workers, *Fabricator*, 1922–25. By 1910 the Greening Wire Company was using only eight men to operate 75 new wire-weaving machines in place of the 75 skilled wire weavers in the plant a decade earlier. In the spinning and weaving departments of the local cotton mills, ring frames, automatic looms, and thread-tying machines were also replacing older, more labour-intensive technology after the turn of the century. *HH*, 8 Oct. 1910, 5; Copeland, *Cotton Manufacturing Industry*, 54–100; Coote, *Graphical Survey*, 5; Lahne, *Cotton Mill Worker*, 13; *CJF*, July 1898, 219; December 1898, 374.

4. *HH*, 8 Oct. 1910, 5 (quotation); *HS*, 20 April 1907, 18 (quotation).

5. The earliest machines were hand-operated devices: the "squeezer," which pressed or "rammed" the sand into the mould by the use of a lever, and the stripping plate, which was used to draw the pattern out of the mould. Experiments began in the late 1880s to apply power to these

processes and to combine ramming and pattern-drawing; a further refinement was known as "jolt-ramming," whereby the mould was dropped sharply by pneumatic pressure to pack the sand. After a lengthy period of experimentation the new machines became commercially viable, and each year the American Foundrymen's Association convention featured more and more complex equipment on display. In 1895 one enterprising pattern-maker in Hamilton, Louis Edworthy, won international attention for his new moulding machine, but, as no more was heard from him, it seems likely that the elaborate mechanism was impractical, like so many others in their experimental phase. *IA*, 4 July 1895, 25; *Hardware and Metal*, 25 May 1895, 5.

6. "Molding Machines: Principles Involved in Their Operation," *CM*, April 1908, 53.

7. OIFR, 1908, 22 (quotation); *HH*, 8 Oct. 1910, 5 (quotation); Stecker, "Founders, Molders, and Molding Machines," 438 (quotation); *IMJ*, September 1909, 647. See also Kennedy, "Banishing Skill from the Foundry"; Kennedy, "A Molderless Foundry." Perhaps that was why International Harvester found labour turnover such a serious problem in its Hamilton foundries. *HHB*, June 1920, 23–24.

8. "Coming of the Molding Machine," *CE*, July 1906, 265 (quotation); "Molding Machines: Principles Involved in Their Operation," *CM*, April 1908, 53–56; May 1908, 57–58; "Molding Machine Practice in a Canadian Foundry," *CM*, June 1908, 65–66; *CM*, July 1908, 46–48, 52; *IC*, July 1908, 1108. *Canadian Machinery* carried numerous descriptive articles and advertisements for the machinery, as did *Canadian Foundryman* when it was launched in 1910. The American Foundrymen's Association (which met in Toronto in 1908) exhibited and discussed the new machinery extensively. Canadian membership in the Association immediately leaped from 17 to 57.

9. "Stripping Plate Machine: Inception and Development," *CF*, June 1918, 123–25, 123; Ozanne, *Labor-Management Relations*, 20–28; McCormick, *Century of the Reaper*, 131, 250 (quotation); *IA*, 1 Sept. 1904, 3. This must have been one of the first installations of moulding equipment in Canada. The new machines could be dangerous. In September 1903, a few months after the Hamilton Harvester plant opened, a worker crushed his finger in one. OIFR, 1903, 48–49.

10. Harris, "Rocky Road," 391–96; *CM*, April 1906, 145–46 (quotation).

11. Gartshore-Thompson and the Berlin Machine works had moulding machines as early as 1908, Bowes-Jamieson by 1911, and Brown-Boggs, Dominion Steel Castings, and Hamilton Malleable Iron Company by 1913. *CM*, February 1908, December 1908, 32; 2 Jan. 1913, 23, 52, 59; 10 July 1913, 41; *CF*, September 1911, 18.

12. *HS*, 23 Feb. 1909, 1; LAC, R244-76-4-E, Vol. 296, File 3148.

13. Harris, "Rocky Road"; Stecker, "Founders, Molders, and Molding Machines," 435; *CF*, March 1916, 58–59; April 1920, 115; October 1923, 30; May 1927, 6–9; July 1927, 6; October 1927, 8–10; May 1928, 17–18, 39 (quotation).

14. *LG*, December 1916, 1801–2; Millard, "Crusade for Science."

15. *CF*, September 1925, 35; May 1927, 6; October 1927, 10; May 1928, 19. In 1918 only 37 firms in Canada had research laboratories, compared to 2,000 in the US. Millard, *Master Spirit of the Age*, 197. On the growing importance of science for industrial production, see Hull, "Science and the Canadian Pulp and Paper Industry," 1–116; Hull, "Working with Figures."

16. Wagoner, *U.S. Machine Tool Industry*, 18. See also Floud, *British Machine Tool Industry*; Rolt, *Tools for the Job*; Rosenberg, "Technological Change"; *CE*, April 1900, 321; *CM*, February 1905, 53; *Canadian Manufacturer*, 28 Jan. 1910, 84.

17. High-speed steel was the brainchild of US managerial theorist Frederick W. Taylor and his associate Maunsel White. In 1906 Taylor took the annual meeting of the American Society of Mechanical Engineers by storm with his paper, "On the Art of Cutting Metals," which *Canadian Machinery* reprinted the next month. Rolt, *Tools for the Job*, 197–201; *CM*, January 1907, 18–21; February 1907, 50–51; E.R. Norris, "Machine Shop Equipment, Methods and Processes," *CM*, 12 Oct. 1916, 393–95; *Canadian Manufacturer*, 28 Jan. 1910, 84; Keith, "Five Years' Development of Machine Tools."

18. "Developments in Machine Shop Practice during a Decade," 282; OBLR, 1900, 37; *LG*, March 1901, 356–57; *MMJ*, April 1908, 319 (quotation).

19. "A Post-War Problem of Labor," *CM*, 12 April 1917, 381; Rodgers, "Evolution and Revolution"; "Tendency in Machine Tool Development," *CM*, 6 Dec. 1917, 630; Rodgers, "Should Be No Post-War Slump in Machine Tools," *CM*, 22 Aug. 1918, 240–41; Rodgers, "More Efficient Methods Follow War Work," *CM*, 26 Dec. 1918, 750–73. Throughout the war *Canadian Machinery* provided extensive reports and commentary on developments in munitions plants. Censorship regulations prevented the journal from identifying the location of companies under discussion.

20. Irish, "'Dilution' of Labor'"; *LN*, 12 Jan. 1917, 3; 19 Jan. 1917, 1; 23 Feb. 1917, 1; 26 Feb. 1917, 1; *LG*, February 1917, 97; *HH*, 30 Nov. 1916, 4; "Female Labor on 8 in. High Explosive Shell Machining," *CM*, 21 Oct. 1915, 384; 8 March 1917, 207 (quotation); Rodgers, "Evolution and Revolution," 679–80 (quotation).

21. G.L. Sprague, "Interest in Your Work an Absolute Necessity," *CM*, 13 Jan. 1921, 39. See also the article by the works engineer at International Harvester, T. Daley, "Machinist Should Be Given a Variety of Work," *CM*, 4 Nov. 1920, 427.

22. *CM*, 11 Dec. 1924, 31.

23. *HS*, 11 Dec. 1895, 1; *LG*, November 1904, 465; June 1909, 1305; LAC, R244-76-4-E, Vol. 296, File: 1909–3153, Vol. 303, File: 12 (111A); *HH*, 12 Sept. 1913, 1; 13 Sept. 1913, 1; 17 Sept. 1913, 1; 19 Sept. 1913, 1; 23 Dec. 1916, 7; *HT*, 6 April 1914, 1; Cumbo, *Italian Presence*.

24. *HT*, 11 April 1902, 1; 14 April 1902, 1; Kilbourn, *Elements Combined*, 121, 124. The choice of Italians is curious, since they were not a significant part of the workforce in US iron and steel mills. See US, Immigration Commission, *Reports*, Vol. 8, 35, 240–44; Vol. 9, 9–17, 122.

25. US, Immigration Commission, *Reports*, Vol. 14, 402, 506–10, 608.

26. *HT*, 20 May 1902, 5 (quotation); 10 Dec. 1903; *HS*, 20 April 1904, 4; 16 April 1907, 9; Makowski, *History and Integration of Poles*, 94.

27. *LN*, 30 Oct. 1914, 1; Harney, "Padrone and the Immigrant"; Harney, "Commerce of Migration." These patterns spanned the continent; Bodnar, *Transplanted*, 57–71; Peck, *Reinventing Free Labor*.

28. AO, RG 7, II-1, Box 3, File: "Reports – Employment Offices (B-N)," Hamilton (quotation); F.H. Bell, "Treat *Machines* Better Than *Men*?" *CF*, May 1921, 32 (quotation); *HH*, 7 Aug. 1918, 4; CC, 1921, Vol. 2, 456; Vol. 4, 401. Calculations are mine.

29. *HS*, 21 March 1907, 112 (quotation); 2 April 1907, 7 (quotation).

30. LAC, R244-76-4-E, Vol. 305, File:16(36), C.W. Sherman to F.A. Acland, 12 July 1916. For identical comments from a spokesperson for Chadwick Brass, see *HH*, 10 Feb. 1916, 2.

31. *HS*, 15 Feb. 1919, 13.

32. *HH*, 4 April 1910, 4. See also Heron, *Working in Steel*, 74–87.

33. The old Sawyer-Massey works had a 10-ton model in its engine and erecting departments by 1903, and the enormous new plants of International Harvester and Canadian Westinghouse that opened the next year made use of several of them. Most of the big new east-end factories included one or more such devices. *Hamilton Spectator Carnival Souvenir* (1903), 116; *CE*, June 1904, 154; *CM*, October 1905, 384, 386; *IA*, 1 Sept. 1904, 1–9; 8 Sept. 1904, 7–12. On the use of these cranes at the London Machine Tool Company, see *CM*, July 1906, 251; at the Berlin Machine Works, *CM*, December 1908, 32; at Hamilton Bridge, *CM*, June 1909, 33–38; at the Ford-Smith Machine Company, *CM*, 15 Jan. 1925, 18; at Canada Iron Foundries, *CF*, October 1929, 9; at the Otis-Fensom Elevator Company, *CM*, July 1927, 6–7; at National Steel Car, *CM*, 19 June 1913, 640; 7 Sept. 1916, 244. See also "Better Foundry Practice," *CF*, September 1925, 34–35.

34. For the railway at the Westinghouse plant, see *CM*, October 1905, 384. See also *CF*, July 1927, 6; and Bell, "Treat *Machines* Better Than *Men*?" 34. For the electric lift truck, see Clement A. Hardy, "Speeding up Handling in the Foundry," *CF*, January 1930, 18. For changes in wartime munitions works, see *CM*, 21 Oct. 1915, 381; F.C. Perkins, "Gravity Carriers and Electric Conveyers," *CM*, 27 Feb. 1919; J.H. Moore, "Speed up Production by Systematic Handling," *CM*, 4 Sept. 1919, 250–52. Networks of chutes were first installed between machines to eliminate loading and unloading from trucks and were soon replaced with "roller conveyors" sloped to use gravity as the motive force or powered with electricity. All production materials in the Wagstaffe canning factory moved along overhead tracks, and the Ewing Bakery (later part of Canada Bread) boasted that every night 25,000 loaves passed through its plant untouched by human hands. *CF*, February 1925, 14; R. Micks, "Getting Maximum Production," *CF*, August 1925,12; *Hamilton Manufacturer*, 1909–10, 57; *HT*, 3 Feb. 1910; 24 June 1913, 11; *IA*, 1 Sept. 1904, 5.

35. Heron, "Hamilton Steelworkers"; Kilbourn, *Elements Combined*, 93; *HS*, 21 March 1907, 12 (quotation); *CF*, September 1913, 142–44 (quotations); *CMJ*, 1 Aug. 1913, 489.

36. Small wonder, then, that between 1916 and 1920, 6,900 employees of the Steel Company produced an average of 325,000 tons of steel per year, while in the 1926–30 period only 5,200 men averaged 415,000 tons. Kilbourn, *Elements Combined*, 119. For a fuller discussion of technological change in the Canadian steel industry in the period, see Heron, *Working in Steel*, 42–50.

37. *IA*, 8 Sept. 1904, 12; *CF*, March 1921, 19; *CM*, 7 Sept. 1916, 244; Boam, comp., *Twentieth Century Impressions of Canada*, 556; *HS*, 12 Aug. 1913, 13.

38. M.L. Begeman, "Economies of Materials Handling," *CTJ*, 22 July 1924, 662 (quotation). The celebrated problem of labour shortages in North America (see Habakkuk, *American and British Technology*) probably accounts for the far more extensive mechanization of unskilled work in Hamilton as compared to Britain. In the 1940s a British delegation was astounded at how extensively the handling of materials in North American factories had been mechanized. See Anglo-American Council on Productivity, *Materials Handling in Industry*.

39. F.H. Bell, "Lifting and Conveying Material in the Foundry," *CF*, March 1921,19 (quotation). See also M.L. Begeman, "Economies of Materials Handling," *CTJ*, 22 July 1924, 662.

40. Craven and Traves, "Labour and Management in Canadian Railway Operations"; Chandler, *Visible Hand*, 79–205.

41. The Ontario Institute of Chartered Accountants was founded in 1883 (and a more specialized Canadian Society of Cost Accountants in 1920), while the Canadian Society of Civil Engineers appeared in 1887 (renamed the Engineering Institute of Canada in 1918). Lee, "Traditions and Change"; Millard, *Master Spirit of the Age*; Calvert, *Mechanical Engineer in America*; Noble, *America by Design*. On the growing interest in "systematic" business management in the late 19th century, see Litterer, "Systematic Management"; Nelson, *Managers and Workers*, 48–54; Jacoby, *Employing Bureaucracy*, 40–44. On cost accounting itself, see Lowe, "Mechanization, Feminization, and Managerial Control," 177–209. At the turn of the century the privately run Hamilton Business College was one of only four in Canada recognized by the Institute of Chartered Accountants to train accountants. *HS*, 25 Aug. 1900, 8.

42. *CF*, 7 Dec. 1916, front cover; *CM*, June 1908, 111. See also frequent advertisements for Charles C. Kawin Company and the David McLain Company.

43. Beginning in July 1905, for example, the *Canadian Engineer* ran a two-year-long series of articles by A.J. Lavoie discussing "the most comprehensive, and at the same time the most *practical* scheme for saving time and accelerating production." See also G.C. Keith, "General Scheme of Cost Keeping," *CM*, April 1905, 131–32; "Systematic Works Management," *CM*, October 1905, 403; G.C. Keith, "Is Piecework a Necessity?" *CM*, April 1907, 122–23; D.B. Swinton, "Day Work vs. Piecework," *CM*, December 1906, 453; "The Art of Handling Men," *CM*, September 1907, 27–29; "Machine Shop Time and Cost System," *CM*, 32–34; Hall, "Economy in Manufacturing"; "The Model Factory," *CM*, February 1907, 586–88; April 1907, 723–25; C.R. Stevenson, "System Applied to Factories," *CM*, December 1907, 420; L.E. Bowerman, "What a Cost System Will Accomplish," *CM*, May 1908, 774–75; Kenneth Falconer, "Cost Finding in the Factory," *CM*, March 1908, 639–40.

44. Hall, "Economy in Manufacturing" (quotation).

45. On the arrival of "time-recorders," see *IA*, 27 April 1899, 14; 20 July 1899, 53; 13 Dec. 1900, 19–20; 7 Aug. 1902, 53; 16 Nov. 1911, 1984; *IC*, May 1902, 337; *CE*, June 1904, 176; December 1908, 433; June 1916, 193, 196; *CM*, August 1905, lxv; September 1905, lxv; November 1908, 39–41; January 1909, 45; 30 Oct. 1919, 446; 23 Sept. 1920, 293; 2 June 1921, 32–33; *CTJ*, 24 May 1921, 279; 16 Aug. 1921, 434; 28 Aug. 1923, 768–69. Advertisements for the time clocks ran regularly in the business press. In one of those ads, in 1915, the International Time Recording Company included ten of Hamilton's largest employers in a list of firms using time clocks. *IC*, November 1915, 762.

46. Hall, "Economy in Manufacturing," 420, 430, 732–33 (quotation).

47. See Nelson, *Frederick W. Taylor*; Braverman, *Labor and Monopoly Capital*, 85–138; Palmer, "Class, Conception and Conflict"; Nelson, *Managers and Workers*, 55–78; Haber, *Efficiency and Uplift*, 52–55; Craven, *"Impartial Umpire,"*

96–100; Heron and Palmer, "Through the Prism of the Strike," 430–34; Lowe, "Rise of Modern Management." Canadian editors reprinted articles from the pens of the movement's leading spokesmen, along with the various pre-war studies of US governmental bodies, and offered their own endorsements. H.L. Gantt, "Straight Line to Profit," *IC*, March 1911, 37–40; H.L. Gantt, "Sidelights on the Industrial Efficiency Question," *CF*, September 1912, 15–17; F.W. Taylor, "Principles of Scientific Management, *IC*, March 1913, 1105–6; "What is Scientific Management?" *IC*, April 1913, 1224–25; Taylor, "How Scientific Management Works," *IC*, May 1913, 1349–50; Harrington Emerson, "The Determination of Man's Natural Aptitude," *CF*, April 1913, 51; Frank G. Gilbreth, "Eliminating Fatigue in Factories," *IC*, September 1916, 621; also *CF*, May 1912, 13–14; June 1912, 13–14; *CM*, February 1911, 58; *IC*, November 1913, 423.

48. Whitaker, "Scientific Management Theory as Political Ideology"; Noble, *America by Design*, 33–34.

49. *HH*, 19 Feb. 1913, 1 (quotation); 20 Feb. 1913, 1; LAC, R244-76-4-E, Vol. 301, File:13 (11); File:13 (15). On International Harvester, see *IA*, 1 Sept. 1904, 1–9; 8 Sept. 1904, 7–12. On Westinghouse see *CE*, June 1904, 154–55; *HH*, 14 Oct. 1905; *CM*, October 1905, 383–88. On the Berlin Machine works, see *CM*, December 1908, 29–32.

50. See, for example, *CM*, July 1906, 249–51; 15 Jan. 1925, 17–25; P.M. Yeates, "A System of Factory Cost Keeping," *IC*, May 1909, 836–38; "A Practical Cost System for a Manufacturing Plant," *CM*, June 1909, 39–41.

51. *MMJ*, June 1913, 588 (quotation); *HS*, 6 March 1912, 4 (quotation); HPL, HTLC Minutes, 18 July 1913, 298 (quotation). The "house-in-day" contractor was able to assuage local unionists' fears, and the Council reversed its decision two weeks later.

52. *ISC*, July 1918, 256; Kilbourn, *Elements Combined*, 84–85 (Steel Company); *IC*, March 1907, 659 (Zimmerknit); *HT*, 5 May 1910, 1 (Imperial Cotton); *CM*, 4 April 1918, 339 (Dofasco); *HH*, 20 May 1918, 4 (Steel Company and Westinghouse); 16 Sept. 1918, 1 (Dominion Power and Dofasco); LAC, R6113-0-X-E, H 1(C), Col. 210, 118553 (Dominion Sheet Metal). A British business journalist visiting Canadian factories in the early years of the century observed that there was "no class of managers that can be called typically Canadian." He saw heavy US influence: "The Canadian managers of to-day are brought from many different lands and localities. Perhaps, on the whole, the greater number of them are imported from the United States." Jeans, *Canada's Resources*, 206.

53. The same year the machinists' business agent also told a conciliation commission, after it had heard testimony from a US-born manager of a Hamilton munitions plant, that "a shop full of Canadians, Scotsmen, Irishmen and Englishmen might find it a real cause of dissatisfaction to be bossed by an American." *IB*, April 1905, 4; August 1906, 4; *HH*, 25 April 1916, 3 (quotation); 4 May 1916, 9 (quotation); 13 Oct. 1916, 7 (quotation).

54. *HHB*, May 1920, 14; Moore, "A Planning System That *Is* a Planning System"; Caddie, "Installing Time Studies."

55. *HS*, 24 Feb. 1921, 6. The YMCA's Industrial Department had been promoting these courses since before the war and expanded them in the postwar years. By 1919 they were part of a general North American pattern of trying to upgrade front-line supervisors at the end of the war. The provincial Trades and Labour Branch also worked with the University of Toronto to run a course for employment managers, as were many other North American universities. *LG*, April 1919, 384; OTLBR, 1920, 79–81; *IC*, July 1919, 244; Jacoby, *Employing Bureaucracy*, 56–59, 144–47, 187; Nelson, *Managers and Workers*, 152.

56. The progress of these innovations can be followed in the Imperial Cotton employees' magazine, *Fabricator*, between 1920 and 1925. See also *HS*, 24 Feb. 1921, 16.

57. LAC, R244-76-4-E, Vol. 342, 29(4); Vol. 353, 80, 180; *Textile Worker*, February 1929, 653; March 1929, 716–17; *CTJ*, 17 May 1928, 436; 7 Feb. 1929, 18, 21; 21 Feb. 1929, 11–12; 7 March 1929, 24; 11 April 1929, 20; *HS*, 1 Feb. 1929, 5; 2 Feb. 1929, 5. The managerial theory behind these innovations is discussed in Rehn, *Scientific Management and the Cotton Textile Industry*, 107–12. The Bedeaux system was an elaborate bonus plan involving a set standard of output and extra pay for work over that amount, intended to speed up work significantly. Not all corporate managers turned to these schemes; in 1930 the plant superintendent of Eaton Knitting said he had "no faith in these cost-reduction experts." Quoted in Lewis, "Workplace and Economic Crisis," 516.

58. In 1923–24 the Chamber enrolled 784 in its classes and expected 1,000 the next winter. HPL, HCC, Education Committee, Minutes, 1923–24; Board of Directors, Minutes, 24 July 1923, 56; 7 Aug. 1923, 62; 16 April 1924, 195; Annual Report, 1923–24, 7; 1925–26, 6–7; 1926–27, 7–8; *LG*, August 1924, 669.

59. CC, 1921, Vol. 4, 400–9; 1931, Vol. 7, 180–85. Calculations are mine. Unfortunately, the 1911 data was not published in a comparable form.

60. Lowe, "Mechanization, Feminization, and Managerial Control"; Lowe, "Class, Job, and Gender"; *HH*, 28 Jan. 1916, 1; 26 Oct. 1916, 14; 6 Feb. 1917, 10; 10 Oct. 1917; Davies, *Women's Place Is at the Typewriter*; *HS*, 7 July 1900, 8; 25 Aug. 1900, 8; 4 July 1904, 5; *Hamilton: The Electric City*, 51–52; *LN*, 1 Aug. 1919, 4.

61. *HH*, 14 Oct. 1905 (clipping in MUA, Westinghouse Fonds, Box 9, F.3, P.J. Myler Scrapbook) (quotation); *CM*, 19 June 1913, 640 (quotation). Westinghouse had established continuous-flow production systems in its plant outside Pittsburgh before arriving in Hamilton. Harris, "Rocky

Road," 391–96. For similar comments on the new Hamilton Bridge plant, see *CM*, 2 Jan. 1913, 35–39. On the creation of the trend-setting automobile assembly line, see Peterson, *American Automobile Workers*; Meyer, *Five Dollar Day*; Hounsell, *From the American System to Mass Production*, 217–62.

62. Nelson, *Managers and Workers*, 11–33. T.A. Somerville and Stewart & McTaggart, for example, hung out their shingles in Hamilton in 1908, and Prack and Perrine, a US architectural firm with an office in Hamilton, was responsible for the design of several new plants or factory extensions. Its connection with the new management movement was clear in its description of itself as being made up of "industrial architects and engineers." *CM*, August 1908, 81; 2 Jan. 1913, 6. Similar services were offered by Copeland-Chatterson-Crain of Toronto, Montreal, Winnipeg, and Ottawa; Business Systems, Ltd. of Toronto; Chapin, Churchill and Company in St. Catharines; and Sherman Services, Ltd., of Toronto. *IC*, September 1906, 89; November 1906, 343, December 1906, 449, 471; August 1916, 463, 519–20; May 1920, 13. *Canadian Engineer* also advised its readers of the Modern Systems Correspondence School in Boston, which could provide "practical assistance in the matter of costs and shop systems." *CE*, 15 Jan. 1909, 82.

63. Stone, "Origins of Job Structures"; Braverman, *Labor and Monopoly Capitalism*; Gordon, Edwards, and Reich, *Segmented Work, Divided Workers*, 100–64.

64. Heron, *Working in Steel*, 63.

65. In 1925 the Policyholders' Service Bureau of Metropolitan Life Insurance Company studied management practices in 54 Canadian foundries and concluded, "A foundry's proportional expenditure for labor in respect of total output is much higher than the average manufacturing plant." *CF*, May 1923, 33–37, 40; July 1923, 17; August 1925, 9; July 1927, 6 (quotation); Stecker, "Founders, Molders, and Molding Machine," 455; Harris, "Rocky Road"; CC, 1911, Vol. 6, 310; 1921, Vol. 4, 402; 1931, Vol. 7, 184.

66. "Developing Present Help," *CM*, 5 Oct. 1916, 372; R.I.N., "Machines and the New Mechanic," *CM*, 9 Nov. 1916, 496; 26 Dec. 1919, 751; Noble, "Social Change in Machine Design." In 1922 the editor of *Canadian Machinery* worried that "few, if any, competent all-round machinists have been made since 1916," and that the industry would soon have to start training new "all-round" men. *CM*, 24 Aug. 1922, 33.

67. *CF*, July 1923, 17. During the 1920s Hamilton's textile plant managers made the same efforts to strip away some of the minor tasks of spinners and weavers in order to concentrate their efforts more narrowly and to intensify their workload. "The purpose of the rearrangement is to separate the work that requires skill from that which does not require skill, and takes up a good deal of the worker's time," the manager of the local Canadian Cottons' plant explained. Taking away the tasks of cleaning the machinery would "naturally enable the spinner to attend more frames." *HS*, 1 Feb. 1929, 5; *CTJ*, 7 Feb. 1929, 18, 21; 21 Feb. 1929, 11–12; Canada, Royal Commission on the Textile Industry, *Report*, 177.

68. *HT*, 7 Oct. 1910, 13. The percentages in census data were 6.8 in 1911, 7.2 in 1921, 7.2 in 1931, and 8.8 in 1941. CC, 1911, Vol. 6, 310; 1921, Vol. 4, 402; 1931, Vol. 7, 184; 1941, Vol. 7, 190. Totals and calculations are mine. Changing census definitions make comparisons across time difficult.

69. Ontario, Department of Labour, *Vocational Opportunities; Bulletin No.4: Garment Making*; Nelson, *American Rubber Workers*, 15–19, 83–86; Heron et al., *All That Our Hands Have Done*, 40–41; LAC, R244-76-4-E, Vol. 378, File 101; Heron, *Working in Steel*, 56–63.

70. *IC*, November 1911, 433; August 1911, 37–38; *HT*, 7 Oct. 1910, 13; *IA*, 6 April 1911, 848–50; Nelson, *Managers and Workers*, 95–99; *CM*, 1 Sept. 1922, 19–20; *LG*, December 1926, 1200. Westinghouse and International Harvester had their apprenticeship programs in place by 1911. International Harvester liked to recruit them "from the sons of the men working with the company, or recommended by these men." Seath, *Education for Industrial Purposes*, 359–60, 365–66 (quotation at 365). By the 1920s Westinghouse had a club for its apprentices with an annual banquet. *HS*, 18 May 1929, 36.

71. Less specialized "manual training" classes had also started up in the public schools five years earlier. Stamp, "Campaign for Technical Education"; ODER, 1904, 1906; Hamilton Technical School, *Preliminary Announcement*, 1909–1910, 5; LAC, R3096-0-8-E, Vol. 16, File:1909–10; File:1911–12, 25 Sept. 1911; *HT*, 7 Oct. 1910, 13 (quotation); *HH*, 8 Oct. 1910, 5 (quotation); 2 Feb. 1911, 5; 25 Oct. 1913, 1; 16 Dec. 1916, 4; HPL, Hamilton Trades and Labor Council, Minutes, 6 Oct. 1911, 103. In 1915 the Trades and Labor Council formally protested the appointment of a local factory superintendent as a workers' representative on the technical education committee. *IB*, 26 Feb. 1915, 3. In 1930 labour representatives were still complaining that their nominees for the advisory committee were being ignored in favour of a Steel Company employee. *HS*, 11 July 1930, 16.

72. Sprague's varied career had included work in the Manufacturing and Engineering Department of the American Locomotive Company, a position as efficiency engineer for the Wisconsin civil service, and service with the US Commission on Industrial Relations. *CM*, 13 Jan. 1921, 39; *HH*, 31 May 1918, 19; *LG*, December 1926, 1200–1; August 1928, 874; LAC, MG 28, I, 230, Vol. 17, File:1918–19, 20 May 1918; Vol. 18, File: 1921–24, 19 May 1922; File: 1924–26, 11 April 1924; Hogan, *Class and Reform*, 138–93; Jacoby,

Employing Bureaucracy, 65–97; Stamp, *Schools of Ontario*, 114–16.

73. See Table 10.

74. See Table 11.

75. The shift away from child labour may help to explain the slight increase in the female percentage of the Hamilton workforce from 21 per cent in 1911 to 23 in 1931 and 26 in 1941. CC, 1911, Vol. 4, 306; 1921, Vol. 4, 400; 1931, Vol. 7, 180; 1941, Vol. 7, 190, 196; Ontario, Department of Labour, *Vocational Opportunities; Bulletin No.6: Textiles*.

76. *HH*, 17 April 1914, 12; 28 April 1914, 9 (quotation); CC, Vol. 4, xxxvi (quotation); LAC, R1176-0-0-E, 2385 (quotation); Social Service Council of Canada, Industrial Life Committee, *Man Out of Work*, 12–18.

77. *HT*, 6 April 1914, 1; *HH*, 12 Nov. 1914, 1. Exceptional circumstances might bring some of these "foreigners" onto the city payroll. In 1906, for example, the *Spectator* reported that the sewers department was having trouble getting men to work on the mountain drain, since the job was cold and wet, and "that it may be necessary to put on Italians." *HS*, 29 Oct. 1906, 1. The next spring a city foreman threatened to hire Italians to replace striking civic labourers. *HH*, 7 May 1907, 12.

78. LAC, R244-76-4-E, Vol. 301, File:13 (11) (quotation); R1449-0-5-E, Vol. 2, File:11, Robert Hobson to J.W. Flavelle, 17 Feb. 1916 (quotation); *HH*, 8 March 1916, 1; American Iron and Steel Institute, *Yearbook*, 1919, 414 (quotation); Arthur Smith, "Methods of Solving the Problem of Foundry Help," *CF*, May 1914, 85 (quotation); Braverman, *Labor and Monopoly Capital*.

79. A reporter, for example, thought the assembling of cars at National Steel Car in 1913 required considerable skill. *HS*, 12 Aug. 1913, 13. For a more detailed discussion of semi-skilled work in the steel plant in Hamilton and other Canadian steel-making centres, see Heron, *Working in Steel*, ch. 2. See also Lazonick, "Technological Change and the Control of Work," 112.

80. Canada, House of Commons, *Journals*, Vol. 45 (1909–10), Appendix, Part 3, 166.

81. *HH*, 8 Oct. 1910, 5; see also B. Greening Wire Co. Limited, *Catalogue No.*10. The same equipment could be found at the Banwell-Hoxie and Frost wire fence plants. "Hamilton – The Electric City of Canada," *Magazine of Industry* (Hamilton), Souvenir Edition, December 1910, 28.

82. *HS*, 2 Feb. 1929, 5; Nuwer, "From Batch to Flow."

83. MUA, Westinghouse Fonds, Box 19, F.32, Letter from John Martindale (n.d.).

84. *CJF*, July 1901, 212 (quotation). For Hamilton Steel and Iron, see *CE*, April 1900, 332; MUA, M.T. Montgomery interview. See also *CJF*, 20, May 1903, 178; September 1903, 258; June 1904, 131; April 1906, 97; August 1906, 175; *LG*, August 1904, 207; *CTJ*, May 1913, 133; 2 April 1918, 130; 13 May 1919, 534; *LN*, 9 July 1920, 1; Roberts,

"Changing Patterns," 58–59. In 1913 the *Canadian Textile Journal* noted that the Hamilton textile mills "find difficulty in maintaining their force and more difficulty in increasing it. The authorities usually interpose no obstacle to the importation of help on contract where the need it evident, but not a great amount is obtained this way and usually the mills have to break in green hands." *CTJ*, December 1913, 361.

85. *HH*, 8 Oct. 1910, 5.

86. *HH*, 11 Nov. 1912, 12; 12 Nov. 1912, 7; 20 Nov. 1912, 1; HPL, HTLC, Minutes, 15 Nov. 1912, 218; *MT*, 13 Feb. 1914, 353; *CM*, 7 Sept. 1916, 243–52 (quotation); *LN*, 23 April 1915, 1; 10 Dec. 1915, 1. The company did import some car builders during the war; *HH*, 5 Feb. 1916, 6.

87. MUA, Westinghouse Fonds, Box 9, F.3, "Report on Plant and Operation," 1909, 2, 7; 1910, 1–2; 1914, 6 (quotation); Roberts, ed., *Organizing Westinghouse*, 5–6.

88. LAC, R1176-0-0-E, 2348 (quotation); *CF*, June 1923, 32 (quotation).

89. Ontario, Department of Labour, *Vocational Opportunities; Bulletin No.4: Garment Making*, 5–6, 12–13; Wright, *Report upon the Sweating System*, 46; Ontario, Department of Labour, *Vocational Opportunities; Bulletin No.6: Textiles*. In 1923 the Ontario Minimum Wage Board learned that "50% of the workers in knitting factories are employed on sewing machines, the operation being heavier than in the ordinary garment factory." AO, RG 7, VIII-1, Vol. 39, 8 Feb. 1923, 68.

90. CC, 1911, Vol. 6, 306–17; 1921, Vol. 4, 400–19; 1931, Vol. 7, 190; 1941, Vol. 7, 196, 200. Totals and calculations are mine.

91. CC, 1931, Vol. 7, 190; 1941, Vol. 7, 196, 200.

92. *ISC*, July 1918, 271; Engineering Institute of Canada, *Journal*, October 1918, 299; February 1919, 76–77; March 1919, 164, 234; February 1920, 71–72; August 1920, 417; January 1921, 45; February 1921, 74; March 1921, 215; July 1922, 476; Millard, *Master Spirit of the Age*.

93. The classic study of this process is Mathewson, *Restriction of Output*.

94. For a discussion of the importance of this phenomenon in corporate-capitalist industry generally, see Littler, "Comparative Analysis of Managerial Structures and Strategies," 171–78.

95. Meredith, *Final Report on Laws Relating to the Liability of Employers*, 36; *MMJ*, September 1915, 840; *HS*, 4 May 1916, 8 (quotation); *Bulletin* (International Machinists' Association), January 1916, 2 (quotation). On the general tendency of incentive wage-payment systems to break down existing work norms, see Hobsbawm, *Labouring Men*, 344–70.

96. Hall, "Model Factory," 588; D.B. Swinton, "Day Work vs. Piecework," *CM*, December 1906, 453; G.C. Keith, "Is Piece-Work a Necessity?" *CM*, April 1907, 122–23; "Machine Shop Time and Cost System," *CM*, September

1907, 34; Nelson, *Managers and Workers*, 52–54, 57–58; Jacoby, *Employing Bureaucracy*, 44–46; *HS*, 17 Feb. 1916, 9 (quotation); *CM*, 31 July 1919, 89 (quotation). In 1917 a group of "foreigners" working for the Hamilton Steel Wheel Company walked out on strike when the company tried to cut their bonus payments. *HH*, 1 March 1917, 2.

97. LAC, R1176-0-0-E , 2338 (quotation); *Clarion*, 1 Aug. 1936, 7 (quotation). The so-called "drive system" of factory supervision is discussed in Slichter, *Turnover of Factory Labor*, 202–3, 375; Nelson, *Managers and Workers*, 43–44; Jacoby, *Employing Bureaucracy*,19–21; Heron, *Workers in Steel*, 93–94.

98. *HT,* 7 Oct. 1910, 13; LAC, R244-76-4-E, Vol. 342, File 29 (4), letter to C.W. Bolton, 25 Feb. 1929 (quotation). A police court case in 1910 brought to light the possibility that a foundry foreman's methods of control could include physical violence. *HS*, 29 Nov. 1910, 14.

99. In 1903 the female employees of the Parisian Steam Laundry applauded their former manager, "whom the girls highly respect," when he dropped in for a visit (the company called the police). In 1907 sewer-pipe workers walked out in support of a foreman fired for raising issues on their behalf. Civic labourers did the same in 1910. In 1921 Tuckett Tobacco workers shut down the plant when their superintendent was discharged. In 1928 175 women in Zimmerknit's finishing department struck over the firing of a popular foreman who had worked for the firm for 20 years and had coached their softball team. *HS*, 20 Nov. 1903, 12; LAC, R244-76-4-E, Vol. 294, File: 2857; Vol. 297, File: 3238; Vol. 327, File 21 (198); Vol. 341, File: 28 (106). See also *HS*, 4 Aug. 1900, 8; 13 April 1909, 1; *CJF*, 1904, 17; *CTJ*, January 1910, 19; Harvester Industrial Council, *Bulletin*, February 1920, 13.

100. Peck, *Reinventing Free Labor*, 59 (quotation), 79; A.W. McDonald, "Labour Turnover in Industrial Plants and What Steps Can Be Taken to Minimize It," Canadian Institute of Mining and Metallurgy, *Bulletin*, September 1920, 707–8 (quotation); *HS*, 30 April 1900, 8; 4 Aug. 1900, 8; 13 April 1909, 1; 9 Oct. 1919, 7; Roberts, ed., *Organizing Westinghouse*, 9; Harney, "Padrone and the Immigrant"; *HH*, 30 July 1907, 1; Kaprielian-Churchill, *Like Our Mountains*, 70; LAC, R244-76-4-E, Vol. 297, File:3231; Roberts, ed., *Baptism of a Union*, 12–15; Brandino, "Italians of Hamilton," 69–70; Patrias, *Patriots and Proletarians*, 66–67; AO, RG 4-32-3188/1931, 10 C, 2275 ("Statement of Strike Committee of the Workers Employed in the National Street [*sic*] Car Co. Sept. 9 1929"); *Worker*, 19 Oct. 1929, 2; Archibald, "Distress, Dissent, and Alienation," 8; Martynowych, *Ukrainians*, 131; Storey, "Workers, Unions, and Steel," 208–11; Freeman, 1005, 29–31; Jacoby, *Employing Bureaucracy*, 173–74. For allegations of sexual harassment in the clothing factories, see Birke: "'Girls Remain Loyal.'"

101. AO, RG 7, II-1, Box 3, File: "Reports – Employment Offices (B-N)," Hamilton; LAC, R1176-0-0-E, 2365 (quotation),

2316 (quotation); McCallum, "Corporate Welfarism," 64–65.

102. Storey, "Workers, Unions, and Steel," 208–11; Freeman, 1005, 29–31; Jacoby, *Employing Bureaucracy*, 180–82.

103. This was also the pattern in New England textile mills and Chicago's packing-houses; see Hareven, *Family Time and Industrial Time*, 38–43; Halpern, "Iron First and the Velvet Glove," 175–77. The superintendent of International Harvester explained that, even with a Planning Department undertaking time studies, foremen still set the piece rate actually paid. *HHB*, November 1920, 19.

104. Heron, "Factory Workers," 531–36; Kristofferson, *Craft Capitalism*; Parr, *Gender of Breadwinners*, 140–42. For Eagle Knitting, see *MT*, 9 Feb. 1894, 994; for Tuckett Tobacco, see *HS*, 24 Dec. 1895, 1; 24 Dec. 1906, 1; *LG*, January 1904, 629; January 1907, 731; for Norton Manufacturing, see *HS*, 24 Dec. 1895, 8; for Hamilton Steel and Iron rolling mills, see *HS*, 5 Feb. 1900, 8; for W.E. Sanford, see *HS*, 12 April 1897, 5; 31 Jan. 1914, 1; *HS*, 24 Feb. 1909, 4; *LN*, 6 Feb. 1914, 1; *CJF*, February 1903, 51; for Gurney Scale, see *HS*, 27 Dec. 1906, 1; for Walter Woods, *HH*, 23 Dec. 1916, 17.

105. Mandell, *Corporation as Family*, 11–24; Tone, *Business of Benevolence*, 16–65; McCallum, "Corporate Welfarism," 47; Canada, House of Commons. *Journals*, 45 (1909–10). Appendix, Part 3; Meredith, *Final Report on Laws Relating to the Liability of Employers*, 32–48. For the larger national campaigns, see Piva, "Workmen's Compensation Movement"; Bliss, *Living Profit*, 55–73.

106. Andrea Tone examined which US firms had introduced welfare measures by 1913 and discovered that they were preponderantly the largest corporations with big clusters of staff in one location in larger cities and with considerable numbers of relatively skilled male workers, notably in the metalworking industries, or large numbers of women workers, who were the most prone to labour turnover. Tone, *Business of Benevolence*, 52–63. For Frost Wire Fence Company, see *LG*, November 1904, 466; December 1904, 327; for Hamilton Bridge, see *CM*, March 1905, 106; for Hamilton Steel and Iron, see Ontario, Inspector of Insurance and Registrar of Friendly Societies, *Report*, 1902, C130; for International Harvester, see *HH*, 4 Jan. 1910, 6; *Harvester World*, November 1909, 14; for Sawyer-Massey, see *HH*, 30 Jan. 1912, 12; 27 April 1912, 5; for National Steel Car, see *HH*, 26 Aug. 1913, 1; for McPherson shoe workers, see *LN*, 13 Feb. 1914, 1 Both *Industrial Canada* and *Hamilton Manufacturer* were enthusiastic about these new "welfare" programs; see *IC*, January 1907, 506; May 1909, 839; September 1909, 121–23; November 1909, 424–27; February 1910, 693–96; March 1910, 786–87; *Hamilton Manufacturer*, 1913, 10.

107. Tone, *Business of Benevolence*, 35 (quotation); *LG*, October 1908, 378; January 1909, 744–45; April 1911, 1056; *HH*, 4

Jan. 1910, 6; 6 Jan. 1910, 8; 28 Jan. 1910, 10; 16 May 1910, 9; 30 Aug. 1910, 6; 15 Dec. 1911, 20; 29 July 1912, 4; 3 Aug. 1912, 1; 14 Jan. 1913, 7; *LN*, 8 Nov. 1912, 1; *Harvester World*, October 1909, 21; December 1909, 24; June 1920, 15; OIFR, 1910, 45–46; *HHB*, January 1920, 32–34; MUA, Westinghouse Fonds, Box 8A, F.4. International Harvester was a leader in "welfare work" across the continent; see Ozanne, *Century of Labor-Management Relations*. In 1911 Westinghouse's general manager raised the idea of "a modern general service or welfare building," but no action was taken until after the war. MUA, Westinghouse Fonds, Box 9, F.3, F.A. Merrick, "Report on Plant and Operation for Year 1911."

108. Dawson, "Relations of Capital and Labour," 172 (quotation); Heron, *Working in Steel*, 98–111; Brandes, *American Welfare Capitalism*, 30–37; Tone, *Business of Benevolence*. International Harvester's response to absenteeism was to hire a returned soldier as a "Look-Up Man" to check in on missing workers. *HHB*, February 1920, 16.

109. For the Steel Company, see Steel Company, *Annual Report*, 1918–19; LAC, R1176-0-0-E, Vol. 3, 2290, 1; HH, 17 May 1920; *ISC*, April 1923, 68; *LG*, January 1929, 18; June 1929, 649–50; Storey, "Workers, Unions, and Steel," 199–213; for Westinghouse, see *Regulations of the Benefit Department of the Canadian Westinghouse Co. Limited* (Hamilton 1923); *Regulations of the Service Pension System* (Hamilton 1923) (copies in AO, RG 7, XV-4, Vol. 3); MUA, Westinghouse Fonds, Box 13, Westinghouse Veteran Employees' Association, Minutes; for International Harvester, see *Harvester World*, 1919–20; *HHB*, 1920; for Canadian Cottons, see *LG*, October 1919, 1121–22; for the elaborate program at Dominion Sheet Metal, see *LG*, July 1919, 755; *LN*, 1 Sept. 1919, 8; *CM*, 31 July 1919, 88–91; *ISC*, September 1919, 220; AO, RG 7, VII-1, Vol. 8; for Union Drawn Steel, see *ISC*, February 1920, 46; for Canadian Cottons, see *CTJ*, 14 Oct. 1919, 472, 480; for Firestone, see *LN*, 31 Oct. 1919, 4; *CLW*, 19 Dec. 1924, 1–2; for Frost Wire, see LAC, R1176-0-0-E, 2514–15; for American Can, see *Service Annuity Plan of the American Can Company and Subsidiary Companies* (n.p. 1924) (copy in AO, RG 7, XV-4, Vol. 3); for Proctor and Gamble, see *HS*, 31 March 1919, 1, 8; *LG*, October 1930, 118; *The Proctor & Gamble Company Pension and Benefit Plan* (Cincinnati 1925) (copy in AO, RG 7, XV-4, Vol. 3); for Hoover, see *HS*, 13 Feb. 1920, 7. See also *LG*, March 1920, 210; HPL, B. Greening Wire Company Fonds; *LN*, 23 Sept. 1920; *Made-in-Hamilton Quarterly*, June 1921, 32; AO, RG 7, VII-1, Vol. 8; Canada, Department of Labour, *Employees' Magazines*, 13, 16, 17, 21; Ontario, Department of Labour, *Survey of Industrial Welfare*; McCallum, "Corporate Welfarism"; Naylor, *New Democracy*, 165–80. In 1921 the Department of Labour publication on company magazines explained that this publication would help with "the downward revision of wages taking place during this readjustment period," making the process "one of peace instead of one accompanied by strikes, disputes and general dissatisfaction." *Employees' Magazines*, 4.

110. *HH*, 27 June 1918; AO, RG 7, II-1, Vol. 3, File: "Reports – Employment Offices (B-N)," Hamilton, 12 Nov. 1919; *CTJ*, 36 (14 Oct. 1919), 483; 39 (19 Dec. 1922), 566.

111. *Fabricator*, 1920–26; *CTJ*, 19 Dec. 1922, 566. For welfare programs at Zimmerknit, see *CTJ*, 2 Sept. 1919, 388; 14 Oct. 1919, 483; 20 Jan. 1920, 33; 3 Sept. 1926, 916; at Canadian Cottons, *CTJ*, 23 Dec. 1919, 605; at Eaton Knitting, *CTJ*, 5 Jan. 1928, 5; *LN*, 25 Dec. 1919, 3; *ND*, 14 Dec. 1922, 4; on the YWCA HPL, YWCA Scrapbook, 39; and, in general, AO, RG 7, VII-1, Vol. 8; and Ontario, Department of Labour, *Survey of Industrial Welfare*; Sangster, "Softball Solution"; Tone, *Business of Benevolence*, 142–65. One company with a large number of female workers, Imperial Cotton, introduced an insurance plan for anyone with three months' service, but in 1925 drastically changed it to cover only those with at least three years' service, thus probably eliminating a large number of women. *Fabricator*, Easter 1920, 14; January 1925, 12.

112. A separate Industrial Council operated at the local International (formerly Oliver Chilled) Plow Works, which the company had taken over. International Harvester Company of Canada, Ltd., *Harvester Industrial Council* (n.p. 1919) (quotation) (copy in AO, RG 7, XV-4, Vol. 3); *HH*, 11 March 1919, 1; 2 May 1919, 1; *HS*, 11 March 1919, 19; 12 March 1919, 6; *LN*, 14 March 1919, 2; 28 March 1919, 1; 29 Aug. 1919, 1; *LG*, 19, April 1919, 440–41; May 1919, 577–81; *CM*, 30 Dec. 1920, 597–600; *CF*, May 1921, 40; Canada, Department of Labour, *Joint Councils in Industry*; Ozanne, *Century of Labor-Management Relations*, 116–161. The plan was the centrepiece of a conference on joint councils organized by the federal Department of Labour early in 1921; see Canada, Department of Labour, *Report of a Conference on Industrial Relations*.

113. LAC, R244-76-4-E, Vol. 319, File 20 (76). The Steel Company seriously considered forming one, but in the end did not; *LG*, January 1919, 46; LAC, R1176-0-0-E, 2290, 2315–16. Another experiment in "industrial democracy" was unfolding at the same time in the building trades, but this one took the form of the British "Whitley Council," which provided for union appointees rather than independent elections. The whole Canadian construction industry was involved, but Hamilton had its own local Industrial Council, which began meeting in 1920. *HH*, 21 July 1920, 1; *LG*, April 1920, 376; June 1920, 628–29; February 1921, 207, 276. Naylor, *New Democracy*, 185–88.

114. RCIRE, Vol. 3, 2289.

115. AO, RG 7, II-1, Vol. 3, File: "Reports – Employment Offices (B-N)," Hamilton, 12 Nov. 1919. These were developments promoted by the Canadian Manufacturers' Association and the new, business-led Canadian Reconstruction

Association, and implemented across the country. Traves, *State and Enterprise*, 15–28, 86–94.

116. *Harvester World*, November 1919, 3 (quotation). Clergymen were particularly impressed with this new public face of industrial capitalism. Allen, *Social Passion*, 141–42; Turkstra, "Christianity and the Working Class," 235.

117. LAC, R244-76-4-E, Vol. 319, File 20 (76); McCallum, "Corporate Welfarism," 63 (quotation).

118. *HH*, 20 June 1916, 7.

119. Ozanne, *Century of Labor-Management Relations*, 120–37; *HS*, 11 March 1919, 19; 12 March 1919, 18; *LN*, 14 March 1919, 2 (quotation); LAC, R1176-0-0-E, 2270–75, 2327–39, 2348–50, 2357–61, 2411, 2481–86 (quotation at 2481), 2538–41.

120. LAC, R1176-0-0-E, 2270–1, 2330–31 (quotation), 2348–49 (quotation), 2358–59, 2412 (quotation), 2481–82 (quotation).

121. *HHB*, April 1920, 6–7, 28; Canada, Department of Labour, *Report of a Conference on Industrial Relations*, 34–35. Harvester workers got a curious version of an "eight-hour day" by continuing to work nine hours, but getting time and a half for the ninth hour. *LN*, 29 Aug. 1919, 2.

122. *HHB*, January 1920, 20–21; February 1920, 4–6, 8 (quotation); April 1920, 15; May 1920, 14; Moore, "A Planning System That *Is* a Planning System"; *CF*, May 1921, 40; *CM*, 21 April 1921, 50 (quotation); *LG*, August 1921, 978–79; Karpelien-Churchill, *Like Our Mountains*, 247, 250–51.

123. One superintendent wrote: "The men got so they paid little attention to the warning whistle, and would come running in on the last minute, punching their clock, and gasping for breath at the same time. Of course it took at least an hour before they could produce at anything like normal, and I had quite a time preventing them discussing at length the events of the noon hour." "Can Welfare Work Be Carried to Excess?" *CM*, 27 April 1922, 29. Gerald Zahavi makes a strong case that workers negotiated within the processes of welfarism to make the system work for them. Andrea Tone and Nikki Mandell argue persuasively that workers nonetheless did not buy into the reciprocity expected by employers in the relationships flowing from welfarism. Zahavi, *Managers and Welfare Capitalism*; Tone, *Business of Benevolence*, 199–225; Mandell, *Corporation as a Family*, 115–30.

124. Ontario, Registrar of Friendly Societies, *Report*, 1916, 132, 148; *HHB*, March 1920, 15; AO, RG 27, VII-1, Vol. 8. In 1919 only roughly one in three of Steel Company's and International Harvester's workers had participated in those firms' limited stock-option plans. LAC, R1176-0-0-E, 2299, 2364. Calculations are mine.

125. LAC, R244-76-4-E, Vol. 370, File 95, Letter dated 13 May 1935; Storey, "Workers, Unions, and Steel."

126. *Harvester Industrial Council*, 7; Nelson, *Managers and Workers*, 144–45.

127. AO, RG 7, VII-1, Vol. 8. On the parallel development in the US, see Jacoby, *Employing Bureaucracy*, 167–205.

128. This conclusion thus contradicts David Brody's influential argument about the role of welfare capitalism in stabilizing the US working class in the 1920s; see "Rise and Decline of Welfare Capitalism."

129. Richard Edwards's suggestion that this period was characterized primarily by capitalists' "technical control" (machine-pacing) of the workforce leans too heavily on a superficial appreciation of the auto industry and minimizes both the new bureaucratization and the residual "simple control" of front-line supervisors. *Contested Terrain*, 111–29. The subsequent book he co-authored with David Gordon and Michael Reich also places great emphasis on mechanization, but adds in the authoritarian supervision of the "drive" system. *Segmented Work, Divided Workers*, 100–64.

130. *CM*, 30 Oct. 1919, 446; 23 Sept. 1920, 293; 2 June 1921, 32–33; *CTJ*, 24 May 1921, 279–80; 16 Aug. 1921, 434–46.

131. There were certainly exceptions. On the Sherman brothers' closer relations with their Dofasco workers, see Storey, "Unionization Versus Corporate Welfare."

132. MUA, Westinghouse Fonds, Box 26, Notice Book, 29 Feb., 13 April 1916; 30 March 1917.

133. *HS*, 6 Jan. 1919, 6 (quotation); 14 Nov. 1921, 6 (quotation); Heron, *Working in Steel*, 88–89. Burlington Steel also ran its rolling mills 24 hours a day in busy periods; *CF*, January 1917, 7. Accurate information on the length of the working day in Hamilton factories is hard to come by, but the uneven data published by the federal Department of Labour, combined with stray references in the press, suggests that, while organized craftsmen, especially in the building trades, were able to get their hours shortened considerably, often to 8 hours per day by 1920, most factory workers were working a 55–hour week in 1911 and, despite some shortening of working hours towards the end of the war, were still putting in 50 to 55 hours by the end of the 1920s. See Canada, Department of Labour, *Wages and Hours of Labour in Canada*, 1901–1920; *CYB*, 1925, 727; 1926, 719; 1931, 795.

134. Heron, *Working in Steel*, 50–72.

135. See, for example, *LG*, April 1919, 380; R.M. Hutton, "Industrial Hygiene in Canadian Factories," *IC*, June 1920, 81–83.

136. OIFR, 1890–1916; for a summary of the accidents in Hamilton, see Table 25. In 1917 the factory inspectorate merged into the new Trades and Labour Branch, and its annual reporting ceased to include the extensive detail formerly provided. OTLBR, 1917.

137. *CM*, 19 June 1913, 643 (quotation). Photographic evidence can be found in the collection of the School of Labour Studies, McMaster University. During its first nine months of operation in 1903 International Harvester

reported 123 serious accidents; 57 were injuries to the hand, with roughly a third of those resulting from working on machinery and another third from objects falling on or otherwise hurting the hand; 13 involved flying objects hitting the eye; 22 injuries were from burns from hot metal, 9 of them to the feet. OIFR, 1903, 42–53. Totals are mine.

138. OIFR, 1916, 82–100. Calculations are mine.

139. OWCBR, 1916, 24 (quotation). For Workmen's Compensation Board statistics, see Table 26. The factory inspectors reported only those accidents that disabled the worker for more than six days. The Compensation Board statistics cover those who lost more than two days' work.

140. The largest categories of non-Anglo-Celtic workers whose injuries were reported to the Workmen's Compensation Board in the years down to 1930 were Southern and Eastern Europeans. OWCBR, 1915–1930; OIFR, 1914, 23; *HS*, 12 Aug. 1913, 13; *HHB*, June 1920, 31; Meredith, *Final Report on Laws Relating to the Liability of Employers*, 36–37; MHSO, ITA-0808-CEC.

141. R.M. Hutton, "Industrial Hygiene in Canadian Factories," *IC*, June 1920, 81–83; *CCJ*, January 1926, 12; Rosner and Markowitz, *Deadly Dust*, 49–74.

142. Tucker, *Administering Danger*.

143. Risk, "'This Nuisance of Litigation.'" In 1903 in Hamilton, according to the *Labour Gazette*, of the ten workers' compensation cases before the courts, "in nearly every instance were they settled out of court by the complainant accepting a proportion of the amount sued for." *LG*, November 1903, 391. In 1908 International Harvester set up a program that encouraged its injured workers to sign a form "agreeing not to hold the company responsible for injuries received at the works," in return for a fixed compensation, but the courts ruled that this document "did not relieve the corporation of responsibility." *HS*, 10 March 1909, 12.

144. LAC, MG R3096-0-8-E, Vol. 16, File: 1911–12, 8 Jan. 1912; Vol. 17, File: 1916–17, 8 Nov. 1916; File: 1920–21, 17 Sept. 1920; Vol. 18, File: 1924–26, 7 April 1925; HPL, HTLC, Minutes, 2 Feb. 1912, 134; *LN*, 27 Nov. 1914, 4 (quotation); *IC*, February 1912, 809–13 (quotation at 810); March 1914, 1033; April 1914, 1135; July 1914, 1530–31; September 1915, 572; October 1915, 668, 671; March 1916, 1176–77; *CM*, 11 June 1914, 567–70; *LG*, November 1918, 1026; February 1919, 205–6; *CTJ*, January 1914, 15; April 1916, 95–97, 115; October 1916, 273–74; 31 March 1927, 281–82; 2 June 1927, 477–78; 23 June 1927, 540.

145. *HS*, 12 Aug. 1913, 13; and Table 25.

146. OWCBR, 1924, 3. For the WCB accident statistics, see Table 26.

11. Standing Up to the Boss

1. The strike as a form of working-class protest had emerged as distinct from the crowd "riot" by the 1870s. Shorter

and Tilly, *Strikes in France*; Cronin, "Strikes and Power"; Palmer, "Labour Protest and Organization."

2. Tilly, Tilly, and Tilly, *Rebellious Century*; Shorter and Tilly, *Strikes in France*; Cronin, "Rethinking the Legacy of Labor."

3. See Friedman, *State-Making and Labor Movements*, 22–63.

4. I explore this "web of dependency" in *Working in Steel*, 98–111.

5. Heron, "Ontario Department of Labour"; Tucker, *Administering Danger*; Craven, *"Impartial Umpire"*; Fudge and Tucker, *Labour before the Law*.

6. Montgomery, *Fall of the House of Labor*, 2.

7. *HT*, 6 April 1907, 1. These comments appeared in a spring when the city saw an unprecedented explosion of militancy among the unskilled.

8. OCUR, 67 (quotations).

9. Brissenden and Frankel, *Labor Turnover*; Jacoby, *Employing Bureaucracy*, 30–37; Meyer, *Five Dollar Day*; Schatz, *Electrical Workers*, 17.

10. *HT*, 2 May 1910, 1; *HH*, 2 March 1912, 22; 9 March 1912, 1; LAC, R3096-0-8-E, Vol. 16, File 1910–11, Executive Committee, Minutes, 29 March 1911; General Meeting, 5 April 1910. In 1906 the Board of Trade had discussed how workingmen hit by high housing costs were leaving (or, as the price of staying, demanding wage increases). *HS*, 17 Oct. 1906, 7.

11. See, for example, the case of nail workers at the Steel Company; *HS*, 26 Oct. 1920, 17.

12. In 1910 the city engineer tried to root out such practices among civic labourers. He argued that "one man would do the digging while the other three would do nothing but smoke their pipes, taking turn and turn about." *HS*, 20 April 1910, 1 (quotation); *HH*, 15 April 1910, 1.

13. Mathewson, *Restriction of Output*; Peterson, "More News from Nowhere."

14. Between 1901 and 1914, 30 per cent of the strikes that I located through reports of the federal Department of Labour and the local press involved no more than 20 workers.

15. Cuts in piece rates: shirt seamstresses in 1897, knitting finishers in 1901, cotton workers in 1907, National Steel Car workers in 1913, and Westinghouse metre assemblers the same year. *CJF*, August 1897, 244; *HS*, 27 Dec. 1901, 1; LAC, R244-76-4-E, Vol. 294, File 2855; Vol. 301, File 13 (11); *HH*, 19 Feb. 1913, 1; 20 Feb. 1913, 1; 24 April 1913, 1.

16. Actions to defend discharged workers: blast-furnace workers in 1901, cotton warpers and machinists in 1903, and teamsters in 1913. In contrast, striking waitresses in a hotel dining room in 1904 insisted that a fellow worker be fired. *HS*, 30 March 1901, 12; 22 April 1903, 1; 6 Aug. 1904, 16; *HT*, 30 March 1901, 1; *CJF*, April 1903, 115; *HH*, 28 March 1913, 3.

17. Work time or safety on the job: moulders over the right to take a cooling-off period in 1903, freight handlers over

having to work late on Saturdays in 1911, and coat pressers over time and a half for overtime in 1912. *HS*, 15 July 1903, 1; 17 July 1903, 1; LAC, R244-76-4-E, Vol. 557, File 3450; Vol. 299, File 3450A. Safety on the job: in 1906 building labourers struck for stronger scaffolding when one of their number fell and died. *LG*, July 1906, 133.

18. Disruptive managerial innovations: knitting-mill cutters in 1902 over changes in work classification imposed by a new foreman, tobacco workers in 1902 and female knitters eight years later over fines for inferior work, civic labourers in 1910 over efforts to get them to shovel more, clothing-factory workers in 1911 over a foreman's attempt to introduce piecework, and Westinghouse's punch-department workers in 1913 over the use of a time clock to monitor their work. *LG*, April 1902, 674; December 1902, 479; *HT*, 29 Nov. 1902, 1; *CJF*, December 1902, 371; LAC, R244-76-4-E, Vol. 297, File 3257; File 3238; Vol. 298, File 3376; Vol. 301, File 13 (11).

19. In 1910 a knitting-mill manager wrote: "There was no strike worthy of the name. Girls left their machines and discussed the question and returned to work in the afternoon with the exception of a very few who came back next morning." The *Herald* added a sexist twist: "Womanlike, they seemed to all want to talk to the head of the firm at once. They became so agitated that Mr. Holton found it necessary to take a walk until they cooled down." LAC, R244-6-4-E, Vol. 297, File 3257.

20. I have developed this argument further in relation to the steel industry in *Working in Steel*, 118–27.

21. See, for example, *LG*, March 1909, 936; June 1913, 1359; *LN*, 23 Feb. 1912, 1; 8 March 1912, 1; 10 May 1912, 1.

22. Heron and Palmer, "Through the Prism of the Strike"; Tomlins, *State and the Unions*, 69–71.

23. *LG*, May 1911, 1355; June 1912, 1175–76; *HH*, 18 April 1912, 1; 9 May 1912, 1; *LN*, 10 May 1912, 1; *IMJ*, June 1912, 45; LAC, R244-76-4-E, Vol. 299, File 3492.

24. *IMJ*, April 1913, 315; *LG*, April 1913, 1060, 1139; July 1913, 87, September 1913, 355; HPL, HTLC, Minutes, 18 April 1913, 257, 261; 2 May 1913, 263, 267; 16 May 1913, 274–75; 6 June 1913, 280; LAC, R244-76-4-E, Vol. 301, File 13 (27); *HH*, 31 Jan. 1913, 1; 17 Feb. 1913, 1; 26 March 1913, 12; 11 April 1913, 4; 21 April 1913, 1; 22 April 1913, 1; 26 April 1913, 1; 5 June 1913, 1; MUA, Westinghouse Fonds, Box 9, F.3, F.A. Merrick, "Report on Plant and Operation Year 1912," 9–10. The strike involved only 38 machine operators out of 276 strikers. The union was attempting to establish a minimum wage of $2.50 per day for these workers, compared with $3.25 for skilled moulders. Westinghouse's concern about the contamination of its handymen by the unionized workers became one of the factors in its decision to build its new foundry, designed for work on moulding machines, at the opposite end of the city from its existing plant. The company issued a

notice reassuring scabs that they would not lose their jobs when strikers returned. MUA, Westinghouse Fonds, Box 26, Notice Book.

25. *LG*, October 1901, 250; Perlman, *Machinists*, 7; Palmer, "Most Uncommon Men," 435–36; *MMJ*, November 1902, 739; July 1914, 700 (quotation); OBLR, 1902, 42. In 1902 the IAM enrolled only 90 of the estimated 300 machinists in the city.

26. Haydu, *Between Craft and Class*, 104. A local union member complained in 1907 that Hamilton machinists were comparatively poorly paid and resistant to organization. *HS*, 28 March 1907, 10; *IB*, April 1911, 1 (quotation).

27. "The average machinist who works ten hours per day ... and who during that ten hours has a speeder standing over him, or the man who has to work all day at top speed to make $3.25, has not energy enough left to drag his weary limbs to an open meeting or to discuss trades unionism if you call upon them," Business Agent Richard Riley lamented in the summer of 1913. *MMJ*, March 1910, 244; May 1910, 441; March 1911, 230; February 1912, 140; 150; March 1912, 442, 449; June 1912, 518; July 1912, 634, August 1912, 730; December 1912, 1125; March 1913, 254; July 1913, 684 (quotation); February 1917, 158; *LN*, 2 Feb. 1912, 1; 9 Feb. 1912, 1; 8 March 1912, 1; 19 April 1912, 3; *HH*, 23 March 1912; IAM, *Bulletin*, October 1914, 4. The Berlin Machine and Tool Works was reported to be requiring men to sign a "yellow-dog," anti-union contract; *LN*, 25 May 1914, 1. The only exception was among the handful who worked for the Toronto, Hamilton, and Buffalo Railway, where, in a new departure for the IAM, its lodge included helpers and specialists. These trends were not far off the pattern of machinists' unionism across North America generally before the war. Montgomery, *Workers' Control in America*, 63.

28. *LN*, 15 May 1914, 1; *IB*, 22 May 1914, 7.

29. *LG*, July 1901, 64; May 1903, 844, 924; LAC, R244-6-4-E, Vol. 294, File 2876; *HS*, 1 June 1901, 1; 30 March 1903, 1; 31 March 1903, 1; 1 May 1903, 1; 4 May 1903, 1; 10 Jan. 1914; *LN*, 29 Nov. 1921, 1; Ashworth, *Helper and American Trade Unions*; Clegg, Fox, and Thompson, *History of British Trade Unions*, Vol. 1, 55–96; AFLP, 1902, 49; 1905, xv. A building labourers' local had emerged briefly in the first decade of the century and was reorganized a decade later as a more general organization open to all outside labourers. By April 1914 it had recruited only 123 members; hundreds more stayed away from its meetings. *LN*, 2 April 1914, 5; *HH*, 25 June 1910, 2; 20 Feb. 1913, 3; 17 March 1913, 7; 10 Jan. 1914, 15; 2 April 1914, 4, 7.

30. Dubofsky, *We Shall Be All*; Leier, *Where the Fraser River Flows*; *HS*, 21 March 1908, 7; *HH*, 23 Feb. 1909, 5; 3 April 1914, 1; 6 April 1914, 7; *HT*, 17 April 1914, 1.

31. *World* (Toronto), 23 Sept. 1913, 3; *HH*, 18 Sept. 1913, 1; 8 Oct. 1913, 1.

32. See, for example, Patrias, *Patriots and Proletarians*; Himka, "Background to Emigration"; Petryshyn, *Peasants in the Promised Land*, 157–61; Bukowczyk, "Transformation of Working-Class Ethnicity."

33. An earlier example of ethnic solidarity occurred late in 1895, when Italian labourers working on construction of the new Toronto, Hamilton, and Buffalo Railway line marched off the job twice beneath "a red handkerchief on a pole" to demand a wage increase. *HS*, 12 Nov. 1895, 8; 13 Nov. 1895, 8; 11 Dec. 1895, 1; 12 Dec. 1895, 1. In April 1907 some 200 labourers at the Hamilton Steel and Iron Company struck for a wage increase and, when successful, decided to stay out for more. Their leader "rushed about the grounds waving a red handkerchief," but when the company called the police to restore order, the men returned to work with their original victory intact. LAC, R244-76-4-E, Vol. 294, File 2857; *HT*, 8 April 1907, 1 (quotation). Two weeks later 300 Italian labourers working on railway construction were unable to get such an increase, partly because they could not convince a gang of "Austrians" to join them. LAC, R244-6-4-E, Vol. 294, File 2868; *LG*, May 1907, 1302; *HS*, 24 April 1907, 1. For the dock workers, see LAC, R244-76-4-E, Vol. 296, File 1909–3162. The *Herald* was commenting on a 1912 strike of immigrant railway labourers; 30 July 1912, 1 (quotation).

34. *HS*, 1 April 1910, 1 (quotation); *HT*, 2 April 1910, 1 (quotation); 12 April 1910, 1; 13 April 1910, 1. For a more detailed account of this strike, see Heron, "Hamilton Steelworkers," 122–24. For the complex role of interpreters in immigrants communities, see Mar, *Brokering Belonging*. That spring the agitation extended to other groups of unskilled labourers. Small strikes erupted in several other Hamilton workplaces without any union leadership – the Toronto, Hamilton, and Buffalo Railway freight sheds, city water and sewer departments, street-railway reconstruction, and Hamilton Brick works. The city engineer alleged, mysteriously, that the sewer labourers' strike "was inspired by someone with a view to getting an increase in pay for laborers throughout the city." LAC, R244-76-4-E, Vol. 557, File 3243; Vol. 297, File 3238; File 3260; *LG*, June 1910, 1372; *HH*, 12 April 1910, 12; 15 April 1910, 1; 21 April 1910, 1; 18 May 1910, 1; 27 May 1910, 16 (quotation); *HT*, 18 May 1910, 12.

35. LAC, R244-76-4-E, Vol. 300, File 3577; *HH*, 29 Aug. 1912, 1; 9 Sept. 1912, 4; 1 May 1912, 1; 2 May 1913, 4.

36. For more on this strike, see Heron, "Working-Class Hamilton," 348–49.

37. In 1910 (a month after the blow-up at the Hamilton Steel and Iron Company), 300 un-unionized male and female workers at Imperial Cotton walked out to get pre-depression wages restored. They gave up after a week. For more detail, see Heron, "Working-Class Hamilton," 443–44.

38. Josephson, *Hillman*, 45–62; Dubofsky, *When Workers Organize*, 49–66, 72–75; Frager, *Sweatshop Strife*; Steedman, *Angels in the Workplace*; Tulchinsky, *Taking Root*, 204–15; McCreesh, *Women in the Campaign to Organize Garment Workers*; Jenen and Davidson, eds., *Needle, a Bobbin, a Strike*. The Hamilton local pulled itself out of the doldrums in 1910 and again in 1911 to head off efforts by local clothing manufacturer Coppley, Noyes, and Randall to introduce piecework and the so-called "team" system of production, which union leaders denounced as the basis of the "sweating" system. In neither case did the women workers play anything more than a passively supportive role when the men struck. LAC, R244-6-4-E, Vol. 298, File 3376; *HH*, 1 Sept. 1910, 1, 10; 2 Sept. 1910, 1; 3 Sept. 1910, 1; 6 Sept. 1910, 1; 7 Sept. 1910, 1; 9 Sept. 1910, 1; 29 Oct. 1910, 1; 20 May 1911, 1; 31 May 1911, 1; *HS*, 1 Sept. 1910, 1; 2 Sept. 1910, 1; 6 Sept. 1910, 1; 7 Sept. 1910, 1; 9 Sept. 1910, 7; *HT*, 1 Sept. 1910, 1. The Hamilton Trades and Labor Council passed a resolution of support for the 1910 dispute that declared the proposed shop methods as "not conducive to good citizenship." HPL, HTCL, Minutes, 2 Sept. 1910, 11–12.

39. *HH*, 12 Oct. 1912, 8; *LN*, 1 Nov. 1912, 1; HPL, HTLC, Minutes, 1 Nov. 1912, 213; *IB*, 24 Jan. 1913, 6; 31 Jan. 1913, 3; *GW*, 24 Jan. 1913, 3; 4 April 1913, 3. At the end of February B.A. Larger, UGWA general secretary, sent a telegram to Hamilton: "Under no circumstances permit cutters, pressers, and tailors of Hamilton to go on strike at this time. We have big strikes on at New York, Philadelphia, Baltimore, Rochester, Boston, and a possibility of Cincinnati walking out. Tell Hamilton garment workers to hold off until we can give them better support. Just now nothing can be done for them." *GW*, 7 March 1913, 2.

40. In Toronto and London clothing workers threatened sympathy strikes if their bosses gave them work from the strike-bound Hamilton companies. LAC, R244-6-4-E, Vol. 301, File 13 (37); *HH*, 8 April 1913, 1; 10 April 1913, 1; 15 April 1913, 19 April 1913; *HS*, 15 April 1913, 1; 19 April 1913, 15; *GW*, 7 March 1913, 2; 18 April 1913, 1.

41. *GW*, 4 April 1913, 3; 25 April 1913, 1; 2 May 1913, 1; 9 May 1913, 1; *HS*, 15–19 April 1913; *HH*, 15–28 April 1913; LAC, R244-76-4-E, Vol. 301, File 13 (37). On the journalistic depiction of female strikers in this period, see McMaster, *Working Girls*, 121–44.

42. *HS*, 15 April 1913, 1; 16 April 1913, 1; 17 April 1913, 1; 18 April 1913, 1; *HT*, 17 April 1913, 1; 19 April 1913, 1; 24 April 1913, 1; Birke: "'Girls Remain Loyal'"; Birke, "'Even Better Than the Boys'"; McCreesh, *Women in the Campaign to Organize Garment Workers*; Jensen and Davidson, eds., *Needle, a Bobbin, a Strike*; Frager, *Sweatshop Strife*; Glenn, *Daughters of the Shtetl*, 167–206. Hamilton's women clothing workers carried out these activities without any help from the kinds of middle-class feminists who joined the fray in other cities. Frager, *Sweatshop Strife*, 138–40;

Steedman, *Angels of the Workplace*, 72–74, 82–83. The clothing workers nonetheless probably benefited from widespread public discussion of the plight of women workers in the city in the winter of 1912–13. *HH*, 13 Jan. 1913, 1; 15 Jan. 1913, 4; 25 Jan. 1913, 7; *IB*, 24 Jan. 1913, 6.

43. Sam Landers argued this case in 1910; see Frager, *Sweatshop Strife*, 111.

44. *HS*, 16 April 1913; *HT*, 19 April 1913.

45. LAC, R244-6-4-E, Vol. 301, File 13 (37); Birke, "'Girls Remain Loyal.'"

46. Some no doubt resented the attitude of Landers, the former Hamilton garment worker who had joined the cautious international leadership of the union as Canadian vice-president, general organizer for Canada, and, for two years, editor of the UGWA's *Weekly Bulletin*. Now, as editor of the new Hamilton *Labor News*, he struck an odd posture as a "neutral" party in case he was "needed later to assist in making an adjustment." *GW*, 8 Aug. 1913, 1; *HH*, 23 April 1913, 14; 25 April 1913, 4 (quotation); 29 April 1913, 1; 17 April 1914, 12 (quotation); 12 April 1916, 1; *HS*, 25 May 1916, 12; *HT*, 18 July 1916, 6. In 1903 during a strike led by a local independent garment workers' union, Landers had intervened to discourage the contractors from settling with the union. In 1914 he supported Altman's attacks. *HH*, 5 Aug. 1916, 13; Heron, "Landers."

47. *HS*, 31 March 1900, 8 (quotation); *IB*, April 1910, 4; 27 Nov. 1914, 4; *HH*, 10 Aug. 1912, 8 (quotation); 17 May 1913, 23 (quotation); *LN*, 25 Sept. 1914, 4.

48. Reported union membership statistics are woefully inadequate. The Department of Labour found 60 locals in Hamilton in 1913, but only 53 in 1914 and 50 in 1916. Of those reporting in 1913, only 36 indicated actual members (3,847); only 32 reported in 1914 (2,684 members). *LOC*, 1913, 12; 1914, 13, 187; 1916, 189.

49. *LN*, 26 March 1915, 1 (quotation).

50. *LN*, 14 April 1916, 1; Bercuson, "Organized Labour and the Imperial Munitions Board."

51. LAC, R1449-0-5-E, Vol. 38, File 1918–19, Mark Irish to Flavelle, 20 June 1918 (quotation); Robin, *Radical Politics and Canadian Labour*, 165 (quotation); Heron and Siemiatycki, "Great War, the State, and Working-Class Canada."

52. LAC, R1449-0-5-E, Vol. 2 File 11, Department of Labour, Basil Magor to J.W. Flavelle, 22 Feb. 1922.

53. *HS*, 8 Aug. 1916, 1 (quotation); *HH*, 23 Jan. 1917, 1 (quotation). The owner of Canadian Steel Goods complained that press reports on labour shortages were only making the problem of workers' independent spirit worse: "Thinking that they now have the situation in their own hands, they hold back and prefer to loiter around in preference to accepting positions which they could fill at good wages, thinking that the factories will eventually give them their demands, whether they are competent or not." *HH*, 12 Aug. 1916, 1.

54. *HH*, 12 Aug. 1916, 1 (quotation); R.H., "The Industrial Slacker," *CF*, May 1918, 105; LAC, R1449-0-5-E, Vol. 2, File Department of Labour, Basil Magor to J. Flavelle, 7 June 1916 (quotation); Dawson, "Relations of Capital and Labour," 172 (quotation).

55. LAC, R1449-0-5-E, Vol. 38, File 1918–19, Mark Irish to Flavelle, 20 June 1918 (quotation); Carnegie, *History of Munitions and Supply*, 252–53 (quotation).

56. *HH*, 6 April 1918, 1; *ODLR*, 1922, 8–9.

57. In a pattern familiar to the Steel Company's managers, the company faced a strike of 250 shell workers and one of 100 labourers in July 1915, a more dramatic, but poorly reported two-week strike of 700 shell workers the following February, a walkout by 150 blast-furnace workers in August 1916, and another by 40 labourers the next spring. All of these were for higher wages and all were unsuccessful. LAC, R244-76-4-E, Vol. 300, File 3577; Vol. 304, File 15 (20); File 16 (27); File 16 (27A); File 16 (37); Vol. 306, File 17 (57); LAC, R1449-0-5-E, Vol. 2, File 11, Department of Labour, Robert Hobson to Flavelle, 17 Feb. 1916; *HH*, 14 Feb. 1916, 1; 16 Feb. 1916, 1; *HS*, 17 Feb. 1916, 9. Dofasco faced similar strikes of immigrant labourers; LAC, R244-76-4-E, Vol. 304, File 16 (27A); Vol. 305, File 17 (48); *HH*, 1 March 1917, 2; 16 April 1917, 2.

58. Haydu, *Between Craft and Class*, 125–43; *MMJ*, September 1915, 840; Rodgers, "Evolution and Revolution," 680 (quotation); for similar comments about the imbalance of machinists' wages and those of the unskilled, see *Typographical Journal*, October 1918, 387–88; *HH*, 3 May 1916, 1; 4 May 1916, 1; "Man-Power Demands and the Supply," *CM*, 25 April 1918, 436; 4 Nov. 1920, 427; *HS*, 22 May 1916, 1; 27 May 1916, 24.

59. *HH*, 3 May 1916, 2 (quotation); 4 May 1916, 9 (quotation); *LN*, 28 Jan. 1916, 1 (quotation).

60. *HH*, 29 Dec. 1917, 1.

61. State Historical Society of Wisconsin, American Federation of Labor Papers, Samuel Gompers Files, Series II, A, Box 23, R. Riley to A. Holder, 4 July 1917 (I am indebted to Myer Siemiatycki for this reference).

62. *CM*, 18 March 1915, 227; *HT*, 18 March 1915, 3; 28 June 1915; IAM *Bulletin*, May 1915, 4; Jan. 1916, 1; April 1916, 4; May 1916, 1; *IB*, 22 Oct. 1915, 1; 19 Jan. 1917, 4; *MMJ*, May 1915, 448; November 1915, 1021; *LN*, 26 March 1915, 1; 14 May 1915, 1; 29 Oct. 1915, 1; 10 Dec. 1915, 1; 28 Jan. 1916, 1; 18 Feb. 1916, 1; 24 March 1916, 1; 31 March 1916, 1; 7 April 1916, 1; Bercuson, "Organized Labour and the Imperial Munitions Board"; Rider, "Imperial Munitions Board," ch. 9; Siemiatycki, "Munitions and Labour Militancy," 134–37.

63. LAC, R1449-0-5-E, Vol. 17, File 1915–16, 5 April 1916.

64. *HS*, 2 May 1916, 1; 4 May 1916, 8, 13; 5 May 1916, 3; *HH*, 3 May 1916, 1, 2; 4 May 1916, 1; 5 May 1916, 1.

65. See, in particular, the voice of an articulate, particularly embittered machinist. *HH*, 4 May 1916, 9.

66. *HH*, 5 May 1916, 1 (quotations); *HT*, 12 June 1916, 12 (quotation); LAC, R1449-0-5-E, Vol. 2, File 11 (Department of Labour 1916). The Commission's report was printed in *LG*, June 1916, 1295–97.

67. LAC, R1449-0-5-E, Vol. 2, File 11 (Department of Labour, 1916), Gerald W. Brown to J.W. Flavelle, 7 June 1916; *HT*, 10 June 1916, 1 (quotation); *HS*, 9 June 1916, 1; 12 June 1916, 1 (quotation); Siemiatycki, "Munitions and Labour Militancy." The less-skilled munitions workers were probably not union members, since the IAM did not recruit them. RCIRE, 2278.

68. *HS*, 12 June 1916, 6; LAC, R174-45-6-E, Vol. 528, File 170–G-1, Labour Troubles: Threatened General Strike of Munitions Workers; Hamilton Strike; Keshen, *Propaganda and Censorship*. For a thorough discussion of the evolution of the strike and its demise, see Siemiatycki, "Munitions and Labour Militancy," 137–51. The strike was not officially declared off until January 1918. LAC, R244-6-4-E, Vol. 304, File 16 (27A), Richard Riley to Bryce Stewart, 4 Jan. 1918. A similar though less dramatic strike was waged that spring against the Toronto, Hamilton, and Buffalo Railway by the machinists, boilermakers, blacksmiths, and car-men in a short-lived coalition known as a "system federation." It was equally unsuccessful and destroyed the federation. LAC, R244-76-4-E, Vol. 557, File 1916–49B.

69. *LN*, 11 May 1917, 27 March 1918; *MMJ*, April 1917, 438. In September 1916 the *Herald* reported that employees in all departments at International Harvester had petitioned the company "several weeks ago" for a nine-hour day and wage increases to make up for the one-hour reduction, but the company provided only a 10 per cent wage hike with no cut in hours. *HH*, 9 Sept. 1916, 1.

70. The preamble of the new organization's constitution rang a clear bell for class struggle and the need for unity among wage-earners: "Modern industrial methods are rapidly wiping out the old craft demarcations, and the resultant conditions dictate the organization of Labor along industrial lines." LAC, R4143-0-4-E, ACWA, *Membership Book and Constitution*, 1915, 10. The union in Hamilton, as elsewhere, would always be active in promoting educational programs with a socialist flavour for its membership. See *HH*, 12 June 1916, 2; *Advance*, 18 May 1917, 7; 21 Jan. 1921, 2; 17 Nov. 1922. Landers accused Isaac Shapiro, a former Hamilton garment worker and the new union's general organizer, of IWW sympathies and snarled from his editor's chair at the *Labor News* that "if such an aggregation with industrial workers' proclivities, as the one endeavoring to form here, ever got a foothold on Hamilton and it spread to other trades, it would be both a calamity to trade unionists and employers of labor in this community." *HH*, 2 Aug. 1916, 12; *LN*, 21 July 1916, 1 (quotation).

71. LAC, R244-6-4-E, Vol. 304, File 16 (19); *HH*, 15, 17, 27 July, 4, 18 Aug. 1916; *HT*, 15 July 1916.

72. *HH*, 17 April 1916, 5; 12 June 1916, 2; 23 March 1917, 9; 27 March 1917, 5; 3 April 1917, 7; 4 April 1917, 1; 5 April 1917, 1; 12 April 1917, 2; 25 Feb. 1919, 1; 25 April 1919; *HS*, 25 Feb. 1919, 1; LAC, R244-6-4-E, Vol. 304, File 16 (19); *Advance*, 16 March 1917, 8; 20 April 1917, 8; 27 April 1917, 7; 18 May 1917, 7; 24 Aug. 1917, 8; 14 Sept. 1917, 8; 21 Sept. 1917, 3; 7 May 1919, 1.

73. In May 1919 clothing manufacturer G.H. Douglas indicated that he ran an open shop and that his firm had not been presented with a set of demands for two years. In July ACWA organizer Shapiro admitted that Hamilton's workers were earning 25 per cent less than those in Toronto and elsewhere. The international was concerned about this situation. LAC, R1176-0-0-E, 2438; *LN*, 25 July 1919; ACWAP, 1920, 174. For the greater success in Montreal and Toronto, see Steedman, *Angels of the Workplace*, 94–98.

74. *IB*, 1 March 1918, 1; *HH*, 17 April 1918, 4; 17 Sept. 1918, 1, 4; 18 Sept. 1918, 1, 4, 7; 20 Sept. 1918, 1; *LOC*, 1918, 43, 95; 1919, 138; *LN*, 22 March 1918, 1; 19 July 1918, 1. Hamilton's police commissioners nervously denied the police the right to affiliate with the larger labour movement. On the blossoming of police unionism across Canada at this point, see Cruikshank and Kealey, "Canadian Strike Statistics," 112. For a count of Hamilton unions at this point, see Table 27.

75. Heron, ed., *Workers' Revolt*; Montgomery, "New Tendencies"; Cronin, "Labor Insurgency." This employer belligerence was part of a national pattern; see Cruikshank and Kealey, "Canadian Strike Statistics," 209–14.

76. The union had restored some informal bargaining clout in the machinery and jobbing foundries, to the extent that one foundry manager was complaining again that "since the Molders' union took possession of my shop I have no say in the running of it." *IMJ*, April 1916, 343; June 1916, 466; June 1918, 448; July 1918, 542; *HH*, 15 Feb. 1916, 12; 3 May 1916, 2 (quotation); 2 Sept. 1916, 1; 4 Sept. 1916, 1; 5 Sept. 1916, 2; 30 Nov. 1916, 1; 21 Dec. 1916, 18; 5 Jan. 1917, 1; 13 March 1918, 7; 3 May 1918, 1; 6 May 1918, 1; 10 May 1918, 4; 16 May 1918, 4; 19 May 1918, 11; 1 June 1918, 9; *IB*, 21 April 1916, 2; 15 Sept. 1916; *LN*, 8 Sept. 1916, 1; 8 Dec. 1916, 1; 29 Dec. 1916, 1; 12 Jan., 18 May 1917; 3 May 1918, 1; 10 May 1918, 1. LAC, R244-76-4-E, Vol. 308, File 18 (80); *LG*, June 1918, 408.

77. *HH*, 18 July 1918, 4 (quotation).

78. LAC, R244-6-4-E, Vol. 308, File 18 (41); *HH*, 24 July 1918, 4; 31 July 1918, 5; *LN*, 2 Aug. 1918, 1; 9 Aug. 1918, 1; 13 Sept. 1918, 1; *IB*, 19 July 1918, 2.

79. Lahne, *Cotton Mill Worker*, 175–200; LAC, R244-76-4-E, Vol. 308, File 18 (51); *HH*, 28 June 1917, 3 Aug. 1918, 2, 3; 6 Aug. 1918, 1; 7 Aug. 1918, 4; 8 Aug. 1918, 4, 7; 9 Aug. 1918, 4; 10 Aug. 1918, 15; 15 Aug. 1918, 6; 16 Aug. 1918, 1; 26 Aug. 1918, 1; 27 Aug. 1918, 1; *HS*, 29 June 1917, 10; *IB*, 31 May 1918, 3; *LN*, 21 June 1918, 1; 28 June 1918, 1; 12 July 1918, 1; 9

Aug. 1918, 1; 16 Aug. 1918, 1; 23 Aug. 1918, 1; 6 Sept. 1918, 4; 4 Oct. 1918, 2; 18 Oct. 1918, 1, 2; *LG*, October 1918, 802–3.

80. LAC, R6113-0-X-E, Vol. 104, 56651 (A.F. Sherwood, "Re I.W.W. and Kindred Organizations," 18 June 1918) (quotation); AO, RG 23, E-30, 1.6; *HH*, 1 Aug. 1918, 1 (quotation); 26 Sept. 1918, 1; Avery, "*Dangerous Foreigners*," 75. On the continued surveillance of radicals, see Horrall, "Royal North-West Mounted Police and Labour Unrest"; Kealey, "State Repression."

81. Cronin and Sirianni, eds., *Work, Community, and Power.*

82. AO, RG 7, II-1, Box 3, File "Reports – Employment Offices (B-N): Hamilton," n.p. In May 1919 the Royal Commission on Industrial Relations heard about local unemployment from many witnesses in its Hamilton hearings.

83. *LN*, 25 Oct. 1918, 1; Naylor, *New Democracy*, 34–41.

84. See, for example, Miller, ed., *New Era in Canada*; Bland, *New Christianity*; Irvine, *Farmers in Politics*; King, *Industry and Humanity*; Leacock, *Unsolved Riddle*; MacIver, *Labor in the Changing World*. For a discussion of this intellectual ferment, see Orwam, *Government Generation*, 80–106.

85. Mainwaring, *International Labour Organization*, 9–19. A Hamilton labour leader, Harry Halford, became a delegate to these international meetings. Heron, "Halford," 83.

86. Reimer, "War, Nationhood, and Working-Class Entitlement"; McCartin, "'American Feeling'"; Kramer and Mitchell, *When the State Trembled.*

87. *HS*, 24 Jan. 1919, 12; 5 Feb. 1919, 5; 17 Feb. 1919, 6; LAC, R1176-0-0-E, 2263–4, 2275–76, 2328, 2347, 2369, 2281, 2356, 2393, 2424, 2483 (quotation), 2525, 2531 (quotation).

88. LAC, R1176-0-0-E, 2281, 2424 (quotations).

89. LAC, R244-76-4-E, Vol. 312, File 19 (108). Machinists, moulders, shoe-workers, painters, and carpenters also pushed the issue that spring. *HH*, 31 March 1919, 1; *HS*, 25 Feb. 1919, 1; *LG*, July 1919, 830–31; August 1919, 946–48; LAC, R244-76-4-E, Vol. 311, File 19 (46).

90. LAC, R1176-0-0-E, 2384; *CF*, March 1921, 41 (quotation); *LN*, 29 June 1917, 2 (quotation); Naylor, *New Democracy*. For a discussion of the wider context of the eight-hour demand, see Cross, "Worktime in International Discontinuity."

91. Heron, ed., *Workers' Revolt*; *LOC*, 1919, 189–91.

92. The strike was against eight firms that made machinery. Moulders in the smaller stove shops were not involved because they had managed to rebuild their union there and by spring 1919 had a new working arrangement with the stove foundrymen's association. The Metal Trades Council played no role comparable to what it did in Winnipeg or Toronto at this point, both because the metalworking unions were too weak and because the moulders had refused to join. LAC, R244-76-4-E, Vol. 312, File 19 (104); *IMJ*, February 1919, 140; March 1919, 222; *IB*, 2 Jan. 1920, 2; Bercuson, *Confrontation at Winnipeg*, 72–74; Naylor, *New Democracy*, 52–59; *LN*, 23 May 1919 (quotation).

93. Heron, "National Contours."

94. By April 1920 the labourers' and steelworkers' unions each reported more than 700 members. *LL*, 23 April 1920, 1. Hamilton saw only 8 strikes throughout 1919, only 4 of them with more than 20 workers. There were 20 in 1920, however, involving a total of 2,622 workers. Calculated from reports by Department of Labour and the local press.

95. LAC, R244-76-4-E, Vol. 319, File 20 (76); Vol. 320, File 20 (125); *LL*, 16 April 1920, 1, 5; *LN*, 7 May 1920, 2; *ND*, 20 May 1920, 2.

96. *LN*, 5 Sept. 1919, 1; 3 Oct. 1919, 1; 31 Oct. 1919, 1; 7 Nov. 1919, 1; 21 Nov. 1919, 1; 28 Nov. 1919, 1; 12 Dec. 1919, 4; 25 Dec. 1919, 3; 20 Feb. 1920, 1; 5 March 1920, 1; 12 March 1920, 1; 15 April 1920, 1; *HS*, 24 Sept. 1919, 20; *ND*, 5 Feb. 1920, 2; 18 March 1920, 1; 29 April 1920, 3; *LL*, 24 Oct. 1919, 1; *AJ*, 11 Sept. 1919, 18; 16 Oct. 1919, 81; 16 Oct. 1919, 3; 11 Dec. 1919, 8; 12 Feb. 1920, 9; 8 April 1920, 8, 18; Heron, *Working in Steel*, 128–38.

97. The Steel Company's workers were not the only targets of this campaign. According to an early member, the Amalgamated's charter "originally covered workers in the old 10" Merchant Mill and the Sheet Mill at Stelco's East End Plant (Hamilton Works), the 20" Bar and 9" Guide Mills in the West End (Ontario Works) and in Burlington Steel's re-rolling mill." Montgomery, "Stelco Story," 5 (quotation). There were apparently enough at Burlington Steel to extract a 7 per cent wage increase for rolling-mill employees in March 1920.

98. MUA, M.T. Montgomery Papers, interview; Steel Company of Canada, *Annual Report* (Hamilton), 1919, n.p.; *AJ*, 20 May 1920, 8; *LN*, 30 Sept. 1920, 1 (quotation); *LL*, 1 Oct. 1920, 7; *HT*, 25 Oct. 1920, 1; Storey, "Workers, Unions, and Steel"; Freeman, 1005, 20–24.

99. LAC, R244-76-4-E, Vol. 320, File 20 (125); *LN*, 7 May 1920, 2; *ND*, 20 May 1920, 2; *AJ*, 6 May 1920, 18; 15 July 1920, 24; 29 July 1920, 13; 23 Sept. 1920, 31; *ND*, 24 June 1920, 1; 1 July 1920, 1; 15 July 1920, 1; *LN*, 25 June 1920, 1; 20 Aug. 1920, 1.

100. The sheet-mill men were hived off into the new Irondale Lodge No.9 and the west-end rolling-mill employees into Unity Lodge No. 10, leaving the original Hamilton Lodge No. 7 as the holding tank for all the remnants. A quarter of a century later a former Canadian member of the Amalgamated believed that "the division of the mills by crafts was its outstanding weakness." Gordon Bishop, "Recollections of the 'Amalgamated'" (typescript; copy in author's possession), 5.

101. *HH*, 29 April 1920, 1.

102. Membership dwindled, and the weakest of the Amalgamated lodges, No. 7, expired in 1923, as did No. 10 by 1925. The last of the three, the sheet-mill men's Irondale Lodge No. 9, limped on until 1932, with its members informally

getting the Steel Company to pay them the Amalgamated scale. *AJ*, 15 July 1920, 24; 4 Nov. 1920, 30, 11 Nov. 1911, 19; 18 Nov. 1920, 14; 17 Feb. 1921, 20; 31 March 1921, 13; 29 Sept. 1921, 18; 24 Nov. 1921, 29; 25 Jan. 1923, 13; *LN*, 9 Dec. 1920, 1; 29 July 1921, 4; *ND*, 24 June, 1 July 1920; *HT*, 25 Oct. 1920; UBC, James Robertson Papers, "Notes from Conversations with Officers of the Steel Company of Canada, Hamilton, Ont., Dec.21/23"; Heron, *Working in Steel*, 148–59.

103. Each of these four strikes was eventually settled by separate negotiations. LAC, R244-76-4-E, Vol. 320, File 20 (116); File 20 (131); File 20 (142); Vol. 321, File 20 (158); *LN*, 19 March 1920, 1; 26 March 1920, 1; 2 April 1920, 1; 16 April 1920, 1; 14 Jan. 1921, 1; *ND*, 1 April 1920, 2; 15 April 1920, 2; 7 July 1920, 1; *HH*, 27 April 1920, 1; *LL*, 30 April 1920, 5; 7 May 1920, 4; 14 May 1920, 7; Naylor, *New Democracy*, 185–88, 201–5.

104. A few months later the builders' labourers gave up and surrendered their union charter. LAC, R244-76-4-E, Vol. 322, File 20 (263); Vol. 323, File 20 (323); Vol. 325, File 21 (87) (quotation); *ND*, 10 June 1920, 1; 17 June 1920, 1; 8 July 1920, 1; 12 Aug. 1920, 1; 7 Oct. 1920, 1; 7 April 1921, 1; *LN*, 25 Feb. 1921, 1; 5 Sept. 1921, 1; 29 Nov. 1921, 1; *LL*, 4 March 1921, 1; 22 April 1921, 1; 27 May 1921, 7; *LG*, April 1919, 437; April 1920, 376; June 1920, 628–29; September 1920, 1108; December 1920, 1604; January 1921, 7; February 1921, 207; September 1921, 1190; Canada, Department of Labour, *Report of a Conference on Industrial Relations*, 36; Canada, Department of Labour, *Joint Councils in Industry*, 9–10.

105. *ND*, 25 Sept., 25 Dec. 1919, 15, 22 April 1920; ACWAP, 1920, 174; *Advance*, 31 Oct., 7 Nov. 1919. Isaac Bainbridge, a former national leader of the defunct Social Democratic Party of Canada, moved to Hamilton in September to take up the job of general organizer for the local clothing workers.

106. Canada, Department of Labour, *Joint Councils in Industry*, 9; Fraser, *Labor Will Rule*, 146–77.

107. *HH*, 5 Jan. 1917, 13; 23 March 1917, 9; 27 March 1917, 5; 12 April 1917, 2; 22 Oct. 1919, 1; *Advance*, 15 June 1917, 7; 23 April 1920, 1; *IB*, 11 Oct. 1918; 28 Dec. 1921, 7; *LN*, 7 May 1920, 1, 28 Jan. 1922, 1; *ND*, 7 April 1921, 1; *LG*, June 1913, 1358. In 1917 the union had won a 10 per cent wage increase for those earning over $10 a week, but a flat $1 – proportionally a much higher increase – for those under that line, including most of the women. Then in 1920 the men got $7 and the women $6 (a striking contrast with the 1913 settlement).

108. *ND*, 2 Sept. 1920, 2; *LN*, 14 Jan. 1921, 1; 21 Jan. 1921, 1; 28 Jan. 1921, 1.

109. *ND*, 3 March 1921, 1; *LN*, 25 Feb. 1921, 1; 28 Jan. 1922, 4; *Advance*, 28 Jan. 1921, 2; 25 Feb. 1921, 3; 4 March 1921, 2; 18 March 1921, 2; 25 March 1921, 1; 27 May 1921, 3; 9 Dec. 1921, 1; 21 July 1922, 1; 28 July 1922, 2; *LL*, 25 Feb. 1921, 1;

18 March 1921, 4; LAC, R244-76-4-E, Vol. 324, File 21 (32); *HS*, 22 Feb. 1922, 1, 15; 23 Feb. 1921,1; 25 Feb. 1921, 1; 10 March 1921, 1; 25 March 1922; ACWAP, 1922, 215; 1924, 14; LAC, R244-76-4-E, Vol. 322, File 20 (249); Vol. 328, File 22 (14); Vol. 330, File 23(2). These conditions encouraged the Toronto-based W.R. Jonston and Company to open a Hamilton plant in what it considered a low-wage, non-union labour market.

110. LAC, R244-76-4-E, Vol. 324, File 21 (32); Vol. 325, File 21 (89); File 21 (95); *ND*, 4 June 1921, 1; *LN*, 29 Nov. 1921, 1; Zerker, *Rise and Fall*, 178–204; Allen, *Social Passion*, 175–96.

111. *LL*, 22 April 1921, 1; *HS*, 11 Dec. 1920, 8 (quotation); *CF*, January 1921, 37 (quotation).

112. On the North American steel industry's hard-core anti-unionism, see Brody, *Steelworkers in America*; Heron, *Working in Steel*; Holt, "Trade Unionism in the British and U.S. Steel Industries." In a tightly knit local business community, the Steel Company's executive officers, especially Hobson, were often the spokespersons for local manufacturers, notably in the 1916 machinists' strike, where federal officials recognized Hobson as the leader of the employers' counteroffensive.

113. In support of the foundry owners' stand against the moulders in 1919, the Employers' Association joined hands with Toronto employers to fight the metal-trades unions and managed to keep their shops "open" until the post-1920 depression eroded the moulders' bargaining strength. In 1920 the foundry employers consolidated their strength in a large new open-shop organization, the Canadian Founders' Association (renamed the Canadian Founders' and Metal Trades' Association a few months later), whose commissioner, C.W. Burgess, kept up a belligerent anti-union campaign well into the 1920s. LAC, R244-76-4-E, Vol. 312, File 19 (104); MG 28, I, 230, Vol. 17, File 1918–19, 11 April 1919; *LN*, 9 May 1919, 2; 16 May 1919, 1; 20 June 1919, 3; 8 Aug. 1919, 1; 12 Sept. 1919, 1; 7 Nov. 1919, 1; 25 Dec. 1919, 1; 13 Feb. 1920, 1; 7 May 1920, 1; 5 June 1920, 1; 29 July 1921, 1; *ND*, 14 Jan. 1920, 2; *CF*, January 1920, 28; *HH*, 29 April 1919, 1; 30 April 1919, 1; 1 May 1919, 1; 2 May 1919, 2; 3 May 1919, 1; 6 May 1919, 1; 7 May 1919, 2; 8 May 1919, 5; 12 May 1919, 4; 17 Feb. 1920, 1; 18 Feb. 1920, 1; *HS*, 28 May 1919, 1; Canada, Department of Labour, *Report on Organization in Industry, Commerce and the Professions*. This time the defeat of the moulders seems to have been permanent; only two of the machinery firms gave in early in 1920, and one of these, the Hamilton Foundry Company, drove out the union in 1925; LAC, R244-76-4-E, Vol. 334, File 25 (10). For Burgess's attacks, see, for example, *CF*, June 1923, 32–34; *MMJ*, January 1925, 25; *CCJ*, December 1924, 37.

114. Hamilton, moreover, lacked the occupational nexuses of metalworker militancy in Canada – the huge railway

shops and shipbuilding yards that became the hotbeds of new organizing and propagandizing for wider workplace solidarities in cities such as Vancouver, Winnipeg, Toronto, Montreal, and Halifax, or Seattle, Glasgow, and Petrograd. The militancy forged in these workplaces grew out of workplace cultures based on all-around skills and proud, "manly" independence – a sharp contrast with the work life of thousands of much more dependent semi-skilled handyman-specialists in Hamilton's metalworking factories, whom the machinists' unions had always been reticent about organizing. The largest group of skilled men accustomed to independent modes of work and action in the city's factories were the moulders. But, unlike the machinists, these men did not belong to a union committed to socialism or to some form of craft amalgamation as a step towards industrial unionism, but rather maintained an aloof distance from other workers, skilled and unskilled – notably refusing to join the revived Metal Trades Council in 1919. Perlman, *Machinists*, 39–56; Laslett, *Labor and the Left*, 144–79; Montgomery, *Workers' Control in America*, 67–82; *LN*, 23 May 1919, 1. On the importance of the railway shopcraft unions, see Bercuson, *Confrontation at Winnipeg*, 192–93; Naylor, *New Democracy*, 52–59; McKay and Morton, "Maritimes," 66: Ewen, "Quebec," 100–1, 110–11; Mitchell and Naylor, "Prairies," 199; Seager and Roth, "British Columbia," 245; Haydu, *Between Craft and Class*, 121–22; Peterson, "One Big Union," 71–72; Montgomery, "New Tendencies"; Cronin, "Labor Insurgency and Class Formation." On the moulders' aloofness, see Helbing, *Departments of the American Federation of Labor*, 48–51; Stockton, *International Molders' Union*, 112–13; Ramirez, *When Workers Organize*, 114–22.

115. In 1912 a west-coast labour leader identified "an element within the trade union movement of Canada, with headquarters at Hamilton, Ont., who refused to accept the activities of socialists among their membership as being just as bone fide and sincere as if their politics were of a different hue." Quoted in *HH*, 16 Nov. 1912. See the Council's attack on a 1912 resolution of the Trades and Labor Congress of Canada convention, which it denounced as "Socialistic propaganda." *HH*, 5 Oct. 1912, 10.

116. In spring 1920 local craft unionists pulled back squeamishly from the incipient general strike of the building trades and the broadening of the strike of the Steel Company operating engineers to other employers. This behaviour had its parallel during the Toronto general strike in 1919, as well as in Calgary during the wave of Western Canadian sympathy strikes that year. Naylor, *New Democracy*, 52–59; Bright, *Limits of Labour*, 145–61.

117. *LL*, 26 Sept. 1919, 2; Siemiatycki, "Labour Contained."

118. *Blacksmiths' Journal*, September 1912, 43.

119. The "Mals" raised more hackles by joining the small nationalist labour congress, the Canadian Federation of Labour, in 1913, through which Flatman spearheaded an abortive effort to launch a national Labour Party in September 1916 before departing with his comrades in evident frustration at the tame and ineffectual CFL leadership. Canadian Federation of Labour, *Proceedings*, 1914, 4, 6; 1915, 4, 8; 1916, 4, 15, 16, 19, 20; 1917, 1, 6–12. Flatman became an active supporter of Hamilton's revitalized Independent Labor Party. In spring 1918 he was the driving force behind an Amalgamation Committee formed by the ASE and the machinists' union, and he campaigned vigorously among other metalworking trades to generate interest in the idea of amalgamating crafts, winning at least a lukewarm reception. *LN*, 1 March 1918, 1; 12 April 1918, 1; 19 April 1918, 1; 5 July 1918, 1; 19 July 1918, 2; 16 Aug. 1918, 2; 24 Jan. 1919, 1.

120. He gave similar attention to the British shops stewards' movement. *LN*, 25 Oct. 1918, 1; 8 Nov. 1918, 1; Hinton, *First Shop Stewards' Movement*.

121. *LN*, 21 March 1919, 2; 9 May 1919, 1.

122. *LN.*, 7 Feb. 1919, 1; PAM, MG 10, A 3, 331 (F.J. Flatman to V. Midgely, 22 April 1919); *Advance*, 25 April 1919, 8 (quotation); *HS*, 28 March 1919, 1. A new machinists' lodge based in the two small railway shops and the three local branches of the ASE (like their comrades in Toronto and Montreal) also voted in favour of the OBU idea. Sympathy could also be expected from the local leadership of the Amalgamated Clothing Workers, who were socialist comrades of the local industrial unionists, and whose international secretary, Sidney Hillman, was making overtures to the leaders of the Western movement during May. Bercuson, *Fools and Wise Men*, 77; *LN*, 21 March 1919, 1; 25 April 1919, 6; *HH*, 10 May 1919, 13; IAM, *Bulletin*, April 1919, 9; PAM, MG 10, A 3, 477–78 (H. Ram to V. Midgely, 2 May 1919) (quotation); 141 (D. Sime to V. Midgely, 3 April 1919), 328 (J. Ferguson to V. Midgely, 22 April 1919), 408 (J.G. Robinson to V. Midgley, 27 April 1919), 457 (A.H. McNamee to V. Midgley, 1 May 1919), 623 (R.J. Johns to V. Midgley, 17 May 1919).

123. AFL organizer John Flett, who had been shocked on returning to Hamilton to find men like Flatman addressing union meetings, also warned the commission about the revolutionary new unionism. *HH*, 14 April 1919, 1 (quotation), 26 May 1919, 1; LAC, R1176-0-0-E, 2382, 2410 (quotation), 2483 (quotations).

124. *ND*, 19 June 1919, 4; 26 June 1919, 4; 3 July 1919, 4; Naylor, *New Democracy*, 69.

125. Naylor, *New Democracy*, 64–66; McKay and Morton, "Maritimes"; *ND*, 17 July 1919, 4; 7 Aug. 1919, 2, 4; 14 Aug. 1919, 3, 4; 21 Aug. 1919, 4; 28 Aug. 1919, 2; *HS*, 29 Sept. 1919, 1.

126. "The Socialists, who for years attempted to destroy the usefulness of the Trade Union movement by every means

possible from the outside, without much success, decided to get into the Trades organizations and bore from within," the *Labor News* snarled. *LN*, 26 Sept. 1919, 2. A year later Harry Halford spoke out as Canada's representative to the new International Federation of Trade Unions against the "revolutionary resolutions" introduced (and passed) at the organization's convention. *LL*, 26 Nov. 1920, 4.

127. *LN*, 13 June 1919, 1; 13 June 1919, 1; 18 July 1919, 4; 25 July 1919, 2; 15 Aug. 1919, 4; 22 Aug. 1919, 2; 5 Sept. 1919, 1.

128. *IB*, 9 May 1919, 1; *LN*, 13 June 1919, 1 (quotation).

129. The international organizer of the textile workers' union who helped launch the Hamilton local in May was described as a well-known "O.B.U. smasher." *HS*, 17, 24, 29 Sept. 1919; *AJ*, 11 Dec. 1919; *LN*, 30 April, 9 July, 13, 20 Aug., 7 Oct. 1920; *ND*, 21 Jan. 1920, 2; 19 Aug. 1920; *HH*, 21 May 1921, 1 (quotation); LAC, R244-76-4-E, Vol. 319, File 20 (76).

130. *LN*, 19 Sept. 1919, 1; 31 Dec. 1919, 1; 30 April 1920, 2; *ND*, 7 Aug. 1919, 2, 4; 14 Aug. 1919, 3, 4; 24 Aug. 1919, 3, 4; 28 Aug. 1919, 2; 23 Oct. 1919, 1; 27 Nov. 1919, 1; *LL*, 7 Nov. 1919, 1; 5 Feb. 1921, 7.

131. Rollo and Halford became key figures in this process. They had been appointed to Robert Borden's new labour advisory group early in 1918, and Rollo would be prominent at the National Industrial Conference in Ottawa in September 1919, while Halford was later a Canadian labour delegate to the International Labour Organization in Geneva. LAC, R6113-0-X-E, Vol. 100, 54035; R3096-0-8-E, Vol. 17, File 1918–19, Executive Committee Meeting, 12 Feb. 1919; *HH*, 8 April 1919, 1 (quotation); *HS*, 8 May 1920, 1; *LN*, 30 April 1920, 1; 14 May 1920, 1; *LL*, 7 May 1920, 4; *ND*, 7 April 1921 (quotation); Canada, National Industrial Conference, *Official Report*, 4. Rollo was praised by one of his labour colleagues as "the go-between for the manufacturers and workers." *LL*, 17 Oct. 1919, 6; 6 Feb. 1920, 4. A few months later he told dinner guests at the new Hoover plant that the non-union company's welfarism was commendable: "If Canadian industrial captains in general took a leaf out of the book of the Hoover Suction Sweeper Company and some other progressive Hamilton firms there would be little unrest in the labor world." *HS*, 13 Feb. 1920, 7.

132. *Worker*, 31 March 1928, 2; 7 July 1928, 2.

133. From 1922 to 1928 Hamilton had only 15 strikes, only 9 of which involved more than 20 workers, and only 3 more than 100 (calculated from reports by the Department of Labour and the local press). The only light in this labour darkness was the reorganization of the garment workers in 1929.

134. LAC, R244-76-4-E, Vol. 342, File 29 (4); Vol. 343, File 29 (87); Vol. 355, File 59; Vol. 368, File 58; AO, Communist Party of Canada Fonds, 10 C, 2275–2437.

135. AO, RG 4-32-3188/1931, 10 C, 2275–2437; *Textile Worker*, February 1929, 653; March 1929, 716–17; *CTJ*, 17 May 1928, 436; 7 Feb. 1929, 18, 21; 21 Feb. 1929, 20; *LN*, 26 Feb. 1929, 1 (quotation); Hall et al., *Like a Family*, 183–236. At the Hamilton Cotton Company, where similar efficiency schemes were being implemented, workers walked out for one day and had to be coaxed back with a wage increase.

136. LAC, R244-76-4-E, Vol. 343, File 29 (87); Vol. 344, File 30 (6); Vol. 353, File 180; Vol. 355, File 59; Vol. 368, File 58; *Worker*, 24 June 1933, 1; Addario, "Fighting Bedeaux"; Lewis, "Workplace and Economic Crisis," 514–15.

137. During the Canadian Cottons strike, local Communist militants repeatedly sniped at the record of cautious leadership by the United Textile Workers and its "craft" structure. As would be clear at Mercury Mills a year later, when workers were encouraged to set up a branch of the Full-Fashioned Hosiery Workers, an affiliate of the UTW, that organization was willing to organize separate locals for different groups of workers within a plant. *HS*, 4 Feb. 1929, 5; 7 Feb. 1930, 7; 10 Feb. 1930, 11; *CTJ*, 7 Feb. 1929, 18. When the short-lived Hamilton Cotton strike was brought to an end by a small wage increase in 1932, the Communists also chided these workers on their loosely organized tactics. *Worker*, 4 Nov. 1933, 4.

138. By August 1925 the Trades and Labor Council had had enough of the Communists' so-called "boring from within" and expelled five radicals, including three from a new labourers' union that the Communists were using as a base in several cities. Four years later the Labor Temple Association barred the Communists from even meeting on its premises, and the Trades and Labor Council introduced a new oath of loyalty to the AFL-led international labour movement. *ND*, 26 Aug. 1920, 3; 9 Sept. 1920, 12; *LN*, 27 Aug. 1920, 1; 28 Aug. 1925, 1; 29 Jan. 1929, 2; *Worker*, 22 Aug. 1925, 4; 2 Feb. 1929, 2; 2 March 1929, 1. These confrontations over Communism were erupting in many unions and labour councils across Canada. Manley, "Does the International Labour Movement Need Salvaging?"; Rodney, *Soldiers of the International*, 107–17.

139. Manley, "Does the International Labour Movement Need Salvaging?"; Buck, *Yours in the Struggle*, 119–23; Manley, "Communism and the Canadian Working Class"; *Worker*, 10 Oct. 1931, 3. By 1935 the WUL would also have some success in organizing leather-jacketmakers and bread-truck drivers in Hamilton; *Worker*, 16 Feb. 1935, 1; 20 Feb. 1935, 1; 23 Feb. 1935, 3; 23 March 1935, 1.

140. *Worker*, 7 July 1928, 2; 6 Oct. 1928, 2; 13 Oct. 1928, 1, 3; 20 Oct. 1928, 2; 27 Oct. 1928, 2; 13 July 1929, 2; 20 July 1929, 2; 10 Aug. 1929, 2; 17 Aug. 1929, 2; 24 Aug. 1929, 2.

141. Manley, "Does the International Labour Movement Need Salvaging?"; Manley, "Communists and Autoworkers"; Pendergast, "Attempt of Unionization"; AO, RG 4-32-3188/1931, 10 C, 2297 (letter from Strikers' Relief

Committee, n.d.) (quotation); 2338 ("Donations Received in Aid of National Steel Car Strikers").

142. *Worker*, 6 May 1935, 1; 7 May 1935, 1; 14 May 1935, 1; 16 May 1935, 2; *Clarion*, 20 June 1936, 1; Storey, "Workers, Unions, and Steel," 182–90.

143. LAC, R244-76-4-E, Vol. 342, File 29 (4); Vol. 353, File 32 (180); Vol. 355, File 59.

144. AO, RG 4-32-3188/1931, 10 C, 2275 (quotation); *HH*, 27 Sept. 1929, 39 (quotation); *HS*, 7 Oct. 1929, 7 (quotation); LAC, R244-76-4-E, Vol. 343, File 29 (987), Charles Aitchison to C.W. Burton, 19 Sept. 1929 (quotation); Vol. 355, File 59 (quotations). The cautious *Labor News* naively blamed the Mercury Mill workers for letting their union fall apart: "If the union had been kept intact, perhaps the objectionable speed-up system would never have been introduced and established." *LN*, 26 June 1933, 2.

145. LAC, R244-76-4-E, Vol. 342, File 29 (4) (quotation in Alex. E. Adam to deputy minister, 11 Feb. 1929); *CTJ*, 21 Feb. 1929, 11.

146. During the 1933 Mercury Mills strike, the Department of Labour's correspondent reported that "our experience with these workers has been in the past, they are afraid to talk" and that even this time they were "very carefull [*sic*] about giving out any information." Initially, to protect against intimidation, they insisted on a delegation of 50 strikers to meet management, but the company said no. LAC, R244-76-4-E, Vol. 355, File 59, M.C. Turnbull, 27 June 1933, 1 Aug. 1933.

147. LAC, R244-76-4-E, Vol. 355, File 59.

148. Even at the Steel Company the men returned to work after ten days with some wage adjustments but no union recognition. LAC, R244-76-4-E, Vol. 368, File 58 (quotation from Toronto *World*, 15 May 1935); *Worker*, 6 May 1935, 1; 7 May 1935, 1; 14 May 1935, 1; 16 May 1935, 2; *Clarion*, 20 June 1936, 1; Storey, "Workers, Unions, and Steel," 182–90.

149. *Young Worker*, October 1929, 1; November 1929, 1, 5; February 1930, 2. In May 1930 the National Steel Car union reorganized as a more broad-based Steel Workers' Industrial Union, but it remained marginal for the next few years. *Worker*, 31 May 1930, 3. In 1932 a Mercury Mills superintendent told a Labour Department official that after the 1930 strike "all employees who took any leading part were shortly after discharged." LAC, R244-76-4-E, Vol. 353, File 32 (180), M.H.C. Turnbull to H.H. Ward, 20 Dec. 1932. LAC, R244-76-4-E, Vol. 355, File 59; *Worker*, 8 July 1933, 1; 15 July 1933, 2. The Hamilton textile industry was still simmering. In October 1933 knitters at the smaller Real Silk Hosiery Mills used a two-day strike to win higher piece rates, and a month later two departments at Hamilton Cotton that walked out to protest the addition of another hour to their workday provoked the company to coax them back quickly with a 10 per cent wage increase. Both strikes followed the old pattern of loose, spontaneous organizing by disgruntled work groups without any union or even any clear decision-making structures (as the Communists pointed out in frustration). The same pattern prevailed in 1936 when a group of weavers at Hamilton Cotton stopped work, convinced the rest of the workforce to join them, and threatened a sit-down strike; the dispute was settled within a day. LAC, R244-76-4-E, Vol. 356, File 115; Vol. 357, File 126; Vol. 380, File 186.

150. The sheet-mill workers' union urged the men to reject the plan, but that was the only department that voted it down (as usual, the large numbers of foreign-born workers were excluded from the vote). The sheet mill then elected the only unionist to the new works council. Storey, "Workers, Unions, and Steel"; *Worker*, 21 May 1935, 4. A few months later McMaster circulated to all company foremen a copy of a leading Canadian banker's speech calling for restraint on wages and greater efficiency, and extolling the benefits of capitalist progress in the face of "Socialist and Communist" critiques. *Worker*, 7 March 1936, 2.

151. Abella, *Nationalism, Communism, and Canadian Labour*, 1–22; *Worker*, 21 May 1935, 4; *Clarion*, 23 Jan. 1936, 2; 30 June 1936, 2; 19 Aug. 1936, 2; 4 March 1937, 3; Storey, "Workers, Unions, and Steel"; Storey, "Unionization Versus Corporate Welfare"; Freeman, 1005. An effort by the Steel Workers Organizing Committee to organize National Steel Car workers in 1937 prompted a brief strike, but no longer-term settlement. LAC, R244-76-4-E, Vol. 391, File 226.

152. The Dominion Glass Company made that clear when two unions in its large Hamilton plant struck in August 1936, bringing out more than 500 workers for union recognition and higher wages. The venerable Flint Glass Workers' Union, an old affiliate of the American Federation of Labor, represented the highly skilled glass mould-makers and machinists, and the Glass Bottle Blowers' Association signed up the rest of the semi-skilled and unskilled workers. After a week, in the face of angry picket-line confrontations with imported strikebreakers, the less-skilled strikers grabbed at a promise of a small wage increase and no discrimination for their strike activities, and scurried back to work. But the skilled men held out for another ten months. All eventually returned on the company's terms, and both unions were crushed. LAC, R244-76-4-E, Vol. 378, File 101; *NC*, 29 Aug. 1936, 1 (quotation), 2; 5 Sept.1936, 2; *Clarion*, 22 Aug. 1936, 1, 7; 24 Aug. 1936, 2; 25 Aug. 1936, 1; 289 Aug. 1936, 1; 31 Aug. 1936, 1; 8 Sept. 1936, 1; 18 Sept. 1936, 3. Elsewhere in Hamilton unions among skilled workers in construction, cap-making, leather-jacket production, and bakeries battled on to retain their wages and right to bargain collectively. Their strikes never involved more than a tiny handful of workers. For the construction trades, see LAC, R244-76-4-E, Vol. 355, File 43

(electricians); File 51 (plasterers); File 57 (bricklayers); File 68 (plumbers). For cap-makers, see LAC, R244-76-4-E, Vol. 355, File 85; Vol. 359, File 17; Vol. 365, File 233; Vol. 371, File 1678; For leather-jacket workers, LAC, R244-76-4-E, Vol. 367, File 11; for bakers, see LAC, R244-76-4-E, Vol. 365, File 259; Vol. 379, File 173; Vol. 392, File 263; File 282; Vol. 396, File 70. New unionists in moving vans, milk trucks, and restaurants, and on the docks also struck for recognition and better wages, generally with only limited success at best; LAC, R244-76-4-E, Vol. 370, File 95; Vol. 371, File 165; Vol. 378, File 106; Vol. 378, File 121; Vol. 379, File 178; Vol. 385, File 80.

153. On the politics of such strikes, see Shorter and Tilly, *Strikes in France*.

154. In 1937, in the context of rancorous debate between craft and industrial unionists inside the AFL, the federation's Ontario organizer lifted the charter of the Hamilton Trades and Labor Council to block an industrial unionist takeover. The two groups then formed separate councils. *Clarion*, 12 Dec. 1936, 3; 11 May 1937, 1; 13 May 1937, 1; Heron et al., *All That Our Hands Have Done*, 144.

155. Several of the construction trades struck in 1933 to stave off wage cuts, but these actions were all within the well-established rituals of collective bargaining in most sectors. Two years later new provincial labour legislation known as the Industrial Standards Act created procedures for establishing common wage rates in construction and other sectors made up of a multitude of relatively small-scale employers. Cox, "Limits of Reform"; Fudge and Tucker, *Labour before the Law*, 188–89.

156. Gerber, *Irony of State Intervention*; Parr, *Gender of Bread-winners*; Holt, "Trade Unionism."

12. The Family Circle

1. Coe and Gates, *Snapshot Photograph*; King, *Say "Cheese"*; Hirsch, *Family Photographs*; Levine and Snyder, eds., *Snapshot Chronicles*; Reynolds, *British Immigrant*, 213. Home photography was no doubt a privilege of better-off workers, and many working-class families would find it hard to scrape together $2.25 for the cheapest Kodak in the 1920s. At that point Kodak still avoided mass advertising on billboards and street cars and preferred to concentrate on the readership of "better" magazines. *HS*, 10 Dec. 1926, 12; Strasser, *Satisfaction Guaranteed*, 102.

2. Bradbury, *Working Families*. The analytical framework for this chapter is deeply indebted to Gillis, *World of Their Own Making*. See also Perrot, ed., *History of Private Life*; Hoggart, *Uses of Literacy*; Orsi, *Madonna of 115 Street*; Cumbo, "As the Twig Is Bent"; Rybczynski, *Home*. The ideals about domesticity expressed in working-class circles by the early 20th century were not new. For their articulation in Southern Ontario labour circles as early as the 1870s, see Burr, *Spreading the Light*, 126–35; and in Britain, McClelland, "Masculinity and the 'Representative Artisan.'"

3. "Theatre of private life, scene of the most personal of learning experiences, and focus of our childhood memories, the home is a fundamental place of commemoration in which our imaginations dwell forever." Michelle Perrot, "At Home," in Perrot, ed., *History of Private Life*, 357.

4. See, for example, Cumbo, "As the Twig Is Bent," 1–83.

5. Sangster, *Dreams of Equality*; Butler, "Mother Russia and the Socialist Fatherland"; Van Goss, "To Organize in Every Neighbourhood."

6. *HS*, 26 Dec. 1910, 8; 27 Dec. 1910, 14; Methodist Church, Board of Management of the Toronto Deaconess Home and Training School, *Annual Report*, 1906–20, in UCA, Methodist Church (Canada), Toronto Conference, Deaconess Board of Management, 78.101C, Box 4; Garvie, *Growing Up*, 31–32; Synge, "Family and Community," ch. 3.1; Gillis, *World of Their Own Making*, 98–104; Restad, *Christmas in America*; Pimlott, *Englishman's Christmas*.

7. Cumbo, *Italian Presence*; *HS*, 29 March 1910, 14 (quotation); *HHB*, January 1920, 20–21; April 1920, 15. Hamilton's Italian residents organized two summertime festas – the feast of St. Anthony on 13 June and the feast of the Madonna on 31 July. MHSO, ITA-09826–FER; ITA-09829–GRI (quotation). For Hungarian cultural celebrations, see Patrias, *Patriots and Proletarians*, 225–27.

8. Cumbo, *Italian Presence*; Ewen, *Immigrant Women*, 236–39.

9. For comparable US patterns before World War One, see Chapin, *Standard of Living*, 191–97. All 175 Armenian labourers in International Harvester's foundry walked out on strike in 1912 when they learned that the company's benefit society intended to bury one of their country-men in an undignified grave with another Armenian; the company quickly relented. Karelian-Churchill, *Like Our Mountains*, 74–75.

10. Synge, "Family and Community," ch. 3.1.

11. This profile of the Spec. Man's chosen households was developed from the information in his daily reports and from *VCHD*, 1907 (all the calculations of totals and percentages are mine). There were 196 visits to Hamilton homes (and then a few more in neighbouring Dundas, which have not been included in this sketch). Because of the changing personnel behind the mask of the "Spec. Man," four households were inadvertently visited twice. More than a third were headed by skilled manual workers (including a handful who had become foremen) and almost another third by semi-skilled and unskilled men (listed in the city directory as "labourers"). Only 10 per cent were in clerical or sales work, and he visited only one professional (a veterinarian), one small-scale manufacturer, and 14 self-employed men, all of whom ran artisanal

businesses (including gardeners, building contractors, a sub-contracting tailor, a shoe repairman, and a blacksmith). Some 10 per cent were women apparently living without a husband.

12. *HS*, 17 April 1907, 7; 15 May 1907, 5.

13. Halttunen, "From Parlor to Living Room"; Cohen, "Embellishing a Life of Labor," 334–36; Jones, "Working-Class Culture," 113; Garvie, *Growing Up*, 4. British working-class housewives disciplined their families to stay out of the parlour, a space that they put great efforts into enhancing as a showplace. Bourke, *Working-Class Cultures*, 66.

14. One night he concluded: "Many southwest end people keep the fronts of their houses shut up and in darkness. They don't spend their evenings in the parlor; probably they surround the range in the kitchen." *HS*, 22 March 1907, 13. For other comments on rows of dark houses without lights in their front windows, see *HS*, 25 March 1907, 7; 15 April 1907, 3.

15. Gillis, *World of Their Own Making*, 90. Newspaper advertisements in this period suggest that dining tables were commonly round and made of heavy oak, and had matching chairs and sideboard.

16. Ewen, *Immigrant Women*, 157–59; Gilliland and Sendbuehler, "To Produce the Highest Type of Manhood and Womanhood."

17. *HS*, 13 April 1907, 1. Synge's working-class interviewees also noted that their fathers were usually home in the evening. Synge, "Family and Community," ch. 3.3. Their evenings would be short. Most of these men would have worked ten-hour days, and, as US economist Paul Douglas wrote in 1930, "The 10-hour day does not leave a great deal of free time.... If we allow 8 hours for sleep, 2 hours for meals, half an hour for transportation, and half an hour for dressing and undressing then the surplus time ... which the worker could spend on himself, was only 3 hours." Douglas, *Real Wages*, 117.

18. *HS*, 21 March 1907, 5; 23 March, 1; 2 April 1907, 7; 11 April 1907, 1; 13 April 1907, 12; 20 April 1907, 7; 22 April 1907, 7; 23 April 1907, 7; 7 May 1907, 11; 8 May 1907, 3.

19. One man was in a militia parade at the armouries. *HS*, 14 May 1907, 7.

20. *HS*, 25 March 1907, 7; 1 April 1907, 7; 22 April 1907, 7; 13 May 1907, 3. One man headed off to the library on his own every week.

21. US studies made the same discovery in this period. Peiss, *Cheap Amusements*, 15–16.

22. *HS*, 9 April 1907, 7; 10 May 1907, 11; 15 May 1907, 5.

23. *HS*, 21 March 1907, 1 (quotation); 19 March 1907, 1 (two female neighbours in the home of a Westinghouse shipper); 8 April 1907 (married daughters in the home of a widow); 13 April 1907, 12 (a female neighbour in the home of a baker); 17 April 1907, 7 (a female neighbour in the home of a clerk from Westinghouse); 18 April 1907, 5 (a female neighbour in the home of a moulder); 27 April 1907, 7 (a female neighbour in the home of a labourer); 7 May 1907, 11 (one female visitor in the home of a widow); 8 May 1907, 3 (two neighbours in the home of a cigar-maker).

24. Synge, "Family and Community."

25. Synge, "Family and Community," ch. 3.1, 3.4, 5.3; see also Morton, *Ideal Surroundings*, 39–40. According to Cohen, American workers in this period also "only invited close friends and family inside." Cohen, "Embellishing a Life of Labor," 336. A British social investigator found the same restraint towards neighbours among working-class families. Reeves, *Round About a Pound a Week*, 33–34. Richard Hoggart made similar observations about English working-class households in the first half of the 20th century: "The hearth is reserved for the family, whether living at home or nearby, and those who are 'something to us,' and look in for a talk or just to sit." Hoggart, *Uses of Literacy*, 34. See also Bourke, *Working-Class Cultures*, 138–51.

26. *HS*, 4 April 1907, 5; 18 April 1907, 5; 19 April 1907, 5; 10 May 1907, 11. In one house all the women of the house were out at an undefined meeting.

27. *HS*, 23 March 1907, 14 (quotation); 25 March 1907, 7; 6 April 1907, 12; 8 April 1907, 7; 11 April 1907, 11; 23 April 1907, 7; 27 April 1907, 7; 30 April 1907, 5; 2 May 1907, 5; 3 May 1907, 5; 4 May 1907, 13; 8 May 1907, 3; 15 May 1907, 5; 25 March 1907, 7.

28. Many claimed to have followed the daily reports on the Spec. Man's perambulations, and one said she liked the *Spectator* because "the advertisements always seemed more complete and because there was such a quantity of news in the paper." *HS*, 8 May 1907, 3.

29. *HS*, 22 March 1907, 13; 27 March 1907, 9; 13 April 1907, 12; 19 April 1907, 7; 20 April 1907, 7; 25 April 1907, 5; 30 April 1907, 5; 2 May 1907, 7; 3 May 1907, 5; 4 May 1907, 13; 6 May 1907, 7; 10 May 1907, 11. One man, a labourer at International Harvester, had built a house out of concrete blocks and painted a mural on the parlour walls; *HS*, 15 April 1907, 3.

30. *HS*, 20 March 1907, 1; 25 April 1907, 5; 30 April 1907, 5.

31. *HS*, 25 March 1907, 7.

32. *HS*, 19 March 1907, 1; 22 March 1907, 13; 25 April 1907, 5 (quotation); see also 17 April 1907, 7.

33. One group was playing dominoes around the dining-room table. *HS*, 5 April 1907, 11.

34. Garvie, *Growing Up*, 3–6; Murphy and Murphy, *Tales from the North End*, 128–29; WAHC, interviews at North End Community Meeting; interviews with Ed Fisher, Jake Isbister, Charles Old, Fred Purser, Lil Seager; Gilliland and Sendbeuhler, "To Produce the Highest Type of Manhood and Womanhood." In 1931 census-takers reported that two-thirds of Hamilton's households had five, six, or seven rooms, which in most cases would have allowed

for the use of rooms described here. Some 20 per cent, however, had fewer than five rooms and would most likely have made the kitchen the main congregating space. Tenants occupied proportionally smaller households than owners – one-third had fewer than five rooms and only three in five had five to seven rooms. CC, 1931, Vol. 5, 1038 (calculations are mine).

35. Rutherford, *Victorian Authority* (quotation at 133); Rutherford, *Making of the Canadian Media*, 38–76; Bruce, *News and the Southams*; HPL, Our Heritage Scrapbook, Vol. 1, 71.

36. Rutherford, *Making of the Canadian Media*; "Tinsley, Richard," *DHB*, Vol. 2, 172–73; Vol. 3, 20–21; Johnston, *Selling Themselves*.

37. Roell, *Piano in America*, 1–28.

38. Garvie, *Growing Up*, 4. In a Pennsylvania steel town a year later, Margaret Byington found many Anglo-Celtic working-class families providing music lessons for their children "so that in the evening they might enjoy such gayeties together.... These quiet family gatherings are apparently the source of much pleasure." Byington, *Homestead*, 110.

39. Kelly, *Downright Upright*; Ehrlich, *Piano*; HS, 6 April 1907, 12. A piano tuner that the Spec. Man interviewed said "more people were buying pianos now than formerly." HS, 10 April 1907, 7.

40. In 1910 the Heintzman and Company ads proposed payments of 50 or 75 cents a week or $5 a month; HS, 22 Aug. 1910, 12; 24 Dec. 1910, 24; 27 Dec. 1910, 8. The leading music stores also sold second-hand pianos, which by 1917 could be priced as low as $35; see, for example, HS, 18 Nov. 1911, 17; 19 May 1917, 9; 25 May 1917, 17; 1 June 1917, 8; 8 June 1917, 21; 23 June 1917, 14. Many of the piano ads nonetheless included scenes of household affluence that would be unlikely to strike a familiar chord among workers; see, for example, HS, 4 Nov. 1911, 17; 8 June 1917, 21; 4 Oct. 1920, 10. A survey of New York working-class families published in 1909 found that fewer than 5 per cent had a piano, and those were concentrated among the higher-income earners. Chapin, *Standard of Living*, 201. Although one of the musical families noted by the Spec. Man was headed by an insurance agent (and former grocer), the other chief breadwinners were a blacksmith, a janitor, a toolmaker, a sub-contracting tailor, and a machinist. The common characteristic among these men, beyond a love of music, was probably relatively steady employment.

41. HS, 19 March, 7; 22 March 1907, 13; 27 March 1907, 9; 18 April 1907, 5; 3 May 1907, 5.

42. This discussion has benefited from a fascinating exchange of messages that appeared on H-LABOR early in 1999 on the complex question of piano ownership. Several of Synge's interviewees remembered music, and sometimes pianos, in their childhood homes; "Family and Community," ch. 3.1. How often the instrument was actually used is suggested by a local CCF club's request for a donated piano in 1934: "In many homes a piano is a useless piece of lumber." NC, 24 Nov. 1934, 6. As for other instruments, Hamilton had several brass bands and small orchestras, including one headed by labour leader Harry Halford; see also Fenwick, "Some Musical Memories," 25–26; Heron, "Halford." In the city's small African-Canadian community, the Washington family members were well-respected performers. WAHC, interview with Floyd Read.

43. Since the mid-19th century a good deal of music publishing in Canada had involved simply republishing US or British works. Kallman, *History of Music*, 113–15, 256–60. But after 1900 considerably more Canadian content appeared; see Argyle, "Rocking with Ragtime"; Steven, "Sounds of the Cities"; "Ragtime," *Encyclopedia of Music in Canada*. By the war years local music stores were selling sheets of popular music for as little as 15 cents a copy (or two for a quarter), and in one case in 1918 for only five cents. HS, 16 Dec. 1911, 10; 1 June 1917, 19; 1 Nov. 1918, 19.

44. The new tunes were promoted as widely as possible through theatres, minstrel shows, vaudeville and movie houses, band concerts, music stores, and dance halls to popularize them and stimulate purchases. Besides hiring "pluggers" to break into song in theatres or music stores, the concerns paid vaudeville stars to sing a new song in their acts and to encourage audiences to join in. In a typical case in 1904, the *Spectator* reported that "It Was Summertime in Dixie Land" had become "the biggest 'song hit'" in the country, being "sung nightly in all the principal theatres from Maine to California." Ewen, *Life and Death*; Jasen, *Tin Pan Alley*; HS, 14 July 1904, 4 (quotation).

45. Ewen, *Life and Death*; Furia, *Poets of Tin Pan Alley*; Tawa, *Way to Tin Pan Alley*; Pessen, "Great Song Writers"; Srigley, "Working Lives and Simple Pleasures," 212, 215–17. Canadian music publishers produced their own ragtime music, including "The Rinaldo Rag" (1909), "The Balloon Rag" (1911), "The Silver Leaf Rag" (1911), "The Ottawa Rag" (1913), and "The Doherty Rag" (1913). Wellinger's rags can be found at LAC, Amicus Nos. 21901676, 22632204, 23070896, 23226665, 23821832; for his other music, see LAC, "Sheet Music from Canada's Past," www.collectionscanada.gc.ca. English immigrants might well have encountered the cheap songbooks that contained many Tin Pan Alley songs and were sold locally in pre–World War Two England; Hoggart, *Uses of Literacy*, 123–37.

46. Roell, *Piano in America*, 29–65; Kelly, *Downright Upright*, 36–41; HS, 11 Nov. 1911, 21; 19 May 1917, 9; 1 June 1917, 8. Prices dropped somewhat in the interwar period, but player-pianos remained far more expensive than simple pianos.

47. Millard, *America on Record*, 17–79; Gellatt, *Fabulous Phonograph*.

48. Similarly, the New York study in the same period found only five working-class households out of 318 surveyed with a gramophone. Chapin, *Standard of Living*, 211.

49. *HH*, 11 Jan. 1917, 6; *HS*, 10 Nov. 1906, 18 (quotation); 18 March 1916, 15; 10 July 1920, 23; *LN*, 5 Jan. 1912, 2 (quotation). For other examples of gramophone advertising, see *HS*, 6 Dec. 1902, 7; 21 Jul 1904, 4, 8; 1 Feb. 1910, 5; 3 Nov. 1911, 15; 9 Nov. 1911, 11; 23 Nov. 1911, 12; 20 May 1913, 12; May 1917, 23; 25 May 1917, 22; 26 Nov. 1920, 9. In 1917 the *Industrial Banner* ran a contest in which those who sent in the largest number of new subscribers would win a gramophone. *IB*, 9 Nov. 1917, 1. Like Henry Ford in car production, gramophone manufacturers saw sales of the machines slump in an apparently saturated market and then plummet in the poor consumerist climate of the 1930s.

50. Kenney, *Recorded Music*, 3–22, 65–87; Millard, *America on Record*, 80–95; Miller, "Talking Machine World," 177–81; Gellatt, *Fabulous Phonograph*; Jasen, *Tin Pan Alley*, 112–92; Cohen, *Making a New Deal*, 104–6; Srigley, "Working Lives and Simple Pleasures," 216–17. For samples of what was being sold in Hamilton in 1920, see *HS*, 10 July 1920, 23; 31 July 1920, 2, 20; 2 Oct. 1920, 8; 11 Oct. 1920, 4. In 1919 a Thiel Detective Agency spy hired by the Steel Company to sniff out militants and radicals reported visiting a north-end music store that catered to Russian immigrants and finding not only records of Russian dance music but also a recording of "the latest Revolutionary song in the Russian language," entitled "Hym Swobada Rossia" (Hymn Freedom of Russia). AO, RG 23, E-30, 1.6, F.H. Whitton to Joseph E. Rogers, 22 Feb. 1919, "Re Investigation, February 14 & 15, 1919," 1.

51. Kenney, *Recorded Music*, 10–11, 14–22, 109–34.

52. According to US sources, piano and record sales slumped dramatically in the interwar period; Roell, *Piano in America*, 199–221; Millard, *America on Record*, 136–75. Statistics on Canadian sales are scanty, but the annual Dominion Bureau of Statistics reporting on the gross value of production and imports of musical instruments indicates a levelling off in the 1920s and a catastrophic collapse in the 1930s. In the early 1920s 68 establishments turned out products worth roughly $10 million; by 1935 just 15 firms were reporting a production value of only $500,000. Similarly, imports of musical instruments, worth more than $2 million during most of the 1920s, plummeted to a mere $300,000 by 1933 and only slowly climbed back up to about $1 million by the end of the decade. See *CYB*, 1922–44.

53. Vipond, *Listening In*, 3–53; MacLennan, "Circumstances beyond Our Control," 3–4; Douglas, *Listening In*, 55–82; Butsch, *Making of American Audiences*, 173–96; Moores, "Box on the Dresser"; CC, 1931, Vol. 5, 980; 1941, Vol. 9, 83.

54. Houghton, "Hamilton's CKOC." In 1931 Ontario stations still averaged less than seven hours a day. Vipond, *Listening In*, 84. CHML originated in 1927 as the voice of prohibitionists; Hanlon, "Lees." For a few years the *Spectator* also owned what was known as a "phantom" station, which broadcast only on another station's wavelength and appears to have been quietly abandoned in the early 1930s.

55. Vipond, *Listening In*, 79–103; MacLennan, "Circumstances beyond Our Control," 98–145; Nolan, "Infant Industry"; Johnston, "Emergence of Broadcast Advertising"; MacLennan, "Toronto's Sound"; Allard, *Straight Up*, 11. A few Canadian stations (notably the powerful CFRB in Toronto) became affiliates of the US networks. Even stations connected to the new government-owned Canadian Radio Broadcasting Commission (CRBC) network, launched in 1932 as a counterweight to the US influence (and reorganized in 1936 as the Canadian Broadcasting Corporation), broadcast US-produced programs. For a time CKOC was part of a 12–station Canadian network, but after such links were shut down in 1932 (by the creation of the CRBC) both Hamilton stations remained completely independent and selectively included some CBC material.

56. McNeill and Wolfe, *Signing On*, 98 (quotation); *HS*, 7 Nov. 1930, 18; 26 Nov. 1932, 13.

57. In 1927 Hamilton's Union Label League announced plans to use "high-class artists" in "entertainment, interspersed with short addresses" to promote the purchase of union-made products. *CCJ*, September 1927, 30. Three years later Westinghouse advertised its radios as a stimulus to "vote intelligently": "Radio thwarts the political charlatan. What is promised in Vancouver over the air must also stand in Halifax. Political partisans cannot distort the issues for local consumption when you hear the actual speeches yourself by radio." *HS*, 22 July 1930, 6. In 1935 the CCF had a regular program known as "The Voice of the CCF." *NC*, 12 Oct. 1935, 8.

58. *Canadian Hotel Review*, December 1933, 19; McNeill and Wolfe, *Signing On*, 96 (quotation); Fairclough, *Saturday's Child*, 29; Fenwick, "Some Musical Memories"; Douglas, *Listening In*, 83–99; Vipond, *Listening In*, 86–89; Allard, *Straight Up*, 51–58; MacLennan, "Circumstances beyond Our Control," 106. When surveyed, US listeners, especially those from lower socio-economic groups, regularly named popular music as their favourite programming. Douglas, *Listening In*, 134; Butsch, *Making of American Audiences*, 197. A study of music played on radio stations in Vancouver, Montreal, and Halifax during the 1930s reported that a substantial majority of the music available, particularly dance music, came from the United States. MacLennan, "Circumstances beyond Our Control," 113–14. Some black musicians such as Bessie Smith, Duke Ellington, and Louis Armstrong built up huge

audiences, although network control worked to tame this "wild," infectious music.

59. MacLennan, "Circumstances beyond Our Control," 115, 119, 124.

60. Vipond, *Listening In*, 79–103; Kuffert, "To Pick You Up or to Hold You"; Smulyan, *Selling Radio*, 93–125; Peers, *Politics of Canadian Broadcasting*, 156–63, McNeil and Wolfe, *Signing On*, 96 (quotation); Nolan, "Infant Industry," 512; Marchand, *Advertising the American Dream*, 88–116.

61. Vipond, "London Listens," 51, 57; Douglas, *Listening In*, 133, 100–23; Pegg, *Broadcasting and Society*, 121–22; MacDonald, *Don't Touch That Dial!* 91–153.

62. Butsch, *Making of American Audiences*, 197. In the 1920s the famous US study of "Middletown" noted mothers' observations that family members no longer went their separate ways in the evening, but "now we all sit around and listen to the radio." Quoted in Cohen, *Making a New Deal*, 133. British social surveyors made similar observations in the 1930s; see Moores, "Box on the Dresser."

63. WAHC, interview with Fred Purser, 23 May 1995.

64. Kuffert, "To Pick You Up or to Hold You"; Moores, "Box on the Dresser"; MacDonald, *Don't Touch That Dial!* 92–112, 234–57. Richard Hoggart suggests that retailers regularly played to English working people's susceptibility to "a personal, friendly and homely manner"; *Uses of Literacy*, 89–91.

65. Mazepa, "Battles on the Cultural Front," 319.

66. Loviglio, *Radio's Intimate Public*.

67. Laverdure, *Sunday in Canada*, 1–2.

68. Bailey et al., *Presbytery of Hamilton*, 120–21.

69. See Table 5.

70. Smyth, "Centenary Methodist Church"; Hanlon, "Moral Order and the Influence of Social Christianity"; Smith, "Dialectics of Faith," 157–58, 213; Turkstra, "Towards an Understanding of the Relationship between the Working Class and Religion"; Addison, "Life and Culture."

71. Moyles, *Blood and Fire*, 3–60; Marks, "Working-Class Femininity and the Salvation Army"; Draper, "People's Religion"; *HH*, 24 June 1907, 5.

72. The early examples were Simcoe St. Methodist (1877), St. Luke's Anglican (1882), Calvin Presbyterian (1887), and St. Lawrence Catholic (1890), followed by, for example, Barton St. Methodist and the Presbyterians' Westminster, Laidlaw Memorial, and St. Giles churches, as well as new ethnically specific parishes of Catholics for Italians and Poles – St. Anthony and St. Stanislaus. The prominent businessmen who were so often the driving force behind these projects evidently believed that workers also needed the moral disciplining of regular church attendance; Smith, "Working-Class Anglicans," 28–30; Addison, "Life and Culture"; Turkstra, "Christianity and the Working Class," 262–63; Gauvreau, "Factories and Foreigners"; Bailey et al., *Presbytery of Hamilton*, 64–65, 95–103, 106,

125–26; *HH*, 16 June 1913, 3. For a parallel development in Montreal, see Trigger, "Protestant Restructuring."

73. This relative class homogeneity makes these new churches different from the socially mixed congregations that Lynne Marks studied in *Revivals and Roller Rinks*.

74. Smith, "Working-Class Anglicans"; Addison, "Life and Culture," 36; Turkstra, "Christianity and the Working Class," 249–51; Gauvreau, "Factories and Foreigners."

75. Addison, "Life and Culture," 73–94; Turkstra, "Christianity and the Working Class," 285–87; Synge, "Immigrant Communities," 38; Smith, "Dialectics of Faith,"53–54; Shadd, *Journey from Tollgate to Parkway*, 206–8. Michael Gauvreau reports that the pastor at Barton St. Methodist used his connections with major east-end employers, including Canadian Westinghouse and International Harvester, to attract recently arrived English workingmen in search of jobs; "Factories and Foreigners."

76. Turkstra, "Christianity and the Working Class," 251–60; Smith, "Working-Class Anglicans," 135–36; Clarke, *Piety and Nationalism*, 62–96; Cumbo, "Salvation in Indifference"; Marks, *Revivals and Roller Rinks*, 22–51; Dirks, "Reinventing Christian Masculinity and Fatherhood"; Braud, "Women's History *Is* American Religious History."

77. Turkstra, "Christianity and the Working Class," 261–64, 274–87; Gauvreau, "Factories and Foreigners."

78. Addison, "Life and Culture," 65.

79. Kenneth Draper has written that one of the most evangelical of the local working-class congregations, the Gospel Tabernacle, "did not present a critique of industrial capitalism, but critiqued a version of Christianity that had implicated itself in wealth and injustice, thereby losing touch with working people"; it "constituted a reform movement in their intention to return Christianity to the people." Draper, "People's Religion," 112; see also Turkstra, "Christianity and the Working Class," 264–69; Christie and Gauvreau, "World of the Common People Is Filled With Religious Fervour." In sharp contrast, Edward Smith indicates that services in the Anglican churches in working-class neighbourhoods were all shaped by high-Anglican ritualism; Smith, "Dialectics of Faith." In the 1920s and 1930s an Italian-Canadian boy was "more than impressed" with a local Catholic priest, Father Bonomi: "his eloquence and his sermons had me enthralled really. Didn't understand what he was talking about but the way his voice modulated and so on, well, you couldn't help but listen. And of course, the singing, the choir, was always good." WAHC, interview with Gene Yachetti.

80. Harrison, "Traditions of Respectability," 185–88.

81. Smith, "Working-Class Anglicans," 133.

82. ACCDNA, *Journal of the Proceedings of the Diocese of Niagara*, 1890–1940; UCCA, *Minutes of the Hamilton Annual Conference of the Methodist Church*, 1891–1926; Cumbo, *Italian Presence*. Dianne Brandino's Italian interviewees

"mentioned yearly church picnics, feast day celebrations, and family weddings as focal points rather than weekly spiritual devotions." Brandino, "Italians in Hamilton," 91.

83. The Anglicans, for example, had to adjust their system of pew rents to allow workers to sublet pews on a service-by-service basis, perhaps only two or three times a year, though this might require the possibly socially awkward step of taking a seat in the midst of the wealthier members of the congregations. Smith, "Dialectics of Faith," 92, 160–61. The poorer working-class families of New York and Montreal were less likely to contribute to churches than were those with higher incomes; Chapin, *Standard of Living*, 207; Reynolds, *British Immigrant*, 220–23.

84. Addison, "Life and Culture," 44.

85. Turkstra, "Constructing a Labour Gospel"; Turkstra, "Christianity and the Working Class," 165–243; *HS*, 1 Oct. 1932, 19; 8 Oct. 1932, 13.

86. Cumbo, "'Cci voli sorti macari a frijiri l'ova'"; Cumbo, "Salvation in Indifference"; Cumbo, *Italian Presence*; Orsi, *Madonna of 115 Street*; Kaprielian-Churchill, *Like Our Mountains*, 311–14. Along with fundamental attachments to some broad Christian principles, Hoggart noted the survival of deeply held beliefs in "fate and destiny" and in numerous superstitions within English working-class families as well; see Hoggart, *Uses of Literacy*, 29–30, 93–99, 114.

87. Turkstra, "Constructing a Labour Gospel."

88. Evangelical Protestant preachers in many cities demonstrated that, even among apparently hard-bitten male absentees from church pews, the intensely emotional appeals of special revivals could tap into powerful religious feelings; see, for example, *HH*, 4 Jan. 1910, 5; 24 Oct. 1910, 5; 26 May 1911, 12; *HS*, 4 Dec. 1907, 16; Draper, "People's Religion"; Turkstra, "Christianity and the Working Class," 258, 266; Gauvreau, "Factories and Foreigners"; Bailey et al., *Presbytery of Hamilton*, 102; Crouse, "They 'Left Us Pretty Much as We Were,'" 51–57; Christie and Gauvreau, *Full-Orbed Christianity*, 37–74; Bederman "'Women Have Had Charge.'"

89. Turkstra, "Relationship between the Working Class and Religion," 28–32; Addison, "Life and Culture," 36–38, 59–61, 87–88; Smith, "Dialectics of Faith," 158–59; Hunter, *Which Side Are You On, Boys*, 5.

90. In 1900, for example, the Presbyterians had 2,588 "scholars" on their Sunday school rolls. Ten years later Hamilton's Anglican churches had 2,721, and in 1921 4,529 (half of them boys). The Methodists signed up 3,976 in 1905 and 5,881 in 1920. In 1920 the Baptists had 1,796 (though considerably fewer showed up each week). In 1909 St. Lawrence Roman Catholic Church had 300 children attending an early-morning mass arranged especially for them each week. *Acts and Proceedings of the Presbyterian Church in Canada*, 1901; *Journal of the Proceedings of the Diocese of Niagara* (Hamilton), 1910, 114; 1921, 126; *Minutes of the Annual Conference of the Methodist Church*, 1906, 1921; *Baptist Year Book*, 1920, 296–97; *HH*, 2 Oct. 1909, 15. At the turn of the century British youth worker Reginald A. Bray commented on what must have been a common experience for the thousands of British immigrants arriving in Hamilton in this period; he was struck by how important religion could be in even the least pietistic families and how attending Sunday school was an "almost universal practice"; see "The Boy and the Family." Many of Synge's Hamilton interviewees remembered Sunday school and churchgoing. Synge, "Family and Community," ch. 3.3. See also Sutherland, *Growing Up*, 69–72.

91. The solidly working-class Barton St. Methodist had 1,624 children on its rolls in 1913; the equally proletarian Calvin Presbyterian enrolled 306 in 1910 and 427 in 1923; Laidlaw Presbyterian signed up 650 in 1920 and 902 two years later (weekly attendance could be much lower, of course – only 377 in 1920 and 600 in 1922 in the last case). These numbers considerably exceeded the adult memberships (in one case, more than half the parents of the students were not church members). Turkstra, "Christianity and the Working Class," 290.

92. Addison, "Life and Culture," 50, 90–91; Gauvreau, "Factories and Foreigners" (statistics); Smith, "Working-Class Anglicans"; and "Dialectics of Faith," 132–33; Addison, "Life and Culture," 50–52, 90–91; Draper, "People's Religion"; Murphy and Murphy, *Tales from the North End*, 53; Hamilton Council of Social Agencies, *Study of Group Memberships*, 12; Dirks, "Serving Church and Nation"; Reed, "Reform Movement of the Sunday School"; Fraser, *Social Uplifters*, 118–19; Sutherland, *Growing Up*, 69–72; McLeod, *Piety and Poverty*.

93. Synge, "Family and Community," ch. 3.1. One of the local Italian Catholic churches held a mass at 8 a.m. on Sunday, known as the "housewife mass," to allow women to attend and then get home to cook the midday meal. MHSO, ITA-09826–FER.

94. McCrossen, *Holy Day, Holiday*; Mirola, "Shorter Hours and the Protestant Sabbath"; Fairclough, *Saturday's Child*, 21–22; Cooper *Rapid Ray*, 15–16.

95. Heron, *Booze*, 152; Reed, "Reform Movement of the Sunday School," 67–76. The 1845 Lord's Day Act banned all forms of commercial activity and labour (except ill-defined "works of necessity" or charity), including hunting, shooting, and fishing, as well as public bathing, drinking, gambling, "noisy" games (such as skittle or football), and other amusements. On mid-19th-century prohibitionist activity, see Heron, *Booze*, 152–53.

96. Meen, "Battle for the Sabbath"; Schrodt, "Sabbatarianism and Sport"; Synge, "Family and Community," ch. 3.1; WAHC, interview with Floyd Read (quotation); MHSO,

ITA–0826–CRE; Cumbo, *Italian Presence*. "Respectable parents did not let their children out of the house on Sunday without shoes or respectable clothes," Brian Harrison writes about British workers." "Traditions of Respectability," 170.

97. The Hamilton Steamboat Company ran regular ferries to Hamilton Beach and on to Toronto. The Hamilton Street Railway Company's charter allowed it to run on Sunday, and electrical radial cars similarly travelled out to the beach (starting in 1896) and Hamilton Mountain (up two incline railways, opened in 1892 and 1900), as well as to Grimsby and other nearby towns. All these lines fell into the hands of the giant Cataract Power Company, which recognized that Sunday business could be lucrative. Cataract's president, John M. Gibson, sat in the Ontario cabinet, which undoubtedly helped to keep any new legislation from threatening that earning power. Mills, *Cataract Traction*; Due, *Intercity Electric Railway Industry*, 61–68; Armstrong and Nelles, *Revenge of the Methodist Bicycle Company*; Manson, *Getting Around Hamilton*, 19–34; Turcotte, *Sand Strip*, 40, 49; Gray, "Gibson"; Cruikshank and Bouchier, "Heritage of the People Closed against Them," 46–47; Henley, *Hamilton, 1889–1890*, 30–31; Henley, *Hamilton: Our Lives and Times*, 22–23.

98. At the turn of the century a one-way ride on the Mount Hamilton Incline Railway cost only 2 cents a passenger (1 cent for children), but a family outing on the radial car to Grimsby that cost 25 cents a head round trip (half price for children) at the turn of the century could eat up a big chunk of a workingman's daily wage. Return trips to Toronto that regularly cost 75 cents before the war (with occasional discounts) were probably completely out of reach. The son of a regularly employed worker at American Can recalled that trips to Dundurn Park were almost weekly, but only sometimes, "when we got a couple of bucks," they would "all go on the radial to the Beach." By the 1920s middle-class reformers were worried that the street-car fare was prohibitive for working-class children; a letter-writer to the *Spectator* lamented workers' "sadly depleted pocket book" to cover "the expenses of such an outing." This was the same pattern uncovered in a New York study in the same period. Synge, "Family and Community," ch. 3.1 (quotation); WAHC, interview with Floyd Read (quotation); Cruikshank and Bouchier, "Blighted Areas and Obnoxious Industries," 476–77, 480 (quotation); Evans, *Hamilton*, 170–71; *HS*, 29 May 1903, 10; 2 April 1909, 16; 29 July 1961, 26; Manson, *Getting Around Hamilton*, 19, 33; Blaine, "*Ride through the Garden of Canada*," 12; Murphy and Murphy, *Tales from the North End*, 32; Chapin, *Standard of Living*, 210–11. Working-class family outings on rail and steamer were also well established in Britain, the United States, and Australia; see Pimlott, *Englishman's Holiday*, 74–95, 151–52, 160–71;

Aron, *Working at Play*, 183–236; White et al., *On Holidays*, 54–87.

99. Meen, "Battle for the Sabbath" (quotation at 100); AO, F885, WCTU 1898 (quotation); Armstrong and Nelles, *Revenge of the Methodist Bicycle Company*, 112 (quotation).

100. Like many other parts of the Canadian craft union movement, the Hamilton Trades and Labor Council had appointed a committee in 1901 to work with the local branch of the Alliance, as part of wage-earners' purely secular struggles to get more time away from the job. *LG*, May 1901, 471; *IB*, November 1905, 3; January 1906, 2; May 1907, 1.

101. Meen, "Battle for the Sabbath"; Laverdure, *Sunday in Canada*, 1–25. The Presbyterian Church's Hamilton Conference had been the sparkplug for the national Sabbatarian movement, and Shearer had become national secretary of the revived Lord's Day Alliance in 1899. A local Methodist clergyman, T.A. Moore, was also recruited as a field secretary.

102. In the midst of the parliamentary deliberations, Shearer assured Hamilton Steel and Iron Company manager Hobson that he would not have to stop running his blast furnaces on Sunday; Canada, House of Commons, *Journals*, 1906, Appendix 1, 133. In 1914 the National Steel Car plant was also operating on Sundays. *HH*, 19 Sept. 1914, 7.

103. A signal victory had been a 1904 legal decision that ice cream was a frivolity that could be sold only in licensed restaurants with other food, and not in drug stores, ice-cream parlours, or confectioneries. Like other local magistrates, Jelfs ruled a year later that such shops could not dodge this ruling by getting a restaurant licence. Henceforth they all decided to close on Sunday, although the Alliance continued to pursue "Sabbath violators" for years after. Few working-class families could ever afford to eat in restaurants in any case. *HS*, 30 May 1900, 8; 9 May 1903, 16; 3 Aug. 1903, 12; 29 April 1907, 12; 8 July 1909, 1; 11 Aug. 1910, 10; 15 Aug. 1910, 10; *Lord's Day Advocate*, December 1904, 7; July 1905, 4, August/September 1905, 6, 11.

104. Greenfield, *Hamilton Public Library*, 26, 43–44, 76–77; *HS*, 20 Sept. 1919, 17. In 1913 a six-month experiment in opening only the public library's reference and reading rooms (but not its circulation service) elicited so little interest that it was ended quickly. Three years later another experiment, this time to serve soldiers, was equally unsuccessful. *LN*, 15 May 1914, 3; *HT*, 31 Jan. 1913, 7; 29 Jan. 1915, 7; *HH*, 11 Feb. 1916.

105. For selections from the parliamentary debate on the new act, see Emery, "Lord's Day Act," 23–51. In March 1907 Hamilton's police magistrate Jelfs had the dubious honour of levelling the country's first conviction under the new act, against a Hamilton news agent who sold US Sunday newspapers (who had already been charged twice before) and who tried the novel device of claiming he was merely

"leasing" the paper to customers. Laverdure, *Sunday in Canada*, 45–67 (quotation at 65); *Lord's Day Advocate*, April 1907, 6; November 1907, 9; January 1908, 11; March 1908, 6; May 1908, 3–5; September 1908, 10; January 1909, 9; April 1909, 6, 8; May 1909, 7, 9; June 1909, 9; *HS*, 4 March 1907, 1; 9 March 1907, 1; 11 March 1907, 1; 18 March 1907, 1; 5 Jan. 1910, 12; 11 Aug. 1910, 10; 15 Aug. 1910, 10; 4 Sept. 1915, 32; 1 June 1917, 32; 20 Sept. 1919, 17; 3 July 1920, 12; 10 July 1920, 12; 4 July 1925, 24; 11 July 1925, 22; 29 July 1961, 26; *HH*, 17 June 1907, 1; 30 Jan. 1909, 7; 16 June 1911, 6 (quotation); 4 July 1918, 4; 18 July 1918, 6; 10 Aug. 1918, 1; 9 Oct. 1920, 15; *LG*, November 1902, 305; Murphy and Murphy, *Tales from the North End*, 31–39. In 1912 a small riot broke out on a north-end wharf when too many tickets were sold for a steamer cruise. *HS*, 25 June 1912, 1. By 1915 steamship companies were advertising "sacred band concerts" at Wabasso Park on Sundays to coax people onto their ferries. *HS*, 31 July 1915, 12. One man born in 1901 told Synge that after the war, "when people began to get cars, it killed all that stuff." The radial lines began closing in the 1920s and were all gone by 1931, largely replaced by buses. Synge, "Family and Community," ch. 5.4; Due, *Intercity Electric Railway Industry*, 52–55, 61–68.

106. *HH*, 17 June 1911, 1.

107. HPL, Hamilton Recruiting League, Minutes, 20 July 1915; 18 Oct. 1915; 16 Nov. 1915; 6 June 1916; 20 June 1916; HPL, Hamilton Military Scrapbooks, Vol. 1 (1914–16); Collinson, *Hamilton Recruiting League*, 27; *LN*, 7 Jan. 1916, 1; *HS*, 11 May 1917, 13; 20 Jan. 1925, 5; 11 Feb. 1925, 5; 22 April 1925, 5; 15 July 1925, 5; 4 March 1930, 7; Laverdure, *Sunday in Canada*, 69–84; Wilson, *Ontario and the First World War*, xlv–xlvi; *HS*, 1 March 1919, 23 (quotation); 29 July 1961, 26; 18 March 1969.

108. On the 19th-century experience, see Heron, "Factory Workers," 539. The local labour movement made the half-holiday a priority, and convinced the Lord's Day Alliance to provide support at least for early closing, which quickly fizzled out. See TFL, MS.Coll. 129, Box 71:1 (Lord's Day Alliance of Canada, Minutes, 1888–1901), 25 June 1901; 71:5 (Minutes – Ontario), Legislative Committee, 4, 29 Jan., 7, 25 Feb. 1901; Item 76 (Ontario Executive Committee, Minutes), 7 Feb. 1901; Item 78 (Ontario Branch, Committees), "Report of the Committee on Saturday Night Early Closing," 7 Nov. 1901. For turn-of-the century strikes in Hamilton for the Saturday half-holiday, see *HT*, 14 April 1902, 1; *LG*, June 1902, 53; May 1903, 925; May 1904, 1105, 113. For reports on shorter hours, OBLR, 1900–14; Canada, Department of Labour, *Wages and Hours of Labour in Canada*, 1901–1920; *Hamilton: The Manufacturing Metropolis*, 10. For reports on Saturday drinking, MPSS. For Kernighan's poem, Heron et al., *All That Our Hands Have Done*, 83. For a parallel decline in US

working hours, see Douglas, *Real Wages*, 112–17. The Steel Company finally ended its 12-hour days in 1930, but to use up the gas it was producing and to take advantage of cheaper weekend electricity rates, it kept the bloom and billet mills running seven days a week. *Clarion*, 23 May 1936, 2.

109. *HS*, 26 May 1903, 1; Heron and Penfold, *Workers' Festival*. Easter and Thanksgiving were less festive and fell in seasons less amenable to outings.

110. McCallum, "Corporate Welfarism," 68. US workers were little better off; Aron, *Working at Play*, 194–205. In Britain somewhat more of them got paid vacations, but still only a small minority; Pimlott, *Englishman's Holiday*, 214–15.

111. The general patterns of public activities on these four holidays were traced through local newspaper reports at five-year intervals from 1890 to 1940.

112. These were certainly moments for dressing up, as special newspaper advertisements for holiday clothing and accessories emphasized (and surviving photographs reveal). Mothers no doubt spent a good part of the day badgering their flock to keep their clothes clean and to stay out of trouble. See, for example, *HS*, 1 Sept. 1900, 1; 22 May 1905, 3; 23 May 1910, 10.

113. See, for example, *HS*, 7 Sept. 1897, 8; 2 Sept. 1901, 8; 4 Sept. 1906, 1. If mothers did not already have a good idea how important their labour was in ensuring the success of these outings, a Canada Bread ad provided a blunt reminder: "You can do much to make or mar the pleasure of a day's outing by the bread you put in the lunch basket." *HS*, 17 July 1920, 12. In Chapin's 1909 study, three-quarters of the New York working-class families surveyed reported taking excursions to parks or friends during the year; *Standard of Living*, 210.

114. Inglis, *Delicious History*, 1–13; Löfgren, *On Holiday*, 91–100.

115. See, for example, *HH*, 16 June 1910, 1 (Hamilton Bridge); 4 July 1910, 8 (Sawyer-Massey); 13 July 1910, 7 (Regal Shirt); 14 July 1910, 12 (Lyon's Tailoring); 18 July 1910, 9 (Tuckett Tobacco); 20 July 1910, 4 (grocers); 22 July 1910, 11 (International Harvester); 26 July 1910, 4 (Journeymen Tailors' Union); 30 July 1910, 4 (Gartshore-Thompson and Otis-Fensom); 16 Aug. 1910, 4 (Chadwick Brothers); 25 June 1912, 1 (street-railway union); 18 July 1912, 4 (grocers); *HS*, 8 Sept. 1903, 1; 8 June 1904, 1 (Coppley, Noyes, and Randall); 11 June 1904, 1 (Kerr and Coomes); 28 June 1904, 8 (Dowswell Manufacturing); 29 June 1904, 1 (Westinghouse); 2 July 1904, 1 (Canada Screw, Otis Elevator, letter carriers); 5 July 1904, 1 (Norton Manufacturing); 14 July 1904 (leather workers); 16 July 1904, 1 (McPherson Shoe, moulders' union, Chadwick Brothers); 22 July 1904, 1 (B. Greening Wire, Canadian Westinghouse); 25 July 1904, 1 (Hamilton Bridge); 6 July 1920, 17; *LN*, 21 May 1912, 4; 7 July 1916, 1 (plumbers' union); 17 Aug. 1917, 1 (female

local of boot and shoe union); 24 Aug. 1917, 1 (moulders' union).

116. Ray Lewis, future Olympic athlete, was a swift runner as a boy and won baskets of groceries for his family in Labour Day races. Palmer, *Culture in Conflict*, 54, 59–60; *HT*, 3 July 1893, 7; 15 Aug. 1893, 5; *HH*, 5 Sept. 1908, 13; 13 Aug. 1912, 5; 3 Sept. 1912, 5; *IB*, July 1907, 1; *LN*, 14 Aug. 1914, 1; 7 Sept. 1915, 4; 31 Aug. 1917, 1; 29 Aug. 1919, 1; 9 Sept. 1920, 1; 8 Sept. 1925, 7; WAHC, interview with Jack Watts; Cooper, *Shadow Runner*, 21; Heron and Penfold, *Workers' Festival*; Clarke, "Religion and Public Space." Hamilton's unions did agree to assemble a labour parade for the 1913 centennial celebrations, but it was held in mid-August as part of more broad-based civic programming, not on Labour Day.

117. See, for example, *HS*, 3 July 1900, 1; 5 Sept. 1905, 5; 21 May 1915, 5; 2 July 1915, 1; 2 July 1920, 17; 26 May 1930, 12; 2 July 1930, 9; 2 July 1935, 13; 25 May 1940, 12. "Of the many holidays during the summer Labor Day is one of the few where there is something going on here to keep citizens at home," the *Spectator* lamented on 5 Sept. 1905.

118. *HS*, 3 Sept. 1892, 8; *HT*, 10 June 1912, 1; 4 July 1925, 11; HPL, Our Heritage Scrapbook, Vol. 2, 28a. Private parks included Mountain View, Claremont, Beaver, and Britannia.

119. Cruikshank and Bouchier, "Blighted Areas and Obnoxious Industries." The city council's only restriction on factory locations was to keep them out of the upper-class area in the southwest corner of the city, a move for which the Local Council of Women took credit. Lyle, *Hamilton Local Council of Women*, 31.

120. *HH*, 17 Aug. 1915, 10; 1 Aug. 1922, 1; HPL, Our Heritage Scrapbook, Vol. 1, 117; Cruikshank and Bouchier, "*Dirty Spaces*."

121. Only the tiny Gore Park in the centre of the city, the small west-end Victoria Park (former site of the famed Crystal Palace), and a six-acre patch of land near the new east-end Westinghouse plant dubbed Woodlands Park, added in 1895.

122. Beveridge, "Hamilton's 'Public' Parks"; Read, "Hamilton Board of Parks Management and Dundurn Park" (quotation at 5). In one of its first steps towards government by non-elected, more elitist commissions, Hamilton's city council replaced its own Parks Committee with a new, quasi-autonomous Board of Parks Management in 1900.

123. "The North End park, instead of being a beauty spot is a disgrace to the city," the Spec. Man wrote in 1907. "For the past few years it has been made a dumping ground for the scavengers and gathers of all kinds of truck and at the present time it presents a most unsightly appearance." *HS*, 27 March 1907, 9; see also HPL, RG 18, Series A (Board of Parks Management, Minutes), 12 Dec. 1900, 7 Aug. 1901, 3 Feb. 1903, 12 Oct. 1904, 10 Aug. 1907, 14 Oct. 1908; Cruikshank and Bouchier, "Blighted Areas and Obnoxious Industries," 470.

124. That same year, 1924, the city council's essentially powerless Town Planning Board (appointed two years earlier) had received a stern lecture from an outside planning expert on the need for more parks, and through the 1920s and 1930s the parks board did eventually acquire some large chunks of undeveloped land on the edges of the city (and, in 1924, a floundering, limited-membership golf course). But the city certainly never seriously contemplated a single large green space on the scale of Toronto's High Park, Montreal's Mount Royal, Vancouver's Stanley Park, Halifax's Point Pleasant, or New York's Central Park. *HH*, 30 Sept. 1922, 15; Terpstra, "Local Politics and Local Planning," 120–27; Couchon, *Reconnaissance Report*. In 1918 the *Herald* suggested that park development was curtailed by real-estate interests that wanted land divided up for building lots. Indeed, in 1910 the merchant prince Stanley Mills had approached the city about buying the Gore in order to build a 15-storey office building, on the roof of which would be a public park. *HH*, 1 March 1918, 6; *HT*, 6 July 1910, 1. Later the parks board chair admitted the exclusiveness of the golf course: "The Golf Links is in no sense a public park accessible to and usable by all classes of the community at all times." HPL, RG 18, Series A, 9 Nov. 1923.

125. Cruikshank and Bouchier, "'Heritage of the People Closed against Them,'" 48; Newlands, "History and Operation of Hamilton's Parks," 9–15; *HH*, 1 Aug. 1922, 1 (quotation); 5 July 1923; 13 July 1923; Murphy and Murphy, *Tales from the North End*, 92–96, 139–47, 235–36; Terpstra, "Local Politics and Local Planning," 121–27.

126. Beveridge, "Hamilton's 'Public' Parks," 4–5; Read, "Hamilton Board of Parks Management and Dundurn Park," 7 (quotation from *HT*); Houghton, "Gore Park"; *HS*, 23 Dec. 1890, 5.

127. HPL, RG 18, 23 April, 2 May 1900, 22 April 1903, 8 Feb. 1905, 8 March 1905, 21 June 1911, 15 May 1912; Our Heritage Scrapbook, Vol. 2, 70–71; *HS*, 23 Dec. 1890, 5; 5 June 1900, 8; 6 July 1900, 8; 6 Aug. 1900, 8; Martin and Segrave, *City Parks of Canada*, 29–31. Much of the new park development of the 1920s and 1930s was devoted to creating a few well-manicured, formal gardens near the entrances to the city in the spirit of the "City Beautiful" movement, as proposed by Noulan Couchon's 1917 report; Terpstra, "Local Politics and Local Planning," 123–25.

128. Several citizens concerned about public access then took the board to court to block this action, but lost their case. HPL, RG 18, Series A, 14, 21 March, 5, 16 April, 2 May 1900; *HS*, 20 June 1900, 8.

129. During the 1890s the Trades and Labor Council had lobbied repeatedly for more parks with athletic facilities.

Kerr, "Rise of Sport"; *HS*, 23 Dec. 1890, 5; HPL, RG 18, Series A, 5 April 1900.

130. *Hamilton: The Electric City*, 48; *HS*, 6 Jan. 1917, 1.

131. Cruikshank and Bouchier, "'Heritage of the People Closed against Them,'" 49; Terpstra, "Local Politics and Local Planning," 123; *ND*, 11 Dec. 1919, 2 (quotation); *HS*, 13 Nov. 1919, 6; 31 Dec. 1927, 5; *HH*, 18 June 1924, 1; 19 June 1924, 3. For a similar confrontation over the use of park space in Vancouver, see McDonald, "'Holy Retreat' or 'Practical Breathing Spot'?"

132. Moore, "Rendezvous for Particular People."

133. The one or two circuses that arrived in Hamilton each year numbered among the nearly 100 touring circus shows moving through North American towns and cities; most of those were eventually absorbed into the Ringling Brothers empire. School children would get notes from their parents to allow them to leave class to watch circus parades. HCCM, 1896–1924 (License Inspector's Reports); *HS*, 16 July 1897, 8; 24 July 1900, 8; 30 July 1900, 8; 2 Aug. 1900, 8; 8 June 1904, 1; 13 July 1904, 8; 14 July 1904, 8; 11 Aug. 1906, 1; 13 Aug. 1906, 7; *HH*, 8 June 1910, 12; 17 May 1911, 1; 18 Aug. 1911, 7; 18 June 1912, 12; 18 June 1913, 1, 4; 26 Aug. 1913, 11; 12 July 1916, 2; 19 May 1919, 7; Davis, *Circus Age*; Oliphant, comp., *Hess Street School*, 38; Beattie, *John Christie Holland*, 47–50; Lenton-Young, "Variety Theatre," 171–76.

134. Kasson, *Amusing the Million*; Register, *Kid of Coney Island*, 85–143; Turcotte, *Sand Strip*, 32; Cruikshank and Bouchier, "'Heritage of the People Closed against Them,'" 47; Henley, *Hamilton: Our Lives and Times*, 64–67; Walden, *Becoming Modern*; *HH*, 11 Feb. 1909, 5; 14 May 1910, 3; 19 May 1910, 5; *HS*, 11 April 1907, 1; 7 May 1907, 26; 14 May 1907, 14; 11 June 1909, 14. Smaller, tamer travelling versions, calling themselves carnivals, also passed through the city regularly, sometimes as a fundraising project for a local group (the Moose from 1914 to 1916 and the Independent Labor Party in 1920, for example). Local politicians and businessmen might also attach such spectacles to industrial exhibitions to promote the city's manufacturing output, such as the Greater Hamilton Exposition in 1909 and another in 1914. In 1903 and 1913 the city itself sponsored week-long "summer carnivals," the second supposedly in honour of its centennial. But the strong opposition of the Canadian Manufacturers' Association and later the Chamber of Commerce to such disruptive amusements suggests little support in the business community for such ventures. *HH*, 4 July 1912, 12; 22 July 1912, 6; 3 July 1913, 14; 27 July 1915, 7; 9 Aug. 1915, 9; 10 Aug. 1915, 4; 8 Aug. 1916, 6; *HS*, 12 Aug. 1920, 8; *LN*, 8 May 1914, 8; 26 June 1914, 5; HPL, ILP Central Branch, Minutes, 27 Aug. 1920; Evans, *Prints of Hamilton*, 67–69; *Greater Hamilton Exposition*, 26; LAC, MG 28, I, 230, Vol. 6, File: 1911–12; File 1913–14; HPL, HCC, Board of Directors, Minutes, 18 Jan. 1921, 128; 8 May 1923, 22.

135. Woody Register argues that the elaborate, respectable amusement park developed in the heart of Coney Island, Luna Park, which after opening in 1903 became the model for hundreds more across the continent, was not aimed primarily at the industrial working class, but rather at the growing numbers of New York's white-collar and middle-class workforce, along with the city's tourists; see Register, *Kid of Coney Island*, 95–97.

136. In New York only a third of families surveyed for Chapin's 1909 study reported spending money on the theatre; Chapin, *Standard of Living*, 210.

137. Levine, *High Brow/Low Brow*; Allen, *Horrible Prettiness*.

138. Henley, *Grand Old Buildings*, 62–63; Brown, "Entertainers of the Road," 125–34. After a wave of criticism the theatre was substantially renovated in 1892. HPL, Our Heritage Scrapbook, Vol. 2, 43–44.

139. In the 1880s Larkin Hall had proclaimed itself the "Canadian Home of Mirth and Mystery," and the Hamilton Dime Museum and Theatre had advertised itself as a place "where the working classes can enjoy a good evening Entertainment at prices within the reach of all," namely, 10 and 20 cents. Through the 1890s other small dime theatres had similar programs, notably the Palace Rink, the Wonderland, and the Standard. *HS*, 10 May 1890, 4: 15 Dec. 1890, 4; 16 Dec. 1890, 8; 24 Dec. 1890, 8; 10 Sept. 1892, 8; 18 Sept. 1893, 8. The minstrel shows are examined in Lott, *Love and Theft*.

140. *HS*, 16 Dec. 1890, 8; 23 Dec. 1890, 1; 24 Dec. 1890, 8; 10 Sept. 1892, 8; 13 Sept. 1892, 8; 16 Jan. 1893, 8; 24 Sept. 1895, 5; 21 Oct. 1895, 1; 23 Feb. 1897, 8; 4 May 1897, 5; 30 Oct. 1897, 5; 16 Jan. 1900, 8; 6 Feb. 1900, 8; 11 May 1900, 8; 21 Nov. 1900, 8; 17 Jan. 1902, 8; 27 Jan. 1902, 8; 28 Jan. 1902, 8; 6 Feb. 1956, 6. The changing definition of "burlesque" in this period is brilliantly analysed in Allen, *Horrible Prettiness*.

141. Snyder, *Voice of the City*; Gilbert, *American Vaudeville*; Kibler, *Rank Ladies*; Lenton-Young, "Variety Theatre." At the turn of the century the street-railway company provided free tickets to summertime vaudeville in Sherman Park (later Nona Park) in the east end (the incline railway did the same for summer-stock shows on Mountain Park), and the Brant House at the Beach ran summertime vaudeville shows on its "Roof Garden." *HS*, 3 July 1900, 8; 4 July 1900, 8; 10 July 1900, 8; 19 July 1900, 8; 23 July 1900, 8; 11 June 1904, 1; 11 June 1904, 1, 4; 13 June 1904, 4; 28 June 1904, 5; Turcotte, *Sand Strip*, 7. The privately owned Mountain View Park was offering summertime vaudeville in 1907, following the annual closing of the regular houses; *HS*, 7 May 1907, 26; 18 May 1907, 15.

142. The Star had been running Saturday-afternoon matinees for the women and children since it opened, but the shows attracted mainly a male audience. *HS*, 18 Sept. 1893, 8; 12 Dec. 1902, 10; 13 Nov. 1903, 12.

143. The performers were drawn from a leading New York agency and regularly announced as well established and wildly popular south of the border. They were supported by a small house orchestra (not simply the tireless pianist who had served all acts at the Star). *VCHD*, 1903, 500; *HS*, 25 Feb. 1905, 20; 8 Sept. 1906, 19 (quotation); 11 Nov. 1906, 5; *HH*, 11 May 1907, 1; 30 Sept. 1914, 12. The quality of the Star's performances had improved sufficiently by 1904 to prompt Canadian Westinghouse to sponsor an outing there for delegates to the Canadian Electrical Association convention; *HS*, 16 June 1904, 4.

144. *HH*, 24 Aug. 1907, 14. In 1910 the "war" ended with a merger.

145. HPL, Henley, "Hamilton in Ragtime" (scrapbook); Henley, *Grand Old Buildings*, 71–72, 84–85, 110–11; Lenton-Young, "Variety Theatre"; Moore, "Rendezvous for Particular People," 126–37 (on Griffin's). English-language legitimate theatre withered away under the pressure of vaudeville's success, and eventually the Grand Opera House fell into line. In 1921, for example, the Grand (having dropped the "Opera House" part of its name) featured the British star Harry Lauder and his vaudeville company. *HS*, 26 Nov. 1921, 5. Unbeknownst to most Hamiltonians, live theatre continued to flourish right through the 1930s in small halls in the new European immigrant neighbourhoods; see, for example, Patrias, *Patriots and Proletarians*, 217–18.

146. *HH*, 18 Jan. 1908, 13.

147. Kibler, *Rank Ladies*, 23–28. Just before the war, as competition stiffened among the sprouting crop of new theatres, the larger houses began to lower prices, so that an evening performance at the Temple ranged from 15 to 50 cents and matinees from 10 to 25. The theatres where movies predominated usually charged 5 to 10 cents for matinees and 10 to 15 cents for evening shows. *HH*, 14 Nov. 1914, 16.

148. Quoted in Snyder, *Voice of the City*, 34. The social composition of theatre audiences has to remain speculative. A 1911 study of New York theatregoers (apparently the only one of its kind) concluded that 60 per cent of the average vaudeville audience and 72 per cent of a movie audience were working class; Snyder, *Voice of the City*, 199.

149. Butsch, *Making of American Audiences*, 114–15; Kibler, *Rank Ladies*, 26–27; Nasaw, *Going Out*, 31; McLean, *American Vaudeville as Ritual*, 48; Jowett, "First Motion Picture Audiences," 199–203; Havig, "Commercial Amusement Audience," 11–12.

150. Recent British immigrants may have been drawn in anticipating a local version of the music halls that so many working people had attended back home. *HH*, 15 April 1910, 1; 30 Aug. 1912, 9, 16; 4 Oct. 1913, 1; 30 Sept. 1914, 12; 17 Nov. 1914, 10; *HT*, 28 Aug.–20 Sept. 1912; *LN*, 20 Sept. 1912, 1 (quotation). Before World War One the city's theatre managers certainly admitted publicly that there were not enough potential customers for all the "big-time"

vaudeville houses in the city. The major economic depression of 1913–15 first prompted a ticket-price war, and then forced one of the brand new theatres to close temporarily and another (Griffin's) to shut down permanently. In 1914 the Savoy even turned back to burlesque to find more customers. The theatre promised that this was "clean, wholesome burlesque" and "a real polite entertainment." *HH*, 4 Oct. 1913, 1; 10 Oct. 1914, 4; 26 Aug. 1915, 9; 26 Feb. 1916, 16; *HS*, 1 Aug. 1914, 1; 8 Aug. 1914, 16.

151. The first Hamilton showing of the celebrated Lumière Cinématographe was in Association Hall from 26 to 28 Nov. 1896, two months after its debut at the Canadian National Exhibition. Gutteridge, *Magic Moments*, 39–126; Morris, *Embattled Shadows*, 13–23; Houghton, ed., "Adults Paid 15 Cents," 49; Steven, "Pleasing the Canadians." A *Spectator* reporter complained that "no one announced the pictures" at one showing in 1897; *HS*, 4 Sept. 1897, 5.

152. *HS*, 16 Dec. 1896, 8; 19 July 1900, 8; 23 July 1900, 8; 31 Jan. 1902, 8; 5 May 1903, 8; 13 Nov. 1903, 12; 10 Dec. 1904, 18; 8 Nov. 1906, 10.

153. *HS*, 23 Feb. 1897, 5; 9 June 1897, 8; 9 June 1897, 8; 4 Sept. 1897, 5; 16 Sept. 1897, 5; 21 Sept. 1897, 8; 6 March 1900, 8; 1 March 1901, 10; 12 Dec. 1902, 10; 18 Feb. 1905, 8; 24 Feb. 1906, 14; 13 Oct. 1906, 20; 8 Nov. 1906, 10; 24 Dec. 1907, 4; 20 Nov. 1908, 10; Houghton, "Adults Paid 15 Cents"; Gutteridge, *Magic Moments*, 51; Fell, "Motive, Mischief, and Melodrama"; Sklar, *Movie-Made America*, 20–30. A few downtown retailers also set up small theatres inside their stores to show the latest productions. *HS*, 6 March 1900, 8; 9 March 1900, 8; 6 April 1909, 7; 24 Dec. 1960, 60. In 1909 the Carey Brothers took over showing movies in Association Hall and dropped the price of the cheapest seats to 5 cents; *HS*, 2 April 1909, 16; 12 Feb. 1910, 13.

154. One of these, the Armory Palm Garden, attached these new attractions to its "ice-cream parlour, refreshment hall, palm lounge, and smoking rooms," alongside its skating rink and dance hall. Another, the Red Mill, created a sensation with its rainbow-coloured glass staircase with water flowing underneath, which led up to a second-floor screening room. When it opened, the Red Mill had a variety of slot machines on its ground floor that could be operated for 1 cent. *HS*, 15 Feb. 1907, 12. The other four were the Unique, the Wonderland (renamed the Colonial in 1909), the Crystal Palace, and the Gayety. *HS*, 25 Jan. 1907, 12; 15 Feb. 1907, 12; 8 June 1907, 24; 15 June 1907, 24; 28 June 1907, 16; 2 July 1907, 14; 2 April 1909, 16 (quotation); *Motion Picture World*, 1 Feb. 1908; *HH*, 18 Jan. 1908, 13; *LN*, 27 Aug. 1915, 3.

155. *HS*, 11 May 1907, 26; *HH*, 18 Jan. 1908, 19. For parallel developments in the United States at precisely the same time, see Sklar, *Movie-Made America*, 18–31; Rabinovitz, *For the Love of Pleasure*, 105–36.

156. Murphy and Murphy, *Tales from the North End*, 211–13. The Unique, Imperial (formerly the Gayety), and Red Mill theatres had first opened in 1907; the Royal came in 1913. *VCHD*, 1907–13. Most of the theatres were initially independently owned, though the Unique was part of a small movie-house chain owned by the vaudeville entrepreneur C.W. Bennett. Moore, "Rendezvous for Particular People," 138–39. A 1910 *Motion Picture Handbook* recommended that the "ideal location" for a nickel theatre was "a densely populated workingmen's residence section, with frontage on a much traveled business street" (quoted in Sklar, *Movie-Made America*, 16). The Britannia opened around 1910, Empire in 1914, Queen's in 1915, Playhouse in 1916, and New Strand in 1917. The 1920s saw another explosion of new east-end theatres – the Kenilworth (renamed the Gregory), Strand, Delta, Main, Cinderella, and Kenmore. The Lyceum also opened on Mount Hamilton and the Regent in the west end. *VCHD*, 1910–1930. Most of these were eventually integrated into large theatre chains, notably Famous Players. Theatre owners also collaborated through trade associations, beginning with the Motion Picture Protective Association of Ontario, founded in 1915. Moore, "Rendezvous for Particular People," 159–60.

157. See, for example, *HS*, 27 Dec. 1918, 20; 3 July 1920, 1; 21 Nov. 1924, 11. By the 1930s the prices ranged between 25 cents at the east-end theatres and 50 cents at the downtown "palaces." *HS*, 4 Nov. 1932, 4.

158. HPL, Our Heritage Scrapbooks, 3 (quotation). The Red Mill seems to have been one of the first to make this transition. It opened with a ground-floor arcade of 100 "peepshow" slot machines and a second-floor theatre with 350 seats. Within a year it had expanded the seating capacity to 600 and added "refined vaudeville" to give patrons "a solid hour of entertainment." *Motion Picture World*, 1 Feb. 1908; *HS*, 29 Oct. 1910, 20. Other small, mixed movie-vaudeville theatres included the Britannia, Colonial, and Unique; *HS*, 26 Feb. 1910, 20; 9 June 1910, 12; 25 June 1910, 20.

159. In 1909 the Savoy decided to shift the balance to give movies priority, as did the Lyric five years later. *HS*, 3 Oct. 1908, 16; 10 Oct. 1908, 7; 17 April 1909, 12; 30 Oct. 1909, 20; 2 April 1910, 24; 9 April 1910, 16; 30 April 1910, 24; 1 Oct. 1910, 20; *HH*, 21 May 1910, 7; 13 Feb. 1914, 15; Bachman, "Still in the Dark," 31–34.

160. See, for example, *HS*, 26 Nov. 1921, 101, where only the Lyric foregrounds its vaudeville acts. Significantly, for the opening ceremonies of Hamilton's most elegant theatres, Loew's and Pantages, the featured guests were movie stars.

161. Morris, *Embattled Shadows*, 23. In 1935 the venerable Grand Opera House was converted to a movie theatre known as the Granada. Well before World War One,

movie production and distribution had followed the path of corporate concentration seen in vaudeville (and so many other industries) as Edison pulled together a cartel of major US and French companies popularly known as the "Trust." The demand for films to supply the vastly larger number of movie houses in the decade before the war stimulated an ambitious crop of independent producers, many of them rooted in immigrant ghettoes in the United States. There were virtually no Canadian filmmakers, and before the war the flickering images presented to the workers who flocked into the new movie houses came from the United States, Britain, and, to a remarkable extent, France. During World War One US control tightened, and a handful of powerful capitalists built vast empires of production, distribution, and theatre exhibition based in the new mecca of cinema, Hollywood, California. By the 1920s most Hamilton audiences sat in theatres controlled by US distributors, especially Famous Players, and watched movies that were showing all over North America. Pendakur, *Canadian Dreams and American Control*, 45–78.

162. Upper-class interest in this more refined product became unmistakably evident when a society wedding party took in a vaudeville show at the Savoy late in 1906, a branch of the elite IODE held a fundraising matinee there for tuberculosis patients two months later, and the St. George's Benevolent Society booked a large bloc of seats the next year. *HS*, 19 Nov 1906, 7; 19 Jan 1907, 22; 25 April 1908, 15.

163. *HS*, 8 Sept. 1906, 19; 31 Aug. 1907, 14; Lenton-Young, "Variety Theatre," 203–4; *HH*, 18 Jan. 1908, 13; 9 Nov. 1912, 24; for similar features of Loew's, see also *HS*, 15 Nov. 1919, 9.

164. Mothers started dropping in on matinees with children during shopping expeditions. In 1916 the Red Mill made Thursday "Ladies' Day" and admitted women free to matinees. That spring the Savoy relaunched its movie programming and during the first week gave women carrying babies free admission. *HH*, 31 July 1916, 4; *HT*, 3 May 1916, 3.

165. Although much more modest in scale, Hamilton's smaller theatres mimicked this model of respectability. Jowett, *Film*, 74–184; *SW*, 1 Feb. 1920, 119–21; 1 Feb. 1921, 141–42; 1 Sept. 1921, 297; 1 July 1922, 206; April 1927, 1; Coxwell, "Safeguarding the Movies"; Norris, "Better Films"; Snyder, *Voice of the City*, 28–29 (quotations), 64–81; Kibler, *Rank Ladies*; McLean, *American Vaudeville as Ritual*, 67–83; Henley, *Grand Old Buildings*, 72; Henley, *Hamilton: Our Lives and Times*, 98–99; *HH*, 15 Nov. 1919, 9 (quotation); 4 Oct. 1921, 5 (quotation). A Hamilton Theatre Managers' Association was formed in 1921. *HS*, 13 May 1921, 12.

166. While Hamilton's Ministerial Association had attacked the old Star vaudeville theatre in 1895 and the WCTU had worried about pictures of prize fights two years later the earliest movies had not provoked any significant outcry.

Indeed, a few churches even used particular films with religious content to attract worshippers. HCCM, 1895, 349; AO, F 885, WCTU, 1897; *HS*, 24 Sept. 1895, 5; 7 Jan. 1907, 5; 4 Sept. 1907, 4; 4 Aug. 1914, 8.

167. Province-wide film censorship had been preceded in 1909 by an amendment to the 1908 Ontario fire-safety act, which empowered local police to act as censors against the presentation of crime and immorality, and then by another amendment in 1910 to give responsibility to the Ontario Provincial Police. The two systems of surveillance persisted somewhat awkwardly until the provincial board of censors was created in 1911. HBEM, 1907, 74; *HT*, 12 July 1907, 1, 11 (quotation); 21 Oct. 1910, 14; 22 Oct. 1910, 6; 4 Nov. 1910, 1; *HH*, 12 July 1907, 1; 22 Oct. 1910, 6; 11 March 1911, 8; 28 June 1911, 2; *HS*, 28 Oct. 1910, 8; Henley, "Hamilton in Ragtime"; Waters, "Moving Picture Shows"; Moore, "Rendezvous for Particular People," 48–111, 174– 241; Dean, *Censored!*; Bowser, *Transformation of Cinema*, 37–52; Koszarski, *Evening's Entertainment*, 198–210.

168. *HT*, 3 Nov. 1911, 11; 28 Aug. 1912, 5; 30 Aug. 1912, 1; 4 Sept. 1912, 12; 6 Sept. 1912, 6; 7 Sept. 1912, 1; 9 Sept. 1912, 7; 10 Sept. 1912, 5; 11 Sept. 1912, 12; 13 Sept. 1912, 12; 18 Sept. 1912, 1; 20 Sept. 1912, 1; *HH*, 3 Nov. 1911, 7; 16 Feb. 1912, 8; 2 March 1912, 13; 30 Aug. 1912, 9, 16; 7 Sept. 1912, 1; 11 Sept. 1912, 1; *LN*, 20 Sept. 1912, 1.

169. See, for example, Cocks, "Moving Pictures as a Factor in Municipal Life"; Thomas, "Community Use of the Moving Picture"; Coxwell, "Safeguarding the Movies"; Norris, "Better Films." Also Christie and Gauvreau, *Full-Orbed Christianity*, 44.

170. Quoted in Snyder, *Voice of the City*, 88; see also Sklar, *Movie-Made America*, 45–46.

171. *LN*, 2 Jan. 1914, 1; 16 Jan. 1914, 8; 27 March 1914, 2; *HH*, 8 March 1923, 5. That was the pattern in Chicago as well; Cohen, *Making a New Deal*, 121–22.

172. *HH*, 15 Sept. 1910, 4.

173. *LN*, 23 Jan. 1914, 2 (quotation); 1 May 1914, 2; *HH*, 13 Dec. 1913; 17 Jan. 1914, 5 (quotation); 3 Feb. 1914, 4. In the decade before the war social surveyors conducted numerous studies of recreation in US cities and discovered that movies had become popular among huge numbers of working people. In one 1914 survey of 1,000 workingmen, 60 per cent said they had attended movies. Havig, "Commercial Amusement Audience," 7–8; see also Rosenzweig, *Eight Hours*, 193–95.

174. *HH*, 19 Jan. 1918, 4; Rosenzweig, *Eight Hours*, 196; Ewen and Ewen, *Channels of Desire*, 81–105; Ewen, *Immigrant Women*, 216–24.

175. Early in 1917, after nine months of administering a new amusement tax, an Ontario government official reported that taxes had been collected across the province on 21 million admissions to cheap seats (worth less than 20 cents). Moore, "Rendezvous for Particular People," 236.

176. US surveys in the 1910s and 1920s found that a significant majority of frequent moviegoers were in their late teens and early twenties. Koszarski, *Evening's Entertainment*, 25–34. In 1912 James Roberts, the local medical officer of health, complained that he knew "a mother of small children to make the rounds of no less than five moving picture shows on a Saturday afternoon." Roberts, "Insanitary Areas," 180.

177. *HH*, 15 Sept. 1910, 4; AO, F 885, WCTU, 1928; Heron, *Booze*. "They are the only theaters which it is possible for the entire family of the wageworker to attend," the *Movie Picture World* stated in 1911 (quoted in Bowser, *Transformation of Cinema*, 123). By the 1920s the editor of that magazine was referring to the movie house as the new "Working Man's Club." Bailie, "Profitable Leisure," 11. Madelon Powers has argued that in the United States respectable outlets like movies were eroding the attraction of the saloon even before prohibition, but my reading of the still vigorous saloon culture both before and after prohibition has prompted me to disagree. Powers, "Decay from Within"; Heron, *Booze*.

178. HPL, Our Heritage Scrapbook, Vol. 1, 139–40.

179. In a classic statement, George Orwell argued, "The movies, the radio, strong tea and the football pools have between them averted revolution." Quoted in Scannell and Cardiff, *Social History of British Broadcasting*, 362. The stifling power of mass culture was a central theme in the writings of the so-called Frankfurt School, especially Theodore Adorno. For a helpful critique of perspectives that emphasize either total cultural "incapsulation" or complete working-class autonomy, see Hall, "Notes on Deconstructing 'The Popular.'"

180. Alan Havig's conclusion about the United States has resonance in Canada: "The entertainment dollar was spent disproportionately by older adolescents and young adults"; see "Commercial Amusement Audience,"12. This is a distinction Roy Rosenzweig downplayed in *Eight Hours*, but that Kathy Peiss emphasized in *Cheap Amusements*.

181. We would do well to heed US historians' conclusions that much of the new mass culture of amusement (including amusement parks and vaudeville and movie "palaces") was aimed at, and most often attracted, mainly white-collar and middle-class patrons. Nasaw, *Going Out*, 31, 40–46, 191, 201, 232; Allen, "Motion Picture Exhibition"; Gomery, "Movie Audiences." Roy Rosenzweig emphasized how infrequently US workers could afford outings; *Eight Hours*, 181.

182. Kenney, *Recorded Music*, 44–64; Miller, "Talking Machine World," 177–81. These pricier classical recordings were aimed at more affluent consumers, and, although the Victor Talking Machine Company did have an educational department, which sent a dozen women across the United

States to promote the use of "better" music in homes, schools, and other educational settings, social reformers in Canada spent little time pondering how to use gramophones as tools for instilling standards of bourgeois taste. Kenney, *Recorded Music*, 92–93.

183. US listener surveys showed a marked decline to a point in 1933 when only just over half the radio owners turned their sets on each evening (networks began scrambling to find programming to win them back). Butsch, *Making of American Audiences*, 198–99; MacDonald, *Don't Touch That Dial!* 29–30; Scannell and Cardiff, *Social History of British Broadcasting*, 356–80. In his oral-history project with US radio listeners, Ray Barfield found some sitting together by the radio, but also plenty of coming and going for favourite shows, often woven into other household activities. Barfield, *Listening to Radio*, 39–57. See also similar British evidence in Pegg, *Broadcasting and Society*, 195–217. Canadian radio audience surveys remained minimal and sporadic until the 1940s; see Vipond, "London Listens"; Eamon, *Channels of Influence*, 49–61, 68–72.

184. Levine, "Folklore of Industrial Society," 1393–95.

185. Levine, "Folklore of Industrial Society"; Snyder, *Voice of the City*, 130–54; Kibler, *Rank Ladies*, 32–40; Butsch, *Making of American Audiences*, 108–20. Caroline Caffin's 1914 study of vaudeville is centrally concerned with how particular performers succeeded in engaging with their audiences. Caffin, *Vaudeville*. Peter Bailey discusses this kind of interactive performative work in British music halls as constructing an audience out of an amorphous crowd. Bailey, *Popular Culture and Performance*, 133.

186. Kibler, *Rank Ladies*, 23–55, 104–9; *HS*, 16 Jan. 1893, 8; 30 Oct. 1897, 5; 22 Sept. 1903, 6; Gilbert, *American Vaudeville*, 204–5. In 1919, after interviewing vaudeville performers at Loew's theatre, a *Herald* reporter discovered their need to play to the gallery, and their feeling that there was nothing "as sweet as the deafening, bewildering sound of a house determined to bring him out again." HPL, Our Heritage Scrapbooks, Vol. 3, 115.

187. Just before the Savoy opened in 1906, the manager even approached Hamilton's board of police commissioners to request a policeman be present to keep order. Six years later, the Temple's manager asked for one at his theatre every afternoon and evening. The police chief was never keen to accept this responsibility. HPL, RG 10 Series S, 7 Nov. 1906, 17 Oct. 1912; *HS*, 7 Nov. 1906, 1; 3 May 1910, 1.

188. Snyder, *Voice of the City*, 33–34, 99–100; Kibler, *Rank Ladies*, 23–45. Donald Garvie later reported that the upper balcony was still known as the seat of the "gods" in the 1920s. Garvie, *Growing Up*, 51.

189. Richard Koszarski, quoted in Hansen, *Babel and Babylon*, 99.

190. Stead, *Film and the Working Class*, 8 (quotation); Rosenzweig, *Eight Hours*, 199–204; Bachman, "Still in the Dark,"

32. A Hamilton man remembered that at the Unique Theatre in the 1920s "periodically someone would throw a stink bomb to the lower level," while at his local theatre, the Regent, children regularly cheered on their cowboy heroes. Garvie, *Growing Up*, 51–52 (quotation); Ross, *Working-Class Hollywood*, 24–26; Butsch, *Making of American Audiences*, 165–72; Koszarski, *Evening's Entertainment*, 45; Rabonovitz, *For the Love of Pleasure*, 117–19; Stamp, *Movie-Struck Girls*, 24–37; Doherty, "This Is Where We Came In"; WAHC, interview with Gene Yachetti; Kaprielian-Churchill, *Like Our Mountains*, 333; Levine, "Folklore of Industrial Society," 1395 (quotation).

191. Lears, "Making Fun of Popular Culture," 1426.

192. In 1895 representatives of the Hamilton Ministerial Association charged that they came from "the Bowery and the low quarters of Buffalo." *HS*, 24 Sept. 1895, 5.

193. Snyder, *Voice of the City*, 42–63; Gilbert, *American Vaudeville* (quotation at 251). Gilbert's fondness for turn-of-the-century vaudeville acts is marked. He argues that after 1910, under the tighter control of the booking syndicate, the routines got less original and more formulaic and lost their vitality.

194. Ross, *Working-Class Hollywood*, 34–55; Rosenzweig, *Eight Hours*, 216–17; Berry, *Screen Style*. For Chaplin's impact in the World War One era, see Horrall, "Charlie Chaplin."

195. Ross, *Working-Class Hollywood*. In 1912, for example, *The Cry of the Children* played at the Red Mill. "The film shows a mill town, children at work, a strike and many other features of interest to the working class," the *Labor News* announced on 3 May 1912.

196. Ewen, *Rise and Fall*; Furia, *Poets of Tin Pan Alley*; Tawa, *Way to Tin Pan Alley*.

197. Kenney, *Recorded Music*, 3–22, 65–87; Millard, *America on Record*, 80–95; Gellatt, *Fabulous Phonograph*; Jasen, *Tin Pan Alley*, 112–92; Cohen, *Making a New Deal*, 104–6.

198. Stead, *Film and the Working Class*, 22–45; Koszarski, *Evening's Entertainment*, 181–90.

199. Nasaw, *Going Out*, 47–61, 100–1, 167–68; MacDonald, *Don't Touch That Dial!* 92–112, 234–57; Kelley, "Notes on Deconstructing 'The Folk,'" 1405.

200. Gilbert, *American Vaudeville*; Snyder, *Voice of the City*, 137–40; Bailey *Popular Culture and Performance*, 128–50.

201. McLean, *American Vaudeville as Ritual*, 106–37; Bowser, *Transformation of Cinema*, 179–84; Sklar, *Movie-Made America*, 104–21; Douglas, *Listening In*, 100–23; MacDonald, *Don't Touch That Dial!* 91–153.

202. Ewen, *Rise and Fall*; Furia, *Poets of Tin Pan Alley*; Tawa, *Way to Tin Pan Alley*.

203. Levine, "Folklore of Industrial Society"; Grimsted, "Melodrama as Echo of the Historically Voiceless"; Clarke, "Pessimism versus Populism"; Jones, *Languages of Class*, 76–89; Stead, *Film and the Working Class*, 233–49; Hansen, *Babel and Babylon*, 90–125; Srigley, "Working Lives and

Simple Pleasures," 219. Richard Hoggart argues: "They know life is not really like that; they do not expect life ever to be like that in some hazy future. But they say it is 'nice to think of' a life like that; and this attitude seems to me near at times to being a kind of vision, a glimpse of another order." Hoggart, *Uses of Literacy*, 196–97.

204. Kenney, *Recorded Music*, 3–22, 65–87; Cohen, *Making a New Deal*, 105–6, 155; Douglas, *Listening In*.

205. Cohen, *Making a New Deal*, 325–31.

206. Heron et al., *All That Our Hands Have Done*, 165.

207. In my 1981 doctoral dissertation, I too readily accepted the argument of Gareth Stedman Jones about working-class London; see Jones, *Languages of Class*, 237.

208. *IB*, January 1906, 2.

13. One of the Girls

1. The controversy was not limited to Hamilton; see, for example, Strange, *Toronto's Girl Problem*; McMaster, *Working Girls*.

2. Public-health nurses complained about the tendency to hold babies too much (see chapter 4). Anna Davin found that this tendency was common among London's working-class families in the early 20th century; see Davin, *Growing Up Poor*, 18.

3. R.T. Steele, "Playgrounds," CCCCP, 1911, 46; *HT*, 5 Aug. 1912, 12; 20 Aug. 1914,4; *HS*, 21 May 1915, 10; Strong-Boag, *New Day Recalled*, 12. The Spec. Man also encountered this practice. *HS*, 30 April 1907, 5.

4. *HS*, 22 Aug. 1910, 12; Synge, "Family and Community," chs. 3.1, 3.4; WAHC, interview with Florence Fisher; Kaprielian-Churchill, *Like Our Mountains*, 332; Zembrzycki, "There Were Always Men in Our House," 100–1.

5. Synge, "Family and Community," ch. 3.5; *HS*, 15 May 1901, 8; 22 Jan. 1902, 8; HBEM, 1932, 70 (quotation); Davin, *Growing Up Poor*, 10–11, 110–11. "I remember that every time a building was being torn down, all the kids of the neighbourhood would get out their wagons and go down to the site in order to collect the scrap wood to heat their house," one Hamilton woman recalled. MHSO, ITA-0982–PAS.

6. In the 1909 Ontario "Third Book" reader (aimed at Grades 5 and 6), for example, amidst the countless tales of military heroism and other daring male adventures, the only female featured in such exploits was the Quebec heroine Madeleine de Verchères. In contrast, another poem expressed a girl's longing for a knight as a lover, and a nature story about deer highlighted the maternal protection that a doe provided to her fawn. Most stories and poems featured only boys or men. Ontario, Minister of Education, *Ontario Readers: Third Book*, 152–58, 281–85, 301–6.

7. HBEM, 1906, 18; 1917, 126; Oliphant, comp., *Hess Street School*, 38; Stamp, *Schools of Ontario*, 57–61.

8. HBEM, 1909, 50; 1911, 137–39; 1912, 34–35, 72–73; 1914, 38–40; Lenskyj, "Training or 'True Womanhood'"; Lenskyj, "Role of Physical Education"; Strathcona Trust, *Syllabus of Physical Exercises for Schools*, 152–56; Morrow, "Strathcona Trust in Ontario." In 1913 the Ontario Department of Education first permitted schools to include sports in girls' compulsory physical education courses, and by 1920 the Hamilton Board of Education was committed to the "encouragement of athletics among the school children" and included girls in the annual sporting competition, including basketball and track and field, organized by the Collegiate Athletic Association (later renamed the Girls' Interscholastic League to include the new technical and commercial students). *HS*, 24 Sept. 1920, 22; 28 Sept. 1920, 16; 16 Jan. 1930, 24.

9. ODLR, 1931, 22.

10. Synge, "Family and Community," ch. 3.3. Enrico Cumbo found evidence of girls' gangs or "clubs" in Toronto in the interwar period; "As the Twig Is Bent," 94–95.

11. After 1900 no more than three or four girls under age 16 were ever committed to trial in Hamilton in one year, and in 13 of the years down to 1925, none appeared. OIPPCR, 1901–25.

12. Myers, *Caught*, 7–10; Cumbo, "As the Twig Is Bent," 28–29.

13. Each year the Methodist deaconesses ran a special summer camp for working-class children (and their mothers) and held large Christmas parties for as many as 350 youngsters. Methodist Church, Board of Management of the Toronto Deaconess Home and Training School, *Annual Report*, 1900–20, in UCA, Methodist Church (Canada), Toronto Conference, Deaconess Board of Management, 78.101C, Box 4.

14. AO, F 885, Ontario WCTU, *Annual Reports*, 1887–1905 (quotation in 1887); Cook, "Educating for Temperance"; Cook, *"Through Sunshine and Shadow,"* 171–80.

15. HYWCAA, Minutes, 1895–1917; Annual Reports, 1893–94, 1896, 1903, 1904, 1907, in Scrapbooks, 1896–1906; *HS*, 21 May 1901, 8; Sebire, *Woman's Place*, 76–78. Compared to the Y's main building, the facilities for the North End Branch were always makeshift and shabby. It apparently got little or no financial support from the central branch and had to hold rummage sales to finance modest redecorating. After running the Saturday-afternoon sessions for more than a decade in the aging Custom House, the disgusted organizers swept the children out in 1905, when "forty Russian Jews" moved into another part of the large building as it made a transition to being temporary housing for immigrants. The children moved along the street to an abandoned office building belonging to the street-railway company, where a seriously leaking roof curtailed activities for a time and the street-railway strike several months later forced a suspension in programming for a few months. HYWCAA, Minutes, 7 March 1905, 4

Dec. 1906; Annual Report, 1907. For a fuller account of this project, see Heron, "The Y and the Working Girl."

16. HT, 18 Dec. 1909, 22; 19 Jan. 1910, 4; 6 April 1911, 6 (quotation); 26 Aug. 1912, 5; 25 June 1914, 10; 20 Aug. 1914, 4 (quotation); HH, 11 July 1913, 1; 28 April 1914, 4; 13 July 1916, 5; HS, 21 May 1915, 5; HPL, Hamilton Playgrounds Association Fonds, Chief Supervisor, General Report, 1919, 19; Hamilton Playgrounds Association, Souvenir Number.

17. HYWCAA, Minutes, 13 Feb. 1912; MacQueen, "Domesticity and Discipline"; Voeltz, "Antidote to 'Khaki Fever'?"; Proctor, On My Honour, 21–26; Alexander, "Motherhood, Citizenship, Continuity, and Change." Some historians suggest that,"part regulatory project and part liberating adventure," the Guides encouraged a kind of "feminine masculinity." Alexander, "Girl Guide Movement, Imperialism, and Internationalism," 59–62; Alexander, "Girl Guide Movement and Imperial Internationalism," 41 (quotation).

18. HYWCAA, Minute Books, 6, 13, 20 Feb., 12 March, 2 April, 14 May 1912; 21 Jan., 13 May, 11 Nov. 1913; 7 April 1914; 8 June 1915; 11 April, 12 Dec. 1916; 13 Nov. 1917; 14 Jan., 8 April 1919; 18 May 1920; GG, SRS 109–3 (Helen Smith Scrapbook, 1928–31); SRS 109–5 (Katherine Panabaker Scrapbook), "Early Days in Guiding in Hamilton"; HH, 19 May 1920, 11; 9 Jan. 1924, 7; Roberts and Klein, "Besieged Innocence," 231 (quotation); Alexander, "Motherhood, Citizenship, Continuity, and Change"; Pedersen, "Keeping Our Girls Good," 107–8; Duff, Highlights of the Hamilton YWCA, 3; Panabaker, Story of the Girl Guides; Jarvis, "Founding of the Girl Guide Movement"; Prang, "Girl God Would Have Me Be"; Marr, "Church Teen Clubs"; CC, 1931, Vol. 2, 272.

19. GG, SRS 109–3 (Helen Smith Scrapbook, 1928–31); SRS 109–5 (Katherine Panabaker Scrapbook), "Early Days in Guiding in Hamilton"; Alexander, "Motherhood, Citizenship, Continuity, and Change"; Proctor, On My Honour. A Toronto visitor told the Hamilton YWCA board in February 1912 that the Guide uniform would cost $5, but Panabaker indicates that when the first uniforms arrived from England two months later, the bill was actually $12. Panabaker, Story of the Girl Guides, 18. Tammy Proctor has examined local records (unavailable in Hamilton) in Britain and concluded that both the Guides and Scouts had many working-class members in the interwar period (typically in separate troops from their middle-class counterparts), in what she sees as a multi-class movement. Class distinctions were often felt in the quality of the uniforms that a child could afford. See Proctor, On My Honour, 34–53.

20. GG, SRS 109–3 (Helen Smith Scrapbook, 1928–31); Alexander, "Motherhood, Citizenship, Continuity, and Change."

21. GG, SRS 109–10 (10th Company Log Book, 1932–36), 27 Sept., 1 Nov., 8 Nov., 15 Nov. 1933; 3 Jan., 7 Feb., 7 March, 28 March, 11 April, 18 April, 2 May, 30 May 1934; 9 Jan., 13 Feb., 15 May 1935.

22. Hinther, "Raised in the Spirit of the Class Struggle," 54–59.

23. This process of trying to balance family responsibility with the desire to use some earnings on fun had a long history; see Bradbury, Working Families, 144–49; Stansell, City of Women, 53; Benson, Household Accounts, 70–76. On Jewish women, see Frager, Sweatshop Strife, 150–51; Glenn, Daughters of the Shtetl, 8–49.

24. Synge, "Family and Community," ch. 5.4; Strange, Toronto's Girl Problem, 136–37.

25. Gabaccia, "Immigrant Women," 68–71; Cohen, Workshop to Office, 10–11; Ewen, Immigrant Women, 109.

26. Synge's working-class interviewees explained that they rarely brought friends home. Her middle-class subjects said they were discouraged from socializing with friends at sites of popular culture. Synge, "Family and Community," chs. 3.1, 6. See also Bailey, From Front Porch to Back Seat, 17–19.

27. OCUR, 170–71.

28. Klein and Roberts, "Besieged Innocence"; "Videre," "A Little Independence"; Sangster, Earning Respect, 97–106; Peiss, Cheap Amusements, 45–55; Enstad, Ladies of Labor, Girls of Adventure; Tentler, Wage-Earning Women, 58–80; Glenn, Daughters of the Shtetl, 132–66. These practices would continue after World War Two; see Sugiman, Labour's Dilemma, 81–87.

29. Lil Seager, who started working at Tuckett Tobacco in 1923, found many people related to each other, including her sisters. "That's what I've often thought about Tuckett's," she recalled years later. "We were family." WAHC, interview with Lil Seager.

30. Bird, "Hamilton Working Women"; WAHC, interviews with Lil Seager, Florence Fisher.

31. Burkholder, Course of Impatience Carningham, 14; Enstad, Ladies of Labor, Girls of Adventure. A former working woman in Peterborough told Sangster that to be treated with respect on the job was to be treated "like ladies." Sangster, Earning Respect, 105. For a discussion of the treatment of "working girls" in Canadian fiction in this period, see McMaster, Working Girls, 44–87.

32. Nan Enstad follows Walter Benjamin in arguing that these women tried to actualize the "wish images" embedded in the products they purchased and thus opened up their "utopian" possibilities. Ladies of Labor, Girls of Adventure, 68–69, 82. On this more positive possibility for the woman's (unfairly low) wage see Kessler-Harris, Woman's Wage, 26–29.

33. HT, 24 Aug. 1917, 1; Peiss, Cheap Amusements, 67; Roberts and Klein, "Besieged Innocence," 211; Bates, "Shop and

Factory"; Sangster, *Earning Respect*, 89; Swyripa, *Wedded to the Cause*, 63–64; Glenn, *Daughters of the Shtetl*, 160–66; Ewen, *Immigrant Women*, 69–71; Cohen, *Workshop to Office*, 70–72; Benson, *Household Accounts*, 69–70; Beaumont, "English View of the Canadian Factory Girl." In 1910 the *Herald* reported that "a number of young men who are in the habit of attending the various picture shows" did not think that signs requesting women to remove their hats were adequate and intended to petition theatre managers to ask them to enforce the rule. One manager admitted that "when approached in regard to the matter the greater number of the ladies got angry and left the theatre." *HH*, 28 March 1910. The demand for these hats meant that the next year census-takers counted 299 milliners in Hamilton; Bates, "Shop and Factory," 132.

34. Sangster, *Earning Respect*, 89.

35. Enstad, *Ladies of Labor, Girls of Adventure*, 10; see also Berry, *Screen Style*, xxiii.

36. Ewen, *Immigrant Women*, 71, 197–202; Cohen, *Workshop to Office*, 70–72.

37. Community leaders within particular ethnic groups could be scathing about young women's fondness for fine clothing; see Swyripa, *Wedded to the Cause*, 92–102. See also Monod, *Store Wars*, 113–14.

38. *LN*, 27 Sept. 1912, 2 (quotation); Enstad, *Ladies of Labor, Girls of Adventure*; Peiss, *Cheap Amusements*, 62–67; Stansell, *City of Women*, 127; Steedman, *Angels of the Workplace*; Synge, "Family and Community," chs. 3.1, 3.6; *HH*, 26 July 1924, 7 (for observations drawn from interviews with young women living in the YWCA residence); Ewen, *Immigrant Women*, 70–71; Wright, "Most Prominent Rendezvous"; Schofield, "Rebel Girls and Union Maids." The Ontario government's 1923 film on factory girls' health, *Her Own Fault*, depicts a young woman "wasting" her lunch break by racing off to find a bargain in a clothing sale.

39. *HH*, 10 Dec. 1919, 1; 17 March 1920, 1; 23 March 1920, 1; 28 May 1920, 7.

40. *HH*, 9 Feb. 1921, 1; 25 March 1922, 1; 24 Aug. 1923, 1; *HS*, 28 March 1922, 1; Strong-Boag, *New Day Recalled*, 14–15. The decision-making meeting involved the school principal, two school inspectors, the Children's Aid Society inspector, and the chair of the school board.

41. *HH*, 26 May 1924, 3 (quotation); Latham, "Packaging Woman"; Gentile, "Queen of the Maple Leaf," 119; Berry, *Screen Style*. For the contrast between women's pre-1920s bathing costumes on Hamilton's beaches and what they sported later, see Turcotte, *Sand Strip*, 51–52; Henley, *Hamilton Back Then*, 51.

42. *HH*, 12 Oct. 1909, 1 (quotation); 1 Oct. 1910, 20; 15 March 1911, 1 (quotation); 30 March 1911, 1; 29 Aug. 1910, 1; 17 Sept. 1912, 5 (quotation); 23 March 1914, 1; 5 Dec. 1915 (quotation); 25 Oct. 1920; 17 Nov. 1920, 1; *HS*, 9 Jan. 1907, 12; 26 July 1900, 8; 6 Oct. 1900, 8; 19 Nov. 1910, 1 (quotation); 28 Dec. 1920, 15; HPL, J. Brian Henley, "Hamilton in Ragtime," 17 July 1976 (quotation); Myers, *Caught*, 46–48; Peiss, *Cheap Amusements*, 57–59.

43. Stansell, *City of Women*, 99.

44. All of this promenading and parading was created spontaneously by young people, and none of it was part of the centennial's official program. *HH*, 12 Aug. 1913, 1; 13 Aug. 1913, 1, 11; 15 Aug. 1913, 3; 18 Aug. 1913, 4; *HS*, 18 Aug. 1903, 1, 7; 19 Aug. 1903, 1; 21 Aug. 1903, 1, 3; 12 Aug. 1913, 1 (quotation); 16 Aug. 1913, 4; 18 Aug. 1913, 1, 5, 6; *HS*, 14 Aug. 1920, 19 (quotation); *HT*, 12 Aug. 1913, 1; 13 Aug. 1913, 4 (quotation); 18 Aug. 1913, 4 (quotation); *Star* (Toronto), 21 Aug. 1903, 1. The thousands of British immigrants who arrived in Hamilton in this period would have been familiar with these youthful street activities because British investigators continued to note them right through the interwar period; see Davies, *Gender, Leisure, and Poverty*, 96–108.

45. Stamp, *Movie-Struck Girls*, 10–40; Kibler, *Rank Ladies*, 30–31, 46–54; Rabinovitz, *For the Love of Pleasure*, 117–18; Synge, "Family and Community," ch. 3.6 (quotation); Murphy and Murphy, *Tales from the North End*, 213 (quotation).

46. The first roller rink, the Palace, burned down in 1903. Five years later there were three: the Armory, Britannia, and Alexandra. Normally they closed in late May for the summer, and a seasonal operation opened in Mountain View Park. *HS*, 15 June 1907, 24; 21 May 1909, 14; *HH*, 18 Jan. 1908, 13; Houghton, "Alexandra"; Henley, *Grand Old Buildings*, 114–15; Marks, *Revivals and Roller Rinks*, 129–30.

47. *HS*, 17 March 1905, 20; 5 Feb. 1907, 12; 12 Feb. 1907, 12; 15 Feb. 1907, 12; 25 Oct. 1907, 20; 13 Jan. 1908, 12; 7 April 1909, 14; 5 Nov. 1909, 16; 9 March 1910, 14; 15 March 1910, 12; 26 Feb. 1916, 16; 28 Nov. 1930, 4; 25 Nov. 1932, 10; LAC, "Sheet Music from Canada's Past," www.collectionscanada.gc.ca (quotation).

48. Palmer, *Culture in Conflict*, 55–59; Peiss, *Cheap Amusements*, 90–93. Such sponsored dances continued, of course; see, for example, a blacksmiths' union dance noted in *LN*, 29 Nov. 1912, 1.

49. *HS*, 9 June 1910, 12; "Report of the License Inspector," HCCM, 1906–14; *HT*, 3 Sept. 1917, 1; *HH*, 16 Dec. 1921, 1. In 1915 a recruiting rally in Gore Park was disrupted by the pounding piano of a third-floor dance hall nearby. *HH*, 24 Aug. 1915, 1. Canadian dance halls have not yet been subjected to the careful research that their US counterparts have attracted; see, in particular, McBee, *Dance Hall Days*.

50. Peiss, *Cheap Amusements*, 93–97; Ewen, *Life and Death of Tin Pan Alley*, 179–87; *HH*, 11 Aug. 1913, 3; 16 Aug. 1913, 1; *HS*, 12 Aug. 1913, 20; 15 Aug. 1913, 1; 18 Aug. 1913, 5. A few months later a newspaper report suggested that

"Hamilton society" had only acknowledged these dances during 1913. *HH*, 5 Jan. 1914, 1, 12. The Savoy Theatre was soon running amateur tango contests. *HH*, 30 Oct. 1914, 10.

51. *HS*, 20 Nov. 1920, 14; 26 Nov. 1921, 16; 29 Nov. 1924, 32; 26 Nov. 1926, 30; 24 Nov. 1928, 15; 7 Oct. 1929, 4; 4 Nov. 1932, 4; *HT*, 31 Aug. 1917, 16; 3 Sept. 1917, 4; MHSO, ITA-0884-VIO; WAHC, interview with Lil Seager; Synge, "Family and Community," ch. 6. By the end of the war some Hamilton hotels, notably the Royal and Royal Connaught, were organizing public dancing and dance classes in a cabaret environment for more upper-class youth. *HT*, 31 Aug. 1917, 16; 3 Sept. 1917, 8; *HH*, 2 Sept. 1922, 19; *Canadian Hotel Review*, December 1933, 4, 19; Miller, *Such Melodious Racket*, 49–50. Katrina Srigley's study of female leisure in working-class Toronto in the 1930s found clear distinctions among particular dance halls based on the entrance fee and therefore the clientele. Srigley, "Working Lives and Simple Pleasures," 242–50. One large Hamilton family, the Washingtons, was regularly performing jazz by the 1930s. Shadd, *Journey from Tollgate to Parkway*, 238.

52. McBee, *Dance Hall Days*, 82–114.

53. *HT*, 12 Jan. 1914, 1; *HS*, 20 Dec. 1919, 36; 16 Nov. 1923, 1; *HH*, 27 Jan. 1914, 3; 20 Feb. 1924; 1 April 1924, 1; 7 April 1924, 3; 4 Feb. 1929; HYWCAA, Minutes, 11 Feb. 1919 (quotation); Sebire, *Woman's Place*, 85; WAHC, interview with Lil Seager; Casey, "Community Recreation"; Tomko, *Dancing Class*; Peiss, *Cheap Amusements*, 93–114. In October 1920 the *Spectator* ran ads for the Alexandra Academy, Sharples Academy, and Bluebird Academy; *HS*, 20 Oct. 1920, 14. For criticism, see, for example, *HH*, 24 April 1911, 1; 19 Aug. 1912, 5; 24 March 1913, 1; 1 Sept. 1913, 1; 5 Jan. 1914, 12; 25 Feb. 1914, 1. The YWCA's new openness did not mean that many dances were held there. Late in 1921 a delegation from the Big Sisters' organization prompted a board discussion about "having regular dances in the building, oftener than we have had formerly, in order primarily to get in touch with these girls who are under the patronage of the Big Sisters." But three years later board members were still expressing scepticism about social evenings that included dancing. HYWCAA, Minutes, 16 Dec. 1921 (quotation), 13 March 1924.

54. *HS*, 28 May 1920, 22; 10 Oct. 1924, 5; 9 Jan. 1925, 5; 2 May 1925, 5; 10 Aug. 1925, 5; McBee, *Dance Hall Days*, 131; Davies, *Leisure, Gender, and Poverty*; Gutzke, "Gender, Class, and Public Drinking"; AO, RG 3-8-0-226 (Liquor Control Operation, 1932). Although she was an active Methodist, the young clerical worker (and future MP) Ellen Fairclough later wrote that in the 1920s she "drank a beer or two." Fairclough, *Saturday's Child*, 33. In the late 1890s a local hotel-owner had experimented with barmaids, brought in from England, but this brief experiment was never repeated; the practice became illegal in

Ontario in 1907 and again in 1934. *HS*, 18 March 1961, 30; Heron, *Booze*, 112, 289, 407n.53.

55. AO, RG 36-8, Box 329, 27 July 1942.

56. Malleck, *Try to Control Yourself*, 162–76; Heron, *Booze*, 288–92; *HS*, 30 Jan. 1930, 28. The Hamilton inspector pressured any holdouts among hotel-keepers to add a ladies' room, and only two still refused. AO, RG 36–8, Box 133, Fischer's (then known as the New Commercial) 8 July 1935; Box 155, Grand, 6 July 1935; Box 390, Wellington, 13 May 1943. A curious anomaly in the LCBO regulations was the ban on female membership in the licensed clubs. The issue blew up first in 1935 when the Germania Club, which had always had a mixed membership, was ordered to stop serving beer to women. Most clubs had women's auxiliaries, but even when those groups held their own meetings and socials on club premises, they were not allowed to have beer. The board was only willing to sanction monthly or biweekly "social evenings" or "ladies' nights." The women evidently chafed under this restraint, especially as the wartime conditions gave them new opportunities and responsibilities. The secretary of His Majesty's Army and Navy Veterans' Society wrote in 1940 that there was "a little agitation on the part of some members or perhaps I should say probably a little spurring on by their women folk asking us to write you . . . to have a little more freedom in this connection." He noted that wives and daughters had joined the "various auxiliary forces, some of them are in uniform," and that "the circumstances today are just a little different to ordinary time and perhaps the women have some right to expect a little more of us than heretofore." The Board refused to change its policy. AO, RG 36-8, Box 420, Canadian Legion No.7, 18 Oct. 1941, 3–6 April 1943, 11 April 1945, 28 Feb. 1949; Box 426, Canadian Legion No. 56, 4 Oct. 1940, 17 Nov. 1940, 22 Nov. 1941; Box 452, Army and Navy Veterans in Canada, 1941; Box 460, British Imperial Club, 26 Feb. 1941; Box 463, Canadian Pensioners' Association of the Great War, 27 Nov., 4 Dec. 1934, 21 May 1940, 3 Dec. 1941; Box 474, Her Majesty's Army and Navy Veterans' Society, 1, 15 May 1939, 13–15 Nov. 1940, 17 Nov. 1941; Box 483, Old Contemptibles' Association, 7 June 1939, 28 April 1942, 20 Sept. 1946; Box 502, Veterans Service League, 14 May 1943. In 1949 the LCBO restricted the number of ladies' nights per month to three.

57. AO, RG 36-8, Box 18, 30 July 1935; Box 350, Savoy, 15 Aug. 1939; Box 367, Strand, 27 April, 19 May 1945.

58. AO, RG 36-8, Box 18, Armory, 22 March 1936, 26, 30 March 1938, 4 Dec. 1940, 16 June 1942, 14 March 1943; Box 28, Bayview, 20 Dec. 1937, 27 Jan. 1943; Box 44, Britannia (formerly Vulcania), 3 April, 22 May 1940; Box 61, Cecil, 9 Nov. 1942, 7 Feb. 1948; Box 93, Corktown (formerly Gurry), 18 April 1938; Box 133, Fischer's (formerly New Commercial), 25 Feb., 15 March, 14 April, 23 June, 3–10,

17 Nov. 1937, 25 March 1938; Box 142, Genesse, 27, 30 June 1936; Box 269, Old City (formerly Dog and Gun), 30 May 1938; Box 155, Grand, 6 July 1935, 30 Aug. 1941; Box 169, Homeside, 19 June 1942, 7–10 Sept. 1945; Box 178, Iroquois (formerly Dominion), 18 Sept. 1941; Box 519, Whitmore (formerly Mart), 29 July, 16 Sept. 1935, 20 Oct. 1936, 22 March 1938.

59. There were also swimming classes in the Y pool.

60. HYWCAA, Minutes, 8 March 1908; Kidd, *Struggle for Canadian Sport*, 98; *HS*, 7 Feb. 1920, 20; 9 Feb. 1920, 14; 12 Feb. 1920, 23; 17 Feb. 1920, 19; 19 Feb. 1920, 18; 28 Feb. 1920, 20, 21; 1 March 1920, 18; 2 March 1920, 19; 4 March 1920, 18; 8 March 1920, 19; 11 March 1920, 18; 19 March 1920, 26; 20 March 1920, 24; 1 April 1920, 26; April 1920, 23; 16 April 1920, 24; 19 April 1920, 18; 23 April 1920, 28. Margaret Lord, a middle-class teacher and leader of women's sports in Hamilton, told athlete and writer Bruce Kidd that basketball was the "sport of entry" into other athletics for most girls." Kidd, *Struggle for Canadian Sport*, 101.

61. *HS*, 21 May 1920, 31; 25 May 1920, 20; 27 May 1920, 20; 31 May 1920, 16; 9 June 1920, 24; 14 June 1920, 18; 25 June 1920, 20; 26 June 1920, 26; 28 June 1920, 18; 29 June 1920, 16; 6 July 1920, 18; 10 July 1920, 20; 12 July 1920, 14; 14 July 1920, 21; 20 Oct. 1920, 20; *HHB*, July 1920, 35; WAHC, interview with Florence Fisher. The teams came from factories with large female work-forces, including Imperial Cotton, Zimmerknit, Chipman-Holton, Eagle Knitting, and American Can. The number of company-sponsored girls' softball teams declined during the 1920s. By 1930 there seems to have been only two, which competed with teams from other Ontario cities. *HS*, 18 Dec. 1926, 25; 29 May 1930, 28.

62. Lenskyj, "Femininity First." When a group of women in the east-end working-class suburb of Homeside formed a football (soccer) club, they had few competitors and played mainly exhibition matches, including one against a group of war amputees, which was intended to be more comedy than serious sport. *HS*, 27 May 1920, 20; 19 June 1920, 30; 27 Aug. 1920, 23; 1 Sept. 1920, 21.

63. *HS*, 4 Feb. 1930, 18; 17 Feb. 1930, 16; 21 Feb. 1930, 27; Kidd, *Struggle for Canadian Sport*, 108, 112, 129, 131, 139; Miller, ed., *Centennial Sports Review*; Macdonald, "Hamilton's Hurdler"; Lenskyj, "We Want to Play."

64. Miller, ed., *Centennial Sports Review*; Strong-Boag, *New Day Recalled*, 31; Kidd, *Struggle for Canadian Sport*, 107–8. "My mother never approved my involvement in sport," Lord told Bruce Kidd repeatedly. Kidd, *Struggle for Canadian Sport*, 140.

65. Kibler, *Rank Ladies*, 55–170; Ewen, *Immigrant Women*, 218; Davis, *Circus Age*, 82–141.

66. Davis, *Circus Age*, 89; Stamp, *Movie-Struck Girls*, 37–40; Berry, *Screen Style*, 22–30.

67. *HS*, 13 May 1907, 3; Synge, "Family and Community," ch. 5.4; ch. 3.1 (quotation). In 1924 a *Herald* reporter concluded from interviews with young women living in the YWCA residence that those earning $12 a week (which was roughly the average female weekly wage at that point; see Table 21) would probably have no more than 50 cents of that sum for entertainment ($25 a year). *HH*, 26 July 1924, 7.

68. Synge, "Family and Community," ch. 3.1.

69. OCPR, 271 (quotation); *HH*, 27 Jan. 1913, 1 (quotation); 13 Nov. 1916, 1 (quotation); Strange, *Toronto's Girl Problem*, 120–24; Peiss, *Cheap Amusements*, 53–55; McBee, *Dance Hall Days*, 106–113; Bailey, *From Front Porch to Back Seat*, 25–56.

70. Cumbo, *Italian Presence*; Cumbo, "As the Twig Is Bent," 27–31; Ewen, *Immigrant Women*, 210–14.

71. Synge, "Family and Community," ch. 5.4; *HS*, 18 March 1969; Peiss, *Cheap Amusements*, 67–72.

72. ODER, 1911–19; *HS*, 1 Feb. 1915, 5; 20 Sept. 1919, 18 (quotation); *HH*, 30 Jan. 1920, 13; *Clarion*, 2 Feb. 1937, 1; HPL, Our Heritage Scrapbook, Vol. 3, 65; Greenfield, *Hamilton Public Library*, 36, 43, 47–48, 66, 69–72.

73. Enstad, *Ladies of Labor, Girls of Adventure*, 17–83.

74. Sangster, "Mobilizing Women."

75. This discussion draws heavily on the insights in Strange, *Toronto's Girl Problem*.

76. *HS*, 28 Feb. 1907, 1; 2 March 1907, 1; 12 Feb. 1910, 1; 4 March 1910, 4; 1 June 1910, 8; *HH*, 22 July 1907, 1; 25 Feb. 1908, 7; 5 Dec. 1910, 1; 22 May 1912, 5; 17 Sept. 1912, 1 (quotation); 18 Sept. 1912, 1; 25 Sept. 1912, 1; 26 Sept. 1912, 1, 6; 4 Oct. 1912, 1; 5 Oct. 1912, 1; 9 Nov. 1912, 4; 14 Nov. 1912, 1; 13 June 1913, 1; 17 June 1913, 1; *HT*, 13 April 1910, 5; *CWRT*, 1 May 1910; 1 May 1912; Lyle, *Hamilton Local Council of Women*, 33; Valverde, *Age of Light, Soap, and Water*, 77–103 (quotation at 95); Strange, *Toronto's Girl Problem*, 96–102. The on-screen exposures of "white slavery" in pre-war movies caused considerable stir as well; Stamp, *Movie-Struck Girls*, 41–101.

77. In 1924 pressure from a committee of youth workers and the police magistrate convinced the Board of Police Commissioners to bar girls under 16 from admission to dance halls and to require all females to have a male "escort." The press reported, "A person who is of known immoral character will not be admitted to any dance hall, and those who do not conduct themselves properly will not be allowed to remain." *HS*, 14 March 1924, 18.

78. PCCA, 1977-3014, Box 2, 2 Nov. 1920, 358.

79. RG A, Series A, 1905-40; Sangster, *Regulating Girls and Women*, 132 (quotation); Strange, *Toronto's Girl Problem*, 116–74; Cassel, *Secret Plague*, 160–64. In a typical vagrancy case a court reporter described two women who "had been for some time hanging about the streets at all hours of the day and night, even frequenting

Chinese restaurants, at all times with questionable characters." *HS*, 29 June 1910, 14. Police Magistrate Jelfs claimed in 1914 that shutting down the "disorderly houses" (a move that he had once argued against) had pushed more young women towards street solicitation: "More young girls had appeared before him of late than at any time in his occupancy of the bench." *HS*, 20 April 1914, 16 (quotation).

80. From 1901 to 1910 the number was about 9 a year; over the next decade, about 11. In 1921 the number jumped up to 30 and remained higher in the 1920s. OIPPCR, 1901-25.

81. *HS*, 20 Sept. 1921, 12; 23 Feb. 1924, 2; 6 Aug. 1925, 5; 8 Nov. 1925, 2; 16 Nov. 1926, 2; 1 Dec. 1926, 8; 22 Nov. 1927, 2; 2 Nov. 1929, 14; 29 Jan. 1934, 2; 13 Feb. 1939, 2.

82. AO, F 885, Ontario, 1902, Report on Purity and Mothers' Meetings; also 1910.

83. *HH*, 12 Jan. 1918, 11; Cassel, *Secret Plague*, 159, 171, 217–18.

84. In 1914 the local Presbyterians reported 976 females among the 1,522 members of the Presbytery's young people's societies (only half of whom were communicants), but these figures lumped together Hamilton participants with those in several other cities, including Niagara Falls. In her study of working women in Peterborough, Sangster also found many whose social networks operated through particular churches, as did Srigley in Toronto. *HS*, 29 April 1910, 7; *HH*, 16 April 1924; PCCA, 1977-3014, Box 2, 3 March 1914, 13; Turkstra, "Christianity and the Working Class," 274–79; Smith, "Working-Class Anglicans," 132, 143; Fairclough, *Saturday's Child*, 21–23, 30–31; Sangster, *Earning Respect*, 90; Srigley, "Working Lives and Simple Pleasures," 223–31. The Girls' Friendly Society was founded in Britain in 1874 and spread across the empire as a religiously based structure for drawing together deferential working-class women with their aristocratic "betters"; Harrison, "For Church, Queen and Family." For a case study of a young woman whose social life revolved around her local Baptist Church, see Gidney, "Dredger's Daughter," 129–31, 136–37.

85. The WCTU also set up distinct branches for evangelically inclined young women, though they seem to have attracted mainly middle-class participants, in rapidly declining numbers. The more socially aloof IODE also tried to set up a girls' club in the east end in 1911, with classes in dramatic dancing and first aid, but ended up a year later simply running a small boarding house and dining room for recently arrived British working girls; the house had only 16 boarders in 1914 and closed in 1920. See Heron, "The Y and the Working Girl."

86. HYWCAA, Minutes, 4 May, 6 Dec. 1904; 14 Feb., 5 Dec. 1905; 4 Jan. 1906; 31 Jan. 1907; 2 June 1908; 4 March, 16 Aug., 12 Sept., 14 Nov., 12 Dec. 1911; 28 May, 12 July, 8 Oct., 12 Nov. 1912, 8 April, 8 July, 13 Oct. 1913; 10 March 1914; 1

June, 12 June, 12 Sept. 1917; Pedersen, "Keeping Our Girls Good," 143.

87. HYWCAA, Minutes Books, 4 Oct., 6 Dec. 1904; 3 Jan., 14 Feb., 7 March, 5 Dec. 1905; 6 March, 20 March, 1 May, 17 July 1906; 2 June, 17 Sept., 2 Nov., 8 Dec. 1908; 2 Feb. 1909; 15 Nov. 1910; 17 Jan., 17 Feb., 4 March, 18 April, 16 Aug., 14 Nov., 12 Dec. 1911; 9 Jan., 23 Jan., 6 Feb., 2 April, 14 May, 10 Sept., 12 Nov. 1912; 8 April, 11 Nov. 1913; 14 Dec. 1915; 11 Jan., 14 March, 10 May 1916; 13 Feb., 13 March, 10 April, 11 Sept. 1917; *HS*, 9 Oct. 1897, 3; *HT*, 27 Sept. 1893 (in HPL, YWCA Scrapbook); Sebire, *Woman's Place*, 76–78.

88. HYWCAA, Minutes, 14 Aug., 11 Sept., 18 Sept., 13 Nov. 1917; 8 Jan., 12 Feb., 9 April, 7 May, 21 May, 9 Oct., 12 Nov. 1918; 14 Jan., 20 May 1919; 20 Jan. 1920; *HS*, 6 Jan. 1919, 15; *HH*, 21 May 1919, 2.

89. Pedersen, "Keeping Our Girls Good," 159–60; Turkstra, "Christianity and the Working Class"; HYWCAA, Minutes, 25 Sept. 1923. As in many other local associations, Hamilton's board of directors was more cautious than were some of the national staff and leaders. The limits of their vision became clear in 1919 when, in response to a call from the National Council of Women to endorse a "Women's Platform" to help guide women voters, the Y directors seemed happy to do so until stumbling over clauses endorsing "Collective Bargaining" and the "Eight-Hour Day." These they refused to accept, as might be expected from the wives of corporate businessmen who were fighting such pro-labour measures on their own turf. The Y would continue to reach out to the managers of local corporations, but never approached the new unions that were recruiting female members at this point. HYWCAA, Minutes, 13 Jan. 1920. In fundraising for expansion, east-end employers were prime targets; see HYWCAA, Minutes, 5 March, 15 April 1924; 11 Feb., 9 Nov. 1926.

90. HYWCA, Minutes, 23 March 1920. The emphasis on clubs in national YWCA discussions dated back to 1910. Pedersen, "Keeping Our Girls Good," 148.

91. HYWCAA, 5 Oct., 9 Nov., 23 Nov., 14 Dec. 1920; 11 Jan., 8 Feb., 8 March, 12 April, 19 May 1921; 10 Jan., 14 Feb., 16 Feb., 22 May, 12 Dec. 1922. The noon-hour meetings seem to have fallen off during the economic slump of the early 1920s, but revived late in 1924. HYWCAA, Minutes, 13 Jan. 1925.

92. HYWCAA, Minutes, 16 Feb., 11 April, 22 May, 14 Nov. 1922; 8 May, 17 May, 11 Sept., 25 Sept., 13 Nov., 11 Dec. 1923; 8 Jan., 12 Feb. (quotation), 19 Feb., 26 Feb., 5 March, 11 March, 13 March, 25 March, 7 April, 15 April, 8 May, 27 May, 10 June, 17 July, 6 Aug., 30 Sept., 14 Oct. 1924; 11 May, 9 Nov. 1926; 10 Jan., 3 Nov., 13 Dec. 1927; *HS*, 6 Jan. 1919, 15; 3 Aug. 1920; *HH*, 21 May 1919, 2; 23 May 1922, 8; 8 Dec. 1923, 6; January 1924; 21 Jan. 1924; 16 Feb. 1924, 6; 20 Feb. 1924, 7; 28 Feb. 1924, 7; 12 April 1924, 7; 5 July 1924; 22 Nov. 1925.

93. HYWCAA, Minutes, 10 Jan., 11 Feb., 14 May 1929; *HH*, 22 Nov. 1928; Casey, "Community Recreation"; Sebire, *Woman's Place*, 83–96.

94. See, for example, YWCA Archives, 3 Sept. 1907, 4 Feb. 1908, 17 Nov. 1911, 26 Jan. 1915.

95. HYWCAA, Minutes, 5 March 1924 (quotations). The discomfort with these new immigrants peeked through in the directors' deliberations; see HYWCAA, Minutes, 19 Feb., 30 Sept. 1924. Discussion about starting some kind of "Canadianization" program never went anywhere.

96. HYWCAA, Minutes, 19 March, 14 April 1931; 11 Sept., 13 Nov., 11 Dec. 1934, 17 Sept. 1935. In 1934 the national YWCA developed a "Nine-Point Plan" for upgrading domestic service to encourage more single unemployed women to take it up. Sabire, *Woman's Place*, 97–106.

97. *HS*, clipping in HYWCA, Scrapbook.

98. In 1916 the YWCA's national magazine published a disparaging assessment: "In many ways these girls are still childish in their attitude, but at the same time they are sensitive and jealous of their rights as self-supporting grown-ups. Their mental calibre is limited and their power of concentration weak, so diversity in the evening's programme is necessary." Quoted in Pedersen, "Keeping Our Girls Good," 150. For similar attitudes in other industrial centres, see Sangster, *Earning Respect*, 91; Morton, *Ideal Surroundings*, 137. The east-end work was supervised by a board committee known as the Industrial Committee, which in October 1924 was substantially expanded with non-board representatives, in recognition of the special needs of the working-class clientele that the new branch would be working with. At a heated special meeting of the board a few months later, which had been called to discuss the increasing tension between the east-end and main branches, one board member declared that "the crux of the situation is in the fact that the Industrial Secretary [Berta Hamilton] and Committee refuse to recognize the authority of the Board of Directors." Two months later, Hamilton resigned. HYWCAA, Minutes, 14 Oct. 1924; 16 March, 6 June, 23 June 1925.

99. Berta Hamilton and a board member on the Industrial Committee were emphatic that poverty was a deterrent to membership among east-end young women; HYWCAA, Minutes, 13 Jan., 10 Feb. 1925.

100. Quoted in Pedersen, "Keeping Our Girls Good," 144.

101. In 1922, for example, the local Y's Industrial Committee reported that the young women from the Imperial Cotton Company wanted swimming and basketball classes, and those from the Moodie, Eaton, and Chipman-Holton plants came in primarily for basketball practice. HYWCAA, Minutes, 9 May, 12 Dec. 1922. For similar attitudes, see Sangster, *Earning Respect*, 91–92.

102. In 1924 the girls of the Blue Triangle Club demanded (and got) representation on the Y's Industrial Committee, and two years later the Pioneer Club, which claimed to represent the east-end membership there, tried (unsuccessfully) to get the Dominion Council to hold a national conference of "industrial girls" the following summer. HYWCAA, Minutes, 11 Nov. 1924; 9 Feb. 1926.

103. *HS*, 16 Aug. 1924, 2.

104. *HS*, 23 May 1925, 2; 22 July 1925; HYWCAA, Minutes, 28 April 1925, 13 April 1926; Sebire, *Woman's Place*, 93–96.

105. *Advance*, 26 Oct. 1917, 5; 9 Dec. 1921, 1; *ND*, 31 Dec. 1919, 2.

106. *Advance*, 28 Dec. 1917, 7; *IB*, 11 Oct. 1918, 2 (quotation); *HH*, 22 Oct. 1919, 5; *HS*, 8 May 1920, 13; *LN*, 25 April 1919, 1 (quotation); 7 May 1920, 1; 23 Dec. 1921, 1; *ND*, 7 April 1921, 1; Mary McNab, "Woman's Place in Citizenship," *ND*, 5 Sept. 1921, 2 (quotation). Hamilton's teachers had their own flash of militancy late in 1919, when, to get higher salaries, they collectively threatened to resign en masse. The protest quickly petered out. *LL*, 12 Dec. 1919, 1.

107. Pedersen, "Keeping Our Girls Good," 153.

108. Many adult women arrived in the city from rural backgrounds that had confined them to their parents' households and had given them none of these outlets into a public life of independent and commercialized sociability. See, for example, Swyripa, *Wedded to the Cause*, 21.

109. Synge, "Family and Community," ch. 5.4 (quotation); Dubinsky, *Improper Advances*, 64–85.

110. Baillargeon found similar courtship patterns in the interwar period in her interviews with Montreal working-class women. Synge, "Family and Community," chs. 3.1, 5.4; WAHC, interview with Ed Fisher; Cumbo, *Italian Presence*; Kaprielian-Churchill, *Like Our Mountains*, 324; Srigley, "Working Lives and Simple Pleasures," 221–22; Baillargeon, *Making Do*, 47–65; Chambers, "Courtship, Condoms, and 'Getting Caught'"; Gidney, "Dredger's Daughter," 137–40; Swyripa, *Wedded to the Cause*, 79–90; Morton, "June Bride as the Working-Class Bride"; Dubinsky, *Second Greatest Disappointment*, 19–53; Gillis, *For Better, For Worse*, 126–28, 179–80, 282; Cohen, *Workshop to Office*, 72–75; D'Emilio and Freedman, *Intimate Matters*, 300; McBee, *Dance Hall Days*, 13–50, 198–233. The Ontario government's passage of the Children of Unmarried Parents Act in 1921 signalled a concern with how frequently premarital sex among working-class couples led to pregnancy; a child conceived before marriage could be declared legitimate if his or her parents subsequently married.

111. WAHC, interviews with Lil Seager, Floyd Read; Bird, "Hamilton Working Women."

112. Kaprielian-Churchill, *Like Our Mountains*, 330 (quotation); Turkstra, "Christianity and the Working Class," 275–79; Bedal and Bartlett, "Women Do Not Speak"; Marks, *Revivals and Roller Rinks*, 52–80.

113. *HS*, 17 May 1895, 8; 11 July 1904, 1; Johnston and Campbell, comps., *Odd Fellowship*, 298–305; Anstead, "Fraternalism," 165–69; Emery and Emery, *Young Men's Benefit*, 31–32; Stubbs, "Visions of the Common Good," 131–32; Pennefather, *Orange and the Black*, 56–58, 144–49; Synge, "Family and Community," ch. 3.1; WAHC, interview with Lil Seager; Cumbo, *Italian Presence;* Clawson, "Nineteenth-Century Women's Auxiliaries." Hamilton's Mary Catherine Cullum led the creation of the first lodge in the Ladies Orange Benevolent Association. The Order of Canadian Home Circles and the Order of Chosen Friends admitted both men and women equally. Anstead, "Fraternalism," 225–26.

114. *Veteran*, December 1919, 34; 19 May 1923, 8; 21 July 1923, 6; *HS*, 6 Aug. 1919, 5; 10 Sept. 1919, 21; 24 Oct. 1919, 18. In 1920 a new Ladies Federation brought together representatives of several veterans' ladies' auxiliaries as a sister organization to the new Discharged Soldiers and Sailors Federation. *Veteran*, 12 March 1920, 7.

115. HPL, Hamilton Trades and Labor Council, Minutes, 4 Nov. 1910, 4 (quotation); *IB*, November 1903, 3; October 1905, 4; January 1909, 3; *LN*, 8 June 1917, 2; 19 Dec. 1919, 2; 25 Feb. 1921, 1; *HT*, 31 May 1910, 4; *Hamilton Labor Directory*, 1911, 31.

116. James Naylor notes how the decision to hive off women into their own organization fit into familiar patterns of organizing among the craftworkers who controlled the ILP. Naylor, *New Democracy*, 149–50.

117. AO, F 885, WCTU, Ontario Union Annual Convention, President's Address, 1891; 1894, 1898, 1900, 1901, 1907; Wentworth County Report, 1893, 1894, 1895, 1897, 1898, 1899, 1901, 1906, 1907; Ontario Franchise Superintendent, Report, 1913, 1915.

118. Cleverdon, *Woman Suffrage Movement*, 30–42; Strong-Boag, *Parliament of Women*, 276.

119. *HH*, 28 April 1910, 4; 5 May 1910; 6 Dec. 1910, 5; 27 March 1912; 20 Nov. 1912, 4; 15 July 1913, 4; 31 March 1914, 13; 23 April 1914, 7. Undoubtedly some women arrived from Britain with experience in working-class women's organizations such as the Women's Cooperative Guild or Women's Trade Union League.

120. *HH*, 13 April 1917, 14; 1 May 1917, 8; 26 March 1918, 14; 23 July 1918, 11; *LN*, 20 April 1917, 1; 27 April 1917, 1; 18 May 1917, 1; 15 June 1917, 1; 21 June 1918, 1; 12 July 1918, 1; 26 July 1918, 1 (quotation); 29 Nov. 1918, 1; 27 Dec. 1918, 1; 17 Jan. 1919, 1; 24 Jan. 1919, 31 Jan. 1919, 1; 28 Feb. 1919, 1; 7 March 1919, 1; 28 March 1919, 1; 4 April 1919, 1; 18 April 1919, 1; 25 April 1919, 1; 16 May 1919, 1; 13 June 1919, 1; 27 June 1919, 4; 28 Nov. 1919, 1; 5 Dec. 1919, 1; 12 Dec. 1919, 1; 19 Dec. 1919, 1; 16 April 1920, 1; *IB*, 4 May 1917, 1, 5; *ND*, 27 Nov. 1919, 1; 11 Dec. 1919, 1.

121. *IB*, 5 Oct. 1917, 2; *LN*, 27 Dec. 1918, 1; 17 Jan. 1919, 1; 7 March 1919, 1; 28 March 1919, 1; 4 April 1919, 1; 11 April

1919, 1 (quotation). No precise membership figures have survived.

122. *HS*, 29 Nov. 1924, 21; *LN*, 29 May 1925, 1; Sangster, *Dreams of Equality*, 26–80; Hobbs and Sangster, eds., *Woman Worker*; Kealey and Whitaker, eds., *R.C.M.P. Security Bulletins: Early Years*, 300; Swyripa, *Wedded to the Cause*; Sangster, "*Robitnytsia*, Ukrainian Communists, and the 'Porcupinism' Debate." The Communist Party's "Third Period," which began in 1929, shut down this emphasis on domesticity in the labour leagues in favour of organizing wage-earning women. Sangster, *Dreams of Equality*, 60–64; Endicott, *Raising the Workers' Flag*, 157–76; Butler, "Mother Russia and the Socialist Fatherland," 164–68.

123. *HS*, 3 Jan. 1921, 18 (quotation); *Worker*, 1 June 1922, 3 (quotation); Smith, *All My Life*, 88; Heron, "Jeffrey"; *NC*, 21 Dec. 1935, 8. In 1919 Inman gave a lecture to the local Theosophists on the unconventional British socialist and sex-reformer Edward Carpenter. *HS*, 21 May 1919, 17.

124. In the 1890s the WCTU had two "Bible women" who convened weekly mothers' meetings among the 200 poor families they visited. Those efforts would be revived at points over the next 30 years. AO, WCTU, Wentworth County, 1887, 1888, 1889, 1891, 1892, 1895, 1897, 1900, 1902, 1904, 1908, 1918, 1926; *Woman's Journal*, January 1892. The Methodists were just as persistent, adding to weekly mothers' meetings for about 30 women an annual short holiday on Hamilton Beach and a special Christmas dinner. Methodist Church, Board of Management of the Toronto Deaconess Home and Training School, *Annual Report*, 1906–20, in UCA, Methodist Church (Canada), Toronto Conference, Deaconess Board of Management, 78.101C, Box 4 (quotation from 1906–7, 61). The YWCA's mothers' meetings were limited to the North End Branch and held only sporadically. HYWCAA, Minutes, 5 Jan., 2 March 1897; 23 Jan. 1912; 27 May 1924.

125. *HH*, 17 Jan. 1914, 5; 3 Feb. 1914, 4.

126. *NC*, 8 Sept. 1934, 7; *Clarion*, 25 Feb. 1937, 3; Morton, *At Odds*, 89–107 (quotation at 93); WAHC, interview with Fred Purser.

127. The ILP and the CCF, for example, made card-playing and dancing regular features of their social occasions; see *LN*, 15 June 1917, 1 (48 tables of euchre); 26 April 1918, 4; 31 March 1918, 1; 31 Jan. 1919, 1; 28 Feb. 1919, 1; 16 May 1919, 12 Dec. 1919, 1; 29 Oct. 1920, 1; 25 Nov. 1920, 1; 28 Jan. 1921, 1; *NC*, 3 Nov. 1934, 6; 5 Jan. 1935, 6. So too did the Conservatives; *HS*, 29 Sept. 1930, 7.

128. *HS*, 21 Oct. 1919, 4.

129. Heron, "Boys and Their Booze"; WAHC, interview with Florence Fisher (quotation); AO, RG 36-8, Box 181, Jockey Club, 1 May 1937. These clubs took on various names: Goodwill and Benevolent Club, Good Time Social and Benevolent Club, Blue Ribbon Social and Benevolent Club, Red Ribbon Club, Monday Night Club, Ye Olde

Tyme Social Club, Union Jack Club, Red Rose Social Club, Queen's Happy Gang Club, and so on.

14. Boys Will Be Boys

1. *HS*, 15 Aug. 1913, 1; 20 Oct. 1924, 5; AO, RG 36-8, Homeside Hotel, 15 Nov. 1945.

2. Connell, *Masculinities*; Tosh, "What Should Historians Do with Masculinity?"; Tosh, "Hegemonic Masculinity and the History of Gender"; Frank, "Hegemonic Heterosexual Masculinity"; Baron, ed., *Work Engendered*; Bradbury, *Working Families*; Horowitz, ed., *Boys and Their Toys?*; Dunk, *It's a Working Man's Town*; Fine, *Story of Reo Joe*; Marks, *Revivals and Roller Rinks*; McClelland, "Masculinity and the 'Representative Artisan'"; Peck, *Reinventing Free Labor*, 117–57.

3. For an early contribution to masculinity studies that did address the process of growing up male (though not historically), see Tolson, *Limits of Masculinity*.

4. Performance as an element in relationships of subordination has been explored by, among others, Bailey, "'Will the Real Bill Banks Please Stand Up?'"; Scott, *Domination and the Arts of Resistance*; Butler, *Gender Trouble*.

5. Connell, *Masculinities*, 59–64.

6. Synge, "Family and Community," ch. 4.

7. Synge, "Family and Community," chs. 3.2, 3.4, 3.5 (quotation); Kaprielian-Churchill, *Like Our Mountains*, 324–25; Cumbo, "As the Twig Is Bent," 13–15. See also Griswold, *Fatherhood in America*, 42–43.

8. Zembrzycki, "There Were Always Men in Our House."

9. In her interviews Baillargeon discovered that Montreal boys in this period were also released from housework. "Little boys were like little kings," one woman recalled. "Very few homes made the boys work. They couldn't be touched. If there was something to be done, the girls did it." Baillargeon, *Making Do*, 42. See also Zembrzycki, "'There Were Always Men in Our House.'"

10. Synge, "Family and Community," ch. 3.2; WAHC, interviews with Florence Fisher, Floyd Read, North End Community Meeting; MHSO, ITA-0982-PAS; Murphy and Murphy, *Tales from the North End*, 122–28; Hunter, *Which Side Are You On, Boys*, 6.

11. Synge was told that the father of an informant would change diapers and sometimes feed the baby after he married, as a result of being from a large family with few girls. Another interviewee, born in 1902 and the eldest child with no older sisters, put up with a lot of teasing when he was sent into the street with a baby buggy at age 12. Synge, "Family and Community," ch. 3.2.

12. *HS*, 22 March 1907, 13; WAHC, interview with Jack Watts; Synge, "Family and Community," ch. 3.3.

13. Turkstra, "Christianity and the Working Class," ch. 4; Gauvreau, "Factories and Foreigners"; Murphy and Murphy, *Tales from the North End*, 53; Dirks, "Serving Church and Nation"; Cumbo, "Salvation in Indifference"; Reed, "Reform Movement of the Sunday School," 74–75.

14. Stamp, "Empire Day"; Morton, "Cadet Movement"; Morrow, "Strathcona Trust"; Moss, *Manliness and Militarism*; Oliphant, comp., *Hess Street School*, 34; Maciejko, "Public Schools and the Workers' Struggles," 224–27; Tosh, "What Should Historians Do with Masculinity?" 196; Bloomfield, "Drill and Dance as Symbols of Imperialism"; Mangan, "Duty unto Death"; HBEM, 2 May 1912, 69; 7 Nov. 1912, 131; 11 Feb. 1932, 55–56, 271–73; 8 June 1933, 175; 4 Oct. 272; 12 Oct. 1933, 252; 6 Feb. 1934, 55–56; ODER, 1913–1934; Oliphant, comp., *Hess Street School*, 24; *HH*, 8 Nov. 1919, 9. Under relentless pressure from CCF school trustee Agnes Sharp, the cadet program was abruptly and permanently shut down in 1934.

15. Garvie, *Growing Up*, 10 (quotation); Hunter, *Which Side Are You On, Boys*, 6.

16. Spencer, "Alternative Vision," 164 (quotation); *LN*, 12 Jan. 1912, 2 (quotation). See also Maciejko, "Public Schools and the Workers' Struggle."

17. The 1909 Ontario "Third Book" reader, for example, was packed with stories and poems about Canadian and overseas adventurers and warrior heroes from many periods ("Hearts of Oak," 55; "The Argonauts," 66–70; "The Minstrel-Boy," 71; "Burial of Sir John Moore," 106–7; "David and Goliath," 117–22; "The Charge of the Light Brigade," 123–25; "Adventure with a Whale," 174–78; "The Bed of Procrustes," 202–8; "Radisson and the Indians," 209–12; "William Tell and His Son," 241–44; "The Song in Camp," 250–52; "King Richard and Saladin," 253–58; "England's Dead," 258–60; "A Roman's Honour," 270–73; "Jacques Cartier," 307–10; "The Battle of Queenston Heights," 332–37). Playground organizers noticed that among the children "the Anglo-Saxon showed a disinclination to mix up with the new arrival." *HT*, 28 Oct. 1911, 5; 29 March 1912, 6 (quotation). Some made a game of spitting on Italian labourers working in trenches. Cumbo, *Italian Presence*.

18. Moss, *Manliness and Militarism*, 61–89; Tosh, "Imperial Masculinity," 76–77.

19. Baldus and Kassam, "Make Me Truthful, Good, and Mild"; Tomkins, *Common Countenance*.

20. Synge, "Family and Community," ch. 3.3; Murphy and Murphy, *Tales from the North End*, 61. One woman told Synge that her working-class mother expected perfect marks in "Attendance," "Punctuality," and "Conduct."

21. Oliphant, comp., *Hess Street School*, 36–39.

22. *HS*, 6 March 1889, 2; BBAA, Scrapbooks, undated clipping (c.1936).

23. Street gangs were certainly not completely new urban formations during this period. On both sides of the Atlantic groups of young artisanal apprentices had banded together and caused various forms of trouble since well back in the 19th century, as had young male Irish

immigrant day labourers. See Wilentz, *Chants Demo-cratic*, 55–56, 256, 262, 300–1; Hogeveen, "'Can't You Be a Man?'"

24. Unsworth, *Church and the Boy*, 4; MHSO, ITA-6489-BOR; The following discussion links the scattered Hamilton evidence to other contemporary and later studies, including Forbush, *Boy Problem*; Puffer, *Boy and His Gang*; Thrasher, *Gang*; Rogers, *Street Gangs*; Cumbo, "As the Twig Is Bent," 95–98; Sutherland, *Growing Up*, 227–28, 238–42; Nasaw, *Children of the City*; Humphries, *Hooligans or Rebels?* 174–208; Davies, "Youth Gangs, Masculinity and Violence."

25. HS, 13 June 1900, 8; 26 July 1900, 8; 14 Aug. 1900, 8; 7 May 1901, 8; HH, 28 Feb. 1914, 1; Murphy and Murphy, *Tales from the North End*, 155–75; WAHC, interview with Fred Purser; Beattie, *John Christie Holland*, 39–40; Cooper, *Shadow Running*, 18; Cumbo, "As the Twig Is Bent," 86–88.

26. Cumbo, *Italian Presence* (quotation); Murphy and Murphy, *Tales from the North End*.

27. OCPR, 251, 264; HT, 10 July 1893, 8; HS, 2 May 1900, 8; 27 May 1901, 8; 4 June 1901, 8; 14 Oct. 1908, 4; 9 March 1909, 10; 8 April 1909, 7; HH, 10 May 1910, 1; 30 March 1911, 1; 27 May 1920, 19; 6 July 1920, 17; 10 March 1923, 1; 23 March 1923, 1; HPL, RG 10, Series S, 31 May 1912. The WCTU was particularly concerned about the widespread use of cigarettes among boys and lobbied to get legislation restricting access. It declared 25 March 1900 to be "Crusade Day Against the Cigarette." See also remarks in OSNDCR, 1900, 13.

28. Murphy and Murphy, *Tales from the North End*, 75–88, 105, 155–75; WAHC, interviews with Jake Isbister, Ed Fisher, Ken Withers.

29. HT, 9 Aug. 1913, 13; HS, 5 June 1900, 8; 13 July 1900, 8; 2 Sept. 1901, 8; OCPR, 260, 269, 280–81, 308, 309; HH, 23 May 1913, 4; Newlands, "History and Operation of Hamilton's Parks"; Halcrow, "Burlington Bay as I Remember It"; HPL, RG 18, Series A, 1900–40; Murphy and Murphy, *Tales from the North End*, 101, 235–36; Cruikshank and Bouchier, "*Dirty Spaces*." In 1900 the police magistrate fined two boys 50 cents each for climbing trees "and otherwise destroying property" in Victoria Park; HS, 14 May 1900, 8.

30. HS, 5 Jan. 1900, 8; 31 March 1900, 8; 6 July 1900, 8; 23 July 1900, 8; 24 July 1900, 8; 3 Feb. 1902, 8; 7 Jan. 1930, 7. In 1909 80 out of 91 juveniles brought to the police court were listed as "intemperate." Nagy, "Juvenile Delinquency," 7.

31. HT, 10 July 1893, 8; HS, 31 March 1900, 8; 19 June 1900, 6. Some also damaged equipment in public parks. HT, 23 July 1903, 4.

32. HS, 1 March 1901, 10; MPSS, 18. Years later a man who grew up in a working-class neighbourhood recalled, "Parents in those days thought that a poolroom was a

den of iniquity, and if you were caught going into one, the seat of your pants would know it for quite a spell." In 1930 the police magistrate was still arguing, "Nearly every boy under 21 who comes before me tells me that he first started with a bad gang he met in a pool room." Oliphant, comp., *Hess Street School*, 37; HS, 19 July 1930, 9.

33. HPL, RG 10, Series S, 7 Nov. 1906, 17 Oct. 1912; HS, 16 Jan. 1893, 8; 30 Oct. 1897, 5; 22 Sept. 1903, 6.

34. OSNDCR, 1900, 13–14; 1901, 8–9; Ontario, Legislative Assembly, *Journals*, 1907, Appendix 1, 11–12; HS, 9 Sept. 1910, 1; 28 Oct. 1910, 16; HH, 22 Oct. 1910, 6; 4 Nov. 1910, 1; 28 June 1911, 12; HT, 5 July 1910, 1; 12 Sept. 1910, 6; 21 Oct. 1910, 1; 22 Oct. 1910, 6; Butsch, *Making of American Audiences*, 151–57; Bachman, "Still in the Dark," 31. In 1925 the police hauled a boy into court for entertaining his friends with a "Wild West" outfit of cowboy hat and holstered gun. HS, 6 June 1925, 5. After new Ontario legislation in 1911 barred children under 15 from attending movies without adult accompaniment, local film exhibitors became furious "since their audiences were for the most part children." A 1916 court case made clear that young adolescents were getting in anyway. Ontario's movie censor claimed that children persuaded adults to buy tickets for them. When Magistrate Jelfs proposed raising the age for admission to 21, a letter to the *Spectator* argued that teenagers who "worked all day to supply bread for a whole family and when some night they wish to have a little amusement" would be "stalled from the theatre." In 1919 an amendment to the provincial legislation allowed children to enter movie theatres unattended on Saturdays. HH, 11 March 1911, 8 (quotation); HS, 4 Jan. 1916, 1; 8 Jan. 1917, 6 (quotation); Moore, "Rendezvous for Particular People," 192, 386; Dymond, *Laws of Ontario Relating to Women and Children*, 127. By the 1930s numerous "scientific" studies by US social scientists had raised alarm bells about the psychological effects of movies on children. Bachman, "Still in the Dark," 26.

35. OCPR, 269, 271, 281, 290; HS, 23 June 1897, 1; 7 Oct. 1897, 8; 12 Jan. 1900, 8; 17 Jan. 1900, 8; 1 Feb. 1900, 8; 20 Feb. 1900, 8; 1 23 March 1900, 8; 1 May 1900, 8; 15 May 1900, 8; 26 May 1900, 8; 29 May 1900, 8; 30 May 1900, 8; 31 May 1900, 8; 4 June 1900, 8; 11 Sept. 1900, 8; 19 Sept. 1900, 8; 15 Dec. 1900, 8; 21 May 1901, 8; 21 Jan. 1902, 8; 28 Jan. 1902, 8; 3 Feb. 1902, 8; 12 Jan. 1910, 12; 15 March 1910, 8; 2 Nov. 1910, 14; 28 June 1920, 7; 3 July 1920, 7; 22 July 1920, 7; 27 July 1920, 12; 27 Jan. 1925, 5; 29 Jan. 1925, 5; 7 Feb. 1925, 5; 10 Feb. 1925, 5; 2 Jan. 1930, 7; 10 Jan. 1930, 7; 13 Jan. 1930, 7; 24 Jan. 1930, 7; 19 Feb. 1930, 7; 4 March 1930, 7; 28 Nov. 1930, 7; 13 Jan. 1973, 23; HT, 10 July 1893, 8; 28 Sept. 1912, 1; Fenton, "Supervised Playgrounds," 160; Murphy and Murphy, *Tales from the North End*, 66, 100, 106, 162–63, 181; Garvie, *Growing Up*, 12; WAHC, interview with Floyd Read; Cooper, *Rapid Ray*, 4; BBAA, Board

of Directors, Minutes, 4 March, 2 Dec. 1935; HPL, RG 10, Series A, 1920–31.

36. Garvie, *Growing Up*, 20; *HS*, 23 June 1897, 1; 7 Oct. 1897, 8; 9 Jan. 1900, 8; 22 June 1900, 8; 24 Aug. 1900, 8; 13 Nov. 1900, 3; 25 Nov. 1900, 8; 16 Jan. 1901, 8; 6 May 1901, 8; 15 May 1901, 8; 18 May 1901, 8; 22 May 1901, 8; 29 May 1901, 8; 31 May 1901, 8; 31 July 1903, 1; 20 March 1907, 16; 1 Nov. 1907, 1; 24 Nov. 1920, 26. In 1906 the *Spectator*'s court reporter sketched the activities of a gang of eight boys who had "lately formed themselves into a society for the purpose of frightening people." Using a gun to stage a holdup, the boys targeted "the class of people they were pleased to designate as 'chumps.'" *HS*, 13 Oct. 1906, 1; 15 Oct. 1906, 1.

37. *HS*, 18 June 1920, 7; see also 25 Aug. 1910, 10; 12 Oct. 1910, 14; 17 Oct. 1912, 1; 19 Aug. 1914, 16; *HH*, 20 July 1917, 2; Murphy and Murphy, *Tales from the North End*, 90; Cooper, *Shadow Runner*, 19; WAHC, interview with Floyd Read; Burkholder, *Story of Hamilton*, 144–46. The aggression and violence never seem to have reached the level of intensity in Hamilton that it did in East London, Manchester, Birmingham, or Glasgow in the same period. Humphries, *Hooligans or Rebels?* 174–76; Davies, "Youth Gangs, Masculinity and Violence."

38. *HS*, 1 Nov. 1898, 1; 1 Nov. 1907, 1; 1 Nov. 1919, 1; 2 Nov. 1925, 5, 17; 1 Nov. 1928, 4; 1 Nov. 1929, 6, 7; Garvie, *Growing Up*, 28 (quotation); Rogers, *Halloween*, 56–62.

39. On the traditions of "misrule," see Davis, "Reasons of Misrule."

40. *HS*, 12 March 1891, 2; 27 Oct. 1908, 7; *HS*, 26 May 1903, 1; Garvie, *Growing Up*, 25–26.

41. *Star*, 21 Aug. 1903, 1; see also *HS*, 18 Aug. 1903, 1, 7; 19 Aug. 1903, 1; 21 Aug. 1903, 1, 8; HPL, Our Heritage Scrapbooks, Vol. 2, 77.

42. *HS*, 12 Aug. 1913, 1, 20; 15 Aug. 1913, 1, 7, 14; 16 Aug. 1913, 1; 18 Aug. 1903, 5; *HH*, 26 Aug. 1913, 11; *HT*, 12 Aug. 1913, 1, 11; 13 Aug. 1913, 1, 4; 14 Aug. 1913, 12; 16 Aug. 1913, 1, 9; 18 Aug. 1913, 5.

43. *HS*, 6 Nov. 1906, 1, 6; 7 Nov. 1906, 1; 8 Nov. 1906, 10; 9 Nov. 1906, 1, 9; 16 Nov. 1906, 1; 24 Nov. 1906, 1, 6, 16. Frederic Thrasher described how a youth gang played the same role in Chicago's race riots of 1919: "When the gang becomes inflamed . . . it may become the nucleus for a mob, as is shown by the Dirty Dozen's invasion of the Black Belt. The superior organization, solidarity, and morale of the gang give the mob an unwonted stability and direct its excited activities to greater destruction. The less active elements in the mob, on the other hand, and even the mere spectators, give moral support to or provide an appreciative audience for the more active nucleus – the gang." Thrasher, *Gang*, 53; see also 203–3.

44. *HS*, 9 Nov. 1906, 1; 24 Nov. 1906, 1; Palmer, *Culture in Conflict*, 214.

45. A few were caught and charged with "gross indecency." HPL, RG 10, Series M, 1904–11. See also *HS*, 13 April 1921, 17. For an analysis of intergenerational sex in this period, see Maynard, "'Horrible Temptations.'"

46. *HS*, 30 July 1900, 8; 18 May 1901, 8; 9 March 1909, 10; 8 April 1909, 7; *HT*, 23 March 1911, 1; 12 Aug. 1913, 1; Dennis, *We Boys Together*, 1–80. Christine Stansell found these attitudes and behaviour towards women on the streets far back in the 19th century; see *City of Women*, 27.

47. See Connell's discussion of "protest masculinity" in *Masculinities*, 109–12.

48. Grant, "'Real Boy' and Not a Sissy."

49. OCPR, 245–311; Hogeveen, "'Can't You Be a Man?'"

50. City council debated the imposition of a curfew law to curb youths' street activities at night, but in the end decided against such a move. *HS*, 23 Feb. 1897, 7. One man recalled his early-20th-century boyhood as a time for getting to know the police force well and learning how to avoid them when engaged in such activities as "chiseling a little gum from a gum box." He also remembered watching out for the truant officer on days when he and his friends skipped school. *HS*, 6 Feb. 1956, 6; 13 Jan. 1973, 23.

51. OCPR, 252, 253, 263, 270, 293; *HS*, 17 Aug. 1900, 8; 4 Sept. 1900, 8; 11 Oct. 1900, 8; 21 Jan. 1901, 8; 22 Jan. 1901, 8; 26 March 1901, 8; 8 May 1901, 8; Wever, "Crime and Punishment in Hamilton," 9–11; Bennett, "Taming 'Bad Boys.'" These boys made up about 5 per cent of the boys age 10 to 16 in Hamilton in 1941. CC, 1941, Vol. 3, 65. Calculation is mine.

52. HPL, Rotary Club of Hamilton, Minutes, 1917–20; HPL, RG 10 Series A, 1920–31; *HH*, 2 Feb. 1921, 9; *HS*, 5 June 1920, 15; 2 Feb. 1921, 3; 26 Jan. 1925, 2; 22 Jan. 1927; 13; HBEM, 1921, 67–68; BBAA, Board of Directors, Minutes, 1929–39; Big Brothers Association of Hamilton, *Annual Report*, 1936, 2; 1937, 2; 1939, 6–8; Canadian Welfare Council, *Study of the Community Fund*, 97–100.

53. The "problem" of working-class boys and their masculine identities provoked widespread debate and a massive outpouring of books and articles across the English-speaking world at the turn of the century and was often related to concerns about solidifying imperial superiority. Girls were largely ignored. For a review of the literature, see Hendrick, *Images of Youth*. For an indication of the impact of these discussions on Hamilton youth workers, see Unsworth, *Church and the Boy*.

54. Ross, *Y.M.C.A. in Canada*, 194; McLeod, "Live Vaccine"; Grant, "'Real Boy' and Not a Sissy."

55. Howell and Lindsay, "Social Gospel and the Young Boy Problem"; Dirks, "'Getting a Grip on Harry'"; Dirks, "Serving Church and Nation"; Springhall, "Building Character."

56. Smith, "Working-Class Anglicans," 143 (quotation); *HS*, 15 Jan. 1907, 9; Addison, "Life and Culture," 63–64; Cumbo, *Italian Presence*; Marr, "Church Teen Clubs." St. Peter's

Anglican Church also had a boxing club; Smith, "Dialectics of Faith," 129.

57. Ross, *Y.M.C.A. in Canada*, 194; Macleod, *Building Character in the American Boy*; HPL, Young Men's Christian Association – East End, Minutes; *HS*, 3 March 1910, 12; 10 March 1910, 12; Marr, "Church Teen Clubs."

58. Hamilton Playgrounds Association, *Souvenir Number* (quotation); *HT*, 13 July 1916, 7 (quotation); Fenton, "Supervised Playgrounds."

59. *HH*, 2 Feb. 1910, 1, 4; 25 Nov. 1920, 12 (quotation); *HT*, 12 March 1910, 1; Dirks, "Canada's Boys"; Moss, *Manliness and Militarism*, 115–17.

60. Allen Warren draws a sharp distinction between the mindless drilling of cadet training and the more varied educational program of scouting; see Warren, "Sir Robert Baden-Powell, the Scout Movement, and Citizenship Training."

61. *HH*, 27 Jan. 1910, 9; 2 Feb. 1910, 1, 4; 19 Feb. 1910, 7; 26 Feb. 1910, 10; 9 April 1910, 26 Oct. 1910; 4; 19 June 1918, 4; 20 April 1920, 9; 22 June 1920, 8 (quotation); 15 Oct. 1920, 5; 20 Oct. 1920, 4; 25 Nov. 1920, 12 (quotation); 26 Nov. 1920, 12; 24 Nov. 1920, 16; 4 Dec. 1920, 3; 6 Dec. 1920, 15; 21 Jan. 1922, 4; 14 Nov. 1923, 11; 22 Oct. 1924, 17 (quotation); *HS*, 11 May 1916, 8; *HT*, 12 March 1910, 1; 24 June 1910, 1; 8 July 1910, 1; 9 July 1912, 1; 13 July 1912, 1; 4 April 1914, 13; 13 April 1914, 3; HPL, HCC, Minutes, 7 Dec. 1920, 106; HPL, Rotary Club of Hamilton, Minutes, 13 March 1919; Dirks, "Canada's Boys – An Imperial or National Asset?"; Moss, *Manliness and Militarism*, 115–17; Springhall, "Boy Scouts, Class, and Militarism"; Macleod, "Act Your Age"; Rosenthal, *Character Factory*; MacDonald, *Sons of the Empire*; Warren, "Popular Manliness"; Proctor, *On My Honour*, 16; Bogardus, *City Boy*, 113–16. The first under-12 "Wolf Cub" packs in Canada were authorized in 1916, and by the mid-1920s had reached about half the membership of the Scouts; Thompson, *Origins and Development of the Wolf Cub Movement*; LAC, R4619-0-9-E, Boy Scouts of Canada, *Annual Reports*, 1916–39.

62. An effort to have a Scout troop in every school never got off the ground. Although the local language suggested concern to channel rougher boyish behaviour, the thrust of the movement seemed to be rescuing middle-class boys from "softness" and cultivating a more vigorous masculinity among them. *HH*, 26 Feb. 1910, 10; 26 Oct. 1912, 8; *HS*, 2 Feb. 1910, 14; 19 Feb. 1910, 9; 11 May 1916, 8; Springhall, "Boy Scouts, Class, and Militarism"; Macleod, "Act Your Age"; Proctor, *On My Honour*, 46–47. Across the whole province Scout membership hovered around 7,000 until 1919 and then dropped to 6,258 in 1920. LAC, R4619-0-9-E, *Annual Reports*, 1916–21.

63. See, for example, HPL, YMCA – East End, Minutes, 9 Nov., 6 Dec. 1915; 10 Jan., 7 Feb., 6 March, 10 April, 8 May, 12 Dec. 1916.

64. William Foote Whyte notes how gang activity moved inside a settlement house in Boston; see *Street Corner Society*, 6–8, 57–58.

65. *HT*, 11 Feb. 1910, 11 (quotation); *HS*, 17 Aug. 1925, 5 (quotation); 22 July 1930, 7; CCCCP, 1911, 48; HPL, Hamilton Playgrounds Association Fonds, Chief Supervisor, General Report, 1919–25; Soldiers' Aid Commission, Minutes, 10 April 1919; Rotary Club of Hamilton, Minutes, 1921; Murphy and Murphy, *Tales from the North End*, 65–66. An Anglican Church choirmaster also had to quell a competition of whistle-blowing among his choir boys as they lined up behind the church; Fenwick, "Some Musical Memories," 24–25.

66. *HS*, 19 Jan. 1925, 5; Coates and McGuiness, *Only in Canada*.

67. *HS*, 6 Aug. 1925, 5; Hamilton Playgrounds Association, *Souvenir Number*; HPL, Playgrounds Scrapbook; *HS*, 22 Nov. 1919, 12; 19 Jan. 1925, 5; 15 May 1925, 17; HPL, HCC, Minutes, 7 Dec. 1920, 106; HPL, Rotary Club of Hamilton, Minutes, 13 March 1919; LAC, R 4619-0-9-E, Boy Scouts of Canada, *Annual Reports*, 1920–39 (quote in 1920, 43); *Annual Reports of the Social Agencies*, 1930, 62–67; Proctor, *On My Honour*; CC, 1941, Vol. 3, 65 (total is mine); Canadian Welfare Council, *Study of the Community Fund*, 97–100. After the initial burst of reorganization, Hamilton's Scout membership did not expand dramatically in the 1920s and slipped slightly to 1,100 in 1927.

68. Hunter, *Which Side Are You On, Boys*, 9–32; WAHC, interview with Bert McClure; Murphy and Murphy, *Tales from the North End*, 194, 210; Hinther, "Raised in the Spirit of the Class Struggle." The Ukrainian youth organization was minuscule by comparison – 11 members in 1926. Kealey and Whitaker, eds., *R.C.M.P. Security Bulletins: Early Years*, 359–60.

69. Roberts, ed., *Organizing Westinghouse*, 2–3. Later in his teens young Alf Ready joined the militia to get onto their track team.

70. Garvie, *Growing Up*, 12. For similar responses to youth programming in a Toronto settlement house, see Cumbo, "As the Twig Is Bent," 273–80. Surveys of children using playgrounds in Worcester, Mass., revealed similar resistance to the discipline imposed on them; see Rosenzweig, *Eight Hours*, 150–51.

71. LAC, R4619-0-9-E, Boy Scouts of Canada, *Annual Reports*, 1924, 43, 46.

72. Maltin and Bann, *Little Rascals*.

73. In her interviews with boys from Hamilton's middle-class families, Synge learned that these children generally did not contribute their earnings to the family coffers. Just before World War One Canada's future prime minister Lester Pearson, son of a Methodist minister, had a paper route in Hamilton, but he was allowed to put his earnings into a bank account. Synge, "Family and Community," ch.

6; Pearson, *Mike*, 13; Rotundo, "Boy Culture"; Macleod, *Building Character*.

74. In 1910 the Children's Aid Society announced a "crusade" against boys under 14 selling newspapers after 10 p.m., and by 1925 parents were being prosecuted for sending their children out to work as newsboys. *HS*, 16 May 1910, 14; 23 May 1910, 14; 8 Aug. 1910, 10; 11 Feb. 1925, 5. On youth employment, see chapter 6.

75. Cowles, *Juvenile Employment System*, 3.

76. Synge, "Transition from School to Work," 254–26; Addams, *Spirit of Youth*, 107–35; Whyte, *Street Corner Society*.

77. Tolson, *Limits of Masculinity*, 47–51.

78. For discussion of these workplace changes, see chapter 10; also Peck, *Reinventing Free Labor*.

79. The use of boys' labour is noted in *Globe* (Toronto), 8 Jan. 1894, 8. In 1929 National Steel Car paid "boys" $6.75 a day, while men got $10. In 1936 Dominion Glass paid boys 25 to 33 cents an hour, and men an average of 58 cents. A year later a local paper-box manufacturer explained to the federal labour department how some young men, originally hired at boys' wages several years earlier, had become stuck by the lack of jobs during the depression. "Normally, after a few years' experience, they would move into better positions in ours or other plants," he wrote. "But these openings had not presented themselves and the personel [*sic*] turnover during this time in our plant was practically nil." The young men were disgruntled at still earning boys' rates. *HS*, 6 Sept. 1929, 7; *Clarion*, 22 Aug. 1937, 7; LAC, R244-76-4-E, Vol. 388, File 175.

80. *HS*, 4 Jan. 1907, 12; *CM*, January 1908, 56–58; March 1908, 42–43; 5 Feb. 1909, 61–62; April 1910, 40; 17 July 1919, 57. The fictional hero of Claudius Gregory's 1933 novel *Forgotten Men* was subjected to this kind of hazing when he started work at a steel plant. Gregory, *Forgotten Men*, 152.

81. For rich discussions of these masculine variants in the workplace, see Parr, *Gender of Breadwinners*; Peck, *Reinventing Free Labor*.

82. See, for example, *HS*, 13 July 1904, 8; 7 Jan. 1910, 16; 22 March 1910, 14; 13 May 1910, 20; 26 May 1910, 8; 11 Oct. 1910, 12; 29 Nov. 1910, 14; 23 Dec. 1910, 9; 30 Dec. 1910, 9; 2 Nov. 1913, 24; 3 Feb. 1920, 16; 14 Dec. 1920, 18; *HH*, 22 Feb. 1909, 10; 29 Dec. 1910, 1; 25 May 1912, 1; 30 Oct. 1912, 7; 22 March 1913, 1; 17 Aug. 1915, 10; 8 July 1916, 1.

83. One old-timer remembered how a spunky gang of 16-year-old boys was recruited to help organize the Westinghouse plant at the end of the 1930s. WAHC, interview with Fred Purser, 23 May 1995.

84. The 1921 census-takers recorded that 99 per cent of males of age 15 to 19 were single, as were 76 per cent of those of age 20 to 24. For those of age 25 to 29, 41 per cent were single, and of age 30 to 34 only 22 per cent. Over the next 20 years these proportions changed little, except for a noticeable drop in the number of bachelors in the 25 to 29 age bracket (the new wartime boom in the early 1940s may well have sparked a new surge of marriages). ORGR, 1890–1924 (there are no published breakdowns by city after this date); CC, 1921, Vol. 2, 184–85; 1931, Vol. 3, 136–37; 1941, Vol. 3, 122 (calculations of percentages are mine). Before 1921 the published census data for Hamilton did not include marital status by age group.

85. Synge, "Transition from School to Work"; Synge, "Young Working Class Women"; Synge, "Family and Community," ch. 3.6; Comacchio, "Dancing to Perdition," 10–11; Nasaw, *Children of the City*, 130–37; Benson, *Household Accounts*, 64–67. During World War One military recruiters were frustrated that mothers were apparently discouraging their sons from signing up in order to keep them bringing home good wages. HPL, Hamilton Military Scrapbooks, Vol. 1 (1914–16). In 1921 a machinist under age 20 took home only $15 a week, while one of age 20 to 24 clutched a pay packet of $22.50, which compared to $26 for such a worker of age 25 to 34. A foundry worker similarly went from $17.50 in his teens to $22 to $26 in each half of his twenties, while a labourer got $14, $18.60, and $20.70 in each of these age brackets. In all three cases they were earning the average wage for their whole occupational group by their mid-twenties. CC, 1921, Vol. 3, 142, 153–54 (calculations are mine).

86. Harney, "Men without Women"; Harney, "Boarding and Belonging." On the issue of sending home wages, a great deal more is known about these patterns among European "sojourners" than about the practices of their Anglo-Celtic workmates.

87. Local unemployment relief policies discriminated against single men. In 1921, for example, the city cut them off completely; a "Young Unemployed Fellow" writing to the *Spectator* concluded they had only two options: "either get married (if you have the money), or go out into the garden and eat worms." *HS*, 2 April 1921, 1; 24 June 1921, 6 (quotation); MacDowell, "Relief Camp Workers."

88. Clark, *Struggle for the Breeches*; Fingard, *Jack in Port*, 96–98; Burley, *Servants of the Honourable Company*; Chudacoff, *Age of the Bachelor*. In 1911 the *Herald* began running the US comic strip that captured this bachelor world: *Mutt and Jeff*.

89. In 1900 Hamilton had 29 amateur baseball clubs; Kerr, "Rise of Sport." See also *HH*, 7 April 1910, 8; 19 April 1910, 9; 2 May 1910, 9; 3 May 1910, 8; 11 May 1910, 1, 11; 28 June 1916, 8; 15 April 1911, 17; *HS*, 15 July 1926, n.p.; *LN*, 12 April 1912, 1; 31 July 1914, 1; 6 Aug. 1915, 2; 30 April 1920, 4; Murphy and Murphy, *Tales from the North End*, 194–98. Palmer, *Culture in Conflict*, 52–54, 163–67; Miller, ed., *Centennial Sports Review*; Metcalfe, *Canada Learns to Play*, 26, 163–68; Morrow, "Baseball"; Howell, *Northern Sandlots*. Steven M. Gelber argues that the fascination with baseball reflected the new rationalized structure of

the industrial-capitalist workplace. Melvin L. Adelman has looked more closely at the origins and patterns of recreational baseball (as opposed to the competitive version oriented to professionalism and spectators), and rejected such an easy congruence with business. Neither, however, investigates closely enough the ways in which the sport grew out of the bachelor cultures of the late 19th and early 20th centuries. Gelber, "Working at Play"; Adelman, "Baseball, Business and the Workplace." For a useful discussion of the distinctive dynamics of casual working-class sports, see Dunk, *It's a Working Man's Town*, 65–100. Cricket, tennis, curling, and yachting remained elite sports in which workingmen were rarely found. Garvie, *Growing Up*, 41–43.

90. *HH*, 8 March 1910, 8; 26 March 1910, 8; 4 April 1910, 9; 8 April 1910, 12; 17 June 1910, 16; 13 Sept. 1910, 4; 12 June 1911, 8; 25 Jan. 1913, 1; 1 Feb. 1913, 1; 28 March 1913, 16; 19 May 1913, 5; 20 April 1914, 10; 1 Aug. 1917, 13; *LN*, 27 Sept. 1912, 3; 1 Nov. 1912, 1. North American football seems to have been a less widespread participatory sport in Hamilton in the early 20th century despite the popularity of the city's professional team, the Tigers (staffed partly by brawny wage-earners). A local sports enthusiast later wrote that on local football teams "many of the names of the players were those of the foremost families of Hamilton." Gaudaur, "Century of Football" (quotation); Bruce, *News and the Southams*, 35–37; Murphy and Murphy, *Tales from the North End*, 182; Kerr, "Rise of Sport," 17–19; HPL, Henley, "Hamilton in Ragtime"; Bailey, *Hamilton*, 71, 83–84; Cosentino, "Football." Like football, hockey developed as a more elite sport in universities and private clubs before the quick emergence of professional teams in the early 20th century (Hamilton had only one pro hockey team, from 1921 to 1925, when the franchise moved to New York following a players' strike). Wesley, *Hamilton's Hockey Tigers*; Miller, ed., *Centennial Sports Review*; Metcalfe, *Canada Learns to Play*, 54–65, 168–72; Gruneau and Whitsun, *Hockey Night in Canada*, 31–106; Simpson, "Hockey." Running was also a significant spectator sport. Miller, ed. *Centennial Sports Review*; HPL, Henley, "Hamilton in Ragtime," 81–82.

91. Reiss, "From Pitch to Putt," 179; Kidd, *Struggle for Canadian Sport*, 20–21; Metcalfe, *Canada Learns to Play*, 85, 88; Gruneau and Whitson, *Hockey Night in Canada*, 80–103.

92. Dunk, *It's a Working Man's Town*, 88.

93. See, for example, *HH*, 26 March 1910, 8; 24 June 1912, 8; 24 Sept. 1918, 10; Murphy and Murphy, *Tales from the North End*, 88, 188–89; Henley, *Hamilton: Our Lives and Times*, 95. A well-behaved crowd in Hamilton was a subject of comment; see *HH*, 13 Nov. 1923, 12.

94. Kidd, *Struggle for Canadian Sport*, 19–20; Kerr, "Rise of Sport," 42; *HH*, 9 March 1910, 8; 22 April 1910, 11; 2 June

1910, 11; 3 June 1910, 1; 17 June 1910, 1; 8 July 1910, 5; 22 Feb. 1911, 1; 24 Feb. 1911, 1; 27 Feb. 1911, 1; 28 Feb. 1911, 1; 2 March 1911, 1; 17 March 1911, 1; *HS*, 12 March 1901, 10; 16 March 1901, 12; 8 June 1917, 28; 26 Oct. 1917, 32; *IB*, May 1906, 4; Murphy and Murphy, *Tales from the North End*, 191–94; Cumbo, *Italian Presence*. In 1910 the city's Board of Control decided that "in future if boxing bouts were held by a responsible athletic organization there would be no particular objection to permits being issued so long as regulations governing the fight were drawn up. But no permit was to be issued for a bout arranged for gain for private individuals." *HS*, 3 June 1910, 1; 10 June 1910, 4. After the war, veterans' groups held boxing matches, and delegates to the international convention of the Amalgamated Association of Iron, Steel, and Tin Workers meeting in Hamilton were treated to some pugilism during a smoker. The Independent Labor Party also held boxing "entertainments" as fundraisers. See *HS*, 15 March 1919, 18; *AJ*, 12 May 1921, 8; HPL, Independent Labor Party, Central Branch, Minutes, 10, 24 March, 12, 29 April 1922. For the masculine identities cultivated in and around boxing rings, see Gorn, *Manly Art*. Wrestling was also a popular spectator sport; see *HS*, 8 June 1900, 8; 21 June 1900, 8; 4 Dec. 1903, 12; 4 Nov. 1905, 20; 2 April 1909, 16.

95. *AJ*, 11 Aug. 1921, 27; *HH*, 10 June 1907, 1; 29 May 1907, 1; 15 March 1910, 11; 20 June 1910, 1; 19 Sept. 1910, 1; 29 Dec. 1910, 1; 3 Feb. 1913, 4; 19 Jan. 1914, 9; 5 June 1916, 1; *HS*, 10 Oct. 1900, 8; 4 Jan. 1901, 1; 20 June 1904, 10; 2 Oct. 1908, 1; 11 April 1910, 12; 28 June 1920, 7; 19 Jan. 1925, 14; *HT*, 11 April 1910, 1; 22 March 1911, 1; 17 Nov. 1919, 1; HPL, RG 10, Series A (Police Department), 1905, 1909, 1911, 1912, 1915; Canada, Royal Commission in Racing Inquiry, *Report*, 38–44; WAHC, interview with Ken Withers; Irwin, "Moral Order Crime" (1907–12 statistics); Kerr, "Rise of Sport," 30–31; Murphy and Murphy, *Tales from the North End*, 47–50; Morton, *At Odds*; see also McKibbin, "Working-Class Gambling." For a lengthy description of a 1925 police raid on a poker game in a social club, see *HS*, 27 March 1925, 5.

96. Hunter, *Which Side Are You On, Boys*, 9; Murphy and Murphy, *Tales from the North End*, 85–88, 155, 179–81; McBee, *Dance Hall Days*, 157–97.

97. There was nonetheless disagreement within the YMCA over whether the ever-popular baseball game was an appropriate physical activity; see Baker, "Disputed Diamonds." International Harvester not only sponsored numerous teams, but also an annual field day for its many employees. *Made-in-Hamilton Quarterly*, January 1921, n.p. In 1931 young Italians organized the Italo-Canadian Recreation Club. Cumbo, *Italian Presence*.

98. Turkstra, "Christianity and the Working Class," ch. 4; Addison, "Life and Culture," 5263–64; Smith, "Dialectics of Faith," 255; Gauvreau, "'Factories and Foreigners'";

Bailey et al., *Presbytery of Hamilton*, 134; Cumbo, *Italian Presence*. The Presbyterians were discouraged by the limited support for the Brotherhood movement across the country; Fraser, *Social Uplifters*, 128–29. In 1912 the *Catholic Register* also expressed disillusionment with the failure to hold on to young men in the clubs created for them; Cumbo, "As the Twig Is Bent," 391–92.

99. O'Brien, "Manhood and the Militia Myth." In Britain, where so many Hamilton workers had been born, respect for the army before the war was low; Fuller, *Troop Morale and Popular Culture*, 32–33.

100. Morton, *When Your Number's Up*; Cook, *Shock Troops*, 179–96; Englander and Osborne, "Jack, Tommy, and Henry Dubb"; Fuller, *Troop Morale and Popular Culture*; Dawson, *Soldier Heroes*. Desmond Morton has calculated that nearly two-thirds of the CEF had been manual workers, that roughly four out of five were bachelors, and nearly seven out of ten were under 30. One in eight who served overseas in the CEF died, and another one in three was wounded. Morton, *When Your Number's Up*, 181, 278–79. "Gangs" made the transition into the army, as military recruiters tapped into civilian friendship circles to encourage group recruitment; Gordon, "Hamilton, 1916."

101. The court case that resulted prompted the magistrate to say that "street fights were becoming altogether too common." Quoted in Wever, "Crime and Punishment," 18. See also *HS*, 2 March 1900, 8; 17 April 1901, 10; 13 May 1901, 8; 25 May 1901, 8; 1 Aug. 1903, 1; 20 Dec. 1920, 27.

102. Murphy and Murphy, *Tales from the North End*, 210–13. On pool rooms, see Fred Howe, "Edwardian Era Pool Shark," *HS*, 15 April 1961, 49.

103. A 1907 law set the legal drinking age at 21, but two years later a *Spectator* reporter noted how "young men and boys" spilled over from Victoria Park into the two saloons across the road: "After the boys are through with their games, they crowd to these places, and the hotels do a thriving business in the summer." The fact that some hotels ran poolrooms adjacent to the barrooms probably allowed younger drinkers to slip in. In 1913 a church-sponsored investigation of local drinking spots worried about a considerable number of "very young" men who "might be minors." Popham, *Working Papers on the Tavern*, 2, 7, 29; *HS*, 30 Dec. 1909, 5; MPSS, 20.

104. Much of the ensuing discussion draws on Heron, "Boys and Their Booze."

105. In April 1913 a Methodist-Presbyterian "census" of all saloons in the hour before closing on one Saturday night found 1,775 drinkers and estimated that probably three times that number would have passed through the barrooms during that hour. MPSS, 19.

106. Gusfield, "Passage to Play."

107. One of the most influential books in the post–World War Two alcohol-studies field, published in 1969, compared the behaviour of drunks across many cultures and discovered that no consistent pattern could be attributed to "the release of inhibitions," as so many writers had previously assumed. The authors concluded that the drunken comportment was culturally constructed and that drunks acted out well-understood scripts of behavioural expectations. See MacAndrew and Edgerton, *Drunken Comportment*.

108. HPL, RG 10, Series A, 1900–5, 1909, 1912–13, 1915; Series M, 1909–10; *HS*, 4 March 1910, 4; 9 May 1910, 14; 6 June 1910, 12; 11 June 1910, 1.

109. Heron, *Booze*, 213–32.

110. Heron, "Boys and Their Booze." Even the old socialist William Barrett, who served as president of the Gospel Temperance Reform Club, urged workers at a 1916 meeting of Social Democrats "to leave the booze alone" because "it muddled the brain."

111. Brewing beer at home for personal and family consumption was still legal in Canada. In 1926, 8,914 home permits were registered in Hamilton by the federal customs department, and by 1934, 175,000 across the province. The ingredients were openly advertised in local newspapers. Distilling spirits at home, however, was illegal, though apparently not difficult. "They just put raisins in water, let it stand and then drink it," one man told the police magistrate in 1920. "Everybody's doing it." Five years later the magistrate admitted, "There are so many different appliances for home brewing these days that it can't be readily decided what is legal and what is not." *HH*, 27 June 1924, 3; *HS*, 8 Jan. 1920, 14; 12 Jan. 1920, 19; 25 Sept. 1920, 27 (quotation); 19 March 1925, 5 (quotation); 18 July 1925, 19; 25 Nov. 1926, 14; Ontario, Legislative Assembly, Newspaper, "Hansard," 28 March 1934 (copy at University of Toronto's Robarts Library). Hamilton was a major centre of bootlegging and rum-running; see Hunt, *Booze, Boats, and Billions*; Hunt, *Whiskey and Ice*; Dubro and Rowland, *King of the Mob*. The neighbourhood bootlegger was typically just a small operation running out of a family home; WAHC, interviews with Mary and Louis Fiori, Jake Isbister, Floyd Read; MHSO, ITA-0826-CRE; ITA-09826-FER.

112. Heron, "Boys and Their Booze," 436–46.

113. See, for example, *HS*, 8 Aug. 1910, 10; *HH*, 27 May 1912, 5; *LN*, 31 May 1912, 1; 27 Feb. 1914, 1; 10 Nov. 1916, 1. In her study of working-class churches in Hamilton, Melissa Turkstra found that single men were far less likely to join. They made up only 7 per cent of the membership of Calvin Presbyterian between 1910 and 1925, for example. This confirms the observation made about late-19th-century Ontario towns in Marks, *Revivals and Roller Rinks*. It is possible, however, that young men dropped in on services at different churches, partly in search of female company, without ever joining. *HS*, 27 March 1907, 9; Synge, "Family and Community," ch. 5.4.

114. In 1907 the Spec. Man found one such fellow boarding in Hamilton: "He works hard all day at the Bridge works, and spends his evenings in the house studying. He is ambitious to become an electrical engineer." *HS*, 27 March 1907, 9.

115. In 1915 the provincial inspector of libraries contradicted a local politician's charge that workers read only fiction: although women liked fiction, he wrote, "the working class as a rule are the readers of a better class of literature and are very exacting in their wants in this direction." *HS*, 1 Feb. 1915, 5.

116. *LN*, 11 Nov. 1920, 3; 28 Jan. 1921, 2; 27 Oct. 1922, 1; 27 Sept. 1923, 2; 28 Aug. 1925, 8; *CLW*, 30 Sept. 1926, 2; 28 April 1927, 3; 29 March 1929, 3; Radforth and Sangster, "Link between Labour and Learning." The Educational Association's local president, Harry Fester, complained in 1925 about "the failure of members of labour organizations" to take these classes. *LG*, May 1925, 476.

117. Synge, "Family and Community," ch. 3.1; McBee, *Dance Hall Days*, 23–29.

118. Dubinsky, *Improper Advances*, 117; Synge, "Family and Community."

119. Garvie, *Growing Up*, 8; Synge, "Family and Community," ch. 5.4; Cruickshank and Bouchier, "*Dirty Spaces*," 66–67; Gauvreau, "Factories and Foreigners."

120. Synge, "Family and Community," ch. 5.4.

121. Heron, "Boys and Their Booze"; Heron, *Booze*, 284–93.

122. Wexman, *Creating the Couple*.

123. Swiencicki, "Consuming Brotherhood"; White, *First Sexual Revolution*, 100; cf., Fowler, *First Teenagers*, 116–33.

124. HPL, RG 10, Series M, 1904–11. The men seemed to be mostly single labourers, varying in age from 15 to 42. Newspaper reporters squeamishly referred to these cases as simply "a serious offense," and provided no details. *HS*, 13 April 1921, 17. For the patterns of furtive sex between men in this period, see Maynard, "'Horrible Temptations'"; Maynard, "'Through a Hole in the Lavatory Wall.'" Any discussion of sexual behaviour here must remain speculative because no detailed surveys were undertaken in Hamilton or any other Canadian city in this period. The most extensive investigations involved cases of venereal disease after about 1917, initially by the military and later by public-health workers. The military investigators discovered that much of the widespread VD had been contracted in sexual activity before enlistment. Cassel, *Secret Plague*, 157. US research is also suggestive. The publication of the massive study of male sexuality by sexologist Alfred Kinsey in 1948 brought to light the pre–World War Two experience of thousands of working-class men who reached adulthood in the 1920s and 1930s. Some three-quarters of the "least-educated" reported pre-marital sex, far more than did middle-class respondents. White, *First Sexual Revolution*, 84–86; see also D'Emilio and Freedman, *Intimate Matters*, 256–65.

125. Their knowledge of sex and sexuality could well have been fragmentary and inaccurate, because the only sexual instruction available came from booklets distributed by Canadian churches and, after 1905, occasional "advanced purity" talks in school rooms by an intimidating lecturer who toured Ontario (with the active support of the Woman's Christian Temperance Union). Both sources placed more emphasis on abstinence and moral probity than on the practicalities of sexual behaviour. Public lectures and films were occasionally available after World War One in the wake of the VD scare. Far more boys and men probably pieced together some rudimentary (often incorrect) knowledge from peers. *CWRT*, 1 May 1910; 1 July 1910; Bliss, "Pure Books on Avoided Subjects"; Stamps, *Schools of Ontario*, 69; Sutherland, *Growing Up*, 94; McLaren, *Bedroom and the State*; Cassel, *Secret Plague*; Hall, *Hidden Anxieties*, 15–62; Thrasher, *Gang*, 220.

126. Givertz, "Sex and Order"; Dubinsky, *Improper Advances*; Dubinsky and Givertz, "'It Was Only a Matter of Passion'"; Cumbo, "As the Twig Is Bent," 22–31; Bailey, *From Front Porch to Back Seat*, 77–96.

127. Bliss, "Pure Books on Avoided Subjects"; Cassel, *Secret Plague*; *HS*, 19 Oct. 1910, 14; *HH*, 6 Nov. 1920, 19.

128. On men seeking out brothels, see *HS*, 31 Dec. 1895, 8; 1 April 1901, 8; 20 June 1904, 10; 6 Nov. 1906, 12; 20 April 1914, 16; *HH*, 16 Feb. 1909, 1; 13 March 1911, 1; 7 Nov. 1912, 3; 27 Jan. 1913, 1; 9 Jan. 1914, 1; 20 April 1914, 14. By 1925 the Hamilton General Hospital's VD clinic was treating nearly 6,000 men. OPBHR, 1920, 228; 1921, 325–28; 1922, 262–63; 1923, 388–89; 1926, 15; Cassel, *Secret Plague*.

129. A 1917 survey of VD cases in Toronto discovered that almost half were contracted out of doors. Cassel, *Secret Plague*, 142.

130. "There is no invention of modern times which could equal the motor car in leading the youths and the maidens astray," a local judge intoned in 1919. *HH*, 28 Aug. 1919, 1.

131. Dubinsky, *Improper Advances*, 74–77; Chambers, "Courtship, Condoms, and 'Getting Caught.'" In the United States, historians of sexuality have noted a sharp increase in pre-marital intercourse in the 1920s; see D'Emilio and Freedman, *Intimate Matters*, 256. Kinsey would later claim that women born after 1900 were two and a half times more likely to engage in pre-marital sex than were those born earlier; White, *First Sexual Revolution*, 15.

132. For examples, see Givertz, "Sex and Order," 107–48.

133. Givertz, "Sex and Order," 110; Dubinsky, *Improper Advances*, 33, 134–38; Dubinsky and Givertz, "'It Was Only a Matter of Passion.'"

134. *HS*, 14 Aug. 1920, 19; Givertz, "Sex and Order," 131. Failure to show sufficient resistant to such male aggression could lead courts to conclude that women had consented. Givertz, "Sex and Order," 132–35.

135. HPL, RG 3, Series A; Struthers, *Limits of Affluence*, 53–62; Snell, *Citizen's Wage*, 36–72; Davies, *In the House of Old*.

136. McBee, *Dance Hall Days*, 45–49.

137. Bederman, "'Women Have Had Charge of the Church Work Long Enough'"; Christie and Gauvreau, *Christian Churches and Their Peoples*, 83–88.

138. Snell, "'White Life for Two'"; Ursel, *Private Lives, Public Policy*, 102, 143–45, 341; Chambers, "Illegitimate Children."

139. Heron, "Boys and Their Booze," 429; Benson, *Household Accounts*, 21–22.

140. What sorts of men would a workingman meet in these lodge meetings? Most studies concluded that late-19th-century orders brought together some mix of middle-class men and skilled manual workers, and seldom their poorer, less-skilled workmates. There were differences between orders – the Masons reaching further up the social scale, and the Odd Fellows further down, while the Ancient Order of United Workmen and the Orange Order had a decidedly proletarian cast. The class composition of different lodges within an order could also vary widely. Table 44 looks at four lodges of Masons and one of Odd Fellows, and reveals that one (Doric) shifted decidedly to more middle-class membership after the turn of the century, while two others (Electric and Tuscan) formed in 1909 and 1919 respectively had only four in ten and three in ten middle-class membership. In all five, there were few labourers, helpers, or teamsters. See Anstead, "Fraternalism," 181–93; Palmer, "Mutuality"; Clawson, *Constructing Brotherhood*; Boucher, "Charity, Hope, and Protection."

141. Hunter, *Which Side Are You On, Boys*, 10; Heron, "Boys and Their Booze."

142. Givertz, "Sex and Order." See also Benson, *Household Accounts*, 20–23.

143. Bederman, *Manliness and Civilization*; Rotundo, *American Manhood*; Kimmel, *Manhood in America*.

144. When a newly elected Independent Labor Party member of the provincial legislation, George Halcrow, was found with a bottle of liquor in his car in 1919 and confessed to social drinking at a party beforehand, party members easily forgave him. *HT*, 30 Oct. 1919, 1; 5 Nov. 1919, 1.

15. Our Kind

1. *HH*, 31 Aug. 1912, 1.

2. Anderson, *Imagined Communities*; Colley, "Britishness and Otherness"; Buckner, "Whatever Happened to the British Empire?"; Buckner "Long Goodbye"; Buckner and Bridge, "Reinventing the British World"; Berger, *Sense of Power*; Cole, "Problem of 'Nationalism' and 'Imperialism'"; Cannadine, "Imperial Canada."

3. *HS*, 21 June 1897, 1, 4 (quotation); 23 June 1897, 5, 8. For an analysis of the even larger Toronto celebrations and of the Sons of England's remarkable Empire-wide singing of the national anthem, see Stubbs, "Visions of the Common Good," 220–43.

4. "Trenholme, Clementina (Fessenden)," *DHB*, Vol. 1, 199; Stamp, "Empire Day."

5. Stamp, *Schools of Ontario*, 92–93; Cumbo, "As the Twig Is Bent," 153–56, 162 (quotation at 155); McGowan, "Toronto's English-Speaking Catholics," 208–9. Schools were so sensitive to this role that at the outset of World War One the Hamilton school board required each teacher to declare that "he or she is pro-British in his or her sympathies, and a Loyal British Subject, or else face dismissal." Stamp, *School of Ontario*, 95.

6. *HS*, 9 Oct. 1905, 5; HPL, Our Heritage Scrapbook, Vol. 1, 139; Best and Fraser, "Chisholm."

7. *HS*, 1 March 1900, 5; 2 March 1900, 5 (quotation); 21 Jan. 1950, n.p.; HPL, Our Heritage Scrapbook, Vol. 2, 17; *CAC*, 9 March 1900 (quotation). For another, more restrained, celebration, see *HS*, 1 June 1900, 8. The press reported none of the harassment of pacifists that appeared during such celebrations in Montreal and Britain at that point. Miller, *Painting the Map Red*, 300; Price, *Imperial War*, 132–77. In Canada generally, the small labour press was ambiguous about the Boer War; see Miller, "English-Canadian Opposition." For a discussion of the limited labour support for that war in Britain, see Pelling, *Popular Politics*, 101–20; Price, *Imperial War*.

8. *HS*, 3 Aug. 1914, 12; 4 Aug. 1914, 1, 14; 5 Aug. 1914, 14; 6 Aug. 1914, 4, 6 (Marion E. Bell, "Sound the Loud Call," and Ernest Hesketh, "The Call of the Blood"), 14; 7 Aug. 1914, 1, 14; 8 Aug. 1914, 1, 8; 10 Aug. 1914, 12; 12 Aug. 1914, 1, 4; 13 Aug. 1914, 12; 14 Aug. 1914, 13; 15 Aug. 1914, 18; 18 Aug. 1914, 9; 20 Aug. 1914, 1, 4; *HT*, 11 Aug., 1914, 1; 12 Aug. 1914, 1; 14 Aug. 1914, 1; 18 Aug. 1914, 1; Rutherdale, *Hometown Horizons*, 34–45 (quotation); Wilson, *Ontario and the First World War*, xvii–xix.

9. Keshen, *Propaganda and Censorship*; *HH*, 3 July 1915, 2; 8 July 1915, 5; 20 March 1916, 4; 24 April 1916, 1; 10 July 1916, 1; *HS*, 8 May 1916, 9; *LN*, 17 March 1916, 1; HPL, Hamilton Military Scrapbook, Vol. 1 (1915–16); Collinson, *Hamilton Recruiting League*, 21–22; Wilson, *Ontario and the First World War*, xxix–li; Gordon, "Hamilton, 1916"; Evans, *Hamilton*, 194–95; Maroney, "Great Adventure"; Bray, "Fighting as an Ally"; Crerar, "Ontario in the Great War."

10. *HH*, 20 March 1916, 4; Wilson, *Ontario and the First World War*, li–lviii; Morton, *When Your Number's Up*.

11. HPL, Hamilton Recruiting League Minutes, 20 July, 10 Aug., 17 Aug. (quotation), 24 Aug., 14 Sept., 16 Sept., 20–21, Sept., 24 Sept., 5 Oct., 18 Oct., 26 Oct., 7 Dec. 1915; *LN*, 23 July 1915, 1; 30 July 1915, 1; *IB*, 23 July 1915, 3. The friction between labour and manufacturers' representatives

within the Recruiting League probably became unbearable once the machinists' strike erupted in spring 1916. Labour participation in the League seemed to disappear after that point.

12. HPL, Hamilton Recruiting League Minutes, 8 Feb., 15 Feb., 22 Feb., 7 March, 6 June 1916; *LN*, 25 Feb. 1916, 1; 17 March 1916, 1; 28 April 1916, 1; 13 Oct. 1916, 1; 12 Jan. 1917, 1; HPL, Hamilton Military Scrapbooks, Vol. 1 (1914–16); *IB*, 25 Feb. 1916, 3; 31 March 1916, 2; *HS*, 10 May 1916, 6; *HH*, 4 July 1917, 2; Collinson, *Hamilton Recruiting League*, 23–24, 26; Heron, "Landers"; Naylor, *New Democracy*, 31–32; Granatstein and Hitsman, *Broken Promises*. Ever the opportunist, Landers in 1915 volunteered to produce a monthly newspaper to promote recruitment, to be known as "The Recruiting Sergeant," which was ultimately rejected by the recruiting league's Publicity Committee as "a waste of money [and] a waste of energy."

13. *HS*, 7 Nov. 1918, 1; *HH*, 7 Nov. 1918, 1; 8 Nov. 1918, 1; 11 Nov. 1918, 6; Henley, "Hamilton in Ragtime." The next year the Prince of Wales' brief sojourn in the city provided another occasion to crank up the imperialist rhetoric in public ceremonies, which once again highlighted the military. But on that October weekend the prince's visit was overshadowed by the imminent provincial election and a referendum on the prohibition of alcohol sales, both of which engaged far more attention in working-class Hamilton. *HS*, 18 Oct. 1919, 1, 15; 20 Oct. 1919, 1, 3; Henley, "Hamilton in Ragtime."

14. Buckner, "Long Goodbye," 194 (quotation); *LL*, 25 June 1920, 1; 13 Aug. 1920, 4 (quotation).

15. Cupido, "Appropriating the Past"; *HS*, 16 Dec. 1918, 11 (quotation); 29 June 1927, 1, 6, 19; 30 June 1927, 5, 10, 17, 20; 1 July 1927, 1, 5, 8, 15, 17; 2 July 1927, 18; 4 July 1927, 5, 12, 19, 23; Cannadine, "Imperial Canada," 10–12; Buckner, "Long Goodbye." On the soldier and his recent war as the embodiment of the Canadian "spirit," see Vance, *Death So Noble*, 226–56. In mid-1918 veterans attending the Great War Veterans' national convention had voted to give "O Canada" precedence over "God Save the Queen," but too few knew the words to be able to sing it. Morton and Wright, *Winning the Second Battle*, 81–82.

16. Avery, *Reluctant Host*, 82–107; Kelley and Trebilcock, *Making of the Mosaic*, 183–215.

17. The IODE named their first chapter after Fessenden. IODE, Fessenden Chapter Minutes.

18. After 1914 the Scouts even had governors general and lieutenant governors as official Chief Scouts and enjoyed annual grants from the Canadian government. LAC, R4619-0-9-E, Boy Scouts of Canada, *Annual Report*, 1915. On the imperialist message, see Alexander, "Girl Guide Movement and Imperial Internationalism."

19. In 1910 the city directory listed only nine men's lodges, one women's lodge, one youth organization (Orange Young Britons), and two groups of Loyal True Blues, as well as five "district" organizations. Large celebrations of the "Glorious Twelfth" of July were held in Hamilton only in 1908 and 1913, and those were regional events with Orangemen from many neighbouring towns and cities. More often a few hundred local Orangemen travelled to other cities. After the war the press regularly claimed that Orange parades drew 12,000 people. The large numbers in 1920s Orange parades included many from surrounding counties. VCHD, 1910, 753; Houston and Smyth, *Sash Canada Wore*; Senior, *Orangeism*; Pennefather, *Orange and the Black*; Jenkins, "Views from 'The Hub of the Empire'"; *HH*, 14 July 1913, 4; 13 July 1923, 11; 12 July 1924, 6; *HS*, 12–13 July 1900, 25. In 1923, 43 of the 111 members of the Ontario legislature were Orangemen, including two of the three ILP representatives. Pennefather, *Orange and the Black*, 137. On the centrality of Protestantism and anti-Catholicism to British identity, see Colley, "Britishness and Otherness," 316–23.

20. LAC, R244-76-4-E, Vol. 299, File 3475, Company report from J. Orr Callaghan, manager, Canada Works.

21. Levitt, *Henri Bourassa and the Golden Calf*; Trofimenkoff, *Dream of Nation*.

22. Quoted in McLaren, *Our Own Master Race*, 52; see also Valverde, *Age of Soap, Light, and Water.*

23. Anderson, "Idea of Chinatown."

24. Quoted in Cumbo, "As the Twig Is Bent," 154.

25. Jacobson, *Whiteness of a Different Color*; Barrett and Roediger, "Inbetween Peoples"; Field, "Ideology and Race"; Frank, "White Working-Class Women"; Backhouse, *Colour-Coded*; Walker, "*Race,*" *Rights, and the Law*, 12–23; Palmer, "Reluctant Hosts." Eric Arnesen's critique of the loose use of the term "whiteness" seems to throw out the baby with the bathwater; there is value in careful use of the term; see Arnesen, "Whiteness and the Historians' Imagination," and several rejoinders in the same issue.

26. Miller, *Skyscrapers Hide the Heavens*; Weaver, "Iroquois," 250; Hill, *Skywalkers*. The aboriginal population documented in the censuses rose from 23 in 1901 to 92 in 1911, 219 in 1921, 329 in 1931, and 426 in 1941. CC, 1901, Vol. 1, 325; 1911, Vol. 2, 372; 1921, Vol. 1, 542; 1931, Vol. 2, 495; 1941, Vol. 3, 180.

27. Fryer, *Black People*, 66–72.

28. Ray Lewis, a Hamilton-born sleeping-car porter and Olympic athlete, later recalled the informal process of church segregation: "What Black families would often find, if they were new to the city and attended services at a predominantly white church, that they would, after a couple of weeks be told that 'there is a nice church on John Street where you will find some friends.' In other words, don't come back." *HS*, 20 Aug. 1900, 8; *HT*, 3 Aug. 1893; AO, F 995, WCTU, Annual Report, 1917, 1923, 1929; *Hamilton: The Birmingham of Canada*, n.p.; Shadd, *Journey from*

Tollgate to Parkway, 184–89, 196, 209–12, 220–36; Beattie, *John Christie Holland*; Cooper, *Shadow Running* (quotation at 17); Winks, *Blacks*, 292–98, 313–20, 355–61; Anstead, "Fraternalism," 229; Walker, *"Race," Rights, and the Law*, 124–37; Walker, "'Race,' and Recruitment"; Weaver, "From Land Assembly to Social Maturity"; Wilson, *Ontario and the First World War*, cviii–cix; Heron, "Boys and Their Booze,"439–40; Malleck, *Try to Control Yourself*, ch. 8; Workers Art and Heritage Centre, Hamilton, website, http://www.museevirtuel-virtualmuseum.ca, "The Souls of Black Folk: Hamilton's Stewart Memorial Community – 5: New Wave: Influx of Caribbean Families in the 1960s-Present Day." In 1939 the Supreme Court ruled that "freedom of commerce" allowed retailers to discriminate against visible minorities. Backhouse, *Colour-Coded*, 254–55.

29.   In 1866 72 black citizens in Hamilton petitioned unsuccessfully to have the lurid, degrading imagery on posters for minstrel shows banned. Shadd, *Journey from Tollgate to Parkway*, 19; Roediger, *Towards the Abolition of Whiteness* (quotation at 65); Roediger, *Wages of Whiteness*; Lott, *Love and Money*; Douglas, *Listening In*, 107. George Lipsitz argues: "With the growth of bureaucratic regimentation in all aspects of social life, methods of carving away limited spheres of autonomy by outwitting those in power became increasingly relevant to more and more people. White Americans may have turned to black culture for guidance because black culture contains the most sophisticated strategies of signification and the richest grammars of opposition available to aggrieved populations." *Rainbow at Midnight*, 305.

30.   *HH*, 14 Nov. 1914, 16; 21 Nov. 1919, 4; *HS*, 7 Feb. 1918, 8; 2 May 1919, 17; 26 Jan. 1922, 16; *Veteran*, 15 April 1922, 17; Cumbo, *Italian Presence*. On minstrelsy moving into amateur theatre: for example, at one Hamilton Conservative Club social event in 1901, the "Smith family of pickaninnies provided a great deal of amusement for the large audience." *HS*, 6 May 1901, 8. On "public processions (like the 1919 Victory Loan parade)": Head of the Lake Historical Society, *Hamilton*, 211, 213. Jolson was still appearing in blackface in 1930, when "Mammy" played in Hamilton. *HS*, 21 July 1930, 4.

31.   Walker, *"Race," Rights and the Law*, 27–28; Calliste, "Race, Gender, and Canadian Immigration." Census-takers counted 450 "Negroes" in Hamilton in 1901, but only 304 in 1911, 375 in 1921, 337 in 1931, and 305 in 1941. CC, 1901, Vol. 1, 325; 1911, Vol. 2, 372; 1921, Vol. 1, 542; 1931, Vol. 2, 495; 1941, Vol. 3, 180. In an apparent move to copy US manufacturers, Dominion Foundries and Steel proposed bringing in 100 blacks from the Southern United States in 1916, but immigration authorities denied their request. LAC, R244-76-4-E, Vol. 304, File 16 (27A), Report of Hugh Sweeney, 24 July 1916.

32.   *LG*, July 1904, 84. Some black families in Hamilton still trace their arrival in the city to Tuckett's turn of the century recruitment; Workers Art and Heritage Centre, Hamilton, website, http://www.museevirtuel-virtualmuseum.ca, "The Souls of Black Folk: Hamilton's Stewart Memorial Community – 5: New Wave: Influx of Caribbean Families in the 1960s-Present Day." A decade earlier a controversy had blown up when the WCTU protested the appointment of a black woman as a police matron in the city jail. Shadd, *Journey from Tollgate to Freeway*, 203. For the Buffalo and Cincinnati experience, see, for example, Carpenter, *Nationality, Color, and Economic Opportunity*; Yans-McLaughlin, *Family and Community*.

33.   Bederman, *Manliness and Civilization*, 1–5.

34.   *HH*, 18 March 1920, 1; 19 March 1920, 1; 20 March 1920, 1; 22 March 1920, 1; 23 March 1920, 1; 25 March 1920, 1; 27 March 1920, 1; *HS*, 19 March 1920, 1; 20 March 1920, 1; 22 March 1920, 1; 23 March 1920, 6; 24 March 1920, 21; 25 March 1920, 1. Magistrate Jelfs recognized the racial dimension of the public reaction and told the press that there would have been an outcry if he had convicted a respectable white man on evidence as flimsy as that presented in the Boyd case.

35.   In 1926 Hamilton had 80 Chinese laundries. For a description of their operation, see Hoe, *Enduring Hardship*, 27–28, 50.

36.   See, for example, *HH*, 19 June 1911, 1; 2 Feb. 1914, 1; *HS*, 16 March 1910, 14; OIFR, 1911, 21–22; Mosher, *Discrimination and Denial*, 126–29, 167–68; Anderson, "Idea of Chinatown." The 1914 legislation on the employment of white women was not actually proclaimed until December 1920, under pressure from organized labour. Backhouse, *Colour-Coded*, 360. Hamilton never did have much of a "Chinatown" – only a slight clustering of grocery stores and laundries. By the 1930s the city had only eight families among the more than 400 Chinese; the rest were bachelors. The population would remain stagnant for many years after. *HS*, 16 Nov. 1936, 7; 6 July 1974, 61.

37.   Wickberg, ed., *From China to Canada*; Walker, *"Race," Rights, and the Law*, 56–86; Mosher, *Discrimination and Denial*, 73–81.

38.   Goutor, *Guarding the Gates*, 35–59; Palmer, *Culture in Conflict*, 178–80.

39.   See Tables 1 and 3.

40.   MUA, International Association of Machinists Fonds, Minutes, 8 Oct. 1913, 51; CC, 1901, Vol. 1, 325; 1911, Vol. 2, 372; 1931, Vol. 2, 495; *HS*, 3 Nov. 1906, 1; 1 June 1916, 1 (quotation); *HH*, 13 June 1917, 2; *LG*, February 1912, 746; *IB*, March 1912, 2; *LN*, 17 May 1912, 2; 29 Jan. 1915, 1; 12 Feb. 1915, 1; 25 Aug. 1916, 1; 7 June 1918, 2 (quotations); *ND*, 17 June 1920, 2; 2 Feb. 1922, 4; Roy, *White Man's Province*, 97; Goutor, *Guarding the Gates*, 60–84 (quotation at 78).

41. Jacobson, *Whiteness of a Different Color*; Barrett and Roediger, "Inbetween Peoples"; Guglielmo, "No Color Barrier."

42. See, for example, *HS*, 30 April 1907, 5; 18 Jan. 1919, 7; 28 Jan. 1919, 13 (quotation); 21 Feb. 1919, 17; 9 May 1919, 6; 1 Oct. 1919, 15 (quotation); *HH*, 13 March 1913, 10; LAC, R1176-0-0-E, 2526–27; *AJ*, 13 Jan. 1921, 18 (quotation); Palmer, *Working-Class Experience*, 212. Another Italian said, "When I grew up Italians were seen as 'niggers.'" MHSO, ITA-6489-BOR. In 1913 a Ukrainian socialist newspaper called Canada's immigrant labourers "white niggers." Petryshyn, *Peasants in the Promised Land*, 162. Gunther Peck has made this argument about the varying "whiteness" of Italians, Greeks, and Mexicans across North America; see *Reinventing Free Labor*, 166–70.

43. Palmer, "Reluctant Hosts." In "From Victorian Values to White Virtues," Douglas Lorimer makes a compelling case that between 1870 and 1914 assimilation and exclusion were distinct and even competing strategies for confronting the "Other" in the Empire. Assimilation was older and rooted in the liberal "civilizing mission" of the British, which would enable the gradual transformation of other cultures to the higher British standards, while the exclusionists who defended racial subordination and exclusion had no such confidence, especially with regard to the "coloured" races.

44. *HH*, 3 June 1910, 7; 29 June 1910, 1; 16 Jan. 1911, 9; 27 Feb. 1911, 9; 19 June 1911, 3; 2 Sept. 1911, 1; 4 March 1912, 1; 21 Sept. 1912, 6; 5 Feb. 1913, 1; 12 April 1914, 14; 14 Feb. 1914, 1; 28 March 1914, 6; 1 April 1914, 14; 5 Sept. 1916, 7; 11 Jan. 1918, 6; 9 July 1918, 12; *HT*, 21 Sept. 1917, 8; 22 Sept. 1917, 5; *HS*, 10 Jan. 1910, 10; 6 Sept. 1910, 12; 21 Sept. 1911, 1; 23 March 1914, 14; 27 Dec. 1919, 11; 22 Dec. 1930, 7; UCCA, Methodist Church (Canada), Board of Home Missions, 78.099C, Box 7, Files 5–8; Methodist Church, Women's Missionary Society, *Annual Reports*, 1917–25; PCCA, 1977-3014, 2 Nov. 1909, 5; 3 May 1910, 2; 5 July 1910, 5; 5 March 1912, 2–3; 5 Nov. 1912, 4; 4 March 1913, 14; 3 April 1914, 11–12; 2 Nov. 1915, 72; 11 July 1916, 108; 7 Nov. 1916, 124; 6 May 1919, 272; 4 Jan. 1921, 362; 3 Jan. 1922, 425; 4 May 1926, 727; 26 April 1927, 795; MPSS, 11; MHSO, ITA-0913-FOU; ITA-09829-GRI; ITA-0811-PIS; ITA-0810-SAR; ITA-0884-VIO; Schissler, "Presbytery of Hamilton," 10–11, 17; Bailey et al., *Presbytery of Hamilton*, 105, 108; Kukushkin, *From Peasants to Labourers*, 156; Parker, "Origins and Early History," 107–8; AO, F 885, WCTU, Annual Report, 1922; *HS*, 23 Feb. 1924, 2. Neighbourhood House closed in 1939. For the parallel experience in Toronto, see Cumbo, "'Impediments to the Harvest.'" Cumbo discusses the concept of *furberia* in "As the Twig Is Bent," 35–38.

45. Barber, "Nationalism, Nativism, and the Social Gospel" (quotation); *HH*, 19 June 1911, 3 (quotation).

46. HBEM, 1907, 102, 113–14, 116, 127; 1908, 11, 39; 1911, 135; 1912, 146–47; 1913, 155; 1914, 11, 135, 154, 171; 1915, 145; 1916, 149, 168, 171, 188, 190; 1917, 9, 25, 30, 191, 210, 229; *HH*, 7 Oct. 1913, 11; 14 Feb. 1914, 6; *HS*, 5 Oct. 1909, 9; 15 Sept. 1916, 13; 10 Nov. 1916, 9; 16 Oct. 1920, 23; 26 Oct. 1921, 22; 6 Dec. 1921, 3. The Hungarian Presbyterian Church also provided English classes; Patrias, *Patriots and Proletarians*, 120.

47. In spring 1919 the president of the East Hamilton Great War Veterans' Association called for compulsory English-language instruction for all "foreigners" under age 45. A few months later a national conference on citizenship urged more assimilative measures, and a new federal immigration act sparked similar debate. The YWCA and the WCTU both showed new concern. *HS*, 7 April 1919, 15; 9 May 1919, 19. Mitchell, "'Manufacture of Souls of Good Quality'"; McLean, "'To Become Part of Us'"; Kelley and Trebilcock, *Making of the Mosaic*, 183–87; AO, F 885, Ontario, Annual Report, Report of Canadianization Superintendent, 1922, 1922, 1925, 1928; *CWRT*, September 1920.

48. *HS*, 15 Nov. 1919, 1; 5 Dec. 1919 (clipping in HPL Canadian Patriotic Fund, Scrapbooks, Vol. 2, 188); 13 Feb. 1920, 9; 14 May 1920, 17; 9 March 1921, 17; 2 April 1922, 1; *HH*, 7 April 1922, 4; HBEM, 1921, 119; 1922, 78, 141, 229; 1923, 161; 1931, 105; HPL, HCC, Board of Directors, Minutes, 15 Feb. 1921, 145; 1 March 1921, 155; 8 March 1921, 161; 8 Dec. 1921, 109; 20 June 1922, 2–3; 1 Aug. 1922, 63–64; 26 June 1923, 43; 8 Jan. 1924, 134; 12 Feb. 1924, 150; Canadianization Committee, Minutes, 31 March 1921, 106; 14 Oct. 1921, 108; 1 Dec. 1921, 110; 2 June 1922; 12 June 1922, 110–11; 17 Oct. 1922, 112–13; 30 Nov. 1922, 114–15; 6 Feb. 1924, 90; *Annual Reports*, 1921, 4, 6; 1926–27, 19; 1930–31, 21; 1935, 9. In 1934 the Chamber of Commerce decided that the night classes had been "probably very desirable" but were now a "luxury." Board of Directors, Minutes, 5 Nov. 1934.

49. Among Italians in Wards Five and Seven, 82.9 per cent were separate-school supporters. Brandino, "Italians," 97, 102–3; Cumbo, *Italian Presence*; Cumbo, "As the Twig Is Bent," 149–242; MHSO, ITA-0808-CEC; ITA-0775-COR; ITA-0913-FOU; ITA-0884-VIO.

50. Swyripa, *Wedded to the Cause*; Cumbo, "As the Twig Is Bent."

51. A new police station that opened in the east end in 1911 took a particular interest in regulating the daily life of the "foreign colony," especially the residents' drinking habits. HPL, Our Heritage Scrapbooks, Vol. 3, 1. For examples of police raids on immigrant boarding houses in search of booze, see *HS*, 12 Jan. 1910, 12; 24 Oct. 1910, 12; 1 Feb. 1916, 1; 1 March 1916, 1.

52. As one Hungarian immigrant explained, "The English were unwilling to do such 'bad' work." Quoted in Patrias,

Patriots and Proletarians, 67; see also Reynolds, *British Immigrant*, 46.

53. Reynolds, *British Immigrant*, 104–6, 109–13; MHSO, ITA-0808-CEC; ITA-0826-CRE; WAHC, interview with Joyce Yakmalian.

54. Goutor, *Guarding the Gates*. In contrast, Australian workingmen had more clout in establishing a more restrictive immigration policy; Cross, "Labour in Settler-State Democracies," 9.

55. *HS*, 11 Oct. 1904, 4. On the late-19th-century experience with immigrant strikebreakers, see Fenton, *Immigrants and Unions*, 77–94.

56. The contemporary American economist Isaac A. Hourwich pointed out in 1912 that, even in a context of labour scarcity, actual competition for the same jobs between Anglo-Celtic and European workers was rare, but that the new immigrants were frequently blamed for the degradation of work. See Hourwich, *Immigration and Labor*, 148–76, 351.

57. *IB*, March 1905, 2 (quotation); *HS*, 17 Jan. 1905, 4 (quotation); 29 Sept. 1929, 31 (quotation); *HT*, 6 April 1914, 1 (quotation).

58. *IB*, December 1903, 2 (quotation); August 1904, 1 (quotations); February 1905, 4 (quotation); March 1905, 2; 31 Dec. 1908, 1; 22 May 1914, 4 (quotation). For a parallel argument about the US labour movement (to which the bulk of Hamilton's unionists were connected), see Collomp, "Unions, Civics, and National Identity."

59. See, for example, *HS*, 11 Feb. 1910, 16; 17 Feb. 1910, 12; 22 March 1910, 14; 29 March 1910, 14.

60. *HS*, 8 Dec. 1908, 6 (quotation); *HH*, 31 May 1911, 4; 10 March 1913, 1 (quotation); 26 July 1918 (quotation). See also *IB*, December 1903, 3; 22 May 1914, 4.

61. Barrett and Roediger, "Inbetween Peoples," 23–24; LAC, R244-0-4-E, Vol. 1, Unemployment 1914, Niagara Fall, Brantford, Hamilton, Toronto, 18 Feb. 1914; R244-6-4-E, Vol. 299, File 3475; Vol. 301, File 13 (15); *HH*, 26 Feb. 1913; 13 March 1913, 10; *LN*, 12 Jan. 1912, 3; TLCCP, 1915, 53.

62. *HH*, 20 Nov. 1914, 15; 9 Dec. 1914, 1; 15 May 1915, 17; 24 May 1916; Morton, "Sir William Otter and Internment Operations"; Melnycky, "Internment of Ukrainians"; Martynovych, *Ukrainians*, 315–34, 420–27, 447n46; Keshen, *Propaganda and Censorship*.

63. *HH*, 14 Feb. 1916, 1; 16 Feb. 1916, 1; 29 Sept. 1916, 1; 8 Jan. 1917, 11; 11 Jan. 1917, 1; 25 April 1917, 1; 30 July 1917, 7; *HS*, 17 Feb. 1916, 9; LAC, R244-76-4-E, Vol. 304, File 16 (27); HPL, RG 10, Series 4, 1915.

64. The police often discovered great hordes of cash on money belts around the waists of these men or tucked away in clothing or suitcases in their rooms. "For this reason," the press noted, "there are more reports of stolen and lost money from the foreign section than any other

part of the city." In August 1916 one European immigrant was robbed of his month's earnings, a whopping $225. A few months later another who had been arrested had $130 in cash and two bank books showing deposits of $2,190 and $400; and in August 1917 a Russian reported the theft of $1,140 from an old tobacco pouch in his boarding house. *HH*, 15 Aug. 1916, 1; 24 April 1917, 1; 13 July 1917, 20; 30 July 1917, 7.

65. *HH*, 27 July 1916, 11; 29 Dec. 1916, 1; 12 April 1917, 2. These complaints were arising across the country; see Makuch, "Ukrainian Canadians and the Wartime Economy."

66. *HT*, 11 Sept. 1917, 11; 22 Sept. 1917, 11; 2 Oct. 1917, 1; 3 Oct. 1917, 4; *LN*, 14 Sept. 1917, 1; 12 Oct. 1917, 1.

67. *LN*, 18 Jan. 1918, 1; *HH*, 22 Jan. 1918, 14; 4 March 1918, 7; 15 March 1918; 16 March 1918, 4; 18 March 1918, 1; 27 March 1918, 2; *HS*, 25 May 1918, 8; *Veteran*, April 1918, 11; Thompson, "Enemy Alien and the Canadian General Election of 1917." In a strike of freight handlers at the TH and B sheds, resentments flared against the hiring of Bulgarians "and other foreigners," who the men alleged were taken on whenever a labour shortage developed. At the same time moulders who were negotiating with the foundrymen for a wage increase that spring complained about "aliens" making $7 to $10 a day on munitions work. By August additional resentment was fuelled by the results of the federal government's registration, which revealed the immigrants' reluctance to move into agricultural labour to help the war effort. LAC, R244-76-4-E, Vol. 558, File 1918–131; *HH*, 7 Aug. 1918, 4; 8 Aug. 1918, 6; *LN*, 3 May 1918, 1.

68. *HH*, 3 April 1918, 1. The police officer who made this statement received a "Black Hand" letter the next day threatening his life for such comments.

69. *HH*, 6 April 1918, 8; 10 April 1918; 13 April 1918, 5; 19 April 1918, 1.

70. *HH*, 15 Nov. 1918, 20; 6 Dec. 1918, 1; 4 Jan. 1919, 1; *HS*, 28 Jan. 1919, 13; 8 Feb. 1919, 1. In midsummer civic labourers struck "until some foreigners who had been employed instead of British-born were discharged." *LL*, 25 July 1919, 3.

71. *HS*, 18 Jan. 1919, 4; 20 Jan. 1919, 1; 21 Jan. 1919, 6; 25 Jan. 1919, 7; 27 Jan. 1919, 14; 28 Jan. 1919, 1; 30 Jan. 1919, 1, 3; 31 Jan. 1919, 1, 6, 16, 18; 8 Feb. 1919, 1; 10 Feb. 1919, 1; 11 Feb. 1919, 6; 17 Feb. 1919, 1; 21 Feb. 1919, 7, 23; 4 March 1919, 1; 6 March 1919, 1; 14 March 1919, 6; *LN*, 14 Feb. 1919, 1.

72. *HH*, 14 Dec. 1918, 1, 11; *ISC*, January 1919, 485; *HS*, 15 Jan. 1919, 15; 28 Jan. 1919, 5; 1 Feb. 1919, 6; 5 Feb. 1919, 13; 14 Feb. 1919, 1; 25 Feb. 1919, 7; 4 March 1919, 11; *CM*, 31 July 1919, 109; Avery, "Ethnic and Class Tensions"; Keshen, *Propaganda and Censorship*, 67, 93.

73. Martynowych, *Ukrainians*, 439; *HS* 16 Sept. 1919, 6 (quotation); 18 Sept. 1919, 9; AO, RG 23, E-30, 1.6 (Strikes and Agitation), 22 July 1919. In 1920 Father Thomas Tarasiuk watched in dismay as the core 60 families of St. Stanislaus

Church undermined the parish's stability by returning to Poland. Wall, "Tarasiuk." See also Reczyńska, *For Bread and a Better Future*, 86–97.

74. *HS*, 15 Jan. 1919, 15; AO, RG 23, E-30, 1.6, 22 Feb. 1919, 2.

75. Avery, *"Dangerous Foreigners,"* 90–115; AO, RG 4-32-3188/1931, 10 C, 2304.

76. Shadd, *Journey from Tollgate to Parkway*, 212–15; Cooper, *Shadow Runner*, 24–25, 32–33, 39–40; Bartley, "Public Nuisance"; Backhouse, *Colour-Coded*, 173–225; Winks, *Blacks in Canada*, 320–35; Jackson, *Ku Klux Klan in the City*, 240–41; Lay, *Hooded Knights*, 39–61. The Klan intervened in a similar way in a miners' strike in the Crowsnest Pass in 1932; Sher, *White Hoods*, 45–46; Endicott, *Raising the Workers' Flag*, 116–17. The Communists raised regular warnings about this anti-labour potential; see, for example, *Worker*, 1 Nov. 1924, 1; 28 Feb. 1925, 1; 8 Aug. 1925, 1.

77. Shadd, *Journey from Tollgate to Parkway*, 215–19; Backhouse, *Colour-Coded*, 175, 180 (quotations); Walker, *"Race," Rights, and the Law*, 135–37; Mosher, *Discrimination and Denial*, 112–14; Sher, *White Hoods*, 26–30.

78. Bartley, "Public Nuisance," 162, 169–70; Pennefather, *Orange and the Black*, 42–43; Houston and Smyth, *Sash Canada Wore*, 155–56, 169–70.

79. Harney, "Ethnicity and Neighbourhoods"; Zucchi, *History of Ethnic Enclaves*.

80. Neave, "Friendly Societies"; Cordery, "Fraternal Orders"; Palmer, "Mutuality"; Stubbs, "Visions of the Common Good." In 1910 the Sons of Scotland also had three "camps" and the Ancient Order of Hibernians had two "divisions." *VCHD*, 1910, 754.

81. Cumbo, *Italian Presence*.

82. We should be careful not to assume that such "parochialism" was unique to European peasant-sojourners. As Linda Colley stresses, local identities remained strong among British people as well; Colley, "Britishness and Otherness," 314–16.

83. Patria, *Patriots and Proletarians*, 78–81; Kaprielian-Churchill, *Like Our Mountains*, 92–93; Rasporich, *For a Better Life*, 112, 115; Cumbo, *Italian Presence*. Donna Gabaccia argues: "For migrants from Italy, home was a place – the patria or paese – not a people, nation, or descent group." *Italy's Many Diasporas*, 7.

84. Bodnar, *Transplanted*, 120–23; Tomassini, "Mutual Benefit Societies"; Hitchins, "Mutual Benefit Societies"; Kaczynska, "Mutual Benefit Societies." On these societies in the United States, see Cohen, *Making the New Deal*, 64–75.

85. Kaprielian-Churchill, "Armenian Village Educational Associations," 65; Martynowych, *Ukrainians*, 275; Tulchinsky, *Taking Root*, 131.

86. By 1916, when they created the United Hebrew Association of Hamilton as an umbrella organization, the local Jewish societies included the Hamilton Israelite Benevolent Society, Hamilton Jewish Relief Society, Hamilton Jewish Loan Society, Hebrew Institute, and the more political Workmen's Circle. In 1933 an even more expansive Jewish federation, the Council of Jewish Agencies, brought together 24 organizations in the city, and the next year the Hamilton Jewish Community House opened. *HH*, 12 June 1916, 9; Foster, "Ethnic Settlement," 98; Kurman, "Hamilton Jewish Community," 9–10; Tulchinsky, *Taking Root*, 96–108, 129–55.

87. Patrias, *Patriots and Proletarians*, 96, 149–52.

88. In 1920 the Prima Societa dissolved, and, shortly after, a Hamilton branch of the Sons of Italy, a North-American-wide organization, was formed to continue the programs of mutual aid and cultural promotion. *HH*, 29 Oct. 1912, 3; 12 June 1913, 1; 23 April 1917, 13; 25 April 1917, 1; 30 April 1917, 9; Cumbo, *Italian Presence*; Brandino, "Italians," 62–63. Years later an elderly Italian remembered how the Sons of Italy paid doctor's bills; MHSO, ITA-09826-FER.

89. In 1912 Poles established the Society of St. Stanislaus Kostka, modelled on (and after a year, affiliated with) US organizations of the same name, with its own library and meeting hall; in 1913 a "nest" of the Polish Falcons Alliance, boasting 62 members, to promote physical fitness and military training along with a nationalist fervour for a liberated Poland; in 1915 a branch of the Sons of Poland for mutual benefit and for celebrating Polish cultural events; and in 1927 a Hamilton branch of the Polish Alliance of Canada, which became one of the largest and most active in Canada. *HH*, 29 March 1913, 16; Makowski, *Poles*, 75–76; Wyrtwal, *Behold! The Polish Americans*, 102–3; Heydenkorn, "Polish Canadian Parish," 39. The Croatians founded the Croatian Fraternal Union, along with the country's first Croatian hall, where a choir, orchestra, and dance company performed. Rasporich, *For a Better Life*, 112.

90. The First Hungarian Society had 86 members in 1927, and the Sons of Racalmuto had more than 100. Patrias, *Patriots and Proletarians*, 96; Cumbo, *Italian Presence*.

91. Jews focused on their own synagogues. As the city's Jewish community expanded, the number of synagogues grew from two at the turn of the century, Anshe Shalom (Reform) and Beth Jacob (Orthodox), which dated well back into the 19th century, to five by the 1930s, including Ohaw Zedec, Anshi Sfard, and Agudas Achim. HPL, Wilesnky, "Report Re the Jewish Community in Hamilton," 15; Kurman, "Hamilton Jewish Community"; Tulchinsky, *Taking Root*, 160–61. Small Orthodox Christian parishes also appeared among the Greek and Russian populations. *HS*, 14 March 1914, 5; *HH*, 2 April 1917, 6; Kukushkin, *From Peasants to Labourers*, 143. African Canadians also rallied around the local African Methodist Episcopal Church;

Workers Art and Heritage Centre, Hamilton, website, http://www.museevirtuel-virtualmuseum.ca, "The Souls of Black Folk: Hamilton's Stewart Memorial Community – 5: New Wave: Influx of Caribbean Families in the 1960s–Present Day."

92. Clarke, *Piety and Nationalism*. For the religious breakdown of the Hamilton population, see Table 5.

93. Perin, *Immigrants' Church*; Lando, "Italian National Catholic Churches"; Cumbo, "As the Twig Is Bent," 38–42; Vecoli, "Prelates and Peasants," 228–29; Radecki and Heydenkorn, *Distinguished Family*, 63, 142; Thomas and Znaniecki, *Polish Peasant*, Vol. 1, 205–88; Green, *For God and Country*, 24–27; Williams, *Southern Italian Folkways*, 135–37.

94. The pre-war depression, wartime constraints, and the postwar exodus of much of the local Polish population prevented the completion of St. Stanislaus until well after the war. In October 1917 a cornerstone was laid for the Ukrainian Catholic Church of the Holy Ghost, and in 1923 a second Italian parish, Our Lady of All Souls, finally opened in the western immigrant community, with more than 1,000 Italians turning out for the dedication. It was the second-largest Italian church in Canada and soon had a wide range of spiritual and recreational programs. Bonomi transferred to All Souls, and his assistant, Charles Mascari, the son of Italian immigrants to Hamilton and Canada's first Canadian-born Italian to be ordained, took over St. Anthony's. Tarasiuk stayed in Hamilton until 1935. Lando, "Italian National Catholic Churches," 67; Cumbo, *Italian Presence* (quotation); Filer, "Bonomi"; *HH*, 8 May 1911, 5; 11 June 1911, 1; 13 June 1911, 1; 14 June 1911, 9; 23 Sept. 1911, 10; 20 May 1912, 5; 2 June 1913, 1; *HS*, 13 June 1910, 1; *HT*, 29 Oct. 1917; Shahrodi, "Early Polish Settlement," 35; Heydenkorn, "Polish Canadian Parish"; Wall, "Tarasiuk"; Foster, "Ethnic Settlement," 86.

95. *HH*, 11 June 1910, 1; 13 June 1911, 1; 14 June 1911, 9; 2 June 1913, 1; 12 June 1913, 1; 14 June 1915, 7; MHSCO, ITA-09826-FER; Cumbo, *Italian Presence*.

96. For a similar process elsewhere, see Zucchi, *Italians in Toronto*; Briggs, *Italian Passage*, 69–94; Bodnar, *Transplanted*, 117–43.

97. After he left Hamilton for Regina in 1910, Protich was charged with influence-peddling around that city's police court. *VCHD*, 1909, 530; *HH*, 11 Feb. 1910, 1; 25 May 1910, 1; 11 May 1911, 12; 2 Jan. 1912, 1; 3 Jan. 1912, 1; 22 Jan. 1912, 1; Weaver, *Crimes, Constables, and Courts*, 76. One of his successors, Armin Czech, had an even more controversial career in Hamilton that highlighted the dual role of the intermediary. Described by the *Herald* as "a smooth Russian who speaks Polish," Czech worked as a court interpreter and ran the "European Information Bureau" in the west end. Late in 1910 he organized a series of meetings

of the city's Polish population "to enlighten the Poles . . . on various matters and particularly with regard to [local] politics." The *Herald* gravely warned the city against "a taste of Tammany," when Controller John Allan, the Tory candidate for mayor, appeared at the first meeting. Czech seemed to be rallying non-English voters (few though they were) against the threat to the workingman's glass of beer posed by the temperance candidate, George H. Lees, and attempting to act as their mediator with established political interests. Allan was defeated, and Czech left the city soon afterwards, but the role of the ethnic intermediary was becoming visible. *HH*, 10 Dec. 1910, 1; 12 Dec. 1910, 1, 6; 13 Dec. 1910, 1; *HS*, 12 Dec. 1910, 1. For the parallel experience in Western Canada, see Martynowych, *Ukrainians*, 237–44.

98. *HH*, 1 March 1917, 2; MHSO, ITA-09826-FER; ITA-0913-FOU; ITA-6489-BOR; Cumbo, *Italian Presence*; Kaprielian-Churchill, *Like Our Mountains*, 108–9.

99. Financial appeals for the Italian Red Cross during 1916 and 1917 also featured public events for the local Italians and similarly encouraged identification with broader Italian nationality. *HH*, 20 Sept. 1913, 1; 24 Sept. 1913, 1; 24 May 1915, 1; 4 June 1915, 2; 11 Sept. 1916, 12; 29 Nov. 1916; 8 Jan. 1917; 23 April 1917, 13; 25 April 1917, 1; 30 April 1917, 9; 1 May 1917, 7; 23 June 1917, 1; 10 July 1917, 12 (quotation); *HS*, 13 June 1913, 1; 16 Aug. 1913, 18; *HT*, 10 Aug. 1914, 1; 12 Aug. 1914, 1; 13 Aug. 1914, 9; 14 Aug. 1914, 6; *LN*, 6 March 1914, 2; HPL, Canadian Patriotic Fund Scrapbooks, Vol. 2, 85; Cumbo, *Italian Presence*; Harney, *Italians in Canada*, 29.

100. *HH*, 31 May 1918, 1; *HS*, 28 Jan. 1919, 1; 29 Jan. 1919, 8; 8 Feb. 1919, 4; 14 Feb. 1919, 23; *HT*, 23 April 1918 (clipping in HPL Scrapbook). On Zionism, see Tulchinsky, *Taking Root*, 181–203.

101. *HH*, 1 July 1927, 5; MHSO, ITA-6489-B); Cumbo, *Italian Presence*; Radecki and Heydenkorn, *Distinguished Family*, 76; Dreisziger, *Struggle and Hope*, 127–28; Rasporich, *For a Better Life*, 155–61. In 1929 an Italian band included the left-wing "Red Flag" in its concert, but refused to play the Fascist March. *Worker*, 3 Aug. 1929, 2. The anti-fascist Order of Italo-Canadians was started in the late 1930s under the leadership of Dr. Vincent Agro and had its own hall in the west-end Italian enclave. Cumbo, *Italian Presence*. Zionist activity in the local Jewish community also increased in the interwar period; HPL, Wilensky, "Report Re the Jewish Community," 15–16.

102. Swyripa, *Wedded to the Cause*; Perin, "Introduction," in Perin and Sturino, eds., *Arrangiarsi*, 17–19; Gabbaccia, *Italy's Many Diasporas*, 8–9.

103. Branches of the two main left-wing Armenian organizations existed in Hamilton by 1907 and a parallel women's group known as the Armenian Revolutionary Federation Red Cross eight years later. Jewish socialists founded the

Workmen's Circle in 1910, and a branch of the Ukrainian Social Democratic Party followed by 1915. A Russian Socialist Revolutionary group had also appeared by that point, and a visiting Russian Orthodox bishop lamented that year that the more than 600 Russians he found had "almost all turned to socialism." Hungarian socialists had been active from the beginning, and in 1925 a Hungarian branch of the Communist Party was organized. Polish radicals emerged in the city in the interwar period as well, by the early 1930s through a strong Communist-led Polish Workers' Association. That decade also saw local Yugoslavian, Lithuanian, and Carpatho-Russian clubs with radical leadership. Kaprielian-Churchill, *Like Our Mountains*, 94–110, 128–41; Kukushkin, *From Peasants to Labourers*, 143 (quotation); Patrias, *Patriots and Proletarians*; Heydenkorn, "Polish Canadian Parish," 38–39; Kealey and Whitaker, eds., *R.C.M.P. Security Bulletins: Depression Years, Part 1*, 319, 333, , 447, 462; *Part 3*, 370–71, 403–4; Petryshyn, *Peasants in the Promised Land*, 163–69; Krawchuk, *Ukrainian Socialist Movement* , 63, 66; Martynowych, *Ukrainians*, 252–60, 274, 276–77, 427–34. The Lithuanian Club had 40 members in 1934.

104. Kaprielian-Churchill, *Like Our Mountains*; Patrias, *Patriots and Proletarians*; Martynowych, *Ukrainians*; *Worker*, 19 April 1924, 2. For an excellent discussion of how Jewish and working-class identity were mutually reinforcing in this period, see Frager, *Sweatshop Strife*, 35–54.

105. Cumbo, "As the Twig Is Bent," 111–21.

106. Hunter, *Which Side Are You On, Boys*, 19.

107. MHSO, ITA-0807-COL; ITA-0913-FOU; ITA-0809-GRO.

108. Loewen and Friesen, *Immigrants in Prairie Cities* (quotation at 35).

109. The later emergence of this second generation in Canada compared to the United States may help to explain the more limited involvement of immigrants in the "workers' revolt" of the 1917–25 period. See Heron, *Working in Steel*; Heron, "National Contours." Cohen provides the most compelling statement about a new more unifying mass culture among US workers in the 1930s in *Making a New Deal*. While Canadian workers embraced similar forms of mass culture, Canada lacked the galvanizing political force of the US New Deal and the widespread success of CIO organizing drives. On Italian-Canadians' appropriation of mass culture and more generally on the second-generation's "Canadianness," see Cumbo, "As the Twig Is Bent." For a schematized outline of migrants' acculturation, see Hoerder, "From Migrants to Ethnics."

110. Cumbo, "As the Twig Is Bent," 258–68.

111. In the United States organizers in packing houses and steel mills recruited blacks and European immigrants much more aggressively. Barrett, "Unity and Fragmentation"; Halpern, "Race, Ethnicity, and Union"; Brody, *Labor in Crisis*; Bodnar, *Transplanted*, 99–104.

112. *HH*, 2 April 1917, 3; 9 June 1917, 8; 2 May 1918, 7.

113. Krawchuk, *Our History*, 148–202; Barrett, "Americanization from the Bottom Up," 1004–17 (quotation); *Worker*, 17 May 1924, 4; 16 May 1925, 1; 15 May 1926, 2; 14 May 1927, 2; *Clarion*, 4 March 1937, 3.

114. Barrett, "Americanization from the Bottom Up," 999–1000.

16. True Blue

1. *IB*, March 1905, 1.

2. *IB*, November 1908, 2 (quotation); Marshall, *Class, Citizenship, and Social Development*; Joyce, *Work, Society, and Politics*; Pugh, "Rise of Labour."

3. The term has been widely debated in British writing; see Newby, "Deferential Dialectic"; Joyce, *Work, Society, and Politics*, 90–133.

4. Lawrence, "Class and Gender." In 1868 Friedrich Engels wrote to Karl Marx: "What do you say to the elections in the factory districts? Once again the proletariat has discredited itself terribly.... It cannot be denied that the increase of working class voters has brought the Tories more than their simple percentage increase; it has improved their relative position." Quoted in Mackenzie and Silver, *Angels in Marble*, 14.

5. *HH*, 9 Dec. 1916, 11.

6. Quoted in Humphries, *"Honest Enough to Be Bold,"* 50. Voting eligibility was set by the federal government between 1885 and 1898, when the provinces again got control. Ontario had opened the polls to all men over 21 in 1888. The Dominion Elections Act of 1920 put responsibility back into federal hands. Evans, *Mowat*, 210; Elections Canada, *History of the Vote*.

7. Elections Canada, *History of the Vote*, 54. Ross McGibbon argues that before 1914 these kinds of restrictions kept a huge proportion of male workers off the voters' lists in Britain; see *Ideologies of Class*, 66–100.

8. According to political scientist Norman Ward, getting onto the voters' list "might depend primarily on the political circumstances in one's riding." He concluded that the franchise law was "for many years a poor source to which to turn for information on the extent of the suffrage in Canada." *HS*, 9 Oct. 1900, 4; 17 Oct. 1900, 4 (quotation); Meredith to Macdonald, 22 Dec. 1883, quoted in Humphries, "Political Career," 38 (quotation); Ward, *House of Commons*, 189 (quotation); AO, F 5, MU312 (form letter from Robert Birmingham to local organizations, 10 May 1897); MU3115, Western Ontario Conservative Association, "Recommendations on Organization to Candidates, and to Presidents and Secretaries of Ridings," 22 Nov. 1901. On the registration work in Hamilton, see, for example, *HS*, 10 Oct. 1900, 1; 17 Oct. 1900, 4; 16 May 1902, 4; 7 Oct. 1904, 1. In Britain the Conservatives tried to use voter registration to reduce voter turnout and

thus improve their electoral fortunes. Green, "Radical Conservatism," 678–80. For a review of the voter restriction in Britain in this period (on which so much Canadian experience was based), see Blewett, "Franchise in the United Kingdom."

9. In 1901 census-takers found nearly 2,000 more males of voting age in Hamilton than the 12,696 who had been registered for the 1900 federal election the previous fall – a 15 per cent gap. CC, 1901, Vol. 4, 10–13; Canada, Clerk of the Crown in Chancery, *Returns on General Elections for the House of Commons of Canada*, 1900, 33–35. The failure of census officials to break down population figures by age in 1911 prevents our knowing exactly how many male adults were eligible to be registered for the federal and provincial elections that year. But the total male population of the city had grown by 17,253, while the registered voters grew by only 6,340 (see Tables 38 and 39). It would be an interesting research question, not pursued here, to determine who might be left off the assessment rolls systematically, such as the subletting tenants in East London in this period; see Brodie, *Politics of the Poor*, 44–74.

10. Elections Canada, *History of the Vote*, 73–74. After the war the revision process seemed to be finished a good month before the vote; see, for example, *HS*, 25 Sept. 1919, 1; 25 Sept. 1924, 4; 23 June 1930, 7.

11. See Table 38.

12. In 1934 the *Spectator* noted that, during the vote counting, the CCF candidate in Wentworth, John Mitchell, was "piling up a heavy majority" in the east-end urban polls, but fell behind when the rural votes came in. "The county voters are not supporters of Mr. Mitchell and in many ridings [*sic*] the vote he secured could be counted on one hand." He ran a strong third in a close three-way race, less than 600 votes behind the victor. *HS*, 20 June 1934, 10.

13. *HS*, 1 June 1908, 7; 17 Oct. 1919, 1; 6 Dec. 1921, 1; 6 Dec. 1926, 1; 29 Oct. 1929, 27; 18 June 1934, 20; 12 Oct. 1935, 6; Elections Canada, *History of the Vote*, 79. In 1929 Tom Moore, president of the Trades and Labor Congress of Canada, told a parliamentary committee that, with no penalties against them, many employers did not give their workers their statutory two hours off. The Congress had been agitating for some time for a holiday on election day. Ward, *House of Commons*, 169; *HS*, 25 Feb. 1922, 6.

14. Cleverdon, *Woman Suffrage Movement*, 44.

15. When William Barrett carried the Socialist Labor Party banner into the mayoralty campaign in 1901 and 1902, the *Spectator* indicated that he did not own enough property in the city to qualify. Three years later Hugh Robinson, a tailor, had to drop off the Workingmen's Political Association slate because of his limited property holdings. Similarly in 1914, after the Independent Labor Party's Rollo narrowly missed election to the provincial legislature in a West Hamilton by-election, his limited property in the city prevented him from running for city council a few months later. *HS*, 2 Jan. 1901, 4; 2 Jan. 1902, 6; 29 Jan. 1903, 1; 21 Jan. 1914, 1; *IB*, 21 Nov. 1914, 2; 24 Jan. 1919, 2. Not surprisingly, recent research on the membership of the Hamilton city council in the early 20th century has found only 14 workers among the 159 councillors between 1895 and 1909. Middleton and Walker, "Manufacturers and Industrial Development," 24.

16. John English found this to be the most common experience with Conservative Members of Parliament. *Decline of Politics*, 40.

17. *LN*, 11 Dec. 1914, 1; 12 Feb. 1915, 1; 26 Feb. 1915, 1; 12 March 1915, 1. Goran Therborn argues that the extension of bourgeois democracy throughout the advanced capitalist world has been primarily the result of working-class agitation; see "Rule of Capital."

18. Ward, *Canadian House of Commons*, 156. In 1931 the Independent Labor Party had to collect $1 from each of 200 supporters to put its candidate into the ring that year. *LN*, 22 May 1931, 2.

19. Most of these constraints also existed in the United States, and help to explain the sharp decline in voter participation there at the turn of the century. Toinet, "Political Participation."

20. English, *Decline of Politics*, 18–30; Humphries, "Political Career, 163 (quotation); *HS*, 2 Nov. 1904, 1; 3 Nov. 1904, 8; 2 Nov. 1904, 1; 21 Oct. 1908, 1; 26 Oct. 1908, 1 (quotation); Siegfried, *Race Question*, 127–28.

21. Hamilton delegates to the annual meeting of the Trades and Labor Congress of Canada had called for an end to numbered ballots; TLCCP, 1896, 22; 1897, 15; 1898, 27.

22. *HS*, 3 Nov. 1904, 8 (quotation); 25 Jan. 1905, 1; 24 Oct. 1908, 9; Humphries, "Political Career," 189–97; LAC, R10811-0-X-E, Vol. 542, 147079 (A. Zimmerman to Sir Wilfrid Laurier, 3 Nov. 1908) (quotation). See also LAC, R10383-0-6-F, Vol. 10, 9916 (A. Zimmerman to W.L.M. King, 27 Oct. 1908); *HH*, 6 Oct. 1910, 1; 11 Dec. 1911, 4 (quotation). The accusations about the free use of liquor to woo voters were legion. See, for example, *HS*, 26 Feb. 1898, 1; 25 Oct. 1900, 1; *HH*, 30 Dec. 1910, 12. In 1910 a prominent civic reformer and Liberal Party member, T. S. Morris, ferreted out practices in the municipal election campaign, where a shot of whiskey in a cab parked near a polling booth had apparently been enough to buy some votes. *HH*, 11 Jan. 1910, 5.

23. *HS*, 22 Feb. 1898, 1; 26 Feb. 1898, 4; 29 March 1900, 8; 2 April 1900, 8; 3 April 1900, 8; 9 April 1900, 8; 14 April 1900, 8; 16 April 1900, 8; 14 Aug. 1900, 8; 17 Aug. 1900, 8; 4 Jan. 1901, 8; 8 June 1908, 1; 9 June 1908, 4; *HH*, 1 Feb. 1910, 1; 20 Feb. 1913, 6; 20 Nov. 1914, 1; Ward, *House of Commons*, 171–88; English, *Decline of Politics*, 18–30.

24. *IB*, June 1903, 1.

25. Humphries, "Sources," 118; *HS*, 5 Dec. 1906, 9; 14 Dec. 1906, 5; *HH*, 20 Nov. 1914, 1.

26. In 1909, when Mackenzie King unveiled his anti-combines legislation to meet the rising public outcry against the merger movement in Canadian business, the Hamilton Board of Trade promptly submitted a resolution proposing instead "a permanent trade tribunal with power to sit in cases of alleged trade combines," to function as "a court of commercial men with power to hear all evidence, a commission similar to the Railway Commission." LAC, R10811-0-X-E, Vol. 601, 163167 (Hamilton Board of Trade to Sir Wilfrid Laurier, 2 Dec. 1909). For a discussion of the conservatism of this regulatory impulse, see Kolko, *Triumph of Conservatism*.

27. Nelles, *Politics of Development*.

28. Commission government was a model of civic administration in which voters would elect on a city-wide basis a small commission to run the city. "No railway, no large industrial concern, no big financial institution would dream of entrusting its interests to a body of voluntary or semi-paid men who have not been well trained for such responsibilities," argued C. R. McCullough, head of a large printing enterprise and editor of the *Hamilton Manufacturer*, in 1912. "A Commission composed of the best men procurable ... will give Hamilton the sort of service that the Steel Company, the Harvester Company, the Westinghouse Company, and numerous other Hamilton concerns get from their officers." *Hamilton, Canada: Its History, Commerce, Industries, Resources*, 103 (quotation); *Hamilton Manufacturer*, 1912, 3.

29. "*HH*, 18 Jan. 1913, 3; *IB*, 24 Jan. 1913, 6 (quotation); *LN*, 20 Dec. 1918, 1 (quotation).

30. English, *Decline of Politics*, 20–21 (quotation); *CW*, 4 March 1909, 8.

31. The official election returns do not break the figures down in a fashion that allow one to isolate the more solidly working-class wards, but the overall decline in voter participation in such a predominantly working-class population can be seen to indicate the abstention of large numbers of workers. *HS*, 8 Jan. 1901, 1; 7 Jan. 1902, 7; 6 Jan. 1903, 9; *CC*, 1901, Vol. 1, 12; 1911, Vol. 1, 322–23; 1921, Vol. 2, 66.

32. See Tables 38 and 39

33. This decline was a province-wide trend; see Piva, "Workers and Tories."

34. *IB*, Jan. 1905, 1; AO, F 5, E. A. Dalley to J. P. Whitney, 7 Dec. 1906.

35. See Tables 38 and 39.

36. *HS*, 23 Sept. 1919, 6; *ND*, 7 Jan. 1920, 1. Before the 1921 federal election the *Spectator* commented that local voters were traditionally "remarkable for the rather small vote polled"; and in a post-mortem on that election the *Labor News* pointed to the same voter lethargy about getting on the voters' list: "The advice was unheeded. On polling day thousands of men and women were unable to vote. Their neglect helped to defeat Labor's standard-bearers." *HS*, 7 Dec. 1921, 1; *LN*, 23 Dec. 1921, 2. In 1926 the Chamber of Commerce spearheaded a campaign involving 26 local organizations to increase voter turnout in municipal elections, but to no avail. *HS*, 27 Nov. 1926, 5; 4 Dec. 1926, 9.

37. For a discussion of political abstention as a conscious political choice, see Campbell, "Voters and Non-Voters."

38. See Tables 40 and 41.

39. *HS*, 8 Jan. 1901, 1. Until 1911 the *Spectator* proudly announced the Tory slate before each municipal vote and in the wake of most elections throughout the period indicated the political complexion of the new council.

40. *HS*, 6 Jan. 1903, 10.

41. McMenemy, "Lion in a Den of Daniels," 2.

42. Crossick, *Artisan Elite*, 199–242 (quotation at 199); Vincent, *Formation of the Liberal Party*, 76–82; Harrison, *Before the Socialists*, 137–209; Kirk, *Change, Continuity, and Class*, 186–98; Shepherd, "Labour and Parliament."

43. The social base of the Liberal Party at the end of the 19th century has never been systematically analysed, but can be pieced together from various secondary sources. See, for example, Skelton, *Life and Letters of Sir Wilfrid Laurier*, Vol. 2, 1–27; Harkness, *Atkinson*; Neatby, *Laurier and a Liberal Quebec*; Stevens, "Laurier and the Liberal Party," 1–191.

44. LAC, R10811-0-X-E, Vol. 76, 23773–75 (E. Williams to A. T. Wood, 27 May 1898). Williams had helped to elect Alexander MacDonald as Britain's first Lib-Lab MP in the 1870s, and had run as an independent labour candidate in Hamilton in 1883. See Kealey and Palmer, *Dreaming*, 206–8.

45. TLCCP, 1896, 8; Gray, "Gibson," 69–70; Evans, *Mowat*, 190–97; Kealey, *Toronto Workers*, 127, 155; Kealey and Palmer, *Dreaming*, 217, 220.

46. HCCM, 1898, 295; Dawson, *King: 1874–1923*, 94–105; Loudon, *Mulock*, 106–34.

47. Prang, *Rowell*, 91–144; LAC, R10383-0-6-F, Vol. 24, 2215 (W.L.M. King to N. W. Rowell, 1 July 1914). Rowell's counterpart in Hamilton was probably Thomas S. Morris, a prominent Liberal alderman and controller with a keen interest in civic and moral reform, especially temperance. *DHB*, Vol. 3, 153–54.

48. Rutherford, *Victorian Authority*; Harkness, *Atkinson*; Bruce, *News and the Southams*, 21, 220–28; *DHB*, Vol. 3, 86–87; Heron, "Landers"; Heron, "Obermeyer." The *Herald*'s active role in promoting Lib-Labism was evident before the 1911 election; see *HH*, 14 Oct. 1911, 4; 16 Oct. 1911, 4; 18 Oct. 1911, 4; 19 Oct. 1911, 1.

49. In the 1887 federal election the Grits in Hamilton collaborated with the Labor Political Association to support Fred Walters, a moulder. Kealey and Palmer, *Dreaming*, 240–41. In the early years of the 20th century similar

arrangements got Lib-Lab MPs elected in three cities. When workers in Winnipeg and Nanaimo, B.C., nominated their own candidates for office in 1900, the Laurier Liberals supported Labourites Arthur Puttee and Ralph Smith as semi-autonomous affiliates of the party and then proceeded to integrate them as regular supporters of the government in the house. Six years later the election of Montreal Labor MP Alphonse Verville followed the same pattern. McCormack, "Arthur Puttee"; Robin, *Radical Politics*, 48–56; Leroux, "Verville." For a detailed description of a similar phenomenon in Britain, see Bealey and Pelling, *Labour and Politics*, 125–59.

50. LAC, R10383-0-6-F, Vol. 8, 7378–80 (P.D. Crerar to King, 2 Aug. 1908; 73780 (King to Crerar, 8 Aug. 1908); Vol. 9, 8222 (King to S. Landers, 15 Sept. 1908); 8223 (Landers to King, 17 Oct. 1908); Vol. 10, 9908, 9910 (A. Zimmerman to King, 31 July 1908, 15 Sept. 1908); LAC, R10811-0-X-E, Vol. 533, 144489–92 (Laurier to Sir John Gibson, 8 Sept. 1908); *HS*, 14 Sept. 1908, 1; *HH*, 4 Sept. 1908, 1. Municipally, Lib-Labism was limited. In the 1902 municipal elections the local Liberal Party listed two independent labour candidates on its official slate published in the *Times* and, when one won, integrated him into the Liberal caucus at City Hall. *HS*, 4 Jan. 1902, 3.

51. *HS*, 6 Dec. 1911, 1; *HH*, 15 Feb. 1911, 9; 16 March 1911, 12; 28 Nov. 1911, 12; 27 Oct. 1914, 1. Despite official labour neutrality, Landers wrote letters to the *Herald* in support of Peebles. Rowell also tried to flatter Studholme. See *HH*, 20 March 1912, 1; 16 April 1912, 5.

52. *HS*, 9 Oct. 1919, 3.

53. *HS*, 22 Sept. 1911, 8 (quotation); *HH*, 22 Nov. 1911, 9 (quotation).

54. *Globe and Mail*, 8 May 1982, 15 (quotation); English, *Decline of Politics*, 41 (quotation). A British Conservative argued at the turn of the century that "instinct rather than intellect" was at the core of the "Tory tradition." Coetzee, *Party or Country*, 5. See also Pugh, *Tories and the People*, 70. Canada's Conservative Party avoided the internal democracy of a party convention until 1927, and six years later Prime Minister Bennett was proposing the reintroduction of titles for Canadians. Glassford, *Reaction and Reform*, 16–44, 99.

55. McKay, "Canada as a Long Liberal Revolution"; Waite, "Political Ideas"; Brown, "Political Ideas"; Graham, "Some Political Ideas"; English, *Decline of Politics*, 54–61; Humphries, "Sources"; Christian and Campbell, *Political Parties and Ideologies*, 76–115; *HS*, 4 Oct. 1900, 4 (quotation).

56. *HS*, 9 Dec. 1911, 1; *VCHD*, 1911–12.

57. Kealey, *Toronto Workers*, 160–71.

58. This discussion of the working-class Tory benefits from insights in the following: Newby, "Deferential Dialectic"; Joyce, *Work, Society and Politics*; Genovese, *Roll, Jordan, Roll*; Thompson, "Eighteenth-Century English Society";

Nordlinger, *Working-Class Tories*; McKenzie and Silver, *Angels in Marble*; Kealey, *Toronto Workers*; Jones, *Languages of Class*; Pugh, *Tories and the People*; Lawrence, "Class and Gender."

59. See Rude, *Crowd in History*, 135–48.

60. Historian Jesse Lemisch, quoted in Newby, "Deferential Dialectic," 142.

61. Piva, "Workmen's Compensation Movement."

62. *HS*, 16 Oct. 1900, 4.

63. Palmer, *Culture in Conflict*, 97–122.

64. *HS*, 3 Oct. 1908, 7 (quotation); 10 Oct. 1908, 6; LAC, R10383-0-6-F, Vol. 9, 8224 (S. Landers to W.L.M. King, 28 Oct. 1908) (quotation).

65. *HS*, 22 Oct. 1925, 18; 30 Oct. 1925, 1; 21 July 1930; 28 Sept. 1935, 5; 4 Oct. 1935, 17; Glassford, "'The Presence of So Many Ladies,'"; 12; Glassford, *Reaction and Reform*.

66. *HH*, 22 Feb. 1911, 5; *HS*, 14 Sept. 1911, 14; Brown, *Robert Laird Borden*, Vol. 1, 190–91; Kilbourn, *Elements Combined*, 91.

67. *HS*, 16 Aug. 1911, 1; 14 Sept. 1911, 1 (quotation); 20 Sept. 1911, 1 (quotation).

68. *HS*, 14 Sept. 1911, 1; *HH*, 18 Aug. 1911, 9 (quotation); 21 Sept. 1911, 1; 22 Sept. 1911, 1. A workingman's letter to the *Herald* supported Peebles' concern about high food prices: "It would be a good thing for us if reciprocity would decrease the cost of living here at least." *HH*, 6 Sept. 1911, 5.

69. *HH*, 16 March 1911, 12; 18 March 1911, 1; LAC, R10383-0-6-F, Vol. C5, 22910 (clipping from Berlin *Telegraph*, 1 Sept. 1911); *HS*, 16 Aug. 1911, 24 (quotation); 20 Sept. 1911, 1. The confusion in the Canadian labour movement over the tariff question in this period is documented in Craven and Traves, "Class Politics," 27.

70. See Morton, *Progressive Party*.

71. The party decided on this new name for itself in 1920 and on the "National Party" as an appropriate abbreviation. The name was dropped in favour of the original "Liberal-Conservative" label in 1922. Williams, *Conservative Party*, 45–46, 50. After the election a local Liberal organizer described to Mackenzie King how "nearly all the leading Liberals left us, men like Sir John Gibson and even the Hon J.V. Teetzel," a former Liberal candidate and retired judge, who wrote to the press to support Conservative leader Arthur Meighen. "There was only a handful of us who stuck to the ship," J.J. Hunt whimpered. A defeated Liberal candidate wrote that "so many of our friends became enamoured with the other side that it was difficult here living a comfortable political life." He admitted victory was impossible: "The other side had the best and strongest political organization I have ever seen in Hamilton in 30 years." LAC, R10383-0-6-F, Vol. 62, 53456–58 (J.J. Hunt to W.L.M. King, 8 Dec. 1921); Vol. 60, 51602–3 (W.T. Evans to King, 8 Dec. 1921). For the local Liberals' ongoing difficulties, see Best and Fraser, "Chisolm."

72. The president of the John McPherson shoe company declared that, without the tariff, "every other shoe factory in Canada will have to go out of business." The Sanford clothing firm and J.R. Moodie knitting company sounded similar warnings, and the president of Hamilton Cotton Company distributed letters to his employees warning that the present tariff was "absolutely necessary if we are to continue in business." *HS*, 23 Nov. 1921, 6; 24 Nov. 1921, 1, 22; 30 Nov. 1921, 1; *ND*, 1 Dec. 1921, 1.

73. Significantly, although an overwhelmingly proletarian city, Hamilton did not produce in this period a single working-class parliamentarian to join the two Western labour MPs who sat in the House of Commons in the 1920s. These westerners had not only emerged from a milieu of radical farm movements, but also hailed from a region whose economic life was not as dependent on manufacturing and whose politics were not dominated by a defence of the tariff. Indeed, the protectionist Tories were a weak force on the Prairies by World War One. Friesen, *Canadian Prairies*; Smith, *Prairie Liberalism*; Macpherson, *Democracy in Alberta*; English, *Decline of Politics*, 37. British Conservatives (Unionists) in this period similarly turned to tariff reform in an effort to attract working-class voters away from their emerging Lib-Lab affinities to a notion of "Tory Democracy." Green, "Radical Conservatism"; Dutton, "Unionist Party."

74. Nelles, *Politics of Development*, 215–55; Armstrong and Nelles, *Monopoly's Moment*.

75. There was a glimmer of anti-corporate rhetoric from the Tories well before a "public power" movement emerged in 1902. The involvement of prominent Hamilton Liberals such as John Gibson and James Dixon in the growing utility field had already brought public denunciations from Conservative opponents that they were not acting in the best interests of the city's industries. In the 1898 provincial campaign the Conservative candidate who would defeat Gibson that year attacked his opponent's promotion of the local gas company and promised that "he would not work for the benefit of the Gas company or the Niagara Power company. (Cheers.)" In 1902 he continued his attacks on the big-business connections of several Liberal Cabinet ministers: "He was not against corporations as such, but he objected to them being favored, as against the people." Some months later the *Spectator* boasted that a Tory mayoralty candidate had "no dangerous entanglements with powerful corporations, whose interests are opposed to the interests of the ratepayers of Hamilton." *HS*, 25 Feb. 1898, 7; 22 May 1902, 10; 3 Jan. 1903, 1. In the 1902 campaign the Conservatives also repeatedly attacked the "text-book ring" that controlled the production of school books. Humphries, *Whitney*, 79–80.

76. Nelles, *Politics of Development*, 256–72. The Conservatives were seizing on public ownership as a policy issue in this period. In the 1904 federal election Borden proposed a state-controlled transcontinental railway as an alternative to Laurier's new program of private railway development through Western Canada, a position that won support from several local labour leaders, including the independent-minded John Flett. A letter from a Liberal workingman in Hamilton in October 1904 urged Laurier to change his railway policy if he wanted to have "a great effect on the voters of Hamilton." *HS*, 19 Oct. 1904, 1; 21 Oct. 1904,1; 29 Oct. 1904, 1; LAC, R10811-0-X-E, Vol. 338, 90559–60 ("A Good Liberal Voter" to Laurier, 7 Oct. 1904); Gray "Barker," 7–8.

77. For Tory opposition to public power elsewhere in Southern Ontario, see Nelles, *Politics of Development*, 272–88; Plewman, *Adam Beck*, 85–87; Bliss, *Canadian Millionaire*, 173–75.

78. Lucas, "Conflict over Public Power," 241, 246.

79. Quoted in Humphries, "Political Career," 345.

80. W.R. Plewman seems to have been the source of a persistent myth that Hendrie was opposed to public power (Plewman, *Adam Beck*, 58; Denison, *People's Power*, 54; Nelles, *Politics of Development*, 560). While Hendrie must indeed have had friends and associates in the Hamilton elite who, like William Southam, held stock in Dominion Power, and while Hendrie was undoubtedly uncomfortable with Beck's flamboyance, he seems to have openly parted company with the private power advocates and campaigned in Hamilton, in his sober, careful fashion, for the Conservative program of public ownership. See, for example, *HH*, 17 July 1911, 1; 18 July 1911, 1.

81. *HS*, 28 July-6 Aug. 1908. Richard Lucas's list of city councillors who supported Dominion Power includes a few Conservatives. "Conflict over Public Power," 240. Lucas's suggestion of four more-or-less equal components in a coalition – labour, city council, temperance forces, and "Conservative reformers and labour ward representatives" – is not convincing. The Hamilton Trades and Labor Council's support was important but, because of the lack of independent working-class aldermen, necessarily limited. City council was a forum for the conflict, not an independent agent; and temperance did not give any focus to a public power fight. Any attempt to identify "reformers" in municipal politics would have to delineate more clearly the principles that united them and take into account the continuing presence of partyism in municipal elections.

82. Gray, "Gibson"; *HH*, 29 Aug. 1911, 6.

83. Lucas, "Conflict over Public Power," 239; J. Pottinger, "The Strike," in *HS*, 12 Nov. 1906, 6; *HH*, 21 July 1911, 1.

84. *HS*, 8 Jan. 1907, 1 (quotation).

85. HPL, HTLC, Minutes, 21 July 1911, 86; *HH*, 21 July 1911, 8; 22 July 1911, 16; 16 Dec. 1916, 17 (quotation); Lucas, "Conflict over Public Power," 246; *IB*, 23 April 1915, 3; 8 Sept. 1916, 4; 13 April 1917, 1.

86. *HS*, 22 May 1934, 12; 9 June 1934, 24.

87. Nelles, *Politics of Development*, 254.

88. Humphries, "Political Career," 509 (quotation); Nelles, *Politics of Development*, 304; *HH*, 22 Nov. 1911, 9. Tory populism was strengthened by the rhetoric of its unofficial adjunct, the Orange Order. The Orange *Sentinel*, for example, advocated "absolute control of railroad, power franchises, and all natural wealth, so that foreign capitalists coming in here may be bound by our laws." Quoted in Roberts, "Studies in the Toronto Labour Movement."

89. Mackenzie and Silver discuss this strain in British Toryism in *Angels in Marble*, 48–71.

90. A more tenuous but undoubtedly useful link was the British Welcome League, a society formed in May 1911 to help new British immigrants get established in the city, and administered by the well-named John Bull, a manufacturer and prominent member of the Ward Eight Conservative organization. *HS*, 8 Dec. 1911; 2 May 1916, 6; *HH*, 18 March 1911, 1; 20 May 1911, 18; 3 Feb. 1912, 15; 13 March 1913, 5; English, *Decline of Politics*, 65.

91. In 1900 the *Spectator* scored Laurier and his minister of public works, Joseph Israel Tarte, for their hesitation to send troops for the South African war and for the alleged French-Canadian efforts to sunder the Empire and impose a French-Catholic hegemony in the country: "The Queen does not rule her Canadian Dominion," the paper thundered, "Tarte does." In 1904 the prime minister's dismissal of Lord Dundonald as commander of the Canadian armed forces and his careless reference to the British gentleman as a "foreigner" sent the Conservative press into paroxysms once again. Stevens, "Laurier," 218–25, 251–56.

92. *HS*, 14 Sept. 1911, 1 (quotation). The efforts to bury partisan differences in Hamilton in 1917 hit many snags. T.J. Stewart won the Union government nomination by calling his own, Tory-dominated, convention. The Liberals were so irate that they ran J.I. McLaren against Stewart, but without success. A bipartisan convention in East Hamilton nominated S.C. Mewburn, already appointed minister of militia in Borden's cabinet.

93. *HS*, 12 Dec. 1917, 13 (quotation); Glassford, *Reaction and Reform*, 79 (quotation).

94. Humphries, "Political Career," 96–179. One of Hamilton's Tory MPs, Samuel Barker, a Protestant, was a generous subscriber to his family's church, St. Patrick's Roman Catholic Cathedral. Humphries, "Political Career," 203. Canadian Tories had long since given up defending an established church, but they were quick in their defence of Protestantism against alleged "papist" aggression. Whitney's predecessor as Ontario Conservative leader, William Meredith, had repeatedly attacked Roman Catholic educational rights in the province, and in the 1894 provincial election the local Conservative organization had not opposed the Protestant Protective Association candidate in Hamilton. The same spirit animated the Ontario Tories in the 1896 controversy over Manitoba schools. In Hamilton the Conservative organization split over the nomination of a candidate committed to remedial legislation for the Catholic minority in Manitoba. The day after the election a disgusted *Spectator* editor complained: "Many anti-remedialists were dissatisfied, and refused to accept the ticket, while many more who were among the most ardent political workers of the party, gave it only a passive support, and abstained from actively assisting in the fight." Humphries, "Political Career," 34–95; Watt, "Anti-Catholicism," 62; Clark, "Conservative Party"; Miller, "Anti-Catholicism"; *HS*, 24 June 1896, 5 (quotation).

95. Oliver, *G. Howard Ferguson*, 39–80; Prang, "Clerics, Politicians, and the Bilingual Schools Issue"; *HS*, 2 May 1916, 6.

96. *HS*, 22 Feb. 1898, 1; 21 Oct. 1904, 1; 3 June 1908, 6.

97. In the 1904 federal campaign, in the context of a longshoremen's strike on the Hamilton docks, a *Spectator* editorial note charged the Liberals with failing to deal with the "alien labour" question: "Laurier has tied [Alien Labour Officer] Ed. Williams' hands behind his back and has gagged Ed.'s mouth. And the foreign cheap labor has taken the bread out of the mouths of the stevedores' wives and children." *HS*, 20 Oct. 1904, 4 (quotations); 26 Oct. 1904, 4.

98. *HS*, 3 Oct. 1908, 7; 7 Oct. 1908, 1; 10 Oct. 1908, 5; 16 Oct. 1908, 5; 20 Oct. 1908, 1 (quotation). The Laurier government had been hesitating to impose quotas and could well have been seen as promoting such immigration. See Ward, *White Canada Forever*, 67.

99. *HS*, 19 July 1930, 17. In a similar pattern British historian Henry Pelling found rising Conservative strength in the districts of Lancashire experiencing large-scale immigration of Irish Catholics – the home communities of many newcomers to Hamilton. Pelling, *Social Geography*, 284–85. British Conservatives also allegedly benefited from reactions to Jewish immigration to East London; Lee, "Conservatism," 88.

100. *HS*, 9 June 1934, 24.

101. See, for example, *HT*, 3 Oct. 1917, 4; 4 Oct. 1917, 4. On the Liberals' cultivation of the European immigrant vote, see Smith, *Prairie Liberalism*, 25–65. The Hamilton Liberals continued to maintain their hold on the European Catholic community in the city well past World War Two; see Jacek, "John Munro"; Jacek et al., "Congruence," 196; Anderson, "Ethnic Behaviour."

102. Spence, *Prohibition in Canada*; Tennyson, "Sir William Hearst and the Ontario Temperance Act"; Hallowell, *Prohibition*; Heron, *Booze*.

103. *HH*, 18 Nov. 1912, 1; 14 Feb. 1916, 4; *LN*, 22 Oct. 1915, 2 (quotation); 7 April 1916, 1; *IB*, 7 April 1916, 3; Prang, *N.W. Rowell*, 106–44; Heron, *Booze*, 213–24. Sixteen unions voted for neutrality and eight against. On the general suspicion of working-class leisure patterns among labour and socialist leaders in this period, see Heron, *Booze*, 219–24.

104. Humphries, "Sources of Ontario 'Progressive' Conservatism"; Stevens, "Laurier," 351; Young, "Conscription, Rural Depopulation, and the Farmers of Ontario"; *HH*, 23 Feb. 1917, 1; *HS*, 30 Nov. 1916, 1.

105. The Hendrie family owned race horses and were pillars of the city's Jockey Club, a mecca for the many workingmen with a passion for gambling. J.J. Scott, who was president of the Jockey Club, and several other local Tories owned the Grant Spring Brewery, while Hendrie held an interest in the Hamilton Distilling Company. Mayor (and MP) Stewart was a shareholder in one of the city's much vilified vaudeville and movie houses, the Red Mill. *HS*, 29 Nov. 1907 (clipping in HPL Scrapbook); LAC, R6113-0-X-E, Vol. 193, 107688 (Sir John Hendrie to Robert Borden, 8 May 1916); *HH*, 2 Aug. 1910, 5; 25 June 1915, 1; 20 June 1917, 6; AO, F 5, E.A. Dalley to Whitney, 7 Dec. 1906. Jon Lawrence describes the British Tories' "deliberate identification with key aspects of urban popular culture, such as the pub, football and racing, [which] was intended to distinguish them from the 'moral reforming' style of Liberal politics." Lawrence, "Class and Gender," 638 (quotation); Lawrence, *Speaking for the People*, 107–8; see also Joyce, *Work, Society, and Politics*, 292–301.

106. Humphries, "Political Career," 356; *HS*, 18 Jan. 1905, 1.

107. *HH*, 23 June 1910, 4; 12 Aug. 1910, 4. In 1910 the former secretary of the Conservative association, C.R. Smith, was hired as the secretary of the hotelmen's association. *HS*, 20 July 1910, 10; 27 Dec. 1910, 6; *HS*, 4 Jan. 1913, 1; 31 Dec. 1914, 1.

108. *HH*, 2 March 1918, 1; 4 March 1918, 10; *LN*, 8 March 1918, 1; Heron, *Booze*, 224–33.

109. *HH*, 3 Jan. 1911, 6; 7 Jan. 1913, 9; 2 Jan. 1915, 4; MPSS, 19; *HS*, 21 Oct. 1919, 1; Johnston, *E.C. Drury*, 157–65.

110. See Table 40. Oliver, "Hearst and the Collapse"; Oliver, *G. Howard Ferguson*, 138–39, 159–69, 269–74, 277–80; Hallowell, *Prohibition*, 131–69; Prang, *N.W. Rowell*, 111; Tennyson, "Sir William Hearst and the Ontario Temperance Act"; *HS*, 16 Aug. 1919, 1; 30 Nov. 1926, 45; 2 Dec. 1926, 1; Heron, *Booze*, 274–76. The Communists scoffed that prohibition was a "red herring" that allowed politicians to avoid talking about unemployment. Sternly assuming that drunkenness would disappear along with capitalism, they declared: "The whole issue is an appeal to the lower instincts of the voter." *Worker*, 15 Nov. 1924, 3; 27 Nov. 1926, 1, 3 (quotation); 18 Dec. 1926, 1 (quotation), 2.

111. Green, "Strange Death"; Lawrence, "Class and Gender," 642–45; Kirk, *Change, Continuity and Class*, 201–5.

112. *Our Journal*, December 1908, 34 (quotation); Callow, ed., *City Boss in America*.

113. In 1912 the Ward Eight Conservative organization had a predominantly working-class membership – 11 workers alongside two manufacturers and one builder. *HH*, 3 Feb. 1912, 15; *VCHD*, 1912.

114. The Primrose League was far larger and more successful than any comparable social groups in the Liberal or Labour parties. Pugh, *Tories and the People*; Pugh, "Popular Conservatism"; Lawrence, "Class and Gender," 638–39.

115. *HS*, 28 Nov. 1900, 8; 14 Sept. 1908, 7; 8 Oct. 1910, 10; 8 Dec. 1926, 11; 26 Sept. 1929, 7; *HH*, 17 June 1911, 9; 28 March 1914, 12; 31 May 1915, 10; 16 Oct. 1916, 11; 21 Oct. 1916, 4.

116. See, for example, *HS*, 21 June 1897, 8; 25 March 1898, 5; 6 June 1900, 8; 26 Sept. 1900, 8; 29 Nov. 1900; 25 March 1901, 8; 26 May 1901, 8; 2 June 1904, 4; 3 June 1904, 1; 30 July 1907, 12; 14 Sept. 1908, 7; 16 Sept. 1908, 1; 19 Sept. 1908, 1; 20 April 1910, 12; 23 June 1910, 12; 8 Oct. 1910, 10. These clubs were also a feature of British Toryism; see Lawrence, *Speaking for the People*, 105–6, 110–12. The Liberals also had a Hamilton club, which they closed in 1918. *HH*, 20 March 1918, 1; 1 April 1918, 1.

117. *HT*, 1 April 1910, 1; *HH*, 29 Sept. 1914, 3; *HS*, 25 Nov. 1905, 20; 20 March 1907, 7; 1 April 1907, 7; 15 Jan. 1908, 3; 8 Dec. 1910, 14; 14 Jan. 1914, 7; 31 Jan. 1914, 1; 16 Feb. 1917, 15; 8 Dec. 1920, 17; Hanlon, "Lamoreaux," 87.

118. *HH*, 18 Feb. 1914, 7; 25 Feb. 1914, 7; 27 March 1914, 18; 28 March 1914, 12; 7 April 1914, 15; 27 April 1914, 6; 17 Dec. 1914, 1 (quotation); 19 Dec. 1914, 35; 1 May 1915, 1; 8 March 1916, 2; *HS*, 31 Jan. 1914, 1; 18 March 1914, 9; 27 April 1914, 5; 15 Aug. 1914, 13; 2 Jan. 1915, 11.

119. Early in 1909 the Conservative Club inaugurated "an educational and progressive campaign" among its members and announced forthcoming addresses by three Tory MLAs on "The Resources of Ontario," "Prison Reform," and "New Ontario." A similar program was beamed at the East Hamilton Conservatives in 1914, with talks on workmen's compensation and "The Conservative Party as a Factor in the Building up of Canada." *HS*, 12 March 1909, 14; 21 April 1914, 5; *HH*, 16 March 1914, 1, 3.

120. "These political heelers do not come into the trades unions to influence workingmen to follow their political party," the *Industrial Banner* noted in 1915, "but they carry on their proselytising in the different fraternal and benevolent societies . . . the same men who would protest in the trade unions allow these same heelers to draw the wool over their eyes in the other societies to which they belong." *IB*, 7 May 1915, 1. One Italian-Canadian man in Hamilton later recalled that such political appeals also happened inside ethnic societies. MHSO, ITA-6489-BOR.

121. *HS*, 2 Oct. 1919, 1; 6 Dec. 1929, 28. Glassford, "'Presence of So Many Ladies.'" The Liberals had a women's association

by 1914, and the ILP in 1917. *HH*, 28 April 1914, 9. A special meeting for women Conservatives during the 1931 federal election campaign featured no female speakers and no issues pitched specially to female ears. It was essentially a rally for campaign workers. *HS*, 25 July 1931, 4.

122. *HS*, 8 Dec. 1926, 11. In 1930 the Conservatives set up another association in the Wentworth County part of the East Hamilton riding. *HS*, 20 Feb. 1930, 22.

123. Brown, *Robert Laird Borden*, Vol. 1, 132–34; Synge, "Family and Community," ch. 6; *IB*, August 1906, 3 (quotation); *HH*, 11 Jan. 1916, 3 (quotation).

124. *HS*, 2 Jan. 1901, 4; 4 Jan. 1902, 4 (quotation); *HT*, 7 Jan. 1902, 4; *HH*, 9 Oct. 1912, 6 (quotation).

125. Stewart, "Political Patronage"; Stewart, *Origins of Canadian Politics*. Contracts for the Board of Education became quite controversial in 1915, when the *Herald* reported that two contractors – a Ward Seven Tory committeeman and a Tory alderman – had earned three-quarters of the $740,000 spent on schools in the preceding decade. The next year the city's Builders' Exchange was so incensed at this patronage system that it considered running its own candidates for city hall. *HH*, 3 June 1915, 1; 25 Nov. 1916, 1.

126. City hall appointments, for example, went to Thomas Towers, once district master of the local Knights of Labor; William McAndrew, an independent-minded printer with Tory connections who had served for ten years as a Ward Six alderman; and Thomas Church, a moulder who also spent a few years in the Tory caucus on city council. John Pryke, whose role as a link between the Tories and the local labour movement extended back to the nine-hours agitation of the 1870s, was secretary of the Hamilton Liberal-Conservative Association in the pre-war period and won a federal position in the local office of the inspector of weights and measures in 1914. Three years later Nathaniel Merigold, a former stove-mounter, a leading figure in the local Orange Order, and a one-time Ward Eight Tory alderman, moved up in the excise office to a $1,200-per-year post. Fred Kellond, a bookbinder at the *Spectator* and active Tory, became a provincial factory inspector in 1907. *HS*, 30 June 1917, 8; 25 Jan. 1919, 1; *HH*, 21 Nov. 1911, 1; 12 June 1912, 1; 25 March 1914, 1; 28 March 1914, 1; 23 Aug. 1915, 1; 10–14 May 1917, 1; *LN*, 6 March 1914, 2; *IB*, March 1911, 4.

127. *HH*, 21 Nov. 1911, 12 June 1912; *IB*, 7 May 1915; see also April 1917. English confirms that such practices were indeed normal. *Decline of Politics*, 75; see also Stewart, "Political Patronage." In an interview in 1979 an elderly north-end resident suggested that private-sector jobs could also require allegiance to the Tories; she said her father, an Irish Catholic and life-long Liberal, "was offered a job in a cotton mill on condition that he become a Conservative." MHSO, ITA-6990-ROB.

128. *HS*, 22 Oct. 1925, 1.
129. Glassford, "'Presence of So Many Ladies.'"
130. Thompson, "Labour and the Modern British Monarchy."
131. *HT*, 27 May 1902, 8.

17. The Classes and the Masses

1. *HH*, 31 Oct. 1914, 15 (quotation); Briggs, "Language of 'Mass' and 'Masses'"; Saville, "Ideology of Labourism"; Heron, "Labourism."

2. *IB*, 3 July 1914, 1.

3. Montgomery, *Citizen Worker*; Fink, *Workingmen's Democracy*; 18–35; Hinton, "Voluntarism versus Jacobinism," 83. James Hinton sums up this attitude to citizenship as "the workingman's capacity to determine his own destiny in association with his fellows, free from the attentions of an interfering, tyrannical, or paternalistic state." Hinton, "Voluntarism versus Jacobinism," 83.

4. Hinton, "Voluntarism versus Jacobinism."

5. *IB*, May 1910, 3.

6. Kealey, *Toronto Workers*, 274–90; Homel, "'Fading Beams'"; CRCRLC, *Report: Evidence – Ontario*, 861; Cook, "Henry George and the Poverty of Canadian Progress"; Schwantes, *Radical Heritage*, 98; McKay, *Reasoning Otherwise*, 142–43; *HS*, 14 Oct. 1897, 1; 4 Nov. 1897, 1; 11 Nov. 1897, 8; 23 Dec. 1897, 1; 13 Jan. 1898, 8; 14 Jan. 1898, 8; 3 Feb. 1898, 1; 10 Feb. 1898, 8; 21 Feb. 1898, 1; 22 Feb. 1898, 1; 28 Feb. 1898, 8; 12 March 1898, 8; 26 March 1898, 8; 17 Nov. 1898, 8; 20 Jan. 1899, 8; 17 Feb. 1899, 8; 16 March 1899, 8; 17 March 1899,1; *CAC*, 9 Feb. 1900, 2; *IB*, Jan. 1898, 8.

7. See Kealey and Palmer, *Dreaming of What Might Be*, 277–329.

8. Hamilton Trades and Labor Council, *Official Programme and Souvenir*, 4.

9. *Globe*, 6 Sept. 1895; *HS*, 14 Jan. 1898, 8; 29 Jan. 1898, 1; 12 March 1898, 1.

10. The platform called for "Proportional representation, initiative and referendum; single tax on land values; government control on natural monopolies in the interest of the whole people; municipal operation of franchises; hours of labour reduced gradually, so as to keep pace with labor-saving machinery; industrial co-operation," as well as the union label and a limited temperance measure. *HS*, 12 March 1898, 8. The platform was redrafted shortly afterward, but the *Spectator* did not publish it. The temperance plank must have disappeared, since the Royal Templars coldly withdrew in May. *HS*, 28 March 1898, 7; 2 April 1898, 1; 23 April 1898, 8; 7 May 1898, 8.

11. H.P. Bonny, a retail clerk, former president of the Canadian Co-operative Commonwealth, and a founding member of the Social Reform Union, headed the Hamilton branch of the League. *HS*, 15 April 1901, 8; 22 May 1901, 8; *HT*, 17 April 1901, 8; 22 May 1901, 8; *CAC*, 9

March 1900, 9 (quotation); 18 March 1900, 4; 30 March 1900, 3.

12. The Hamilton delegates to the 1896 convention of the Trades and Labor Congress of Canada vigorously defended the SLP's right to representation in the Congress. John Flett argued that no one "who had carefully considered the platform of the Socialistic labor party would oppose their representation." In March 1899 the head table at a local SLP banquet included temperance reformer W.W. Buchanan and representatives of the East and West End Workingmen's Clubs. TLCCP 1896; *Globe*, 21 Sept. 1896, 6; *HS*, 23 March 1899, 1; 7 Sept. 1900, 8; 2 Feb. 1901, 8; *CAC*, 25 March 1899, 3. The *CAC* included the Hamilton SLP in its list of "Progressive Organizations" on 15 April 1899, 2.

13. McCormack, "Origins and Extent of Western Labour Radicalism," 45; Herreshoff, *Origins of American Marxism*; McKay, *Reasoning Otherwise*, 136–38. In 1901 an SLP speaker in Hamilton "scored the Socialist League and did not take much stock in the 'love' plank in their platform." The League, he said, "played hypocrite" when it said "the Nazarene worked all things through love, for the Scriptures showed He always fed the people first and then taught them." *HS*, 7 Sept. 1900, 8; *HT*, 2 May 1901, 8.

14. Kirk, *Comrades and Cousins*, 44–51; Green, "'Strike at the Ballot Box.'"

15. *HS*, 20 May 1901, 8; *HT*, 5 Aug. 1901, 8; *HH*, 20 Aug. 1910, 2 (quotation); *IB*, May 1910, 3 (quotation). Hamilton's Philip Obermeyer fought back against the socialist tirades from his labour page in the *Herald*: "If a man's trade unionism has to take second place to his economic belief, it is well to make the issue clear, and those who don't subscribe to the doctrines of the Socialist Party of Canada cannot be blamed if they decline to hold out any more olive branches to the irreconcilables." *HH*, 23 July 1910, 2. The "impossibilism" of the SPC in these years is discussed in McCormack, *Reformers, Rebels, and Revolutionaries*, 53–76; Homel, "Simpson," 152–564; Robin, *Radical Politics and Canadian Labour*, 44–61, 92–103; McKay, *Reasoning Otherwise*, 151–69.

16. *HT*, 7 Jan. 1902, 1; 22 May 1902, 8 (quotation); *HS*, 7 Sept. 1900, 8; 2 Feb. 1901, 8; 16 Sept. 1901, 4; 17 Sept. 1901, 8; 23 Sept. 1901, 1.

17. *HS*, 2 Jan. 1900, 1, 5; 3 Jan. 1900, 3; 8 Jan. 1901, 1. The mayor was irate: "If Barrett had run as a labor candidate and polled the same vote it would have been all right, but to outsiders it would appear that the Socialists are very strong in Hamilton, and the effect may be bad." *HS*, 3, 8 Jan. 1900; *HT*, 2 Jan. 1902, 8; 4 Jan. 1902, 12; 7 Jan. 1902, 1 (quotation).

18. *HT*, 2 May 1902, 1; 5 May 1902, 5; 8 May 1902, 1; 12 May 1902, 6; 13 May 1902, 8; 22 May 1902, 8; 26 May 1902, 8; 27 May 1902, 8; 28 May 1902, 1; 30 May 1902, 1; 11 May

1911, 1; 17 June 1902, 8; 25 June 1902, 8; *HS*, 27 May 1902, 5, 19; 17 June 1902, 8; 13 Dec. 1902, 1; 15 Dec. 1902; *IB*, July 1902, 1.

19. In 1907 the leading socialists who caught the attention of the press were still Rodehouse and Gordon. The socialists kept up their propaganda efforts, preaching to the unemployed, initiating a short-lived local of the Industrial Workers of the World in 1908, and bringing Eugene Debs and Daniel De Leon to the city to speak, but their fortunes remained gloomy as they continued the SLP custom of denouncing trade unionists and reformists. Ten days after the end of the street-railway strike in 1906, and only a week after Studholme's upset victory, they managed to attract only ten men to a meeting. In 1908 Lockhart Gordon again ran in the provincial election, this time against Studholme, and picked up only 24 votes. His running mate in West Hamilton, William Armstrong, won a total of only 253. *Western Clarion*, 10 June 1905, 1; 5 Sept. 1905, 1; 4 Nov. 1905, 1; 25 Nov. 1905, 4; 17 Feb. 1906, 4; 2 June 1906, 4; *HS*, 3 Feb. 1906, 6; 10 Dec. 1906, 7; 1 April 1907, 1; 21 March 1908, 1; 27 March 1908, 9 June 1908, 1; 26 Nov. 1908; *HH*, 27 Feb. 1909, 1; *CW*, 4 March 1909, 8. On the British Independent Labour Party in this period, see Howell, *British Workers and the Independent Labour Party*.

20. Hamilton evidently lacked that growing body of disenchanted middle-class citizens who had provided the backbone of so much of the social-reform activity in Toronto in the 1890s. With none of the headquarters of religious or other voluntary organizations and, by 1900, none of the periodicals that flowed from them, Hamilton reformers had more difficulty constructing the radical intellectual culture that thrived in the Queen City at the close of the century. Homel, "Fading Beams." Efforts to explain the weakness of radical socialism in North America that focus on the political legacies that grew from real confrontations in ongoing historical processes are more fruitful than those that highlight broad transhistorical value systems. For the most recent statement of the latter, see Lipset and Marks, *It Didn't Happen Here*.

21. Heron, "Labourism"; Kirk, *Comrades and Cousins*, 23–30.

22. The Ontario Executive Committee, which included the Hamilton tailor Hugh Robinson, similarly found both mainstream parties "run directly in the interest of moneyed corporations." Labour had become "the laughing stock of dishonest politicians." TLCCP, 1903, 56 (quotation); 1904, 22 (quotation); *HS*, 29 Aug. 1904, 2 (quotation). A new assault by employers in the late 1890s had already convinced the British Trades Union Congress to endorse a new labour party in 1899 and to back the Labour Representation Committee, founded the next year. Union support for the new British party soared even higher after the famous Taff Vale decision, which so

directly threatened the unions' existence. In Western Canada and the United States, and in Nova Scotia, coal miners' bitter disputes with coal masters also produced new sympathy for socialist politics. Even in the Eastern United States, homeland of the cautious AFL, the hostility of employers and the indifference of politicians brought a call in 1906 for "the independent use of the ballot by the trade unionists and workmen." Pelling, *Origins of the Labour Party*, 192–215; Saville, "Trade Unions and Free Labour"; Dubofsky, *We Shall Be All*; McCormack, *Reformers, Rebels, and Revolutionaries*, 35–76; Reed, *Labor Philosophy of Samuel Gompers*, 105–6; Roberts "Studies in the Toronto Labour Movement."

23. *HS*, 3 Jan. 1899, 3, 5; 20 Dec. 1901, 15; 21 Dec. 1901, 13; 7 Jan. 1902, 7; *IB*, November 1899, 1; *IMJ*, February 1902, 92; September 1905, 730. For more detail on these campaigns, see Heron, "Working-Class Hamilton," 596–98.

24. The determination flowed out of the Congress meeting into other cities as well; see Heron, "Labourism," 52–53.

25. *IB*, November 1903, 1; *HS*, 26 Oct. 1903, 1; 2 Nov. 1903, 1. Whitcombe left the city within the next two years.

26. *HS*, 28 Dec. 1903, 1; 29 Dec. 1903, 9; 5 Jan. 1904, 1.

27. *HS*, 3 June 1904, 1; 9 June 1904, 1; 20 June 1904, 1; 28 June 1904, 5; 24 Sept. 1904, 1; 5 Oct. 1904, 1; 7 Oct. 1904, 1; 27 Dec. 1904, 1, 5; 29 Dec. 1904, 1; 31 Dec. 1904, 1, 7; 3 Jan. 1905, 1; 2 Jan. 1906, 1. One of the defeated candidates was appointed to the council later in 1904 after an incumbent's death, but the *Spectator* pointed out, "It is rarely his voice has been heard either in committee or council." *HS*, 31 Dec. 1904, 1.

28. TLCCP, 1906, 80–86; Homel, "James Simpson," 327–28; Robin, *Radical Politics*, 79–90; Greene, "'Strike at the Ballot Box'"; *HS*, 27 Oct. 1906, 1; 5 Nov. 1906, 12; 9 Nov. 1906, 6. Although he was working in New York, the ever-ambitious Landers let it be known that he was interested in the nomination. He got no support. *HS*, 31 Oct. 1906, 1, 6; 7 Nov. 1906, 1.

29. The recently deceased Conservative MLA, Henry Carscallen, had ruffled many local feathers by his independent attitude to patronage, especially after the Whitney government had taken office at Queen's Park in 1905. Moreover, cracks had begun to appear in party unity as some of the younger, more populist Tories, notably alderman T.J. Stewart, challenged their party elders. The most important disaffected Conservative was William Southam, the wealthy publisher of the *Spectator*, whose pique prompted him to answer Whitney's conciliatory gestures in November with cool words that there was still "something wrong somewhere." In the subsequent municipal election Southam's paper backed the Liberal candidate for mayor in opposition to Stewart. AO, MU3120, S. Barker to Whitney, 22 Sept. 1906; Whitney to Barker, 24 Sept.

1906; W. Southam to Whitney, 6 Nov. 1906 (quotation); *HS*, 5 Nov. 1906, 12; 16 Nov. 1906, 1, 5.

30. *HS*, 10 Nov. 1906, 1; 16 Nov. 1906, 1; 19 Nov. 1906, 1; 26 Nov. 1906, 6; 28 Nov. 1906, 12; 29 Nov. 1906, 1; 30 Nov. 1906, 1; 1 Dec. 1906, 1; 3 Dec. 1906, 6. In desperation the *Spectator* argued at different points in the campaign that Studholme was in the pocket of the Liberals, that the Liberals had capitulated to labourist strength, and that the Liberals were pulling back and refusing to co-operate. There were even suggestions in *Spectator* editorials that the aged Studholme was simply hoping for a sinecure from the Liberal pork barrel. None of these contradictory charges were ever sustained.

31. A mass rally on 30 November featured Toronto's idiosyncratic maverick Tory MP W.F. Maclean, Toronto labour lawyer J.G. O'Donoghue, and Trades and Labor Congress president Alphonse Verville as guest speakers. *HS*, 19 Nov. 1906, 1, 3, 6; 20 Nov. 1906, 1; 21 Nov. 1906; 12, 29 Nov. 1906, 1, 12. A local Tory later told the premier that closing the Normal School had been "a very great blow to many people in East Hamilton, as the scholars boarded among the people down there and were quite a source of revenue to them." The same Conservative informant indicated that the resentment against these measures had been building for at least a year. AO, F 5, MU 3121, Dalley to Whitney, 7 Dec. 1906.

32. *HS*, 5 Dec. 1906, 6; AO, F 5, E.A. Dalley to J.P. Whitney, 7 Dec. 1906 (quotations). After the election Whitney consoled Scott: the "fact that the large majority of voters in East Hamilton are labour men clears the air with regard to the situation and shows that the labour men simply acted together in consequence of the Strike." AO, F 5, Whitney to J.J. Scott, 5 Dec. 1906.

33. *IB*, 5 Dec. 1906, 1 (quotation); AO, F 5, Dalley to Whitney, 7 Dec. 1906 (quotation). For the election results, see Table 40.

34. *HS*, 19 Dec. 1906, 1 (quotation); 8 Jan. 1907, 1.

35. Labour politics in Ontario (and elsewhere in Canada and Britain at the time) was highly decentralized. The 600 delegates who arrived in Toronto in April 1907 to found the Ontario ILP chose Rollo as president, but, like the party's British namesake, the organization had little or no co-ordination through a central office before 1917. Each city or town created its own political unit, which then affiliated with the ultimately short-lived provincial body, which disappeared after a few years. After a curiously long delay, Hamilton workers organized their own branch, No. 5, on 25 Nov. 1907. Unlike the British Labour Representation Committee (renamed the Labour Party in 1906), the ILP based its membership on the affiliation of individuals, not organizations. A man could join if he subscribed to the party's program and paid 50 cents a year. Hamilton's unions helped to launch the local party and then quickly

withdrew into strict political neutrality. *IB*, April 1907,
1; Pelling, *Origins of the Labour Party*, 120–21; McKibbin,
Evolution of the Labour Party, 20–47; Heron, "Rollo."

36. The Hamilton ILP more than once was denied a hall or
rink for its rallies. See, for example, *HH*, 7 Dec. 1911, 1.

37. For a reflection on how this little band held things
together, see *HH*, 23 Sept. 1911, 17.

38. *HS*, 12 March 1909, 1; *HH*, 30 March 1909, 9; 13 Jan. 1910;
12 Feb. 1910, 1; 18 March 1910, 5; 11 June 1910, 2; 11 Feb.
1911, 17; 11 March 1911, 15; 20 Oct. 1911, 15; 23 Dec. 1911, 8;
9 March 1912, 1; 16 Oct. 1912, 8; 20 Jan. 1913, 9; 6 May 1918,
5; 18 July 1919; 20 Dec. 1919, 5; 28 Nov. 1921, 17; 18 June
1923, 15; *IB*, January 1912, 1; *LN*, 15 March 1912,1; 12 June
1912; 25 Oct. 1912, 1; 23 May 1919, 4. These efforts certainly
pale alongside the accomplishments of the German Social
Democrats or even some of the US Socialist Party and
British Labour Party activity. See Nettl, "German Social
Democratic Party," 76–78; Miller, "Casting a Wide Net";
Cox, "Labour Party in Leicester," 201–3. Probably the most
famous "movement culture" within the British labour
movement was Robert Blatchford's Clarion Fellowship.

39. *HS*, 26 Nov. 1907, 4; 12 Dec. 1907, 3; 17 Dec. 1907, 3; 28
Dec. 1907, 1; 7 Jan. 1908, 6. The ILP's candidate in 1912
was Harry Halford, who lost by 45 votes. *HH*, 13 April
1912, 12; 29 April 1912, 6; *LN*, 19 April 1912, 1; 26 April
1912, 1; 3 May 1912, 2.

40. *HH*, 25 Oct. 1911, 1; 11 Nov. 1911, 8; 15 Nov. 1911, 8; 21 Nov.
1911, 5; 22 Nov. 1911, 5; 24 Nov. 1911, 1; 25 Nov. 1911, 1; 5
Dec. 1911, 7; 12 Dec. 1911, 1, 12; 23 Dec. 1911, 8; 9 March
1912, 1; 13 March 1912; 29 April 1912, 6; *LN*, 12 Jan. 1912,
3; 2 Feb. 1912; 15 March 1912, 1; 19 April 1912, 1; 26 April
1912, 1; 3 May 1912, 2; 20 Dec. 1912; *IB*, July 1908; November 1911, 1; January 1912, 1. Roberts's account of his visit to
Hamilton was reprinted in *LN*, 2 Feb. 1912, 1. In the Crown
Point area of the South Wentworth riding, Barrett actually
ran second with 150 votes, against 271 for the Conservatives and 149 for the Liberals.

41. *IB*, 26 June 1914, 1; 3 July 1914, 1; *LN*, 13 May 1914, 1; 5
June 1914, 1; 12 June 1914, 1, 4, 8; 19 June 1914, 1, 4; 26 June
1914,1, 4; 3 July 1914, 1.

42. *HH*, 24 Oct. 1914, 1, 6; 26 Oct. 1914, 5; 28 Oct. 1914, 1; 31
Oct. 1914, 9, 15; 3 Nov. 1914, 2; 4 Nov. 1914, 2; 5 Nov. 1914,
2, 7; 7 Nov. 1914, 15; 9 Nov. 1914, 4; 10 Nov. 1914, 4; 13 Nov.
1914, 1; 14 Nov. 1914, 7; 16 Nov. 1914, 2; 18 Nov. 1914, 1, 9; 19
Nov. 1914, 1, 7; *LN*, 30 Oct. 1914, 1; 6 Nov. 1914, 1; 13 Nov.
1914, 1, 5, 8; 20 Nov. 1914, 1, 4; *IB*, 13 Nov. 1914, 3; 20 Nov.
1914, 1; 4 Dec. 1914, 2.

43. LAC, R10383-0-6-F, Vol. 11, 9558 (A. Studholme to W.L.M.
King, 6 Oct. 1908) (quotation); *Ottawa Journal*, quoted in
HH, 2 March 1912, 19; *HH*, 3 April 1909, 17.

44. After 1914 Studholme often appeared on platforms across
Ontario to promote new ILP organizations. But in Hamilton he was increasingly eclipsed by the younger labourists

who began to win seats in local municipal government.
His health began to fail in 1915, but he insisted on attending legislative sessions and maintaining his many
speaking engagements. The warm tribute paid to him by
all segments of Hamilton's population on his death in July
1919 bespoke the deep-rooted respect he had accumulated
in the community. Four years later local labour leaders
gathered to dedicate a new centre for labour meetings and
organizations, named in his honour the Allan Studholme
Memorial Labor Temple. *ND*, 7 June 1923, 2. For a fuller
account of Studholme's life and legislative career, see
Heron, "Studholme."

45. In 1908 the *Industrial Banner* lavished praise on the
Hamilton paper for its support, and in 1912 the new *Labor
News* called it "the people's paper." A banner in the 1911
ILP victory parade described the paper as "the Workingman's friend," and the crowd cheered heartily outside its
offices. *IB*, July 1908, 1; *LN*, 5 Jan. 1912, 2 (quotation); *HH*,
12 Dec. 1911, 12 (quotation).

46. *HH*, 25 Oct. 1911, 1 (quotation); 7 Nov. 1911, 1; *LN*, 25 Oct.
1912, 1 (quotation); 13 Feb. 1914, 4; 1 May 1914, 1; 30 Oct.
1914, 1. On the general phenomenon of the labourist "cultural baggage" brought over with British immigrants, see
McCormack, "British Working-Class Immigrants."

47. *HH*, 4 Jan. 1912, 1; 19 Jan. 1912, 11; 2 March 1912, 22; 2 Aug.
1912, 11; 11 Dec. 1912, 7; 17 Dec. 1912, 4; 19 Dec. 1912, 1; 20
Dec. 1912, 4; 9 Jan. 1913, 1; 16 Jan. 1913, 4; 21 Jan. 1913, 12;
4 Feb. 1913, 13; 13 Feb. 1913, 7; 24 Feb. 1913, 7; 24 March
1913, 2; 14 April 1913; 9 May 1913, 13; 24 Jan. 1914, 6; 26
March 1914, 12; *HT*, 8 Jan. 1914, 5; *HS*, 26 March 1914, 15.
The district also had Homeside and Mount Hamilton
Improvement societies. *HH*, 5 Jan. 1913, 3; 7 Feb. 1913, 4;
3 Jan. 1914, 1.

48. On the formation of Liberal and Conservative clubs in the
east end, see *LN*, 13 Feb. 1914, 1.

49. *LN*, 19 June 1914, 1 (quotation), 4 (quotation); 3 July 1914, 1
(quotation); 6 Nov. 1914, 1 (quotation); *HH*, 5 Nov. 1914, 1;
6 Nov. 1914, 1 (quotation). The Tories charged Rollo with
trying to introduce "class representation." *LN*, 12 Nov.
1914, 6.

50. *LN*, 7 Aug. 1914, 4 (quotation); 15 Oct. 1914, 1; *HH*, 15 Oct.
1914, 4 (quotation). 31 Oct. 1914, 15 (quotation).

51. *IB*, quoted in *LN*, 7 May 1915, 1.

52. *LN*, 15 Jan. 1915, 1; 14 May 1915, 1; 21 May 1915, 1; 28 May
1915, 1; 11 June 1915, 1; 13 Aug. 1915, 1.

53. *LN*, 18 Feb., 17 March, 8 April, 29 Dec. 1916; 15 March
1918; 31 Jan., 19 Dec. 1919; 20 Aug. 1920; 28 March, 22
April 1922; *HH*, 22 Feb. 1917, 22 March 1918; HPL, Independent Labor Party, Central Branch, Minutes, 25 Feb.
1921, 30–31.

54. *IB*, 10 July 1914, 3; *LN*, 3 July 1914, 1; 2 Oct. 1914, 1; 16 Oct.
1914, 1; 30 Oct. 1914, 1; 29 March 1918, 1; 31 Jan. 1919, 1;
HH, 28 Jan. 1918, 6; 8 Feb. 1918, 2; *HS*, 31 Jan. 1919, 1.

55. *LN*, 4 Dec. 1914, 1; 11 Dec. 1914, 4; 1 Jan. 1915, 1; 8 Jan. 1915, 1; 11 June 1915, 1; 9 July 1915, 1; 17 Dec. 1915, 1; 24 Dec. 1915, 1; 14 Jan. 1916, 4; 17 Nov. 1916, 1; 24 Nov. 1916, 1; 8 Dec. 1916, 1; 15 Dec. 1916, 1; 22 Dec. 1916, 1; 29 Dec. 1916, 1; *IB*, 7 Jan. 1916, 1; 17 Nov. 1916, 1; 4 Jan. 1918, 2; *HH*, 9 Dec. 1914, 2; 31 Dec. 1914, 14, 15; 9 July 1915, 12; 8 Jan. 1916, 6; 12 Jan. 1916, 1; 11 Nov. 1916, 5; 1 Dec. 1916, 11; 16 Dec. 1916, 10; 22 Dec. 1916, 5; 29 Dec. 1916, 1; 3 Jan. 1917, 1; 9 Jan. 1917, 1; *HS*, 21 Dec. 1917, 1. On Halcrow, see Heron, "Halcrow." For the detailed results of these ILP municipal campaigns, see Table 42. The various parties agreed to acclamation of all municipal office-holders for 1918.

56. *LN*, 26 Oct. 1917, 1; 2 Nov. 1917, 1; 9 Nov. 1917, 1; 30 Nov. 1917, 1; 7 Dec. 1917, 1; 14 Dec. 1917, 1; *IB*, 16 Nov. 1917, 1; 23 Nov. 1917, 12; 30 Nov. 1917, 2, 4; 7 Dec. 1917, 4; 28 Dec. 1917, 4; 4 Jan. 1918, 2; *HH*, 18 Jan. 1918, 1; *HS*, 4 Dec. 1917, 7; 7 Dec. 1917, 10; 13 Dec. 1917, 19; Robin, *Radical Politics*, 136–37. For the statistical results, see Table 41.

57. *IB*, 30 Nov. 1917, 4 (quotation).

58. *IB*, 30 Nov. 1917, 4 (quotation).

59. *LN*, 14 Dec. 1917, 1 (quotations); 25 Jan. 1918, 1; 25 Oct. 1918, 1; Fudge and Tucker, *Labour before the Law*, 96–101; Conner, *National War Labor Board*.

60. Heron and Siemiatycki, "Great War, the State, and Working-Class Canada"; Heron, "National Contours."

61. *LN*, 20 Dec. 1918, 1 (quotation). Other labour groups across North America mimicked Wilson's "Fourteen Points"; see, for example, Strouthous, *US Labor and Political Action*, 178–80.

62. *LN*, 13 Dec. 1918, 1; 20 Dec. 1918, 12; 3 Jan. 1919, 1; *HH*, 7 Dec. 1918, 7; 23 Dec. 1918, 1; 31 Dec. 1918, 1; 2 Jan. 1919, 1, 6 (quotation); *HS*, 2 Jan. 1919, 6 (quotation). By September 1919 the appointment process had also given the ILP three more members on the school board, one on the Board of Health, and one on the local housing commission. *LN*, 3 Sept. 1919, 2.

63. *LN*, 7 March 1919, 4; 14 March 1919, 1; *HS*, 21 Feb. 1919, 1; 7 March 1919, 6, 23; 8 March 1919, 13; 4 March 1919, 9; 17 March 1919, 1 (quotation).

64. *IB*, 8 Aug. 1919, 1; *ND*, 25 Dec. 1919, 1; *LL*, 21 Nov. 1919, 1; 9 Jan. 1920, 1; 16 Jan. 1920, 1 (quotation).

65. Oliver, *Public and Private Persons*, 18–43; Tennyson "Ontario General Election of 1919"; English, *Decline of Politics*, 224–27; Naylor, *New Democracy*, 215–19.

66. *LN*, 8 Aug. 1919, 1; 15 Aug. 1919, 1, 2; 12 Sept. 1919, 1; 26 Sept. 1919, 6; 17 Oct. 1919, 1; *LL*, 10 Oct. 1919, 1, 3; *HS*, 22 Sept. 1919, 5; 2 Oct. 1919, 22; 3 Oct. 1919, 19; 4 Oct. 1919, 6; 6 Oct. 1919, 7.

67. *HS*, 14 Oct. 1919, 14 (quotation); *LN*, 10 Oct. 1919, 2 (quotation), 4 (quotation).

68. *HS*, 21 Oct. 1919, 1 (quotation), 6 (quotation). For the ILP members joining the coalition government, see Naylor, *New Democracy*, 215–44.

69. The British and Australian parallels are the most obvious, but there were also new Labour parties in the United States, at the local and state level in several major states and briefly in a national party in 1919–20. Shapiro, "'Hand and Brain'"; Strouthous, *US Labor and Political Action*.

70. That unity was also evident in Britain, but in the United States the Socialist Party of America kept its distance from the new Labour party movement, although many individual socialists shifted their allegiance. Weinstein, *Decline of Socialism*, 222–29.

71. *CW*, 16 June 1910, 3; 14 July 1910, 3; 13 Oct. 1910, 3; 8 Dec. 1910, 3; 2 Feb. 1911, 3; 6 April 1911, 3; 22 June 1911, 3; 7 Nov. 1912, 3; 23 Jan. 1913, 2; 4 Sept. 1913; *HH*, 11 April 1910, 2; 29 Aug. 1910, 7; 16 Jan. 1911, 9; 18 March 1911, 1; 28 April 1911, 5; 1 May 1911, 3; 17 June 1911, 15; 18 March 1912, 11; 26 Oct. 1912, 14; 14 Dec. 1912, 13; 17 Dec. 1912, 12; 18 Dec. 1912, 9; 22 Jan. 1913, 9; 12 April 1913, 9; McKay, *Reasoning Otherwise*, 174–78.

72. *CW*, 18 Sept. 1913, 4; 25 Sept. 1913, 4; 9 Oct. 1913, 3; 23 Oct. 1913, 2; 11 Dec. 1913, 3; 25 Dec. 1913, 4; 15 Jan. 1914, 3; 29 Jan. 1914, 3; 12 March 1914, 4; 9 April 1914, 2; *HT*, 28 March 1914, 5; *HS*, 9 April 1914, 1; 20 April 1914, 11; *LN*, 17 April 1914, 1; 24 April 1914, 1. On 17 June 1913 the *Herald* published a letter from an outraged citizen who objected to literature "of such a nature as would tend to undermine the belief in revealed religion" being distributed on the Sabbath.

73. *CW*, 29 Jan. 1914, 3; 18 June 1914, 4 (quotations); *HH*, 10 Sept. 1914, 4; 3 June 1915, 1; 4 June 1915, 15; 14 Feb. 1916, 4; 3 April 1916, 10; 1 May 1916, 9; *IB*, 21 April 1916; *Canadian Forward*, 27 Jan. 1917, 5; 10 Feb. 1917, 3; 24 Feb. 1917, 5; 10 May 1917, 4. The closer co-operation between the Social Democrats and the labourists was evident elsewhere, notably in Toronto, where the SDP's James Simpson won a seat on the city's Board of Control in 1914. Homel, "James Simpson"; McKay, *Reasoning Otherwise*, 193–98.

74. *IB*, 6 July 1917, 1–2 (quotation).

75. *IB*, 28 Oct. 1916, 4, 8 (quotation); *CW*, 7 Nov. 1912, 3; 1 May 1913, 3; 31 July 1913, 3; 28 Aug. 1913; 6 Aug. 1914; 20 Aug. 1914; 3 Sept. 1914; 1 Oct. 1914; *IB*, 6 April 1917, 2 (quotation); 12 July 1917 (quotation).

76. *HH*, 9 June 1917, 3; 12 July 1917, 1; 14 July 1917, 3; *LN*, 29 June 1917, 1.

77. *IB*, 23 Nov. 1917, 12; 30 Nov. 1917, 2; 7 Dec. 1917, 1; *LN*, 30 Nov. 1917, 1; 7 Dec. 1917, 1; 14 Dec. 1917, 1 (quotation); *HS*, 28 Nov. 1917, 6; 3 Dec. 1917, 16; 4 Dec. 1917, 7; 6 Dec. 1917, 20; 7 Dec. 1917, 10.

78. In the ensuing months he energetically promoted the sales of subscriptions to the *Banner* in the Hamilton area. *IB*, 28 Dec. 1917, 4; 4 Jan. 1918, 2; 15 March 1918, 4; 12 April 1918, 4.

79. See, for example, the editorials "Labor Power," *LN*, 3 May 1918, 1; "To Live upon Unpaid Labor," *LN*, 17 May 1918, 1; and "Labor Must Realize Its Power," *LN*, 31 May 1918, 1.

80. See in particular his two-part article, "Safety First in Municipal Politics," *LN*, 20 Dec. 1918, 3; 27 Dec. 1918, 1.

81. *LN*, 9 Aug. 1918.

82. *Canadian Forward*, 10 April 1918, 4; *LN*, 28 June 1918, 1; Naylor, *New Democracy*, 105–11. The *Herald* was so disturbed by this new vein of labour journalism that it denounced Gordon Nelson, the nominal editor of the *Labor News*, as a closet Bolshevik. *HH*, 31 Dec. 1918, 1.

83. *LN*, 15 Feb. 1918, 1; 29 March 1918, 1; 26 April 1918, 1; 7 June 1918, 1; 14 June 1918, 1; 19 July 1918, 1; 16 Aug. 1918, 1; 20 Sept. 1918, 1; 18 Oct. 1918, 1; 31 Jan. 1919, 1; 16 Jan. 1920, 1; 2 April 1920, 1; *IB*, 22 March, 30 Aug. 1918; *ND*, 11 Dec. 1919, 2; 31 Dec. 1919; 18 March 1920, 1; *HH*, 22 March 1918, 15; 10 May 1918, 4; *LL*, 16 Jan. 1920, 2. On labour churches in Canada, see Allen, *Social Passion*, 159–74.

84. *HS*, 31 Jan. 1919, 1; *LN*, 7 March 1919, 4; 25 April 1919, 1 (quotations); 2 May 1919, 6; 9 May 1919, 2; 30 May 1919, 1; *HH*, 10 May 1919, 7; 28 May 1919, 11.

85. *LN*, 31 Jan. 1919, 1 (quotation).

86. *LN*, 12 Dec. 1919, 1; 25 Dec. 1919, 1; 9 Jan. 1920, 1; 18 Nov. 1930, 1; 2 Dec. 1920, 1; 9 Dec. 1920, 1; 16 Dec. 1920, 1; 6 Jan. 1921, 1; HPL, ILP, Central Branch, Minutes, 12 Nov.–10 Dec. 1920; 11 March 1921.

87. *HS*, 21 Nov. 1921, 11; 25 Nov. 1921, 1; 28 Nov. 1921, 21; 1 Dec. 1921, 11; 5 Dec. 1921, 20; 7 Dec. 1921, 1 (quotation); HPL, ILP, Central Branch, Minutes, 30 Sept.–3 Nov. 1921; *LN*, 29 Nov. 1921, 1; 23 Dec. 1921, 1; *ND*, 1 Dec. 1921, 2. Etherington's politics had created the same kind of animosity within his church that J.S. Woodsworth, William Irvine, A.E. Smith, and Salem Bland faced in this period.

88. HPL, ILP, Central Branch, Minutes, 9 Dec. 1921; *LN*, 23 Dec. 1921, 1; 28 Jan. 1922, 1; *ND*, 5 Jan. 1922, 1; 4 Jan. 1923, 1.

89. *ND*, 5 July 1923, 1.

90. See Table 42.

91. Heron, ed., *Workers' Revolt*.

92. *LN*, 30 Nov. 1917, 1 (quotation); 25 April 1919 (quotations); 18 Nov. 1920, 1; 29 April 1921, 2; *IB*, 1 Feb. 1918, 1; *ND*, 25 Nov. 1920, 1; 7 April 1921, 2; 1 Dec. 1921, 4; *HS*, 23 April 1921, 12; HPL, ILP, Central Branch, Minutes, 3 Nov. 1921.

93. *LN*, 25 Dec. 1919, 1 (quotation).

94. *ND*, 10 July 1919, 1; 9 Oct. 1919, 2 (quotations). Flatman was not alone in this reorientation of his radicalism; see Peterson, "One Big Union."

95. The Association managed to garner only 11 per cent of the vote when it ran ILP alderman Sam Lawrence in the 1925 federal election (when only half the voters went to the polls), and decided to sit out the federal contest a year later. For the provincial election that year it nominated an outsider, A.E. Smith, the Communist clergyman who had recently migrated from Manitoba and now headed the CLP's Ontario Section. The local organization collapsed soon after his crushing defeat (with only 3 per cent of the vote). The next year the Ontario Section finally split irrevocably, and the right wing immediately formed a new Labor Party of Ontario, with support from the remnants of the East Hamilton ILP. *HH*, 16 July 1924; 20 Dec. 1924; *LN*, 27 July 1923; 30 Jan. 1925, 4; 31 July 1925, 1; 27 Aug. 1926, 1; 28 Jan. 1927, 1; *CLW*, 31 July 1924, 2; 23 Oct. 1925, 2; 31 Aug. 1926, 1; HPL, ILP, Central Branch, Minutes, 27 Oct., 10 Nov. 1922; 28 March 1924–26 June 1925; *Worker*, 25 July 1925, 1, 2; 17 April 1926, 1, 4; 14 Aug. 1926, 1; 30 April 1917, 2, 5; 19 Nov. 1927, 1, 4; 17 March 1928, 3; 24 March 1928, 2; 21 April 1928, 1; Smith, *All My Life*, 87; Rodney, *Soldiers*, 97–106. Lawrence remained involved in the Labor Representation Political Association and on the provincial council of the CLP. The Hamilton lodge of the Iron, Steel, and Tin Workers and the Hamilton Workmen's Circle also sent delegates to the last meeting of the Ontario section in April 1928.

96. See Table 38.

97. *IB*, 6 July 1917, 1.

98. See Saville, "Ideology of Labourism"; Heron, "Labourism."

99. Ashcraft, "Liberal Political Theory," 250 (quotation); Thompson, *Making of the English Working Class*, 105 (quotation); Jones, *Languages of Class*, 90–178; Biagini and Reid, "Currents of Radicalism."

100. HPL, ILP, Central Branch, Minutes, 9 Nov. 1921.

101. This was the ingredient that was missing from the particular political mix that created Western labour radicalism in this period; defending the manufacturing interest was not a crucial component in the political economy of the West. Heron, "Labourism," 68–70.

102. In his own article, Halford called for "absolute unity and co-operation between business man, farmer and wage earner" to buy Canadian. *ND*, 28 Jan. 1920, 2; 7 April 1920, 1 (quotation). The *Labor News* was equally, if less stridently, committed to the "Made-in-Canada" movement. See, for example, 19 March 1920, 1.

103. *LN*, 22 Aug. 1919, 1; 9 April 1920, 2 (quotation); 30 April 1920, 1; *ND*, 8 April 1920, 2; 29 April 1920, 2; 20 May 1920, 1; *IB*, 25 Nov. 1921, 3; *HS*, 29 Nov. 1921, 20 (quotation).

104. Representation had been a central strand in 19th-century working-class radicalism; Lawrence, "Popular Radicalism," 167–70.

105. *HS*, 29 Dec. 1903, 9 (quotation); *HH*, 11 Nov. 1911, 7 (quotation); *IMJ*, December 1913, 1048 (quotation); *LN*, 14 Dec. 1917, 1; 3 Jan. 1918, 1 (quotation).

106. *LN*, 10 Jan. 1919, 3; 17 Jan. 1919, 1 (quotation); 28 Nov. 1922, 1 (quotation); *HH*, 13 Jan. 1919, 1; 14 Jan. 1919, 6; *ND*, 14 Jan. 1920, 1.

107. *LN*, 30 June 1916, 1 (quotation); 24 Feb. 1922, 2 (quotation).

108. Saville, "Ideology of Labourism," 222.

109. *LN*, 24 Jan. 1919, 2; 28 Feb. 1919, 2 (quotation); *ND*, 7 Jan. 1920, 2 (quotation).

110. *LN*, 12 Dec. 1919, 1; *ND*, 4 Dec. 1919, 2 (quotation).

111. *LN*, 2 April 1920, 2; HPL, ILP, Central Branch, Minutes, 23 Dec. 1921; 28 Nov. 1923.

112. *LN*, 2 Dec. 1920, 1; 9 Dec. 1920, 1; 28 Nov. 1922, 1; *ND*, 4 Jan. 1923, 4; ILP, Central Branch Minutes, 26 Jan. 1923, 9 Feb. 1923, 23 Feb. 1923. O'Heir stayed on city council as an independent and then as a Conservative. *HS*, 2 Dec. 1924, 1.

113. *ND*, 4 Jan. 1923, 4; 1 Feb. 1923, 1; 5 July 1923, 1, 2; *CLW*, 2 Aug. 1923, 3; 17 Dec. 1923, 2; 28 Aug. 1924, 2; 26 March 1925, 2; *LOC*, 1926, 206; *Worker*, 10 Oct. 1925, 2; *HS*, 18 July 1930, 11.

114. Halcrow's criticisms continued and escalated until he was displaced as the ILP's house leader in February 1922. Naylor, *New Democracy*, 215–44; *ND*, 28 Jan. 1920, 1 (quotation); 5 Sept. 1921, 1; 1 Oct. 1921, 1; *LL*, 12 April 1920, 7; *LN*, 29 July 1921, 1; HPL, ILP, Central Branch, Minutes, 22 July 1921, 26 Aug. 1921, 14 Oct. 1921, 28 Oct. 1921, 11 March 1922; *HS*, 28 Sept. 1921, 1; 9 Feb. 1922, 4; *HH*, 3 March 1922 (quotation).

115. *ND*, 5 April 1923, 2; *LN*, 27 April 1923, 1; 25 May 1923, 1; 21 June 1923, 4 (quotation).

116. *HS*, 14 June 1923, 1; HPL, ILP, Central Branch, Minutes, 11 May 1923 (quotation).

117. *ND*, 23 Oct. 1919, 2 (quotation).

18. Unassailable Rights

1. *HS*, 31 Jan. 1919, 5.

2. On the creation of a public sphere of discourse outside the state in the 19th century, see Calhoun, ed., *Habermas and the Public Sphere*. For a stimulating discussion of the working-class intervention into the bourgeois public sphere, see Hurd, "Class, Masculinity, Manners, and Mores."

3. See, for example, *WG*, 15 Oct. 1921, 2.

4. See, for example, *HS*, 9 Feb. 1921, 1.

5. Quoted in Owram, *Government Generation*, 100.

6. Traves, *State and Enterprise*.

7. Allen, *Social Passion* (quotations at 73–74); Turkstra, "Christianity and the Working Class," 24–164.

8. During the 1906 street-railway strike and the 1916 machinists' battle, several had intervened to promote an arbitrated solution. Just before the war, under the crusading leadership of the city's lone Congregationalist minister and head of the interdenominational Ministerial Association, W.E. Gilroy, some had also placed themselves at the forefront of public agitation to address the severe unemployment crisis. Turkstra, "Christianity and the Working Class," 165–231.

9. Turkstra, "Christianity and the Working Class," 81–82 (quotation); Allen, *Social Passion*. Early in 1920 *Social Welfare* undertook a major survey of company welfare programs in 53 plants. *SW*, 1 Aug. 1920, 316–17.

10. Turkstra, "Christianity and the Working Class," 231–41; Allen, *Social Passion*; Moir, *Enduring Witness*, 213 (quotation); Heron, "Etherington"; Christie and Gauvreau, "World of the Common People"; Christie and Gauvreau, *Full-Orbed Christianity*.

11. Hamilton industrialists and labour leaders continued this kind of dialogue in the National Industrial Conference, the larger, but equally ineffective forum called together in September by the federal government to discuss labour relations. LAC, R3096-0-8-E, Vol. 12 (CMA, Executive Council), 27 Feb. 1919; 27 March 1919; *HH*, 1 Feb. 1919, 1; 13 Feb. 1919, 1; 18 Feb. 1919, 1; *LN*, 21 Feb. 1919, 1; *HS*, 22 Feb. 1919, 19; 24 Feb. 1919, 6, 9; 26 Feb. 1919, 17; 28 Feb. 1919, 1; 7 March 1919, 21; 26 Aug. 1919, 1; Naylor, *New Democracy*, 196–97; Fudge and Tucker, *Labour before the Law*, 122. The local government Employment Bureau's report for 1919 noted that the Triangle Committee "failed to accomplish the objects for which it was organized and was discontinued." OTLBR 1919, 21.

12. This was not an entirely surprising development because as far back as 1902 many prominent Hamilton businessmen had signed an open letter against prohibition, and ten years later 31 local industrialists and merchants had similarly denounced the drastic reduction of liquor licences in the city. Heron, *Booze*, 197. In 1924 Hamilton's Moderation League had George C. Thomson, a prominent lawyer, and industrialists George M. Hendrie and W.B. Champ as its chief officers, and executives of Tuckett Tobacco, Hamilton Bridge Works, Steel Company of Canada, Canada Steel Goods, Dominion Canners, and Canadian Westinghouse, along with several corporate lawyers and merchants, on its steering committee. *HS*, 11 Oct. 1924, 5.

13. Heron, *Booze*, 196–99 (including quotations); *HS*, 16 Aug. 1919, 1.

14. Lawrence, "Class and Gender," 646; Hallowell, *Prohibition*, 80 (quotation).

15. Charles, *Service Clubs*; *HH*, 19 April 1924 (quotation); 10 May 1924; 5 Feb. 1927; 20 June 1928; 21 March 1930; 18 Jan. 1933 (clippings in HPL Scrapbook); *HS*, 19 Jan. 1925, 5 (quotation); 11 April 1925; 6 Aug. 1925, 5; 1 May 1926; 2 Feb. 1927; 7 July 1938 (clippings in HPL Scrapbook); HPL, HCC, Board of Directors, Minutes, 19 Oct. 1920. The Kinsmen club was founded in Hamilton in 1920 as a local organization among younger businessmen and professionals; it soon expanded across Canada as a more nationalistic organization. Coates and McGuinness, *Only in Canada*.

16. *HS*, 18 Jan. 1925, 5.

17. The Chamber undertook an energetic recruitment drive, adopted a new constitution in mid-May, and held

the first meeting of its new board of directors at the end of the month. *HS*, 3 Feb. 1920, 16; 17 April 1920, 6 (quotations); 1 May 1920, 26; 10 May 1920, 22; 13 May 1920, 22; HPL, HCC, Board of Directors, Minutes, 25 May 1920.

18. *LN*, 14 May 1920, 1 (quotation). The Trades and Labor Council's appointee was one of its most conservative members, Fester, who as editor of *New Democracy* approached the Chamber about placing a letter in its Christmas issue "giving reasons why Chambers of Commerce are not antagonistic to labor interests." HPL, Hamilton Chamber of Commerce, Board of Directors, Minutes, 9 Aug. 1920, 7 Dec. 1920.

19. *HS*, 29 April 1920, 21 (quotations). At one of the Chamber's well-publicized lunches, a guest speaker from Chatham proclaimed the virtues of industrial councils as a means of promoting labour-management co-operation; *HS*, 10 Feb. 1921, 9.

20. HPL, HCC, Board of Directors, Minutes, 3 May 1921, 10 May 1921, 30 May 1922.

21. The Chamber was thus a kissing cousin of the "Citizens' Committees" that appeared in Western Canada and the United States, notably during the Winnipeg General Strike, to establish an organizing centre outside the state to appropriate some state functions and to direct governments along appropriate lines. See Mitchell, "'To Uphold Organized Society'"; Kramer and Mitchell, *When the State Trembled*.

22. *HS*, 6 Oct. 1920, 22. By 1925 the Chamber was advertising a "Business Training Course" of 11 weekly lectures on topics related to Canadian resource development. *HS*, 28 Oct. 1925, 26.

23. HPL, HCC, Board of Directors, Minutes, 1920–39; on municipal government, see 26 July, 27 Nov., 9 Dec. 1921, 11 April 1922.

24. *HS*, 2 April 1919, 1; Morton, "'Kicking and Complaining'"; Cook, *Shock Troops*, 581–610. The city's dispersal centre opened only in March and closed in July. *HS*, 10 March 1919, 11; 15 July 1919, 15.

25. The local newspapers published news about returning troops every week. See, for example, *HS*, 15 Nov. 1918, 7; 4 Dec. 1918, 1; 19 Dec. 1919, 1; 22 Jan. 1919, 19; 27 Jan. 1919, 3; 6 March 1919, 11; 29 March 1919, 1; 8 April 1919, 1; 26 April 1919, 5; 9 June 1919, 4.

26. *HS*, 11 April 1918, 13; HPL, Soldiers' Aid Commission, Minutes; Morton and Wright, *Winning the Second Battle*, 105–19.

27. Morton, *Fight or Pay*; Morton, *When Your Number's Up*; Morton and Wright, *Winning the Second Battle* (quotation at 117); Brown, "Shell Shock." See, for example, letters to the editor from W. Herron and W. Tye; *HS*, 19 Dec. 1918, 5; 29 April 1920, 21.

28. *HS*, 2 April 1918, 1 (quotation); see also 8 Nov. 1918, 3, 6.

29. *HH*, 5 Jan. 1917, 2, 9; 3 June 1917, 8; *Veteran*, December 1917, 24; Morton, *Winning the Second Battle*, 70–72.

30. The Army and Navy Veterans had existed since the late 19th century, incorporating veterans of earlier wars. The Great War Veterans' Association restricted its membership to those who had served overseas (a restriction challenged by the East Hamilton branch soon after its formation in the fall of 1918). The Veterans of France, a purely local group made up of disgruntled members of the Great War Veterans, was organized in November 1918 to include only those who actually served in a battle zone ("first degree"), with an auxiliary status for those who got no further than England ("second degree"). The Originals, a purely social group formed in April 1919, took in only those from the First Contingent sent overseas. The Honourably Discharged Soldiers' Association took in those who had not seen service in the war zone, and the Grand Army of Canada opened its ranks to all veterans regardless of where they had served. *HS*, 25 May 1918, 1; 16 Sept. 1918, 3; 30 Nov. 1918, 3; 3 Dec. 1918, 10; 4 Dec. 1918, 9; 5 Feb. 1919, 19; 16 April 1919, 23; 23 April 1919, 17.

31. In April 1919 a proposal from the Veterans of France that representatives of all these organizations meet quarterly to discuss common concerns went nowhere. Over the summer public discussion about the need for more unity continued, and in August three of the smaller groups agreed to form a Soldiers' and Sailors' Welfare League. The Great War Veterans voted to stay out, however. *HS*, 16 April 1919, 23; 3 June 1919, 13; 6 June 1919, 17; 7 June 1919, 7; 11 June 1919, 17; 13 June 1919, 21; 16 June 1919, 7; 25 July 1919, 18; 29 July 1919, 7; 30 July 1919, 6; 31 July 1919, 7; 2 Aug. 1919, 5; 5 Aug. 1919, 13; 6 Aug. 1919, 5.

32. The secretary of the Great War Veterans, Richard Dawson, told a reporter in the summer of 1917 that "the returned soldiers had had enough of the regimental method of organization while with the fighting forces," and declared his opposition to "any officer assuming leadership" by right rather than merit. *HH*, 14 July 1917, 1.

33. *HS*, 6 June 1919, 31.

34. *HS*, 12 Dec. 1918, 19; 23 Jan. 1919, 5; 30 Jan. 1919, 8; 8 Feb. 1919, 3; 8 March 1919, 5; 21 March 1919, 26; 22 March 1919, 8; 1 May 1919, 21; 6 May 1919, 16; 29 May 1919, 17; 15 Aug. 1919, 8.

35. *HS*, 20 Jan. 1919, 9; 21 Feb. 1919, 13; 22 Feb. 1919, 19; 26 March 1919, 14; 31 March 1919, 10; 4 April 1919, 20; 21 April 1919, 19; 17 July 1919, 10; 30 Dec. 1919, 10.

36. *HS*, 19 Feb. 1918, 1; 10 April 1918, 19; 16 April 1918, 12; 30 Jan. 1919, 8; 27 March 1919, 19; 29 May 1919, 17; 26 Nov. 1919, 18; 24 Feb. 1920, 1.

37. *HS*, 2 April 1919, 23; 21 April 1919, 19; 22 April 1919, 13; 23 April 1919, 17; 6 May 1919, 16; 7 Aug. 1919, 6; 3 Feb. 1920, 19.

38. *Veteran*, December 1917, 9–10.

39.   *HS*, 23 May 1918, 19.

40.   In January 1918 the Great War Veterans' local executive had a colonel, two majors, a sergeant major, a sergeant, a corporal, and a private. A few months later the national executive had six officers and six enlisted men. William Hendrie had served on the local executive for some time and was elected a national vice-president at that point. In the demobilization period in 1919 he often led veterans' parades. *HS*, 6 Aug. 1918, 8; 17 July 1919, 1.

41.   *HS*, 14 Nov. 1918, 19. "I fear that if we get into the political game we shall be like the ass that donned the lion's skin," Hendrie warned in 1918. "We have lots of roar, but we haven't got much bite yet. We don't want to antagonize our own friends." *HS*, 25 March 1918, 13. Governments recognized the importance of such a stabilizing force in civil society, and in Ontario doled out a $50,000 grant to the Great War Veterans. *HS*, 23 May 1918, 1.

42.   *HS*, 10 June 1919, 13; 17 June 1919, 9.

43.   *HS*, 7 March 1918, 1 (quotation); 12 April 1919, 8 (quotation); 5 June 1919, 17 (quotation); *Veteran*, December 1917, 10 (quotation).

44.   To the extent that it is possible to identify executive members of the Great War Veterans' branches from newspaper accounts and then find them in city directories, the Central group was dominated by white-collar clerical workers, with a handful of powerful men like William Hendrie and Heming, while the East Hamilton and Mount Hamilton branches had working-class leadership. Albert Peart, a news agent, was initially president of the east-end group, but by the fall of 1919 William Jordon, an electrician, had taken over, and William Herron, a bricklayer, was vice-president. At that point, the Mount Hamilton executive was also filled with blue-collar workers. *HS*, 16 Oct. 1918, 15; 14 Nov. 1918, 19; 26 Nov. 1918, 19; 7 Jan. 1919, 11; 22 Jan. 1919, 11; 5 Feb. 1919, 19; 22 April 1919, 13; 12 June 1919, 17; 28 June 1919, 7; 1 Aug. 1919, 18; 5 Sept. 1919, 1; 12 Sept. 1919, 4; *VCHD*, 1919–21.

45.   At the Great War Veterans' national convention in Vancouver in July, delegates adopted a hard-hitting resolution against profiteers and "capitalistic combines which sought by economic pressures to control the governing bodies of Canada." It called for "recovery, by income or other taxes, of excessive profits, the removal of exemption from taxation of Victory bonds over one thousand dollars, and conscription of wealth." *HS*, 26 June 1919, 16 (quotation); 7 July 1919, 5 (quotation).

46.   At their national convention, the Great War Veterans' conservative leadership managed to deflect the surging interest in gratuities into a resolution calling on the federal government to establish a joint commission with the association to study the scheme. Citing financial stringency, Robert Borden and his cabinet flatly rejected such an idea. Privately government officials scoffed at the idea

of handouts to men who needed to learn to survive on their own labour power in peacetime labour markets. *HS*, 21 June 1919, 10 (quotation); 23 Sept. 1919, 6 (quotation); 9 July 1919, 12 (quotation).

47.   In the face of such sentiments arising in similar meetings across the country, the Borden government turned the issue over to a parliamentary committee. During September and October delegations of veterans duly arrived in Ottawa to present their case, and Great War Veterans' leaders proposed an elaborate compromise for a means-tested gratuity. But the committee refused to bite. The gratuity was rejected. *HS*, 8 Sept. 1919, 7; 9 Sept. 1919, 1; 11 Sept. 1919, 23; 12 Sept. 1919, 4; 12 Sept. 1919, 4 (quotation). The only Hamilton veteran to appear before the committee was Peart, who was speaking on behalf of a mass meeting of Imperial Reservists, and who urged the government to tax the "unearned increment" of profiteering businesses. Canada, House of Commons, *Journals*, 56 (1920), Appendix, 673–81.

48.   *HS*, 15 Sept. 1919, 7, 14; 17 Sept. 1919, 1, 20; 18 Sept. 1919, 6 (quotation); 4 Oct. 1919, 4; 8 Oct. 1919, 24; 9 Oct. 1919, 4; 16 Oct. 1919, 24; 17 Oct. 1919, 18; 29 Oct. 1919, 18; 3 Nov. 1919, 5; *LL*, 19 Sept. 1919, 2; Morton and Wright, "Bonus Campaign."

49.   *HS*, 13 Nov. 1919, 4; 17 Nov. 1919, 15; 18 Nov. 1919, 10; 19 Nov. 1919, 17; 26 Nov. 1919, 18; 5 Dec. 1919, 17. In a similar spirit of openness, the Great War Veterans voted solidly in a national referendum to open their ranks to ex-soldiers who did not serve overseas. *HS*, 29 Nov. 1919, 26.

50.   *HS*, 3 Jan. 1920, 4; 13 Jan. 1920, 17; 22 Jan. 1920, 3; 23 Jan. 1920, 27; 26 Jan. 1920, 13; 28 Jan. 1920, 17; 29 Jan. 1920, 12; 3 Feb. 1920, 19; 9 Feb. 1920, 1; 12 Feb. 1920, 5; 17 March 1920, 22. The petition was presented to parliament in March.

51.   *HS*, 5 April 1920, 7; 24 April 1919, 26; 26 April 1919, 17. The Great War Veterans had declined Flynn's offer to join the merger. *HS*, 24 March 1920, 21. Over the next several months both the Honourably Discharged Soldiers and Sailors and the Originals merged into the local Great War Veterans, which reaffirmed its unwillingness to merge with other groups in 1922. *Veteran*, 28 Jan. 1922, 12; 18 Nov. 1922, 8. The East End Branch had ceased functioning by the end of 1922 and had to be revived. *HS*, 9 Dec. 1922, 8; 16 Dec. 1922, 13; 23 Dec. 1922, 9.

52.   *HS*, 28 Aug. 1919, 4; 4 Sept. 1919, 12; 17 Oct. 1919, 1, 18 Oct. 1919, 7 (quotation).

53.   *HS*, 27 Sept. 1919, 1; 29 Sept. 1919, 1; 1 Oct. 1919, 15; 3 Oct. 1919, 19; 6 Oct. 1919, 7, 11; 8 Oct. 1919, 15; 9 Oct. 1919, 13; 10 Oct. 1919, 1; 11 Oct. 1919, 3 (quotation); 14 Oct. 1919, 13; 15 Oct. 1919, 1; *LN*, 5 Aug. 1919, 2; 10 Oct. 1919, 1; 24 Oct. 1919, 1; *LL*, 10 Oct. 1919, 1, 3; 17 Oct. 1919, 1. The *Spectator* was particularly surprised at the size of Halcrow's victory in Ward 8, popularly known as "Little England," which

had "set the pace in enlistments for the rest of the city," but where "strangely, the soldier candidate was snowed under." *HS*, 21 Oct. 1919, 1.

54. *HS*, 29 Nov. 1919, 26; 2 Dec. 1919, 9; 30 Dec. 1919, 4; 21 Jan. 1920, 19; *Veteran*, February 1920, 17. The editor of the *Veteran* did a careful comparison of the labour and farmer platforms and that of the Great War Veterans to help focus that discussion. *Veteran*, March 1920, 13.

55. They had helped launch the Soldiers' and Sailors' Labor Party in August, but, after Landers co-opted it and changed the name to Political League, it disappeared into the Discharged Soldiers' and Sailors' Federation. The ILP had approached the East Hamilton Great War Veterans about jointly nominating William Herron, a returned soldier and ILP member, but the association turned to Landers instead. The ILP also endorsed the gratuity demanded at Flynn's mass meeting in mid-September, but an effort to get the United Veterans' League endorsement foundered in mid-October. Discussions continued into November. *LN*, 8 Aug. 1919, 1; 15 Aug. 1919, 1; 12 Sept. 1919, 1; 19 Sept. 1919, 1; *HS*, 3 Oct. 1919, 19; 6 Oct. 1919, 7; 15 Oct. 1919, 1; 8 Nov. 1919, 11; *LL*, 21 Nov. 1919, 1.

56. See, for example, the letter to the editor in *HS*, 30 Dec. 1919, 6.

57. *HS*, 8 Nov. 1919, 11; 26 Dec. 1919, 4; 27 Dec. 1919, 13; 29 Dec. 1919, 13; 7 Jan. 1920, 23; *Veteran*, February 1920, 16.

58. *HS*, 24 Jan. 1920, 3; 20 March 1920, 12; 1 April 1920, 1 (quotation).

59. *HS*, 19 May 1920, 19; 4 Sept. 1920, 6; 7 Sept. 1920, 7; 16 Sept. 1920, 8; 21 Sept. 1920, 20; 24 Sept. 1920, 16; 26 Oct. 1920, 6; HPL, ILP, Central Branch, Minutes, 9 Nov. 1920, 14; 26 Nov. 1920, 17–18; 6 Dec. 1920, 19; 10 Dec. 1920, 22; *LN*, 2 Dec. 1920, 1; 9 Dec. 1920, 1; 21 Jan. 1920, 2. The Great War Veterans became uncomfortable with the partnership with labour, and the Central Branch pulled out of the federation. *HS*, 8 Dec. 1920, 17; 15 Dec. 1920, 27; 30 Dec. 1920, 1.

60. *HS*, 6 Oct. 1921, 10.

61. See, for example, *Veteran*, 22 Jan. 1922, 12; 15 April 1922, 17–18; 23 Dec. 1922, 9; 13 Jan. 1923, 8; 3 March 1923, 8; 31 March 1923, 8; 14 Feb. 1925, 8; 14 March 1925, 8; 27 June 1925,14; 22 Aug. 1925, 8; 9 Jan. 1926, 8; 10 April 1926, 9.

62. Morton and Wright, *Winning the Second Battle*, 130–201; *Veteran*, 8 Nov. 1924, 11. As an indication of the political shift that had taken place, the wife of Arthur Meighen, leader of the national Conservative Party, was made honorary president of the East Hamilton Branch in 1924; *Veteran*, 24 Jan. 1925, 8; 28 Feb. 1925, 9. In 1929 the executive of the Central Branch of the Legion included as honorary presidents Lieut.-General Sir George Norton Cory, industrialist-politician Major S.C. Mewburn, Col. George S. Rennie, businessman Col. C.R. McCullough,

Col. John I. McLaren, and Lieut-Col. J.E. Davey. *HS*, 4 Feb. 1930, 10.

63. Archibald, "Distress, Dissent, and Alienation," 18.

64. *HH*, 19 March 1917, 2; 26 March 1917, 1; 2 April 1917, 3; 4 April 1917; 7 May 1917; 8 May 1917; 2 June 1917, 1; 4 June 1917, 4; 9 June 1917, 8; 2 May 1918, 7; 4 May 1918, 1; 7 May 1918, 13; 8 May 1918, 1; *LN*, 3 May 1918, 1; AO, RG 23, E-30, 1.6; Kealey, "State Repression of Labour." From the editor's chair at the *Labor News*, Flatman published favourable reports on developments in Russia during 1917; *LN*, 6 April 1917, 2; 6 July 1917, 2; 14 Sept. 1917, 1.

65. Angus, *Canadian Bolsheviks*, 36–48, 63–65.

66. Kealey, "State Repression of Labour"; Angus, *Canadian Bolsheviks*, 36–48; *HH*, 27 Nov. 1918, 1 (quotation); 7 Dec. 1918, 1; 9 Dec. 1918, 1; *LN*, 6 Dec. 1918, 2 (quotation).

67. UTL, Ms Col 179, Box 1, File: Constitutions, Documents, Manifestoes, etc.; Box 11, File: May Day – Undated; *HH*, 16 Dec. 1918, 11; 30 April 1919, 1; 7 May 1919, 1; 10 May 1919, 13; 7 Jan. 1919, 4; Robin, *Radical Politics*, 146; Avery, "Radical Alien," 217; *HS*, 2 Jan. 1919, 6; 9 Jan. 1919, 4; 11 Jan. 1919, 7; 16 Jan. 1919, 9; 14 Feb. 1919, 1; 17 Feb. 1919, 12; 18 Feb. 1919, 16; 25 Feb. 1919, 7, 9; 4 March 1919, 1, 15; 5 March 1919, 23; 13 March 1919, 19; *LN*, 24 Jan. 1919, 1; Milligan, "'Seemingly Onerous Restrictions,'" 65–67. The November and May leaflets were reprinted in Angus, *Canadian Bolsheviks*, 331–38. The weak impact of revolutionaries in the city is reflected in the complete absence of any Hamilton names on the Dominion Police's 1919 list of "Chief Agitators in Canada"; Kealey and Whitaker, eds., *R.C.M.P. Security Bulletins: Early Years*, 362–82.

68. LAC, R6113-0-X-E, Vol. 112, 61050 (Percy Reid to J.A. Calder, 19 Jan. 1920) (quotation); Kealey and Whitaker, eds., *R.C.M.P. Security Bulletins*, Vol. 1, 92 (quotation); *HS*, 8 Jan. 1920, 1; *LL*, 1 Oct. 1920, 7 (quotation); Kolasky, *Shattered Illusion*; Krawchuk, *Our History*. On two occasions in October 1920 a government spy attended meetings of Russians in Hamilton in which the discussion of forming a Communist Party foundered on the fear of deportation. Kealey and Whitaker, eds., *R.C.M.P. Security Bulletins: Early Years*, 233, 251.

69. Kealey and Whitaker, eds., *R.C.M.P. Security Bulletins: Early Years*, 47, 61, 81, 90, 91, 92, 135, 199, 250, 269–70, 289; Angus, *Canadian Bolsheviks*, 63–80; Buck, *Yours in the Struggle*, 89–108; Rodney, *Soldiers of the International*, 29–46; Communist Party, *Canada's Party of Socialism*, 10–23.

70. *ND*, 6 May 1921, 2; 2 March 1922, 1, 2; 6 April 1922, 1, 2; 4 May 1922, 1; *LN*, 28 April 1922, 1; *HS*, 27 Feb. 1922, 3; 3 April 1922, 2; 2 May 1922, 1, 6; *WG*, 26 Nov. 1921, 1; 17 Dec. 1921, 1, 4; 7 Jan. 1922, 1; 11 Jan. 1922, 1; *Worker*, 1 April 1922, 4; 15 April 1922, 4; 1 May 1922, 2; 15 May 1922, 1, 4; Rodney, *Soldiers of the International*, 50; Sangster,

"*Robitsinytsia*, Ukrainian Communists, and the 'Porcupinism' Debate"; Heron, "Lawrence." The Communists' national newspaper reported in May 1922 that a Bulgarian Branch of the party had been formed, though nothing more was heard of it. *Worker*, 15 May 1922, 3. The Chamber of Commerce had worried about the emergent Communist movement late in 1921, but ultimately decided to take no action. HPL, HCC, Board of Directors, Minutes, 8 Nov. 1921, 24 Jan. 1922. From his editor's chair at *New Democracy*, Fester published blistering front-page attacks on the new Workers' Party; see 2 May 1922, 1, 2; 6 April 1922, 1; 4 May 1922, 1.

71. Party organizer Tim Buck later wrote: "In its early stages, our Party was, in many respects, more of a left-wing movement within the trade union movement than a parliamentary or political party." Buck, *Yours in the Struggle*, 113.

72. *ND*, 5 April 1923, 2; *HH*, 28 April 1923; *HS*, 2 May 1923, 29; 2 May 1924, 10; *Worker*, 22 Nov. 1924, 3; 16 May 1925, 1; 13 June 1925, 1; 20 June 1925, 2; 27 June 1925, 2; 4 July 1925, 3; 11 July 1925, 2; 25 July 1925, 1; 3 Oct. 1925, 2; 15 May 1926, 2; 3 Sept. 1927, 2; 10 Sept. 1927, 2; 8 Oct. 1927, 2; 29 Oct. 1927, 3; 1 Sept. 1928, 3; 22 Sept. 1928, 3; 5 Jan. 1929, 2; 16 Feb. 1929, 4 (quotation); 20 April 1929, 2; 18 May 1929, 2; *LOC*, 1924, 204; 1925, 162, 208–9; 1926, 213; 1927, 233; 1928, 183; 1929, 179; 1930, 183; Hunter, *Which Side Are You On, Boys*, 18–20; Angus, *Canadian Bolsheviks*; Communist Party, *Canada's Party of Socialism*, 24–65.

73. AO, Communist Party of Canada Fonds, 5B0529 (29 Feb. 1928), 2A1202 (11 June 1931), 2A1205 (11 June 1931), 2A1275 (14 July 1931). From 1919 to 1929 the RCMP kept files on 2,590 Canadians, only 21 of whom were in Hamilton, the majority of them Anglo-Canadian; Kealey and Whitaker, eds., *R.C.M.P. Security Bulletins: Early Years*, 383–487. Nationally the party had fewer than 1,400 members in 1931; Angus, *Canadian Bolsheviks*, 199.

74. See, for example, *HS*, 14 Oct. 1921, 20; 18 Oct. 1921, 5.

75. HPL, HCC, Board of Directors, Minutes, 15 June, 31 Aug., 12 Oct., 14 Dec. 1920, 8 Feb. 1921; *HS*, 13 Dec. 1920, 1, 6; 22 Dec. 1920, 1; 23 Dec. 1920, 19; 27 Dec. 1920, 10; 28 Dec. 1920, 1; 6 Jan. 1921, 1; 11 Jan. 1921, 11; *LL*, 8 Oct. 1920, 1; Smith, "Cooper."

76. HPL, HCC, Board of Directors, Minutes, 1 May, 28 June, 12 July, 23 Aug., 6 Sept., 13 Dec., 16 Dec., 22 Dec., 27 Dec. 1921, 3 Jan., 10 Jan., 14 Feb. (quotations), 21 March, 16 May 1922, 6 March 1923; *HS*, 30 Sept. 1921, 19; 21 Jan. 1930, 18; Wills, *Marriage of Convenience*.

77. *HS*, 11 Dec. 1920, 8; 13 Dec. 1920, 1.

78. *HS*, 11 Dec. 1920, 26; 13 Dec. 1920, 15; 14 Dec. 1920, 1 (quotation); 15 Dec. 1920, 15; 17 Dec. 1920, 17; 18 Dec. 1920, 58; 21 Dec. 1920, 16; 22 Dec. 1920, 10; 29 Dec. 1920, 18; 30 Dec. 1920, 5 (quotation).

79. *HS*, 6 Jan. 1921, 1; 7 Jan. 1921, 1; 8 Jan. 1921, 10; 1 Feb. 1921, 1 (quotation); 5 Feb. 1921, 1; 10 Feb. 1921, 1; 4 July 1921, 3; 9 Aug. 1921, 1; 10 Sept. 1921, 1; *LL*, 24 Dec. 1920, 7; 4 Feb. 1921, 9.

80. A local radical said that the Soldiers' and Workers' Association was still alive and well the following December, but it seemed to have followed the same path to marginality that other veterans' groups took that year. *HS*, 20 Dec. 1920, 21; 30 Dec. 1920, 5; 7 Jan. 1921, 1; 1 Feb. 1921, 1; 5 Feb. 1921, 1; 9 Feb. 1921, 18; 15 April 1921, 1; *WG*, 17 Dec. 1921, 4; *LL*, 22 April 1921, 1. The Trades and Labor Council distanced itself from this agitation and provided no support for their legal defence. *HS*, 19 Feb. 1921, 1.

81. *HS*, 20 Sept. 1921, 1 (quotation); 21 Oct. 1921, 2; 21 Jan. 1922, 9; 23 Jan. 1922, 1; 2 Feb. 1922, 1; 9 Feb. 1922, 1; 21 Feb. 1922, 12; 7 April 1922, 23; *LN*, 28 Oct. 1921, 1; *ND*, 5 Sept. 1921, 3; *WG*, 5 Nov. 1921, 1; 12 Nov. 1921, 1; HPL, ILP, Central Branch, Minutes, 23 Dec. 1921, 8 Feb. 1922.

82. *HS*, 23 Jan. 1922, 1; 27 Feb. 1922, 3; 27 March 1922, 13; *ND*, 2 March 1922, 1; 6 April 1922, 2; *Worker*, 1 April 1922, 1, 4. The new Communist movement made organizing the unemployed a priority.

83. *LN*, 28 April 1922, 1; *HS*, 29 April 1922, 23; 1 May 1922, 1, 10; 2 May 1922, 1 (quotation), 17; *Worker*, 15 May 1922, 1 (quotation).

84. *HH*, 24 March 1925; *HS*, 16 Nov. 1923, 5; 12 March 1925, 5; *Worker*, 1 Nov. 1924, 4; 21 March 1925, 2; 9 May 1925, 2; 13 June 1925, 1; 20 June 1925, 2; 27 June 1925, 2; 4 July 1925, 3; 11 July 1925, 2; 25 July 1925, 1; 15 Aug. 1925, 1; 26 Dec. 1925, 2. The references made by the Communist press to the Unemployed Association in Hamilton stop at the end of 1925.

85. *HS*, 16 Dec. 1929, 7; 4 Feb. 1930, 10; 6 Feb. 1930, 7; 11 Feb. 1930, 16; 13 Feb. 1930, 21 (quotation); 14 Feb. 1930, 7; 19 Feb. 1930, 27; 11 March 1930, 18; 12 March 1930, 4 (quotation); 7 April 1930, 7; 8 April 1930, 27 (quotation); 19 July 1930, 7; *Worker*, 25 Feb. 1933, 4; Campbell, "'We Who Have Wallowed in the Mud of Flanders.'" Premier Howard Ferguson announced in 1930 that unemployed immigrants would not be eligible for provincially funded relief. Avery, *Reluctant Host*, 109. Hamilton's veterans kept alive an "assistance committee," which reported in 1937 that 1,000–1,500 were still unemployed. *Clarion*, 4 Jan. 1937, 3.

86. These business leaders put particular stress on the need for better accommodation for the single unemployed. They were happy to leave the single unemployed woman to the care of the YWCA, but, as they advised the Board of Control, it was "most undesirable in the interests of the community to allow a large number of such men to wander on streets, [and] crowd the reading rooms of the library and the Y.M.C.A." They recommended much expanded accommodation, dining hall, and recreational space, most of which the Board agreed to provide. The facilities for these men provoked a protest from some of them early in 1936 over vermin-infested beds, poor food,

and unhealthy premises. HPL, HCC, Board of Directors, Minutes, 13 Jan., 29 Jan., 24 Feb., 8 Sept., 27 Oct., 24 Nov., 8 Dec. 1930, 31 Oct. 1931, 17 Oct. 1932, 27 Nov. 1933; Unemployment Committee, Minutes, 19 Sept., 13 Oct. (quotation), 4 Nov., 17 Nov. 1930, 21 Jan. 1931; *NC*, 19 Jan. 1936, 1–2. Some of the single unemployed were shipped to Northern Ontario relief camps run by the provincial government. MacDowell, "Relief Camp Workers." If they were not citizens, they might also be deported.

87. Manley, "'Starve, Be Damned!'"; Bright, "The State, the Unemployed, and the Communist Party."

88. *Worker*, 26 July 1930, 1, 4; 30 Aug. 1930, 3. A few weeks later the Communists faced a challenge from a new Un-employed Workers' Council of Hamilton, sponsored by left-wing ILPers, notably Lawrence, and headed by two renegades from the Communist group (similar social-democratic activity with the unemployed was emerging in other cities). Communist correspondents to the *Worker* lodged frequent complaints against the efforts of these "social-fascist" interlopers holding meetings on the same square and getting a more sympathetic hearing at city hall. The new group had apparently faded from the scene by late winter. *Worker*, 27 Sept. 1930, 3; 11 Oct. 1930, 3; 25 Oct. 1930, 4; 1 Nov. 1930, 2; 8 Nov. 1930, 2; 15 Nov. 1930, 4; 22 Nov. 1930, 1; 29 Nov. 1930, 4 (quotation); 28 Feb. 1931, 1; *HS*, 27 Oct. 1930, 8.

89. Later that month a local organizer for the Young Communist League, Harry Binder, was arrested for distributing leaflets for a meeting to protest the arrests – "obviously another method that the Hamilton police are using to crush the revolutionary movement," a local com-rade wrote. Betcherman, *Little Band*; Smith, *All My Life*, 98–122; Glassford, *Reaction and Reform*, 121–24; *HS*, 24 March 1930, 23; 25 March 1930, 7; 15 April 1930, 7; 17 April 1930, 33; 21 April 1930, 7; 29 July 1930, 10; 30 July 1930, 7; 31 July 1930, 7; *Worker*, 19 April 1930, 1; 26 April 1930, 1; 24 May 1930, 1; 7 June 1930, 4; 5 July 1930, 2; 19 July 1930, 2; 1 Nov. 1930, 1, 2; 19 Nov. 1930, 1, 4; 22 Nov. 1930, 1; *Young Worker*, April 1930, 1; May 1930, 1; July 1930, 2. Cohen's continuing role with the Unemployed Association got him into trouble with the party leadership for using language in public letters that was insufficiently class-conscious; a few months later he had to publish a self-criticism and a promise "to adhere in the future to the line necessary for a revolutionary working class." *Worker*, 13 Sept. 1930, 4.

90. AO, MS1740, File "Unemployment Situation 1931," William Stewart to Henry, 13 Aug. 1931 (quotations); Hamilton Board of Control to Henry, 12 Sept. 1931. On this shift in party policy towards a greater emphasis on defending the family home, see Manley, "'Starve, Be Damned!'"; Bright, "State, the Unemployed, and the Communist Party"; Gosse, "'To Organize in Every Neighbourhood.'"

91. *Worker*, 28 Feb. 1931, 1; 13 June 1931, 3 (quotation).

92. *Worker*, 24 Oct. 1931, 3; 31 Oct. 1931, 4 (quotation); 12 Dec. 1931, 3.

93. *Worker*, 6 Feb. 1932, 3; 20 Feb. 1932, 4; 5 March 1932, 3; 12 March 1932, 2; 23 April 1932, 3; 28 May 1932, 4; 5 Nov. 1932, 2; 14 April 1934, 3; 21 April 1934, 2; Kealey and Whitaker, eds., *R.C.M.P. Security Bulletins: Depression Years, Part 2*, 173–74.

94. *Worker*, 7 Nov. 1931, 1; 16 Jan. 1931, 3; 12 March 1932, 2; 16 April 1932, 1, 3; 23 April 1932, 1.

95. *Worker*, 23 April 1932, 3; 14 May 1932, 4; *HS*, 2 May 1932, 12; Archibald, "Small Expectations and Great Adjust-ments," 383 (quotation).

96. *Worker*, 14 May 1932, 4; 21 May 1932, 2 (quotation).

97. *Worker*, 16 July 1932, 1, 2; 23 July 1932, 1; 20 Aug. 1932, 3; 3 Sept. 1932, 3; 22 Oct. 1932; 29 Oct. 1932, 5; 5 Nov. 1932, 2; 12 Nov. 1932, 4; 26 Nov. 1932, 5; 28 Jan. 1933, 3.

98. *Worker*, 4 March 1933, 3; 25 March 1933, 1; 22 April 1933, 2; Hunter, *Which Side Are You On, Boys*, 21 (quotation); Archibald, "Small Expectations and Great Adjustments," 372. Much to the disgust of the Communists, the local Workers' Ex-Servicemen's League slipped into "reform-ist" hands early in 1933 and later had to be reorganized. Nationally it was collapsing in several cities. *Worker*, 18 March 1933, 3; 1 April 1933, 3; 29 April 1933, 5; 8 July 1933, 4; 22 Sept. 1934, 2; Kealey and Whitaker, eds., *R.C.M.P. Security Bulletins: Depression Years, I*, 34, 37–39, 46–47, 52, 123, 138–39, 219, 241, 251, 256–57, 272–73, 310, 400–1.

99. *Worker*, 8 April 1933, 1, 4; 15 April 1933, 2; 29 April 1933, 5; 6 May 1933, 1, 3; 13 May 1933, 2; 20 May 1933, 2; 3 June 1933, 3. The sponsor of the 1 May demonstration was the United Front May Day Conference, but the Trades and Labor Council and ILP (whose leaders were still being denounced as "fakirs' and "misleaders") refused to participate.

100. *Worker*, 3 June 1933, 1, 3; 10 June 1933, 1; 24 June 1933, 2; 1 July 1933, 4; 23 Sept. 1933, 2.

101. A meeting of the Canadian Labor Defence League in the Labour Temple early in 1934 had Lawrence and CCF alderman Fred Reed on the platform, and by Labour Day the Communists had succeeded in putting together a Hamilton Conference of Allied Organizations on Wel-fare and Relief that included the East Hamilton ILP and Lawrence. In 1935 a local branch of the Canadian League Against War and Fascism brought CCFers and Commun-ists together as well, and later that year they co-operated in running candidates in the federal and municipal elections. Kealey and Whitaker, eds., *R.C.M.P. Security Bulletins: Depression Years, I*, 181; *II*, 106–7, 186, 189–90, 263, 433, 626; *III*, 196; *HS*, 29 May 1933, 1; *Worker*, 22 July 1933, 2; 5 Aug. 1933, 1; 12 Aug. 1933, 2; 19 Aug. 1933, 1; 19 Aug. 1933, 2; 2 Sept. 1933, 2; 16 Sept. 1933, 2; 18 Jan. 1935, 4; 2 Feb. 1935, 4; 9 Feb. 1935, 4; 21 March 1935, 4; 15 April

1935, 4; 18 April 1935, 1; 2 May 1935, 2; 16 May 1935, 2; 17 Sept. 1935, 3; 24 Sept. 1935, 2; *Clarion*, 17 Nov. 1936, 2; *NC*, 14 March 1936, 1; 28 March 1936, 6; 25 July 1936, 2; 1 Aug. 1936, 2; 5 Sept. 1936, 2; Manley, "'Starve, Be Damned!'" There were nonetheless bumps on the road to the "popular front": early in 1937 a woman was expelled from the CCF for seconding the nomination of a Communist aldermanic candidate a few months before. *Clarion*, 25 Feb. 1937, 4.

102. *Worker*, 16 May 1931, 3; 13 Feb. 1932, 3; 1 April 1933, 3; 8 April 1933, 2; HPL, HCC, Board of Directors, Minutes, 10 April, 24 April, 19 June, 11 Sept., 25 Sept. 1933, 7 Jan. (quotations), 18 March, 18 Nov. 1935, 25 Jan. 1937, 7 Feb. 1938; Community Garden Plot Committee, Minutes, 21 Feb. 1934. The number of men who cultivated gardens each year declined after 1934: 5,157 in 1933, 5,217 in 1934, 3,490 in 1935, 3,940 in 1936, 2,512 in 1937, 2,240 in 1938.

103. LAC, R244-76-4-E, Vol. 372, File 1; *NC*, 2 Feb. 1935, 1; 5 Feb. 1936, 6 (quotation); 25 April 1936, 2; 12 Sept. 1936, 2; 26 Sept. 1936, 2; *Worker*, 17 Sept. 1935, 3; 1 March 1936, 2; *Clarion*, 4 Aug. 1936, 2; 8 Aug. 1936, 2; 11 Sept. 1936, 1. By late 1936 the Hamilton and District Workers' Association had small east-end and west-end branches, supported by both the CCF and the Communists. By the end of the decade a Workers' Progressive Association was representing the unemployed. *Clarion*, 28 Oct. 1936, 3; 18 April 1938, 4; 25 April 1939, 3.

104. HPL, HCC, Board of Directors, Minutes, 24 April (quotation), 11 Sept. (quotation) 1933, 2 Feb. 1934 (quotation), 7 Jan. (quotations), 18 Nov. 1935, 25 Jan. 1937, 7 Feb. 1938.

105. Glassford, *Reaction and Reform*, 72–97.

106. In the late 1920s the ILP had undergone a minor revival, starting with Lawrence's election to the Board of Control in 1928. In 1931 the party had four alderman and a controller on city council and one school trustee. *LN*, 28 Nov. 1930, 1; 20 Dec. 1930, 2.

107. *HS*, 20 July 1931, 4, 6; 21 July 1931, 6, 7, 19; 25 July 1931, 4; 28 July 1931, 2, 11; 28 July 1931, 7; 30 July 1931, 3, 17; 31 July 1931, 13, 25; 1 Aug. 1931, 3, 7; 4 Aug. 1931, 10; 5 Aug. 1931, 9, 13; 6 Aug. 1931, 9, 11; 7 Aug. 1931, 4, 13; 8 Aug. 1931, 7, 9, 13, 24 (quotation); 11 Aug. 1931, 6 (quotation), 15, 27; *LN*, 24 April 1931, 1; 22 May 1931, 1; 24 June 1931, 2; 30 July 1931, 1; 28 Aug. 1931, 1.

108. *NC*, 1 Sept. 1934, 7; 8 Sept. 1934, 7; 22 Sept. 1934, 5; 15 Dec. 1934, 6; Heron, "Mitchell"; Caplan, *Dilemma of Canadian Socialism*; Morley, *Secular Socialists*.

109. *HS*, 20 June 1934, 1, 10; *NC*, 23 March 1935, 1 (quotation). Mitchell was a seasoned organizer who arrived in Hamilton in 1929 after many years of experience as a leader in the Scottish miners' union and the British Labour Party. He was said to have "a knowledge of economics, philosophy and history of socialism possessed by comparatively few." His organizational skills and oratorical prowess

helped to get him elected to city council. In 1934 he also became president of the CCF's Ontario section, and travelled across the province speaking on behalf of the party. *NC*, 4 Aug. 1934, 5; 16 Feb. 1935, 6 (quotation); 23 March 1935, 1.

110. *NC*, 3 Nov. 1934, 6; 17 Nov. 1934, 6; 24 Nov. 1934, 6; 1 Dec. 1934, 3; 15 Dec. 1934, 6; 16 Feb. 1935, 6; 4 May 1935, 6; 17 Aug. 1935, 8; 1 Oct. 1935, 13; 12 Oct. 1935, 8; 19 Oct. 1935, 7; 7 Dec. 1935, 8; 14 Dec. 1935, 8; Saywell, *"Just Call Me Mitch."* Stevens began and ended his cross-country campaign in Hamilton. Wilbur, *H.H. Stevens*, 184–203. For the municipal election results, see Tables 42 and 43. The Conservatives held West Hamilton in a 1937 by-election. The ILP's Central Branch (renamed simply the Hamilton Branch) was still denouncing CCF candidates in the 1940 federal election.

111. *NC*, 28 March 1936, 6; 25 April 1936, 2; 22 Aug. 1936, 3; 12 Sept. 1936, 1; 5 Dec. 1936, 1; 12 Dec. 1936, 1, 6; 16 Jan. 1937, 6; *HS*, 7 Oct. 1937, 1; Abella, *Nationalism, Communism, and Canadian Labour*, 1–40; Saywell, *"Just Call Me Mitch,"* 139–65, 343–60. In an odd déjà-vu, the 40-year-old Socialist Labor Party re-emerged to run candidates in two Hamilton ridings in 1937, gathering only a scattering of votes. *HS*, 29 Sept. 1937, 7; 26 Sept. 1937, 6.

112. Struthers, *No Fault of Their Own*; Owram, *Government Generation*, 135–53; Pal, "State, Class, and Reserve Labour"; Pierson, "Gender and Unemployment Insurance Debates"; *Clarion*, 10 Jan. 1938, 1; 31 Jan. 1938, 1.

113. Kealey and Whitaker, eds., *R.C.M.P. Security Bulletins: Depression Years, II*, 19,112.

114. Manley, "'Starve, Be Damned!'" 491.

19. Lunch-Bucket Politics

1. The earliest versions were improvised from any metal pails or boxes with lids. In the second half of the 19th century, manufacturers began to produce specially designed lunch pails with compartments and drinking cups (see, for example, 1901 *Editions of T. Eaton Co. Limited. Catalogues*, 188). Tobacco companies also produced square versions covered with colourful advertising of their products. The Thermos company popularized the iconic rectangular box shape after it brought its "vacuum flask" onto the market in 1904. Typically lunch buckets got dented, chipped, and personalized over the years. See Smithsonian National Museum of American History website, "Taking America to Lunch: The First Generation," http://americanhistory.si.edu/lunchboxes/section1.htm.

Bibliography

Primary – Archival

Ambrose McGhee Medical Museum (Hamilton)

RG 1, A-A, Hamilton Medical Society, Minute Books; Hamilton Academy of Medicine, Executive Committee, Minutes

RG 1, A-C, Petitions to Stop Lodge Practice, 1936–37

RG 1-C-I, *Bulletin of the Hamilton Medical Society*

RG 1, D-E, Box 1, General Practitioners Section, Minutes

RG 2-E, AA Numbers Collection, Victor A. Cecilioni, RM Stringer

RG 2-G, Babies' Dispensary Guild, Scrapbook; Fred Bowman, "Autobiography"; A.P. McKinnon, Call Lists 1917; William James McNichol, Account Book, 1912–18; A.E. Walkey, Call Lists, 1908–16

Archives of Ontario (Toronto)

F 5 (Sir James Whitney Fonds)

F 885 (Canadian Woman's Christian Temperance Union Fonds)

F 980 (Henry Cody Fonds)

MU 4989, C-1 (Minister of Education Papers)

RG 3-8 (George S. Henry Correspondence)

RG 4-32-3188/1931 (Communist Party of Canada)

RG 7-12 (Department of Public Works, Trades and Labour Branch, Office of the Deputy Minister, General Subject Files, 1916–20)

RG 7-57, (Research Branch, Senior Investigator, Industrial Welfare, 1926–29)

RG 7-76, (Ontario, Department of Labour, Minimum Wage Board, Minutes)

RG 7-116, Employee Handbooks on Pension, Insurance, and Benefit Plans, 1917–26; Company Publications, News Leaflets, and Magazines, 1925–26

RG 7-12-0-21, File: Mothers' Allowance, "Mothers' Pension Allowance, Hamilton Enquiry, Thursday February 20, 1919"

RG 7-12-0-153, "Placement on Northern Development Highway Projects by Districts," 1 Dec. 1931

RG 7-111 (Employment Service Council of Ontario, 1920–23)

RG 23-50-1 (Ontario Provincial Police, Criminal Investigations, Strikes and Agitations)

RG 29-135-1-6 (Ministry of Social and Family Services, Administration – Municipal Affairs, 1931–40), "Report of the Unemployment Situation and How It Is Being Handled" (1932)

RG 36-8 (Liquor Control Board of Ontario, Establishment Files)

Big Brothers Association of Hamilton Archives (Hamilton)

Board of Directors, Minutes

Scrapbooks

Girl Guides of Canada, Escarpment Branch Archives (Hamilton)

SRS 109-3 (Helen Smith Scrapbook, 1928–31)

SRS 109-5 (Katherine Panabaker Scrapbook), "Early Days in Guiding in Hamilton"

SRS 109-10 (10th Company Log Book, 1932–36)

Hamilton Health Association Archives (McMaster University)

Hamilton Health Association, *Annual Reports*

Hamilton Public Library, Local History and Archives Department (Hamilton)

Aged Women's Home, Minutes

Canadian Patriotic Fund, Hamilton and Wentworth Branch, Scrapbooks. "Report of the Relief Committee, October 1914 to January 2 1918" (typescript)

B. Greening Wire Company Fonds

Hamilton Board of Trade, Minutes

Hamilton Chamber of Commerce, Minutes; *Annual Reports*

Hamilton Orphan Asylum, Aged Women's Home, and Ladies' Benevolent Society, Minutes; *Annual Reports*

Hamilton Playgrounds Association Fonds

Hamilton Recruiting League, Minutes

Hamilton Trades and Labor Council, Minutes

IODE, Paardeburg Chapter, Annual Reports, 1915–40

Independent Labor Party, Central Branch, Minutes

Labour and Labouring Classes, Recollections of John Peebles, 7 Feb. 1946

"Report of Some Housing Conditions" (typescript, Hamilton, 1938)

RG 3, Series A (Hospital and House of Refugee Committee, Minutes)

RG 10, Series A (Annual Reports); Series M (Police Registers); Series S (Board of Police Commissioners, Minutes)

RG 12, Series A (Board of Health Minutes)

RG 13, Series A (Hospital Board of Governors Minutes)

RG 18, Series A (Board of Parks Management, Minutes)

Rotary Club of Hamilton, Minutes

Scrapbooks (various)

Soldiers' Aid Commission, Minutes

St. George's Benevolent Society of Hamilton, Minutes

Wilensky, D. "Report Re the Jewish Community in Hamilton and Its Social Service Organization" (typescript, March 1931)

Young Men's Christian Association – East End, Minutes

Hamilton YWCA Archives (Hamilton)

Annual Reports

Minute Books

Scrapbooks

Imperial Order Daughters of the Empire,
Municipal Chapter Archives (Hamilton)
Minute Books

Library and Archives Canada (Ottawa)
R174-45-6-E (Chief Press Censor's Fonds)
R200-275-4-E (Tariff Commission, 1905–6)
R224-0-4-E, Vol. 1, Unemployment, 1914; Niagara Falls,
    Brantford, Hamilton, Toronto; Hamilton, 1914–16
R244-76-4-E (Strikes and Lockouts Files)
R1449-0-5-E (Sir Joseph Flavelle Fonds)
R3096-0-8-E (Canadian Manufacturers' Association Fonds)
R3735 (Hamilton Cotton Company Fonds), 3–9; (Tariff Advis-
    ory Board Reference No. 64 [Second Hearing], 1927); 3–18
    (Welfare Committee Minutes, 1914–17)
R4143-0-4-E (American Labour Unions' Constitutions
    and Proceedings)
R4619-0-9-E (Boy Scouts of Canada Fonds)
R6113-0-X-E (Sir Robert Borden Fonds)
R10383-0-6-F (William Lyon Mackenzie King Fonds)
R10811-0-X-E (Sir Wilfrid Laurier Fonds)
R1176-0-0-E (Commission to Inquire into and Report upon
    Industrial Relations in Canada Fonds), Minutes

McMaster University Archives (Hamilton)
International Association of Machinists Fonds
M.T. Montgomery Fonds
Westinghouse Fonds

Multicultural History Society of Ontario (Toronto)
ITA-0806-COL (Interview with Urbano Colangelo)
ITA-0807-COL (Interview with Berlino Colangelo)
ITA-0808-CEC (Interview with Vittorio Cecilioni)
ITA-0809-GRO (Interview with John Grosso, 14 July 1977)
ITA-0810-SAR (Interview with S.U. Sardo, 4 Sept. 1977)
ITA-0811-PIS (Interview with Joe Pissolante, 27 Sept. 1977)
ITA-0815-ANO (Anonymous interview, 1977–79)
ITA-0826-CRE (Interview with Peter Cremasco, 1 July 1977)
ITA-0830-SAL (Interview with Pietro Di Savatore, 6 Sept. 1977)
ITA-0883-ANO (Anonymous interview, 1977–79)
ITA-0884-VIO (Interview with C. Viola, 11 Feb. 1978)
ITA-0913-FOU (Interview with L. Fournier, 16 Nov. 1977)
ITA-0982-PAS (Interview with Donna Pasquale, 13 April 1983)
ITA-09826-FER (Interview with Frank Ferri, 10 April 1983)
ITA-09829-GRI (Interview with Gianbattista Grittani,
    31 March 1983)
ITA-6489-BOR (Interview with Alfred Borsellino, 11 Dec. 1979)
ITA-6990-ROB (Interview with Ann Marie Robson, January 1979)

Presbyterian Church of Canada Archives (Toronto)
1977-3014 (Presbytery of Hamilton, Minutes)
1988-4002-3-9 (Calvin Presbyterian Church, Ladies Aid,
    Minutes, March 1922 – December 1931)

Provincial Archives of Manitoba (Winnipeg)
MG 10, A 3 (One Big Union Papers)

State Historical Society of Wisconsin (Madison)
American Federation of Labor Papers, Samuel Gompers Files,
    Series II, A, Box 23, R. Riley to A. Holder, 4 July 1917 (I am
    indebted to Myer Siemiatycki for this reference)

Thomas Fisher Rare Books Library (Toronto)
MS.Coll. 129 (Lord's Day Alliance Papers)
Ms Col 179 (Robert Kenney Fonds)

United Church of Canada Archives (Toronto)
Local History Files, Hamilton Presbytery
Methodist Church (Canada), Board of Home Missions,
    78.099C, Box 7, Files 5–8 (Italian Work, 1909–25)
Methodist Church (Canada), Toronto Conference, Deaconess
    Board of Management
Methodist Church, Women's Missionary Society, *Annual
    Reports* (Toronto), 1917–25

University of British Columbia Library,
Special Collections (Vancouver)
James Robertson Papers, "Notes from Conversations with Offi-
    cers of the Steel Company of Canada, Hamilton, Ont., Dec.
    21/23" (I am grateful to Gene Homel for this reference)

Workers' Arts and Heritage Centre (Hamilton)
Garnet W. Dickenson Account Book
Interviews:
Charles Old
Mary and Louis Fiori
Ed Fisher
Florence Fisher
Bert McClure
North End Community
Fred Purser
Floyd Read
Lil Seager
Jack Watts
Ken Withers
Joyce Yakmalian

Primary – Books and articles

Aberdeen and Temair, Ishbel Gordon, Marchioness of. *Through
    Canada with a Kodak*. Edinburgh: W.H. White 1893.
Ames, Herbert Brown. *The City Below the Hill: A Sociological
    Study of a Portion of the City of Montreal, Canada*. Toronto:
    University of Toronto Press 1972 (1897).
Anglo-American Council on Productivity. *Materials Handling
    in Industry: Summary of a Report on the Investigation in the
    United States of America*. London: Anglo-American Council
    on Productivity n.d.

Annual Reports of the Social Agencies, Members of the Hamilton Community Fund, 1929. N.p. n.d. *1930*. N.p. n.d.

Ashworth, John H. *The Helper and American Trade Unions*. Baltimore: Johns Hopkins University Press 1915.

B. Greening Wire Co. Limited. *Catalogue No.10*. Hamilton: B. Greening Wire Co. 1909.

Beaumont, John. "English View of the Canadian Factory Girl." *CTJ*, November 1911. Pp.285–86.

"Bett Button Looks Back." [Proctor and Gamble] *Moonbeams*, February 1968. Pp.15–16.

Bertram, Alexander. "Development of the Machine Tool Industry." *CM*, 29 Dec. 1921. P. 153.

Bland, Salem. *The New Christianity, or the Religion of the New Age*. Toronto: University of Toronto Press 1973 [1920].

Blue Ribbon Limited. *Blue Ribbon Cook Book*. Winnipeg: Blue Ribbon Limited 1905 (CIHM 78120).

Boam, Henry J., comp. *Twentieth Century Impressions of Canada: Its History, People, Commerce, Industries, and Resources*. London: Sells 1914.

Bogert, John N. "Union Labels." In Hamilton Trades and Labor Council. *Official Programme and Souvenir*. Pp.9–10.

Bray, Reginald A. "The Boy and the Family." In E.J. Urwick, ed. *Studies of Boy Life in Our Cities*. London: J.M. Dent 1904. Pp.65–69.

Bridle, Augustus. "A Shack-Town Christmas." *Canadian Magazine*, December 1909. Pp.129–34.

Brissenden, Paul Frederick, and Emil Frankel. *Labor Turnover in Industry: A Statistical Analysis*. New York: Macmillan 1922.

Bruegernan, Vera. "With the Babies' Dispensary." *CN*, May 1926. P. 256.

Burgar, Gertrude. "Difficulties in Re-Establishing Discharged Sanatorium Patients in the Community." CCSWP, 1934. Pp.92–94.

Burkholder, Mabel. *The Course of Impatience Carningham*. Toronto: Musson Book Company [1911].

——————. *The Story of Hamilton*. 2nd ed. Hamilton: n.p. 1939.

Butler, Elizabeth Beardsley. *Women and the Trades: Pittsburgh 1907–1908*. New York: Arno 1969 [1911].

Byington, Margaret. *Homestead: Households of a Mill Town*. New York: Charities Publication Committee 1910.

Caddie, A. "Installing Time Studies." *CM*, 23 April 1925. Pp.13–16. 30 April 1925. Pp.16, 40–42.

Caffin, Caroline. *Vaudeville: The Book*. New York: Mitchell Kennerley 1914.

Canada, Board of Inquiry into Cost of Living. *Report*. 2 vols. Ottawa: King's Printer 1915.

Canada, Census and Statistics Office, Department of Trade and Commerce. *Census of Canada, 1911*. Ottawa: C.H. Parmelee 1912.

Canada, Clerk of the Crown in Chancery. *Returns on General Elections for the House of Commons of Canada, 1900*. Ottawa: Queen's Printer 1901.

Canada, Department of Agriculture. *Census of Canada, 1891*. Ottawa: S.E. Dawson 1893; *1901*. Ottawa: S.E. Dawson 1902–6.

Canada, Department of Labour. *Employees' Magazines in Canada*. Ottawa: Department of Labour 1921.

——————. *The Employment of Children and Young Persons in Canada*. Ottawa: King's Printer 1930.

——————. *Joint Councils in Industry*. Ottawa: Department of Labour 1921.

——————. *Labour Organizations in Canada*. Ottawa: Department of Labour 1911–40.

——————. *Report of a Conference on Industrial Relations*. Ottawa: King's Printer 1921.

——————. *Report on Organization in Industry, Commerce and the Professions in Canada*. Ottawa: King's Printer 1923.

——————. *Wages and Hours of Labour in Canada, 1901–1920*. Ottawa: King's Printer 1921.

——————. *Wages and Hours of Labour in Canada, 1920–1929*. Ottawa: King's Printer 1930.

Canada, Dominion Bureau of Statistics. *Census of Canada, 1921*. Ottawa: F.A. Acland 1924.

Canada, Dominion Bureau of Statistics. *Census of Canada, 1931*. Ottawa: E. Cloutier 1942.

Canada, Dominion Bureau of Statistics. *Census of Canada, 1931, Unemployment among Wage-earners, Bulletin No. 6: Hamilton, Ontario*. Ottawa: E. Cloutier 1942.

Canada, Dominion Bureau of Statistics. *Census of Canada, 1941*. Ottawa: E. Cloutier 1947.

Canada, Dominion Bureau of Statistics. *Family Income and Expenditure in Canada, 1937–1938*. Ottawa: King's Printer 1941.

Canada, House of Commons. *Journals*, 42 (1906), Appendix 1 (Select Committee to Which Was Referred Bill No. 12 Respecting the Lord's Day, *Minutes of Proceedings and Evidence*).

——————. 45 (1909–10). Appendix, Part 3 ("Proceedings of a Special Committee on Bill No.21, 'An Act Respecting Hours of Labour on Public Works,' Comprising Reports, Evidence and Correspondence, December 9, 1909 – May, 1910").

——————. 56 (1920), Appendix ("Soldiers' Civil Re-Establishment").

——————. 61 (1924). Appendix 4 ("An Old Age Pension System for Canada").

Canada, House of Commons, Special Committee on Old Age Pensions. *Proceedings*. Ottawa: King's Printer 1912.

Canada, National Industrial Conference of Dominion and Provincial Governments with Representative Employers and Labour Men, on the Subject of Industrial Relations and Labour Laws, and for the Consideration of the Labour Features of the Peace Treaty. *Official Report of Proceedings and Discussions Together with Various Memoranda Relating to the Conference and the Report of the Royal Commission on Industrial Relations*. Ottawa: King's Printer 1919.

Canada, *Postal Census of Manufactures, 1916*. Ottawa: J. de Laborquerie Tache 1917.

Canada, Royal Commission on the Liquor Traffic. *Minutes of Evidence, Vol. 4, Part 1: Province of Ontario*. Ottawa: S.E. Dawson 1895.

Canada, Royal Commission on Price Spreads. *Minutes of Evidence*. Ottawa: King's Printer 1934.

Canada, Royal Commission on the Relations of Labour and Capital. *Report: Evidence – Ontario*. Ottawa: Queen's Printer 1888.

Canada, Royal Commission on Racing Inquiry. Report. Ottawa: King's Printer 1920.

Canada, Royal Commission on the Textile Industry. *Report*. Ottawa: King's Printer 1938.

Canadian Patriotic Fund, Hamilton and Wentworth Branch. *Five Years of Service, 1914–1919*. N.p. n.d..

Canadian Welfare Council. *A Study of the Community Fund and Its Member Agencies in Hamilton, 1937*. Ottawa: Canadian Welfare Council 1937.

Canadian Who's Who. London: Times Publishing Company 1910–40.

Carpenter, Niles. *Nationality, Color, and Economic Opportunity in the City of Buffalo*. Buffalo: University of Buffalo 1927.

Casey, Jean. "Community Recreation in the Y.W.C.A." CCSWP, 1930. Pp.221–23.

Cassidy, H.M. *Unemployment and Relief in Ontario, 1929–1932: A Survey and Report*. Toronto: J.M. Dent 1932.

Cauchon, Noulan. *Reconnaissance Report on Development of Hamilton*. N.p. 1917.

Chandler, G.S. "Agency Autonomy and the Community Chest." CCSWP, 1932. Pp.132–34.

Chapin, Robert Coit. *The Standard of Living among Workingmen's Families in New York City*. New York: Charities Publication Committee 1909.

Cheasley, Clifford Henry. *The Chain Store Movement in Canada*. Orillia, Ont.: McGill University, Department of Economics and Political Science [1930].

Charlesworth, Hector, ed. *A Cyclopaedia of Canadian Biography*. Toronto: Hunter-Rose 1919.

Cocks, Orrin G. "Moving Pictures a Factor in Municipal Life." *Canadian Municipal Journal*, November 1914. P. 447.

Cody, W.L. "The Scope and Function of the Medical Staff of the Babies' Dispensary, Hamilton." *PHJ*, November 1915. Pp.545–46.

Collinson, J.H. *The Hamilton Recruiting League*. Hamilton: Hamilton Recruiting League 1918.

Commons, J.R. "A Comparison of Day Labor and the Contract System on Municipal Works." *AF*, January 1897–February 1898.

Coote, James A. *A Graphical Survey of the Canadian Textile Industries*. Montreal: McGill University 1936.

Copeland, Melvin Thomas. *The Cotton Manufacturing Industry of the United States*. Cambridge, Mass.: Harvard University 1912.

Cowles, J.P. *The Juvenile Employment System of Ontario*. Ottawa: Canadian Council on Child Welfare 1923.

Coxwell, Mona. "Safeguarding the Movies." *SW*, June 1925. Pp.169–70.

Cummings, Mrs Willoughby. "The Care of the Destitute Poor." In CCCCP, 1900.

Dallyn, F.A. "Diarrhoea and Enteritis: The Comparative Statistics of the Municipalities in the Province of Ontario, 1902–1914." OPBHR, 1915. Pp.9–18.

Dalzell, A.G. *Housing in Canada II: The Housing of the Working Classes*. Toronto: Social Service Council of Canada 1928.

Davis, Jr., Michael M., and Andrew R. Warner. *Dispensaries: Their Management and Development*. New York: Macmillan 1918.

Dawson, A.O. "The Relations of Capital and Labour." *SW*, 1 April 1920. Pp.171–73.

Day, F.E.H. "Gastro-Intestinal Diseases among Steel Workers." *CPHJ*, November 1939. Pp.555–57.

"Developments in Machine Shop Practice during a Decade." *CM*, 20 March 1913. Pp.281–87.

Dickey, R.M. "The Houses of Hamilton." *SW*, 1 Oct. 1920. P. 20.

Donald, W.J.A. *The Canadian Iron and Steel Industry: A Study in the Economic History of a Protected Industry*. Boston: Houghton Mifflin 1915.

Douglas, Paul H. *American Apprenticeship and Industrial Education*. New York: Columbia 1921.

——————. *Real Wages in the United States, 1890–1926*. Boston: Houghton Mifflin Company 1930.

Dublin, Louis I. *A Family of Thirty Million: The Story of Metropolitan Life Insurance Company*. New York: Metropolitan Life Insurance Company 1943.

—————— et al. *The Mortality Experience of Industrial Policyholders, 1916–1920: A Contribution to the Public Health Movement in America*. New York: Colonial Life Insurance Company et al. 1923.

——————, Edwin W. Kopf, and George H. Van Buren. *Cancer Mortality among Insured Wage-Earners and Their Families: The Experience of the Metropolitan Life Insurance Company Industrial Department, 1911–1922*. New York: Metropolitan Life Insurance Company 1925.

——————. *Mortality Statistics of Insured Wage-Earners and Their Families: Experience of the Metropolitan Life Insurance Company Industrial Department, 1911 to 1916, in the United States and Canada*. New York: Metropolitan Life Insurance Company 1919.

—————— and Alfred J. Lotka. *Twenty-Five Years of Health Progress: A Study of the Mortality Experience among the Industrial Policyholders of the Metropolitan Life Insurance Company, 1911 to 1935*. New York: Metropolitan Life Insurance Company 1937.

Dymond, Allan M. *The Laws of Ontario Relating to Women and Children*. Toronto: King's Printer 1923.

The 1901 Editions of T. Eaton Co. Limited. Catalogues for Spring and Summer, Fall and Winter. Don Mills: Stoddart Publishing 1991.

Egg-o Baking Powder Company. *Helpful Recipes and Helpful Hints.* Hamilton: Egg-o Baking Powder Company 1919 (CIHM 74198).

Emery, G.N. "The Lord's Day Act of 1906 and the Sabbath Observance Question." In J.M. Bumsted, ed. *Documentary Problems in Canadian History, Volume 2: Post-Confederation.* Georgetown, Ont.: Irwin-Dorsey Limited 1969. Pp.23–51.

Engels, Frederick. *The Housing Question.* New York: International Publishers n.d.

Fenton, J. Hubert. "Supervised Playgrounds." Canadian Club of Hamilton. *Addresses, 1913–14.* Hamilton: Labor News Printery 1914.

Forbush, William Byron. *The Boy Problem.* Boston: Pilgrim Press 1907.

Frey, John P. and John R. Commons. "Conciliation in the Stove Industry." United States, Bureau of Labor. *Bulletin*, January 1906. Pp.124–96.

Gill, L.W. "Specialized Training for an Industrial Life." *LG*, August 1928. P. 873.

Gompers, Samuel. *Seventy Years of Life and Labour: An Autobiography.* New York: Dutton 1925.

Greenway, H.F. "Housing in Canada." In CC, 1931, Vol. 12. Pp.410–578.

Gregory, Claudius. *Forgotten Men.* Hamilton: Davis Lisson 1933.

Halcrow, John James. "Burlington Bay as I Remember It." *Wentworth Bygones*, 9 (1971). Pp.56–61.

Hall, H.C. L. "Economy in Manufacturing." *IC*, February 1906. Pp.430–31. June 1906. Pp.732–35. September 1906. Pp.103–5.

Hamilton, Canada: Its History, Commerce, Industries, Resources. Hamilton: Lister 1913.

Hamilton, Canada: The City of Opportunity. Hamilton n.d.

Hamilton Community Chest. *Twenty-Five Years in Review.* Hamilton: Hamilton Community Chest 1952.

Hamilton Community Fund, *Report*, 1928.

Hamilton Council of Social Agencies. *A Study of Group Membership and Other Recreational Activities, As Reported by Public School Students.* Hamilton: Hamilton Council of Social Agencies 1941.

Hamilton Health Association, *Annual Report*s.

Hamilton Labor Directory. Hamilton: Hamilton Trades and Labor Council 1911, 1913.

Hamilton Orphan Asylum, Aged Women's Home, and Ladies' Benevolent Society. *Annual Report.* Hamilton, 1891–1926.

Hamilton Playgrounds Association. *Souvenir Number: An Historical Review.* [Hamilton: n.p. 1931].

Hamilton: The Birmingham of Canada. Hamilton: Times Printing Company [1892].

Hamilton, Canada: The City of Opportunity. Hamilton: City of Hamilton n.d.

Hamilton: The Electric City. Hamilton: Hamilton Times [1906].

Hamilton, The Manufacturing Metropolis of Canada. Hamilton: n.p. 1910.

Hamilton Spectator Carnival Souvenir. Hamilton: Spectator Publishing 1903.

Hamilton Technical School. *Preliminary Announcement, 1909–1910.* Hamilton: Board of Education 1909.

Hamilton Trades and Labor Council. *Official Programme and Souvenir of the Labor Day Demonstration Held at Dundurn, Hamilton, Ont., September 6th, 1897.* Hamilton: Hamilton Trades and Labor Council 1897.

Hamilton Young Women's Christian Association. *A Centre for Girls, 1889–1929.* N.p., n.d.

Hanna, M.E. "Clean Milk for Babies." *CN*, July 1911. Pp.347–49.

Hardie, A.D. "The Inter-Relation between Community Chests, Councils of Social Agencies, and Social Service Exchanges." *CCSWP*, 1928. Pp.112–16.

Helbing, Albert Theodore. *The Departments of the American Federation of Labor.* Baltimore: Johns Hopkins University 1931.

Hilbert, F.W. "Trade Union Agreements in the Iron Molders' Union." In Jacob H. Hollander and George E. Barnett, eds. *Studies in American Trade Unionism.* New York: Henry Holt and Company 1912. Pp.219–60.

Hobbs, Margaret, and Joan Sangster, eds. *The Woman Worker, 1926–1929.* St. John's: Canadian Committee on Labour History 1999.

Hodgins, Frank Egerton. *Report on the Care and Control of the Mentally Defective and Feeble-Minded in Ontario.* Toronto: King's Printer 1919.

Hogert, John H. "Union Labels." In Hamilton Trades and Labor Council. *Labor Day Souvenir, 1897.* P. 11.

Holbrook, J.H. "The Fight Against Tuberculosis." CCCCP, 1911. Pp.80–88.

————. "The First Regular Open Air School in Canada." *PHJ*, March 1913. Pp.141–46.

————. "Tuberculosis from the Nurse's Standpoint." *CN,* July 1912. Pp.382–87.

Hoodless, Adelaide. "The Social Influence of the Home." CCCCP, 1901.

Hourwich, Isaac A. *Immigration and Labor: The Economic Aspects of European Immigration to the United States.* New York: Putnam 1912.

Houston, W.R. ed. *Directory of Directors in Canada, 1912.* Toronto: Houston S. Standard Publications 1912.

Irish, Mark H. "'Dilution' of Labor in Canadian Munition Plants." *CM*, 28 Dec. 1916. Pp.717–19.

Irvine, William. *The Farmers in Politics.* Toronto: McClelland and Stewart 1920.

Jackson, Gilbert E. "Cycles of Unemployment in Canada." *CCJ*, October 1926. Pp.21–24.

Jarvis, Julia. "The Founding of the Girl Guide Movement in Canada, 1910." *OH*, 62, no. 4 (December 1970). Pp.213–19.

Jeans, James Stephan. *Canada's Resources and Possibilities, with Special Reference to the Iron and Allied Industries, and the Increase of Trade with the Mother Country*. London: British Iron Trade Association 1904.

Jelfs, George Frederick. *Man's Natural, Moral, and Social Duties*. Hamilton: Cloke's Bookstore 1925.

Johnston, W. Sandfield, and C.T. Campbell, comps. *Odd Fellowship in Ontario up to 1923*. Toronto IOOF, Grand Lodge of Ontario 1923.

Kappelle, A.P. "The Administrative Set-Up for Local Welfare Service." CCSWP, 1938. Pp.192–95.

_____. "City of Hamilton Set-Up – Public Welfare Department." *Child and Family Welfare*, July 1934. Pp.48–52.

_____. "Public Relief and Care of the Sick." CCSWP, 1940. Pp.152–55.

Keith, G.C. "Five Years' Development of Machine Tools in Canada." *CM*, January 1910. Pp.27–32.

Kennedy, Thomas F. "Banishing Skill from the Foundry." *International Socialist Review*, February 1911. Pp.469–73.

_____. "A Molderless Foundry." *International Socialist Review*, April 1911. Pp.610–12.

King, W.L. Mackenzie. *Industry and Humanity: A Study of the Principles Underlying Industrial Reconstruction*. Toronto: University of Toronto Press 1973 [1918].

_____. *Report to the Honourable Postmaster General on the Methods Adopted in Canada in the Carrying Out of Government Clothing Contracts*. Ottawa: Queen's Printer 1898.

Lahne, Herbert J. *The Cotton Mill Worker*. New York: Farrar Rinehart 1944.

Langrill, A.D. "The Hospital from the Viewpoint of the Medical Superintendent." *CN*, September 1910. Pp.392–93.

Leacock, Stephen. *The Unsolved Riddle of Social Justice*. London: J. Lane 1920.

Leake, Albert H. *Industrial Problems, Methods, and Dangers*. Boston: Houghton Mifflin 1913.

_____. *Vocational Education of Girls and Women*. New York: Macmillan 1918.

Leven, Maurice, Harold G. Moulton, and Clark Warburton. *America's Capacity to Consume*. Washington, D.C.: Brookings Institution 1934.

London, Jack. *John Barleycorn*. New York: Century Company 1913.

Loudon, William James. *Sir William Mulock: A Short Biography*. Toronto: Macmillan 1932.

Lovering, W.H. "How Much Should Be Given by the Fund." In Canadian Patriotic Fund. *Report of the Proceedings at a Conference of Representatives of Branches of the Canadian Patriotic Fund in Eastern Canada Held at Toronto May 16, 17 & 18 1916*. N.p. 1916. Pp.24–29.

Lozier, Robert T. "Variable Motor Speeds and Their Relation to New Shop Methods." *CE*, July 1903. Pp.189–91.

Lyle, Elizabeth. *Hamilton Local Council of Women, Part One, 1893–1919: A Record of Twenty-Six Years of Activity*. Hamilton: Local Council of Women 1920.

MacDougall, John. *Rural Life in Canada: Its Trends and Tasks*. Toronto: University of Toronto Press 1973 [1913].

MacIver, R.M. *Labor in the Changing World*. Toronto: E.P. Dutton and Company 1919.

MacMurchy, Helen. *Care of the Feeble-Minded in Ontario, 1907*. Toronto: King's Printer 1907.

_____, ed. *Handbook of Child Welfare Work in Canada*. Ottawa 1923.

_____. *Reports on the Feeble-Minded in Ontario*. Toronto: King's Printer 1907–20.

Mathewson, Samuel B. *Restriction of Output among Unorganized Workers*. New York: Viking Press 1931.

McCormick, Cyrus. *The Century of the Reaper: An Account of Cyrus Hall McCormick, the Inventor of the Reaper; of the McCormick Harvesting Machine Company, the Business He Created; and of the International Harvester Company, His Heir and Chief Memorial*. Boston: Houghton Mifflin 1931.

McCready, Margaret S. "Analysis of Weekly Relief Food Orders in a Southern Ontario City." *CPHJ*, February 1934. Pp.67–72.

_____. "Relief Diets." CCSWP, 1934. Pp.54–58.

McKinnon, N.E., and Mary A. Ross. "Whooping Cough: The Public Health Problem." *CPHJ*, November 1934. Pp.533–37.

McVean, Sarah. "The Pageant of Motherhood." *CPHJ*, November 1930. P. 579.

Meikeljohn, M.L. "Anti-Tuberculosis Work in Canada." *CN*, November 1907. Pp.581–85.

Meredith, Sir William Ralph. *Final Report on Laws Relating to the Liability of Employers to Make Compensation to Their Employees for Injuries Received in the Course of Their Employment Which Are in Force in Other Countries*. Toronto: King's Printer 1913.

Methodist Church of Canada, Department of Temperance and Moral Reform, and Presbyterian Church of Canada, Board of Social Service and Evangelism. *Report of a Preliminary and General Social Survey of Hamilton*. N.p. [Hamilton] 1913.

Middleton, Jesse Edgar, and Fred Landon. *The Province of Ontario – A History, 1615–1927*. 4 vols. Toronto: Dominion Publishing Company 1926–28.

Miller, J.O., ed. *The New Era in Canada: Essays Dealing with the Upbuilding of the Canadian Commonwealth*. Toronto: J.M. Dent and Sons 1917.

Montgomery, M.T. "Stelco Story." United Steelworkers of America, *Information*, August- September 1954. P.5.

Moore, J.H. "A Planning System That *Is* a Planning System." *CM*, 17 June 1920. Pp.563–66.

Morgan, Henry James, ed. *The Canadian Men and Women of the Time*. Toronto: W. Briggs 1912.

Mullen, J. Heurner. "Child Welfare in a Democracy." *PHJ*, October 1918. Pp.446–48.

_____. "History of the Organization of the Babies' Dispensary Guild, Hamilton (Inc.)." *PHJ*, November 1915. Pp.542–44.

Murray, R.H. "The Extent of Pasteurization in Canada." *CPHJ*, January 1934. Pp.30–31.

National Council of Women of Canada, *Women of Canada: Their Life and Work*. Ottawa: National Council of Women 1975 [1900].

Nieman, Flora L. "How Can Skilled Nurses Be Secured in the Homes of the Workingman?" *CN*, February 1909. Pp.92–95.

Norris, D.N. "Better Films." *SW*, June 1925. Pp.172–73.

Ogilvie Flour Mills Company Limited. *Ogilvie's Book for a Cook*. Montreal: Ogilvie Flour Mills Company 1905 (CIHM 80162).

Ontario, Commissioners Appointed to Enquire into the Prison and Reformatory System of Ontario. *Report*. Toronto: Warwick and Sons 1891.

Ontario, Department of Health. *The Baby*. Toronto: Ontario Department of Health n.d.

_____, Division of Medical Statistics. *A Survey of Public General Hospitals in Ontario*. Toronto: Ontario Department of Health 1940.

Ontario, Department of Labour. *Survey of Industrial Welfare in Ontario*. Toronto: King's Printer 1929.

_____. *Vocational Opportunities in the Industries of Ontario: A Survey; Bulletin No.4: Garment Making*. Toronto: Ontario Department of Labour 1920.

_____. *Vocational Opportunities in the Industries of Ontario: A Survey; Bulletin No.6: Textiles*. Toronto: Ontario Department of Labour 1920.

Ontario, Housing Committee. *Report*. Toronto: n.p. 1919.

Ontario, Inspector of Charities and Hospitals. *Annual Reports*.

Ontario, Inspectors of the Hospitals for the Insane. *Annual Reports*.

Ontario, Inspector of Prisons and Public Charities. *Annual Reports*.

Ontario, Legislative Assembly, *Journals*, 41 (1907), Appendix 1 ("Report of Committee on Child Labour, 1907").

_____, Milk Commission Appointed to Enquire into the Production, Care and Distribution of Milk. *Report 1909*. Toronto: L.K. Cameron 1910.

Ontario, Minimum Wage Board. *Annual Reports*.

Ontario. Minister of Education. *The Ontario Readers: Third Book*. Toronto: T. Eaton Company 1909.

Ontario, Minister of Public Welfare. *Annual Reports*.

Ontario, Mothers' Allowance Commission. *Annual Reports*.

Ontario, Provincial Board of Health. *Annual Reports*.

Ontario, Registrar General. *Annual Reports*.

Ontario, Registrar of Friendly Societies. *Annual Reports*.

Ontario, Superintendent of Neglected and Dependent Children. *Annual Reports*.

Ontario, Trades and Labour Branch. *Annual Reports*.

Ontario, Workmen's Compensation Board. *Annual Reports*.

Parry, R.Y. "Keeping Babies Well." *CCCCP*, 1911. Pp.65–70.

Pettit, E. Phyllis. "The Integration of Case Work and Group Work." *CCSWP*, 1937. Pp.138–40.

Phair, J.T. and A.H. Sellers. "A Study of Maternal Deaths in the Province of Ontario." *CJPH*, December 1934.

Power, Mary. "The Hamilton Diphtheria Exhibit." *CPHJ*, April 1932. Pp.198–200.

Puffer, J. Adams. *The Boy and His Gang*. Boston: Houghlin Mifflin 1912.

Reed, Louis S. *The Labor Philosophy of Samuel Gompers*. New York: Columbia University Press 1930.

Reeves, Maud Pember. *Round About a Pound a Week*. London: Virago 1979 [1913].

Rehn, Henry Joseph. *Scientific Management and the Cotton Textile Industry*. Chicago: n.p. 1934.

Renton, Miss. "Dispensary and Work amongst Down-Town Tuberculosis Patients." *CN*, July 1912. Pp.374–76.

Reynolds, Lloyd G. *The British Immigrant: His Social and Economic Adjustment in Canada*. Toronto: Oxford University Press 1935.

Rice, Margery Spring. *Working-Class Wives: Their Health and Conditions*. London: Virago 1981 [1939].

Roberts, James. "A Campaign against Diphtheria." *CCSWP*, 1930. Pp.42–49.

_____. "Housing Situation, Hamilton." *Canadian Municipal Journal*, July 1912. Pp.255–56.

_____. "Insanitary Areas." *PHJ*, April 1912. Pp.177–82.

_____. "Public Health Organization." *PHJ*, June 1922. Pp.241–50.

_____. "Queries and Answers." *PHJ*, September 1913. P. 505.

_____. "Radio Talk on Immunization." *PHJ*, October 1927. Pp.484–85.

_____. *Report of the Medical Officer of Health on Amalgamation of Health Service in the City of Hamilton*. [Hamilton: n.p. 1932].

_____. "Tuberculosis in Hamilton." *Bulletin of the Hamilton Academy of Medicine*, November 1931. Pp.10–14.

_____. "Twenty-Three Years of Public Health." *PHJ*, December 1928. Pp.552–58.

Rodgers, J.H. "Evolution and Revolution in Machine Shop Practice." *CM*, 28 June 1917. Pp.677–82.

Rogers, Kenneth H. *Street Gangs in Toronto: A Study of the Forgotten Boy*. Toronto: Ryerson Press 1945.

Ross, Mary A. "The Mortality in Ontario of Four Communicable Diseases of Childhood." *CPHJ*, July 1932. Pp.331–41.

_____. "Typhoid Fever Mortality in Ontario, 1880–1931." *CPHJ*, January 1935. Pp.73–84.

Ross, Victor, and A. St. L. Trigge. *A History of the Canadian Bank of Commerce, with an Account of the Other Banks Which Now Form Part of Its Organization*. 3 vols. Toronto: Oxford University Press 1920–34.

Sadlier, John. "The Problem of the Molder." *IA*, 6 June 1901. P. 266.

Scott, Jean Thomson. *The Conditions of Female Labour in Ontario*. Toronto: Warwick 1892.

Seath, John. *Education for Industrial Purposes: A Report*. Toronto: L.K. Cameron 1911.

Siegfried, Andre. *The Race Question in Canada*. Toronto, 1907; 1966.

Skelton, Oscar Douglas. "General Economic History, 1867–1912." In Adam Shortt and Arthur G. Doughty, eds. *Canada and Its Provinces*. Toronto: T. & A. Constable at the Edinburgh University Press for the Publishers' Association of Canada 1914. Vol. 9. Pp.95–274.

――――――. *Life and Letters of Sir Wilfrid Laurier*. Abridged edition, 2 vols. Toronto, 1965.

Slichter, Sumner H. *The Turnover of Factory Labor*. New York: D. Appleton 1919.

Smith, A.E. *All My Life: An Autobiography*. Toronto: Progress Books 1949.

Smith, Helen M.W. "Child Welfare." *CN*, October 1914. Pp.593–95.

――――――. "Keeping Babies Well." *CCCCP*, 1911. Pp.70–73.

――――――. "The Possibilities of Women's Work in Relation to the Babies' Dispensary, Hamilton." *PHJ*, November 1915. Pp.548–49.

Social Service Council of Canada, Industrial Life Committee. *The Man Out of Work: A Report on a Study of Five Hundred Unemployed Men*. N.p.: Social Service Council of Canada 1927.

The Society Blue Book of Toronto and Hamilton. New York: Dau Publishing Company 1906, 1910–12, 1920.

Spedden, Ernest. *The Trade Union Label*. Baltimore: Johns Hopkins University Press 1910.

Spence, Ruth Elizabeth. *Prohibition in Canada*. Toronto: Ontario Branch of the Dominion Alliance 1919.

St. Giles Presbyterian Church, Ladies' Aid and Friends. *Choice Recipes*. Hamilton: F.G. Smith 1909 (CIHM 84009).

Stecker, Margaret Loomis. "The Founders, the Molders, and the Molding Machine." In J.R. Commons, ed. *Trade Unionism and Labor Problems*. 2nd series. Boston: Ginn and Company 1921. Pp.433–57.

Steel Company of Canada, *Annual Reports*. Hamilton: Steel Company of Canada 1910–40.

Stewart, Bryce M. "The Housing of Our Immigrant Workers." Canadian Political Science Association, *Papers and Proceedings* (Ottawa 1913).

Stockton, Frank T. *The International Molders' Union of North America*. Baltimore: Johns Hopkins University Press 1921.

Strathcona Trust, Executive Council. *Syllabus of Physical Exercises for Schools*. Toronto: Copp Clark Company 1911.

Struthers, Lina Rogers. *The School Nurse: A Survey of the Duties and Responsibilities of the Nurse in the Maintenance of Health and Physical Perfection and the Prevention of Disease among School Children*. New York: Putnam 1917.

Thomas, Ernest. "The Community Use of the Moving Picture." *SW*, 1 Sept. 1919. Pp.278–79.

Thompson, T. Phillips. *The Labor Reform Songster*. Philadelphia: Journal of the Knights of Labor Print 1892.

Thomson, Jean. *The Conditions of Female Labour in Ontario*. Toronto: University of Toronto 1892.

Thrasher, Frederic M. *The Gang: A Study of 1,313 Gangs in Chicago*. Chicago: University of Chicago Press 1926.

Tite, W. "Married Women in Industry." *CCJ*, October 1924. Pp.40–42.

Trades and Labor Congress of Canada. *Official Book, 1901*. N.p. 1901.

United States. Immigration Commission. *Reports*. 41 vols. Washington, D.C.: Immigration Commission 1907–10.

Unsworth, J.K. *The Church and the Boy*. N.p. [Hamilton] 1903. (CIHM 80639.)

Victoria Order of Nurses for Canada, Board of Governors. *Reports*, 1908–10. Ottawa: Copeland-Chatterson-Crain 1909–11.

――――――. *How to Take Care of Babies during Hot Weather*. N.d. n.p.

"Videre." "A Little Independence: Factory Girls, 1912." In Irving Abella and David Millar, eds. *The Canadian Worker in the Twentieth Century*. Toronto: Oxford University Press 1978. Pp.167–78.

Wales, Henry C. "Medical Relief in the Province of Ontario." *CCSWP*, 1937. Pp.86–90.

Walters, Chester S. "The Duty of the City to the Child: What Can Be Accomplished by a 'Baby Week.'" *PHJ*, November 1915. Pp.540–41.

Ward, Harold Bernard. "Hamilton, Ontario, as a Manufacturing Center." PhD thesis, University of Chicago 1934.

Waters, George A. "Moving Picture Shows." *Canadian Municipal Journal*, October 1912. Pp.391–93.

Who's Who in Canada. Toronto International Press 1910–40.

Willetts, Gilson. *Workers of the Nation: An Encyclopedia of the Occupations of the American People and a Record of Business, Professional and Industrial Achievement at the Beginning of the Twentieth Century*. 2 vols. New York: P.F. Collier and Son 1903.

Willett, Mabel Hurd. *The Employment of Women in the Clothing Trade*. New York: Columbia University Press 1902.

Williams, Cecil. "Textile Classes for Hamilton in Near Prospect." *CTJ*, 4 July 1929. Pp.13–14.

Wills, T.H. "Account of Work for the Feeble-Minded in Hamilton, Ontario." *Canadian Journal of Mental Hygiene*, October 1919. Pp.237–41.

Wright, A.W. *Report upon the Sweating System in Canada*. Ottawa: Queen's Printer 1896.

Primary – Periodicals

Advance (New York).

Amalgamated Journal (Pittsburgh).

American Federationist (Washington, D.C.).

American Iron and Steel Institute, *Yearbook* (New York).

Annual Financial Review (Montreal).
Broom Maker (Galesburg, Ill.).
Bulletin (International Machinists' Association, Winnipeg).
Canada Year Book (Ottawa).
Canadian Congress Journal (Ottawa).
Canadian Engineer (Toronto).
Canadian Forward (Toronto).
Canadian Foundryman (Toronto).
Canadian Hotel Review (Toronto).
Canadian Institute of Mining and Metallurgy, *Bulletin* (Montreal).
Canadian Journal of Fabrics (Montreal).
Canadian Labor World (Hamilton).
Canadian Machinery (Toronto).
Canadian Manufacturer (Toronto).
Canadian Mining Journal (Gardenvale, Que.).
Canadian Mining Review (Ottawa).
Canadian Nurse (Ottawa).
Canadian Public Health Journal (Toronto).
Canadian Textile Journal (St-Laurent, Que.).
Canadian White Ribbon Tidings (London, Ont.).
Citizen and Country (Toronto).
Clarion (Toronto).
Cotton's Weekly (Cowansville, Que.).
Engineering Institute of Canada, *Journal* (Montreal).
Fabricator (Hamilton).
Galaxy (Hamilton).
Garment Worker (New York).
Globe (Toronto).
Hamilton Harvester Bulletin (Hamilton).
Hamilton Manufacturer (Hamilton).
Hardware and Metal (Montreal and Toronto).
Herald (Hamilton).
Industrial Banner (London; Toronto).
Industrial Canada (Toronto).
Iron Age (New York).
Iron and Steel of Canada (Gardenvale, Que.).
Iron Molders' Journal (Cincinnati).
Labor Leader (Toronto).
Labor News (Hamilton).
Labour Gazette (Ottawa).
Lord's Day Advocate (Toronto).
Magazine of Industry (Hamilton), Souvenir Edition, December 1910.
Made in Hamilton Quarterly (Hamilton).
Monetary Times (Montreal).
Motorman and Conductor (Detroit).
New Commonwealth (Toronto).
New Democracy (Hamilton).
Ontario Labor News (Toronto).
Public Health Journal (Toronto).
Social Welfare (Toronto).
Spectator (Hamilton).

Star (Toronto).
Stelco Flashes (Hamilton).
Templar Quarterly (Hamilton).
Times (Hamilton).
Veteran (Ottawa).
Worker (Toronto).
Workers' Guard (Toronto).
Young Worker (Toronto).

Primary – Proceedings

Amalgamated Clothing Workers of America.
American Federation of Labor (Washington, D.C.).
Canadian Conference on Charities and Corrections (Toronto).
Canadian Council on Social Work (Ottawa).
Canadian Federation of Labour (Ottawa).
International Association of Machinists.
National Trades and Labor Congress of Canada (Montreal).
Trades and Labor Congress of Canada (Ottawa).
United Garment Workers of America. Toronto 1906.

Secondary

Abella, Irving Martin. *Nationalism, Communism, and Canadian Labour: The CIO, the Communist Party, and the Canadian Congress of Labour, 1935–1956.* Toronto: University of Toronto Press 1973.
Acheson, Thomas William. "Changing Social Origins of the Canadian Industrial Elite, 1880–1910." In Glenn Porter and Robert Cuff, eds. *Enterprise and National Development: Essays in Canadian Business and Economic History.* Toronto: Hakkert 1973. Pp.51–79.
_____. "The Maritimes and 'Empire Canada.'" In David Jay Bercuson, ed. *Canada and the Burden of Unity.* Toronto: Macmillan 1977. Pp.87–114
_____. "The Social Origins of Canadian Industrialism: A Study in the Structure of Entrepreneurship." PhD thesis, University of Toronto 1971.
Acton, Janice, et al., eds. *Women at Work: Ontario, 1850–1930.* Toronto: Women's Press 1974.
Adario, Andrea. "Fighting Bedeaux and Other Hardships in the Textile Industry: The Mercury Mills Strike of 1933." Unpublished paper, York University 1994.
Addison, George Nelson. "Life and Culture of Three 'Blue Collar' Churches in Hamilton, Ontario, 1875–1925." MA thesis, Queen's University 1999.
Adelman, Melvin L. "Baseball, Business and the Workplace: Gelber's Thesis Reexamined." *JSH*, 23, no. 2 (Winter 1989). Pp.285–301.
Alexander, Kristine. "The Girl Guide Movement, Imperialism and Internationalism in Interwar England, Canada, and India." PhD dissertation, York University 2010.
_____. "The Girl Guide Movement and Imperial Internationalism during the 1920s and 1930s." *Journal of*

the History of Childhood and Youth, 2, no. 1 (Winter 2009). Pp.37–63.

_____. "Motherhood, Citizenship, Continuity, and Change: The Girl Guides and Imperialism in Interwar Canada." Major Research Paper, Department of History, York University 2003.

Allard, T.J. *Straight Up: Private Broadcasting in Canada: 1918–1958*. Ottawa: Canadian Communications Foundation 1979.

Allen, Richard. *The Social Passion: Religion and Social Reform in Canada, 1914–28*. Toronto: University of Toronto Press 1973.

Allen, Robert C. *Horrible Prettiness: Burlesque and American Culture*. Chapel Hill: University of North Carolina Press 1991.

_____. "Motion Picture Exhibition in Manhattan, 1906–1912: Beyond the Nickelodeon." In Fell, ed. *Film Before Griffith*. Pp.162–75.

Ames, John H. "The Bank of Hamilton, 1872–1923: A History of a Local Bank as Part of the Triad of Finance, Boosterism, and Business that Built Modern Hamilton." Unpublished paper (WC).

Anderson, Benedict. *Imagined Communities: Reflections on the Origin and Spread of Nationalism*. London: Verso 1983.

Anderson, Grace M. "Ethnic Behaviour and the Ethnic-Religious Variable: A Study of a Federal Election in Hamilton, Ontario." *Canadian Journal of Economics and Political Science*, 32, no. 1 (February 1966). Pp.27–37.

Anderson, Kay J. "The Idea of Chinatown: The Power of Place and Institutional Practice in the Making of a Racial Category." In Gerald Tulchinsky, ed. *Immigration in Canada: Historical Perspectives*. Toronto: Copp Clark Longman 1994. Pp.223–48.

Andrews, Margaret W. "The Emergence of Bureaucracy: The Vancouver Health Department, 1886–1914." *Journal of Urban History*, 12, no. 2 (February 1986). Pp.131–55.

_____. "Epidemics and Public Health: Influenza in Vancouver, 1918–19." *BC Studies*, 34 (Summer 1977). Pp.21–44.

_____. "Medical Attendance in Vancouver, 1886–1920." In Shortt, ed. *Medicine in Canadian Society*. Pp.417–45.

Angus, Ian. *Canadian Bolsheviks: The Early Years of the Communist Party of Canada*. Montreal: Vanguard Publications 1981.

Annau, Catherine. "Eager Eugenicists: A Reappraisal of the Birth Control Society of Hamilton." *HS/SH*, 27, no. 53 (May 1994). Pp.111–34.

_____. "Promoting Prophylactics: The Birth Control Society of Hamilton's Very Public Profile." *OH*, 90, no.1 (Spring 1998). Pp.49–67.

Ansell, Christopher K., and Antoine Joseph. "The Mass Production of Craft Unionism: Exploring Workers' Solidarity in Late Nineteenth-Century France and America." *Politics and Society*, 26, no. 4 (December 1998). Pp.575–602.

Anstead, Christopher J. "Fraternalism in Victorian Ontario: Secret Societies and Cultural Hegemony." PhD dissertation, University of Western Ontario 1992.

Archibald, W. Peter. "Distress, Dissent, and Alienation: Hamilton Workers in the Great Depression." *UHR*, 21, no. 1 (October 1992). Pp.3–32.

_____. "Do Status Differences among Workers Make a Difference during Economic Crises? The Case of Depression Hamilton." *CRSA*, 35, no.2 (May 1998). Pp.125–63.

_____. "Small Expectations and Great Adjustments: How Hamilton Workers Most Often Experienced the Great Depression." *CJS*, 21, no. 3 (Summer 1996). Pp.359–402.

Argyle, Ray. "Rocking with Ragtime." *Beaver*, 88, no. 3 (June/July 2008). Pp.25–28.

Armstrong, Christopher, and H.V. Nelles. *Monopoly's Moment: The Organization and Regulation of Canadian Utilities, 1830–1930*. Toronto: University of Toronto Press 1986.

_____. *The Revenge of the Methodist Bicycle Company: Sunday Streetcars and Municipal Reform in Toronto, 1888–1897*. Toronto: Peter Martin Associates 1977.

Arnesen, Eric. "Whiteness and the Historians' Imagination." *ILWCH*, 60 (Fall 2001). Pp.3–32.

Arnup, Katherine. *Education for Motherhood: Advice for Mothers in Twentieth-Century Canada*. Toronto: University of Toronto Press 1994.

Aron, Cindy S. *Working at Play: A History of Vacations in the United States*. New York: Oxford University Press 1999.

Aronowitz, Stanley. *How Class Works: Power and Social Movement*. New Haven, Conn.: Yale University Press 2003.

Artibise, Alan F.J. "In Pursuit of Growth: Municipal Boosterism and Urban Development in the Canadian Prairie West, 1871–1913." In Gilbert A. Stelter and Alan F.J. Artibise, eds. *Shaping the Urban Landscape: Aspects of the City-Building Process*. Ottawa: Carleton University Press 1982. Pp.116–47.

Ashcraft, Richard. "Liberal Political Theory and Working-Class Radicalism in Nineteenth-Century England." *Political Theory*, 21, no. 2 (May 1993). Pp.249–72.

Atherton, James J. "The Department of Labour and Industrial Relations 1900–1911." MA thesis, Carleton University 1972.

Avery, Donald. "British-Born 'Radicals' in North America: The Case of Sam Scarlett." *CES*, 10, no. 2 (1978). Pp.65–85.

_____. "*'Dangerous Foreigners': European Immigrant Workers and Labour Radicalism in Canada, 1896–1932*. Toronto: McClelland and Stewart 1979.

_____. "Ethnic and Class Tensions in Canada, 1918–20: Anglo-Canadians and the Alien Worker." In Swyripa and Thompson, eds. *Loyalties in Conflict*. Pp.79–98.

_____. "The Radical Alien and the Winnipeg General Strike of 1919." In Carl Berger and Ramsay Cook, eds. *The West and the Nation: Essays in Honour of W.L. Morton*. Toronto: McClelland and Stewart 1976.

_____. *Reluctant Host: Canada's Response to Immigrant Workers, 1896–1994*. Toronto: McClelland and Stewart 1995.

Avolio, Franco. "Hamilton's Social Landscape of Bootlegging in the Late 1920s." (WC.)

Ayers, Pat, and Jan Lambertz. "Marriage Relations, Money, and Domestic Violence in Working-Class Liverpool, 1919–39." In Lewis, ed. *Labour and Love*. Pp.195–219.

Babcock, Robert H. *Gompers in Canada: A Study in American Continentalism before the First World War*. Toronto: University of Toronto Press 1974.

Bacher, John C. *Keeping to the Marketplace: The Evolution of Canadian Housing Policy*. Montreal and Kingston: McGill-Queen's University Press 1993.

Backhouse, Constance. *Colour-Coded: A Legal History of Racism in Canada, 1900–1950*. Toronto: University of Toronto Press 1999.

—————. "Physicians, Abortions, and the Law in Early Twentieth-Century Ontario." *CBMH*, 10, no.2 (1993). Pp.229–49.

Bachman, Gregg. "Still in the Dark – Silent Film Audiences." *Film History*, 9, no. 1 (1997). Pp.23–48.

Bailey, Beth L. *From Front Porch to Back Seat: Courtship in Twentieth-Century America*. Baltimore: Johns Hopkins University Press 1989.

Bailey, Peter. *Popular Culture and Performance in the Victorian City*. Cambridge: Cambridge University Press 1998.

—————. "'Will the Real Bill Banks Please Stand Up?': Towards a Role Analysis of Mid-Victorian Working-Class Respectability." *JSH*, 12, no.2 (Summer 1979). Pp.336–51.

Bailey, T. Melville. *Hamilton: Chronicle of a City*. Hamilton: Windsor Publications 1983.

————— et al. *The Presbytery of Hamilton: 1836–1967*. Hamilton: Presbytery of Hamilton, Presbyterian Church of Canada 1967.

Bailie, Douglas. "'Profitable Leisure': The Motion Picture Industry's Fight against Amusement Taxes in Canada, 1918–1930." Paper presented to the Canadian Historical Association, 2000.

Baillargeon, Denyse. "Care of Mothers and Infants in Montreal between the Wars: The Visiting Nurses of Metropolitan Life, Les Gouttes de lait, and Assistance maternelle." In Dodd and Gorham, eds. *Caring and Curing*. Pp.164–67.

—————. "'If You Had No Money, You Had No Trouble, Did You?': Montreal Working-Class Housewives during the Great Depression." In Wendy Mitchinson et al., eds. *Canadian Women: A Reader*. Toronto: Harcourt Brace and Company 1996. Pp.251–68.

—————. *Making Do: Women, Family, and Home in Montreal during the Great Depression*. Waterloo, Ont.: Wilfrid Laurier University Press 1999.

—————. *Un Québec en mal d'enfants: la médicalisation de la maternité, 1910–1970*. Montreal: Les éditions du remue-ménage 2004.

Baker, William J. "Disputed Diamonds: The YMCA Debate over Baseball in the Late 19th Century." *Journal of Sport History*, 19, no. 3 (Winter 1992). Pp.257–62.

Baldus, Bernd, and Meenz Kassam. "Make Me Truthful, Good, and Mild: Values in Nineteenth-Century Ontario Textbooks." *CJS*, 21, no. 3 (Summer 1996). Pp.327–40.

Barber, Marilyn. *Immigrant Domestic Servants in Canada*. Ottawa: Canadian Historical Association 1991.

—————. "Nationalism, Nativism and the Social Gospel: The Protestant Church Response to Foreign Immigrants in Western Canada, 1897–1914." In Richard Allen, ed. *The Social Gospel in Canada*. Ottawa: National Museum of Man 1975. Pp.186–226.

—————. "The Women Ontario Welcomed: Immigrant Domestics for Ontario Homes, 1870–1930." In Michael J. Piva, ed. *A History of Ontario: Selected Readings*. Toronto: Copp Clark Pitman 1988. Pp.144–60.

Barfield, Ray. *Listening to Radio, 1920–1950*. Westport, Conn.: Praeger 1996.

Barman, Jean. "'Knowledge Is Essential for Universal Progress but Fatal to Class Privilege': Working People and the Schools in Vancouver during the 1920s." *LLT*, 22 (Fall 1988). Pp.9–66.

—————. "Neighbourhood and Community in Interwar Vancouver: Residential Differentiation and Civic Voting Behaviour." *BC Studies*, 69–70 (Spring-Summer 1986). Pp.97–141.

Baron, Ava. "Masculinity, the Embodied Male Worker, and the Historian's Gaze." *ILWCH*, 69 (Spring 2000). Pp.143–60.

—————, ed. *Work Engendered: Toward a New History of American Labor*. Ithaca, N.Y.: Cornell University Press 1991.

Barrett, James R. "Americanization from the Bottom Up: Immigration and the Remaking of the Working Class in the United States, 1880–1930." *JAH*, 79, no. 3 (December 1992). Pp.996–1020.

—————. "Unity and Fragmentation: Class, Race, and Ethnicity on Chicago's South Side, 1900–1922." *JSH*, 18, no. 1 (Fall 1984). Pp.37–55.

—————, and David Roediger. "Inbetween Peoples: Race, Nationality, and the 'New Immigrant' Working Class." *Journal of American Ethnic History*, 16, no. 3 (Spring 1997). Pp.3–44.

Bartlett, Eleanor. "Real Wages and the Standard of Living in Vancouver, 1901–1929." *BC Studies*, 51 (Autumn 1981). Pp.3–62.

Baskerville, Peter. "Familiar Strangers: Urban Families with Boarders, Canada, 1901." *Social Science History*, 25, no. 3 (Fall 2001). Pp.321–46.

—————. *A Silent Revolution? Gender and Wealth in English-Canada, 1860–1930*. Montreal and Kingston: McGill-Queen's University Press 2008.

—————, and Eric Sager. *Unwilling Idlers: The Urban Unemployed and Their Families in Late Victorian Canada*. Toronto: University of Toronto Press 1998.

Bates, Barbara. *Bargaining for Life: A Social History of Tuberculosis, 1876–1938*. Philadelphia: University of Pennsylvania Press 1992.

Bates, Christina. "Shop and Factory: The Ontario Millinery Trade in Transition, 1870–1930." In Alexandra Palmer, ed. *Fashion: A Canadian Perspective*. Toronto: University of Toronto Press 2004. Pp.113–38.

Bator, Paul Adolphus. "The Health Reformers Versus the Common Canadian: The Controversy over Compulsory Vaccination against Smallpox in Toronto and Ontario, 1900–1920." *OH*, 75, no. 4 (December 1983). Pp.349–73.

Bealey, Frank, and Henry Pelling. *Labour and Politics, 1900–1906: A History of the Labour Representation Committee*. London: Macmillan 1958.

Beattie, Jessie L. *John Christie Holland: Man of the Year*. Toronto: Ryerson Press 1956.

Beaujot, Roderic, and Kevin McQuillan. *Growth and Dualism: The Demographic Development of Canadian Society*. Toronto: Gage 1982.

Beckert, Sven. *The Moneyed Metropolis: New York City and the Consolidation of the American Bourgeoisie, 1850–1896*. Cambridge: Cambridge University Press 2001.

Beckham, Sue Bridwell. "The American Front Porch: Women's Liminal Space." In Motz and Browne, eds. *Making the American Home*. Pp.69–88.

Bedel, Penny, and Ross Bartlett. "The Women Do Not Speak: The Methodist Ladies' Aid Societies and World War I." Canadian Methodist Historical Society. *Papers*, 10 (1995). Pp.63–86.

Bederman, Gail. *Manliness and Civilization: A Cultural History of Gender and Race in the United States, 1880–1917*. Chicago: University of Toronto Press 1995.

————. "'The Women Have Had Charge of the Church Work Long Enough': The Men and Religious Forward Movement of 1911–1912 and the Masculinization of Middle-Class Protestantism." *American Quarterly*, 41, no. 3 (September 1989). Pp.432–65.

Belisle, Donica. "Negotiating Paternalism: Women and Canada's Largest Department Stores, 1890–1960." *Journal of Women's History*, 19, no. 1 (Spring 2007). Pp.58–81.

————. *Retail Nation: Department Stores and the Making of Modern Canada*. Vancouver: UBC Press 2011.

————. "Rise of Mass Retail: Canadians and Department Stores, 1890 to 1940." PhD dissertation, Trent University 2007.

————. "Toward a Canadian Consumer History." *L/LT*, 52 (Fall 2003). Pp.181–206.

Belshaw, John Douglas. *Colonization and Community: The Vancouver Island Coalfield and the Making of the British Columbian Working Class*. Montreal and Kingston: McGill-Queen's University Press 2002.

Benn, Adam. "Steel City Shutdown: The 1918 Quarantine in Hamilton." In Herring, ed. *Anatomy of a Pandemic*. Pp.121–33.

Benner, Penney. *100 Years for Children, 1894–1994: The Children's Aid Society of Hamilton-Wentworth, "Celebrating 100 Years for Children."* [Hamilton: Children's Aid Society 1994].

Bennett, Paul W. "Taming 'Bad Boys' of the 'Dangerous Class': Child Rescue and Restraint at the Victoria Industrial School, 1887–1935." *HS/SH*, 21, no. 41 (1988). Pp.71–96.

————. "Turning 'Bad Boys' into 'Good Citizens': The Reforming Impulse of Toronto's Industrial Schools Movement, 1883 to the 1920s." *OH*, 78, no. 3 (September 1986). Pp.209–32.

Benson, John. *Entrepreneurism in Canada: A History of 'Penny Capitalists.'* Lewiston, N.Y.: Edward Mellen Press 1990.

————. "Retailing in Hamilton, Ontario, 1891–1941." *British Journal of Canadian Studies*, 5, no. 2 (1990), 396–413.

Benson, Susan Porter. "Gender, Generation, and Consumption in the United States: Working-Class Families in the Interwar Period." In Susan Strasser, Charles McGovern, and Matthias Judt, eds. *Getting and Spending: European and American Consumer Societies in the Twentieth Century*. New York: Cambridge University Press 1998. Pp.223–40.

————. *Household Accounts: Working-Class Family Economies in the Interwar United States*. Ithaca, N.Y.: Cornell University Press 2007.

————. "Living on the Margin: Working-Class Marriages and Family Survival Strategies in the United States, 1919–1941." In De Grazia with Furlough, eds. *Sex of Things*. Pp.212–43.

Bercuson, David J. *Confrontation at Winnipeg: Labour, Industrial Relations, and the General Strike*. Montreal and Kingston: McGill-Queen's University Press 1974.

————. "Organized Labour and the Imperial Munitions Board." *RI/IR*, 28, no. 3 (July 1973). Pp.602–16.

————. *Fools and Wise Men: The Rise and Fall of the One Big Union*. Toronto: McGraw-Hill Ryerson 1978.

Berger, Carl C. *A Sense of Power: Studies in the Ideas of Canadian Imperialism, 1867–1914*. Toronto: University of Toronto Press 1970.

Berger, Michael L. "The Car's Impact on the American Family." In Wachs and Crawford, eds. *Car and the City*. Pp.57–74.

Berry, Sarah. *Screen Style: Fashion and Femininity in 1930s Hollywood*. Minneapolis: University of Minnesota Press 2000.

Best, John C., and Robert L. Fraser. "Chisolm James." *DHB*, 3. Pp.28–33.

Betcherman, Lita-Rose. *The Little Band: The Clashes between the Communists and the Political and Legal Establishment in Canada, 1928–1932*. Ottawa: Deneau 1982.

Beveridge, Scott G. "Hamilton's 'Public' Parks." Unpublished paper, McMaster University (WC).

Biggs, C. Lesley. "The Case of the Missing Midwives: A History of Midwifery in Ontario from 1795–1900." In Arnup, Levesque, and Pierson, eds. *Delivering Motherhood*. Pp.20–35.

Biagini, Eugenio, and Alistair J. Reid, eds. *Currents of Radicalism: Popular Radicalism, Organised Labour, and Party Politics in Britain, 1850–1914*. Cambridge: Cambridge University Press 1991.

——————. "Currents of Radicalism, 1850–1914." In Biagini and Reid, eds. *Currents of Radicalism*. Pp.1–19.

Bird, Pat. "Hamilton Working Women in the Period of the Great Depression." *Atlantis*, 8, no.2 (Spring 1983). Pp.125–36.

Birke, Michael. "'Even Better Than the Boys': Gender Relations, Femininity, and Masculinity in the 'Uprisings' in the Garment Industry, 1909 to 1913." Major Research Paper, York University 1995.

——————. "'Girls Remain Loyal': Gender Relations in the Hamilton Garment Workers' Strike of 1913." Unpublished graduate paper, York University 1994.

Blaine, William E. *"Ride through the Garden of Canada": A Short History of the Hamilton, Grimsby & Beamsville Electric Railway Company, 1894–1931*. Grimsby, Ont.: Author 1967.

Bledstein, Burton J. "Introduction: Storytellers to the Middle Class." In Bledstein and Johnston, eds. *Middling Sorts*. Pp.1–25.

—————— and Robert D. Johnston, eds. *The Middling Sorts: Explorations in the History of the American Middle Class*. New York: Routledge 2001.

Blewett, Neal. "The Franchise in the United Kingdom, 1885–1918." *Past and Present*, 32 (December 1965). Pp.27–56.

Bliss, Michael. *A Canadian Millionaire: The Life and Business Times of Sir Joseph Flavelle, Bart., 1858–1939*. Toronto: Macmillan 1978.

——————. "Canadianizing American Business: The Roots of the Branch Plant." In Ian Lumsden, ed. *Close the 49th Parallel etc: The Americanization of Canada*. Toronto: University of Toronto Press 1970. Pp.27–42.

——————. *A Living Profit: Studies in the Social History of Canadian Business, 1883–1911*. Toronto: McClelland and Stewart 1974.

——————. "'Pure Books on Avoided Subjects': Pre-Freudian Sexual Ideas in Canada." CHAHP, 1970. Pp.89–108.

Bloomfield, Anne. "Drill and Dance as Symbols of Imperialism." In J.A. Mangan, ed. *Making Imperial Mentalities: Socialization and British Imperialism*. Manchester: Manchester University Press 1990. Pp.74–95.

Bloomfield, Elizabeth. "Boards of Trade and Canadian Urban Development." *UHR*, 12, no. 2 (October 1983). Pp.77–99.

Blumin, Stuart M. *The Emergence of the Middle Class: Social Experience in the American City, 1760–1900*. Cambridge: Cambridge University Press 1989.

Bodnar, John. "Immigration, Kinship, and the Rise of Working-Class Realism in Industrial America." *JSH*, 14, no. 1 (Autumn 1980). Pp.45–65.

——————. *The Transplanted: A History of Immigrants in Urban America*. Bloomington: Indiana University Press 1985.

Bonnett, Alastair. "How the British Working Class Became White: The Symbolic (Re)formation of Racialized Capitalism." *Journal of Historical Sociology*, 11, no. 3 (September 1998). Pp.316–40.

Bose, Christine E. "Household Resources and U.S. Women's Work: Factors Affecting Gainful Employment at the Turn of the Century." *American Sociological Review*, 49, no. 3 (August 1984). Pp.474–90.

Bothwell, Robert S. and John S. English. "Pragmatic Physicians: Canadian Medicine and Health Care Insurance, 1910–1945." In Shortt, ed. *Medicine in Canadian Society*. Pp.479–93.

Bottles, Scott L. "Mass Politics and the Adoption of the Automobile in Los Angeles." In Wachs and Crawford, eds. *Car and the City*. Pp.194–203.

Bouchier, Nancy B., and Ken Cruikshank. "'Sportsmen and Pothunters': Environment, Conservation, and Class in the Fishery of Hamilton Harbour, 1858–1914." *Sport History Review*, 28, no. 1 (May 1997). Pp.1–18.

——————. "The War on the Squatters, 1920–1940: Hamilton's Boathouse Community and the Re-Creation of Recreation on Burlington Bay." *L/LT*, 51 (Spring 2003). Pp.9–46.

Bourdieu, Pierre. *Distinction: A Social Critique of the Judgement of Taste*. Cambridge, Mass.: Harvard University Press 1984.

——————. *Outline of a Theory of Practice*. Cambridge: University of Cambridge 1977.

——————. "What Makes a Social Class? On the Theoretical and Practical Existence of Groups." *Berkeley Journal of Sociology*, 32 (1987). Pp.1–17.

Bourke, Joanna. *Working-Class Cultures in Britain, 1890–1960: Gender, Class and Ethnicity*. London: Routledge 1994.

Boutilier, Beverly. "Helpers or Heroines? The National Council of Women, Nursing, and 'Woman's Work' in Late Victorian Canada." In Dodd and Gorham, eds. *Caring and Curing*. Pp.17–48.

Bowden, Sue, and Avner Offer. "The Technological Revolution That Never Was: Gender, Class, and Diffusion of Household Appliances in Interwar England." In De Grazia with Furlough, eds. *Sex of Things*. Pp.244–74.

Bowser, Eileen. *The Transformation of Cinema, 1907–1915*. New York: Charles Scribner's Sons 1990.

Bradbury, Bettina. "The Fragmented Family: Family Strategies in the Face of Death, Illness, and Poverty, Montreal 1860–1885." In Joy Parr, ed. *Childhood and Family in Canadian History*. Toronto: McClelland and Stewart 1982. Pp.109–28

——————. "The Home as Workplace." In Craven, ed. *Labouring Lives*. Pp.412–78

——————. *Working Families: Age, Gender, and Daily Survival in Industrializing Montreal*. Toronto: McClelland and Stewart 1993.

Braithwaite, Catherine, Peter Keating, and Sandi Vicer. "The Problem of Diphtheria in the Province of Quebec: 1894–1909." *HS/SH*, 29, no. 57 (May 1996). Pp.71–95.

Brand, Dionne. "We Weren't Allowed to Go into Factory Work until Hitler Started the War." In Peggy Bristow, ed. *"We're*

Rooted Here and They Can't Pull Us Up": Essays in African Canadian Women's History. Toronto: University of Toronto Press 1994. Pp.171–91.

Brandino, Diane. "The Italians of Hamilton, 1921–1945." MA thesis, University of Western Ontario 1977.

Braud, Ann. "Women's History *Is* American Religious History." In Thomas A. Tweed, ed. *Retelling U.S. Religious History*. Berkeley: University of California Press 1997. Pp.87–107.

Braverman, Harry. *Labor and Monopoly Capitalism*. New York: Monthly Review Press 1974.

Bray, R. Matthew. "'Fighting as an Ally': The English-Canadian Response to the Great War." *CHR*, 61, no.2 (June 1980). Pp.151–68.

Braybrook, Kevin. "The First Apartment Dwellers in the City of Hamilton: A Social Profile." Unpublished paper (WC).

Briggs, Asa. "The Language of 'Mass' and 'Masses' in Nineteenth-Century England." In David E. Martin and David Rubinstein, eds. *Ideology and the Labour Movement: Essays Presented to John Saville*. London: Croom Helm 1979. Pp.62–93.

Bright, David. *The Limits of Labour: Class Formation and the Labour Movement in Calgary, 1883–1929*. Vancouver: UBC Press 1998.

————. "Loafers Are Not Going to Subsist upon Public Credulence: Vagrancy and the Law in Calgary, 1900–1914." *LLT*, 36 (Fall 1995). Pp.37–58.

————. "The State, the Unemployed, and the Communist Party in Calgary, 1930–5." *CHR*, 78, no. 4 (December 1997). Pp.537–65.

Broadfoot, Barry. *Ten Lost Years, 1929–1939: Memories of Canadians Who Survived the Depression*. Toronto: Doubleday Canada 1973.

Brodie, Marc. *The Politics of the Poor: The East End of London, 1885–1914*. Oxford: Clarendon Press 2004.

Brody, David. *In Labor's Cause*. New York: Oxford University Press 1993.

————. *Labor in Crisis: The Steel Strike of 1919*. Philadelphia: J.B. Lippincott 1965.

————. "The Rise and Decline of Welfare Capitalism." In Brody. *Workers in Industrial America: Essays on the Twentieth Century Struggle*. New York: Oxford University Press 1980. Pp.82–119.

————. *Steelworkers in America: The Nonunion Era*. New York: Harper and Row 1960.

Brookes, Alan A., and Catharine A. Wilson. "'Working Away' from the Farm: The Young Women of North Huron, 1910–30." *OH*, 77, no.4 (December 1985). Pp.281–300.

Brookes, Barbara. "Women and Reproduction c.1860–1919." In Lewis, ed. *Labour and Love*. Pp.149–71.

Brown, Mary M. "Entertainers of the Road." In Ann Saddlemyer, ed. *Early Stages: Theatre in Ontario, 1800–1914*. Toronto: University of Toronto Press 1990. Pp.123–65.

Brown, Robert Craig. "The Political Ideas of Robert Borden." In Hamelin, ed. *Les idées politiques des premiers ministres*. Pp.87–106.

————. *Robert Laird Borden: A Biography*. 2 vols. Toronto: Macmillan 1975–80.

————, and Ramsay Cook. *Canada, 1896–1921: A Nation Transformed*. Toronto: McClelland and Stewart 1974.

Brown, Tom. "Shell Shock in the Canadian Expeditionary Force, 1914–1918: Canadian Psychiatry in the Great War." In Charles G. Rowland, ed. *Health, Disease, and Medicine: Essays in Canadian History*. Toronto: Clark Irwin for the Hannah Institute for the History of Medicine 1984. Pp.308–32.

Brownlee, Jamie. *Ruling Canada: Corporate Cohesion and Democracy*. Halifax: Fernwood Publishing 2005.

Bruce, Charles. *News and the Southams*. Toronto: Macmillan 1968.

Bryden, Kenneth. *Old-Age Pensions and Policy-Making in Canada*. Montreal and Kingston: McGill-Queen's University Press 1974.

Buck, Tim. *Yours in the Struggle: Reminiscences of Tim Buck*. Ed. William Beeching and Phyllis Clarke. Toronto: NC Press 1977.

Buckner, P.A. "The Long Goodbye: English Canadians and the British World." In Buckner and R. Douglas Francis, eds. *Rediscovering the British World*. Calgary: University of Calgary Press 2005. Pp.181–207.

————. "Whatever Happened to the British Empire?" *JCHA*, 4 (1993). Pp.1–31.

————, and Carl Bridge. "Reinventing the British World." *Round Table*, 92, no. 368 (2003). Pp.77–88.

————, and R. Douglas Francis, eds. *Rediscovering the British World*. Calgary: University of Calgary Press 2005.

Buckley, Suzann, and Janice Dickin McGinnis. "Venereal Disease and Public Health Reform in Canada." *CHR*, 63, no. 3 (September 1982). Pp.337–54.

Bukowczyk, John J. "The Transformation of Working-Class Ethnicity: Corporate Control, Americanization, and the Polish Immigrant Middle Class in Bayonne, New Jersey, 1915–1925." *LH*, 25, no. 1 (1984). Pp.53–82.

Burke, Stacie D.A. "Transitions in Household and Family Structure in 1901 and 1991,' In Sager and Baskerville, eds. *Household Counts*. Pp.17–58.

Burley, Edith I. *Servants of the Honourable Company: Work, Discipline, and Conflict in the Hudson's Bay Company, 1770–1879*. Toronto: Oxford University Press 1997.

Burnett, John. *A Social History of Housing, 1815–1985*. London: Methuen 1986.

Burr, Christina. *Spreading the Light: Work and Labour Reform in Late-Nineteenth-Century Toronto*. Toronto: University of Toronto Press 1999.

Butler, Judith. *Gender Trouble: Feminism and the Subversion of Identity*. New York: Routledge: 1999.

Butler, Nancy. "Mother Russia and the Socialist Fatherland: Women and the Communist Party of Canada, 1931–1941, with Specific Reference to the Activism of Dorothy Livesay and Jim Watts." PhD dissertation, Queen's University 2010.

Butsch, Richard. *The Making of American Audiences: From Stage to Television, 1750–1990*. Cambridge: Cambridge University Press 2000.

———, ed. *For Fun and Profit: The Transformation of Leisure into Consumption*. Philadelphia: Temple University Press 1990.

Calder, Lendol. *Financing the American Dream: A Cultural History of Consumer Credit*. Princeton, N.J.: Princeton University Press 1999.

Calhoun, Craig, ed. *Habermas and the Public Sphere*. Cambridge: MIT Press 1992.

Calliste, Agnes. "Race, Gender, and Canadian Immigration Policy: Blacks from the Caribbean, 1900–1932." *JCS*, 28, no. 4 (Winter 1993–94). Pp.131–48.

Callow, Jr., Alexander B., ed. *The City Boss in America: An Interpretive Reader*. New York: Oxford University Press 1976.

Calvert, Monte A. *The Mechanical Engineer in America, 1830–1910: Professional Cultures in Conflict*. Baltimore: Johns Hopkins University Press 1967.

Campbell, Douglas F. "Class, Status, and Crisis: Upper-Class Protestants and the Founding of the United Church of Canada." *JCS*, 29, no. 3 (Autumn 1994). Pp.63–84.

Campbell, Gail. "Voters and Non-Voters: The Problem of Turnout in the Nineteenth Century; Southwestern Ontario as Case Study." *Social Science History*, 11, no. 2 (Summer 1987). Pp.187–210.

Campbell, Jane. "'The Balance Wheel of the Industrial System': Maximum Hours, Minimum Wages, and Workmen's Compensation Legislation in Ontario, 1900–1939." PhD dissertation, McMaster University 1981.

Campbell, Lara. "'We Who Have Wallowed in the Mud of Flanders': First World War Veterans, Unemployment, and the Development of Social Welfare in Canada, 1929–1939." *JCHA*, 11, no. 1 (2000). Pp.125–49.

Campbell, Marjorie Freeman. *The Hamilton General Hospital School of Nursing, 1890–1955*. Toronto: Ryerson Press 1956.

———. *A History of Beth Jacob Congregation, 1886–1969*. [Hamilton]: n.p. 1969.

———. *Holbrook of the San*. Toronto: Ryerson Press 1953.

Cannadine, David. "Imperial Canada: Old History, New Problems." In Colin M. Coates, ed. *Imperial Canada, 1867–1917*. Edinburgh: University of Edinburgh, Centre of Canadian Studies 1997. Pp.1–19.

Canning, Kathleen. "The Body as Method? Reflections on the Place of the Body in Gender History." In Canning. *Gender History in Practice*. Pp.168–89.

———. *Gender History in Practice: Historical Perspectives on Bodies, Class, and Citizenship*. Ithaca, N.Y.: Cornell University Press 2006.

———. "Gender: Meanings, Methods, and Metanarratives." In Canning. *Gender History in Practice*. Pp.3–62.

Caplan, Gerald L. *The Dilemma of Canadian Socialism: The CCF in Ontario*. Toronto: McClelland and Stewart 1973.

Carnes, Mark C., and Clyde Griffen, eds. *Meanings for Manhood: Constructions of Masculinity in Victorian America*. Chicago: University of Chicago Press 1990.

Cassel, Jay. "Public Health in Canada." In Dorothy Porter, ed. *The History of Public Health and the Modern State*. Amsterdam: Wellcome Trust 1994. Pp.276–312.

———. *The Secret Plague: Venereal Disease in Canada, 1838–1939*. Toronto: University of Toronto Press 1987.

Challinor, Raymond. *The Origins of British Bolshevism*. London: Croom Helm 1977.

Chambers, Edward J. "Canadian Business Cycles since 1919: A Progress Report." *Canadian Journal of Economics and Political Science*, 24, no. 2 (May 1958). Pp.166–89.

Chambers, Lori. "Courtship, Condoms, and 'Getting Caught': Working-Class Sexual Behaviour in Ontario, 1921–1969." Paper presented to the Canadian Historical Association meeting, 1995.

———. "Illegitimate Children and the Children of Unmarried Parents Act." In Edgar-Andre Montigny and Lori Chambers, eds. *Ontario Since Confederation: A Reader*. Toronto: University of Toronto Press 2000. Pp.235–59.

———. *Married Women and Property Law in Victorian Ontario*. Toronto: University of Toronto Press 1997.

———. *Misconceptions: Unmarried Motherhood and the Ontario Children of Unmarried Parents Act, 1921–1969*. Toronto: University of Toronto Press 2007.

Chan, Andrea H.W., and Hagen F. Kluge. "The Epidemic Spreads through the City." In Herring, ed. *Anatomy of a Pandemic*. Pp.41–55.

Chandler, Alfred D. *The Visible Hand: The Managerial Revolution in American Business*. Cambridge: Belknap Press 1977.

Charles, Jeffrey A. *Service Clubs in American Society: Rotary, Kiwanis, and Lions*. Urbana: University of Illinois Press 1993.

Chauncey, George. *Gay New York: Gender, Urban Culture, and the Making of the Gay Male World, 1890–1940*. New York: Basic Books 1994.

Chodo, Marc, and Richard Harris. "The Local Culture of Property: A Comparative History of Housing Tenure in Montreal and Toronto." Association of American Geographers, *Annals*, 80, no.1 (March 1990). Pp.73–95.

Christian, William, and Colin Campbell. *Political Parties and Ideologies in Canada: Liberals, Conservatives, Socialists, Nationalists*. Toronto: 1974.

Christie, Nancy. *Engendering the State: Family, Work, and Welfare in Canada*. Toronto: University of Toronto Press 2000.

———, ed. *Households of Faith: Family, Gender, and Community in Canada, 1760–1969*. Montreal and Kingston: McGill-Queen's University Press 2002.

_____, and Michael Gauvreau. *Christian Churches and Their Peoples, 1840–1965*. Toronto: University of Toronto Press 2010.

_____. *A Full-Orbed Christianity: The Protestant Churches and Social Welfare in Canada, 1900–1940*. Montreal and Kingston: McGill-Queen's University Press 1996.

_____. "The World of the Common People Is Filled with Religious Fervour." In G.A. Rawlyk, ed. *Aspects of the Canadian Evangelical Experience*. Montreal and Kingston: McGill-Queen's University Press 1997. Pp.337–50.

Chudacoff, Howard P. *Age of the Bachelor: Creating an American Subculture*. Princeton, N.J.: Princeton University Press 1999.

Chunn, Dorothy E. *From Punishment to Doing Good: Family Courts and Socialized Justice in Ontario, 1880–1940*. Toronto: University of Toronto Press 1992.

Clark, Anna. "Domesticity and the Problem of Wifebeating in Nineteenth-Century Britain: Working-Class Culture, Law, and Politics." In D'Cruze, ed. *Everyday Violence in Britain*. Pp.27–39.

_____. *Struggle for the Breeches: Gender and the Making of the British Working Class*. Berkeley: University of California Press 1997.

Clark, Lovell C. "The Conservative Party in the 1890s." CHAAR, 1961. Pp.58–74.

Clarke, Brian. *Piety and Nationalism: Lay Voluntary Associations and the Creation of an Irish-Catholic Identity in Toronto, 1850–1895*. Kingston and Montreal: McGill-Queen's University Press 1993.

_____. "Religion and Public Space in Protestant Toronto, 1880–1900." In Marguerite Van Die, ed. *Religion and Public Life in Canada: Historical and Comparative Perspectives*. Toronto: University of Toronto Press 2001. Pp.69–86.

Clarke, John. "Pessimism versus Populism: The Problematic Politics of Popular Culture." In Butsch, ed. *For Fun and Profit*. Pp.28–44.

Clawson, Mary Ann. *Constructing Brotherhood: Class, Gender, and Fraternalism*. Princeton, N.J.: Princeton University Press 1989.

_____. "Fraternal Order and Class Formation in the Nineteenth-Century United States." *Comparative Studies in Society and History*, 27, no. 4 (October 1985). Pp.672–95.

_____. "Nineteenth-Century Women's Auxiliaries and Fraternal Orders." *Signs*, 12, no. 1 (Autumn 1986). Pp.40–61.

Clegg, H.A., Alan Fox, and A.F. Thompson. *A History of British Trade Unions since 1889, Volume 1: 1889–1910*. Oxford: Clarendon Press 1964.

Clement, Wallace. *Canadian Corporate Elite: An Analysis of Economic Power*. Toronto: McClelland and Stewart 1975.

Cleverdon, Catherine. *The Woman Suffrage Movement in Canada*. Toronto: University of Toronto Press 1950.

Clifford, Geraldine Joncich. "'Marry, Stitch, Die or Do Worse': Educating Women for Work." In Harvey Kantor and David Tyack, eds. *Work, Youth, and Schooling: Historical Perspectives on Vocationalism in American Education*. Stanford, Cal.: Stanford University Press 1982. Pp.223–68.

Clow, Barbara. *Negotiating Disease: Power and Cancer Care, 1900–1950*. Montreal and Kingston: McGill-Queen's University Press 2001.

Coates, Ken, and Fred McGuinness. *Only in Canada: Kinsmen and Kinettes*. Winnipeg: Peguis Publishers 1987.

Cody, William M. "Who Were the Five Johns?" *Wentworth Bygones*, 5 (1964). Pp.14–17.

Coe, Brian, and Paul Gates. *The Snapshot Photograph: The Rise of Popular Photography, 1888–1939*. London: Ash and Grant 1977.

Coetzee, Frans. *For Party or Country: Nationalism and the Dilemmas of Popular Conservatism in Edwardian England*. New York: Oxford University Press 1990.

Cohen, Andrew Wender. "Obstacles to History? Modernization and the Lower Middle Class in Chicago, 1900–1940." In Bledstein and Johnston, eds. *Middling Sorts*. Pp.189–200.

Cohen, G.A. *Karl Marx's Theory of History: A Defence*. Princeton, N.J.: Princeton University Press 1978.

Cohen, Lizabeth A. "The Class Experience of Mass Consumption: Workers as Consumers in Interwar America." In Richard Wightman Fox and T.J. Jackson Lears, eds. *The Power of Culture: Critical Essays in American History*. Chicago: University of Chicago Press 1993. Pp.135–60.

_____. "Embellishing a Life of Labor: An Interpretation of the Material Culture of American Working-Class Homes, 1885–1915." In Dirk Hoerder, ed. *Labor Migration in the Atlantic Economies: The European and North American Working Classes during the Period of Industrialization*. Westport, Conn.: Greenwood Press 1985. Pp.321–52.

_____. *Making a New Deal: Industrial Workers in Chicago, 1919–1939*. Cambridge: Cambridge University Press 1990.

Cohen, Miriam. *Workshop to Office: Two Generations of Italian Women in New York City, 1900–1950*. Ithaca, N.Y.: Cornell University Press 1992.

_____, and Michael Hanagan. "The Politics of Gender and the Making of the Welfare State, 1900–1940: A Comparative Perspective." *JSH*, 24, no. 3 (Spring 1991). Pp.469–84.

Cole, Douglas. "The Problem of 'Nationalism' and 'Imperialism' in British Settler Colonies." *Journal of British Studies*, 10, no. 2 (May 1971). Pp.160–82.

Colley, Linda. "Britishness and Otherness: An Argument." *Journal of British Studies*, 31, no. 4 (October 1992). Pp.309–29.

Collomp, Catherine. "Unions, Civics, and National Identity: Organized Labor's Reaction to Immigration, 1881–1897." In Marianne Debouzy, ed. *In the Shadow of the Statue of Liberty: Immigrants, Workers, and Citizens in the American Republic, 1880–1920*. Urbana: University of Illinois Press 1992. Pp.229–55.

Comacchio, Cynthia. "Mechanomorphosis: Science, Management, and 'Human Machinery' in Industrial Canada, 1900–45." *L/LT*, 41 (Spring 1998). Pp.35–67

_____. *Nations Are Built of Babies: Saving Ontario's Mothers and Children, 1900–1940*. Montreal and Kingston: McGill-Queen's University Press 1993.

_____. "'A Postscript for Father': Defining a New Fatherhood in Interwar Canada." *CHR*, 78, no. 3 (September 1997). Pp.385–408.

Communist Party of Canada. *Canada's Party of Socialism: History of the Communist Party of Canada, 1921–1976*. Toronto: Progress Books 1982.

Connell, Robert W. *Masculinities*. Berkeley: University of California Press 1995.

Conner, Valerie Jean. *The National War Labor Board: Stability, Social Justice, and the Voluntary State in World War I*. Chapel Hill: University of North Carolina Press 1983.

Constant, Jean-François, and Michel Ducharme, eds. *Liberalism and Hegemony: Debating the Canadian Liberal Revolution*. Toronto: University of Toronto Press 2009.

Cook, Ramsay. "Henry George and the Poverty of Canadian Progress." *CHAHP*, 1977. Pp.142–57.

Cook, Sharon Anne. "Educating for Temperance: The Woman's Christian Temperance Union and Ontario Children, 1880–1916." *Historical Studies in Education*, 5, no. 2 (Fall 1993). Pp.251–77.

_____. *"Through Sunshine and Shadows": The Woman's Christian Temperance Union, Evangelicalism, and Reform in Ontario, 1874–1930*. Montreal and Kingston: McGill-Queen's University Press 1995.

Cook, Tim. *Shock Troops: Canadians Fighting the Great War, 1917–1918*. Toronto: Penguin 2008.

Cooper, John. *Rapid Ray: The Story of Ray Lewis*. Toronto: Tundra Books 2002.

_____. *Shadow Running: Ray Lewis, Canadian Railway Porter and Olympic Athlete*. Toronto: Umbrella Press 1999.

Copp, Terry. *The Anatomy of Poverty: The Condition of the Working Class in Montreal, 1897–1929*. Toronto: McClelland and Stewart 1974.

Cordery, Simon. "Fraternal Orders in the United States: A Quest for Protection and Identity." In Van der Linden, ed. *Social Security Mutualism*. Pp.83–109.

Cortiula, Mark W. "The Social Transformation of the Hospital in Hamilton: 1880–1917." PhD dissertation, University of Guelph 1992.

Cosentino, Frank. "Football." In Morrow et al. *Concise History*. Pp.140–68.

Cowan, Ruth Schwartz. *More Work for Mother: The Ironies of Household Technologies from the Open Hearth to the Microwave*. New York: Basic Books 1983.

Cox, David. "The Labour Party in Leicester; A Study in Branch Development." *IRSH*, 6, Part 2 (1961). Pp.197–211.

Cox, Mark. "The Limits of Reform: Industrial Regulation and Management Rights in Ontario, 1930–7." *CHR*, 68, no. 4 (December 1987). Pp.552–75.

Craven, Paul. *"An Impartial Umpire": Industrial Relations and the Canadian State, 1900–1911*. Toronto: University of Toronto Press 1980.

_____, ed. *Labouring Lives: Work and Workers in Nineteenth-Century Ontario*. Toronto: University of Toronto Press 1995.

_____, and Tom Traves. "The Class Politics of the National Policy, 1872–1933." *JCS*, 14, no. 3 (Fall 1979). Pp.14–38.

_____. "Labour and Management in Canadian Railway Operations: The First Decade." Paper presented to the Commonwealth Labour History Conference, Coventry, England 1981.

Crawford, Margaret. *Building the Workingman's Paradise: The Design of American Company Towns*. London: Verso 1995.

Crerar, Adam. "Ontario and the Great War." In Mackenzie, ed. *Canada and the First World War*. Pp.230–71.

_____. "Ties That Bind: Agrarian Ideals and Life in Ontario, 1890–1930." PhD dissertation, University of Toronto 1999.

Crompton, Rosemary. *Class and Stratification: An Introduction to Current Debates*. 2nd ed. London: Polity Press 1998.

Cronin, James E. "Labor Insurgency and Class Formation: Comparative Perspectives on the Crisis of 1917–1920 in Europe." In Cronin and Sirianni, eds. *Work, Community, and Power*. Pp.20–48.

_____. "Rethinking the Legacy of Labor, 1890–1925." In Cronin and Sirianni, eds. *Work, Community, and Power*. Pp.3–19.

_____. "Strikes and Power in Britain, 1870–1914." *IRSH*, 32 (1987), Part 2. Pp.144–67.

_____, and Carmen Sirianni, eds. *Work, Community, and Power: The Experience of Labor in Europe and America, 1900–1925*. Philadelphia: Temple University Press 1983.

Cross, Gary. *An All-Consuming Century: Why Commercialism Won in Modern America*. New York: Columbia University Press 2000.

_____. "Labour in Settler-State Democracies: Comparative Perspectives on Australia and the US, 1860–1920." *Labour History*, 70 (May 1996). Pp.1–24.

_____. *Time and Money: The Making of Consumer Culture*. London: Routledge 1993.

_____. "Worktime in International Discontinuity, 1886–1940." In Gary Cross, ed. *Worktime and Industrialization: An International History*. Philadelphia: Temple University Press 1988. Pp.155–82.

Crossick, Geoffrey. *An Artisan Elite in Victorian Society: Kentish London, 1840–1880*. London: Croom Helm 1978.

_____. "The Labour Aristocracy and Its Values: A Study of Mid-Victorian Kentish London." *Victorian Studies*, 19, no. 3 (March 1976). Pp.301–28.

_____, ed. *The Lower Middle Class in Britain, 1870–1914*. London: Croom Helm 1977.

_____. "The Petite Bourgeoisie in Nineteenth-Century Britain: The Urban and Liberal Case." In Geoffrey Crossick and Heinz-Gerhard Haupt, eds. *Shopkeepers and Master Artisans in Nineteenth-Century Europe*. London: Methuen 1984. Pp.62–94.

_____ and Heinz-Gerhard Haupt. *The Petite Bourgeoisie in Europe, 1780–1914*. London: Routledge 1995.

Crouse, Eric. "They 'Left Us Pretty Much as We Were': American Saloon/Factory Evangelists and Canadian Working Men in the Early Twentieth Century." Canadian Society of Church History, *Historical Papers*, 1999. Pp.51–57.

Crowley, Terry. "Madonnas Before Magdalenes: Adelaide Hoodless and the Making of the Canadian Gibson Girl." *CHR*, 67, no. 4 (December 1986). Pp.520–47.

Crozier, Colin. "Jelfs, George Frederick." *DHB*, 3. Pp.97–99.

Cruikshank, Douglas, and Gregory S. Kealey. "Canadian Strike Statistics, 1891–1950." *L/LT*, 20 (Fall 1987). Pp.85–145.

Cruikshank, Ken, and Nancy B. Bouchier. "Blighted Areas and Obnoxious Industries: Constructing Environmental Inequality on an Industrial Waterfront, Hamilton, Ontario, 1900–1960." *Environmental History*, 9, no. 3 (July 2004). Pp.464–96.

_____. "Dirty Spaces: Environment, the State, and Recreational Swimming in Hamilton Harbour, 1870–1946." *Sports History Review*, 29, no. 1 (May 1998). Pp.59–76.

_____. "'The Heritage of the People Closed against Them': Class, Environment, and the Shaping of Burlington Beach, 1870s–1980s." *UHR*, 30, no. 1 (October 2001). Pp.46–47.

Cumbo, Enrico Carson. "'As the Twig Is Bent, the Tree's Inclined': Growing Up Italian in Toronto, 1905–1940." PhD thesis, University of Toronto 1995.

_____. "'Cci voli sorti macari a frijiri l'ova': The Notion of Fate in Sicilian Popular Belief." *Canadian Ethnic Studies*, 30, no. 2 (June 1998). Pp.73–94.

_____. "'Impediments to the Harvest': The Limitations of Methodist Proselytization of Toronto's Italian Immigrants, 1905–1925." In Mark George McGeowan, ed. *Catholics at the "Gathering Place": Historical Essays on the Archdiocese of Toronto, 1841–1991*. Toronto: Canadian Catholic Historical Association 1993. Pp.155–76.

_____. "Italians in Hamilton, 1900–40." *Polyphony*, 7, no.2 (Fall/Winter 1985). Pp.28–36.

_____. *The Italian Presence in Hamilton: A Social History: 1870–2000*. N.p.: Author n.d.

_____. "Salvation in Indifference: Gendered Expressions of Italian-Canadian Immigrant Catholicity, 1900–1940." In Christie, ed. *Households of Faith*. Pp.205–33.

Cuneo, Carl J. "State, Class, and Reserve Labour: The Case of the 1941 Canadian Unemployment Insurance Act." *CRSA*, 16, no. 2 (May 1979). Pp.47–70.

Cupido, Robert. "Appropriating the Past: Pageants, Politics, and the Diamond Jubilee of Confederation." *JCHA*, 9 (1998). Pp.155–86.

Curtis, Bruce, D.W. Livingstone, and Harry Smaller. *Stacking the Deck: The Streaming of Working-Class Kids in Ontario Schools*. Toronto: Our Schools/Ourselves Education Foundation 1992.

Dahlie, Jorgen, and Tissa Fernando, eds. *Ethnicity, Power, and Politics in Canada*. Toronto: Methuen 1981.

Dalley, D. Norman. *A History of the Hamilton Branch of the Victorian Order of Nurses for Canada*. Hamilton: Victorian Order of Nurses 1966.

Darroch, Gordon. "Families, Fostering, and Flying the Coop: Lessons in Liberal Cultural Formation." In Sager and Baskerville, eds. *Household Counts*. Pp.197–246.

Daunton, M.J. "Cities of Homes and Cities of Tenements: British and American Comparisons." *JUH*, 14, no.3 (May 1988). Pp.283–319.

_____, ed. *Housing the Workers, 1850–1914: A Comparative Perspective*. London: Leicester University Press 1990.

_____. "Rows and Tenements: American Cities, 1880–1914." In Daunton, ed. *Housing the Workers*. Pp.249–86.

Davey, Ian E. "Educational Reform and the Working Class: School Attendance in Hamilton, Ontario, 1851–1891." PhD dissertation, University of Toronto 1975.

Davidoff, Leonore. "The Separation of Home and Work? Landladies and Lodgers in Nineteenth- and Twentieth-Century England." In Sandra Burman, ed. *Fit Work for Women*. London: Croom Helm 1979. Pp.64–97.

Davies, Andrew. *Leisure, Gender, and Poverty: Working-Class Culture in Salford and Manchester, 1900–1939*. Buckingham, England: Open University Press 1992.

_____. "Youth Gangs, Masculinity and Violence in Late Victorian Manchester and Salford." *JSH*, 32, no.2 (Winter 1998). Pp.349–69.

Davies, Margery W. *Women's Place Is at the Typewriter: Office Work and Office Workers, 1870–1930*. Philadelphia: Temple University Press 1982.

Davies, Megan. *In the House of Old: A History of Residential Care in British Columbia*. Montreal and Kingston: McGill-Queen's University Press 2003.

_____. "'Services Rendered, Rearing Children for the State': Mothers' Pensions in British Columbia, 1919–1931." In Barbara K. Latham and Roberta J. Pazdro, eds. *Not Just Pin Money: Selected Essays on the History of Women's Work in British Columbia*. Victoria: Camosun College 1984. Pp.249–63.

Davies, Stephen. "'Reckless Walking Must Be Discouraged': The Automobile Revolution and the Shaping of Modern Urban Canada to 1930." *UHR*, 18, no. 2 (October 1989). Pp.123–38.

Davin, Anna. *Growing Up Poor: Home, School, and Street in London, 1870–1914*. London: Rivers Oram Press 1996.

_____. "Imperialism and Motherhood." *HWJ*, 5 (Spring 1978). Pp.9–88.

Davis, Clark. "The Corporate Reconstruction of Middle-Class Manhood." In Bledstein and Johnston, eds. *Middling Sorts*. Pp.201–16.

Davis, Janet M. *The Circus Age: Culture and Society under the American Big Top*. Chapel Hill: University of North Carolina Press 2002.

David, Mike. *Prisoners of the American Dream: Politics and Economy in the History of the US Working Class*. London: Verso 1986.

Davis, Natalie Zemon. "The Reasons of Misrule." In Davis. *Society and Culture in Early Modern France*. Stanford, Cal.: Stanford University Press 1975. Pp.97–123.

Dawson, Graham. *Soldier Heroes: British Adventure, Empire, and the Imagining of Masculinities*. London: Routledge 1994.

Dawson, R. MacGregor. *William Lyon Mackenzie King: A Political Biography, 1874–1923*. Toronto: University of Toronto Press 1958.

Day, Jeanna. "The Creation of a Neighbourhood: West Mount Survey." Unpublished paper (WC).

D'Cruze, Shari, ed. *Everyday Violence in Britain, 1850–1950: Gender and Class*. London: Longman 2000.

Dean, Malcolm. *Censored! Only in Canada: The History of Film Censorship – The Scandal off the Screen*. Toronto: Virago Press 1981.

Dean, Mitchell. *Governmentality: Power and Rule in Modern Society*. London: Sage Publications 1999.

Dear, M.J., J.J. Drake, and L.G. Reeds, eds. *Steel City: Hamilton and Region*. Toronto: University of Toronto Press 1987.

De Grazia, Victoria, with Ellen Furlough, eds. *The Sex of Things: Gender and Consumption in Historical Perspective*. Berkeley: University of California Press 1996.

Dehli, Kari. "'Health Scouts' for the State: School and Public Health Nurses in Early Twentieth-Century Toronto." *Historical Studies in Education*, 2, no. 2 (Fall 1990). Pp.247–64.

D'Emilio, John, and Estelle Freedman. *Intimate Matters: A History of Sexuality in America*. New York: Harper and Row 1988.

Denison, Merrill. *Harvest Triumphant: The Story of Massey-Harris: A Footnote to Canadian History*. Toronto: McClelland and Stewart 1949.

_____. *The People's Power: The History of Ontario Hydro*. Toronto: McClelland and Stewart 1960.

Denning, Michael. "The End of Mass Culture." *ILWCH*, 37 (Spring 1990). Pp.4–18.

Dennis, Richard. "Apartment Housing in Canadian Cities, 1900–1940." *UHR*, 26, no. 2 (1998). Pp.17–31.

Dick, William M. *Labor and Socialism in America: The Gompers Era*. Port Washington, N.Y: Kennikat Press 1972.

Dirks, Patricia. "Canada's Boys – An Imperial or National Asset? Responses to Baden-Powell's Boy Scout Movement in Pre-War Canada." Paper presented to the British World Conference, Calgary, 2003.

_____. "'Getting a Grip on Harry': Canada's Methodists Respond to the 'Big Boy' Problem." Canadian Methodist Historical Society, *Papers* 1990. Pp.67–82.

_____. "Reinventing Christian Masculinity and Fatherhood: The Canadian Protestant Experience, 1900–1920." In Christie, ed. *Households of Faith*. Pp.290–316.

_____. "Serving Church and Nation: Methodist Sunday Schools in Canada's Century." Canadian Methodist Historical Society, *Papers* 1995. Pp.46–62.

Dodd, Dianne E. "Advice to Parents: The Blue Books, Helen McMurchy, MD, and the Federal Department of Health, 1920–1934." *CBMH*, 8 (1991). Pp.203–30.

_____. "Delivering Electrical Technology to the Ontario Housewife, 1920–1939: An Alliance of Professional Women, Advertisers, and the Electrical Industry." PhD dissertation, Carleton University 1988.

_____. "The Hamilton Birth Control Clinic of the 1930s." *OH*, 74, no.1 (March 1983). Pp.71–86.

_____. "Women in Advertising: The Role of Canadian Women in the Promotion of Domestic Electrical Technology in the Interwar Period." In Marianne Gosztonyi Ainley, ed. *Despite the Odds: Essays on Canadian Women and Science*. Montreal: Véhicule Press 1990. Pp.134–51.

_____. "Women's Involvement in the Canadian Birth Control Movement of the 1930s: The Hamilton Birth Control Clinic." In Arnup, Levesque, and Pierson, eds. *Delivering Motherhood*. Pp.150–72.

_____ and Deborah Gorham, eds. *Caring and Curing: Historical Perspectives on Women and Healing in Canada*. Ottawa: University of Ottawa Press 1994.

Dolman, Claude E. "Landmarks and Pioneers in the Control of Diphtheria." *CJPH*, 64, no. 4 (July/August 1973). Pp.317–36.

Doucet, Michael J. "Working Class Housing in a Small Nineteenth Century Canadian City: Hamilton, Ontario, 1852–1881." In Gregory S. Kealey and Peter Warrian, eds. *Essays in Canadian Working Class History*. Toronto: McClelland and Stewart 1976. Pp.83–105.

Doucet, Michael, and John Weaver. *Housing the North American City*. Kingston and Montreal: McGill-Queen's University Press 1991.

Draper, Kenneth L. "A People's Religion: P.W. Philpott and the Hamilton Christian Workers' Church." *HS/SH*, 36, no. 71 (May 2003). Pp.99–121.

Dreisziger, N.F., with M.L. Kovacs, Paul Brődy, and Bennett Kovris. *Struggle and Hope: The Hungarian-Canadian Experience*. Toronto: McClelland and Stewart 1982.

Dubinsky, Karen. *Improper Advances: Rape and Heterosexual Conflict in Ontario, 1880–1929*. Chicago: University of Chicago Press 1993.

_____. *The Second Greatest Disappointment: Honeymooning and Tourism at Niagara Falls*. Toronto: Between the Lines 1999.

_____ and Adam Givertz. "'It Was Only a Matter of Passion': Masculinity and Sexual Danger." In McPherson, Morgan, and Forestall, eds. *Gendered Pasts*. Pp.65–79.

Dubofsky, Melvyn. *We Shall Be All: A History of the Industrial Workers of the World*. New York: Quadrangle 1969.

Dubro, James, and Robin F. Rowland. *King of the Mob: Rocco Perri and the Women Who Ran His Rackets*. Toronto: Viking 1987.

Due, John F. *The Intercity Electric Railway Industry in Canada*. Toronto: University of Toronto Press 1966.

Duff, Frances I. *Highlights of the Hamilton YWCA, 1889–1964*. Hamilton: Hamilton YWCA n.d.

Dunk, Thomas W. *It's a Working Man's Town: Male Working-Class Culture in Northwestern Ontario*. Montreal and Kingston: McGill-Queen's University Press 1991.

Dunn, Timothy A. "Teaching the Meaning of Work: Education in British Columbia, 1900–1929." In David C. Jones et al., eds. *Shaping the Schools of the Canadian West*. Calgary: Detselig Enterprises 1979. Pp.236–56.

Dutton, D.J. "The Unionist Party and Social Policy, 1906–1914." *Historical Journal*, 24, no. 4 (December 1981). Pp.871–84.

Dyhouse, Carol. "Working-Class Mothers and Infant Mortality in England, 1895–1914." *JSH*, 12, no. 2 (Winter 1978). Pp.248–67.

Eaman, Ross A. *Channels of Influence: CBC Audience Research and the Canadian Public*. Toronto: University of Toronto Press 1994.

Edel, Matthew, Elliott D. Sclar, and Daniel Luria. *Shaky Palaces: Home Ownership and Social Mobility in Boston's Suburbanization*. New York: Columbia University Press 1984.

Edsforth, Ronald. *Class Conflict and Cultural Consensus: The Making of a Mass Consumer Society in Flint, Michigan*. New Brunswick, N.J.: Rutgers University Press 1987.

Edwards, Richard. *Contested Terrain: The Transformation of the Workplace in the Twentieth Century*. New York: Basic Books 1979.

Ehrlich, Cyril. *The Piano: A History*. London: J.M. Dent and Sons 1976.

Elections Canada. *A History of the Vote in Canada*. Ottawa: Chief Electoral Officer of Canada 1997.

Eley, Geoff, and Keith Nield. *The Future of Class in History: What's Left of the Social?* Ann Arbor: University of Michigan Press 2007.

Emery, George. *Facts of Life: The Social Construction of Vital Statistics, Ontario, 1869–1952*. Montreal and Kingston: McGill-Queen's University Press 1993.

_____, and J.C. Herbert Emery. *A Young Man's Benefit: The Independent Order of Odd Fellows and Sickness Insurance in the United States and Canada, 1860–1920*. Montreal and Kingston: McGill-Queen's University Press 1999.

Encyclopedia of Music in Canada. (www.thecanadianencyclopedia.com).

Endicott, Stephen L. *Raising the Workers' Flag: The Workers' Unity League of Canada, 1930–1936*. Toronto: University of Toronto Press 2012.

Englander, David, and James Osborne. "Jack, Tommy, and Henry Dubb: The Armed Forces and the Working Class." *Historical Journal*, 21, no. 3 (September 1978). Pp.593–621.

English, John. *The Decline of Politics: The Conservatives and the Party System, 1901–20*. Toronto: University of Toronto Press 1977.

Ennals, Peter, and Deryck W. Holdsworth. *Homeplace: The Making of the Canadian Dwelling over Three Centuries*. Toronto: University of Toronto Press 1998.

Enstad, Nan. *Ladies of Labor, Girls of Adventure: Working Women, Popular Culture, and Labor Politics at the Turn of the Twentieth Century*. New York: Columbia University Press 1999.

Epp, Abrahm Ernest. "Co-operation among Capitalists: The Canadian Merger Movement, 1909–1913." PhD dissertation, Johns Hopkins University 1973.

Evans, A. Margaret. *Sir Oliver Mowat*. Toronto: University of Toronto Press 1992.

Evans, Gary. *The Prints of Hamilton: A Nostalgic View of the Ambitious City*. Burlington, Ont.: North Shore Publishing 1999.

_____. *The Prints of Time: Old Photographs from the Spectator's Archives*. Burlington, Ont.: North Shore Publishing 1996.

Evans, Lois C. *Hamilton: The Story of a City*. Toronto: Ryerson Press 1970.

Ewbank, Douglas C., and Samuel H. Preston. "Personal Health Behaviour and the Decline in Infant Mortality: The United States, 1900–1930." In *What We Know about Health Transition: The Cultural, Social, and Behavioural Determinants of Health*. Canberra: Health Transition Centre, Australian National University 1990.

Ewen, David. *The Life and Death of Tin Pan Alley: The Golden Age of American Music*. New York: Funk and Wagnalls 1964.

Ewen, Elizabeth. *Immigrant Women in the Land of Dollars: Life and Culture on the Lower East Side, 1890–1925*. New York: Monthly Review Press 1985.

Ewen, Stuart. *Captains of Consciousness: Advertising and the Social Roots of the Consumer Culture*. New York McGraw-Hill 1976.

_____, and Elizabeth Ewen. *Channels of Desire: Mass Images and the Shaping of American Consciousness*. New York: McGraw-Hill 1982.

Fahrni, Magdalena. "The Rhetoric of Order: Respectability, Deviance, and the Criminalizing of Class in Ontario, 1880–1914." MA thesis, Queen's University 1993.

Fairclough, Ellen Louks. *Saturday's Child: Memoirs of Canada's First Female Cabinet Minister*. Toronto: University of Toronto Press 1995.

Featherstone, Lisa. "Infant Ideologies: Doctors, Mothers, and the Feeding of Children in Australia, 1880–1910." In Warsh and Strong-Boag, eds. *Children's Health Issues*. Pp.131–59.

Feldberg, Georgina D. *Disease and Class: Tuberculosis and the Shaping of Modern North American Society*. New Brunswick, N.J.: Rutgers University Press 1995.

Fell, John L. ed. *Film before Griffith*. Berkeley: University of California Press 1983.

_____. "Motive, Mischief, and Melodrama: The State of Film Narrative in 1907." In Fell, ed. *Film before Griffith*. Pp.272–83.

Fenton, Edwin. *Immigrants and Unions, A Case Study: Italians and North American Labor, 1870–1920*. New York: Arno Press 1975.

Fenwick, G. Roy. "Some Musical Memories." *Wentworth Bygones*, 6 (1965). Pp.24–30.

Ferns, Thomas H. "Theaker, John." *DHB*, 3. Pp.209–13.

Field, Barbara J. "Ideology and Race in American History." In J. Morgan Kousser and James M. McPherson, eds. *Region, Race, and Reconstruction: Essays in Honor of C. Vann Woodward*. New York: Oxford University Press 1982. Pp.143–77.

Filer, S. Patricia. "Bonomi, John F." *DHB*, 3. Pp.13–14.

Fine, Lisa M. "Rights of Men, Rites of Passage: Hunting and Masculinity at Reo Motors of Lansing, Michigan, 1945–1975." *JSH* 33, no.4 (Summer 2000). Pp.805–23.

_____. *The Story of Reo Joe: Work, Kin, and Community in Autotown, USA*. Philadelphia: Temple University Press 2004.

Fingard, Judith. *Jack in Port: Sailortowns of Eastern Canada*. Toronto: University of Toronto Press 1982.

Fink, Leon. "Labor, Liberty, and the Law: Trade Unionism and the Problem of American Constitutional Order." *JAH*, 74, no. 3 (December 1987). Pp.904–25.

Finkel, Alvin. *Business and Social Reform in the Thirties*. Toronto: James Lorimer 1979.

Flink, James J. *The Automobile Age*. Cambridge: MIT Press 1990.

Floud, Roderick. *The British Machine Tool Industry, 1850–1914*. Cambridge: Cambridge University Press 1976.

Foner, Philip S. *History of the Labor Movement in the United States, Volume III: The Policies and Practices of the American Federation of Labor, 1900–1909*. New York: International Publishers 1964.

Forbath, William E. *Law and the Shaping of the American Labor Movement*. Cambridge, Mass.: Harvard University Press 1991.

Forestall, Nancy. "Gendered Terrains: Family and Community Life in a Northern Ontario Mining Community." Unpublished manuscript.

Forster, Ben. *A Conjunction of Interests: Business, Politics, and Tariffs, 1825–1879*. Toronto: University of Toronto Press 1986.

Foster, Matthew James. "Ethnic Settlement in the Barton Street Region of Hamilton, 1921 to 1961." MA thesis, McMaster University 1965.

Fowke, Vernon C. *The National Policy and the Wheat Economy*. Toronto: University of Toronto Press 1957.

Fowler, David. *The First Teenagers: The Lifestyle of Young Wage-Earners in Interwar Britain*. London: Woburn Press 1995.

Frader, Laura L., and Sonya O. Rose. "Introduction: Gender and the Reconstruction of European Working-Class History." In Frader and Rose, eds. *Gender and Class in Modern Europe*. Ithaca, N.Y.: Cornell University Press 1996. Pp.1–33.

Frager, Ruth A. "Labour History and the Interlocking Hierarchies of Class, Ethnicity, and Gender: A Canadian Perspective." *International Review of Social History*, 44 (1999). Pp.217–47.

_____. "No Proper Deal: Women Workers and the Canadian Labour Movement, 1870–1940." In Linda Briskin and Lynda Yanz, eds. *Union Sisters: Women in the Labour Movement*. Toronto: Women's Press 1983. Pp.44–64.

_____. *Sweatshop Strife: Class, Ethnicity, and Gender in the Jewish Labour Movement of Toronto, 1900–1939*. Toronto: University of Toronto Press 1992.

_____, and Carmela Patrias. *Discounted Labour: Women Workers in Canada, 1870–1939*. Toronto: University of Toronto Press 2005.

Frank, Blye. "Hegemonic Heterosexual Masculinity." *Studies in Political Economy*, 24 (Autumn 1987). Pp.159–70.

Frank, Dana. *Purchasing Power: Consumer Organizing, Gender, and the Seattle Labor Movement, 1919–1929*. New York: Cambridge University Press 1994.

_____. "Where Are the Workers in Consumer-Worker Alliances? Class Dynamics and the History of Consumer-Labor Campaigns." *Politics and Society*, 31, no. 3 (September 2003). Pp.363–79.

_____. "White Working-Class Women and the Race Question." *ILWCH*, 54 (Fall 1998). Pp.80–102.

Frank, David. *J.B. McLachlan: A Biography*. James Lorimer 1999.

Fraser, Brian J. *The Social Uplifters: Presbyterian Progressives and the Social Gospel in Canada, 1875–1915*. Waterloo, Ont.: Wilfrid Laurier University Press 1988.

Fraser, Steven. *Labor Will Rule: Sidney Hillman and the Rise of American Labor*. Ithaca, N.Y.: Cornell University Press 1991.

Freeman, Bill. *1005: Political Life in a Union Local*. Toronto: James Lorimer and Company 1982.

_____, and Marsha Hewitt, eds. *Their Town: The Mafia, the Media, and the Party Machine*. Toronto: James Lorimer 1979.

Friedman, Gerald. *State-Making and Labor Movements: France and the United States, 1876–1914*. Ithaca, N.Y.: Cornell University Press 1998.

Friesen, Gerald. *The Canadian Prairies: A History*. Toronto: University of Toronto Press 1987.

Fryer, Peter. *Black People in the British Empire: An Introduction*. London: Pluto Press 1988.

Fudge, Judy, and Eric Tucker. *Labour before the Law: The Regulation of Workers' Collective Action in Canada, 1900–1948*. Toronto: Oxford University Press 2001.

Fuller, J.G. *Troop Morale and Popular Culture in the British and Dominion Armies, 1914–1918*. Oxford: Clarendon Press 1990.

Furia, Philip. *The Poets of Tin Pan Alley: A History of America's Great Lyricists*. New York: Oxford University Press 1990.

Gabaccia, Donna. *From the Other Side: Women, Gender, and Immigrant Life in the U.S., 1820–1990*. Bloomington and Indianapolis: Indiana University Press 1994.

———. "Immigrant Women: Nowhere at Home?" *Journal of American Ethnic History*, 10, no. 4 (Summer 1991). Pp.61–87.

———. *Italy's Many Diasporas*. Seattle: University of Washington Press 2000.

———. "Women of the Mass Migrations: From Minority to Majority, 1820–1930." In Hoerder and Moch, eds. *European Migrants*. Pp.90–111.

Gagan, David, and Rosemary Gagan. "'Evil Reports' for 'Ignorant Minds'? Patient Experience and Public Confidence in the Emerging Modern Hospital: Vancouver General Hospital, 1912." *CBMH*, 18, no. 2 (2001). Pp.356–57.

———. *For Patients of Moderate Means: A Social History of the Voluntary Public General Hospital in Canada, 1890–1950*. Montreal and Kingston: McGill-Queen's University Press 2002.

Gagan, Rosemary. "Disease, Mortality, and Public Health, Hamilton, Ontario, 1900–1914." MA thesis, McMaster University 1981.

———. "Roberts, James." *DHB*, 3. Pp.175–78.

Gardner, Todd. "The Slow Wave: The Changing Residential Status of Suburbs in the United States, 1850–1940." *JUH*, 27, no. 3 (March 2001). Pp.293–312.

Garvie, Donald A. *Growing Up in the City*. Dundas, Ont.: Darm Publishing n.d.

Gaudaur, J.G. "A Century of Football Marked by Grid Supremacy: Toronto and Hamilton Launch Inter-City Rivalry." In Miller, ed. *Centennial Sports Review*.

Gauvreau, Michael. "Factories and Foreigners: Church Life in Working-Class Neighbourhoods in Hamilton and Montreal, 1890–1930." In Michael Gauvreau and Ollivier Hubert, eds. *The Churches and Social Order in Nineteenth- and Twentieth-Century Canada*. Montreal and Kingston: McGill-Queen's University Press 2006. Pp.225–73.

Gelber, Steven M. "Working at Play: The Culture of the Workplace and the Rise of Baseball." *JSH*, 16, no. 4 (Summer 1983). Pp.3–22.

Gellatt, Roland. *The Fabulous Phonograph, 1877–1977*. New York: Collier Books 1977.

Genovese, Eugene D. *Roll, Jordan, Roll: The World the Slaves Made*. New York: Pantheon Books 1974.

Gentile, Patrizia. "Queen of the Maple Leaf: A History of Beauty Contests in Twentieth Century Canada." PhD dissertation, Queen's University 2006.

Gibson, John Murray. *The Victorian Order of Nurses for Canada: Fiftieth Anniversary, 1897–1947*. Montreal: Victorian Order of Nurses for Canada 1947.

Gidney, Catherine. "The Dredger's Daughter: Courtship and Marriage in the Baptist Community of Welland, Ontario, 1934–1944." *L/LT*, 54 (Fall 2004), 121–49.

Gidney, R.D., and W.P.J. Millar. *Inventing Secondary Education: The Rise of the High School in Nineteenth-Century Ontario*. Toronto: University of Toronto Press 1990.

———. *Professional Gentlemen: The Professions in Nineteenth-Century Ontario*. Toronto: University of Toronto Press 1994.

Gilbert, Douglas. *American Vaudeville: Its Life and Times*. New York: Dover Publications 1968 [1940].

Gilliland, Jason A., and Matt Sendbuehler. "'...To Produce the Highest Type of Manhood and Womanhood': The Ontario Housing Act, 1919 and a New Suburban Ideal." *UHR*, 26, no. 2 (March 1998). Pp.42–55.

Gillis, John R. *For Better, For Worse: British Marriages, 1600 to the Present*. New York: Oxford University Press 1985.

———. *A World of Their Own Making: Myth, Ritual, and the Quest for Family Values*. Cambridge, Mass.: Harvard University Press 1996.

Gittins, Diana. "Marital Status, Work and Kinship, 1850–1930." In Lewis, ed. *Labour and Love*. Pp.249–67.

Givertz, Adam. "Sex and Order: The Regulation of Sexuality and the Prosecution of Sexual Assault in Hamilton, Ontario, 1880–1929." MA thesis, Queen's University 1992.

Glassford, Larry A. "'The Presence of So Many Ladies': A Study of the Conservative Party's Response to Female Suffrage in Canada, 1918–1939." Unpublished paper, Canadian Historical Association meeting, 1996.

Gleason, Mona. "Race, Class, and Health: School Medical Inspection and 'Healthy' Children in British Columbia, 1890 to 1930." *CBMH*, 19, no.1 (2002).

Glenn, Susan A. *Daughters of the Shtetl: Life and Labor in the Immigrant Generation*. Ithaca, N.Y.: Cornell University Press 1990.

Glickman, Lawrence B. *A Living Wage: American Workers and the Making of Consumer Society*. Ithaca, N.Y.: Cornell University Press 1997.

Glynn, Desmond. "'Exporting Outcast London': Assisted Emigration to Canada, 1886–1914." *HS/SH*, 15, no.29 (May 1982). Pp.209–38.

Golz, Annalee E. "'If a Man's Wife Does Not Obey Him, What Can He Do?' Marital Breakdown and Wife Abuse in Late Nineteenth-Century and Early Twentieth-Century Ontario." In Louis Knafla and Susan W.S. Binnie, eds. *Law, Society, and the State: Essays in Modern Legal History*. Toronto: University of Toronto Press 1995. Pp.323–50.

Gomery, David. "Movie Audiences, Urban Geography, and the History of the American Film." *Velvet Light Trap*, 19 (Spring 1983). Pp.23–29.

Goodson, Ivor F., and Christopher J. Anstead. *Through the Schoolhouse Door: Working Papers*. London, Ont.: RUCCUS and Garamond Press 1993.

Gordon, David M., Richard Edwards, and Michael Reich. *Segmented Work, Divided Workers: The Historical Transformation of Labor in the United States*. New York: Cambridge University Press 1982.

Gordon, Linda. "Social Insurance and Public Assistance: The Influence of Gender in Welfare Thought in the United States, 1890–1935." *AHR*, 96, no.1 (February 1992). Pp.19–54.

Gordon, Robert D. "Hamilton, 1916: Recruiting and the Clubs System." Unpublished paper (WC).

Gospel, Howard F., and Craig R. Littler, eds. *Managerial Strategies and Industrial Relations: An Historical and Comparative Study*. London: Heinemann Educational 1983.

Gorn, Elliott J. *The Manly Art: Bare-Knuckle Prize Fighting in America*. Ithaca, N.Y.: Cornell University Press 1986.

Goss, Van. "'To Organize in Every Neighbourhood, in Every Home': The Gender Politics of American Communists between the Wars." *Radical History Review*, 50 (Fall 1991), Pp.109–41.

Goutor, David. *Guarding the Gates: The Canadian Labour Movement and Immigration, 1872–1934*. Vancouver: UBC Press 2007.

Gowans, Alan. *The Comfortable House: North American Suburban Architecture, 1890–1930*. Cambridge, Mass.: MIT Press 1986.

Graebner, William. *A History of Retirement: The Meaning and Function of an American Institution, 1885–1978*. New Haven, Conn.: Yale University Press 1980.

Graham, Roger. "Some Political Ideas of Arthur Meighen." In Hamelin, ed. *Les idées politiques des premiers ministres*. Pp.107–20.

Gramsci, Antonio. *Prison Notebooks*. New York: Columbia University Press 1992.

Granatstein, J.L., and J.M. Hitsman. *Broken Promises: A History of Conscription in Canada*. Toronto: Oxford University Press 1977.

Grant, Julia. "A 'Real Boy' and Not a Sissy: Gender, Childhood, and Masculinity, 1890–1940." *JSH*, 37, no. 4 (Summer 2004). Pp.829–51.

Gray, Carolyn. "Barker, Samuel." *DHB*, 2. Pp.5–9.
———. "Gibson, Sir John Morison." *DHB*, 3. Pp.66–77.
———. "Stinson, Marion Elizabeth (Ottaway; Crerar)." *DHB*, 2. Pp.156–59.

Gray, Robert. *The Labour Aristocracy in Victorian Edinburgh*. Oxford: Clarendon 1976.

Green, E.H.H. "Radical Conservatism: The Electoral Genesis of Tariff Reform." *HJ*, 28, no. 3 (September 1985). Pp.667–92.
———. "The Strange Death of Tory England." *Twentieth Century British History*, 2, no. 1 (1991). Pp.67–88.

Greene, Julia. "'The Strike at the Ballot Box': The American Federation of Labor's Entrance into Election Politics, 1906–1909." *LH*, 32, no. 2 (Spring 1991). Pp.165–92.

Greenfield, J. Katharine. *Hamilton Public Library, 1889–1963: A Celebration of Vision and Leadership*. Hamilton: Hamilton Public library 1989.

Grimsted, David. "Melodrama as Echo of the Historically Voiceless." In Tamara K. Hareven, ed. *Anonymous Americans: Explorations in Nineteenth-Century Social History*. Englewood Cliffs, N.J.: Prentice-Hall 1971. Pp.80–98.

Griswold, Robert L. *Fatherhood in America: A History*. New York: Basic Books 1993.

Gruneau, Richard, and David Whitsun. *Hockey Night in Canada: Sport, Identities, and Cultural Politics*. Toronto: Garamond Press 1993.

Gryfe, Arthur. "The Taming of Diphtheria: Ontario's Role." *Annals of the Royal Society of Physicians and Surgeons of Canada*, 20, no. 2 (March 1987). Pp.115–19.

Guglielmo, Thomas A. "'No Color Barrier': Italians, Race and Power in the United States." In Jennifer Guglielmo and Salvatore Salerno, eds. *Are Italians White? How Race Is Made in America*. New York: Routledge 2003. Pp.29–43.

Gusfield, Joseph R. "Passage to Play: Rituals of Drinking Time in American Society." In Mary Douglas, ed. *Constructive Drinking: Perspectives on Drink from Anthropology*. New York: Cambridge University Press 1987. Pp.73–90.

Gutteridge, Robert W. *Magic Moments: First 20 Years of Moving Pictures in Toronto (1894–1914)*. Toronto: Gutteridge-Pratley Publications 2000.

Gutzke, David W. "Gender, Class, and Public Drinking in Britain during the First World War." *HS/SH*, 27, no. 54 (November 1994). Pp.367–91.

Habakkuk, H.J. *American and British Technology in the Nineteenth Century: The Search for Labor-Saving Inventions*. Cambridge: Cambridge University Press 1967.

Haber, Samuel. *Efficiency and Uplift: Scientific Management in the Progressive Era, 1890–1920*. Chicago: University of Chicago Press 1964.

Hall, Carl A.S. "Electrical Utilities in Ontario under Private Ownership, 1890–1914." PhD dissertation, University of Toronto 1968.

Hall, Jacquelyn Dowd, et al. *Like a Family: The Making of a Southern Cotton Mill World*. New York: W.W. Norton and Company 1987.

Hall, John R. ed. *Reworking Class*. Ithaca, N.Y.: Cornell University Press 1997.

Hall, Lesley A. *Hidden Anxieties: Male Sexuality, 1900–1950*. London: Polity Press 1991.

Hall, Stuart. "Notes on Deconstructing 'The Popular.'" In Samuel, ed. *People's History and Socialist Theory*. Pp.227–40.

Hallowell, Gerald A. *Prohibition in Ontario, 1919–1923*. Ottawa: Ontario Historical Society 1972.

Halpern, Rick. "The Iron Fist and the Velvet Glove: Welfare Capitalism in Chicago's Packinghouses, 1921–1933." *JAS*, 26, no. 2 (August 1992). Pp.59–83.

——————. "Race, Ethnicity, and Union in the Chicago Stockyards, 1917–1922." *ILWCH*, 37, no. 1 (1992). Pp.25–58.

——————, and Jonathan Morris., eds. *American Exceptionalism? US Working-Class Formation in an International Context*. London: Macmillan 1997.

——————. "The Persistence of Exceptionalism." In Halpern and Morris, eds. *American Exceptionalism?*

Halttunen, Karen. "From Parlor to Living Room: Domestic Space, Interior Decoration, and the Culture of Personality." In Simon J. Bonner, ed. *Consuming Visions: Accumulation and Display of Goods in America, 1880–1920*. New York: W.W. Norton and Company 1989. Pp.157–89.

Hamelin, ed. Marcel. *Les idées politiques des premiers ministres du Canada; The Political Ideas of the Prime Ministers of Canada*. Ottawa: Les éditions de l'Université d'Ottawa 1969.

Hamilton, Diane. "The Cost of Caring: The Metropolitan Life Insurance Company's Visiting Nurse Service, 1909–1953." *Bulletin of the History of Medicine*, 63, no. 3 (Fall 1989). Pp.414–34.

Hamilton Association for the Advancement of Literature, Science, and Art. *100th Anniversary, 1857–1957*. Hamilton: Hamilton Association for the Advancement of Literature, Science, and Art 1958.

Hamilton Local Council of Women. *Fifty Years of Activity, 1893–1943*. Hamilton: Local Council of Women 1944.

Hammerton, A. James. *Cruelty and Companionship: Conflict in Nineteenth-Century Married Life*. London: Routledge 1992.

Hanlon, Peter. "Lamoreaux, James Wilmot." *DHB*, 2. Pp.86–87.

——————. "Lees, George Harman." *DHB*, 3. Pp.111–16.

——————. "Moral Order and the Influence of Social Christianity in an Industrial City, 1890–1899: A Social Profile of the Protestant Lay Leaders of Three Hamilton Churches – Centenary Methodist, Central Presbyterian, and Christ's Church Cathedral." PhD dissertation, McMaster University 1984.

Hann, Russell. *Farmers Confront Industrialism: Some Historical Perspectives on Ontario Agrarian Movements*. Toronto: New Hogtown Press 1975.

Hansen, Miriam. *Babel and Babylon: Spectatorship in American Silent Film*. Cambridge, Mass.: Harvard University Press 1991.

Hareven, Tamara K. *Family Time and Industrial Time: The Relationship between the Family and Work in a New England Industrial Community*. Cambridge: Cambridge University Press 1982.

Harkness, Ross. *J.E. Atkinson of the Star*. Toronto: University of Toronto Press 1963.

Harney, Robert F. "Boarding and Belonging." *UHR*, 2–78 (October 1978). Pp.8–37.

——————. "The Commerce of Migration." *Canadian Ethnic Studies*, 9, no. 1 (1977). Pp.42–53.

——————. "Men without Women: Italian Immigrants in Canada, 1885–1930." *Canadian Ethnic Studies*, 9, no.1 (1979). Pp.29–47.

——————. "The Padrone and the Immigrant." *Canadian Review of American Studies*, 5, no. 2 (Fall 1974). Pp.101–18.

Harris, Howell John. "The Rocky Road to Mass Production: Change and Continuity in the U.S. Foundry Industry, 1890–1940." *Enterprise and Society*, 1, no. 2 (June 2000). Pp.391–437.

Harris, Richard. "Canada's All Right: The Lives and Loyalties of Immigrant Families in a Toronto Suburb, 1900–1945." *Canadian Geographer*, 36, no.1 (Spring 1992). Pp.13–30.

——————. *Class and Housing Tenure in Modern Canada*. Toronto: Centre for Urban Studies, Research Paper no.153 1984.

——————. *Creeping Conformity: How Canada Became Suburban, 1900–1960*. Toronto: University of Toronto Press 2004.

——————. "The End Justified the Means: Boarding and Rooming in a City of Homes, 1890–1951." *JSH*, 26, no. 2 (Winter 1992). Pp.331–58.

——————. "The Home in Working-Class Life." Unpublished paper, 1988.

——————. "The Flexible House: The Housing Backlog and the Persistence of Lodging, 1891–1951." *Social Science History*, 18, no.1 (Spring 1994). Pp.31–53.

——————. *The Growth of Home Ownership in Toronto, 1899–1913*. Toronto: Centre for Urban Studies Research Paper no.163 1987.

——————. "Residential Segregation and Class Formation in Canadian Cities: A Critical Review." *Canadian Geographer*, 28, no.2 (Summer 1984). Pp.186–96.

——————. "Self-Building and the Social Geography of Toronto, 1901–1913: A Challenge for Urban Theory." Institute of British Geographers. *Transactions*, 15, no. 4 (1990). Pp.387–402.

——————. "Self-Building in the Urban Housing Market." *Economic Geography*, 67, no.1 (1991). Pp.1–21.

——————. "Working-Class Home Ownership and Housing Affordabilty across Canada in 1931." *HS/SH*, 19, no.37 (May 1986). Pp.121–38.

——————. "A Working-Class Suburb for Immigrants, Toronto, 1909–1913." *Geographical Review*, 81, no.3 (1991). Pp.318–32.

——————, and Chris Hammett. "The Myth of the Promised Land: The Social Diffusion of Home Ownership in Britain and North America." Association of American Geographers. *Annals*, 77, no. 2 (June 1987). Pp.173–90.

——————, and Peter J. Larkham, eds. *Changing Suburbs: Foundation, Form, and Function*. London: Spon Press 1999.

——————, and Robert Lewis. "The Geography of North American Cities and Suburbs, 1900–1950." *JUH*, 27, no. 3 (March 2001). Pp.262–92.

_____, and Doris Ragonetti. "Where Credit Is Due: Residential Mortgage Finance in Canada, 1901 to 1954." *Journal of Real Estate Finance and Economics*, 16, no. 2 (September 1998). Pp.223–38.

_____, and Matt Sendbuehler. "Hamilton's East End: The Early Working-Class Suburb." *Canadian Geographer*, 36, no.4 (Winter 1992). Pp.381–86.

_____. "The Making of a Working-Class Suburb in Hamilton's East End, 1900–1945." *JUH*, 20, no. 4 (August 1994). Pp.486–511.

Harrison, Brian. "For Church, Queen and Family: The Girls' Friendly Society, 1874–1920." *Past and Present*, 61 (November 1973). Pp.107–38.

_____. "Traditions of Respectability in British Labour History." In Brian Harrison. *Peaceable Kingdom: Stability and Change in Modern Britain*. Oxford: Clarendon Press 1982.

Harrison, Royden. *Before the Socialists: Studies in Labour and Politics 1861–1881*. London: Routledge and Kegan Paul 1965.

Havig, Alan. "The Commercial Amusement Audience in Early 20th-Century American Cities." *Journal of American Culture*, 5, no. 1 (Spring 1982). Pp.1–19.

Hay, Keith A.J. "Early Twentieth Century Business Cycles in Canada." *Canadian Journal of Economic and Political Science*, 32, no. 3 (August 1966). Pp.354–65.

Haydu, Jeffrey. *Between Craft and Class: Skilled Workers and Factory Politics in the United States and Britain, 1890–1922*. Philadelphia: Temple University Press 1988.

Hayter, Charles R.R. "Medicalizing Malignancy: The Uneasy Origins of Ontario's Cancer Program, 1929–34." *CBMH*, 14, no. 2 (1997). Pp.195–213.

Head of the Lake Historical Society. *Hamilton, Panorama of Our Past: A Pictorial History of the Hamilton-Wentworth Region*. Hamilton: Head of the Lake Historical Society n.d.

Helm, Norman C. *In the Shadow of the Giants: The History of the Toronto, Hamilton and Buffalo Railway*. Cheltenham,Ont.: Boston Mills Press 1978.

Henley, Brian. *The Grand Old Buildings of Hamilton*. Hamilton: The Spectator 1994.

_____. *Hamilton, 1889–1890: "From the Light-Lit Bay to the Lordly Hill."* Hamilton: Hamilton Public Library n.d.

_____. *Hamilton: Our Lives and Times*. Hamilton: The Spectator 1993.

Heron, Craig. *Booze: A Distilled History*. Toronto: Between the Lines 2003.

_____. "The Boys and Their Booze: Masculinities and Public Drinking in Working-Class Hamilton, 1890–1946." *CHR*, 86, no. 3 (September 2005). Pp.411–52.

_____. "The Crisis of the Craftsman: Hamilton's Metal Workers in the Early Twentieth Century." *L/LT*, 6 (Autumn 1980). Pp.7–48.

_____. "Etherington, Edward James." *DHB*, 3. Pp.46–47.

_____. "Factory Workers." In Craven, ed. *Labouring Lives*. Pp.479–590.

_____. "Halcrow, George G." *DHB*, 4. Pp.112–13.

_____. "Halford, Harry John." *DHB*, 3. Pp.82–83.

_____. "Hamilton Steelworkers and the Rise of Mass Production." *CHAHP*, 1982. Pp.103–31.

_____. "Harold, Marg, and the Boys: The Relevance of Class in Canadian History." *JCHA*, Vol. 20, no.1 (2009). Pp.1–26.

_____. "The High School and the Household Economy in Working-Class Hamilton, 1890–1940." *HSE*, 7, no. 2 (Fall 1995). Pp.217–59.

_____. "Hobson, Robert." *DCB*, Vol. 15.

_____. "Jeffrey, Janet (Inman)." *DHB*, 3. Pp.96–97.

_____. "Labourism and the Canadian Working Class." *L/LT*, 13 (Spring 1984). Pp.45–76.

_____. "Landers, Samuel." *DHB*, 3. Pp.105–6.

_____. "Lawrence, Samuel." *DHB*, 4. Pp.150–54.

_____. "Mitchell, Humphrey." *DHB*, 4. Pp.193–96.

_____. "National Contours: Solidarity and Fragmentation." In Heron, ed. *Workers' Revolt*. Pp.268–304.

_____. "The New Factory Regime and Workers' Struggles in Canada, 1890–1940." Paper presented to the Australian Canadian Labour History Conference, Sydney, 1988.

_____. "Obermeyer, Philip." *DHB*, 3. P. 160.

_____. "The Ontario Department of Labour and Class Relations in Ontario before World War II." Paper presented to Ontario Ministry of Labour, Symposium: Past Present and Future, Toronto, 1994.

_____. "The Second Industrial Revolution in Canada, 1890–1930." In Deian R. Hopkin and Gregory S. Kealey, eds. *Class, Community, and the Labour Movement: Wales and Canada, 1850–1930*. Aberystwyth: Llafur and Committee on Canadian Labour History 1989. Pp.48–66.

_____. "Studholme, Allan." *DCB*, Vol. 14 (1998).

_____. "Working-Class Hamilton 1895–1930." PhD dissertation, Dalhousie University 1981.

_____, ed. *The Workers' Revolt in Canada, 1917–1925*. Toronto: University of Toronto Press 1998.

_____. *Working in Steel: The Early Years in Canada, 1883–1935*. Toronto: McClelland and Stewart 1988.

_____, Shea Hoffmitz, Wayne Roberts, and Robert Storey. *All That Our Hands Have Done: A Pictorial History of the Hamilton Workers*. Oakville, Ont.: Mosaic Press 1981.

_____, and Bryan D. Palmer. "Through the Prism of the Strike: Industrial Conflict in Southern Ontario, 1901–14." *CHR*, 58, no.4 (December 1977). Pp.423–58.

_____, and Steve Penfold. *The Workers' Festival: A History of Labour Day in Canada*. Toronto: University of Toronto Press 2005.

_____, and Myer Siemiatycki. "The Great War, the State, and Working-Class Canada." In Heron, ed. *Workers' Revolt*. Pp.11–42.

_____, and Robert Storey, eds. *On the Job: Confronting the Labour Process in Canada*. Montreal and Kingston: McGill-Queen's University Press 1986.

_____. "On the Job in Canada." In Heron and Storey, eds. *On the Job*. Pp.3–46.

Herreshoff, David. *The Origins of American Marxism: From the Transcendentalists to De Leon*. New York: Monad Press 1973.

Herring, D. Ann, ed. *Anatomy of a Pandemic: The 1918 Influenza in Hamilton*. Hamilton: Allegra Print and Imaging [2006].

Hessen, Robert. "The Bethlehem Steel Strike of 1910." *LH*, 15, no. 1 (Winter 1974). Pp.3–18.

Heydenkorn, Benedykt. "The Polish Canadian Parish as a Social Entity: A Hamilton Example." *Polyphony*, 6, no. 2 (Fall-Winter 1984). Pp.37–39.

Hiebert, Daniel. "Class, Ethnicity, and Residential Structure: The Social Geography of Winnipeg, 1900–1921." *Journal of Historical Geography*, 17 (1991). Pp.56–86.

Hill, Richard. *Skywalkers: A History of Indian Ironworkers*. Brantford, Ont.: Woodlands Indian Cultural Educational Centre 1987.

Himka, John-Paul. "The Background to Emigration: Ukrainians of Galicia and Bukovyna, 1848–1914." In Lupul, ed. *Heritage in Transition*. Pp.11–31.

Hinther, Rhonda L. "Raised in the Spirit of the Class Struggle: Children, Youth, and the Interwar Ukrainian Left in Canada." *L/LT*, 60 (Fall 2007). Pp.43–76.

Hinton, James. *The First Shop Stewards' Movement*. London: George Allen and Unwin 1973.

_____. "Voluntarism versus Jacobinism: Labor, Nation, and Citizenship in Britain, 1850–1950." *ILWCH*, 48 (Fall 1995). Pp.68–90.

Hirsch, Julia. *Family Photographs: Content, Meaning, and Effect*. New York: Oxford University Press 1981.

Hitchins, Keith. "Mutual Benefit Societies in Hungary, 1930–1941." In Van der Linden, ed. *Social Security Mutualism*. Pp.359–83.

Hobbs, Margaret. "Equality and Difference: Feminism and the Defense of Women Workers during the Great Depression." *L/LT*, 32 (Fall 1993). Pp.201–23.

_____. "Gendering Work and Welfare: Women's Relationship to Wage-Work and Social Policy in Canada during the Great Depression." PhD dissertation, Ontario Institute for Studies in Education 1995.

_____. "Rethinking Antifeminism in the 1930s: Gender Crisis or Workplace Justice? A Response to Alice Kessler-Harris." *Gender and History*, 5, no. 1 (Spring 1993). Pp.4–15.

_____, and Ruth Roach Pierson. "'A Kitchen That Wastes No Steps . . .': Gender, Class, and the Home Improvement Plan, 1936–40." *HS/SH*, 21, no. 41 (May 1988). Pp.9–37.

Hobsbawm, E.J. *Labouring Men: Studies in the History of Labour*. London: Weidenfeld and Nicolson 1964.

_____. *Primitive Rebels: Studies in Archaic Forms of Social Movement in the 19th and 20th Centuries*. New York: W.W. Norton and Company 1959.

Hoe, Ban Seng. *Enduring Hardship: The Chinese Laundry in Canada*. Ottawa: Canadian Museum of Civilization 2003.

Hoerder, Dirk. "From Migrants to Ethnics: Acculturation in a Societal Framework." In Hoerder and Moch, eds. *European Migrants*. Pp.211–62.

_____. "Immigration and the Working Class: The Remigration Factor." *ILWCH*, 21 (Spring 1982). Pp.28–41.

_____. "An Introduction to Labor Migration in the Atlantic Economies, 1815–1914." In Hoerder, ed. *Labor Migration in the Atlantic Economies: The European and North American Working Classes during the Period of Industrialization*. Westport, Conn.: Greenwood Press 1985. Pp.3–31.

_____, and Leslie Page Moch, eds. *European Migrants: Global and Local Perspectives*. Boston: Northeastern University Press 1996.

Hogan, David John. *Class and Reform: School and Society in Chicago, 1880–1930*. Philadelphia: University of Pennsylvania Press 1985.

Hogeveen, Bryan. "'Can't You Be a Man?': Rebuilding Wayward Masculinities and Regulating Juvenile Deviance in Ontario, 1860–1930." PhD dissertation, University of Toronto 2003.

Hoggart, Richard. *The Uses of Literacy: Aspects of Working-Class Life, with Special References to Publications and Entertainments*. London: Chatto and Windus 1971.

Holdsworth, Deryck W. "Cottages and Castles for Vancouver Home-Seekers." *BC Studies*, 69–70 (Spring-Summer 1986). Pp.11–32.

_____. "House and Home in Vancouver: Images of West-Coast Urbanism, 1886–1929." In Gilbert A. Stelter and Alan F.J. Artibise, eds. *The Canadian City: Essays in Urban History*. Toronto: McClelland and Stewart 1977. Pp.186–211.

Holman, Andrew Carl. "Corktown, 1832–1847: The Founding of Hamilton's Pre-Famine Catholic Irish Settlement." MA thesis, McMaster University 1989.

_____. *A Sense of Their Duty: Middle-Class Formation in Victorian Ontario Towns*. Montreal and Kingston: McGill-Queen's University Press 2000.

Holt, James. "Trade Unionism in the British and U.S. Steel Industries, 1880–1914: A Comparative Study." *LH*, 18, no. 1 (Winter 1977). Pp.5–35.

Homel, Gene Howard. "'Fading Beams of the Nineteenth Century': Radicalism and Early Socialism in Canada's 1890s." *L/LT*, 5 (Spring 1980). Pp.7–32.

_____. "James Simpson and the Origins of Canadian Social Democracy." PhD dissertation, University of Toronto 1978.

Horowitz, Daniel. *The Morality of Spending: Attitudes toward the Consumer Society in America, 1875–1940*. Chicago: Ivan R. Dee 1985.

Horowitz, Roger, ed. *Boys and Their Toys? Masculinity, Class, and Technology in America*. New York: Routledge 2001.

Horrall, Andrew. "Charlie Chaplin and the Canadian Expeditionary Force." In Briton C. Busch, ed. *Canada and the Great War: Western Front Association Papers*. Montreal and Kingston: McGill-Queen's University Press 2003. Pp.27–45.

Horrall, S.W. "The Royal North-West Mounted Police and Labour Unrest in Western Canada, 1919." *CHR*, 61, no. 2 (June 1980). Pp.169–90.

Houghton, Bob. "Hamilton's CKOC Noted For Recording Many Radio Firsts." In Houghton, ed. *More of First Here*. Pp.12–14.

Houghton, Margaret. "Gore Park." In Missett et al. *Downtown Hamilton*. Pp.7–14.

————. "Adults Paid 15 Cents to See City's First Film at Palace Rink." In Houghton, ed. *First Here*. Pp.49–52.

————. "The Alexandra: Roller Skaters Packed the Hall." In Houghton, ed. *Vanished Hamilton, II*. Pp.17–18.

————, ed. *First Here*. Burlington, Ont.: North Shore Publishing 2008.

————, ed. *More of First Here*. Burlington, Ont.: North Shore Publishing 2009.

————, ed. *Vanished Hamilton, II*. Burlington, Ont.: North Shore Publishing 2006.

Hounshell, David A. *From the American System to Mass Production, 1800–1932: The Development of Manufacturing Technology in the United States*. Baltimore: Johns Hopkins University Press 1984.

Houston, Cecil J., and William J. Smyth. *The Sash Canada Wore: A Historical Geography of the Orange Order in Canada*. Toronto: University of Toronto Press 1980.

Howell, Colin. *Northern Sandlots: A Social History of Maritime Baseball*. Toronto: University of Toronto Press 1995.

Howell, David. *British Workers and the Independent Labour Party, 1888–1906*. Manchester: Manchester University Press 1983.

Howell, David, and Peter Lindsay. "Social Gospel and the Young Boy Problem, 1895–1925." In Morris Mott, ed. *Sports in Canada: Historical Readings*. Toronto: Copp Clark Pitman 1989. Pp.220–33.

Hoy, Suellen. *Chasing Dirt: The American Pursuit of Cleanliness*. New York: Oxford University Press 1995.

Hughes, Annmarie. "Representations and Counter-Representations of Domestic Violence on Clydeside between the Two World Wars." *Labour History Review*, 69, no.2 (August 2004). Pp.169–84.

Hull, James P. "Science and the Canadian Pulp and Paper Industry, 1903–1933." PhD dissertation, York University 1985.

————. "Working with Figures: Industrial Measurement as Hegemonic Discourse." *Left History*, 9, no.1 (Fall/Winter 2003). Pp.62–78.

Humphries, Charles W. *"Honest Enough to Be Bold": The Life and Times of Sir James Pliny Whitney*. Toronto: University of Toronto Press 1985.

————. "The Political Career of Sir James P. Whitney." PhD dissertation, University of Toronto 1966.

————. "The Sources of Ontario 'Progressive' Conservatism." *CHAHP*, 1967. Pp.118–29.

Humphries, Jane. "Class Struggle and the Persistence of the Working Class Family." *Cambridge Journal of Economics*, 1, no.3 (September 1977). Pp.241–58

————. "The Working Class Family, Women's Liberation and Class Struggle: The Case of Nineteenth Century British History." *Review of Radical Political Economics*, 9, no.3 (Fall 1977). Pp.25–41.

Humphries, Stephen. *Hooligans or Rebels? An Oral History of Working-Class Childhood and Youth, 1889–1939*. Oxford: Basil Blackwell 1982.

Hunt, C.W. *Booze, Boats, and Billions: Smuggling Liquid Gold!* Toronto: McClelland and Stewart 1988.

————. *Whiskey and Ice: The Saga of Ben Kerr, Canada's Most Daring Rumrunner*. Toronto: Dundurn Press 1995.

Hunter, Peter. *Which Side Are You On, Boys: Canadian Life on the Left*. Toronto: Lugus Productions 1988.

Hurd, Madeleine. "Class, Masculinity, Manners, and Mores: Public Space and Public Sphere in Nineteenth-Century Europe." *Social Science History*, 24, no. 1 (Spring 2000). Pp.75–110.

Hurl, Lorna F. "Overcoming the Inevitable: Restricting Factory Labour in Late Nineteenth-Century Ontario." *L/LT*, 21 (Spring 1988). Pp.87–123.

————. "The Toronto Housing Company, 1912–1923: The Pitfalls of Painless Philanthropy." *CHR*, 64, no.1 (March 1984). Pp.28–53.

Huzel, James P. "The Incidence of Crime in Vancouver during the Great Depression." *BC Studies*, 69–70 (Spring-Summer 1986). Pp.211–48.

Iacovetta, Franca, with Paula Draper, eds. *A Nation of Immigrants: Women, Workers, and Communities in Canadian History, 1840s–1960s*. Toronto: University of Toronto Press 1998.

Inglis, Fred. *The Delicious History of the Holiday*. New York: Routledge 2000.

Irwin, Tom. "Moral Order Crime in Hamilton: 1907–1912." Unpublished paper (WC).

Jacek, Henry. "John Munro and the Hamilton East Liberals: Anatomy of a Modern Machine." In Freeman and Hewitt, eds. *Their Town*. Pp.62–73.

————— et al. "The Congruence of Federal-Provincial Campaign Activity in Party Organizations: The Influence of Recruitment Patterns in Three Hamilton Ridings." *Canadian Journal of Political Science*, 5, no. 2 (June 1972). Pp.190–205.

Jackson, Kenneth T. *The Ku Klux Klan in the City*. New York: Oxford University Press 1967.

Jacobson, Matthew Frye. *Whiteness of a Different Color: European Immigrants and the Alchemy of Race*. Cambridge, Mass.: Harvard University Press 1998.

Jacoby, Sanford M. *Employing Bureaucracy: Managers, Unions, and the Transformation of Work in American Industry, 1900–1945*. New York: Columbia University Press 1985.
_____, and Sunil Sharma. "Employment Duration and Industrial Labor Mobility in the United States, 1880–1980." *Journal of Economic History*, 52, no.1 (March 1992). Pp.161–79.

Jaggard, Robert, and Glynn Cracknell. *75 Years: A History of Division 107, Amalgamated Transit Union*. [Hamilton: Amalgamated Transit Union, Local 107 1974].

James, Marquis. *The Metropolitan Life: A Study in Business Growth*. New York: Viking Press 1947.

Jasen, David A. *Tin Pan Alley: The Composers, the Songs, the Performers, and Their Times: The Golden Age of American Popular Music from 1886 to 1956*. New York: Donald I. Fine 1988.

Jeffreys, James B. *The Story of the Engineers, 1800–1945*. London: Lawrence and Wishart 1945.

Jenkins, William. "Views from 'The Hub of the Empire': Loyal Orange Lodges in Early Twentieth-Century Toronto." In David A. Wilson, ed. *The Orange Order in Canada*. Dublin: Four Courts Press 2007. Pp.128–45.

Jensen, Joan M., and Sue Davidson, eds. *A Needle, a Bobbin, a Strike: Women Needleworkers in America*. Philadelphia: Temple University Press 1984.

Johnson, Lesley. "Radio and Everyday Life: The Early Years of Broadcasting in Australia, 1922–1945." *Media, Culture, and Society*, 3, no. 2 (April 1981). Pp.167–78.

Johnson, Paul. *Saving and Spending: The Working-Class Economy in Britain, 1870–1939*. Oxford: Clarendon Press 1985.

Johnston, Charles M. *E.C. Drury, Agrarian Idealist*. Toronto: University of Toronto Press 1986.
_____. *The Head of the Lake: A History of Wentworth County*. Hamilton: Wentworth County Council 1967.

Johnston, Robert D. "Conclusion: Historians and the American Middle Class." In Bledstein and Johnston, eds. *Middling Sorts*. Pp.296–306.

Johnston, Russell. "The Emergence of Broadcast Advertising in Canada, 1919–1932." *Historical Journal of Film, Radio and Television*, 17, no. 1 (1997). Pp.29–47.
_____. *Selling Themselves: The Emergence of Canadian Advertising*. Toronto: University of Toronto Press 2001.

Jones, Andrew, and Leonard Rutman. *In the Children's Aid: J.J. Kelso and Child Welfare in Ontario*. Toronto: University of Toronto Press 1981.

Jones, Esyllt Wynne. "Searching for the Springs of Health: Women and Working Families in Winnipeg's 1918–19 Influenza Epidemic." PhD dissertation, University of Manitoba 2002.

Jones, Gareth Stedman. *Languages of Class: Studies in English Working-Class History, 1832–1982*. Cambridge: Cambridge University Press 1983.

Josephson, Matthew. *Sidney Hillman: Statesman of American Labor*. Garden City, N.Y.: Doubleday 1952.

Jowett, Garth. *Film: The Democratic Art*. Boston: Little, Brown and Company 1976.
_____. "The First Motion Picture Audiences." In Fell, ed. *Film Before Griffith*. Pp.196–206.

Joyce, Patrick, ed. *Class*. Oxford: Oxford University Press 1995.
_____. *Visions of the People: Industrial England and the Question of Class, 1848–1914*. Cambridge: Cambridge University Press 1991.
_____. *Work, Society and Politics: The Culture of the Factory in Later Victorian England*. New Brunswick, N.J.: Rutgers University Press 1980.

Kaczynska, Elzbieta. "Mutual Benefit Societies in Partitioned Poland, 1815–1914." In Van der Linden, ed. *Social Security Mutualism*. Pp.385–401.

Kalbach, Warren E., and Wayne W. McVey. *The Demographic Bases of Canadian Society*. Toronto: McGraw-Hill Ryerson 1971.

Kallmann, Helmut. *A History of Music in Canada, 1534–1914*. Toronto: University of Toronto Press 1960.

Kaprielian-Churchill, Isabel. "Armenian Village Educational Associations." *Polyphony*, 2, no. 1 (Winter 1979). Pp.64–6.
_____. *Like Our Mountains: A History of Armenians in Canada*. Montreal and Kingston: McGill-Queen's University Press 2005.

Kasson, John F. *Amusing the Million: Coney Island at the Turn of the Century*. New York: Hill and Wang 1978.

Katz, Michael B. *In the Shadow of the Poorhouse: A Social History of Welfare in America*. New York: Basic Books 1986.
_____. *The People of Hamilton, Canada West: Family and Class in a Mid-Nineteenth-Century City*. Cambridge, Mass.: Harvard University Press 1975.
_____, Michael J. Doucet, and Mark J. Stern. *The Social Organization of Early Industrial Capitalism*. Cambridge, Mass.: Harvard University Press 1982.

Katznelson Ira. "Working-Class Formation: Constructing Cases and Comparisons." In Katznelson and Zolberg, eds. *Working-Class Formation*. Pp.3–41.
_____, and Aristide R. Zolberg, eds. *Working-Class Formation: Nineteenth-Century Patterns in Western Europe and the United States*. Princeton, N.J.: Princeton University Press 1986.

Kaye, Harvey J. *The British Marxist Historians*. London: Polity Press 1984.

Kealey, Gregory S. "'The Honest Workingman' and Workers' Control: The Experience of Toronto Skilled Workers, 1860–1892." *L/LT*, 1 (1976). Pp.32–68.
_____. "Labour and Working-Class History in Canada: Prospects for the 1980s." *L/LT*, 7 (1981). Pp.67–94.
_____. "State Repression of Labour and the Left in Canada, 1914–20: The Impact of the First World War." *CHR*, 73, no. 3 (September 1992). Pp.281–94.
_____. "The Structure of Canadian Working-Class History." In Kealey. *Workers and Canadian History*. Montreal

and Kingston: McGill-Queen's University Press 1995. Pp.329–44.

_____. "Work Control, the Labour Process, and Nineteenth-Century Canadian Printers." In Heron and Storey, eds. *On the Job*. Pp.75–101.

_____, and Peter Warrian, eds. *Essays in Canadian Working Class History*. Toronto: McClelland and Stewart 1976.

_____, and Reg Whitaker, eds. *R.C.M.P. Security Bulletins: The Early Years, 1919–1929*. St. John's: Canadian Committee on Labour History 1994.

_____. *R.C.M.P. Security Bulletins: The Depression Years*. St. John's: Canadian Committee on Labour History 1993.

Kealey, Linda. "Women and Labour during World War I: Women Workers and the Minimum Wage in Manitoba." In Mary Kinnear, ed. *First Days, Fighting Days: Women in Manitoba History*. Regina: Canadian Plains Research Centre, University of Regina 1987. Pp.76–99.

Kelley, Ninette, and Michael Trebilcock. *The Making of the Mosaic: A History of Canadian Immigration Policy*. Toronto: University of Toronto Press 1998.

Kelley, Robin D.G. "Notes on Deconstructing 'The Folk.'" *AHR*, 97, no. 5 (December 1992). Pp.1400–8.

Kelly, Wayne. *Downright Upright: A History of the Canadian Piano Industry*. Toronto: Natural Heritage/Natural History Inc 1991.

Kendall, Walter. *The Revolutionary Movement in Britain, 1900–21: The Origins of British Communism*. London: Weidenfeld and Nicolson 1969.

Kenneally, James. *Women and American Trade Unions*. St. Alban's, Vt.: Eden Press 1978.

Kenney, William Howland. *Recorded Music in American Life: The Phonograph and Popular Memory, 1890–1945*. New York: Oxford University Press 1999.

Kerr, Gordon B. "The Rise of Sport in Hamilton, 1860–1900." Unpublished paper (WC).

Keshen, Jeffrey A. *Propaganda and Censorship during Canada's Great War*. Edmonton: University of Alberta Press 1996.

Kessler-Harris, Alice. "Gender Ideology in Historical Reconstruction: A Case Study from the 1930s." *Gender and History*, 1, no. 1 (Spring 1989). Pp.31–49.

_____. *Gendering Labor History*. Urbana: University of Illinois Press 2007.

_____. *In Pursuit of Equity: Women, Men, and the Quest for Economic Citizenship in 20th-Century America*. Oxford: Oxford University Press 2001.

_____. *A Woman's Wage: Historical Meanings and Social Consequences*. Lexington: University of Kentucky Press 1990.

Kett, Joseph E. "The Adolescence of Vocational Education." In Harvey Kantor and David Tyack, eds. *Work, Youth, and Schooling: Historical Perspectives on Vocationalism in American Education*. Stanford, Cal.: Stanford University Press 1982. Pp.80–113.

Kibler, M. Alison. *Rank Ladies: Gender and Cultural Hierarchy in American Vaudeville*. Chapel Hill: University of North Carolina Press 1999.

Kidd, Bruce. *The Struggle for Canadian Sport*. Toronto: University of Toronto Press 1996.

Kilbourn, William. *The Elements Combined: A History of the Steel Company of Canada*. Toronto: Clarke Irwin 1960.

Kimmel, Michael. *Manhood in America: A Cultural History*. New York: Free Press 1996.

King, Graham. *Say 'Cheese'! The Snapshot as Art and Social History*. London: Collins 1986.

Kinnear, Mary. *In Subordination: Professional Women, 1870–1970*. Montreal and Kingston: McGill-Queen's University Press 1995.

Kirk, Neville. *Comrades and Cousins: Globalization, Workers and Labour Movements in Britain, the USA and Australia from the 1880s to 1914*. London: Merlin Press 2003.

_____. "History, Language, Ideas, and Post-Modernism: A Materialist View." *Social History*, 19, no. 2 (May 1994). Pp.221–40.

_____. *Labour and Society in Britain and the USA*. 2 vols. Aldershot, England: Scolar Press 1994.

Knowles, Norman. "'Christ in the Crowsnest': Religion and the Anglo-Canadian Working Class in the Crowsnest Pass, 1898–1918." In Michael Behiels and Marcel Martel, eds. *Nation, Ideas, and Identities: Essays in Honour of Ramsay Cook*. Don Mills, Ont.: Oxford University Press 1997. Pp.57–71.

Kolasky, John. *The Shattered Illusion: The History of Ukrainian Pro-Communist Organizations in Canada*. Toronto: PMA Books 1979.

Kolko, Gabriel. *The Triumph of Conservatism: A Reinterpretation of American History, 1900–1916*. New York: Free Press of Glencoe 1963.

Koszarski, Richard. *An Evening's Entertainment: The Age of the Silent Feature Picture, 1915–1928*. Berkeley: University of California Press 1990.

Koven, Seth, and Sonya Michel. "Womanly Duties: Maternalist Politics and the Origins of Welfare States in France, Germany, Great Britain, and the United States, 1880–1920." *AHR*, 95, no. 4 (October 1990). Pp.1076–1108.

Kramer, Reinhold, and Tom Mitchell. *When the State Trembled: How A.J. Andrews and the Citizens' Committee Broke the Winnipeg General Strike*. Toronto: University of Toronto Press 2010.

Krawchuk, Pater. *Our History: The Ukrainian Labour-Farmer Movement in Canada, 1907–1991*. Toronto: Lugus 1996.

_____. *The Ukrainian Socialist Movement in Canada (1907–1918)*. Toronto: Progress Books 1979.

Kristofferson, Robert R. *Craft Capitalism: Craftworkers and Early Industrialization in Hamilton, Ontario, 1840–1872*. Toronto: University of Toronto Press 2007.

Kuffert, Len. "'To Pick You Up or to Hold You': Intimacy and Golden-Age Radio in Canada." Paper presented to Canadian Historical Association, 2006.

Kukushkin, Vadim. *From Peasants to Labourers: Ukrainian and Belarusan Immigration from the Russian Empire to Canada*. Montreal and Kingston: McGill-Queen's University Press 2007.

Kurman, Louis A. "The Hamilton Jewish Community." *Wentworth Bygones*, 8 (1969). Pp.8–12.

Ladd-Taylor, Molly, ed. *Raising a Baby the Government Way: Mothers' Letters to the Children's Bureau, 1915–1932*. New Brunswick, N.J.: Rutgers University Press 1986.

Latham, Angela J. "Packaging Woman; The Concurrent Rise of Beauty Pageants, Public Bathing, and Other Performances of Female 'Nudity.'" *Journal of Popular Culture*, 29, no. 3 (Winter 1995). Pp.149–67.

Laverdure, Paul. *Sunday in Canada: The Rise and Fall of the Lord's Day*. Yorkton, Sask.: Gravelbooks 2004.

Lawrence, Jon. "Class and Gender in the Making of Urban Toryism, 1880–1914." *English Historical Review*, 108, no. 428 (July 1993). Pp.629–52.

———. "Popular Radicalism and the Socialist Revival in Britain." *Journal of British Studies*, 31, no. 2 (April 1992). Pp.163–86.

———. *Speaking for the People: Party, Language, and Popular Politics in England, 1867–1914*. Cambridge: Cambridge University Press 1998.

Lay, Shawn. *Hooded Knights on the Niagara: The Ku Klux Klan in Buffalo, New York*. New York: New York University Press 1995.

Lazonick, William H. "Industrial Relations and Technical Change: The Case of the Self-Acting Mule." *Cambridge Journal of Economics*, 3, no. 3 (September 1979). Pp.231–62.

———. "Technological Change and the Control of Work: The Development of Capital-Labour Relations in US Mass Production Industries." In Gospel and Littler, eds. *Managerial Strategies and Industrial Relations*. Pp.111–36.

Leadbeater, David. *Setting Minimum Living Standards in Canada: A Review*. Ottawa: Economic Council of Canada, Working Paper no. 38 1992.

Lears, T.J. Jackson. "The Concept of Cultural Hegemony: Problems and Possibilities." *AHR*, 90, no. 3 (June 1985). Pp.567–93.

———. *Fables of Abundance: A Cultural History of Advertising in America*. New York: Basic Books 1994.

———. "Making Fun of Popular Culture." *AHR*, 97, no. 5 (December 1992). Pp.1417–26.

Lee, Alan J. "Conservatism, Traditionalism, and the British Working Class, 1880–1918." In David E. Martin and David Rubinstein, eds. *Ideology and the Labour Movement: Essays Presented to John Saville*. London: Croom Helm 1979. Pp.84–102.

Lee, Gloria L. "Traditions and Change in the Canadian Accounting and Engineering Professions." *British Journal of Canadian Studies*, 7, no. 2 (1992). Pp.326–44.

Lee, Jenny. "The Redivision of Labour: Women and Wage Regulation in Victoria, 1896–1903." In Susan Magarey et al., eds. *Debutante Nation: Feminism Contests the 1890s*. St. Leonards, Australia: Allen and Unwin 1993. Pp.27–38.

Lehrer, Susan. *Origins of Protective Labor Legislation for Women, 1905–1925*. Albany: State University of New York 1987.

Leier, Mark. *Where the Fraser River Flows: The Industrial Workers of the World in British Columbia*. Vancouver: New Star Books 1990.

Lenskyj, Helen. "Femininity First: Sport and Physical Education for Ontario Girls, 1890–1930." In Morris Mott, ed. *Sports in Canada: Historical Readings*. Toronto: Copp Clark Pitman 1989. Pp.187–200.

———. "The Role of Physical Education in the Socialization of Girls in Ontario, 1890–1930." PhD dissertation, University of Toronto 1983.

———. "Training for 'True Womanhood': Physical Education for Girls in Ontario Schools, 1890–1920." *HSE*, 2, no. 2 (Fall 1990). Pp.205–23.

———. "We Want to Play . . . We'll Play: Women and Sport in the Twenties and Thirties." *Canadian Woman Studies*, 4, no. 3 (May 1983). Pp.15–18.

Lenton-Young, Gerald. "Variety Theatre." In Saddlemyer, ed. *Early Stages*. Pp.166–213.

Leroux, Eric. "Verville, Alphonse." *DCB*, Vol. 15.

Leslie, Genevieve. "Domestic Service in Canada, 1880–1920." In Acton et al., eds. *Women at Work*. Pp.71–125.

Levine, Barbara, and Stephanie Snyder, eds. *Snapshot Chronicles: Inventing the American Photo Album*. New York: Princeton Architectural Press 2006.

Levine, Lawrence W. "The Folklore of Industrial Society: Popular Culture and Its Audiences." *AHR*, 97, no. 5 (December 1992). Pp.1369–99.

———. *Highbrow/Lowbrow: The Emergence of Cultural Hierarchy in America*. Cambridge, Mass.: Harvard University Press 1988.

Levitt, Joseph. *Henri Bourassa and the Golden Calf: The Social Program of the Nationalists of Quebec (1900–1914)*. Ottawa: Les Editions de l'Université d'Ottawa 1969.

Lewis, Jane. "Dealing with Dependency: State Practices and Social Realities, 1870–1945." In Jane Lewis, ed. *Women's Welfare, Women's Rights*. London: Croom Helm 1983. Pp.17–37.

———, ed. *Labour and Love: Women's Experience of Home and Family, 1850–1940*. Oxford: Basil Blackwell 1986.

———. *The Politics of Motherhood: Child and Maternal Welfare in England, 1900–1939*. London: Croom Helm 1980.

———. "The Prevention of Diphtheria in Canada and Britain, 1914–1945." *JSH*, 20, no. 1 (Fall 1986). Pp.163–76.

———. "The Working-Class Wife and Mother and State Intervention, 1870–1918." In Lewis, ed. *Labour and Love*. Pp.99–120.

Lewis, Norah L. "Goose Grease and Turpentine: Mother Treats the Family Illnesses." In Veronica Strong-Boag and Anita

Clair Fellman, eds. *Rethinking Canada: The Promise of Women's History*. 2nd ed. Toronto: Copp Clark Pitman 1991. Pp.234–48.

Lewis, Robert. "Redesigning the Workplace: The North American Factory in the Interwar Period." *Technology and Culture*, 42, no. 4 (October 2001). Pp.665–84.

_____. "The Workplace and Economic Crisis: Canadian Textile Firms, 1929–1935." *Enterprise and Society*, 10, no. 3 (September 2009). Pp.498–528.

Lichtenstein, Nelson, and Howell John Harris, eds. *Industrial Democracy in America: The Ambiguous Promise*. Cambridge: Cambridge University Press 1993.

Lilley, Patricia. "'These Walls Around Me': Asylum for the Insane at Hamilton: 1876–1896." Major Research Paper, Department of History, York University n.d..

Lipset, Seymour Martin, and Gary Marks. *It Didn't Happen Here: Why Socialism Failed in the United States*. New York: W.W. Norton 2000.

Little, Margaret Hillyard. "The Blurring of Boundaries: Private and Public Welfare for Single Mothers in Ontario." *SPE*, 47 (Summer 1995). Pp.89–109.

_____. *"No Car, No Radio, No Liquor Permit": The Moral Regulation of Single Mothers in Ontario, 1920–1997*. Toronto: Oxford University Press 1998.

Lisowka, Anna. "Healing and Treatment: Who Answered the Call of the Sick?" In Herring, ed. *Anatomy of a Pandemic*. Pp.89–103.

Litterer, Joseph A. "Systematic Management: The Search for Order and Integration." *Business History Review*, 25 (1961). Pp.461–76.

Littler, Craig R. "A Comparative Analysis of Managerial Structures and Strategies." In Gospel and Littler, eds. *Managerial Strategies and Industrial Relations*.

Liverant, Bettina. "The Promise of a More Abundant Life: Consumer Society and the Rise of the Managerial State." *JCHA*, 2008. Pp.229–51.

Lockwood, David. *The Blackcoated Worker: A Study in Class Consciousness*. London: Unwin 1966.

Loeb, Lori. "Beating the Flu: Orthodox and Commercial Responses to Influenza in Britain, 1889–1919." *Social History of Medicine*, 18, no.2 (1995). Pp.203–24.

Loewen, Royden, and Gerald Friesen. *Immigrants in Prairie Cities: Ethnic Diversity in Twentieth-Century Canada*. Toronto: University of Toronto Press 2009.

Löfgren, Orvar. *On Holiday: A History of Vacationing*. Berkeley: University of California Press 1999.

Lonnee, Bruce. "The City of Hamilton's Maitre D' to Industry: A Study of the Industrial Commissioner's Officer." Unpublished paper (WC).

Lorimer, Douglas. "From Victorian Values to White Virtues: Assimilation and Exclusion in British Racial Discourse, c.1870–1914." In Buckner and Francis, eds. *Rediscovering the British World*. Pp.109–34.

Lott, Eric. *Love and Theft: Blackface Minstrelsy and the American Working Class*. New York: Oxford University Press 1993.

Loviglio, Jason. *Radio's Intimate Public: Network Broadcasting and Mass-Mediated Democracy*. Minneapolis: University of Minnesota Press 2005.

Lowe, Graham S. "The Administrative Revolution in the Canadian Office: An Overview." In Katherina L.P. Lundy and Barbara D. Warme, eds. *Work in the Canadian Context: Continuity Despite Change*. Toronto: Butterworths 1981.

_____. "Class, Job, and Gender in the Canadian Office." *LL/T*, 10 (Autumn 1982). Pp.11–37.

_____. "Mechanization, Feminization, and Managerial Control in the Early Twentieth-Century Canadian Office." In Heron and Storey, eds. *On the Job*. Pp.178–80.

_____. "The Rise of Modern Management in Canada." *Canadian Dimension*, 14, no. 3 (December 1979). Pp.32–38.

_____. *Women in the Administrative Revolution*. Toronto: University of Toronto Press 1987.

Lucas, Richard. "The Conflict over Public Power in Hamilton, Ontario, 1906–1914." *OH*, 68, no. 4 (December 1976). Pp.236–46.

Lupul, Manoly R., ed. *A Heritage in Transition: Essays in the History of Ukrainians in Canada*. Toronto: McClelland and Stewart 1982.

Luxton, Meg. *More Than a Labour of Love: Three Generations of Women's Work in the Home*. Toronto: Women's Press 1980.

MacAndrew, C., and R.B. Edgerton. *Drunken Comportment*. Chicago: Aldine 1969.

MacCuaig, Stuart. *Women's Art Association of Hamilton: The First Hundred Years*. Hamilton: Art Gallery of Hamilton 1996.

Macdonald, Cathy. "Hamilton's Hurdler – Betty Taylor." *Canadian Woman Studies*, 4, no. 3 (May 1983). Pp.19–21.

MacDonald, Cheryl. *Adelaide Hoodless, Domestic Crusader*. Toronto: Dundurn Press 1986.

MacDonald, J. Fred. *Don't Touch That Dial! Radio Programming in American Life, 1920–1960*. Chicago: Nelson-Hall 1979.

MacDonald, Robert H. *Sons of the Empire: The Frontier and the Boy Scout Movement, 1890–1918*. Toronto: University of Toronto Press 1993.

MacDougall, Heather. *Activists and Advocates: Toronto's Health Department, 1883–1983*. Toronto: Dundurn Press 1990.

MacDowell, Laurel Sefton. "Canada's 'Gulag': Project #51 Lac Seul (A Tale from the Great Depression)." *JCS*, 28, no.2 (Summer 1993). Pp.130–58.

_____. "Relief Camp Workers in Ontario during the Great Depression of the 1930s." *CHR*, 76, no.2 (June 1995). Pp.205–28.

Maciejko, Bill. "Public Schools and the Workers' Struggle: Winnipeg, 1914–1921." In Nancy M. Sheehan et al., eds. *Schools in the West: Essays in Canadian Educational History*. Calgary: Detselig Enterprises 1986. Pp.222–27.

Macintyre, Stuart. *A Proletarian Science: Marxism in Britain, 1917–1933*. Cambridge: Cambridge University Press 1980.

MacKenzie, David, ed. *Canada and the First World War: Essays in Honour of Robert Craig Brown*. Toronto: University of Toronto Press 2005.

MacKinnon, Mary. "Relief Not Insurance: Canadian Unemployment Relief in the 1930s." *Explorations in Economic History*, 27, no.1 (January 1990). Pp.46–83.

Mackintosh, W.A. *The Economic Background to Dominion-Provincial Relations*. Toronto: McClelland and Stewart 1964.

MacLennan, Anne Frances. "Circumstances beyond Our Control: Canadian Radio Program Schedule Evolution during the 1930s." PhD dissertation, Concordia University 2001.

_____. "Toronto's Sound: Urban Radio Programming in the 1930s." Paper presented to the Canadian Historical Association, 2006.

MacLennan, David. "Beyond the Asylum: Professionalization and the Mental Hygiene Movement in Canada, 1914–1928." *CBMH*, 4, no. 1 (1987). Pp.7–23.

Macleod, David I. "Act Your Age: Boyhood, Adolescence, and the Rise of the Boy Scouts of America." *JSH*, 16, no.2 (Winter 1982). Pp.3–20.

_____. *Building Character in the American Boy: The Boy Scouts, YMCA, and Their Forerunners, 1870–1920*. Madison: University of Wisconsin Press 1983.

_____. "A Live Vaccine: The YMCA and Male Adolescence in the United States and Canada, 1870–1920." *HS/SH*, 11, no.21 (May 1978). Pp.5–25.

Macpherson, C. B. *Democracy in Alberta: Social Credit and the Party System*. Toronto: University of Toronto Press 1962.

MacQueen, Bonnie. "Domesticity and Discipline: The Girl Guides in British Columbia, 1910–1943." In Barbara K. Latham and Roberta J. Pazdro, eds. *Not Just Pin Money: Selected Essays on the History of Women's Work in British Columbia*. Victoria: Camosun College 1984. Pp.221–35.

Magney, William H. "The Methodist Church and the National Gospel, 1884–1914." United Church of Canada, *Bulletin*, 20 (1968). Pp.3–95.

Main, O.W. *The Canadian Nickel Industry: A Study in Market Control and Public Policy*. Toronto: University of Toronto Press 1955.

Mainwaring, John. *The International Labour Organization: A Canadian View*. Ottawa: Canada, Minister of Labour 1986.

Makowski, William Boleslaus. *History and Integration of Poles in Canada*. Lindsay, Ont.: Canadian Polish Congress 1967.

Makuch, Amdrij. "Ukrainian Canadians and the Wartime Economy." In Swyripa and Thompson, eds. *Loyalties in Conflict*. Pp.69–77.

Malcolmson, Robert. *Life and Labour in England 1700–1770*. New York: St. Martin's Press 1981.

Malleck, Dan. *Try to Control Yourself: The Regulation of Public Drinking in Post-Prohibition Ontario, 1927–44*. Vancouver: UBC Press 2012.

Maltin, Leonard, and Richard W. Bann. *The Little Rascals: The Life and Times of Our Gang*. New York: Crown 1992.

Mandell, Kikki. *The Corporation as Family: The Gendering of Corporate Welfare, 1890–1930*. Chapel Hill: University of North Carolina Press 2002.

Mangan, J.A. "Duty unto Death: English Masculinity and Militarism in the Age of the New Imperialism." In Mangan, ed. *Tribal Identities: Nationalism, Europe, Sport*. London: Frank Cass 1996. Pp.10–38.

Mangan, J.A., and James Walvin, eds. *Manliness and Morality: Middle-Class Masculinity in Britain and America, 1800–1940*. New York: St. Martin's Press 1987.

Manley, John. "Communism and the Canadian Working Class during the Great Depression: The Workers' Unity League, 1930–1936." PhD dissertation, Dalhousie University 1984.

_____. "Communists and Autoworkers: The Struggle for Industrial Unionism in the Canadian Automobile Industry, 1925–1936." *L/LT*, 17 (Spring 1986). Pp.105–33.

_____. "'Communists Love Canada': The Communist Party of Canada, the 'People,' and the Popular Front, 1933–1939." *JCS*, 36, no. 4 (Winter 2002). Pp.59–86.

_____. "Does the International Labour Movement Need Salvaging? Communism, Labourism, and the Canadian Trade Unions, 1921–1928." *L/LT*, 41 (Spring 1998). Pp.147–80.

_____. "'Starve, Be Damned!' Communists and Canada's Urban Unemployed , 1929–39." *CHR*, 79, no. 3 (September 1998). Pp.466–91.

Manning, Vanessa. "The 1918 Influenza Epidemic as an Agent of Transformation." In Herring, ed. *Anatomy of a Pandemic*. Pp.185–99.

Manson, Bill. *Getting Around Hamilton: A Brief History of Transportation In and Around Hamilton, 1750 to 1950*. Burlington, Ont.: North Shore Publishing 2002.

Mar, Lisa Rose. *Brokering Belonging: Chinese in Canada's Exclusion Era, 1885–1945*. Toronto: University of Toronto Press 2010.

Marchand, Roland. *Advertising the American Dream: Making Way for Modernity, 1920–1940*. Berkeley: University of California Press 1985.

Mardiros, Anthony. *William Irvine: The Life of a Prairie Radical*. Toronto: James Lorimer 1979.

Marks, Gary. *Unions in Politics: Britain, Germany, and the United States in the Nineteenth and Early Twentieth Centuries*. Princeton, N.J.: Princeton University Press 1989.

Marks, Lynne. "Indigent Committees and Ladies Benevolent Societies." *SPE*, 47 (Summer 1995). Pp.61–87.

_____. *Revivals and Roller Rinks: Religion, Leisure, and Identity in Late-Nineteenth-Century Small-Town Ontario*. Toronto: University of Toronto Press 1996.

_____. "Working-Class Femininity and the Salvation Army: Hallelujah Lasses in English Canada, 1882–1892." In Veronica Strong-Boag and Anita Clair Fellman, eds. *Rethinking Canada: The Promise of Women's History*. 2nd ed. Toronto: Copp Clark Pitman, 1991. Pp.182–205.

Maroney, Paul. "'The Great Adventure': The Context and Ideology of Recruiting in Ontario, 1914–1917." *CHR*, 77, no.1 (March 1996). Pp.62–79.

Marquardt, Richard. *Enter at Your Own Risk: Canadian Youth and the Labour Market*. Toronto: Between the Lines 1998.

Marr, M. Lucille. "Church Teen Clubs, Feminized Organizations? Tuxis Boys, Trail Rangers, and Canadian Girls in Training, 1919–1939." *HSE*, 3 no. 2 (Fall 1991), 249–67.

Marshall, T.S. *Class, Citizenship, and Social Development*. New York: Anchor Books 1965.

Martin, Linda, and Kerry Segrave. *City Parks of Canada*. Oakville, Ont.: Mosaic Press 1983.

Martynowych, Orest T. *Ukrainians in Canada: The Formative Years, 1891–1924*. Edmonton: Canadian Institute of Ukrainian Studies Press 1991.

Masters, D.C. *Henry John Cody: An Outstanding Life*. Toronto: Dundurn Press 1995.

Matters, Diane L. "The Boys' Industrial School: Education for Juvenile Offenders." In J. Donald Wilson and David C. Jones, eds. *Schooling and Society in Twentieth Century British Columbia*. Calgary: Detselig Enterprises 1980. Pp.53–70.

Maurutto, Paula. *Governing Charities: Church and State in Toronto's Catholic Archdiocese, 1850–1950*. Montreal and Kingston: McGill-Queen's University Press 2003.

May, Martha. "Bread before Roses: American Workingmen, Labor Unions, and the Family Wage." In Ruth Milkman, ed. *Women, Work, and Protest: A Century of US Women's Labor History*. Boston: Routledge and Kegan Paul 1985. Pp.1–21.

————. "The 'Good Managers': Married Working Class Women and Family Budget Studies, 1895–1915." *LH*, 25, no. 3 (Summer 1984). Pp.351–72.

————. "The Historical Problem of the Family Wage: The Ford Motor Company and the Five Dollar Day." *Feminist Studies*, 8, no.2 (Summer 1982). Pp.399–424.

Mayer, Arno J. "The Lower Middle Class as Historical Problem." *Journal of Modern History*, 47, no.3 (September 1975). Pp.409–36.

Maynard, Stephen. "'Horrible Temptations': Sex, Men, and Working-Class Male Youth in Urban Ontario, 1890–1935." *CHR*, 78, no.2 (June 1997). Pp.191–235.

————. "'Through a Hole in the Lavatory Wall': Homosexual Subcultures, Police Surveillance, and the Dialectics of Discovery, Toronto, 1890–1930." *Journal of the History of Sexuality*, 5, no. 2 (October 1994). Pp.207–42.

Mazepa, Patricia. "Battles on the Cultural Front: The (De) Labouring of Culture in Canada, 1914–1944." PhD dissertation, Carleton University 2003.

McAree, J.V. *Cabbagetown Store*. Toronto: Ryerson Press 1953.

McBee, Randy D. *Dance Hall Days: Intimacy and Leisure among Working-Class Immigrants in the United States*. New York: New York University Press 2000.

McCalla, Douglas. "The Decline of Hamilton as a Wholesale Centre." *OH*, 65, no. 4 (December 1973). Pp.247–54.

McCallum, Margaret E. "Assistance to Veterans and Their Dependants: Steps on the Way to the Administrative State, 1914–1929." In W. Wesley Pue and Barry Wright, eds. *Canadian Perspectives on Law and Society: Issues in Legal History*. Ottawa: Carleton University Press 1988. Pp.164–65.

————. "Corporate Welfarism in Canada, 1919–39." *CHR*, 71, no. 1 (March 1990). Pp.46–79.

————. "Keeping Women in Their Place: The Minimum Wage in Canada, 1910–1925." *L/LT*, 17 (Spring 1986). Pp.29–59.

McCallum, Todd. "'Not a Sex Question'? The One Big Union and the Politics of Radical Manhood." *L/LT*, 42 (Fall 1998). Pp.15–54.

McCalman, Pamela. "Respectability and Working-Class Politics in Late-Victorian London." *Historical Studies*, 19, no. 74 (1980). Pp.108–24.

McCann, Larry. "Suburbs of Desire: The Suburban Landscape of Canadian Cities, c.1900–1950." In Harris and Larkham, eds. *Changing Suburbs*. Pp.111–45.

McCartin, Joseph A. "'An American Feeling': Workers, Managers, and the Struggle over Industrial Democracy in the World War I Era." In Lichtenstein and Harris, eds. *Industrial Democracy*. Pp.67–86.

McClelland, Keith. "Masculinity and the 'Representative Artisan' in Britain, 1850–80." In Roper and Tosh, eds. *Manful Assertions*. Pp.74–91.

McConnachie, Kathleen Janet Anne. "Science and Ideology: The Mental Hygiene and Eugenics Movements in the Inter-War Years, 1919–1939." PhD dissertation, University of Toronto 1987.

McCormack, A. Ross. "Arthur Puttee and the Liberal Party, 1899–1904." *CHR*, 51, no. 6 (June 1970). Pp.141–63.

————. "Cloth Caps and Jobs: The Ethnicity of English Immigrants in Canada, 1900–1914." In Jorgen Dahlie and Tissa Fernando, eds. *Ethnicity, Power, and Politics*. Toronto: Methuen 1981. Pp.38–55.

————. "Networks among British Immigrants and Accommodation to Canadian Society: Winnipeg, 1900–1914." *HS/SH*, 17, no. 34 (November 1984). Pp.357–74.

————. "The Origins and Extent of Western Labour Radicalism: 1896–1919." PhD dissertation, University of Western Ontario 1973.

————. *Reformers, Rebels, and Revolutionaries: The Western Canadian Radical Movement, 1899–1919*. Toronto: University of Toronto Press 1977.

McCreesh, Carolyn D. *Women in the Campaign to Organize Garment Workers, 1880–1917*. New York: Garland 1985.

McCririck Donna, and Graeme Wynn. "Building 'Self-Respect and Hopefulness': The Development of Blue-Collar Suburbs in Early Vancouver." In Wynn, ed. *People, Places, Patterns, Processes: Geographical Perspectives on the Canadian Past*. Toronto: Copp Clark Pitman 1990. Pp.267–84.

McCrossen, Alexis. *Holy Day, Holiday: The American Sunday.* Ithaca, N.Y.: Cornell University Press 2000.

McCuaig, Katherine. *The Weariness, the Fever, and the Fret: The Campaign against Tuberculosis in Canada, 1900–1950.* Kingston and Montreal: McGill-Queen's University Press 1999. Pp.3–31.

McCullough, A.B. *The Primary Textile Industry in Canada: History and Heritage.* Ottawa: Minister of the Environment 1992.

McDonald, Robert. "'Holy Retreat' or 'Practical Breathing Spot'? Class Perceptions of Vancouver's Stanley Park, 1910–1913." *CHR,* 64, no. 2 (June 1984). Pp.127–53.

McKibbin, Ross. *The Evolution of the Labour Party, 1910–1924.* Oxford: Oxford University Press 1974.

McGinnis, Janice P. Dickin. "The Impact of Epidemic Influenza: Canada, 1918–1919." In Shortt, ed. *Medicine in Canadian Society.* Pp.447–77.

McGowan, Mark. "Toronto's English-Speaking Catholics, Immigration, and the Making of a Canadian Catholic Identity, 1900–30." In Terrence Murphy and Gerald Stortz, eds. *Creed and Culture: The Place of English-Speaking Catholics in Canadian Society, 1750–1930.* Montreal and Kingston: McGill-Queen's University Press 1993. Pp.204–45.

McKay, Ian. "Canada as a Long Liberal Revolution: On Writing the History of Actually Existing Canadian Liberalism, 1840s–1940s." In Jean-François Constant and Michel Ducharme, eds. *Liberalism and Hegemony: Debating the Canadian Liberal Revolution.* Toronto: University of Toronto Press 2009. Pp.347–452.

————. "Capital and Labour in the Halifax Baking and Confectionery Industry during the Last Half of the Nineteenth Century." *L/LT,* 3 (1978). Pp.63–108.

————. *Reasoning Otherwise: Leftists and the People's Enlightenment in Canada, 1890–1920.* Toronto: Between the Lines 2008.

————, and Suzanne Morton. "The Maritimes: Expanding the Circle of Resistance." In Heron, ed. *Workers' Revolt.* Pp.43–86.

McKenzie, Robert, and Allan Silver. *Angels in Marble: Working Class Conservatives in Urban England.* Chicago: University of Chicago Press 1968.

McKibbin, Ross. "Working-Class Gambling, 1880–1939." In McKibbin. *The Ideologies of Class: Social Relations in Britain, 1880–1950.* Oxford: Oxford University Press 1991. Pp.101–38.

McKinnon, Mary. "Relief Not Insurance: Canadian Unemployment Relief in the 1930s." *Explorations in Economic History,* 27, no.1 (January 1990). Pp.46–83.

McLaren, Angus. "Illegal Operations: Women, Doctors, and Abortions, 1886–1939." *JSH,* 26, no. 4 (Summer 1993). Pp.797–816.

————. *Our Own Master Race: Eugenics in Canada, 1885–1945.* Toronto: McClelland and Stewart 1990.

————, and Arlene Tigar McLaren. *The Bedroom and the State: The Changing Practices and Politics of Contraception and Abortion in Canada, 1880–1980.* Toronto: McClelland and Stewart 1986.

McLean, Albert F., Jr. *American Vaudeville as Ritual.* Lexington: University of Kentucky Press 1965.

McLean, Lorna. "'Deserving' Wives and 'Drunken' Husbands: Wife Beating, Marital Conduct, and the Law in Ontario." *HS/SH,* 35, no.69 (May 2002). Pp.59–81.

————. "'To Become Part of Us': Ethnicity, Race, Literacy and the Canadian Immigration Act of 1919." *CES,* 36, no. 2 (2004). Pp.1–28.

McLeod, Hugh. *Piety and Poverty: Working Class Religion in Berlin, London, and New York, 1870–1914.* New York: Holmes and Meier 1996.

McMaster, Lindsey. *Working Girls in the West: Representations of Wage-Earning Women.* Vancouver: UBC Press 2008.

McMenemy, John M. "Lion in a Den of Daniels: A Study of Sam Lawrence, Labour in Politics." MA thesis, McMaster University 1965.

McNall, Scott W., Rhonda F. Levine, and Rick Fantasia, eds. *Bringing Class Back In: Contemporary and Historical Perspectives.* Boulder, Col.: Westview Press 1991.

McNaught, Kenneth. *A Prophet in Politics: A Biography of J.S. Woodsworth.* Toronto: University of Toronto Press 1959.

————. "J.S. Woodsworth and a Political Party for Labour, 1896–1921." In Donald Swainson, ed. *Historical Essays on the Prairie Provinces.* Toronto: McClelland and Stewart 1970. Pp.230–53.

McPherson, Kathryn. *Bedside Matters: The Transformation of Canadian Nursing, 1900–1990.* Toronto: Oxford University Press 1996.

————, Cecilia Morgan, and Nancy M. Forestall, eds. *Gendered Pasts: Historical Essays in Femininity and Masculinity in Canada.* Toronto: Oxford University Press 1999.

McShane, Clay. *Down the Asphalt Path: The Automobile and the American City.* New York: Columbia University Press 1994.

Meacham, Standish. *A Life Apart: The English Working Class, 1890–1914.* Cambridge, Mass.: Harvard University Press 1977.

Meeling, S.R. "The Concept of Social Class and the Interpretation of Canadian History." *CHR,* 46, no. 3 (September 1965). Pp.201–18.

Meen, Sharon Patricia. "The Battle for the Sabbath: The Sabbatarian Lobby in Canada, 1890–1912." PhD dissertation, University of British Columbia 1979.

Melnycky, Peter. "The Internment of Ukrainians in Canada." In Swyripa and Thompson, eds. *Loyalties in Conflict.* Pp.1–24.

Metcalfe, Alan. *Canada Learns to Play: The Emergence of Organized Sport, 1807–1914.* Toronto: McClelland and Stewart 1987.

Meyer, Stephen. *The Five Dollar Day: Labor Management and Social Control in the Ford Motor Company, 1908–1921.* Albany: State University of New York 1981.

Middleton, Diana J., and David F. Walker. "Manufacturers and Industrial Development Policy in Hamilton, 1890–1910." *UHR*, 8, no. 3 (February 1980). Pp.20–46.

Miliband, Ralph. *Parliamentary Socialism: A Study in the Politics of Labour*. London: Merlin Press 1972.

_____. *The State in Capitalist Society*. London: Quartet Books 1984.

Millard, Andre. *America on Record: A History of Recorded Sound*. Cambridge: Cambridge University Press 1995.

Millard, J. Rodney. "The Crusade for Science: Science and Technology on the Home Front, 1914–1918." In MacKenzie, ed. *Canada and the First World War*. Pp.300–22.

_____. *The Master Spirit of the Age: Canadian Engineers and the Politics of Professionalism*. Toronto: University of Toronto Press 1988.

Miller, Carman. "English-Canadian Opposition to the South African War as Seen through the Press." *CHR*, 55, no. 4 (December 1974). Pp.427–32.

_____. *Painting the Map Red: Canada and the South African War, 1899–1902*. Montreal and Kingston: McGill-Queen's University Press 1993.

Miller, Ivan, ed. *Centennial Sports Review, Hamilton Canada: Sports over the Century*. Hamilton: Centennial Sports Committee 1967.

Miller, J.R. "Anti-Catholicism in Canada: From the British Conquest to the Great War." In Terrence Murphy and Gerald Stortz, eds. *Creed and Culture: The Place of English-Speaking Catholics in Canadian Society,1750–1930*. Montreal and Kingston: McGill-Queen's University Press 1993. Pp.25–48.

_____. *Skyscrapers Hide the Heavens: A History of Indian-White Relations in Canada*. Toronto: University of Toronto Press 1989.

Miller, Karl Hagstrom. "Talking Machine World: Selling the Local in the Global Music Industry, 1900–20." In A.G. Hopkins, ed. *Global History: Interactions between the Universal and the Local*. New York: Palgrave Macmillan 2006. Pp.160–90.

Miller, Sally. "Casting a Wide Net: The Milwaukee Movement to 1920." In Donald T. Critchlow, ed. *Socialism in the Heartland: The Midwestern Experience, 1900–1925*. Notre Dame, Ind.: University of Notre Dame Press 1986. Pp.18–45.

Milligan, Ian. "'Seemingly Onerous Restrictions': Sedition in Ontario, 1914–1919." Major Research Paper, Department of History, York University 2007.

Mills, Allen. "Single Tax, Socialism, and the Independent Labour Party of Manitoba." *L/LT*, 5 (Spring 1980). Pp.33–56.

Mills, C. Wright. *White Collar: The American Middle Classes*. New York: Oxford University Press 1956.

Mills, John M. *Cataract Traction: The Railways of Hamilton*. Toronto: Upper Canada Railway Society and Ontario Electric Railway Historical Association 1971.

Mirola, William A. "Shorter Hours and the Protestant Sabbath: Religious Framing and Movement Alliances in Late-Nineteenth-Century Chicago." *Social Science History*, 23, no. 3 (Fall 1999). Pp.395–433.

Missett, Dennis, et al. *Downtown Hamilton: The Heart of It All*. Hamilton: Fountain Foundation 1995.

Mitchell, Tom. "'The Manufacture of Souls of Good Quality': Winnipeg's 1919 National Conference on Canadian Citizenship, English-Canadian Nationalism, and the New Order after the Great War." *JCS*, 31, no. 4 (Winter 1996–97). Pp.5–28.

_____. "'To Uphold Organized Society': The Canadian and American *Citizens' Committee* as an Anti-Labour Organization, 1901–1937." Paper presented to Northern Great Plains History Conference 2008.

Mitchinson, Wendy. *Giving Birth in Canada, 1900–1950*. Toronto: University of Toronto Press 2002.

Moffatt, Ken. *A Poetics of Social Work: Personal Agency and Social Transformation in Canada, 1920–1939*. Toronto: University of Toronto Press 2001.

Moir, John S. *Enduring Witness: A History of the Presbyterian Church in Canada*. Toronto: Presbyterian Publications [1974].

Monod, David. "Ontario Retailers in the Early Twentieth Century: Dismantling the Social Bridge." *JCHA*, 1993. Pp.207–27.

_____. *Store Wars: Shopkeepers and the Culture of Mass Marketing, 1890–1939*. Toronto: University of Toronto Press 1996.

Montgomery, David. *Citizen Worker: The Experience of Workers in the United States with Democracy and the Free Market during the Nineteenth Century*. Cambridge: Cambridge University Press 1993.

_____. *The Fall of the House of Labor: The Workplace, the State, and American Labor Activism, 1865–1925*. Cambridge: Cambridge University Press 1987.

_____. "New Tendencies in Union Struggle and Strategies in Europe and the United States, 1916–1922." In Cronin and Sirianni, eds. *Work, Community, and Power*. Pp.88–116.

_____. *Workers' Control in America: Studies in the History of Work, Technology, and Labor Struggles*. Cambridge: Cambridge University Press 1979.

Montigny, Edgar-Andre. "Families, Institutions, and the State in Late-Nineteenth-Century Ontario." In Montigny and Chambers, eds. *Ontario since Confederation*. Pp.74–93.

_____. *Foisted Upon the Government? State Responsibilities, Family Obligations, and the Care of the Dependent Aged in Late Nineteenth-Century Ontario*. Montreal and Kingston: McGill-Queen's University Press 1997.

_____, and Lori Chambers, eds. *Ontario since Confederation: A Reader*. Toronto: University of Toronto Press 2000.

Moore, Paul Samuel. "A Rendezvous for Particular People: Showmanship, Regulation, and Promotion of Early Film-Going in Toronto." PhD dissertation, York University 2004.

Moores, Shaun. "'The Box on the Dresser': Memories of Early Radio and Everyday Life." *Media, Culture, and Society*, 10, no.1 (January 1988). Pp.23–40.

Morawask, Ewa. "Labor Migration of Poles in the Atlantic World Economy, 1880–1914." In Hoerder and Moch, eds. *European Migrants*. Pp.170–208.

Morley, J.T. *Secular Socialists: The CCF/NDP in Ontario, A Biography*. Kingston and Montreal: McGill-Queen's University Press 1984.

Morris, Peter. *Embattled Shadows: A History of Canadian Cinema, 1895–1939*. Montreal: McGill-Queen's University Press 1978.

Morrow, Don. "Baseball." In Morrow et al. *Concise History*. Pp.109–39.

——————, et al. *A Concise History of Canadian Sport*. Toronto: Oxford University Press 1989.

——————. "The Strathcona Trust in Ontario, 1911–1939." *Canadian Journal of History of Sport and Physical Education*, 8, no.1 (May 1977). Pp.72–90.

Morton, Desmond. "The Cadet Movement in the Moment of Canadian Militarism, 1909–1914." *JCS*, 13, no. 2 (Summer 1978). Pp.56–68.

——————. *Fight or Pay: Soldiers' Families in the Great War*. Vancouver: UBC Press 2004.

——————. "'Kicking and Complaining': Demobilization Riots in the Canadian Expeditionary Force, 1918–19." *CHR*, 61, no. 3 (September 1980). Pp.334–60.

——————. "Resisting the Pension Evil: Bureaucracy, Democracy, and Canada's Board of Pension Commissioners, 1916–33." *CHR*, 68, no.2 (June 1987). Pp.199–224.

——————. "Sir William Otter and Internment Operations in Canada during the First World War." *CHR*, 55, no. 1 (March 1974). Pp.32–58.

——————. *When Your Number's Up: The Canadian Soldier in the First World War*. Toronto: Random House 1993.

——————, and Glenn Wright. "The Bonus Campaign, 1919–21: Veterans and the Campaign for Re-Establishment." *CHR*, 64, no. 2 (June 1983). Pp.147–67.

——————. *Winning the Second Battle: Canadian Veterans and the Return to Civilian Life, 1915–1930*. Toronto: University of Toronto Press 1987.

Morton, Suzanne. *At Odds: Gambling and Canadians, 1919–1969*. Toronto: University of Toronto Press 2003.

——————. *Ideal Surroundings: Domestic Life in a Working-Class Suburb in the 1920s*. Toronto: University of Toronto Press 1995.

——————. "The June Bride as the Working-Class Bride: Getting Married in a Halifax Working-Class Neighbourhood in the 1920s." In Bettina Bradbury, ed.

Canadian Family History: Selected Readings. Toronto: Copp Clark Pitman 1992. Pp.360–79.

Morton, W.L. *The Progressive Party in Canada*. Toronto: University of Toronto Press 1950.

Moscovitch, Allan, and Jim Albert, eds. *The Benevolent State: The Growth of Welfare in Canada*. Toronto: Garamond Press 1987.

Mosher, Clayton James. *Discrimination and Denial: Systemic Racism in Ontario's Legal and Criminal Justice Systems, 1892–1961*. Toronto: University of Toronto Press 1998.

Moss, Mark. *Manliness and Militarism: Educating Young Boys in Ontario for War*. Toronto: Oxford University Press 2001.

Motz, Marilyn Ferris, and Pat Browne, eds. *Making the American Home: Middle-Class Women and Domestic Material Culture, 1840–1940*. Bowling Green, Ohio: Bowling Green State University Popular Press 1988.

Moyles, R.G. *Blood and Fire in Canada: A History of the Salvation Army in the Dominion of Canada, 1882–1976*. Toronto: Peter Martin Associates 1977.

Murphy, Lawrence, and Philip Murphy. *Tales from the North End*. Hamilton: Authors 1981.

Myers, Tamara. *Caught: Montreal's Modern Girls and the Law, 1869–1945*. Toronto: University of Toronto Press 2006.

Nagy, Nancy A. "Juvenile Delinquency in Hamilton: 1895 and 1909." Unpublished paper (WC).

Nasaw, David. *Children of the City: At Work and At Play*. Garden City, N.Y.: Anchor Press 1985.

——————. *Going Out: The Rise and Fall of Public Amusements*. New York: Basic Books 1993.

Nava, Mica. "Consumerism Reconsidered: Buying and Power." *Cultural Studies*, 5, no. 2 (May 1991). Pp.158–74.

Naylor, David. *Private Practice, Public Payment: Canadian Medicine and the Politics of Health Insurance, 1911–1966*. Montreal and Kingston: McGill-Queen's University Press 1986.

Naylor, James. *The New Democracy: Challenging the Social Order in Industrial Ontario, 1914–25*. Toronto: University of Toronto Press 1991.

——————. "Southern Ontario: Striking at the Ballot Box." In Heron, ed. *Workers' Revolt*. Pp.144–75.

——————, and Tom Mitchell. "The Prairies: In the Eye of the Storm." In Heron., ed. *Workers' Revolt*. Pp.176–230.

Naylor, Tom. *The History of Canadian Business, 1867–1914*. 2 vols. Toronto: James Lorimer 1975.

Neatby, H. Blair. *Laurier and a Liberal Quebec: A Study in Political Management*. Toronto: McClelland and Stewart 1973.

Neave, David. "Friendly Societies in Great Britain." In Van der Linden, ed. *Social Security Mutualism*. Pp.41–64.

Nelles, H.V. *The Politics of Development: Forests, Mines, and Hydro-Electric Power in Ontario, 1849–1941*. Toronto: Macmillan 1974.

Nelson, Barbara J. "The Origins of the Two-Channel Welfare State: Workmen's Compensation and Mothers' Aid." In

Linda Gordon, ed. *Women, the State, and Welfare*. Madison: University of Wisconsin Press 1990. Pp.123–51.

Nelson, Daniel. *American Rubber Workers and Organized Labor, 1900–1941*. Princeton, N.J.: Princeton University Press 1988.

———. *Frederick W. Taylor and the Rise of Scientific Management*. Madison: University of Wisconsin Press 1980.

———. *Managers and Workers: Origins of the New Factory System in the United States, 1880–1920*. Madison: University of Wisconsin Press 1975.

Nerbas, Don. *Dominion of Capital: The Politics of Big Business and the Crisis of the Canadian Bourgeoisie, 1914–1947*. Toronto: University of Toronto Press 2013.

Nettl, Peter. "The German Social Democratic Party, 1890–1914, as a Political Model." *Past and Present*, 30 (April 1965). Pp.65–95.

Newby, Howard. "The Deferential Dialectic." *Comparative Studies in Society and History*, 17, no. 2 (April 1975). Pp.139–64.

Newlands, T.J. "The History and Operation of Hamilton's Parks." *Wentworth Bygones*, 9 (1971). Pp.9–15.

Nickles, Shelley. "More Is Better: Mass Consumption, Gender, and Class Identity in Postwar America." *American Quarterly*, 54, no.4 (December 2002). Pp.581–622.

Nicolaides, Becky M. "'Where the Working Man Is Welcomed': Working-Class Suburbs in Los Angeles, 1900–1940." *Pacific Historical Review*, 68, no. 4 (November 1999). Pp.517–59.

Noble, David. *America by Design: Science, Technology, and the Rise of Corporate Capitalism*. New York: Oxford University Press 1977.

———. "Social Change in Machine Design: The Case of Automatically Controlled Machine Tools, and a Challenge for Labor." *Politics and Society*, 8, nos. 3–4 (1978). Pp.313–47.

Nolan, Michael. "An Infant Industry: Canadian Private Radio, 1919–36." *CHR*, 70, no.4 (December 1989). Pp.496–518.

Norcliffe, Glen. *The Ride to Modernity: The Bicycle in Canada, 1869–1900*. Toronto: University of Toronto Press 2001.

Nordlinger, Eric A. *The Working-Class Tories: Authority, Deference and Stable Democracy*. London: MacGibbon and Kee 1967.

Nuwer, Michael. "From Batch to Flow: Production Technology and Work-Force Skills in the Steel Industry, 1880–1920." *Technology and Culture*, 29, no. 4 (October 1988). Pp.808–38.

Nye, Russell B. "Saturday Night at the Paradise Ballroom: Or, Dance Halls in the Twenties." *Journal of Popular Culture*, 7 (Summer 1973). Pp.14–22.

O'Brien, Mike. "Manhood and the Militia Myth: Masculinity, Class and Militarism in Ontario, 1902–1914." *L/LT*, 42 (Fall 1998). Pp.115–41.

Oliphant, Donald M., comp. *Hess Street School: 1882–1974: A Pictorial History*. Hamilton: Aggus 1974.

Oliver, Peter. *G. Howard Ferguson: Ontario Tory*. Toronto: University of Toronto Press 1977.

———. *Public and Private Persons: The Ontario Political Culture, 1914–1934*. Toronto: Clarke Irwin 1975.

———. "Sir William Hearst and the Collapse of the Ontario Conservative Party." In Oliver. *Public and Private Persons*. Pp.18–43.

———. *"Terror to Evil Doers": Prisons and Punishments in Nineteenth-Century Ontario*. Toronto: University of Toronto Press 1998.

Oppenheimer, Jo. "Childbirth in Ontario: The Transition from Home to Hospital in the Early Twentieth Century." In Arnup, Levesque, and Pierson, eds. *Delivering Motherhood*. Pp.62–67.

Orloff, Ann Shola. *The Politics of Pensions: A Comparative Analysis of Britain, Canada, and the United States, 1880–1940*. Madison: University of Wisconsin Press 1993.

Osterman, Paul . "Education and Labor Markets at the Turn of the Century." *Politics and Society*, 9, no.1 (1979). Pp.108–15.

Ostry, Aleck. "The Early Development of Nutrition Policy in Canada." In Warsh and Strong-Boag, eds. *Children's Health Issues*. Pp.191–206.

Owram, Doug. *The Government Generation: Canadian Intellectuals and the State, 1900–1945*. Toronto: University of Toronto Press 1986.

Oxford Dictionary of English Idioms. 3rd ed. Oxford: Oxford University Press 2009.

Ozanne, Robert. *A Century of Labor-Management Relations at McCormick and International Harvester*. Madison: University of Wisconsin Press 1967.

Pal, Leslie A. *State, Class, and Bureaucracy: Canadian Unemployment Insurance and Public Policy*. Kingston and Montreal: McGill-Queen's University Press 1988.

Palmer, Bryan D. "Class, Conception and Conflict: The Thrust for Efficiency, Managerial Views of Labor and the Working Class Rebellion, 1903–22." *Review of Radical Political Economy*, 7 (Summer 1975). Pp.31–49.

———. *A Culture in Conflict: Skilled Workers and Industrial Capitalism in Hamilton, Ontario, 1860–1914*. Montreal and Kingston: McGill-Queen's University Press 1979.

———. "'Give Us the Road and We Will Run It': The Social and Cultural Matrix of an Emerging Labour Movement." In Kealey and Warrian, eds. *Essays in Canadian Working Class History*. Pp.106–24.

———. "Labour Protest and Organization in Nineteenth-Century Canada, 1820–1890." *L/LT*, 20 (Fall 1987). Pp.61–84.

———. "Most Uncommon Men: Craft and Culture in Historical Perspective." *L/LT*, 1 (1976). Pp.5–31.

———. "Mutuality and the Masking/Making of Difference: Mutual Benefit Societies in Canada, 1850–1950." In Van der Linden, ed. *Social Security Mutualism*. Pp.111–46.

———. *Working-Class Experience: Rethinking the History of Canadian Labour, 1800–1991*. Toronto: McClelland and Stewart 1992.

Palmer, Howard. "Reluctant Hosts: Anglo-Canadian Views of Multiculturalism in the Twentieth Century." In Canadian

Conference on Multiculturalism. *Multiculturalism as State Policy: Conference Report*. Ottawa: Canadian Consultative Council on Multiculturalism 1976.

Panabaker, Katherine. *The Story of the Girl Guides in Ontario*. Toronto: Ryerson Press 1966.

Parker, Ethel (Dodds). "The Origins and Early History of the Presbyterian Settlement Houses." In Richard Allen, ed. *The Social Gospel in Canada*. Ottawa: National Museums of Canada 1975. Pp.86–121.

Parr, Joy. "Gender History and Historical Practice." In Joy Parr and Mark Rosenfeld, eds. *Gender and History in Canada*. Toronto: Copp-Clark 1996. Pp.8–27.

_____. *The Gender of Breadwinners: Women, Men, and Change in Two Industrial Towns, 1880–1950*. Toronto: University of Toronto Press 1990.

_____. "Household Choices as Politics and Pleasure in 1950s Canada." *ILWCH*, 55 (Spring 1999). Pp.112–28.

_____. *Labouring Children: British Immigrant Apprentices to Canada, 1869–1924*. Montreal: McGill-Queen's University Press 1980.

Paterson, Ross. "Housing Finance in Early 20th Century Suburban Toronto." *UHR*, 20, no.3 (February 1992). Pp.63–72.

Patrias, Carmela. *Patriots and Proletarians: Politicizing Hungarian Immigrants in Interwar Canada*. Montreal and Kingston: McGill-Queen's University Press 1994.

_____. *Relief Strike: Immigrant Workers and the Great Depression in Crowland, Ontario, 1930–1935*. Toronto: New Hogtown Press 1990.

Peck, Gunther. *Reinventing Free Labor: Padrones and Immigrant Workers in the North American West, 1880–1930*. New York: Cambridge University Press 2000.

Pedersen, Diana L. "'Keeping Our Girls Good': The Young Women's Christian Association of Canada, 1870–1920." MA thesis, Carleton University 1981.

Peers, Frank. *The Politics of Canadian Broadcasting, 1920–1951*. Toronto: University of Toronto Press 1969.

Pegg, Mark. *Broadcasting and Society, 1918–1939*. London: Croom Helm 1983.

Pelling, Henry. *The Origins of the Labour Party, 1880–1900*. Oxford: Oxford University Press 1965.

_____. *Popular Politics and Society in Late Victorian Britain*. London: Macmillan 1968.

_____. *Social Geography of British Elections, 1885–1910*. London: Macmillan 1967.

Pendakur, Manjunath. *Canadian Dreams and American Control: The Political Economy of the Canadian Film Industry*. Toronto: Garamond Press 1990.

Pendergast, James A. "The Attempt of Unionization in the Automobile Industry in Canada, 1928." *OH*, 70, no. 4 (December 1978). Pp.245–62.

Penfold, Steven. "'Have You No Manhood in You?': Gender and Class in the Cape Breton Coal Towns, 1920–1926." *Acadiensis*, 23, no. 2 (Spring 1994). Pp.21–44.

Penell, Michael R. "'The Relics of Barbarism': Resisting Public Health Efforts." In Herring, ed. *Anatomy of a Pandemic*. Pp.135–48.

Pennefather, R.S. *The Orange and the Black: Documents in the History of the Orange Order Ontario and the West, 1890–1940*. N.p.: Orange and Black Publications 1984.

Penny, Harry L. *One Hundred Years and Still Sailing! A History of Hamilton Yachts, Yachtsmen, and Yachting – 1888–1988*. Hamilton: Hamilton Yacht Club 1988.

Perin, Roberto. *The Immigrants' Church: The Third Force in Canadian Catholicism, 1880–1920*. Ottawa: Canadian Historical Association 1998.

_____, and Franc Sturino, eds. *Arrangiarsi: The Italian Immigration Experience in Canada*. Montreal: Guernica 1989.

Perlman, Joel. "After Leaving School: The Jobs of Young People in Providence, R.I., 1880–1915." In Ronald K. Goodenow and Diane Ravitch, eds. *Schools in Cities: Consensus and Conflict in American Educational History*. New York: Holmes and Meier 1983. Pp.3–43.

Perlman, Mark A. *The Machinists: A New Study in American Trade Unionism*. Cambridge, Mass.: Harvard University Press 1961.

Perrot, Michelle, ed. *A History of Private Life, Volume IV: From the Fires of Revolution to the Great War*. Cambridge, Mass.: Harvard University Press 1990.

Pessen, Edward. "The Great Songwriters of Tin Pan Alley's Golden Age: A Social, Occupational, and Aesthetic Inquiry." *American Music*, 3, no.2 (Summer 1985). Pp.180–97.

Peterson, Jim. "'More News from Nowhere': Utopian Notes of a Hamilton Machinist." *L/LT*, 17 (Spring 1986). Pp.169–223.

Peterson, Joyce Shaw. *American Automobile Workers, 1900–1933*. Albany: State University of New York Press 1987.

Peterson, Larry. "The One Big Union in International Perspective: Revolutionary Industrial Unionism, 1900–1925." In Cronin and Sirianni, eds. *Work, Community, and Power*. Pp.49–87.

Petryshyn, Jaroslav. "Canadian Immigration and the North Atlantic Trading Company, 1899–1906: A Controversy Revisited." *JCS*, 32, no. 3 (Autumn 1997). Pp.55–76.

_____. *Peasants in the Promised Land: Canada and the Ukrainians, 1891–1914*. Toronto: James Lorimer 1985.

Phillips, Jim. "Poverty, Unemployment, and the Administration of the Criminal Law: Vagrancy Laws in Halifax, 1864–1890." In Philip Girard and Jim Phillips, eds. *Essays in the History of Canadian Law, Volume III: Nova Scotia*. Toronto: University of Toronto Press 1990. Pp.128–62.

Phillips, W.G. *The Agricultural Implement Industry in Canada: A Study in Competition*. Toronto: University of Toronto Press 1956.

Piedalue, Gilles. "Les groupes financiers au Canada, 1900–1930: étude préliminaire." *RHAF*, 30, no.1 (juin 1976). Pp.3–34.

Pierson, Ruth Roach. "Gender and Unemployment Insurance Debates in Canada, 1934–1940." *L/LT*, 25 (Spring 1990). Pp.77–103.

Pimlott, J.A.R. *The Englishman's Christmas: A Social History*. Hassocks, UK: Harvester Press 1978.

———. *The Englishman's Holiday: A Social History*. London: Faber and Faber 1947.

Pitsula, James M. "The Treatment of Tramps in Late Nineteenth-Century Toronto." *CHAHP*, 1980. Pp.116–32.

Piva, Michael J. *The Condition of the Working Class in Toronto – 1900–1921*. Ottawa: University of Ottawa Press 1979.

———. "Workers and Tories: The Collapse of the Conservative Party in Urban Ontario, 1908–19." *UHR*, 3–76 (February 1977). Pp.23–39.

———. "The Workmen's Compensation Movement in Ontario." *OH*, 67, no. 1 (March 1975). Pp.39–56.

Plewman, W. R. *Adam Beck and the Ontario Hydro*. Toronto: Ryerson Press 1947.

Polanyi, Karl. *The Great Transformation: The Political and Economic Transformation of Our Times*. Boston: Beacon Hill Press 1957.

Pope, Mara. "The Essence of Altruism: The Spirit of Volunteerism in Hamilton during the 1918 Influenza Pandemic." In Herring, ed. *Anatomy of a Pandemic*. Pp.105–19.

Popham, Robert E. *Working Papers on the Tavern, 2: Legislative History of the Ontario Tavern, 1774–1974*. Toronto: Addiction Research Foundation, Substudy No. 809 1976.

Powers, Madelon. "Decay from Within: The Inevitable Doom of the American Saloon." In Susanna Barrows and Robin Room, eds. *Drinking: Behavior and Belief in Modern History*. Berkeley: University of California Press 1991. Pp.112–31.

Prang, Margaret. "Clerics, Politicians, the Bilingual Schools Issue in Ontario, 1910–1917." In Craig Brown, ed. *Minorities, Schools, and Politics*. Toronto: University of Toronto Press 1969. Pp.85–111.

———. "The Girl God Would Have Me Be: The Canadian Girls in Training, 1915–39." *CHR*, 66, no. 2 (June 1985). Pp.154–84.

———. *N.W. Rowell: Ontario Nationalist*. Toronto: University of Toronto Press 1975.

Pratt, Geraldine. "Housing Tenure and Social Cleavages in Urban Canada." Association of American Geographers. *Annals*, 76, no.3 (September 1986). Pp.366–80.

Price, Richard. *An Imperial War and the British Working Class: Working-Class Attitudes and Reactions to the Boer War, 1899–1902*. London: Routledge and Kegan Paul 1972.

Proctor, Tammy M. *On My Honour: Guides and Scouts in Interwar Britain*. Philadelphia: American Philosophical Society 2002.

Proulx, David. *Pardon My Lunch Bucket: A Look at the New Hamilton . . . with a Bit of Old Thrown In*. Hamilton: Corporation of the City of Hamilton [1971].

Pucci, Antonio. "At the Forefront of Militancy: Italians in Canada at the Turn of the Century." *Polyphony*, 7, no. 2 (Fall/Winter 1985). Pp.37–42.

Pugh, Martin. "Popular Conservatism in Britain: Continuity and Change, 1880–1987." *Journal of British Studies*, 27, no. 3 (July 1988). Pp.254–82.

———. "The Rise of Labour and the Political Culture of Conservatism, 1890–1945." *History*, 87, no.288 (October 2002). Pp.514–37.

———. *The Tories and the People, 1880–1935*. Oxford: Basil Blackwell 1985.

Purdy, Sean. "'This Is Not a Company; It Is a Cause': Class, Gender and the Toronto Housing Company, 1912–1920." *UHR*, 21, no.2 (March 1993). Pp.75–91.

Rabinovitz, Lauren. *For the Love of Pleasure: Women, Movies, and Culture in Turn-of-the-Century Chicago*. New Brunswick, N.J.: Rutgers University Press 1998.

Radecki, Henry, and Benedykt Heydenkorn. *A Member of a Distinguished Family: The Polish Group in Canada*. Toronto: McClelland and Stewart 1976.

Radforth, Ian. *Bushworkers and Bosses: Logging in Northern Ontario, 1900–1980*. Toronto: University of Toronto Press 1987.

———, and Joan Sangster. "'A Link between Labour and Learning': The Workers' Educational Association in Ontario, 1917–1951." *L/LT*, 8/9 (Autumn 1981/Spring 1982). Pp.41–78.

Ramirez, Bruno. *Crossing the 49th Parallel: Migration from Canada to the United States, 1900–1930*. Ithaca, N.Y.: Cornell University Press 2001.

———. *On the Move: French Canadian and Italian Migrants in the North American Economy, 1860–1914*. Toronto: McClelland and Stewart 1991.

———. *When Workers Fight: The Politics of Industrial Relations in the Progressive Era, 1898–1916*. Westport, Conn.: Greenwood Press 1978.

Rasporich, Anthony W. *For a Better Life: A History of the Croatians in Canada*. Toronto: McClelland and Stewart 1982.

Read, J.G. "The Hamilton Board of Parks Management and Dundurn Park, 1900–1910." Unpublished paper (WC).

Ready, Alf. *Organizing Westinghouse: Alf Ready's Story*. Ed. Wayne Roberts. Hamilton: McMaster University Labour Studies Program 1979.

Reasons, Charles E. *Assault on the Worker: Occupational Health and Safety in Canada*. Toronto: Butterworths 1980.

Reczyṅska, Anna. *For Bread and a Better Future: Emigration from Poland to Canada, 1918–1939*. Toronto: Multicultural History Society of Ontario 1996.

Reed, Susan. "The Reform Movement of the Sunday School of the Methodist Church of Canada, As It Applies to Ontario, 1884–1924." MA thesis, University of Toronto 1988.

Register, Woody. *The Kid of Coney Island: Fred Thompson and the Rise of American Amusements*. New York: Oxford University Press 2001.

Reimer, Chad. "War, Nationhood, and Working-Class Entitlement: The Counter-Hegemonic Challenge of the 1919 Winnipeg General Strike." *Prairie Forum*, 18, no. 2 (Fall 1993). Pp.219–37.

Reiss, Steven A. "From Pitch to Putt: Sport and Class in Anglo-American Sport." *Journal of Sport History*, 21, no. 2 (Summer 1994). Pp.138–84.

Restad, Penne L. *Christmas in America: A History*. New York: Oxford University Press 1995.

Richardson, Theresa R. *The Century of the Child: The Mental Hygiene Movement and Social Policy in the United States and Canada*. Albany: State University of New York Press 1989.

Rider, Peter Edward. "The Imperial Munitions Board and Its Relationship to Government, Business, and Labour." PhD dissertation, University of Toronto 1974.

Risk, R.C.B. "'This Nuisance of Litigation': The Origins of Workers' Compensation in Ontario." In David H. Flaherty, ed. *Essays in the History of Canadian Law, Volume 2*. Toronto: University of Toronto Press 1981. Pp.18–91.

Robbins, Jessica M. "Class Struggles in the Tubercular World: Nurses, Patients, and Physicians, 1903–1915." *Bulletin of the History of Medicine*, 71, no. 3 (1997). Pp.412–34.

Roberts, Barbara Ann. *Whence They Came: Deportation from Canada, 1900–1935*. Ottawa: University of Ottawa Press 1988.

Roberts, Elizabeth. *A Woman's Place: An Oral History of Working-Class Women, 1890–1940*. Oxford: Basil Blackwell 1984.

Roberts, R.D. "The Changing Patterns in Distribution and Composition of Manufacturing Activity in Hamilton between 1861 and 1921." MA thesis, McMaster University 1964.

Roberts, Wayne. "Artisans, Aristocrats, and Handymen: Politics and Trade Unionism among Toronto Skilled Building Trades Workers, 1896–1914." *L/LT*, 1 (1976). Pp.92–121.

_____. *Honest Womanhood: Feminism, Femininity and Class Consciousness among Toronto Working Women, 1893–1914*. Toronto: New Hogtown Press 1976.

_____. "Studies in the Toronto Labour Movement, 1896–1914." PhD dissertation 1977.

_____. "Toronto Metal Workers and the Second Industrial Revolution, 1889–1902." *L/LT*, 6 (Autumn 1980). Pp.49–72.

_____, ed. *Baptism of a Union: The Stelco Strike of 1946*. Hamilton: McMaster University Labour Studies Program 1981.

_____, ed. *Organizing Westinghouse: Alf Ready's Story*. Hamilton: McMaster University Labour Studies Program 1979.

_____, and Alice Klein. "Besieged Innocence: The 'Problem' and Problems of Working Women – Toronto, 1896–1914." In Acton et al., eds. *Women At Work*. Pp.211–59.

Robertson, Heather. *Driving Force: The McLaughlin Family and the Age of the Car*. Toronto: McClelland and Stewart 1995.

Robin, Martin. *Radical Politics and Canadian Labour, 1880–1930*. Kingston: Queen's University, Industrial Relations Centre 1968.

Rodney, William. *Soldiers of the International: A History of the Communist Party of Canada, 1919–1929*. Toronto: University of Toronto Press 1968.

Roediger, David. *Towards the Abolition of Whiteness: Essays on Race, Politics, and Working-Class History*. London: Verso 1994.

_____. *The Wages of Whiteness: Race and the Making of the American Working Class*. London: Verso 1991.

Roell, Craig H. *The Piano in America, 1890–1940*. Chapel Hill: University of North Carolina Press 1989.

Roger, Nicholas. *Halloween: From Pagan Ritual to Party Night*. New York: Oxford University Press 2000.

Rolt, L.T.C. *Tools for the Job: A Short History of Machine Tools*. London: B.T. Batsford 1965.

Rooke, Patricia T., and R.L. Schnell. *Discarding the Asylum: From Child Rescue to the Welfare State in English Canada (1800–1950)*. Lanham, Md.: University Press of America 1983.

Roper, Michael, and John Tosh, eds. *Manful Assertions: Masculinities in Britain Since 1800*. London: Routledge 1991.

Rose, Sonya O. "Class Formation and the Quintessential Worker." In Hall, ed. *Reworking Class*. Pp.133–66.

Rosenberg, Charles E. *Explaining Epidemics and Other Studies in the History of Medicine*. New York: Cambridge University Press 1992.

_____. "Framing Disease: Illness, Society, and History." In Rosenberg, ed. *Explaining Epidemics*. Pp.305–18.

_____. "Social Class and Medical Care in Nineteenth-Century America: The Rise and Fall of the Dispensary." In Rosenberg. *Explaining Epidemics*. Pp.155–77.

Rosenberg, Nathan. "Technological Change in the Machine Tool Industry, 1840–1910." *Journal of Economic History*, 23 (1963). Pp.414–43.

Rosenthal, Michael. *The Character Factory: Baden-Powell and the Origins of the Boy Scout Movement*. New York: Pantheon Books 1986.

Rosenzweig, Roy. *Eight Hours for What We Will: Workers and Leisure in an Industrial City, 1870–1920*. Cambridge: Cambridge University Press 1983.

Rosner, David, and Gerald Markowitz. *Deadly Dust: Silicosis and the Politics of Occupational Disease in Twentieth-Century America*. Princeton, N.J.: Princeton University Press 1991.

Ross, Ellen. "'Fierce Questions and Taunts': Married Life in Working-Class London, 1870–1914." *Feminist Studies*, 8, no. 3 (Fall 1982). Pp.575–99.

_____. "Good and Bad Mothers: Lady Philanthropists and London Housewives before the First World War." In Kathleen D. McCarthy, ed. *Lady Bountiful Revisited: Women, Philanthropy, and Power*. New Brunswick, N.J.: Rutgers University Press 1990. Pp.174–98.

_____. *Love and Toil: Motherhood in Outcast London, 1870–1918*. New York: Oxford University Press 1993.

_____. "'Not the Sort That Would Sit on the Doorstep': Respectability in Pre-World War I London Neighbourhoods." *ILWCH*, 27 (Spring 1985). Pp.39–59.

_____. "Survival Networks: Women's Neighbourhood Sharing in London." *HWJ*, 15 (1983), 4–27.

Ross, Murray G. *The Y.M.C.A. in Canada: The Chronicle of a Century*. Toronto: Ryerson Press 1951.

Rothman, Sheila M. *Living in the Shadow of Death: Tuberculosis and the Social Experience of Illness in American History*. Baltimore: Johns Hopkins University Press 1994.

Rotundo, E. Anthony. *American Manhood: Transformations in Masculinity from the Revolution to the Modern Era*. New York: Basic Books 1993.

_____. "Boy Culture: Middle-Class Boyhood in Nineteenth-Century America." In Carnes and Griffen, ed. *Meanings for Manhood*. Pp.15–36.

Rouillard, Jacques. *Les travailleurs du coton, 1900–1915*. Montreal: Les presses de l'Université du Québec 1974.

Rouse, W.R., and A.F. Burghardt. "Climate, Weather, and Society." In Deer, Drake, and Reeds, eds. *Steel City*. Pp.34–47.

Rowan, Caroline. "Child Welfare and the Working-Class Family." In Mary Langan and Bill Schwarz, eds. *Crises in the British State, 1880–1930*. London: Hutchinson 1985. Pp.226–39.

Rowbotham, Judith. "'Only When Drunk': The Stereotyping of Violence in England, c.1850–1900." In D'Cruz, ed. *Everyday Violence in Britain*. Pp.155–69.

Roy, Patricia. *A White Man's Province*. Vancouver: University of British Columbia Press 1989.

Royce, Marion. *Eunice Dyke: Health Care Pioneer*. Toronto: Dundurn Press 1983.

Rudé, George. *The Crowd in History: A Study of Popular Disturbances in France and England, 1730–1848*. New York: John Wiley and Sons 1964.

Ruffilli, Dean C. "The Car in Canadian Culture, 1898–1983." PhD dissertation, University of Western Ontario 2006.

Rury, John L. "Vocationalism for Home and Work: Women's Education in the United States, 1880–1930." *History of Education Quarterly*, 24, no. 1 (Spring 1984). Pp.29–33.

Rutherdale, Robert. *Hometown Horizons: Local Responses to Canada's Great War*. Vancouver: UBC Press 2004.

Rutherford, Paul. *The Making of the Canadian Media*. Toronto: McGraw-Hill Ryerson 1978.

_____. *A Victorian Authority: The Daily Press in Late-Nineteenth-Century Canada*. Toronto: University of Toronto Press 1982.

Rybczynski, Witold. *Home: A Short History of an Idea*. New York: Penguin Books 1987.

Ryder, N.B. "The Interpretation of Origin Statistics." *Canadian Journal of Economics and Political Science*, 21, no. 4 (November 1955). Pp.466–79.

Saddlemyer, Ann. *Early Stages: Theatre in Ontario, 1800–1914*. Toronto: University of Toronto Press 1990.

Sager, Eric W. "Inequality, Earnings, and the Canadian Working Class in 1901." In Sager and Baskerville, eds. *Household Counts*. Pp.339–70.

_____, and Peter Baskerville, eds. *Household Counts: Canadian Households and Families in 1901*. Toronto: University of Toronto Press 2007.

Samuel, Raphael, ed. *People's History and Socialist Theory*. London: Routledge and Kegan Paul 1981.

_____. "Workshop of the World: Steam Power and Hand Technology in Mid-Victorian Britain." *HWJ*, 3 (Spring 1977). Pp.6–72.

Sangster, Joan. *Dreams of Equality: Women on the Canadian Left, 1920–1950*. Toronto: McClelland and Stewart 1989.

_____. *Earning Respect: The Lives of Working Women in Small-Town Ontario, 1920–1960*. Toronto: University of Toronto Press 1995.

_____. "Mobilizing Women for War." In Mackenzie, ed. *Canada and the First World War*. Pp.157–93.

_____. *Regulating Girls and Women: Sexuality, Family, and the Law in Ontario, 1920–1960*. Toronto: Oxford University Press 2001.

_____. "*Robitnytsia*, Ukrainian Communists, and the 'Porcupinism' Debate." *L/LT*, 56 (Fall 2005). Pp.51–89.

_____. "The Softball Solution: Female Workers, Male Managers and the Operation of Paternalism at Westclox, 1923–60." *L/LT*, 32 (Fall 1993). Pp.167–99.

Sauter, Udo. "Measuring Unemployment in Canada: Federal Efforts before World War Two." *HS/SH*, 15, no. 30 (1982). Pp.475–89.

_____. "The Origins of the Employment Service of Canada, 1900–1920." *L/LT*, 6 (1980). Pp.89–112.

Saville, John. "The Ideology of Labourism." In Robert Benewick, R.N. Berki, and Bhikhu Parekh, eds. *Knowledge and Belief in Politics: The Problem of Ideology*. London: Allen and Unwin 1973. Pp.213–26.

_____. "Trade Unions and Free Labour: The Background to the Taff Vale Decision." In Asa Briggs and John Saville, eds. *Essays in Labour History*. London: Macmillan 1967. Pp.317–50.

Saywell, John. *Housing Canadians: Essays in the History of Residential Construction in Canada*. Ottawa: Economic Council of Canada 1975.

_____. *"Just Call Me Mitch": The Life of Mitchell F. Hepburn*. Toronto: University of Toronto Press 1991.

Scannell, Paddy, and David Cardiff. *A Social History of British Broadcasting: Volume One, 1922–1939, Serving the Nation*. Oxford: Basil Blackwell 1991.

Scarrow, Howard A. *Canada Votes: A Handbook of Federal and Provincial Election Data*. New Orleans: Hauser Press 1962.

Scates, Bruce. "'Knocking Out a Living': Survival Strategies and Popular Protest in the 1890s Depression." In Susan

Magarey et al., eds. *Debutante Nation: Feminism Contests the 1890s*. St. Leonards, Australia: Allen and Unwin 1993. Pp.38–39.

Schatz, Ronald W. *The Electrical Workers: A History of Labor at General Electric and Westinghouse, 1923–1960*. Urbana: University of Illinois Press 1983.

Schissler, J.P. "The Presbytery of Hamilton, 1875–1925." In Bailey et al. *Presbytery of Hamilton*. Pp.9–15.

Schofield, Ann. "Rebel Girls and Union Maids: The Woman Question in the Journals of the AFL and IWW, 1905–1920." *Feminist Studies*, 9, no. 2 (Summer 1983). Pp.335–58.

Schrodt, Barbara. "Sabbatarianism and Sport in Canadian Society." *Journal of Sport History*, 4, no.1 (Spring 1977). Pp.22–33.

Schull, Joseph. *The Century of the Sun: The First Hundred Years of Sun Life Assurance Company of Canada*. Toronto: Macmillan 1971.

Schultz, Patricia V. *The East York Workers' Association: A Response to the Great Depression*. Toronto: New Hogtown Press 1975.

Schwantes, Carlos A. *Radical Heritage: Labor, Socialism, and Reform in Washington and British Columbia, 1885–1917*. Seattle: University of Washington Press 1979.

Scobey, David. "Anatomy of the Promenade: The Politics of Sociability in Nineteenth-Century New York." *Social History*, 17, no. 2 (May 1992). Pp.203–27.

Scott, James C. *Domination and the Arts of Resistance*. New Haven, Conn.: Yale University Press 1990.

Scott, Joan. *Gender and the Politics of History*. New York: Columbia University Press 1988.

Seager, Allen, and Rodney Fowler. "Burnaby: The First Fifty Years." In L.J. Evenden, ed. *"The Suburb of Happy Homes": Burnaby – Centennial Themes*. Burnaby, B.C.: Community and Economic Development Centre and Centre for Canadian Studies, Simon Fraser University 1995. Pp.17–40.

_____, and David Roth. "British Columbia and the Mining West: A Ghost of a Chance." In Heron, ed. *Workers' Revolt*. Pp.231–67.

Sears, Alan. "Before the Welfare State: Public Health and Social Policy." *Canadian Review of Sociology and Anthropology*, 32, no. 2 (May 1995). Pp.169–88.

Sebire, Dawn. *A Woman's Place: The History of the Hamilton Young Women's Christian Association*. Hamilton: YWCA n.d. [c.1991].

Seccombe, Wally. "Patriarchy Stabilized: The Construction of the Male Breadwinner Wage Norm in Nineteenth-Century Britain." *Social History*, 11, no. 1 (January 1986). Pp.53–76.

_____. *Weathering the Storm: Working-Class Families from the Industrial Revolution to the Fertility Decline*. London: Verso 1993.

Semple, Neil. "'The Nurture and Admonition of the Lord': Nineteenth-Century Canadian Methodism's Response to 'Childhood.'" *HS/SH*, 14, no. 27 (May 1981). Pp.157–75.

Senior, Hereward. *Orangeism: The Canadian Phase*. Toronto: McGraw-Hill Ryerson 1972.

Seretan, L. Glen. *Daniel DeLeon: The Odyssey of an American Marxist*. Cambridge, Mass.: Harvard University Press 1979.

Sewell, Jr., William H. "How Classes Are Made: Critical Reflections on E.P. Thompson's Theory of Working-Class Formation." In Harvey J. Kaye and Keith McClelland, eds. *E.P. Thompson: Critical Perspectives*. Philadelphia: Temple University Press 1990. Pp.59–66.

_____. "Toward a Post-Materialist Rhetoric for Labor History." In Lenard R. Berlanstein, ed. *Rethinking Labor History: Essays on Discourse and Class Analysis*. Urbana: University of Illinois Press 1993. Pp.15–38.

Shadd, Adrienne. *The Journey from Tollgate to Parkway: African Canadians in Hamilton*. Toronto: Natural Heritage Books 2010.

Shahrodi, Zofia. "The Early Polish Settlement in Hamilton." *Polyphony*, 6, no. 2 (Fall-Winter 1984). Pp.33–36.

Shapiro, Stanley. "'Hand and Brain': The Farmer-Labor Party of 1920." *LH*, 26, no. 3 (Summer 1985). Pp.405–22.

Shepherd, John. "Labour and Parliament: The Lib-Labs as the First Working-Class MPs, 1885–1906." In Biagini and Reid, eds. *Currents of Radicalism*. Pp.187–213.

Sher, Julian. *White Hoods: Canada's Ku Klux Klan*. Vancouver: New Star Books 1983.

Shergold, Peter. *Working-Class Life: The 'American Standard' in Comparative Perspective, 1899–1913*. Pittsburgh: University of Pittsburgh Press 1982.

Shorter, Edward, and Charles Tilly. *Strikes in France, 1830–1968*. New York: Cambridge University Press 1974.

Shortt, S.E.D. "'Before the Age of Miracles': The Rise, Fall, and Rebirth of General Practice in Canada, 1890–1940." In Charles D. Roland, ed. *Health, Disease, and Medicine: Essays in Canadian History*. Toronto: Clark Irwin for the Hannah Institute for the History of Medicine 1984. Pp.123–52.

_____. "Social Change and Political Crisis in Rural Ontario: The Patrons of Industry, 1889–1896." In Donald Swainson, ed. *Oliver Mowat's Ontario*. Toronto: Macmillan 1972. Pp.211–35.

_____. ed. *Medicine in Canadian Society: Historical Perspectives*. Montreal and Kingston: McGill-Queen's University Press 1981.

Siemiatycki, Myer. "Labour Contained: The Defeat of a Rank and File Workers' Movement in Canada, 1914–1921." PhD dissertation, York University 1986.

_____. "Munitions and Labour Militancy: The 1916 Hamilton Machinists' Strike." *L/LT*, 3 (1978). Pp.131–51.

Simmons, Christina. "'Helping the Poorer Sisters': The Women of the Jost Mission, Halifax, 1905–1945." *Acadiensis*, 14, no.1 (Autumn 1984). Pp.3–27.

Simmons, Harvey G. *From Asylum to Welfare*. Toronto: National Institute on Mental Retardation 1982.

Simpson, Wayne. "Hockey." In Morrow et al. *Concise History*. Pp.140–68.

Sklar, Martin J. *The Corporate Reconstruction of American Capitalism, 1890–1916*. Cambridge: Cambridge University Press 1988.

Sklar, Robert. *Movie-Made America: A Cultural History of American Movies*. New York: Vintage Books 1976.

Smith, David E. *Prairie Liberalism: The Liberal Party in Saskatchewan, 1905–71*. Toronto: University of Toronto Press 1976.

Smith, Edward Arthur Warwick. "Cooper, William Henry." *DHB*, 4. Pp.52–53.

——————. "The Dialectics of Faith: Laity, Clergy, and Church in Three Hamilton Anglican Parishes, 1880–1914." PhD dissertation, University of Guelph 2000.

——————. "Working-Class Anglicans: Religion and Identity in Victorian and Edwardian Hamilton, Ontario." *HS/SH*, 36, no. 71 (May 2003). Pp.28–30.

Smulyan, Susan. *Selling Radio: The Commercialization of American Broadcasting, 1920–1934*. Washington, D.C.: Smithsonian Institution Press 1994.

Smyth, Elizabeth M. "Centenary Methodist Church, 1899: A Study of the Congregational and Lay Leadership of the 'Church in the Heart of Hamilton.'" MA thesis, McMaster University 1976.

Snell, James. *The Citizen's Wage: The State and the Elderly in Canada, 1900–1951*. Toronto: University of Toronto Press 1996.

——————. "Filial Responsibility Laws in Canada: An Historical Study." *Canadian Journal on Aging*, 9, no. 3 (1990). Pp.268–77.

——————. *In the Shadow of the Law: Divorce in Canada, 1900–1939*. Toronto: University of Toronto Press 1991.

——————. "'The White Life for Two': The Defence of Marriage and Sexual Morality in Canada, 1890–1914." *HS/SH*, 16, no. 31 (May 1983). Pp.111–28.

——————, and Cynthia Comacchio Abeele. "Regulating Nuptiality: Restricting Access to Marriage in Early Twentieth-Century English-Speaking Canada." *CHR*, 64, no.4 (December 1988). Pp.466–89.

Snyder, Robert W. *The Voice of the City: Vaudeville and Popular Culture in New York*. New York: Oxford University Press 1989.

"The Souls of Black Folk: Hamilton's Stewart Memorial Community." www.virtualmuseum.ca/pm_v2.php?id=story_line&lg=English&fl=0&ex=00000636&sl=5137&pos=.

Spalding, L.T. *The History and Romance of Education (Hamilton), 1816–1950*. [Hamilton 1950].

Spelt, Jacob. *Urban Development in South-Central Ontario*. Toronto: McClelland and Stewart 1972.

Spencer, David Ralph. "An Alternative Vision: Main Themes in Moral Education in Canada's English-Language Working-Class Press, 1870–1910." PhD dissertation, University of Toronto 1990.

Spiesman, Stephen A. "Munificent Parsons and Municipal Parsimony: Voluntary vs. Public Poor Relief in Nineteenth Century Toronto." *OH*, 64, no.1 (March 1973). Pp.33–49

Splane, Richard B. *Social Welfare in Ontario, 1791–1893: A Study of Public Welfare Administration*. Toronto: University of Toronto Press 1965.

Spragge, Shirley. "A Confluence of Interests: Housing Reform in Toronto, 1900–1920." In Alan F.J. Artibise and Gilbert A. Stelter, eds. *The Usable Urban Past: Planning and Politics in the Modern Canadian City*. Toronto: Macmillan 1979. Pp.247–67.

Springhall, J.O. "The Boy Scouts, Class, and Militarism in Relation to British Youth Movements, 1908–1930." *IRSH*, 17 (1972). Pp.3–23.

——————. "Building Character in the British Boy: The Attempt to Extend Christian Manliness to Working-Class Adolescents, 1880–1914." In Mangan and Walvin, eds. *Manliness and Morality*. Pp.52–74.

Srigley, Katrina Penelope. "Working Lives and Simple Pleasures: Single, Employed Women in a Depression-Era City, 1929–1939." PhD dissertation, University of Toronto 2005.

Stamp, Robert Miles. "The Campaign for Technical Education in Ontario, 1876–1914." PhD dissertation, University of Western Ontario 1970.

——————. "Canadian High Schools in the 1920s and 1930s: The Social Challenge to the Academic Tradition." CHAHP, 1978. Pp.76–93.

——————. "Empire Day in the Schools of Ontario: The Training of Young Imperialists." *JCS*, 8, no.3 (August 1973). Pp.32–42.

——————. *Ontario Secondary School Program Innovations and Student Retention Rates: 1920s–1970s: A Report to the Ontario Study of the Relevance of Education and the Issue of Dropouts*. Toronto: Queen's Printer 1988.

——————. *The Schools of Ontario, 1876–1976*. Toronto: University of Toronto Press 1982.

Stamp, Shelley. *Movie-Struck Girls: Women and Motion Picture Culture after the Nickelodeon*. Princeton, N.J.: Princeton University Press 2000.

Stansell, Christine. *City of Women: Sex and Class in New York, 1780–1860*. Urbana: University of Illinois Press 1987.

Starr, Paul. *The Social Transformation of American Medicine*. New York 1982.

Steedman, Mercedes. *Angels of the Workplace: Women and the Construction of Gender Relations in the Canadian Clothing Industry, 1890–1940*. Toronto: Oxford University Press 1997.

Steinberg, Marc W. "Culturally Speaking: Finding a Commons between Post-Structuralism and the Thompsonian Perspective." *Social History*, 21, no. 2 (May 1996). Pp.193–214.

——————. "Talkin' Class: Discourse, Ideology, and Their Roles in Class Conflict." In McNall, Levine, and Fantasia, eds. *Bringing Class Back In*. Pp.261–84.

Stern, Mark J. *Society and Family Strategy: Erie County, New York, 1850–1920*. Albany: State University of New York 1987.

Steven, Peter. "Pleasing the Canadians: A National Flavour for Early Cinema, 1896–1914." *Canadian Journal of Film Studies*, 12, no. 2 (Fall 2003). Pp.5–21.

_____. "Sounds of the Cities." *Beaver*, 88, no. 3 (June/July 2008). Pp.29–31.

Stevens, Paul Douglas. "Laurier and the Liberal Party in Ontario, 1887–1911." PhD dissertation, University of Toronto 1966.

Stevens, Peter. "Getting Away from It All: Family Cottaging in Postwar Ontario." PhD dissertation, York University 2010.

Stewart, Gordon T. *The Origins of Canadian Politics: A Comparative Approach*. Vancouver: UBC Press 1986.

_____. "Political Patronage under Macdonald and Laurier, 1878–1811." *American Review of Canadian Studies*, 10, no. 1 (Spring 1980). Pp.3–26.

Stokes, Melvyn, and Richard Maltby, eds. *American Movie Audiences: From the Turn of the Century to the Early Sound Era*. London: British Film Institute 1999.

Storey, Robert Henry. "From Invisibility to Equality? Women Workers and the Gendering of Workers' Compensation in Ontario, 1900–2005." *L/LT*, 64 (Fall 2009). Pp.75–106.

_____. "Industrialization in Canada: The Emergence of the Hamilton Working Class, 1850–1870s." MA thesis, Dalhousie University 1975.

_____. "Unionization Versus Corporate Welfare: The "Dofasco Way."" *L/LT*, 12 (Autumn 1983). Pp.7–42.

_____. 'Workers, Unions, and Steel: The Reshaping of the Hamilton Working Class, 1935–1948." Ph.D. dissertation, University of Toronto 1981.

Stott, R.M. *Hamilton's Doctors, 1863–1935: Guardians of the City's Health*. Hamilton: Hamilton Academy of Medicine Foundation 1995.

Strange, Carolyn. "From Modern Babylon to a City upon a Hill: The Toronto Social Survey Commission of 1915 and the Search for Sexual Order in the City." In Roger Hall, William Westfall, and Laurel Sefton MacDowell, eds. *Patterns of the Past: Interpreting Ontario's History*. Toronto: Dundurn Press 1988. Pp.255–77.

_____. *Toronto's Girl Problem: The Perils and Pleasures of the City, 1880–1930*. Toronto: University of Toronto Press 1995.

Strasser, Susan. *Never Done: A History of American Housework*. New York: Pantheon 1982.

_____. *Satisfaction Guaranteed: The Making of the American Mass Market*. Washington, D.C.: Smithsonian Institution Press 1989.

Strebel, Elizabeth Grottle. "Imperialist Iconography of Anglo-Boer War Film Footage." In Fell, ed. *Film Before Griffith*. Pp.264–71.

Stricker, Frank. "Affluence for Whom? – Another Look at Prosperity and the Working Classes in the 1920s." *LH*, 24, no. 1 (Winter 1983). Pp.5–33.

Strong-Boag, Veronica. "Keeping House in God's Country: Canadian Women at Work in the Home." In Heron and Storey, eds. *On the Job*. Pp.124–51.

_____. *The New Day Recalled: Lives of Girls and Women in English Canada, 1919–1939*. Toronto: Copp Clark Pitman 1988.

_____. *The Parliament of Women: The National Council of Women of Canada, 1893–1929*. Ottawa: National Museum of Man 1976.

_____. "'Wages for Housework': Mothers' Allowances and the Beginnings of Social Security in Canada." *JCS*, 14, no.1 (Spring 1979). Pp.24–34.

Strouthous, Andrew. *US Labor and Political Action, 1918–24: A Comparison of Independent Political Action in New York, Chicago, and Seattle*. New York: St. Martin's Press 2000.

Struthers, James. *Limits of Affluence: Welfare in Ontario, 1920–1970*. Toronto: University of Toronto Press 1994.

_____. *No Fault of Their Own: Unemployment and the Canadian Welfare State, 1914–1941*. Toronto: University of Toronto Press 1983.

_____. "'Lord Give Us Men': Women and Social Work in English Canada, 1918–1953." In Moscovitch and Albert, eds. *Benevolent State*. Pp.111–25.

_____. "A Profession in Crisis: Charlotte Whitton and Canadian Social Work in the 1930s." In Moscovitch and Albert, eds. *Benevolent State*. Pp.126–43.

Stuart, Mervyn. "Ideology and Experience: Public Health Nursing and the Ontario Rural Child Welfare Project, 1920–25." *CBMH*, 6, no.2 (1989).

Stubbs, Todd Russell. "Visions of the Common Good: Britishness, Citizenship, and the Public Sphere in Nineteenth-Century Toronto." PhD dissertation, York University 2007.

Sturino, Franc. "Italian Emigration: Reconsidering the Links in Chain Migration." In Perin and Sturino, eds. *Arrangiarsi*. Pp.63–90.

Sugiman, Pamela. *Labour's Dilemma: The Gender Politics of Auto Workers in Canada, 1937–1979*. Toronto: University of Toronto Press 1994.

_____. "Privilege and Oppression: The Configuration of Race, Gender, and Class in Southern Ontario Auto Plants, 1939 to 1949." *L/LT*, 47 (Spring 2001). Pp.3–62.

Sutcliffe, Joseph Harry, and Paul Phillips. "Real Wages and the Winnipeg General Strike: An Empirical Investigation." Unpublished paper.

Sutherland, Neil. *Growing Up: Childhood in English Canada from the Great War to the Age of Television*. Toronto: University of Toronto Press 1997.

_____. "'We Always Had Things to Do': The Paid and Unpaid Work of Anglophone Children between the 1920s and the 1960s." *L/LT*, 25 (Spring 1990). Pp.105–41.

Swiencicki, Mark A. "Consuming Brotherhood: Men's Culture, Style, and Recreation as Consumer Culture, 1880–1930." *JSH*, 31, no.4 (Summer 1998). Pp.773–808.

Swyripa, Frances. *Wedded to the Cause: Ukrainian-Canadian Women and Ethnic Identity, 1891–1991*. Toronto: University of Toronto Press 1993.

_____, and John Herd Thompson, eds. *Loyalties in Conflict: Ukrainians in Canada during the Great War*. Edmonton: University of Alberta, Canadian Institute of Ukrainian Studies 1983.

Sylvester, Kenneth M. "Rural to Urban Migration: Finding Household Complexity in a New World Environment." In Sager and Baskerville, eds. *Household Counts*. Pp.147–79.

Synge, Jane. "Changing Conditions for Women and Their Consequences in Hamilton and Its Rural Environs, 1900–1930: An Empirical Study Based on Life History Interviews." Paper presented to the Working Sexes Symposium, University of British Columbia 1976.

_____. "Family and Community in Hamilton." Unpublished manuscript (WC).

_____. "Immigrant Communities – British and Continental European – in Early Twentieth Century Hamilton, Canada." *Oral History*, 4, no. 2 (Autumn 1976). Pp.38–51.

_____. "Self-Help and Neighbourliness: Patterns of Life in Hamilton, 1900–1920." In Irving Abella and David Millar, eds. *The Canadian Worker in the Twentieth Century*. Toronto: Oxford University Press 1978. Pp.97–104.

_____. "The Transition from School to Work: Growing up Working Class in Early 20th Century Hamilton, Ontario." In K. Ishwaran, ed. *Childhood and Adolescence in Canada*. Toronto: McGraw-Hill Ryerson 1979. Pp.249–69.

_____. "Work and Family Support Patterns of the Aged in the Early Twentieth Century." In Victor W. Marshall, ed. *Aging in Canada: Social Perspectives*. Don Mills, Ont.: Fitzhenry and Whiteside 1980. Pp.140–44.

_____. "Young Working Class Women in Early 20th Century Hamilton – Their Work and Family Lives." In A.H. Turrittin, ed. *Proceedings of the Workshop on Blue-Collar Workers and Their Communities*. Toronto: York University 1976. Pp.137–45.

Szreter, Simon. "The Importance of Social Intervention in Britain's Mortality Decline c.1850–1914: A Re-interpretation of the Role of Public Health." *Social History of Medicine*, 1, no.1 (April 1988). Pp.1–37.

Philip Taft, *The A.F. of L. in the Time of Gompers*. New York: Harper 1957.

Taschereau, Sylvie. "'Behind the Store': Montreal Shopkeeping Families between the Wars." In Bettina Bradbury and Tamara Myers, eds. *Negotiating Identities in 19th- and 20th-Century Montreal*. Vancouver: UBC Press 2005. Pp.235–58.

Tawa, Nicholas E. *The Way to Tin Pan Alley: American Popular Song, 1866–1910*. New York: Schirmer Books 1990.

Taylor, Graham D., and Peter Baskerville. *A Concise History of Business in Canada*. Toronto: Oxford University Press 1994.

Tebbutt, Melanie. *Making Ends Meet: Pawnbroking and Working-Class Credit*. London: Methuen 1984.

Tennyson, Brian D. "The Ontario General Election of 1919; The Beginnings of Agrarian Revolt." *JCS*, 6, no. 1 (February 1969). Pp.26–36.

_____. "Sir William Hearst and the Ontario Temperance Act." *OH*, 55, no. 4 (December 1963). Pp.233–45.

Terpstra, Nicholas. "Local Politics and Local Planning: A Case Study of Hamilton, Ontario, 1915–1930." *UHR*, 14, no. 2 (October 1985). Pp.121–27.

Thane, Pat. "Women in the British Labour Party and the Construction of State Welfare, 1906–1939." In Seth Koven and Sonya Michel, eds. *Mothers of a New World: Maternalist Politics and the Origins of Welfare States*. London: Routledge 1993. Pp.343–77.

Therborn, Goran. "The Rule of Capital and the Rise of Democracy." *New Left Review*, 103 (May-June 1977). Pp.3–41.

_____. "Why Some Classes Are More Successful Than Others." *New Left Review*, 138 (1983). Pp.37–55.

Thernstrom, Stephan. *Poverty and Progress: Social Mobility in a Nineteenth-Century City*. Cambridge, Mass.: Harvard University Press 1964.

Thistlethwaite, Frank. "Migration from Europe Overseas in the Nineteenth and Twentieth Centuries." In Herbert Moller, ed. *Population Movements in Modern European History*. New York 1964. Pp.73–92.

Thomas, John D. "Servants of the Church: Canadian Methodist Deaconess Work, 1890–1926." *CHR*, 65, no.3 (September 1984). Pp.371–95.

Thompson, E.P. *Customs in Common: Studies in Traditional Popular Culture*. New York: New Press 1993.

_____. "Eighteenth-Century English Society: Class Struggle Without Class?" *Social History*, 3, no. 2 (May 1978). Pp.133–65.

_____. *The Making of the English Working Class*. London: Penguin 1968.

Thompson, J.A. "Labour and the Modern British Monarchy." *South Atlantic Quarterly*, 70 (1971). Pp.341–9.

Thompson, John F., and Norman Beasley. *For Years to Come: A Story of International Nickel of Canada*. New York and Toronto: Putnam 1960.

Thompson, John Herd. "Bringing in the Sheaves: The Harvest Excursionists, 1890–1929." *CHR*, 59, no. 4 (December 1978). Pp.467–89.

_____. "The Enemy Alien and the Canadian General Election of 1917." In Swyripa and Thompson, eds. *Loyalties in Conflict*. Pp.25–45.

_____. *The Harvests of War: The Prairie West, 1914–1918*. Toronto: McClelland and Stewart 1978.

Thompson, Ronald T.F. *The Origins and Development of the Wolf Cub Movement in Canada, Parts I – IV, 1914–1940*. Victoria: author 1971.

Thwaites, James Douglas. "The International Association of Machinists in Canada." MA thesis, Carleton University 1966.

Tillotson, Shirley. *Contributing Citizens: Modern Charitable Fundraising and the Making of the Welfare State, 1920–66*. Vancouver: UBC Press 2008.

Tilly, Charles. *From Mobilization to Revolution*. Reading, Mass.: Addison-Wesley 1978.

——————, Louise Tilly, and Richard Tilly. *The Rebellious Century*. Cambridge, Mass.: Harvard University Press 1975.

Todd, Selina. "Breadwinners and Dependants: Working-Class Young People in England, 1918–1955." *IRSH*, 52 (2007). Pp.57–87.

Toinet, Marie-France. "Political Participation of the American Working Class at the End of the Nineteenth Century." In Marianne Debouzy, ed. *In the Shadow of the Statue of Liberty: Immigrants, Workers, and Citizens in the American Republic, 1880–1920*. Urbana: University of Illinois Press 1992. Pp.293–310.

Tolson, Andrew. *The Limits of Masculinity*. London: Tavistock Press 1977.

Tomassinin, Luigi. "Mutual Benefit Societies in Italy, 1861–1922." In Van der Linden, ed. *Social Security Mutualism*. Pp.225–71.

Tomes, Nancy. *The Gospel of Germs: Men, Women, and the Microbe in American Life*. Cambridge, Mass.: Harvard University Press 1998.

——————. "A 'Torrent of Abuse': Crimes of Violence between Working-Class Men and Women in London, 1840–1875." *JSH*, 11 (1978). Pp.328–45.

Tomkins, S.M. "The Failure of Expertise: Public Health Policy in Britain during the 1918–19 Influenza Epidemic." *Social History of Medicine*, 5 (1992). Pp.435–54.

Tomko, Linda J. *Dancing Class: Gender, Ethnicity, and Social Divides in American Dance, 1890–1920*. Bloomington: Indiana University Press 1999.

Tomkins, George S. *A Common Countenance: Stability and Change in the Canadian Curriculum*. Scarborough, Ont.: Prentice-Hall Canada 1986.

Tomlins, Christopher L. *The State and the Unions: Labor Relations, Law, and the Organized Labor Movement in America, 1880–1960*. Cambridge: Cambridge University Press 1985.

Tone, Andrea. *The Business of Benevolence: Industrial Paternalism in Progressive America*. Ithaca, N.Y.: Cornell University Press 1997.

Tosh, John. "Hegemonic Masculinity and the History of Gender." In Stefan Dudink, Karen Hagerman, and John Tosh, eds. *Masculinities in Politics and War: Gendering Modern History*. Manchester: University of Manchester Press 2004. Pp.41–58.

——————. "Imperial Masculinity and the Flight from Domesticity in Britain, 1880–1914." In Timothy P. Foley et al. *Gender and Colonialism*. Galway: Galway University Press 1995.

——————. "What Should Historians Do with Masculinity? Reflections on Nineteenth-Century Britain." *HWJ*, 38 (Fall 1994). Pp.179–202.

Trachtenberg, Alan. *The Incorporation of America: Culture and Society in the Gilded Age*. New York: Hill and Wang 1982.

Traves, Tom. *The State and Enterprise: Canadian Manufacturers and the Federal Government, 1917–1931*. Toronto: University of Toronto Press 1979.

Trigger, Rosalyn. "Protestant Restructuring in the Canadian City: Church and Mission in the Industrial Working-Class District of Griffintown, Montreal." *UHR*, 31, no. 1 (Fall 2002). Pp.5–18.

Troen, Selwyn K. "The Discovery of the Adolescent by American Educational Reformers, 1900–1920: An Economic Perspective." In Lawrence Stone, ed. *Schooling and Society: Studies in the History of Education*. Baltimore: Johns Hopkins University Press 1976. Pp.241–43.

Trofimenkoff, Susan Mann. *The Dream of Nation: A Social and Intellectual History of Quebec*. Montreal: McGill-Queen's University Press 2002.

Tsuzuki, Chushichi. *H.M. Hyndman and British Socialism*. Oxford: Oxford University Press 1961.

Tuck, Joseph Hugh. "Canadian Railways and the International Brotherhoods: Labour Organization in the Railway Running Trades in Canada, 1865–1914." PhD dissertation, University of Western Ontario 1975.

Tucker, Eric. *Administering Danger in the Workplace: The Law and Politics of Occupational Health and Safety Regulation in Ontario, 1850–1914*. Toronto: University of Toronto Press 1990.

——————. "Making the Workplace 'Safe' in Capitalism: The Enforcement of Factory Legislation in Nineteenth-Century Ontario." *L/LT*, 21 (Spring 1988). Pp.45–86.

——————. "Who's Running the Road? Street Railway Strikes and the Problem of Constructing a Liberal Capitalist Order in Canada, 1886–1914." *Law and Social Inquiry*, 35, no. 2 (Spring 2010). Pp.451–85.

——————, and Judy Fudge. "Forging Responsible Unions: Metal Workers and the Rise of the Labour Injunction in Canada." *L/LT*, 37 (Spring 1996). Pp.81–119.

Tulchinsky, Gerald. *Taking Root: The Origins of the Canadian Jewish Community*. Toronto: Lester Publishing 1992.

Turcotte, Dorothy. *The Sand Strip: Burlington/Hamilton Beaches*. St. Catharines, Ont.: Stonehouse Publications 1987.

Turkstra, Melissa. "Christianity and the Working Class in Early Twentieth Century English Canada." PhD dissertation, York University 2005.

——————. "Constructing a Labour Gospel: Labour and Religion in Early Twentieth-Century Ontario." *L/LT*, 57 (Spring 2006). Pp.93–130.

_____. "Towards an Understanding of the Relationship between the Working Class and Religion." MA Cognate Paper, Department of History, McMaster University 1998.

_____. "Working-Class Churches in Early Twentieth-Century Hamilton: Fostering a Distinctive Working-Class Identity and Culture." *HS/SH*, 41, no. 82 (November 2009). Pp.459–504.

Ungar, Molly. "Trenholme, Clementina (Fessenden)." *DHB*, 3. Pp.214–16.

Ursel, Jane. *Private Lives, Public Policy: 100 Years of State Intervention in the Family*. Toronto: Women's Press 1992.

Valverde, Marianna. *The Age of Soap, Light, and Water: Moral Reform in English Canada, 1885–1925*. Toronto: McClelland and Stewart 1991.

_____. "The Mixed Social Economy as a Canadian Tradition." *SPE*, 47 (Summer 1995). Pp.33–60.

Vance, Jonathan F. *Death So Noble: Memory, Meaning, and the First World War*. Vancouver: UBC Press 1997.

Van der Linden, Marcel, ed. *Social Security Mutualism: The Comparative History of Mutual Benefit Societies*. Bern: Peter Lang 1996.

Van Tine, Warren. *The Making of the Labor Bureaucrat: Union Leadership in the United States, 1870–1920*. Amherst, Mass.: University of Massachusetts Press 1973.

Varty, Carmen Nielson. "The City and the Ladies: Politics, Religion, and Female Benevolence in Mid-Nineteenth-Century Hamilton, Canada West." *JCS*, 38, no. 2 (Spring 2004). Pp.151–71.

Veltmeyer, Henry. *Canadian Class Structure*. Toronto: Garamond Press 1986.

Vincent, John. *The Formation of the Liberal Party, 1857–1868*. London: Constable 1966.

Vipond, Mary. *Listening In: The First Decade of Canadian Broadcasting, 1922–1932*. Montreal and Kingston: McGill-Queen's University Press 1992.

_____. "London Listens: The Popularity of Radio in the Depression." *OH*, 88, no. 1 (March 1996), 47–63.

Voeltz, Richard A. "The Antidote to 'Khaki Fever'? The Expansion of the British Girl Guides during the First World War." *Journal of Contemporary History*, 27, no. 4 (October 1992). Pp.627–38.

Wachs, Martin, and Margaret Crawford, eds. *The Car and the City: The Automobile, the Built Environment, and Daily Urban Life*. Ann Arbor: University of Michigan Press 1992.

Wagoner, Harless D. *The U.S. Machine Tool Industry from 1900 to 1950*. Cambridge, Mass.: M.I.T. Press 1968.

Waite, P.B. "The Political Ideas of John A. Macdonald." In Hamelin, ed. *Les idées politiques des premiers ministres*. Pp.51–67.

Walden, Keith. *Becoming Modern in Toronto: The Industrial Exhibition and the Shaping of a Late Victorian Culture*. Toronto: University of Toronto Press 1997.

Walker, James St. G. "'Race' and Recruitment in World War I: Enlistment of Visible Minorities in the Canadian Expeditionary Force." *CHR*, Vol. 70, no.1 (January 1989). Pp.1–26.

_____. *"Race," Rights, and the Law in the Supreme Court of Canada: Historical Case Studies*. Waterloo, Ont.: Wilfrid Laurier University Press 1997.

Wall, Shelly. "Tarasiuk, Thomas." *DCB*, Vol. 3.

_____. "Williams, Edward Howard." *DHB*, 2. Pp.186–87.

Walsh, John C., and Steven High. "Rethinking the Concept of Community." *HS/SH*, 32, no. 64 (November 1999). Pp.255–73.

Walters, Pamela Barnhouse. "Occupational and Labor Market Effects on Secondary and Postsecondary Educational Expansion in the United States: 1922 to 1979." *American Sociological Review*, 49, no. 5 (October 1984). Pp.659–71.

Ward, Norman. *The Canadian House of Commons: Representation*. Toronto: University of Toronto Press 1963.

Ward, W. Peter. *White Canada Forever: Popular Attitudes and Public Policy towards Orientals in British Columbia*. Montreal and Kingston: McGill-Queen's University Press 1978.

Warren, Allen. "Popular Manliness: Baden-Powell, Scouting, and the Development of Manly Character." In Mangan and Walvin, ed. *Manliness and Morality*, 199–219.

_____. "Sir Robert Baden-Powell, the Scout Movement, and Citizenship Training in Great Britain, 1900–1920." *English Historical Review*, 101, no. 399 (April 1986). Pp.376–98.

Warsh, Cheryl Krasnick, and Veronica Strong-Boag, eds. *Children's Health Issues in Historical Perspective*. Waterloo, Ont.: Wilfrid Laurier University Press 2005.

Watt, James T. "Anti-Catholicism in Ontario Politics: The Role of the Protestant Protective Association in the 1894 Election." *OH*, 69, no. 2 (June 1967). Pp.57–67.

Weaver, John C. *Crimes, Constables, and Courts: Order and Transgression in a Canadian City, 1816–1970*. Montreal and Kingston: McGill-Queen's University Press 1995.

_____. "From Land Assembly to Social Maturity: The Suburban Life of Westdale (Hamilton), Ontario, 1911–1951." *HS/SH*, 11, no. 22 (November 1978). Pp.411–40.

_____. *Hamilton: An Illustrated History*. Toronto: James Lorimer and Company 1982.

_____. "The Location of Manufacturing Enterprises: The Case of Hamilton's Attraction of Foundries, 1830–1890." In Richard A. Jarrell and Arnold E. Ross, eds. *Critical Issues in the History of Canadian Science, Technology, and Medicine*. Thornhill, Ont.: HSTC 1983.

_____. "Social Control, Martial Conformity, and Community Entanglement: The Varied Beats of the Hamilton Police, 1895–1920." *UHR*, 19, no.2 (October 1990). Pp.113–27.

Weaver, Sally M. "The Iroquois: The Grand River Reserve in the Late Nineteenth and Early Twentieth Centuries, 1875–1945."

In Edward S. Rogers and Donald B. Smith, eds. *Aboriginal Ontario: Historical Perspectives on the First Nations*. Toronto: Dundurn Press 1994. Pp.213–57.

Weinstein, James. *The Decline of Socialism in America, 1912–1925*. New York: Vintage 1969.

Weldon, J.C. "Consolidations in Canadian Industry, 1900–1948." In L.A. Skeotch, ed. *Restrictive Trade Practices in Canada*. Toronto: University of Toronto Press 1966.

Wesley, Sam, with David Wesley. *Hamilton's Hockey Tigers*. Toronto: James Lorimer and Company 2005.

Westley, Margaret W. *The Remembrance of Grandeur: The Anglo-Protestant Elite of Montreal*. Montreal: Libre Expression 1990.

Wever, Cathy. "Crime and Punishment in Hamilton: Jelfs and Social Control." Unpublished paper (WC).

Wexman, Virginia Wright. *Creating the Couple: Love, Marriage, and Hollywood Performance*. Princeton, N.J.: Princeton University Press 1993.

Whitaker, Reginald. "Introduction," to William Irvine, *The Farmers in Politics*. Toronto: McClelland and Stewart 1976. Pp.v–xxxv.

_____. "Scientific Management Theory as Political Ideology." *SPE*, 2 (Autumn 1979). Pp.75–108

White, Kevin. *The First Sexual Revolution: The Emergence of Male Heterosexuality*. New York: New York University Press 1993.

White, Michelle. "Work, Protest, and Community Power in Nineteenth-Century Hamilton." Unpublished paper, Department of History, York University 1994.

White, Richard, with Sarah-Jane Ballard, Ingrid Bown, Meredith Lake, Patricia Leehy, and Lila Oldmeadow. *On Holidays: A History of Getting Away in Australia*. North Melbourne: Pluto Press Australia 2005.

Whyte, William Foote. *Street Corner Society*. Chicago: University of Chicago Press 1943.

Wickberg, Edgar, ed. *From China to Canada: A History of the Chinese Communities in Canada*. Toronto: McClelland and Stewart 1982.

Wilbur, Richard. *H.H. Stevens, 1878–1973*. Toronto: University of Toronto Press 1977.

Wild, Marjorie. *Elizabeth Bagshaw*. Markham, Ont.: Fitzhenry and Whiteside 1984.

Wilentz, Sean. *Chants Democratic: New York City and the Rise of the American Working Class, 1788–1850*. New York: Oxford University Press 1984.

Wilkins, Mira. *The Emergence of Multinational Enterprise: American Business Abroad from the Colonial Era to 1914*. Cambridge, Mass.: Harvard University Press 1970.

Williams, Clifford J. *Decades of Service: A History of the Ontario Ministry of Community and Social Services: 1930–1980*. Toronto: Ministry of Community and Social Services 1984.

Williams, John R. *The Conservative Party of Canada: 1920–1949*. Durham, N.C.: Duke University Press 1956.

Williams, Raymond. "Base and Superstructure in Marxist Cultural Theory." *New Left Review*, 82 (November-December 1973). Pp.3–16.

_____. *Keywords: A Vocabulary of Culture and Society*. London: Fontana 1986.

Willrich, Michael. "Home Slackers: Men, the State, and Welfare in Modern America." *JAH*, 87, no. 2 (September 2000). Pp.460–89.

Wills, Gale. *A Marriage of Convenience: Business and Social Work in Toronto, 1918–1957*. Toronto: University of Toronto Press 1995.

Wilson, Barbara M., ed. *Ontario and the First World War, 1914–1918: A Collection of Documents*. Toronto: University of Toronto Press 1977.

Wilson, Leonard G. "The Historical Decline of Tuberculosis in Europe and America: Its Causes and Significance." *Journal of the History of Medicine*, 45, no. 3 (July 1990). Pp.366–96.

Wilson, John. "The Ontario Political Culture." In Donald C. MacDonald, ed. *Government and Politics of Ontario*. Toronto: Macmillan 1975. Pp.211–34.

Wilson, Ralph Holland. *Chedoke: More Than a Sanatorium*. Hamilton: Hamilton Health Sciences 2006.

Wingfield, Alexander H. *The Hamilton Centennial, 1846–1946*. Hamilton: Hamilton Centennial Committee 1946.

Winks, Robin W. *The Blacks in Canada: A History*. 2nd ed. Montreal and Kingston: McGill-Queen's University Press 1997.

Wood, Ellen Meiksins. *Democracy against Capitalism: Renewing Historical Materialism*. Cambridge: Cambridge University Press 1995.

Woods, Robert. "Mortality and Sanitary Conditions in the 'Best Governed City in the World' – Birmingham, 1870–1910." *Journal of Historical Geography*, 4, no.1 (January 1978). Pp.35–56.

Wright, Cynthia Jane. "'The Most Prominent Rendezvous of the Feminine Toronto': Eaton's College Street and the Organization of Shopping in Toronto, 1920–1950." PhD dissertation, University of Toronto 1993.

Wright, Eric Olin. *Classes*. London: Verso 1985.

Wright, Gwendolyn. *Building the Dream: A Social History of Housing in America*. New York: Pantheon 1981.

_____. *Moralism and the Model Home: Domestic Architecture and Cultural Conflict in Chicago, 1873–1913*. Chicago: University of Chicago Press 1980.

Wyman, Mark. *Round-Trip to America: The Immigrants Return to Europe, 1880–1930*. Ithaca, N.Y.: Cornell University Press 1993.

Wytrwal, Joseph A. *Behold! The Polish Americans*. Detroit: Endurance Press 1977.

Yans-McLaughlin, Virginia. *Family and Community: Italian Immigrants in Buffalo, 1880–1930*. Urbana: University of Illinois Press 1982.

Yeo, Stephen. "A New Life: The Religion of Socialism in Britain, 1883–1896." *HWJ*, 4 (Autumn 1977). Pp.5–56.

Young, W.R. "Conscription, Rural Depopulation, and the Farmers of Ontario, 1917–19." *CHR*, 52, no.3 (September 1972). Pp.289–320.

Zembrzycki, Stacey. "'There Were Always Men in Our House': Gender and Childhood Memories of Working-Class Ukrainians in Depression-Era Canada." *L/LT*, 60 (Fall 2007). Pp.77–105.

Zucchi, John E. *A History of Ethnic Enclaves in Canada*. Ottawa: Canadian Historical Association 2007.

_____. *Italians in Toronto: Development of a National Identity, 1875–1935*. Montreal and Kingston: McGill-Queen's University Press 1988.

_____. "Mining, Railway Building, and Street Construction: Italians in Ontario before World War One." *Polyphony*, 7, no. 2 (Fall/Winter 1985). Pp.7–13.

Zunz, Olivier. *The Changing Face of Inequality: Urbanization, Industrial Development, and Immigrants in Detroit, 1880–1920*. Chicago: University of Chicago Press 1982.

_____. *Making America Corporate, 1870–1920*. Chicago: University of Chicago Press 1990.

Zweig, Michael. *The Working Class Majority: America's Best Kept Secret*. Ithaca, N.Y.: ILR Press 2000.

Index

Canadian Broadcasting Corporation, 631n55
Canadian Building and Construction Industries, National Joint Conference Board, 291
Canadian Chamber of Commerce, 541
Canadian City Bureau, 516
Canadian Club, 30, 433
Canadian Coloured Cottons, 560n16
Canadian Conference on Charities and Correction, 193, 575n114, 603n73
Canadian Congress Journal, 118; women's page, 571n38, 581n195
Canadian Co-operative Commonwealth, 477, 672n11
Canadian Co-operative Concern, 163
Canadian Cottons, 242, 249, 257, 283; strike at, 296, 297, 298, 299, 300, 360, 529, 626n
Canadian Council on Child Welfare, 579n176
Canadian Drawn Steel, 514, 561n31, 561n47
Canadian Electrical Association, 638n143
Canadian Engineer, 209, 232
Canadian Expeditionary Force, 33, 110, 401, 414, 422, 440, 656n100
Canadian Federation of Labour, 625n119
Canadian Founders Association, 624n113
Canadian Founders' and Metal Trades Association, 250, 624n113
Canadian Foundryman, 233, 236, 238, 239, 245, 292
Canadian Girls in Training, 351
Canadian Home Market Association, 460
Canadian Iron Corporation. *See* Canadian Iron Foundries
Canadian Iron Foundries, 254, 560n16
Canadian Iron Foundry Company, 221, 254
Canadianization, 427
Canadian Knitting, 561n32
Canadian Labor Defence League, 529, 536, 683n101
Canadian Labor Party, 482, 500, 528; Ontario Section, 377, 498, 501, 677n95
Canadian Labor World, 507
Canadian League Against War and Facism, 683n101
Canadian Legion, 524, 543, 681n62
Canadian Locomotive Company, 22

Canadian Machinery, 144, 231, 234, 250, 263, 267, 284, 610n19, 613n66
Canadian Machinery Corporation, 560n16
Canadian Manufacturers' Association, 22, 32, 37, 220, 230, 241, 460, 504, 512, 513, 608n65, 609n1, 616n115; Declaration of Principles, 220; Hamilton Branch of, 23, 37, 46, 227–28, 247, 269, 274, 284, 295, 561n46, 592n81, 637n134; Parliamentary Committee, 220; Technical Education Committee of, 143, 247
Canadian Medical Association, 95
Canadian National Exhibition, 332
Canadian Northern Railway, 22
Canadian Pacific Railway, 560n19
Canadian Patriotic Fund, 24, 59, 117, 119, 151, 180, 185, 189, 197, 198, 288, 326, 415, 416, 518, 604n86; Relief Committee of, 180–81, 185, 190, 194, 197
Canadian Radio Broadcasting Commission, 631n55
Canadian Reconstruction Association, 22, 503, 513, 616n115
Canadian Socialist League, 478, 672n11, 673n13
Canadian Society of Civil Engineers, 611n41
Canadian Society of Cost Accountants, 611n41
Canadian Steamship Lines, 560n16
Canadian Steel Goods, 458, 514, 621n53, 678n12
Canadian Street Railway Association, 225
Canadian Textile Journal, 141, 260, 614n84
Canadian Welfare Council, 188, 192, 602n49, 603n66
cancer, 75, 90, 95, 105, 268, 573n83, 578n156
canning industry, 15, 127, 130
Cantor, Eddie, 343, 344
capitalism, phases of, 8, 14–16; corporate, 8, 17, 20, 113, 230, 274, 473; monopoly, 8, 17
capitalist class. *See* bourgeoisie
car-builders, 250, 281, 614n86
card-playing, 360, 370, 372, 374, 378, 379, 407, 442, 471, 489, 519, 649n127
carnivals, 406, 489, 517, 637n134; summer, 388, 560n26, 637n134

Caroline St. Mission, 368
Carpatho-Russians, 665n103
Carpenter, Annie (Cascaden), 27
Carpenter, Edward, 649n123
carpenters, 174, 211, 227, 262, 275, 375, 468, 606n24, 623n89
Carroll, William, 143, 165, 598n62
Carscallen, Henry, 674n29
Carson, John, 214
Casa d'Italia, 441
Cassaday, Annie, 375, 376
Cassidy, Harry, 187, 197
Cataract Power Company, 15, 18, 22, 221–26, 237, 463, 483, 483, 608n56, 634n97
Catholic Athletic Club, 393
Catholic Church, Roman, 439, 444
Catholic Hockey League, 392
Catholic Register, 325, 656n98
Catholics, Roman, 69, 70, 72, 176, 178, 198, 200, 319, 320, 321, 322, 323, 325, 345, 374, 375, 378, 382, 404, 411, 413, 420, 425, 427, 428, 439, 454, 511, 574n102, 582n9, 599n6, 670n94, 632n72, 633n90, 662n73, 664n94, 670n101; hostility to, 419, 435, 436, 444, 466. *See also* St. Elizabeth Nurses Association; St. Joseph's Hospital; St. Vincent de Paul Society; saints days; separate schools, Roman Catholic
Cauchon, Nolan, 636n127
censorship, 285, 287, 417, 431, 610n19
census, 39, 108, 110, 122; 1901, 43, 124, 319, 582n15, 582n16, 666n9; 1911, 39, 45, 104,108, 122, 124, 127, 564n23, 582n15, 590n34, 666n9; 1921, 44, 76, 122, 124, 135, 585n45, 589n18, 591n45; 1931, 76, 107, 119, 122, 124, 142, 143, 146, 182, 316, 351, 567n72; 1941, 51, 59, 64, 104, 117, 124, 146, 316, 572n54; 1951, 571n32
Centenary Methodist Church, 322, 512
Centennial Industrial Exhibition, 15
Central Bureau of Family Welfare, 44, 187, 191, 192, 193, 195, 200, 201
Central Bureau of Social Agencies, 187, 191, 195, 201, 530. *See also* Central Bureau of Family Welfare; Family Service Bureau
Central Prison, 608n71
Central School, 124
Central Presbyterian Church, 26, 27, 320
Chadwick Brass, 129

chain stores, 114, 143, 163, 598n62

Champ, H.H., 166, 236

Champ, W.B., 458, 678n12

Chaplin, Charlie, 341, 343, 388

charitable homes, 94, 176, 183, 201, 550; inspection of, 176; residents' fees, 600n15; state funding of, 176, 178

charities, 6, 38, 54, 79, 84, 92, 93, 94, 96, 108, 152, 161, 162, 173–202, 308, 338, 374, 378, 461, 510, 515, 546; co-operation among, 186, 551, 602n44, 602n50; directors of, 24, 27; ethnic, 188, 599n6, 663n86; government funding for, 76, 174, 186; state programs as, 174, 175, 183; investigators/visitors for, 73,186, 188–92, 194, 195, 200, 201, 101, 550, 602n60; work and, 193; workers for, 93, 112, 117, 166, 184, 186, 189, 193, 195, 196, 309. See also relief; soup kitchens; social work; social workers; welfare programs

chemical industry, 145

chemists, 29, 233, 251

Chicago, 18, 43, 225, 232, 235, 276, 278, 285, 431, 439

chickens, 112, 113, 168, 311, 349, 586n55

Chief Press Censor, 431

childbirth, 79–80, 552; registration, 578n146. See also mortality, infant; maternal; pregancy

child labour, 8, 71, 112, 116, 123, 124, 126, 137, 189–90, 210, 247–48, 267, 342, 486, 548, 551, 588n4, 588n8, 589n17, 591n48, 591n81, 614n75; on strike, 605n10

child-rearing, 58, 69–74, 92, 93, 94, 98, 348, 378, 382, 572n56, 642n2

children, number per family, 572n54

Children of Unmarried Parents Act, 182, 585n51, 648n110

Children's Aid Society, 24, 33, 72, 99, 124, 143, 176, 181, 189, 194, 195, 348, 350, 357, 390, 394, 549, 603n66, 644n40, 654n74

Children's Protection Act, 124

child-saving, 3, 24, 29, 31, 72, 177, 309, 385, 390, 549

Chinatown, 421, 660n36

Chinese, 40, 53, 151, 326, 385, 400, 420, 421, 424–25, 426, 443, 445, 466, 548, 660n35, 660n36; head tax on, 424

Chinese Immigration Act, 424

Chipman-Holton Knitting Company, 561n32, 561n47, 588n84, 646n61, 648n101

Christ Church Cathedral, 26, 320

christenings, 53, 308, 321, 323

Christian Workers' Church, 320

Christmas, 41, 135, 150, 152, 255, 256, 263, 308, 309, 317, 321, 388, 443, 471, 515, 642n13, 649n124; baskets for poor, 176, 187, 308, 604n97

Church, Thomas, 481

Church of England. See Anglicans

Church of St. John the Evangelist, 477

churches, and charity, 175, 187, 188; and labour, 223, 322; and new immigrants, 427; and popular culture, 640n166; and recreation, 328, 362, 368, 380, 391, 392, 393, 399, 400, 405, 423; and socializing, 374; as agents of morality, 59; attendance at, 6, 322, 344, 407, 551, 554; Bible classes, 368; buildings of, 3, 5, 7, 29, 52, 337, 347, 387, 547; congregations/parishes of, 54, 92, 151, 255, 313, 315, 319–20, 322, 345, 364, 372, 374, 472, 551; elite, 26, 27; fees for, 160, 162, 322; Labour, 498; mission, 320, 322, 368, 426, 435, 552; religious services of, 89, 317, 321, 326, 344, 369, 374, 511

Churchill, Winston, 454

cigarettes. See smoking

cigar-makers, 207, 208, 211, 212, 216, 294, 461, 468, 478, 605n4; strike, 286

circuses, 332, 333, 345, 353, 637n133

Citizen and Country, 478, 673n12

Citizens' Committees, 679n21

citizenship, 33, 139, 168–69, 198, 200, 289, 293, 397, 411–12, 420, 427, 430, 441, 452, 475–76, 509, 510, 515, 516–17, 519–10, 532, 542, 543, 661n47, 672n3; economic, 102; for women, 351, 369, 371, 376, 380; "social," 543

Citizens' League, 366

Citizens' Liberty League, 469, 514, 520

Citizens' Relief Committee, 186, 530

"City Beautiful" movement, 636n127

city council, 32, 139, 163, 176, 188, 218, 222, 330, 427, 458, 480, 517, 539, 652n45; eligibility for election to, 169, 449, 666n15; partisan politics on, 452, 453, 472, 481, 483, 490, 499, 505

city engineer, 182, 218, 286, 618n12, 620n34

City Hospital. See Hamilton General Hospital

class, definition of, middle, 4–5; upper, 4; working, 4–7

class consciousness, 5–7, 547

class, formation of, 4–7

cleaners, 119, 120, 122, 126, 248, 422

cleanliness, 93, 169, 194, 194

clergymen, 4, 6, 29, 70, 150, 153, 155, 156, 160, 306, 307, 321, 322, 324, 335, 343, 352, 357, 364, 415, 419, 499, 511, 512, 517, 549, 554, 594n10, 677n95; and charity, 175, 185, 187, 199, 201, 356, 375, 376, 599n7; and corporate welfarism, 617n116; and new immigrants, 426, 443; Catholic, 41, 70, 323, 426, 427, 439, 632n79; Jewish, 427

clerical workers, 2, 30, 121, 131–32, 133, 146, 197, 239, 242–43, 270, 317, 400, 401, 492, 591n54, 593n94, 594n108, 645n54; and feminization, 242–43, 251, 590n38; and mechanization, 342–43, 251; unemployment among, 583n31

Cleveland, 9, 423, 554

clinics, baby, 6, 24, 33, 84–85, 91, 92, 93, 94, 97, 99, 119, 550, 552; out-patient, 95–96, 98; public-health, 5; tuberculosis, 83

closed shop, 291

clothing, working-class, 54, 65–66, 93, 115, 121, 128, 150, 151, 153, 154, 155, 156, 162, 164, 171, 319, 322, 345, 355, 356–57, 360, 364, 366, 380, 405, 546, 552, 644n33, 644n37, 644n38; cost of 160, 161, 597n43, 597n57, 635n112; supplied by charity, 161, 176, 191, 196

clothing industry, 6, 15, 20, 23, 27, 105, 114, 118, 126, 131, 207, 211, 227, 458, 502, 549, 563n7; subcontracting in, 118, 207, 440, 621n46

clothing workers, 129, 207, 245, 283, 288, 454, 562n66, 585n42; business agent, 285, 292, 372; strikes, 217, 264, 278–80, 281, 285, 292, 303, 355, 356, 488, 619n17, 619n18, 620n38, 620n39, 620n40, 620n42, 627n152; union, 211, 213, 214, 215, 216, 218, 227, 251, 266, 285–86, 291–92, 356, 444, 606n24, 622n70, 624n105; women, 217, 291, 354, 372, 606n38, 618n15, 620n38, 620n41, 620n42

Coats, Robert, 564n27

Hamilton Technical Institute, 140, 143, 404, 427
Hamilton Temperance Federation, 468
Hamilton Theatre Managers' Association, 639n165
Hamilton Tigers, 360, 655n90
Hamilton Trades and Labor Council, and alcohol, 468, 469; and Chamber of Commerce, 516, 517, 679n18; and charity, 190; and conciliation, 214, 228; and domestic labour, 99; and elections, 449, 451, 461; and female suffrage, 375; and high cost of living, 163; and housing, 46, 598n72; and immigration, 424, 432, 433–34, 563n9; and International Harvester, 19, 235, 262; and international unionism, 605n18; and Labour Day, 328; and managerial change, 241, 274; and medical fees, 95, 96; and old-age pensions, 193; and organizing, 298; and parks, 330, 636n129; and politics, 293, 300, 477, 482, 501, 526, 528, 531, 532, 626n138, 682n80, 683n99; and popular culture, 335; and Sabbatarianism, 634n100; and school fees, 125; and school-leaving age, 140; and solidarity, 223, 295; and tariffs, 504; and technical education, 613n71; and unskilled workers, 217, 281, 302; and war, 416; Declaration of Principles, 477; female delegates to, 218; membership, 212, 217, 296; municipal program (1906), 483; officers of, 227, 294, 417, 486, 500, 540; 562n66; spilt over industrial unionism, 301, 541, 628n154
Hamilton Trades Assembly, 218
Hamilton Unemployed Association, 507, 531, 682n84, 683n88
Hamilton United Relief Association, 186
Hamilton-Wentworth riding, 448
Hand, Gladys, 363
Handicraft Schools, 87, 88
handymen, 230, 234, 250, 266, 288, 289, 488, 619n24
Hardie, Keir, 484, 486, 487
Harvest Excursion, 41, 109, 397
Haslam, Edgar, 530, 531
Hatch, Arthur F., 23, 458, 514, 561n47
hawking. See peddling
Hawkins, Mary (Chambers), 28, 187, 530
Hawkins, William, 431

health care, 4, 76–98, 546; impact of unemployment on, 95, 176; state-run, 84, 90, 96, 100, 580n190
health insurance, 524, 540
Heaps, A.A., 182
Hearst, William, 469, 492, 508
heart disease, 75, 90, 105, 573n83, 578n156
Hebrew Institute, 663n86
hegemony, 5–6, 14, 23, 32–33, 34, 94, 150, 262,272, 446–47, 545
helpers, 132, 289, 389, 395, 605n4, 619n27
Helping Hand Club, 600n8
Heming, Charles, 520, 680n44
Henderson, Nora Frances, 344, 573n71
Henderson, Rose, 376
Hendrie, George M. , 678n12
Hendrie, John S., 24, 25, 32, 458, 561n37, 561n39, 605n10671n105; as politician, 34, 453, 463, 468, 469, 472, 479, 485, 669n80, 673n17
Hendrie, Lily, 352
Hendrie, William, 514, 520, 521, 680n40, 680n41, 680n44
Hendrie Cartage Company, 227
Hepburn, Mitchell, 541
Herald, 312; labour column in, 214, 246, 248, 455, 477, 673n15; on election procedures, 450; on female suffrage, 375; on independent labour politics, 482, 486, 488, 492, 675n45, 677n82; on new immigrants, 428, 431, 444, 664n94; on popular culture, 334, 337, 338, 359, 400; on Sabbatarianism, 326; on slums,, 175; political slant of, 455, 463–64, 472; on World War One, 496
Herron, William, 681n55
Hess Street Public School, 123, 134
high schools, 124; absenteeism in, 135, 143; academic, xi (Table 33), 25, 134–36, 139, 140, 142, 144, 146, 147; commercial, xi (Table 35), 131, 132, 137, 138, 140, 142, 144, 146, 592n65; dropouts from, xi (Table 37), 6, 135, 138, 143, 593n99, 594n110; enrolment in, xi (Tables 31–32), 134–36, 144; guidance in, 144, 247; night classes in, 138, 139, 141, 144, 591n54, 592n75, 593n84; part-time classes, in, 139; Roman Catholic, 140; technical, xi (Table 34), 136–38, 139, 142, 144, 145, 146, 149, 234, 246–47

High School of Commerce, 140; strike at, 144
Highfield School, 26, 392
high-speed steel, 233, 610n17
high-steel ironworkers, 421
Hillman, Sidney, 625n122
Hobson, Robert, as business leader, 13, 18, 19, 21, 34, 228; as industrialist, 220, 233, 248, 254, 268, 277, 289, 513, 560n28, 561n37, 561n39, 624n112, 634n102; community service of, 180, 186, 252, 560n24; politics of, 32, 460; private life of, 17, 25
hockey, 259, 317, 318, 392, 393, 399, 655n90
Holbrook, J.H., 82, 83, 89–90, 91, 578n154
Holton, W.A., 561n47
holidays, 6, 232, 263, 307, 327, 328, 338, 359, 398, 399, 402, 547, 554; Civic Holiday, 238; Dominion Day, 237, 418, 548; Easter, 263, 308, 321, 635n109; Thanksgiving, 635n109; Victoria Day, 327, 388, 412. See also Christmas; Labour Day; vacations, paid
Holy Angels School, 428
Holy Name Society, 404
home, significance of, 167–70, 305–8
Home for Aged Women, 76, 177
Home for the Aged and Infirm, 177, 188, 193, 406, 600n19
Home for the Friendless and Infants Home, 600n12
home ownership, working-class, 44, 48–49, 127, 128, 162, 163, 166–70, 307, 546, 551, 552, 554, 568n73, 598n68; by skilled workers, 567n72, 586n56; by unskilled workers, 567n72; company loans for, 259, 598n66; meaning of, 167–70
Homeside, 47, 646n62
Homeside Improvement Society, 675n47
Homestead, Pa., 242
homosexuality, 59, 389, 390, 405, 652n45, 657n124
homosociability, 310, 400, 401, 406, 407–8, 515, 547
honeymoons, 374
Honorary Advisory Council on Industrial and Scientific Research, 233; Committee on Industrial Fatigue, 268
Honourably Discharged Soldiers' Association, 519, 679n30, 680n51

Hoodless, Adelaide (Hunter), 27, 67, 71, 79, 350, 571n41
Hoover Company, 258, 626n131
Hospital Committee, 79
hospitals, 79–81, 98, 175, 186, 517, 575n105; clinics in, 95–96; directors of, 24, 451; fees, 80; maternity services of, 79, 80–81, 552; private care in, 80, 575n106; public wards in, 79, 80, 98, 575n105, 575n107, 600n12; semi-private care in, 80, 575n108
hostels, 103, 179, 199, 201, 546; for women, 199
hotels, 361, 362, 379, 401, 403, 422, 469, 576n121, 604n94, 645n51, 656n103
hotel workers, 116, 121, 422
hours of work, 2, 4, 158, 218, 258, 264, 265, 275, 284, 398, 488; impact of, 447; legislation on, 213, 289, 476, 493; lengthening of, 296, 297; reduction of, 221, 220, 261, 285, 288, 322, 346, 477, 540, 672n10. *See also* overtime; shift work; short time; working day; work week
household appliances, 63–69, 155, 161, 171
household economies. *See* family economies
household furnishings, 150, 151, 153, 154, 160, 161, 167, 169, 310
households, conflict within, 7, 566n63; European immigrant, 45–6, 62, 69, 73, 76, 77, 86, 88, 97, 118, 126, 141, 151, 157, 168, 176, 309, 318, 354; working-class, 43–46, 57–122
house-in-a-day, 212, 241, 612n51
housekeeping. *See* domestic labour
House of Refuge, 76, 103, 177, 178, 188, 189, 193, 472. *See also* Home for the Aged and Infirm
housework, 63–69, 126; standards for, 67–69
housing, working-class, 4, 42–51, 150, 151, 171, 193, 194; affordable, 151, 159–60, 170, 518, 618n10; company, 46; construction of, 46–51, 551, 566n52, 568n75; "co-operative," 46, 167; economic uses of, 598n71; for new immigrants, 38, 50, 642n15; government programs for, 44, 46–47, 50, 167, 486, 491; in shacks, 44, 45, 50, 53, 119, 168; interior spaces in, 169, 629n34 (*see also* bedrooms; dining

rooms; kitchens; parlours; verandahs); overcrowding in, 43–44, 50, 51, 74, 82, 90, 93, 118, 169, 309, 428, 566n51; row, 43; owner-built, 449, 166, 158, 568n75; pre-fabricated, 49, 166; shortages, 43–44, 46–47, 48, 53, 168, 506, 566n50; size, 565n49, 568n81. *See also* building code; building contractors; covenants; home ownership; landlords; mortgages; real estate; renters; rents; subdivisions
Housing Act (1918), 166
Housing Committee (1912), 46
Housing Commission (1919), 47, 498, 519
Hungarians, 40, 152, 277, 339, 426, 438, 441, 442, 587n78, 661n46, 661n52, 665n103
Hunger March, 535
Hunter, Peter, 443, 572n56, 586n57
hunting, 112, 402, 408, 546, 586n54
Hurst, Alfred, 506
hydro-electricity, 15, 18, 32, 69, 491, 493; campaign for public ownership of, 64, 462–65, 467
hygiene, 71, 73, 83, 86, 92, 385

ice-cream, 326, 387, 489, 634n103
ice-cutting, 109, 329
illegitimacy, 182, 585n51, 648n110
illness, 43, 74, 98, 105, 108, 111, 120, 122, 126, 173, 174, 175, 176, 185, 186, 190, 198, 256, 309, 311, 319, 321, 348, 374, 408, 438, 517, 546, 555
immigrants, 5, 112, 465; Canadianization of, 264, 550, 648n95; British, 9, 39, 51, 175, 185, 246, 305, 309, 369, 382, 399, 424, 429, 488, 495, 564n19; European, xi (Table 2), 38–40, 45–46, 48, 51, 52, 104, 109, 133, 184, 195, 198, 199, 231, 232, 235, 236, 248, 252, 255, 262, 264, 268, 273, 275, 281, 283, 284, 286, 294, 295, 313, 315, 323, 326, 337, 339, 341, 356, 370, 382, 385, 395, 396, 411, 424, 425, 429, 434, 435, 443, 465, 466, 473, 488, 518, 530, 540, 542, 548, 551, 582n9, 599n4, 614n77, 615n96, 627n150, 662n64, 662n70; US, 9, 246, 250, 564n24; women among, 42, 43, 45, 564n29, 565n41. *See also* Armenians; Bulgarians; Chinese; Croatians; Germans; Greeks; Hungarians; Irish; Italians; Lithuanians; Macedonians;

Poles; Romanians; Russians; Scots; Ukrainians
immigration, 9; controversies over, 106, 434–35, 476, 486, 524, 532; offices, 5; policy, 31, 37, 38, 39, 429, 434, 435, 565n34; promotion by private agencies, 38, 548
Imperial Cotton Company, 20, 242, 250, 560n17, 563n10, 620n37; corporate welfare at, 258, 259, 263, 362, 369, 377, 589n29, 505n14, 598n66, 616n111, 646n61, 648n101
Imperial Order Daughters of the Empire, 24, 27, 81, 99, 419, 598n63, 639n162, 659n17; girls' club, 647n85; Visiting and Relief Committee, 600n8
Imperial Munitions Board, 130, 163, 242, 384, 286; Labour Department, 129, 234, 282, 283
import substitution, 16
improvement societies, 54, 487, 675n47
incentive wages, 103, 211, 241, 250, 253–54, 264, 270, 459. *See also* piecework; premium bonus
incline railways, 634n97, 634n98
income, middle-class, 562n76
income, working-class family, 51, 55, 58, 74, 80, 84, 87, 91, 92, 93, 95, 101, 108–9, 162, 408, 562n76, 584n40, 597n47; children's contribution to, 127–47, 151, 162, 192, 198, 202, 373, 396, 397, 409, 548, 593n94, 597n47, 653n73; insecurity of, 135, 151, 352, 398; men's share of, 111; peak years of, 168; stable, 151; wives' contributions to, 116–22; non-waged sources of, 112–16, 122
Independent Labor Party, Hamilton, xi (Tables 42–43), 36, 96, 99, 125, 169, 190, 289, 294, 300, 322, 326, 372, 375, 417, 424, 447, 453, 456, 458, 470, 475–508, 509, 513, 538, 539, 543, 553, 554, 625n119, 666n15, 666n15, 675n39, 676n62, 683n99, 684n106; and Chamber of Commerce, 516, 529–30; and health, 581n205; and new immigrants, 431; and tariffs, 461; and veterans, 523–24, 530, 681n55; baseball teams, 489; Central Branch, 408, 492, 498, 499, 500, 501, 504, 506, 507, 540, 684n110; city councillors, 425, 430, 455, 490, 492, 500, 505, 506, 507, 528, 540, 541, 684n106; controllers, 491, 492, 498, 499, 506,

233, 235, 277, 610n24; as strikers, 277; clubs of, 423, 439, 440, 441, 655n97; community of, 54, 76, 150, 164, 268, 324, 344, 354, 364, 374, 411, 440, 569n91, 572n56, 587n80, 597n55, 661n49, 664n99; discrimination against, 53, 421, 425, 429, 431, 444, 466, 614n77, 650n17, 661n42; family size, 572n54; *festas* of, 308, 321, 438, 628n7; fraternal societies of, 152, 199, 374, 438, 440, 663n88, 663n90; in boarding houses, 45, 46; newspaper for, 53, 440; Protestant missions to, 426, 427; Roman Catholic churches of, 320, 322, 411, 439, 632n72, 632n79, 633n93; women among, 42, 564n29

Italo-Canadian Recreation Club, 655n97

"Jacobinism," 476

jail, 33, 61, 62, 71, 103, 112, 173, 178, 199, 472, 534, 536

Jameson, Eric, 113

janitors, 108, 248

Jarvis, C.H., 92, 93

jazz, 314, 317, 339, 359, 423

Jelfs, George, 32, 60, 62–63, 111, 432, 569n93, 571n25, 634n103, 634n105, 651n34, 660n34

jewellers, 455

Jews, 40, 53, 114, 150, 198–99, 279, 321, 326, 342, 345, 354, 423, 429, 438, 440, 441, 442, 444, 445, 466, 495, 525, 531, 572n54, 642n15, 663n86, 664n101, 664n103; synagogues of, , 663n91

job control, 207–10, 213, 229, 233, 244, 274, 276, 284, 547, 549

job ladders. *See* labour markets, internal

Johnson, Jack, 423

joint-stock companies. *See* corporations

Jolson, Al, 422, 423, 660n30

Jordon, William, 522, 680n44

journalists, 3, 19, 29, 121, 129, 130, 131, 173, 229, 235, 236, 239, 273, 279, 284, 295, 309, 310, 385, 388, 411, 414, 415, 428; socialist, 478

Journeymen Tailors Union, 213, 216

Judicial Committee of the Privy Council, 325

Junior Catholic Women's League, 368

Junior Health League, 576n116

justices of the peace, 440

Jutten, Tom, 485, 602n51

juvenile court, 72, 367, 390, 393, 549, 550

juvenile delinquency, 3, 32, 74, 88, 367, 390, 548

Juvenile Delinquents Act, 367

Kanadai Magyar Munkas, 442

Kappelle, A.P., 192

Karl Marx Club, 495

Kashtan, William, 534

Kaye, A.W., 189

Khan, The. *See* Kernighan, Richard

Keghi, 38

Keith theatre chain, 334, 336

Kellond, Fred, 672n126

Kenilworth, 47

Kernighan, Richard, 101, 112, 128, 327

Keystone Studios, 343

Kimlik, Fred, 526

kin, 43, 51, 58, 59, 150, 232, 265, 308, 309, 310, 311, 324, 359; support from, 49, 102, 165, 174, 175, 176, 177, 181, 185, 255, 546, 551, 555, 570n12, 596n33, 599n4

kindergarten, 126, 426

King, William Lyon Mackenzie, 182, 184, 215, 259, 454, 455, 456, 460, 486, 539, 541, 667n26, 668n71

Kingston, 22, 38, 449; Penitentiary, 534

Kinmel, Wales, 517

Kinsey, Alfred, 657n124

Kinsmen Club, 30, 393, 515, 678n15

kitchens, 170, 310, 311, 319, 630n34

Kitchener-Waterloo, 9, 455

Kiwanis Club, 24, 195, 393, 515

Knight, A.F., 242

Knight, Joe, 294

Knights of Labor, 211, 218, 454, 455, 477, 672n126

Knights of Pythias, 152; Pythian Sisters, 374

knitting, home, 119, 349, 374, 599n8; factory, 128, 130, 132, 248, 249, 251, 266, 353, 614n89, 618n15, 619n18, 619n19, 627n149

knitting mills, 15, 20, 251, 347

Knox Presbyterian Church, 322, 404

Ku Klux Klan, 435, 444, 663n76; women's branch, 435

laboratories, 233, 610n15

Labor Educational Association of Ontario, 480

Laborers' and Hod Carriers' International Union, 295

Labor Hall, 212, 276

Labor News, 486, 487, 500, 677n82; on Buy-Canadian, 503; on censorship, 285; on independent labour politics, 488, 494, 497, 505, 506, 681n64; on new immigrants, 425, 465; on organizing, 217, 281, 289, 295; on popular culture, 337, 344; on radicalism, 294, 498; on strikes, 621n46, 627n144; on tariffs, 504; on unemployment, 107; on war, 416, 417; on women, 356, 375; on workplace safety, 269; on works councils, 262,

Labor Party of Ontario, 677n95

Labor Representation Political Association, 501, 677n95

Labor Temple, Allan Studholme Memorial, 292, 675n44

Labor Temple Association, 626n138

labour aristocracy, 162

Labour Church, 498

Labour Day, 211, 219, 328, 339, 477, 512, 605n17, 636n116, 636n117

labourers, 141, 196, 479; and charity,179; and labour turnover, 274; and home ownership, 168, 522, 629n29; and World War One, 284; builders', 218, 226, 619n17; civic, 23, 227, 286, 288, 294, 472, 618n12, 619n18; hiring of, 252; strikes of, 277, 488, 614n77, 615n99, 620n33, 620n34, 621n57, 662n70; unemployment of, 183; unions of, 227, 291, 295, 302, 444, 619n29, 623n94, 624n104, 626n138; wages of, 507, 585n42, 593n94; work of, 210, 218, 232, 233, 247–48, 250, 252, 266, 270, 395, 396, 428, 548. *See also* unskilled workers

labour force participation, xi (Table 16)

Labour Gazette, 107, 109, 120, 235, 455, 564n27, 582n15, 618n143

labourism, 467, 475–76, 481, 486, 492, 496, 499, 501–5, 511, 539. *See also* Independent Labor Party

labour markets, 6, 206, 234, 239, 302; gender and, xi (Table 12); female, 251; internal, 104, 250, 252, 253, 254, 259, 303, 396; male, 103–4; segmented, 6, 140, 248, 411, 422, 430, 434, 436, 443, 553, 662n56; unskilled, 210, 217, 583n21; youth, 127–33, 138, 143, 164

labour recruitment, 6, 8, 37, 103–4, 230, 247; of employees' families, 255,

Royal Commission on Industrial Relations, 95, 154, 184, 248, 250, 260, 262, 263, 288, 294, 579n181, 580n183, 623n82

Royal Commission on Price Spreads, 143, 598n62

Royal Commission on the Relations of Labour and Capital, 208–9, 210

Royal Commission on Technical Education, 245, 246, 249

Royal Commission to investigate munitions workers' grievances, 284–85

Royal Guardian Society, 277

Royal Hamilton Yacht Club, 26, 329, 562n59

Royal Templars of Temperance, 468, 477, 672n10

Royal Thistle Curling Club, 562n59

Russell, James, 420

Russia, 39, 279, 418, 442, 467, 498

Russian Revolution, 286, 287, 430, 444, 496, 497, 520, 525, 553, 681n64

Russian Socialist Revolutionaries, 665n103

Russians, 53, 248, 286, 425, 429, 430, 441, 442, 525, 526, 536, 564n22, 631n50, 662n64, 663n91, 664n97, 665n103, 681n68

Ryerson, Egerton, 139

Sabbatarians, 324–27, 488, 547, 549, 634n100, 634n101, 634n102, 634n103, 634n104, 634n105, 676n72

Sacco, Nicola, 528

Sacred Heart School, 428

safety, company programs for, 257, 263, 269, 552; strikes over, 275, 299, 619n17

sailing, 331

St. Andrew's Society, 200, 419, 599n6

St. Ann's School, 428, 439

St. Anthony of Padua Roman Catholic Church, 320, 411, 439, 632n72

St. Anthony's Day, 411, 438, 439, 440

St. David's Presbyterian Church, 320, 323

St. Elizabeth Nurses Association, 574n102

St. George's Benevolent Society, 38, 176, 185, 189, 192, 419, 599n6, 602n55, 604n84, 639n162

St. Giles Presbyterian Church, 632n72

Saint John, N.B., 568n81

St. Joseph's Hospital, 79, 80, 575n106, 575n109, 575n112

St. Lawrence Roman Catholic Church, 320, 632n72, 633n90

St. Luke's Anglican Church, 320, 322, 352, 368, 632n72; Boys' Club, 391; Brotherhood of St. Andrews, 400

St. Mary's Roman Catholic Cathedral, 439

St. Mary's Orphan Asylum, 178, 600n15, 600n18

St. Mary's School, 428

St. Matthew's Anglican Church, 477

St. Patrick's Day, 428

St. Patrick's Girls' Clubhouse, 368

St. Patrick's Roman Catholic Cathedral, 670n94

St. Peter's Anglican Church, 653n56

St. Peter's Infirmary, 177

St. Stanislas Roman Catholic Church, 320, 439, 632n72, 662n73, 664n94

St. Vincent de Paul Society, 72, 200, 427, 599n6

saints days, 308, 321, 328, 411, 438, 439, 628n7, 633n82

saloons, 3, 6, 7, 12, 149, 310, 319, 327, 332, 333, 336, 338, 360, 379, 382, 401, 404, 407, 408, 409, 414, 438, 469, 547, 551, 552, 609n77, 640n177, 656n103, 656n100. See also alcohol; beverage rooms; "blind pigs"; prohibition; temperance movement

Salvation Army, 179, 320, 357, 599n6, 603n72; and immigration, 38; employment bureau for women, 120; hostel, 103, 179, 199, 306; Rescue Home, 600n12, 600n15

Samaritan Club, 175, 576n116, 603n66

"San." See Hamilton Health Association, Sanatorium

Sanford, W.E., 27

Sanford Manufacturing, 15, 16, 207, 216, 669n72

Sanzone, Salvatore, 440

Saturday afternoon, 307, 327, 328, 338; half-holiday on, 266, 547, 635n108

savings, 108, 113, 152, 153, 162, 171, 180, 197, 309, 564n30; accounts, 152, 153, 595n14. See also insurance; war bonds

Savoy Theatre, 333, 334, 336, 638n150, 639n159, 639n162, 641n187

Sawyer-Massey Company, 15, 20, 22, 220, 264, 610n33

scabs. See strikebreakers

Scalabrini, 439

Scarlet, Sam, 565n37

scarlet fever, 74, 75, 80, 83

Scarrone, Leopoldo, 440

scavenging, 71, 115, 127, 165, 348, 383, 589n19, 642n5

school attendance, 64, 67, 98, 124, 126, 194, 348, 551, 589n18, 591n55, 591n58, 591n59, 592n61; exemptions, 124, 139. See also Adolescent School Attendance Act; truancy; truant officer

school attendance officer, 139, 140, 143, 176, 348, 394

school board. See Hamilton Board of Education

school fees, 125, 163, 491, 588n9

school-leaving age, 64, 121, 124, 138–43, 164, 247, 248, 348, 394, 591n55, 592n81, 603n76

school medical officer, 87, 88

School of Domestic Science and Art, 137

schools, 5, 54, 70–71, 74, 124–47, 306, 381, 387; curriculum, 642n6, 650n17; imperialism in, 412; half-day schedules in, 125; military drills in, 349; overcrowding in, 125; parents expectations of, 650n20; private, 25–6, 591n49; sports in, 642n8

science in production, 233

Scots, 39, 113, 177, 200, 320, 360, 413, 419, 572n56, 599n6

Scott, J.J., 482, 483, 671n105, 674n32

Scott Park, 329, 331

seasonality, 105–6, 109, 151, 183, 402, 583n18

Seattle, 625n114

second-hand stores, 164, 165, 166, 387, 587n63, 597n59

sedition, 287

"segmented class formation," 445

self-employment, 113, 164, 197, 562n66, 586n57, 586n58, 587n65

semi-skilled workers, 103, 108, 132, 168, 248–50, 270, 275, 282, 296, 300, 302, 320, 396, 409, 428, 476, 553, 614n79, 625n114. See also handymen; specialists

Senate, 32, 504

Sennett, Mack, 343

separate schools, Roman Catholic, 124, 126, 134, 135, 137, 140, 146, 349, 385, 392, 412, 413, 413, 427, 428, 444, 591n49, 591n59, 661n49

separate spheres, 116, 117

Serato, Manuel Pardinas, 41

Serbs, 53

servants, domestic, 5, 25, 26, 28, 38, 45, 118, 120, 121, 130, 131, 132, 156, 182, 197, 199, 319, 326, 369, 370, 380, 423, 648n96; decline of as proportion of wage-earning women, 353, 354, 590n34, 590n35

service clubs, 514, 530, 533

settlement houses, 352, 370, 426, 444

sewer-pipes-makers, 227

sewers, 50, 64, 74, 329

sewing, 65–66, 154, 171, 311, 369, 374, 587n80; classes, 92, 119, 350, 351, 370, 378, 599n8; for relief, 535; for wages, 119, 128, 145, 198, 208, 249, 251, 350

sex, premarital, 373, 380, 405, 405–6, 657n124, 657n131

sexual assault, 59, 118, 406, 432, 433

sexual harassment, 255, 279, 424

sexualities, 59–60, 69, 87, 88, 118, 342, 343, 350, 359, 363, 364, 367, 373, 405, 423–24, 657n125, 657n134

Sharp, Agnes, , 650n14

Shapiro, Isaac, 622n70, 622n73

Shaw, Duncan, 487

Shearer, John G., 325, 634n101, 634n102

sheet-metal workers, 211, 291

Sherman, Clifton W., 236, 561n47

Sherwood, A.F., 286

shift work, 104, 265, 310, 398, 617n133

shipbuilding, 625n114

shoe repairmen, 29

shoe shining, 127

shoe workers, 208, 213, 217

shop-floor bargaining, 274–75, 278

shopkeepers, 4, 14, 28, 29, 40, 52, 113, 114, 119, 226, 320, 326, 343, 386, 437, 438, 440, 443, 457, 506

shopping, 52, 65, 73, 152, 156, 165, 306, 310, 356, 378, 379, 437, 479

short time, 105, 106, 202, 250, 530

showmen, 7, 332, 344, 363, 552

Sicilians, 6, 38, 53, 59

sidewalks, 50

silicosis, 268

Silverman, Morris, 652n66

Simcoe St. Methodist Church, 632n72

"simple control," 617n129

Simpson, James, 498, 676n73

singing, 259, 313, 315, 333, 335, 340, 341, 342, 343, 345, 350, 351, 352, 355, 369, 370, 388, 402, 404, 409, 412, 414, 418, 423, 443, 496, 630n44, 632n79

single men, 108, 402, 432, 448, 565n45, 582n8; and charity, 178, 184, 198, 546; and churches, 656n113; and relief, 102, 110, 183, 199, 531, 533, 537, 581n2, 603n73, 654n87, 682n86; and old age, 177

Single Men's Unemployed Association, 537

single mothers, 71, 162, 174, 181–81, 189, 307, 565n42

single tax, 477, 497, 500, 502

Single Tax Association, 477

single women, 24, 38, 43, 45, 102, 117, 133, 151, 198, 355, 366, 373, 377, 587n68, 587n70, 587n71; unemployment of, 118, 199, 648n96, 682n86

Sisters of Service, 83

Sisters of St. Joseph, 600n15

Six Nations, 421

skating, 331, 358, 405, 406

skill, 207–10, 230–34, 244–53

skilled workers, xi (Table 11), 8, 37, 109, 113, 138, 145, 206, 210, 217, 230, 241, 244, 252, 264, 270, 274, 320, 554; and politics, 476, 483, 454, 456, 458; and women, 477; privileges of, 79, 132, 134, 137, 168, 211, 428; wages of, 95, 103, 110, 127, 162, 548

Slavs, 236, 428, 445, 586n60

sleeping car porters, , 659n28

Slovaks, 40

slump. See depression, economic

slums, 44, 45, 51, 175, 352, 433

smallpox, 75, 83, 88, 96

Smelter Workers Union, 607n46

Smith, A.E. , 677n95

Smith, Bessie, 344

Smith, Helen, 93

Smith, R.L., 187, 200

Smith, Ralph, 216, 668n49

"smokers," 290, 471, 484, 489, 495, 519, 655n94

smoking, 111, 149, 151, 155, 171, 210, 216, 290, 326, 366, 387, 391, 392, 401, 402, 308, 618n12; boys and, 651n27; women and, 357, 380, 552

Snider, Colin, 79, 434

"snitching," 54, 185, 602n51

Snowden, Mrs. Philip, 375

snow-shovelling, 109, 110, 143

soap operas, 318, 342, 343

soccer, 39, 54, 256, 258, 328, 331, 399, 471, 487, 646n62

social assistance, two-tiered, 179, 201

Social Democratic Party, 286, 471, 495–97, 498, 525, 526, 528, 624n105, 656n110; alliance with labourists,' 496, 526, 676n73; Ukrainian, 339, 442, 443, 525, 526, 665n103

"social hygiene," 367

social insurance, 180

Socialist Labor Party, 478, 666n15, 673n11, 673n13, 684n111

Socialist Party of America, 502, 675n38, 676n70

Socialist Party of Canada, 478, 480, 495, 673n15

socialists, xi (Table 43), 3, 4, 34, 257, 262, 263, 276, 277, 279, 286, 293, 294, 339, 343, 438, 445, 474, 476, 512, 529, 548, 553, 622n70, 625n114, 625n115, 625n122, 625n126, 673n17, 673n19, 673n20; Armenian, 442, 480; Christian, 414, 478; Hungarian, 442; Jewish, 279, 441, 442, 480, 525; Marxist, 478–80, 490, 495–98, 500, 502, 526; Polish, 442; Russian, 442, 525; Ukrainian, 339, 442, 480, 525, 661n42

social purity, 366

Social Purity League, 366

Social Relief Auxiliary, 175

Social Reform Union, 478, 672n11

Social Service Council of Canada, 511

Social Service Exchange, 187, 188

social structures of accumulation, 8

social survey, Methodist and Presbyterian (1913), 35, 45, 402, 656n105

Social Welfare, 511

social work, 6; professionalization of, 28, 187, 191, 200, 201, 549, 603n66

social workers, 3, 7, 29, 72, 92, 99, 104, 106, 108, 120, 149, 150, 155, 167, 175, 192, 193, 195, 201, 307, 315, 426, 550, 562n69, 576n116, 602n49

Society of St. Stanislaus Koska, 663n89

softball. See baseball

sojourning, 6, 40–42, 45, 52, 53, 102, 108, 109, 118, 236–37, 273, 437, 438, 443, 444, 445, 551, 564n27, 564n30, 654n86

"soldiering." See restriction of output

Soldiers' Aid Commission, 181, 189, 190, 392, 415, 518, 582n10

soldiers, 185, 349, 375, 384, 400–1, 415–16, 418, 493, 517; and labour, 226,

Tilden, John, 23, 214, 481, 606n27

time clocks, 104, 205, 240, 241, 265, 354, 374, 409, 445, 550, 611n45, 619n18

Times, 199, 273, 312, 330, 357, 455, 482; and hydro-electric development, 463; and new immigrants, 429, 432

Tin Pan Alley, 314, 315, 341, 342, 343, 630n44

Tinsley, Joseph, 312

tire-builders, 246

tobacco industry, 105, 116, 126, 206, 207, 208, 256, 395, 502, 569n91

tobacco workers, 129, 216, 362; strikes, 286, 423, 619n18

toilets, 64, 67; privies as, 64, 82, 169

toolmakers, 245, 246, 247, 283

Toronto, 9, 17, 20, 25, 30, 83, 125, 160, 219, 278, 284, 289, 332, 405, 449, 512, 520, 528, 533, 566n62, 568n81, 576n123, 590n34, 620n40, 623n92, 625n114, 625n122; general strike, 625n116

Toronto General Trusts, 22

Toronto, Hamilton, and Buffalo Railway, 15, 43, 210, 235, 619n27, 620n33, 620n34, 622n68, 662n67

Toronto Housing Company, 46

Toronto *Star*, 435, 455

Towers, Thomas, 672n126

town planning, 49

Town Planning Board, 44, 636n124

toys, 152

track and field, 257, 349, 363, 391, 653n69, 655n90

Trades and Labor Congress of Canada, 116, 214, 220, 289, 293, 325, 425, 431, 454, 481, 482, 500, 563n15, 571n38, 605n18, 605n22, 666n13, 666n21, 673n11, 674n31; Ontario Executive Committee, 480, 598n72, 673n22

Trade Union Educational League, 298

train station, 38, 385, 414

tramps, 179, 306, 341

transiency, xi (Table 4), 36–37, 39–42, 45, 55, 103, 109, 122, 162, 183, 199, 201, 236–37, 257, 268, 273, 277, 278, 281, 307, 397, 426, 431, 438, 442, 448, 546, 565n37, 565n38, 565n39, 609n77

Travellers' Aid, 38, 366

Triangle Committee, 513, 678n11

truancy, 71, 124, 394; notices to parents, 126

truant officer, 72, 73, 124, 126, 139, 194, 348, 390, 392, 652n50. *See also* school attendance officer

truck drivers, 109

tuberculosis, 25, 27, 75, 77, 81–82, 86, 91, 95, 96, 105, 175, 182, 201, 517, 549, 550, 573n82, 574n115, 576n116; sanatorium for, 81–82, 98, 89–90, 96,, 575n125; treatment of, 89–90, 578n154. *See also* Hamilton Health Association; Samaritan Club

Tuckett, George, 15, 32, 256

Tuckett Tobacco Company, 15, 22, 129, 206, 207, 208, 216, 294, 362, 458, 561n39, 587n70, 589n29, 605n4, 615n99, 643n29, 660n32, 678n12; strike at, 286

Turks, 53, 431

Twentieth Century Club, 471

typhoid, 88

typists, 243, 251, 354, 562n77

Ukrainian Catholic Church of the Holy Ghost, 664n94

Ukrainian Labour Temple, 352, 393, 442, 527, 528; Children's School, 352–53; Women's Section, 376, 377, 553

Ukrainians, 40, 287, 339, 352–53, 376, 377, 393, 426, 442, 443, 445, 525, 526, 527, 528, 553, 564n22, 653n68, 661n42, 664n94, 665n103; and World War One, 431, 433, 434, 441

Underground Railroad, 421

Unemployed Council, 532

unemployed workers, 102, 104, 106, 174, 175, 185, 196, 197, 401, 402, 414, 429, 433, 489, 513, 540, 599n2; organizing of, 115, 200, 201, 488, 501, 507, 519, 527, 530–38, 539, 553, 554, 682n82, 682n84, 683n88, 684n103

Unemployed Workers' Association, 533, 534; Grievance Committee, 535

Unemployed Workers' Council, 683n88

unemployment, male, xi (Tables 23–24), 31, 41, 95, 104–10, 114, 135, 146, 151, 155, 168, 174, 184, 192, 193, 201, 217, 264, 272, 276, 287, 288, 296, 316, 383, 404, 429, 460, 473, 499, 509, 510, 517, 529, 532, 539, 541, 542, 552, 582n15, 582n16, 583n29, 623n82, 671n110, 678n8; ad-hoc committee on, 530; among unionists, 107, 582n15; among factory workers, 583n22; among youth, 394,

397, 591n46; impact of, 447, 501, 525, 554; international comparison of, 583n28; make-work projects for, 115, 174, 183, 186, 193, 198, 199, 200, 201, 202, 477, 530, 546

unemployment insurance, 184, 199, 200, 507, 524, 532, 534, 540, 541–42, 554

Unemployment Insurance Act, 541

Union government, 32, 282, 417, 432, 462, 466, 467, 467, 490, 491, 493, 497

unionization, xi (Table 27), 162, 211, 270, 273

Union Drawn Steel, 461, 560n27

Union Label League, 151, 216, 375, 631n57

union labels, 151, 215, 216, 218, 227, 279, 286, 295, 454, 502, 547, 672n10

Union Park, 48, 50, 567n70

unions, 7, 54, 149, 151, 162, 232, 271–303, 310, 313, 320, 322, 328, 345, 359, 378, 382, 396, 408, 412, 443, 509, 537, 547, 551; and courts, 32; and recreation, 399, 400; benefit plans of, 108, 175, 583n34; bureaucratization of, 213, 216–17, 553; business, 213; craft, 103, 108, 140, 151, 160, 210–19, 227, 230, 246, 247, 253, 254, 272, 275, 278, 279, 284, 285, 290, 293, 296, 302, 328, 429, 430, 468, 478, 480, 481, 489, 492, 500, 501, 502, 541, 547, 548, 553, 554, 584n40; industrial, 164, 256, 275, 278, 285, 290, 293, 294, 298, 300, 301, 377, 492, 496, 501, 532, 541, 543, 553, 554, 625n114; international, 211, 213, 605n18, 626n138; jurisdictional boundaries of, 212, 217, 219; membership, 621n48; organizing of, 211, 219, 276, 289, 295, 410, 417, 480, 513; provincial organizations of, 213, 214, 606n24; women and, 371–72, 380, 396

union staff, 213, 222, 226, 280. *See also* business agents

United Booking Office, 336

United Church of Canada, 319, 599n7

United Communist Party of America, 527

United Community Service League, 602n48

United Farmers of Ontario, 469, 493

United Front May Day Conference, 683n99

United Garment Workers of America, 213, 214, 216, 217, 278–80, 285, 606n38, 621n46

Westinghouse, George, 220
Westinghouse Air Brake Company, 18
Westminster Presbyterian Church, 632n72
Whitcombe, C.E., 477, 478, 481
White, Thomas, 32
white-collar workers, 108, 110, 127, 145, 162, 251–52, 258, 270, 335, 368, 385, 392, 436, 591n54, 597n54, 637n135, 640n181
whiteness, 102, 151, 175, 211, 236, 239, 309, 366, 384, 395, 400, 420, 421, 424, 425–36, 434, 443, 467, 473, 476, 546, 661n42
"white slavery," 366, 566n57, 646n76
Whitley councils, 291, 613n113
Whitney, James P., 222, 225, 450, 452, 457, 463, 469, 481, 483, 670n94, 674n29, 674n31
Whitton, Charlotte, 579n176
Whitton, F.H., 260, 283
whooping cough, 74, 75, 89, 573n79
Wickson, Garnet W., 160
widows, 24, 43, 79, 117, 119, 175, 179, 181, 182, 185, 189, 190, 201, 202, 286, 309, 535, 587n71. *See also* mothers' allowance
wife abuse. *See* domestic violence
Wilcox, C.S., 561n37
"Wild West" shows, 332
Wilkes, Alf, 451
Williams, Edward, 454, 667n44, 670n97
Willison, John, 503
Wilson, Woodrow, 491
Windsor, 9, 568n81
Winnipeg, 9, 22, 83, 160, 222, 225, 433, 442, 526, 527, 528, 568n81, 590n34, 625n114, 668n49; General Strike, 289, 295, 500, 512, 520, 623n92, 679n21
wire-drawers, 248, 364, 431
wire industry, 23, 609n3
wire weavers, 205, 249, 609n3
Witton, J.G., 247
Wobblies. *See* Industrial Workers of the World
Woman's Christian Temperance union, 62, 71, 99, 119, 175, 325, 338, 366, 367, 375, 378, 600n8, 639n166, 651n27, 657n125, 660n32, 661n47; children's programs of, 350; day nursery of, 120, 588n84; employment service of, 120; mothers' meetings, 378, 649n124;

Royal Mary Union, 422; young women's group, 647n85
Woman Worker, 376
Women Citizens' League, 424
Women's Art Association, 27
women's auxiliaries, 78, 165, 175, 374, 379, 415, 599n8, 645n56; of political parties, 471; of union, 375; of veterans' wives, 374–75, 649n114
Women's Canadian Club, 26, 598n63
Women's Canadian Ku Klux Klan, 435
Women's Cooperative Guild, 99, 649n119
Women's Exchange, 119
Women's Independent Labor Party, 99–100, 372, 375–76, 490, 553; Mount Hamilton branch, 95, 117, 166, 377
Women's International Union Label League, 375
Women's Labor League, 100, 376–77, 528, 529, 535, 553
Women's Liberal Association, 28
Women's Trade Union League, 281, 649n119
"women's wage," 132
women workers, xi (Tables 12, 17, 21), 5, 6, 8, 102, 112, 116–18, 128–33, 242–43, 248, 249, 250–51, 252, 281, 341, 347, 376, 548, 614n75; and corporate welfare, 258, 259; and unions, 217–18, 278, 291–92, 649n122; male attitudes to, 116, 278, 284, 301; militancy among, 116, 251, 275, 278–81
Wood, A.T., 17, 21
Woodlands Park, 406, 536, 537, 540, 543, 636n121
Woodsworth, J.S., 182
work camps, 199, 398, 683n86
Worker, 298, 300, 529, 535
workers' compensation, 23, 132, 146, 179–80, 183, 197, 198, 256, 257, 268–69, 486, 554, 604n89, 618n143; and women, 179, 197; pensions, 197
Workers' Economic Conference, 536
Workers' Educational Association, 339, 369, 371, 657n116
Workers' Ex-Servicemen's League, 536, 683n98
Workers' International Educational Association, 527
Workers' Party, 377, 527, 531, 682n70
Workers' Progressive Association, 684n103

Workers' Protective Association, 536, 539
workers' revolt, 100, 12, 133, 184, 264, 293, 512
Workers' Society, 438
Workers' Unity League, 298, 299, 301, 533, 534, 537, 626n139
work groups, 210, 274–75, 283, 296, 297, 302, 303, 355, 396, 547, 553, 555
working day, 617n133; eight-hour, 256, 261, 252, 288–89, 292, 299, 455, 486, 492, 494, 495, 505, 507, 511, 524, 553, 623n89, 647n84; nine-hour, 18, 275, 284–85, 346, 617n121, 622n69; ten-hour, 394, 458, 629n17; twelve-hour, 220, 266, 635n108. *See also* hours of work
"working girls." *See* women workers
workingmen's clubs, 375, 471, 477, 481, 464, 487, 673n12
Workingmen's Liberal Conservative Union, 458
Workingmen's Political Association, 481, 505, 666n15
working mothers, 93, 120, 189, 198, 309, 383, 551
Workmen's Circle, 279, 441, 495, 531, 663n86, 665n103, 677n95
Workmen's Compensation Act, 179, 459, 508
Workmen's Compensation Board, 146, 180, 185, 267–68, 269, 575n108, 618, 139
workplace contractualism, 217
works councils, 116, 259–60, 261, 262–63, 288, 300, 301, 517, 616n112, 679n19
work week, 266, 547, 634n102, 635n108; 40–hour, 291; 44–hour, 292, 516; 50–hour, 300; six-day, 60–hour, 327
World War One, 412; economy, 44, 107, 113, 126, 131, 135, 152, 242, 281, 315, 443, 662n64; deaths in, 416, 517; enthusiasm for, 24, 282, 287, 414–15, 416; labour shortages during, 117, 234, 243, 281, 425, 429, 431, 621n53, 662n67; military recruitment for, 110, 326, 415–17, 490, 496, 644n49, 656n100; mobilization for, 33, 491; national registration for, 235, 282, 416, 564n25, 662n67; rationing during, 151, 491; strikes during, 416. *See also* Canadian Patriotic Fund; censorship; Hamilton Recruiting League; Imperial Munitions Board; munitions